Summary of Contents

Professional Java Server Programming
J2EE Edition

Subrahmanyam Allamaraju
Karl Avedal
Richard Browett
Jason Diamond
John Griffin
Mac Holden
Andrew Hoskinson
Rod Johnson
Tracie Karsjens
Larry Kim
Andrew Longshaw
Tom Myers
Alexander Nakimovsky
Daniel O'Connor
Sameer Tyagi
Geert Van Damme
Gordan van Huizen
Mark Wilcox
Stefan Zeiger

Wrox Press Ltd. ®

Professional Java Server Programming
J2EE Edition

Published by Wrox Press Ltd,
Arden House, 1102 Warwick Road, Acocks Green,
Birmingham, B27 6BH, UK
Printed in the United States
ISBN 1-861004-65-6

Trademark Acknowledgements

Wrox has endeavored to provide trademark information about all the companies and products mentioned in this book by the appropriate use of capitals. However, Wrox cannot guarantee the accuracy of this information.

Credits

Authors
Subrahmanyam Allamaraju
Karl Avedal
Hans Bergsten
Richard Browett
Jason Diamond
John Griffin
Mac Holden
Andrew Hoskinson
Rod Johnson
Tracie Karsjens
Larry Kim
Andrew Longshaw
Tom Myers
Alexander Nakhimovsky
Daniel O'Connor
Andrew Patzer
Sameer Tyagi
Geert Van Damme
Gordon van Huizen
Mark Wilcox
Stefan Zeiger

Technical Architect
Craig A. Berry

Technical Editors
Richard Huss
Allan Jones
Robert Shaw
Chanoch Wiggers

Category Manager
Paul Cooper

Author Agents
Emma Batch
Velimir Ilic

Project Administrator
Chandima Nethisinghe

Index
Adrian Axinte
Martin Brooks
Andrew Criddle
Bill Johncocks

Technical Reviewers
Yogesh Bhandarkar
Jason Bock
Carl Burnham
Gavin Cornwell
Vikram David
Linda DeMichiel
Kevin Farnham
Kevlin Henney
David Hudson
Andrew Jones
Meeraj Moidoo Kunnumpurath
Carol McDonald
Jim MacIntosh
Eric Ma
Jacob Mathew
Vinay Menon
Joe Meirow
Yasir Feroze Minhas
Stéphane Osmont
Bryan Plaster
Phil Powers-DeGeorge
David Schultz
Michael Slinn
Deepak Thomas
John Timney
Paul Warren
Andrew Watt
David Whitney

Production Project Coordinator
Pip Wonson

Illustrations
Shabnam Hussain
Mark Burdett

Additional Layout & Illustrations
Tom Bartlett

Cover
Shelley Frazier

Proof Readers
Chris Smith
Bernard Simon
Peter Carrington

About the Authors

Subrahmanyam Allamaraju

Subrahmanyam is a Senior Engineer with BEA Systems. His interest in modeling lead him from his Ph.D. in Electrical Engineering to object-oriented programming, and then to distributed computing and software architecture. In this process, he drifted from his one-time home - the Indian Institute of Technology, to Computervision, and Wipro Infotech, and later to BEA Systems. You can find more about his current activities at his home `http://www.Subrahmanyam.com`.

Subrahmanyam would like to thank Varaa for her hand in code samples (in the face of tight deadlines), and sharing his frustration as well as exhiliration.

Karl Avedal

Karl Avedal has been a Java developer since the language was publicly launched in 1995. With the advent of Java server side technologies like servlets, he quickly turned his attention to the server and worked a lot with CORBA, before his first contacts with EJB in 1998. He is now a developer with the Orion Application Server team (`http://www.orionserver.com`). He is also taking part in the development of the J2EE 1.3 specification as well as the JSP 1.2 and Servlet 2.3 specifications as a member of expert groups for these standards.

Thank you Anna-My for always supporting me!

Richard Browett

Richard Browett is currently European Technical Director for Persistence Software Inc., technically based in London but more frequently to be found on the way to, or from, an airport somewhere in the world.

Richard has spent the last 25 years working on computer systems of one form or another and over the last five of those years has been getting his kicks designing, building and trouble shooting large-scale, high-performance, distributed systems.

Dedicated to my beautiful, loving wife Lynn, who has the patience of a saint - your love and support keep me sane.

Jason Diamond

Jason Diamond loves you.

John Griffin

John Griffin is a software consultant specializing in large-scale distributed application architecture and development. In 1997, John founded Aries Software Technologies, Inc., an IT consulting company providing software solutions and testing services to the financial and healthcare industries. John has designed, built and deployed n-tier applications using CORBA and/or Java for many Fortune 500 companies, spanning platforms from handhelds to mainframes.

For my parents Theresa and John and my brother Daniel. Thank you so much for your love, support and guidance.

Mac Holden

Mac Holden has over 15 years experience in the Information Technology Industry. For the last 10 years he has been running his own software house based in South East Asia. The company initially concentrated on development and implementation of Client Server systems and then moved increasingly into web-based applications written in Java. He first became interested in Java in its alpha days as a means of connecting remote locations such as mines and oil rigs to their head offices. Mac is also the chief designer and developer of a pure Java application development tool called JdJ Servlet Builder which creates database aware servlets from HTML forms.

Andrew Hoskinson

Andy Hoskinson is a senior technical director for US Interactive, a leading Internet professional services firm. He develops enterprise-class, n-tier Internet and wireless applications using a variety of different technologies, including J2EE. Prior to joining US Interactive, he was an Internet architect at Plural, Inc., and was also a part-time Java instructor in the George Washington University Center for Career Education Information Technology program. Andy is a Sun Certified Java Programmer, and a frequent contributor to various technical publications. He lives in Arlington, Virginia with his wife Angie. Andy can be reached at andy@hoskinson.net.

Rod Johnson

Rod Johnson is an enterprise Java architect specializing in scalable web applications. He is currently designing a J2EE solution for FT.com, Europe's largest business portal.

After an arts degree majoring in music and computer science, Rod completed a Ph.D. in musicology before returning to software development.

Rod has worked with Java on both client and server since its release, and has concentrated on Internet development since 1996. His main interests are J2EE architecture, EJB, and OO web development.

Rod divides his time between London and Sydney, and enjoys tennis, skiing and playing the piano. He can be reached at rod.johnson@bigfoot.com.

Thanks to Kerry for her love and encouragement.

Tracie Karsjens

Tracie Karsjens is a consultant with Javelin Solutions, a Minneapolis-based consulting firm. She has been working with Java since 1996, and her experience covers every tier of enterprise Java applications. She is a strong advocate for extreme programming practices such as refactoring and unit testing for improving code. She is a Sun Java-certified programmer and architect.
When not working, Tracie spends time at home with her husband Timothy and their two cats. She wishes to thank her husband for his support and understanding while she was working on this book. She also wishes to thank her parents for their longstanding support and encouragement.

Larry Kim

Larry Kim is the Product Manager for the JRun Server at the Allaire Corporation. He has an undergraduate degree in Electrical Engineering from the University of Waterloo, and is pursuing graduate studies in distributed computing.

Dedicated to Clement Wong, Dan Smith, Tom & Paul Reilly, Edwin Smith, Spike Washburn, and Scott Stirling.

Andrew Longshaw

Andy Longshaw is a Principal Technologist with Content Master Ltd. In this role he is responsible for the creation of various types of technical content such as training courses and whitepapers. Andy has designed, created and delivered technical training and consultancy on many aspects of Java, XML, component systems and e-commerce. Andy also gives conference sessions on Java, XML and middle-tier component architectures. There is an unconfirmed rumor that some people stay awake during these sessions. He can be contacted as andyl@contentmaster.com or andy@longshaw.demon.co.uk.

To Sarah, Adam and Joshua who inspire everything that I do, and to my parents who ensured that I was educated enough to write this.

Tom Myers

Tom taught computer science at the University of Delaware and at Colgate before becoming a full-time programmer (while occasionally teaching a course or two at Colgate). He is the author of Equations, Models and Programs: A Mathematical Introduction to Computer Science (Prentice Hall 1988) and several theoretical articles.

Alexander Nakhimovsky

Alexander Nakhimovsky has been a member of Colgate's Computer Science department in 1985. He is the author of several Russian language textbooks, a book and numerous articles on linguistics, and several articles on computational linguistics, in addition to ventures into other fields in frequent collaboration with Alice Nakhimovsky.

Daniel O'Connor

Daniel O'Connor is an independent software developer currently working on management applications using Enterprise JavaBeans technology. He is a member of the board of directors for jBoss, an open-source application server featuring an EJB container. Prior experience includes assisting in the development of Friedman Corporation's application server for its ERP product, and working on CAD/CAM software for Cutting Edge, Inc. (now a division of GGT).

I would like to dedicate my efforts in this book to my mother and father, who have given me so much.

Sameer Tyagi

Sameer writes regularly for online and print publications. He has over four years of experience in software design and development and specializes in server side Java based distributed applications. (N-tier architectures, JDBC, JNDI, EJB, JMS, RMI, JSP, Servlets *et al.*) He has a Bachelors in Electronic Engineering and numerous other certifications.

He is a Java addict who gets his fix by jumping head on into almost anything that compiles into bytecodes and is known to blame that newly discovered area of the brain called the Javasphere for such stimuli.

When he's not going through another latte flavor, he can be found flying around at 15000 ft in a small Cessna.

Geert Van Damme

Geert Van Damme lives in Leuven (Belgium) with his wife Sofie and his little son Jules. He studied Mathematical Psychology and Philosophy but ended up working in the IT business after a short while. In 1997 he started his own development and consulting company Darling, currently focusing on server side Java. Since then he works as an independant consultant on a number of projects, mainly from his home office. Geert can be reached at geert.vandamme@darling.be.

You can leave your name on my Graffiti wall at http://www.gojasper.be/wall.jsp

Gordon van Huizen

Gordon Van Huizen has designed and developed solutions for Website generation, distributed electronic forms systems, network-based object licensing and real-time data merging and imaging. As Director of Product Management for Progress Software, he has been responsible for systems engineering of Progress' JMS-based messaging server, Progress SonicMQ, and is currently responsible for the company's product strategies for the application of messaging technology. Gordon has the tremendous fortune of performing this work from his home in Berkeley, California, which he shares with his wife Diana Gaston and a troublesome feline named Zoë.

My chapter is dedicated to Diana, as well as to my mother, and the memory of my father. They have all helped shape the way I view the workings of this world, and they each continue to inspire me forward.

Mark Wilcox

Mark is the Web Administrator for the University of North Texas. He's also a frequent author and speaker on a variety of Internet topics. You can reach him at mark@mjwilcox.com.

To my lovely wife, Jessica. Thanks to our parents for bringing us up right.

Stefan Zeiger

Stefan Zeiger has been working as a freelance Java programmer since 1997 and studying computer science at the Technical University of Darmstadt since 1996. He is the author of the *NetForge* web server software and the popular online servlet tutorial *Servlet Essentials*.

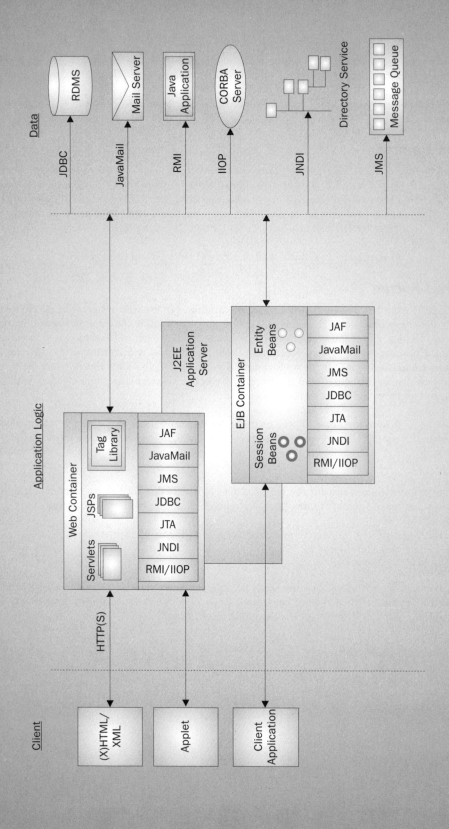

Table of Contents

Table of Contents

Table of Contents

Table of Contents

Table of Contents

Table of Contents

Table of Contents

Table of Contents

Table of Contents

Table of Contents

Table of Contents

Table of Contents

Table of Contents

Table of Contents

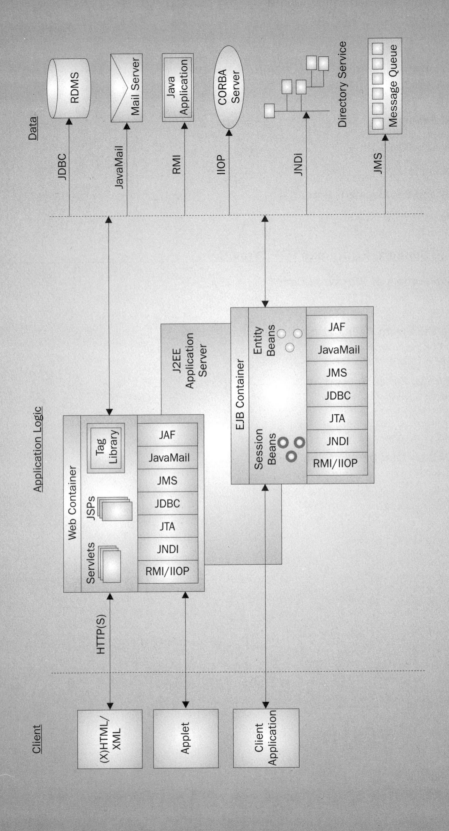

Introduction

Welcome to the second edition of *Professional Java Server Programming – the J2EE Edition*. For those of you who have read the first edition of the book, you'll see that quite a lot had changed; and it's only been a year since the first edition was published!

The J2EE Edition

Since the release of the first edition in the fall of '99, probably the single most significant change in the Java server-side landscape has been the release of the **Java 2 Platform, Enterprise Edition (J2EE)**. Although we covered many of the elements of J2EE in the first edition of the book, many things have changed.

J2EE represents a serious attempt by Sun to make Java, not just a viable language, but more importantly a viable *platform* for enterprise development. As you will see over the course of this book, J2EE is not simply a collection of APIs, but also defines a runtime architecture to develop to. The beauty of this architecture for enterprise Java developers is that one of its primary goals is to make the developer's life easier by encapsulating a lot of the fundamental yet messy, low-level semantics, of enterprise development such as connection pooling and even transactions, into a **container-based architecture**. All you have to do is get on with writing your business logic.

Take a look at the following diagram summarizing the whole enterprise as seen by J2EE – this diagram will appear between every chapter so you'll always know where you are:

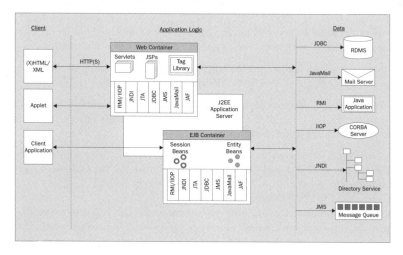

So rather than a simple update of the first edition, we have completely evolved the content to reflect the changing state of server-side Java development.

Who is this Book For?

This book is aimed at professional Java programmers who, although they may not have much practical experience of, are at least familiar with the fundamental concepts of network and web programming. It also assumes familiarity with the Java language and the core APIs – through reading Ivor Horton's Beginning Java 2, or some other tutorial book that covers similar ground. However, all concepts that relate to server-side Java programming will be covered assuming no prior knowledge.

Having said that, some familiarity with the basic server-side Java technologies is recommended as this book covers a large area of ground very quickly and does not claim to be exhaustive in all areas.

What's Covered in this Book

In this book, we discuss three things:

❑ The rules in the technology's specifications that developers must follow to write enterprise components

❑ The benefits and limits of the typical real-world vendor implementations of the J2EE specification

❑ The resulting practical aspects of real-word design using the J2EE technologies

The book has the following basic structure:

❑ We'll start with a look at the latest demands placed on a Java enterprise developer and how Jave (more particularly J2EE) rises to meet these challenges. You'll also get your first real taste of the J2EE container architecture.

❑ After we're up to speed on the J2EE architecture we'll start by looking at some of the fundamental technologies in enterprise development: RMI, JDBC, JNDI, and XML.

❑ Then we'll get back into J2EE more explicitly by looking at how to develop web components using Java servlets.

❑ Once we understand the servlet technology we'll look at how JavaServer Pages takes it and extends to provide a more felxible means of creating dynamic web content.

❑ We'll then take a step further back into the enterprise by looking at the sophisticated component technology of Enterprise JavaBeans.

❑ Once we've finished our tour through the three component technologies in J2EE, we'll spend some time looking at some of the issues of developing for the enterpise domain, such as security, performance and scalability.

❑ Finally, we'll look at how we can integrate our Java applications with other non-Java tecnologies such as COM and CORBA and how to use the Java Message Service for message-based integration.

There are also several appendicies containing additional useful information regarding configuring and installing some of the software you'll need, as well as topics such as internationalization.

What You Need to Use this Book

Most of the code in this book was tested with the Java 2 Platform, Standard Edition SDK (JDK 1.3) and the Java 2 Platform, Enterprise Edition SDK 1.2.1 Reference Implementation. However, for many of the chapters, either the reference implementation is not sufficient or you need some additional software:

Web Container

In order to run the web components used in this book you will need a web container that supports the servlet 2.2 and the JSP 1.1 specifications. We used:

❑ J2EE RI which includes Tomcat 3.0, we used Tomcat 3.1 for some additional features that the 3.0 version does not support, http://www.apache.org/

❑ Allaire's JRun 3.0, http://commerce.allaire.com/download/

See Appendix A for installation and configuration instructions.

EJB Container

For the EJB chapters you will also need an EJB container supporting version 1.1 of the EJB specification. We used:

❑ jBoss 2.0 Application Server, http://www.jboss.org

❑ Orion Application Server, http://www.orionserver.com

There is also one chapter on the EJB 2.0 specifiction. However, this specification is only at the public draft stage so is not widely implemented. A few of the application server vendor's, such as BEA, have implemented a beta patch for their app server that supports the current public draft but please note that things are likely to change before the specification is finalized.

Databases

Several of the chapters also require access to a database. For these chapters we used a mixture of:

❑ Cloudscape (an in-process version comes with the J2EE RI), http://www.cloudscape.com

❑ Microsoft Access 2000

❑ Microsoft SQL Server 7.0

❑ HypersonicSQL, http://hsql.oron.ch/

Additional Software

Finally, there are a few additional pieces of software that a couple of chapters also require:

❑ Sun's JNDI SDK, which is included with JDK 1.3

❑ XML parser and XSLT engine – xp and xt from James Clark, http://www.jclark.com/xml

❑ The Java API for XML Parsing (JAXP), http://java.sun.com/xml/

❑ IBM Parser for XML and the Lotus XSL processor, http://alphaworks.ibm.com

❑ Xalan XSLT Processor and Xerces XML Parser, `http://xml.apache.org`

❑ Java Secure Sockets Extension (JSSE), 1.0.1, `http://java.sun.com/products/jsse/`

❑ Allaire Tag Library, `http://commerce.allaire.com/download/`

❑ LDAP server – Netscape's iPlanet Directory Server version 4.11, `http://www.iplanet.com`

❑ Messaging server – SonicMQ, `http://www.sonicmq.com`

❑ Unit testing framework – JUnit, `http://www.junit.org`

❑ SMTP and/or POP3 service

The code in the book will work on a single machine, provided it is networked (that is, it can see `http://localhost` through the local browser).

The complete source code from the book is available for download from:

`http://www.wrox.com`

Conventions

To help you get the most from the text and keep track of what's happening, we've used a number of conventions throughout the book.

For instance:

> **These boxes hold important, not-to-be forgotten information that is directly relevant to the surrounding text.**

While the background style is used for asides to the current discussion.

As for styles in the text:

❑ When we introduce them, we **highlight** important words.

❑ We show keyboard strokes like this: *Ctrl-A*.

❑ We show filenames and code within the text like so: doGet()

❑ Text on user interfaces and URLs are shown as: Menu.

We present code in three different ways. Definitions of methods and properties are shown as follows:

```
protected void doGet(HttpServletRequest req, HttpServletResponse resp)
                throws ServletException, IOException
```

Example code is shown:

```
In our code examples, the code foreground style shows new, important,
    pertinent code
while code background shows code that's less important in the present context,
    or has been seen before.
```

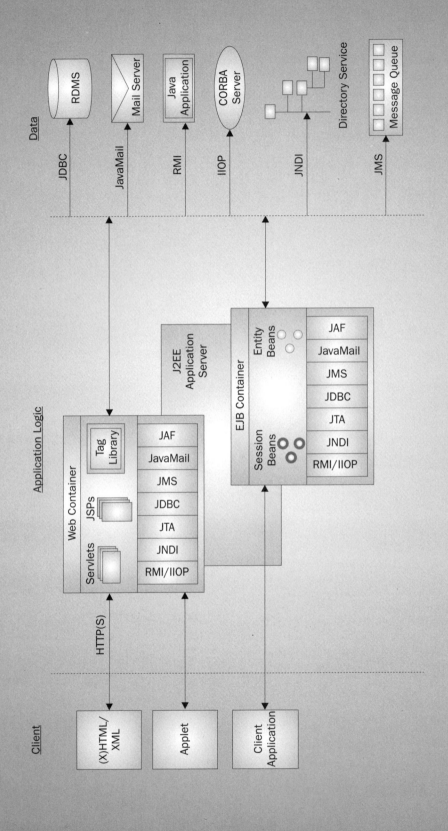

Java and the J2EE Platform

Java, as a programming language is still young. However, the evolution of Java from a means of developing applets for running in browsers, to a programming model capable of driving today's enterprise applications has been remarkable. Java has been around for only five years, yet it has attracted a very high level of interest in the technical and business communities, fuelling a considerable range of applications.

From its inception, Java has triggered new programming models and technologies in different domains – ranging from devices, to telephony applications, to the enterprise. At the same time, Java has acted as a catalyst in making certain technology domains take more robust and secure shapes. Java's enterprise computing platform, a.k.a. the **Java 2 Platform, Enterprise Edition (J2EE)** is one such domain.

There were times in the history of Java, when debates on whether Java is a programming language or a platform used to surface in the media as well as technical circles. However, J2EE is one of the most successful attempts by Sun and its associates at making Java credible as a *platform* for enterprise computing.

But what's J2EE? Why is it relevant? Why should you choose this technology for building enterprise-level applications – from client-server to Internet to mobile? This chapter gives one perspective, and assists you in answering these questions. We hope that the rest of this book will help you to successfully build and manage such applications.

In this introductory chapter, we'll focus on:

❑   The J2EE technical architecture

❑   What makes J2EE credible as a platform

❑   What are the challenges it addresses

❑   What technologies constitute the J2EE platform

First however, let us start with the challenges of developing applications for the enterprise today.

The Enterprise Today

With the advent of the Internet, many businesses realized that a whole new market had opened up to be exploited, however, we doubt if many had realized what a radical effect it would have on the economy. Through the Internet and the recent growth of e-commerce, an organization's information assets have now become more valuable. This shift to an information economy is forcing many businesses to rethink even their most basic business practices. In order to maintain a competitive edge, the adoption of new technologies has become a key factor in a company's ability to best exploit its information assets. More importantly, adapting these new technologies to work in tandem with the existing, legacy systems has become one of the foremost requirements of the enterprise.

One place these shifts in business practices have been felt most keenly is at the application development level. The funding and the time allocated to application development has been shrinking, while demands for complexity have increased. Although the emphasis on information is a small hurdle for developers, the whole revolution is being driven by the rapidly changing technological and economic landscape, which has created some new challenges for today's enterprise application developers:

❑   **Responsiveness**
Although timeliness has always been important, the high-paced, fast-changing information-driven economy means that responding quickly to new directions and information is critical in establishing and maintaining a competitive edge.

❑   **Programming Productivity**
Direct adoption of new technologies is insufficient unless they are properly utilized to their full potential and appropriately integrated with other relevant technologies. Thus, the ability to develop and then deploy applications as effectively and as quickly as possible is also important. Achieving this can be complicated by the sheer variety of technologies and standards that have been developed over the years, requiring highly developed skill sets, the acquiring of which and keeping up with which is a problem in itself. Moreover, the rapid pace of change in 'standards' themselves poses significant challenges to ensuring efficient meshing of technologies.

❑   **Reliability and Availability**
In today's internet economy downtime can be fatal to the success of a business. The ability to get your web-based operations up and running, and to keep them running, is critical to success. As if that wasn't enough, you must also be able to guarantee the reliability of your business transactions so that they will be processed completely and accurately.

❑   **Security**
The Internet has not only exponentially increased the number of potential users but also the value of a company's information, thus the security of that information has become of prime concern. What's more as technologies become more advanced, applications more sophisticated, and enterprises more complex, the ability to implement an effective security model become increasingly difficult.

❏ **Scalability**
The ability for the application to grow to meet new demand both in its operation and user base is important when an application's potential user base may be millions of individual users through the Internet. To scale effectively requires not only the ability to handle a large increase in the number of clients but also effective use of system resources.

❏ **Integration**
Although information has grown to be a key business asset, much of this information exists as data in old and outdated information systems. In order to maximize the usefulness of this information, applications need to be able to integrate with the existing information system – not necessarily an easy task as current technologies have often advanced far ahead of some of these legacy systems. The ability to combine old and new technologies is key to the success of developing for today's enterprises.

None of these problem domains is especially new to the enterprise developer! But solving these problems in a comprehensive and economical manner is still crucial. You may be aware that there have been several technologies to address one or more of the above demands. However, what has been missing is a comprehensive platform with a rich infrastructure and numerous architectural possibilities that also promotes a rapid development environment.

System Architecture

When discussing enterprise application development, it is appropriate to introduce the concept of **n-tier architecture**. Typical client/server systems are based on the 2-tiered architecture, whereby there is a clear separation between the data and the presentation/business logic. These are generally data driven, with the application existing entirely on the client machine while the database server is deployed somewhere in the organization. While this approach allows us to share data across the enterprise, it does have many drawbacks.

2-Tier Architecture

In a traditional 2-tiered application, the processing load is given to the client PC while the server simply acts as a traffic controller between the application and the data. As a result, not only does the application performance suffer due to the limited resources of the PC, but the network traffic tends to increase as well. When the entire application is processed on a PC, the application is forced to make multiple requests for data before even presenting anything to the user. These multiple database requests can heavily tax the network.

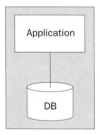

Another problem with a 2-tiered approach is that of maintenance. Even the smallest of changes to an application might involve a complete rollout to the entire user base. Even if it's possible to automate the process, you are still faced with updating every single client installation. What's more, some users may not be ready for a full rollout and ignore the changes while another group insists on making the changes immediately. This can result in different client installation using different versions of the application.

3-Tier Architecture

To address these issues, the software community developed the notion of a 3-tier architecture. An application is broken up into three separate logical layers, each with a well-defined set of interfaces. The first tier is referred to as the **presentation layer** and typically consists of a graphical user interface of some kind. The middle tier, or **business layer**, consists of the application or business logic and the third tier – the **data layer** – contains the data that is needed for the application.

The middle tier (application logic) is basically the code that the user calls upon (through the presentation layer) to retrieve the desired data. The presentation layer then receives the data and formats it for display. This separation of application logic from the user interface adds enormous flexibility to the design of the application. Multiple user interfaces can be built and deployed without ever changing the application logic, provided the application logic presents a clearly defined interface to the presentation layer.

The third tier contains the data that is needed for the application. This data can consist of any source of information, including an enterprise database such as Oracle or Sybase, a set of XML documents (data that has been stored in documents conforming to the XML specification), or even a directory service like an LDAP server. In addition to the traditional relational database storage mechanism, there are many different sources of enterprise data that your applications can access.

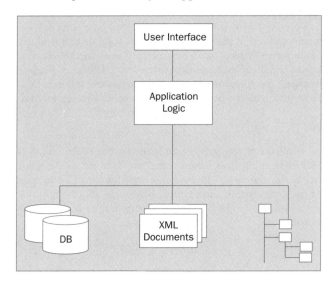

However, we're not quite finished with our subdivision of the application. We can take the segregation one final step to create an n-tier architecture.

n-Tier Architecture

As the title suggests, there is no hard and fast way to define the application layers for an n-tier system. In fact, an n-tier system can support a number of different configurations. In an n-tier architecture the application logic is divided by function rather than physically.

n-tier architecture then breaks down like this:

❏ A **user interface** that handles the user's interaction with the application; this can be a web browser running through a firewall, a heavier desktop application or even a wireless device

❏ **Presentation logic** that defines what the user interface displays and how a user's requests are handled – depending on what user interfaces are supported you may need to have slightly different versions of the presentation logic to handle the client appropriately

❏ **Business logic** that models the application's business rules, often through the interaction with the application's data

❏ **Infrastructure services** that provide additional functionality required by the application components, such as messaging, transactional support, etc.

❏ The **data layer** where the enterprise's data resides

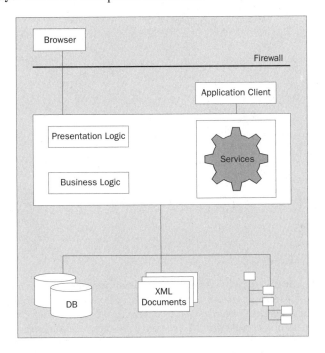

Applications based on this architecture are employing the **Model-View-Controller (MVC)** pattern. What this ultimately means is that the data (the model) is separated from how the information is presented (the view). In between this is the application/business logic (the controller) that controls the flow of the information. Therefore, an application is designed based on these three functional components (model, view, and controller) interacting with each other.

Enterprise Architecture

So far we have really been concentrating on a single application's architecture, however, we are in danger of considering these applications as "stovepipes". In other words, we might end up with many different applications – possibly even with different architectures – all of which don't communicate with one another. In an enterprise, we are looking to create a more cohesive whole.

Rather than a change in architecture – enterprise architecture is basically just n-tier – we need a change in perception. To turn an n-tier system into an enterprise system, we simply extend the middle tier by allowing for multiple **application objects** rather than just a single application. These application objects must each have an interface that allows it to work together with the others.

An interface can be thought of as a contract. Each object states through its interface that it will accept certain parameters and return a specific set of results. Application objects communicate with each other using their interfaces:

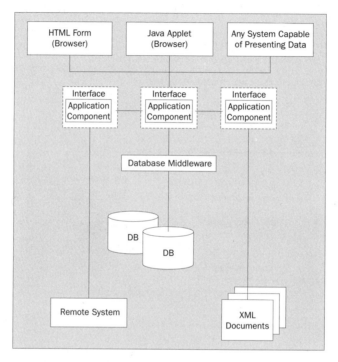

With enterprise architecture, we can have multiple applications using a common set of components across an organization. This promotes the standardization of business practices by creating a single set of business functions for the entire organization to access. If a business rule changes, then changes have to be made to the business object only and, if necessary, its interface and subsequently any object that accesses the interface.

It is important to note that when designing an object and its interface, it is a good idea to make the interface as generic as possible to avoid changes later on. Since other objects communicate with the interface and not the object itself, changes to the object, and not the interface, are relatively simple and quick.

Is Java the Answer?

So far we have discussed system architecture from an implementation agnostic perspective and there exist many potential paths that you can take to actually implement your enterprise. Microsoft has Windows DNA (and the new .net architecture), Sun has J2EE, Oracle has the Oracle 8i Internet Platform, and so on. With so many choices for server-side development, you are probably wondering what makes Java such a great choice.

Platform Independence

With a enterprise's information spread disparately across many different platforms and applications it is important to leverage a programming language that can work equally well throughout the enterprise without having to resort to awkward, inefficient translation mechanisms. A unifying programming model also reduces the difficulties encountered from integrating many of the different technologies that grow up specific to certain platforms and applications.

Reusability

Code reuse is the holy grail of all programming. Segregating an application's business requirements into component parts is one way to achieve reuse; using object-orientation to encapsulate shared functionality is another. Java uses both. Java is an object-oriented language and, as such, provides mechanisms for reuse. However, unlike objects, components require a more complex infrastructure for their construction and management. Basic object-oriented concepts do not provide such a framework; however, the Enterprise Edition of Java provides a significantly stringent architecture for the reuse of components.

Modularity

When developing a complete server-side application, your programs can get large and complex in a hurry. It is always best to break down an application into discreet modules that are each responsible for a specific task. When you do this, it makes your application much easier to maintain and understand. Java servlets, JavaServer Pages, and Enterprise JavaBeans provide ways to modularize your application – breaking your application down into tiers and into tasks.

Despite the above features in its favor, it was not until early 2000 that Java developed a unifying programming model for applications on the enterprise scale – not that it lacked the capabilities but rather it was disorganized. Sun recognized this shortcoming and released the **Java 2 Platform, Enterprise Edition (J2EE)**.

> **The idea behind the J2EE platform is to provide a simple, unified standard for distributed applications through a component-based application model.**

We will spend the rest of the chapter, and indeed the rest of the book, looking at what J2EE brings to server-side development with Java.

Java, to thousands of developers, represents an extraordinary technology that provides tremendous potential in virtually every aspect of development. With this new technology come the inevitable quirks born of experience. It would be disingenuous of any technical author to aver that Java is a flawless technology, or that it assumes a de-facto presence as the technology of choice for any application. The developer, whether long-experienced in Java or a newcomer to its simplest advantages, must be well aware of the caveats carried with it. Java, as a language, is maturing. The ancillary technologies in many cases, are often still very much "green" with youth. Specifications change rapidly, evolving to solve earlier weaknesses while often introducing (or exposing) others. Is this to diminish Java? Certainly not. Rather, it is to celebrate Java's success and the demands placed upon it; and to warn the reader that Java solutions provide great opportunity, but not without risk. Implementation of immature elements of technology carries with it obvious risks, but with great potential rewards.

The J2EE Platform

As you'll see in the rest of this book, J2EE is one of the best solutions that we've had so far for meeting the demands of today's enterprise. J2EE specifies both the infrastructure for managing your applications, and the service APIs for building them.

The J2EE platform is essentially a distributed application server environment – a Java environment that provides the following:

❑   A runtime infrastructure for hosting applications

❑   A set of Java extension APIs to build applications

The applications that you can develop with the above may be programs to drive web pages, or components to implement complex database transactions, or even Java applets – all distributed across the network.

The J2EE Runtime

While J2EE bundles together APIs that have been in existence in one form or the other for quite some time, the most significant aspect of J2EE is its abstraction of the **runtime infrastructure**. Note that the J2EE specification does not specify how a J2EE runtime should/could be built. Instead, the J2EE specifies roles and interfaces for applications, and the runtime onto which applications could be deployed. This results in a clear demarcation between applications and the runtime infrastructure. This demarcation allows the runtime to abstract most of the infrastructure services that enterprise developers have traditionally attempted to build on their own. As a result, J2EE application developers could just focus on the application logic and related services, while leveraging the runtime for all infrastructure related services.

It is interesting to note that application development in a fast-paced environment, such as the Internet, typically leads to designs that are short-lived. Design decisions made for short-lived applications reflect this in their lack of reference to the long-term.

On the other hand, when you consider long-term design aspects, you may find it difficult to trade off short-term demands. There are technologies that lend themselves to rapid development, and then there are technologies that let you build applications taking care of such long-term concerns as reusability, cost of maintenance, etc. Often the two do not mix; however J2EE is flexible enough to allow you to build applications that include both. This is because it lets you build each layer of your application loosely coupled to all other layers. Each layer can therefore evolve to meet respective evolutionary needs.

Apart from specifying a set of standard APIs, the J2EE architecture also provides a uniform means of accessing these services via its runtime environment. Before we see details of J2EE's approach, let's take a look at traditional distributed computing.

Until the advent of J2EE, distributed computing was, in general, considered as client-server programming. You wrote a server application implementing an interface, a client application to connect to the server, and then start both the server and the client! Although this process seems so simple, in practice there are several critical hurdles in this process, depending on the technology you're using.

For instance, consider a CORBA object request broker for building distributed applications. The typical procedure for building the server-side CORBA objects would start from specifying an interface (using the Interface Definition Language, or IDL) for each object. Subsequent steps include compiling this IDL to generate stubs and skeletons for the language of your choice, implementing the object based on the skeleton, then writing the client application, preparing your environment, etc. Here the stub is the class that represents the CORBA object on the client side. The skeleton is where the server-side logic is implemented. This procedure in itself is not complicated and could fairly be automated.

Now consider that your servers as well as clients require access to services such as distributed transactions, messaging, etc. To utilize such services, you'll be required to add a significant amount of plumbing code to your applications. More often than not, you'll be required to set up and configure different middleware solutions, and make API calls to the vendor-specific APIs to access the services. Apart from services such as relational database access, most of these services are either proprietary or non-standard. The result is that your applications will be more complex, time consuming and expensive to develop, manage, and maintain.

Apart from having to manage all these different APIs, there is another critical demand on server-side applications. On the serverside, resources are scarce. For example, you cannot afford to create the same number of objects that you can typically afford to create in client-side applications. Other server-side resources that require special attention include threads, database connections, security, transactions, etc. Custom-building an infrastructure that deals with these resources has always been a challenge. This task is almost impossible in the Internet economy. Would you care to build a connection pool, or an object cache, or an "elegant" object layer for database access, when your development lifecycle is only three months?

Since these server-side requirements are common across a wide variety of applications, it is more appropriate to consider a platform that has built-in solutions. This lets you separate these infrastructure-level concerns from the more direct concern of translating your application requirements to software that works. The J2EE runtime addresses such concerns. You leave it to the J2EE server vendor to implement these features for you in a standards compliant manner.

As mentioned above, the J2EE does not specify the nature and structure of the runtime. Instead, it introduces what is called a **container**, and via the J2EE APIs, specifies a contract between containers and applications. You'll see more details of this contract at appropriate places later in this book.

Before looking into more details of J2EE containers, let's have a brief look at the J2EE APIs.

The J2EE APIs

Distributed applications require access to a set of enterprise services. Typical services include transaction processing, database access, messaging, etc. The J2EE architecture unifies access to such services in its enterprise service APIs. However, instead of having to access these services through proprietary or non-standard interfaces, in J2EE application programs can access these APIs via the container.

A typical commercial J2EE platform (or J2EE application server) includes one or more containers, and access to the enterprise APIs specified by the J2EE.

Note that J2EE application servers need not implement these services; containers are only required to provide access to each service implementation via a J2EE API. For example, a J2EE implementation might delegate the Java Messaging Server API calls to a commercial message oriented middleware solution. Yet another implementation might include a message oriented middleware solution within a container.

The specification of the J2EE platform defines a set of Java standard extensions that each J2EE platform must support:

❑ **Java DataBase Connectivity (JDBC) 2.0 Extension:** Also called the **JDBC 2.0 Optional Package**. This API improves the standard JDBC 2.0 API by adding better means of obtaining connections, connection pooling, distributed transactions, etc.

❑ **Remote Method Invocation over the Internet Inter-ORB Protocol (RMI-IIOP) 1.0:** Provides an implementation of the usual Java RMI API over IIOP. This bridges the gap between RMI and CORBA applications.

❑ **Enterprise Java Beans (EJB) 1.1:** Specifies a component framework for multi-tier distributed applications. This provides a standard means of defining server-side components, and specifies a rich runtime infrastructure for hosting components on the server side.

❑ **Java Servlets 2.2:** The Java Servlet API provides object-oriented abstractions for building dynamic web applications.

❑ **JavaServer Pages (JSP) 1.1:** This extension further enhances J2EE web applications by providing for template-driven web application development.

❑ **Java Message Service (JMS) 1.0:** JMS provides a Java API for message queuing, and publish and subscribe types of message-oriented middleware services.

❑ **Java Naming and Directory Interface (JNDI) 1.2:** The JNDI API standardizes access to different types of naming and directory services available today. This API is designed to be independent of any specific naming or directory service implementation. J2EE also specifies a JNDI service provider interface (SPI), for naming and directory service providers to implement.

❑ **Java Transaction API 1.0:** This API is for implementing distributed transactional applications.

❑ **JavaMail 1.1:** This API provides a platform-independent and protocol-independent framework to build Java-based mail applications.

We will take a more detailed look at these APIs later in the chapter.

All the above APIs are specifications, independent of implementation. That is, one should be able to access services provided by these APIs in a standard way, irrespective of how they are implemented.

J2EE Architecture – Containers

As discussed in the previous section, a typical commercial J2EE platform includes one or more containers. But what's a container? A J2EE container is a runtime to manage application components, and to provide access to the J2EE APIs. Beyond the identity associated with the runtime, J2EE does not specify any identity for containers. This gives a great amount of flexibility to achieve a variety of features within the container runtime.

The following figure shows the architecture of J2EE:

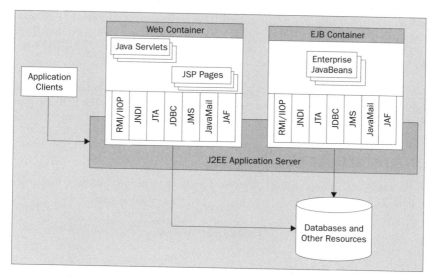

This architecture shows two containers:

❑   A **web container** for hosting Java servlets and JSP pages

❑   An **EJB container** for hosting Enterprise JavaBean components

Apart from these two, the J2EE also specifies two more containers – an applet container to run applets, and an application client container for running standard Java application clients. In this book, our focus is limited to web and EJB containers only.

In the above figure, the vertical blocks at the bottom of each container represent the J2EE APIs. Apart from access to these infrastructure-level APIs, each container also implements the respective container-specific API (Java Servlet API for the web container, and the EJB API for the EJB container).

The stacks of rectangles (servlets, JSP pages, and EJBs) in this figure are the programs that you develop and host in these containers. In the J2EE parlance, these programs are called **application components**.

> So we can also say that a container is a Java 1.2 (Java 2 Standard Edition 1.2) runtime for application components.

In this architecture, there are primarily two types of clients:

❑ **Web clients** normally run in web browsers. For these clients, the user interface is generated on the serverside as HTML or XML, and is downloaded and then rendered by the browsers. These clients use HTTP to communicate with web containers. Application components in web containers include Java servlets and JSP pages. These components implement the functionality required for web clients. Web containers are responsible for accepting requests from web clients, and generating responses with the help of the application components.

❑ **EJB clients** are applications that access EJB components in EJB containers. There are two possible types of EJB clients. The first category is application clients. Application clients are stand-alone applications accessing the EJB components using the RMI-IIOP protocol. The second category of application clients are components in the web container. That is, Java servlets and JSP pages can also access the EJB components via the RMI-IIOP protocol in the same way as the application clients.

In either case, clients access application components via the respective container. Web clients access JSP pages and Java servlets via the web container, and EJB clients access the EJB components via the EJB container.

Container Architecture

Having seen the core constituents of J2EE, let's now go back to our architecture discussions and see the architecture of a J2EE container:

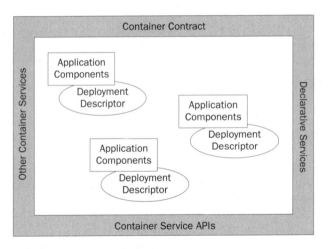

In this architecture, as a developer, you are required to provide the following:

❑ **Application components**:
As discussed in the previous section, application components include servlets, JSPs, EJBs, etc. In J2EE, application components can be packaged into archive files.

❑ **Deployment descriptors:**
A deployment descriptor is an XML file that describes the application components. It also includes additional information required by containers for effectively managing application components.

The rest of this figure forms the container. The architecture of a container can be divided into four parts:

- **Component contract:**
  A set of APIs specified by the container that your application components are required to extend or implement.

- **Container service APIs:**
  Additional services provided by the container, which are commonly required for all applications in the container.

- **Declarative services:**
  Services that the container interposes on your applications, based on the deployment description provided for each application component.

- **Other container services:**
  Other run time services, related to component lifecycle, resource pooling, garbage collection, etc.

Let's now discuss each of the above in detail.

Component Contracts

As we mentioned earlier, the basic purpose of the container in the J2EE architecture is to provide a runtime for application components. That is, instances of the application components are created and invoked within the JVM of the container. This makes the container responsible for managing the lifecycle of application components. However, for the application components to be manageable within the container runtime, the application components are required to abide by certain **contracts** specified by the container.

To better understand this aspect, consider a Java applet. Typically, a Java applet is downloaded by the browser and instantiated and initialized in the JVM of the browser. That is, the applet lives in the runtime provided by the JVM of the browser.

However, in order for the container to be able to create, initialize, and invoke methods on application components, the application components are required to implement or extend certain Java interfaces or classes. For example, considering the applet example again, a Java applet is required to extend the `java.applet.Applet` class specified by the JDK. The JVM of the browser expects your applets to extend this class. This enables the browser's JVM to call `init()`, `start()` `stop()`, and `destroy()` methods on your applets. These methods control the lifecycle of an applet – without your applet extending the `java.applet.Applet` class, the browser JVM has no means on calling these methods to control the lifecycle of your applet.

In J2EE, all application components are instantiated and initialized in the JVM of the container. In addition, since J2EE application components are always remote to the client, clients cannot directly call methods on these components. Since the container process is the only entry point into the application components, all application components are required to follow the contract specified by the container. In J2EE, the contract is in the form of interfaces and classes that your classes implement or extend, with additional rules that the component definition should follow.

Let's look at the various contracts specified by the J2EE:

In the case of web containers, web application components are required to follow the Java Servlet and JSP APIs. In this model, all Java servlets are required to extend the `javax.servlet.http.HttpServlet` class, and implement certain methods of this class such as `doGet()`, `doPost()`, etc. Similarly, when compiled, classes corresponding to JSP pages extend the `javax.servlet.jsp.HttpJspPage` class.

In the case of EJB containers, all enterprise beans are required to have `javax.ejb.EJBHome` and `javax.ejb.EJBObject` interfaces specified, while implementing either a `javax.ejb.SessionBean` or `javax.ejb.EntityBean` interface. As you'll see in Chapter 18, the component specifications and implementations are also required to follow certain rules. Apart from the interfaces, all such rules form part of the component contract for EJB components.

Container Service APIs

As discussed earlier, the J2EE platform defines a set of Java standard extensions that each J2EE platform must support. J2EE containers provide a service-level abstraction of the APIs. As a result, you can access the service APIs such as JDBC, JTS, JNDI, JMS, etc. within the container, as though the underlying container were implementing them.

> **A container in the J2EE architecture provides a federated view of various enterprise APIs specified in the J2EE platform.**

In J2EE, application components can access these APIs via appropriate objects created and published in a JNDI service or implementation. For example, when you want to use JMS within your application components, you configure your J2EE platform to create JMS connection factories, message queues and topics and publish these objects in the JNDI service. Your applications can then look in the JNDI, obtain references to these objects, and invoke methods. In this process, it does not matter if your J2EE platform has a JMS implementation built-in or it is using a third-party messaging middleware solution.

Let's consider Java applets again. For example, if you want to play an audio file from an applet, you call the `play()` method defined in the superclass, `java.applet.Applet`, with a URL pointing to the audio file. In this case, the functionality for playing audio files is implemented by the superclass. This is one of the approaches for code reuse. A better alternative to this approach is to delegate this functionality to a common component. Such a component need not be a part of the same inheritance hierarchy. All that is required is a reference to an object implementing this functionality. Once your application is able to get a reference to such an object, you can delegate the "play" functionality to that object. A significant advantage of this approach is that it allows other objects from more than one inheritance hierarchy to access the "play" functionality.

In the case of distributed applications this gets complicated, as the services are remote. Just as an analogy, consider the same audio component running as a separate server! How do you get hold of a reference to such a component? The solution is to let the J2EE platform create the audio component, and publish its name in a naming service (JNDI) available to your application. This provides a simplified method of access to the service APIs. This also allows you to plug in different implementations of these services without disturbing the applications using the services.

All the J2EE service APIs use the above approach for providing services to the applications.

The following are the key implications of this approach:

❑ As a single standard that can sit on top of a variety of existing database systems, transaction processing systems, naming and directory services, etc. the service APIs eliminate the inherent heterogeneity involved in bringing these technologies together in your applications.

❑ In J2EE, these services are also integrated tightly with the programming model. In later chapters, you'll see how to access these APIs seamlessly from your application components and clients.

❑ The J2EE platform also specifies a uniform mechanism for accessing these services.

Declarative Services

One of the important features of the J2EE architecture is its ability to dynamically interpose services for application components. This is based on declarations specified outside your application components. The J2EE architecture provides a simple means of specifying such declarations. These are called **deployment descriptors**.

> **A deployment descriptor defines the contract between the container and component. You are required to specify a deployment descriptor for each group of application components.**

For example, a set of EJB components can be described together in a single deployment descriptor file. Similarly, in the case of web containers, each web application is required to have a deployment descriptor specified.

Depending on the type of the component, certain types of services (such as transactions, security, etc.) can be specified in the deployment descriptor. The purpose of this approach is to minimize the application programming required in order to make use of such services.

The standard method of invoking J2EE services is via **explicit invocation**. For example, to implement transactions for database access, you can programmatically start a transaction before accessing the database, and commit or rollback the transaction once the business methods are completed. In the case of **declarative invocation**, your application components need not explicitly start and stop transactions. Instead, you can specify in the deployment descriptor that your business methods should be invoked within a new transaction. Based on this information, the container can automatically start a transaction whenever the business methods in your applications are invoked.

> **In simple terms, a declarative service is a service or action that is performed by the container on your behalf.**

How does this approach work? J2EE containers are by nature distributed and the application components are remote to clients. Accordingly, requests to application components and responses back from application components occur across process and network boundaries.

In addition, since application components are maintained in the container runtime, the container process is responsible for receiving the requests, and delegating the incoming requests to appropriate application components. For instance, in the case of the EJB container, the container receives all client requests, and delegates them to appropriate EJB objects deployed on the container. Similarly, in the case of web containers, the web container receives HTTP requests, and delegates them to servlets and JSP pages. The following diagram depicts a simplified view of this invocation. In this figure, the remote interface is what the clients use to communicate with the EJB on the container. Note that the container process handles all requests and responses to and from the application components:

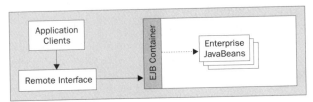

This approach gives the container an ability to **interpose** a new service before transferring a request to the application component. In the case of declarative transactions, the container can start the transaction before delegating the incoming request to your business method implication, and end the transaction as soon as your method returns.

What's the advantage of this approach? You can interpose new services without changing the application component. That is, this facility allows you to postpone decisions about such services to the runtime, instead of the design time. In other words, the container can selectively enhance your components based on the deployment descriptor.

For EJB containers, the declarative services include transactions and security. Both these can be specified in deployment descriptors. In the case of web containers, you can specify the required security roles for accessing components within web applications.

Other Container Services

The following are some of the runtime services that containers provide:

- **Lifecycle management of application components:**
  This involves creating new instances of application components and pooling or destroying them when the instances are no longer required.

- **Resource pooling:**
  Containers can optionally implement resource pooling such as object pooling and connection pooling.

- **Population of the JNDI name space based on the deployment names associated with EJB components:**
  This information is typically supplied at deployment time. We'll discuss more about deployment in the next section.

- **Population of the JNDI name space with objects necessary for utilizing container service APIs:**
  Some of the objects include data source objects for database access, queue and topic connection factories for obtaining connections to JMS, and user transaction objects for programmatically controlling transactions.

❑ **Clustering:**
In J2EE, containers can be distributable. A distributable container consists of a number of JVMs running on one or more host machines. In this setup, application components can be deployed on a number of JVMs. Subject to the type of load-balancing strategy and the type of the component, the container can distribute the load of incoming requests to one of these JVMs. Clustering is essential for enhancing the scalability and availability of applications.

Now that we have covered the architecture of J2EE applications, let's take a closer look at some of the various technologies included in the J2EE platform.

J2EE Technologies

Having discussed all the architecture of the J2EE platform, we now want to cover the collection of technologies that provide the mechanics we need to build large, distributed enterprise applications. This large collection, of quite disparate technologies, can be divided according to use:

❑ **The component technologies:**
These technologies are used to hold the most important part of the application – the business logic. There are three types of components, JSP, servlets, and Enterprise JavaBeans; we will look at each of these in a moment.

❑ **The service technologies:**
These technologies provide the application's components with supported services to function efficiently.

❑ **The communication technologies:**
These technologies, which are mostly transparent to the application programmer, provide the mechanisms for communication among different parts of the application, whether they are local or remote.

Let's now examine how the J2EE APIs and associated technologies can be categorized.

Component Technologies

With any application, the most important element is modeling the necessary business logic through the use of components – application level reusable units. Earlier in the chapter, we described a container as hosting the runtime for application components, so although the container may be able to supply many of the services and much of the communication infrastructure, it is ultimately the responsibility of the developer to create the application components. However, these components will be dependent upon their container for many services, such as life-cycle management, threading, security, etc. This allows you to concentrate on providing the requisite business functionality without getting into details of low-level container-level semantics.

The J2EE platform provides three technologies for developing components.

> One thing that should be made clear is that the J2EE platform does not specify that an application need make use of all three types of component technologies – in many cases using Enterprise JavaBeans may well be overkill.

Web Components

These can be categorized as any component that responds to an HTTP request. A further distinction that can be drawn is based on the hosting container for the application components. As we saw earlier in the chapter, the two basic server-side containers are the web container and the EJB container.

Servlets

Servlets are server-side programs that allow application logic to be embedded in HTTP request-response process. Servlets provide a means to extend the functionality of the web server to enable dynamic content in HTML, XML, or other web languages. With the release of J2EE, the Servlets specification reached version 2.2.

We'll be working with servlets in Chapters 7 to 10.

JavaServer Pages

JavaServer Pages (JSP) provides a way to embed components in a page, and to have them do their work to generate the page that is eventually sent to the client. A JavaServer Page can contain HTML, Java code, and JavaBean components. JavaServer Pages are in fact an extension of the servlet programming model – when a user requests a JSP page, the web server compiles the JSP page into a servlet. The web server then invokes the servlet and returns the resulting content to the web browser. Once the servlet has been compiled from the JSP page, the web server can simply return the servlet without having to recompile each time. Thus, JavaServer Pages provides a powerful and dynamic page assembly mechanism that benefits from the many advantages of the Java platform.

Compared to servlets, which are pure Java code, JavaServer Pages are merely text-based documents until the web server compiles them into the corresponding servlets – this allows a clearer separation of application logic from presentation logic; that allows application developers to concentrate on business matters and web designers to concentrate on presentation. With the release of J2EE, the JSP specification reached version 1.1. Chapters 11 through 14 discuss JSP in detail.

JSP also allows a further degree of modularization within your J2EE applications. JSP provides a standard, XML-based interface for defining your own custom tags and packaging them in a tag library.

A typical architecture for a web application may look like this:

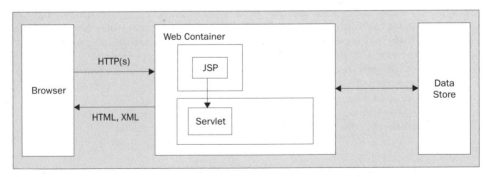

Enterprise JavaBean Components

The remaining component technology is **Enterprise JavaBeans (EJBs)**, at the time of writing in version 1.1, but version 2.0 is due soon. The EJB architecture is a distributed component model for developing secure, scalable, transactional, and multi-user components. To put it simply, they are reusable software units containing business logic. Just as JSPs allows the separation of application and presentation logic, EJBs allow separation of application logic from system-level services thus allowing the developer to concentrate on the business domain issues and not system programming. These enterprise bean business objects take two basic forms – again you are not required to implement both – session beans and entity beans. We'll see EJBs in action in Chapters 18 to 23.

Session Beans

Session beans themselves come in two types. A **stateful session bean** is a transient object used to represent a client's interaction with the system – it performs the client's requests in the application, accessing a database etc., and when the client's operations are complete it is destroyed (that is, it exists for the length of the client session) – one example of this is an online shopping cart. Alternatively, a **stateless session bean** maintains no state between client requests. Generally, this type of session bean is used to implement a specific service that does not require client state, for instance, a simple database update.

Entity Beans

An **entity bean** on the other hand is a persistent object that models the data held within the data store, that is, it is an object wrapper for the data. Compared to session beans that can be used by any client, entity beans can be accessed concurrently by many clients but must maintain a unique identity through a primary key. In fact under the J2EE container architecture you can elect whether to have the persistent state of the entity bean managed for you by the container or whether to implement this yourself in the bean itself.

Service Technologies

As we have discussed, some of the J2EE services for the application components are managed by the containers themselves, thus allowing the developer to concentrate on the business logic. However, there will be times when developers find it necessary to programmatically invoke some services themselves.

JDBC

Although all data access should be accessible through the single standard API of the Connector architecture in the future, database connectivity is probably one of the key services that developers implement in their application component.

The **Java Database Connectivity (JDBC)** API (J2EE adds an extension to the core JDBC API that comes with the Java 2 Standard Edition to add advanced features such as connection pooling and distributed transactions) provides the developer with the ability to connect to relational database systems. As we will see in Chapter 3, it allows the transactional querying, retrieval, and manipulation of data from a JDBC-compliant database.

Java Transaction API and Service

The **Java Transaction API (JTA)** is a means for working with transactions and especially distributed transactions independent of the transaction manger's implementation (the **Java Transaction Service**

(**JTS**)). Under the J2EE platform, distributed transactions are generally considered to be container controlled so you, as the developer, shouldn't have to be too concerned with transactions across your components – having said that, though, the J2EE transaction model is still somewhat limited, so at times it may be necessary to do the hard work yourself.

JNDI

The role of the **Java Naming and Directory Interface (JNDI)** API in the J2EE platform is two-fold:

❑ Firstly, it provides the means to perform standard operations to a directory service resource such as LDAP, Novell Directory Services, or Netscape Directory Services.

❑ Secondly, a J2EE application utilizes JNDI to look up interfaces used to create, amongst other things, EJBs, and JDBC connections.

In Chapter 4, we'll see how to use JNDI to access a directory service resource.

Communication Technologies

The final technology grouping is those technologies that provide the means for the various components and services within a J2EE application to communicate with each other – a distributed application would be pretty ineffectual if these technologies didn't provide the 'glue' to hold it all together.

Internet Protocols

As we are talking about n-tier applications in this book, our client will very often be a browser potentially situated anywhere in the world. A client's requests and the server's responses are communicated over three main protocols.

HTTP

HTTP or **Hypertext Transfer Protocol** is a generic, stateless, application-level protocol, which has many uses beyond simply hypertext capabilities. It works on a request/response basis – a client sends a request to the server in the form of a request method, URI (Uniform Resource Identifier) and protocol version, followed by a MIME-like message containing request modifiers, client information, and possible body content over a connection with a server. The server in turn responds with a status line followed by a MIME-like message containing server information, entity meta-information, and possible entity-body content.

TCP/IP

TCP (Transmission Control Protocol) over **IP (Internet Protocol)** are actually two separate protocols but are typically combined into a single entity. IP is the protocol that takes care of making sure that data is received by both endpoints in communication over the Internet. When you type the address of a web site into your browser, IP is what ensures your requests and the fulfillment of those requests make it to the proper destinations. For efficiency, the data being sent back and forth between a client and a web server is broken into several pieces, or packets. All of these packets do not have to take the same route when they are sent between the client and the web server. TCP is the protocol that keeps track of all these packets and makes sure they are assembled in the same order they were dispatched and are error free. Therefore, TCP and IP work together to move data around on the Internet. For this reason, you will almost always see these two protocols combined into TCP/IP.

SSL

Secure Socket Layer (SSL) uses cryptography to encrypt the flow of information between the client and server. This also provides a means for both parties to authenticate each other. Secure HTTP (HTTPS) is usually distinguished from regular unencrypted HTTP by being served on a different port number, 443, by default.

Remote Object Protocols

In applications where the components are often distributed across many tiers and servers, some mechanism for using the components remotely is required – preferably such that the client isn't aware that the component is not local to itself.

RMI and RMI-IIOP

Remote Method Invocation (RMI) is one of the primary mechanisms in distributed object applications. It allows you to use interfaces to define remote objects. You can then call methods on these remote objects as if they were local. The exact wire level transportation mechanism is implementation specific: Sun uses the Java Remote Method Protocol (JRMP) on top of TCP/IP but other implementations such as BEA WebLogic etc. have their own protocol.

RMI-IIOP is an extension of RMI but over IIOP (Inter-ORB Protocol), which allows you to define a remote interface to any remote object that can be implemented in any language that supports OMG mapping and ORB. In the next chapter, we'll take a more in-depth look at how to write distributed applications with RMI.

JavaIDL

Through the use of **JavaIDL**, a Java client can invoke method calls on CORBA objects. These CORBA objects need not be written in Java but merely implement an IDL-defined interface.

JMS

In the enterprise environment, the various distributed components may not always be in constant contact with each other. Therefore, there needs to be some mechanism for sending data asynchronously. The **Java Message Service (JMS)** provides just such functionality to send and receive messages through the use of message-oriented middleware (MOM).

JavaMail

An alternative asynchronous process to messaging is JavaMail. JavaMail also allows the sending and receiving of messages; however, it is more oriented towards the user rather than parts of an application. JavaMail supports the most widely used Internet mail protocols such as IMAP4, POP3, and SMTP but compared to JMS it is slower and less reliable.

XML

Although the XML parsing APIs such as JAXP are not currently included by the J2EE specification – future versions should include them, however – XML is widely used internally in J2EE. Moreover, XML is rapidly becoming a key technology in today's enterprises.

XML (Extensible Markup Language) influences how we view, process, transport, and manage data. The data description mechanisms in XML mean it is a great way to share information because:

❏ It is open; XML can be used to exchange data with other users and programs in a platform-independent manner.

❏ It is self-describing; this makes it an effective choice for business-to-business and extranet solutions.

❏ You can share data between programs without prior coordination.

As its name suggests, XML is extensible which has allowed the easy and rapid construction of custom tag-sets specific to corporations, scientific disciplines, and other such domains. One of the strengths of XML is the sharing of such "vocabularies", all of which use the same basic syntax, parsers, and other tools. Shared XML vocabularies provide more easily searchable documents and databases, and a way to exchange information between many different organizations and computer applications.

> *For example, IBM's Bean Markup Language (BML) is an XML-based component configuration markup language that is customized for the JavaBean component model. BML can be used to describe the creation of new JavaBeans, access and/or configure existing JavaBeans, bind events from one bean to another, and call arbitrary methods in other beans.*

XML plays a significant role in the construction of J2EE applications:

❏ As we have mentioned previously, the J2EE architecture provides the means for a container to provide services at runtime through a declarative mechanism defined in a deployment descriptor. This deployment descriptor file is an XML document.

❏ XML can also be used to integrate your J2EE application with legacy systems.

❏ You can return XML instead of HTML to display application data to the client.

XML can be far more than just a description mechanism though:

❏ **Transforming XML**
Transformations allow a programmer to map an XML document in one form into another form based on a set of rules. XML transformations are used to translate between similar XML vocabularies as well as translating XML documents into other text-based file formats like comma-delimited values.

❏ **XML and Databases**
Although the XML data model is inherently hierarchical whereas databases are essentially relational – creating some mapping difficulties – it does provide a mechanism of integrating existing data into new systems. Many database vendors are now adding native support for XML into their engines in recognition that programmers need ways to interface XML and databases.

❏ **Server-to-Server Communication**
Complex enterprise applications are often built on and utilize differing server software running on distributed computing technologies. XML provides a layer of abstraction in order to integrate these dissimilar systems – XML can be obtained from one server, manipulated, and then passed to another server in a way that it can understand the request.

We'll be looking at the role that XML can play in J2EE applications at various points throughout the book, starting with a much closer look at XML in Chapters 5 and 6.

Developing J2EE Applications

The J2EE specification specifies the following steps in the application development and deployment process:

1. **Application component development:**
During this step you model the business rules in the form of application components.

2. **Composition of application components into modules:**
In this step, the application components are packaged into modules. This phase also involves providing deployment descriptors for each module.

3. **Composition of modules into applications:**
This step integrates multiple modules into J2EE applications. This requires assembling one or more modules into a J2EE application, and supplying it with the descriptor files.

4. **Application deployment:**
In the final step the packaged application is actually deployed and installed on the J2EE platform application server(s).

The J2EE platform specifies multiple levels for packaging, customization, and installation. Packaging is the process of composing applications out of application components. J2EE specifies a three-level packaging scheme for composing components into applications. These are application components, modules, and applications.

What is the purpose of these stages for application development and deployment? In J2EE, application architecture starts with decomposing the application into modules, and modules into application components. This is a top-down process towards building fine-grained building blocks. Once the development of these building blocks is achieved, we need to construct higher-level constructs from these fine-grained blocks. The notion of application packaging and deployment in multiple levels attempts to achieve this. In this process, we compose fine-grained application components into modules, and then modules into applications.

J2EE Application Development and Deployment Roles

Before we look at the development and deployment process in a bit more detail, let's take a sidetrack for the moment to examine who should be doing what. The J2EE specification as well as defining a process also defines a number of roles in development of J2EE applications:

❑ **J2EE Product Provider:**
The J2EE Product provides the base J2EE platform upon which you develop your applications – this will be your relevant server vendor who implements the container architecture and the J2EE APIs defined by the J2EE specification.

❑ **Application Component Provider:**
Essentially the application developer who creates the application functionality, although it is possible to sub-divide the role into specific areas of expertise, such as web developer, EJB developer, etc.

❑ **Application Assembler:**
As we will see shortly, the application assembler takes the application components and packages them together through a series of modules and descriptor files so they can be deployed to the production servers.

❑ **Deployer:**
The deployer installs the packaged application, and configures it for the particular operating environment on which the application will be running.

❑ **System Administrator:**
Responsible for maintaining and administering the application once it has been deployed.

❑ **Tool Provider:**
Provides tools that are of use in the development and deployment of application components.

Obviously, the definition of the above roles will not divide neatly among individuals and should only be considered a typical setup to provide some guidance.

Application Component Development

In J2EE, the development process starts with designing and developing application components. We'll be spending most of the book looking at this so there's no need to go any further here.

Composition of Application Components into Modules

A module is used to package one or more related application components of the same type. Apart from the application components, each module also includes a deployment descriptor describing the structure of the module. There are three types of modules in J2EE:

❑ **Web Modules:**
A web module is a deployable unit consisting of Java Servlets, JSP pages, JSP tag libraries, library JAR files, HTML/XML documents, and other public resources such as images, applet class files, etc. A web module is packaged into a **Web Archive file**, also called a **WAR** file. A WAR file is similar to a JAR file, except that a WAR file contains a WEB-INF directory with the deployment description contained in a web.xml file. We'll see more details of web modules and their packaging in later chapters.

❑ **EJB Modules:**
An EJB module is a deployable unit consisting of EJBs, and associated library JAR files, and resources etc. EJB modules are packaged into JAR files, with a deployment descriptor (ejb-jar.xml) in the META-INF directory of the JAR file.

❑ **Java Modules:**
A Java module is a group of Java client classes packaged into JAR files. The deployment descriptor for a Java module is an application-client.xml file.

Composition of Modules into Applications

The highest level of packaging is in the form of applications. A J2EE application consists of one or more modules composed into an **Enterprise Archive (EAR) file**. An EAR file is similar to a JAR file, except that it contains an application.xml file (located in the META-INF directory) describing the application:

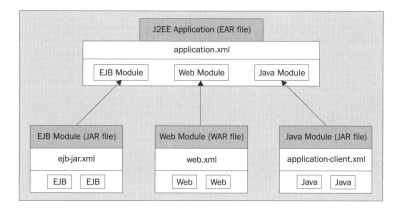

What is the role of multiple descriptor files in the above? Fine-grained application components can be customized while integrating them into modules. This necessitates a deployment descriptor in a module. However, not all information related to final deployment onto a J2EE platform will/may be available at the time of assembling modules. In addition, we need a means of specifying which modules make up the application. The `application.xml` file lets you achieve this.

The advantage of this structure is that it allows reuse at different levels. Application components can be reused across multiple web modules. For example, web components related to user login can be packaged to different web modules responsible for online ordering, customer service, etc. Similarly, modules can be reused across multiple applications. An EJB module for shopping cart management need not be restricted to a single application, but can be packaged into multiple online commerce applications.

> *Note that without such a reusable means of packaging, the goal of component reuse will only be partially met! By defining the above structure, the J2EE allows more refined reuse of application components.*

Application Deployment

Finally, application deployment is the process of installing and customizing packaged modules onto a J2EE platform. This process involves two steps:

❑ To prepare the application for installing on to a J2EE application server. This involves copying the EAR files onto the application server, generating additional implementation classes with the help of the container, and finally installing the application onto the server.

❑ To configure the application with application server specific information. An example is creating data sources and connection factories, as the actual creation of these objects is application server specific.

Summary

You should now have a better idea of the topology of the J2EE landscape. In particular, we have seen how J2EE extends the traditional multi-tier architecture of distributed computing to include the concept of containers. We discussed the constituents of this container architecture, with relation to:

❏ The component contract

❏ Container services

❏ Declarative services

❏ Other runtime facilities

The following are the key points of this discussion:

❏ J2EE is a container centric architecture. A container is more than a simple runtime. It provides several levels of abstractions. In later chapters, you will see how these abstractions simplify application development.

❏ J2EE recognizes the need for composing components into modules, and modules into applications. This is an attempt to standardize reuse of application components and modules.

❏ J2EE represents a very intuitive approach to building applications. The deployment process is the reverse of a typical top-down design process.

Having finished our introductory look at the J2EE perspective of server-side Java programming, we will start our more detailed journey with a closer look at writing distributed Java applications with RMI.

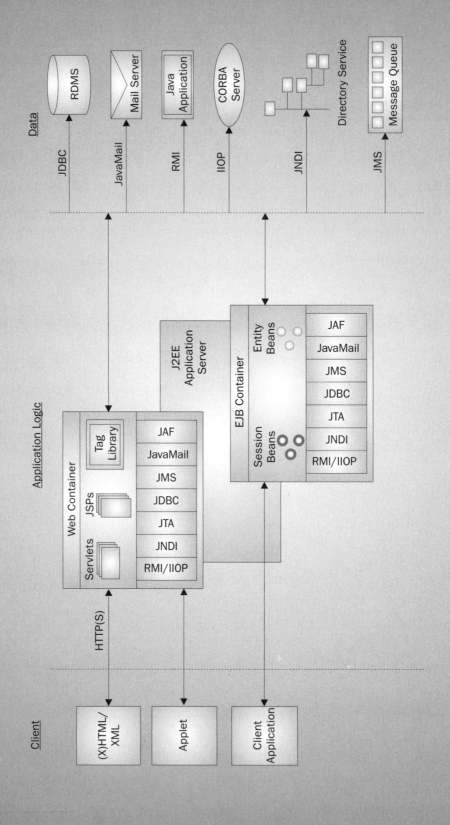

2

Distributed Computing Using RMI

Distributed computing has become a common term in today's programming vocabulary. It refers to the application design paradigm in which the programs, the data they process, and the actual computations are spread over a network, either to leverage the processing power of multiple computers or due to the inherent nature of the application, for example, an application comprised of smaller applications spread across different locations.

Remote Method Invocation (RMI) allows object-to-object communication between different Java Virtual Machines (JVM). JVMs can be located on the same or separate computers – yet one JVM can invoke methods belonging to an object stored in another JVM. This enables applications to call object methods located remotely, sharing resources and processing load across systems. Methods can even pass objects that a foreign virtual machine has never encountered before, allowing the dynamic loading of new classes as required.

In this chapter we will look at:

❑   How the RMI architecture allows us to use objects transparently of their location

❑   How to develop applications that use RMI

❑   How to dynamically and lazily load objects

❑   Encrypting the communication across SSL

❑   Extending RMI over IIOP

However, before we look at the RMI architecture we should very quickly look at some alternatives to RMI for remote method invocation.

RMI Alternatives

If you want two Java applications executing within different virtual machines to communicate with each other there are a couple of other Java-based approaches that can be taken besides RMI:

❑   Sockets

❑   Java Messaging Service (JMS)

Basic network programming with sockets is flexible and sufficient for communication between programs. However, it requires all the involved parties to communicate via application-level protocols, designing for which is involved and can be error-prone. For example, consider a collaborative application, any application, even a simple chat: for multiple clients to participate you would first need to design some sort of protocol then use sockets to communicate in that protocol with the server.

Having said that keep in mind that RMI is a distributed system that internally uses sockets over TCP/IP.

The difference between RMI and JMS is that in RMI the objects stay resident and are bound to the virtual machines (although method arguments and returns as well as stubs travel across the network) whereas in JMS the messages (objects) *physically* travel asynchronously across the network from one JVM to another.

We'll be looking at JMS in detail in Chapter 28.

The RMI Architecture

Before we look at how the RMI mechanism works, we should define some terms that we will be coming across often. As per the RMI specifications:

> **To quote the specifications "...In the Java distributed object model, a remote object is one whose methods can be invoked from another Java virtual machine, potentially on a different host. An object of this type is described by one or more remote interfaces, which are Java interfaces that declare the methods of the remote object. Remote method invocation (RMI) is the action of invoking a method of a remote interface on a remote object...".**

RMI's purpose is to make objects in separate JVMs look and act like local objects. The JVM that calls the remote object is usually referred to as a client and the JVM that contains the remote object, a server. One of the most important aspects of the RMI design is its intended *transparency*. Applications do not know whether an object is remote or local. A method invocation on a remote object has the same syntax as a method invocation on a local object, though under the hood there is a lot more going on than meets the eye.

> **It is important to note that in RMI the term "server" does not refer to a physical server or application but to a single remote object having methods that can be remotely invoked. Similarly, the term "client" does not refer to a client machine but actually refers to the object invoking a remote method on a remote object. Thus, the same object can be both a client and a server.**

Although obtaining a reference to a remote object is somewhat different from doing so for local objects, once you have the reference, you use the remote object as if it were local. The RMI infrastructure will automatically intercept the method call, find the remote object, and process the request remotely. This location transparency even includes garbage collection.

> **A remote object is always accessed via its remote interface, in other words the client invokes methods on the object only after casting the reference to the remote interface.**

The RMI implementation is essentially built from three abstraction layers:

❑ **The Stubs/Skeletons Layer**
This layer intercepts method calls made by the client to the interface reference and redirects these calls to a remote object.

❑ **The Remote Reference Layer**
This layer handles the details relating to interpreting and managing references made by clients to the remote objects. It connects clients to remote objects that are running and exported on a server by a one-to-one connection link. In the Java 2 SDK, this layer was enhanced to support the activation framework, which is discussed later.

❑ **The Transport Layer**
This layer is based on TCP/IP connections between machines in a network. It provides basic connectivity, as well as some firewall penetration strategies.

The diagram below shows these three layers, along with the breakup of the transport layer. The descriptions on the side represent the OSI layers (OSI is concisely described at `http://www.webopedia.com/TERM/O/OSI.html`):

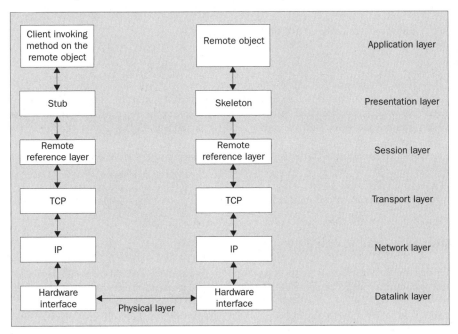

This layered architecture provides implementation flexibility without affecting the application architecture. Each of the layers can be enhanced or replaced without affecting the rest of the system. For example, the transport layer implementation can be changed by a vendor to UDP (User Datagram Protocol) instead of TCP without affecting the upper layers.

The Stub and Skeleton Layer

To achieve location transparency, RMI introduces two special kinds of objects known as **stubs** and **skeletons** that serve as an interface between an application and the rest of the RMI system and performs the marshalling and unmarshalling of the data. This layer's purpose is to transfer data to the Remote Reference Layer via marshalling and unmarshalling. Marshalling refers to the process of converting the data or object being transferred into a byte stream, and un-marshalling the reverse: converting the stream into an object or data. This conversion is achieved via **object serialization**.

The stub and skeleton layer of RMI lies just below the actual application and is based on the Proxy design pattern. In the RMI use of the Proxy pattern, the stub class plays the role of the proxy for the remote service implementation. The skeleton is a helper class that is generated by RMI to help the object communicate with the stub across the RMI link. The skeleton carries on a conversation with the stub; it reads the parameters for the method call from the link, makes the call to the remote service implementation object, accepts the return value, and then writes the return value back to the stub.

In short, the Proxy pattern forces method calls to occur through a proxy that acts as a surrogate, delegating all calls to the actual object in a manner transparent to the original caller.

> *Details about the Proxy design pattern are beyond the scope of this book and can be found in Design Patterns, Elements of Reusable Object-Oriented Software Erich Gamma et al ISBN: 0-201-63361-2 or Patterns in Java: a Catalog of Reusable Design Patterns ISBN: 0471333158.*

Let us look at stubs and skeletons in a little more in detail.

Stubs

The stub is a client-side object that represents (or acts as a proxy for) the remote object. The stub has the same interface, or list of methods, as the remote object, but when the client calls a stub method, the stub forwards the request via the RMI infrastructure to the remote object, which actually executes it. The following lists the sequence of tasks performed by the stub in detail:

- ❑ Initiates a connection with the remote VM containing the remote object
- ❑ Marshals (writes and transmits) the parameters to the remote VM
- ❑ Waits for the result of the method invocation
- ❑ Unmarshals (reads) the return value or exception returned
- ❑ Returns the value to the caller

The stub hides the serialization of method parameters (parameters should be serializable) and the network-level communication in order to present a simple invocation mechanism to the caller.

In the remote VM, each remote object may have a corresponding skeleton (in JDK 1.2-only environments, skeletons are not required).

Skeletons

On the server side, the skeleton object takes care of all of the details of "remoteness" so that the actual remote object doesn't need to worry about them. In other words, you can pretty much code a remote object the same way as if it were local – the skeleton insulates the remote object from the RMI infrastructure. During remote method requests, the RMI infrastructure automatically invokes the skeleton object so it can do its magic. The following lists the sequence of the skeleton's tasks in detail:

❑ Unmarshals (reads) the parameters for the remote method (remember these were marshaled by the stub on the client side)

❑ Invokes the method on the actual remote object implementation

❑ Marshals (writes and transmits) the result (return value or exception) to the caller (which is then marshaled by the stub)

The JDK contains the `rmic` *tool that creates the class files for the stubs and skeletons.*
Details about `rmic` *can be found packaged with the JDK or online at:*
`java.sun.com/j2se/1.3/docs/tooldocs/tools.html`

The Remote Reference Layer

The Remote Reference layer defines and supports the invocation semantics of the RMI connection. This layer provides a **JRMP (Java Remote Method Protocol)** specific `java.rmi.server.RemoteRef` object that represents a handle to the remote object. A `RemoteStub` uses a remote reference to carry out a remote method invocation to a remote object.

In JDK 1.1.x the stub objects use a series of methods in this `RemoteRef` *class,* `newCall()`,
`invoke()`, *and* `done()` *in that order to forward the method calls to the server. In JDK1.2 stubs no longer use these methods but use a single method,* `invoke(Remote, Method, Object[], long)` *on the remote reference to carry out parameter marshalling, remote method execution and un-marshalling of the return value.*

The Java 2 SDK implementation of RMI adds a new semantic for the client-server connection: **activatable remote objects** (as we shall see later). Other types of connection semantics are possible. For example, with multicast, a single proxy could send a method request to multiple implementations simultaneously and accept the first reply (this improves response time and possibly improves availability). In the future, Sun is expected to add additional invocation semantics to RMI.

The Transport Layer

The Transport layer makes the stream-based network connections over TCP/IP between the JVMs, and is responsible for setting and managing those connections. Even if two JVMs are running on the same physical computer, they connect through their host computer's TCP/IP network protocol stack. RMI uses a wire-level protocol called Java Remote Method Protocol (JRMP) on top of TCP/IP (an analogy is HTTP over TCP/IP).

JRMP is specified at:
`java.sun.com/products/jdk/1.2/docs/guide/rmi/spec/rmi-`
`protocol.doc.html.`

It is important to note that JRMP is specific to the Sun "implementation". Alternate implementations, such as BEA Weblogic, NinjaRMI, ObjectSpace's Voyager, etc. do not use JRMP, but instead use their own wire-level protocol. Sun and IBM have jointly developed the next version of RMI, called RMI-IIOP, which is available with Java 2 SDK Version 1.3 (or separately). Instead of using JRMP, RMI-IIOP uses the Object Management Group (OMG) Internet Inter-ORB Protocol, IIOP, to communicate between clients and servers.

In JDK 1.2 the JRMP protocol was modified to eliminate the need for skeletons and instead use reflection to make the connection to the remote service object. You only have to generate skeleton classes in JDK 1.1.x compatible system implementations. To generate stubs for the JDK 1.2 stub-only protocol use the `-v1.2` option with `rmic`.

For a detailed description of how JRMP was modified to remove skeletons see the `CallData`, `Operation`, and `Hash` descriptions in the JRMP specification.

The RMI Transport layer is designed to make a connection between clients and server, even in the face of networking obstacles. While the Transport layer prefers to use multiple TCP/IP connections, some network configurations only allow a single TCP/IP connection between a client and server (for example, some browsers restrict applets to a single network connection back to their hosting server). In this case, the Transport layer multiplexes multiple virtual connections within a single TCP/IP connection.

The Transport layer in the current RMI implementation is TCP-based, but again a UDP-based transport layer could be substituted in a different implementation.

Locating Remote Objects

We haven't answered one crucial question until now. How does a client find the object? Clients find remote services by using a naming or directory service. This may seem like circular logic. How can a client find the naming service? Simple, a naming or directory service is run on a host and port number that the client is already aware of (a well known port on a public host). RMI can transparently look up these different directory services, with the **Java Naming and Directory Interface (JNDI)** – which we'll cover in Chapter 4.

The RMI naming service, a **registry**, is a remote object that serves as a directory service for clients by keeping a hashtable-like mapping of names to other remote objects. It is not necessary to have a single registry on a particular physical host. An object is free to start its own registry. The behavior of the registry is defined by the interface `java.rmi.registry.Registry`. RMI itself includes a simple implementation of this interface called the RMI Registry, (the `rmiregistry` tool with the JDK can also be started programmatically). The RMI Registry runs on each machine that "hosts" remote objects and accepts queries for services, by default on port 1099.

In simple words, a remote object is associated with a name in this registry. Anytime the client wants to invoke methods on this remote object, it obtains a reference to it by looking up the name. The lookup returns a remote reference, a stub, to the object. RMI also provides another class, the `java.rmi.Naming` class that serves as the client's interaction point with the object serving as the registry on the host for this lookup:

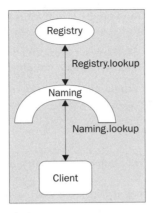

> Don't confuse the `java.rmi.Naming` with the JNDI context. Although they provide
> the same services the `Naming` class specifically locates objects in the RMI registry.
> Sun provides a JNDI provider for RMI that allows clients to lookup RMI objects using
> a JNDI context. The JNDI-based RMI registry can be downloaded from
> `http://java.sun.com/products/jndi`

The `Naming` class's methods take, as one of their arguments, a name that is URL formatted
`java.lang.String`, of the form:

`public static void bind (String name, Remote obj)`	Binds the remote object to a string name. The name itself is in the RMI URL format described below.
`public static String[] list (String name)`	Returns an array of the names bound in the registry.
`public static Remote lookup (String name)`	Returns a reference, a stub, for the remote object associated with the specified name.
`public static void rebind (String name, Remote obj)`	Rebinds the specified name if it is already in use to a new remote object. This could be dangerous if different applications use the same name in the registry but is helpful in development.
`public static void unbind (String name)`	Removes the binding with specified name.

The methods in the `Naming` class and `Registry` interface have identical signature and throw a variety
of exceptions (see next section on exceptions). Here is what happens when a client invokes a lookup for
a particular URL in the `Naming` class:

❑ A socket connection is opened to the host on the specified port (using a client socket factory if
   necessary, see the later section in this chapter for Socket Factories).

❑ Since the registry implementation on the host itself is a remote object, a stub to that remote registry is returned from the host. The stub acts as the client proxy for the registry.

❑ Subsequently the `Registry.lookup()` is performed on this stub and returns another stub, for the remote object that was registered with it on the server.

❑ Once the client has the stub to the requested object, it interacts directly with the object on the port to which it was exported.

The URL takes the form:

```
rmi://<host_name>[:<name_service_port>]/<service_name>
```

❑ The `host_name` is a name recognized on the local area network (LAN) or a DNS name on the Internet

❑ The `name_service_port` needs to be specified only if the naming service is running on a port other than the default 1099

❑ The `service_name` is the string name that the remote object is associated with in the registry

To facilitate this on the host machine, a server program exposes the remote object service by:

❑ Creating a local object

❑ Exporting that object to create a listening service, that waits for clients to connect and request the service

❑ Registering the object in the RMI Registry under a public name

The code below summarizes these steps:

```
// Create the object. Exporting happens in the constructor.
   HelloServer obj = new HelloServer();

// Bind the object to a name in the registry that has been started beforehand.
   Naming.rebind("/HelloServer", obj);
```

Similar to the `Naming` class there is another class, the `java.rmi.registry.LocateRegistry`, that has various methods for directly getting a reference to the registry and for starting the registry. To reiterate, starting the registry (either by the tool or programmatically) is nothing but exporting the remote object that implements the `Registry` interface.

> The method **LocateRegistry.getRegistry(String host)** does not contact the registry on the host, but rather just looks up the host to make sure it exists. So, even though this method succeeded, this does not necessarily mean that a registry is running on the specified host. It just returns a stub that can then access the registry.

The JDK has a tool called `rmiregistry` that starts the registry on the host with the following command:

```
rmiregistry -J-Djava.security.policy=<policy file>
```

or to start with default values:

```
start rmiregistry
```

Remember the registry is an object running in a JVM. The –J flag is used to pass parameters, such as the **policy file**, to the JVM.

> *You can also programmatically start the registry with the*
> `LocateRegistry.createRegistry(int port)` *method or the more detailed*
> `LocateRegistry.createRegistry(int port, RMIClientSocketFactory csf,`
> `RMIServerSocketFactory ssf)`. *Both these methods return the stub, implementing the*
> *interface* `java.rmi.registry.Registry`.

Policy Files

Code is granted permissions in what is called a policy file. If you look in the `%JAVA_HOME%/jre/lib/security` directory, you will find the default policy file for your JVM named `java.policy`. This file can be edited either manually or by using the policytool program found in the `%JAVA_HOME%/bin` directory.

RMI Exceptions

As mentioned earlier, RMI is a distributed system that uses sockets over TCP/IP. In such a networked environment, many things could go wrong. It is important that the client be able to recover when problems occur. For example, you don't want a client to indefinitely wait for an input on the socket if the network goes down, or the host cannot be reached.

So that the client is aware of such conditions, every remote method must throw the `java.rmi.RemoteException` (or one of its super classes such as `java.io.IOException` or `java.lang.Exception`). The `RemoteException` is a generic exception and there are specialized sub-classes that are thrown (and caught) for specific conditions. These are listed in the table below:

Exception Thrown	Description
AccessException	Thrown by certain methods of the `java.rmi.Naming` class (specifically `bind()`, `rebind()`, and `unbind()`) and methods of the `ActivationSystem` interface, which we shall encounter soon, to indicate that the caller does not have permission to perform the action requested by the method call.
AlreadyBoundException	Thrown if an attempt is made to bind an object in the registry to a name that already has an associated binding.
ConnectException	Thrown if a connection is refused to the remote host for a remote method call.

Table continued on following page

Exception Thrown	Description
ConnectIOException	Thrown if an IOException occurs while making a connection to the remote host for a remote method call.
MarshalException	Thrown if a java.io.IOException occurs while marshalling the remote call header, arguments, or return value for a remote method call.
NoSuchObjectException	Thrown if an attempt is made to invoke a method on an object that no longer exists in the remote virtual machine. If this exception is thrown then it means that the object was garbage-collected or unexported. A common occurrence is if the "only/all" clients repeatedly fail to renew their leases, and the leases expire, for example, if the network is clogged with traffic or goes down. Also keep in mind that the stub with the client is valid only as long as the RMI server is alive)
	If you don't want the remote objects to be garbage-collected then you should keep alive in the server JVM by storing a reference to the implementation object in a static variable. As a locally reachable object, it won't be garbage-collected even in the event of extended unreachability of clients.
NotBoundException	Thrown if an attempt is made to look up or unbind in the registry a name that has no associated binding.
RemoteException	A RemoteException is the common super class for a number of communication-related exceptions that may occur during the execution of a remote method call.
ServerError	Thrown as a result of a remote method call if the execution of the remote method on the server machine throws a java.lang.Error.
ServerException	Thrown as a result of a remote method call if the execution of the remote method on the server machine throws a RemoteException.
StubNotFoundException	Thrown if a valid stub class could not be found for a remote object when it is exported.
UnexpectedException	Thrown if the client of a remote method call receives, as a result of the call, a checked exception that is not among the checked exception types declared in the throws clause of the method in the remote interface.
UnknownHostException	Thrown if a java.net.UnknownHostException occurs while creating a connection to the remote host for a remote method call.
UnmarshalException	Can be thrown while unmarshalling the parameters or results of a remote method call if: ❑ An exception occurs while unmarshalling the call header ❑ If the protocol for the return value is invalid ❑ An IOException occurs while unmarshalling parameters (on the server side) or the return value (on the client side)

Developing Applications with RMI

Writing client-server applications using RMI involves six basic steps:

1. Defining a remote interface

2. Implementing the remote interface

3. Writing the client that uses the remote objects

4. Generating stubs (client proxies) and skeletons (server entities)

5. Starting the registry and registering the objects

6. Running the server and client

Let's look at each step by developing a simple application as an example to help us in understanding each step.

Defining the Remote Interface

An interface manifests the exposed operations and the client programmer need not be aware of the implementation (the interface in this case also serves as a marker to the JVM). A remote interface by definition is the set of methods that can be invoked remotely by a client:

❑ The remote interface must be declared public or the client will get an error when it tries to load a remote object that implements the remote interface, unless that client is in the same package as the remote interface

❑ The remote interface must extend the `java.rmi.Remote` interface

❑ Each method must throw a `java.rmi.RemoteException` (or a superclass of `RemoteException`)

❑ If the remote methods have any remote objects as parameters or return types, they must be interface types not the implementation classes

Note the `java.rmi.Remote` *interface has no methods. It's just used as a marker by the JVM, in a similar fashion to how the* `java.io.Serializable` *interface is used to mark objects as being serializable.*

For our example, we'll define our remote interface like this:

```
public interface HelloInterface extends java.rmi.Remote {

    // This method is called by remote clients and is implemented by the
    // remote object
    public String sayHello() throws java.rmi.RemoteException;
}
```

> **If your object implements other interfaces, keep them distinct from the remote interface. You can also minimize the number of objects registered in the registry with a factory design pattern or a single factory object.**

Implementing the Remote Interface

The implementation class is the actual class that provides the implementation for methods defined in the remote interface. The `java.rmi.server.RemoteObject` extends the functionality provided by the `java.lang.Object` class into the remote domain by overriding the `equals()`, `hashcode()` and `toString()` methods.

> *Remember the generic* `java.rmi.server.RemoteObject` *is an abstract class and describes the behavior for remote objects.*

The abstract subclass `java.rmi.server.RemoteServer` describes the behavior associated with the server implementation and provides the basic semantics to support remote reference semantics. (For example, create and export to a particular port etc.)

`java.rmi.server.RemoteServer` has two subclasses:

❑   `java.rmi.server.UnicastRemoteObject` class defines a non-replicated remote object whose references are valid only while the server process is alive.

❑   `java.rmi.activation.Activatable` is the concrete class that defines behavior for on demand instantiation of remote objects. (See the later section on Activation.)

The following diagram shows the two subclasses and their contained methods with relation to the `java.rmi.server.RemoteServer` class:

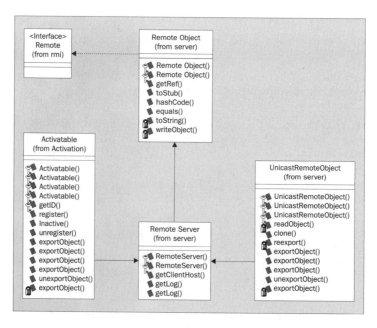

An object can exhibit remote behavior as a result of either of the following:

❑ The class extends `java.rmi.RemoteServer` or one of its subclasses (including other remote objects). The class must however invoke one of the superclass constructors so that it can be exported

❑ The class explicitly exports itself via by passing itself ("`this`") to different forms of the `UnicastRemoteObject.exportObject()` methods

The term "exporting" encapsulates the semantics that involve a remote object's ability to accept requests. This involves listening on a TCP (server) socket. It should be kept in mind that multiple objects can listen on the same port. See the section on Sockets for more information.

In addition to these, the class must implement one or more remote interfaces that define the remote methods.

> **A remote class can define any methods but only methods from the implemented class can be invoked remotely.**

The `HelloServer` remote object implementation class for our example:

```
import java.io.*;
import java.rmi.*;
import java.rmi.server.*;
import java.util.Date;

public class HelloServer extends UnicastRemoteObject implements HelloInterface
{
    public HelloServer() throws RemoteException {
        super();    // Call the superclass constructor to export this object
    }

    public String sayHello() throws RemoteException {
        return "Hello World, the current system time is " + new Date();
    }
}
```

Writing the Client That Uses the Remote Objects

The client performs a lookup on the registry on the host and obtains a reference to the remote object. Note that casting to the remote interface is critical. In RMI, clients always interact with the interface, never with the object implementation:

```
import java.rmi.*;

public class HelloClient {

    public static void main(String args[]) {
        if (System.getSecurityManager() == null)
            System.setSecurityManager(new RMISecurityManager());
```

```
        try {
            HelloInterface obj = (HelloInterface) Naming.lookup("/HelloServer");
            String message = obj.sayHello();
            System.out.println(message);
        } catch (Exception e) {
            System.out.println("HelloClient exception: " + e);
        }
    }
}
```

Generating Stubs and Skeletons

Now that we have the remote interface and the implementation, we can generate the stubs and skeletons (or only stubs in Java 2) with the `rmic` tool after we have compiled the classes:

```
rmic -v1.2 HelloServer
```

The –v1.2 flag suppresses skeleton generation.

Registering the Object

Now that we have the interface and the implementation, we need to make this object available to clients by binding it to a registry. This will allow clients to look up the object on the host by a String name. The stubs and skeletons (if any) are needed for registration. After all, it is the object stub that is going to be passed around from the registry to clients.

> It is often misunderstood that the object must be bound to a registry for it to be used. Not true. The object is available for use the moment it is successfully exported. It could behave as a client, invoke a method on another object, and pass itself to that object. See the section on callbacks later in this chapter.

The following code shows how to register the above object:

```
import java.rmi.*;

public class RegisterIt {

    public static void main(String args[]) {
        try {
            // Instantiate the object
            HelloServer obj = new HelloServer();
            System.out.println("Object instantiated: " + obj);
            Naming.rebind("/HelloServer", obj);
            System.out.println("HelloServer bound in registry");
        } catch (Exception e) {
            System.out.println(e);
        }
    }
}
```

There are two methods in the `java.rmi.Naming` class that can bind an object in the registry. The `bind()` method that binds an object to a string name and throws a `java.rmi.AlreadyBoundException` if the binding already exists. The `rebind()` method used above replaces any pre-existing binding with the new one.

The registry must be running for the object to bind. It can be started by the tool, or programmatically as explained before. We start the executable:

```
rmiregistry -J-Djava.security.policy=registerit.policy
```

The security policy is needed because of the Java 2 security model. The registry needs permissions to open sockets, which are restricted to standard extensions in the default policy file.

Our policy file for this example grants all permissions:

```
grant {
    // Allow everything for now
    permission java.security.AllPermission;
};
```

Of course, you wouldn't use this policy in a production environment.

> *By default there is a single system-wide policy file, and a single user policy file. The system policy file is by default located at:*
> *%JAVA_HOME%/lib/security/java.policy (Solaris)*
> *%JAVA_HOME%\lib\security\java.policy (Windows)*
> *The user policy file is by default located at:*
> *%USER_HOME%/.java.policy (Solaris)*
> *%USER_HOME%\.java.policy (Windows)*
> *Look at the tool documentation with your JDK for details about policies if you're not familiar with them.*

Also, keep in mind that while starting the registry all classes and stubs must be available in the classpath, or the classpath should be not be set at all, to support dynamic loading (see later section on Bootstrapping).

Running the Client and Server

To run the client you need to open yet another command window (that should make three) and run the `HelloClient` class specifying our security policy file:

```
Java -Djava.security.policy=registerit.policy HelloClient
```

```
C:\WINNT\System32\cmd.exe                                              _ □ ×

C:\ProJavaServer\Chapter02\DevApps>java -Djava.security.policy=registerit.policy HelloClient
Hello World, the current system time is Sat Jul 29 13:15:13 GMT+01:00 2000

C:\ProJavaServer\Chapter02\DevApps>_
```

The RMISecurityManager

The `java.rmi.RMISecurityManager` extends the `java.lang.SecurityManager` class and provides the security context under which RMI applications execute. If no security manager has been set, stubs and classes can only be loaded from the local classpath and not from the host or code base (see the section later on Dynamic Downloading). This protects applications from downloading unsecure code via remote method invocations.

In JDK 1.2 there really is no need to subclass `RMISecurityManager` due to the policy based access control.

Remember the security manager in JDK 1.2 calls `AccessController.checkPermission(Permission)` by default and refers to a policy file for permission checking.

There really is no reason to set the security manager to `RMISecurityManager` if an RMI program has a purely server role on all of its communication links. `RMISecurityManager` (and user-defined security managers obtained by extending `RMISecurityManager`) are for subjecting the classes that are dynamically loaded by a client application to security control. If the client has access to the object definitions for the host there is no reason to use `RMISecurityManager` on the clientside either.

Parameter Passing in RMI

The normal semantics for methods in a single JVM are governed by two rules:

> **If the type being passed is a primitive, then the parameter or result is passed by value.**
> **If, however, the type being passed is an object, the object is passed by reference.**

When a primitive data type is passed as a parameter to a method the JVM simply copies the value and passes the copy to (or returns it from) the method. An object on the other hand, resides in heap memory and is accessed by one (or more) references. When passed to a method, a copy of the reference variable is made (increasing the reference count to the object by one), placed on the stack and the copy is passed around.

Inside the method, code uses the copy of the reference to access the object and invoking any method on the reference changes the state of the original object. Altering the reference itself does not affect the original object; however, altering the object that the reference points to alters the object that was initially created.

So when remote method invocation involves passing parameters or accepting a return value, what semantics are used? The answer depends on whether the parameters are primitive data types, objects, or remote objects.

Primitive Parameters

When a primitive data type is passed as a parameter to, or returned from, a remote method, the RMI system passes it by value. A copy of the primitive data type is sent to the remote method and the method returns a copy of the primitive from its JVM. These values are passed between JVMs in a standard, machine-independent format allowing JVMs running on different platforms to communicate with each other reliably.

Object Parameters

A reference to an object doesn't make sense across multiple JVMs since the reference points to a value in the heap and different JVMs do not share heap memory. RMI sends the object itself, not its reference, between JVMs. It is the object that is passed by value, not the reference to the object. Similarly, when a remote method returns an object, a copy of the whole object is returned to the calling program.

A Java object can be simple, or it could refer to other Java objects in a complex tree-like structure. Since RMI must send the referenced object and all objects it references using RMI object serialization, it thereby transforms an object into a linear format that can then be sent over the network. Object serialization essentially flattens an object and any objects it references. Serialized objects can be de-serialized in the memory of the remote JVM and made ready for use by a Java program.

Passing large object trees can use a lot of CPU time and network bandwidth. Try keeping object arguments to, and results from, remote methods simple for optimization. Objects being passed around must implement the `java.io.Serializable` or the `java.io.Externalizable` interface.

Remote Parameters

Passing remote objects as method arguments or return types is a little different from passing other objects. A client program can obtain a reference to a remote object through the RMI Registry program or it can be returned to the client from a method call. (See the HelloWorld example later in the Distributed Garbage Collector section). Passing remote objects is very important, especially for remote callbacks.

Consider the following code:

```
HelloInterface obj = (HelloInterface) Naming.lookup("/HelloServer");
MsgInterface msg = obj.getMsg();
```

What happens when the `MsgInterface` itself is a remote object that has been exported on the server?

RMI does not return a copy of the remote object. It substitutes the stub for the remote object, serializes it, and sends it to the client. Just as a note, if the client sends this remote object back to the server as another argument, the object is still treated as a remote object on the server and not local to the server (even though it is). Though this may seem like a performance overhead, it is crucial to preserve the integrity of the semantics.

Consider another case; what happens when of the remote methods returns a reference to "this":

```
public class ThisServer extends UnicastRemoteObject implements HelloInterface
{
    public ThisServer()throws RemoteException {
        super();
    }
```

```
    public HelloInterface someMethod() throws RemoteException {
        return this;
    }
}
```

In the server code, this refers to the actual server implementation living in the server's JVM. However, clients have no direct contact with the other JVM; they deal with the server's object's proxy, the stub. Behind the scenes, RMI always checks the input and output parameters from a remote method to see if they implement `Remote`, if they do they are transparently replaced with the corresponding stub. This gives clients the illusion that they are working with the local objects because even things like "`this`" can be exchanged between different JVMs.

> **Remember, the class files themselves are never serialized, just the names of the classes. All classes should be capable of being loaded during de-serialization using the normal class loading mechanisms.**

The Distributed Garbage Collector

One of the design objectives for the RMI specifications was to keep the client's perspective of remote objects the same as other objects within its own JVM. This implies that remote objects should also be subjected to garbage collection.

The RMI system provides a reference counting distributed garbage collection algorithm based on Modula-3's Network Objects. Internally, the server keeps track of which clients have requested access to the remote object. When a reference is made, the server marks the object as dirty and when all clients have dropped the reference, it is marked as being clean. A clean object is marked for garbage collection and reclaimed when the garbage collector runs.

In addition to the reference counting mechanism on the server, when a client obtains a reference, it actually has a lease to the object for a specified time. If the client does not refresh the connection, by making additional dirty calls to the remote object before the lease term expires, the distributed garbage collector then assumes that the remote object is no longer referenced by that client (the reference is considered to be dead) and the remote object may be garbage collected.

A remote object can implement the `java.rmi.server.Unreferenced` interface. This has one method `unreferenced()` which is invoked when there are no longer any clients holding a live reference. This enables the DGC to check whether any remote references are still in use.

> **The lease time is controlled by the system property `java.rmi.dgc.leaseValue`. (value is in milliseconds and defaults to 10 minutes).**

Of course all this dirty, clean, and leasing is never visible to users or clients. The DGC (distributed garbage collector) mechanism is completely transparent. The DGC mechanism is hidden in the stubs-skeleton layer and is abstracted in the `java.rmi.dgc` package.

It is important to remember that a remote object can be garbage-collected, leaving it unavailable to clients (typically resulting in a `java.rmi.ConnectException`). Due to these garbage collection semantics, a client must be prepared to deal with remote objects that have "disappeared". On the server, if you don't want your object to "disappear" always hold an explicit reference so that it is not garbage-collected.

Remember, that the registry itself (itself a remote object) acts as a client to the server object and hence holds a lease to the object. So even if all the "actual" clients get disconnected from a server, the method `unreferenced()` may not be invoked on a server object while the registry holds a lease.

Consider the following modified version of the same HelloWorld example that demonstrates how distributed garbage collection works and how the `unreferenced()` method can be used. We discussed this in an earlier section about parameter passing how a client can get a reference to a remote object as a result of a method invocation. This example uses that concept.

We modify the interface to return a remote object instead of a String:

```
import java.rmi.*;

public interface HelloInterface extends java.rmi.Remote {
    public MsgInterface getMsg() throws RemoteException, Exception;
}
```

The remote object implementation of this interface is also simple:

```
import java.io.*;
import java.rmi.*;
import java.rmi.server.*;
import java.util.Date;

public class HelloServer extends UnicastRemoteObject implements HelloInterface {

    public HelloServer() throws RemoteException {
        super();
    }

    public MsgInterface getMsg() throws RemoteException, Exception {
        return (MsgInterface)new MsgServer();
    }
}
```

The `MsgInterface` is also simple. It has no methods and is just used to mark the object being passed around as remote:

```
import java.io.Serializable;
import java.rmi.server.*;

public interface MsgInterface extends java.rmi.Remote {}
```

The simple implementation of this interface is designed to trap the events of the object by printing out information when the object is created, no longer referenced, finalized, and then deleted. This object also implements the `Unreferenced` interface and implements the `unreferenced()` method. The `unreferenced()` method will be called when there are no client references to the object; `finalize()` is called just before the object is garbage-collected:

```
import java.io.Serializable;
import java.rmi.server.*;
import java.rmi.*;

public class MsgServer extends UnicastRemoteObject
            implements MsgInterface, Serializable, Unreferenced {

    // Set a counter for the number of instances of this class that are created.
    private static int counter;
    // Hold an id for the object instance
    private int id;

    public MsgServer() throws RemoteException {
        super();
        System.out.println("Created Msg:" + counter);
        counter++;
        setId(counter);
    }

    public void finalize() throws Throwable {
        super.finalize();
        System.out.println( "Finalizer called for Msg: " + id );
    }

    public void unreferenced() {
        System.out.println("The unreferenced()method called for Msg: " + id);
        // If we need we can call unexportObject here since no one is using it
        // unexportObject(this, true);
    }

    private void setId(int id) {
        this.id=id;
    }
}
```

The registration program remains the same as in the previous example:

```
import java.rmi.*;

public class RegisterIt {

    public static void main(String args[]) {
        try {
            HelloServer obj = new HelloServer();
            Naming.rebind("/HelloServer", obj);
            System.out.println("HelloServer bound in registry");
        } catch (Exception e) {
            System.out.println(e);
        }
    }
}
```

We modify the client to create multiple instances of the remote object `MsgServer()` on the server (we explicitly instantiate an object in the `getMsg()` method). We need to do this for this demonstration because the JVM runs the distributed garbage collector, like the usual garbage collector, only when it feels like there is a need to reclaim memory:

```
import java.rmi.*;

public class HelloClient {

    public static void main(String args[]) {
        if (System.getSecurityManager() == null)
            System.setSecurityManager(new RMISecurityManager());

        try {
            HelloInterface obj = (HelloInterface) Naming.lookup("/HelloServer");
            for(int i = 0; i < 100; i++) {
                MsgInterface msg = obj.getMsg();
            }
        } catch (Exception e) {
            System.out.println("HelloClient exception: " + e);
        }
    }
}
```

Start the server after compiling the classes and generating the stubs and skeletons (for both `HelloServer` and `MsgServer`) with the following (changing the `codebase` path as appropriate):

```
java -Djava.rmi.dgc.leaseValue=1000 RegisterIt
```

Again you might want to experiment with the lease value property as well as the −ms and −mx options to set the heap memory for this example. The following is the output when executed with default values:

```
C:\WINNT\System32\cmd.exe - java -Djava.rmi.dgc.leaseValue=1000 RegisterIt
Created Msg:0
Created Msg:1
Created Msg:2
Created Msg:3
Created Msg:4
Created Msg:5
Created Msg:6
Created Msg:7
Created Msg:8
Created Msg:9
Created Msg:10
Created Msg:11
Created Msg:12
Created Msg:13
The unreferenced() method called for Msg: 1
The unreferenced() method called for Msg: 6
The unreferenced() method called for Msg: 4
The unreferenced() method called for Msg: 5
The unreferenced() method called for Msg: 3
Created Msg:14
Created Msg:15
Created Msg:16
The unreferenced() method called for Msg: 2
The unreferenced() method called for Msg: 8
Created Msg:17
```

The leaseCheckInterval in `sun.rmi.transport.DGCImpl` *is read in from the*
`sun.rmi.dgc.checkInterval` *property without taking into account the current value of the*
`leaseValue` *variable. This causes a five-minute delay in removing unused objects, even if the*
`leaseValue` *is set to a lower value. Workaround: Set the* `sun.rmi.dgc.checkInterval`
property to half of the setting of `java.rmi.dgc.leaseValue`.

Dynamically Loading Classes

We talked earlier about how references, stubs, parameters, and socket factories are sent to the client over the wire and how the class definitions are not. Dynamic class loading addresses the latter, making definitions available.

Dynamic class loading has been around for a long time in Java and this ability to dynamically load and instantiate classes is a very powerful concept in Java. Applets for example are downloaded to the client browser from a web server and are executed in the clients JVM. This gives the client's runtime the ability to access applications that have never been installed in their system.

It is assumed that the reader is familiar with how applets work and how the `codebase` property is used for them. To summarize, `codebase` is the location from which the class loader loads classes into the JVM. This means that classes can be deployed in a central place, such as a web server, for a distributed system and all applications in the system can download the class files to operate.

There are two important system properties in RMI:

❑ `java.rmi.server.codebase`
This specifies the URL (a `file://`, `ftp://`, or `http://` location) where the classes can be accessed. If an object is passed around as a method argument or return type the client JVM needs to load the class files for that object. When RMI serializes the object it inserts the URL specified by this property alongside the object.

❑ `java.rmi.server.useCodebaseOnly`
This property is used to notify the client that it should load classes only from the codebase location.

Let us revisit the process of exporting and registering a remote object and put it under a magnifying glass:

❑ When instantiating the remote object and registering it with the registry (our `RegisterIt.java` programs in previous examples), the codebase is specified by the `java.rmi.server.codebase` property.

❑ When the `bind()` call is made the registry uses this codebase to locate the stub for the object. Remember, the registry itself is a client to the object. Once this is successful the registry binds the object to a name and the codebase is saved along with the reference to the remote object in the registry.

❑ When a client requests a reference to the remote object the registry returns the stub to the client. The client looks for the class definition of the stub in its local `CLASSPATH` (the `CLASSPATH` is always searched before the codebase) and if it is found the client loads the local class. If the stub class definition is not there in the `CLASSPATH`, the client will attempt to retrieve the class definition from the remote object's codebase which was stored in the registry.

❑ The class definitions for the stub and any other classes that it needs, such as socket factories, are downloaded to the client JVM from the `http` or `ftp` codebase.

❑ When all the class definitions are available the stub's proxy method calls to the object on the server.

Using the two properties and the downloading mechanism discussed, five potential configurations can be set up to distribute classes:

❑ **Closed**
There is no dynamic loading and all classes are located in the respective JVMs and loaded from the local classpath (`java.rmi.server.codebase` not set).

❑ **Dynamic client side**
On the client, some classes are loaded from the local classpath and others from the codebase specified by the server.

❑ **Dynamic server side**
This is similar to the dynamic client-side configuration. Some classes on the server are loaded locally and others from the codebase specified by the client (for example, in the case of callbacks from the server to client).

❑ **Bootstrapped client**
All of the client code is loaded from the codebase via a small program on the client (bootstrap loader).

❑ **Bootstrapped server**
Same as above, only on the server side. The server uses a small program (bootstrap loader).

There are two classes, the `java.rmi.RMISecurityManager` and `java.rmi.server.RMIClassLoader` that check the security context before loading the class. The RMI system will not download any classes from remote locations if no security manager has been set. The `RMIClassLoader` has one important method:

```
public static Class loadClass (String codebase, String name)
```

This method loads the class from the specified codebase. Other overloaded forms of this method take a URL for a codebase or a string list of multiple URLs.

Let's take the HelloWorld example and set it up in the bootstrapped client and bootstrapped server configuration. This configuration is usually the most popular one due to its flexibility. We will download:

❑ All the classes on the client including the client class itself to the client from the web server

❑ All the server classes including the server class itself from a central web server.

We will only need one simple bootstrap class for the client and one for the server.

First, let's tweak the `HelloClient` class a little so that it connects to the server when instantiated:

```
import java.rmi.*;

public class HelloClient {
```

```
    public HelloClient() {
        try {
            HelloInterface obj = (HelloInterface)
                Naming.lookup("rmi://localhost/HelloServer");
            String message  = obj.sayHello();
            System.out.println(message);
        } catch (Exception e) {
            System.out.println("HelloClient exception: " + e);
        }
    }
}
```

That's it. We leave the remote implementation and interface the same as our initial example.

Now let's write a bootstrap class (instead of the `RegisterIt.java` we used earlier) that starts the server. It accesses the `codebase` property and loads the server class from the codebase using `RMIClassLoader`:

```
import java.rmi.Naming;
import java.rmi.Remote;
import java.rmi.RMISecurityManager;
import java.rmi.server.RMIClassLoader;
import java.util.Properties;

public class DynamicServer {

    public static void main(String args[]) {

        // Create and install a security manager
        if (System.getSecurityManager() == null) {
            System.setSecurityManager(new RMISecurityManager());
        }

        try {
            Properties p = System.getProperties();
            String url = p.getProperty("java.rmi.server.codebase");
            Class serverclass = RMIClassLoader.loadClass(url, "HelloServer");
            Naming.rebind("/HelloServer",(Remote)serverclass.newInstance());
            System.out.println("HelloServer bound in registry");
        } catch (Exception e) {
            System.out.println(e);
        }
    }
}
```

When the downloaded class is instantiated with a `newInstance()`, the constructor for the class is invoked (our `HelloServer()` constructor) and the object is exported in the constructor and registered with the registry.

There is a similar bootstrap program for the client that accesses the `codebase` property and loads the client class. When the downloaded client class is instantiated, it connects to the server and looks up the object.

```
import java.rmi.RMISecurityManager;
import java.rmi.server.RMIClassLoader;
import java.util.Properties;

public class DynamicClient {

    public DynamicClient() throws Exception {
        Properties  p = System.getProperties();
        String url = p.getProperty("java.rmi.server.codebase");
        Class clientClass = RMIClassLoader.loadClass(url, "HelloClient");
        // Start the client
        clientClass.newInstance();
    }

    public static void main (String args[]) {
        System.setSecurityManager(new RMISecurityManager());
        try {
            DynamicClient dc = new DynamicClient();
        } catch (Exception e) {
            System.out.println(e);
        }
    }
}
```

Compile all the classes and generate the stubs. Now we need to place the HelloWorld class files in a web server so that the DynamicServer can download them at runtime. For this example, we will use a small test HTTP server from Sun called ClassFileServer (also included in the sourcecode).

Place the four class files for the HelloWorld example in a directory under the HTTP server.

First start the RMI registry as before then start the HTTP server. For ClassFileServer it would be something like this:

```
java ClassFileServer 8080 c:\projavaserver\chapter02\dynamic\webserver\
                              public_html
```

Where the first parameter specifies the port that the server runs on, and the second parameter is the source for the files to be served.

Then run the DynamicServer specifying the codebase as the web server:

```
java -Djava.security.policy=registerit.policy
      -Djava.rmi.server.codebase=http://localhost:8080/ DynamicServer
```

Finally run the DynamicClient, again providing the codebase:

```
java -Djava.security.policy=registerit.policy
      -Djava.rmi.server.codebase=http://localhost:8080/ DynamicClient
```

```
C:\WINNT\System32\cmd.exe                                             _ □ ×
C:\ProJavaServer\Chapter02\Dynamic>java -Djava.security.policy=registerit.policy -Djava.rmi.server.c
odebase=http://localhost:8080/ DynamicClient
Hello World, the current system time is Sat Jul 29 14:40:35 GMT+01:00 2000

C:\ProJavaServer\Chapter02\Dynamic>_
```

To summarize:

❑ When you start the `DynamicServer` it accesses the codebase, downloads the implementation class, and exports the object.

❑ The registry uses the codebase to download the stub and bind the object, keeping track of the codebase used.

❑ When you start the `DynamicClient`, it again contacts the codebase and downloads the client class and the stub and invokes a method on the server object.

Notice that all the HelloWorld client, server, and stub files are in one location. The only distribution for the server is one class and the only file needed for client distribution is one class.

Remote Callbacks

We've discussed earlier how a client can get a reference to a remote object as a result of a method invocation. In fact, we actually saw how a remote object can be dynamically passed around in the DGC example earlier. Remember that I had initially emphasized that a client and server are terms used to describe roles, not physical locations or architectures. A client also can be a remote object. In many situations, a server may need to make a remote call to a client, for example, progress feedback or administrative notifications. A good example would be a chat application where all clients are remote objects:

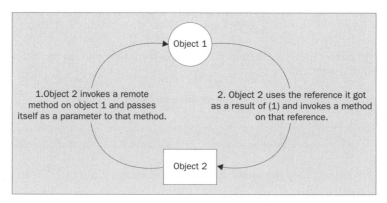

There is nothing really special about peer-to-peer communication or callbacks between remote objects. All that happens is a remote reference is passed around and methods are invoked on that reference.

Let us take the same HelloWorld example we looked at first and modify it to demonstrate callbacks.

The remote interface, `HelloInterface`, has one method that takes a `ClientInterface` as an argument:

```
public interface HelloInterface extends java.rmi.Remote {
    String sayHello(ClientInterface app) throws java.rmi.RemoteException;
}
```

For the client, the `ClientInterface` too is simple with only one method:

```
public interface ClientInterface extends java.rmi.Remote {
    void popup(String msg) throws java.rmi.RemoteException;
}
```

The `HelloServer` implements the `HelloInterface` and invokes the `popup()` method on the `ClientInterface` as shown below:

```
import java.io.*;
import java.rmi.*;
import java.rmi.server.*;
import java.util.Date;

public class HelloServer extends UnicastRemoteObject implements HelloInterface
{
    public HelloServer()throws RemoteException {
        super();
    }
    public String sayHello(ClientInterface ca) throws RemoteException {
        ca.popup("This is a message from the server!");
        return "Hello World, the current system time is " + new Date();
    }
}
```

The client that invokes methods on the server needs to be a remote object itself. Let us write a simple applet to demonstrate this. The applet exports itself and starts listening for incoming calls by explicitly invoking the `UnicastRemoteObject.exportObject(this)` method (Note: an overloaded form of this method allows you to specify the port as well):

```
import java.applet.*;
import java.awt.*;
import java.io.Serializable;
import java.rmi.*;
import java.rmi.server.*;

public class CallbackApplet extends Applet implements
                                        ClientInterface, Serializable {

    String message = "-n/a-";
    Frame f =new Frame();
    Label l1= new Label("                    ");

    public void init() {
```

```
        f.add(l1);
        try {
            // Export the object
            UnicastRemoteObject.exportObject (this);
            String host = "rmi://" + getCodeBase().getHost()+ "/HelloServer";
            HelloInterface obj = (HelloInterface)Naming.lookup(host);
            message = obj.sayHello((ClientInterface)this);
        } catch (Exception e) {
            System.out.println("HelloApplet exception: " + e);
        }
    }

    // Display the message in the applet
    public void paint(Graphics g) {
        g.drawString(message, 25, 50);
    }

    // Implement the interface
    public void popup(String txt) throws RemoteException {
        l1.setText(txt);
        f.setSize(100,100);
        f.show();
    }
}
```

When the applet is loaded it locates the server object and invokes the remote method. It passes itself as an argument to that method. As a result of this, the stub is transported to the server and the server can now reverse roles. It acts as a client to this applet and can invoke the popup() method.

We need a simple HTML page for this applet too:

```
<HTML>
<APPLET CODEBASE="http://localhost:8080/Callbacks" CODE="CallbackApplet.class"
        WIDTH=300 HEIGHT=266>
</APPLET>
</HTML>
```

That's it. We generate the stubs for the client and server, by executing rmic on CallbackApplet and HelloServer. Start the registry, and register the HelloServer with it using the same RegisterIt class as earlier.

The applet must be loaded from a web server on the host (remember unsigned applets can connect back to the host) and you can use either your own web server or the sample ClassFileServer used in the preceding example. All the classes needed by the client should be accessible on the web server. The stub class file definitions of the CallbackApplet should also be either available on the server objects' CLASSPATH (or should be dynamically loaded as we have seen earlier).

You can run the example in appletviewer with:

```
appletviewer -J-Djava.security.policy=registerit.policy
             http://localhost:8080/Callbacks/Applet.html
```

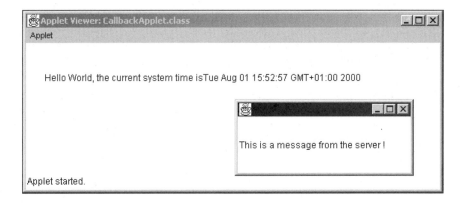

Object Activation

The remote objects discussed so far are instances of a `java.rmi.UnicastRemoteObject` class, and have one main aspect. They are accessible all the time, even when there are no clients executing. Consider the scenario when the number of remote objects, or the amount of resources used by them, on a server is high. This was identified as a major performance bottleneck in Java 2 so the concept of object activation was introduced.

> **Object activation allows remote objects to be executed on a as-needed basis, i.e. when an 'activatable' remote object is accessed (via a method invocation) if that remote object is not currently executing the system initiates the objects execution inside an appropriate JVM. RMI uses lazy activation, this is where the activation of an object is deferred until a client first use, the first method invocation.**

So, what is the difference between an activatable object and the usual remote object from a client's perspective? None! To the client the entire activation mechanism is transparent and the client is never aware of what is happening behind the scenes.

The references to the remote object themselves can be thought of as lazy or faulting references. References to activatable objects contain persistent handle information that allows the activation subsystem to know that the object should be started if it is not already running. After an activatable reference is used the first time, the Remote Reference layer switches to a regular remote reference so that it doesn't have to go through the activation system subsequently.

Since the activation system can switch the lazy reference to a live remote reference, references to an activatable object are always available. However, references to a remote object don't survive a crash, or a restart.

To understand the actual semantics of using the activation model, let us first familiarize ourselves with a few terms:

63

❑ **Activator**
   The Activator is a major component on the server. It facilitates remote object activation by keeping track of all the information needed to activate an object and is responsible for starting instances of JVMs on the server if needed.

❑ **Activation Group**
   An Activation Group creates instances of objects in its group, and informs its monitor about the various active and passive states. The closest analogy to an activation group is a thread group. An Activation Group is essentially a complete, separate instance of the JVM that exists solely to host groups of activated objects. This fresh JVM is started as needed by the Activator. There can be multiple Activation Groups.

❑ **Activation Monitor**
   Every Activation Group has an Activation Monitor that keeps track of an object's state in the group and the group's state as a whole. The Activation Monitor is created when the group is made active.

❑ **Activation System**
   The Activation System provides a means for registering groups and activatable objects to be activated within those groups. This works closely with the Activator, which activates objects registered via the Activation System, and the Activation Monitor, which obtains information about active and inactive objects, and inactive groups.

Entity	Implementation	Implemented as
Activator	`java.rmi.activation.Activator`	Interface – notice that the Activator is a remote object itself
Activation Group	`java.rmi.activation.Activation Group`	Abstract class
Activation Monitor	`java.rmi.activation.Activation Monitor`	Interface
Activation System	`java.rmi.activation.Activation System`	Interface

The activation mechanism uses identifiers and descriptors; if it seems overwhelming at first keep this in mind:

❑ Every activatable object has an ID and a descriptor.

❑ Every activatable object belongs to an Activation Group. The group itself has an ID and a descriptor.

The Activation Group

An Activation Group as mentioned before, is used to maintain a group of activatable objects. The Activation Group is associated with a group identifier (`java.rmi.activation.ActivationGroupID`) and group descriptor (`java.rmi.activation.ActivationGroupDesc`) that identify and describe the Activation Group respectively.

An Activation Group is created explicitly as a result of invoking the
`ActivationGroup.createGroup()` method:

```
public static ActivationGroup createGroup(ActivationGroupID id,
                                          ActivationGroupDesc desc,
                                          long incarnation)
```

Where:

❑   `id` – The Activation Group identifier

❑   `desc` – The Activation Group's descriptor

❑   `incarnation` – The Activation Group's incarnation number (zero on a group initial creation)

The `ActivationGroupID` besides identifying the group uniquely within the Activation System also
contains a reference to the group's Activation System. This allows the group to interact with the system
as and when necessary. All objects with the same `ActivationGroupID` are activated in the same JVM.

An `ActivationGroupDesc` contains the information necessary to create or recreate the group in
which to activate objects. It contains:

❑   The group's class name. Remember that `java.rmi.activation.ActivationGroup` is an
    abstract class and the Activator (`rmid`) internally provides its concrete implementation (for
    example the class `sun.rmi.server.ActivationGroupImpl`).

❑   The location of the group's class.

❑   A marshaled object that can contain group specific initialization data.

The `ActivationGroupDesc` contains an inner class `CommandEnvironment` that specifies the startup
environment options for the `ActivationGroup` implementation classes. This allows exact control over
the command options used to start the child JVM – a null `CommandEnvironment` refers to the `rmid`
default values.

An `ActivationGroupDesc` can be created using one of the two constructors specified below:

❑   Construct a group descriptor that uses system default for group implementation and code location:

```
ActivationGroupDesc(Properties overrides,
                    ActivationGroupDesc.CommandEnvironment cmd)
```

❑   Specify an alternative group implementation and execution environment to be used for the group:

```
ActivationGroupDesc(String className, String location,
                    MarshalledObject data, Properties overrides,
                    ActivationGroupDesc.CommandEnvironment cmd)
```

*In the pre JDK 1.2 Beta4 versions, an `ActivationGroup` was created as a result of creating
default `ActivationGroupDesc` or activating the first object in a group.*

We have taken a whirlwind tour of the Activation Groups here. Let us look at some code that summarizes the creation of Activation Groups:

```
// Create the group descriptor
Properties env = new Properties();
env.put("java.security.policy", "file://c:/activation/registerit.policy");
ActivationGroupDesc mygroupdes = new ActivationGroupDesc(props, null);

// Get a reference to the activation system
ActivationSystem mysystem= ActivationGroup.getSystem();

// Register the group description with the activation system and get the group id
ActivationGroupID groupid = mysystem.registerGroup(mygroupdes);

// Now that we have the id and the descriptor we can explicitly create the group
ActivationGroup.createGroup(groupid, mygroupdes, 0);
```

ActivationID

Just as the `ActivationGroupID` is an ID for the group, the `ActivationID` is an ID for the object. Once the object is registered with the activation system, it is assigned an `ActivationID`. It contains two crucial pieces of information:

❑ A remote reference to the object's Activator

❑ A unique identifier for the object

We will see how to register the object in a later area.

Activation Descriptor

Every activatable object has a unique identifier containing a reference to the Activator that the object is associated with (`ActivationGroupID`) and an ID that uniquely identifies the object (`ActivationID`). The Activation Descriptor contains all the information the system needs to activate an object:

❑ The Activation Group identifier for the object

❑ The name of the class being activated

❑ The location of the class for the object

❑ An optional marshaled object that contains initialization data

Remember all the descriptors and identifiers we talked about until now were associated with the group. Once the group is created we have an identifier for that group in the system. So all that is needed to recreate/activate the object at any time is the Activation Group identifier and the class detail.

The Activation Descriptor can be created by using one of four constructors:

❑ Constructs an Activation Descriptor for the object with the given `groupID` and `className` that can be loaded from the code location, with the optional initialization information data and restart specifics for if the object is activated on demand or restarted when the Activator is restarted:

```
ActivationDesc(ActivationGroupID groupID, String className, String location,
               MarshalledObject data, boolean restart)
```

❑ Same as above but without the restart information:

```
ActivationDesc(ActivationGroupID groupID, String className, String location,
               MarshalledObject data)
```

❑ Again similar to the first, except that the Activation Group defaults to the current `ActivationGroupID` for the current instance of the JVM. It is worth noting that this constructor will throw an `ActivationException` if no current Activation Group has been explicitly created for this JVM:

```
ActivationDesc(String className, String location, MarshalledObject data,
               boolean restart)
```

❑ Simpler form of above, again without the restart information:

```
ActivationDesc(String className, String location, MarshalledObject data)
```

One of the cool things about activation is the restart flag in the constructors above; `rmid` remembers the remote objects that have registered with it and can recreate them when it (or the machine itself) restarts. This is possible because `rmid` keeps a log. By default this is in a log in the directory from which `rmid` was started and can be configured with the `-log` option. When `rmid` starts, it consults this log to gather information and restart any objects that were configured for restart.

Once the `ActivationDesc` has been created, it can be registered in one of the following ways:

❑ By invoking the static `Activatable.register(ActivationDesc desc)` method.

❑ By instantiating the object itself using the first or second constructor of the `Activatable` class. This registers and exports the object.

❑ By exporting the object explicitly via `Activatable`'s first or second `exportObject()` method that takes an `ActivationDesc`, the `Remote` object implementation and a port number as arguments. This registers and exports the object.

Behind the scenes, here is what happens:

❑ When a stub is generated for an activatable object, it contains special information about the object. This information includes the activation identifier and information about the remote reference type of the object.

❑ This stub for the object uses the activation identifier and calls the Activator to activate the object associated with the identifier. (The stub is the lazy/faulting reference.)

❑ The Activator locates the object's Activation Descriptor and Activation Group. If the Activation Group in which this object should be does not exist, the Activator starts an instance of a JVM, creates an Activation Group and then forwards the activation request to that group.

❑ The Activation Group loads the class for the object and instantiates the object (using special constructors that take several arguments, as we shall soon see).

When the object is activated, the Activation Group returns an object reference to the Activator (this is a serialized or marshaled reference). The Activator records the activation identifier and reference pairing and returns the live reference to the stub. The stub then forwards method invocations via this live reference directly to the remote object. (The live reference is like any other remote reference.)

Let us summarize everything we have covered until now, as we redo the HelloWorld example we covered earlier to make it activatable.

Making Objects Activatable

As we have seen there are a few cooperating entities in the activation framework that make everything possible:

- ❏ The object itself.

- ❏ The wrapper program that registers the object. This is similar to the `RegiserIt.java` program we used earlier. It typically makes a few method calls to the Activation System to provide details about how the object should be activated.

- ❏ The third entity is the activation daemon that records information like the registry, about when and what to do with the objects. (This daemon is `rmid`.)

Keeping these entities in mind, the steps to make an object activatable can be summarized as follows:

- ❏ The object should extend the `java.rmi.activation.Activatable` class instead of `UnicastRemoteObject` (there is an alternative to this as we shall see later).

- ❏ The object should include a special constructor that takes two arguments, its activation identifier of type `ActivationID`, and its optional activation data, a `java.rmi.MarshalledObject`. This is unlike non-activatable remote objects, which include a no argument constructor. This special constructor is called by the RMI system when it activates the object.

- ❏ Create an Activation Descriptor (`java.rmi.activation.ActivationDesc`) and register it with the Activator (`rmid`).

It is worth noting that the remote interface of the object does not need to be changed or modified in any way.

This makes sense, after all, we are only changing the implementation of the object instance, not how the outside world sees the object.

Step 1: Create the Remote Interface

This is no different from what we had earlier:

```
import java.rmi.*;

public interface HelloInterface extends Remote {
    public String sayHello() throws RemoteException;
}
```

Step 2: Create the Object Implementation

This class extends `java.rmi.activation.Activatable` and implements the remote interface (since Activatable extends `RemoteObject`). Furthermore, it must contain a two-argument constructor that takes the `ActivationID` and `MarshalledObject` as arguments. This constructor should call the appropriate superclass constructors to ensure initialization:

```
import java.rmi.*;
import java.rmi.activation.*;
import java.util.Date;

public class HelloServer extends Activatable implements HelloInterface {

    public HelloServer(ActivationID id, MarshalledObject data)
            throws RemoteException {
        // Register the object with the activation system
        // then export it on an anonymous port
        super(id, 0);
    }

    public String sayHello() throws RemoteException {
        return "Hello World, the current system time is " + new Date();
    }
}
```

Step 3: Register the Object with the System

This class contains all the information necessary to register the object, without actually creating an instance of the object:

```
import java.rmi.*;
import java.rmi.activation.*;
import java.util.Properties;

public class RegisterIt{

    public static void main(String args[]) throws Exception {
        try {
        //Install a SecurityManager
        System.setSecurityManager(new RMISecurityManager());

        // Create the group
        Properties env = new Properties();
        env.put("java.security.policy",
                "file://c:/projavaserver/chapter02/activatable/
                activation/registerit.policy");
        ActivationGroupDesc mygroupdes = new ActivationGroupDesc(env, null);
        ActivationGroupID mygroupid = ActivationGroup.getSystem().
                                    registerGroup(mygroupdes);
        ActivationGroup.createGroup(mygroupid, mygroupdes, 0);

        // Create the details about the activatable object itself
        ActivationDesc objectdesc = new ActivationDesc("HelloServer",
```

```
                        "file://c:/projavaserver/chapter02/activatable", null);

        // Register the activation descriptor with the activator
        HelloInterface myobject = (HelloInterface)Activatable.
                               register(objectdesc);

        // Bind the stub to a name in the rmiregistry
        Naming.rebind("helloObject", myobject);

        // Exit
        System.exit(0);

        }catch(Exception e) {
            System.out.println("Exception "+ e);
        }
    }
}
```

That's it!

We can just use the old client that we wrote for our initial example and execute it with the same policy and startup arguments:

```
import java.rmi.*;

public class HelloClient{

    public static void main(String args[]) {

        if (args.length < 1) {
            System.out.println ("Usage: java HelloClient <host>");
            System.exit(1);
        } else

        try {
            HelloInterface server = (HelloInterface)Naming.lookup("rmi://"
                                + args[0] + "/helloObject");
            System.out.println(server.sayHello());
        } catch (Exception e) {
            e.printStackTrace();
        }
    }
}
```

Compile the files then generate the stubs and skeletons for the remote object. Start the registry and then start the Activation System using the rmid utility:

```
rmid -J-Djava.security.policy=registerit.policy
```

Now we can execute the RegisterIt.class file:

```
java -Djava.security.policy=registerit.policy
     -Djava.rmi.server.codebase=file://c:/projavaserver/chapter02/activatable/
     RegisterIt
```

Finally, we can use the client:

```
java HelloClient localhost
```

There should be 3 to 4 DOS windows for this example:

- ❑ rmiregistry
- ❑ rmid
- ❑ RegisterIt
- ❑ HelloClient

Although the last two could be done in one window.

Alternative to Extending the Activatable Class

Sometimes it may be not be possible to extend the Activatable class if the remote object needs to extend another class. For example, if you are writing an applet that you want to make activatable or a remote object your applet would need to extend `java.applet.Applet` and in Java there is no such thing as multiple inheritance.

We saw earlier that it was possible to make an object remote by exporting the object directly using one of the export methods in the `java.rmi.UnicastRemoteObject` class rather than extending the UnicastRemoteObject class itself.

There is a similar alternative for activatable objects. While talking about Activation Descriptors I mentioned an `exportObject()` method. It is possible to register and export an object by invoking any of the export methods in the `java.activation.Activatable` class.

Let us rewrite our activatable `HelloServer` class to demonstrate this, keeping everything else the same:

```
import java.rmi.*;
import java.rmi.activation.*;
import java.util.Date;

public class HelloServer implements HelloInterface {
```

71

```
    public HelloServer(ActivationID id, MarshalledObject data)
            throws RemoteException {
      // Register and export it on an anonymous port
      Activatable.exportObject(this, id, 0);
      // OR
      /*
      Activatable.exportObject(this, id, 0,
                          new SomeRMIClientSocketFactory csf(),
                          new SomeRMIServerSocketFactory())
      OR
      Activatable.exportObject(this, ".", data, false, 0);
      OR
      Activatable.exportObject(this, ".", data, false, 0,
                          new SomeRMIClientSocketFactory(),
                          new SomeRMIServerSocketFactory());
      */
   }

    public String sayHello() throws RemoteException {
      return "Hello World, the current system time is " + new Date();
   }
}
```

Starting Multiple JVMs Other Than rmid

rmid or the Activator itself is a remote object and executes in a JVM. Every object that is activated is activated in its Activation Group's JVM but sometimes it may be desirable to spawn a separate JVM for each activatable object. This is straightforward if you keep in mind what was mentioned when talking about the ActivationGroupID, "All objects with the same ActivationGroupID are activated in the same JVM".

To start multiple JVMs, the object must have a different ActivationGroupID or in other words must be in a separate Activation Group. The code below shows how the same HelloServer object is registered differently so that each object has a different ActivationGroupID (and hence a different Activation Group).

The class that registers the activatable objects:

```
import java.rmi.*;
import java.rmi.activation.*;
import java.util.Properties;

public class RegisterIt {
   public static void main(String[] args) {
      try {
         //Install a SecurityManager
         System.setSecurityManager(new RMISecurityManager());

         // create another one for a new VM
         Properties env = new Properties();
         env.put("java.security.policy",
               "file://c:/projavaserver/chapter02/activatable/multiVM/
                registerit.policy");
```

```
        ActivationGroupDesc mygroupdes = new ActivationGroupDesc(env, null);
        ActivationGroupID mygroupid =
                     ActivationGroup.getSystem().registerGroup(
                                              mygroupdes);
        ActivationGroup.createGroup(mygroupid, mygroupdes, 0);
        ActivationDesc objectdesc = new ActivationDesc("HelloServer",
             "file://c:/projavaserver/chapter02/activatable/multiVM/",
             null);
        HelloInterface myobject = (HelloInterface)Activatable.register(
                                 objectdesc);
        Naming.rebind("helloObject",myobject);

        // Register another group's id
        ActivationGroupID mygroupid_2 = ActivationGroup.getSystem().
                                registerGroup(mygroupdes);
        ActivationDesc objectdesc_2 = new ActivationDesc("HelloServer",
             "file://c:/projavaserver/chapter02/activatable/multiVM /",
             null);
        HelloInterface myobject_2 = (HelloInterface)Activatable.register(
                                 objectdesc_2);
        Naming.rebind("helloObject_2", myobject_2);

        System.exit(0);

    } catch (Exception e) {
        System.out.println(e);
        e.printStackTrace();
    }
  }
}
```

The client starts the new JVM on the server because of the lazy activation (activation the first time the method is invoked):

```
import java.rmi.*;

public class HelloClient {

    public static void main(String args[]) {
        if (args.length < 1) {
           System.out.println ("Usage: java HelloClient <host>");
           System.exit(1);
        }
        try{
           HelloInterface obj = (HelloInterface)Naming.lookup(
                          "rmi://" + args[0] + "/helloObject");
           System.out.println(obj.sayHello());

           // Spawn the second VM on the server!
           HelloInterface obj_2 = (HelloInterface)Naming.lookup(
                          "rmi://" + args[0] + "/helloObject_2");
           System.out.println(obj_2.sayHello());
```

```
        }catch (Exception e) {
            System.out.println("HelloClient exception: " + e.getMessage());
            e.printStackTrace();
        }
    }
}
```

If you run this example, and take a look at the processes running when you run the client, you'll see that two Java VMs are used:

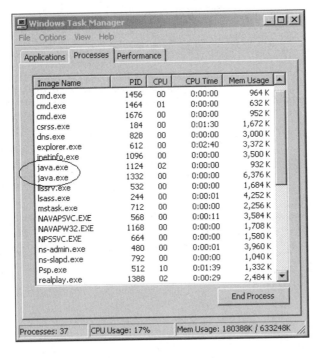

Deactivation

Activation allows an object to be started on demand; however, it does not automatically deactivate an object. The decision to deactivate the object is left to the object itself. An activatable object can deactivate itself by invoking the `Activatable.inactive(ActivationID id)` method.

It is important to know the difference between un-registering and deactivating an object. Deactivation is a temporary state, allowing the Activation System to restart the object later, whereas un-registering the object by `Activatable.unregister(ActivationID id)` permanently removes it from the Activation System.

Another useful method is the `Activatable.unexportObject(Remote obj, boolean force)` method that can be used to unexport the object. The boolean is used to force the object to be unexported even if there are pending or in-progress calls.

> While activation can be a big improvement in performance when the number of objects in a system is large, by relieving the drain on the resources, you should take care while deciding how and when to use it. The overhead required to create and reactivate an inactive object is large. It can involve creating a new JVM, loading, verifying classes, and deserializing a persistent object state. An object should typically decide on a safe time to stay alive. A good deactivating strategy could be based on the time since the last call was made

The following section assumes that the reader is familiar with TCP/IP sockets and networking in Java.

Custom Sockets and SSL

A socket is an endpoint for communication. Two collaborating sockets, one on the local machine and the other on the remote machine, form a connection. (Sockets are not the same as connections.)

There are two types of sockets: connection sockets, and listening sockets. A connection socket exists on each end of an open TCP connection and is abstracted by the `java.net.ServerSocket` and `java.net.Socket` classes. A listening socket is not associated with any TCP connection, but only exists as an abstraction to allow the TCP kernel to decide which incoming connections are accepted, and who gets the newly accepted connection socket.

At any time, RMI has a small number of listening sockets, one for each listened-to port; usually one because RMI exports all objects on the "default" port (unless a specific port is specified in the `export()` method discussed earlier). RMI also creates connection sockets for outgoing connections and incoming connections.

The number of outgoing connections only depends on the number of concurrent outgoing calls. The simple rule is:

- ❑ If a thread wants to make a remote call, and all the connections to the endpoint are in use, then RMI opens a new connection to carry the call.

- ❑ If a connection is free (meaning: there's no call in progress using that connection), then RMI will reuse it for the next remote call.

RMI spawns one thread to listen to each listening socket (also usually one). When RMI accepts a new connection, it creates a new thread: one thread handles the new connection, and the other goes back to accept a new connection. When the connection closes, its associated thread also exits.

The connection-handling threads spawned by RMI are not serialized in any way. If the calls arrive at the same time they will be run in concurrent threads. The calls are still allowed to synchronize on Java objects but RMI does not do such synchronization automatically (the remote object is responsible for its own synchronization either by synchronized methods or synchronized locking).

A common point of confusion is that if a remote stub is returned by a remote call, the client can sometimes be seen to make two connections to the server. This happens because the distributed garbage-collection subsystem needs to make a `DGC.dirty()` call to notify the server that a new entity holds a reference to the remote object.

You can use `netstat` *(or* `netstate.exe` *packaged in Windows) to monitor listening sockets. The following figure shows the sockets just after the registry is started on 1099.* `HelloServer` *is exported to 2000 and is binding with the registry. The left column lists the open sockets on the machine. The first line is for the registry, the second for the object. The third shows that a socket has been opened by the object to the registry; the last line shows the socket opened by the registry to the object.*

A significant enhancement that was added in the RMI release with Java 1.2 was the ability to use custom socket factories based on the Factory design pattern. Instead of using the conventional sockets over TCP/IP, each object has the ability to use its own socket type. This allows the object to process data (rather than simply passing it), either before it is sent to, or after it has been received from the socket.

In JDK 1.1.x, it was possible to create a custom `java.rmi.RMISocketFactory` subclass that produced a custom socket, other than the `java.net.Socket`, for use by the RMI transport layer. However, it was not possible for the installed socket factory to produce different types of sockets for different objects. For example in JDK 1.1, an RMI socket factory could not produce SSL (Secure Sockets Layer) sockets for one object and use the Java Remote Method Protocol (JRMP) directly over TCP for a different object in the same JVM. In addition, before 1.2, it was necessary for `rmiregistry` to use only your custom socket protocol.

The socket factory affected the whole system and not just a single object.

Details about the Factory design pattern are beyond the scope of this book and can be found in Design Patterns, Elements of Reusable Object-Oriented Software Erich Gamma et al. ISBN: 0-201-63361-2 or Patterns in Java: a Catalog of Reusable Design Patterns ISBN: 0471333158.

To see what this statement actually means, let us first see where in the RMI architecture sockets are involved, their types and purpose:

Location	Server socket	Client sockets
RMI registry	Opens a server socket (default port 1099) and waits for requests from: ❑ Servers to bind, re-bind and un-bind object implementations ❑ Clients who want to locate servers	Uses a client socket to establish a connection to a server object right after it has registered.

Location	Server socket	Client sockets
RMI servers (Remote implementation)	Opens a server socket on a user specified port via the `exportObject()` method or defaults to a random local port. It is used to accept connections from the client's (stub's) send responses.	A client socket is used while connecting to the registry, in particular to register the server implementation.
RMI clients (objects invoking remote methods)	Not used.	Client sockets are used for the communication with the RMI registry, to locate the server implementation and to make the actual RMI method call to the server.

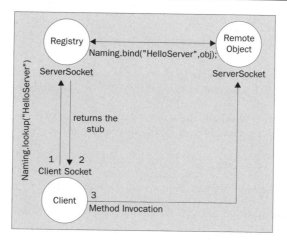

When a client performs a "lookup" operation, a connection is made to the server socket on the `rmiregistry`. In general, a new connection may or may not be created for a remote call. The RMI Transport layer caches connections for future use. If there are any existing connections, and at least one of them is free, then it is reused, otherwise the current implementation creates additional sockets on demand. For example, if an existing socket is in use by an existing call then a new socket is created for the new call. Usually there are at least two sockets open since the distributed garbage collector needs to make remote calls when remote objects are returned from the server. A client has no explicit control over the connections to a server, since connections are managed at the RMI Transport layer level. Connections will time out if they are unused for a period.

As you can see, there are several communication points and sockets being used in this three-way communication among the client, the registry, and the object. It is also important to note that the registry is only needed to locate an object by its name. Once the object is located there is direct communication between the object and the client.

An object can specify what factory classes are needed for anyone to communicate with its socket type through the `java.rmi.server.UnicastRemoteObject` (or `java.rmi.server.Activatable` for that matter) constructor. Instances of these factories are used to create instances of the desired sockets types:

```
protected UnicastRemoteObject(int port, RMIClientSocketFactory csf,
                              RMIServerSocketFactory ssf)
```

As explained in the previous table, once the client has located an object, it uses a client socket to connect to the server socket that the object is listening on. The client socket factory must implement the `java.rmi.server.RMIClientSocketFactory` interface. The client socket is created from this instance of the `RMIClientSocketFactory` by invoking the `createSocket()` method that returns an instance of the custom socket type to the specified server and port:

```
public Socket createSocket(String host, int port)
```

The server socket factory must implement the `java.rmi.server.RMIServerSocketFactory` interface and provide an implementation for the `createServerSocket()` method. The server socket is created (to start listening for incoming calls) by invoking the method implementation in the server socket factory class:

```
public ServerSocket createServerSocket(int port)
```

This is particularly useful when you want to encrypt the communication between the objects. For example using SSL or TLS. Let us look at an example of how this can be done.

First we would need a couple of things, the foremost being a security provider that provides an implementation of the SSL protocol in Java. Many third party products available do this.

> **SSL and TLS both provide encryption and certification. Actually, Transport Layer Security (TLS) is the new Internet Engineering Task Force (IETF) standard and is based on SSL.**

SSL specifications can be found at `http://home.netscape.com/eng/security`.
TLS specifications can be found in RFC 2246 at: `www.ietf.org/rfc/rfc2246.txt`
Details about open source SSL implementations (SSLeay/OpenSSL) can be found at
`www.openssl.org/`.

Sun provides the **Java Secure Sockets Extension (JSSE)** that implements a Java version of SSL and TLS protocols and includes functionality for data encryption, server authentication, message integrity, and optional client authentication. The example discussed here uses JSSE, details about which can be seen at `http://java.sun.com/products/jsse/`.

There is going to be a performance overhead and the communication is going to be very slow due to the complexity of the handshake and the encryption involved. How the provider implements the algorithms (natively etc.) would also affect performance. For example, a native implementation such the GoNative Provider (`www.rtfm.com/puretls/gonative.html`) is faster then its pure counterpart.

Let us first try to see what part of the communication we want/need to encrypt. The naming registry is implemented as a standard RMI service so attempts to register and look up services will involve network connections being established. If you need the communication with the registry to take place over secure sockets then obviously the naming registry to would need to listen on secure server sockets.

A straightforward way to do this is to have your server start its own naming registry. This registry will then benefit from the server's SSL support. The server would need to invoke and set a socket factory explicitly and start the registry:

```
RMISocketFactory.setSocketFactory (some vendor provided factory);
LocateRegistry.createRegistry(someport);
```

The SSL socket factory can then be installed on the client before looking up the object and everything will be SSL-secured.

> **Since the same port cannot listen on two types of sockets, it would be necessary to run two registries: a secure one and a normal one, if you need to look up on different protocols. Most vendors provide a secure registry implementation with the Java-SSL implementation that can be used if you are not programmatically starting the registry.**

In most cases, it is only the communication between the objects that is important and needs encryption; not the lookup, this is what we will look at in the following example. In order for communication to occur over SSL/TLS we need two things: keys and certificates. To see more information on these, see the links to the SSL and TLS documentation.

Before we do anything else, we generate the keys and certificates using the JDK utility `keytool`. This is a certificate management tool used to manage public/private key pairs and associated certificates to be used in self-authentication, and data integrity and authentication services, using digital signatures. In a commercial environment you would probably use `keytool` to generate a certificate request and use that request to obtain a certificate from a certificate authority (CA) like Verisign (www.verisign.com). For our purposes, we will generate a self-signed certificate (a certificate from the CA, authenticating its own public key). In other words, we will use our own keys and certificates using the `-genkey` option in keytool.

Run the `keytool` utility with parameters something like this:

```
keytool -genkey -dname "cn=ProJavaServer, ou=Java, o=Wrox Press, c=US"
        -alias wrox -keypass secret -storepass secret -validity 365
        -keystore c:\projavaserver\chapter02\SSL\.keystore
```

You can check the certificate by using `keytool` in a different way:

```
keytool -list -keystore c:\projavaserver\chapter02\SSL\.keystore
        -storepass secret
```

This generates a keystore called "wrox" that contains the keys and the self signed certificate and has the password "secret".

> *Please refer to the tool documentation packaged with JDK for details about how to use keytool, keys, and certificates in the Java 2 security architecture.*

Finally, we also export the generated certificate into a file `clientimport.cer` for use by clients using `keytool`:

```
keytool -export -keystore c:\projavaserver\chapter02\SSL\.keystore
        -storepass secret -file clientimport.cer -alias wrox
```

> **Please remember that we are not using browser based SSL anywhere in these examples. If you want to do that then you need to generate certificates with the RSA algorithm (use – `keyalg` option in `keytool`).**
>
> **For this you would need to install a provider that provides the RSA algorithm implementation since the JDK 1.2 keytool does not support it. (The JSSE provider provides an implementation and RSA support is in-built in JDK 1.3.)**
>
> **A freeware JCE implementation at `http://www.openjce.org` is a good security API provider.**

Let us now revisit and rewrite the HelloWorld example we used earlier, to secure the object-to-object communication.

The remote interface remains unchanged:

```
import java.rmi.Remote;
import java.rmi.RemoteException;

public interface HelloInterface extends Remote {
    public String sayHello() throws RemoteException;
}
```

We now write the remote implementation of this interface:

```
import java.rmi.*;
import java.rmi.server.UnicastRemoteObject;
import java.util.Date;

public class HelloServer extends UnicastRemoteObject implements HelloInterface
{
    public HelloServer() throws RemoteException {
        super(0, new MyClientSocketFactory(), new MyServerSocketFactory());
    }

    public String sayHello() {
        return "Hello World, the current system time is " + new Date();
    }
}
```

Notice that the only difference is that we pass our own custom factories that will be used for this object instead of the default factories.

We now use the same program we used earlier to register this remote object:

```
import java.rmi.*;

public class RegisterIt {

    public static void main(String args[]) {
        try {
            // Instantiate the object
            HelloServer obj = new HelloServer();
            System.out.println("Object instantiated" + obj);
            Naming.rebind ("/HelloServer", obj);
            System.out.println("HelloServer bound in registry");
        } catch (Exception e) {
            System.out.println(e);
        }
    }
}
```

The pieces we passed so easily are the socket factories. Let us look at them in detail now. The MyServerSocketFactory class is used to create instances of the server socket on the port that the object was exported on. This class must implement the java.rmi.server.RMIServerSocketFactory interface and should be serializable (to facilitate possible transportation over the network). The secure interchange between the client and the server involves an exchange of keys and certificates and the socket created must first initialize communication with the client before exchanging any data. The JSSE implementation allows us to do this in a few lines of code. We open the keystore (we generated) from the file using its password, initialize the SSL/TLS implementation, and return an instance of a secure socket:

```
import java.io.*;
import java.net.*;
import java.rmi.server.*;
import java.security.*;
import javax.net.ssl.*;
import javax.security.cert.*;
import com.sun.net.ssl.*;

public class MyServerSocketFactory implements RMIServerSocketFactory,
                                              Serializable {
    // Implement the interface method
    public ServerSocket createServerSocket(int port) throws IOException {
        SSLServerSocketFactory ssf = null;
        try {
            // Set up key manager to do server authentication
            char[] passphrase = "secret".toCharArray();
            // Get a context for the protocol. We can use SSL or TLS as needed.
            SSLContext ctx = SSLContext.getInstance("TLS");
            KeyManagerFactory kmf = KeyManagerFactory.getInstance("SunX509");

            // Open the keystore with the password and initialize the SSL context
            // with this keystore.
```

```
        KeyStore ks = KeyStore.getInstance("JKS");
        ks.load(new FileInputStream(".keystore"), passphrase);
        kmf.init(ks, passphrase);
        ctx.init(kmf.getKeyManagers(), null, null);
        ssf = ctx.getServerSocketFactory();
    } catch (Exception e) {
        e.printStackTrace();
    }
    return ssf.createServerSocket(port);
    }
}
```

The client socket factory is used to create instances of the client sockets that connect to the instances of the server sockets generated from the above factory. It is assumed that the JSSE provider is also installed on the client machine:

```
import java.io.*;
import java.net.*;
import java.rmi.server.*;
import javax.net.ssl.*;

public class MyClientSocketFactory implements RMIClientSocketFactory,
                                              Serializable {

    public Socket createSocket(String host, int port) throws IOException {

        // We get the default SSL socket factory.
        SSLSocketFactory factory =
                    (SSLSocketFactory)SSLSocketFactory.getDefault();
        SSLSocket socket = (SSLSocket)factory.createSocket(host, port);
        return socket;
    }
}
```

The client too remains unchanged:

```
import java.rmi.Naming;
import java.rmi.RemoteException;

public class HelloClient {

    public static void main(String args[]) {
        if (args.length < 1) {
            System.out.println ("Usage: java HelloClient <host>");
            System.exit(1);
        }

        try {
            HelloInterface obj =(HelloInterface)Naming.lookup(
                                      "rmi://" + args[0] + "/HelloServer");
            System.out.println("Got a remote reference" + obj);
            System.out.println(obj.sayHello());
        } catch (Exception e) {
```

```
            System.out.println(e);
        }
    }
}
```

The policy file we use is the same:

```
grant {
    permission java.security.AllPermission;
};
```

That's it. We can now compile the classes and generate the stubs using the `rmic` packaged with the JDK.

Two small configuration details need to be examined before executing the example. In order for the client to interact and exchange keys and certificates with the server, it must trust the provider of the digital certificate. In other words, since our certificate is self-generated the client VM should:

❑   Explicitly import the certificate into the keystore it is using and mark it as a trusted certificate

❑   Use the same keystore that we use on the server

For the second option, the JSSE provider must be installed on the client machine (if it is different form the server):

❑   Either statically in the `java.security` file

❑   Or dynamically using
     `Security.addProvider(new com.sun.net.ssl.internal.ssl.Provider());`

The client can import the certificate from the file we generated earlier, `clientimport.cer`, into the keystore it is using and mark it as trusted using `keytool` with the `-import`:

```
keytool -import -file clientimport.cer -alias wrox
```

```
C:\WINNT\System32\cmd.exe                                                    _ □ ×
C:\ProJavaServer\Chapter02\SSL>keytool -export -keystore c:\projavaserver\chapter02\SSL\.keystore -s
torepass secret -file clientimport.cer -alias wrox
Certificate stored in file <clientimport.cer>

C:\ProJavaServer\Chapter02\SSL>keytool -import -file clientimport.cer -alias cab
Enter keystore password:  secret
Owner: CN=ProJavaServer, OU=BTUS, O=Wrox Press, C=US
Issuer: CN=ProJavaServer, OU=BTUS, O=Wrox Press, C=US
Serial number: 3982fcde
Valid from: Sat Jul 29 16:48:46 GMT+01:00 2000 until: Sun Jul 29 16:48:46 GMT+01:00 2001
Certificate fingerprints:
        MD5:   10:3F:B4:38:BD:76:35:81:CB:67:64:86:3D:EE:EF:86
        SHA1:  4F:E0:64:98:E8:A5:62:53:F9:88:55:F4:D4:AD:CF:1E:6F:2C:28:98
Trust this certificate? [no]:  y
Certificate was added to keystore

C:\ProJavaServer\Chapter02\SSL>_
```

Once this is done we first start the registry on the server (execute `rmiregistry`) then register the object with the registry:

```
java -classpath %classpath% -Djava.security.policy=ssl.policy
    -Djava.rmi.server.codebase=file://c:/projavaserver/chapter02/SSL/
    RegisterIt
```

> **Remember to carefully install the JSSE. Put the JAR files in your
> %JAVA_HOME%\lib\ext location and install the provider in your java.security file
> (see the README file for more details). If you have multiple runtime environments be
> sure to edit the right security file. The easiest solution is to set the PATH to point only to
> the JDK you are using. There is a JRE installation that goes with the JDK (default
> installation c:\Program files\JavaSoft on windows) so you actually have two
> virtual machines.**

Now run the client and specify the keystore to use using the JSSE javax.net.ssl.trustStore property.
This is the keystore into which the certificate has been imported or the same keystore as the server:

```
java -Djava.security.policy=ssl.policy -Djavax.net.ssl.trustStore=.keystore
    HelloClient localhost
```

If you want the client to be an applet, a few configuration issues need to be resolved first:

❑   The client must have a JDK 1.2 JVM. At the time this article was written Netscape 6 beta was
    the only browser with limited JDK 1.2 support. Hence, you would probably need to install the
    Java plug-in software.

❑   The client JVM must have the appropriate keystore and certificates installed.

❑   The client JVM should have the right policy, allowing sockets to be opened back to the server.

❑   The client JVM should have the security provider installed, or have the right security
    permissions so that a security provider can be installed dynamically.

Let us look at the applet below. It is simple, the same as discussed earlier, except that it is an applet. It is important to realize that the applet has nothing to do with the browser's SSL configuration. The SSL connection happens at the RMI socket level. The client socket factory class is downloaded dynamically and the secure connection made to the server:

```java
import java.applet.*;
import java.awt.*;
import java.rmi.*;
import java.security.*;

public class SSLHelloApplet extends Applet {

    String message = "-n/a-";

    HelloInterface obj = null;
    // Get a reference to the object in applet initialization
    public void init() {
        try {
            Security.addProvider(new com.sun.net.ssl.internal.ssl.Provider());
            String host="rmi://" + getCodeBase().getHost() + "/HelloServer";
            HelloInterface obj = (HelloInterface)Naming.lookup(
                                    "rmi://localhost/HelloServer");
            message = obj.sayHello();
        } catch (Exception e) {
            System.out.println(e);
        }
    }
    // Display the message in the applet
    public void paint(Graphics g) {
        g.drawString(message, 25, 50);
    }
}
```

Below is the HTML page for the above applet. This page is converted using the HTML converter tool packaged with the Java plug-in. When a client comes across this page, if a compatible version does not exist, it will prompt you to download the plug-in from the URL specified. (The Sun web site in this case):

```html
<HTML>
<HEAD>
<TITLE>Hello World</TITLE>
<HEAD>

<BODY>
<CENTER> <H1>Hello World</H1> </CENTER>

The message from the HelloServer is:
<P>
<!--"CONVERTED_APPLET"-->
<!-- CONVERTER VERSION 1.3 -->
<OBJECT CLASSID = "clsid:8AD9C840-044E-11D1-B3E9-00805F499D93"
        WIDTH = 500 HEIGHT = 120 CODEBASE =
        "http://java.sun.com/products/plugin/1.3/jinstall-13-win32.cab#
        Version=1,3,0,0">
```

```
<PARAM NAME = CODE VALUE = "SSLHelloApplet" >
<PARAM NAME = CODEBASE VALUE = "http://localhost/hello/" >

<PARAM NAME="type" VALUE="application/x-java-applet;version=1.3">
<PARAM NAME="scriptable" VALUE="false">
<COMMENT>
<EMBED TYPE = "application/x-java-applet;version=1.3" CODE = "SSLHelloApplet"
       CODEBASE = "http://localhost/hello/" WIDTH = 500 HEIGHT = 120
       SCRIPTABLE=false PLUGINSPAGE =
              "http://java.sun.com/products/plugin/1.3/plugin-install.html">
<NOEMBED></COMMENT>

</NOEMBED></EMBED>
</OBJECT>

<!--
<APPLET CODE = "SSLHelloApplet" CODEBASE = "http://localhost/hello/" WIDTH = 500
       HEIGHT = 120>
</APPLET>
-->
<!--"END_CONVERTED_APPLET"-->

</BODY>
</HTML>
```

When the page above is accessed, the browser determines that a plug-in (JRE) is needed to load this component and prompts you to download it from the location that was specified in the PLUGINSPAGE parameter – this is of course assuming it isn't already installed:

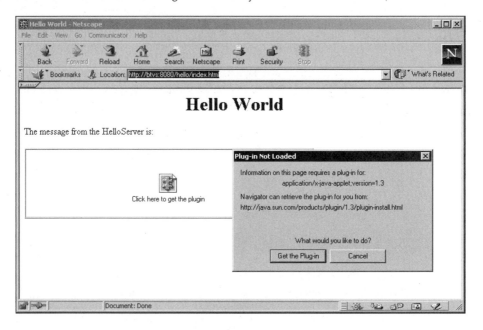

Once you download and install the plug-in and enable it from its console on your machine you can access the same page. The browser will now load it in the new Java 1.3 JVM (instead of the browsers default JVM).

Make sure to add the necessary runtime parameters for the plug-in using the Java Plug-in applet in Control Panel. You need to add the -Djava.security.policy and -Djavax.net.ssl.trustStore parameters:

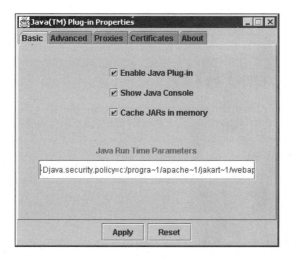

The result should be this:

The same URL can be accessed using appletviewer:

```
appletviewer -J-Djava.security.policy=ssl.policy
             -J-Djavax.net.ssl.trustStore=.keystore
             http://localhost:8080/hello/index.html
```

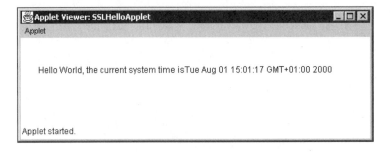

RMI, Firewalls, and HTTP

If you have worked in any networked enterprise, then you are probably familiar with how firewalls block all network traffic, with the exception of that intended for certain "well-known" ports. They are however necessary to protect the security of the network.

Since the RMI Transport layer opens dynamic socket connections between the client and the server, the JRMP traffic is typically blocked by most firewall implementations. RMI provides a workaround to this.

There are three main methods to bypass firewalls:

- ❑ HTTP-tunneling
- ❑ SOCKS
- ❑ Downloaded socket factories.

HTTP Tunneling

To get across firewalls, RMI makes use of **HTTP tunneling** by encapsulating the RMI calls within an HTTP POST request. This method is popular since it requires almost no setup, and works quite well in firewall environments that permit handling of HTTP through a proxy, but disallow regular outbound TCP connections. There are two forms of HTTP-tunneling:

HTTP-to-Port

If a client is behind a firewall and RMI fails to make a normal connection to the server, the RMI Transport layer automatically retries by encapsulating the JRMP call data within an HTTP POST request.

Since almost all firewalls recognize the HTTP protocol, the specified proxy server should be able to forward the call directly to the port on which the remote server is listening. It is important that the proxy server configuration be passed to the client JVM. Once the HTTP-encapsulated JRMP data is received at the server, RMI can automatically unwrap the HTTP tunneled request and decode it. The reply is then sent back to the client as HTTP-encapsulated data:

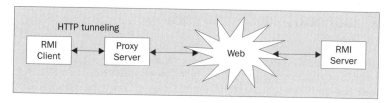

The proxy server configuration can be passed using properties as:

```
java -Dhttp.proxyHost=hostname -Dhttp.proxyPort=portnumber HelloClient
```

HTTP tunneling can be disabled by setting the property `java.rmi.server.disableHttp=true`.

HTTP-to-CGI

If the server cannot be contacted from the client, even after tunneling, because it is also behind a firewall, the RMI Transport layer uses a similar mechanism on the server. The RMI Transport layer places JRMP calls in HTTP requests and sends those requests, just as above. However, instead of sending them to the server port it sends them to `http://hostname:80/cgi-bin/java-rmi?forward=<port>`. There must be an HTTP server listening on port 80 on the proxy, which has the `java-rmi.cgi` script. The `java-rmi.cgi` in turn invokes a local JVM, unwraps the HTTP packet, and forwards the call to the server process on the designated port. RMI JRMP-based replies from the server are sent back as HTTP packets to the originating client port where RMI again unwraps the information and sends it to the appropriate RMI stub.

> *The* `java-rmi.cgi` *script is packaged with JDK and can be found in the* bin *directory. To avoid any DNS resolution problems at startup, the host's fully qualified domain name must be specified via a system property as:*
>
> `java.rmi.server.hostname=www.host.domain`
>
> *A servlet implementation of the cgi called a servlet handler is available from Sun at* `http://java.sun.com/j2se/1.3/docs/guide/rmi/archives/rmiservlethandler.zip.`

Another alternative to the `java-rmi.cgi` is using a port redirector (such as, DeleGate proxy) on port 80 that accepts connections and immediately redirects them to another port.

Although HTTP tunneling is an alternative, it should be avoided because:

- ❑ There is significant performance degradation. While tunneling, the RMI application will not be able to multiplex JRMP calls on a single connection, due to the request-response HTTP paradigm.

- ❑ Using the `java-rmi.cgi` script (or servlet) is a big security loophole on the server. The script redirects any incoming request to any port, completely circumventing the firewall.

- ❑ RMI applications tunneling over HTTP cannot use callbacks.

The SOCKS Protocol

SOCKS is a networking proxy protocol that enables hosts on one side of a SOCKS server to gain full access to hosts on the other side of the SOCKS server without requiring direct IP reachability. The SOCKS server redirects connection requests from hosts on opposite sides of a SOCKS server (the SOCKS server authenticates and authorizes the requests, establishes a proxy connection, and relays data).

By default, JDK sockets use a SOCKS server if available and configured. Server sockets however do not support SOCKS so this approach is only useful for outgoing calls from the client to the server.

Downloaded Socket Factories

We have already discussed at length how custom sockets can be used. The factory classes can be coded to work around the firewall. **Dynamically downloaded socket factories** provide a good alternative to HTTP tunneling, but the code to bypass the firewall must be hard-coded in the factories. This is OK if you have a fixed network configuration and know how that particular firewall works. However, different clients can have different firewalls and there is the question of access rights to provide this tunneling and of course, changing factory classes.

RMI Over IIOP

RMI over Internet Inter-Orb Protocol (IIOP) integrates Common Object Request Broker Architecture (CORBA) compliant distributed computing directly into Java. RMI over IIOP, developed jointly by IBM and Sun, is a new version of RMI for IIOP that combines RMI's easy programming features with CORBA's interoperability.

RMI and CORBA have developed independently as distributed-objects programming models. RMI was introduced to provide a simple programming model for developing distributed objects whereas CORBA is a well-known distributed-object programming model that supports a number of languages. The IIOP protocol connects CORBA products from different vendors, ensuring interoperability among them.

> The OMG (Object Management Group `http://www.omg.org/`) is the official keeper of information for CORBA and IIOP, including the CORBA 2.0 specifications available at `http://www.omg.org/corba/corbiiop.htm`. The IDL to Java mappings are also available at `http://developer.java.sun.com/developer/earlyAccess/jdk12/idltojava.html`.

RMI-IIOP is, in a sense, a marriage of RMI and CORBA, since remote interfaces can be written in Java, and implemented using Java RMI APIs. These interfaces however can be implemented in any other language that is supported by an OMG mapping and a vendor supplied ORB for that language. Similarly, clients can be written in other languages, using IDL derived from the Java remote interfaces.

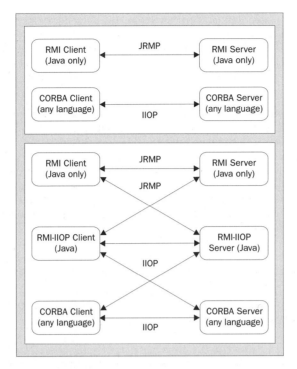

The figure above summarizes the RMI-IIOP marriage. It may seem that the arrows connecting the JRMP clients/servers to the RMI-IIOP clients/servers are misplaced because they are different protocols. These arrows are actually in the right place because RMI-IIOP supports both JRMP and IIOP protocols.

One of the initial design objectives was to make migration to IIOP easy, and not have a third distributed model for developers to learn. The server object created using RMI-IIOP API can be exported as (and client objects can connect to) either a JRMP or IIOP supporting object by simply changing deployment time properties (without changing/recompiling code).

RMI-IIOP also supports dual export; meaning that a single server object can be exported to support both JRMP and IIOP simultaneously.

Interoperability with CORBA

An RMI-IIOP client cannot necessarily access all existing CORBA objects. The semantics of CORBA objects defined in IDL are a superset of those supported by RMI-IIOP objects, which is why an existing CORBA object's IDL cannot always be mapped into an RMI-IIOP Java interface. It is only when a specific CORBA object's semantics happen to correspond with those of RMI-IIOP that an RMI-IIOP client can call a CORBA object. The connection between the RMI-IIOP client and CORBA server is sometimes – (but not always) possible.

However, this issue should not be over emphasized because it only applies when dealing with existing CORBA objects. Looking at the lower half of the above figure, if you design a new object with an RMI-IIOP Java interface.

- ❑ The CORBA implementation: You can automatically generate its corresponding IDL with the `rmic` tool. From this IDL file you can implement it as a CORBA object (in any language like C++). This C++ object is a pure CORBA object that can be called by a CORBA client as well as a RMI-IIOP client without any limitations. To the RMI-IIOP client, this C++ CORBA object appears as a pure RMI-IIOP object because it is defined by an RMI-IIOP Java interface.

- ❑ The RMI-IIOP implementation: The object appears as a CORBA object to a CORBA client because a CORBA client accesses it through its IDL and as an RMI object to RMI clients because they access it through its RMI-IIOP Java interface.

In short, the difference between a CORBA object and an RMI-IIOP object is only an implementation matter.

One of the reasons for the above mentioned issue with existing objects is that two significant enhancements to the CORBA 2.3 specifications were actually made to bring about the RMI-IIOP and CORBA interoperability. OMG accepted the:

- ❑ Objects by Value specification: This is already defined in Java in the form of object Serialization and is intended to make other languages implement a similar protocol.

- ❑ Java-to-IDL Mapping specification: This is the mapping used to convert RMI Java interfaces into CORBA IDL definitions. It should not be confused with the IDL-to-Java mapping already defined in CORBA 2.2.

> **Both of these specifications are available at OMG; they are also accessible at http://java.sun.com/products/rmi-iiop/index.html.**
> **OMG has officially accepted both specifications for CORBA 2.3 and JDK 1.3 to include both RMI-IIOP and an IDL-to-Java compiler.**

RMI-IIOP and Java IDL

The first question most developers ask is: "So is RMI being phased out in favor of RMI-IIOP?" The answer is no! The second question is: "Is RMI-IIOP a replacement for Java IDL?" Again, no! An RMI-IIOP client cannot necessarily access an existing CORBA object. If you do want to use Java to access CORBA objects that have already been written, Java IDL is your best choice. With Java IDL, which is also a core part of the Java 2 Platform, you can access any CORBA object from Java. Sun's recommendation for usage of RMI-IIOP and Java IDL is if you want to use Java to access existing CORBA resources use Java IDL. If, conversely, you want to export Java RMI resources to CORBA users you should use RMI-IIOP. That is also the reason why RMI-IIOP is the specified communication model in the J2EE specifications, allowing the EJBs and objects to be accessible to CORBA clients.

Writing Programs with RMI-IIOP

There are some development differences in syntax though the overall model remains the same; significantly, RMI-IIOP uses the JNDI API to locate and register objects. Although the development procedure for RMI-IIOP is almost the same as that for RMI (JRMP), the runtime environment is significantly different, in that communication is made through a CORBA 2.3-compliant ORB, using IIOP for communication between servers and clients. Let us look at the differences briefly.

On the Server

There is no significant change in development procedure for RMI objects in RMI-IIOP. The basic steps and their order is still the same as outlined earlier in the initial HelloWorld example, with some changes that also reflect the use of JNDI to look up and bind objects.

- ❑ import statements – in HelloServer we need:

  ```
  import javax.rmi.PortableRemoteObject;
  ```

  and in RegisterIt we need:

  ```
  import javax.naming.*;
  ```

- ❑ Implementation class of a remote object:

  ```
  public class HelloServer extends PortableRemoteObject implements HelloInterface
  ```

  The PortableRemoteObject is similar to the UnicastRemoteObject but provides the base functionality in the IIOP domain.

- ❑ Create the JNDI context and bind to it:

  ```
  Context ctx = new InitialContext();
  ctx.rebind("/EgServer", obj);
  ```

  This binds the object to the JNDI context just as the Namind.bind() method did.

- ❑ Generate a tie for IIOP with rmic -iiop:
  With the -iiop option the rmic compiler generates the stubs and tie classes that support the IIOP protocol. Without this -iiop option, rmic generates a stub and a skeleton for the JRMP protocol or only stubs if you also use the –v1.2 option (remember skeletons are not needed in 1.2).

- ❑ Run tnameserv.exe as a name server:
  This server provides the IIOP CosNaming services to for clients to lookup objects.

- ❑ Generate IDL with rmic -idl for CORBA clients (if your object is also going to be accessed by CORBA clients.)

- ❑ While starting the server the two important environment variables for the JNDI context must be set up.

  a. java.naming.factory.initial. This is the name of the class to use as the factory for creating the context.

  b. java.naming.provider.url. This is the URL to the naming service similar to the rmi:// URL format described earlier. The rmi:// is replaced by iiop:// and the default port is 900 instead of the 1099 for the registry.

These properties can be specified either while starting the server as shown below or by hard-coding values into java.util.Properties and passing that to the InitialContext:

```
java -Djava.naming.factory.initial=com.sun.jndi.cosnaming.CNCtxFactory
    -Djava.naming.provider.url=iiop://localhost:900 RegisterIt
```

In the Client

The client has the same import statement and uses the JNDI context to obtain a reference to the object, rather than using the registry. The JNDI `lookup()` method returns a `java.lang.Object`, which must then be cast using the `narrow()` method of `PortableRemoteObject`.

❑   import statement:

```
import javax.rmi.PortableRemoteObject;
import javax.naming.InitialContext;
```

❑   Look up the remote object by name from the JNDI context:

```
InitialContext ctx = new InitialContext (); // Create the JNDI context
Object obj = ctx.lookup("/EgServer");
HelloInterface myobj = (HelloInterface) PortableRemoteObject.narrow(obj,
                                                HelloInterface.class);

String message = myobj.sayHello();
```

Again, the properties for the JNDI context must be passed to the client applications at runtime. That's basically it! To recap, `HelloInterface` is unchanged from the original. `HelloServer` now reads as follows:

```
import java.rmi.*;
import java.util.Date;
import javax.rmi.PortableRemoteObject;

public class HelloServer extends PortableRemoteObject implements HelloInterface
{
    public HelloServer() throws RemoteException {
        super();     // Call the superclass constructor to export this object
    }

    public String sayHello() throws RemoteException {
        return "Hello World, the current system time is " + new Date();
    }
}
```

`RegisterIt` now contains this code:

```
import java.rmi.*;
import javax.naming.*;

public class RegisterIt {

    public static void main(String args[]) {
        try {
            // Instantiate the object
            HelloServer obj = new HelloServer();
            System.out.println("Object instantiated: "  + obj);

            Context ctx = new InitialContext();
            ctx.rebind("/EgServer", obj);
```

```
              System.out.println("HelloServer bound in registry");
          } catch (Exception e) {
              System.out.println(e);
          }
      }
  }
```

and finally, `HelloClient` reads like this:

```
import java.rmi.*;
import javax.rmi.PortableRemoteObject;
import javax.naming.InitialContext;

public class HelloClient {

    public static void main(String args[]) {
        if (System.getSecurityManager() == null)
            System.setSecurityManager(new RMISecurityManager());
        try {

            InitialContext ctx = new InitialContext (); // Create the JNDI context
            Object obj = ctx.lookup("/EgServer");
            HelloInterface myobj = (HelloInterface)
                            PortableRemoteObject.narrow(obj,
                                            HelloInterface.class);

            String message = myobj.sayHello();
            System.out.println(message);
        } catch (Exception e) {
            System.out.println("HelloClient exception: " + e);
        }
    }
}
```

> **Sun provides a step-by-step guide packaged with the JDK on conversion of existing RMI programs and applets. This can also be accessed online at http://java.sun.com/j2se/1.3/docs/guide/rmi-iiop/rmi_iiop_pg.html**

We have swept through quite a lot in the preceding section. Let us recap what we have just described. We have talked about what steps are involved in writing the RMI-IIOP server and client, the differences between them and how the same server object can be written for both RMI-JRMP and RMI-IIOP clients. What we haven't talked about is how a CORBA client can request services of this object or how the RMI-IIOP client can access a CORBA object. Let us examine this a little.

Once the Java interface is written (`HelloInterface`) you can use the rmic with the `-idl` option to generate its IDL source.

In our case `rmic -idl HelloInterface` produces the following `HelloInterface.idl` file:

```
/**
 * HelloInterface.idl
 * Generated by rmic -idl. Do not edit
 * Friday, July 21, 2000 5:44:25 PM EDT
 */
#include "orb.idl"
#ifndef __HelloInterface__
#define __HelloInterface__

    interface HelloInterface {

        ::CORBA::WStringValue sayHello( );
    };
#pragma ID HelloInterface "RMI:HelloInterface:0000000000000000"

#endif
```

This .idl file can be used by any vendor-provided CORBA 2.3-compliant IDL compiler; you can generate a stub in your language of choice (we talk about C++ since it's a very common language for CORBA objects) to generate the stub classes for that language.

The same compiler can be used to generate skeleton/tie classes and the C++ server objects written to these classes, and IDL can be accessed with the RMI-IIOP clients that we wrote.

RMI-IIOP and J2EE

RMI/IIOP provides the following benefits to developers over RMI/JRMP:

❑ Interoperability with objects written in other languages via language-independent CORBA IDL.

❑ Transaction and security contexts can be propagated implicitly because of the use of IIOP, which can implicitly propagate context information.

❑ IIOP-based firewall support via IIOP proxies that can pass IIOP traffic in a controlled and manageable way.

With IIOP as the transport protocol, Java RMI finds the support it needs to promote industrial-strength distributed application development, within a Java environment only. RMI/IIOP nevertheless has some weaknesses of its own compared to RMI/JRMP:

❑ No distributed garbage collection support is present. The RMI DGC interfaces do not represent object IDs as CORBA does, so those interfaces are not sufficient for CORBA/IIOP. You cannot rely on Java RMI/JRMP's features while using RMI/IIOP.

❑ Java's casting operator cannot be used in your clients directly after getting a remote object reference. Instead, you need to use a special method to get the right type.

❑ You are not allowed to inherit the same method name into your remote interface from different base remote interfaces.

❑ All constant definitions in remote interfaces must be of primitive types or Strings and evaluated at compile time.

So, what's the idea behind making RMI-IIOP the de facto protocol in J2EE?

EJB is a key constituent of J2EE; EJB components live within EJB containers, which provide the runtime environments for the components. EJB containers are developed by different vendors based on the EJB specifications (which use RMI semantics). Vendors are free to choose the implementation for their containers. To help interoperability for EJB environments that include systems from multiple vendors, Sun has defined a standard mapping of EJB-to-CORBA, based on the specification of Java-to-IDL from OMG. That is, EJB interfaces are inherently RMI/IIOP interfaces.

> **Sun's EJB-to-CORBA mapping can be accessed at**
> `http://java.sun.com/products/ejb/index.html`

EJBs are a model for creating distributed enterprise applications that can be deployed in a heterogeneous environment. Standard RMI with the JRMP fails to deliver on some aspects:

❑ It's a Java only solution, and EJBs should also be accessible to other clients in an enterprise environment.

❑ It does not support transaction and security context propagation across distributed JVMs (in fact, it does not support context propagation at all).

❑ Is not as scalable as IIOP.

RMI/IIOP overcomes these limitations of RMI/JRMP. The EJB-to-CORBA mapping not only enables on-the-wire interoperability among multiple vendors' implementations of the EJB container, but also enables non-Java clients to access server-side applications written as EJBs through standard CORBA APIs. EJB-to-CORBA mapping by the EJB containers is not a requirement in the current specification of EJB 1.1, but the EJB 2.0 specifications propose intercontainer operability using RMI/IIOP.

Summary

We have talked about a lot in this chapter, ranging from the basic RMI architecture to HTTP-tunneling. If it overwhelms you, take it slow. Go through the examples and execute them. Write some test applications and that should get you on the move.

Keep in mind that because RMI-IIOP is the model for J2EE, JRMP is still very much alive. If your application requires just Java-Java communication then RMI-JRMP is a feasible solution.

The close association of RMI-IIOP with EJB and its inclusion (starting with the Java 1.3 release) in the core JDK establishes it as a foundation technology for enterprise middleware.

In hindsight, RMI has come a long way from its initial days when no distributed model existed in Java. Today it is the core of the Java distributed model in J2EE and is the base for future technologies like those of JINI and JavaSpaces, which are transforming the way in which devices and systems are going to be networked together. Though outside the scope of this chapter, JINI essentially takes the RMI model and architecture a quantum leap forward.

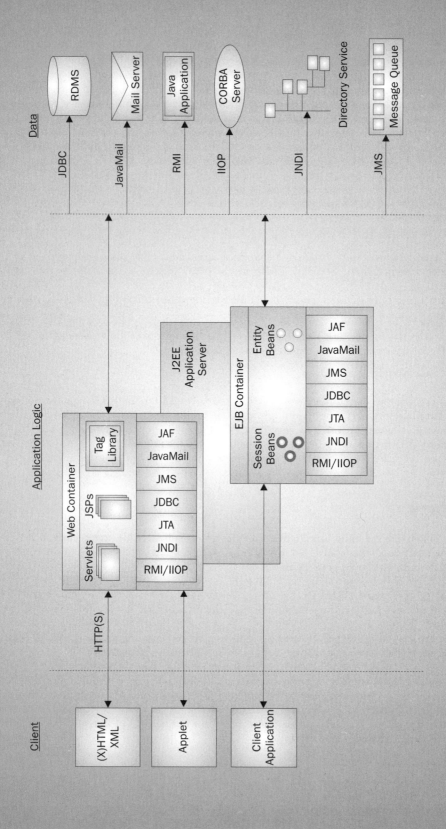

Database Programming with JDBC

3

Databases constitute one of the primary data resources in enterprise applications. The **Java Database Connectivity (JDBC) API** facilitates access to relational data from Java. This API provides cross-vendor connectivity and data access across relational databases from different vendors.

JDBC is essentially an API for executing SQL statements, and extracting the results. Using this API, we can write database clients (from applets to servlets and EJBs) that connect to a relational database, execute SQL statements, and process the results extracted. The structure of this API itself is very simple to use, provided you are conversant with SQL and the underlying relational database semantics.

The JDBC API provides a set of generic database access methods for SQL-compliant relational databases. JDBC abstracts much of the vendor-specific details and generalizes the most common database access functions. The result is a set of classes and interfaces of the `java.sql` package that can be used with any database providing JDBC connectivity through a vendor-specific JDBC driver in a consistent way. Application programmers mostly use the interfaces as implemented by the driver vendor. With a little care to ensure the application conforms to the most commonly available database features, we should be able to reuse an application with another database simply by switching to a new JDBC driver.

Database connectivity does not begin and end at connecting to databases and executing statements. In an enterprise-level application environment such as the J2EE there are additional concerns to be met – such as optimizing network resources by employing connection pooling, and implementing distributed transactions. While the concepts behind these latter concerns are rather advanced, in this chapter you'll find that addressing them is not complex.

In this chapter, we'll discuss the JDBC 2.0 API, which represents the latest update of the JDBC API. The JDBC 2.0 API has two parts:

❏ **JDBC 2.1 Core API**
  This API is specified in the `java.sql` package, and is part of the Java 2, Standard Edition (J2SE). The previous versions of this API focused primarily on basic database programming services such as such as creating connections, executing statements and prepared statements, running batch queries, etc. However, currently the API also supports batch updates, scrollable resultsets, transaction isolation, and the new SQL:1999 datatypes such as BLOB and CLOB in addition to the SQL2 datatypes.

❏ **JDBC 2.0 Optional Package API**
  This API is specified in the `javax.sql` package, and is distributed with the enterprise edition of Java 2 a.k.a. J2EE. The optional package API addresses Java Naming and Directory Interface (JNDI) based data sources for managing connections, connection pooling, distributed transactions, and rowsets. Of these, the first three features are currently required by the J2EE specification. That is, J2EE application servers should support the `javax.sql` package with JNDI based database connections, connection pooling and distributed transactions.

The following are the goals of this chapter:

We will first give an overview of the JDBC API. While doing so, we will not attempt to cover general database programming concepts. Basic knowledge of SQL programming and client-server application development is a prerequisite for this chapter. We will limit ourselves to an overview of some of the facilities of the JDBC API. Rather than attempting to discuss lengthy examples on the JDBC API, this chapter will present short code snippets that illustrate the usage. Here is a list of topics that will be covered to meet this end:

❏ Database connectivity using JDBC drivers

❏ How various SQL operations can be performed using the standard JDBC API: this includes obtaining database connections, sending SQL statements to a database, and retrieving results from database queries

❏ Mapping SQL types in the Java programming language

❏ New features in the JDBC 2.1 core API that include scrollable result sets, and batch updates

The second goal is to discuss database related issues that concern J2EE application architecture and development. The topics for discussion include:

❏ Working with the JDBC 2.0 Optional Package API and JNDI to obtain database connections

❏ Connection pooling, including discussion on traditional connection pooling vs. data source based connection pooling

❏ Distributed transactions and how the Optional Package API, along with the Java Transaction API, enables distributed transactions

❏ Rowsets: When compared to basic JDBC, rowsets provide a higher-level of abstraction for database access – we'll discuss different types of rowsets as implemented in Sun's early access release

While the first set of topics discusses micro-level database programming issues (revolving around connections and result sets), the second set extends towards macro-level concerns such as transactions and connection pooling.

Database Drivers

Before we go into the details of the JDBC API, it is important to understand how the JDBC abstracts database connectivity from Java applications.

A database vendor typically provides a set of APIs for accessing the data managed by the database server. Popular database vendors such as Oracle, Sybase, Informix, etc. provide proprietary APIs for client access. Client applications written in native languages such as C/C++ can make these API calls for database access directly. The JDBC API provides a Java-language alternative to these vendor-specific APIs. Although this eliminates the need to access vendor-specific native APIs for database access, the implementation of the JDBC layer may still need to make these native calls for data access. This is where the concept of a driver comes from. A **JDBC driver** is a middleware layer that translates the JDBC calls to the vendor-specific APIs.

The Java Virtual Machine uses the JDBC driver to translate the generalized JDBC calls into vendor-specific database calls that the database understands. Depending on whether you're using the standard JDBC API, or the Optional Package API, there are different approaches for connecting to a database via the driver. Irrespective of this, for accessing data, you'll need a database driver supplied either by the database vendor, or by a J2EE server provider.

Let's now consider different approaches for connecting from your application to a database server via a database driver. Note that the following classification is an industry standard, and commercial driver products are categorized based on this classification.

Type 1 – JDBC-ODBC Bridge

ODBC (Open Database Connectivity) is Microsoft's API for database drivers, and is very popular on Windows platforms. ODBC is a Windows API standard for SQL by Microsoft that was further enhanced by Visigenic and Intersol to provide ODBC SDKs for non-windows platforms. ODBC is based on the X/Open Call-Level Interface (CLI) specification, a standard API for database access. CLI is intended to be vendor, platform, and database neutral and this is where ODBC diverges. The ODBC API defines a set of functions for directly accessing the data, without the need for embedded SQL in client applications. The JDBC API is originally based on the ODBC API.

> *Embedded SQL was one of the approaches considered for database access by the SQL Access Group. This involves embedding SQL statements in applications programmed in high-level languages, and preprocessing them to generate native function calls.*

The first category of JDBC drivers provides a bridge between the JDBC API and the ODBC API. This bridge translates the standard JDBC calls to corresponding ODBC calls, and sends them to ODBC data source via ODBC libraries as shown overleaf:

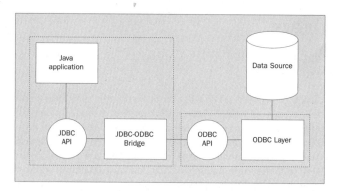

The **JDBC-ODBC bridge** translates all JDBC API calls into equivalent ODBC calls. The driver then delegates these calls to the data source. The process boundaries are marked with a broken line. That is, the Java classes for the JDBC API and the JDBC-ODBC bridge are invoked within the client application process. Similarly, the ODBC layer executes in another process. This configuration requires the client application to have the JDBC-ODBC bridge API, the ODBC driver, and the native language level API (such as the OCI library for Oracle) installed on each client machine.

Due to the multiple layers of indirection for each data access call, this solution for data access is inefficient for high-performance database access requirements. Not only does the system have to pass the database call through multiple layers, but it also limits the functionality of the JDBC API to that of the ODBC driver. Using a bridge to an ODBC data source is not a preferred solution, but in some cases it might be the only solution. For instance, a Microsoft Access database can only be accessed using the JDBC-ODBC bridge.

> *The standard JDK includes classes for the JDBC-ODBC bridge*
> *(`sun.jdbc.odbc.JdbcOdbcDriver`), and there is no need for additional installation – apart*
> *from having to configure the ODBC driver by creating data source names (DSNs).*

Type 2 – Part Java, Part Native Driver

The second alternative is the Type 2 driver. Type 2 drivers use a mixture of Java implementation and vendor-specific native APIs for data access. This is similar to the Type 1 driver architecture, except that there is one less layer to go through and so it is much faster. When a database call is made using JDBC, the driver translates the request into vendor-specific API calls. The database will process the request and send the results back through the API, which will forward them back to the JDBC driver. The JDBC driver will format the results to conform to the JDBC standard and return them to the program:

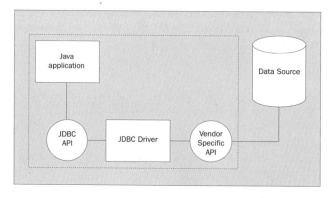

In this approach too, the native JDBC driver (part Java, part native code) must be installed on each client along with the vendor-specific native language API. The native code uses vendor-specific protocols for communicating with the database. The improved efficiency makes this a preferred method over the use of Type 1 drivers and also means that potentially we have use of the full functionality of the vendor's API.

Type 3 – Intermediate Database Access Server

Type 3 drivers are based on intermediate (middleware) database servers with the ability to connect multiple Java clients to multiple database servers. In this approach, clients connect to various database servers via an intermediate server that acts as a gateway for multiple database servers. While the specific protocol used between clients and the intermediate server depends on the middleware server vendor, the intermediate server can use different native protocols to connect to different databases. The Java client application sends a JDBC call through a JDBC driver to the intermediate data access server. The middle-tier then handles the request using another driver (for example, a Type 2 driver) to complete the request:

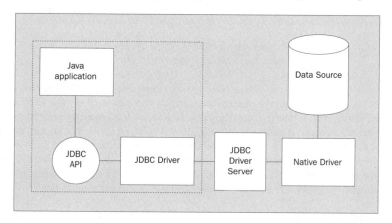

Architecturally this is a very flexible alternative, as the intermediate server can abstract details of connections to database servers. J2EE application servers such as BEA's WebLogic include Type 3 drivers.

Type 4 – Pure Java Drivers

This is a pure Java alternative to Type 2 drivers. These drivers convert the JDBC API calls to direct network calls using vendor-specific networking protocols by making direct socket connections with the database (such as Tabular Data Stream for Sybase and Oracle Thin JDBC Driver). This is the most efficient method of accessing databases, both in performance and development time. It is also the simplest to deploy since there are no additional libraries or middleware to install as shown overleaf. All major database vendors (Oracle, Sybase, and Microsoft, etc.) provide Type 4 JDBC drivers for their databases and they are also available from third party vendors.

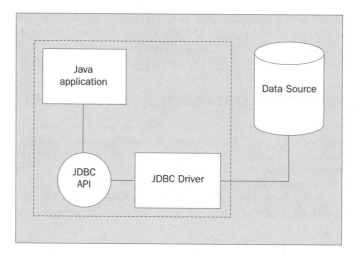

For a complete list of JDBC drivers under the above categories, refer to
`http://industry.java.sun.com/products/jdbc/drivers`.

To get started with JDBC applications, you need to install a driver of one of the above types. You'll also need a database server. However, for the sake of simplicity, in this chapter, we'll use the Cloudscape database for demonstrating the JDBC API. If you're using the J2EE Reference Implementation from Sun, your installation already includes the Cloudscape database at `%J2EE_HOME%\lib\cloudscape\cloudscape.jar` where `%J2EE_HOME%` is the directory where you installed the J2EE. You can also obtain an evaluation copy of Cloudscape at `http://www.cloudscape.com`. In order to the JDBC API and the Cloudscape database, you should add the `cloudscape.jar` file to your `CLASSPATH`. Refer to the Cloudscape documentation for instructions on using the CloudView, a GUI for accessing the Cloudscape database.

Cloudscape is a small footprint database management system built into Java. Cloudscape can be used in one of two modes – embedded mode, and client-server mode. In the embedded mode, Cloudscape executes within the client application process. This is the simplest mode for database management, as this does not involve any setup, apart from including the Cloudscape classes in your `CLASSPATH`. The second mode is the client-server mode, which lets you access Cloudscape in the traditional client-server manner. For Cloudscape, there is no need for additional database drivers, as Cloudscape is an all Java implementation, and JDBC calls are mapped to Cloudscape Java API calls within the same process. In client-server mode, these calls are further mapped to RMI calls to the Cloudscape server process.

> *If you wish to use another database such as Oracle, Microsoft Access, or similar, make sure that you follow the instructions given by the database vendor to setup the database, and install the applicable database driver.*

The JDBC 2.1 Core API

The JDBC 2.1 Core API is specified in the `java.sql` package. This package includes classes provided with the J2SE, and interfaces implemented by driver providers.

The following table provides an overview of the `java.sql` package. In this table, interfaces are shown in bold, and the classes/interfaces are categorized based on their role in the JDBC API.

Class/Interface	Purpose
DriverManager	Load a driver and connect to a database
Driver	
DriverPropertyInfo	
Connection	
Statement	Set up and execute SQL statements
PreparedStatement	
CallableStatement	
ResultSet	Retrieve and update results
Array	Map between SQL data types and Java language types
Blob	
Clob	
Date	
Ref	
Struct	
Time	
Timestamp	
Types	
SQLData	Map user-defined SQL types to Java classes
SQLInput	
SQLOutput	
DatabaseMetadata	Obtain meta-information about database and results
ResultSetMetaData	
SQLException	Handle SQL error, warning, and driver-level exceptions
SQLWarning	
DataTruncation	
BatchUpdateException	
SQLPermission	Provide security

All the classes in the above table are implemented in the J2SE itself, and abstract higher level database independent operations. Except the interfaces for user-defined SQL types, the remaining interfaces, implemented by driver vendors, provide access to database-specific semantics, such as connections, statements, result sets, etc.

In the following sections, we'll discuss some of the most commonly used classes and interfaces of this API. In particular, we will learn:

- ❑ How to load a database driver

- ❑ How to open a database connection

- ❑ How to send SQL statements to databases for execution

- ❑ How to extract results returned from a database query

- ❑ What prepared statements are

- ❑ The role of JDBC types

- ❑ Handling exceptions and warnings

Loading a Database Driver and Opening Connections

In the JDBC core API, the `java.sql.Connection` interface represents a connection with a database. This is specified as an interface because the actual implementation of a connection is network protocol and vendor dependent. In a single application, we can obtain one or more connections for one or more databases using different JDBC drivers. Each driver implements the `java.sql.Driver` interface. One of the methods that this interface defines is the `connect()` method that establishes a connection with the database, and returns a `Connection` object that encapsulates the database connection.

Instead of directly accessing classes that implement the `Driver` interface, the standard approach for obtaining connections is to register each driver with the `java.sql.DriverManager`, and use the methods provided on this class to obtain connections. Before going into the details of this approach, let's discuss how JDBC represents database locations.

JDBC URLs

The notion of a URL in JDBC is very similar to the way URLs are used otherwise. In order to see the rationale behind JDBC URLs, consider an application using several databases each being accessed via a different database driver. In such a scenario, how do we uniquely identify a driver? Moreover, databases use different types of parameters for obtaining connections. How are parameters specified while making connections?

JDBC URLs provide a way of identifying a database driver. A JDBC URL represents a driver, and additional driver-specific information to locate a database and to connect to it. The syntax of the JDBC URL is as follows:

```
jdbc:<subprotocol>:<subname>
```

This has three parts separated by colons:

- ❑ Protocol: In the above syntax, `jdbc` is the protocol. This is the only allowed protocol in JDBC.

- ❑ Sub-protocol: The sub-protocol is used to identify a database driver, or the name of a database connectivity mechanism, chosen by the database driver providers.

- ❑ Subname: The syntax of the subname is driver-specific. A driver may choose any syntax appropriate for its implementation.

For example, for a Cloudscape database called "Movies", the URL to connect to it is:

```
jdbc:cloudscape:Movies
```

Alternatively, if we were using Oracle via the JDBC-ODBC bridge, our URL would be:

```
jdbc:odbc:Movies
```

where `Movies` is a System DSN set up using our ODBC driver administrator.

As you see from the above syntax, JDBC URLs are flexible enough to specify-driver specific information in the subname.

DriverManager

The purpose of the `java.sql.DriverManager` class in JDBC is to provide a common access layer on top of different database drivers used in an application. In this approach, instead of using individual Driver implementation classes directly, applications use the `DriverManager` class to obtain connections. This class provides three static methods to obtain connections.

However, the `DriverManager` requires that each driver required by the application must be registered before use, so that the `DriverManager` is aware of it.

The JDBC approach for loading database drivers seems obscure when you take a cursory glance at the following code snippet, which loads the Cloudscape's database driver. In JDBC, you try to load the database driver using the current `java.lang.ClassLoader` object:

```
try {
  Class.forName("COM.cloudscape.core.JDBCDriver");
} catch (ClassNotFoundException e) {
  // Driver not found.
  ...
}
```

How does this code load the driver? At runtime, the `ClassLoader` locates and loads the class `COM.cloudscape.core.JDBCDriver` from the `CLASSPATH` using the bootstrap class loader. While loading a class, the class loader executes any static initialization code for the class. In JDBC, each driver provider is required to register an instance of the driver with the `java.sql.DriverManager` class during this static initialization. The `java.sql.DriverManager` is a static class, and provides the `public static void registerDriver(java.sql.Driver)` method for this purpose.

Alternatively, we can also specify a list of drivers using the Java properties mechanism. For example, the following snippet would allow the `DriverManager` class to load the list of drivers when an attempt is made to establish a connection:

```
System.setProperty("jdbc.drivers", "COM.cloudscape.core.JDBCDriver");
```

Multiple drivers can be specified as a list separated by colons (:).

Once a driver has been registered with the DriverManager, we can use its static methods to get connections. The DriverManager class specifies the following methods:

Methods to Manage Drivers

The following methods manage drivers. Note that these methods are meant for driver implementation, and tools that manipulate drivers:

```
public static void registerDriver(Driver driver)
```

This method is used to register a driver with the DriverManager. A newly loaded driver class should call this method to make itself known to the DriverManager. Classes implementing the Driver interface call this method during the static initialization to register a class. Once registered, the driver manager holds a reference to the driver until it is deregistered. For security reasons, the driver manager associates the caller's class loader with each driver, so that classes loaded from a class loader will have access only to those drivers that are registered by classes loaded by the same class loader.

```
public static void deregisterDriver(Driver driver)
```

This method deregisters a driver from the driver manager.

```
public static Driver getDriver(String url)
```

Given a JDBC URL, this method returns a driver that can understand the URL.

```
public static Enumeration getDrivers()
```

This method returns an enumeration of all registered JDBC drivers registered by classes using the same class loader.

Methods to Obtain Connections

The driver manager has three variants of getConnection() methods to establish connections. These are all static methods. The driver manager delegates these calls to the connect() method on the Driver interface.

Depending on the type of the driver and the database server, a connection may involve a physical network connection to the database server, or a proxy to a connection. Embedded databases require no physical connection. Whether or not there is a physical connection involved, the connection object is the only object that an application uses to communicate with the database. All communication must happen within the context of one or more connections.

Let's now consider the different methods for getting a connection:

```
public static Connection getConnection(String url) throws SQLException
```

The DriverManager retrieves an appropriate driver from the set of registered JDBC drivers. The database URL is specified in the form of jdbc:subprotocol:subname.

```
public static Connection getConnection(String url, java.util.Properties info)
        throws SQLException
```

This method requires a URL and a java.util.Properties object. The Properties object contains each required parameter for the specified database. Two commonly used properties for the Cloudscape are autocommit=true and create=false. We can specify these properties along with the URL as jdbc:cloudscape:Movies;autocommit=true;create=true, or we can set these properties using the Properties object, and pass the Properties object in the above getConnection() method:

```
String url = "jdbc:cloudscape:Movies";
Properties p = new Properties();
p.put("autocommit", "true");
p.put("create","true");
Connection connection = DriverManager.getConnection(url, p);
```

Note these properties are driver specific, and you should refer to your driver documentation for the list of required properties.

```
public static Connection getConnection(String url, String user, String password)
        throws SQLException
```

The third variant takes user and password as the arguments in addition to the URL. The third simply takes the URL as its only argument. Whether we would get a connection with this method or not depends on whether the database accepts connection requests without authentication. Here is an example. The following code uses an ODBC driver, where Movies is a DSN setup in the ODBC configuration. This DSN corresponds to a database that requires a user name and password for getting a connection:

```
String url = "jdbc:odbc.Movies ";
String user = "catalog_admin";
String password = "catalog_admin";

Connection conn = DriverManager.getConnection(url, user, password);
```

Note that all these methods are synchronized, implying that more than one application thread cannot directly get hold of the same java.sql.Connection object. These methods throw a SQLException if the driver fails to obtain a connection.

Sometimes it is necessary to specify the maximum time that a driver should wait while attempting to connect to a database. The following two methods can be used to set/get the login timeout:

```
public static void setLoginTimeout(int seconds)
public static int getLoginTimeout()
```

Methods for Logging

The following methods access or set a PrintWriter object for logging purposes:

```
public static void setLogWriter(PrintWriter out)
public static PrintWriter getLogWriter()
```

In addition, client applications can also log messages using the following method:

`public static void println(String message)`

This method is used in conjunction with the `PrintWriter` set by the `setLogWriter()` method to print log messages.

Driver

In JDBC, each driver is identified using a JDBC URL, and each driver should implement the `java.sql.Driver` interface. For instance in Cloudscape, the `COM.cloudscape.core.JDBCDriver` class implements the `java.sql.Driver` interface, which specifies the following methods:

```
public boolean acceptsURL(String url)
public Connection connect(String url, Properties info)
public int getMajorVersion()
public int getMinorVersion()
public DriverPropertyInfo getPropertyInfo(String url, Properties info)
public boolean jdbcCompliant()
```

The driver manager class uses these methods. In general, client applications need not access the driver classes directly.

Establishing a Connection

To communicate with a database using JDBC, we must first establish a connection to the database through the appropriate JDBC driver. The JDBC API specifies the connection in the `java.sql.Connection` interface. This interface has the following public methods:

Methods for creating statements:

- ❑ `createStatement()`
- ❑ `createStatement ()`
- ❑ `prepareStatement()`
- ❑ `prepareCall()`

This method obtains database information:

- ❑ `getMetaData()`

Methods for transaction support:

- ❑ `setAutoCommit()`
- ❑ `getAutoCommit()`
- ❑ `commit()`
- ❑ `rollback()`
- ❑ `setTransactionIsolation()`
- ❑ `getTransactionIsolation()`

Methods for testing connection status and closing:

- ❏ isClosed()
- ❏ close()

Methods to set or test various properties, clear values, and retrieve any warnings generated:

- ❏ setReadOnly()
- ❏ isReadOnly()
- ❏ clearWarnings()
- ❏ getWarnings()

And finally, methods to convert SQL strings into database specific SQL and for setting or getting views and user defined types:

- ❏ nativeSQL()
- ❏ setCatalog(String catalog)
- ❏ getCatalog()
- ❏ setTypeMap(Map map)
- ❏ getTypeMap()

The categories in the above list attempt to break the methods into logical groups according to functionality. In the next few sections, we'll discuss most of these methods.

Here's an example of establishing a JDBC connection to the Cloudscape Movies database:

```
Connection connection;
String url = "jdbc:cloudscape:Movies;create=true"

try {

  connection = DriverManager.getConnection(url);

  // Data access using the connection object
  . . .
} catch (SQLException e) {
        // Deal with error here
} finally {
  try {

    connection.close();
  } catch(SQLException e) { }
}
```

In this example, the URL specifies the JDBC URL; create=true indicates that Cloudscape should create the Movies database if it does not exist. You should also always catch the SQLException, and try to close the connection after using the connection for data access.

In the JDBC API, there are several methods that throw a SQLException. In this example, the connection is closed in the `finally` block, so that the system resources can be freed up regardless of the success or otherwise of any database operations.

Creating and Executing SQL Statements

We can use this Connection object to execute SQL statements by creating a Statement, a PreparedStatement, or a CallableStatement. These objects abstract regular SQL statements, prepared statements, and stored procedures respectively. Once we obtain one of these statement objects, we can execute the statement and read the results through a ResultSet object.

As shown the list above, the following methods create statement objects:

```
Statement createStatement() throws SQLException
```

This method creates a Statement object, which we can use to send SQL statements to the database. SQL statements without parameters are normally executed using Statement objects.

```
Statement createStatement(int resultSetType, int resultSetConcurrency)
            throws SQLException
```

This variant of createStatement() requires a result set type, and result set concurrency arguments. The java.sql.ResultSet interface specifies three constants as result types. We'll see more details of these parameters (including concurrency) later in this chapter.

The createStatement() method takes no arguments (except for type and concurrency where applicable) and returns a Statement object. The ultimate goal of a Statement object is to execute a SQL statement that may or may not return results. We will see an example soon.

```
public PreparedStatement prepareStatement(String sql) throws SQLException
```

We can get a PreparedStatement object by calling this method on a Connection.

```
public CallableStatement prepareCall(String sql) throws SQLException
```

This method is used to call a database stored procedure.

The Statement interface has the following methods:

Methods for executing statements:

- ❑ execute()
- ❑ executeQuery()
- ❑ executeUpdate()

Methods for batch updates:

- ❏ `addBatch()`
- ❏ `executeBatch()`
- ❏ `clearBatch()`

Methods for result set fetch size and direction:

- ❏ `setFetchSize()`
- ❏ `getFetchSize()`
- ❏ `setFetchDirection()`
- ❏ `getFetchDirection()`

Method to get current result set:

- ❏ `getResultSet()`

Methods for result set concurrency and type:

- ❏ `getResultSetConcurrency()`
- ❏ `getResultSetType()`

Other methods:

- ❏ `setQueryTimeout()`
- ❏ `getQueryTimeout()`
- ❏ `setMaxFieldSize()`
- ❏ `getMaxFieldSize()`
- ❏ `cancel()`
- ❏ `getConnection()`

`Statements` also support the same methods for transaction support as the `Connection` object, together with the `close()` method.

There are two sub-interfaces, `PreapredStatement` and `CallableStatement`, that are used for calling precompiled SQL statements and database stored procedures. These two interfaces specify additional methods for preparing statements and calling stored procedures.

An Example: Movie Catalog

In order to illustrate the JDBC API, let's consider a simple movie catalog. The database for this example consists of a table called `CATALOG`.

Let's consider a Java class `CreateMovieTables` that creates a `CATALOG` table, and inserts the data into the table. In this example, we retrieve the data from a text file, `catalog.txt` and insert into the `CATALOG` table.

Create the Movies Table

The initialize() method loads the driver, and obtains a connection. createTable() creates the table.

You can use the following method on the Statement object to insert data:

int executeUpdate(String sql) throws SQLException

executeUpdate() is used to execute SQL statements that do not return any results, for example INSERT, UPDATE, or DELETE statements. This method returns an integer that denotes the number of rows affected:

```
public class CreateMovieTables
{
  static String driver = "COM.cloudscape.core.JDBCDriver";
  static String url = "jdbc:cloudscape:";
  Connection connection = null;
  Statement statement = null;
  ...

  public void initialize() throws SQLException, ClassNotFoundException
  {
    Class.forName (driver);

    connection = DriverManager.getConnection(url + "Movies;create=true");
  }

  public void createTable() throws SQLException
  {
    statement = connection.createStatement();

    statement.executeUpdate("CREATE TABLE CATALOG(TITLE VARCHAR(256),
                            LEAD_ACTOR VARCHAR(256), LEAD_ACTRESS
                            VARCHAR(256), TYPE VARCHAR(20), RELEASE_DATE
                            DATE)");
  }
```

In this code, the variables connection and statement are instance variables of CreateMovieTables class. The createTable() method obtains a connection from the DriverManager. For Cloudscape, we specify the protocol as "jdbc:cloudscape:Movies;create=true". When we create a table for the first time using this URL, the Cloudscape DBMS creates a subdirectory under the current working directory called "Movies" to store the data. Refer to Cloudscape documentation for specifying a different directory. In case you want to cleanup your database, you may remove this directory, and recreate all the tables. You can access the Cloudscape documentation online at http://www.cloudscape.com/support/documentation.html.

After getting a connection, the next step is to create a statement. We pass a SQL statement for creating the table using the executeUpdate() method on the statement. As you see from the SQL statement above, the CATALOG table has five columns.

Inserting Data

The `insertData()` method of the `CreateMovieTables` class reads movie records from a text file, and inserts them into the database:

```
public void insertData() throws SQLException, IOException
{
  BufferedReader br = new BufferedReader(new FileReader("catalogue.txt"));

  try {
    do  {

        title = br.readLine();
        leadActor = br.readLine();
        leadActress = br.readLine();
        type = br.readLine();
        dateOfRelease = br.readLine();

        String sqlString = "INSERT INTO CATALOGUE VALUES('" + title +
                           "','" + leadActor + "','" + leadActress +
                           "','" + type + "','" + dateOfRelease + "')";

        statement.executeUpdate(sqlString);
      } while(br.readLine() != null); // This reads the termination line

  } catch (EOFException e) {
  } finally {
      statement.close();
      br.close();
  }
}
```

The format of the input file is `title`, `leadActor`, `leadActress`, `type`, and `dateOfRelease` entered in separate lines, followed by a separator line as shown below:

```
Austin Powers
Mike Myers
Liz Hurley
Comedy
1999-04-01
--------------
```

In the code above, the only statement that is relevant for our discussion is the `statement.executeUpdate()` method call to insert the data into the CATALOG table. Note that we did not catch the `SQLException` here. Instead we're letting the caller of this method catch the `SQLException`.

Methods for Exception Handling

As mentioned previously, most of the methods on JDBC interfaces/classes throw `SQLException` to indicate failures. However, depending on the drivers and databases that you're using, there could be several layers and sources of errors. In order to accommodate this, the `SQLException` can be nested, by embedding several exceptions in a linked list. We can use the `getNextException()` on the

SQLException class to retrieve all such exceptions. The following code snippet recursively traverses through the available exceptions. This approach could prove to be informative for handling exceptions in our JDBC applications:

```
} catch(SQLException sqlException) {

    while(sqlException != null)
    {
        System.err.println(sqlException.toString());
        sqlException = sqlException.getNextException();
    }
}
```

You can similarly retrieve warnings (including vendor-specific) received or generated by the driver using the getWarnings() method on the connection:

```
SQLWarning warnings = connection.getWarnings();

while(warnings != null) {
    System.err.println(connection.getWarnings());
    warnings = warnings.getNextWarning();
}
```

Here is the complete source:

```
import java.sql.*;
import java.io.*;

// This class requires a text file called catalog.txt containing the
// input data.

public class CreateMovieTables {

    static String driver = "COM.cloudscape.core.JDBCDriver";
    static String url = "jdbc:cloudscape:";

    String title, leadActor, leadActress, type, dateOfRelease;
    Connection connection;
    Statement statement;

    public void initialize() throws SQLException, ClassNotFoundException
    {
        Class.forName(driver);

        connection = DriverManager.getConnection(url + "Movies;create=true");
    }

    public void createTable() throws SQLException
    {
        statement = connection.createStatement();
```

```
      statement.executeUpdate("CREATE TABLE CATALOGUE(TITLE VARCHAR(256),
                             LEAD_ACTOR VARCHAR(256), LEAD_ACCTRESS
                             VARCHAR(256), TYPE VARCHAR(20),
                             RELEASE_DATE DATE)");
    }

  public void insertData() throws SQLException, IOException
  {
    BufferedReader br = new BufferedReader(new FileReader("catalogue.txt"));

    try {
      do {
        title = br.readLine();
        leadActor = br.readLine();
        leadActress = br.readLine();
        type = br.readLine();
        dateOfRelease = br.readLine();
        System.err.println(title + " " + dateOfRelease);

        String sqlString = "INSERT INTO CATALOGUE VALUES('" + title +
                      "','" + leadActor + "','" + leadActress +
                      "','" + type + "','" + dateOfRelease + "')";
        statement.executeUpdate(sqlString);
        statement.close();

      } while(br.readLine() != null); // This reads the termination line
    } catch (EOFException e) {
    } finally {
      br.close();
    }
  }

  public void close() throws SQLException
  {
    try {
        connection.close();
    } catch(SQLException e)  {
      throw e;
    }
  }

  public static void main(String arg[])
  {
    CreateMovieTables movies = new CreateMovieTables();

    try {
      movies.initialize();
      movies.createTable();
      movies.close();
    } catch(SQLException sqlException) {
      while(sqlException != null)
      {
        sqlException.printStackTrace();
        sqlException = sqlException.getNextException();
      }
    }
```

```
        } catch(IOException ioException)  {
          ioException.printStackTrace();
        } catch(Exception e) {
          e.printStackTrace();
        }
    }
  }
```

For the purpose of demonstration, this class is structured in terms of small methods each of which perform specific JDBC functions. In this class, the `initialize()` method loads the driver, and creates a connection. The `createTable()` method creates a table using the `executeUpdate()` method on the `java.sql.Statement`. The `insertData()` method reads a number of records from a text file, and inserts them into the table. The `main()` method of this class is the controller that calls the other methods in sequence. Note that the `main` method calls the `close()` method to close the statement and the connection.

For most of the remaining examples in this chapter, we follow the above class as a template. If you want to experiment with the JDBC API, you should add new methods in this class.

Querying the Database Using the ResultSet Interface

The `Statement` object returns a `java.sql.ResultSet` object that encapsulates the results of execution. This is an interface that is implemented by driver vendors. You can scroll through the result set using this cursor for reading the results in the `ResultSet`. The JDBC API 1.0 allowed only forward scrolling. That is, after reading a row in the result set, there is no provision for going back in the `ResultSet`.

The following method, `executeQuery`, in the `java.sql.Statement` interface, allows you to execute SQL SELECT statements:

public ResultSet executeQuery (String sql) throws SQLException

There is also a generic `execute()` method that can return multiple results:

public boolean execute(String sql) throws SQLException

This method can be used to execute stored procedures that are a known to give multiple results, or unknown SQL strings (for example, SQL statements read from another source at runtime).

The JDBC API 2.1 introduced two more types of `ResultSets` that allow scrolling through the result in both forward and reverse directions. Not all database vendors support this feature currently, however. We'll discuss scrolling later in this chapter.

Methods to Retrieve Data

The `java.sql.ResultSet` interface provides several methods for retrieving fields of different types. Depending on your schema, you should use appropriate methods to retrieve the data:

getAsciiStream()	getTimestamp()	getTime()	getBigDecimal()
getBoolean()	getBinaryStream()	getString()	getMetaData()
getDate()	getBytes()	getByte()	getClob()
getInt()	getFloat()	getDouble()	getWarnings()
getShort()	getObject()	getLong()	getBlob()

Most of these methods require either the column name (as a string) or the column index as the argument. The syntax for the two variants of the getString() method is shown below:

```
public String getString(int columnIndex) throws SQLException;
public String getString(String columnName) throws SQLException;
```

Let's get back to our movie catalog. Now we have created a table, let's create another class, QueryMovieTables, to implement different types of queries. The following method, queryAll(), retrieves all the data from the CATALOG table:

```
public void queryAll() throws SQLException
{
  System.out.println("Query All");
  Statement statement = connection.createStatement();

  String sqlString = "SELECT CATALOGUE.TITLE, CATALOGUE.LEAD_ACTOR,
                      CATALOGUE.LEAD_ACCTRESS, CATALOGUE.TYPE,
                      CATALOGUE.RELEASE_DATE FROM CATALOGUE";

  ResultSet rs = statement.executeQuery(sqlString);

  while(rs.next())
  {
    System.out.println(rs.getString("TITLE") + ", " +
                       rs.getString("LEAD_ACTOR") + ", " +
                       rs.getString("LEAD_ACCTRESS") + ", " +
                       rs.getString("TYPE") + ", " +
                       rs.getDate("RELEASE_DATE"));
  }
}
```

This method first creates a Statement object, which it then uses to call executeQuery() with a SQL SELECT statement as an argument. The java.sql.ResultSet object returned contains all the rows of the CATALOG table matching the SELECT statement. Using the next() method of the ResultSet object, we can iterate through all the rows contained in the result set. At any given row, we can use one of the getXXX methods in the table above to retrieve the fields of the row.

ResultSetMetaData Interface

The ResultSet interface also allows us to find out the structure of the result set. The getMetaData() method helps us to retrieve a java.sql.ResultSetMetaData object that has several methods to describe result set cursors:

getCatalogName()	getScale()
getTableName()	getPrecision()
getSchemaName()	isNullable()
getColumnCount()	isCurrency()
getColumnName())	isSearchable()
getColumnLabel()	isCaseSensitive()
getColumnType()	isSigned()
getColumnTypeName()	isAutoIncrement()
getColumnClassName()	isReadOnly()
getColumnDisplaySize()	isDefinitelyWritable()

Given a result set, we can use the getColumnCount() method to get the number of columns in the result set. Using this column number, we can get the meta-information of each column.

For example, the following method prints the structure of the ResultSet:

```
public void getMetaData() throws SQLException
{
  System.out.println("MetaData of ResultSet");
  Statement statement = connection.createStatement();

  String sqlString = "SELECT * FROM CATALOG";

  ResultSet rs = statement.executeQuery(sqlString);

  ResultSetMetaData metaData = rs.getMetaData();

  int noColumns = metaData.getColumnCount();

  // Column numbers start from 1.
  for(int i = 1; i < noColumns + 1; i++)
  {
      System.out.println(metaData.getColumnName(i) + " " +
                         metaData.getColumnType(i));
  }
}
```

The above method gets the number of columns in the result set, and prints the name and type of each column. In this case, the column names are TITLE, LEAD_ACTOR, LEAD_ACTRESS, TYPE, and RELEASE_DATE. Note that the types of column are returned as integers. For example, all VARCHAR type columns will have the column type as 12, while DATE type has a type 91. These types are constants defined in the java.sql.Types interface. Also note that the column numbers start from 1 instead of 0.

Prepared Statements

If the same SQL statement is executed many times with different paramaters, it is more efficient to use a PreparedStatement object. A PreparedStatement object can hold precompiled SQL statements. The following methods on the java.sql.Connection interface let us create PreparedStatement objects:

```
PreparedStatement prepareStatement(String sql) throws SQLException
PreparedStatement prepareStatement(String sql, int resultSetType,
                                   int resultSetConcurrency)
       throws SQLException
```

For example, in the insertData() method of the CreateMovieTables class, the SQL INSERT statement is executed a number of times. This statement must be compiled before it is executed. Compilation is a time-consuming process that typically involves parsing of the statement, binding with the tables and columns, any optimization, and code generation; it may be better to use a PreparedStatement as an alternative. With prepared statements, this compilation is done only once.

To allow us to specify the data, prepared statements are parameterized, with each parameter represented as a question mark ('?').

We can replace the insertData() method of the CreateMovieTables class with the following to make use of the PreparedStatement object:

```
public void insertPreparedData () throws SQLException, IOException
{

   BufferedReader br = new BufferedReader(new FileReader("catalogue.txt"));

   PreparedStatement preparedStatement = connection.prepareStatement(
       "INSERT INTO" CATALOGUE(title, lead_actor, lead_acctress, type,
       release_date)VALUES(?, ?, ?, ?, ?)");

   SimpleDateFormat dateFormat = new SimpleDateFormat("yyyy-MM-dd");

   try {
     do {
       preparedStatement.clearParameters();
       title = br.readLine();
       leadActor = br.readLine();
       leadActress = br.readLine();
       type = br.readLine();
       dateOfRelease = br.readLine();
       Date date = new Date(dateFormat.parse(dateOfRelease).getTime());

       preparedStatement.setString(1, title);
       preparedStatement.setString(2, leadActor);
       preparedStatement.setString(3, leadActress);
       preparedStatement.setString(4, type);
       preparedStatement.setDate(5, date);

       preparedStatement.executeUpdate();
```

```
        } while(br.readLine() != null);
    } catch (EOFException e) {
    } catch (java.text.ParseException pe) {
        pe.printStackTrace();

    } finally {
        preparedStatement.close();
        br.close();
    }
}
```

Once the `PreparedStatement` is created, use the `setXXX` methods to set parameters for the `PreparedStatement`. For instance, we use the `setString()` method for setting VARCHAR parameters. Similarly, for setting SQL DATE type, we can use the `setDate()` method. These methods take the column number as the first argument.

Also note that the date object requires special treatment. There are four different objects that we can use for representing date and time. The `java.util.Date` class was the only date object available prior to the JDBC API. However, the `java.sql` package introduces three more classes:

public class Date extends java.util.Date

This `Date` class corresponds to the SQL DATE type. Therefore, we should use `java.sql.Date` in our JDBC programming to conform to the JDBC types:

public class Time extends java.util.Date

This class corresponds to the SQL TIME DATE type:

public class TimeStamp extends java.util.Date

Neither of the `java.sql.Date` and `java.sql.Time` classes captures the precision of SQL TIMESTAMP type. The `java.sql.TimeStamp` class fills this gap. Time stamp objects can hold TIMESTAMP nanoseconds, in addition to the standard dates.

The JDBC API also provides facilities for invoking stored procedures. The `java.sql.CallableStatement` interface can be used for creating statements for executing stored procedures. The following methods on the `java.sql.Connection` interface create `CallableStatement` objects:

```
CallableStatement prepareCall(String sql) throws SQLException
CallableStatement prepareCall(String sql, int resultSetType,
                              int resultSetConcurrency) throws SQLException
```

In practice, a stored procedure is not appropriate in a J2EE environment, as it couples the application very closely with a specific database.

Mapping SQL Types to Java

SQL data types and Java data types are not equivalent. While SQL types include types such as VARCHAR, NUMBER, TIMESTAMP, etc., data types in Java evolved from programming languages such as C and C++. This disparity between SQL types and Java data types has been addressed by the specification of generic SQL types, and their mapping to and from Java data types. The JDBC SQL types are specified in the `java.sql.Types` interface, as constants.

There are two occasions where we require this mapping information: While setting input parameters for prepared statements (using `setXXX()` methods in the `PreparedStatement` interface), and secondly while getting results from `ResultSet` objects (using `getXXX()` methods in the `ResultSet` interface). In both these cases, drivers map the types across JDBC and Java types.

The following table summarizes the JDBC types, and their mapping to Java types and SQL data types:

JDBC Type	Purpose	SQL Type	Java Type
ARRAY	Represents SQL type ARRAY	ARRAY	`java.sql.Array` (new in JDBC 2.1)
BIGINT	64-bit signed integer	BIGINT	`long`
BINARY	Small, fixed length binary value	No correspondence. Check your driver documentation	`byte[]`
BIT	Single bit value (0 or 1)	BIT	`boolean`
BLOB	Represents SQL type BLOB for storing binary large objects	BLOB	`java.sql.Blob` (new in JDBC 2.1)
CHAR	Small, fixed length character string	CHAR	`String`
CLOB	Represents SQL type CLOB for storing character large objects	CLOB	`java.sql.Clob` (new in JDBC 2.1)
DATE	Date consisting of day, month, and year	DATE	`java.sql.Date`
DECIMAL	Fixed precision decimal values	DECIMAL	`java.math.BigDecimal`
DISTINCT	For custom mapping of user defined types	DISTINCT	User defined

Table continued on following page

JDBC Type	Purpose	SQL Type	Java Type
DOUBLE	Double-precision floating point numbers with 15 digit mantissa	DOUBLE PRECISION	`double`
FLOAT	Double-precision floating point numbers with 15 digit mantissa	FLOAT	`double`
INTEGER	32-bit signed integer	INTEGER	`int`
JAVA_OBJECT	For storing Java objects	No correspondence	`Object`
LONGVARBINARY	Large, variable length binary value	No correspondence. Check your driver documentation	`byte[]`
LONGVARCHAR	Large, variable length character string	No correspondence. Check your driver documentation	`String`
NULL	To represent NULL values	NULL	`null` for Java objects, `0` for numeric primitives, and `false` for Boolean
NUMERIC	Fixed precision decimal values	NUMERIC	`java.math.BigDecimal`
OTHER	For storing/retrieving database specific types	No correspondence. Meant for database/driver specific types	`Object`
REAL	Single-precision floating point numbers with 7 digit mantissa	REAL	`float`
REF			
SMALLINT	16-bit signed integer	SMALLINT	`short`
STRUCT			
TIME	Time consisting of hours, minutes, and seconds	TIME	`java.sql.Time`
TIMESTAMP	Time-stamp consisting of DATE, TIME, and a nano-second field	TIMESTAMP	`java.sql.TimeStamp`

JDBC Type	Purpose	SQL Type	Java Type
TINYINT	8-bit unsigned integer	TINYINT	short
VARBINARY	Small, variable length binary value	No correspondence. Check your driver documentation	byte[]
VARCHAR	Small, variable-length character string	VARCHAR	String

While this table summarizes all possible mapping between SQL and Java, in practice the support for these mappings varies from driver to driver. Moreover, since not all database vendors conform to all the SQL types, and there are also several vendor-specific SQL types in vogue, you should consult your database and driver documentation for conformance to this mapping. If portability of your application is a concern, you should try to keep your SQL conformed to the most commonly used data types.

Transaction Support

In some applications, we might like to group together a series of statements that need to either all succeed or all fail. In such cases, a group of SQL operations constitute one unit of work. The notion of transaction is important to preserve the integrity of business transactions that span multiple SQL operations. When multiple statements are executed in a single transaction, all operations can be committed (made permanent in the database) or rolled back (that is, changes to the database are undone).

When a new Connection object is created, it is set to commit every transaction automatically. This means that every time a statement is executed, it is committed to the database and cannot be rolled back. The following methods in the Connection interface are used to demarcate transactions and either rollback or commit them to the database:

```
void setAutoCommit(boolean autoCommit) throws SQLException
void commit() throws SQLException
void rollback() throws SQLException
```

In order to begin a transaction, we call setAutoCommit(false). This will give us control over what is committed and when. A call to the commit() method will commit everything that was done since the last commit was issued. Conversely, a rollback() call will undo any changes since the last commit.

Consider a business use case consisting of three steps each involving executing SQL statement, and additional logic implemented in the application: create an order, update inventory, and create shipping record. Business logic may require that all succeed together or else all should fail.

The failure of the creation of a shipping record may dictate that an order may not be created. In such cases, effects of SQL statements corresponding to the first two tasks (creating an order, and updating the inventory) should be undone – or rolled back.

The following code fragment illustrates this scenario:

```
Connection connection = null;

// Get a connection
...
try {
  // Begin a transaction
  connection.setAutoCommit(false);

  Statement statement = connection.createStatement();

  // Create an order
  statement.executeUpdate("INSET INTO ORDERS(ORDER_ID, PRODUCT_ID, ...)
                          VALUES(...)");

  // Update inventory
  statement.executeUpdate("UPDATE TABLE INVENTORY SET QUANTITY = QUANTITY - 1
                          WHERE PRODUCT_ID = ...");

  // Create shipping record
  if(...)
  {
    // Business logic succeeded
    statement.execute("INSERT INTO SHIP_RECORD(...) VALUES (...)");
    connection.commit();
  } else {
    // Business logic failed. Can not proceed with this order
    connection.rollback();
  }
}  catch (SQLException e)  {
  // Handle exceptions here
}  finally {
  // Close the statement and connection
}
```

In this snippet, once the rollback() method is called, the database restores the ORDERS and INVENTORY tables to their previous state. commit() makes the changes done by the INSERT and UPDATE statements permanent.

We'll discuss transactions in more detail later in this chapter.

Scrollable and Updatable Result Sets

Prior to JDBC 2.1 (that is up to JDBC 1.2), a result set object created by executing a statement is by default forward, only scrollable. That is, we can traverse through the result set using the next() method only. next() returns false when the last record is reached and no more details can then be retrieved.

The JDBC 2.1 API (included in the J2SE API 1.2 onwards) provides more flexible means of accessing results from result set objects. These enhancements are categorized into the following:

❑ **Scrollable result sets:**
   The JDBC 2.1 result set objects are scrollable. Scrollable result sets have the ability to move the cursor backwards, and also support absolute positioning of the cursor at a particular row in the result set.

❑ **Scroll sensitivity:**
The JDBC 2.1 API also specifies scroll-sensitive and scroll-insensitive result sets. A scroll-insensitive set represents a static snapshot of the results when the query was made. On the other hand, a scroll-sensitive result set is sensitive to changes made to the data after the query has been executed, thus providing a dynamic view of the data as it changes.

❑ **Updatable result sets:**
By default, result sets are read-only. That is, contents of the result set are read-only and can not be changed. The JDBC 2.1 API also introduces updatable result sets. When a result set is updated, the update operation also updates the original data corresponding to the result set.

The `java.sql.ResultSet` has additional methods to support these features. These are discussed in the following subsections.

Scrollable ResultSets

The `java.sql.ResultSet` interface specifies three types of result sets:

❑ `TYPE_FORWARD_ONLY` – A result set of this type supports forward-scrolling only.

❑ `TYPE_SCROLL_INSENSITIVE` – A result set of this type supports scrolling in both directions.

❑ `TYPE_SCROLL_SENSITIVE` – A result set of this type is sensitive to updates made to the data after the result set has been populated. For instance, if your query returns 10 rows, and if another application removes two of the rows, your result set will only have 8 rows.

Before we use the methods on the `java.sql.ResultSet` interface for scrolling through the result sets, we should make sure that the JDBC driver supports these features. The `java.sql.DatabaseMetadata` interface provides several methods to discover the capabilities of the database driver.

To find out what result set types are supported use `supportsResultSetType()`. For instance, the following code snippet should tell us the extent of the driver's support for these types:

```java
public void testScrollable() throws SQLException
{
  boolean supports;

  DatabaseMetaData md = connection.getMetaData();

  supports = md.supportsResultSetType(ResultSet.TYPE_FORWARD_ONLY);

  if(supports) {
    System.out.println("TYPE_FORWARD_ONLY - Supports");
  } else {
    System.out.println("TYPE_FORWARD_ONLY - Does not support");
  }

  supports = md.supportsResultSetType(ResultSet.TYPE_SCROLL_INSENSITIVE);
  if(supports) {
    System.out.println("TYPE_SCROLL_INSENSITIVE - Supports");

  } else {
    System.out.println( "TYPE_SCROLL_INSENSITIVE - Does not support");
  }
```

```
        supports = md.supportsResultSetType(ResultSet.TYPE_SCROLL_SENSITIVE);

    if(supports) {
      System.out.println("TYPE_SCROLL_SENSITIVE - Supports");
    } else {
      System.out.println("TYPE_SCROLL_SENSITIVE - Does not support");
    }
  }
```

For scroll-sensitive result sets, the following methods on `java.sql.DatabaseMetadata` return the level of sensitiveness:

```
public boolean othersUpdatesAreVisible(int type) throws SQLException
```

This method returns `true` if changes made by other transactions will be visible for a scroll-sensitive result set.

```
public boolean othersDeletesAreVisible(int type) throws SQLException
```

`othersDeletesAreVisible()` returns `true` if deletions made by other transactions are visible in a scroll-sensitive result set.

```
public boolean othersInsertsAreVisible(int type) throws SQLException
```

`othersInsertsAreVisible()` returns `true` if insertions made by other transactions are visible in a scroll-sensitive result set.

Similarly the `java.sql.DatabaseMetadata` interface specifies `ownUpdatesAreVisible()`, `ownDeletesAreVisible()`, and `ownInsertsAreVisible()` methods to find out if changes made to the result are visible to this result set.

The `java.sql.ResultSet` interface supports the following methods for scrolling through the result sets. These methods are grouped according to their usage.

Cursor Position Related Methods

```
public boolean isBeforeFirst() throws SQLException
public boolean isAfterLast() throws SQLException
```

`isBeforeFirst()` returns `true` if the cursor position is before the first row of the result set. `isAfterLast()` returns `true` if the cursor position is after the last row of the result set.

```
public boolean isFirst() throws SQLException
public boolean isLast() throws SQLException
```

`isFirst()` returns `true` if the cursor is at the first row of the result set. `isLast()` returns `true` if the cursor is at the last row of the result set.

```
public void beforeFirst() throws SQLException
public void afterLast() throws SQLException
```

These two methods returns true if the cursor position is before the first row or after the last row of the result set respectively.

Methods for Scrolling

```
public boolean first() throws SQLException
public boolean last() throws SQLException
```

These methods move the cursor to the first row and last row of the result set respectively.

```
public boolean absolute(int row) throws java.sql.SQLException
```

absolute() moves the cursor to the specified row in the result set. The row argument can be positive or negative. A negative argument moves the cursor in the backward direction, while a positive argument moves the cursor in the forward direction.

```
public boolean relative(int rows) throws SQLException
```

This method moves the cursor by the specified number of rows relative to the current position of the cursor. This method should not be called when the cursor position is invalid. For instance, after calling next() recursively till next() returns false (signifying the end of the resultset), we should not call relative(), as the current position is outside the result set. Before calling relative(), we should bring the cursor to a valid potion using the absolute(), first(), or last() methods.

```
public boolean previous() throws SQLException
```

previous() moves the cursor to the previous row, relative to the current position. Unlike the relative() method, this method can be called even when there is no current row. For instance, after calling next() recursively till next() returns false, we can call previous() to bring the cursor to the last row.

Fetch Direction and Size

```
public void setFetchDirection(int direction) throws SQLException
```

This method lets us set a fetch direction. The java.sql.ResultSet interface specifies three fetch direction constants – ResultSet.FETCH_UNKNOWN, ResultSet.FETCH_FORWARD, and ResultSet.FETCH_REVERSE. These types indicate the current fetch direction for the results.

The result set may internally optimise the result structures for the specified type of scrolling.

```
public int getFetchDirection() throws SQLException
```

This method returns the current fetch direction.

```
public void setFetchSize(int rows) throws SQLException
```

This method gives a hint to the JDBC driver as to the number of rows that should be fetched from the database. Note that, when fetch size is set to 1, the result set may fetch the data from the database whenever we call next(). By setting to a larger fetch size, we may be able to use fetches more optimally.

`public int getFetchSize() throws SQLException`

This method returns the current fetch size.

Note that inappropriate setting of fetch direction and size may affect performance. The values we set should consider the number of expected rows in the result set, and its intended usage.

The following examples illustrate these methods – note that the results of this code depend on driver support:

```
public void queryByScrollableResultSet() throws SQLException
{
  connection.setAutoCommit(false);

  Statement statement = connection.createStatement(
                                  ResultSet.TYPE_SCROLL_INSENSITIVE,
                                  ResultSet.CONCUR_READ_ONLY);

  ResultSet scroller= statement.executeQuery("SELECT CATALOGUE.TITLE,
                    CATALOGUE.LEAD_ACTOR, CATALOGUE.LEAD_ACCTRESS,
                    CATALOGUE.TYPE, CATALOGUE.RELEASE_DATE FROM CATALOGUE");
```

In order to test the methods for scrollable result sets, first create a result set. The above snippet populates a result set object scroller.

```
int type = scroller.getType();
  switch(type) {
    case ResultSet.TYPE_FORWARD_ONLY :
      System.out.println("Type = TYPE_FORWARD_ONLY");
      break;
    case ResultSet.TYPE_SCROLL_SENSITIVE :
      System.out.println("Type = TYPE_SCROLL_SENSITIVE");
      break;
    case ResultSet.TYPE_SCROLL_INSENSITIVE :
      System.out.println("Type = TYPE_SCROLL_INSENSITIVE");
      break;
}

System.err.println("Current fetch size: " + scroller.getFetchSize());
scroller.setFetchSize(2);
System.err.println("Fetch size reset to: " + scroller.getFetchSize());
```

The code above indicates the level of support for scrollable result sets, and allows us to change the fetch size. In the same way we can find the level of support for concurrency.

The following code scrolls through the result set in both backward and forward directions. As mentioned previously, the results of this code depend on driver support. As of writing, Cloudscape 3.5 supports read-only scrollable result sets:

```
   int count = 0;
   System.out.println("Scrolling forward from the beginning ...");
   while(scroller.next())
   {
      System.out.println(count++ + ": " +
                        scroller.getString("TITLE") + ", " +
                        scroller.getString("TYPE"));
   }

   scroller.first();
   System.out.println("Scroller moved to first.");

   scroller.absolute(count/2);
   System.out.println("Scroller moved to " + count/2);
   System.out.println("Scrolling forward ...");
   while(scroller.next())  {
      System.out.println("     " + scroller.getString("TITLE") + ", "
                        + scroller.getString("TYPE"));
   }

   scroller.first();
   System.out.println("Scroller moved to first.");

   int fetchDirection = scroller.getFetchDirection();
   switch(fetchDirection)  {
      case ResultSet.FETCH_UNKNOWN:
         System.out.println("Current fetch direction: FETCH_UNKNOWN");
         break;
      case ResultSet.FETCH_FORWARD:
         System.out.println("Current fetch direction: FETCH_FORWARD");
         break;
      case ResultSet.FETCH_REVERSE:
         System.out.println("Current fetch direction: FETCH_REVERSE");
         break;
   }
   scroller.setFetchDirection(ResultSet.FETCH_REVERSE);
   System.out.println("Fetch direction set to FETCH_REVERSE");
   scroller.absolute(-count/3);
   System.out.println("Scroller moved to " + (-count/3));

   System.out.println("Scrolling forward ...");
   while(scroller.next())  {
      System.out.println("     " + scroller.getString("TITLE") + ", " +
                        scroller.getString("TYPE"));
   }

   scroller.previous();
   scroller.relative(-2);
   System.out.println("Scroller moved by -2 rows relative to the current" +
                     "position");

   System.out.println("Scrolling forward ...");
   while(scroller.next())  {
      System.out.println("     " + scroller.getString("TITLE") + ", " +
                        scroller.getString("TYPE"));
   }

   scroller.close();
}
```

Updatable Result Sets

By default, result sets are read-only. That is, contents of the result set are read-only and cannot be changed. The JDBC 2.1 API also introduces updateable result sets. When a result set is updated, the update operation also updates the original data corresponding to the result set.

The `java.sql.ResultSet` interface specifies two constants to indicate whether the result set is read-only or updateable:

❑ CONCUR_READ_ONLY – If the type of the result set is CONCUR_READ_ONLY, we cannot use any of the methods discussed below to insert, update, or delete rows in the result set.

❑ CONCUR_UPDATABLE – When the type of the result set is CONCUR_UPDATABLE, we can insert, update, or delete rows in the result set.

We can find out the concurrency types by calling the `getConcurrency()` method on the result set.

The `java.sql.ResultSet` interface specifies the following set of methods for updating results.

Updating a Row

The following set of `updateXXX()` methods allows us to update the elements of the current row in the result set:

updateAsciiStream()	updateTimestamp()	updateTime()
updateBigDecimal()	updateBoolean()	updateBinaryStream()
updateString()	updateMetaData()	updateDate()
updateBytes()	updateByte()	updateClob()
updateInt()	updateFloat()	updateDouble()

These methods require the column name (as a string) or column index as the first argument, and an object of type XXX. For example, there are two variants of `updateTimestamp()` methods

```
public void updateTimestamp(int columnIndex, Timestamp x)
public void updateTimestamp(String columnName, Timestamp x)
```

After calling these methods, we should call the `updateRow()` method to update the changes. Alternatively, we can call the `cancelRowUpdates()` method to cancel all the updates done so far.

The `rowsUpdated()` method lets us know whether the current row has been updated. The returned value depends on whether the result set can detect updates or not.

Deleting a Row

We can use the `deleteRow()` method to delete the current row from the result set as well as the underlying database. The `rowDeleted()` method indicates whether a row has been deleted. Note that a deleted row may leave a visible hole in a result set. The `rowDeleted()` method can be used to detect such holes.

Inserting a Row

To insert a row in the result set, and the underlying database, we should first use the moveToInsertRow(), and then one or more of updateXXX() methods.

A call to the moveToInsertRow() method moves the cursor to the insert row. The insert row is a special buffer row associated with an updateable result set. After moving the cursor to this row, we can use the usual updateXXX() methods to set the elements of this row. At the end of these calls, we should call insertRow() to finally insert the row in the database.

Batch Updates

Apart from scrollable result sets, the JDBC API 2.1 also specifies support for batch updates. This feature allows multiple update statements (INSERT, UPDATE, or DELETE) in a single request to the database. Batching large numbers of statements can result in significant performance gains.

For example, we can redo the table for the Movies database but this time we can performs all INSERT statements in a single batch. We can also use prepared statements in a batch. When compared to the insertData() method in the example, the only differences in this implementation are the calls to the addBatch() method and executeBatch() method on the statement for batch update:

```
public void insertBatchData() throws SQLException, IOException
{
  BufferedReader br = new BufferedReader(new FileReader("catalogue.txt"));
  statement = connection.createStatement();

  try {
    do {
      title = br.readLine();
      if(title == null) break;
      leadActor = br.readLine();
      leadActress = br.readLine();
      type = br.readLine();
      dateOfRelease = br.readLine();

      String sqlString = "INSERT INTO CATALOGUE VALUES('" + title + ',''"
                         + leadActor + "','" + leadActress + "','"
                         + type + "','" + dateOfRelease + "')";

      statement.addBatch(sqlString);
    } while(br.readLine() != null);

    statement.executeBatch();

  } catch (EOFException e) {
  } finally {
      statement.close();
      br.close();
  }
}
```

Why does this result in better performance? Instead of executing n number of statements, we're performing all such updates in a single statement. This reduces the overhead on the database server, as it otherwise would have to allocate and maintain resources (cursors etc.) for each statement.

The JDBC 2.0 Optional Package API

The core JDBC API is based on the client-server programming paradigm. As discussed in the previous sections, typical JDBC programming includes the following steps:

❑ Load the database driver (using the driver's class name)

❑ Obtain a connection (using the JDBC URL for the database)

❑ Create and execute statements

❑ Use result sets to navigate through the results

❑ Close the connection

This model is exactly that of ODBC, if you are familiar with it. This programming model is well suited to desktop clients with long-held connections and localized database transactions. However, it is not sufficient for distributed applications. The JDBC 2.0 Optional Package API (previously called Standard Extension) provides the following facilities:

❑ JNDI-based lookup for accessing databases via logical names: Instead of each client trying to load the driver classes in their respective local virtual machines using JNDI-based lookup allows us to access the database resources using logical names assigned to these resources.

❑ Connection pooling: The JDBC Optional Package API specifies an additional intermediate layer for implementing connection pooling. That is, the responsibility for connection pooling is shifted from application developers to driver and application server vendors.

❑ Distributed transactions: Similarly, JDBC driver/application server vendors can support distributed transactions.

❑ Rowsets: `Rowset` is a JavaBeans compliant object that encapsulates database result sets and access information. A rowset may be connected or disconnected. Note that, in the JDBC 2.1 API, `ResultSets` are connected. That is, the connection is open while the object exists. However, rowsets allow us to encapsulate a set of rows, without necessarily maintaining a connection. Rowsets also allow us to update the data, and propagate the changes back to the underlying database.

These facilities simplify JDBC programming in a distributed paradigm such as J2EE. Excepting rowsets, JNDI, distributed transactions, and connection pooling services require minimal changes to client applications. These services are now the responsibility of the JDBC driver and the J2EE application server. JDBC driver vendors and J2EE application server vendors can make use of the intermediate layers in this API and build these services.

Most of the classes and interfaces in this package are intended for application server and database driver vendors to implement in their products. The number of classes and interfaces that we will require to develop client applications is small. Therefore, in the rest of this chapter, our focus will be on gaining an insight into these services, and not on how to use these services for developing client applications. Wherever applicable, we'll provide code snippets that illustrate the programming aspects.

To test the concepts discussed in this chapter, you should either have the J2EE reference implementation from Sun Microsystems (available for download at `http://java.sun.com/j2ee`) or a commercial J2EE application server (with support for the JDBC Optional Package API). You will also need the drivers that support them. You should note, however, that not all driver and application server vendors currently support all the facilities in this API. Nonetheless, it is important to understand how these services could be designed. For an up-to-date list of vendors that support these features, please refer to the driver database at `http://industry.java.sun.com/products/jdbc/drivers`.

In this section, we'll discuss the following:

❑　Data sources: how this mechanism works, and how it simplifies database access.

❑　Connection pooling: We'll discuss facilities for connection pooling in the JDBC 2.0 Optional Package API.

❑　Distributed transactions: We'll discuss the background and concepts associated with distributed transactions. We'll then see how the JDBC 2.0 Optional Package API, along with the Java Transaction API manage distributed transactions.

❑　Rowsets and the Sun Microsystems reference implementation.

JDBC Data Sources

The JDBC 2.0 Optional Package API replaces the static `java.sql.DriverManager` class, although it is still provided for backward compatibility. The replacement is the `javax.sql.DataSource` interface as the primary means of creating database connections. With respect to programming, the following are the noticeable factors:

❑　Instead of explicitly loading the driver manager classes in the run-time of the client application, we use a centralized JNDI service lookup to obtain the `java.sql.DataSource` object.

❑　Instead of using the `java.sql.DriverManager` class, we'll use a `javax.sql.DataSource` interface, which provides similar facilities for getting database connections.

This approach isolates client applications from the responsibility of database driver initialization. This means that we need not hard code the driver class and that client applications need not be aware of database driver classes and the database URL. These now become the responsibility of the server administrator who configures data sources. As we'll see later in this chapter, this decoupling also allows additional services such as connection pooling and transaction support to be enabled without affecting client applications.

The javax.sql.DataSource Interface

The `javax.sql.DataSource` interface is a factory for creating database connections. The `javax.sql.DataSource` interface provides the following methods:

The getConnection() Method

```
public Connection getConnection() throws SQLException
public Connection getConnection(String username, String password)
    throws SQLException
```

These methods return a connection to a data source. Note the return type of this method is a `Connection` object. This is the same as that returned by the `java.sql.DriverManager` interface. Note that, when we retrieve a `Connection` object from the `java.sql.DriverManager` class, it is likely that the `Connection` object directly encapsulates a network connection. However, as we shall see later in this chapter, the `Connection` object need not directly encapsulate a physical database connection. Instead, the connection object can delegate most of its operations to another layer that can implement connection pooling and distributed transactions.

The getLoginTimeout() Method

```
public int getLoginTimeout() throws SQLException
```

This method returns the time interval in seconds the data source will wait while trying to get a database connection.

The setLoginTimeout() Method

```
public void setLoginTimeout(int seconds) throws SQLException
```

This method specifies the time interval in seconds the data source should wait while trying to obtain a database connection.

Note that the JDBC driver will have a default timeout interval.

The getLogWriter() Method

```
public PrintWriter getLogWriter() throws SQLException
```

This method returns the current `java.io.PrintWriter` object to which the `DataSource` object writes the log messages. Note that by default, unless a `PrintWriter` object is set using the `setLogWriter()` method, logging is disabled and so the method will return `null`.

The setLogWriter() Method

```
public void setLogWriter(LogWriter out) throws SQLException
```

This method sets a `java.io.LogWriter` for logging purposes. For example, we can create a `PrinterWriter` object with `System.out` as the output stream, and set it for logging, as shown below:

```
PrintWriter logWriter = new PrintWriter(System.out);

// dataSource is the DataSource object
datasource.setLogWriter(logWriter);
```

Note that all these methods throw `java.sql.SQLException`.

As we see from the list of methods above, this interface is very simple, and its main responsibility is to create connections.

However, there are two questions concerning its usage: Who creates an object implementing this interface? How can application clients obtain this instance, so that applications can get connections? The next subsection answers these questions.

JNDI and Data Sources

In the JDBC Optional Package API, a data source is considered as a network resource, retrieved from a JNDI service. We'll learn more about JNDI in the next chapter, but for the present, consider a JNDI service as a network repository of objects. A JNDI service implements the **Java Naming and Directory Interface (JNDI) API**, and provides a uniform means of accessing any network repository of objects. In a JNDI service, applications can bind objects with names. Other applications can retrieve these objects using these names. Both the applications that *bind* objects to names in the JNDI service, and the applications that look up these names in the JNDI service can be remote. The JDBC Optional Package API allows application server vendors and driver vendors to build database resources based on this approach.

The following diagram gives an overview of this approach:

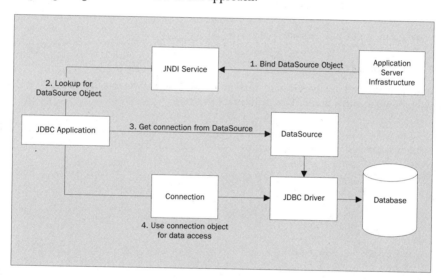

This diagram shows the schematic of how objects implementing the `javax.sql.DataSource` interface are made available in a JNDI service, and how JDBC application clients can look up these objects, and create connection objects.

Apart from JDBC application clients, and database resources, the above figure shows two more components – a JNDI service, and an application that binds the `javax.sql.DataSource` objects in the JNDI service. A JNDI service is a provider of the JNDI API. Typically, the application that binds the `javax.sql.DataSource` objects in the JNDI service is an application server (possibly implementing all J2EE services).

The following are the responsibilities of each of the blocks in the above figure:

❑ The driver vendor or the application server ('infrastructure' in the figure above) implements the `javax.sql.DataSource` interface.

❑ The application server creates an instance of the object implementing the `javax.sql.DataSource` interface, and binds it with a logical name (specified by the application server administrator) in the JNDI service indicated by Step 1.

❑ The JDBC application (client) does a lookup in the JNDI service using this logical name, and retrieves the object implementing the `javax.sql.DataSource` interface. This is the second step in the above diagram.

❑ The JDBC application (client) uses the data source object and obtains database connections, as indicated by Step 3. The data source implementation may use the JDBC driver to retrieve a connection.

❑ The JDBC application (client) uses the connection object for all its database access, using the standard JDBC API, the final step in the sequence.

Let's see the details of the first three steps.

Creating a Data Source

This is a simple process, and involves instantiating an object that implements the `javax.sql.DataSource` interface, and binding it with a name. This is illustrated below:

```
XDataSource x = new XDataSource(...);
// Set properties for the DataSource

// Create a context
try {

   Context context = new InitialContext();
   context.bind("jdbc/Orders", x);

} catch(NamingException ne) {
     // Failed to create the context or bind.
}
```

In the above code snippet, XDataSource is a class that implements the `javax.sql.DataSource` interface. Note that the actual name of this class is irrelevant for the application developer. Instead we use the logical name assigned to the data source. In the above example, this is `jdbc/Orders`.

The InitialContext class is a class implementing the `javax.naming.Context` interface of the JNDI API. As we'll see in Chapter 4, depending on the environment (client-side or server-side) where we create the initial context, we may have to use the InitialContext constructor that takes a Hashtable object as an argument. This Hashtable should contain certain environment attributes that govern how the initial context is created. Some of the most commonly attributes include `java.naming.provider.url`, `java.naming.security.principal`, and `java.naming.security.credentials`. These attributes specify a provider (a URL pointing to a JNDI service) of the JNDI service, the identity (called the principal) of the application or the user on behalf of whom this context is being created, and the credentials of the `principal`. While the first

attribute specifies location of the JNDI service, the second and third attributes specify the identity of the caller. These latter arguments may be used for implementing security and access control for the JNDI. For a complete list of these attributes, refer the documentation of the `javax.naming.Context` interface (available online at
`http://java.sun.com/products/jndi/1.2/javadoc/javax/naming/Context.html`).

Note that both the constructor of the `javax.naming.InitialContext` class and the bind method throw `javax.naming.NamingException`.

It is also worth mentioning that the above step is taken care of by the J2EE application server provider. That is, when we start a J2EE application server, the J2EE application server instantiates classes that implement the `javax.sql.DataSource` interface, and binds these objects with logical names in the JNDI service. Note that most of the J2EE application servers also include a JNDI service, and therefore, it may not be necessary to set up one outside the application server.

While some of the J2EE application vendors implement the `javax.sql.DataSource` interface over existing JDBC drivers, there are `javax.sql.DataSource` implementations from different database vendors. At the time of configuring a J2EE application server, we'll be required to add the data source configuration for the database drivers that we plan to use. There are different scenarios:

❏ Application server implementing the `javax.sql` package with third party JDBC driver: In this case, we'll be required to specify the `java.sql.Driver` class while configuring the application server.

❏ JDBC driver vendor implementing the `javax.sql` package: We'll be required to specify the class that implements the `javax.sql.DataSource` interface. We can obtain this information from the driver vendor and the documentation.

In either case, note that there is additional layer between traditional database drivers and the API that we use for getting connections.

Retrieving a Data Source

Once the application server has bound a data source object into the JNDI service, any JDBC client application in the network can retrieve the data source object using the logical name associated with the data source. The following code snippet illustrates this:

```
// Create a context
try
{
    Context context = new InitialContext();
    DataSource dataSource = (DataSource) context.lookup("jdbc/x");
}
catch(NamingException ne)
{
    // Failed to create the context or lookup.
}
```

The process is very simple – we create an `InitialContext` object, and perform a lookup using the logical name assigned during the server configuration.

Since a JNDI service typically exists on a different VM and possibly in a different machine, the `lookup()` operation will typically be a remote operation. From this, we may guess that data source implementation classes implement the `java.io.Serializable` interface.

Key Features

Note the following key features of this approach:

❑ There is no need for each client application to initialize JDBC drivers. As discussed previously, JDBC drivers require initialization in each client application. This will not be necessary with the Optional Package API. Instead the application server is required to make the data source objects available in the JNDI service.

❑ The client application need not be aware of the driver details. The only information required is a logical name. This makes the application code independent of drivers and JDBC URLs.

❑ Since this approach uses a JNDI service to locate data source objects using logical names, this approach provides a location independent lookup of data sources. Data source objects can be created, deployed, and managed in a JNDI service, independent of all application clients.

The Movie Catalog Revisited

Let's now modify the movie catalogue application from earlier in the chapter, to use a data source. There are just two changes to be made to the `CreateMovieCatalog.java` and `QueryMovieCatalog.java` files. These are discussed below:

```
import java.sql.*;
import java.io.*;
import java.text.*;
import javax.sql.*;      // Import the Optional Package API
import javax.naming.*;   // Import the JNDI API
```

Note the two additional import statements to import the `javax.sql`, and `javax.naming` packages.

The other change is in the `initialize()` method in which we had originally loaded the driver, and created a connection. Instead of these, we should now obtain a `javax.sql.DataSource` object, and create a connection:

```
public void initialize() throws SQLException, NamingException
{
   // Rather than registering the driver as below
   /*    Class.forName (driver);   */
   // lookup and obtain a DataSource object from JNDI
   Context initialContext = new InitialContext();
   dataSource = (DataSource) initialContext.lookup("jdbc/Cloudscape");

   // Replace
   //     connection = DriverManager.getConnection(url);
   // with using the DataSource object to obtain a connection.
   connection = dataSource.getConnection();
}
```

The first statement creates a `javax.naming.Context` object. The `InitialContext` class implements the `javax.naming.Context` interface and provides the starting point for resolution of names in the JNDI service.

In the above example, we use initialContext to look up jdbc/Cloudscape. This is a name that we specify while configuring the application server, so that the application server can create an instance of javax.sql.DataSource, and bind with the name jdbc/Cloudscape in the JNDI service. jdbc is the standard naming sub-context for all data source objects.

The lookup method returns an object implementing the javax.sql.DataSource interface. Since the lookup() method returns a java.lang.Object, we need to cast it to javax.sql.DataSource.

The rest of the database operations are done as usual. In order to test this application, we require a J2EE application server that supports data sources for client applications.

Connection Pooling

A server application, by definition, performs a service for one or more clients. As the number of clients increases, so too does the importance of serving the clients as efficiently as possible.

One of the techniques used for efficiently serving clients' requests is reusing resource expensive objects as much as possible. There's always an overhead with creating an object – memory must be allocated, the object must be initialized, and the JVM must keep track of the object so that it can be garbage-collected when it's no longer needed. So in general it's a good idea to minimize the number of objects we create in applications. This is more so in server-side applications (such as web applications), where the number of clients and client requests is not easily predictable.

In addition, network-related objects are more expensive to create than others. If we can reuse such an object the server's performance can be improved dramatically.

Object pooling is a technique for managing and reusing sets of objects. Creating Connection objects is one of the most expensive operations in terms of resources. In JDBC, a Connection object represents a native database connection (except in in-process databases – which are not very common in production systems). The database server must allocate communication and memory resources as well as authenticate the user and set up a security context for every connection. Although there are several parameters that dictate the time for obtaining a connection, it's not unusual to see connection times of one or two seconds. By sharing a set of connections among clients, instead of trying to create them as and when required, we can improve the load on resources and therefore the responsiveness of the application.

A database connection pool benefits most of the server-side applications that access a database. Use a connection pool if the following characteristics describe your application:

❑ Users access the database through a small set of common database user accounts. The alternative is that each user uses a specific account. In Internet-centric applications, common user accounts are the norm.

❑ A database connection is only used for the duration of a single request, as opposed to the combined duration of multiple requests from the same session.

If the first criterion is not true, it will not be possible to use a connection pool, although it may be possible to redesign the application to use a generic account. If the requirements of the application and any existing database allow us to move the user access control from the database to the application this would be preferred. This could be done with the addition of an Access Control List (ACL).

The second criterion is more interesting. One typical e-commerce application allows users to add items to a shopping cart at their leisure while they browse through the site. When the users finish the shopping they checkout and pay for the contents of the cart. We can design this application in at least two ways:

❑ The shopping cart is a database table. When the user enters the site we get a database connection and keep it until the user checks-out or leaves the site (or after session timeout). Each item added to the cart means adding a row to the table. If the user checks-out we commit the database transaction, and if the user leaves without buying we rollback the transaction. If this is the design the application follows, there is no need for a connection pool, as each connection is associated with the data updates in the cart, and cannot be shared. This is a very poor design choice in general.

❑ The shopping cart content is kept in a regular in-memory object associated with the user. For example, in a servlet/JSP-based web application this object can be kept in the HttpSession. Each item added to the cart means adding the item to the in-memory object. If the user checks-out we get a database connection, add all items from the in-memory object as rows in a database table and commit the transaction. If the user leaves without buying we simply drop the in-memory object. This model satisfies the criterion above so we can use a connection pool.

The JDBC Optional Package API provides a data source based connection pooling that is transparent to client applications. As we shall see shortly, in this approach, connection pooling can be enabled and configured by an administrator of a J2EE application server supporting this feature.

The traditional approach has long been programmatically adding connection pool support. Note that there are several variants of this traditional approach available – such as the DBConnectionPool discussed in the first edition of this book (also available in a short article form at http://www.webdevelopersjournal.com/columns/connection_pool.html), and the DBConnectionBroker (available at http://javaexchange.com). Although such pools offer a range of services, in principle they are very similar. Before discussing the concepts behind the JDBC Optional Package API support for connection pooling, let's examine how traditional connection pooling is done.

Traditional Connection Pooling

In this approach, an application:

❑ Obtains a reference to the pool or an object managing several pools

❑ Gets a connection from a pool

❑ Uses the connection

❑ Returns the connection to the pool

The application is fully aware that it's using a pooled connection, so it should never close the connection. It should instead return the connection to the pool.

The implementation of the classic model typically consists of a class (say, ConnectionPool) managing a set of JDBC connection objects. Such a class provides methods for initializing the pool (to set the number of connections to be opened at startup, JDBC URL, maximum number of connections etc.) to get connections and to return connections. Clients of this class first initialize the pool before getting connections. The following diagram illustrates this:

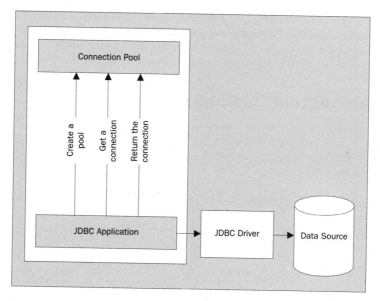

As we see from the figure above, connection pooling is treated as client's responsibility. The client application creates the pool, retrieves connections, and frees the connections again. Apart from this, this approaches requires a strict contract from the application client developer:

❑ The client application should not close the connections; it should only return them back to the pool. However, such a contract cannot be strictly be enforced on client applications. If the client inadvertently closes the connection before returning it to the pool, the connection will be unusable, and the pool will remove the reference to the connection, and recreate it if necessary.

❑ When the client uses the connection object within a transaction, and forgets to end (commit or rollback) the transaction, the connection pool cannot detect this. This leads to application transactions getting mixed up, and loss of consistency of data.

Although these points can be taken care of by careful coding practices, implementation of robust connection pooling is still a responsibility of the client application.

This classic connection pool is valid only for clients that share the same runtime. This is a client-side pool. Within the scope of this book, there are two possibilities under which multiple clients share the same environment:

❑ J2EE web applications deployed on a single container. In this case, multiple servlets and JSP objects will be invoked in different threads – but in the same runtime (provided the container is not distributed).

❑ A multi-threaded server application providing business methods for database access for the clients.

When connections are required from different client applications, the classic pool is not the right choice. For such cases, a server-side connection pool would be more appropriate. As we'll see in the next section, the JDBC Optional Package API specifies connection pools that meet this requirement. Currently, most of the J2EE application servers provide this feature.

Leaving aside the details of which classes are used to hold connections, this approach is neither robust nor scalable. The fundamental flaw in classic connection pooling is that such a pool does not work with distributed transactions. It also plays havoc with container-managed environments such as web containers since it forces you have connection held in static variables, onto which the container can not enforce access control.

JDBC 2.0 Connection Pooling

The JDBC2.0 Optional Package API provides a transparent means of connection pooling. With this approach, the application server and/or the database driver handle connection pooling internally. As long as we use data source objects for getting connections, connection pooling will automatically be enabled once we configure the J2EE application server.

Before we go into details of this approach, here is a schematic view:

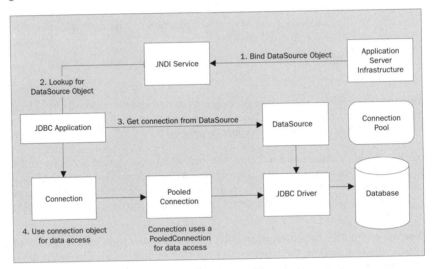

When compared to the figure on page 137, the only change is the additional connection pool maintained by the application server in coordination with the JDBC driver. This means that there is no additional programming requirement for JDBC client applications. Instead, the administrator of the J2EE server will be required to configure a connection pool on the application server. The exact syntax and the names of classes are implementation dependent. However, with a JDBC 2.0 compliant application server and database driver, the server administrator typically specifies the following:

❑　A class implementing the `javax.sql.ConnectionPoolDataSource` interface

❑　A class implementing the `java.sql.Driver` interface

❑　Size of the pool (minimum and maximum sizes)

❑　Connection time out

❑　Authentication parameters (login, password etc.)

In the rest of this section, we will discuss the interfaces related to connection pooling, and how connection pooling is implemented using these interfaces.

The purpose of this section is to give you an insight into the JDBC 2.0 connection pooling. Apart from configuring the J2EE server to enable connection pooling, the client applications need not implement or access these interfaces directly.

The `javax.sql` package specifies three interfaces and one class for implementing connection pooling:

`javax.sql.ConnectionPoolDataSource, javax.sql.PooledConnection, javax.sql.ConnectionEventListener,` and `javax.sql.ConnectionEvent.`

The javax.sql.ConnectionPoolDataSource Interface

This interface is similar to the `javax.sql.DataSource` interface. Instead of returning `java.sql.Connection` objects, this interface returns `javax.sql.PooledConnection` objects. That is, the connection pool data source is a factory of pooled connection objects. The following methods return `javax.sql.PooledConnection` objects:

```
public javax.sql.PooledConnection getPooledConnection()
        throws java.sql.SQLException

public javax.sql.PooledConnection
                getPooledConnection (String user, String password)
        throws java.sql.SQLException
```

The remaining methods in this interface are the same as those in the `javax.sql.DataSource` interface.

Even after we configure connection pooling, applications still use `javax.sql.DataSource` objects for getting connection objects as we've seen in the `initialize()` method of the Movie Catalog application. It is the `javax.sql.DataSource` object that uses the `javax.sql.ConnectionPoolDataSource` in order to create and maintain a connection pool. This is a part of the data source implementation (provided by the driver or server vendor). The connection pool remains transparent to the application code. Once the administrator sets up the connection pool, we'll automatically start to use pooled connections.

The javax.sql.PooledConnection Interface

When connection pooling is enabled, objects implementing the `javax.sql.PooledConnection` interface hold a physical database connection.

This interface is a factory of `javax.sql.Connection` objects. This interface specifies the following methods:

```
public java.sql.Connection getConnection() throws java.sql.SQLException
```

This method returns a `java.sql.Connection` object. However, the returned `Connection` object is actually a handle (or proxy) for the physical connection held by the `javax.sql.PooledConnection` object.

```
public void close() throws java.sql.SQLException
```

This method closes the connection to the database.

But what's the difference between a pooled connection and a connection?

❏ Firstly, the connection is a physical connection in JDBC client applications. With JDBC connection pooling, the Connection object does not hold a physical database connection. What the application gets is an abstraction of a regular Connection object. The Connection object uses the physical connection held by the pooled Connection object for all its data access.

❏ Secondly, when we call the close() method, the physical connection is not closed. The data source implementation merely removes the association between the Connection object and the pooled Connection object. We can therefore close the connection after using it, after which the data source reuses the pooled connection.

❏ Thirdly, we need not return the Connection object to any pool. We merely close it, as we would do without connection pooling.

In other words, the Connection object is a wrapper over the pooled connection. When the data source returns a connection, the data source maintains an association between the returned Connection object and the pooled connection object, so that calls on the connection object are delegated to the pooled connection object.

The javax.sql.PooledConnection interface has two more methods for handling the association between the connection and the pooled Connection. Remember that, when the Connection object is closed, the Connection pool should be notified, so that the pooled connection can be reused:

```
public void addConnectionEventListener(ConnectionEventListener listener)
public void removeConnectionEventListener(ConnectionEventListener listener)
```

These two methods are used by the connection pool implementation to add and remove Connection event listeners.

The javax.sql.ConnectionEventListener Interface

The ConnectionEventListener interface has two methods:

```
public void connectionClosed(ConnectionEvent event)
```

This method is invoked when the application calls the close() method. The connection pool marks the connection for reuse.

```
public void connectionErrorOccurred(ConnectionEvent event)
```

This method is invoked when fatal connection errors occur. The connection pool may close the connection on this event.

The javax.sql.ConnectionEvent Class

This class represents connection-related events.

Note that this event handling mechanism is similar to AWT events. The connection pool adds connection event listeners to the pooled connection, and connection listeners are notified when connection events occur.

Connection Pooling Implementation

The JDBC 2.0 Optional Package API does not specify any specific algorithm for connection pooling. The interfaces that we discussed above are hooks for implementing a connection pool. In a typical implementation, the following steps occur when we call getConnection() on the data source:

❑   The data source first checks for a free pooled connection object. If there is one, the connection pool returns a pooled Connection object to the data source. The data source then calls getConnection() on the pooled Connection object, which returns a Connection object.

❑   If there is no free pooled Connection object available in the connection pool, the data source uses a connection pool data source, to get a new pooled connection.

As we can see, the javax.sql.ConnectionPoolDataSource interface is a factory for javax.sql.PooledConnection objects. Further, the javax.sql.PooledConnection interface is a factory for java.sql.Connection objects. The javax.sql.DataSource implements the connection pool, and coordinates pooled connections and regular connections with the help of the interfaces discussed above.

Since a connection is purely a handle to a pooled connection (that holds the network connection), a connection may be created and closed a number of times using the same pooled connection. Moreover, the client API (the javax.sql.DataSource and java.sql.Connection interfaces) remains the same – this is because the connection pooling details are never exposed to the application.

To reiterate, the main advantage of this approach is its simplicity – for both client application developers, and system administrators. System administrators can enable/reconfigure the connection pool independently of all applications.

Distributed Transactions

While discussing the JDBC 2.1 core API, we've briefly discussed transactions. The java.sql.Connection interface has two methods – commit() and rollback(), to commit and recover from changes made respectively. We control the transaction boundaries (that is beginning and ending) of transactions by calling setAutoCommit(false) at the beginning of a transaction, and by calling either the rollback() or the commit() method to end the transaction.

Such transactions are called local transactions. In a local transaction, client applications perform database read and write/update operations over a single connection object.

However, in certain scenarios, we may have more than one client (for example two different servlets, or EJB components) participating in a transaction. Alternatively, the client may have to perform database operations across multiple databases in the same transaction. How would we implement such features?

This is where distributed transactions fit in. The JDBC 2.0 Optional Package API, together with the **Java Transaction API (JTA)**, can be used to implement distributed transactions.

In this section, we'll see an overview of distributed transactions, and see the relevant interfaces in JDBC 2.0 and JTA.

What is a Transaction?

Enterprise applications often require concurrent access to distributed data shared among multiple components, to perform operations on data. Such applications should maintain integrity of data (as defined by the business rules of the application) under the following circumstances:

❑ **Distributed access to a single resource of data:**
For example, we may have two application components implementing two parts of a business transaction – both using the same database, but different connections.

❑ **Access to distributed resources from a single application component:**
For example, a component updating multiple databases in a single business transaction. This operation would require multiple Connection objects.

In both these cases, the methods provided by the core JDBC API are not adequate. This is because the methods provided on the java.sql.Connection for starting and ending transactions are associated with a single Connection object. In the above situations, however, this is not the case.

The concept of a transaction, and a transaction manager (or a transaction processing service) simplifies developing such applications to maintain integrity of data in a unit of work as described by the **ACID** properties, guaranteeing that a transaction is never incomplete, the data is never inconsistent, concurrent transactions are independent, and the effects of a transaction are persistent. For more information on transactions refer to Chapter 21.

Brief Background

In the distributed transaction processing domain, the X/Open Distributed Transaction Processing (DTP) model is the most widely adopted model for building transactional applications. Almost all vendors developing products related to transaction processing, relational databases, and message queuing, support the interfaces defined in the DTP model.

This model defines three components:

❑ Application programs

❑ Resource managers

❑ Transaction manager

This model also specifies functional interfaces between application programs and the transaction manager (known as the TX interface), and between the transaction manager and the resource managers (the XA interface). Using TX compliant transaction managers and XA compliant resource managers (such as databases), we can implement transactions with the two-phase commit and recovery protocol to comply with the requirements for transactions.

Object Transaction Service (OTS) is another distributed transaction processing model specified by the Object Management Group (OMG). This model is based on the X/Open DTP model, and replaces the functional TX and XA interfaces with CORBA IDL interfaces. In this model, the various objects communicate via CORBA method calls over Internet Inter ORB Protocol (IIOP). IIOP was specified by the OMG specifically to implement CORBA solutions over the Internet. Yet, the OTS model is interoperable with the X/Open DTP model. An application using transactional objects could use the TX interface with the transaction manager for transaction demarcation.

Within the J2EE architecture, the JDBC 2.0 Optional Package API and the Java Transaction API provide interfaces for implementing distributed transactions. In addition, the Java Transaction Service (JTS) specifies a Java mapping of the OTS.

Transaction Processing – Concepts

Before we proceed to look into the relevant APIs in the JDBC, and JTA, let's briefly discuss some of the concepts associated with distributed transactions.

Transaction Demarcation

A transaction can be specified by what is known as transaction demarcation. Transaction demarcation enables work done by distributed components to be bound by a global transaction. For example, for local transactions, as soon as we create a transaction, and call setAutoCommit(false), we start a transaction. Similarly, a call to commit() or rollback() ends the transaction.

However, this is not true for distributed transactions. The most common approach to demarcation is to mark the thread executing the operations for transaction processing. This is called programmatic demarcation. The transaction so established can be suspended by unmarking the thread, and be resumed later by marking the thread again. In order to mark and resume the transaction, the transaction context has to be explicitly propagated to the thread where the transaction is resumed. However, with component transaction processing systems such as EJB containers, this becomes the responsibility of the container.

The transaction demarcation ends after a commit or a rollback request to the transaction manager. The commit request directs all the participating resources managers to make the effects of the operations of the transaction permanent. The rollback request instructs the resource managers to undo the effects of all operations on the transaction.

An alternative to programmatic demarcation is declarative demarcation. Component-based transaction-processing systems such as application servers based on the Enterprise JavaBeans specification and Microsoft Transaction Server support declarative demarcation. In this technique, components are marked as transactional at the deployment time. This has two implications. Firstly, the responsibility of demarcation is shifted from the application to the container hosting the component. For this reason, this technique is also called **container-managed demarcation**. Secondly, the demarcation is postponed from application build time (static) to the component deployment time (dynamic).

We'll learn about programmatic and container-managed transactions in Chapter 21.

Transaction Context and Propagation

Since multiple application components and resources participate in a transaction, it is necessary for the transaction manager to establish and maintain the state of the transaction as it occurs. This is usually done in the form of transaction context.

Transaction context is an association between the transactional operations on the resources, and the components invoking the operations. During the course of a transaction, all the threads participating in the transaction share the transaction context. Thus the transaction context logically envelopes all the operations performed on transactional resources during a transaction. The underlying transaction manager usually maintains the transaction context transparently. For instance, a Java client or an EJB component implementing transactions need not explicitly propagate the context. The underlying J2EE container handles this.

Resource Enlistment

Resource enlistment is the process by which resource managers inform the transaction manager of their participation in a transaction. This process enables the transaction manager to keep track of all the resources participating in a transaction. The transaction manager uses this information to coordinate transactional work performed by the resource managers and to drive two-phase commit and recovery protocol.

At the end of a transaction (after a commit or rollback) the transaction manager delists the resources. Thereafter, association between the transaction and the resources does not hold.

Two-Phase Commit

This protocol between the transaction manager and all the resources enlisted for a transaction ensures that either all the resource managers commit the transaction or they all abort. In this protocol, when the application requests the transaction be committed, the transaction manager issues a prepare request to all the resource managers involved. Each of these resources will send a reply in turn indicating whether it is ready to commit its operations.

Only when all the resource managers are ready for a commit, does the transaction manager issue a commit request to all the resource managers. Otherwise, the transaction manager issues a rollback request and the transaction will be rolled back.

How can the resource manager or transaction manager request for a rollback when the application has decided that the transaction should be committed? This could happen, for example, when one of the resources that participated in the transaction is not reachable due to network or system failures. This could also happen if one of the resources holding locks on certain data can no longer hold the lock due to a timeout. The two-phase commit makes sure that each of the participating resources can actually commit the transaction.

Building Blocks of Transaction Processing Systems

Any typical transaction processing architecture involves a transaction manager and a resource manager for each resource. These components abstract most of the transaction-specific issues from applications, and share the responsibility of implementation of transactions.

Application Components

Application components are clients for the transactional resources. These are the programs with which the application developer implements business transactions.

With the help of the transaction manager, these components create global transactions, propagate the transaction context if necessary, and operate on the transactional resources within the scope of these transactions. These components are not responsible for implementing semantics for preserving the ACID properties of transactions. However, as part of the application logic, these components generally make a decision whether to commit or rollback transactions.

The following are the typical responsibilities of an application component:

- ❑ Create and demarcate transactions

- ❑ Propagate transaction context

- ❑ Operate on data via resource managers

Resource Managers

A resource manager is a component that manages persistent and stable data storage systems, and participates in the two-phase commit and recovery protocols with the transaction manager. Examples are database systems, message queues, etc.

In addition, a resource manager is typically a driver or a wrapper over a storage system, with interfaces for operating on the data (for the application components). This component may also, directly or indirectly, register resources with the transaction manager so that the transaction manager can keep track of all the resources participating in a transaction. This process is called resource enlistment. The resource manager should also implement supplementary mechanisms (for example, logging) that make recovery possible.

Resource managers provide two sets of interfaces: one set for the application components to get connections and perform operations on the data, and the other set for the transaction manager to participate in the two-phase commit and recovery protocol.

The following are the typical responsibilities of resource managers:

- ❑ Enlist resources with the transaction manager

- ❑ Participate in two-phase commit and recovery protocol

Transaction Manager

The transaction manager is the core component of a transaction-processing environment. Its primary responsibilities are to create transactions when requested by application components, allow resource enlistment and delisting, and to perform the commit/recovery protocol with the resource managers.

A typical transactional application begins a transaction by issuing a request to a transaction manager to initiate a transaction. In response, the transaction manager starts a transaction and associates it with the calling thread. The transaction manager also establishes a transaction context. All application components and threads participating in the transaction share the transaction context. The thread that initially issued the request for beginning the transaction, or, if the transaction manager allows, any other thread may eventually terminate the transaction by issuing a commit or rollback request.

Before a transaction is terminated, any number of components and/or threads may perform transactional operations on any number of transactional resources known to the transaction manager. If allowable by the transaction manager, a transaction may be suspended and resumed before finally completing it.

Once the application issues the commit request, the transaction manager prepares all the resources for a commit operation (by conducting a vote), and based on whether all resources are ready, issues a commit or rollback request.

The following are the typical responsibilities of a transaction manager:

❑ Establish and maintain transaction context

❑ Maintain association between a transaction and the participating resources

❑ Initiate and conduct two-phase commit and recovery protocol with the resource managers

❑ Make synchronization calls to the application components before beginning and after end of a two-phase commit and recovery process

JDBC 2.0 Distributed Transactions

The distributed transaction support in the JDBC 2.0 Optional Package API specifies the responsibilities of a database driver (equivalent to a resource manager in the above discussion). Similar to connection pooling, the JDBC 2.0 Optional Package API specifies two more interfaces – javax.sql.XADataSource and javax.sql.XAConnection. Note that, as per the convention followed by the X/Open DTP model, interfaces starting with letters "XA" stand for interfaces for resource managers – that is, database drivers, or application servers supporting distributed transactions.

The javax.sql.XADataSource Interface

This is a transactional data source. This interface is a factory for javax.sql.XAConnection objects, and is similar to the javax.sql.DataSource interface. However, instead of creating javax.sql.Connection objects, an implementation of this interface creates javax.sql.XAConnection objects. The javax.sql.XAConnection is a transactional connection interface.

The following are the key methods in this interface:

```
public javax.sql.XAConnection getXAConnection()
        throws java.sql.SQLException
public javax.sql.XAConnection getXAConnection (String user, String password)
        throws java.sql.SQLException
```

The remaining methods in this interface are the same as those in the javax.sql.DataSource interface.

The javax.sql.XAConnection Interface

This interface provides support for distributed transactions. This interface extends the javax.sql.PooledConnection interface, and naturally enough supports all the methods specified in the javax.sql.PooledConnection interface. In addition to these methods, the javax.sql.XAConnection interface specifies the following additional method:

```
public javax.transaction.xa.XAResource getXAResource()
        throws java.sql.SQLException
```

What's the purpose of this method? To better understand the purpose of this method, let's consider the transaction processing concepts discussed in the previous section.

Application components in distributed transactions may access the data through multiple database connections. That is, a transaction consists of several connections, with each connection operating (reading, updating, or deleting) on a specified set of database resources. As discussed in the previous section, each resource must be enlisted, so that the transaction manager can keep track of all resources that may have been modified during the transaction. The JTA specifies the `javax.transaction.xa.XAResource` interface for this purpose. For each `Connection` object, the transaction manager obtains a `javax.transaction.xa.XAResource`, and enlists it under the current transaction.

The `javax.transaction.xa` package is a part of the Java Transaction API (JTA).

Before we go on to look at how we can implement distributed transactions, we must consider one additional interface.

The javax.transaction.UserTransaction Interface

Programmatic transaction demarcation is done with the use of the `UserTransaction` interface. This is unnecessary in container-managed environments such as EJB containers.

This interface is not a part of the JDBC 2.0 Optional Package API, but of the Java Transaction API (JTA). We can access this API online at `http://java.sun.com/products/jta/javadocs-1.0.1/index.html`.

This `UserTransaction` interface encapsulates most of the functionality of a transaction manager, and is meant for application server (or transactional middleware) vendors to implement.

The methods exposed by this interface provide the means to explicitly begin and end transactions:

```
public void begin() throws NotSupportedException, SystemException
```

With the help of this method, we can create a new transaction. The `NotSupportedException`, and `SystemException` are part of the `javax.transaction` package. The `javax.transaction.NotSupportedException` is thrown when the transaction manager cannot start a transaction. As an example, this might happen if we're attempting to start a second transaction within the same thread. The `javax.transaction.SystemException` is thrown in case of unexpected errors.

```
public void commit()
        throws RollbackException, HeuristicMixedException,
               HeuristicRollbackException, java.lang.SecurityException,
               java.lang.IllegalStateException, SystemException
```

`Commit()` explicitly commits all the database operations performed so far within the current transaction. The underlying transaction manager uses the two-phase commit and recovery process to complete the commit process.

```
public void rollback() throws java.lang.IllegalStateException,
                              java.lang.SecurityException,
                              SystemException
```

We can use this method to rollback the current transaction.

Of the above three methods, the first method marks the start of a transaction boundary, while the second and third methods explicitly end a transaction. These methods are used in explicit transaction demarcation.

```
public void setRollbackOnly()
         throws java.lang.IllegalStateException, SysemException
```

`setRollbackOnly()` allows an application to enforce roll back, and the transaction should not be committed from that point on. After this method, if we try to call the `commit()` method above, the application will receive the `javax.transaction.RollbackException`.

```
public int getStatus() throws SystemException
```

This method returns the current status of the transaction. These status values are defined in the `javax.transaction.Status` interface.

```
public void setTransactionTimeout(int seconds) throws SystemException
```

We can specify the timeout interval for the transaction with `setTransactionTimeout()`. This allows the transaction manager to reclaim the pending transaction and rollback all changes in case the client remains inactive beyond this interval.

Steps for Implementing Distributed Transactions

The following steps are required for programmatic demarcation of transactions. In container-managed (declarative) transactions, the only step is the configuration.

Configuration

The first step is to configure the application server, and the database driver. Similar to the `javax.sql.ConnectionPoolDataSource`, and `javax.sql.PooledConnection` interface, the interfaces should be implemented by application server vendors and database driver vendors. Therefore, the application server environment should be configured to use the `javax.sql.XADataSource` interface. However, most of the J2EE application server vendors have their own implementations of this API, in which case we may not be required to do this configuration.

Beginning a Transaction

In order to begin a transaction, we should obtain an object implementing the `javax.transaction.UserTransaction` interface. The standard approach for retrieving this object is to perform a lookup in the JNDI service. The following code snippet illustrates this:

```
import javax.sql.*;         // Import the Optional Package API
import javax.naming.*;      // Import the JNDI API
import javax.transaction.*; // Import the JTA

...

    try
    {
        Context initialContext = new InitialContext();
        UserTransaction ut = (UserTransaction)
                    initialContext.lookup("javax.transaction.UserTransaction");

        ut.begin()
    }
```

Notice we import the `javax.transaction` package in addition to the `javax.sql`, and `javax.naming` packages.

In the above snippet, the JNDI lookup looks for `javax.transaction.UserTransaction`. This is the standard name associated with the `javax.transaction.UserTransaction` interface. The application server, which implements this interface, binds an object implementing this interface in the JNDI service.

Database Operations

Apart from certain constraints on calling specific methods on the `java.sql.Connection` object, the rest of the procedure for JNDI lookup for a data source object, creating connections, and executing SQL statements over statements is the same. The following code snippet gives a snapshot:

```
// Create a context
...

try
{

    Context context = new InitialContext();
    DataSource dataSource = (DataSource) context.lookup("jdbc/x");
}
catch(NamingException ne)
{
    // Failed to create the context or lookup.
}

Connection connection = dataSource.getConnection();

...

// Perform usual database operations

...
```

155

```
// Rollback the transaction in case of any failure of business condition
if(...)
{
    // Get the UserTransaction.
    ut.setRollbackOnly()
}

connection.close()

// Do something that uses another data source and another
// connection object
doSomeThing();

...
```

The above code is similar to what we would do in local database transactions! However, the implementation of the application logic can decide to raise a condition for rollback of the transaction.

Let's see what happens when we call the getConnection() method on the data source. With our application server configured for distributed transactions, the data source object uses the underlying implementation of the javax.sql.XADataSource interface for creating javax.sql.XAConnection objects. Note that an XA connection is a special type of pooled connection (javax.sql.XAConnection extends the javax.sql.PooledConnection interface). The data source therefore obtains a connection from this javax.sql.XAConnection object by calling the getConnection() method, and returns it to the application. Notice that this is exactly what happens with connection pooling.

However, there is one additional step. That is resource enlistment. Before returning a connection, the underlying transaction manager obtains the javax.transaction.XAResource object from the XA connection, and enlists for the transaction. The javax.transaction and javax.transaction.xa packages have other packages that help in resource enlistment, and two-phase commit and recovery process. However, as an application developer, we are only concerned with the javax.transaction.UserTransaction interface.

Ending a Transaction

The procedure for ending a transaction is similar to the way we start a transaction. We now call the commit() method on the UserTransaction object to end the transaction. We may need to perform an additional JNDI lookup to retrieve the UserTransaction object if the transaction is being closed from a different method or object from the one that started the transaction.

Special Precautions

Within a transaction, we should not perform the following:

❏   We should not call the commit() and rollback() methods on connection objects. This is because the user transaction object controls the transaction boundaries. These methods throw java.sql.SQLException when called within a transaction.

❑ We should not enable auto-commit on `Connection` objects. Note that auto-commit is contrary to the notion of transactions. When we retrieve a connection under a transaction, the connection will have auto-commit turned off by default, and an attempt to enable it by calling the `setAutoCommit()` method throws `java.sql.SQLException`.

RowSets

The final feature of the JDBC 2.0 Optional Package API we will examine is the `RowSet` class.

In simple terms a `RowSet` is a JavaBean compliant component that encapsulates database access including the result. The `javax.sql.RowSet` interface represents rowsets. In order to see the benefits of rowsets, let's consider a simple database access to fetch a set of rows. Let's first see how we would achieve this without using rowsets:

```
// Create a connection
connection = DriverManager.getConnection("jdbc:HypersonicSQL:Movies");
connection.setAutoCommit(false);

// Create a statement
Statement statement = connection.createStatement();

// Execute a query
ResultSet rs = statement.executeQuery("SELECT * FROM CATALOGUE");

while(rs.next())
{
    // Scroll though and process the results
}
```

In this approach, there are at least three objects that represent different aspects of a query operation – a `java.sql.Connection` object for database connectivity, a `java.sql.Statement` object for executing a statement, and a `java.sql.ResultSet` object to hold the returned values.

Instead consider an approach where the same query operation is encapsulated by one single object:

```
JdbcRowSet rowSet = new JdbcRowSet();

rowSet.setCommand("SELECT * FROM CATALOGUE WHERE TYPE = 'ROMANCE'");
rowSet.setUrl("jdbc:HypersonicSQL:Movies");
rowSet.setUsername("sa");
rowSet.setPassword("");
rowSet.execute();

while(rowSet.next())
{
    // Scroll through and process the results.
}
```

The above code illustrates one possible application of rowsets. In this code, the `JdbcRowSet` class is part of the `sun.jdbc.rowset` package. This package is a reference implementation of the `RowSet`

specification. You can download this along with examples from
`http://developer.java.sun.com/developer/earlyAccess/crs`.

Apart from this encapsulation, the main feature of a rowset is that a `RowSet` object can be used as a JavaBean component. As a bean, a rowset provides a set of mutators for setting properties, and a complementary set of accessors to get the values of those properties. In the above example, we programmatically call the setters to set the properties of the `RowSet`. Instead, we could use a visual programming environment to create a `RowSet` object and set its properties.

`RowSet` objects also support JavaBean style events. `RowSet` objects generate events when certain changes occur in the state of the `RowSet`. Interested objects can register themselves as listeners for these events, and be notified as events occur.

> *In essence, a* `RowSet` *object is a JavaBeans component, having certain properties that can be manipulated by setters, and a set of events that interested objects can listen to. A* `RowSet` *object also encapsulates the results of executing a statement.*

The `javax.sql.RowSet` interface can be implemented as a separate layer on top of an existing JDBC layer. Sun's reference implementation is in fact such a layer, and we can use it on top of any JDBC 2.1 compliant JDBC driver.

The javax.sql.RowSet Interface

```
public interface RowSet extends java.sql.ResultSet
```

The `javax.sql.RowSet` interface extends the `java.sql.ResultSet`. This is because a rowset also encapsulates a set of rows (results) sperately from the properties. As discussed previously, the `java.sql.ResultSet` interface offers a rich set of methods for accessing result rows. Therefore, all the methods that are applicable for a result set are applicable for rowsets too.

Properties

The `javax.sql.RowSet` interface provides a set of JavaBeans properties that can be set at design time. With the help of these properties, the `RowSet` object can connect to a data source and retrieve a set of results at run time. The following are some of the commonly required parameters:

- ❑ URL: A JDBC URL.

- ❑ DataSource name: Name of the datasource. Depending on the implementation, the rowset may use either URL or the datasource name for obtaining a connection.

- ❑ User name: User name for obtaining a connection.

- ❑ User password: Password for obtaining a connection.

- ❑ Transaction isolation: Transaction isolation level. This is a property of `java.sql.Connection`, which specifies a set of constants for isolation level.

- ❑ Command: The SQL statement. The command can also be a prepared statement string.

Events

RowSet objects can generate three types of events:

- ❏ Cursor movement events: These are generated when the cursor is moved. For example, calling a previous() method on the rowset object would generate an event.

- ❏ Row change events: These events are generated when rows in a rowset are changed. For instance, deleting a row would generate an event.

- ❏ RowSet change events: These events are generated when the entire contents of the rowset changes. For instance, calling the execute() would change the entire contents of a rowset.

For application objects to be notified of these events, the JDBC Optional Package API specifies the javax.sql.RowSetListener interface:

```
public interface RowSetListener extends java.util.EventListener
```

This interface specifies three methods:

```
public void cursorMoved(RowSetEvent event)
public void rowChanged(RowSetEvent event)
public void rowSetChanged(RowSetEvent event)
```

The RowSet object calls these methods when one of the listed events occurs.

Application objects implementing the javax.sql.RowSetListener interface can register and deregister for these events with the rowset, using the following methods on javax.sql.RowSet:

```
public void addRowSetListener(RowSetListener listener);
public void removeRowSetListener(RowSetListener listener);
```

These methods are similar to the methods that we find in AWT. We can dynamically add more than one listener. We can also remove these listeners dynamically.

When the Listener objects are notified, the Listener objects receive the RowSet object encapsulated in the javax.sql.RowSetEvent.

Command Execution and Results

After setting the properties, and the listeners, we can call the execute() method on the rowset to populate the results, and use any of the methods specified in the java.sql.ResultSet interface for scrolling, and modifying the results. The execute() method internally obtains a database connection, prepares a statement, and creates a result set.

Creating and using RowSet objects is very simple, and follows the JavaBeans model. In order to populate a result set there are three tasks that we are required to do:

- ❏ Create a RowSet object

- ❏ Set its properties

- ❏ Execute it

159

Types of Rowsets

As of writing, the JDBC 2.0 Optional Package API specification does not "specify" standard interfaces implementing the `javax.sql.RowSet` interface. The specification does, however, identify three possible implementations. Although currently these are not part of the specification, in future, they could be added to the specification as part of a revised set of interfaces.

The following are three possible implementations of this interface:

- ❑ Cached rowsets (`sun.jdbc.rowset.CachedRowSet`)
- ❑ JDBC rowsets (`sun.jdbc.rowset.JdbcRowSet`)
- ❑ Web rowsets (`sun.jdbc.rowset.WebRowSet`)

These are specified in the `sun.jdbc.rowset` package. This package is not a part of either the standard API, or the Optional Package API. Currently, Sun provides a reference implementation of these rowsets in an Early Access release (currently release 4), which can be downloaded from Sun's Java Developer Connection web site (`http://java.sun.com/jdc`).

All the above classes extend from the `sun.jdbc.rowset.BaseRowSet`, and implement the javax.sql.RowSet interface. The `BaseRowSet` class provides the common implementation for properties, events, and methods for setting parameters for rowsets (since rowsets implement the `java.sql.ResultSet` interface).

Apart from the reference implementation, some of the JDBC driver vendors are beginning to support implementations for these types of rowsets. For a list of drivers supporting rowsets, see `http://industry.java.sun.com/products/jdbc/drivers`.

In the following subsections, let's briefly discuss each of these.

Cached Rowsets

A JDBC result set is a connected object. That is, as long as the result set is open (and before we call the `close()` method on it), the result set maintains a connection to the database. This is acceptable if we're holding the result set for short intervals. However, when we intend to use result set objects for significant periods of time, holding the connection would consume unacceptable levels of network resources. For instance, if a result set has 1000 rows and the web application is displaying 10 results per page, we may be required to hold the `Statement` object for a significantly large time frame. This is not desirable. In order to address this, we'll have to transfer the result to custom objects, so that we can release the statement and the connection immediately after executing the statement.

The **cached rowset** addresses this problem. Once a cached rowset has been created and the results populated, the statement and the `Connection` objects can be closed. The cached rowset maintains the result rows in a "disconnected" manner. When we update or modify the rowset, the cached rowset connects to the database and performs the updates on the database and therefore limits the cost in resources.

The `sun.jdbc.rowset.CachedRowSet` class defines cached rowsets:

```
public class CachedRowSet extends BaseRowSet
                          implements javax.sql.RowSet,
                                     javax.sql.RowSetInternal,
                                     java.io.Serializable,
                                     java.lang.Cloneable
```

A cached rowset is a disconnected, serializable, cloneable, and scrollable container for rows of data. It extends `sun.jdbc.rowset.CachedRowSet` and implements the `javax.sql.RowSet`, `RowSetInternal`, `java.io.Serializable`, and `java.lang.Cloneable` interfaces. It is disconnected, therefore it does not hold a connection object. Since it is serializable and cloneable, we can create copies of cached rowsets and transfer them across the wire. For instance, an EJB component can create and return a cached rowset to a client across the network. The client can modify the rowset and send it back to the component, and the component can perform updates. In order for the applications to populate and access/modify the state of cached rowsets, the cached rowset also implements the `javax.rowset.RowSetInternal` interface.

Cached rowsets are suitable in at least two scenarios:

❑　The client application intends to hold the results for a significantly long time interval. This is true for web applications as well as client-server applications executing queries with possibly large number of rows in the result.

❑　The client has neither capacity nor the resources for connecting to a database. For instance, networked devices such as PDAs and other thin clients do not have resources to connect to databases. In such cases, a server-side application can create a cached rowset, and send it across the network to the thin client. The client can scroll through the rowset, and may also save it for later use. The client can send a copy of the results back to the server-side application whenever it updates it.

In effect, the cached rowset gives the ability to create "downloadable" result sets.

The procedure for creating and using cached rowsets is similar to that seen at the beginning of this section:

```
CachedRowSet rowSet = new CachedRowSet();

rowSet.setCommand("SELECT * FROM CATALOGUE WHERE TYPE = 'ROMANCE'");
rowSet.setUrl("jdbc:cloudscape:Movies;create=true");
rowSet.setUrl("jdbc:HypersonicSQL:Movies");
rowSet.setUsername("sa");
rowSet.setPassword("");
rowSet.execute();

while(rowSet.next())
{
   // Scroll through the results .
}
```

The cached rowset gets populated when the `execute()` method is called.

The updateXXX() methods are those specified in the java.sql.ResultSet interface, and are meant for updateable result sets.

Since cached rowsets are disconnected, the database does not enforce any concurrency control on the data held by the cached rowset. In order to maintain optimimum concurrency, the current implementation of a cached rowset caches the original value of the data. This copy represents the state of the cached rowset when the execute() was last called. We can access the original data by calling the getOriginal() and getOriginalRow() methods on the cached rowsets. These methods return result set objects corresponding to the rowset and the current row respectively.

Since the rowset is disconnected, we should call the acceptChanges() method to update the rowset:

```
rowSet.acceptChanges();
```

This method re-establishes a connection to the database, and makes the necessary updates to the database. If the original data held in the cached rowset does not match the data in the database, this method does not update the database with the changed values. Note that this method throws SQLException in the case of failures while making the changes.

JDBC Rowsets

The **JDBC rowset** is a connected rowset. The purpose of the JDBC rowset is to provide a JavaBean type layer on top of java.sql.ResultSet. This is defined in the sun.jdbc.rowset.JdbcRowSet class:

```
public class JdbcRowSet extends BaseRowSet implements javax.sql.RowSet
```

In this class specification, unlike a cached rowset, a JDBC rowset is connected, is not serializable, and neither is it cloneable. It provides whatever features the underlying java.sql.ResultSet interface provides, with the added advantage of presenting itself like a JavaBean.

Web Rowset

As of this writing, the rowset specification is not final and the implementation is being delivered as early access releases. The early access release implementation itself is not complete. In this section, let's therefore focus on the concepts behind **web rowsets**, without the programming detail.

The following represents the intended structure of this rowset type. The web rowset is intended for web-based applications. For this reason, the primary way in which it deviates from the CachedRowSet (which it extends) is that it communicates with other components by the use of XML over HTTP. The sun.jdbc.rowset.WebRowSet class represents a client-server implementation of the rowset interface.

```
public class WebRowSet extends CachedRowSet
```

The web rowset implementation is expected to include the above class, a Java servlet, and a protocol for transmitting tabular data using XML as the data format.

The intended scenario for using web rowsets is as follows: A web client (possibly with Java or JavaScript support) retrieves a set of results using a sun.odbc.rowset.WebRowSet object. When the execute() method on the web rowset is called, it calls a servlet on the server-side (which performs

162

database access) to populate a result set. Once the rowset is updated, the web rowset object sends the updated data to a server-side implementation of the rowset as XML data over the HTTP protocol. The server-side implementation then updates the database. Web rowsets use incremental caching of data, so that data can be retrieved in chunks from the server-side. As the client browses through the web rowset, additional data is downloaded from the server-side.

Although specification as well as implementation of this class is currently incomplete, the goal of this web rowset class is as follows.

Over the Internet, it is not always possible to connect to a database server. Proxies and firewalls will often not allow this. Even if the proxy/firewall configurations allow this, opening up a database over the Internet posses a security threat. In order to avoid this, the server-side implementation of the web rowset would act as a proxy for the database. Therefore, the client-side implementation uses the server-side implementation to retrieve and update results. The main implication of this architecture is that it makes the database clients thin, and clients can use the HTTP protocol (instead of TCP/IP based connection-full database protocols).

When the web client creates a web result set and executes a command, the client-side implementation of the web rowset sends this request to the server-side implementation over HTTP. The server-side implementation would connect to the database, execute the command, and populate the rowset. The server-side implementation would then serialize the data into XML, and send it back to the client-side implementation over HTTP.

This process is repeated when the client modifies the rowset, and calls `acceptChanges()`. The client-side implementation would send a serialized (XML) copy of the rowset to the server-side implementation over HTTP, and the server-side implementation would perform the actual updates.

This mechanism relies on the HTTP and XML for exchanging commands and data between client- and server-side implementations. This eliminates the need for the client to connect to the database server over the Internet.

Based on this approach, we can expect more refined implementations for thin clients.

Summary

The purpose of this chapter has been to provide an overview of database programming using the JDBC API, and then introduce certain advanced concepts related to transactions and databases that are more relevant in an enterprise platform such as J2EE.

As mentioned at the beginning of this chapter, the goal of the first part of this chapter has been to discuss how to perform typical SQL operations using this API. The JDBC API is quite extensive and provides more facilities than can be covered in one chapter. Most of these features (such as batch updates, scrollable result sets, etc.) are comparatively new, and most of the database vendors are only beginning to support these features. We're encouraged to check the documentation from the vendor before we plan to implement these features.

To summarize, in the first part, we've discussed the following in this chapter:

❑ Database drivers, and how to load JDBC drivers

❑ Creating tables, and inserting data

❑ Prepared statements

❑ Mapping between SQL and Java types

❑ Batch updates

❑ Scrollable result sets

In the second part of this chapter, we've discussed four features specified in the JDBC 2.0 Optional Package API:

❑ Now, the JDBC client applications need not be hard-wired to specific JDBC drivers, and to use vendor-specific JDBC URLs. Instead, the data source object, combined with the JNDI-based binding and lookup decouples vendor-specific database details from the client applications.

❑ The JDBC 2.0 Optional Package API shifts the responsibility of connection pooling to J2EE application servers and JDBC drivers. With this approach, connection pooling is a matter of configuring the application server – there is no need to implement custom connection pools, as this mechanism offers a more reliable means of connection pooling.

❑ As we've seen in the previous section, distributed transaction processing has never been so simple. Using the `javax.transaction.UserTransaction` interface, we can explicitly demarcate transactions, while still using the standard JDBC API for database access.

❑ Rowsets are an addition to the Optional Package API. The goal of rowsets is to provide for more flexible, bean-like data access. Sun is also working on Java Data Objects (JDO), presumably based on Microsoft's Active Data Objects. JDOs are expected to complement the JDBC API and provide database access at a higher level without using SQL. The JDO API is currently under development, and we could expect more advanced data access facilities in future. Look for announcements at `http://java.sun.com/products/jdbc`.

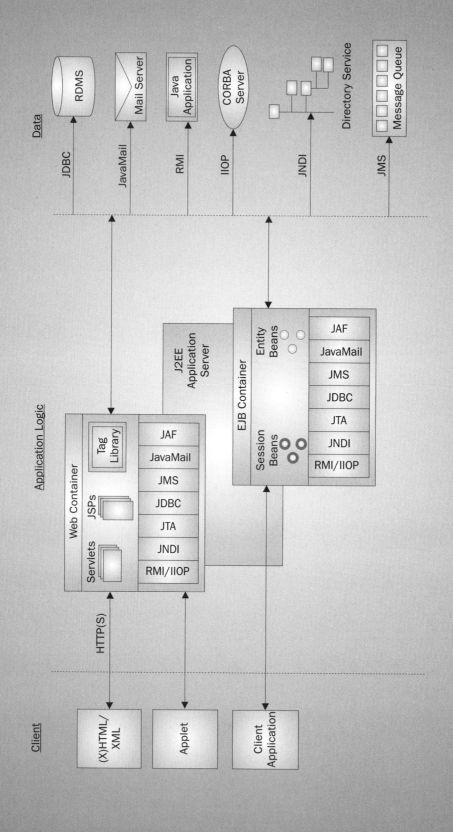

JNDI and LDAP

The **Java Naming and Directory Interface (JNDI)** is designed to simplify access to the directory infrastructure used in the development of advanced network applications. **Directories** are special types of databases that provide quick access to their data stores. Databases are traditionally thought of as the *relational* data storage model, as in Oracle or Microsoft's SQL Server. By contrast a directory database stores its information *hierarchically*.

Traditionally, you had to use different APIs to access different directory services such as **LDAP (Lightweight Directory Access Protocol)** or Sun's **NIS (Network Information Service)**. However, JNDI supplies a standard API to access any type of directory. In addition, JNDI also allows you to store and retrieve Java objects on the network.

In this chapter we are going to cover:

- ❏ What directory and naming services are
- ❏ What LDAP is
- ❏ How to use LDAP to work with a directory service
- ❏ How to manage directory information with JNDI

Finally, we're going to look at an example application, demonstrating the practical applications of JNDI and LDAP.

Naming and Directory Services

Before we look at how to use JNDI it would be appropriate to first cover the basics of naming and directory services.

Naming Services

> **A naming service is a service that provides for the creation of a standard name for a given set of data.**

It does not allow you to search or manipulate the objects in the service beyond adding, changing, or deleting the names of the objects.

The key concept to remember about a naming service is that it provides a **unique name** for every entry that is registered (in JNDI this is called **binding**) for the service. Every naming service will have one or more **context**s.

> **A context is simply a name that is used to make it easier to manage entries in the naming service and to allow reuse of common names.**

There are two types of contexts, **root context** and **sub-context**. A root context is the base name of an entry. Under a file system (which is the most common naming and directory service we use), the root context is the base from which all other directories and files are stored. Thus under UNIX the root context is '/'. Under Windows it generally is C:\ (though each drive letter could also be a root context). In DNS (more on this in a moment), the root contexts are the top-level domains like 'com' or 'edu'. In RMI a root context would be the base of the class hierarchy (if the class hierarchy is wilcox.mark.abc, then the root context would be 'wilcox').

A sub-context is a name that adds another level to the root context. You can have more than one sub-context. The sub-context is simply used to help subdivide the namespace either to provide more flexibility in management or to allow several objects to share the same 'common name'. For example to allow for more than one server to be named www, we have second-level domains like 'wrox.com' and 'yahoo.com'. Thus, www.yahoo.com and www.wrox.com can share the same common name of www, but are considered to be two unique systems on the Internet. The same thing occurs in a file system by creating sub-directories.

After the sub-context is simply the name of the object stored in the naming service. In DNS hostname (www). In a file system this is the name of the file (myfile.txt) In RMI it's the Java class this is the name.

www.wrox.com is an example of a **Fully Qualified Domain Name (FQDN)**. A FQDN is unique name constructed from a *hostname* (www), zero or more *sub-domain names* (there are none in www.wrox.com) and a *domain name* (wrox.com).

Directory Services

> **A directory service is a naming service that includes meta-data describing the object referenced by that name. This enables you to search the directory service on the meta-data to find the object without knowing its name.**

A directory service will always have a naming service, but a naming service doesn't necessarily have to have a directory service. An example of a directory service in the physical world is a telephone book. A telephone book allows us to look up the telephone number of a person or business very quickly if we know the name of the person or business whose number we want (assuming we understand how the directory is basically organized).

There is a plethora of directory (and pseudo-directory) services already in use on our networks today. One directory service we use every day on the Internet is the **Domain Naming Service (DNS)**, which takes a FQDN and returns that FQDN's IP address. All Internet communication uses the Internet Protocol suite (consisting of TCP, UDP, and IP); for successful communication between two computers, each system must know the IP address of the other.

IP addresses currently consist of 32 bit numbers, for example 198.137.240.92, while a FQDN is of a form like www.yahoo.com. Computers are better at dealing with numbers, but humans (most humans anyway), are better at remembering names. Every time you try to connect to an Internet server using its name, your computer must first get the server's IP address via DNS or your computer's hosts file.

It is most likely your organization also uses one or more of the following types of directory service:

- ❑ Novell Directory Services (NDS)
- ❑ Network Information Services (NIS/NIS+)
- ❑ Windows NT Domains
- ❑ Active Directory Services (ADS)

Each of these directory services provides more information than the simple name-to-IP mapping we get from DNS. Each one also allows us to store information about users (userid, passwords, names, etc.), user groups (for access control), and computers (such as their Ethernet and IP addresses). NDS and ADS allow more functions (such as the location of network printers, software, and so on) than either NIS or NT Domains.

As there are so many directory services, and we have so many systems on our networks, some larger problems have arisen, which essentially boil down to two issues:

- ❑ Keeping track of users
- ❑ Keeping track of network resources, such as computers and printers

For example, you may find that your users will need access to a Novell system (which uses NDS) for file and print sharing, an account on a Windows NT box for running Microsoft-based applications, and finally an account on an UNIX box (using NIS) for e-mail and web page publication.

Unfortunately for network managers, none of these directory services interact with each other. Thus you usually must manage all these accounts separately. This can mean that a user has a different userid and password for each directory service. It also leads to 'orphan' accounts, which are accounts that belong to people who are longer with your organization, yet still have open access to these systems. This creates a security hole that can be exploited by the former organizational member or by someone who hacks that account.

Each directory service also has its own particular protocol, which makes it very difficult for the traditional application developer to interact with several different directory services. Fortunately there is one protocol that comes to our rescue.

Enter LDAP

The **Lightweight Directory Access Protocol (LDAP)** was developed in the early 1990s as a standard directory protocol. Since LDAP is now the most popular directory protocol, and JNDI can access LDAP, we'll be spending most of our time talking about how to harness LDAP to improve your Java applications with JNDI.

> *LDAP v3 provides new features for referrals (allowing servers to return referrals to other servers), security (using the Simple Authentication and Security Layer, or SASL), Unicode support, and extensibility.*

LDAP defines how clients should access data on the server; it does not specify how the server should store the data. Most often you'll interact with a server that's been specifically built for LDAP, such as openLDAP or iPlanet Directory server. However, LDAP can become an interface to any type of data store. Because of this, most popular directory services now have an LDAP interface of some type, including NIS, NDS, Active Directory, and even Windows NT Domains.

Before we dig into the parts of LDAP and how to use LDAP within your Java applications, let's take a brief look at the current uses of LDAP.

There are three basic applications of LDAP:

- ❑ Access Control
- ❑ White Pages Services
- ❑ Distributed Computing Directory

So what do these mean?

Access Control

All applications dictate who can use them; this can range from allowing anyone who can click on the application's icon to start it up, to allowing only a person who matches a particular retinal scan. Most applications lie somewhere between these two extremes.

Access control can be broken into two parts: **authentication** and **authorization**.

Authentication

> **Authentication is determining who the person using a piece of software is.**

Due to the nature of computing, we can never be 100% certain of a user's identity, but various authentication mechanisms improve the odds that the person is who they claim to be.

All forms of authentication require the use of a shared secret. The most common form is a standard password, where the user gives a username and a password, and the username is used to look up the person's record in a database. (This database can be a simple flat file like the UNIX `passwd` file, or a directory service like LDAP.) If the password given is the same as the one stored in the database, then we assume that person is who they say they are.

Password-based authentication is the simplest but one of the least secure, because passwords are written down, sniffed in transit over the Internet, or easily cracked when a person gains unauthorized access to the password database. In today's networked world the biggest threat to passwords (outside of asking the user personally for their password) is sending them over the network 'in the clear'. Thus it's best to protect passwords when they travel over the network.

LDAP has the capability to support a wide range of authentication services, including password, digital certificates, and the Simple Authentication and Security Layer (SASL) protocol.

Authorization

After you have authenticated someone, you need to determine what they are allowed to do. For example you might decide that only members of the Dwarfs have the right to access the Snow White files. You might also add finer granularity than just simply saying someone has access or not. For example you might say that members of the Jedi Council have full rights over items in the Force database, while members of the Jedi Knights have the ability to edit certain elements in the Force database, and that apprentices have only the ability to read the Force database.

You can use LDAP to develop sophisticated authorization policies.

White Pages Services

White pages services are services that enable someone to look up users based on attributes contained in their entries. For example you can look up Mark Wilcox's e-mail address, return the telephone number of the Engineering office, the building number of Human Resources, etc. They are called 'white pages' because this type of information is similar to the type of information you find in the white pages of US telephone books.

These types of services are the most public of all LDAP operations and are what many, if not most, people use LDAP for.

Under Java we're putting it second, because most white pages services are provided through an LDAP client found in an e-mail package, like Netscape Messenger or Microsoft Outlook, instead of through a Java application.

I find that Java applications normally perform this function either as the back-end for a web page LDAP interface, or to provide workflow services in an enterprise Java application. For example, John enters an electronic purchase order request for 100 widgets from Acme Widgets. The purchasing application has a business rule that says after a person enters a PO request it must be sent to the PO authorization person for their group. So the application looks up in the LDAP directory to find out who the PO authorizer is for John's group, and sends them an e-mail notification using the authorizer's LDAP e-mail attribute.

Distributed Computing Directory

One of the fastest growing segments of server programming is distributed network programming. This is where an application uses code that actually resides separately from the running application. The code can be either in a separate JVM (or similar engine like a CORBA server), or on a different physical machine located on the other side of the world.

We often use this type of programming to make it easier to reuse existing legacy code or to improve application performance by offloading heavy processing onto a separate machine.

In Java we have three distributed architectures available to us:

❑   Remote Method Invocation (RMI)

❑   Common Object Request Broker Architecture (CORBA)

❑   Enterprise Java Beans (EJB)

All three use a registry service that a client application uses to locate the distributed code. EJB, because the specification was developed after JNDI, uses JNDI for its registry services.

RMI and CORBA use their own independent registry services. One of the problems with these services is that they don't provide a mechanism to search their registry to discover what objects are available for use. With JNDI and LDAP you can provide indirect references to these services. For example, you can have an entry with a name of 'Real Time Stock Quote Service' that has an attribute that contains the actual network location of the RMI or CORBA object.

This type of service makes your code easier to understand and also gives you more flexibility in your application. For example, if you need to move a particular distributed object to a new server you only have to change its location in LDAP, instead of having to change all of the applications that reference that object. All of the client applications will update their locations automatically the next time they reference the object.

Since, as you'll find out later, LDAP can also store other descriptive attributes in an entry, you could store better descriptions of your object in the directory to build a 'white pages' for objects. I've talked to several people who've actually been a part of projects for their companies to develop centralized code libraries. Most of them had said that developing the code has been the easy part, making the code easy to find has been the hard part. My normal reaction to this is to tell them to think about using LDAP as a class directory.

Going back to our stock quote object example, we could add other elements to its description. For example we could add details such as the development language used (such as Java, C, C++), a note about its purpose (such as "This object provides a real time stock quote for any stock listed in the NASDAQ or NYSE when given a particular ticker symbol"), and the name of the developer or development team.

Application Configuration

You could also use LDAP to store configuration information about an application. This is particularly helpful if the same user accesses the same application but on different machines, and it would be helpful to provide the same configuration information regardless of the machine being used.

LDAP Data

The data in an LDAP directory store is organized in a tree, called a **Directory Information Tree (DIT)**. Each 'leaf' in the DIT is called an **entry**. The first entry in a DIT is called the **root entry**.

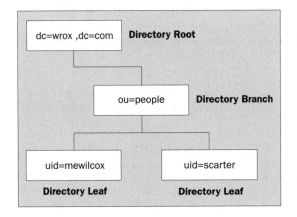

An entry is composed of a **Distinguished Name (DN)** and any number of attribute/value pairs. The DN is the name of an entry, and must be unique. It's like the unique key of a relational database table. A DN also shows the relation of the entry to the rest of the DIT, in a manner similar to the way the full path name of a file shows the relation of a particular file on your hard-drive to the rest of the files on your system. A path to a file on your system reads left-to-right when reading from root to file, whereas a DN reads right-to-left when reading from root to entry.

Here is an example of a DN:

```
uid=scarter, ou=people, o=wrox.com
```

The leftmost part of a DN is called a **Relative Distinguished Name (RDN)** and is made up of an attribute/value that is in the entry. The RDN in the example above would be `uid=scarter`.

LDAP attributes often use mnemonics as their names. Here are some of the more common LDAP attributes and what they define:

LDAP Attribute	Definition	Example
cn	common name	cn=Mark Wilcox
sn	surname	sn=Wilcox
givenname	first name	givenname=Mark
uid	userid	uid=mewilcox
dn	Distinguished Name	uid=mewilcox,ou=people,dc=wrox,dc=com
		cn=Mark Wilcox,ou=people,o=wrox Inc.,c=UK
mail	e-mail address	mail=mark@mjwilcox.com

Any attribute can have one or more values if defined by the **schema**.

> **The schema is the rules that defines the objectclasses and attributes in the LDAP server.**

For example, a user can have more than one e-mail address, so they could have more than one value for their `mail` attribute. Attributes are referred to in name/value pairs, and the attribute values can contain either text or binary data.

There is also a special attribute called **objectclass**. This attribute is similar to a table in a traditional database. An objectclass defines which attributes can be used in a given entry in the directory. It separates attributes into two types, `required`, which means attributes that must be present in the entry, and `allowed`, which means optional attributes.

For example here is the schema for the `inetOrgPerson` objectclass. This is one of the more common objectclasses in use today by many different LDAP servers. I'm presenting this in the standard schema format as defined in LDAP v3:

```
( 2.16.840.1.113730.3.2.2 NAME 'inetOrgPerson' DESC 'Standard ObjectClass' SUP
'organizationalPerson' MUST ( objectclass $ sn $ cn ) MAY
    ( aci $ description $ seealso $ telephonenumber $ userpassword $
    destinationindicator $ facsimiletelephonenumber $
    internationalisdnnumber $ l $ ou $ physicaldeliveryofficename $
    postofficebox $ postaladdress $ postalcode $
    preferreddeliverymethod $ registeredaddress $ st $ street $
    teletexterminalidentifier $ telexnumber $ title $ x121address $
    audio $ businesscategory $ carlicense $ departmentnumber $
    displayname $ employeetype $ employeenumber $ givenname $
    homephone $ homepostaladdress $ initials $ jpegphoto $ labeleduri $
    manager $ mobile $ pager $ photo $ preferredlanguage $ mail $ o $
    roomnumber $ secretary $ uid $ x500uniqueidentifier $
    usercertificate $ usersmimecertificate $ userpkcs12 )
)
```

The first string of digits is the objectclass' **Object Identifier** or **OID**. This OID must be unique in the schema. The next component is the name of the objectclass, followed by an optional description:

```
( 2.16.840.1.113730.3.2.2 NAME 'inetOrgPerson' DESC 'Standard ObjectClass'
SUP 'organizationalPerson'
```

The SUP field means the name of the objectclass' superclass, because in LDAP objectclasses can be extended just like you can extend a class in Java, except that in LDAP, you only add attributes, not behavior.

After the SUP field we get the MUST field, which is the list of the required attributes. After this is the MAY field, which defines the list of optional attributes.

The $ is used to separate the attributes because this is a tradition in LDAP. The tradition dates back to the original X.500 server which was developed on particular piece of hardware that couldn't print the $, thus it was chosen as the text delimiter because it was guaranteed never to show up in any of the original X.500 data values

Here is an example LDAP entry represented in the **LDAP Data Interchange Format (LDIF)**, which is the most common way to show LDAP data in human readable format:

```
dn: uid=scarter, ou=People, o=wrox.com
cn: Sam Carter
sn: Carter
givenname: Sam
objectclass: top
objectclass: person
objectclass: organizationalPerson
objectclass: inetOrgPerson
ou: Accounting
ou: People
l: Sunnyvale
uid: scarter
mail: scarter@wrox.com
telephonenumber: +1 408 555 4798
facsimiletelephonenumber: +1 408 555 9751
roomnumber: 4612
```

Attributes also have **matching rules**, which tell the server how it should consider whether a particular entry is a 'match' or not for a given query.

The possible matching rules are:

Matching Rule	Meaning
DN	Attribute is in the form of a Distinguished Name.
Case Insensitive String (CIS)	Attribute can match if value of the query equals the attribute's value, regardless of case.
Case Sensitive String (CSS)	Attribute can match if value of the query equals the attribute's value, including the case.
Telephone	Is the same as CIS except that things like '-' and '()' are ignored when determining the match.
Integer	Attribute match is determined using only numbers.
Binary	Attribute matches if the value of the query and the value of the attribute are the same binary values (for example searching a LDAP database for a particular photo).

The definitions of attributes, attribute matching rules, and the relationship between objectclasses and attributes are defined in the server's schema. 'Out of the box', the server already contains a pre-defined schema, but you can extend the schema (as long as the server supports the LDAP v3 protocol as defined in RFC 2251) to include your own attributes and objectclasses.

LDAP has growing momentum both as the standard protocol for electronic address books and as the central directory service for network services. For more information about LDAP see Implementing LDAP, *ISBN 1-861002-21-1, from Wrox Press.*

Introducing JNDI

While LDAP is growing in popularity and in usage, it's still a long way from being ubiquitous. Other directory services such as NIS (primarily developed by Sun) are still in widespread use. Another issue for the developers of Java was that for Java to succeed as an enterprise development language, it needed to support existing distributed computing standards such as the **Common Object Request Broker Architecture (CORBA)**, which is heavily used in large organizations that have many different types of applications interacting with each other. CORBA is a language- and platform-independent architecture (as opposed to RMI which is strictly only Java) for enabling distributed application programming (where an application on one machine can access a function of a different application located on a different machine as if it was calling an internal function). CORBA uses a naming service for defining the location of the available objects.

So it was decided to make things easier for Java application developers, by creating a standard API for interacting with naming and directory services, similar to what Java application developers have for databases in JDBC. This API is very important for the long-term development of Java, particularly the Enterprise JavaBeans (EJB) initiative.

A key component of EJB is the ability to store and retrieve Java objects on the network. A directory service (most likely LDAP) is going to be the primary data store for Java objects, in particular Java objects that are fairly stable (that is, they are retrieved from the network more often than stored on the network). This is because, when loading objects (such as a person's record, or binary data like a serialized Java object) from the network, you want to be able to locate them quickly, and a directory service enables the very fast lookup and retrieval of data.

Let's look in more detail at the relationships between directory services, JNDI, and LDAP.

The diagram below shows the relationship between a client and a variety of directory services. Each directory service requires its own API, which adds complexity and code bloat to our client application:

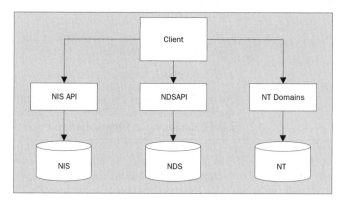

Our next example shows how we could simplify this for the application developer with JNDI. With JNDI, we still have multiple servers and multiple APIs underneath, but to the application developer, it is effectively a single API:

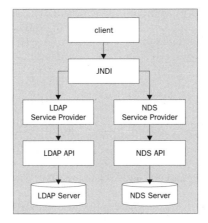

There are definite pros for using a single, standardized API for programming directory service applications:

❑   One is that because Sun has made it a standard part of Java, it's integrated into many facets of the Java platform, which we'll discuss later.

❑   Second, it makes it easier to change out service providers (you can think of a JNDI service provider as being like a directory service driver), just like you can change out JDBC drivers.

However, there are a few cons:

❑   One is that not all service providers are created equal, just like all JDBC database drivers are not created equal.

❑   Second, you are programming at a higher level than the protocol level, so sometimes you can't use protocol features that you might have been accustomed to.

❑   Third, because each directory service protocol is different, you must still factor these differences into your application, even if you're using the same API and a proper service provider.

Thus I prefer to stick to a standard protocol like LDAP so that I can pick the best service provider without having to worry about differences in directory server protocols.

Here is an example of using JNDI and LDAP together for a more elegant solution:

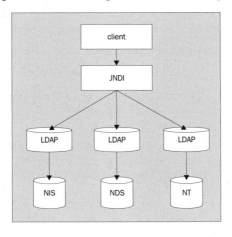

In this final version, we use JNDI to communicate with an LDAP server(s). The developer needs to worry about only one particular protocol (LDAP) and API (JNDI). In this example, we are relying on the vendors to provide LDAP interfaces to their respective protocols. This is not such a far-fetched idea: for each of these popular directory services, there are products that allow you to communicate with them via LDAP.

Using JNDI

Now that you have a basic understanding of directory services, JNDI, and LDAP, it's time to get our hands dirty by looking at an example.

To use JNDI as described in this chapter you will need the following:

- ❑ Sun's Java Development Kit 1.1 or higher (JNDI is shipped as a standard part of JDK 1.3)

- ❑ The JNDI Software Development Kit 1.2 (available from `java.sun.com/jndi/`)

- ❑ The JNDI LDAP Service Provider 1.2.2 (also available from the JNDI site)

- ❑ An LDAP v3 compliant directory server (I used Netscape's iPlanet Directory Server from `http://www.iplanet.com/downloads/`)

JNDI does now ship with JDK 1.3, including the LDAP, COS (a.k.a. the CORBA naming service), and RMI service providers. You do, however, need to get the `ldapbp.jar` and `providerutil.jar` files from the JNDI 1.2.2 distribution to get all of the LDAP functionality, including the ability to use LDAP controls, and to store or retrieve RMI objects in an LDAP server, which we'll need later on in the chapter.

Installing JNDI

Here are the steps I followed to get things working on my system (Windows NT):

- ❑ Install iPlanet Directory Server (or your favorite LDAP v3 server) – See Appendix B for instructions. All the examples you will see in this chapter are using the `arius.com` sample data that comes with the iPlanet install.

- ❑ Download JNDI 1.2.

- ❑ Unzip JNDI 1.2 into a directory called `jndi2`.

- ❑ Unzip the JNDI zip file into a directory called `jndi` inside the `jndi2` directory.

- ❑ Unzip the LDAP zip file into a directory called `ldap` inside the `jndi2` directory.

- ❑ Make a directory called `jar` in your `jndi2` directory.

- ❑ Copy all of the `*.jar` files in the `jndi/lib` and `ldap/lib` directories to the `jndi2/jar` directory (not really necessary but makes it easier to remember the paths to the JAR files when we do the next step).

- ❑ Add the paths to each of the JAR files to your CLASSPATH environment variable (for example, on a Windows system the extra entries might be: `C:\jndi2\jar\ldap.jar;` `C:\jndi2\jar\providerutil.jar;C:\jndi2\jar\jndi.jar;`).

Optionally in JDK 1.2 or later you can simply copy the JAR files into your `java_home/jre/lib/ext` directory and you don't have to fuss with your CLASSPATH variable.

Once you have followed these steps, you are ready to use JNDI and LDAP.

JNDI Service Providers (JNDI Drivers)

We've briefly talked about service providers already, but here we'll talk about them in more detail.

> **A service provider is a driver that enables you to communicate with a directory service, similar to the way in which a JDBC driver enables you to communicate with a database.**

For a service provider to be available for use in JNDI, it must implement the `Context` interface. (Actually most of the service providers you will use will likely implement the `DirContext` interface, which extends the `Context` interface to enable directory services.)

What this means is that you only have to learn JNDI itself to know the API calls to connect to a naming or directory service, while the service provider worries about the ugly details (such as the actual network protocol, and encoding/decoding values).

Unfortunately, service providers are not a magic bullet. You must know something about the underlying directory service so that you can correctly name your entries and build the correct search queries.

> *Unlike relational databases, directory services do not share a common query language such as SQL. A common query language for directory services may be developed through the Directory Services Markup Language (DSML) group which is attempting to define an XML standard for directory services, but I think the focus is now on providing LDAP interfaces to existing directory services as the way to provide a consistent directory service query language.*

In JNDI 1.2, service providers can support a concept of **federation**, where a service provider can pass an operation to another service provider if the first provider does not understand the naming or operation scheme. For example, if you wanted to find out the MX record for a particular domain from DNS (the MX record contains the preferred destination e-mail server for a domain), but your initial service provider was LDAP, it would not be able to answer the request. If federation were enabled, the LDAP service provider would be able to pass the request to the next provider on the federation list, which if it were a DNS service provider would be able to handle the request for you. If a service provider capable of handling the request cannot be found, your operation will throw an exception.

Ideally this should be transparent to the application programmer. However, since this is a new feature, it has not been widely implemented and tested.

> **So to sum up, a service provider enables your JNDI applications to communicate with a naming/directory service. The rest of the interfaces, classes, and exceptions all revolve around your interaction with a service provider.**

How to Obtain JNDI Service Providers

When you download the JNDI Software Development Kit (SDK) from Sun, it will come with a number of service providers (an SDK comes with the API plus documentation and extras like service providers). These include providers for LDAP, NIS, COS (CORBA Object Service), RMI Registry, and File

179

System. Many different vendors also provide service providers for other directory services, or as replacements for the default providers Sun ships. For example, Novell has a service provider for NDS, while both IBM and Netscape have written alternative service providers for LDAP.

Here we show how easy it is to switch between service providers. For example to use the default Sun LDAP service provider you would make a call like this:

```
//Specify which class to use for our JNDI provider
env.put(Context.INITIAL_CONTEXT_FACTORY,
        "com.sun.jndi.ldap.LdapCtxFactory");
```

Now to switch to using IBM's LDAP service provider, you would simply replace `"com.sun.jndi.ldap.LdapCtxFactory"` with the full package name of the IBM LDAP service provider, like this:

```
//Specify which class to use for our JNDI provider
env.put(Context.INITIAL_CONTEXT_FACTORY,
        "com.ibm.jndi.LDAPCtxFactory");
```

Developing Your Own Service Provider

You may also need to implement your own service provider, in particular if you need to use a directory service (such as Windows NT domains or Banyan Vines) that doesn't already have an existing service provider.

In the JNDI SDK, Sun provides an example of how to write a service provider. The JNDI tutorial contains information on how to write a service provider and is available at: `http://java.sun.com/products/jndi/tutorial/index.html`.

Another option to investigate is Netscape's LDAP service provider, which is available as an open-source project at `http://www.mozilla.org/directory/`.

Basic LDAP Operations

In the rest of this chapter we'll see how to perform basic LDAP operations with JNDI. We'll end with a final application that shows how to use JNDI in multiple roles, such as authentication and object discovery.

Before you can perform any type of operation on an LDAP sever, you must first obtain a reference and a network connection to the LDAP server. You must also specify how you wish to be bound to the server – either anonymously or as an authenticated user. Many Internet accessible LDAP servers allow some type of anonymous access (generally read-only abilities for attributes like e-mail addresses and telephone numbers), but LDAP also supports very advanced security features via **Access Control Lists (ACLs)**, that are dependent upon who the connection is authenticated as.

Standard LDAP Operations

There are a few standard procedures when using LDAP:

- ❏ Connect to the LDAP server
- ❏ Bind to the LDAP server (you can think of this step as authenticating)
- ❏ Perform a series of LDAP operations:
    - ❏ Search the server
    - ❏ Add a new entry
    - ❏ Modify an entry
    - ❏ Delete an entry
- ❏ Disconnect from the LDAP server

We'll go through each of these steps in turn.

Connecting to the LDAP Server

When using JNDI, you must first obtain a reference to an object that implements the `DirContext` interface. In most applications we will use an `InitialDirContext` object, which takes a hash table as a parameter. This hash table can contain a number of different references – at the very least it should contain a reference to a field with the key `Context.INITIAL_CONTEXT_FACTORY` with a value of the fully qualified class name of the service provider, and a field with the key `Context.PROVIDER_URL` with a value containing the protocol, hostname, and port number to the LDAP server like this: `ldap://localhost:389`. Note that port 389 is the default LDAP port.

In the next few sections we'll present some code snippets to demonstrate some basic concepts and we'll put it all together at the end with some applications.

For example, let's start by creating a `Hashtable` to store the environment variables that JNDI will use to connect to the directory service.

```
Hashtable env = new Hashtable();
```

Next, we specify the fully qualified package name of our JNDI provider as specified in the API. Here we are using (only because it ships with SDK) the standard Sun LDAP service provider that comes with the JNDI SDK:

```
//Specify which class to use for our JNDI provider
env.put(Context.INITIAL_CONTEXT_FACTORY,
        "com.sun.jndi.ldap.LdapCtxFactory");
```

Next we specify the hostname and port number to our LDAP server:

```
// Specify host and port to use for directory service
env.put(Context.PROVIDER_URL, "ldap://localhost:389");
```

Finally, we get a reference to our initial directory context with a call to the `InitialDirContext` constructor, giving it our `Hashtable` as its only parameter. A directory context tells JNDI what service provider we will be using, what naming/directory server we will be connecting to, what location we will we be accessing the directory from initially (the search base), and any authentication information:

```
//Get a reference to a directory context
DirContext ctx = new InitialDirContext(env);
```

Authentication (LDAP Bind)

In LDAP authentication is called **binding** because an authenticated connection is bound to a particular entry in the directory. This binding should not be confused with a JNDI bind which associates an object to a particular name in a naming or directory service (regardless of whether it's LDAP or not).

If you use the default values, the connection will be authenticated as an anonymous user, without many privileges on the server. Many LDAP servers provide some type of read access to their directory data (for address book applications). Specifically, the type of access an application has to the LDAP server is dependent upon the Access Control Lists (ACLs) of the LDAP server. Which ACLs apply to an operation is determined by how the application is authenticated.

LDAP allows for an extremely flexible security model. ACLs determine what particular access is available to an entry(s) by an application.

For example, an LDAP server may have several layers of rights for any given entry:

❑   Anonymous users can see an employee's e-mail address and telephone number.

❑   The employee can see their entire entry, but only modify certain attributes such as telephone number, password, and office room number.

❑   A user's manager can update an employee's telephone number and office room number, but nothing else. They can also see the employee's entire record.

❑   A small group, the Directory Administrators, have full rights to the entire server including the ability to add or remove any entry.

As an entry can have several ACLs defined, it is possible for an entry to have several different 'views' to an application simply by changing the binding (who the application is authenticated as).

> *LDAP also supports **Transport Security Layer (TSL**, also still known as **Secure Socket Layer/SSL)** for protecting content 'over the wire' or to improve authentication via client certificates. Finally, LDAP supports the **Simple Authentication and Security Layer (SASL)** protocol that enables you to use other authentication/encryption mechanisms such as Kerberos without 'breaking' the protocol.*

You can specify authentication by storing the Context.SECURITY_AUTHENTICATION, Context.SECURITY_PRINCIPAL, and Context.SECURITY_CREDENTIALS in the hash table passed to the InitialDirContext constructor.

To specifically bind to the server we must provide the environment with the method for our authentication (such as 'simple', SSL, or SASL). Then we must specify the DN of the entry we wish to bind as, and the entry's password:

```
Hashtable env = new Hashtable();

//This sends the id and password as plain text over the wire
```

```
env.put(Context.SECURITY_AUTHENTICATION, "simple");
env.put(Context.SECURITY_PRINCIPAL, MGR_DN);
env.put(Context.SECURITY_CREDENTIALS, MGR_PW);

//Get a reference to a directory context
DirContext ctx = new InitialDirContext(env);
```

Simple

'Simple' security means that you will only authenticate to the server using standard plain-text userids and passwords, without any encryption on the network. This is by far the most common, and least secure, of the various authentication methods. It is insecure for two reasons:

❑ Userids and passwords are transmitted to the server over a public network, where anyone can steal them off the network

❑ There is nothing to guarantee that the person who types in the userid and password is the actual owner of that userid and password (although you can never truly combat this)

SSL/TLS

The Secure Socket Layer protocol was developed by Netscape Communications to improve the security of web-based transactions. It has become an official standard called Transport Layer Security (TLS), but is still often referred to as SSL. TLS is defined in RFC 2246.

SSL allows you to encrypt your entire transaction over the network, making it very hard for anyone to steal the information (such as your userids and passwords). Most servers that implement SSL also support client-certificates (text files that are used to vouch for the identity of the server and client) for user authentication. Instead of presenting a userid and password to the server, you can present a certificate. If the certificate you present matches an allowed certificate, you are granted access.

Certificates are considered more secure, because they are hard to fake. However, certificates are typically stored as a file on a local user's machine, which means that if the client machine is compromised, a certificate can be used just like a stolen userid and password. If certificates are stored locally, then a mechanism must be developed to recover them if the machine they are stored on crashes or is upgraded. Certificates can be stored on smart cards instead of files on a local machine, for more security and reliability. Finally, the issuing and managing of client certificates is still in the early stages of development (the technology is there in the forms of standards and APIs, but the policies and procedures are not in place yet in any great numbers).

SASL

The **Simple Authentication and Security Layer** is an Internet standard (RFC 2222) for implementing authentication mechanisms besides simple or SSL.

There are two popular SASL mechanisms:

❑ In **MD5**, a MD5 hash is built of the password a user enters on the client, the userid and MD5-hashed password are sent to the server, and are compared to see if they match. If the userid and MD-5-hashed password sent from the client match those stored on the server, then the client is allowed access. MD5 doesn't encrypt the transaction, and it doesn't solve the problem of 'who typed in the password'. Indeed, if the MD5-hashed password is stolen on its way to the server, a hacker could use that to gain access to the system, just as if it was a plain-text password. It does, however, make it harder to guess what the password originally was, so if a hacker does steal the password, they won't easily be able to guess what the password was to try and to use it to gain access to other systems.

❑ **Kerberos** encrypts the transaction, and in a Kerberos-aware network it is very easy to implement a single-logon environment because of the way Kerberos works.

Under Kerberos, you have a master server that everyone originally authenticates to called the Ticket Granting Server or TGS, which issues a ticket to the user upon successful authentication. This ticket is valid for a given time, generally the length of the average work-day, so that a user doesn't have to login repeatedly to the TGS. Applications that are Kerberos enabled consult the user's master ticket. If the master ticket is still valid, they will grant an application ticket. This application ticket is normally valid for a period of time that is shorter than the master ticket so that it can time out users after a period of inactivity or to reduce the amount of damage that can be done in the event of a compromised TGS.

However, managing a Kerberos network is very expensive in time and resources, so many places haven't implemented Kerberos yet (though this may change after Windows 2000 is more widely deployed because it ships with a Kerberos implementation by default).

You can easily write your own SASL mechanisms, if your LDAP server supports them. Thus if you wanted to add support for other public key encryption schemes like PGP or El-Gamal you could.

Searching an LDAP Server

The most used operation on any LDAP server is the search operation. You might search an LDAP server to find the e-mail address or telephone number of a friend or colleague. Or you might need to look up an entry's DN in order to authorize their access. Or you might be trying to find all Java classes that are part of the com.sun package tree. You can search on any attribute in an entry, except for the Distinguished Name because the DN is not truly an attribute, but rather is treated as a separate component.

Any advanced LDAP applications use searching as their core functionality. Essentially, all search functions take an LDAP connection handle, the base to start the search from, the scope of the search, and a search filter. A search filter is like a SQL query in that you tell the server the criteria to use to find matching entries. Searches always use an attribute name and a value to look for. Filters can use Boolean logic and wildcards. Some servers, such as the iPlanet Directory Server, support even more advanced query abilities such as 'sounds like', but this will vary on a server-by-server basis.

Example LDAP Filters

Some typical LDAP filters are:

Search to Perform	Filter
Find all users with the last name Carter	sn = Carter
Find all users with last names starting with 'Ca'	sn = Ca*

Search to Perform	Filter

Find all entries that have the word 'Managers' in their common name attribute and are also of type 'groupOfUniqueNames'	`(&(cn = * Managers * )`
	`(objectclass=groupofUniqueNames)`
	`)`

LDAP Search Base and Scope

If you remember back to earlier in the chapter, we learned that LDAP is organized as a tree. When searching the LDAP server, you can define where in this tree you wish to start your search by specifying the **search base**. The search base is simply the DN of the entry you wish to make your starting point.

For example if you want to start at the root you could specify:
`dc=wrox, dc=com`

If you wanted to search only for people in your organization you might specify:
`ou=people, dc=wrox, dc=com`

You can then define a search scope to limit the breadth of your search under your search base.

There are three search scopes:

Scope	Meaning
LDAP_SCOPE_SUBTREE	Starts at the base entry and searches everything below it, including the base entry.
LDAP_SCOPE_ONELEVEL	Searches only the level of the tree immediately below the base entry. Does not include the base entry.
LDAP_SCOPE_BASE	Searches just the base entry, useful if you want to just get the attributes/values of one entry.

The first figure below illustrates a search using LDAP_SCOPE_SUBTREE:

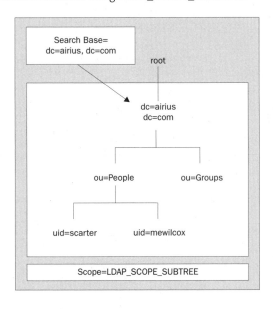

185

Secondly, we have an example of a search using LDAP_SCOPE_ONELEVEL:

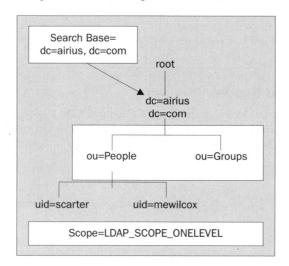

Finally, here is a search using LDAP_SCOPE_BASE:

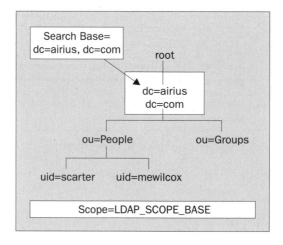

Searching with JNDI

Our first example will show a very simple search, where the search filter is 'sn=Carter'. This will return back all entries that have a surname (the attribute specified by the mnemonic 'sn') of Carter. This first example is an anonymous search.

The examples here are non-GUI based. There is nothing to prevent them from being included in a GUI.

```
// Standard anonymous search
import java.util.Hashtable;
import java.util.Enumeration;

import javax.naming.*;
```

```java
import javax.naming.directory.*;

public class JNDISearch {

  // Initial context implementation
  public static String INITCTX = "com.sun.jndi.ldap.LdapCtxFactory";
  public static String MY_HOST = "ldap://localhost:389";
  public static String MY_SEARCHBASE = "o=Airius.com";
  public static String MY_FILTER = "(sn=Carter)";

  public static void main(String args[]) {
    try {

      // Hashtable for environmental information
      Hashtable env = new Hashtable();

      // Specify which class to use for our JNDI provider
      env.put(Context.INITIAL_CONTEXT_FACTORY, INITCTX);

      // Specify host and port to use for directory service
      env.put(Context.PROVIDER_URL, MY_HOST);

      // Get a reference to a directory context
      DirContext ctx = new InitialDirContext(env);

      // Specify the scope of the search
      SearchControls constraints = new SearchControls();
      constraints.setSearchScope(SearchControls.SUBTREE_SCOPE);

      // Perform the actual search
      // We give it a searchbase, a filter and a the constraints
      // containing the scope of the search
      NamingEnumeration results = ctx.search(MY_SEARCHBASE,
                                      MY_FILTER, constraints);

      // Now step through the search results
      while (results != null && results.hasMore()) {
        SearchResult sr = (SearchResult) results.next();

        String dn = sr.getName();
        System.out.println("Distinguished Name is " + dn);

        Attributes attrs = sr.getAttributes();

        for (NamingEnumeration ne = attrs.getAll();
             ne.hasMoreElements(); ) {
          Attribute attr = (Attribute) ne.next();
          String attrID = attr.getID();

          System.out.println(attrID + ":");
          for (Enumeration vals = attr.getAll();
               vals.hasMoreElements(); ) {
            System.out.println("\t" + vals.nextElement());
          }
        }
      }
```

```
        System.out.println("\n");
      }
    } catch (Exception e) {
      e.printStackTrace();
      System.exit(1);
    }
  }
}
```

The output from this code example is shown in the screenshot below:

```
C:\WINNT\System32\cmd.exe                                          _ □ ×

C:\ProJavaServer\Chapter05>java JNDISearch
Distinguished Name is uid=scarter,ou=People
givenname:
        Sam
telephonenumber:
        +1 408 555 4798
sn:
        Carter
ou:
        Accounting
        People
l:
        Sunnyvale
roomnumber:
        4612
mail:
        scarter@airius.com
facsimiletelephonenumber:
        +1 408 555 9751
objectclass:
        top
        person
        organizationalPerson
```

How the Search Program Works

We perform a search using the search() method of an object that implements the DirContext interface (such as the InitialDirContext class). The minimum requirement for this is the search base and a filter. There are other parameters we can use to help manage the results. If the search is successful, a NamingEnumeration object will be returned.

Once we get the initial context (which we store in the variable ctx), we next specify the scope of our search, which is set in the SearchControls object, which is an optional parameter to the search() method of a DirContext object. If we don't specify a scope, JNDI will assume a scope of 'subtree', so this next line is actually redundant but, for the record, this is how you specify the scope:

```
// Specify the scope of the search
SearchControls constraints = new SearchControls();
constraints.setSearchScope(SearchControls.SUBTREE_SCOPE);
```

After specifying the scope we can perform the actual search:

```
// Perform the actual search
NamingEnumeration results = ctx.search(MY_SEARCHBASE, MY_FILTER,
                                        constraints);
```

The `NamingEnumeration` class is equivalent to the `SearchResults` class in the iPlanet Directory SDK for Java. Each element in a `NamingEnumeration` object will contain a single `SearchResult` object, which we can retrieve like this:

```
SearchResult sr = (SearchResult) results.next();
```

We can get the DN of an entry like this:

```
String dn = sr.getName();
```

To get the attributes of an entry you use the `getAttributes()` method of the `SearchResult` class:

```
Attribute attr = (Attribute) ne.next();
```

This will return a concrete object that implements the `Attributes` interface (the `InitialDirContext` class returns a `BasicAttributes` object).

After we have an `Attributes` object (remember this is a collection class), we can then step through its elements using a `NamingEnumeration` object:

```
for (NamingEnumeration ne = attrs.getAll();
     ne.hasMoreElements();){
  Attribute attr = (Attribute) ne.next();
  String attrID = attr.getID();

  System.out.println(attrID + ":");
  for (Enumeration vals = attr.getAll(); vals.hasMoreElements(); ) {
    System.out.println("\t" + vals.nextElement());
  }
}
```

The `NamingEnumeration` class gives us methods that we can use to step through each attribute that was returned in our search. Each element in the `NamingEnumeration` object will contain an `Attribute` object that represents an attribute and its values.

The `getID()` method of the `Attribute` interface returns the name of the attribute, and the `getAll()` method will return back a standard Java `Enumeration` object, which we can then access to get the values of the individual attribute.

In every LDAP server, there are certain attributes that are not going to be available to anonymous users because the of access controls on the server. There are also certain attributes that may only be available to certain authenticated, privileged users – pay scale, for example, may only be visible to human resources staff.

Authenticated Searching

The next example shows how we can do an authenticated search:

```
// Standard authenticated search

import java.util.Hashtable;
import java.util.Enumeration;

import javax.naming.*;
import javax.naming.directory.*;

public class JNDISearchAuth {

  // Initial context implementation
  public static String INITCTX = "com.sun.jndi.ldap.LdapCtxFactory";
  public static String MY_HOST = "ldap://localhost:389";
  public static String MGR_DN = "uid=kvaughan, ou=People, o=airius.com";
  public static String MGR_PW = "bribery";
  public static String MY_SEARCHBASE = "o=Airius.com";

  public static String MY_FILTER = "(sn=Carter)";

  public static void main(String args[]) {
    try {
      //Hashtable for environmental information
      Hashtable env = new Hashtable();

      //Specify which class to use for our JNDI provider
      env.put(Context.INITIAL_CONTEXT_FACTORY, INITCTX);

      //Security Information
      //authenticates us to the server
      env.put(Context.SECURITY_AUTHENTICATION, "simple");
      env.put(Context.SECURITY_PRINCIPAL, MGR_DN);
      env.put(Context.SECURITY_CREDENTIALS, MGR_PW);

      //Get a reference to a directory context
      DirContext ctx = new InitialDirContext(env);

      SearchControls constraints = new SearchControls();
      constraints.setSearchScope(SearchControls.SUBTREE_SCOPE);
  ...
```

This is exactly the same as the first example, except that we have authenticated ourselves to the server.

Here are the lines where we specified the DN and password to the application:

```
      //Security Information
      //Authenticates us to the server
      env.put(Context.SECURITY_AUTHENTICATION, "simple");
      env.put(Context.SECURITY_PRINCIPAL, MGR_DN);
      env.put(Context.SECURITY_CREDENTIALS, MGR_PW);
```

If you try compiling and running this example, you'll see that it produces the same output as before. Note that by default the LDAP server returns all of the attributes for a search. There may, however, be occasions when we don't want this, because we are only concerned with particular attributes.

Restricting the Attributes Displayed

In our third example, we ask to only be shown the common name (cn) and e-mail address (mail) attributes:

```java
// Search return with specified results
import java.util.Hashtable;
import java.util.Enumeration;

import javax.naming.*;
import javax.naming.directory.*;

public class JNDISearchRestAttribs {

  // Initial context implementation
  public static String INITCTX = "com.sun.jndi.ldap.LdapCtxFactory";
  public static String MY_HOST = "ldap://localhost:389";
  public static String MY_SEARCHBASE = "o=Airius.com";
  public static String MY_FILTER = "(sn=Carter)";

  // Specify which attributes we are looking for
  public static String MY_ATTRS[] = {
    "cn", "mail"
  };

  public static void main(String args[]) {
    try {

      // Hashtable for environmental information
      Hashtable env = new Hashtable();

      // Specify which class to use for our JNDI provider
      env.put(Context.INITIAL_CONTEXT_FACTORY, INITCTX);
      env.put(Context.PROVIDER_URL, MY_HOST);

      // Get a reference to a directory context
      DirContext ctx = new InitialDirContext(env);

      SearchControls constraints = new SearchControls();
      constraints.setSearchScope(SearchControls.SUBTREE_SCOPE);

      NamingEnumeration results = ctx.search(MY_SEARCHBASE, MY_FILTER,
                                             constraints);

      while (results != null && results.hasMore()) {
        SearchResult sr = (SearchResult) results.next();
        String dn = sr.getName() + ", " + MY_SEARCHBASE;

        System.out.println("Distinguished Name is " + dn);
```

```
            Attributes ar = ctx.getAttributes(dn, MY_ATTRS);

        if (ar == null) {
          System.out.println("Entry " + dn
                            + " has none of the specified attributes\n");
        } else {
          for (int i = 0; i < MY_ATTRS.length; i++) {
            Attribute attr = ar.get(MY_ATTRS[i]);
            if (attr != null) {
              System.out.println(MY_ATTRS[i] + ":");
              for (Enumeration vals = attr.getAll();
                   vals.hasMoreElements(); ) {
                System.out.println("\t" + vals.nextElement());
              }
            }
            System.out.println("\n");
          }
        }
      }
    } catch (Exception e) {
      e.printStackTrace();
      System.exit(1);
    }
  }
}
```

Since we have just specified the common name and mail attributes this time, the resulting output from the code should look like this:

The difference between this code and our earlier example searches is that we now limit the number of attributes to be retrieved.

First we created a String array that listed the attributes we wanted:

```
public static String MY_ATTRS[] = {
  "cn", "mail"
};
```

To retrieve this set of attributes we use the `getAttributes()` method of the `DirContext` interface, providing the DN of a specific entry and the array of attributes:

```
Attributes ar = ctx.getAttributes(dn, MY_ATTRS);
```

This will return an `Attributes` object.

We can retrieve a particular `Attribute` object from an `Attributes` object like this:

```
Attribute attr = ar.get("cn");
```

I want to point out that retrieving a specific set of attributes from an individual entry is very quick, but not very practical for general searching. In a general LDAP search, the end user is not going to know the existing Distinguished Names of the entries they are looking for. So we will have to search the LDAP server and retrieve a set of entries. In JNDI (as opposed to the iPlanet Directory SDK for Java), this search will return all of the attributes associated with each individual entry. If we then make a subsequent call to `getAttributes()` to retrieve a subset of attributes like in the previous example, this will require another call to the LDAP server to get back the subset of attributes. This is inefficient, because it requires us to use extra memory for all of the attributes and extra bandwidth for the extra communication. The extra memory is required because your application must hold the data of the LDAP search results for you to process. To improve performance in your Java applications, you want to reduce the amount of extraneous memory used because the JVM's garbage collector can be slow to react, and can slow your application to a crawl as it reclaims memory.

Working with LDAP Entries

We can also use JNDI to add new entries to the server, delete entries, and modify existing entries.

Adding Entries

Using JNDI to add entries to a LDAP server is in fact more difficult than it is with other LDAP SDKs. This is because JNDI's primary goal is to read/write Java objects to the network. A consequence of this is that a programmer must go through some extra hoops, such as creating a Java class for each type of entry to be added to the LDAP server. Here we'll look at how to add and modify a simple entry in the LDAP server, but later in the chapter we'll look also at how to use the LDAP server as an object store.

To store an entry in a LDAP server using JNDI, you must bind an object to a Distinguished Name (DN). This means that each object we store in the server (whether a simple person entry or a serialized Java class) must have a DN associated with it. Remember that a DN is the unique name that each entry in a LDAP server must possess. If you switch to a different directory service (such as NDS) you will still be required to have a unique name for each object. This will become second nature over time; remember that you do this (provide an unique name) each time you save a file to your hard disk. No two files in the same directory can share the same name; if you wish to have two files named `myfile.txt` you must store them in separate directories, otherwise one version will overwrite the other.

To store even a simple entry in the LDAP server, we must create a class that implements the `DirContext` interface. This interface defines how the object (whether a person or a serialized Java class) should be stored in and retrieved from the directory server. For example, if you have a Person object, your class will specify how to build its DN, how to store the available attributes (full name, e-mail address, telephone number, userid, password, etc.), and provide various mechanisms to handle the retrieved data. The `DirContext` also provides for much more sophisticated data handling techniques, and is the basic interface for building a directory service provider.

As with any other LDAP SDK, an 'add' operation can only be performed by an authenticated user who has rights to add a new entry into the server. LDAP security can be set up so that users can only add entries into particular parts of the directory tree.

Our next code sample shows a very simple `Person` class that implements the `DirContext` interface. Most of the methods in the interface are not actually implemented (except to throw exceptions), because we don't need them for our very simple example here.

The methods that we implement here, `getAttributes()` and the constructor, enable us to store/retrieve the data in a `Person` class as traditional LDAP entries. The rest of the methods that we don't fully implement are methods primarily used to build full service providers.

> *New objects must also conform to the LDAP server's schema, or the entries will not be added (your application will throw an LDAP exception).*

It will be easier to explain how to add an entry with JNDI if I explain the code as we go along.

First is our class declaration, note that we state that we will implement the methods for the `DirContext` interface:

```
// Person class
import java.util.*;

import javax.naming.*;
import javax.naming.directory.*;

public class Person implements DirContext {
    String type;
    Attributes myAttrs;
```

Next, we have our constructor, which takes several `String` parameters that we will use to build an `inetOrgPerson` object class. I've chosen the `inetOrgPerson` objectclass because it is the most common example you'll see when you use LDAP (regardless of server vendor):

```
public Person(String uid, String givenname, String sn, String ou,
              String mail) {
    type = uid;
```

We will use the `BasicAttributes` class to store our attributes and their values using the `BasicAttribute` class. By specifying `true` in the `BasicAttributes` constructor, we are telling it to ignore the case of attribute names when doing attribute name lookups:

```
    myAttrs = new BasicAttributes(true);
```

To add a multi-valued attribute we need to create a new `BasicAttribute` object, which requires the name of the attribute in its constructor. We then add the values of the attribute with the `add()` method:

```
Attribute oc = new BasicAttribute("objectclass");
oc.add("inetOrgPerson");
oc.add("organizationalPerson");
oc.add("person");
oc.add("top");

Attribute ouSet = new BasicAttribute("ou");
ouSet.add("People");
ouSet.add(ou);

String cn = givenname+" "+sn;
```

Finally, we add all of our attributes to the `BasicAttributes` object:

```
myAttrs.put(oc);
myAttrs.put(ouSet);
myAttrs.put("uid", uid);
myAttrs.put("cn", cn);
myAttrs.put("sn", sn);
myAttrs.put("givenname", givenname);
myAttrs.put("mail", mail);
}
```

When `getAttributes()` is called, it will return our `BasicAttributes` object when requested by a name in the form of a `String`:

```
public Attributes getAttributes(String name) throws NamingException {
  if (! name.equals("")) {
    throw new NameNotFoundException();
  }
  return myAttrs;
}
```

This method does the same thing as the first `getAttributes()`, but is only called when the name is passed a `Name` object:

```
public Attributes getAttributes(Name name) throws NamingException {
  return getAttributes(name.toString());
}
```

The following method returns only the attributes listed in the `String` array `ids`. The name should be a DN:

```
public Attributes getAttributes(String name,
                                String[] ids) throws NamingException {
  if (! name.equals("")) {
    throw new NameNotFoundException();
  }
```

```
    Attributes answer = new BasicAttributes(true);
    Attribute target;
    for (int i = 0; i < ids.length; i++) {
      target = myAttrs.get(ids[i]);
      if (target != null) {
        answer.put(target);
      }
    }
    return answer;
  }
```

The next method is the same as the other getAttributes(), except it takes a Name object:

```
  public Attributes getAttributes(Name name,
                                  String[] ids) throws NamingException {
    return getAttributes(name.toString(), ids);
  }
```

toString() is used for serialization:

```
  public String toString() {
    return type;
  }
```

The following methods (you can find the complete set in the full source code as there are too many to list here) are used to implement methods that a JNDI service provider (such as the InitialDirContext class) would use to provide an application with services such as reading entries from the directory or for authenticating to the server:

```
  // Not used for this example

  public Object lookup(Name name) throws NamingException {
    throw new OperationNotSupportedException();
  }

  public Object lookup(String name) throws NamingException {
    throw new OperationNotSupportedException();
  }

  public void bind(Name name, Object obj) throws NamingException {
    throw new OperationNotSupportedException();
  }
  ...
```

And here is the program that uses the Person class to add an entry for Mark Wilcox to the LDAP server, most of which we've seen before:

```
  // Adding an object to an LDAP server
  import java.util.Hashtable;
  import java.util.Enumeration;
```

```
import javax.naming.*;
import javax.naming.directory.*;

public class JNDIAdd {

  // initial context implementation
  public static String INITCTX = "com.sun.jndi.ldap.LdapCtxFactory";
  public static String MY_HOST = "ldap://localhost:389";
  public static String MGR_DN = "uid=kvaughan, ou=People, o=airius.com";
  public static String MGR_PW = "bribery";
  public static String MY_SEARCHBASE = "o=Airius.com";

  public static void main(String args[]) {
    try {

      // Hashtable for environmental information
      Hashtable env = new Hashtable();

      // Specify which class to use for our JNDI provider
      env.put(Context.INITIAL_CONTEXT_FACTORY, INITCTX);

      env.put(Context.PROVIDER_URL, MY_HOST);
      env.put(Context.SECURITY_AUTHENTICATION, "simple");
      env.put(Context.SECURITY_PRINCIPAL, MGR_DN);
      env.put(Context.SECURITY_CREDENTIALS, MGR_PW);

      // Get a reference to a directory context
      DirContext ctx = new InitialDirContext(env);

      Person p = new Person("mewilcox", "Mark", "Wilcox", "ou=Accounting",
                            "mewilcox@airius.com");

      ctx.bind("uid=mewilcox,ou=People,o=airius.com", p);
      System.out.println("Mark Wilcox has been added!");
    } catch (Exception e) {
      e.printStackTrace();
      System.exit(1);
    }
  }
}
```

First we must create a new Java object that implements the DirContext interface, such as our Person class:

```
Person p = new Person("mewilcox", "Mark", "Wilcox", "ou=Accounting",
                      "mewilcox@airius.com");
```

Then we associate a name (specifically the DN of the entry) with this object in our current context with the bind() method of the DirContext interface:

```
ctx.bind("uid=mewilcox,ou=People,o=airius.com", p);
```

The `InitialDirContext` interface will actually perform an LDAP 'add' operation, taking all of the attributes we placed in our Java class and encoding them for transfer into a LDAP server.

Since we used the `BasicAttribute` class to build our attributes, they will be stored/retrieved as standard LDAP data and not as pure Java objects. This means that if you store your LDAP data this way any other LDAP client, whether written in C, Perl, or Visual Basic, will still be able to access it.

If you have a look in your directory now you will see a new entry for **Mark Wilcox**:

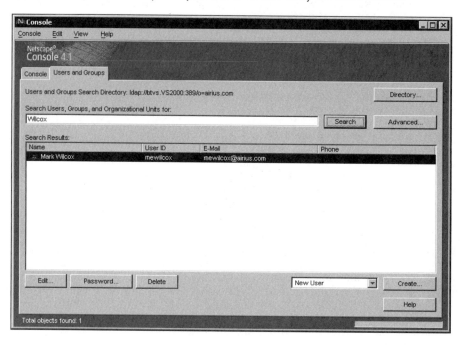

Modifying an Entry

Just as soon as you add an entry to an LDAP server, you'll likely need to modify it. This could be for a variety of reasons, including changing a user's password, updating an application's configuration, etc.

Modifications to an entry are made with the `ModificationItem` and `BasicAttribute` classes. When you make a modification, it can be either an ADD, a REPLACE, or a DELETE operation. A REPLACE will add an attribute if it doesn't exist yet.

> **You should also be aware that if you perform a REPLACE on an attribute that has multiple values, if you don't send the extra values along with your replacement value, they will all be removed.**

Again, an authenticated user must perform any modifications, and the rights the bound entry has on a particular entry will determine which modifications can be performed. For example, users can generally change their own passwords but nothing else, while administrative assistants usually can change telephone numbers and mailing addresses also. Finally, it usually takes a database administrator to change things like a user's userid.

The code below demonstrates how we can modify the attributes of the Mark Wilcox entry that we added in the previous example:

```java
// Modifying an entry
import java.util.Hashtable;
import java.util.Enumeration;

import javax.naming.*;
import javax.naming.directory.*;

public class JNDIMod {

    // Initial context implementation
    public static String INITCTX = "com.sun.jndi.ldap.LdapCtxFactory";
    public static String MY_HOST = "ldap://localhost:389";
    public static String MGR_DN = "uid=kvaughan, ou=People, o=airius.com";
    public static String MGR_PW = "bribery";
    public static String MY_SEARCHBASE = "o=Airius.com";

    public static void main(String args[]) {

        try {

            // Hashtable for environmental information
            Hashtable env = new Hashtable();

            // Specify which class to use for our JNDI provider
            env.put(Context.INITIAL_CONTEXT_FACTORY, INITCTX);

            env.put(Context.PROVIDER_URL, MY_HOST);
            env.put(Context.SECURITY_AUTHENTICATION, "simple");
            env.put(Context.SECURITY_PRINCIPAL, MGR_DN);
            env.put(Context.SECURITY_CREDENTIALS, MGR_PW);

            // Get a reference to a directory context
            DirContext ctx = new InitialDirContext(env);

            ModificationItem[] mods = new ModificationItem[2];

            Attribute mod0 = new BasicAttribute("telephonenumber",
                                                "940-555-2555");
            Attribute mod1 = new BasicAttribute("l", "Waco");

            mods[0] = new ModificationItem(DirContext.REPLACE_ATTRIBUTE, mod0);
            mods[1] = new ModificationItem(DirContext.ADD_ATTRIBUTE, mod1);

            // DirContext.DELETE_ATTRIBUTE not shown here
            ctx.modifyAttributes("uid=mewilcox,ou=People,o=airius.com", mods);
            System.out.println("Modification worked!");
        } catch (Exception e) {
            e.printStackTrace();
            System.exit(1);
        }
    }
}
```

To modify an entry we use the `ModificationItem` class. The `ModificationItem` constructor takes a modification type (ADD, REPLACE, or DELETE) and an `Attribute` object such as `BasicAttribute`. For example, in the above code we added a new attribute, locality (the l attribute), with a new value of `"Waco"`, to the entry:

```
Attribute mod1 = new BasicAttribute("l", "Waco");
mods[1] = new ModificationItem(DirContext.ADD_ATTRIBUTE, mod1);
```

The actual modification is performed by the `DirContext` method `modifyAttributes()`:

```
ctx.modifyAttributes("uid=mewilcox,ou=People,o=airius.com", mods);
```

Again, this modifies the entry in the LDAP server using traditional LDAP and not as a Java object, so that any other client can still access this data.

Deleting an Entry

Eventually, you may need to remove entries from your LDAP server. This is easily accomplished by calling the `destroySubContext()` method of the `DirContext` interface, with the distinguished name of the entry that needs to be removed. Normally, delete operations can be performed only by the LDAP database administrators.

Here is an example of deleting an entry:

```
// Delete Entry

import java.util.Hashtable;
import java.util.Enumeration;

import javax.naming.*;
import javax.naming.directory.*;

public class JNDIDel {

    // Initial context implementation
    public static String INITCTX = "com.sun.jndi.ldap.LdapCtxFactory";
    public static String MY_HOST = "ldap://localhost:389";
    public static String MGR_DN = "uid=kvaughan, ou=People, o=airius.com";
    public static String MGR_PW = "bribery";
    public static String MY_SEARCHBASE = "o=Airius.com";

    public static String MY_ENTRY = "uid=mewilcox, ou=People, o=airius.com";

    public static void main(String args[]) {
        try {

            // Hashtable for environmental information
            Hashtable env = new Hashtable();

            // Specify which class to use for our JNDI provider
            env.put(Context.INITIAL_CONTEXT_FACTORY, INITCTX);
```

```
        env.put(Context.PROVIDER_URL, MY_HOST);
        env.put(Context.SECURITY_AUTHENTICATION, "simple");
        env.put(Context.SECURITY_PRINCIPAL, MGR_DN);
        env.put(Context.SECURITY_CREDENTIALS, MGR_PW);

        // Get a reference to a directory context
        DirContext ctx = new InitialDirContext(env);

        ctx.destroySubcontext(MY_ENTRY);
        System.out.println("Deletion successful");
      } catch (Exception e) {
        e.printStackTrace();
        System.exit(1);
      }
    }
  }
```

The only important difference in the code in this example and the rest of our examples is this line:

```
        ctx.destroySubcontext(MY_ENTRY);
```

This removes the entry from the LDAP server.

Storing and Retrieving Java Objects in LDAP

One of JNDI's strongest features is its ability to use LDAP as a network object store. What this means is that you can use LDAP to store Java objects that you need either to share between different applications, or to store for later use.

There are several reasons why you would like to use LDAP as your data store:

❑   Leverage an existing centralized resource

❑   Leverage existing open standards

❑   LDAP is available on the network 'out of the box'

❑   LDAP is designed for extremely quick read access

❑   LDAP has strong security built in

JNDI allows you to store several types of Java related objects into the LDAP server.

The option you use to store your objects will depend upon the application you are building, and how you need to access the data.

Traditional LDAP

I personally think that at least half of the time you (or at least your organization) will want to access the data in the directory service from a variety of clients using a number of different languages. A popular use of a directory service is for user authentication. Obviously, storing user authentication data in a format that only

Java can use reduces the number of types of applications that can use the directory for authentication. This in turn raises the cost of doing business, because you then need another directory service for providing authentication services to applications that can't access Java objects.

A number of applications won't need authentication, but could benefit from a directory service's address book features. For example, your e-mail program can use it to find the e-mail addresses of co-workers, your marketing department can use it to build mail-merged form letters, and your web developers can use it to make a custom portal for each customer. Each of these applications could be built using Java as the development language, but they probably won't be. More importantly, your company reduces its overhead by maintaining consistent data about its people and clients in a central database.

One of the neat things about storing data in this fashion is that you can treat each entry like an object in Java, but other languages don't have to be object-oriented in order to access the data.

Serialized Java Objects

If you have a growing number of Java applications that need access to a central repository of pre-built Java objects, then use Java's serialization to store those objects into the LDAP server. Then when an application needs a particular object (for example, a 3D rendering engine) it can retrieve it from the LDAP server when it's needed, then release it. Another nice feature of this is that when you update the rendering engine, all of the applications that are using the engine will have access to the update without having to patch the applications themselves.

Java References

Finally if you are in an all-Java environment you might wish to take advantage of **Java References**. References reduce the storage and bandwidth requirements of storing and retrieving entries, because they don't store the entire object in the directory, only key components that are needed to rebuild the object in a factory class. Often the component stored is a URL that points to the real location of the object.

For example, if you create a standard `Printer` object, you can build a `PrinterFactory` that will take as parameters:

- ❑ Network location
- ❑ Color options (monochrome, color, etc.)
- ❑ Specialties (postscript, graphic plotter, etc.)

These parameters can be passed to `PrinterFactory` and will always return a `Printer` object that your application can use to print. This approach reduces bandwidth and storage, because only the above parameters need to be stored. It's easier to deal with as an application programmer, because part of the reference is the fully qualified package name of the actual factory. You don't then have to include it with your application, just to make sure the JVM can find the package.

If you want to read more about using JNDI and LDAP as a Java object store, you can see the official JNDI site at `http://java.sun.com/jndi/`.

DSML

As we mentioned earlier, there is a standard XML representation for directory data called **Directory Services Markup Language** or **DSML**. A consortium of directory service providers including Oracle, Novell, Sun-Netscape Alliance, and Microsoft has developed DSML. Its purpose is to standardize the representation of all types of directory service data, not just LDAP, in an XML format. The DSML consortium has a web site at `http://www.dsml.org` where you can find more information about the project.

As DSML is so new, and because it doesn't yet have any syntax for describing directory service updates, it's not yet widely disseminated. However, starting with Sun LDAP provider version 1.2.2, you can get access to DSML output from a `java.net.URL` object when searching an LDAP server using LDAP URLs. Sun is also working on a complete DSML service provider for JNDI. At the time of this writing, it was available on the Java Developers site as part of the early release program. Code under the early release program is only available to registered Java developers (the registration is free). Once the code is fully released, expect to find it on the public JNDI site.

A Bank Account JNDI Application

So far we have covered a lot of ground. However, most of the examples have been more pedagogical in nature than presented in actual context. Our final example, while still more of a teaching example than a real application ready for you to use in your next project, does show JNDI and LDAP in a truer context.

Our example will be a client-server banking application using RMI. The object of the application is to simply show you how much money you have in your bank account.

We are using JNDI for three parts of the application:

❑   As the RMI object lookup

❑   For user authentication

❑   For user demographic information

The only part we won't use JNDI for is to retrieve the account information. In real life this information would be retrieved from a database; in order for us to concentrate on the JNDI parts, I'm just returning a random number.

The reason why we don't store the actual account amount in LDAP is not a limitation of LDAP, but rather for performance reasons. Most directory services are optimized for reads, and write performance usually suffers (or at least is the least optimal operation). Thus, it's not wise to use a directory service to store information that is updated often. Things like names, userids, and passwords don't change often; thus they are good candidates for directory information.

> *Now a quick note before we continue. While this application should work in JDK 1.2, I did develop it using JDK 1.3. If you're using JDK 1.3, the basic JNDI classes are included by default. However, you will still need the LDAP 'booster pack' contained in the* `ldapbp.jar` *file in the Sun LDAP 1.2.2 service provider SDK (available at* `java.sun.com/jndi`*).*

Using LDAP with RMI

It is rather simple to develop distributed Java applications with RMI. However, there's one problem with normal RMI development, and that is it's difficult to dynamically update the location of your RMI server objects in your RMI clients.

Just a quick note, I've already mentioned 'RMI server' several times in this section and I'll mention it several more times before we're done. What I mean by RMI server, is the distributed RMI object(s) that a client uses in the course of their application. Normally these objects aren't true servers, but it makes it easier to keep track of which objects we're talking about.

Too many times we end up hard-coding this information into our clients. Slightly better is to provide the location of the RMI server object via a resource file or a command-line parameter. These are better than hard coding, because at least you can update the RMI server location without having to recompile. However, all of these require a lot of work if you need to change the location. For example if you hard-coded the RMI server's URL, you must edit the source and recompile (and maybe redistribute). With resource files and command line parameters, you must tell users to change their old values.

However, there's a solution to these ills, and that is to store the RMI server's location (which is actually the URL to its location in a particular RMI registry) in a central location that can be updated whenever necessary, such as a network directory service like LDAP (or even a networked file system like NFS or NTFS shares). When the RMI server's location is changed in the directory, all of the clients will be updated automatically without user intervention.

If you store the location in a true directory service then you can also search that directory service if you're looking for an object but don't know its name (for example you can ask the server to return all entries that contain the attribute `javaclass`); this is the primary benefit of storing references in a directory service as opposed to the file system. Other benefits are standardized access and access controls to the objects, but usually you can tweak other directory mechanisms (such as NTFS shares) to provide security and access mechanisms.

In fact, JNDI has a special class, called a `Reference`, that is specifically designed to store distributed object location information. You can think of a `Reference` object as an indirect pointer to an object.

For example, an RMI location is specified using an RMI URL like `rmi://localhost/MyBank`. If you stored this reference in an LDAP server via the JNDI `Reference` class, you would give the object a name that conforms to the directory server's rules (for example you must give it a valid DN), such as `dn: cn=MyBank,o=airius.com`.

Thus, an RMI client would connect to the LDAP server, asking to get the Java class that is actually stored in the RMI server object (such as the object at `rmi://localhost/MyBank`). JNDI is smart enough to realize that once it retrieves the entry from the LDAP server that it's actually a Java `Reference` object, so it retrieves the RMI URL stored in this object (this information is contained in an LDAP attribute called `javareferenceaddress`). It then connects to the RMI registry specified in the RMI URL, and returns a reference to the RMI server object.

Here's the really complicated code that does this:

```
JNDIRemoteBankInterface j =
        (JNDIRemoteBankInterface)ctx.lookup("cn=MyBank");
```

I was joking about it being really complicated: this code is all there is to it. Once this method returns, you have a reference to a remote object, regardless of whether the object was stored directly in the directory service, or if it was a reference to an object that resided somewhere else.

Here's the LDIF (LDAP Data Interchange Format) for a Java Reference LDAP entry:

```
dn: cn=MyBank,o=airius.com
objectclass: top
objectclass: javaContainer
objectclass: javaObject
objectclass: javaNamingReference
javareferenceaddress: #0#URL#rmi://localhost/MyBank
javaclassname: MyBank
cn: MyBank
```

Application Background

We are going to use the concepts outlined in the above section for our Bank application. There are multiple distributed components involved in making this application work:

❑ **RMI client:** This is the interface the user interacts with

❑ **RMI server:** This provides the mechanism the client uses to retrieve the account information

❑ **LDAP server:** This provides the URL to the RMI server object, authentication services, and user demographic information

❑ **RMI registry:** This allows the RMI client and RMI server to communicate with each other

The diagram below gives a visual overview of what happens:

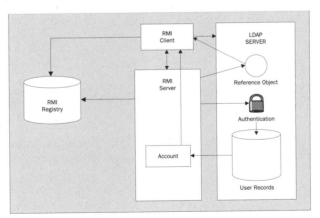

The steps to a working application are:

❑ First, the `JNDIRemoteBankServer` (RMI server) must start up. During startup it registers its RMI location to the LDAP server as a `Reference` object, and then it registers itself with the local RMI registry.

❑   Next, the `JNDIRemoteBankClient` (RMI client) starts up. It must first locate the RMI server object's RMI location, by retrieving the `Reference` object from the LDAP server. Then it connects to the RMI server object using the RMI URL contained in the `Reference` object retrieved from the LDAP server.

❑   The client then passes the username and password to the RMI server object, to retrieve the account information. This process authenticates the user to the LDAP server.

❑   If that succeeds, it retrieves the user's full name from the LDAP server, and then gets the user's account amount.

❑   This is put into an `Account` object that is returned to the RMI client, which then displays the information to the user.

While this does sound a bit overwhelming, we'll show you all of the steps you need to make this work.

Our application requires four classes:

❑   `JNDIRemoteBankInterface` – the interface we need to implement for our remote objects

❑   `JNDIRemoteBankServer` – the remote object

❑   `JNDIRemoteBankClient` – the local object

❑   `Account` – The data object passed from the server to the client

The names pretty much describe themselves. We'll talk about them in more detail as we examine their code.

JNDIRemoteBankInterface

```
import java.rmi.*;
import java.util.Vector;

import Account;

public interface JNDIRemoteBankInterface extends Remote {
  public Account getAccount(String username,
                            String password) throws RemoteException;
}
```

This class simply defines the interface any of our server objects must implement. For our example application, it's extremely simple so that we can focus on the JNDI aspects.

JNDIRemoteBankServer

This class defines the remote object that we will access to provide the bulk of the work. As this is our remote object we must implement our remote interface and because it might be stored in the directory server, we make it `Serializable` as well:

```
import java.rmi.*;
import java.rmi.server.*;
import java.util.*;
```

```
import javax.naming.*;
import javax.naming.directory.*;

import java.io.*;

import Account;

public class JNDIRemoteBankServer extends UnicastRemoteObject
  implements JNDIRemoteBankInterface, Serializable {

  public static String INITCTX = "com.sun.jndi.ldap.LdapCtxFactory";
  public static String MY_HOST = "ldap://localhost:389";
  public static String MY_BASE = "ou=people,o=airius.com";

  public JNDIRemoteBankServer() throws RemoteException {}
```

The bulk of our code is to provide an implementation of the getAccount() method declared in JNDIRemoteBankInterface:

```
public synchronized Account getAccount(String username, String password)
        throws RemoteException {
  Account accountObj = new Account();
  String fullName = null;
  int amount = -1;
  Random account = new Random();
  try {
    Hashtable env = new Hashtable();
    env.put(Context.INITIAL_CONTEXT_FACTORY, INITCTX);

    // Specify host and port to use for directory service
    env.put(Context.PROVIDER_URL, MY_HOST);
    env.put(Context.SECURITY_AUTHENTICATION, "simple");

    StringBuffer dnBuffer = new StringBuffer();
    dnBuffer.append("uid=");
    dnBuffer.append(username);
    dnBuffer.append(",");
    dnBuffer.append(MY_BASE);

    env.put(Context.SECURITY_PRINCIPAL, dnBuffer.toString());
    env.put(Context.SECURITY_CREDENTIALS, password);
```

Next we obtain the InitialDirContext object. If the user entered an incorrect username or password, this will throw a NamingException, which we catch later:

```
    DirContext ctx = new InitialDirContext(env);
    SearchControls constraints = new SearchControls();
    constraints.setSearchScope(SearchControls.SUBTREE_SCOPE);
```

Here we retrieve the user's full name from their LDAP entry and put it into an Account object. We also randomly generate the amount that's in their account and put that number in the Account object as well:

```
    // Get the user attributes
    StringBuffer searchFilter = new StringBuffer();
    searchFilter.append("uid=");
    searchFilter.append(username);

    NamingEnumeration results = ctx.search(MY_BASE,
                                    searchFilter.toString(),
                                    constraints);

    // now step through the search results
    while (results != null && results.hasMore()) {
      SearchResult sr = (SearchResult) results.next();
      Attributes attrs = sr.getAttributes();
      Attribute attr = attrs.get("cn");

      fullName = (String) attr.get();
      amount = account.nextInt() * 1000;
      accountObj.setFullName(fullName);
      accountObj.setAmount(amount);
    }
    return accountObj;
  } catch (NamingException e) {
    System.err.println(e.toString());
  }
  return null;
}
```

We're now getting to the point where we are storing the reference to our RMI location into the LDAP server, from our `main()` method:

```
public static void main(String args[]) {
  Hashtable env = new Hashtable(11);
  env.put(Context.INITIAL_CONTEXT_FACTORY, INITCTX);
  env.put(Context.PROVIDER_URL, MY_HOST + "/o=airius.com");

  env.put(Context.SECURITY_AUTHENTICATION, "simple");
  env.put(javax.naming.Context.SECURITY_PRINCIPAL,
          "cn=Directory Manager");
  env.put(javax.naming.Context.SECURITY_CREDENTIALS, "password");

  // Only works on local machine; change hostname for network access
  String rmiurl = "rmi://localhost/MyBank";

  try {
```

Most LDAP servers require you to authenticate to the server before you can write to the server. You will need to change the above bolded password to whatever you set your Directory Manager password to. Also, in this example, I'm just adding the example directly off the root of the DIT. In practice you might want to create a separate branch for all of your Java objects. Doing so makes it easier to keep things organized:

```
// Create the initial context
DirContext ctx = new InitialDirContext(env);
```

The next line creates an instance of `StringRefAddr`, which is a class that represents the string form of an address. It will store its object's data in the LDAP server using the schema we saw earlier:

```
// Create reference containing (future) location of object
Reference ref = new Reference("MyBank",
                              new StringRefAddr("URL", rmiurl));
```

Then we store the actual object in the directory server:

```
// Bind to directory
ctx.bind("cn=MyBank", ref);
```

Next, we create an instance of the `JNDIRemoteBankServer` so that we can register it with the `rmiregistry` service:

```
// Create object to be bound
JNDIRemoteBankInterface j = new JNDIRemoteBankServer();
```

Now we bind to the RMI registry. Notice that we didn't have to create a different context or new object to do this. JNDI handled this for us through the use of federation, which allows a particular service provider (in this case LDAP) to pass off a request to a different service provider if it gets a request it doesn't understand:

```
// Bind to RMI Registry
// (the RMI URL will redirect request to the RMI registry provider).
ctx.rebind(rmiurl, j);
```

For this to work your LDAP server must support the schema described in RFC 2713. Check with your LDAP server to see how to do this. The iPlanet Directory Server 4.0 already does support this schema.

Finally, we close the context and catch any exceptions:

```
    // Close the context when we're done
    ctx.close();

    System.out.println("MyBank is now open!");
  } catch (NamingException e) {
    System.out.println("Operation failed: " + e);
  } catch (RemoteException e) {
    System.out.println("Operation failed: " + e);
  }
 }
}
```

JNDIRemoteBankClient

This class is what the end user will use:

```
import java.rmi.*;
import java.util.*;

import javax.naming.*;
import javax.naming.directory.*;

import Account;

// Our example client for interfacing with RMI via LDAP
public class JNDIRemoteBankClient {
```

The `main()` method requires two command-line arguments, username and password:

```
public static void main(String args[]) {
  if (args.length < 2) {
    System.out.println("usage is JNDIRemoteBankClient username password");
    System.exit(1);
  }

  // Check that we can look it up via the directory

  try {
    Hashtable env = new Hashtable(11);
    env.put(Context.INITIAL_CONTEXT_FACTORY,
            "com.sun.jndi.ldap.LdapCtxFactory");
    env.put(Context.PROVIDER_URL, "ldap://localhost:389/o=airius.com");
    DirContext ctx = new InitialDirContext(env);
```

Now we look up the object from the LDAP server, which in turn obtains a reference from the `rmiregistry` that contains the object of our desire. An important note is that in my particular LDAP server I allowed anonymous access to the Java object. You may not want to do this if you are storing objects that need to be restricted to certain people, or to provide an audit trail (for example to determine who retrieved a reference to the MyBank object via LDAP):

```
    JNDIRemoteBankInterface j =
      (JNDIRemoteBankInterface) ctx.lookup("cn=MyBank");
    Account a = (Account) j.getAccount(args[0], args[1]);
    if (a.getFullName() != null) {
      System.out.println("Hello, " + a.getFullName());
      System.out.println("You have this much money in your account $"
                        + a.getAmount());
    } else {
      System.out.println("An error occurred. Check with your bank " +
                        "technical support to see what the problem is");
    }
  } catch (Exception e) {
    System.out.println("ERROR! : " + e.toString());
    System.exit(1);
  }
  }
}
```

The Account Class

This is the data object that is passed from the server to the client. It doesn't actually do anything, except provide a mechanism to get and set its data members:

```java
import java.util.*;
import java.io.*;

public class Account implements Serializable {

  private String fullName = null;
  private int amount = -1;

  public Account() {}

  public void setFullName(String fullName) {
    this.fullName = fullName;
  }

  public void setAmount(int amount) {
    this.amount = amount;
  }

  public String getFullName() {
    return fullName;
  }

  public int getAmount() {
    return amount;
  }
}
```

Running the Application

❑ First you need to compile all of these classes.

❑ Second, because this is a RMI application, you need to run `rmic` on your server class, using `rmic JNDIRemoteBankServer`.

❑ Third, you need to copy your client classes, `JNDIRemoteBankInterface.class`, `JNDIRemoteBankClient.class`, `Account.class`, and `JNDIRemoteBankServer_stub.class` to wherever you want your client application to run.

❑ On the client computer, you need to edit the `java.policy` file (located in the `/jre/lib/security` directory) so that the JVM will enable you to connect to RMI server (otherwise the default permissions won't let you run an RMI client). To enable RMI clients to connect to server objects on the same machine, I added the line:

```
permission java.net.SocketPermission "localhost:1024-", "accept, connect";
```

❑ Next you must start `rmiregistry`:

    ❑ On UNIX systems you'll use `rmiregistry &`

- ❑ On Windows NT/2000 you'll use `start rmiregistry` from a command or DOS prompt

❑ Then you can start your server with `java JNDIRemoteBankServer`.

❑ To run your client type `java JNDIRemoteBankClient username password`. The username and password must match a valid user in your LDAP server.

Here's what you should see:

```
C:\WINNT\System32\cmd.exe                                                    _ □ ✕

C:\ProJavaServer\Chapter05\MyBank>java JNDIRemoteBankClient scarter sprain
Hello, Sam Carter
You have this much money in your account $-1094754288

C:\ProJavaServer\Chapter05\MyBank>_
```

If your client fails, on the other hand, you will see the message "An error occurred. Check with your bank technical support to see what the problem is".

Here's what the server says:

```
C:\WINNT\System32\cmd.exe - java JNDIRemoteBankServer                         _ □ ✕

C:\ProJavaServer\Chapter05\MyBank>javac JNDIRemoteBankServer.java

C:\ProJavaServer\Chapter05\MyBank>rmic JNDIRemoteBankServer

C:\ProJavaServer\Chapter05\MyBank>start rmiregistry

C:\ProJavaServer\Chapter05\MyBank>java JNDIRemoteBankServer
MyBank is now open!
```

You will need to delete or unbind the `MyBank` *entry for each time you run the server otherwise you will get an LDAP error.*

RMI Without the Registry

If you have access to an LDAP server that has the RFC 2713 schema installed, you can also store serialized objects directly in the LDAP server.

Now why would you do such a thing? Well if you don't want to run or can't run the `rmiregistry` service is one reason. Another reason would be if you wanted to implement better security for your objects via LDAP because the current `rmiregistry` doesn't provide any security mechanisms beyond whatever mechanisms your object provides.

We can get away from the `rmiregistry` if two properties are true:

❑ The RMI client has some way of finding the remote RMI object

❑ There is an active object of the remote RMI object on the remote JVM

The LDAP server provides the first of these properties, and your remote RMI client in its main() method provides the second. As long as the remote server object keeps an active instance of itself without being garbage-collected, everything works.

After saying this, you might be wondering why, if this is the case, you would ever want to run the rmiregistry? The answer is that rmiregistry comes with the Sun Java SDK (thus if you don't have an LDAP server or don't want to use LDAP for this purpose you don't have to) and, more importantly, it always provides an active reference to your remote RMI objects for RMI clients when a request comes in. Otherwise each RMI remote object is forced to do this itself, which can become cumbersome at the very least. At the worst, things just stop working. One other reason to keep rmiregistry is that most LDAP servers are not optimized for storing large amounts of binary information like Java objects.

Storing Java Objects in the Directory

Just like storing Reference objects in the directory was fairly trivial, so is storing the physical object in the directory. All you must do is make sure that your RMI server object is serializable. When you would normally bind to the RMI registry, you now give it a LDAP DN instead of an RMI URL. JNDI knows to store this in to a LDAP server as a LDAP JavaObject.

During this process, the current state of your object is written out to a byte stream and a new LDAP JavaObject entry is created in the directory. The copy of your data is stored in this entry in the javaserializeddata attribute.

Changes to the Server

Thus if you wanted to store a copy of the JNDIRemoteBankServer object into the directory instead of storing a Reference to it in the directory, you only need to change a few lines of code in the main() routine:

```
// Create reference containing (future) location of object
// Reference ref = new Reference("MyBank", new StringRefAddr("URL",
//                                                      rmiurl));

// Create object to be bound
JNDIRemoteBankInterface j = new JNDIRemoteBankServer();

// Bind to directory
ctx.bind("cn=MyBank2", j);

// Bind to RMI Registry
// (the RMI URL will redirect request to the RMI registry provider).
// ctx.rebind(rmiurl, j);
```

If you look at the code you notice that I simply commented out all of the code that was used for creating a Reference object and the binding to the RMI registry. The other change I made was to change the ctx.bind() call from:

```
ctx.bind("cn=MyBank", ref);
```

to this:

```
ctx.bind("cn=MyBank2", j);
```

I did change the name of the object DN, but I did this simply so that I could keep both a `Reference` and `JavaObject` of the same object in my directory for teaching purposes. You are free to name the entry whatever you wish, as long as it conforms to the rules regarding LDAP DNs.

After you have stored your object in the directory, here's what it would look like if you printed out as LDIF (note that LDIF prints binary data as Base64):

```
dn: cn=MyBank2,o=airius.com
javaserializeddata:: rO0ABXNyABlqYXZhLnJtaS5NYXJzaGFsbGVkT2JqZWN0fL0el+1j/D4C
AANJAARoYXNoWwA1bG9jQn10ZXN0AAJbQlsACG9iakJ5dGVzcQB+AAF4cLyaIhZwdXIAAltCrPMX+AYIVO
ACAAB4cAAAALes7QAFc3IAGUpORElSZW1vdGVCYW5rU2VydmVyX1N0dWIAAAAAAAAAAgIAAHhyABpqYXZh
LnJtaS5zZXJ2ZXIuUmVtb3RlU3R1Yun+3MmL4WUaAgAeHIAHIAHGphdmEucm1pLnNlcnZlci5SZW1vdGVPYm
plY3TTYbSRDGEzHgMAAHhwdzIAClVuaWNhc3RSZWWYACTEyNy4wLjAuMQAA
Ca4AAAAAAAAAABymFQAADfRQyDxIAAAHg=
objectclass: top
objectclass: javacontainer
objectclass: javamarshalledobject
objectclass: javaObject
javaclassnames: JNDIRemoteBankServer
javaclassnames: java.rmi.server.UnicastRemoteObject
javaclassnames: java.rmi.server.RemoteServer
javaclassnames: java.rmi.server.RemoteObject
javaclassnames: java.lang.Object
javaclassnames: java.rmi.Remote
javaclassnames: java.io.Serializable
javaclassnames: JNDIRemoteBankInterface
cn: MyBank2
```

Modifying the RMI Client

You will need to change the context lookup to `MyBank2` for the client to run as before:

```
JNDIRemoteBankInterface j =
                    (JNDIRemoteBankInterface) ctx.lookup("cn=MyBank2");
```

Running the Application

To run this version of the application, follow the same steps as for the `Reference` example above, except that you do not need to start the `rmiregistry` application.

Building an Object Directory

I've already talked briefly about using LDAP as an object directory. What I mean by this is that you can use LDAP's search facilities to search for particular types of Java objects.

Here's a couple of examples, using our `JNDIRemoteBankServer` as an example.

Our first example would be to answer the request, "Show me all of the entries that are JavaObjects". Using the standard `ldapsearch` command line tool, you could enter the request:

```
ldapsearch -b "o=airius.com" "objectclass=javaobject" cn
```

The search would return me a list of all of the entries listed by their `commonname` attribute:

```
C:\WINNT\System32\cmd.exe                                              _ □ ×

C:\Netscape\Server4\shared\bin>ldapsearch -b "o=airius.com" "objectclass=javaobject" cn
dn: cn=MyBank,o=airius.com
cn: MyBank

dn: cn=MyBank2,o=airius.com
cn: MyBank2

C:\Netscape\Server4\shared\bin>
```

You could also look in the directory for the names of entries that are `JNDIRemoteBankServer` Java objects:

```
ldapsearch -b "o=airius.com" "javaclassnames=JNDIRemoteBankInterface"  cn
```

The result would be:

```
C:\WINNT\System32\cmd.exe                                              _ □ ×

C:\Netscape\Server4\shared\bin>ldapsearch -b "o=airius.com" "javaclassnames=JNDIRemoteBankInterface"
 cn
dn: cn=MyBank2,o=airius.com
cn: MyBank2

C:\Netscape\Server4\shared\bin>_
```

While these are simple examples, they do hint at the possibilities. I think tools like this will be needed to make it easier to develop and manage distributed applications, which are one of the fastest growing areas of application development.

Summary

Naming and directory services are an important component of network programming. In the past to use directory services you had to rely on vendors' proprietary protocols and corresponding APIs. Now thanks to LDAP and JNDI, you can use an open-standard protocol and a standardized API. With JNDI you can still use the same API, even if you must switch to a different protocol.

With JNDI you can create your basic directory service applications such as an e-mail address book, perform user authentication, or manage computer resources such as network printers.

JNDI also enables you to create Java specific applications such as storing and retrieving serialized Java objects from the directory. Thus you can store things like database connection information in a central location and only have to update it once if you need to make an update such as changing the name of the database server.

In the next chapter we will continue our journey through some of the fundamental elements of enterprise programming with an exploration of the relatively new technology of XML.

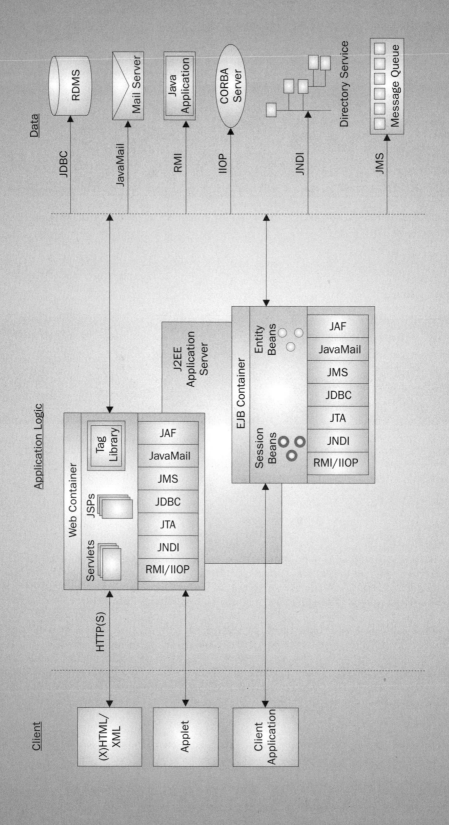

5

XML Beginnings

Since its release in December 1997, **XML**, the **eXtensible Markup Language** has been a huge success: it is used widely and in many different ways, some of them initially intended, others quite surprising. It is an easy guess that XML can only continue to grow in importance.

XML is a large topic because it comprises a number of technologies and specifications in addition to the familiar markup with tags and attributes within angular brackets. Even within XML proper, there is a small sublanguage for writing XML Document Type Definitions (DTDs). There are stylesheets, written in at least two different languages. There are namespace conventions, and an upcoming XML Schema specification. Finally, there are a great many XML applications, from SVG (Scalar Vector Graphics), to JSP (yes, JSPs can be XML documents), RDF (Resource Description Framework, a meta-language for describing web resources), and multiple languages for industry, finance, sciences, news, and entertainment.

With a big topic like that, we'll have to do more than one pass over it. The first two sections will be primers: on XML, and on XML technologies. After that, we will proceed as follows:

- ❑ Well-formed documents and the well-formedness constraint
- ❑ The logical structure of an XML document without a DTD
- ❑ XML documents with DTDs
- ❑ DTDs and entities
- ❑ DTDs, parsers, and validation
- ❑ XML namespaces

❑   Styling XML with CSS

❑   Styling XML with XSLT

We start, as we said, with a primer on XML itself.

A Primer on XML

Let's begin by looking at what an XML document is, some simple examples, and the main reasons for XML's success. It is important to understand these reasons, because they will show what XML is good for and how it may continue to grow in importance.

XML and XML Documents

It is not easy to answer the question, "What is XML?" because XML is not a single technology but a group of related technologies that continually adds new members. However, the central notion of XML, the **XML document**, can be defined quite precisely; in fact, it is so defined in the very first paragraph of the XML 1.0 specification. Here's our own version of that definition, which we will expand and explain in a moment:

> **An XML document is an information unit that can be viewed in two ways: as a linear sequence of characters that contains character data and markup, or as an abstract data structure that is a tree of nodes.**

To switch from the linear view to the structure view, you need an **XML processor**, also known as an **XML parser**. The markup must conform to certain simple requirements (**well-formedness constraints**) so that the parser can construct the tree unambiguously and quickly, using only the information in the markup.

A character sequence whose markup conforms to those requirements is called a **well-formed XML document**. If the markup fails those requirements then what you have is not an XML document at all but a complete failure. (The XML parser will not correct or ignore your errors the way that HTML parsers in web browsers correct or ignore HTML errors.)

In addition to character data and markup, an XML document may have a formally defined 'grammar' that expresses constraints on the document's content. Such a grammar is called a **Document Type Definition** or **DTD**. A document that has a DTD and conforms to its constraints is called a **valid document**. A parser that knows how to check documents against their DTDs is called a **validating parser**, while a parser that only checks whether the document is well-formed is called a **non-validating parser**.

Some Simple Examples

Let's look at some examples to illustrate the concepts we have introduced. They are all complete, well-formed XML documents. The first example is close to a bare minimum: strictly speaking, the first line (the declaration) is optional, but it is strongly recommended, and you will rarely see an XML document without it:

```
<?xml version="1.0" ?>
<greeting>Hello, XML</greeting>
```

The next example introduces attributes and a bit more structure:

```
<?xml version="1.0" ?>
<exchange>
  <greeting mode="warm" >Hello, XML</greeting>
  <response>Hello, what can I do for you?</response>
</exchange>
```

The tree for this example may look somewhat like this:

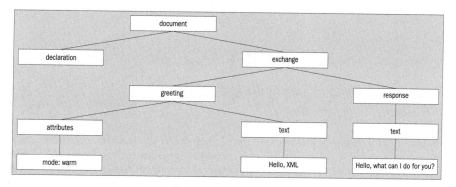

Note that the following is also a well-formed document:

```
<?xml version="1.0" ?>
<exchange>
  <response>Hello, what can I do for you?</response>
  <greeting mode="abracadabra">Hello, XML</greeting>
</exchange>
```

If you want to impose a bit more structure on your document (for example, the `<greeting>` tag must precede the `<response>` tag, or the `mode` attribute can only be one of warm, luke-warm, cool, and cold), you provide a DTD:

```
<?xml version="1.0" ?>
<!DOCTYPE exchange [
<!ELEMENT exchange (greeting, response)>
<!ELEMENT greeting (#PCDATA)>
<!ELEMENT response (#PCDATA)>
<!ATTLIST greeting
  mode (warm|luke-warm|cool|cold) "warm" <!--"warm" is the default -->
>
]>
<exchange>
  <greeting mode="warm" wording="semi-formal">Hello, XML</greeting>
  <response>Hello, what can I do for you?</response>
</exchange>
```

We will go through every detail of this DTD later in the chapter.

Clarification on Entities, and a Bit of Terminology

When we said earlier that, when viewed as text, an XML document is a linear sequence of characters, we cheated a little. An XML document may also contain **references** to individual characters, character strings and text files; these strings and files can, in turn, contain further such references:

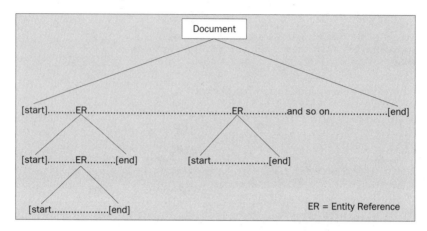

Before the document becomes a linear sequence of characters, all such references need to be replaced with what they refer to (their referents). In XML terminology, these referents are called **entities**: **character entities** if they refer to characters, and **general parsed entities** if they refer to strings or text files to be included in the document. The action of replacing a reference with whatever it refers to is called 'resolving an entity'. (As you will see, a Java XML parser API usually includes an `EntityResolver` interface.) After all the entities are resolved, the document does indeed become a linear sequence of characters.

You will see examples of all possible kinds of entities later in the chapter.

A Note on XML Processors/Parsers

XML **parsing** is discussed in Chapter 6, but we should say a few words about XML parsers right now. As long as you're working with HTML, you probably don't think much about the parser: it's a proprietary binary program, bloated and ugly, that is sitting inside the browser on your desktop. Much of its code is written to anticipate and correct ungrammatical HTML.

XML parsers are small and strict: their attitude to grammatical errors is totally negative. This attitude is precisely defined in the XML specification, which has an entire section on what 'conformant XML processors' must do in response to different kinds of errors. There is a test suite, developed and maintained by OASIS (Organization for the Advancement of Structured Information Standards, `http://www.oasis-open.org`) that is designed to test the parser's compliance with the XML specification. If the parser lets an error pass by, it gets a bad grade on the test.

There are two main reasons for this strict attitude:

❑ One has to do with the 'intended audience' of XML parsers. While HTML parsers mediate between the browser and the human user, XML parsers are mostly used to mediate between computer applications or components within an application. XML data is often generated by computer programs; for humans, there are XML editors that watch out for syntactic correctness. Strict discipline is therefore possible, and saves a good deal of processing time.

❑ It also saves space. Unlike HTML parsers that come as part of a multi-megabyte desktop browser, XML parsers are expected to be able to function in very tight places, such as embedded processors and wireless devices. (WML, the Wireless Markup Language, is an XML application.) It would be impossible for such devices to carry large browsers simply to be able to cater to human sloth.

As you work through the rest of this chapter, it is important to keep in mind the place of XML parsers in the scheme of things:

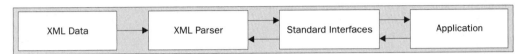

Why XML is Great

We can now summarize the main reasons why XML is such a powerful and versatile tool:

❑ It is very easy, both technically and practically, to switch between the 'linear text' and 'tree of nodes' views. Technically, it is quite easy to write an XML processor that checks whether the document is well-formed or not, and constructs a tree of nodes if it is. It is equally easy to write an XML processor that performs the opposite task. As a result, XML processors are fast, reliable, ubiquitous, and free.

❑ Explicit public standards define not only the inputs to XML processors (XML documents) but also their outputs (representations of the document tree and APIs for working with them). Applications don't have to worry about which processor they use, and can concentrate on using and transforming the documents as data objects.

❑ Free and standard processors make it easy to linearize an XML tree structure, send it to another software component (perhaps over the network), and reconstruct it on the other end. No special arrangements are needed between the sender and the recipient: XML data is always network-ready.

❑ XML data comes with a lot of information about itself (metadata). At a minimum, it has named elements and attributes. It can also have a DTD that provides, in effect, a contract between the provider and the consumer of XML data. That contract is enforced by the validating parser; the application doesn't have to worry about it. When an XML Schema is in place, even more aspects of data interchange can be pushed out of applications into Schema-validating XML processors.

❑ Documents can be considered as trees of labeled nodes, perhaps further decorated with attributes. Trees are well suited for describing many kinds of structured data, operations on trees are well understood, and they are easy to search and transform. (Lisp programmers, among others, have been working with similar data objects for decades.) XML has already developed a standard language for referring to sets of tree nodes (**XPath**) and a standard language for describing tree transformations (**XSLT**).

In more technical language, XML has:

❑   A simple, well-understood data model closed under a large set of useful operations

❑   A human-readable serialization format to go with it

❑   Lots of metadata, including machinery for defining languages (vocabularies and grammar rules)

❑   Standard APIs for processing XML data within applications

Together, these features make XML an ideal instrument for bringing computer programs and human agents together. The first pre-requisite for collaboration is an agreement on a common vocabulary and syntax. XML makes this difficult effort more concrete (you just have to agree on a DTD) and more rewarding (because once the common language is in place, the entire infrastructure of XML is immediately available for free).

Main Uses of XML

So, what is XML actually used for? The following uses are the most prominent:

❑   Creating documents for publishing on the Web and elsewhere

❑   Encoding data, including data extracted from relational databases

❑   Configuring computer programs

❑   Developing domain-specific vocabularies and DTDs

A long list of XML languages (also called XML applications) can be found at
`http://www.oasis-open.org/cover/`.

Java and XML; XML within J2EE

Java and XML work extremely well together. On the one hand, as we described above, the abundance of free and well-designed tools is what makes XML so successful. It so happens that most of them are written in Java: XML tools are the first kind of systems software that has always been written in Java first, before C or C++ or other versions appeared. On the other hand, XML gave Java a powerful push that finally propelled it into the family of firmly established languages.

Why do they fit together so well? The answer boils down to two main points: both are cross-platform and network-ready. It is a very natural thing to do to have Java classes exchange XML data across components and applications over the network. In addition, thanks to Java Reflection capabilities, it is a very natural thing to do to configure Java classes based on XML data. Java classes themselves can be instantiated, configured, and used within JSPs that can also incorporate XML as template data.

All these possibilities make XML a "natural" for any distributed Java application, including J2EE applications. Beyond the specific uses of XML within the J2EE platform, there is this general underlying synergy of Java and XML in any kind of Web application. Specific uses are also numerous and likely to increase in number as the J2EE platform develops further. (For instance, it is quite likely that, in addition to CORBA and RMI/IIOP, J2EE will start using SOAP, an XML-based protocol for remote procedure calls and other interactions between objects over the network.)

Sun's J2EE FAQ (http://java.sun.com/j2ee/faq.html) is quite clear on this point:

> **Q: Is XML supported in J2EE?**
> **XML is an essential component in the J2EE platform. J2EE will provide a framework for business-to-business data interchange using XML. Currently, JavaServer Pages framework can be used to generate and consume XML between servers or between server and client. In addition, Enterprise JavaBeans component architecture uses XML to describe its deployment properties, giving Enterprise JavaBeans data portability in addition to its code portability.**

XML within the EJB Container: Deployment Descriptors

J2EE is structured around containers into which application-specific components (such as EJBs) are deployed. XML provides standardized cross-platform data formats for exchanging data across containers, and also to specify the way a component interacts with its container. This second task is performed by a deployment descriptor, an XML file that conforms to a specific DTD. An example of a deployment descriptor can be found at http://developer.java.sun.com/developer/onlineTraining /EJBIntro/EJBIntro.html. As the tutorial explains, the descriptor specifies the type of bean (session or entity) and the classes used for the remote, home, and bean class. It also contains the security, transaction, and persistence information: who can use which method (the security roles), the transactional attributes of each method, and whether persistence in the entity beans is handled automatically or is preformed by the bean itself.

XML within the Web Container: web.xml

Within the web container, XML is similarly used for configuring the components within the container. A web.xml configuration file holds information on:

❑ Servlet names and mappings

❑ Session configuration

❑ taglib mappings from the URL on the page to the .tld file

❑ Supported MIME types

❑ Various contex parameters such as webmaster's e-mail

XML for Integrating Legacy Data

A significant aspect of enterprise computing is integrating legacy data. This is where XML can also play an important role, providing a bridge between a multitude of proprietary legacy formats and the formats expected by the application. XML is extremely well suited for this role because, once you put your data in one XML format, switching between XML formats is very easy. (See below on XSLT.) So, to integrate legacy data, you only have to provide one conversion, from the legacy format to an appropriate XML format, which can probably be a generic XML "interligua" from which other XMLs can be produced as required, using either specialized Java filters, or XSLT (eXtensible Stylesheet Language for Transformations).

Those J2EE servers that implement Java Messaging Service (JMS) for asynchronous message passing between components will mostly likely use XML for defining message formats. This will fit in well with the scheme for legacy data integration outlined in the preceding paragraph.

XML and EDI

Although EDI (Electronic Data Interchange) is not part of the J2EE platform, it is an essential part of enterprise computing. EDI, more specifically, is an established standard (about 10 years old) for exchanging business data between enterprises. Since it was defined in pre-commercial-internet times, the standard is somewhat unwieldy and very expensive:

❑   EDI uses custom networks whose bandwidth is very expensive.

❑   EDI uses compressed and difficult-to-read data formats, with no metadata included.

❑   EDI solutions are hard to program and maintain.

Because of these limitations, only a small percentage of enterprises, large companies all of them, have established EDI connections. While this automated data interchange occurs amongst them, up to 80% of their suppliers still have to use paper. This is where XML can bring about a decisive change because of its low cost, both in development and maintenance. Several companies and consortia are developing XML-EDI inter-operability solutions, including the XML-EDI Group, Ariba, CommerceOne, and XML Solutions.

To sum up, XML is indispensable for enterprise computing in general, and especially enterprise computing based on the J2EE platform.

We can now proceed to a more systematic overview of XML, beginning with a primer that will place XML in its proper context and briefly characterize several related technologies and specifications that make up the XML family.

A Primer on XML Technologies

There are two common misconceptions about XML: that it is a language, and that it is 'extensible HTML'.

Although called a language, XML is really a technology for *defining* languages, where a 'language' is a set of **tags** and **attributes** with various constraints on them. XML can be defined as a collection of meta-constraints and a meta-language for defining markup languages.

Think of HTML for a moment: you probably know that the <HTML> element consists of <HEAD> and <BODY>, in that order, and <HEAD> can contain a <TITLE> but <BODY> cannot. On the other hand, <BODY> can contain <P>, <TABLE>, and so on, but <HEAD> cannot contain them. These tags are, in a sense, the vocabulary of HTML, and the constraints on the usage of those tags are HTML's grammar rules. HTML parsers embedded in browsers know those rules and use them to parse HTML pages.

> *They also frequently choose not to enforce those rules, on the principle that "the customer is always right". XML parsers are much more strict, as discussed below.*

The Standardization Process and the Role of W3C

Both XML itself and its related technologies are developed and approved by the **World Wide Web Consortium** (**W3C**; see http://www.w3.org), with copious informal input from the XML developers' list, xml-dev@lists.xml.org. The development process usually starts with the formation of a Working Group (WG) that publishes a Requirements Document. The specification goes through several Working Drafts (WD), until there is enough stability and consensus within the WG to release it as Candidate Recommendation. At this point, work on a reference implementation usually begins. After a while, if all goes well, the Candidate Recommendation becomes a Proposed Recommendation, and is submitted for a final round of comments. The final stage of the process is for the Director, Tim Berners-Lee, to put his signature to the document, thus making it the official Recommendation.

This process has worked quite well on many occasions. There have been occasional outbursts of complaints from developers that the review process is too secretive, and closed to people who cannot pay membership fees. In response to such complaints, there have been recent changes to make the process more transparent. In particular, in April-June 2000 there was a very open discussion of the Namespace specification, easily the most controversial of the W3C Recommendations. The discussion accumulated almost 3000 messages in two months, and now (July 2000) seems to be moving towards a resolution. Anybody interested in the inner workings of W3C and the XML developer community should take a look at those discussions, or join xml-dev.

SGML and XML

HTML rules are defined in **SGML (Standard Generalized Markup Language)**, an international publishing standard in existence since 1986. Its notation for defining grammar rules is called a **DTD (Document Type Definition)**. The standard that defines HTML is a DTD developed by the World Wide Web Consortium (W3C); that DTD, together with the other W3C specifications, can be found on the W3C web site at http://www.w3.org/TR/.

XML is a successor to SGML, simplified and adapted for the Internet. A long list of XML-defined languages (also called **XML applications**) can be found at http://www.oasis-open.org/cover/xml.html. For instance, XML has been used to define a successor to HTML called XHTML. The diagram below shows the relationship between SGML, XML, HTML, and XHTML:

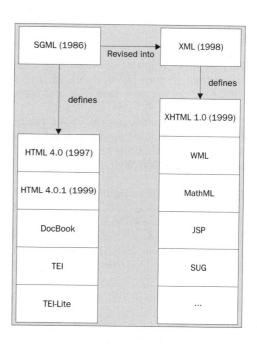

*XML has also been used to define **WML**, the **Wireless Markup Language**, so it is not accurate to think of WML as an 'alternative' to XML: WML is an XML application.*

DTDs and XML Schema

XML inherited from SGML the DTD mechanism for defining grammar rules. DTDs are written in a little language of their own that does not itself conform to XML rules. All the XML applications so far have been defined using a DTD, but this is about to change when DTDs are replaced with the **XML Schema** language. XML Schema several advantages over DTDs:

- ❑ It uses XML syntax, and so can be produced and edited using standard XML tools
- ❑ It is a more detailed system of data types (in DTDs, everything is character data)
- ❑ Users can define their own data types, including structured data types
- ❑ XML Schema is more modular, and easier to reuse

At the time of writing (July 2000), XML Schema is in Working Draft, and the latest version can be found at `http://www.w3c.org/TR/`. Even when the XML Schema specification is complete, DTDs are likely to remain in use, and in spite of their limitations they remain a great tool for language definition. Many useful DTDs can be found at `http://www.xml.org/`. This web site, maintained by OASIS, is building a central repository for DTDs and other XML resources.

XML Styling

As you probably know, you can include style information in HTML pages. For instance, you can include a `<style>` element like this in your document's `<head>`:

```
<style>
  H1 {text-color: green; font-size: small}
</style>
```

This will make your `<H1>` headers appear in small green letters. You don't have to include style information, because HTML has a fixed set of tags (it's an SGML application), and for each tag there is a default style definition built into your favorite browser.

Since XML allows you to define your own element tags and attributes, it follows that before you can display your document you have to provide a stylesheet, to specify how your elements are to be displayed. Otherwise, the best a browser can do is what IE 5 does on XML documents with no style definition: it displays their tree structure, without any differentiation between individual elements.

There are two style languages that work with XML documents. One is the older and more familiar **CSS (Cascading Stylesheets)** that can also be used with HTML; the example above was CSS. The other is **XSL**, the **eXtensible Stylesheet Language**. XSL consists of two parts, one for formatting and display and the other for transformations (**XSLT**). The formatting part is still in Working Draft, but XSLT has been a Recommendation since November 1999. It is a very powerful language for rearranging and modifying the contents of your document.

Stylesheets and Current Browsers

Since the formatting part of XSL is still in draft and not implemented by any browsers, you have to use a combination of XSLT and CSS to display your XML documents. Browser support is currently uneven:

❑　You can use XSLT on the server to transform your XML document into HTML or XHTML for display in the browser. As always, you can optionally add CSS styling to your HTML page.

❑　IE 5 has built-in XSLT support. Initially, it supported an old draft incompatible with the standard version, but if you download the latest version of MSXML you can let the browser transform your XML document into HTML for display.

❑　Mozilla 6 allows you to associate CSS stylesheets directly with XML documents, without transforming them into HTML first.

The most flexible strategy at the moment is to use XSLT (on the server or in the browser, if the browser supports it) to do structural transformations on your document and convert it to HTML, then attach a CSS stylesheet to the HTML page. We will show examples of this later in the chapter.

Namespaces

XML is designed to be modular and extensible, and so you should to be able to reuse modules from other DTDs in your own work. This raises a problem of potential name conflicts: once all Internet users can define their tags, the chances are high that the same tags will be used by different people to mean different things. The function of **XML Namespaces** is to prevent name conflicts between your tags and somebody else's. When new XML applications are designed (such as XSLT or JSP), their tags are usually associated with a specific namespace. A section later in this chapter will show you how this is done.

The table below lists the specifications covered in this chapter, all of them to be found at `http://www.w3.org/TR/`.

Specification	Date
XML 1.0	February 1998
Namespaces in XML	January 1999
Associating Stylesheets with XML Documents	June 1999
XSLT 1.0	November 1999
XPath 1.0 (used within XSLT)	November 1999

In a single chapter, we could not possibly cover all this material full detail, and so we will concentrate on the main points. The first of them is the notion of a well-formed document, a key to XML success, and the single most important difference between SGML and XML.

Well-Formedness Constraints

There are a number of well-formedness constrains scattered through XML 1.0, but these three are the most important, and probably the only ones you will ever need:

❑   All attribute values must be quoted

❑   Elements must form a tree

❑   The tree structure must be explicitly shown by the document's markup

The first two constraints also apply to SGML languages, including HTML (although HTML parsers don't choose to enforce them).

Attribute Quoting

The first constraint is easy enough to understand. The important point is that the quote characters (double quote and single quote) cannot be used in an XML document for any other purpose. If you want to include them in the document's data, they have to be escaped.

Tree Structure

The second constraint implies two requirements:

❑   **There must be a root element**
The root is an element that contains all other elements, but itself is not contained in another element. In tree terms, all other elements in the page are the root's children or more distant descendants, but the root itself does not have a parent element. In terms of markup, it means that, apart from initial declarations, all of the document's content must be contained in a single element. This is familiar from HTML, where the root of every page is the <html> element.

❑   **All other elements have one and only one parent**
In terms of markup, the single-parent requirement means that elements cannot partially overlap: they must either not overlap at all, or one of them must contain the other. This is another constraint that applies equally to XML and SGML, but is not always enforced by HTML browsers.

The no-overlap constraint is easy to state in terms of tags: for no two tags <a> and <b> is it ever legal to have:

```
<a>...<b>...</a>...</b>
```

Explicit Tree Structure in Markup

The third constraint means that the start and end of every element must be clearly indicated in markup. For non-empty elements, it means that they must always have an end tag. Empty elements may also have an end tag, or they can use an alternative syntax:

```
<br /> <!-- equivalent to <br></br> -->
```

Note that in documents marked up in this way, the well-formedness constraint is very easy to check in a single pass over the document, using a stack:

❑ As you encounter a start tag, push it on the stack

❑ As you encounter a matching end tag, pop the start tag off the stack

❑ If the stack is empty at the end then the document is well-formed

❑ If at any time during the pass, you come across an end tag that does not match the start tag at the top of the stack, the document is not well-formed

❑ If you reach the end of the document and there are still some start tags sitting on the stack, the document is not well-formed

Note a very important fact: we don't need to know the 'grammar rules' of the document in order to check for well-formedness in this way. All we do is compare start and end tags.

This last markup requirement is what most clearly separates SGML (including HTML) from XML (including XHTML). XML documents can be parsed, quickly and reliably, into a tree, in the absence of a DTD, but SGML documents need a DTD to be parsed. The notion of well-formedness does not apply to SGML documents: there can be perfectly valid SGML documents that are not well-formed in the XML sense. Let's consider a simple example.

An HTML/XHTML/XML Example

Here's a very simple HTML page:

```
<html><head><title>HTML Example</title></head>
<body>
  <p>a paragraph followed by a list
  <ul>
    <li>item one
    <li>item two
  </ul>
  <p>Another paragraph with a line break <BR>in the middle.
</body></html>
```

This is a valid HTML 4.0 document. However, it is not well-formed in the XML sense:

❑ An XML parser would assume that <ul> is a child rather than a sibling of <p>,

❑ It would keep the <p> element open while working through <ul>

❑ It would assume that the second <li> is a child of the first

❑ It would choke on </body>, because it will try to match it with the latest open tag, which is <br>.

The reason an HTML parser can parse this page correctly is because it consults the HTML DTD which says, among other things, that an <li> cannot contain another <li> (and therefore the second <li> implicitly closes the first), and that <br> is empty.

In XHTML (but also acceptable to HTML parsers), this document would come out as:

```
<html><head><title>HTML Example</title></head>
<body>
  <p>a paragraph followed by a list</p>
  <ul>
    <li>item one</li>
    <li>item two</li>
  </ul>
  <p>Another paragraph with a line break <br></br>in the middle.</p>
</body></html>
```

This is a valid HTML document, a valid XHTML document (with respect to the XHTML DTD), and a well-formed XML document that can be processed by an XML parser with no reference to a DTD.

> Note that in the XHTML file, all markup is in lowercase, and has to be that way. XML (unlike SGML) is case sensitive, and all XHTML tags are declared to be in lower case.

Why is well-formedness so important? The reasons are pragmatic:

❑ XML documents without DTDs are easy to create: anybody with HTML skills can learn to write XML very quickly, which explains the common perception that XML is easy.

❑ The parser can be small and fast.

❑ A document can be processed and made available to an application even if its DTD happens to be on a different server that is down at the moment.

From HTML to XHTML

To illustrate the permissiveness of HTML browsers, our example page can be stripped to almost nothing, as below, and both the Netscape and Microsoft browsers will still show it as if it were a full grammatical document:

```
<p>a paragraph followed by a list
    <li>item one
    <li>item two
```

Yes, this is the entire page, there's nothing else in the file. As you can imagine, this means a lot more work for parser writers, and for the parsers themselves. This is fine if you have a powerful desktop and a multi-megabyte browser, but what if you want to view your page from a PalmPilot?

A moment ago we showed an HTML page that was also XHTML but, as the crippled page above shows, not all of them are like that. Suppose you want to convert an HTML page to XHTML. Two kinds of changes may be needed: those to fix ungrammatical HTML, and changes that stem from the differences between SGML and XML. Changes of the first kind are too numerous to catalog; changes of the second kind are listed in the XHTML 1.0 Recommendation, Section 4. This is probably the best place to look for a practical summary of differences between SGML and XML syntax, because XHTML is a rewrite of an SGML application to conform to XML rules.

For both kinds of changes, the best remedy is HTML Tidy, a program written by Dave Raggett of W3C (`http://www.w3c.org/People/Raggett/Tidy/`). This is a tool both for detecting and correcting a wide range of HTML markup errors and for converting existing HTML content to well-formed XML. To give you an example of what HTML Tidy can do, it converts the bad HTML example above into:

```
<!DOCTYPE html PUBLIC "-//IETF//DTD HTML 2.0//EN">
<html>
<head>
<meta name="generator" content="HTML Tidy, see www.w3.org">
<title></title>
</head>
<body>
<p>a paragraph followed by a list</p>

<ul class="noindent">
<li>item one</li>

<li>item two</li>
</ul>
</body>
</html>
```

Why would you want to convert an HTML page to XHTML? The answer is simple: you can still display it in the browser, but you can also use all the new XML machinery on it. You can give it to a parser and get yourself a Java object to work on. Or you can run XSLT stylesheets on it to transform it in various ways before sending it to the browser.

With the well-formedness constraints dealt with, let's move on to think about the structure of XML documents.

The Logical Structure of an XML Document

At the beginning of this chapter we said that an XML document can be viewed either as a linear sequence of characters (after all entity references are resolved) or as a tree. XML 1.0 expresses this idea by saying that an XML document has **physical content** and **logical structure**: the characters form the physical content, and the logical structure is the tree. We will discuss the logical structure and physical content of DTD-less XML documents first, as a simpler case. Most of what we say here will apply to documents with DTDs as well, but they have some additional options and constraints.

XML Documents Without a DTD

Schematically, a document without a DTD follows this outline:

❑   XML declaration (optional but highly recommended)

- ❏ Optional comments and Processing Instructions (PIs)
- ❏ The root element's start tag
- ❏ All other elements, comments, and PIs
- ❏ The root element's closing tag

The document below illustrates this outline and all the points covered in this section.

A Kitchen-Sink Document Without a DTD

Consider a screen shot first. It is produced from an XML document, accompanied by a very simple CSS stylesheet:

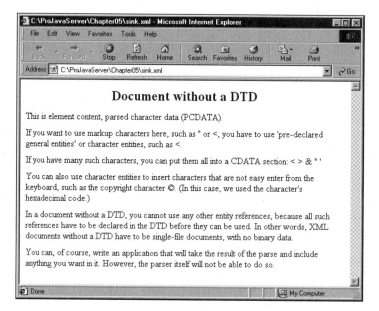

The document illustrates the topics that we will cover in the remainder of the section:

- ❏ The XML declaration, including Unicode character encoding
- ❏ Element content (PCDATA) and attribute values (CDATA)
- ❏ Comments and Processing Instructions (PIs)
- ❏ Using character entities and pre-declared entities to escape markup characters
- ❏ Using CDATA sections for the same purpose

XML Declarations and Character Encodings

The declaration line of the document above is as follows:

```
<?xml version='1.0' encoding='utf-8'?>
```

The version attribute is required; the encoding attribute is optional but frequently useful. It has to do with how Unicode characters in your document are represented in actual bytes of binary data. Unicode characters, as you probably know, use integers from 0 to xFFFF to represent characters. The simplest way to represent them is to allocate two bytes (16) bits for each character. This representation is called utf-16, and all XML processors are required to support it. However, if your characters are mostly Latin-1 (or ASCII), then utf-16 is extremely wasteful. In addition, it is not backward compatible with the ASCII encoding. For these reasons, an alternative, utf-8, has been developed. This uses variable-length encodings (from one to three bytes) for different characters. For the Latin-1 character set it uses the same single-byte encoding as the familiar ASCII table.

If your declaration does not specify the encoding, the parser tries to figure it out from the first few bytes of the document, and usually does a good job of it.

Comments and Processing Instructions

In our document, the declaration is immediately followed by a comment and a Processing Instruction (PI):

```
<!-- The line above is the XML declaration. Nothing can precede it, not even
comments.  Otherwise, comments can appear both between elements and in
element content.  Same for Processing Instructions (PIs), illustrated by the
next line.
-->
<?xml-stylesheet href="sink.css" type="text/css"?>
```

Comments and PIs use special markup, as shown below:

Kind of component	Delimited by
Comments	`<!-- ... -->`
Processing instructions (PIs)	`<? ... ?>`

Character data within comments and PIs is not parsed: when the parser encounters the opening marker, it suspends its normal operation and only looks for the end marker (--> or ?>). They differ in their intent and in what the processor does when the end marker is found. Comments are not usually passed on to the application, but PIs are.

PIs were initially (in SGML) intended for invoking some application other than the XML processor to do some computation on a part of your document. For instance, suppose you have an equation-solving program and you want to invoke it in the middle of your XML document. You might say:

```
<?SolveIt equation="3*x+4=10" ?>
```

The first string after the opening marker is called the PI's **target**; it must identify the application to use. The remaining strings are data to be passed to the application. It is up to your application to extract the target and the data from the PI and perform whatever action it calls for.

PIs are an SGML legacy that is not treated warmly in the XML community. Their drawbacks are:

❑   They use non-standard syntax (PIs are not elements)

❑ There is no connection between XML content and PIs: you cannot nest a PI within a specific element, or otherwise control where it will appear in the resulting data structure

PIs are used, at least for now, to link stylesheets into documents. This how it is used in our example document, with the string `xml-stylesheet` is as target. The example in the document above shows a CSS stylesheet, but XSL stylesheets are linked in exactly the same way. The only difference is that their type is `"text/xsl"`.

We will see the CSS stylesheet used with this document later in the chapter.

The Root Element and its Contents

The rest of our document, as expected, is contained in a single root element. It contains two children, an `<empty-element>` and a `<non-empty-element>`. Comments and PIs also make their appearance, both between and within elements:

```
<rootElement><!-- start tag of root element -->
<h1>Document without a DTD</h1>
  <empty-element
    intent="show 'quotes within quotes' in attributes"
  />
  <!-- PI between elements follows --> <?ProcessSomething using this data?>

  <non-empty-element>
    <!-- comments can appear here, too. --><?So can PIs?>
    This is element content, parsed character data (PCDATA).
    <br />
    If you want to use markup characters here, such as &quot; or &lt;,
    you have to use &apos;pre-declared general entities&apos; or character
    entities, such as &#60;.
    <br />
    If you have many such characters, you can put them all into a
    <![CDATA[CDATA section: < > & " ']]>
    <br />
    You can also use character entities to insert characters that are not
    easy enter from the keyboard, such as the copyright character &#xA9;.
    (In this case, we used the character's hexadecimal code.)
    <br />
    In a document without a DTD, you cannot use any other entity references,
    because all such references have to be declared in the DTD before they
    can be used.  In other words, XML documents without a DTD have to be
    single-file documents, with no binary data.
    <br />
    You can, of course, write an application that will take the result
    of the parse and include anything you want in it.
    However, the parser itself will not be able to do so.
  </non-empty-element>
</rootElement><!-- closing tag of root element -->
```

The main point of this code is to show how markup characters can be inserted into document content.

Character Entities and Pre-Declared Entities

Ultimately, XML documents consist of characters, or **character data (CDATA)**. This comes in two flavors:

❑   Element content that is going to be parsed (**PCDATA**)

❑   Quoted attribute values that are not going to be parsed (**CDATA**)

Both are shown in the document above. Note that although attribute values are not parsed, you are still not allowed to use the two most important markup characters, < and &, within them.

Within element content, there are five characters that need to be escaped: <, >, ", ', and &. To insert them as data, you can refer to them using either their numerical code, or use a special pre-declared name. In either case, you delimit the reference by & . . . ;. This explains why & is a special character: it indicates the beginning of an entity reference.

As the XML source of our document shows, the same character (for example, the right angle bracket) can be referred to in three ways:

❑   Using a pre-declared general entity: >

❑   Using the decimal code within a character entity: <

❑   Using the hexadecimal code within a character entity: <

The five markup characters, and their pre-declared names and decimal codes are:

Character	Number	Name
<	60	lt ('less-than')
>	62	gt ('greater-than')
"	34	quot
'	39	apos
&	38	amp

CDATA Sections

CDATA sections are used to escape character strings that may contain markup characters that you don't want to be interpreted by the parser. Suppose, to take a concrete example, you want to include some Java code in your XML file. You could put your code in an element, such as <java> ... </java>, and it will be very easy for the processor to find it and separate it for special treatment.

The problem is that your code is likely to contain special markup characters, as in the example below. CDATA sections help with this problem:

```
<java>
  <![CDATA[
    while(a>b && b<a)
      doIt();
  ]]>
</java>
```

CDATA sections are similar to comments and PIs, in that their contents are not parsed: you can use any characters within them, including < and &. The difference is that CDATA sections are always part of element content, and their contents are shown by the browser. CDATA sections, unlike comments, are passed on to the application and can be retrieved for processing.

You have to make sure that your CDATA section does not contain a]]> sequence; the following would cause a problem:

```
if(arr[indexArr[4]]>5) ...
```

The parser would interpret such a sequence as the closing marker of the CDATA section. To fix this problem, insert a space between]] and >, or separate the]]> sequence into two CDATA sections.

This completes our discussion of documents without DTDs; DTDs offer many more possibilities and complexities.

XML Documents with DTDs

It is time for a complete picture. Logically, an XML document may contain the following five kinds of components:

Kind of component	Delimited by

Declarations in the DTD	`<!DOCTYPE[...]>`
	`<!ELEMENT ...>`
	`<!ATTLIST ...>`
	`<!ENTITY ...>`
	`<!NOTATION ...>`

Elements	`<tag ...>...</tag >` or `<tag .../>`
CDATA sections	`<![CDATA[...]]>`
Comments	`<!--...-->`
Processing instructions (PIs)	`<?...?>`

The last four rows should look familiar; the first shows all the things you can declare within a DTD:

❑ **DOCTYPE** gives the name of your document type. DOCTYPE is declared (if it is declared) at the very beginning of the document, before the root element. The declaration contains either the DTD itself, or a reference to an external file that contains the DTD.

❑ **ELEMENT** declarations contain the name of the element declared and a description of its content. The description uses a version of **EBNF** (the **Extended Backus-Naur Formalism** for specifying syntax of programming languages), but they are quite easy to read even if you're unfamiliar with EBNF.

❑ **ATTLIST** declarations declare attributes for a given element. For each attribute, you specify its name, type, whether it is required or optional, and sometimes a default value.

❏ **ENTITY** declarations declare names for entities; the name is followed by either the corresponding entity value (an **internal entity**) or by a reference to an external file that contains the value. There are two kinds of entities you can declare: **parameter entities** for use within the DTD itself, and **general entities** for use in the document. The pre-declared entities you have seen are internal general entities.

❏ **NOTATION** declarations are used together with declarations of external general entities that contain either binary data (such as GIF) or text data that is not XML (such as L_AT_EX), to tell the application how to process non-XML data that needs to be included in the document. They are rarely used, because MIME types declared within attributes can serve the same purpose.

A Simple Example: DOCTYPE, ELEMENT, and ATTLIST

Let us return to an example from the beginning of the chapter and use it to explore the possibilities of DTDs:

```
<?xml version="1.0" ?>
<!DOCTYPE exchange [
<!ELEMENT exchange (greeting, response)>
<!ELEMENT greeting (#PCDATA)>
<!ELEMENT response (#PCDATA)>
<!ATTLIST greeting
  mode (warm|luke-warm|cool|cold) "warm"
  wording CDATA "IMPLIED"
>
]>
<exchange>
  <greeting mode="cool">
    Hello, XML.
  </greeting>
  <response>Hello, what can I do for you?</response>
</exchange>
```

Variations on DOCTYPE

This document has an internal DTD. We could, instead, cut out the DTD content within the square brackets and place it, without the brackets, into an external file. If we called this file `exchange.dtd` the `DOCTYPE` declaration would look like this:

```
<!DOCTYPE exchange SYSTEM "exchange.dtd">
```

We could also place that file on a server somewhere else, and specify its location using a URL:

```
<!DOCTYPE exchange SYSTEM "http://myserver.com/dtds/exchange.dtd">
```

Whether we are using file names (perhaps with a directory path) or URLs, `SYSTEM` identifiers use a location to identify a resource. This has the drawback that if a resource is moved, the identifier is no longer valid. An alternative is to have identifiers that are associated with the resource directly, via some registry, independently of the resource location. You may have seen `DOCTYPE`s declared like this:

```
<?xml version="1.0" ?>
<!DOCTYPE html PUBLIC "-//W3C//DTD XHTML 1.0 Strict//EN"
"http://www.w3.org/TR/xhtml1/DTD/strict.dtd">
```

PUBLIC identifiers are an attempt to have location-independent identifiers. The system of registries for them is not quite ready yet, and so, if you do provide a PUBLIC identifier, you must also provide a SYSTEM one (without the keyword SYSTEM), as in the example above. See http://www.xml.org/registry/ for more information on the web resource registry effort.

ELEMENT Declarations

Element declarations follow this pattern:

```
<!ELEMENT name content-model>
```

There are four possible content models:

- ❏ The value EMPTY means that the element may contain neither text nor child elements

- ❏ The value ANY allows the element to contain any combination of text and child elements that does not violate XML's well-formedness constraint

- ❏ The children-only content model allows the element to contain specified child elements, but not text

- ❏ The mixed content model allows a specified combination of text (#PCDATA) and child elements

Here are examples of all four possibilities:

```
<!ELEMENT br EMPTY>                       <!-- no content -->
<!ELEMENT container ANY>                  <!-- anything goes -->
<!ELEMENT exchange (greeting, response)>  <!-- children only -->
<!ELEMENT p (#PCDATA|a|ul|b|i|em)*>       <!-- text mixed with children -->
```

Items separated by commas indicate sequence; a vertical bar indicates alternatives. The repetition-factor characters *, +, and ? are used in the usual way to indicate 'zero or more', 'one or more', and 'zero or 1'. You can combine all these devices to express complex models, such as:

```
<!ELEMENT recipe
(descr,(ingredient,amount)+,directions,origin?,(note|caution)*>
```

This means: "a recipe consists of a description, followed by one or more ingredient-amount pairs, followed by directions, followed by an optional indication of origin, followed by any number (including 0) of notes and cautions, in any order".

Mixed vs. Children-Only Content, and the Treatment of Whitespace

Given the element below, can you tell whether it has mixed or children-only content?

```
<poem>
    <line>Telemachos, my son.  The Trojan war</line>
    <line>is over.  Who won, I don't remember.</line>
    <line>The Greeks, I'd bet.  Who else except the Greeks</line>
    <line>would leave so many dead so far from home.</line>
</poem>
```

The answer is that you (and the parser) cannot tell: the element would match either of the two declarations below:

```
<!ELEMENT poem (line)* >
<!ELEMENT poem (#PCDATA|line)* >
```

One reason why the parser might want to know has to do with whitespace. If the content model is mixed, then the white space (line breaks and indents) is part of the text content of the element and should be passed on to the application. If the content model is children-only, however, the whitespace is not part of the document and should not be passed on to the application unless there is a specific instruction to preserve it. Such an instruction would be a special attribute, as explained in the next section.

Attribute Declarations

Attribute declarations follow this pattern:

```
<!ATTLIST element-name attribute-definitions>
```

where each attribute definition has this form:

```
attribute-name attribute-type default-declarations
```

Here's an example:

```
<!ELEMENT multiAttribute 'EMPTY'>
<!ATTLIST multiAttribute
  name      CDATA          #REQUIRED
  nickname  ID             #REQUIRED
  bfriend   IDREF          #IMPLIED
  penname   NMTOKEN        #IMPLIED
  authors   NMTOKENS       #REQUIRED
  answer    (YES|NO)       "NO"
  method    CDATA          #FIXED "TAXI"
  goto      (DISCO|MOVIES) #REQUIRED
>
```

In these attribute definitions, the first column is the attribute's name, the second is its type, and the third indicates whether it is required or optional and whether it has a default value. The possible types are:

❏ CDATA: text in quotes

❏ ID: also text, but its value must be unique in the document

❏ IDREF: text that is equal to the value of an ID attribute of some element in the document

❏ NMTOKEN: restricted text that contains only 'name characters'; cannot contain whitespace

❏ NMTOKENS: a comma-separated list of NMTOKEN items

❏ (YES|NO): enumerated type consisting of two values, "YES" and "NO", with "NO" as the default

The possible required/default indications are:

- ❏   #REQUIRED: the attribute is required
- ❏   #IMPLIED: the attribute is optional
- ❏   #FIXED plus a default value: the attribute must always have the specified default value
- ❏   A default value

Reserved Attribute Names

Names that begin with the letters 'x' 'm' 'l', in any combination of capitals and lower-case, are reserved by W3C for attributes with special pre-defined meanings. One such is xml:lang, an attribute that specifies the language of the element; another is the xml:space attribute that, if you use it, should be declared as follows:

```
<!ATTLIST xml:space (default|preserve) "default">
```

This gives instructions to the parser on how to treat whitespace in element content. The default value is "default"; in other words, follow the default conventions. If you explicitly set it to "preserve", the parser will preserve whitespace even in the element-only content model, for example:

```
< poem title="Chickobee" xml:space="preserve">
<!-- the layout of your poem will be preserved
     even though you declared it as <!ELEMENT poem (line)* >
-->
```

DTD and Entities

One remaining type of declaration is ENTITY. :

Entity type	Location	Parsed/unparsed
General entities, used in document	internal	–
	external	parsed or unparsed (non-XML)
Parameter entities, used in DTD	internal	–
	external	parsed only

This table does not mention character entities, or the five pre-declared entities that we have already discussed. They do not need a declaration, and can be used either in the DTD or in the document. All other entities have to be declared in the DTD before they are used, with the declaration specifying whether the entity is to be used in the DTD or in the document.

Parameter Entities vs. General Entities

If the entity reference is to be used in the DTD, it is called a **parameter entity**, whereas if it is to be used in the document, it is called a **general entity**. It is an error to put a parameter entity reference in the document. It is not an error to use a general entity reference in the DTD **in defining the value of another entity**, but that reference will not be 'resolved' (replaced with the entity value) until it is used in the document. Does this sound a bit tricky? An example later in this section will help to explain.

Parameter entities are declared and referenced differently. Here is a simple example of both:

```
<!-- within the DTD -->

<!ENTITY   GenEntity "I am general">
<!ENTITY % ParEntity "I am parameter">
%ParEntity; <!-- parameter entity reference in DTD,
                 replaced by its value -->


<!-- DTD has ended, document has started -->

&GenEntity; <!-- general entity reference in the document,
                 replaced by its value -->
```

❑ Parameter entity *declarations* have the % character following the keyword ENTITY, while general entity declarations do not have any character between the keyword and the declared name of the entity.

❑ Parameter entity *references* start with the % character, while general entity references start with the & character.

Internal and External Entities

Put simply, internal entities are strings and external entities are files. Correspondingly, an entity definition is a string that is either the *value* of an internal entity or an *identifier* for an external entity. So far, we have only seen internal entities.

External general entities can be either **parsed** or **unparsed**. Unparsed general entities contain either binary data (such as a JPEG image), or character data that is not XML (such as a T$_E$X document). An unparsed general entity definition would be followed by an NDATA declaration that specifies the data format of the entity; the declared NDATA name would have to be previously declared as NOTATION. As we mentioned before, this a rarely-used feature, and there is a better alternative using MIME.

External Identifiers – SYSTEM and PUBLIC

Everything we said about SYSTEM and PUBLIC identifiers with regard to external DTDs applies to external entities.

An Example of Entity Declarations and References

Replacing a general entity reference in the document is fairly straightforward: replace the reference with the entity text, recursively replacing any entity references in the entity text.

Replacing entity references *in the DTD* can be quite tricky, especially if general entities are used in defining parameter entities. The rule is that only character and parameter entities are replaced within the DTD; general entity references are preserved in the replacement text, together with the delimiting characters around them. Consider this example:

```
<!ENTITY % pub "SomePublisher" >
<!ENTITY rights "All rights reserved" >
<!ENTITY book "A Book by a Famous Author, &#xA9; 1999 %pub;. &rights;" >
```

The character entity reference `&#xA9;` and the parameter entity reference `%pub;` will be expanded in the DTD, so the replacement text for the general entity `book` is going to be:

```
A Book by a Famous Author,
© 1999 SomePublisher. &rights;
```

The general-entity reference `&rights;` will get expanded in the process of expanding the general reference `&book;` somewhere within the document.

Read Well-Known DTDs

Ultimately, DTDs are tools for data modeling. Data modeling is an art, and one of the ways to learn it is by studying examples of good practices. There are many excellent DTDs already written, and you would do well to curl up in bed with one of them occasionally, and read it from cover to cover. Some of the most famous ones are:

❑ The HTML 4.01 and XHTML DTDs at `http://www.w3.org`

❑ The DocBook DTD at `http://www.oasis-open.org/docbook/`

❑ The TEI (Text Encoding Initiative) DTD for scholarly texts at `http://www.uic.edu/orgs/tei/`

Among other things, they show very imaginative uses of entity declarations, conditional inclusion of entities, and other techniques. There are also many excellent books on XML that cover the subject of data modeling and DTD design in some detail. *Professional XML* from Wrox Press, ISBN 1-861003-11-0 is a good starting point.

DTDs, Parsers, and Validation

To remind you of the terminology, an XML document has to be well-formed; any XML parser will check for well-formedness and reject ill-formed documents. A document that, in addition, conforms to the rules of a DTD is called a valid document. A parser that knows how to check a document against a DTD is called a validating parser; otherwise, it's a non-validating parser.

Parsers and DTDs

Even non-validating parsers can make use of a DTD if it is present. For instance, they can supply the default values of attributes, and expand internal entity references; some of them will go so far as to expand external entity references as well. However, they will not check for conformance to the rules: for this you need a validating parser.

There are many more non-validating parsers than validating ones. The best-known validating parsers are from Sun, IBM, Oracle, Microsoft, and Apache; most of them come with source code; the Apache parser, Xerces, is Open Source, available from `http://xml.apache.org`.

Using a DTD and a validating parser shifts some work from the application to the parsing process. Recall that a parser sits between the XML data and an application that wants to use it, and makes the data available to the application via a standard API. If the parser additionally validates the data against a set of rules, the application doesn't have to check those rules itself. A DTD is like a contract between the producer of XML data and an application that consumes it, and a validating parser enforces that contract.

XML Schemas, coming soon from the W3C standardization process, go even further in this direction, because they can impose more detailed and powerful constraints on XML data.

XML Schemas

DTDs are wonderful, but they are far from perfect. Their most important drawbacks are:

❑ Their syntax is not XML, and so XML parsers cannot parse them into component parts very easily

❑ They have a very primitive system of data types

❑ They are not modular, so it's not easy to reuse parts of a DTD

❑ They are not easily extensible; there's nothing like inheritance in the DTD world

XML Schemas are intended to give XML all these features. Work on XML Schema started in 1998, with a Requirements document in February 1999 and five Working Drafts since then. It may become Proposed Recommendation by the time you read this, but it will be a while before browsers will start implementing it. In the meantime, you can 'schema-validate' your documents against schemas using a schema validator from IBM, Oracle, or W3C; or you can use the Xerces parser from Apache that implements an alpha version of Schema support. (See `http://www.xml.com/pub/Guide/Schema` for links.)

Within an XML Schema, you can define types like this:

```
<xsd:simpleType name="fourDigit" base="xsd:string">
  <xsd:pattern value="[12]\d{3}"/> <!-- no items from first millenium -->
</xsd:simpleType>

<xsd:complexType name="collection">
  <xsd:element name="item" minOccurs="0" maxOccurs="unbounded">
    <xsd:complexType><!-- definition of item type goes here -->
      ...
      <xsd:attribute name="type" type="fourDigit"/>
    </xsd:complexType>
  </xsd:element>
</xsd:complexType>
```

Note that, unlike DTDs, Schemas are themselves XML documents, with markup, elements, attributes, and comments. Element tags, you will notice, consist of two parts separated by a colon; if you haven't seen this convention before, be aware that this has to do with Namespaces (coming up next).

There is an excellent primer on XML Schemas at `http://www.w3.org/TR/xmlschema-0/`. Schemas and schema validation are definitely the way to go in the medium-to-long range future. For now, it's DTDs and (plain) validation.

DTD Validators

If you want to use a validating parser yourself, you have to run a Java (or C++ or ...) program; we'll show you how in the next chapter. In the meantime, if you simply want to check your document against a DTD, you can do that without programming by using one of several XML validators available on the Web. We find the one at Brown University particularly useful (`http://www.stg.brown.edu/service/xmlvalid/`).

To illustrate its action, we went to the above URL and entered the directory path to the `exchange.xml` document from the beginning of this section. However, we had introduced two errors in the document, so it looked like this (see if you can catch the errors before the validator does):

```xml
<?xml version="1.0" ?>
<!DOCTYPE exchange [
<!ELEMENT exchange (greeting, response)>
<!ELEMENT greeting (#PCDATA)>
<!ELEMENT response (#PCDATA)>
<!ATTLIST greeting
  mode (warm|luke-warm|cool|cold) "warm"
  wording CDATA "IMPLIED"
>
]>
<exchange>
  <greeting mode="exuberant">
    Hello, XML
  </greeting>
  <response mode="frosty">
    Hello, what can I do for you?
  </response>
</exchange>
```

The validator came back with the following screen:

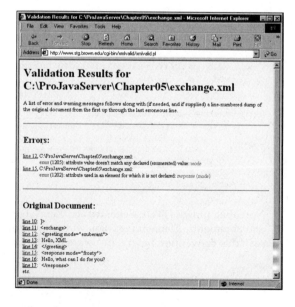

This is a wonderful tool for testing your XML-authoring skills; there are also validating editors that validate your documents as you compose them.

XML Namespaces

XML Namespaces form a mechanism for avoiding name conflicts in XML documents. The notions of a name conflict and a (partitioned) name space are well-known to programmers: all programming languages have some conventions to confine a set of names to an enclosed namespace, so that the same names can peacefully coexist in different namespaces without a conflict.

In Java, to take an example close to our heart, a package is a namespace for its classes and interfaces, a class is a namespace for its variables and methods, and a method is a namespace for its local variables. In C and C++, you in addition have a 'global' namespace, which really means "in the same file but outside any function or class definition". This usage dates from before the Internet, when the word 'global' didn't quite have the same literal ring to it. An XML document does indeed need to worry that somebody, somewhere else on the globe, may use the same name for a different purpose. XML Namespaces address this problem.

Truth be told, the danger of an actual conflict is, at this point, more theoretical than real. Tools for reusing other people's markup (such as Modularized XHTML and XML Schema) are not quite ready, and reuse is mostly done by cut-and-paste. However, important XML applications have been and are being released quite often, and the authors of those applications must make sure that their markup will not come into conflict with other markups in the foreseeable future, and preferably never. For instance, when the language of XML Schemas is released and becomes widely used, we want to make sure that its element names are not in conflict with any XML document they come in contact with. When JSPs were released as an XML application it was essential to have their tags distinct from any XML material that might be embedded in a JSP. Exactly the same concern applies to XSLT stylesheets that mix XSLT processing tags with template XML material. For these and many other reasons, the Namespaces specification had to be released before these essential applications.

The Main Idea – A Prefix and a URI

As a first approximation, we can try to ensure uniqueness of names by associating a namespace with a unique prefix. For instance, all names in XSLT would begin with `xsl:`, while all names in JSPs would begin with `jsp:`. However, this just pushes the problem a little bit back: how do you make sure that your prefix is unique on the Web, now and in the future? Fortunately, there is already a mechanism in place for giving unique names to web resources: the URI (Universal Resource Identifier), of which the URL is the most familiar example. So the Namespace Recommendation follows this strategy:

❑ A set of element names within an XML document can be assigned to a globally-unique namespace. The names may not contain a colon character.

❑ A namespace is uniquely identified by a URI; there are no assumptions made about that URI beyond the general requirement that it should be unique and persistent. For instance, it does not have to contain the list of all the names in the namespace. In other words, *it takes no part in the validation process.* Some people consider this a great weakness of the namespace mechanism as it now stands. (See the next section.)

❑ URIs are too long to use as a prefix, and they do not conform to XML name syntax. So, within a given document a short prefix, conforming to XML syntax, is associated with the URI that identifies the desired namespace. The fully qualified name consists of a prefix (serving as a proxy for the namespace URI), followed by a colon, followed by a name within the namespace (a 'local name'). As mentioned, local names may not contain a colon.

❑ After the document is parsed, the prefix is mapped to the URI to provide globally-unique fully-qualified names.

To take a concrete example, all XSLT stylesheets are XML documents whose root element is `<xsl:stylesheet>`. This sort of name, with a colon in the middle separating a namespace prefix from the 'local name', is called a **Qualified Name**, or **QName** for short. The root element has an attribute whose name is also a QName, `xmlns:xsl`. It is this attribute-value pair that establishes a correspondence between a prefix (`xsl`) and a unique URI:

```
<xsl:stylesheet version="1.0"
  xmlns:xsl="http://www.w3.org/1999/XSL/Transform"
>
```

Note that the URI must be unique but the prefix might not be. In fact, stylesheets intended for IE 5 associate the same `xsl:` prefix with a different URI that points to the actual web location of an old Working Draft of the XSLT specification. By contrast, the URI above is not a real web location: if you follow that link you will arrive at an almost empty page containing a single sentence: "This is the XSLT namespace".

A Big Caveat

This nearly blank page makes an important point (which IE 5's use of a real URL obscures).

> **The only purpose of the URI in a Namespace declaration is to provide a unique name.**

There is no implication that the name 'means' anything, or that dereferencing that name (following the link in the case of a URL) will get you some place interesting or important for the understanding of the local names within the Namespace. As the Recommendation says: "It is not a goal [of the Namespaces Recommendation] that it [the namespace URI] be directly usable for retrieval of a schema (if any exists)". This is elaborated by James Clark in `http://www.jclark.com/xml/xmlns.htm` (required reading on namespaces):

> *"The role of the URI in a universal name is purely to allow applications to recognize the name. There are no guarantees about the resource identified by the URI... It would of course be very useful to have namespace-aware validation: to be able to associate each URI used in a universal name with some sort of schema (similar to a DTD) and be able to validate a document using multiple such URIs with respect to the schemas for all of the URIs. The XML Namespaces Recommendation does not provide this."*

This feature of XML Namespaces has been very clearly stated by very intelligent people on many occasions, and yet there are a number of equally intelligent people who refuse to accept it as a final word. It does indeed seem wasteful that we associate a bunch of names with a web resource and yet refuse to use that resource in any way to say something about those names. The reason is that in order to define what exactly the namespace URI says about the names within the namespace, we have to agree on what it ought to say, and this is one area where agreement is difficult to achieve.

As mentioned earlier in the chapter, namespaces evoke strong passions. A recent discussion of whether relative URIs should be allowed as namespace identifiers produced 3,000 messages in less than two months. (See the archives of xml-uri@w3.org.) It is quite likely that when the XML Schema Recommendation is in place, the question of whether the namespace URI should house a Schema for its names will be re-opened, and a lot of passionate argument will ensue.

The Scope of the Namespace Declaration

To repeat, a namespace declaration takes the form of an attribute-value pair. The scope of that declaration is the entire content of the element that owns that attribute. In other words, the namespace prefix is inherited: if the processor encounters an element with a prefix but without an xmlns attribute, it goes to the parent, then grandparent, and so on, until the namespace declaration is found. If it is not found, a **NameSpace Constraint (NSC)** is violated. Note that this is not a validity constraint: the parser checks validity earlier, if at all.

The Default Namespace

Namespace inheritance saves a bit of typing. You can save even more typing by declaring a **default namespace**. In other words, the namespace of un-prefixed identifiers doesn't have to be local and undeclared: you can associate it with a global namespace identified by a URI. The syntactic convention is to use the xmlns attribute without the trailing colon-prefix part:

```
<fin xmlns='http://ecommerce.org/schema'>
    <!-- The namespace identified by http://ecommerce.org/schema
         is the default namespace for the fin element-->
    <!-- 'price' and 'x-rate' are in that namespace   -->
  <price units='Euro'>32.18</price>
  <x-rate>0.97</x-rate>
</fin>
```

In this version, the declared namespace becomes the 'default' for the element in which it is declared and its descendants. Unqualified local element names are assumed to belong to the default namespace.

What if you want to block some children elements from being in the default namespace, so that their (unqualified) names belong to the local namespace? In order to achieve that, you give them an xmlns attribute and set it to the empty string. An example from the Recommendation (clearly composed by a beer lover and an Anglophile) illustrates:

```
<?xml version='1.0'?>
<Beers>
  <!-- the default namespace is HTML -->
  <table xmlns='http://www.w3.org/TR/REC-html40'>

    <th><td>Name</td><td>Origin</td><td>Description</td></th>
    <tr>
```

```
        <!-- no default namespace inside table cells -->
        <td><brandName xmlns="">Huntsman</brandName></td>
        <td><origin xmlns="">Bath, UK</origin></td>
        <td>
          <details xmlns=""><class>Bitter</class><hop>Fuggles</hop>
            <pro>Wonderful hop, light alcohol, good summer beer</pro>
            <con>Fragile; excessive variance pub to pub</con>
          </details>
        </td>
      </tr>
    </table>
</Beers>
```

Namespaces and Attribute Names

So far, we have been talking exclusively about element names (or tags). What about attributes? Here things get a little trickier, because attribute names are already partitioned into namespaces by elements: it is perfectly common for two different elements to have attributes with the same name. So, in a default namespace, attribute names without prefixes are treated differently from element names without prefixes: they are assumed to just be local names.

This is sometimes described by saying that an XML namespace is not just one flat thing, the way namespaces are in programming languages, but rather consists of three sub-spaces: element names, attribute names with prefixes, and attribute names without prefixes. Each of these three parts forms a namespace in the traditional sense.

What this means in practice is that if you're using a default namespace with unqualified local names then your attributes will not come from that default namespace: they will simply be local names. The only way to have your attributes to belong to a global namespace is to declare a prefix for it, and use that prefix to qualify your attribute names.

Here's an example to illustrate the point. As you know, it is illegal for an element to have two attributes with identical names and different values. In the example, the default namespace is the same as the namespace associated with the prefix n1. However, the `<good>` element in this document is legal because the default namespace does not apply to attribute names:

```
<!-- http://www.w3.org is both the default and bound to n1 -->
<x xmlns:n1="http://www.w3.org"
   xmlns="http://www.w3.org" >

  <bad   a="1"
         a="2"/>  <!-- Cannot have two attributes with the same name -->
  <good a="1"
      n1:a="2"/> <!-- Unprefixed 'a' is in the local, not default namespace
                    it does NOT have an expanded name with a URI prefix -->
</x>
```

If both namespaces had prefixes associated with them, the element would be illegal, as in:

```
<!-- http://www.w3.org is bound to n1 and n2 -->
<x xmlns:n1="http://www.w3.org"
```

```
    xmlns:n2="http://www.w3.org" >
  <bad n1:a="1"
       n2:a="2"/> <!-- Both map to the same expanded name -->
</x>
```

In summary, attributes of the same element cannot have the same name, but you can have attributes with the same local part and namespace prefix mapping to different URIs.

Namespaces and DTDs

There are two ways to avoid using qualified names: have no namespace declaration at all, or have one default namespace. Default namespaces do much more than save keystrokes: they make it possible to use namespaces *without rewriting the DTDs.*

The big problem is that namespaces and DTDs are totally unrelated. When the parser checks prefixed names for validity, it is totally unaware of the significance of the prefix-colon convention. If the DTD declares an <author> element, and the document uses <bk:author>, the document is not valid. If you have a DTD and a collection of documents that conform to it, and you have decided to put all the element names in those documents in a namespace, you have to rewrite the DTD – *unless you make it the default namespace.* The names will remain unchanged, and the parser won't notice that they belong to a namespace. (You do have to declare the xmlns attribute on the elements that have it. Although it is a declaration from the namespace point of view, for the XML parser it's just an attribute like any other, and needs to be declared if the document is validated.)

As before, this may change when XML Schemas arrive on the scene, and parsers become both Namespace and Schema aware. This is not likely to happen for another year, at least.

Styling XML with CSS

Cascading StyleSheets (CSS) is, by Internet standards, an old technology: CSS2 was released as Recommendation in May 1998, and CSS1 goes back all the way to December 1996. CSS stylesheets were initially designed to be used with HTML, but porting the same idea to XML seems a very natural thing to do. CSS1 works well with XML both in IE 5 and Mozilla (but not Netscape, which remains blissfully unaware of XML). Support for CSS2 is limited to Mozilla (beginning with version 6).

We will limit our discussion of using CSS with XML to two example that illustrate the main principles of the stylesheet language.

A CSS1 Example, and an Explanation

Recall an earlier example where we used character entities to render markup characters as data. We repeat it here for convenience, together with the screen shot. Our interest is now on the stylesheet, so we will clip some material, including all comments and PIs, out of the document:

```
<?xml version='1.0' encoding='utf-8'?>

<?xml-stylesheet href="sink.css" type="text/css"?>
<rootElement>
```

249

```
   <h1>Document without a DTD</h1>
   <empty-element
     intent="show 'quotes within quotes' in attributes"
   />

   <non-empty-element>
     This is element content, parsed character data (PCDATA).

     MUCH MORE TEXT

   </non-empty-element>
</rootElement>
```

Our interest is in how the stylesheet renders this document as shown in the screen shot below.

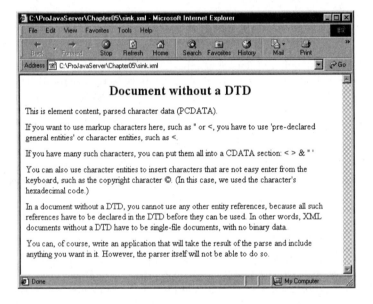

Here is the stylesheet:

```
rootElement, h1, empty-element, non-empty-element, br {
   display: block;
   margin-bottom: .6em;
}

h1 {
   font-weight:bold;
   font-size:large;
   text-align:center;
}
```

You will probably agree that this is very readable. All we need is a little terminology to describe in analytical terms what's going on.

Selectors and Declarations

A CSS stylesheet consists of a set of rules; each rule consists of selectors, and a declaration in curly brackets. A declaration is a set of property-value pairs separated by semicolons, and within each pair the property is separated from its value by a colon. That's all there is to it; the rest is a multitude of detail. In particular, you need to know the syntax of selectors, and you need to know what properties there are, and their possible values.

Let's start by considering the second rule in our stylesheet:

```
h1 {
    font-weight:bold;
    font-size:large;
    text-align:center;
}
```

The selector is h1, which means that the rule will apply to <h1> elements *and their children, if there are children and they do not redefine inherited properties.* This is what the adjective 'cascading' refers to: property settings are inherited from elements to their children. Children are free to define more properties, and their children inherit a larger cascade of properties.

The Syntax of Selectors

The first rule's selector has some structure to it: it's a comma-separated list:

```
rootElement, h1, empty-element, non-empty-element, br {
    display: block;
    margin-bottom: .6em;
}
```

This means that the declaration that follows applies to all elements on that list. The syntax of selectors is summarized in the following table:

Pattern	Meaning
*	Matches any element
E	Matches any E element (that is, an element of type E)
E F	Matches any F element that is a descendant of an E element
E > F	Matches any F element that is a child of an element E
E:first-child	Matches element E when E is the first child of its parent
E:link E:visited	Matches element E if E is the source anchor of a hyperlink of which the target is not yet visited (:link) or already visited (:visited)
E:active E:hover E:focus	Matches E during certain user actions

Pattern	Meaning
E:lang(c)	Matches element of type E if it is in (human) language c (the document language specifies how language is determined)
E + F	Matches any F element immediately preceded by an element E
E[foo]	Matches any E element with the foo attribute set (whatever the value)
E[foo="warning"]	Matches any E element whose foo attribute value is exactly equal to "warning"
E[foo~="warning"]	Matches any E element whose foo attribute value is a list of space-separated values, one of which is exactly equal to "warning"
E[lang|="en"]	Matches any E element whose lang attribute has a hyphen-separated list of values beginning (from the left) with "en"
DIV.warning	HTML only; the same as DIV[class~="warning"]
E#myid	Matches any E element whose ID is equal to "myid"

Properties and Values

Let's take a look at the declaration of the first rule again. It sets two properties:

```
display: block;
margin-bottom: .6em;
```

In CSS1, display has four possible values, namely none, inline, block, and list-item:

❑   none means that the element identified by the selector becomes invisible.

❑   inline means that display continues on the same line.

❑   block means that both the element and whatever follows it starts on a new line. In more precise terminology, whatever is a block sits in its own box, separate from what precedes and follows. A document is rendered as a sequence of such boxes, with each box having margins and padding on all four sides.

❑   list-item means that this is a block element, but preceded (inline) by a list-item marker; you can control the shape and placement of the marker by such properties as list-style-type, list-style-image, and list-style-position.

The second property-value pair above sets the bottom margin of each element, in effect setting them off as paragraphs. An em is a unit of length equal to the current font size, in points. In other words, it's a unit that shrinks and expands together with the current font.

As we said, the rest of CSS1 and even CSS2 is mostly learning the properties and their values. One major innovation of CSS2 is a greatly expanded list of possible values for the display property: it now includes table and list, among others. In other words, you can format your output as lists and tables in CSS rather than in markup. Unfortunately, only Mozilla 6 supports (a good part of) CSS2. Besides, CSS2 shares the general limitations of CSS stylesheets:

❑ Their syntax is not XML, so they have to be the final stage of a processing chain: whatever comes out of them has to be dumped to output.

❑ While they can make elements disappear (`display:none`), and they can output them in various places and various ways, they have no way to change structure: rename the elements, filter them by some criteria, sort them, add new elements, and output well-formed XML.

The first of these limitations is going to be lifted soon, as W3C develops a DOM (Document Object Model) for CSS stylesheets and a Simple API for CSS, see `http://www.w3.org/TR/SAC/`. They are patterned after DOM and SAX APIs for XML processing, which we will discuss in the next chapter. Their intended effect is to make it possible to parse a CSS stylesheet into Java (or some other language) objects so it can be subject to further processing.

The second limitation is fundamental. The strength of the CSS language is that it cleanly separates data from presentation. As such, it does not modify data. By contrast, XSLT (eXtensible Stylesheet Lanuage for Trasformations) is designed to filter and rearrange XML data. CSS, no matter how much further developed, is not in competition with XSLT: they complement each other. What CSS does compete with is XSL-FO, the Formatting Objects part of XSL. The relationship between XSLT and XSL-FO will be discussed in more detail shortly.

Namespaces and CSS

Since both CSS1 and CSS2 predate Namespaces, the relationship between CSS stylesheets and namespaces remains undefined, and different browsers behave differently when a CSS stylesheet is attached to a document containing qualified names. IE 5.0 will refuse to deal with qualified names, whether the stylesheet selectors are prefixed or not, and will render the document as plain text, ignoring the markup together with the stylesheet. Mozilla 6 will recognize the stylesheet *provided the selectors are unqualified names, with namespace prefixes stripped off.*

It is probably a good idea to stay away from the CSS + XML + namespaces combination for the time being. A plausible strategy is to use an XSLT stylesheet on the server to convert a namespaced document to one that does not contain qualified names (perhaps, simply, to an XHTML document), before displaying it in the browser with or without a CSS stylesheet. One more reason to learn XSLT.

Styling XML with XSLT

The history of XSL (eXtensible Stylesheet Language) has been brief but eventful. Work on XSL started in 1997, with the goal of producing a stylesheet language for specifying how an XML document is to be displayed in the browser. That goal has not yet been reached. In the meantime, two other specifications, both having to do with *transforming* rather than *formatting* XML, became Recommendations in November 1999, even though they did not exist as independent projects until fairly late in that year. As the XSL project unfolded, different parts of it grew at different speeds, and their relative importance and state of preparedness changed. Eventually, XSLT and XPath got carved out into separate products and completed, while the document formatting part is still in Working Draft.

It was obvious from the beginning that a stylesheet language was needed for XML to function: if users can define their own elements, they have to be able to specify how those elements will look when displayed in the browser window or other media. Similarly, the intent to make the stylesheet language more powerful than CSS existed from the beginning. CSS, as we have seen, has a good deal of control over *how* different elements are displayed, but very little control over *what* gets displayed and in what order. XSL was intended to be able to add, remove, and reorder the elements of the document tree so that, for instance, the stylesheet could handle multiple reports from a database table, showing different fields and sorting records in different ways.

Initially, the tree-transformation part of XSL was just an aid to the formatting part, but it proved to be easier to develop and to build a consensus about. As XML's role was evolving from a tool for document markup to being (also) a tool for data interchange between applications and components of applications, the transformation 'module' was developing an independent significance, totally unrelated to formatting and display, and the single XSL split into XSL for Formatting and XSL for Transformation (XSLT).

The XSLT part was taken over by James Clark, who brought it to a swift completion while at the same time producing xt, a fully compliant reference implementation of the XSLT processor. Several other implementations rapidly followed, and XSLT use spread rapidly. For a thorough coverage of the language, see *XSLT Programmer's Reference*, Wrox Press, ISBN 1-861003-12-9, by Michael Kay, the creator of Saxon, which is one of the most widely used XSLT processors.

What's XPath?

In order to transform trees, you have to be able to refer to tree paths, both in absolute terms (starting from the root) and relative to the current position in the tree. So XSLT needed a 'sub-language' whose expressions would specify sets of paths that satisfy a certain condition, or match a certain pattern. As work on XSLT unfolded, this sub-language was growing in size and sophistication, and becoming more and more like a 'regular expression language' for tree paths. At some point it was realized that exactly the same sub-language is needed for XLink/XPointer, a specification for hypertext links between XML documents and parts of documents. Here again, the idea was to make the linking facility more powerful and flexible than HTML's <A> or <LINK> tags, so that both the source and the target(s) of a link can be specified in structural terms. The result was that the sub-language for tree path description became separated from both XSLT and XLink/XPointer, and assumed independent existence under the name of XPath. In our example stylesheet below, we'll point out XPath expressions.

Trying Out XSLT

The easiest way to try out XSLT is to use the command line. To run an XSLT processor, you have to give it at least two arguments: the XML data file and the stylesheet. Usually, you want to save the results to a file (rather than see them flash by on screen) so you provide a third argument to specify output, as in:

```
java com.jclark.xsl.sax.Driver stamps.xml italy.xsl italy.htm
```

This assumes that you have downloaded and unpacked both the xp and xt distributions from http://www.jclark.com/xml, and placed xp.jar and xt.jar in the CLASSPATH. There are other ways to get xt working, but this is probably the simplest.

XML Data

Since this chapter is almost over, we are going to introduce, as XML data, a document that will be much used in the next chapter on XML parsing. It is the catalog of a stamp collection, consisting of `<item>` elements as follows:

```
<?xml version="1.0"?>
<?xml-stylesheet href="stamps.css" type="text/css"?>

<collection xmlns:html="http://www.w3.org/TR/REC-html40">
  <item type="stamp">
    <num>S-1873-001</num>
    <country>Italy</country>
    <year>1973</year>
    <price>
      <currency>lira</currency>
      <amount>100</amount>
    </price>
    <purchase-price>
      <currency>US</currency>
      <amount>$50</amount>
    </purchase-price>
    <image>stamps/italy/1873-001.html</image>
  </item>
  <!-- many more items -->
</collection>
```

Our goal is to transform this file, `stamps.xml`, into an HTML file that contains only records of stamps from a specific country. Assuming that the XML file and the XSLT stylesheet `italy.xsl` are in the same directory, the command shown above will create an HTML file, `italy.htm`, that contains only Italian stamps.

A Stylesheet Walkthrough

In outline, the stylesheet `italy.xsl` consists of six parts:

1. Declarations and top-level parameters

2. Match the root of the document tree

3. The first block of XHTML material for output

4. Match "stamps from given country" elements, and collect them in a variable

5. If the count of collected elements is 0, output an appropriate message

6. For each collected element, output a `<div>` element with whatever data is desired

Overleaf is the stylesheet, divided into parts by comments:

```
<?xml version="1.0" encoding="ISO-8859-1"?>

<!-- Part 1 -->
<xsl:stylesheet version="1.0"
  xmlns:xsl="http://www.w3.org/1999/XSL/Transform"
  xmlns="http://www.w3.org/TR/xhtml11/strict"
>
<xsl:output method="xml"/>

<!-- Part 2 -->
<xsl:template match="/">

<!-- Part 3 -->
<html><head>
   <title>Stamps of Italy</title>
   <link rel="stylesheet" type="text/css" href="stamphtm.css" />
</head><body>
<p>
    This is an example of generating HTML from an XML document,
using XSLT to select and CSS to format the data. We are presenting
stamps from Italy, if any.
</p>

<!-- Part 4 -->
<xsl:variable name="stamp-country"
    select="//item[@type='stamp']/country[text()='Italy']" />

<!-- Part 5 -->
<xsl:if test="count($stamp-country)=0">
  <p>Sorry, no stamps for Italy.</p>
</xsl:if>

<!-- Part 6 -->
<xsl:for-each select="$stamp-country" >
  <div class="num">
     Stamp item number: <xsl:value-of select="../num"/>
  </div>
</xsl:for-each>

</body></html>    <!-- close off open elements in output file -->

</xsl:template>    <!-- close off the match-root template -->
</xsl:stylesheet> <!-- end of stylesheet -->
```

Before we comment on the stylesheet's individual parts, let's try to get a general idea of how a stylesheet goes about its business: the **XSLT processing model**. The main point to keep in mind is that a stylesheet's job is to transform one document tree into another tree. The stylesheet starts with declarations and other preliminaries. Once processing begins, it proceeds as follows:

❑ The stylesheet selects a set of nodes for processing. The selection is done using an XPath expression. For instance, the expression " / " selects just one node, the root. The selected nodes form the **current list**.

The expression `"//item[@type='stamp']"` selects all the descendants of the 'currently selected' node whose element name is `item` and whose `type` attribute has the value `"stamp"`. If the currently selected node is the root, then the expression selects all such nodes in the document.

❏ Output corresponding to the current node list is created by processing this list; 'processing' usually means **instantiating a template** associated with the pattern. Typically, the code looks something like this:

```
<xsl:template match="[ expression specifying which nodes to process]">
  [template material; may contain more XSLT markup]
</xsl:template>
```

In the course of processing the current node list, new source nodes can be added to that list, usually by either an `<xsl:apply-templates/>` or an `<xsl:for-each>` element. (Both have a `select` attribute whose value is an XPath expression specifying which nodes to select.)

The entire transformation process begins by processing a list containing just the root node, and ends when the source node list is empty. This picture is a bit over-simplified, but adequate for now. The resulting XHTML output is:

```
<?xml version="1.0" encoding="utf-8"?>
<html xmlns="http://www.w3.org/TR/xhtml1/strict"><head><title>Stamps of
Italy</title><link rel="stylesheet" type="text/css"
href="stamphtm.css"/></head><body><p>
    This is an example of generating HTML from an XML document,
using XSLT to select and CSS to format the data. We are presenting
stamps from Italy, if any.
</p><div class="num">
    Stamp item number: S-1973-001</div><div class="num">
    Stamp item number: S-1973-002</div></body></html>
```

Part 1: Declarations and Top-Level Parameters

An XSLT stylesheet that outputs XHTML starts with a set of declarations similar to:

```
<?xml version="1.0" encoding="ISO-8859-1"?>

<xsl:stylesheet version="1.0"
  xmlns:xsl="http://www.w3.org/1999/XSL/Transform"
  xmlns="http://www.w3.org/TR/xhtml1/strict"
>
<xsl:output method="xml"/>
```

The first line is the standard XML declaration, because an XSLT stylesheet is an XML file. XSLT, although a programming language, uses XML syntax for its expressions.

The second line is the opening tag of the root element of the document. As you can see, the Document Type is xsl:stylesheet. Two namespace declarations follow, one for XSLT elements, the other for XHTML elements. The second declaration is a default declaration (no prefix), which means that unqualified, prefix-less names are to be interpreted as belonging to the http://www.w3.org/TR/xhtml1/strict namespace.

Note that the output method has to be "xml" rather than "html", so that if you construct an empty element on output, it will be closed with the /> sequence. For instance, if the output method were "html", the closing bracket of the <link... /> element in Part 3 would come out the HTML way.

Part 2: Match the Root of the Document Tree

Part 2 simply puts the root node on the current node list. The rest of the stylesheet is contained within this <xsl:template> element:

```
<xsl:template match="/">
```

Part 3: The First Block of XHTML Material for Output

Part 3 is just filler XHTML material that is passed on to output unchanged:

```
<html><head>
  <title>Stamps of Italy</title>
  <link rel="stylesheet" type="text/css" href="stamphtm.css" />
</head><body>
<p>
   This is an example of generating HTML from an XML document,
using XSLT to select and CSS to format the data. We are presenting
stamps from Italy, if any.
</p>
```

Part 4: Match and Collect Elements

Part 4 matches elements representing stamps from given country, and collects them in a variable:

```
<xsl:variable name="stamp-country"
   select="//item[@type='stamp']/country[text()='Italy']" />
```

The XPath expression in the select attribute selects all nodes that are <country> elements such that:

❑   Their text content is Italy

❑   Their parent is an <item> element whose type attribute has the value "stamp"

The set of all such nodes becomes the value of the stamp-country variable, and can be referred to as $stamp-country.

Parts 5 and 6: Output the Collected Elements, or a Message

Parts 5 and 6 check how many elements we collected. If there were none, we output an appropriate message, or otherwise we output a <div> element for each stamp, containing the stamp's number.

These parts of the stylesheet work with $stamp-country:

```
<xsl:if test="count($stamp-country)=0">
  <p>Sorry, no stamps for Italy.</p>
</xsl:if>

<xsl:for-each select="$stamp-country" >
  <div class="num">
    Stamp item number: <xsl:value-of select="../num"/>
  </div>
</xsl:for-each>
```

As you can see, XPath has functional expressions, such as count(), and XSLT has conditional templates, such as <xsl:if>. In the last select expression, we select a <num> element that is a sibling of the currently selected <country> element.

The rest of the stylesheet outputs the closing XHTML tags and closes its own <xsl:template> and <xsl:stylesheet> tags:

```
</body></html>

</xsl:template>
</xsl:stylesheet>
```

A Slight Variation

The following stylesheet produces exactly the same output but uses the recursive <apply-templates> structure instead of the iterative <for-each>. There are other small variations, but the main ideas are the same:

```
<xsl:stylesheet
  xmlns:xsl="http://www.w3.org/1999/XSL/Transform"
  xmlns="http://www.w3.org/TR/xhtml1/strict"
  version="1.0"
>
<xsl:output method="html"/>
<xsl:template match="/">
<html><head>
  <title>Stamps of Italy</title>
  <link rel="stylesheet" type="text/css" href="stamphtm.css" />
</head><body>
<p>
   This is an example of generating HTML from an XML document,
using XSLT to select and CSS to format the data.
</p>
<xsl:apply-templates /> <!-- material from other templates goes here -->
</body></html>
</xsl:template>

<xsl:template match="//item[@type='stamp']">
<xsl:if test="country[text()='Italy']">
  <div class="num">
    Stamp item number: <xsl:value-of select="num"/>
  </div>
```

```
</xsl:if>
</xsl:template>
</xsl:stylesheet>
```

A Bit More Power

Finally, we'll add a few features, as follows:

- ❏ The name of the country will be a parameter that the user can specify on the command line, with Mongolia as the default.

- ❏ The XML file will have a declared namespace and prefix-qualified names in it. The prefix will be excluded on output.

- ❏ The body of the `<xsl:for-each>` loop will be a 'subroutine call' on a named template.

There are other small variations but mostly the stylesheet follows the same outline as the first example. To test, run this command:

```
java com.jclark.xsl.sax.Driver nsstamps.xml nscountry.xsl nsout.htm country=Italy
```

The value entered on the command line becomes the value of the country parameter of the stylesheet:

```
<xsl:stylesheet  version="1.0"
  xmlns:xsl="http://www.w3.org/1999/XSL/Transform"
  xmlns="http://www.w3.org/TR/xhtml1/strict"
  xmlns:nss="http://www.n-topus.com"
  exclude-result-prefixes="nss">

<xsl:param name="country" select="'Mongolia'"/>
<xsl:output method="xml"/>
<xsl:template match="nss:collection"><!-- match collection child of root -->
<html><head>
  <title>Stamps of <xsl:value-of select="$country" /></title>
<link rel="stylesheet" type="text/css" href="stamphtm.css" />

</head><body>
<p>
   This is an example of generating HTML from an XML data
   table, using XSL to select and format the data. We are presenting
   stamps from <xsl:value-of select="$country" />, if any.
</p>
<xsl:variable name="stamp-country"
   select="nss:item[@type='stamp']/nss:country[text()=$country]" />

<xsl:if test="count($stamp-country)=0">
<p>
  Sorry, no stamps for <xsl:value-of select="$country" />.
</p>
</xsl:if>
```

```
<xsl:for-each select="$stamp-country" >
  <xsl:call-template name="show-stamp">
    <xsl:with-param name="stamp" select=".."/>
    <!-- select parent of country -->
  </xsl:call-template>
</xsl:for-each>
</body></html>
</xsl:template>
<xsl:template name="show-stamp">
  <xsl:param name="stamp" />
  <div class="num">
    stamp num: <xsl:value-of select="$stamp/nss:num"/>
  </div>
</xsl:template>
</xsl:stylesheet>
```

Finally, `nsstamps.xml` looks like this:

```
<?xml version="1.0"?>
<?xml-stylesheet href="nsstamps.css" type="text/css"?>

<nss:collection xmlns:nss="http://www.n-topus.com">
  <nss:item type="stamp">
    <nss:num>S-1873-001</nss:num>
    <nss:country>Italy</nss:country>
    <nss:year>1973</nss:year>
    <nss:price>
      <nss:currency>lira</nss:currency>
      <nss:amount>100</nss:amount>
    </nss:price>
    <nss:purchase-price>
      <nss:currency>US</nss:currency>
      <nss:amount>$50</nss:amount>
    </nss:purchase-price>
    <nss:image>stamps/italy/1873-001.html</nss:image>
  </nss:item>
  <!-- ... more items -->
</nss:collection>
```

Even with these additions, we have barely scratched the surface of what XSLT can do for you, especially since you can insert Java method calls in an XSLT stylesheet. For more detail, read Michael Kay's excellent *XSLT Programmer's Reference*, Wrox Press, ISBN 1-861003-12-9.

Coming Attractions

If we had infinite space, we would cover XSLT in some detail: it is a very powerful and flexible programming tool, ranging in scope from simple templates that can be authored by a non-programmer to a mechanism for embedding procedure calls in Java and other languages. Within the next year or so, it will be joined by several other, equally important tools that are in various stages of readiness at W3C. Some of the most important are:

❑ **XML Schema:** We have already talked about this; it is coming soon, and will be very useful for giving more structure to your document and for structure reuse.

❑ **XPointer/XLink:** A language for describing hypermedia links on the web, including two-directional links, multiple-target links, and out-of-document links. The goal is to allow each web user to create links between documents that are created by other people. The links can point very precisely to a location in the document, including time-defined locations in time-based media. A single link can point to a 'node-set', a collection of precisely defined locations. The project is in Working Draft.

❑ **Resource Definition Framework (RDF):** An XML application for describing web resources in a unified manner. It is hoped that given such descriptions, a more meaningful approach to searching and navigating the web can be developed, so we can ask questions like: "Show me web resources that are about the same subject matter (even if they use different keywords)". RDF has been a Recommendation for some time, but supporting machinery is not quite ready.

❑ **XML Query Language:** With XSLT, you can search documents in memory, but existing XSLT processor technology has no facilities for searching large collections. It is possible that existing XSLT stylesheets will eventually run on huge documents faster than they now run on small ones, because there will be no parsing stage and faster-than-linear matching will be not only possible but commonplace. It is also not impossible that the XML Query language, under development in the XML Query Working Group, will have little resemblance to XSLT/XPath.

Since XML is increasingly used as a data storage format, and the Web in its entirety is likely to become a large collection of XML data, a query language and a standard organization of storage are urgently needed. The XML Query Working Group is by far the largest at W3C, and has already published a Requirements draft and a Data Model draft.

❑ **CC/PP:** an XML application to describe "Composite Capability/Preference Profiles...: A user side framework for content negotiation". Device capabilities and user profiling have always been important, but they will be crucial for the success of small wireless devices, where a lot of information has to come from the user context. This is a Working Draft, but will probably move quickly with the rapid spread of wireless Internet services.

These and other ideas are all ultimately based on the amazing growth of XML.

Summary

In this chapter we have barely scratched the surface of the many uses of XML, because our primary task was to show its internals and how you work with it. We have covered, in some detail:

❑ Why XML is important: structured documents, structured data, ease of use, embedded meta-information, ease of transition between the linearized and the structured view, and universal acceptance.

❑ Well-formed documents, and the uses and limitations of well-formedness.

❑ DTDs and validity: we worked our way through some simple DTDs, and showed why DTDs are extremely useful but also how they are limited. Watch out for XML Schema!

❑ An overview of the XML 1.0 Recommendation. We have covered all the major features, leaving out rarely used features.

❑ Namespaces, the tool for avoiding name conflicts on the Web. When used for that purpose, it is widely accepted, but the proposals (or even hints of proposals) to use namespaces for pointing to the document's schema, its RDF description, or some other important information about the document evoked a strong controversy. See `http://lists.w3.org/Archives/Public/xml-uri/` for the ongoing discussion and further links.

❑ XSLT, a powerful XML-transformation language that is useful both for preparing your document for output and as a filter-transformer between software components that exchange XML data.

This background gives you all the knowledge and skills to start using XML parsers in web applications, which is the subject of the next chapter.

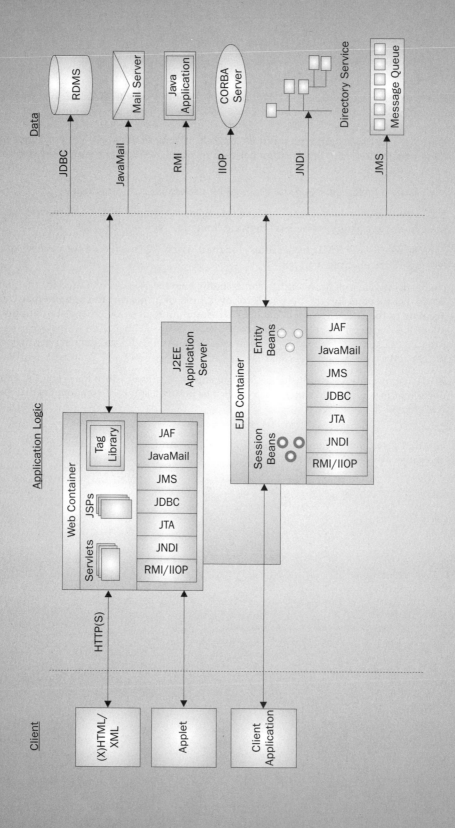

XML Parsing with DOM and SAX

The purpose of parsing an XML document is to make some interfaces available to an application that needs to make use of the document; using those interfaces, the application can inspect, retrieve, and modify the document's contents. The XML parser thus sits in the middle between an XML document and an application that uses it:

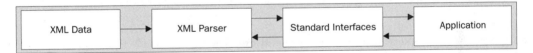

An XML parser is a well-understood, highly efficient, and very predictable piece of software. Its relationship with the XML document is precisely specified in the XML Recommendation, as discussed in Chapter 5. Its obligations towards the application are precisely specified in two standard APIs that form the main subject of this chapter.

Obviously, it would be very bad if the interfaces exposed by the parser were parser-specific: the world of Java XML applications would become partitioned into fiefdoms committed to a specific parser. To prevent this from happening, there are two specifications that spell out the interfaces that an application can expect from the parser:

- ❑ **SAX** – the **Simple API for XML**
- ❑ **DOM** – the **Document Object Model**

Why two standards? This has to do with the space-time tradeoff, so common in programming. DOM describes the document as a data structure, a tree of nodes. The parser constructs such a data structure and gets out of the way. Your application can traverse the tree, edit it, do what you like with it, *as long as you can store it in memory all at once* (and it can be huge).

SAX requires a modest amount of memory (proportional to the depth of the document tree), because SAX lays out the document in time, as a sequence of events. It associates an event with each tag (opening or closing), and with each block of text. You just write the event handlers and sit back to watch the document pass by. SAX is a very efficient and flexible tool, but it becomes awkward to use if the way you process a given element depends on earlier or later elements in the document.

Note that either of the two packages could be implemented using the other one. You could generate the SAX events by traversing a DOM data structure; later in the chapter we will show how, and explain why you would want to do such a thing. Conversely, you could generate the DOM data structure by appropriate SAX event handlers. Many XML parsers, including the one used in this chapter, work this way.

The Origins of DOM and SAX

DOM is a standard produced by the World Wide Web consortium, W3C. They call their standards 'Recommendations' because they are not a recognized standards body, just an industry consortium that wields a lot of power (and, by and large, commands a lot of respect). The DOM Level 1 Recommendation that is currently implemented by most parsers was released in October 1998. (DOM Level 2 became a Candidate Recommendation on May 10, 2000 but it is still a fair distance from becoming a fully approved and implemented standard.)

As people started using DOM for document processing, some drawbacks of the DOM approach became obvious. For example, it takes a good deal of time, and a lot of memory space, to construct a representation for a very large document. Until it is constructed, you cannot do anything with it. Even if all you want to do is a little fix on the second child of the root node, you still have to parse the entire document and construct a huge tree before you can get to your little fix.

> If your document fills gigabytes, the DOM approach is simply not practical.

SAX came about in response to these and similar criticisms that were frequently voiced on the xml-dev mailing list. The person who actually got it done is David Megginson, (http://www.megginson.com). SAX is even less of a formal standard than W3C Recommendations – it is not backed by any consortia – but it has been very widely accepted, both by individual developers and by the likes of IBM and Sun. (It is included, in total, in Sun's javax.xml package.) The version currently implemented by most browsers is 1.0. Megginson released SAX2, which includes support for Namespaces, in May 2000. We don't use its additional features in this chapter.

How Does JAXP Fit In?

As you may know, Sun Microsystems has recently published yet another Java-XML API, **Java API for XML Parsing**, or **JAXP** for short. Is this yet a third alternative, in competition with DOM and SAX? The answer is 'no'; JAXP just tries to standardize some aspects of Java XML parsing that DOM and SAX do not cover.

In order for an application to start working with XML data using DOM or SAX, the application must:

❑ Obtain a parser object

❑   Obtain a source of XML data

❑   Give that source to the parser to parse

These actions take only a few lines of code, but those lines are parser-specific. JAXP 1.0, released in March 2000, is an attempt by Sun to standardize that part of Java XML applications, so they are truly portable without any intervention by a programmer. As of this writing, most parsers are not yet JAXP-compliant, but one important parser, Xerces from Apache, has already joined in, and others are likely to follow after JAXP is folded into the standard Java SDK. We use JAXP classes in this chapter.

The Specific Parser

SAX and DOM are just interfaces and abstract classes and provide default 'do-nothing' implementations; to get anything done (like parse a document) the interfaces have to be implemented or default implementations extended. JAXP itself does not do that: it consists of four abstract classes that provide factory methods for obtaining instances of a parser and an XML data source. Specific implementations have to extend the abstract classes. As part of the JAXP distribution, Sun provides a reference implementation, in the com.sun.xml package, that contains three sub-packages: parser (which implements SAX interfaces), tree (which implements DOM interfaces) and util. This is the concrete implementation we are using.

Chapter Outline

Given this overall picture, in this chapter we will proceed as follows:

❑   Summaries of SAX and JAXP, and a simple example

❑   Summary of DOM, and another simple example

❑   Two utility classes for larger applications

❑   An application using DOM: DomSearcher

❑   An overview of DOM

❑   An application using SAX: Sax2Writer

❑   An application that converts a DOM Node into a SAX document: Dom2Sax

❑   SAX filters: the concept and an example

As you can see from this outline, the chapter is organized as a spiral: instead of giving you a big lump of information all at once, we return to the same topic (DOM, for example) several times, in different contexts, each time presenting it in more depth.

SAX, JAXP, and a Simple Example

We'll start by briefly describing the contents of the SAX distribution, especially the Parser and DocumentHandler interfaces. Next, we'll briefly describe the contents of the JAXP distribution, especially its javax.xml.parsers package. Finally, we'll give a very simple example of SAX use that shows both SAX and JAXP in action, which counts the number of elements in an XML document.

SAX Overview

To understand how SAX works, visualize the parsing process as a steady progression through the text of the document, with notifications of certain important events being sent to a `DocumentHandler` object. These events are things such as "the document has started", "an element has started", "an element has ended", "the character content of an element has been found", and so on.

> **SAX provides standard names for callback functions that are triggered by these events.**

Writing a SAX application mostly consists of implementing these callbacks.

The standard SAX Java distribution consists of two packages, containing eleven classes and interfaces in the `org.xml.sax` package, and another three classes in the `org.xml.sax.helpers` package. (There are also five demo classes showing example applications.) The two packages are included in the JAXP distribution, properly documented in its javadoc-generated documentation.

The SAX classes and interfaces fall into four groups:

❏ **Interfaces implemented by the parser:**
`Parser` and `AttributeList` (required), and `Locator` (optional). These are implemented by the parser writer. One of the `Parser` methods is `setDocumentHandler()`, which registers a document handler object with the parser. During parsing, the parser calls appropriate methods of its document handler. For instance, when the parser finds the start tag of an element, it calls the document handler's `startElement()` method.

❏ **Interfaces implemented by the application:**
`DocumentHandler`, `ErrorHandler`, `DTDHandler`, and `EntityResolver`. These four interfaces are all optional, but most SAX applications implement at least some methods of `DocumentHandler`. Instead of implementing `DocumentHandler` directly, applications frequently extend the `HandlerBase` class and override its methods. `HandlerBase` implements all four interfaces.

❏ **Standard SAX classes:**
`SAXException`, `SAXParseException`, `InputSource`, and `HandlerBase`. These are all fully implemented by SAX. (The two `Exception` classes also show up in DOM applications because, as you know, in Sun's `com.sun.xml` package a SAX parser is used to construct a DOM object.)

❏ **Optional Java-specific helper classes in the `org.xml.sax.helpers` package:**
`ParserFactory`, `AttributeListImpl`, and `LocatorImpl` (also fully implemented by the SAX Java distribution).

More on DocumentHandler

It is the `DocumentHandler` interface that declares the event handling methods of SAX. The most important of them are:

Receive notification of character data:
```
void characters(char[] ch, int start, int length)
```

Receive notification of the beginning of a document:

```
void startDocument()
```

Receive notification of the end of a document:

```
void endDocument()
```

Receive notification of the beginning of an element:

```
void startElement(java.lang.String name, AttributeList atts)
```

Receive notification of the end of an element:

```
void endElement(java.lang.String name)
```

Receive notification of a processing instruction:

```
void processingInstruction(java.lang.String target, java.lang.String data)
```

When you use SAX, you have to think in terms of an unfolding process, a sweep through the text to be parsed. If you come across an element or an attribute list that you want to use later, you have to save a copy of it. (Don't save a *reference* to it, because it will change in the next event handler call.)

The Structure of JAXP

JAXP consists of four packages: two for standard SAX distribution, one for standard DOM distribution, and the remaining one for JAXP proper, the `javax.xml.parsers` package:

Package	Origin
org.xml.sax	SAX distribution
org.xml.sax.utils	SAX distribution
org.w3c.dom	DOM in Java
javax.xml.parsers	JAXP distribution

We will discuss DOM and SAX packages in separate sections; here we'll give a brief overview of the `javax.xml.parsers` package. Its structure is clean and symmetrical. In addition to an exception class and an error class (`ParserConfigurationException` and `FactoryConfigurationError`), it has four classes, two for SAX and two for DOM. In each category, there is a factory class that builds an object of the other class that the application actually uses. So we have:

❑ For SAX: `SAXParser` and `SAXParserFactory`

❑ For DOM: `DocumentBuilder` and `DocumentBuilderFactory`

All four are abstract classes, and to get anything parsed, you need concrete classes that extend them and implement their methods. The identities of factory classes are determined by two system properties:

❑ `javax.xml.parsers.DocumentBuilderFactory`

❑ `javax.xml.parsers.SAXParserFactory`

In the `com.java.xml` package, these properties are set to classes that form the Sun reference implementation. To use JAXP with another concrete parser, that parser will have to extend the factory methods and make sure that the instances they return implement the JAXP signatures. One parser that has done this is the Xerces parser from Apache. In other words, if you are using Xerces and have its JAXP library installed (`org.apache.xerces.jaxp`), our JAXP code will work using the Apache parser, and you won't have to do anything. That's portability in action: before JAXP came about, some modifications in the parsing part of the code were necessary.

A Simple Example: Count the Elements

Our first example is a simple program that parses a document and counts the number of elements in it. It is a command line application that is invoked like this:

```
java CountSax doc.xml
```

The output lists the number of elements in the XML file given as argument on the command line.

Program Structure

The program consists of two parts. The `main()` method uses JAXP abstract classes to obtain a parser instance and call its `parse()` method. The second part uses the methods of `DocumentHandler` to count the elements, as follows:

- In `startDocument()`, we set the element count to 0
- In `startElement()`, we increment the element count
- In `endDocument()`, we output the element count

```java
import java.io.*;

import org.xml.sax.*;

import javax.xml.parsers.SAXParserFactory;
import javax.xml.parsers.SAXParser;

public class CountSax extends HandlerBase {
  public static void main(String argv[]) throws Exception {
    if (argv.length != 1) {
      System.err.println("Usage: cmd filename");
      System.exit(1);
    }

    // JAXP methods

    SAXParserFactory factory = SAXParserFactory.newInstance();
    SAXParser saxParser = factory.newSAXParser();
    saxParser.parse(new File(argv[0]), new CountSax());
  }

  static private int eltCount = 0;
```

```
  // DocumentHandler methods
  public void startDocument() {
    eltCount = 0;
  }

  public void startElement(String name, AttributeList attrs) {
    eltCount++;
  }

  public void endDocument() {
    System.out.println("Total number of elements: " + eltCount);
  }
}
```

We will elaborate on the JAXP part of the program, especially on this crucial line of code:

```
saxParser.parse(new File(argv [0]), new CountSax());
```

Variations on Parsing

The line above uses the `parse()` method of the `javax.xml.SAXParser` class. This method takes two arguments: a source of XML data (a `File` object, in this case), and a `HandlerBase` to use in processing the data. In addition to `File`, the source of XML data can be:

❑   A URI string

❑   A `java.io.InputStream` object

❑   An `org.sax.InputSource` object

For instance, if we wanted to use the URI version in our program, we would replace the line above with:

```
String uri = "file:" + new File(argv[0]).getAbsolutePath();
saxParser.parse(uri, new CountSax());
```

Similarly, we could open an input stream to read from the our file and give it as the first argument to `parse()`; or we could construct an `org.xml.sax.InputSource` object from our file and give it as the first argument to `parse()`.

What happens if our system ID for the source of XML data is not a file name but a URL? The best approach in this case is to create an `InputSource` object for parsing, because in the process of creating that object all external parsed references will be resolved. Alternatively, you can simply give the URL as a `String` argument to the `parse()` method.

The last variation to consider is when we have `String` input that can be either a file name or a URI. In this case, we'll have to test to see which one we have and act accordingly. One way to package this task is as follows:

```
File inF = new File(argv[0]);
if (inF.exists()) {    // we have a file name
  saxParser.parse(inF, new CountSax());
```

```
        } else {                    // we have a URI, we hope
          saxParser.parse(argv[0], new CountSax());
        }
```

The org.xml.sax.Parser Class

In our example, we use the JAXP SAXParser class and its parse() method. That class is actually a wrapper around a Parser class that implements the org.xml.sax.Parser interface. If you don't want to use JAXP, you will use some other class that implements that interface. The interface defines its own parse() method, and in this section we show how to use it, in case you don't want to commit to javax.xml. Here is a version of our simple example that does not use JAXP at all. In this version, InputSource and Parser are from org.xml.sax, and ParserFactory is from org.xml.sax.helpers:

```
import java.io.*;

import org.xml.sax.*;
import org.xml.sax.helpers.*;

public class CountSax extends HandlerBase {
  public static void main(String argv[]) throws Exception {
    if (argv.length < 1) {
      System.err.println("Usage: cmd filename");
      System.exit(1);
    }

    // replacement for JAXP methods
    InputSource input;
    String uri;
    OutputStreamWriter out;

    // Set up output stream
    out = new OutputStreamWriter(System.out, "UTF8");

    // Turn the filename into an XML input source
    uri = "file:" + new File(argv[0]).getAbsolutePath();
    input = new InputSource(uri);

    // Get an instance of the non-validating parser.
    org.xml.sax.Parser parser;
    parser = ParserFactory.makeParser("com.sun.xml.parser.Parser");
    parser.setDocumentHandler(new CountSax());

    // Parse the input, generate SAX events
    parser.parse(input);
  }

  // Other variables and methods as before...
}
```

In order to switch to a different parser, you would have to replace the class name given as argument to makeParser(). By contrast, switching from one JAXP parser to another requires no changes.

DOM and Our Example Revisited

We will now re-implement the element-counting application using DOM. As we said, DOM presents a document as a tree of **nodes**, where each node is the root of a sub-tree, possibly empty. In implementing trees, it is quite common to treat the root of the entire tree in the same way as its internal nodes, so that you can process the entire tree and its sub-trees in a uniform way, frequently using a recursive procedure. The common pattern is to call some procedure on the root of the tree and then recursively call it on the root's children. The procedure bottoms out on those nodes that are roots of empty sub-trees.

The way it's done in the org.w3c.dom package is that it has a Node interface, and a Document interface that extends Node. The output of parse() is an object that implements the Document interface, and you can apply both Document and Node methods to it. For our simple application, we will only need the properties and methods of org.w3c.dom.Node.

Node Types

The first thing to note about Nodes is that they can be of different **types** corresponding to the component types of an XML document: element, attribute, CDATA section, Processing Instruction, and so on. Each DOM node type is associated with a public static short integer constant that is given a symbolic name. For instance, there is an ELEMENT_NODE constant within the Node interface, declared as:

```
public static final short ELEMENT_NODE
```

The Node interface also has a getNodeType() method. If you have a Node object called node and you want to check whether it is an element node or not, you can do this:

```
boolean isElement = (node.getNodeType() == Node.ELEMENT_NODE);
if (isElement) {
  doOneThing();
} else {
  doAnotherThing();
}
```

Node Methods

Node is the largest interface within DOM. Its many methods fall into the following groups:

- **Methods to access information about the current node:**
  getNodeName(), getNodeType(), getNodeValue(), getOwnerDocument(), hasChildNodes()

- **Methods to clone and modify the current node:**
  cloneNode(), setNodeValue()

- **Methods to modify the node's children:**
  appendChild(), removeChild(), replaceChild(), insertBefore()

- **Methods to move around in the tree:**
  getAttributes(), getChildNodes(), getFirstChild(), getLastChild(), getNextSibling(), getPreviousSibling(), getParentNode()

For our simple application, we will only need the methods in the last group. All we need to do is visit every node in the tree, check to see if it is an element node, and if so, increment the element count. Before we do that, we have to go through the process of parsing a file and creating an `org.w3c.dom.Document` object.

Element Counting with DOM

In the code below, we start with the `main()` method, proceed to the JAXP part that does the parsing and in the end show the DOM part that does the element counting. In this case, we allow multiple file names on the command line:

```
import org.w3c.dom.*;
import org.xml.sax.*;    // parser uses SAX methods to build DOM object
import javax.xml.parsers.DocumentBuilderFactory;
import javax.xml.parsers.DocumentBuilder;

public class CountDom {

  /* the main method, just a test driver */
  public static void main(String[] args) throws Exception {
    for (int i = 0; i < args.length; i++) {
      String arg = args[i];
      System.out.println(arg + " elementCount: " + getElementCount(arg));
    }
  }

  /* parse the file, create Document, call getElementCount(Node) */
  public static int getElementCount(String fileName) throws Exception {
    Node node = readFile(fileName);   // parse file, return Document as Node
    return getElementCount(node);   // use DOM methods to count Elements
  }

  /* create File object from file name, call readFile(File) */
  public static Document readFile(String fileName) throws Exception {
    if (null == fileName) {
      throw new Exception("no fileName for readFile()");
    }
    return readFile(new File(fileName));
  }

  /* parse File, return Document */
  public static Document readFile(File file) throws Exception {
    Document doc;
    try {
      DocumentBuilderFactory dbf = DocumentBuilderFactory.newInstance();
      dbf.setValidating(true);
      DocumentBuilder db = dbf.newDocumentBuilder();
      doc = db.parse(file);
      return doc;
    } catch (SAXParseException ex) {
      throw (ex);
    } catch (SAXException ex) {
      Exception x = ex.getException();   // get underlying Exception
      throw ((x == null) ? ex : x);
```

```
    }
  }

  /*
   * use DOM methods to count elements: for each subtree
   * if the root is an Element, set sum to 1, else to 0
   * add element count of all children of the root to sun
   */
  public static int getElementCount(Node node) {
    if (null == node) {
      return 0;
    }
    int sum = 0;
    boolean isElement = (node.getNodeType() == Node.ELEMENT_NODE);
    if (isElement) {
      sum = 1;
    }
    NodeList children = node.getChildNodes();
    if (null == children) {
      return sum;
    }
    for (int i = 0; i < children.getLength(); i++) {
      sum += getElementCount(children.item(i));   // recursive call
    }
    return sum;
  }
}
```

As with SAX, the parse() method of DocumentBuilder can take four types of arguments: File, InputStream, String uri, and InputSource. So, we could again treat our filename either by creating a URI from it or by opening an InputStream to the file.

This concludes the preliminary part of the chapter, in which we made a first pass over the general issues of Java XML parsing, SAX, DOM, and JAXP. We now proceed to three more substantial applications.

Overview of This Chapter's Applications

The remainder of this chapter presents three applications:

❑   The first is pure DOM: it is called DomSearch, and it shows how to traverse a DOM tree looking for a specific pattern of elements and attributes. After this application, we will be ready for in-depth coverage of DOM. DomSearch makes use of the other two applications, Sax2Writer and Dom2Sax.

❑   The second application is pure SAX: it is called Sax2Writer, and it shows how to send the contents of an XML document (specified as a URI or an input source) to a java.io.Writer, without any loss of information.

❑   Finally, Dom2Sax is a SAX parser that traverses a DOM tree and generates the same SAX events that it would in traversing the linear text of an XML file. This is not an entirely novel idea – John Cowan implemented such a class as part of his SAX Filter package, http://www.ccil.org/~cowan/XML/ – but we have re-implemented it here both for its educational value (it uses both DOM and SAX extensively), and because it will be useful (together with Sax2Writer) in a larger case study presented later in the book.

Two Utility Classes

The remaining DOM and SAX applications of this chapter have some features in common and use the same utility classes to support them. To avoid repetition, we will go over those features and utilities in this early section.

One general feature that we frequently build into our code is that the same application should be useable both locally, from the command line, and over the Web, as a middle-tier application. The primary motivation is self-discipline: if your code cannot know whether it receives input locally or over the Web, you have to write it this way, in terms of more abstract sources and sinks of data. This is good for your code because it make it more modular and more reusable. In addition, it is frequently convenient to have a local 'driver' for a quick test of your class before you put it into the distributed environment of the Web.

In support of this (and in support of other needs) we have developed two utility classes that are used in the applications in this chapter: PropDict and Logger.

- ❏   PropDict is a straightforward extension of the Properties class that can also be initialized from a javax.servlet.HttpRequest object

- ❏   Logger is a simple utility that saves logging output to a file

Both classes are included with the chapter code.

The PropDict Class

PropDict is a convenience class for storing and retrieving Strings. It extends java.util.Properties (itself derived from Hashtable). PropDict mostly interacts with the outside world through its getDef() and setDef() methods. The reason we extend Properties rather than use the class directly is because we want a couple of additional features:

- ❏   We make it possible to place a limit on the size of the returned String. The limit is set by the outLimit variable. Ultimately, we want to be able to control the amount of output sent to the browser. This is sometimes useful for desktop browsers, and is crucial for the microbrowsers of WAP devices. This feature is built into the getDef() method, which is like the getProperty() method of Properties except it keeps track of outLimit.

- ❏   We define a setDef() method, overloaded so that in addition to a single name-value pair, it can take an array of such pairs (a 2-dimensional array of Strings), or two parallel arrays of names and values, or a properties file, or, indeed, an HttpServletRequest object arriving from a servlet or a JSP page. We explain how it works below: you don't need to know anything about servlets to understand what it does.

PropDict Code

We present the PropDict class in this order:

- ❏   Imports and declarations, including outLimit

- ❏   getDef() methods

- ❏   Explanation concerning HttpServletRequest

- ❏   setDef() methods

- ❏   Constructors (using the setDef() methods)

Imports and Declarations

We import the `java.util` package that contains `Properties`, and `HttpServletRequest`, in order to be able to initialize our `PropDict` from an HTTP request (that is, from information submitted via an HTML form):

```java
import java.util.*;
import javax.servlet.http.HttpServletRequest;

public class PropDict extends Properties {

  int outLimit;

  public void setOutLimit(int outLimit) {
    this.outLimit = outLimit;
  }

  public int getOutLimit() {
    return outLimit;
  }
```

The `outLimit` variable is for controlling the amount of output, in bytes. You will see it used in `getDef()` methods in a moment. If `outLimit` is set to −1, there is no limit.

getDef() Methods

These methods are patterned after the `getProperty()` method of the `Properties` class. The most common case takes two arguments: the name of the 'property' and a default value to return if the name has no definition. If only one argument is given, the default value is the empty string:

```java
public String getDef(String name) {
  return getDef(name, "");
}

// output as much as outLimit allows; update outLimit
public String getDef(String name, String dflt) {
  String val = getProperty(name, dflt);
  if (val == null) {
    val = "";
  }
  if (outLimit < 0) {
    return val;
  }
  int len = val.length();
  if (len > outLimit) {    // too much, output substring
    val = val.substring(0, outLimit);
    outLimit = 0;
  } else {
    outLimit -= len;
  }
  return val;
}
```

```
// given an array of names and an array of defaults,
// return an array of "definitions"
public String[] getDef(String[] names, String[] dflt) {
  String[] vals = new String[names.length];
  for (int i = 0; i < vals.length; i++) {
    vals[i] = getDef(names[i], dflt[i]);
  }
  return vals;
}

// same with a single default for all names
public String[] getDef(String[] names, String dflt) {
  String[] vals = new String[names.length];
  for (int i = 0; i < vals.length; i++) {
    vals[i] = getDef(names[i], dflt);
  }
  return vals;
}

// same, with "" as default
public String[] getDef(String[] names) {
  return getDef(names, "");
}
```

A Word about HttpServletRequest

Before we can go into setDef() methods, we need a word of explanation about servlets. Servlets play the same role in a web application as CGI scripts or ASP pages: they mediate between the server and the application's server-side components. One of their main tasks is to make the information submitted by the client (via an HTML form) available on the server side. This information is provided to the servlet as a Java object that implements the HttpServletRequest interface. That interface declares the getParameterNames() and getParameter() methods (among others) to extract the request data from the object. For instance, if the HTML form has an input element named "occupation" and the user entered "nurse" in it before submitting the form, then:

```
request.getParameter("occupation")
```

Will return the string "nurse". (Here, request is the object that implements the HttpServletRequest interface.)

This is all you need to know to see how an HttpServletRequest object can be wrapped into a PropDict. You will learn all about servlet programming in Chapters 8 to 10.

setDef() Methods

There are several setDef() methods. The most basic one simply calls the setProperty() method inherited from the parent class. The rest use this basic method, within a loop that iterates over the contents of some object; one of such objects is an HttpServletRequest:

```
public void setDef(String name, String val) {
  setProperty(name, val);
}
```

```
// create a PropDict from an array of name-value pairs
public void setDef(String[][] pairs) {
  for (int i = 0; i < pairs.length; i++) {
    setDef(pairs[i][0], pairs[i][1]);
  }
}

// create a PropDict from two parallel arrays of String
public void setDef(String[] names, String[] vals) {
  int len = names.length;
  if (len > vals.length) {
    len = vals.length;
  }
  for (int i = 0; i < len; i++) {
    setDef(names[i], vals[i]);
  }
}

// create a PropDict from a Properties object
public void setDef(Properties P) {
  Enumeration pNames = P.propertyNames();
  while (pNames.hasMoreElements()) {
    String name = (String) pNames.nextElement();
    setDef(name, P.getProperty(name));
  }
}

// create a PropDict from an HttpServletRequest object
public void setDef(HttpServletRequest req) {
  java.util.Enumeration enum = req.getParameterNames();
  while (enum.hasMoreElements()) {
    String name = (String) enum.nextElement();
    String val = req.getParameter(name);
    setDef(name, val);
  }
}
```

Constructors

The constructors take the same set of arguments as setDef(), and call that method:

```
public PropDict(int outLimit) {
  this.outLimit = outLimit;
}

public PropDict() {
  this(-1);
}

public PropDict(String[][] pairs) {
  this(-1);
  setDef(pairs);
}
```

```
    public PropDict(String[] names, String[] vals) {
      this(-1);
      setDef(names, vals);
    }

    public PropDict(Properties P) {
      this(-1);
      setDef(P);
    }

    public PropDict(HttpServletRequest req) {
      this(-1);
      setDef(req);
    }
  }
```

Web Applications and Local Applications

When we create applications that can be used either locally or over the Web, we use a `PropDict` object to insulate the main part of the application from the part that receives user input. In the web application, there is always a servlet that receives request information from the browser. Before this information is passed on to the rest of the application, it is packaged as a `PropDict` object. Similarly, the local application always packages its input (either from the command line or from a properties file) as a `PropDict` object. In either case, the rest of the application receives its data wrapped in a `PropDict`, and is totally ignorant of where that object is coming from.

The Logger Class

Logging is a very personal thing, because it is closely tied up with debugging. We hesitate to impose our `Logger` on you. We think it's good but you may have your own ideas. If you don't like our `Logger`, or don't like the very idea of using somebody else's `Logger`, replace it with your own arrangements. Just remember that we need a general utility that will make sense both in local and distributed applications. All our `Logger` does is saves the logging output to a file. It can be used in either a local or a web-based application.

Most of the time, the `Logger` uses its `logIt()` method, with `clearLog()` a distant second. `logIt()` can be used with one argument, a `String`, or two arguments, a `String` and a `Throwable`. The string gets written to the log file, followed by the stack trace if the second argument is present.

The Log File

The name of the log file is kept in the `fileName` variable. The value of that variable can be set at construction, or using the `setFileName()` method. There is also a default file name and a system property to hold the log file name. The name of the system property is kept in the `fileProp` variable. In summary, you have the following options:

- ❑ Do nothing and use the default file name
- ❑ Specify the file name as a system property
- ❑ Give the desired file name as argument to the constructor
- ❑ Set the file name dynamically, using the `setFileName()` method

280

You can have more than one logger. Our loggers are thread-safe.

Control of Logging

Logger has built-in machinery for turning itself off. If the integer variable debugLevel is set to 0 or a negative number, Logger produces no output. In this version, debugLevel functions as a binary switch – the logger is either on or off – but a more fine-grained control can be easily programmed.

The value of debugLevel can be specified at construction or using the setDebugLevel() method. There is also a setDebug() method that can take "true" and "false" strings as well as a boolean; it sets debugLevel to 0 or 1.

The Logger Code

The Logger class is very straightforward:

```java
import java.io.*;
import java.util.Date;

public class Logger {    // may be shared across threads

  static String fileProp = "Logger.file";
  static String debugProp = "Logger.debugLevel";
  static String defaultFileName = "dbLog.log";
  String fileName;    // the identity of the log file
  int debugLevel;     // to turn on or off; can be used for
                      // fine-grained control

  public Logger(String fName) {
    fileName = fName;
    debugLevel = Integer.parseInt(System.getProperty(debugProp, "1"));
  }

  public Logger() {
    this(System.getProperty(fileProp, defaultFileName));
  }

  public synchronized void setFileName(String fName) {
    fileName = fName;
  }

  public synchronized void setDebugLevel(int n) {
    debugLevel = n;
  }

  public synchronized void setDebug(boolean b) {
    debugLevel = b ? 1 : 0;
  }

  public synchronized void setDebug(String str) {
    // str is "true" or "false"
    setDebug((new Boolean(str)).booleanValue());
  }
```

```
public synchronized void clearLog() {
  // clear the log file, insert current date
  if (debugLevel <= 0) {
    return;
  }
  try {
    PrintWriter pw = new PrintWriter(new FileWriter(fileName, false));
    String str = (new Date()).toString();
    pw.println(str);
    pw.close();
  } catch (IOException e) {}
}

public synchronized void logIt(String str) {
  if (debugLevel <= 0) {
    return;
  }
  try {
    PrintWriter pw = new PrintWriter(new FileWriter(fileName, true));
    pw.println(str);
    pw.close();
  } catch (IOException e) {}
}

public synchronized void logIt(String str, Throwable ex) {
  if (debugLevel <= 0) {
    return;
  }
  try {
    PrintWriter pw = new PrintWriter(new FileWriter(fileName, true));
    pw.println(str);
    ex.printStackTrace(pw);
    pw.close();
  } catch (IOException e) {}
}
}
```

You will see both `PropDict` and `Logger` used in the applications in this chapter.

A DOM Application

One common thing to do with XML document trees is to walk through them. That is, we visit each 'node' in the document tree in turn. Usually, the walk is not random but follows one of three orders: **preorder**, **inorder** or **postorder**:

❏ In a **preorder** traversal, you visit the root before you (recursively) do a complete walk of its subtrees

❏ In **inorder** traversal, you visit the root after walking the left substree and before walking the rest of them

❏ In **postorder** traversal, you visit the root after walking all its subtrees

Our next application, DomSearch, walks the tree (using a postorder or 'depth-first' traversal) in search of a specific pattern of elements and attributes. The user supplies both the name of the document to search and the pattern to search for. The set of patterns that the application can recognize is quite restricted; the user can specify the tag name of the element to look for, the value of one of its attributes, and the tag name of its parent element. The default is to look for <item type="stamp"> which has a child <country>Italy</country>, in an XML file that looks like this:

```
<?xml version="1.0"?>
<?xml-stylesheet href="stamps.css" type="text/css"?>
<!-- XML data description -->
<collection xmlns:html="http://www.w3.org/TR/REC-html40">
  <item type="stamp">
    <num>S-1873-001</num>
    <country>Italy</country>
    <year>1873</year>
    <price>
      <currency>lira</currency>
      <amount>100</amount>
    </price>
    <purchase-price>
      <currency>US</currency>
      <amount>$50</amount>
    </purchase-price>
    <image>stamps/italy/1873-001.html</image>
  </item>
  <!-- many more items like this -->
</collection>
```

After each search, the application sends back the node it has found, formatted according to the stylesheet referenced in the XML document. This is done by our custom application, Dom2Sax, which uses SAX callbacks to output the contents of a DOM node. This way we cover both DOM and SAX. Our DOM and SAX examples work together in the context of a larger application, although each can be pressed into useful service independently, in other contexts.

Local and Web

DomSearch illustrates the technique of creating applications that can be used both locally and on the Web. In this chapter we will use it as a command-line application using the main() method, but we could equally well have written a servlet to act as the user interface. We will see DomSearch again in Chapter 15, where we access it from a JavaServer page.

The DomSearch Class

In outline, DomSearch consists of the following parts:

❑ **Initialize:** this includes parsing an input source

❑ **Reset:** use user input (wrapped in a PropDict) to reset property values

❑ **Walk and search:** this is where DOM interfaces are used

We will look at these parts of DomSearch in a moment, but first we will show how user input is passed to the application from the command line: the main() method of DomSearch.

The main() Method

This is a simple driver that takes command-line arguments in the form `propName=propValue` and uses them to populate the `PropDict`:

```java
import java.io.*;
import java.util.Properties;
import org.w3c.dom.*;
import org.xml.sax.*;
import javax.xml.parsers.DocumentBuilderFactory;
import javax.xml.parsers.DocumentBuilder;

public class DomSearch {

  public static void main(String[] args) throws Exception {

    // create a new DomSearch object, give it a new PropDict and
    // initialize it from the default values in PropDict
    DomSearch ds = new DomSearch();
    ds.setDict(new PropDict());
    ds.initFromDict();

    // process user input and add it to the PropDict
    int i = -1;
    while (++i < args.length) {
      String arg = args[i];
      int loc = arg.indexOf('=');
      if (0 < loc) {
        ds.setDef(arg.substring(0, loc), arg.substring(loc + 1));
      } else {
        System.out.print(arg + ": ");
        System.out.println(ds.doCommand(arg));
        ds.write();
      }
    }
  }
}
```

As you can see, `DomSearch` doesn't know or care where its data is coming from as long as it is wrapped in a `PropDict`. Once the `PropDict` is in place, `DomSearch` is ready for action, because the `PropDict` contains the name of the file to process and the initial search conditions. To start the program, run the command:

```
java DomSearch fileName=stamps.xml initFile
```

This will print out the entire contents of the document. To see the items that match the default settings of search parameters, run this command:

```
java DomSearch initFile nextMatch
```

This will print the next matching item. To show the second matching item, run:

```
java DomSearch initFile nextMatch nextMatch
```

To change the values of search parameters, run a command like:

```
java DomSearch innerTag=country innerCVal=Germany initFile nextMatch
```

In a web application, the DomSearch class is completely unchanged, except that the main() method is not used: the name-value pairs come from HTML forms via a request object converted into a PropDict.

Overview

It might be useful to rise above the code at this point and take a larger view of the DomSearch class. Its many methods can be divided into groups as follows:

❑   Constructor, set, and get methods.

❑   Initialize/update methods: initFile(), initFromDict(), and updateFromDict()
These are called by the servlet either at the beginning of a session (initFile(), initFromDict()) or at each request (updateFromDict()). initFile() can also be called if the user asks for it, to create another document.

❑   doCommand()
This is the central dispatching point; depending on the user's selection, initFile(), nextMatch(), or resetNode() is called, or an error message is returned.

❑   initFile() helpers: readFile() and readDoc()
readFile() prepares the URI; readDoc() does DOM parsing and creates a document.

The remaining methods assume that a document is available. They search for its stylesheet link or for a specific node, and they output the result of the search:

❑   getStylesheet() and isStylesheet() are for finding the stylesheet node, a Processing Instruction. getStylesheet() uses successor() to traverse and isStylesheet() to test.

❑   nextMatch() does the search. Its helpers are: gotAMatch(), hasChildWithTextVal(), isElementWithName(), hasAttributeWithNameVal().

❑   Output methods: write(), writeNode().

With the main() method and the class structure dealt with, we can proceed to the remainder of DomSearch, where all the DOM processing is done. With the PropDict is in place, DomSearch can call doCommand() and write().

doCommand()

Depending on the current value of domCmd, this method calls one of the following:

❑   initFile()
Call readFile() to parse the XML document and store the resulting Document object in two variables, node and original

❑   nextMatch()
Walk the tree using the successor() method until a match is found, or the successor is the original node from which the walk started

❑ resetNode()
    Reset node to original

Where does domCmd come from? It can be an argument to doCommand(), or it can be stored in the
PropDict, under the key "domCmd". Here is the doCommand() code:

```
protected String doCommand() {    // assumes values read in from dict
  try {
    if ("initFile".equalsIgnoreCase(domCmd)) {
      return initFile();
    } else if ("nextMatch".equalsIgnoreCase(domCmd)) {
      return nextMatch();
    } else if ("reset".equalsIgnoreCase(domCmd)) {
      resetNode();
      return "";
    } else {
      return "error: invalid command [" + domCmd
            + "]\n should be initFile,nextMatch,or reset";
    }
  } catch (Exception ex) {
    return ("error: DomSearch.doCommand " + ex);
  }
}
```

There is also a version that takes a String argument:

```
public String doCommand(String cmd) {
  setDef("domCmd", cmd);
  updateFromDict();
  return doCommand();
}
```

We are going to trace these methods and, in the process, see some JAXP-style XML parsing and DOM
processing. Every line that has a DOM method will have a comment to that effect.

initFile(), readFile(), and readDoc()

These methods do the parsing, in three stages:

❑ The initFile() method is called in the beginning of the session, or in response to the user's
    request to switch to another document

❑ initFile() calls readFile(), which converts a file name into a URI and calls readDoc()

❑ readDoc() finally does the actual parsing and document building

We have also added a readInputSource() method which we'll need in Chapter 15.

```
protected String initFile() throws Exception {

  // process XML document, store the resulting Document node reference
  // both in the (current) node and in the original (to be able to reset)
  node = original = readFile(fileName);
```

```
    styleNode = getStyleSheet(node);
    matchCount = 0;
    return "";
}

public static Document readFile(String fileName)
        throws Exception {    // recall CountDom, same processing
    if (null == fileName) {
      throw new Exception("no fileName for DomSearch.readFile");
    }
    String uri = "file:" + new File(fileName).getAbsolutePath();
    return readDoc(uri);
}

public static Document readDoc(String uri) throws Exception {
    Document doc;
    try {    // Create a DOM object using JAXP abstract classes
      DocumentBuilderFactory dbf = DocumentBuilderFactory.newInstance();
      DocumentBuilder db = dbf.newDocumentBuilder();
      doc = db.parse(uri);
      return doc;
    } catch (SAXParseException ex) {    // an example of Logger in action
      (new Logger()).logIt(" SAXParse error in DomSearch.readDoc(" + uri
      + ")" + ", line " + ex.getLineNumber() + ", the uri is "
      + ex.getSystemId(), ex);
      throw (ex);
    } catch (SAXException ex) {          // do some logging
      throw (ex);
    }
}

public static Document readInputSource(InputSource in) throws Exception {
    if(null == in)
      throw new Exception("No inputsource for DomSearch.readInputSource");
    Document doc;
    try {
      DocumentBuilderFactory dbf = DocumentBuilderFactory.newInstance();
      DocumentBuilder db = dbf.newDocumentBuilder();
      doc = db.parse(in);
      return doc;
    } catch(SAXParseException ex) {
      (new Logger()).logIt(" SAXParse error in DomSearch.readInputSource"
                  + ", line " + ex.getLineNumber() +
                  ", uri=?=" + ex.getSystemId(), ex);
      throw(ex);
    } catch(SAXException ex) {
      Exception x = ex.getException();
      (new Logger()).logIt(" SAX err in DomSearch.readInputSource",
                  (x == null)? ex : x);
      throw((x == null) ? ex : x);
    }
}
```

readDoc() does parsing exactly as stipulated by JAXP. The only tricky part of this code is how we obtain the node whose content identifies the CSS stylesheet for the document. Here we are going to see some DOM methods.

Getting the Stylesheet: getStyleSheet(), isStyleSheet(), and Successor()

Recall that stylesheets are linked to documents by **Processing Instructions (PI)**; in the `stamps.xml` document, it looks like this:

```
<?xml-stylesheet
href="file:///C:/jakarta-tomcat/webapps/examples/WEB-INF/classes/stamps.css"
type="text/css"?>
```

DOM specifies that PIs are made available to the application as Nodes of the 'PI' type. (See below how node types are handled.) The first string after the PI's opening bracket (`xml-stylesheet`) is the name of that `Node`. Therefore, we can find the stylesheet node by this procedure:

❑ Traverse the tree visiting each node

❑ If a PI node is found whose name is `xml-stylesheet`, quit and return that node

❑ Otherwise return `null` when all nodes have been visited

To carry out this procedure we need three functions:

❑ `successor()` systematically visits each node in the tree

❑ `isStyleSheet()` checks to see whether the currently visited node is the stylesheet node, and returns `true` or `false`

❑ `getStyleSheet()` sets the procedure in motion

We will show `getStyleSheet()` and `isStyleSheet()` here. The traversal method is also used in the `nextMatch()` method, and is discussed there:

```java
public static Node getStyleSheet(Node nd) {

  // loop forever while traversing the tree using the successor() method
  // quit the loop when the stylesheet node is found or successor is null
  // indicating we have visited all nodes
  for (; ; ) {
    nd = successor(nd);
    if (isStyleSheet(nd)) {
      return nd;
    }
    if (nd.getParentNode() == null) {   // DOM
      return null;
    }
  }
}

public static boolean isStyleSheet(Node nd) {
  if (nd.getNodeType() != Node.PROCESSING_INSTRUCTION_NODE) {   // DOM
    return false;
  }
  if (nd.getNodeName().equals("xml-stylesheet")) {   // DOM
    return true;
  }
  return false;
}
```

Three DOM methods are used in this code, in addition to our own `successor()`:

❑   `getParentNode()` does the obvious thing.

❑   `getNodeType()` returns an integer, one of twelve integer constants that are declared in the Node interface. `PROCESSING_INSTRUCTION_NODE` is declared as:

```
public static final short PROCESSING_INSTRUCTION_NODE = 7;
```

❑   Finally, `getNodeName()` returns a `String`; the exact value depends on the type of the node. For elements, it's the tag name; for attributes, the attribute name; and for PIs, it's the first string after the opening `<?` bracket, technically known as 'PI Target'. So, we retrieve the node name and compare it to `"xml-stylesheet"`, to see whether we have found the processing instruction that is a link to the stylesheet.

Once we have found it, we can take the PI apart to find the name of the stylesheet file. This is done in `Dom2Sax`, using SAX methods.

nextMatch()

`nextMatch()` follows the same traversal logic as `getStyleSheet()`: it uses `successor()` to get to the next node and a predicate (a method that returns a `boolean`) to test the next node. If it comes back to the original empty-handed it sends back an empty string; otherwise it sends back a string that indicates the number of the match:

```
protected String nextMatch() throws Exception {
  do {
    node = successor(node);
  } while (!gotAMatch() && node != original);
  if (node == original) {
    matchCount = 0;
    return "";
  }
  return Integer.toString(++matchCount);
}
```

How do we test for a match? This is where DOM methods come handy. The code here is a bit verbose but fairly obvious: there are three nodes to check out, and we have a method for each:

```
protected boolean gotAMatch() {
  if (!isElementWithName(node, outerTag)) {
    return false;
  }
  Element elt = (Element) node;
  if (!hasAttributeWithNameVal(elt, outerAttr, outerAVal)) {
    return false;
  }
  return hasChildWithTextVal(elt, innerTag, innerCVal);
}

// Is the node an element node with name equal to second argument?
public static boolean isElementWithName(Node node, String name) {
  if (node == null) {
```

```
      return false;
    }
    if (node.getNodeType() != Node.ELEMENT_NODE) {
      return false;
    }
    if (!node.getNodeName().equals(name)) {
      return false;
    }
    return true;
  }

  // Does the node have an attribute with the same name and value
  // as the second and third arguments?
  public static boolean hasAttributeWithNameVal(Element elt, String name,
                                                String val) {
    String att =
      elt.getAttribute(name);    // by now we know elt is an Element node
    return att != null && att.indexOf(val) >= 0;
  }

  // Does the node have a child with the same name as the second argument?
  public static boolean hasChildWithTextVal(Element elt, String name,
                                            String val) {
    NodeList children = elt.getChildNodes();
    if (null == children) {
      return false;
    }
    for (int i = 0; i < children.getLength(); i++) {
      Node child = children.item(i);
      if (child.getNodeName().equals(name)) {

        // text node is a child of element node
        Node innerText = child.getFirstChild();
        if (innerText == null) {
          continue;    // seek another child of same name
        }
        if (innerText.getNodeType() != Node.TEXT_NODE) {
          continue;
        }
        if (innerText.getNodeValue().indexOf(val) >= 0) {
          return true;
        }
      }
    }
    return false;
  }
```

Finding the Successor

This is where the traversal actually takes place and the order is determined:

```
  public static Node successor(Node node) {
    Node trial = node;
    if (trial.hasChildNodes()) {                    // DOM
      return trial.getFirstChild();                 // DOM
    }
```

```
    while (true) {                              // no children, back up
      Node parent = trial.getParentNode();    // DOM
      if (null == parent) {
        return trial;                          // no child, no parent, no place to go
      }
      if (trial.getNextSibling() != null) {
        return trial.getNextSibling();
      }
      trial = parent;
    }
  }
```

Note that as long as our 'current node' has children, we go down to the first child. This is called **depth-first traversal.** When there are no children, we try to find the next sibling by first finding the parent, then finding the current node's 'child index', then finding a child of the same parent with that index plus one. Many variations are possible; a very common one is to try the next sibling before trying a child; this is called **breadth-first traversal**.

resetNode()

This method is called when the user selects the reset option in the form. The result is simply not to search any further, return to the original node and set `matchCount` to 0.

```
public void resetNode() {
  node=original;
  matchCount=0;
}
```

Output Methods

This group consists of four methods: two versions of `write()` (with and without an argument), `writeNode()`, and `writeDate()`. To understand how they work, you should know that a `DomSearch` object has three variables (among others): the current node `node`, the stylesheet node `styleNode`, and a `Dom2Sax` object `out` that knows how to write a DOM node to an output character stream. In reading through the code below, remember that the variable `out` (not to be confused with `System.out`) is a `Dom2Sax` object. This object traverses a DOM subtree and uses an internal `Sax2Writer` to write out the contents of the subtree to a Java character stream.

`Dom2Sax` is constructed either in the `writeNode()` method (if it is a local application) or in the servlet (if it is a web application). It receives a `java.io.Writer` object at construction, either a `Writer` wrapped around `System.out`, or the writer that the servlet uses to send data back to the client:

```
public void write(java.io.Writer writer) throws Exception {
  setWriter(writer);
  write();
}

public void write() throws Exception {
  try {
    if (null == node) {
      throw new Exception("can't write null node in DomSearch");
    }
```

```
        writeNode(node);
      } catch (IOException ex) {
        lg.logIt("DomSearch.write ", ex);
      }
    }

    public void writeNode(Node node) throws Exception {
      if (null == out) {                              // local app, not servlet
        setWriter(new PrintWriter(System.out, true));// sets Dom2Sax
      }
      if (styleNode == null || node == original) {
        out.parse(node);       // output as if node were an XML file to be echoed
      } else {
        out.parseOpen();
        out.parseRec(styleNode);       // put styleNode out as part of document
        out.parseRec(node);
        out.parseClose();
      }

    public void writeData() throws Exception {
      out.parseRec(node);
    }
  }
```

As you can see, `write(Writer)` calls `write()` with no arguments; `write()` with no arguments calls `writeNode()`; and `writeNode()` calls the parsing methods of `Dom2Sax`. Those methods use the callback methods of SAX interfaces to write out the node(s) to an output stream. We will discuss those methods and the entire `Dom2Sax` class in the SAX section.

Constructor and Get/Set Methods

Finally, here is the rest of `DomSearch`:

```
    String outerTag, outerAttr, outerAVal, innerTag, innerCVal, domCmd,
          fileName;

    protected PropDict dict;
    protected Document original;
    protected Node styleNode;
    protected Node node;
    protected int matchCount = 0;
    protected Dom2Sax out;
    Logger lg;

    public DomSearch() {
      lg = new Logger();
    }

    public void setDict(PropDict defs) {
      dict = defs;
    }

    public PropDict getDict() {
      return dict;
    }
```

```java
public void setDef(String name, String val) {
  dict.setDef(name, val);
  updateFromDict();
}

public void setWriter(Writer writer) throws IOException {
  out = new Dom2Sax(writer);
}

public void setSaxOutput(Dom2Sax ds) {
  out = ds;
}

public Node getNode() {
  return node;
}

// initialize to sample values
public void initFromDict() {
  outerTag = dict.getDef("outerTag", "item");
  outerAttr = dict.getDef("outerAttr", "type");
  outerAVal = dict.getDef("outerAVal", "stamp");
  innerTag = dict.getDef("innerTag", "country");
  innerCVal = dict.getDef("innerCVal", "Italy");
  domCmd = dict.getDef("domCmd", "initFile");
  fileName = dict.getDef("fileName",
                    "stamps.xml");   // in default directory!
}
;

// allow override, but keep old values as defaults.
public void updateFromDict() {
  outerTag = dict.getDef("outerTag", outerTag);
  outerAttr = dict.getDef("outerAttr", outerAttr);
  outerAVal = dict.getDef("outerAVal", outerAVal);
  innerTag = dict.getDef("innerTag", innerTag);
  innerCVal = dict.getDef("innerCVal", innerCVal);
  domCmd = dict.getDef("domCmd", domCmd);
  fileName = dict.getDef("fileName", fileName);
}

public void initFromDict(PropDict d){
  setDict(d); initFromDict();
}
public void updateFromDict(PropDict d){
  setDict(d); updateFromDict();
}

public String doCommand(String cmd) {
  setDef("domCmd", cmd);
  updateFromDict();
  return doCommand();
}

// Other methods shown earlier
}
```

Let's move on and look in more detail at DOM. Many details of this overview will be needed in Dom2Sax, because it uses both DOM and SAX extensively.

DOM in Depth

The notion of the **Document Object Model**, or **DOM**, first became widely known with the release of 4th generation browsers, as part of Dynamic HTML. Within that context, DOM meant a set of naming conventions and APIs for working with objects in the web page. Its area of application was the web browser.

Although DOM was supposed to be language-independent and standard across browsers, in practice the two major browsers simply implemented their DOMs as they wanted them to be, in JavaScript and, in the case of Microsoft, also in VBScript. A more narrowly defined HTML DOM, without an event model, was codified by W3C as DOM Level 0 in late 1997. The IE 4 DOM is very close to that specification; the NC 4 DOM, released a few months earlier, is substantially different. In the future, both IE and NC are expected to be in compliance with the current and forthcoming levels of DOM.

DOM Level 1

The current DOM is Level 1, released in October 1998. Its coverage includes both XML (that is, all XML languages) and HTML 4.0. Since XML can be used for data interchange between applications anywhere, DOM is not just for browsers any more.

DOM Level 1 consists of two parts: Core DOM, and HTML DOM. Core DOM is further subdivided into Fundamental interfaces and Extended interfaces. All DOM-compliant processors, including XML parsers and HTML browsers, must implement the fundamental interfaces: they specify the structure and behavior of Document, Node, and other fundamental structural elements of any SGML/XML document. Extended interfaces specify those items that are never found in an HTML document but can be part of an XML document: DTD, Processing Instructions, Entities and Entity references, and so on. A compliant XML processor must implement Core DOM in its entirety. A compliant HTML processor must implement the Fundamental interfaces of the Core and the HTML DOM. In summary:

❑   DOM = Core + HTML

❑   Core = Fundamental + Extended

❑   For XML: all Core

❑   For HTML: Fundamental + HTML

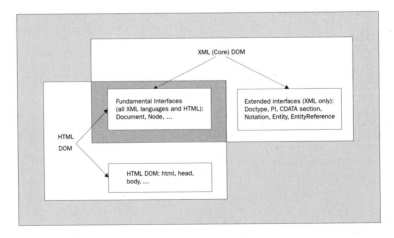

XML, DOM, and Language Bindings

Core DOM ultimately goes back to the XML specification. It is the first step from the specification to a computer program that can create or process documents that conform to the XML specification.

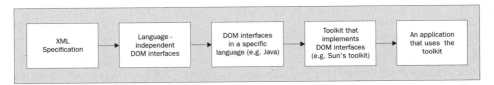

DOM specifies interfaces that are eventually implemented in some programming language. The interfaces imply an abstract data structure of a tree that consists of nodes. A DOM tree is not the same as a tree of document elements: for instance, it contains nodes for comments and processing instructions, and the text content of an element is wrapped in a separate text node that is a child of the element's node.

DOM does not specify data structures: it specifies objects, their containment relationships, and their collaborations (for example, an object may have a method that returns another object). This said, it is still useful to visualize the `Document` object as a tree consisting of nodes, where each node is itself a tree. Whether or not it is implemented as a tree or some other way is up to the program that builds the DOM structure; in our case, the `DocumentBuilder` object in the `javax.xml.parsers` package.

Node Types in DOM

Here's a complete list of node types in DOM (quoted from `http://www.w3.org/TR/REC-DOM-Level-1/level-one-core.html`). Twelve types of `Node` are recognized; they are listed below together with the sub-nodes they can contain:

Node type	Can contain
Document	Element (maximum of one), ProcessingInstruction, Comment, DocumentType
DocumentFragment	Element, ProcessingInstruction, Comment, Text, CDATASection, EntityReference
DocumentType	No children
EntityReference	Element, ProcessingInstruction, Comment, Text, CDATASection, EntityReference
Element	Element, Text, Comment, ProcessingInstruction, CDATASection, EntityReference
Attr	Text, EntityReference
ProcessingInstruction	No children
Comment	No children
Text	No children

Table continued on following page

Node type	Can contain
CDATASection	No children
Entity	Element, ProcessingInstruction, Comment, Text, CDATASection, EntityReference
Notation	No children

With the exception of DocumentFragment these are, of course, the familiar components of an XML document. Notice that the document type declaration, comments, CDATA sections, and parsed text all become nodes in the resulting tree.

Numeric Constants for Node Types

For programming needs, DOM associates each node type with an integer constant that has a symbolic name:

```
const unsigned short   ELEMENT_NODE                   = 1;
const unsigned short   ATTRIBUTE_NODE                 = 2;
const unsigned short   TEXT_NODE                      = 3;
const unsigned short   CDATA_SECTION_NODE             = 4;
const unsigned short   ENTITY_REFERENCE_NODE          = 5;
const unsigned short   ENTITY_NODE                    = 6;
const unsigned short   PROCESSING_INSTRUCTION_NODE    = 7;
const unsigned short   COMMENT_NODE                   = 8;
const unsigned short   DOCUMENT_NODE                  = 9;
const unsigned short   DOCUMENT_TYPE_NODE             = 10;
const unsigned short   DOCUMENT_FRAGMENT_NODE         = 11;
const unsigned short   NOTATION_NODE                  = 12;
```

In Java, as you saw, they come out as public static final short variables of the Node interface. You can obtain the value of that variable by getNodeType(). (See below on the Java binding.)

DOM Features Not in the XML 1.0 Specification

Since DOM is a step closer to processing than the XML specification, it includes several features that meet computational needs. They are:

- ❑ An exception, DOMException, which contains standard names and numerical codes for several common error conditions.

- ❑ A DOMImplementation interface, for providing information about the implementation, via the hasFeature() method. You can also find out the DOM version on which the implementation is based.

- ❑ NodeList and NamedNodeMap, two interfaces for dealing with collections of Nodes.

- ❑ DocumentFragment, a 'lightweight' interface that extends Node and represents a piece of the document that can be cut and pasted and otherwise moved around.

On Document Fragments

DocumentFragment nodes do not have to be well-formed XML documents. For example, a document fragment might have only one child that is a Text node. No XML production allows such a structure, but it may be quite useful in an application. A DocumentFragment may also contain several top nodes (in other words, form a forest of trees) that can be moved around together and inserted as siblings.

At the time of writing, DocumentFragment is a Working Draft, http://www.w3.org/TR/WD-xml-fragment. However, the Status section of the draft says:

> *"The XML Fragment Working Group, with this 1999 June 30 Working Draft considers its charter discharged. This is the XML Fragment WG's W3C Working Draft as revised to reflect comments received during Last Call review. This draft is technically ready to go to Proposed Recommendation, but the WG decided to hold at this stage to await some implementation experience and to allow possibly related work in other WGs to progress further before submitting this draft for PR."*

As with many other current W3C projects, the 'related work' that is holding back the Fragment recommendation certainly includes XML Schemas, intended as a replacement for DTDs. It would be useful to be able to validate a fragment, but DTD declarations, which do not follow XML syntax, are difficult to embed in a specific document or its fragment. The June 30 Working Draft prominently displays (in red italics) the Working Group's decision to stay away from inline inclusion of DTD declarations (Section 4, Fragment Context Information Set).

In practical terms, it is unlikely that you will see many Fragment Nodes for a while. To the best of our knowledge, the DOM interface DocumentFragment has not been implemented in any existing Java XML processors.

DOM Bindings

DOM is programming-language-independent. It is described in English in the main body of the Recommendation; however, in addition to English prose (translated into several other languages), it had to be specified in some formal notation. That notation is, in fact, yet another language, designed for specifying interfaces in a programming-language-independent way. That language is called, reasonably enough, the **Interface Definition Language** or **IDL**. There are several such languages in existence, including one that Microsoft uses to specify COM interfaces, and another one from Object Management Group (OMG) that is used to specify CORBA interfaces. W3C uses the OMG language but makes it clear that the choice does not imply any kind of taking sides in the COM-CORBA contest.

> *See Chapter 29 for more on IDL and CORBA.*

So, DOM interfaces are twice removed from the actual implementation. To get to an implementation, you first have to choose a programming language and translate DOM interfaces into the appropriate constructs of that language: abstract classes in C++, interfaces in Java, objects and properties in JavaScript, and so on. This process is called **language binding**: the language-independent interfaces of DOM are bound to constructs in a specific language. No actual code is written in the process, only declarations. In the second stage of implementation, the language-specific constructs, such as Java interfaces, are implemented in actual working code. That code is used in application programming.

To ensure that different DOM implementations in at least some languages are broadly compatible with each other, W3C itself provides the first stage of implementation – language binding – for two languages, Java and JavaScript (ECMA Script). We will spend most of the time looking at the Java binding, but one example of an interface definition in IDL is in order.

An Example of IDL and Java Bindings

The central concept of DOM is a **Node**. We think of it as a node in a tree, so that the entire tree is a node, and every node within it is a (sub)tree. The DOM recommendation defines a **Node interface** from which other, more specific interfaces are derived: for instance, Document and Element derive from Node. The Node interface itself is too big to serve as an example, but let's look at Document:

The Document Interface in IDL

```
interface Document : Node
{
    readonly attribute    DocumentType           doctype;
    readonly attribute    DOMImplementation       implementation;
    readonly attribute    Element                 documentElement;

    Element                       createElement(in DOMString tagName)
                                          raises(DOMException);
    DocumentFragment              createDocumentFragment();
    Text                          createTextNode(in DOMString data);
    Comment                       createComment(in DOMString data);
    CDATASection                  createCDATASection(in DOMString data)
                                          raises(DOMException);
    ProcessingInstruction         createProcessingInstruction(in DOMString target,
                                                      in DOMString data)
                                              raises(DOMException);
    Attr                          createAttribute(in DOMString name)
                                          raises(DOMException);
    EntityReference               createEntityReference(in DOMString name)
                                              raises(DOMException);
    NodeList                      getElementsByTagName(in DOMString tagname);
};
```

IDL uses the term 'attribute' where we would say 'variable' in Java or 'data member' in C++. As you can see, DOM specifies that a Document object must have three attributes. Most of this material goes back to the XML specification. For instance, the XML spec says that a document can have a DTD and a single element, and this is reflected in the attributes declared in the interface.

In addition to attributes, this interface declares a number of methods. With minor corrections for class names (DOMString becomes String), they are very similar to Java method declarations, as you will see in the Java binding below.

Java Binding for the Document Interface

DOM says absolutely nothing about the data types or data structures: DocumentType can be a string, an integer or an enumerated type; Element can be a tree, a hash table, or (in FORTRAN) an array. All these decisions are up to the implementer, and the Java binding provided by W3C, while making some choices, tries to leave most of them to the implementer also. For instance, the Java interface does not declare any variables to correspond to IDL attributes, but only declares access methods that return the appropriate objects. (This is the way it should be, really, because variables should be private, access methods public, and the programmer should program to public interfaces.)

```
package org.w3c.dom;

public interface Document extends Node {
```

```
    public DocumentType getDoctype();
    public DOMImplementation getImplementation();
    public Element getDocumentElement();
    public Element createElement(String tagName) throws DOMException;
    public DocumentFragment createDocumentFragment();
    public Text createTextNode(String data);
    public Comment createComment(String data);
    public CDATASection createCDATASection(String data);
    public ProcessingInstruction createProcessingInstruction(String target,
            String data) throws DOMException;
    public Attr createAttribute(String name) throws DOMException;
    public EntityReference createEntityReference(String name)
            throws DOMException;
    public NodeList getElementsByTagName(String tagname);
}
```

Note how an IDL's `attribute` corresponds to a `public getXX()` method, not to a specific data type. The `readonly` qualifier of IDL simply means that there is no corresponding `setXX()` method. Of the three `getXX()` methods, the first two don't do much.

The Structure of the Java Binding

DOM Core Java binding (Fundamental and Extended together) is only 210 lines of code, and makes an easy reading. It consists of one class and seventeen interfaces.

DOMException

The only class in the Java binding is `DOMException`. It extends `RuntimeException` and defines a number of public static codes for different error conditions. These are copied directly from IDL (where they are called `const unsigned short`):

```
    public static final short INDEX_SIZE_ERR                = 1;
    public static final short DOMSTRING_SIZE_ERR            = 2;
    public static final short HIERARCHY_REQUEST_ERR         = 3;
    public static final short WRONG_DOCUMENT_ERR            = 4;
    public static final short INVALID_CHARACTER_ERR         = 5;
    public static final short NO_DATA_ALLOWED_ERR           = 6;
    public static final short NO_MODIFICATION_ALLOWED_ERR   = 7;
    public static final short NOT_FOUND_ERR                 = 8;
    public static final short NOT_SUPPORTED_ERR             = 9;
    public static final short INUSE_ATTRIBUTE_ERR           = 10;
```

Java Binding Interfaces

Among the interfaces, four are top-level (`DOMImplementation`, `Node`, `NodeList`, and `NamedNodeMap`), and the remaining thirteen are sub-interfaces of `Node`. `Node` is by far the most important interface; it defines the methods (such as `getFirstChild()` or `insertBefore()`) that do most of the work in accessing and changing the components of a document.

The Node interface and its descendants arrange themselves into a tree as follows:

As we said above in the IDL section, IDL associates each node type with an integer constant, as for example:

```
const unsigned short ELEMENT_NODE = 1;
```

In Java, it comes out as:

```
public static final short ELEMENT_NODE = 1;
```

You have seen ELEMENT_NODE and PROCESSING_INSTRUCTION_NODE used in the code of this chapter.

CharacterData

CharacterData, which groups together Text and Comment nodes, is not given a separate node type. The reason text nodes, comments, and CDATA sections are grouped together is because they all need the same methods for access and editing:

```
public interface CharacterData extends Node {
    public String getData() throws DOMException;
    public void setData(String data) throws DOMException;
    public int getLength();
    public String substringData(int offset, int count) throws DOMException;
    public void appendData(String arg) throws DOMException;
    public void insertData(int offset, String arg) throws DOMException;
    public void deleteData(int offset, int count) throws DOMException;
    public void replaceData(int offset, int count,
                      String arg) throws DOMException;
}
```

These are the methods you would use if you decided to implement an XML editor.

NodeList and NamedNodeMap

`NodeList` defines an ordered sequence of nodes, indexed by integers, zero based. In order to work with such a sequence, you need to know its length, and you need to be able to access a node by its index in the sequence. Those are the two methods of the interface:

```
int getLength()        // Returns the value of the length property.
Node item(int index)   // Returns the indexth item in the map.
```

`NodeList` is read-only; `NamedNodeMap` is read/write. `NamedNodeMap` defines an associative array of 'named items' that can be accessed by name. There are three methods that can be used to get, set, and remove the named items:

```
Node getNamedItem(String name)     // Retrieves a node specified by name
Node removeNamedItem(String name)  // Removes a node specified by name
Node setNamedItem(Node arg)        // Add a node using its nodeName attribute
```

`NamedNodeMap` does not extend `NodeList`, and `NamedNodeMaps` are not maintained in any particular order. However, `NamedNodeMap` does have `getLength()` and `item()` methods, with the same signatures as in `NodeList`. This makes it possible to do a `for` loop on the elements of a `NamedNodeMap`:

```
public void echoAttributes(NamedNodeMap attrs,
                           Writer out) throws IOException {
  int N = attrs.getLength();
  for (int i = 0; i < N; i++) {
    echoNode(attrs.item(i), out);
  }
}
```

Attributes are frequently stored in a `NamedNodeMap` variable because the `Node` interface has a `getAttributes()` method that returns the node's attributes as a `NamedNodeMap`. You will see `NamedNodeMap` used this way in the `Dom2Sax` application.

DOMImplementation

This is a one-line interface that allows you to check availability of features in versions:

```
public interface DOMImplementation {
  public boolean hasFeature(String feature, String version);
}
```

This concludes our discussion of DOM. For further details, read the DOM Java binding, a mere 210 lines of code. It is, of course, available on the Web from the W3C at `http://www.w3.org`, and it is included, in javadoc format, in the Sun JAXP distribution.

A SAX Application

This chapter actually contains two applications that use SAX. The first application in this section, `Sax2Writer`, simply writes out a document to a specified character stream. The other application,

Dom2Sax, is a bit more intricate: it writes a DOM (sub)tree as a sequence of SAX events directed to an internal DocumentHandler. That DocumentHandler can be a Sax2Writer, in which case Dom2Sax in effect writes the contents of a DOM subtree to a character stream.

In either case, Dom2Sax uses a fair amount of DOM and a good deal of SAX.

SAX Reminders

As we mentioned in the overview earlier in the chapter, the main components of a SAX application are: a parser, an InputSource and a DocumentHandler. The parser has a parse() method that expects an InputSource or a URI argument. Calling this method, parser.parse(), results in a stream of events that are processed by the callback methods of the DocumentHandler. Instead of implementing the DocumentHandler interface directly, our SAX application class extends HandlerBase, a class in the SAX distribution that provides default implementations of DocumentHandler methods. You will see all this in action in a moment.

Sax2Writer

The code of Sax2Writer naturally falls into four groups:

❑ Imports, declarations, constructors, set methods

❑ parse() and newParser(); the parse() method calls parser.parse()

❑ Callback methods of DocumentHandler

❑ emit() and nl() methods for output

We'll go through them in order after we present the main() method so you can try it out.

The main() Method

Sax2Writer is typically used from inside applications but we have provided a main() method to try it out (and to test). The method takes one argument that specifies the source of XML data; you can also use it without any arguments, with XML data piped in, as indicated in the commentDocument interface:

```java
public static void main(String argv[]) throws Exception {
    if (argv.length > 1) {
        System.err.println("Usage: java Sax2Writer filename");
        System.err.println("   or: java Sax2Writer");
        System.err.println(" e.g., type MyXmlDoc.xml | java Sax2Writer");
        System.exit(1);
    }
    Sax2Writer s2W = new Sax2Writer();
    String valid = System.getProperty("javax.xml.parsers.validation",
                                      "false");
    s2W.setParser(newParser(valid));
    PrintWriter pW = new PrintWriter(System.out);
    s2W.setWriter(pW);
    if (argv.length == 1) {
        String uri = "file:" + new File(argv[0]).getAbsolutePath();
        s2W.parse(uri);
    } else {
        s2W.parse(new InputSource(System.in));
    }
}
```

Imports, Declarations, Constructors, Set Methods

This is how it starts:

```
import java.io.*;
import org.xml.sax.*;
import javax.xml.parsers.SAXParserFactory;     // JAXP abstract class
import javax.xml.parsers.SAXParser;            // JAXP abstract class

public class Sax2Writer extends HandlerBase {

  // echo an XML document to a Writer.
  private Writer out;
  private Parser parser;
  String lineEnd = "\n";
  Logger lg;

  public Sax2Writer() {
    lg = new Logger();
    lineEnd = System.getProperty("line.separator");
  }

  public Sax2Writer(Parser p, Writer outWriter) throws IOException {
    this();
    setParser(p);
    setWriter(outWriter);
  }

  public void setWriter(Writer w) {
    out = w;
  }

  public void setParser(Parser p) {
    parser = p;
    parser.setDocumentHandler(this);
  }
}
```

Nothing unexpected here. Notice how a SAX parser gets itself a `DocumentHandler`. Now it needs something to parse.

The parse() Method and newParser()

There are two versions: one takes a URI, the other an `InputSource`. (`InputSource` itself can be constructed from a URI, a byte stream (perhaps with encoding specified), or a character stream.) Both methods call `parser.parse()`:

```
public void parse(InputSource in) {
  try {
    parser.parse(in);
  } catch (Exception ex) {
    lg.logIt("Sax2Writer err: ", ex);
  }
}
```

```
public void parse(String uri) {
  try {
    parser.parse(uri);
  } catch (Exception ex) {
    lg.logIt("Sax2Writer err: ", ex);
  }
}
```

How do we get ourselves a parser? Using JAXP classes, of course:

```
public static Parser newParser(String validate) throws Exception {
  SAXParserFactory spf = SAXParserFactory.newInstance();
  if (validate.equalsIgnoreCase("true")) {
    spf.setValidating(true);
  }
  SAXParser sp = spf.newSAXParser();
  Parser parser = sp.getParser();
  return parser;
}
```

Now we have all we need to parse a document; time to decide what we want to do with it. In this case, we will simply echo its contents to the writer.

DocumentHandler Methods

Our DocumentHandler methods use the emit(), emitQuote() and nl() methods. (emit() and nl() are borrowed, with modifications, from Sun's Java XML tutorial, http://java.sun.com/xml, while emitQuote() is local to this chapter.) They are used as follows:

❑ emit() emits strings

❑ nl() emits a system-specific newline character or character sequence

❑ emitQuote() emits strings that may contain characters that need to be 'escaped', or sent to output as character entities or general entities:

```
public void startDocument() throws SAXException {
  emit("<?xml version='1.0' encoding='UTF-8'?>");
  nl();
}

public void endDocument() throws SAXException {
  nl();
}

public void startElement(String tag,
                          AttributeList attrs) throws SAXException {
  emit("<");
  emit(tag);
  if (attrs != null) {
    for (int i = 0; i < attrs.getLength(); i++) {
      emit(" ");
      emitQuote(attrs.getName(i));
```

```
            emit("=\"");
            emitQuote(attrs.getValue(i));
            emit("\"");
        }
    }
    emit(">");
}

public void endElement(String tag) throws SAXException {
    emit("</");
    emit(tag);
    emit(">");
    nl();
}

public void characters(char buf[], int offset,
                        int len) throws SAXException {
    emitQuote(buf, offset, len);
}

public void processingInstruction(String target,
                                  String data) throws SAXException {
    emit("<?");
    emit(target);
    emit(" ");
    emit(data);
    emit("?>");
    nl();
}
```

Output Methods

The only thing left is the technical detail of emit(), nl(), and emitQuote():

```
protected void emit(String s) throws SAXException {
    try {
        out.write(s);
    } catch (IOException e) {
        throw new SAXException("I/O error", e);
    }
}

protected void nl() throws SAXException {
    try {
        out.write(lineEnd);
        out.flush();
    } catch (IOException e) {
        throw new SAXException("I/O error", e);
    }
}
```

The emitQuote() method goes through a String or a character array and 'escapes' every character that needs to be escaped:

```
protected void emitQuote(String s) throws SAXException {
  for (int i = 0; i < s.length(); i++) {
    emitQuote(s.charAt(i));
  }
}

protected void emitQuote(char[] buf, int off,
                         int len) throws SAXException {
  int last = off + len - 1;
  for (int i = off; i <= last; i++) {
    emitQuote(buf[i]);
  }
}

protected void emitQuote(char c) throws SAXException {
  try {
    if (c == '&') {
      out.write("&amp;");
    } else if (c == '"') {
      out.write("&quot;");
    } else if (c == '<') {
      out.write("&lt;");
    } else if (c == '>') {
      out.write("&gt;");
    } else if (c == '\'') {
      out.write("&apos;");
    } else if (c < 127) {
      out.write(c);
    } else {    // use a character entity
      out.write("&#");
      out.write(Integer.toString(c));
      out.write(";");
    }
  } catch (IOException e) {
    throw new SAXException("I/O error", e);
  }
}
```

There is nothing conceptually difficult or profound about these, but you have to see them once. For reasons of efficiency, they should be used with buffered writers; note that our nl() calls flush(), and endDocument() calls nl().

You will see these output methods again in the Dom2Sax application that forms a part of DomSearch. Dom2Sax's structure is very similar to Sax2Writer, but it outputs the contents of a DOM node rather than the entire document. This creates interesting possibilities: you can use Dom2Sax to combine nodes coming from different documents into a single document. We will explore these possibilities in Chapter 14.

Dom2Sax

To recapitulate, Dom2Sax takes a DOM node and parses it into a sequence of SAX callbacks. The HandlerBase object that implements those callbacks is a Sax2Writer (recall that Sax2Writer extends HandlerBase), and so the result is that the DOM node is written out as an XML document to whatever Writer is used by the Sax2Writer object. As before, it can be a Writer wrapped around System.out, or a Writer that the servlet uses to send information back to the client.

We will again divide the code into sections. In outline, Dom2Sax consists of:

- Imports, declarations, and constructors
- Set methods
- Several top-level parse methods
- The recursive parse and its helpers (this is the core of the class)
- parseOpen() and parseClose()

Finally, we will discuss possible uses of Dom2Sax in a larger application.

Imports, Declarations, and Constructors

The imports this time include more of SAX, and so do the variables. The class itself implements the org.xml.sax.Parser interface with its parse() method:

```
import java.io.*;

import org.xml.sax.*;
import org.xml.sax.helpers.AttributeListImpl;
import org.w3c.dom.*;

public class Dom2Sax implements Parser {

  DocumentHandler documentHandler;
  DTDHandler dTDHandler;
  EntityResolver entityResolver;
  ErrorHandler errorHandler;
  java.util.Locale locale;

  Logger lg;

  Node topNode = null;    // root of subtree to be parsed;

  // settable by another program (via setNode())

  public Dom2Sax() {
    lg = new Logger();
  }

  public Dom2Sax(HandlerBase hB) {
    this();
    setHandlerBase(hB);
  }

  public Dom2Sax(Writer w) throws IOException {
    this();
    setHandlerBase(new Sax2Writer(this, w));
  }
```

As you can see, if the constructor is given a Writer as argument, it constructs a Sax2Writer object and uses it as the HandlerBase. Other kinds of HandlerBase are also possible.

Set Methods

There are set methods for all SAX variables of the class. Since `HandlerBase` implements four interfaces (`DocumentHandler`, `DTDHandler`, `EntityResolver`, and `ErrorHandler`), `setHandlerBase()` calls four other `setXXX()` methods:

```
public void setDocumentHandler(DocumentHandler h) {
  documentHandler = h;
}

public void setDTDHandler(DTDHandler h) {
  dTDHandler = h;
}

public void setEntityResolver(EntityResolver r) {
  entityResolver = r;
}

public void setErrorHandler(ErrorHandler h) {
  errorHandler = h;
}

public void setLocale(java.util.Locale locale) {
  this.locale = locale;
}

public void setHandlerBase(HandlerBase hB) {
  setDocumentHandler(hB);
  setDTDHandler(hB);
  setEntityResolver(hB);
  setErrorHandler(hB);
}

public void setNode(Node node) {
  topNode = node;
}
```

The `setLocale()` method is there in case you want to switch to another `Locale`. `setNode()` is useful when `Dom2Sax` is called into service by another program that expects it to use a URI or `InputSource` as input, and will insist on providing such, while we really want `Dom2Sax` to parse a DOM subtree starting at a given node that we provide. We do not encounter this situation in this chapter, but in Chapter 15 we want `Dom2Sax` output events to be fed into an XSLT processor, and then we have to use this feature. In general, a class that claims to be a parser has to be prepared to be called as a parser, with an `InputSource` or a URI as argument.

parse() Methods

As declared in the `Parser` interface, the `parse()` method can take an `InputSource` or a URI `String` as its argument. However, we don't want our `Dom2Sax` to work on entire documents, so we program the method to parse the subtree under `topNode` when given an `InputSource` or a `String`:

```
public void parse(InputSource source) throws IOException, SAXException {
  if (topNode != null) {
    parse(topNode);
```

```
    } else {
        throw new SAXException("Dom2Sax running without DOM tree");
    }
}

public void parse(java.lang.String fileName)
        throws IOException, SAXException {
    if (topNode != null) {
        parse(topNode);
    } else {
        throw new SAXException("Dom2Sax running without DOM tree");
    }
}
```

The only thing that Dom2Sax is willing to parse() is a Node (org.w3c.dom.Node):

```
public void parse(Node node) throws IOException, SAXException {
    parseOpen();      // calls documentHandler.startDocument()
    parseRec(node);
    parseClose();     // calls documentHandler.endDocument()
}
```

Since a Node is a tree, we need a recursive procedure to parse it. To make it look like a document, we surround the 'recursive parse' with startDocument() and endDocument(), called from parseOpen() and parseClose(), respectively. You saw an example of this in the very end of DomSearch; we repeat it here for convenience:

```
public void writeNode(Node node) throws Exception {
    if (null == out) {    // local app, not servlet
        setWriter(new PrintWriter(System.out, true));
    }
    if (styleNode == null || node == original) {
        out.parse(node);       output as if node were an XML file to be echoed
    } else {
        out.parseOpen();
        out.parseRec(styleNode);     // put styleNode out as part of document
        out.parseRec(node);
        out.parseClose();
    }
}
```

Recursive Parse and its Helpers

This is the most interesting part of the class, and the core of its functionality. This is also where you will see a good deal of DOM and SAX working together. We'll start with parseRec(), then proceed to its helpers, parseChildren() and toAttrList(). parseChildren() calls parseRec(), in a pattern of 'mutual recursion'; toAttrList() converts a DOM NamedNodeMap of attributes into a SAX AttributeListImpl object, which is a SAX way of representing attributes.

parseRec() is an if ... else statement, a dispatch on the node type. As you work through this code, note a consistent pattern: we extract information from a DOM node using DOM methods and give it to SAX methods to obtain SAX entities. Consider first one branch in isolation: if the node is an element node, we want to call startElement(). That method requires two arguments, the element's tag, and its attribute list as a NamedNodeMap. So we go like this:

```
    if (nodeType == Node.ELEMENT_NODE) {
        documentHandler.startElement(node.getNodeName(),
                                    toAttrList(node.getAttributes())));
        parseChildren(node);
        documentHandler.endElement(node.getNodeName());
    } else if ...
```

Here is the method in its entirety:

```
public void parseRec(Node node) throws IOException, SAXException {
    short nodeType = node.getNodeType();
    if (nodeType == Node.ELEMENT_NODE) {
        documentHandler.startElement(node.getNodeName(),
                                    toAttrList(node.getAttributes())));
        parseChildren(node);
        documentHandler.endElement(node.getNodeName());
    } else if (nodeType == Node.PROCESSING_INSTRUCTION_NODE) {
        ProcessingInstruction pi = (ProcessingInstruction) node;
        documentHandler.processingInstruction(pi.getTarget(), pi.getData());
    } else if (nodeType == Node.ATTRIBUTE_NODE) {

        // this shouldn't be here;
        // attributes are done within the element node
        throw new SAXException("trying to recursively write attribute node");
    } else if (nodeType == Node.TEXT_NODE) {
        char[] chars = node.getNodeValue().toCharArray();
        documentHandler.characters(chars, 0, chars.length);
    } else {    // this may have ELEMENT_NODE children; log it and pass on.
        lg.logIt("Dom2Sax does not yet handle node " + node.getNodeName()
                + " of type " + nodeType + " with value "
                + node.getNodeValue());
        parseChildren(node);
    }
}                       // end of parseRec()
```

Next we look at `parseChildren()`; it collects the current node's children in a `NodeList` and calls `parseRec()` on each one of them:

```
public void parseChildren(Node node) throws IOException, SAXException {
    NodeList children = node.getChildNodes();
    for (int i = 0; i < children.getLength(); i++) {
        parseRec(children.item(i));
    }
}
```

Finally, `toAttrList()` converts a `NamedNodeMap` into an `AttributeList`, which is a SAX interface implemented by `AttributeListImpl`, a class in `org.xml.sax.helpers`. On the DOM side, it uses `item(i)`, `getNodeName()`, and `getNodeValue()`; on the SAX side, it uses `addAttribute()`, which takes three arguments: the name, the type, and the value of the attribute to add:

```
public static AttributeList toAttrList(NamedNodeMap nnm) {
    if (null == nnm) {
        return null;
    }
```

```
    AttributeListImpl attrs = new AttributeListImpl();
    for (int i = 0; i < nnm.getLength(); i++) {
      Node node = nnm.item(i);
      attrs.addAttribute(node.getNodeName(), "CDATA", node.getNodeValue());
    }
    return attrs;
  }
```

The main() Method

As with the other applications in this chapter, Dom2Sax can be run locally, from the command line. We provide a driver that uses DomSearch to obtain a DOM Node and gives that node to a Dom2Sax for output:

```
public static void main(String argv[]) throws Exception {
  if (argv.length != 1) {
    System.out.println("usage: java Dom2Sax xmlFile");
    System.exit(1);
  }
  Dom2Sax dmW = new Dom2Sax(new PrintWriter(System.out));
  dmW.parse(DomSearch.readFile(argv[0]));
}
```

parseOpen() and parseClose()

Finally, we provide two public methods that call the startDocument() and endDocument() methods of Dom2Sax's DocumentHandler:

```
public void parseOpen() throws IOException, SAXException {
  documentHandler.startDocument();
}

public void parseClose() throws IOException, SAXException {
  documentHandler.endDocument();
}
}   // end of Dom2Sax class
```

Their intended use is to make it possible for other applications to bracket calls on parse(Node) with a call on startDocument() and a call on endDocument(). For instance, a method that outputs an XML document (or, indeed, a code fragment in a JSP page) might contain this sequence:

```
dom2W.setWriter(writer);
dom2W.parseOpen();
theJSPWriter.println("<!DOCTYPE myDocType [lots of stuff]>");
theJSPWriter.println(aStyleSheetLink);
dom2W.parseRec(aBean.gimmeADomNode(arga,argb,argc));
writer.println("<anEmptyElement attr=\"it doesn't have to be empty\" />");
dom2W.parseRec(bBean.gimmeAnotherDomNode(argb,argz,argq));
dom2W.parseClose();
```

We will give an example of how this tactic can be used in the Chapter 15.

SAX Parsing of Java Objects and SAX Filters

Before we conclude this chapter, we would like to give a more detailed discussion of an important idea introduced by Dom2Sax: 'parsing' of Java objects that are not XML character data and markup. After the discussion, we will illustrate the idea with an application that strings together earlier examples.

Here is a summary of our Dom2Sax class that brings out the concepts we want to discuss:

❑   Dom2Sax implements the Parser interface and owns a reference to an object that implements the DocumentHandler interface.

❑   Dom2Sax operates on a certain data structure (a DOM Node). It moves around the data structure and sends out SAX events **as if it encountered XML markup**. In fact, there is no markup, and there is no XML text, only a data structure.

❑   The events are processed by the DocumentHandler that is owned by Dom2Sax. In other words, the application is both the parser that generates the events and the DocumentHandler that has the callbacks.

This is, of course, different from the more traditional situation in which a parser (say, Apache's Xerces) is written to respond specifically to 'lexical' events such as the </ character sequence, and the DocumentHandler's callbacks process specifically those events.

Parsing Objects that are Not XML Text

The main intended use of a SAX parser is to parse XML text that contains markup. The text may come from a local file or a URL, or from several external sources; but, in any case, after all parsed entities are resolved, the input to the parser is a linear sequence of Unicode characters that is a mixture of character data and markup.

The parser contains a component called a 'lexical analyzer' that looks at those characters and says things like: "I have found a left bracket that is not followed by the slash character: this must be the beginning of a start tag; I am going to accumulate the characters up to the next whitespace into the current tag name", and so on. At the direction of its lexical analyzer, the parser calls its DocumentHandler's methods, such as startElement(). This is what Sun's SAX parser, and Xerces, and the parser inside Mozilla or IE 5 are doing when given an XML document to work on.

Dom2Sax implements Parser, and it owns a DocumentHandler. Just like real parsers that process XML text, it calls its DocumentHandler's methods, such as startElement(). However, there is no XML text and there is no lexical analyzer. In the case of Dom2Sax, this may be obscured by the fact that a DOM subtree has (most likely) resulted from parsing XML text. However, the technique is more general: we could 'parse' an integer array, for example. Here's a class, IntArrayParser, with a DocumentHandler variable and a parse() method:

```
import java.io.*;
import org.w3c.dom.*;
import org.xml.sax.*;
import org.xml.sax.helpers.AttributeListImpl;

class IntArrayParser implements Parser {
  int[] intArray = {
```

```
    1, 2, 3
  };
  DocumentHandler docHandler;
  char[] charData;
  int currentDataLength;
  AttributeListImpl attribs = new AttributeListImpl();   // empty attr. list

  // here we actually set up the data to be parsed;
  public void setIntArray(int[] newVal) {
    intArray = newVal;
  }


  // these are the required methods of Parser implementations
  public void parse(String uri) throws SAXException {
    parse();
  }
  public void parse(InputSource in) throws SAXException {
    parse();
  }
  public void setDocumentHandler(DocumentHandler handler) {
    docHandler = handler;
  }
  public void setDTDHandler(DTDHandler handler) {}
  public void setEntityResolver(EntityResolver resolver) {}
  public void setErrorHandler(ErrorHandler handler) {}
  public void setLocale(java.util.Locale locale) {}

  // end of required methods
  // this is the point of this example
  public void parse() throws SAXException {

    // parse an integer array intArray,
    // outputting each element of the array as an XML <num> element
    docHandler.startDocument();
    docHandler.startElement("numbers", attribs);

    // empty attr list, but we could populate it

    for (int i = 0; i < intArray.size; ++i) {
      docHandler.startElement("num", attribs);

      // place current array element as sequence of charcters
      // into charData; return the number of characters in the sequence
      charData = Integer.toString(intArray[i]).toCharArray();
      docHandler.characters(charData, 0, charData.length);
      docHandler.endElement("num");
    }   // end of for loop
    docHandler.endElement("numbers");
    docHandler.endDocument();
  }
```

```
    // An example of using this Parser, using a Sax2Writer object to
    // produce output
    public static void main(String argv[]) throws Exception {
      Sax2Writer s2W = new Sax2Writer();
      s2W.setParser(new IntArrayParser());
      PrintWriter pW = new PrintWriter(System.out);
      s2W.setWriter(pW);

      // IntArrayParser uses its own internal data rather than any document
      // we supply here:
      s2W.parse("");
    }
  }
```

This code produces the same stream of SAX events that a 'normal' parser would produce from parsing the following XML document:

```
<numbers>
  <num>1</num>
  <num>2</num>
  <num>3</num>
</numbers>
```

We can summarize by saying that we took a Java object (an array of integers) and linearized it as a sequence of SAX events, so the object can be processed as XML data. With an array of integers, it's just a pedagogical exercise, but consider doing the same thing to a `ResultSet` object returned by a database query. (We will do that in Chapter 15.) Running a SAX parser on an arbitrary data structure is a general and powerful technique; we will call it 'virtual parsing'. We finish this chapter with a complete worked example.

A Virtual Parsing Example

Our final example of this chapter, `CountSubElts`, brings together three earlier examples to illustrate the idea of virtual parsing. We will continue using DOM trees as objects that our parser will parse. As a source of DOM trees, we will use `DomSearch`: we'll have it parse a real bona fide XML file and return a DOM tree. However, we will not ask it to search for anything; instead, we will use its `successor()` method within a `while` loop to systematically produce each and every subtree of the initial DOM tree.

We will give each subtree to `Dom2Sax`, to get a stream of SAX events. However, we don't want to give that stream to a `Sax2Writer`; we want to give it to a different `DocumentHandler` that will do some computation on it. We happen to have one such lying around: `CountSax`, which we introduced at the beginning of this chapter and which counts the number of elements in a 'document' given to it. `CountSax`, of course, doesn't know or care whether that 'document' comes from a real file or a Java object. So, we will set the `DocumentHandler` of `Dom2Sax` to an instance of `CountSax`, and it will count the number of elements in each subtree of the initial DOM tree. The diagram below shows how the pieces are wired together:

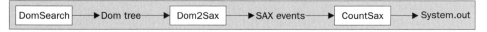

The wiring is done in the `CountSubElts` class, which can be run from the command line as follows:

```
java CountSubElts binary.xml
```

If `binary.xml` contains this data:

```
<a>
   <b>
      <c>C</c>
      <d>D</d>
   </b>
   <e>
      <f>F</f>
      <g>G</g>
   </e>
</a>
```

Then the output from the command above will be:

Here is the code of `CountSubElts`:

```java
import java.io.*;
import org.w3c.dom.*;
import org.xml.sax.*;

public class CountSubElts {

   // a variable for each component
   protected DomSearch domSearch;
   protected Dom2Sax dom2Sax;
   protected CountSax countSax;

   /* the constructor instantiates the components and wires them together */
   public CountSubElts() {
```

```
        domSearch =
          new DomSearch();          // obeys commands, reads files into DOM trees
        dom2Sax = new Dom2Sax();    // takes us from DOM to SAX
        domSearch.setSaxOutput(dom2Sax);          // connect DomSearch to Dom2Sax
        domSearch.initFromDict(new PropDict());   // start with defaults

        countSax = new CountSax();                // takes us from SAX to output
        dom2Sax.setHandlerBase(countSax);         // connect Dom2Sax to CountSax
    }

    // pass all commands and definitions into the start of the pipe:

    public String doCommand(String cmd) {
      return domSearch.doCommand(cmd);
    }

    public void setDef(String name, String val) {
        // calls setDef() of DomSeach that calls setDef() of its PropDict
        // We use it below to set fileName in DomSearch
        domSearch.setDef(name, val);
    }

    // "traverse" uses the successor method of DomSearch
    // to do a preorder examination of all subtrees of current node.
    // We call writeNode() on each, sending the subtree to Dom2Sax
    // which sends it to CountSax.
    public void traverse() throws Exception {
      Node startNode = domSearch.getNode();
      Node currentNode = domSearch.successor(startNode);
      while (startNode != currentNode) {
         System.out.print(currentNode.getNodeName() + " ");
         domSearch.writeNode(currentNode);
         currentNode = domSearch.successor(currentNode);
      }
    }

    public static void main(String[] argv) throws Exception {
      CountSubElts countSubElts = new CountSubElts();

      // set fileName in DomSearch
      countSubElts.setDef("fileName", argv[0]);

      // call doCommand() of DomSearch; the file gets parsed into DOM tree
      String err = countSubElts.doCommand("initFile");

      countSubElts.traverse();
    }
}
```

Extending the Chain: SAX Filters

We could extend the processing chain by giving CountSax another variable that is a DocumentHandler (or a HandlerBase). Instead of writing to System.out, CountSax would pretend to be a parser and send events to its DocumentHandler. The diagram illustrates this setup:

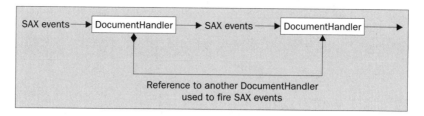

A class that is a `DocumentHandler` and owns a reference to another `DocumentHandler` is called a filter. The entire computational model is similar to Unix pipes of filters, except Unix filters work on a linear sequence of lines in a text file, while SAX filters work on tree-structured data.

The idea of filters was apparently first implemented by John Cowan, `http://www.ccil.org/~cowan/XML/`. It is incorporated in SAX2, which has an `XMLFilter` interface and a class that implements it, `XMLFilterImpl`.

The code download for this chapter contains a fully-worked example implementing the filter idea.

Summary

In this chapter, you have seen several examples of applications that use XML data. To remind you of the general picture, all such applications use an XML parser that sits between an XML data source and the application that wants to use it:

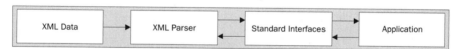

Every aspect of instantiating and using an XML parser is highly predictable. The way the parser behaves with respect to an XML document is specified in the XML 1.0 Recommendation. A general way of obtaining an instance of a parser and calling its `parse()` method is specified in Sun's JAXP. Most importantly, the interfaces that become available to the application after the document is parsed are described in the DOM and SAX specifications. The parser makes the XML data available to the application in one of two standard ways: as a tree structure of nodes, or as a stream of events with standard event-handler signatures.

We have covered SAX, DOM, and JAXP and given several examples of their use. Although basic in their size and content, the three major classes developed in this chapter – `DomSearch`, `Sax2Writer`, and `Dom2Sax` – work together to produce an application of reasonable scope. Moreover, each one of them, especially `Dom2Sax`, can be reused as self-standing modules in other applications. The reason they are easy to reuse is that they expect inputs in standard generic formats (an XML document or a DOM node), and they produce outputs in standard generic formats (an XML document traveling down a character stream).

One consequence of this generality is that all three classes can be used either locally, from the command line, or in a distributed application, controlled by a servlet. We have also presented a `PropDict` class that makes such dual-capacity applications easy to write, and a `Logger` class that facilitates logging (and therefore debugging) of both local and distributed applications. In Chapter 15 we will further investigate the possibilities resulting from this modular design.

The next chapter will start our examination of the Java technologies for dynamic web content generation, with an introduction to the Java Servlet API and web containers.

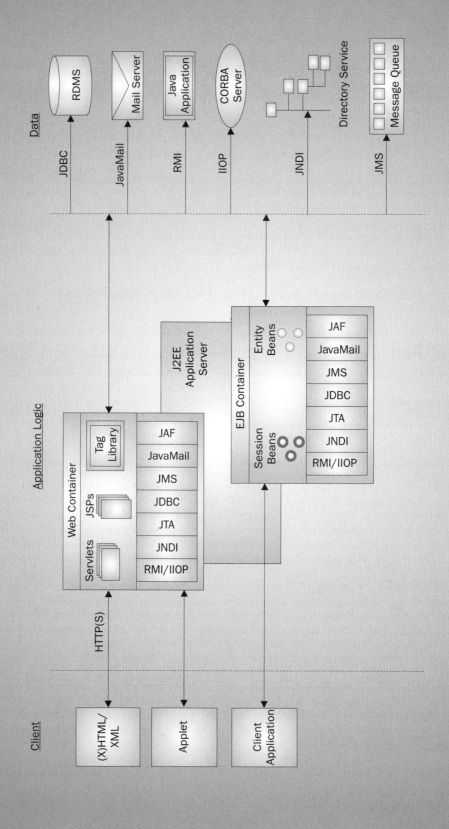

7

Introduction to Web Containers

As we've discussed in Chapter 1, in the J2EE architecture, there are essentially two types of clients – **web clients**, and **application clients**. Before discussing what constitutes web clients, let's look at application clients first.

Application clients date to the client-server era. In traditional client-server architecture, application clients drive the user interaction (typically via a GUI) as well as the bulk of application logic (including database access). For this reason, application clients are called as "fat" clients. With fat clients, users' desktop computers process the application logic. However, in a multi-tier architecture, application clients can delegate part of the application logic and database access to middle-tier components (such as Enterprise JavaBeans). Despite this scope for distribution of application logic to middle-tier components, application clients remain fat and require installation on each user's desktop.

With the advent of the Internet, web clients have been replacing traditional stand-alone application clients. The main driver behind this change is the nature of web clients. In web-client based architectures, the user-interaction layer is separated from the traditional client layer. Web browsers or similar "general-purpose" applications manage the user interaction, leaving the rest of the responsibilities of the client layer to applications on the web server side. Such responsibilities include logic for driving the user interface, interaction with components in the middle-tier, and databases. In this architecture, for an end user, the browser is the client for all web-based applications. Since such a "general-purpose" client does not impose any special requirements (apart from network access) on the client-desktop, web clients are also called "thin" clients.

The following features characterize web clients:

❑   A browser or a similar application to manage user interaction. For an end-user, this is the client-layer.

❑ HTML (with JavaScript and/or DHTML), XHTML or XML (with XSL) as the means of user interface definition.

❑ HTTP/HTTPS as the information exchange protocol between the web clients and web applications. The web application programs on the web server side execute the application logic on behalf of browser clients.

The J2EE architecture offers a feature-rich and flexible programming model for building dynamic web applications. As discussed in Chapter 1, the J2EE architecture provides **web containers**, the Java Servlet API, and the JavaServer Pages API for building and managing web applications. While the web container provides the basic runtime environment and a framework for providing runtime support for web applications, the Java servlet and JSP technologies form the core material for developing web applications.

This chapter introduces you to J2EE web containers in three distinct steps:

❑ In the first step you will see the basic anatomy of a web container. Starting from a brief introduction to HTTP, the emphasis is on introducing the concepts of web containers, Java servlets, and JSP pages. You'll continue to learn more about these topics in the subsequent chapters.

❑ The second step walks you through a simple, but complete web application. The emphasis in this step is on the various phases in the life cycle of a web application development.

❑ The third step discusses in detail the inner working of the above web application.

The primary goal of these steps is to discuss the basics of web application development.

The HTTP Protocol

In distributed application development, the application-level or wire-level communication protocol determines the nature of clients and servers. This is true in the case of web-based applications as well. The complexity of features possible in your web browser and on the web server (say, the on-line store you frequent) depends on the underlying protocol – that is, the **Hypertext Transfer Protocol (HTTP)**.

> **HTTP is an application-level protocol (generally implemented over TCP/IP connections). The HTTP is a stateless protocol based on requests and responses. In this paradigm, client applications (such as your web browser) send requests to the servers (such as the web server of an online store) to receive information (such as downloading a catalog), or to initiate specific processing on the server (such as placing an order).**

If you're new to HTTP, refer to Appendix C for the basic details of the HTTP.

HTTP Request Methods

As an application level protocol, HTTP defines certain types of requests that clients can send to servers. The protocol also specifies how the requests and responses be structured.

HTTP/1.0 specifies three types of request methods: **GET**, **POST**, and **HEAD**. HTTP/1.1 has five additional request methods: **OPTIONS**, **PUT**, **TRACE**, **DELETE**, and **CONNECT**. Of these, the GET and POST requests meet most of the common application development needs.

The GET Request Method

Of all the types of requests, the GET request is the simplest and most frequently used request method for accessing static resources such as HTML documents, images etc. GET requests can also be used to retrieve dynamic information, by using additional query parameters in the request URL. For instance, you can send a parameter name=joe appended to a URL as http://www.domain.com?name=joe. The web server can use this parameter name=joe, to send content specific to "joe."

The POST Request Method

The POST method is commonly used for accessing dynamic resources. Typically, POST requests are meant to transmit information that is request dependent, and are used when you need to send large amounts of complex information to the server. The POST request allows the encapsulation of multi-part messages into the request body. For example, you can use POST requests to upload text or binary files. Similarly, you can use POST requests in your applets to send serializable Java objects, or even raw bytes to the web server. POST requests therefore offer a wider choice in terms of the contents of a request.

There are certain differences between GET and POST requests. With GET requests, the request parameters are transmitted as a query string appended to the request URL. In the case of POST requests, the request parameters are transmitted within the body of the request. This has two ramifications. Firstly, since a GET request contains the complete request information appended to the URL itself, it allows browsers to bookmark the page and revisit later. Depending on the type and how sensitive the request parameters are, this may or may not be desirable. Secondly, some servers might pose restrictions on the length of request URL. This limits the amount of information that can be appended to the request URL. Note that HTTP/1.1 does not impose any upper limit on the length. However, servers/clients complying only to HTTP/1.0 may not support unreasonably long lengths.

Of these three methods, GET and HEAD method requests are expected (as a matter of convention) to be **idempotent** – that is, they should not be programmed to modify the information on the server. An idempotent request is one that can safely be reapplied without changing the any data on the server side. Such requests are meant for pure information retrieval.

Along with the type of the request, the client application also specifies the resource that it needs as part of the request header. For example, when you type http://java.sun.com/index.html in the location/address bar of your browser, the browser sends a GET request to the web server identified by java.sun.com for the resource index.html. In the HTTP lexicon, a **URI** (**Universal Resource Identifier**) specifies a resource. The URI is the part of the URL excluding the domain name. In our example, the resource is the index.html file located on the document root of the web server serving the java.sun.com domain.

HTTP Response

In response to a HTTP request, the server responds with the status of the response, and some meta-information describing the response. All these are part of the response header. Except for the case of the HEAD request, the server also sends the body content that corresponds to the resource specified in the request. In the http://java.sun.com/index.html URL, your browser receives the content of the `index.html` file as part of the message, and renders it. The body content is typically what you'll be interested in. But never forget that the content header fields in the response contain useful information that you may want to check in certain conditions. Some of the header fields include: `"Date"`, `"Content-Type"`, `"Expires"`, etc. For example, the header field `"Expires"` of a page can be set to a date equal to the same date set in the `"Date"` header field to indicate that browsers should not cache the page. When you're developing web applications with sensitive content, you may want to set such fields. We will see some examples of this later in the book.

In HTTP, servers and clients use **MIME (Multi-Purpose Internet Mail Extensions)** to indicate the type of content in requests and responses. Examples of MIME types are `text/html`, `image/gif`, etc. Here, the first part of the header indicates the type of data (such as, text and image), while the second part indicates the standard extension (such as `html` for text, and `gif` for image). MIME is an extension of the e-mail protocol to allow exchange of different kinds of data files over the Internet. HTTP servers (web servers) use MIME headers at the beginning of each transmission. Browsers use this information to decide how to parse or render the response. Browsers also use MIME headers while transmitting data in the body of requests, to describe the type of data being sent. For example, the default MIME type encoding for POST requests is `application/x-www-form-urlencoded`.

Before we conclude this section, let's look at the key features of HTTP:

❑ HTTP is a very simple and lightweight protocol.

❑ In this protocol, the clients always initiate requests. The server can never make a callback connection to the client.

❑ The HTTP requires the clients to establish connections prior to each request, and the servers to close the connection after sending the response. This guarantees that the client cannot hold on to a connection even after receiving the request. Also note that either the client or the server can prematurely terminate a connection.

For more information on HTTP and related aspects, refer to Appendix C.

HTTP was originally meant for serving static information. We need to consider certain additional issues in order to be able to build dynamic applications that communicate over HTTP with clients. In this chapter, we'll see how to address some of the basic issues using J2EE web containers.

Web Containers and Web Applications

Web applications are server-side applications. For any server-side application development, the following are the most essential requirements:

❑ A programming model and an API: For the development of applications.

❑ Server-side runtime support: This includes support for applicable network services, and a runtime for executing the applications.

❑ Deployment support: Deployment is the process of installing the application on the server. Deployment could also include customizing the application.

For building and running web applications, the J2EE specification provides the following to meet each of the above requirements:

- **Java Servlets and JavaServer Pages**
  Java servlets and JavaServer Pages are the building blocks for developing web applications in J2EE. In the J2EE lexicon, Java servlets and JSP pages are called the **web components**.

- **Web Applications**
  A web application is a collection of Java servlets, JavaServer Pages (JSP pages), other helper classes and class libraries, static resources such as HTML, XHTML, or XML documents, images, etc.

- **A Web Container for Hosting Web Applications**
  The web container is essentially a Java runtime providing an implementation of the Java Servlet API, and other facilities for JSP pages. The web container is responsible for initializing, invoking, and managing the life cycle of Java servlets and JavaServer Pages.

- **Packaging Structure and Deployment Descriptor**
  The J2EE specification defines a packaging structure for web applications. The specification also defines a deployment descriptor for each web application. The deployment descriptor is an XML file that lets you customize the web application at deployment time.

The diagram below shows the J2EE web container with two web applications deployed on the same container:

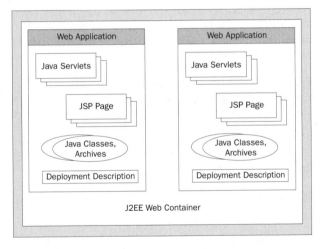

In this section, I'll discuss some of the basic features of servlets, JSP pages, and deployment descriptors. The purpose of this discussion is to give you an overview of what is involved in web application development. In the subsequent chapters, you'll learn more details.

Java Servlets

Java servlets allow application logic to be embedded in the HTTP request-response process. Java servlets are specified in the Java Servlet API Specification 2.2 available at http://java.sun.com/products/servlet.

To better understand the role of application logic in the request-response process, consider a web-based mail server. When you log in to your favorite web-based mail server, the server should be able to send a page with links to your mail, your mail folders, your address book, etc. This information is dynamic, in the sense that each user expects to see their own mailbox. To generate such content, the server must execute complex application logic to retrieve your mail and compose a page.

While clients can send client-specific or context information in the requests to the server, how can the server decide how the content should be generated? HTTP does not define a standard means for embedding application logic during the response generation phase. There is no programming model specified for such tasks. HTTP defines how clients can request information, and how servers can respond. HTTP is not concerned with how the response could be generated.

This is where server-side technologies such as Java servlets and JavaServer Pages come into the picture. With these technologies you can *embed* custom application logic during one or more stages of the request processing and response generation.

> **Java servlets are small, platform independent server-side programs that programmatically extend the functionality of the web server. The Java Servlet API provides a simple framework for building applications on such web servers.**

Java servlets are not user-invokable applications. Instead, the web container in which the web application containing the servlets is deployed invokes the servlets. When a servlet has been invoked, the web container exchanges the incoming request information with the servlet, such that the servlet can analyze the incoming request, and generate responses dynamically. The web container in turn interfaces with the web server by accepting requests for servlets, and transmitting responses back to the web server.

When compared to CGI, and proprietary server extensions such as NSAPI or ISAPI, the servlet framework provides a better abstraction of the HTTP request-response paradigm by specifying a programming API for encapsulating requests, responses, sessions, etc. In addition, servlets have all the advantages of the Java programming language, including platform independence. Java servlet-based applications can be deployed on any web server with built-in (in-process) or connector-based (out-of-process) web containers, irrespective of the operating system and the hardware platform. The various types of possible web container configurations are discussed later in this section.

In order to better understand how a servlet interacts with a web server via a web container, consider the basic invocation process with the web server receiving an HTTP request.

As you've seen in the previous section, the HTTP protocol is based on a request-response paradigm. In this paradigm, a browser (or client) connects to a web server and sends an HTTP request over the connection. Based on the request URL, the following sequence of events happens. Note that this sequence is not "all inclusive", but only demonstrates a typical sequence.

This sequence is illustrated below. In this figure, the rightward arrows indicate requests, while leftward arrows indicate responses:

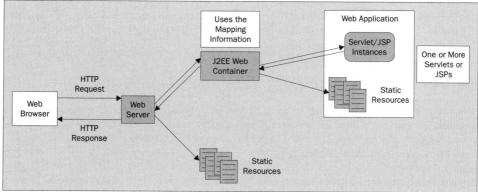

❑ Firstly, the web server has to figure out if the incoming request corresponds to a web application in the web container. This requires an implicit understanding between the web server and the web container. Web containers use the notion of a **servlet context** to identify web applications. You can specify the context when you're deploying the application onto the container.

❑ Once the application figures out that the web container should handle the request, the web server delegates the request to the web container. You can think of this process as the web server invoking a local/remote method on the web container, with the request information.

❑ Once the web container receives the request, it should decide which application should handle this request. In a J2EE web application, an HTTP request can be mapped to a servlet, or a JSP page, or any static resource based on URL patterns. Static resources include HTML/XML pages, images, applet class/JAR files, etc. Note that all these are part of the web application. When you package and deploy a web application, you also specify this mapping information. The web container uses this mapping information to map each incoming request to a servlet, a JSP, or a static resource. If the resource is mapped to a static resource, all that the web container has to do is to pass that resource as is to the web server, and this forms the body of the response that the web server sends to the browser.

❑ However, if the web container determines, based on the mapping information, that the request should be handled by a servlet, the container creates or locates a servlet instance, and delegates the request. In later chapters, we'll see how the web container creates or locates a servlet instance, and what factors govern this process.

❑ When the container delegates the request to a servlet, the container also passes objects encapsulating the HTTP request and HTTP response to the servlet instance. For a servlet instance, these objects represent the request and response streams from the browser. The servlet can read the request information, and write response to these streams. For writing response, the servlet can use the `java.io.PrintWriter` object associated with the response, and write content (using `println` methods) to the response. This is equivalent to writing content to the already opened connection from the web browser.

In order to build and deploy a servlet based application, there are two steps that you'll be required to do:

❑ Write the servlet with the required application logic. This is the development phase.

❑ Provide a context and optional URL pattern mapping information during the deployment phase. This mapping information is used in identifying the appropriate servlet from a web application to handle the request.

JavaServer Pages

Dynamic content generation can be achieved in two ways: programmatic content generation, or template-based content generation. While Java servlets fall into the first category, **JavaServer Pages (JSP)** belong to the second category. JSP pages are specified in the JavaServer Pages 1.1 Specification, available at `http://java.sun.com/products/jsp`.

JavaServer Pages technology is an extension of the Java servlet technology. However, unlike servlets, which are pure Java programs, JSP pages are text-based documents. A JSP page contains two parts:

❑ HTML or XML for the static content

❑ JSP tags and scriptlets written in the Java programming language to encapsulate the logic that generates the dynamic content

Since a JSP page provides a general representation of content that can produce multiple views depending on the results of JSP tags and scriptlets, a JSP page acts like a template for producing content.

A template is basically an HTML/XHTML/XML page with special placeholders (JSP tags and scriptlets) embedded. These placeholders contain special processing information for the underlying template processor (or content generator). In a JSP page, the usual XML/HTML/XHTML tags allow you to define the static structure and content of a page. The additional JSP tags and scriptlets embedded in the page let you include programming logic to be executed during page generation.

The key advantage of this technology is that it enables you to keep the content design and development activities loosely coupled with the design and development of the application logic. If, .on the contrary, you choose to develop the content purely with Java servlets, the above two activities will be coupled strongly. This is undesirable because such lumped applications are not easy to maintain.

In template-driven technologies such as Active Server Pages (ASP), the templates are evaluated at run-time. That is, the template processor dynamically converts the special tags into normal content. This is a run-time process, and every time the page is requested, the template processor interprets the template again and again.

Unlike the above, the JSP technology is based on page-compilation. Instead of interpreting the JSP page, the web container converts it into a servlet class, and compiles it. This process typically happens when the web container invokes a JSP page for the first time in response to a request or at container startup. Web containers also allow you to precompile JSPs into servlets. Most of the containers available today repeat this process whenever the page is modified. This is called the page translation phase. The container invokes the generated/compiled servlet for subsequent requests to the JSP. This is the request-processing phase as indicated in the figure:

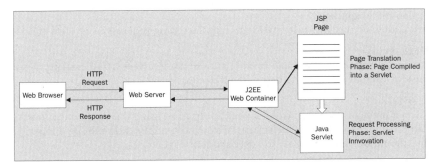

In this figure, the unfilled arrow represents the page compilation process. Once the JSP page is compiled into a servlet, the rest of the request processing and response generation is the same as described in the previous section.

The above architecture leads to very useful and flexible applications using JSPs and servlets:

❑   You can use servlets alone for application logic and content generation.

❑   You can also use JSP pages alone for application logic and content generation.

❑   You can combine these with application logic handled by the servlet, and content generation handled by JSP pages.

Deployment Descriptors

Deployment descriptors are an important part of J2EE web applications. Deployment descriptors help in managing the deployment configuration of web applications. For web containers, the deployment descriptor is an XML file called web.xml stored in the /WEB-INF directory of the web application. The Java Servlets specification specifies a document type definition (DTD) for the deployment descriptor. This is available at http://java.sun.com/j2ee/dtds/web-app_2_2.dtd.

If you've not already done so, refer to Chapter 5 for more discussion on XML and DTD.

A deployment descriptor has several purposes:

❑   **Initialization of parameters for servlets and web applications**
This allows you to minimize the amount of hard coding of initialization values within your web applications. For example, if your servlet requires access to a database, the best place to specify the server details including the login and password is the deployment descriptor. This allows you to configure your applications without having to recompile the servlets.

❑   **Servlet/JSP Definitions**
Each servlet/precompiled JSP used in your web application should be defined in the deployment descriptor. This entry includes the name of the servlet or JSP, class of the servlet or JSP, and an optional description.

❑ **Servlet/JSP Mappings**
Web containers use this information to map incoming requests to servlets and JSPs.

❑ **MIME Types**
Since each web application can contain several content types, you can specify the MIME types for each of these in the deployment descriptor.

❑ **Security**
You can manage access control for your application using the deployment descriptor. For example, you can specify which pages of your web application require a login, what the login page should be, and what role the user should have, etc.

Other customizable elements include welcome pages, error pages, session configuration, etc. You'll learn more about this in Chapter 10.

Structure of Web Applications

A web application has four parts:

❑ A public directory

❑ A WEB-INF/web.xml file

❑ A WEB-INF/classes directory

❑ A WEB-INF/lib directory

The public area is the root of the application, excluding the WEB-INF directory. If you're familiar with web servers such as Apache, this is equivalent to the htdocs directory where you would keep all your HTML files. The web container can serve any of the files under the public area.

The WEB-INF directory is a private area. The container will not serve contents of this directory to users. The files in this are meant for container use. The contents include the deployment descriptor (web.xml file), a classes directory, and a lib directory. The classes directory is meant for all compiled classes of your servlets and other utility classes. If your application has packaged JAR files (for example, a third-party API packaged as a JAR file), you can copy such JAR files into the lib directory. The web container uses these two directories to locate servlet and other dependent classes.

Types of Web Containers

Before we go into the details of web containers, it is worth noting something about the nature of web containers here. There are essentially three ways you could configure web containers. From Chapter 1, recall that a web container can either implement the underlying HTTP services, or delegate such services to external web servers:

❑ **Web container in a J2EE application server**:
Most of the commercial J2EE application servers such as WebLogic, Inprise Application Server, iPlanet Application Server, WebSphere Application Server, etc. now include web containers built in.

❑ **Web containers built into web servers**:
This is the case with pure Java web servers such as Sun's Java WebServer that contains integrated web containers. Jakarta TomCat (from `http://jakarta.apache.org`), which is the web container reference implementation, also falls into this category. TomCat includes a web server along with a web container.

❑ **Web container in a separate runtime**:
In the non-J2EE world, this is the most common scenario. Web servers such as Apache, or Microsoft IIS require a separate Java runtime to actually run servlets, and a web server plug-in to integrate the Java runtime with the web server. The plug-in handles communication between the web server and the web container. Commercially available servlet/JSP engines such as JRun from Allaire, and ServletExec from New Atlanta (now part of Unify's eWave product family) also provide plug-ins to integrate with web servers. Note that these two servlet engines are now part of J2EE application servers. TomCat can also be configured to work in this manner with Apache web server, Microsoft's IIS, and the Netscape Enterprise Server. On the other hand, Sun's iPlanet web server (formerly the Netscape Enterprise Server) also bundles servlet/JSP engines as a separate runtime.

The choice of one of these depends entirely on the requirements of your application. For instance, if you were only interested in building a new Java-based web application, you would possibly choose the second or the third configuration. However, the first configuration is becoming increasingly common with the unification of web and enterprise computing standards via the J2EE.

Your First Web Application

Having seen the broad description of the J2EE web container architecture, and web applications, let's start with our first web application.

While it is customary to start with a "Hello World" application, let's slightly change the approach, so that I can walk you through at least some of the basic aspects of developing web applications with J2EE.

Our web application has two objectives:

❑ Prompt the user for a name and an e-mail address

❑ Print a welcome greeting based on the time of the day

Although various combinations of servlets and JSP pages can be used for developing this application, let's consider an architecture involving the following:

❑ An HTML page with a form to collect the name and e-mail address of the user

❑ A servlet to process the request and generate HTML to display a greeting message

❑ A deployment descriptor

While initially you might find this list complex, once you complete this exercise, you will realize how simple and intuitive the process is.

Prepare the Web Container

This exercise requires a web container (formerly called as servlet/JSP engine) complying with the Java Servlet Specification 2.2, and JSP 1.1. There are several commercial products available in the market, and you might want to use one of those. However, in this chapter, I recommend that you use Tomcat from `http://jakarta.apache.org`. This is a reference implementation of the Java Servlets and JSP pages. (`http://jakarta.apache.org`).

For the example in this chapter, I assume that you're using Tomcat under a Windows platform. In this example, `%TOMCAT_HOME%` refers to the directory where you installed Tomcat. For instance, on my desktop, `%TOMCAT_HOME%` is `c:\opt\jakarta-tomcat`. If you're on a Unix platform, your `$TOMCAT_HOME` might be `/opt/jakarta-tomcat`.

TomCat requires JDK 1.1 or later. Once you install Tomcat, run the examples provided with the server to make sure that your setup is correct.

Create the HTML File

Create an HTML file with the following content, and save it as `%TOMCAT_HOME%\webapps\greeting\index.html`. Note the content for the `<FORM>` tag. This tag has a `POST` request for a form collecting "name" and "email":

```
<HTML>
  <HEAD>
    <TITLE>ProJava Registration</TITLE>
  </HEAD>
  <BODY>

    <H1>Welcome</H1>

    <FORM ACTION="/greeting/servlet/GreetingServlet" METHOD="POST">
      <P>Your Name <INPUT TYPE="text" SIZE="40" NAME="name"></P>
      <P>Your Email <INPUT TYPE="text" SIZE="40" NAME="email">
      <INPUT TYPE="submit" VALUE="Submit"></P>
    </FORM>
  </BODY>
</HTML>
```

Create a Servlet

The next step is to create a servlet. This servlet processes the HTTP `POST` request from the `index.html` file that you created previously.

Create a Java class called `GreetingServlet` in `GreetingServlet.java` under `%TOMCAT_HOME%\webapps\greeting\src`. Here is the complete source code:

```
// Import Servlet packages
import javax.servlet.*;
import javax.servlet.http.*;
```

```java
// Import other Java packages
import java.io.*;
import java.util.*;

public class GreetingServlet extends HttpServlet {

  protected void doPost(HttpServletRequest request,
                        HttpServletResponse response) throws ServletException,
                        IOException {

    // Get parameters from the request.
    String name = request.getParameter("name");
    String email = request.getParameter("email");

    // Compute a greeting message
    String message = null;
    GregorianCalendar calendar = new GregorianCalendar();
    if(calendar.get(Calendar.AM_PM) == Calendar.AM) {
        message = "Good Morning";
    }
    else {
        message = "Good Afternoon";
    }

    // Set MIME type for the response
    response.setContentType("text/html");

    // Obtain a print writer object
    PrintWriter out = response.getWriter();

    // Write the content
    out.println("<HTML>");
    out.println("<BODY>");
    out.println("<P>" + message + ", " + name + "</P>");

    out.println("<P>  Thanks for registering your email (" + email +
                ") with us.</P>");
    out.println("<P> - The Pro Java Team. </P>");

    out.println("</BODY>");
    out.println("</HTML>");

    out.close();
  }
}
```

Don't worry too much about what the code is doing at this point, as we'll be looking at how to code servlets in great detail over the next few chapters. For now we're just trying to get you up and running.

Compile the Source

To be able to compile the servlet, you should have `%TOMCAT_HOME%\lib\servlet.jar` in your CLASSPATH. Also create a `WEB-INF` subdirectory under `%TOMCAT_HOME\webapps\greeting` and a `classes` subdirectory under `%TOMCAT_HOME\webapps\greeting\WEB-INF`.

Issue the following command to compile the servlet from the source directory (`%TOMCAT_HOME%\webapps\greeting\src`):

```
javac -d ..\WEB-INF\classes\ *.java
```

This command compiles the Java classes, and creates the class files under the `%TOMCAT_HOME%\webapps\greeting\WEB-INF\classes` directory.

Write the Deployment Descriptor

The last step is to write a deployment descriptor. Create the file `web.xml` in the `%TOMCAT_HOME%\webapps\greeting\WEB-INF\` directory and copy the following code into it:

```
<?xml version="1.0" encoding="ISO-8859-1"?>
<!DOCTYPE web-app
    PUBLIC "-//Sun Microsystems, Inc.//DTD Web Application 2.2//EN"
    "http://java.sun.com/j2ee/dtds/web-app_2.2.dtd">

<web-app>
  <servlet>
    <!-- Servlet alias -->
    <servlet-name>Registration</servlet-name>

    <!-- Fully qualified Servlet class -->
    <servlet-class>GreetingServlet</servlet-class>
  </servlet>
</web-app>
```

Test the Application

You're now ready to test the application. If you've setup Tomcat correctly, and made sure the demo web applications of Tomcat run trouble free, you should be able to enter the "greeting" web application by typing `http://localhost:8080/greeting/`. Your browser should look like the following:

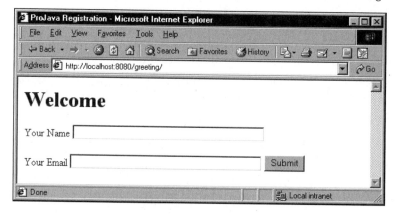

Enter your name, and e-mail address, and click on Submit. Your browser should display the following greeting from The Pro Java Server team. The actual greeting message depends on what time you run this application:

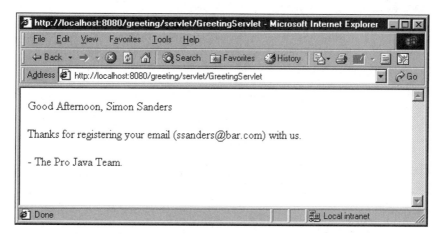

This makes our first web application.

The Making of Your Web Application

In this example, we've created the following files:

- ❑ %TOMCAT_HOME%\webapps\greeting\index.html
- ❑ %TOMCAT_HOME%\webapps\greeting\src\GreetingServlet.java
- ❑ %TOMCAT_HOME%\webapps\greeting\WEB-INF\web.xml
- ❑ %TOMCAT_HOME%\webapps\greeting\WEB-INF\classes\GreetingServlet.class

These files make up your first web application.

The rest of the discussion in this section is divided into two parts: the first part explains the source code, and the second, the structure of the web application.

How the Application Works

The figure overleaf shows what transpires between the web browser and the web application. The numbered arrows indicate the sequence in which requests and responses are processed.

In this example, the browser sends to two HTTP requests to the web container. In response to the first request (http://localhost:8080/greeting), the web container (TomCat) serves the index.html under %TOMCAT_HOME%\webapps\greeting\index.html. In the current configuration, the URI path "greeting" maps to a web application located at %TOMCAT_HOME%\webapps\greeting. In general, web servers/containers consider the "index.html" as the default welcome file in any directory under the URL path. The numbered arrows (1), (2), and (3) show this sequence:

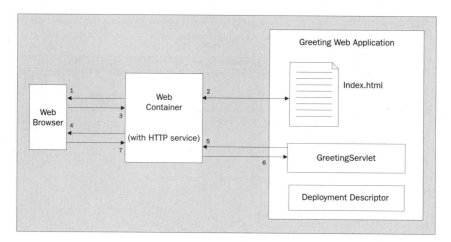

The second request (`http://localhost:8080/greeting/servlet/GreetingServlet`) to the web container is the HTTP POST request with `name` and `email` parameters. Based on the path "`greeting/servlet`", the resource "`Registration`", and the servlet definition in the deployment descriptor, the web container delegates this request to the `GreetingServlet`. The servlet then does the following tasks:

❑ Extracts the request parameters: This involves extracting the "`name`" and "`email`" parameters from the request.

❑ Executes application logic: In our example, this involves generating a greeting message.

❑ Generates the response: After processing the request, the servlet generates an HTML document with the greeting message.

The browser receives the response generated in this way by the servlet. This sequence is shown by numbered arrows (4), (5), (6), and (7). In brief, this is how web containers delegate requests to servlets in web applications. You'll learn more details of this process in Chapters 8 and 9.

The rest of this subsection provides you an overview of how the `GreetingServlet` performs the three tasks mentioned above.

Import the Servlet Packages

The Java Servlet API consists of two packages: `javax.servlet`, and `javax.servlet.http`. Note that all `javax` packages are part of the of the Java 2 SDK, Enterprise Edition.

Of these two packages, the `javax.servlet` package contains servlet classes and interfaces that are independent of HTTP. The rest of the classes that are specific for HTTP are part of the `javax.servlet.http` package.

Apart from the above two, the `GreetingServlet` class also needs to import the `java.io` and `java.util` packages, as we shall see shortly:

```
// Import Servlet packages
import javax.servlet.*;
import javax.servlet.http.*;
```

```
// Import other Java packages
import java.io.*;
import java.util.*;
```

Class Declaration

All servlets are required to implement the `javax.servlet.Servlet` interface. However, for servlets in web applications, the `javax.servlet.http.HttpServlet` class provides an implementation of this interface. So, the `GreetingServlet` class can extend the `HttpServlet` class:

```
public class GreetingServlet extends HttpServlet {
    ...
}
```

Service the HTTP POST Request

In the `GreetingServlet` servlet, the `doPost()` method handles the HTTP POST request. This method takes a `HttpServletRequest` object that encapsulates the information contained in the request, and a `HttpServletResponse` object encapsulating the HTTP response.

Our implementation of the `doPost()` method includes two tasks: to extract the FORM parameters from the HTTP request, and to generate the response.

Extract Parameters from HttpServletRequest

We can use the `getParameter()` method of the `HttpServletRequest` interface to extract parameters from the HTTP request:

```
// Get parameters from the request.
String name = request.getParameter("name");
String email = request.getParameter("email");
```

The first call extracts the parameter named name in the `<FORM>` tag of the `index.html` file. Here is a recap:

```
<P>Your Name <INPUT TYPE="text" SIZE="40" NAME="name"></P>
```

The `getParameter()` method looks into all the available parameters in the request, and extracts a parameter called name. Similarly, we can extract the email parameter. Note that these parameters can be extracted in any particular order. For instance, we can first extract the email parameter and then extract the name parameter.

This ends the request processing part. The next step is to prepare for the response.

Generate Response

The next step is to prepare for the dynamic content to be generated to the user. In the response, we're interested in displaying a greeting message, such as:

Good Afternoon, Simon Sanders

Thanks for registering your email (ssanders@bar.com) with us.

- The Pro Java Team.

In this example, the servlet uses the response stream associated with the response object to directly print the content. Note that JSP pages provide a better alternative for dynamic content generation. However, for the sake of simplicity, let's use servlets instead.

The following code snippet computes a greeting message depending on the current time of the day. Note that this is the only application logic performed in this application. As you'll see in Chapters 9 and 10, you can perform more complex application logic (such as database access) at this point:

```
// Compute a greeting message
String message = null;
GregorianCalendar calendar = new GregorianCalendar();
if(calendar.get(Calendar.AM_PM) == Calendar.AM) {
  message = "Good Morning";
}
else {
  message = "Good Afternoon";
}
```

Note that this is a crude form of greeting message. The servlet uses a `java.util.GregorianCalendar` object for finding out if the time of the day corresponds to AM or PM, and accordingly returns a message string.

After computing this message, the servlet is ready for generating the response. This involves the following steps:

❑   To set a content type (MIME) for the response. In the present example, this is `"text/html"`.

```
// Set MIME type for the response
response.setContentType("text/html");
```

❑   To obtain a `java.io.PrintWriter` object from the response object:

```
// Obtain a print writer object
PrintWriter out = response.getWriter();
```

❑   To print the response using the print writer object:

```
out.println("<HTML>");
out.println("<BODY>");
out.println("<P>" + message + ", " + name + "</P>");

out.println("<P>  Thanks for registering your email (" + email +
            ") with us.</P>");
out.println("<P> - The Pro Java Team. </P>");
out.println("</BODY>");
out.println("</HTML>");
```

❑   To close the print writer object:

```
out.close();
```

These steps result in the HTML document that is displayed in the browser in response to the POST request.

The Deployment Descriptor

In our example application, the deployment descriptor file (web.xml) includes the configuration information.

The first line in the deployment descriptor is an XML declaration specifying the version of the XML and the encoding used:

```
<?xml version="1.0" encoding="ISO-8859-1"?>
```

This is followed by the document type declaration specifying the URI for the DTD used for this application. For more details on XML and DTDs, see Chapter 5:

```
<!DOCTYPE web-app
    PUBLIC "-//Sun Microsystems, Inc.//DTD Web Application 2.2//EN"
    "http://java.sun.com/j2ee/dtds/web-app_2.2.dtd">
```

In the case of web applications, the DTD is web-app_2.2.dtd specified as part of the J2EE specification for web applications. The above two blocks are standard for all your web applications.

The actual definition of servlets is always enclosed within <web-app> tags. Within the <servlet> tag, note the two entries for the name of the servlet and the fully qualified Java class. The <servlet> tag lets the web container know the name used to refer to a servlet:

```
<web-app>
  <servlet>
    <!-- Servlet alias -->
    <servlet-name>Registration</servlet-name>

    <!-- Fully qualified Servlet class -->
    <servlet-class>GreetingServlet</servlet-class>
  </servlet>
</web-app>
```

Recall that the FORM in index.html posts the request to a relative URL, /greeting/servlet/GreetingServlet. To better understand how the container uses the above definitions, change the <FORM> tag in index.html to the following:

```
<FORM ACTION="/greeting/servlet/Registration" METHOD="POST">
  <P>Your Name <INPUT TYPE="text" SIZE="40" NAME="name"></P>
  <P>Your Email <INPUT TYPE="text" SIZE="40" NAME="email">
  <INPUT TYPE="submit" VALUE="Submit"></P>
</FORM>
```

Also change the <servlet> tag in the web.xml file to:

```
<servlet>
  <servlet-name>Registration</servlet-name>
  <servlet-class>GreetingServlet</servlet-class>
</servlet>
```

Restart Tomcat, and launch the application again. You should see the same results. This explains the purpose of the `<servlet>` tag in the `web.xml` file. The `<servlet-name>` is an alias for the actual class name. This feature allows you to change the servlet class files without changing the HTML and/or other servlets. Note that you can deploy the same servlet more than once in the same web application. To do so, you just need to use different names.

Location of the Application

Having seen the detailed source of the web application, let's now examine the structure of this application. Here is the structure we used:

```
%TOMCAT_HOME%\webapps
                        \greeting
                                \src
                                    \GreetingServlet.java
                                \index.html
                                \WEB-INF
                                        \web.xml
                                        \classes
                                                \GreetingServlet.class
```

Firstly, look at the `src` directory. This directory need not be here. It can be anywhere. So, exclude this from the current discussion.

Under the `webapps` directory, we have the `greeting` sub-directory. Recall that the URL you used to access this application is `http://localhost:8080/greeting`. In this URL, the path is `greeting` and is the same as the name we used for the directory for our application. For the sake of convenience, we used the directory name as the name of the application.

However, the above organization clutters your TomCat installation directory. A better approach is to keep this above directory under your working directory. Consider `c:\ProJavaServer\Chapter07` as your working directory. Move the greeting directory from `%TOMCAT%\webapps` into `c:\ProJavaServer\Chapter07`. The resulting structure should be as follows:

```
c:\ProJavaServer\Chapter07
                        \greeting
                                \index.html
                                \WEB-INF
                                        \web.xml
                                        \classes
                                                \GreetingServlet.class
```

Open the `%TOMCAT_HOME%\conf\server.xml` file. Look for a `<ContextManager>` ... `</ContextManager>` block. Add the following entry just before the closing `</ContextManager>` tag. This defines a context for the greeting web application. TomCat inspects content of this directory at server startup.

```
<Context path="/greeting"
         docBase="c:\ProJavaServer\Chapter07\greeting">
</Context>
```

Restart the Tomcat server, and launch the application as you did earlier. It should work the same!

Now, examine the above XML. The <Context> tag has two attributes. The first attribute is a path pointing to /greeting. This is the same as the path in the URL. The second attribute is a docBase attribute pointing to where your application is located. In our case, it is c:\ProJavaServer\Chapter07.

Therefore, the above tag instructs Tomcat to map all requests beginning with a path /greeting to the web application located at c:\ProJavaServer\Chapter07\greeting. This is how you can deploy a web application onto a web container.

This is the approach you should follow for all your web applications in this book. This lets you manage your source/HTML/class files easily, without cluttering the Tomcat installation directory.

Note that the <Context> tag, as well as the webapps subdirectory are server-dependent. Different containers may use different approaches for deploying applications. Refer to the documentation of the particular container you are using for the exact syntax and procedure.

Summary

The notion of web containers is simple yet powerful. Web containers allow you to build dynamic web applications using a very simple Servlet API, and JSP pages.

In this chapter, we've covered the following:

❑　Basics of HTTP, types of requests, and details of the request-response paradigm of HTTP.

❑　Introduction to the two web container technologies – Java servlets, and JSP pages - and deployment descriptors.

❑　Steps involved in building a simple web application to collect data from users and generate a response.

These topics just cover the basics of web application development. The purpose of the above coverage is just to introduce you to web containers and demonstrate the stages involved in building web applications. The next step is to consider the details of java servlets, JSP pages, including web containers, and the steps involved in building web applications.

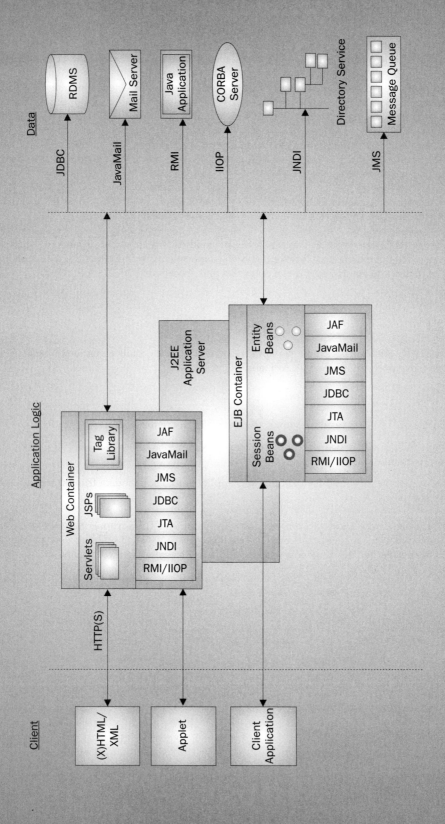

8

Servlet Programming

Servlets are the basic building blocks of web applications. Servlets provide a common programming model that is also the foundation for JSP pages. In the previous chapter, we've seen an overview of web applications and web containers, programming requirements, and the basic structure of web applications. The focus in the previous chapter was more on how web applications (in particular servlets) can be programmed to enhance the HTTP request-response process. The second goal in the previous chapter was to introduce the basic principles of web containers and web applications.

The goal of this chapter and the next is to introduce you to the Java Servlet API, version 2.2, which can be downloaded from `http://java.sun.com/products/servlet`. This API includes two packages: the `javax.servlet` and `javax.servlet.http` packages. Note that the `javax.servlet` package has two subpackages for JSP pages (`javax.servlet.jsp`), and JSP custom tags (`jsp.servlet.jsp.tagext`). These packages will be covered in Chapters 11 and 12.

I'll introduce the Java Servlet API in three steps:

❏   Servlet implementation

❏   Requests and responses

❏   Session, context, and servlet collaboration

In this chapter, our agenda is to discuss the first and second steps, while we'll discuss the third step in the next chapter. Specifically, in this chapter we'll cover the following:

❏   Classes and interfaces for servlet implementation, including servlet exceptions

❏   Servlet configuration

- ❑ The servlet lifecycle
- ❑ Requests and responses
- ❑ The servlet programming model, with an example

Note that this chapter is not meant to be a reference for the `javax.servlet` and `javax.servlet.http` packages. Instead, it walks you through these packages, and the concepts behind these, based on how you'll be using the API while developing applications. I strongly advise you to keep the Servlet API documentation handy while reading this chapter. You can access this documentation online at `http://java.sun.com/products/servlet/2.2/javadoc/index.html`.

Overview of the Java Servlet API

The servlet API is specified in two Java extension packages: `javax.servlet` and `javax.servlet.http`. Of these, the classes and interfaces in the `javax.servlet` package are protocol independent, while the second package, `javax.servlet.http`, contains classes and interfaces that are specific to HTTP. Some of the classes/interfaces in the `javax.servlet.http` extend those specified in the `javax.servlet` package.

The figure below shows the UML class diagram of the core classes of the `javax.servlet` package, and some of their associations. The directed continuous arrows depict associations, while broken directed arrows indicate dependencies. Note that the container maintains all these associations, as long as you're using the `javax.servlet.http` package. However, if you're building specialized servlets extending the classes in the `javax.servlet` package, you'll have to maintain some of the associations yourself.

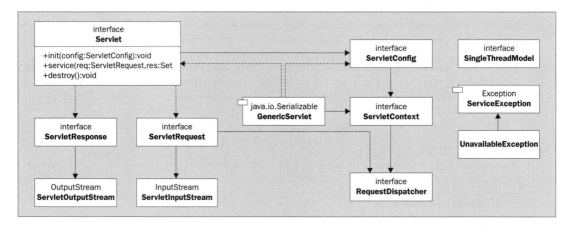

The following figure shows the classes/interfaces from the `javax.servlet.http` package. In this figure, the gray rectangles are classes/interfaces from the `javax.servlet` package:

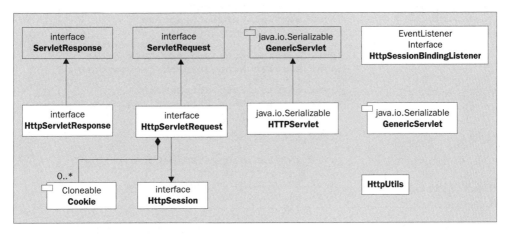

However what's the purpose of all these interfaces and classes? Consider the following basic questions:

- As discussed in the previous chapter, servlets are container-managed. How does the container manage the lifecycle of servlets? How can your servlets participate in this lifecycle?

- How to implement application logic? Application logic in servlets corresponds to the logic in response to HTTP requests.

- How do we read HTTP requests and generate HTTP responses?

- How do we deal with exceptions in servlets?

- How can servlets interact with their environment?

We'll not attempt to answer these questions right now, but while progressing through this chapter, you should come back to this list, and be able to answer them.

The table below provides an overview of the Java Servlet API. In this table, interfaces are shown in bold:

Purpose	Class/Interface

Servlet Implementation	**`javax.servlet.Servlet`**
	`javax.servlet.SingleThreadModel`
	`javax.servlet.GenericServlet`
	`javax.servlet.http.HttpServlet`

Servlet Configuration	**`javax.servlet.ServletConfig`**
Servlet Exceptions	`javax.servlet.ServletException` `javax.servlet.UnavailableException`

Table continued on following page

Purpose	Class/Interface
Requests and Responses	**javax.servlet.ServletRequest** **javax.servlet.ServletResponse** javax.servlet.ServletInputStream javax.servlet.ServletOutputStream **javax.servlet.http.HttpServletRequest** **javax.servlet.http.HttpServletResponse**
Session Tracking	**javax.servlet.http.HttpSession** **javax.servlet.http.HttpSessionBindingListener** javax.servlet.http.HttpSessionBindingEvent
Servlet Context	**javax.servlet.ServletContext**
Servlet Collaboration	**javax.servlet.RequestDispatcher**
Miscellaneous	javax.servlet.http.Cookie javax.servlet.http.HttpUtils

Web container providers (such as Tomcat, WebLogic, JRun etc.) implement most of the interfaces and classes in the above table. In fact, there are one abstract class (javax.servlet.http.HttpServlet) and one interface (javax.servlet.http.HttpSessionBindingListener) that are left for you to implement while building web applications. The container creates the rest of the runtime objects that are part of your application. Why is it so?

A web container is an application framework with a runtime environment. In a framework, application objects are created and invoked by the runtime. While invoking methods on the application objects, the container has to construct the objects for the arguments. For instance, consider the GreetingServlet of the previous chapter. In this servlet, the container creates and passes the HttpServletRequest and HttpServletResponse objects as arguments to the doPost() method. In the same fashion, the container creates all other objects (such as ServletConfig, ServletContext, HttpSession etc.) that a servlet can directly or indirectly access.

Note that the table above categorizes the classes/interfaces in the javax.servlet and javax.servlet.http packages, based on their role in web application development. Let's look at this categorization in more detail:

❑ **API for Servlet Implementation**
The classes/interfaces in this category are meant for implementing servlets. You'll find two interfaces (javax.servlet.Servlet and javax.servlet.SingleThreadModel) and two abstract classes (javax.servlet.GenericServlet, and javax.servlet.http.HttpServlet) in this category for building servlets. For instance, the GreetingServlet class in the previous chapter extends the javax.servlet.HttpServlet class. To develop your own servlets, you'll be implementing one or more methods in these classes/interfaces. When you deploy servlets, the web container invokes these methods to control the lifecycle of servlets, and to execute application logic.

❑ **Servlet Configuration**
The javax.servlet.ServletConfig interface belongs to this category. The servlet API provides various means of accessing the ServletConfig object associated with a servlet. This object provides access to certain initialization parameters that can be configured while deploying a servlet. You'll find some examples of how this can be done later in the chapter.

❑ **Servlet Exceptions**
   The Java Servlet API specifies two exceptions: `javax.servlet.ServletException` and
   `javax.servlet.UnavailableException`. Typically, your servlets throw these exceptions,
   and the container catches them and performs appropriate error handling.

❑ **API for Requests and Responses**
   There are four interfaces (`javax.servlet.ServletRequest`,
   `javax.servlet.ServletResponse`, and `javax.servlet.http.HttpServletRequest`,
   `javax.servlet.http.HttpServletResponse`) and two abstract classes
   (`javax.servlet.ServletInputStream`, and `javax.servlet.ServletOutputStream`)
   in this category. These objects provide methods to access, and the underlying input and output
   streams associated with the client connection. Using these objects, you can read data from the
   input, and write data back to the client.

❑ **Servlet Context**
   The notion of servlet context is closely associated with the notion of a web application. The
   interface `javax.servlet.ServletContext` allows servlets in an application to share data.
   It also provides methods using which servlets can access the host web container.

❑ **Servlet Collaboration**
   The servlet API also provides an interface (`javax.servlet.http.RequestDispatcher`)
   with which a servlet can invoke another servlet, a JSP, or even a static resource such as an
   HTML page. This mechanism helps you to control the flow of logic across multiple servlets
   and JSP pages programmatically, and is discussed in detail in Chapter 11.

❑ **Other Miscellaneous API**
   Under this category, you'll find two classes: `javax.servlet.http.HttpUtils`, which
   provides miscellaneous helper methods, and `javax.servlet.http.Cookie`, which you can
   use to create cookies. You'll find some examples of these classes in the next chapter.

In the following sections, we'll discuss the first four categories in detail.

Servlet Implementation

Let's start by looking at the classes and interfaces used for implementing servlets themselves.

The Servlet Interface

```
public interface Servlet
```

This interface specifies the contract between the web container and a servlet. In the object-oriented
paradigm, an object can communicate with another object as long as the first object can reference the
second object with a known interface – it need not know the name of the actual implementing class. In
the case of the servlet API, the `javax.servlet.Servlet` is the interface that containers use to
reference servlets.

When you write a servlet, you must either directly or indirectly implement this interface. You will most
likely always implement the interface indirectly by extending either the
`javax.servlet.GenericServlet` or `javax.servlet.http.HttpServlet` classes.

When implementing the `javax.servlet.Servlet` interface, the following five methods must be implemented:

```
public void init(ServletConfig config)
public void service(ServletRequest request, ServletResponse response)
public void destroy()
public ServletConfig getServletConfig()
public String getServletInfo()
```

The init() Method

```
public void init(ServletConfig config) throws ServletException
```

Once the servlet has been instantiated, the web container calls the `init()` method. The purpose of this method is to allow a servlet perform any initialization required, before being invoked against HTTP requests. The container passes an object of type `ServletConfig` to the `init()` method; as we shall see later, a servlet can access its configuration data using the `ServletConfig` object. The `init()` method throws a `ServletException` in the event of the `init()` method not completing normally.

The servlet specification guarantees that the `init()` method will be called exactly once on any given instance of the servlet, and the `init()` method will be allowed to complete (provided that it does not throw a `ServletException`) before any requests are passed to the servlet.

Some of the typical tasks that can be implemented in the `init()` method are:

❑ Read configuration data from persistent resources such as configuration files

❑ Read initialization parameters using the `javax.servlet.ServletConfig` object

❑ Initializing one-time activites such as registering a database driver, a connection pool, or a logging service

The service() Method

```
public void service(ServletRequest request, ServletResponse response)
        throws ServletException, IOException
```

This is the entry point for executing application logic in a servlet. The container calls this method in response to incoming requests. Only after the servlet has been successfully initialized will the `service()` method be called. The `service()` method accepts two arguments, implementing the `javax.servlet.ServletRequest` and `javax.servlet.ServletResponse` interfaces respectively. In the UML class diagram for the `javax.servlet` package, the broken arrows indicate this dependency relationship. The request object provides methods to access the original request data, and the response object provides methods with which the servlet can build a response.

The destroy() Method

```
public void destroy()
```

The container calls this method before removing a servlet instance out of service. This might occur if it needs to free some memory or the web server is being shut down. Before the container calls this method, it will give the remaining `service()` threads time to finish executing (subject to some timeout period), so that the destroy() method is not called while a service() call is still underway. After the destroy() method is called, the container does not route requests to the servlet.

Activities that can be implemented in the destroy() method include:

❑ Performing cleanup tasks, such as unregistering a database driver, closing a connection pool, or even informing another application/system that the servlet will no longer be in service

❑ Persisting any state associated with a servlet

The getServletConfig() Method

```
public ServletConfig getServletConfig()
```

You should implement this method to return the ServletConfig that was passed to the servlet during the init() method.

The getServletInfo() Method

```
public String getServletInfo()
```

This method should return a String object containing information about the servlet (for example, author, creation date, description, etc.). You should implement this method to return a meaningful string. This is available to the web container, should it wish to display, for example, a list of servlets installed together with descriptions.

The GenericServlet Class

```
public abstract class GenericServlet implements Servlet,
                                                 ServletConfig,
                                                 Serializable
```

The GenericServlet class provides a basic implementation of the Servlet interface. This is an abstract class, and all subclasses should implement the service() method. This abstract class has the following methods in addition to those declared in javax.servlet.Servlet, and javax.servlet.ServletConfig:

```
public init()
public void log(String message)
public void log(String message, Throwable t)
```

The init(ServletConfig config) method stores the ServletConfig object in a private transient instance variable (called config). You can use the getServletConfig() method to access this object. However, if you choose to override this method, you should include a call to super.init(config). Alternatively, you can override the overloaded no-argument init() method in the GenericServlet class.

The GenericServlet class also implements the ServletConfig interface. This allows the servlet developer to call the ServletConfig methods directly without having to first obtain a ServletConfig object. These methods are getInitParameter(), getInitParameterNames(), getServletContext(), and getServletName(). Each of these methods delegates the calls to the respective methods in the stored ServletConfig object.

The GenericServlet class also includes two methods for writing to a servlet log, which call the corresponding methods on the ServletContext. The first method, log(String msg), writes the name of the servlet and the msg argument to the web container's log. The other method, log(String msg, Throwable cause), includes a stack trace for the given Throwable exception in addition to the servlet name and message. The actual implementation of the logging mechanism is container specific, although most of the containers use text files for logging purposes. For instance, Tomcat uses %TOMCAT_HOME%\log\servlet.log as the log file.

The SingleThreadModel Interface

```
public interface SingleThreadModel
```

The servlet API specifies a special **marker interface** called javax.servlet.SingleThreadModel. (A marker interface is a Java interface without any methods.)

During the lifetime of a servlet that does not implement this interface, the container may send multiple service requests in different threads to a single instance. This means that implementation of the service() method should be thread-safe. However, what's the alternative if the service() method of a servlet is not thread-safe?

The Java Servlet API specifies the SingleThreadModel interface for this purpose. Your servlets can implement the SingleThreadModel interface (in addition to implementing the javax.servlet.Servlet interface or extending one of its implementation classes) in order to inform the container that it should make sure that only one thread is executing the servlet's service() method at any given moment.

For SingleThreadModel servlets, containers may follow one of the following approaches to ensure that each servlet instance is invoked in a separate thread:

❑ **Instance Pooling**
In this approach, the container maintains a pool of servlet instances. For each incoming request, the container allocates a servlet instance from the pool, and upon completion of the service, the container returns the instance to the pool.

❑ **Request Serialization**
In this approach, the container maintains a single instance of the servlet. However, since the container cannot send multiple requests to the instance at the same time, the container serializes the requests. This means that new requests will be kept waiting while the current request is being served.

Note that, in reality a combination of these two approaches is more pragmatic, so that the container could maintain a reasonable number of instances in the pool, while still serializing requests if the number of requests exceeds the number of instances in the pool.

Note that the SingleThreadModel is resource intensive, particularly, if a large number of concurrent requests are expected for the servlet. The effect of the SingleThreadModel is that the container invokes the service() method in a synchronized block. This is equivalent to using the synchronized keyword for the servlet's service() method.

However, in cases where only a few statements of the service() method are not thread-safe, you should consider reducing the scope of synchronization, and explicitly synchronize such blocks using the synchronized key word. Depending on how short such synchronization blocks are, this approach could improve performance.

Always consider redesigning your applications, so that you can completely avoid the SingleThreadModel or thread synchronization, and when you cannot avoid these, be aware of the performance implications.

The HttpServlet Class

```
public abstract class HttpServlet extends GenericServlet implements Serializable
```

The HttpServlet class extends GenericServlet, and provides an HTTP-specific implementation of the Servlet interface. This will most likely be the class that all of your servlets will extend. This class specifies the following methods:

```
public void service(ServletRequest request, ServletResponse response)
protected void service(HttpServletRequest request, HttpServletResponse response)
protected void doGet(HttpServletRequest request, HttpServletResponse response)
protected void doPost(HttpServletRequest request, HttpServletResponse response)
protected void doDelete(HttpServletRequest request, HttpServletResponse response)
protected void doOptions(HttpServletRequest request, HttpServletResponse response)
protected void doPut(HttpServletRequest request, HttpServletResponse response)
protected void doTrace(HttpServletRequest request, HttpServletResponse response)
```

The service() Methods

The HttpServlet has two variants of this method:

```
public void service(ServletRequest request, ServletResponse resposnse)
        throws ServletException, IOException
```

This is an implementation of the service() method in the GenericServlet. This method casts the request and response objects to HttpServletRequest and HttpServletResponse, and calls the following overloaded service() method. You should not therefore override the above method.

```
protected void service(HttpServletRequest request, HttpServletResponse response)
        throws ServletException, IOException
```

This overloaded method takes HTTP-specific request and response objects, and is invoked by the first method above. HttpServlet implements this method to be a dispatcher of HTTP requests. As you'll see later in this chapter, the javax.servlet.ServletRequest interface provides a getMethod() method that returns the type of the HTTP method associated with the request. For instance, for GET requests, this method returns a "GET" as a string. The service() method uses this string to delegate the request to one of the methods doGet(), doPost(), doOptions(), doDelete(), doPut(), and doTrace(). This method should therefore never be overridden.

The sequence of method calls when the container receives a request for a servlet is:

- ❑ The container calls the public `service()` method

- ❑ The public `service()` method calls the protected `service()` method after casting the arguments to `HttpServletRequest` and `HttpServletResponse` respectively

- ❑ The protected `service()` method calls one of the `doXXX()` methods, depending on the type of the HTTP request method

The doXXX() Methods

The `HttpServlet` class implements the following protected methods, one for each of the HTTP request methods:

```
protected void doGet(HttpServletRequest request, HttpServletResponse response)
        throws ServletException, IOException
protected void doPost(HttpServletRequest request, HttpServletResponse response)
        throws ServletException, IOException
protected void doDelete(HttpServletRequest request, HttpServletResponse response)
        throws ServletException, IOException
protected void doOptions(HttpServletRequest request, HttpServletResponse response)
        throws ServletException, IOException
protected void doPut(HttpServletRequest request, HttpServletResponse response)
        throws ServletException, IOException
protected void doTrace(HttpServletRequest request, HttpServletResponse response)
        throws ServletException, IOException
```

The signature of each of these `doXxx()` methods is the same as the protected `service()` method above – each takes `HttpServletRequest` and `HttpServletResponse` arguments, and throws `ServletException` and `IOException`.

The `HttpServlet` class provides proper implementations for the TRACE and OPTIONS methods, and there is no need for your servlets to override `doTrace()` and `doOptions()`.

For the rest of the four methods the `HttpServlet` class provides implementations that return HTTP errors. In case of HTTP 1.0 compliant containers, these methods return an HTTP error with status code 400, indicating that the request sent by the client is syntactically incorrect. For HTTP 1.1 compliant containers, these methods returns an HTTP error with status code 405, indicating that the requested HTTP method is not allowed for this servlet. This class uses the `getProtocol()` method of the `javax.servlet.ServletRequest` interface to determine the protocol.

Depending on your application, you should determine the HTTP methods to be supported by your servlet, and accordingly override the corresponding `doXXX()` methods (except those for the TRACE and OPTIONS methods).

The getLastModified() Method

```
protected long getLastModified(HttpServletRequest req)
```

This method should return the time that the servlet was last modified in milliseconds since January 1, 1970 00:00:00 GMT. The default implementation returns a negative number (-1) indicating that the time of modification is unknown.

HTTP 1.1 has the notion of conditional GET requests. The If-Modified-Since header is one of the headers that makes a request conditional. Clients confirming to the HTTP 1.1 can send this header with a date field (for example: If-Modified-Since: Sat, 01 Jan 2000 00:00:00 GMT). This header indicates to the server that if the requested resource has not been modified since the time indicated in the header, the server can serve a cached page without regenerating the page. In the case of servlets, the web container need not invoke the doGet() method. Note that browsers confirming to the HTTP 1.0 do not support this header.

Your servlets can override this method to control caching of pages generated by the doGet() method.

Servlet Configuration

In the Java Servlet API, javax.servlet.ServletConfig objects represent the configuration of a servlet. The configuration information contains initialization parameters (a set of name/value pairs), the name of the servlet, and a javax.servlet.ServletContext object, which gives the servlet information about the container. The initialization parameters and the name of a servlet can be specified in the deployment descriptor (the web.xml file), for example:

```
<web-app>
  <servlet>
    <servlet-name>Admin</servlet-name>
    <servlet-class>com.wrox.admin.AdminServlet</servlet-class>
    <init-param>
        <param-name>email</param-name>
        <param-value>admin@admin.wrox.com</param-value>
    </init-param>
    <init-param>
        <param-name>helpURL</param-name>
        <param-value>/admin/help/index.html</param-value>
    </init-param>
  </servlet>
<web-app>
```

This example registers a servlet with name Admin, and specifies two initialization parameters, email and helpURL. The web container reads this information, and makes it available to the com.wrox.admin.AdminServlet via the associated javax.servlet.ServletConfig object. If you want to change these parameters, you can do so without having to recompile the servlet. You'll learn more about this approach in Chapter 10.

Note that the deployment descriptor mechanism has been introduced in the servlet 2.2 specification. Web containers (then called servlet engines) complying with older versions of the specification provide vendor-specific means (such as properties files) to specify the initialization parameters.

The ServletConfig Interface

```
public interface ServletConfig
```

This interface specifies the following methods:

```
public String getInitParameter(String name)
public Enumeration getInitParameterNames()
public ServletContext getServletContext()
public String getServletName()
```

The getInitParameter() Method

```
public String getInitParameter(String name)
```

This method returns the value of a named initialization parameter, or `null` if the specified parameter does not exist. In the above example, calling the `getInitParameter()` method with `"email"` as an argument returns the value `"admin@admin.wrox.com"`.

The getInitParameterNames() Method

```
public Enumeration getInitParameterNames()
```

This method returns an enumeration of all the initialization parameters of a servlet. Using this enumeration, you can obtain the names of all enumeration parameters one after the other. If there are no initialization parameters specified, this method returns an empty enumeration. In the above example, calling `getInitParameterNames()` returns an enumeration containing two `String` objects: `"email"` and `"helpURL"`.

The getServletContext() Method

```
public ServletContext getServletContext()
```

This method returs a reference to the `ServletContext` object associated with the web application. The `javax.servlet.ServletContext` is covered in more detail in the next chapter.

The getServletName() Method

```
public String getServletName()
```

This method returns the name assigned to a servlet in its deployment descriptor. If no name is specified, this returns the servlet class name instead.

Obtaining a Reference to ServletConfig

In the Java Servlet API, a servlet can obtain a reference to the `javax.servlet.ServletConfig` object in the following ways:

During Servlet Initialization

As discussed previously, the `init()` methods of the `Servlet` interface and the `GenericServlet` class have an argument of type `javax.servlet.ServletConfig`. During initialization of a servlet, the web container creates this argument, and passes to the `init()` method. When you're overriding this `init()` method, you can access the `javax.servlet.ServletConfig` object.

However, when you're overriding the above `init()` method in the `GenericServlet` class, you should explicitly invoke `super.init()` as follows:

```
public init(ServletConfig config) {
  super.init(config);

  // Initialization here
}
```

The call to super.init(config) ensures that the GenericServlet class receives a reference to the ServletConfig object. The implementation of the GenericServlet class actually maintains a reference to the ServletConfig object (as a private transient instance variable), and requires that super.init(config) be called in subclasses.

Using the getServletConfig() Method

Servlets can also access the ServletConfig object by calling the getServletConfig() method. This method is specified in the javax.servlet.Servlet interface.

Alternatively, servlets extending the GenericServlet, or its subclass HttpServlet can also call the methods of the ServletConfig interface directly. This is because the GenericServlet also implements the ServletConfig interface.

Servlet Exceptions

The javax.servlet package specifies two exception classes: javax.servlet.ServletException, and javax.servlet.UnavailableException.

The ServletException Class

```
public class ServletException extends java.lang.Exception
```

This is a generic exception, which can be thrown by the init(), service(), doXXX(), and destroy() methods. The class provides the following constructors:

```
public ServletException()
public ServletException(String message)
```

While creating objects of type ServletException, you can embed any application-level exception (called as 'root-cause'). The containers use the root-cause exception for logging purposes. For instance, you can embed a java.sql.SQLException in a javax.servlet.ServletException. There are two additional constructors to support root-cause exceptions:

```
public ServletException(Throwable cause)
public ServletException(String message, Throwable cause)
```

The getRootCause() method returns the root-cause exception:

```
public Throwable getRootCause()
```

The UnavailableException Class

```
public class UnavailableException extends ServletException
```

`javax.servlet.UnavailableException` is a special type of servlet exception. Since this servlet extends the `javax.servlet.ServletException`, all servlet methods that can throw a `javax.servlet.Exception` can also throw a `javax.servlet.UnavailableException`.

The purpose of this is to indicate to the web container that the servlet is either temporarily or permanently unavailable.

This class specifies the following constructors:

```
public UnavailableException(String message)
```

This constructs a new permanently unavailable exception with the given message:

```
public UnavailableException(String message, int seconds)
```

This constructs a new unavailable exception with the given message. The `seconds` argument indicates the duration in seconds for which the servlet is unavailable.

We shall discuss later the exact behavior of the container for temporary and permanent failures.

The Servlet Lifecycle

As discussed previously, the container is a runtime that manages the servlets. Of the various responsibilities of a container, lifecycle management is the most crucial. In the case of servlets, the lifecycle events are specified in the `javax.servlet.Servlet` interface of the servlet API. Although the lifecycle management is a container's responsibility you, as a servlet developer, should make sure that your servlets follow the lifecycle model, and that your servlets are not implemented in a way that contradicts this.

The `Servlet` methods relevant to the servlet lifecycle are `init()`, `service()`, and `destroy()`. The lifecycle starts with the container calling the `init()` method, and ends with the container calling the `destroy()` method.

Basically, the lifecycle of a servlet contains the following stages:

- ❑ **Instantiation**: The web container creates an instance of the servlet.
- ❑ **Initialization**: The container calls the instance's `init()` method.
- ❑ **Service**: If the container has a request for the servlet, it calls the servlets instance's `service()` method.
- ❑ **Destroy**: Before destroying the instance, the container calls the servlet instance's `destroy()` method.
- ❑ **Unavailable**: The instance is destroyed and marked for garbage collection.

The UML state diagram below shows the possible transitions in the servlet lifecycle:

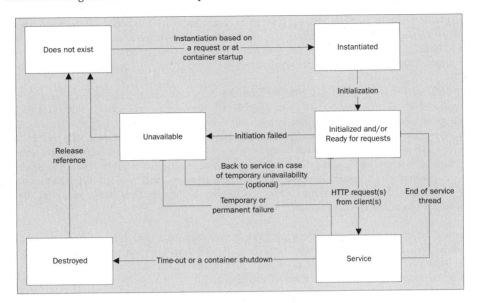

Each rectangle in this diagram represents a possible state of a servlet instance. Arrows between rectangles represent transition from one state to another.

The container creates a servlet instance in response to an incoming HTTP request, or at container startup. After instantiation, the container initializes the instance by invoking its init() method. After initialization, the servlet instance is ready to serve incoming requests. The purpose of this initialization process is to load any initialization parameters required for the servlet. We'll see how this can be accomplished in the next section.

During the initialization process, a servlet instance can throw a ServletException, or an UnavailableException. The UnavailableException is a subclass of ServletException. While the ServletException can be used to indicate general initialization failures (such as failure to find initialization parameters), UnavailableException is for reporting non-availability of the instance for servicing requests. For example, if your servlet depends on an RMI server, and you're verifying if the server is reachable for service, your servlet instance can throw a UnavailableException to indicate that it is temporarily or permanently unavailable. If your servlet instance determines that the unavailability should be temporary, it may indicate so while constructing the UnavailableException, by specifying the number of seconds of unavailability to the exception's constructor. When such a failure occurs, the container suspends all requests to your servlet for the specified period of time, and brings it back to an available state at the end of the period.

The container guarantees that before the service() method is called, the init() method will be allowed to complete, and also that before the servlet is destroyed, its destroy() method will be called.

The servlet may throw a ServletException or an UnavailableException during its service() method, in which case the container will suspend requests for that instance either temporarily or permanently. It is important for you to design your servlets considering temporary or permanent failures.

There is nothing to stop a web container performing the entire servlet lifecycle each time a servlet is requested. In practice, web containers load and initialize servlets during the container startup, or when the servlet is first called, and keep that servlet instance in memory to service all the requests it receives. The container may decide at any time to release the servlet reference, thus ending the servlet's lifecycle. This could happen, for example, if the servlet has not been called for some time, or if the container is shutting down. When this happens, the container calls the `destroy()` method.

In the typical servlet lifecycle model, the web container creates a single instance of each servlet. But what happens if the servlet's `service()` method is still running when the web container receives another request? For servlets that do not implement the `javax.servlet.SingleThreadModel` interface, the container invokes the same servlet instance in each request thread. Therefore, it is always possible that the `service()` method is being executed in more than one service thread, requiring that the `service()` method be thread-safe. Apart from not-accessing thread-safe resources (such as writing to files), you should also consider keeping your servlets stateless (that is, do not define any attributes in your servlet classes). When you define instance variables in your servlets, make sure that such variables are manipulated in a thread-safe manner.

We've previously discussed the behavior of servlets implementing the `javax.servlet.SingleThreadModel` interface. Recall that, for such servlets, the container could either serialize requests, or maintain a pool of servlet instances and allocate each request to a different instance in the pool, or use a combination of these two.

The following diagram shows the sequence of events showing a servlet being loaded, servicing two requests in quick succession, and then being unloaded when the server is shut down:

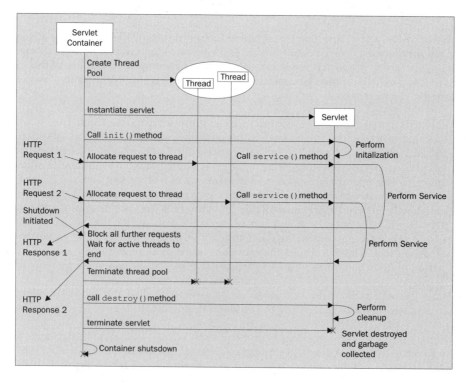

There is yet another situation where a container could create more than one instance of a servlet: this is the case when a servlet class is added in the deployment descriptor more than once, possibly with different initialization parameters.

You might find the above instantiation approaches complex. In order to avoid problems, I suggest that your servlets should make little or no assumption about instantiation. For example, you should not assume that the same servlet instance is used for all requests/clients, or that only one thread at a time is executing a `service()` method.

The Servlet Lifecycle – FreakServlet

Let's now consider an example, to better understand the servlet lifecycle. The example consists of a single servlet called FreakServlet, which demonstrates the various states in the lifecycle of a typical servlet, including unavailability. You'll shortly see why this is called a FreakServlet.

Enter the following source in
`C:\ProJavaServer\Chapter08\FreakServlet\src\FreakServlet.java`:

```
// FreakServlet.java

// Import servlet packages
import javax.servlet.*;
import javax.servlet.http.*;

// Import other Java packages
import java.io.*;
import java.util.*;

public class FreakServlet extends HttpServlet {
  java.util.Vector states;
  java.util.Random random;
  int waitInterval;
  public static final int DEFAULT_WAIT_INTERVAL = 10;

  public FreakServlet() {
    states = new java.util.Vector();
    random = new java.util.Random();
    waitInterval = DEFAULT_WAIT_INTERVAL;
    states.add(createState("Instantiation"));
  }

  public void init() throws ServletException {
    states.add(createState("Initialization"));
    String waitIntervalString =
      getServletConfig().getInitParameter("waitInterval");
    if (waitIntervalString != null) {
      waitInterval = new Integer(waitIntervalString).intValue();
    }
  }
```

```
   protected void doGet(HttpServletRequest request,
                        HttpServletResponse response) throws ServletException,
                        IOException {
      if (random.nextBoolean()) {

         // Not available for waitInterval seconds.
         states.add(createState("Unavailable from doGet"));
         throw new UnavailableException("Unavailable from doGet",
                                         waitInterval);
      }

      states.add(createState("Service"));

      response.setContentType("text/html");
      PrintWriter out = response.getWriter();

      // Send acknowledgment to the browser
      out.println("<HTML>");
      out.println("<META HTTP-EQUIV=\"Pragma\" CONTENT=\"no-cache\">");
      out.println("<HEAD><TITLE>");

      out.println("FreakServlet: State History");
      out.println("</TITLE></HEAD>");
      out.println("<BODY>");
      out.println("<H1>FreakServlet: State History</H1>");

      out.println("<a href=\"/lifeCycle/servlet/freak\">Reload</a></p>");

      for (int i = 0; i < states.size(); i++) {
         out.println("<p> " + states.elementAt(i) + "</p>");
      }

      out.println("</BODY></HTML>");
      out.close();
   }

   public void destroy() {
      states.add(createState("Destroy"));
      log("Flushing state history of LifeCycleTest servlet.");
      for (int i = 0; i < states.size(); i++) {
         log(states.elementAt(i).toString());
      }
   }

   private String createState(String message) {
      return "[" + (new java.util.Date()).toString() + "] " + message;
   }
}
```

Create a web.xml file under C:\ProJavaServer\Chapter08\freakServlet\WEB-INF\ with the following <servlet> and <error-page> definitions:

```xml
<?xml version="1.0" encoding="ISO-8859-1"?>

<!DOCTYPE web-app
  PUBLIC "-//Sun Microsystems, Inc.//DTD Web Application 2.2//EN"
  "http://java.sun.com/j2ee/dtds/web-app_2.2.dtd">

<web-app>
  <servlet>
    <servlet-name>freak</servlet-name>
    <servlet-class>FreakServlet</servlet-class>
    <init-param>
      <param-name>waitInterval</param-name>
      <param-value>5</param-value>
    </init-param>
  </servlet>

  <error-page>
    <exception-type>javax.servlet.UnavailableException</exception-type>
    <location>/unavailable.html</location>
  </error-page>
</web-app>
```

Add the following entry in `%TOMCAT_HOME%\conf\server.xml`:

```xml
<Context path="/lifeCycle"
        docBase="c:\ProJavaServer\Chapter08\freakServlet">
</Context>
```

Now, compile the servlet into the `C:\ProJavaServer\Chapter08\freakServlet\WEB-INF\classes` directory. Refer to the previous chapter for instructions.

Also copy the following HTML into
`C:\ProJavaServer\Chapter08\freakServlet\unavailable.html`:

```html
<HTML>
  <META HTTP-EQUIV="Pragma" CONTENT="no-cache">
  <HEAD>
    <TITLE>FreakServlet Unavailable</TITLE>
  </HEAD>

  <BODY>
    <H1>FreakServlet Unavailable</H1>

    <P>FreakServlet is temporarily unavailable. Please try
      <A HREF="/lifeCycle/servlet/freak">again</A>.</P>
  </BODY>
</HTML>
```

You're now ready to test this servlet. Start Tomcat, and type
`http://localhost:8080/lifecycle/servlet/freak` in your browser's address/location box to load the servlet. Reload the URL a few times by using your browser's reload/refresh button. There are two types of responses that you could see in the browser. You will either see the list of states in the lifecycle of the FreakServlet:

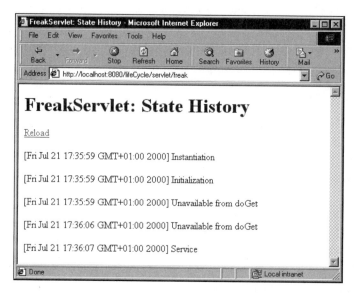

or you will see the response when the servlet enters the unavailable state:

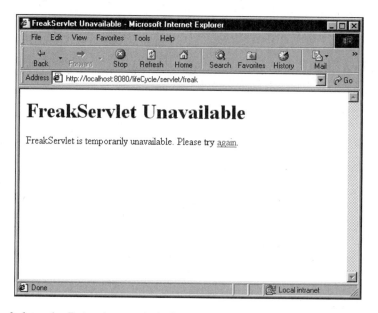

In either case, click on the Reload or again links in the brower to invoke this servlet a number of times.

To complete the lifecycle of this FreakServlet, shutdown Tomcat. To shutdown, do not kill the server (with *Ctrl-C*). Instead use the shutdown program found in the %TOMCAT_HOME%\bin directory. This gives Tomcat a chance to close any pending log buffers.

Open the `servlet.log` file under `%TOMCAT_HOME%\bin\logs\servlet.log` file, and look for log messages similar to these:

```
freak: [Fri Jul 21 17:35:59 GMT+01:00 2000] Instantiation
freak: [Fri Jul 21 17:35:59 GMT+01:00 2000] Initialization
freak: [Fri Jul 21 17:35:59 GMT+01:00 2000] Unavailable from doGet
freak: [Fri Jul 21 17:36:06 GMT+01:00 2000] Unavailable from doGet
freak: [Fri Jul 21 17:36:07 GMT+01:00 2000] Service
freak: [Fri Jul 21 17:36:23 GMT+01:00 2000] Service
freak: [Fri Jul 21 17:36:23 GMT+01:00 2000] Service
freak: [Fri Jul 21 17:36:24 GMT+01:00 2000] Unavailable from doGet
freak: [Fri Jul 21 17:36:51 GMT+01:00 2000] Destroy
```

The above list summarizes all the states of this servlet. Note that the sequence that you'll see may not be the same exactly. This is due to the random nature of this servlet.

Now let's see how these messages are generated.

Instantiation

This state corresponds to the construction of the servlet instance by the container. Refer to the constructor of `FreakServlet`:

```java
public FreakServlet() {
  states = new java.util.Vector();
  random = new java.util.Random();
  waitInterval = DEFAULT_WAIT_INTERVAL;
  states.add(createState("Instantiation"));
}
```

This constructor initializes a `Vector` and a random number generator. In this exercise, the `Vector` `states` is used to store the states as they occur. Each state is represented as a string prepended by a date string. The random number generator is used to randomly throw `UnavailableException` from the `doGet()` method. A 'freak' servlet!

Initialization

This is the second state in any servlet. Refer to the `init()` method of the `FreakServlet`:

```java
public void init() throws ServletException {
  states.add(new State("Initialization"));
  String waitIntervalString =
    getServletConfig().getInitParameter("waitInterval");
  if (waitIntervalString != null) {
    waitInterval = new Integer(waitIntervalString).intValue();
  }
}
```

This method adds another state called "Initialization" to the state history. It also extracts a parameter "waitInterval" from the servlet configuration. The FreakServlet uses this number while throwing UnavailableExceptions. Note that we specified an initialization parameter (<init-param>) in the deployment descriptor:

```
<init-param>
  <param-name>waitInterval</param-name>
  <param-value>5</param-value>
</init-param>
```

This specifies an initialization parameter with name "waitInterval" with value "5".

When the web container loads a web application, it also loads the initialization parameters associated with the application. Upon loading the application, the container creates a ServletConfig object for each servlet in the application. You can obtain this ServletConfig object via the getServletConfig() method, and extract the initialization parameters. The getInitParameter() method may return a null value if the requested parameter is not found in the deployment descriptor.

Also note that only string parameters are allowed in the deployment descriptor. In the case of FreakServlet, since we're interested in an integer time interval, we should programmatically convert the extracted string "5" into an int.

Note that the above two states occur only once during the lifetime of a servlet instance.

Service

This is the third state in the servlet lifecycle. Refer to the implementation of the doGet() method. This method generates a random boolean, and if the boolean is true, throws an UnavailableException, indicating that this servlet will not be available for processing requests for the next waitInterval seconds:

```
if (random.nextBoolean()) {

  // Not available for waitInterval seconds.
  states.add(createState("Unavailable from doGet"));
  throw new UnavailableException("Unavailable from doGet",
                                waitInterval);
}
```

Before throwing the exception, the servlet adds a state called "Unavailable from doGet". In this case, you would see the browser output saying the servlet was unavailable. This page shows an error page indicating that the FreakServlet is unavailable. How is this page displayed?

Once the container receives the UnavailableException (or any exception mentioned in the throws clause of the service() method), the container verifies if an error page is specified in the deployment descriptor for that exception. In the case of FreakServlet, the deployment descriptor has the entry:

```
<error-page>
  <exception-type>javax.servlet.UnavailableException</exception-type>
  <location>/unavailable.html</location>
</error-page>
```

This specifies the location of the error page for the `UnavailableException`. Upon finding this mapping information, the container displays the error page whenever this exception is thrown. You can extend this mechanism to display friendly messages in the case of other exceptions. If you do not specify error pages, and your servlet throws an exception, depending on the implementation of the container, you may get not-so-friendly messages. In the case of Tomcat, you'll see a stack trace pointing to the source of the exception. Here is a sample stack trace:

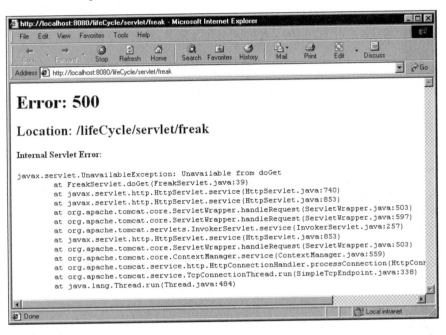

If the generated random number is `false`, `FreakServlet` generates a page displaying the states recorded so far. It uses methods in the `HttpServletRequest` interface to set the content type of the response, and generate the HTML. Refer to the implementation again:

```
states.add(createState("Service"));

response.setContentType("text/html");
PrintWriter out = response.getWriter();

// Send acknowledgment to the browser
out.println("<HTML>");
out.println("<META HTTP-EQUIV=\"Pragma\" CONTENT=\"no-cache\">");
out.println("<HEAD><TITLE>");

out.println("FreakServlet: State History");
out.println("</TITLE></HEAD>");
out.println("<BODY>");
out.println("<H1>FreakServlet: State History</H1>");

out.println("<a href=\"/lifeCycle/servlet/freak\">Reload</a></p>");
```

```
    for (int i = 0; i < states.size(); i++) {
      out.println("<p> " + states.elementAt(i) + "</p>");
    }

    out.println("</BODY></HTML>");
    out.close();
  }
```

There are four steps for generating the response:

- ❏ The first step is to set the content type for the response. The receiving application (the browser) uses this information to know how to treat the response data. In this case, since we're generating HTML output, the content type is being set to "text/html".

- ❏ The second step is to get a `PrintWriter` object from the response. `PrintWriter` is a class from the `java.io` package that extends the `java.io.Writer` abstract class. In the case of servlets, the container constructs the `PrintWriter` object from the `java.io.OutputStream` object associated with the underlying network connection from the client. With TCP/IP based implementations, containers usually get a `java.io.OutputStream` object from the socket, use that object to create the `PrinterWriter` object, and associate it with the `HttpServletResponse` object. As a result, from within the servlet, you'll be able to write to the output stream associated with the network association.

- ❏ Note the META tags in the HTML generated above. This tag indicates to the browser that it should not cache this page. You'll find a similar tag in `unavailable.html`. Without these tags, you'll notice that your browser does not reload the page when you click on the **Reload** or **again** links.

- ❏ The `PrintWriter` class has several methods to print various data types to the associated stream. In this case, we use the `println()` method with a `java.lang.String` argument.

Finally, remember to close the `PrintWriter` object at the end.

Destroy

This is the final stage in the servlet lifecycle. In the case of `FreakServlet`, the `destroy()` method is called before shutting down Tomcat. The `FreakServlet` has a simple implementation for this state:

```
public void destroy() {
  states.add(createState("Destroy"));
  log("Flushing state history of LifeCycleTest servlet.");
  for (int i = 0; i < states.size(); i++) {
    log(states.elementAt(i).toString());
  }
}
```

This method adds a state called `"Destroy"` to the `states` Vector, and logs the complete state history using the `log()` method of the `HttpServlet` class. In general, most of the web containers use a text file for logging messages, although more complex implementations are possible. In the case of Tomcat, log messages are dumped into the `%TOMCAT_HOME%\bin\logs\servlet.log` file.

If you kill the Tomcat server without properly shutting down, you will not be able to observe the destroy state, as the kill message kills the Java virtual machine running the web container. You may also lose unflushed log messages in this process.

This ends our discussion on the servlet lifecycle. A final note on the usage of various servlet API methods/objects during the lifecycle:

❑ Objects of classes such as `ServletConfig`, `ServletContext`, `HttpServletRequest`, and `HttpServletResponse` are valid only between the `init()` and `destroy()` method calls. That is, you should not use these objects before `init()` is called, or after `destroy()` is called. For example, your constructor should not use the `log()` method, because the `log()` method is implemented by the `ServletContext` object associated with your servlet. Your servlet instance will not have a valid reference to a `ServletContext` object before the call to `init()`.

❑ Also notice the `Vector` that we're using is an instance variable in the `FreakServlet`. Since this is not a `SingleThreadModel` servlet, the container creates only one instance of this servlet, and routes all requests in concurrent execution threads to the `doGet()` method. Since this `states` vector is an instance variable, read and write operations on this object should be thread-safe. In the case of the `java.util.Vector` class, the `add()` and `size()` methods are synchronized. Because of this, multiple-users of the `FreakServlet` can can interact with its lifecycle, and yet see the most up-to-date state history

API for Requests and Responses

The `javax.servlet.HttpServletRequest` and `javax.servlet.HttpServletResponse` interfaces are the classes that servlets depend on for accessing HTTP requests and responses. However, as shown in the UML class diagram at the beginning of this chapter, the complete list of interfaces and classes for dealing with requests and response is:

❑ `javax.servlet.ServletRequest`

❑ `javax.servlet.ServletResponse`

❑ `javax.servlet.ServletInputStream`

❑ `javax.servlet.ServletOutputStream`

❑ `javax.servlet.http.HttpServletRequest`

❑ `javax.servlet.http.HttpServletResponse`

With the exception of `javax.servlet.ServletInputStream` and `javax.servlet.ServletOutputStream`, these are interfaces. The `HttpServletRequest` and `HttpServletResponse` interfaces are more specialized versions of the `ServletRequest` and `ServletResponse` interfaces for HTTP. The two classes can be used to read from and write to the input and output streams respectively.

The ServletRequest Interface

```
public interface ServletRequest
```

This interface specifies an abstraction of client requests for a servlet. The web container creates an instance of this object while calling the service() method of the GenericServlet or the HttpServlet. The the complete list of methods in this interface is as follows:

```
public Object getAttribute(String name)
public Object setAttribute(String name, Object attribute)
public Enumeration getAttributeNames()
public void removeAttribute(String name)
public Locale getLocale()
public Enumeration getLocales()
public String getCharacterEncoding()
public int getContentLength()
public String getContentType()
public ServletInputStream getInputStream()
public String getParameter(String name)
public Enumeration getParameterNames()
public Enumeration getParameterValues()
public String getProtocol()
public String getScheme()
public String getServerName()
public int getServerPort()
public BufferedReader getReader()
public String getRemoteAddr()
public String getRemoteHost()
public Boolean isSecure()
public RequestDispatcher getRequestDispatcher(String path)
```

Since this interface has quite a lot of methods, let's group them based on their usage, and discuss some of the most commonly required methods.

Methods for Request Parameters

The following methods can be used to access the request parameters. In the case of HTTP requests, these methods can be used for both GET and POST requests.

The getParameter() Method

```
public String getParameter(String key)
```

This will attempt to locate a parameter with the given key (case-sensitive) in the request and return its value. If there are multiple values for the given parameter, then this method returns the first value in the list. This method returns null if the key is not found in the request.

The getParameterValues() Method

```
public String[] getParameterValues(String key)
```

If a parameter can return multiple values, such as a set of check boxes, a multi-selection list, or even multiple controls with the same name, this method returns an array containing the parameter values.

The getParameterNames() Method

```
public Enumeration getParameterNames()
```

This method returns an enumeration of all of the parameter names for the request. If the request has no parameters, it returns an empty enumeration.

Methods for Request Attributes

Apart from request parameters, web containers or servlets/JSPs can attach attributes to requests. The servlet API specification specifies three different approaches for storing and retrieving attributes. One of them is attaching attributes to request objects. The other two are approaches use the HttpSession, and ServletContext (to be discussed in the next chapter) for storing and retrieving attributes. As you will see in Chapter 11, the JSP specification specifies an additional mechanism using PageContext to store and retrieve attributes. Each of these approaches provides the notion of a scope for the attributes to exist. In the case of attributes attached to request objects, the lifetime of these attributes is that of the request itself.

In the servlet parlance, an attribute is a named Java language object. While setting an attribute, you assign a name to the attribute, and while retrieving the attribute, specify the same name. Names are String objects.

The purpose of attributes in the request scope is to allow the container or another servlet to send additional data to a servlet or a JSP. For the application developer, this is useful when using the RequestDispatcher object to forward requests from one servlet to another. You'll learn more about this approach in Chapter 11.

The following methods can be used to manage attributes in the request context.

The getAttribute() Method

```
public Object getAttribute()
```

This method returns the value of the named attribute (or null if the named attribute does not exist).

The getAttributeNames() Method

```
public Enumeration getAttributeNames()
```

This method returns an enumeration of all the attributes contained in the request. It returns an empty enumeration if there are no attributes in the request.

The setAttribute() Method

```
public void setAttribute(String name, Object o)
```

This method sets a named attribute.

The removeAttribute() Method

```
public void setAttribute(String name, Object o)
```

This method removes the named attribute from the request.

Methods for Input

As discussed previously, the `ServletRequest` holds a reference to the underlying client connection. Using the following methods, you can access the stream/writer objects associated with the request.

The getInputStream() Method

```
public ServletInputStream getInputStream() throws java.io.IOException
```

This method can be used to access the body of the request using a `ServletInputStream` object.

The getReader() Method

```
public java.io.BufferedReader getReader() throws java.io.IOException
```

This method can be used to access the body of the request using a buffered reader object.

Note that only one of the above methods can be invoked on a given `ServletRequest` object.

The HttpServletRequest Interface

```
public interface HttpServletRequest extends ServletRequest
```

The most commonly used methods in this interface are the methods for accessing request parameters. To understand how to use these methods of this interface, consider how HTTP allows data to be passed to the web server. As discussed in the previous chapter, HTTP allows you to submit parameters along with a request. In a GET request, these parameters are appended to the request URL in the form of a query string, whereas in a POST request the parameters are sent within the body of the request in x-www-form-urlencoded format. In any case, these parameters are represented as key-value pairs. HTTP does not require that the keys are unique – so for some keys, there can be a list of values. Examples include multiple selection listboxes or checkbox groups.

When you build an HTML form for GET or POST requests, you specify certain controls using <INPUT> tags. Each control has a TYPE, such as CHECKBOX, TEXT, or SUBMIT, and can also have a NAME and/or a VALUE. The NAME attribute defines the key by which the value returned to the server will be known. The VALUE attribute has different effects on different controls. Obviously, if we give more than one <INPUT> tag the same name, we could have several key/value pairs with the same key as part of our request. The following table shows the values submitted to the server for different types of form controls:

Control Type	Description	Value Returned
TEXT	Single line text input field, with VALUE attribute as default content.	Text entered by user, or the default.
TEXTAREA	Multiple line text area, with VALUE attribute as the default content.	Text entered by the user, or the default.
PASSWORD	Single line password entry field (shows * instead of character entered).	Text entered by user.

Control Type	Description	Value Returned
CHECKBOX	Standard checkbox.	If checked: VALUE attribute (or "on" if not specified). If *not* checked: no key/value pair returned.
RADIO	Standard radio button – all buttons with the same NAME form a button group, so only one can be selected.	VALUE attribute of selected radio button only.
SELECT	Used to create a list of items from which the user can select. Can be single-valued or multi-valued.	User selected items or the default(s).
SUBMIT	Submit button, with VALUE attribute as button caption.	None, unless NAME attribute is supplied. Default for VALUE is "Submit".
HIDDEN	Form field that is not visible in the browser and thus cannot be modified by the user.	VALUE attribute.

There are other controls, but these will do for now. The most common reason for having multiple controls with the same NAME is to be able to build sets of radio buttons and check boxes, and multiple-selection SELECT controls. The radio button set will return the single selected VALUE, and check boxes or multiple-selection SELECT controls will return all of the selected VALUEs.

Any object that implements the HttpServletRequest interface (such as the HTTP request object passed in from the web container) will give the servlet access to all of the request data through its methods.

Note that since the HttpServletRequest interface is meant to encapsulate HTTP, this interface (in combination with the methods provided in the ServletRequest interface) provides numerous methods for accessing the HTTP request:

```
public String getAuthType()
public Cookie[] getCookies()
public long getDateHeader(String name)
public String getHeader(String name)
public Enumeration getHeaders(String name)
public Enumeration getHeaderNames()
public int getIntHeader(String name)
public String getMethod()
public String getContextPath()
public String getPathInfo()
public String getPathTranslated()
public String getQueryString()
public String getRemoteUser()
public boolean isUserInRole(String role)
public java.security.Principal getUserPrincipal()
public String getRequestedSessionId()
public boolean isRequestedSessionIdValid()
```

```
public boolean isRequestedSessionIdFromCookie()
public boolean isRequestedSessionIdFromURL()
public String getRequestURI
public String getServletPath()
public HttpSession getSession()
public HttpSession getSession(boolean create)
```

The following are some of the most commonly used methods specified in the `HttpServletRequest` interface. You'll encounter some of the remaining methods in the next chapter.

Methods for Request Path and URL

The first group of methods allows a servlet to obtain the URL and request path with which it was invoked.

The getPathInfo() Method

```
public String getPathInfo()
```

This method returns any extra path information associated with the request URL. In general, you invoke a servlet using its alias or the class name. For instance, you can access a servlet `MyServlet` using the URL `http://host:port/myApp/MyServlet`, where `myApp` is the application context. However, you can send additional path information to the servlet, say, as `http://host:port/myApp/MyServlet/wrox`. In this case, `/wrox` is the additional path information. The servlet can use the `getPathInfo()` to obtain this path information.

This method returns `null` if there is no additional path in the request.

The getPathTranslated() Method

```
public String getPathTranslated()
```

This method translates the extra path information into a real path. For instance, in the above example, if the `MyServlet` class is located in the `c:\work\myApp\WEB-INF\classes` directory, this method returns `c:\work\myApp\wrox` as the translated path.

This method returns `null` if there is no additional path in the request.

The getQueryString() Method

```
public String getQueryString()
```

This method returns the query string associated with the request.

The getRequestURI() Method

```
public String getRequestURI()
```

This method returns the URI path associated with the request. In the above example, this method would return `/myApp/MyServlet/wrox`.

The getServletPath() Method

```
public String getServletPath()
```

This method returns the URI path associated with the servlet. This excludes any extra path information and query string. For instance, in the above example, this method would return /myApp/MyServlet as the servlet path.

Methods for HTTP Headers

The next group of methods allows servlets to read HTTP headers sent with the request.

The getHeader() Method

```
public String getHeader(String name)
```

This method returns the value of the named header from the HTTP request. This method returns null if the request does not include the specified header.

The getHeaders() Method

```
public Enumeration getHeaders()
```

This method returns an enumeration of all request header values.

The getHeaderNames() Method

```
public Enumeration getHeaderNames()
```

This method returns an enumeration of names of request headers.

The getMethod() Method

```
public String getMethod()
```

This method returns the type of the HTTP request, such as GET, POST, etc.

Apart from these methods, there are several methods specific to HTTP sessions. We shall discuss some of these methods in the next chapter.

The ServletResponse Interface

```
public interface ServletResponse
```

This is the response counterpart of the ServletRequest object, and abstracts most of the methods necessary for constructing responses from servlets. This interface specifies the following methods:

```
public String getgetCharacterEncoding()
public ServletOutputStream getOutputStream()
public PrintWriter getWriter()
public void setContentLength(int length)
```

```
public void setContentType(String type)
public void setBufferSize(int size)
public int getBufferSize()
public void reset()
public boolean isCommitted()
public void flushBuffer()
public void setLocale()
public Locale getLocale()
```

The following are some of the most commonly used methods of this interface.

Methods for Content Type and Length

These methods allow the servlet to set the response's MIME content type and the content length.

The setContentType() Method

```
public void setContentType(String type)
```

This method sets the content type of the response. If you're using the `PrintWriter` object (discussed below) to generate the response, before writing the response, you should call `setContentType()` to set the MIME type of the HTTP response. In the case of HTML, the MIME type should be set to `"text/HTML"`.

The setContentLength() Method

```
public void setContentLength(int size)
```

This method can be used to set the Content-Length header of the content.

Methods for Output

The following methods are useful for generating text or binary content in the response.

The getOutputStream() Method

```
public ServletOutputStream getOutputStream() throws java.io.IOException
```

This method returns a `ServletOutputStream` object that can be used for writing binary data in the response. This `ServletOutputStream` class is a subclass of `java.io.OutputStream`. On a given `HttpServletResponse` object, you should call this method only once. If you try to call this method more than once, you will encounter an `IllegalStateException`.

The getWriter() Method

```
public java.io.PrintWriter getWriter() throws java.io.IOException
```

This method returns a `PrintWriter` object that can be used to send character text in the response. The `PrintWriter` automatically translates Java's internal Unicode characters into the correct encoding so that they can be read on the client machine. For information on how to change the encoding to deal with international character sets, see Appendix D. With the `PrintWriter` object, you would typically write data to the response object using its `println(String string)` method. Similar to the `getOutputStream()` method, this method also should not be called more than once on a given `HttpServletResponse` object.

Moreover, only one of the above two methods should be called on any `HttpServletResponse` object.

Methods for Buffered Output

You can also send buffered response from your servlets. The following methods are useful for controlling the buffering.

In case you're sending large amount of data in the response, you should consider setting the buffer size to smaller values, so that the user can start receiving the data quickly.

Buffering also allows you to abort the content generated so far, and restart the generation.

The setBufferSize() Method

```
public void setBufferSize(int size)
```

This method sets the preferred buffer size for the body of the response. Note that the web container will use a buffer at least as large as the size requested.

The getBufferSize() Method

```
public int getBufferSize()
```

This method returns the actual buffer size used for the response.

The flushBuffer() Method

```
public void flushBuffer() throws java.io.IOException
```

This method forces any content in the buffer to be written to the client.

The isCommitted() Method

```
public boolean isCommitted()
```

This method returns a boolean indicating if the response in the buffer has been committed.

The reset() Method

```
public void reset()
```

This method is useful for resetting the buffer thereby discarding the content in the buffer.

The HttpServletResponse Interface

```
public interface HttpServletResponse extends ServletResponse
```

The web container provides an object that implements this interface and passes it into the servlet through the service() method. The servlet can modify response headers and return results through the HttpServletResponse object. This interface includes the following methods:

```
public void addCookie(Cookie cookie)
public boolean containsHeader(String name)
public String encodeURL(String url)
public String encodeRedirecURL(String name)
public void sendError(int status)
public void sendError(int status, String message)
public void sendRedirect(String location)
public void setDateHeader(String headerName, long date)
public void setHeader(String headerName, String value)
public void addHeader(String headerName, String value)
public void addDateHeader(String headerName, long date)
public void setIntHeader(String headerName, int value)
public void setStatus(int statusCode)
```

Apart from these methods, this interface also specifies a set of error codes that correspond to standard HTTP errors. Refer to the API documentation for this list.

The following are some of the basic methods for writing content in the response.

Methods for Error Handling

This group of methods allows a servlet to send an error message or to set the HTTP status code.

The sendError() Method

```
public void sendError(int status)
```

Servlets can use this method to indicate standard HTTP status codes. As seen in the case of FreakServlet, you can specify error pages for different HTTP errors and servlet exceptions. If there is a matching page for the specified status code, the container sends the specified page to the client. If there is no page specified, the container sends its default error page indicating the status code and a corresponding message.

The sendError() Method

```
public void sendError(int status, String message)
```

This message is similar to the sendError(status) method, except that it also accepts a status message. You can use this message to indicate specific failures.

The setStatus() Method

```
public void setStatus(int status)
```

This method can be used to send HTTP status codes that are not errors.

The sendRedirect() Method

```
public void sendRedirect(String location)
```

This method sends a redirect response to the client. The client receives the HTTP response code 302 indicating that temporarily the client is being redirected to the specified location. If the specified location is relative, this method converts into an absolute URL before redirecting.

Servlet Programming – Tech Support Application

Having seen an overview of the servlet API and the servlet lifecycle, let's now consider another application that involves:

❑ **Collecting a technical support request**
   This part of the application illustrates obtaining parameters from HTTP requests.

❑ **Storing the support request in a database**
   This part of the application illustrates a thread-safe approach for generating sequence numbers, and storing data in the database.

❑ **Generating a confirmation page**

This application requires a database for storing the technical support requests. In the current configuration, I assume that you're using the Cloudscape database.

> *Cloudscape 3.5 Free Developer Edition can be downloaded from*
> `http://www.cloudscape.com/`. *Other databases can be used by changing parameters in the deployment descriptor (see later).*

For this example, we will be creating a technical support request application for a fictitious company called XYZ Corporation. In order to develop this application, we will:

❑ Prepare an HTML page with a form to collect the technical support request

❑ Prepare the database tables, by creating the schema for the database tables

❑ Create a sequencer class to generate sequence numbers for support requests.

❑ Create the `TechSupportServlet` servlet to process the form, insert the request into the tables, and generate a confirmation page

Setting up the HTML Page

The purpose of this page is to provide a form for submitting technical support requests. You'll find that the controls used can be applied to numerous other forms. The following HTML contains the form for collecting technical support request data; copy this under `c:\ProJavaServer\chap08\techSupport\techsupp.html`:

```
<HTML>
<HEAD>
  <TITLE>XYZ Corporation, IT Department</title>
</HEAD>
```

```
<BODY>
  <H1>Technical Support Request</H1>
  <HR><BR>
  <CENTER>
    <FORM ACTION="/techSupport/servlet/techSupport" METHOD="POST">
    <TABLE ALIGN="center" WIDTH="100%" CELLSPACING="2" CELLPADDING="2">
      <TR>
        <TD ALIGN="right">First Name:</TD>
        <TD><INPUT TYPE="Text" NAME="firstName" ALIGN="LEFT" SIZE="15"></TD>
        <TD ALIGN="right">Last Name:</TD>
        <TD><INPUT TYPE="Text" NAME="lastName" ALIGN="LEFT" SIZE="15"></TD>
      </TR>
      <TR>
        <TD ALIGN="right">Email:</TD>
        <TD><INPUT TYPE="Text" NAME="email" ALIGN="LEFT" SIZE="25"></TD>
        <TD ALIGN="right">Phone:</TD>
        <TD><INPUT TYPE="Text" NAME="phone" ALIGN="LEFT" SIZE="15"></TD>
      </TR>
      <TR>
        <TD ALIGN="right">Software:</TD>
        <TD>
          <SELECT NAME="software" SIZE="1">
            <OPTION VALUE="Word">Microsoft Word</OPTION>
            <OPTION VALUE="Excel">Microsoft Excel</OPTION>
            <OPTION VALUE="Access">Microsoft Access</OPTION>
          </SELECT>
        </TD>
        <TD ALIGN="right">Operating System:</TD>
        <TD>
          <SELECT NAME="os" size="1">
            <OPTION VALUE="95">Windows 95</OPTION>
            <OPTION VALUE="98">Windows 98</OPTION>
            <OPTION VALUE="NT">Windows NT</OPTION>
          </SELECT>
        </TD>
      </TR>
    </TABLE>

    <BR>Problem Description
    <BR>
    <TEXTAREA NAME="problem" COLS="50" ROWS="4"></TEXTAREA>

    <HR><BR>

    <INPUT TYPE="Submit" NAME="submit" VALUE="Submit Request">
  </FORM>
  </CENTER>
</BODY>
</HTML>
```

This form has the following controls:

❑ A TEXT control called firstName to collect the first name

❑ A TEXT control called lastname to collect the last name

❑ A TEXT control called email to collect the e mail address

❑ A TEXT control called phone to collect the phone number

- ❑ A SELECT control called software for displaying a combo box with software applications
- ❑ A SELECT control called os for displaying a combox box with operating systems

Although you can view this HTML page in a browser directly from the file system (from c:\ProJavaServer\chap08\techSupport\techsupp.html), you can add the following <Context> definition to %TOMCAT_HOME%\conf\server.xml at this stage:

```
<Context path="/techSupport"
         docBase="c:\ProJavaServer\Chapter08\techSupport">
</Context>
```

Enter the URL http://localhost:8080/techSupport/techsupp.html in your browser's address/location area to load this page.

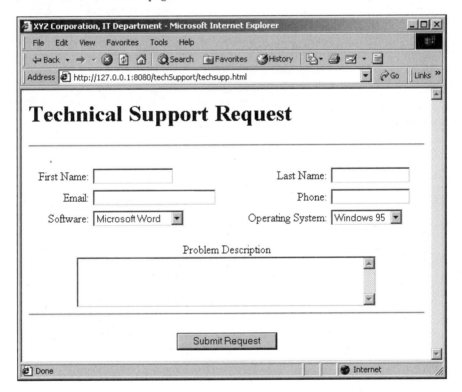

Prepare the Database

Before proceeding to write the servlet, we should prepare the database tables storing the technical support requests. Use your database vendor provided tools (such as CloudView for Cloudscape, or SQL Plus for Oracle) to create the database. If you're using Cloudscape as your database, make sure that the database is created at c:\ProJavaServer\Chapter08\techSupport\WEB-INF\db:

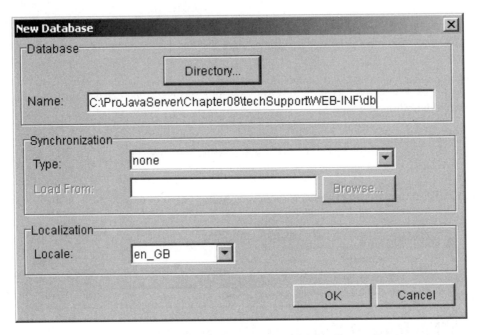

Then execute the following SQL statements to create the tables for this application:

```
--
-- Table for storing the technical support requests
--

CREATE TABLE SUPP_REQUESTS(REQUEST_ID        INTEGER PRIMARY KEY,
                           FIRST_NAME        VARCHAR(40),
                           LAST_NAME         VARCHAR(40),
                           EMAIL             VARCHAR(40),
                           PHONE             VARCHAR(15),
                           SOFTWARE          VARCHAR(40),
                           OS                VARCHAR(40),
                           PROBLEM           VARCHAR(256));


--
-- Sequencer table for generating sequence numbers for REQUEST_ID
--
CREATE TABLE SEQ_NO(NEXT_NO                   INTEGER);

INSERT INTO SEQ_NO VALUES(0);
```

In Cloudscape, you use CloudView as shown opposite:

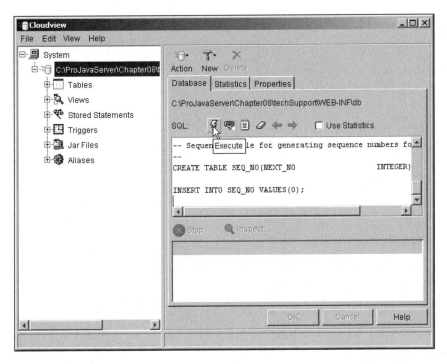

The schema for this application has two tables: a SUPP_REQUESTS table and a SEQ_NO table. While the SUPP_REQUESTS table is meant for storing the technical support requests, the purpose of the SEQ_NO table is to hold the current sequence number. The purpose of this sequencer will be clear shortly.

Creating a Sequencer

In order to assign a unique ID for each technical support request, we need to generate unique sequence numbers. Although it is possible to generate such numbers using database triggers, for this exercise let's consider a Java class that can generate unique numbers. Enter the following Java code in c:\ProJavaServer\Chapter08\techSupport\src\Sequencer.java:

```java
// Imports Java packages
import java.sql.*;

public class Sequencer {

  static String updateStatementStr =
    "UPDATE SEQ_NO SET NEXT_NO = NEXT_NO + 1";
  static String selectStatementStr = "SELECT NEXT_NO FROM SEQ_NO";

  // Get the next number
  public static int getNextNumber(String protocol) throws SQLException {
    Connection connection = DriverManager.getConnection(protocol);

    PreparedStatement updateStatement =
      connection.prepareStatement(updateStatementStr);
    PreparedStatement selectStatement =
      connection.prepareStatement(selectStatementStr);
    connection.setAutoCommit(false);
```

```
    // Increment the sequencer
    updateStatement.executeUpdate();

    // Retrieve the sequencer number
    ResultSet rs = selectStatement.executeQuery();
    rs.next();
    int next = rs.getInt(1);

    rs.close();
    updateStatement.close();
    selectStatement.close();

    connection.commit();
    connection.close();

    return next;
  }
}
```

This class has one static method, getNextNumber(), which accepts a database URL and returns the next possible sequence number. This method increments the NEXT_NO field in the SEQ_NO table, reads the incremented number, and returns. Note that the update and select statements are executed within a transaction (with auto-commit-mode set to false), so that the database serializes access to the NEXT_NO. This would ensure that multiple servlet request threads can access the getNextNumber() method without any conflict.

Writing the Servlet

Since the form in our HTML page has a POST request, we need to implement a servlet with the doPost() method overridden. In order to process the technical support request, the following are the tasks that this method should perform:

❑   initialize the servlet to load the database driver

❑   extract form input from the HttpServletRequest, using the getParameter() methods

❑   insert the data into a database table

❑   generate a confirmation page to the user with a reference number

The outline of the TechSupportServlet class is as follows:

```
// Import Servlet packages
import javax.servlet.*;
import javax.servlet.http.*;

// Import other Java packages
import java.io.*;
import java.sql.*;

public class TechSupportServlet extends HttpServlet {
  String protocol;

  // Methods will go here ...

}
```

Initialize the Servlet

In this example, we use the standard JDBC (`java.sql`) approach for registering the driver and obtain the connections. The `init()` method of the servlet performs this task:

```java
public void init() throws ServletException {
  String driver = getServletConfig().getInitParameter("driver");
  protocol = getServletConfig().getInitParameter("protocol");

  if (driver == null || protocol == null) {
    throw new UnavailableException("Driver not specified.");
  }

  try {
    Class.forName(driver);
  } catch (ClassNotFoundException cnfe) {
    throw new UnavailableException("Driver <" + driver
                              + "> not found in the classpath.");
  }
}
```

This method reads two servlet initialisation parameters, `driver` and `protocol`, from the deployment descriptor, and registers the driver. If the initialization parameters are not specified in the deployment descriptor, or if the driver class could not be found, this method throws permanent `UnavailableExceptions`, indicating this servlet cannot process any requests.

Extract the Form Data

To collect the data that the user entered into the form, we use the `HttpServletRequest` object's `getParameter(String key)` method. The only argument to this method is a `String` specifying the name of the parameter to be extracted. The following statements in the `doGet()` method of this servlet extract the form parameters from the `HttpServletRequest`:

```java
protected void doPost(HttpServletRequest req, HttpServletResponse res)
        throws ServletException, IOException {
  String firstName = req.getParameter("firstName");
  String lastName = req.getParameter("lastName");
  String email = req.getParameter("email");
  String phone = req.getParameter("phone");
  String software = req.getParameter("software");
  String os = req.getParameter("os");
  String problem = req.getParameter("problem");
```

Note that reading parameters from requests is simple. If the specified parameter is found in the request, the `getParameter()` method returns a valid `String` object. However, if the form does not contain the specified parameter at all, this method returns `null`. Note that JDBC drivers and databases expect legal field values (including non-null) in the SQL statements and prepared statements, and you may have to check for such conditions before executing JDBC statements.

Insert the Technical Support Request

After collecting the form parameters, the next step is to execute a SQL statement to insert this data. Note that this process requires generating a sequence number, for which we use the `Sequencer` class created previously:

```
int requestId = 0;
Connection connection = null;
String insertStatementStr =
  "INSERT INTO SUPP_REQUESTS VALUES(?, ?, ?, ?, ?, ?, ?, ?)";
try {
  connection = DriverManager.getConnection(protocol);

  PreparedStatement insertStatement =
    connection.prepareStatement(insertStatementStr);

  requestId = Sequencer.getNextNumber(protocol);

  insertStatement.setInt(1, requestId);

  insertStatement.setString(2, firstName);
  insertStatement.setString(3, lastName);
  insertStatement.setString(4, email);
  insertStatement.setString(5, phone);
  insertStatement.setString(6, software);
  insertStatement.setString(7, os);
  insertStatement.setString(8, problem);
  insertStatement.executeUpdate();
} catch (SQLException sqle) {
  throw new ServletException("Database error", sqle);
}
finally {
  if (connection != null) {
    try {
      connection.close();
    } catch (SQLException sqle) {}
  }
}
```

This method uses a `java.sql.PreparedStatement` for executing the INSERT statement. The steps for inserting the data into the SUPP_REQUESTS table are:

❑   Obtain a database connection using the `DriverManager`

❑   Prepare a statement for the INSERT

❑   Generate a sequence number using the static `getNextNumber()` method of the `Sequencer` class

   Note that this method requires the JDBC protocol string as an argument.

❑   Set parameters for the prepared statement

❑   Execute the prepared statement

❑   Close the database connection in the `finally` block; this is to make sure that the connection is always closed

Generate the Response

The last step in the `TechSupportServlet` is to generate the response for the user:

```
        // Prepare the response
        PrintWriter out = res.getWriter();

        res.setContentType("text/html");

        out.println("<HTML><HEAD><TITLE>");
        out.println("Tech Support: Request Confirmation");
        out.println("</TITLE></HEAD>");
        out.println("<BODY>");
        out.println("<H1>Tech Support: Request Confirmation</H1>");
        out.println("<P>Thank you for your request. Your request with the following
                       reference number has been received.</P>");
        out.println("<P>Request Reference: " + requestId + "</P>");
        out.println("<P>Please note this number for future references.</P>");
        out.println("<P>Your request will be attended to within 24 hours.</P>");
        out.println("<P>Administrator <br>Techsupport team. </P>");
        out.println("</BODY></HTML>");

        out.close();
    }
```

This completes the servlet.

Compile the Source

Compile the source files `TechSupportServlet.java` and `Sequencer.java` to create the class files under the `WEB-INF\classes` subdirectory under `c:\ProJavaServer\chap08\techSupport`.

Deployment Descriptor

Create the following deployment descriptor for the TechSupport application:

```xml
<?xml version="1.0" encoding="ISO-8859-1"?>

<!DOCTYPE web-app PUBLIC "-//Sun Microsystems, Inc.//DTD Web Application 2.2//EN"
    "http://java.sun.com/j2ee/dtds/web-app_2.2.dtd">

<web-app>

  <welcome-file-list>
    <welcome-file>techsupp.html</welcome-file>
  </welcome-file-list>

  <servlet>
    <servlet-name>techSupport</servlet-name>
    <servlet-class>TechSupportServlet</servlet-class>

    <init-param>
      <param-name>driver</param-name>
      <param-value>COM.cloudscape.core.JDBCDriver</param-value>
    </init-param>

    <init-param>
```

```
        <param-name>protocol</param-name>
        <param-value>
jdbc:cloudscape:C:/ProJavaServer/Chapter08/techSupport/WEB-INF/db;autocommit=true
        </param-value>
      </init-param>
    </servlet>
  </web-app>
```

Replace the driver and protocol values to suit your configuration.

Note the following key points in this deployment descriptor:

❑ **Welcome File**
   In this deployment descriptor, `techsupp.html` is the welcome file for this application. So, instead of entering the URL `http://localhost:8080/techSupport/techsupp.html`, you can just type `http://localhost:8080/techSupport/` in your browser to load this file. We'll discuss more about welcome files in Chapter 10.

❑ **Initialization Parameters**
   The name of the driver and the JDBC protocol are the two initialization parameters for this servlet. Note that if you've more than one servlet using the same set of initialization parameters, a better way is to specify such parameters as context parameters. We'll discuss more about context parameters in Chapters 9 and 10.

Tech Support in Action

There is one final step to perform before we can test this application. That is to make sure that Tomcat is setup correctly to load the database driver. Shutdown Tomcat, open `%TOMCAT_HOME%\bin\tomcat.bat` in your favourite editor, and add the two highlighted lines before and after the `CLASSPATH` settings as follows:

```
set CLOUDSCAPE_CP=%CLOUDSCAPE_INSTALL%\lib\cloudscape.jar
set CLASSPATH=.
set CLASSPATH=%TOMCAT_HOME%\classes
set CLASSPATH=%CLASSPATH%;%TOMCAT_HOME%\lib\webserver.jar
set CLASSPATH=%CLASSPATH%;%TOMCAT_HOME%\lib\jasper.jar
set CLASSPATH=%CLASSPATH%;%TOMCAT_HOME%\lib\xml.jar
set CLASSPATH=%CLASSPATH%;%TOMCAT_HOME%\lib\servlet.jar
set CLASSPATH=%CLASSPATH%;%JAVA_HOME%\lib\tools.jar
set CLASSPATH=%CLASSPATH%;%CLOUDSCAPE_CP%
```

Note that you should not modify the lines in between if they are different from the above.

Start the Tomcat server, and enter the URL `http://localhost:8080/techSupport`, and fill the form as shown opposite:

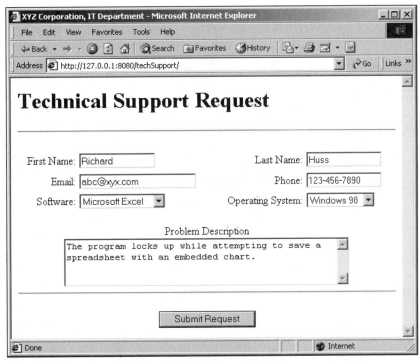

Upon submitting this form, the browser should generate the following response:

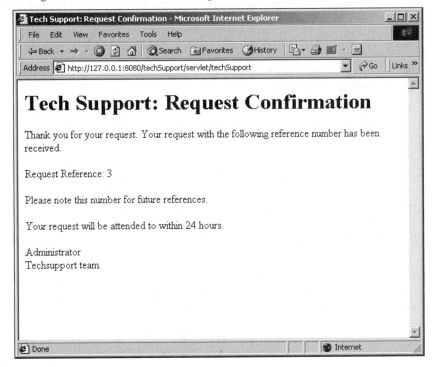

You may use your database vendor provided tools to open the database tables to find that the data has successfully been added. In the case of Cloudscape, you can use the CloudView application to open the database:

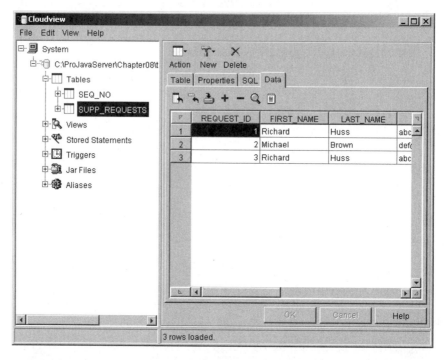

Make sure to shutdown Tomcat before launching CloudView. This is because, in the default configuration, Cloudscape allows only one application to access the database files.

Note on Database Connections

Note that we opened the database connection in the servlet's doPost() method, instead of the init() method, although opening a database connection could be considered a one-time activity. But what happens if you declare the connection as an instance variable, and open it in the init() method, and close it in the destroy() method? There is one pitfall with such an approach, particularly when you turn-off the auto-commit mode for the connection. In the non-auto-commit mode, recollect that the commit() or rollback() operation on the connection is done at the end of each transaction. When the servlet receives multiple requests, the same instance (and therefore the same connection object) will be used to serve all requests. However, since there is only one connection, the database sees only one transaction, instead of one transaction per request thread. This would lead to incorrect commit/rollback operations occurring in multiple request threads. In order to avoid this, you should consider opening and closing connections within the service methods.

As mentioned previously, we are using the standard JDBC approach for obtaining connections, and such connections are not pooled. On the other hand, the JDBC Optional Package API (the javax.sql package) provides a more efficient mechanism for obtaining database connections. This mechanism includes a transparent means of creating connection pools, and creating connections using the javax.sql.DataSource object. For details, refer to Chapter 3.

The Tomcat web container that we're using for this application does not include facilities for creating connections in this fashion. However, most of the J2EE application servers include this feature, in which case you could replace the statement:

```
connection = DriverManager.getConnection(protocol);
```

with the following:

```
Context initialContext = new InitialContext();
DataSource dataSource =
(DataSource)initialContext.lookup("jdbc/Cloudscape");
connection = dataSource.getConnection();
```

Here, `jdbc/Cloudscape` is the name of the data source object. Replace this with the correct name of the data source object in your configuration, and remove the code for database driver registration from the servlet. Refer to the documentation of your J2EE server for details on how to configure data source objects and connection pooling.

Summary

The Java Servlet API is both simple and powerful. It allows us to extend the functionality of any web server, with the help of a simple programming model.

The objective of this chapter has been to introduce the servlet API and the lifecycle of servlets, and to demonstrate how to write servlet based web applications. In this process, we've covered the following:

❑   When building a servlet, you need to implement the `Servlet` interface. You can do this by extending either `GenericServlet` or `HttpServlet`.

❑   The `HttpServlet` class extends `GenericServlet`, and provides additional HTTP-specific functionality.

❑   Servlets can implement the `SingleThreadModel` interface for enforcing synchronized access to the service methods. However, servlets that do not implement this interface should make sure that any servlet instance variables are accessed in a thread-safe manner. We've discussed the implications with the `FreakServlet` and the `TechSupportServlet`.

❑   The servlet lifecycle involves the `init()`, `service()`, and `destroy()` methods. The `FreakServlet` demonstrates the states associated with the lifecycle of a servlet instance.

❑   We use deployment descriptors to specify initialization parameters. This helps us avoid hard-coding such parameters within the servlets.

❑   You can use error pages to automatically send pre-designed HTML pages in response to HTTP errors and exceptions. This is a very flexible approach, and it is a good practice to do adequate error handling to prevent unfriendly container-generated messages from being sent to clients.

In the next chapter we'll take a look at the remaining part of the servlet API, which deals with sessions, context, and servlet collaborations.

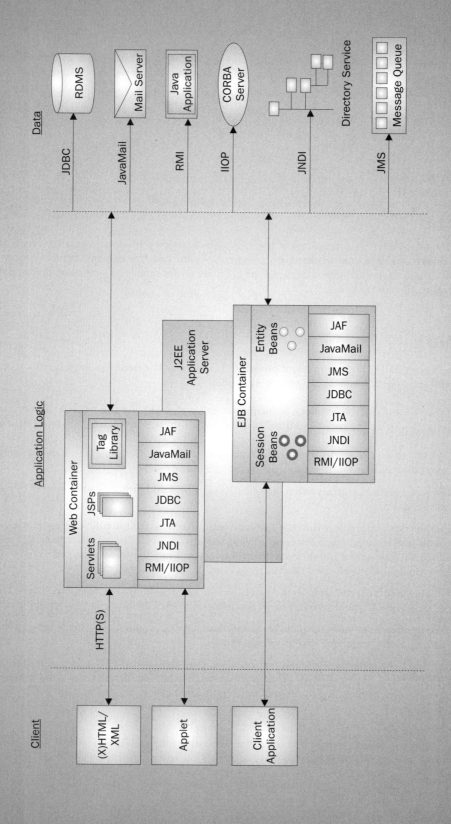

9

Servlet Sessions, Context, and Collaboration

In the previous two chapters we've covered the basic aspects of the servlet API. In particular, we've discussed the lifecycle of servlets, and the APIs for reading requests, and writing responses back to clients. These aspects of the servlet API equip you to build servlets that generate dynamic web pages.

The Tech Support servlet application discussed in the previous chapter gives you an idea of the general structure of a servlet. A servlet receives a request object, extracts parameters (if any) from it, processes any application logic (which may depend on the request parameters), and finally generates the response. Extending this model, you could build larger web applications by having several servlets, with each servlet performing a well-defined independent task.

This model is adequate as long as the application logic in each of these servlets is atomic – that is, as long as the application logic depends only on the parameters in the request (and, if applicable, any persistent data such as data stored in a relational database). For instance, in the Tech Support application the servlet gets all the support request data from the request, and as part of the application logic, writes the request data to a database, and sends a confirmation back. Now consider a familiar online application – an online store.

In a typical online store, the main application that drives the store is a shopping cart. An online shopping cart provides you with a browsable interface to a catalog. You can select items in the catalog, and add them to a shopping cart. Once you have added all the required items to the cart, you proceed for checkout, and place an order for the items in the cart.

However, such an application is not as plain as it appears. Where is the shopping cart maintained? Since the client is 'thin', it is the responsibility of the server to maintain the cart – not only for you, but for all the users who may simultaneously be browsing the catalog and adding items to their respective shopping carts. In order for this mechanism to work, the server should be able to distinguish each user from all other users, and accordingly maintain each shopping cart. How do we build such a feature in a web application?

This is a typical requirement for web applications, where a 'user activity' happens across multiple requests and responses, and the server is required to associate some form of uniqueness with the users. In the first part of this chapter, we'll discuss what is called or **session tracking** to address this requirement. We'll discuss some session tracking approaches, particularly those used by the Java Servlet API.

As well as session tracking, we will consider another useful facility that the servlet API provides. As we discussed in Chapter 8, servlets are part of web applications, and the notion of web applications is built on what is called **servlet context**. In simple terms, a context is a view of the web application and the web container. Servlets in an application can use this context to exchange information, or collaborate with other servlets, access resources, log events, etc. In the second part of this chapter, we'll discuss the servlet APIs related to servlet context.

To demonstrate how session tracking and servlet context let you build complex web applications, we'll also study an online chat application – where multiple users can visit the site, create chat rooms, join a chat room, and exchange messages with other members in a chat room.

Finally, the Technical Support example from the last chapter will be revised to demonstrate a further useful servlet facility: **servlet collaboration**, which can be used to make a number of servlets work together to generate the response to a request.

> *Although the discussion in this chapter centers on servlets, it is also applicable to JSP based web applications.*

Statelessness and Sessions

HTTP is a **stateless** protocol. In this protocol, a client opens a connection and requests some resource or information. The server responds with the requested resource (if available), or sends an HTTP error status. After closing the connection, the server does not remember any information about the client. So, the server considers the next request from the same client as a fresh request, with no relation to the previous request. This is what makes HTTP a stateless protocol.

A protocol is **stateful** if the response to a given request can be programmed to depend not only on the current request, but also on the outcome of previous requests.

Typically, in a stateful protocol, multiple client requests and responses are sent across a single network connection between the client and server. Based on this connection, the server can identify such requests as forming a single session. For instance, consider the file transfer protocol (FTP). FTP is a stateful protocol, with multiple client requests and responses over a single connection in a given session. In this case, the connection is established with the first OPEN command, and is closed after the EXIT command (unless, of course, a network failure terminates the connection). Accordingly, the FTP server can associate all the client requests within a single session with the client. The server can also make decisions based on the state of the session. For example, an FTP server may limit the number of GET (for file download) requests within a session.

But why is it important to be stateful? A stateful protocol helps you develop complex application logic across multiple requests and responses. Let's consider an online bank. When you request a page containing balances of all your accounts, the server should be able to verify that you're a genuine account holder, and that you've established your credentials with the online bank. However, when the protocol is stateless, you'll be required to send your credentials with every request – in fact, each business transaction will be required to occur in a single request. This is not suitable for long business transactions that ought to happen across multiple requests, such as the online bank, or the shopping cart we discussed a moment ago.

For implementing flexible business transactions across multiple requests and responses, we need two facilities:

❑   **Session:**
    The server should be able to identify that a series of requests from a single client form a single working 'session'. By associating a specific request with a specific working session, the shopping cart or the online banking application can distinguish one user from another.

❑   **State:**
    The server should be able to remember information related to previous requests and other business decisions that are made for requests. That is, the application should be able to associate state with each session. In the case of the shopping cart application, possible state could include the user's favorite item categories, user profile, or even the shopping cart itself.

However, in the case of HTTP, connections are closed at the end of each request, and hence HTTP servers cannot use the notion of connections to establish a session. HTTP is a stateless protocol, concerned with requests and responses, which are simple, isolated transactions. This is perfect for simple web browsing, where each request typically results in downloading static content. The server does not need to know whether a series of requests come from the same or from different clients, or whether those requests are related or distinct. But this is not the case with web applications, where we need the ability to perform business transactions across multiple requests and responses.

With HTTP, in a transaction that spans multiple requests and responses, the web server cannot determine that all the requests are from the same client. A client, therefore, cannot establish a dialogue with the web server to perform a business transaction. However, the goal of HTTP has been to provide speedy and light information retrieval across the Internet, and a stateless protocol is the most suitable for such requirements.

Apart from being able to track users based on the notion of sessions, the server should also be able to remember any necessary information within a session. That is, the application programmer should be able to specify what data should be remembered within a given session – so that the application can use such information to make more informed decisions. This is very useful for transactions or processes spanning multiple requests and responses. With stateful protocols, the server associates a state with the connection: it remembers who the user is, and what it is that they're doing, with the help of the connection. However, this cannot be achieved with HTTP, as the lifetime of a connection is limited to a single request.

Over time, several strategies have evolved to address session tracking, and to manage state within a session. The Java Servlet API provides facilities for tracking sessions and maintaining state within a given session. With the help of these facilities, the server can associate all of the requests together and know that they all came from the same user. It can also associate a state with the connection: it remembers who the user is, and what it is that they're doing.

Note that HTTP 1.1 provides for 'persistent connections', in which case clients and servers can use the same connection object for multiple requests/responses. When supported by both clients and servers, persistent connections reduce the latency associated with creating TCP/IP connections. Persistent connections are useful in cases where requests and responses occurring in a quick succession can be optimized using a single connection instead of one connection per request. However, persistent connections do not carry over session state. The discussion in this chapter remains the same with persistent connections.

Approaches to Session Tracking

There are essentially four approaches to session tracking:

- ❑ URL rewriting
- ❑ Cookies
- ❑ Hidden form fields
- ❑ Sessions using the Secure Sockets Layer (SSL).

  Note that some books suggest user authentication as a means of session tracking. But user authentication is an application-level decision, and not all applications require user authentication for all resources in a web application.

Although the above four approaches differ in implementation details, all are based on one simple trick – that is to exchange some form of a **token** between the client and the server.

Consider a client C and a server S. When C sends a request to S for the first time, S gives C a unique token. Whenever C visits S again, it submits the token along with the request. S can now recognize C from this token.

This is the essence of session tracking:

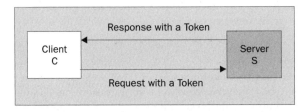

This simple technique for session tracking can be adapted in different ways, based on how such a token can be represented and exchanged. Let's now the consider the above four approaches, and how these approaches represent the tokens, and how these tokens are exchanged in these approaches:

- ❑ **URL Rewriting:**
  In this approach, the token is embedded in each URL. In each dynamically generated page, the server embeds an extra query parameter, or extra path information, in each URL in the page. When the client submits requests using such URLs, the token is retransmitted to the server. This approach is called URL rewriting, as it involves rewriting URLs in the response content to embed the extra token.

❑ **Hidden Form Fields:**
This approach is similar to URL rewriting. Instead of rewriting each URL, the server embeds hidden fields in each form. When the client submits a form, the additional fields will also be sent in the request. The server can use these parameters to establish and maintain a session.

❑ **Cookies:**
Cookies were invented by Netscape, and are one of the most refined forms of token that clients and servers can exchange. Unlike URL rewriting or using hidden form fields, cookies can be exchanged in request and response headers, and therefore do not involve manipulating the generated response to contain a token.

❑ **Secure Socket Layer Sessions:**
SSL is an encryption technology that runs on top TCP/IP and below application-level protocols such as HTTP. SSL is the technology used in the HTTPS protocol. SSL allow SSL-enabled servers to authenticate SSL-enabled clients, and to maintain an encrypted connection between the client and server. In the process of establishing an encrypted connection, both the client and server generate what are called 'session keys', which are symmetric keys used for encrypting and decrypting messages. Servers based on the HTTPS protocol can use the client's symmetric key to establish a session.

But how can we choose between these approaches, and establish and maintain sessions in our web applications? The answer is that, with servlets, it is the *web container's* responsibility to provide the basic facilities for creating and maintaining sessions. The servlet specification allows web containers to use URL rewriting, cookies, or SSL sessions for session tracking. The actual technique used for establishing and tracking a given session depends on both the server's, and the client's capabilities to participate in sessions. The servlet API also provides you with an interface, objects of which let you manipulate session lifecycle and associate state with sessions. There are certain guidelines that make sure that session tracking is functional irrespective of the technique used for session tracking.

Before looking at the servlet API's facilities for session tracking, let's discuss the first three approaches in more detail.

URL Rewriting

As we've discussed in the previous chapters, an HTTP request consists of the location of the server resource (URL), followed optionally by a query string containing pairs of parameters and values. An example of a URL is:

```
http://www.myserver.com/servlet/getSchedule;uid=joe?begPeriod=3&endPeriod=6
```

In this example, the server is `www.myserver.com`, the resource path is `/getSchedule;uid=joe`, and the query string is `beg_period=3&end_period=6`. Typically, browsers generate such responses upon submitting forms with `ACTION` type `GET`. As we've seen in the previous chapter, extra path information in the URL, as well as the query parameters, can be extracted from the `HttpServletRequest` object from within your servlet.

URL rewriting uses the same technique to embed a client-specific unique token within each URL. For example, in the following, each URL path has an appended string `uid=joe`, where `uid` is a parameter unique for each user, with value `joe`:

```
<UL>
  <LI><A HREF="http://www.myserver.com/servlet/usrmenu;uid=joe">User
      Prefs</A></LI>
  <LI><A HREF="http://www.myserver.com/servlet/tsEntry;uid=joe">Time
      Sheets</A></LI>
  <LI><A HREF="http://www.myserver.com/servlet/exEntry;uid=joe">Exp
      Form</A></LI>
</UL>
```

For the moment, assume that the servlet generated this dynamic content, postponing the question of how this can be done with the servlet API. When the servlet generates (with the help of servlet API) the above snippet, it embeds the `uid` within each URL as a query parameter. When the user clicks on any of these hyperlinks, the `uid` is passed along with the request to the web container. The web container can now obtain the value of the `uid` parameter from the request. As discussed in the previous section, the server sent the token as part of the URL, and the client sent it back along with the request, thus giving the container the ability to track the session of `joe`.

This approach is called URL rewriting since it involves rewriting all the URLs to include a unique token in the URL path. Although we used a parameter `uid` in the above example, the name of the parameter specified in the servlet specification is `jsessionid`. The actual URLs generated resemble the following:

```
http://www.myserver.com/servlet/usrmenu;jsessionid=123456789
```

URL rewriting requires that all pages in the application be dynamically generated. URL rewriting cannot be enforced for static HTML pages, because the unique URL path parameter (the `jsessionid`) is dynamic and differs from user to user.

Hidden Form Fields

In this approach, the unique token is embedded within each HTML form. For example, the following HTML specifies an input control of type `HIDDEN`:

```
<INPUT TYPE="HIDDEN" NAME="uid" VALUE="joe">
```

When the request is submitted, the server receives the token as part of the request. Note that, similar to URL rewriting, the above content should be dynamically generated embedding the hidden parameter. In addition, each request should include a FORM submission, and hence may not be applicable to all types of pages.

The servlet specification doesn't use this approach.

Cookies

Cookies are the most commonly used means of tracking client sessions. Cookies were initially introduced by Netscape, and this technology was later standardized in RFC 2109 (http://www.faqs.org/rfcs/rfc2109.html). You can also read the Netscape's preliminary specification at http://www.netscape.com/newsref/std/cookie_spec.html.

> **A cookie is a small piece of textual information sent by the server to the client, stored on the client, and returned by the client for all requests to the server.**

A cookie contains a **name-value** pair with certain additional attributes, exchanged in the response and request headers.

Web servers send a cookie by sending the `Set-Cookie` response header in the following format:

```
Set-Cookie: NAME=VALUE; Comment=COMMENT; Domain=DOMAINNAME; Max-age=SECONDS;
Path=PATH; secure; Version=1*DIGIT
```

Here NAME is the name of the cookie, and VALUE is the value of NAME, Max-age specifies the maximum life of the cookie, Domain (optional) and Path (optional) specify the URL path for which the cookie is valid, and secure (optional) specifies if the cookie can be exchanged over HTTP. For cookies implemented as per RFC 2109, the Version should be set 1. The Version should be set to 0 for cookies implemented as per the original Netscape specification. Comment is an optional parameter that can be used to document the intent of the cookie.

Here is an example of a cookie:

```
Set-cookie: uid=joe; Max-age=3600; Domain=".myserver.com"; Path="/"
```

The above response header sends a cookie with name uid and value joe. The lifetime of this cookie is 3600 seconds, and is valid for the myserver.com domain for the URL path /. The browser should discard this cookie after 3600 seconds.

When a browser client receives the above response header, it can either reject it or accept it. For instance, you can configure your browser to accept or reject cookies. Let's consider that the browser accepts this cookie. When the browser sends a request to the http://www.myserver.com domain within the next one hour, it also sends a request header:

```
Cookie: uid=joe
```

The server can read this cookie from the request, and identify that the request corresponds to a client identified by uid=joe. This completes the token exchange necessary for tracking sessions.

A cookie is specific to a domain or a sub-domain, and can be set by the domain attribute in the cookie. Browsers use the domain and path attributes to determine if a cookie should be sent in the request header, and with what name-value attributes. Once accepted by a browser, the browser stores the cookie against the domain and the URL path.

If the client chooses to reject a cookie, the client does not send the cookie back to the server in the request header, and therefore the server fails to track the user session.

Note that, the main advantage of this approach is that the cookies are not mixed with the HTML content and the HTTP request and response bodies. The container can transparently set cookies in the response headers, and extract cookies from request headers.

The servlet API specification requires that web containers implement session tracking using the cookie mechanism. In this approach, the web container automatically sets a session tracking cookie with name jsessionid. When the container receives client requests, it checks for the existence of this cookie, and accordingly tracks sessions.

However, since servers can transparently set cookies, which are stored in the user's computer and sent back to the server, cookies cause security concerns for many users. Refer to http://www.w3.org/Security/Faq/wwwsf7.html and http://www.ciac.org/ciac/bulletins/i-034.shtml for an overview of security concerns with cookies. In order to address such concerns, browsers allow you disable cookies. When cookies are disabled, servlet containers use URL rewriting to track sessions. We'll see an example in the next section.

Apart from session-tracking cookies, your web applications can explicitly set cookies in the response. Using the servlet API, you can add several cookies in the response, and extract cookies from the response.

The servlet API provides a class called javax.servlet.http.Cookie that represents a cookie from the perspective of the servlet. The servlet can create a new cookie, set its name and value, set max-age dates and so on, and then add the cookie to the HttpServletResponse object to be sent back to the browser. Cookies can also be retrieved from the HttpServletRequest object, and their values read. For the purpose of our present discussion, using the following code in your servlet you can set the above cookie:

```
// Create a new cookie with name and value arguments
Cookie c = new Cookie("uid", "joe");

// Set the life of the cookie
c.setMaxAge(60*60);   //Expires in 1 hour
c.setDomain(".myserver.com");
c.setPath("/");

// Send the cookie to the browser to be stored on the client machine
response.addCookie(c);
```

Similarly, you can retrieve cookies from requests using the getCookies() method on the HttpServletResponse interface.

Possible applications for setting explicit cookies include targeted marketing, site personalization, usage tracking, etc.

Session Tracking with the Java Servlet API

In the Java Servlet API, the javax.servlet.http.HttpSession interface encapsulates the notion of a session. Web containers provide an implementation of this interface.

Since the notion of a session is associated with client requests, the HttpServletRequest interface provides the getSession() method, which you can use to access the HttpSession object associated with the client making the request. If you refer back to the class diagram for the javax.servlet.http package in Chapter 8, you'll notice an arrow between HttpServletRequest and the HttpSession interfaces. This means that, given an HttpServletRequest object, you can obtain the HttpSession object.

In order to associate state with sessions, the HttpSession interface provides methods using which you can set and get attributes from HttpSession objects. We will cover these methods a little later in this chapter.

As we mentioned, web containers use either cookies or URL rewriting for establishing sessions. While most web containers rely on cookies alone for establishing sessions, some use cookies by default, and use URL rewriting when clients reject cookies. The actual creation of sessions is transparent to the application programmer. That is, you do not need explicitly to create, set, or get cookies, or rewrite URLs for session tracking. As you will see later, the only requirement is that you should encode all URLs in the response.

The servlet API for session tracking consists of the following:

- Methods on the `javax.servlet.http.HttpServletRequest` interface for creating and accessing `HttpSession` objects

- A `javax.servlet.http.HttpSession` interface to represent sessions, wich includes methods to associate state with sessions, and to configure and invalidate sessions

- Methods on the `javax.servlet.http.HttpServletResponse` interface to encode URLs such that the web container can use URL rewriting when cookies are rejected by client browsers

- The `javax.servlet.http.HttpSessionBindingListener` interface and the `javax.servlet.http.HttpSessionBindingEvent` class, to represent events associated with sessions

We'll discuss each of these in the following sections.

Session Creation and Tracking

The methods from the `HttpServletRequest` interface for creating and tracking `HttpSession` objects are:

```
public HttpSession getSession(boolean create);
public HttpSession getSession();
```

Each of these methods returns the `HttpSession` object associated with the current request. If there is no session associated with the current request, the second method creates one. This could happen when the client refuses to join a session, for instance when the user disables cookies in their browser. The first method takes an additional `boolean` argument, to indicate whether the container should attempt to create a new session if there is no session associated with the current request. If this argument is `false`, and if there is no session associated with the request, this method returns `null`.

From a servlet's perspective, session creation/tracking involves calling one of these two methods to obtain an `HttpSession` object. However, from the web container's perspective, there is more to it. As we discussed in the previous section, session creation involves establishing a token (based on a cookie, or the URL path parameter, or an SSL session key) that can be exchanged between the client and the server, and associating such a token with an `HttpSession` object. The web container receives the token as part of the request. When the `getSession()` method is called the container retrieves the `HttpSession` object, based on this token.

In other words, session creation/tracking means that the web container is able to associate a request with a client, and the `HttpSession` object represents this association. The web container maintains this object for the duration of the client session, or a configurable timeout period. Since there can be several clients sending requests to the container, the container maintains separate `HttpSession` objects for each client. Consequently, you can associate state with each `HttpSession`, as you'll see shortly.

The HttpSession Interface

```
public interface HttpSession
```

This interface from the `javax.servlet.http` package encapsulates the notion of a session. An object of this type can be obtained using the `getSession()` method of the `HttpServletRequest` object. Note that, as with most of the other servlet API interfaces discussed so far, it is up to containers to provide an implementation of this interface.

The `HttpSession` interface has the following methods:

```
public Object getAttribute(String name)
public Enumeration getAttributeNames()
public long getCreationTime()
public String getId()
public long getLastAccessedTime()
public int getMaxInactiveInterval()
public void invalidate()
public boolean isNew()
public void removeAttribute(String name)
public void setAttribute(String name)
public void setMaxInactiveInterval(int interval)
```

These methods can be divided into two categories:

❑   Methods for session lifetime:
      `getCreationTime()`, `getId()`, `getLastAccessTime()`, `getMaxInactiveInterval()`, `invalidate()`, `isNew()`, and `setMaxInactiveInterval()`

❑   Methods for associating attributes (state) with sessions:
      `getAttribute()`, `getAttributeNames()`, `removeAttribute()`, and `setAttribute()`

Methods for Session Lifetime

Since sessions are maintained on the server side, and since HTTP is a stateless protocol, the web container cannot determine if the client intends to continue to use the web application. For example, consider a web-based mail application, such as Hotmail. After reading the mails for a while, you may close the browser without actually logging out from the mail account.

> **The server cannot detect this.**

Secondly, as the number of users for a web application increases, the number of sessions will increase too. Each session consumes memory on the server side, so it is unwise to keep sessions alive forever.

In order to effectively manage session lifetime, the servlet API provides several methods:

The getCreationTime() Method

```
public long getCreationTime()
```

This method returns the time that the session was created, in milliseconds since January 1, 1970 00:00:00 GMT.

The getId() Method

```
public String getId()
```

This method returns a `String` containing a unique identifier assigned to this session. This string is implementation-dependent.

The getLastAccessedTime() Method

```
public long getLastAccessedTime()
```

This method returns the time that the session was last accessed by the client, in milliseconds since January 1, 1970 00:00:00 GMT. This method can be used to determine the inactivity between two consecutive requests from a client.

The getMaxInactiveInterval() Method

```
public int getMaxInactiveInterval()
```

Returns the length of time in seconds that the session will remain active between requests before expiring.

The setMaxInactiveInterval() Method

```
public int setMaxInactiveInterval(int interval)
```

Sets the length of time in seconds that the session will remain active between requests before expiring. You can use this method to programmatically set the session inactivity interval. The web container makes sure that the session is automatically invalidated after expiry of this interval.

Alternatively, you can use the `<session-timeout>` tag in the deployment descriptor to specify the maximum inactivity period:

```
<session-config>
  <session-timeout>
    300
  </session-timeout>
</session-config>
```

While the second approach allows you to specify the inactivity interval for the application, the first approach allows you to programmatically change this. Upon reaching this interval, the web container automatically invalidates the session.

The isNew() Method

```
public boolean isNew()
```

Returns `true` if the session has been created on the server, but the client does not yet know about, or has not yet joined, the session. A client is considered to join a session when the client returns session tracking information previously sent by the server. When the client refuses to join the session, this method returns `true`, indicating that it is a new session. This can happen, for example, when the web container uses cookies alone for session tracking, and the client refuses to accept cookies.

399

The invalidate() Method

```
public void invalidate()
```

You can use this method to terminate sessions. For example, you can use explicit session invalidation for implementing a logout feature in your application. When the user chooses to log out, your server can invalidate the session, so that the user can no longer be associated with that session. Next time, when your servlet calls the getSession() method on the HttpServletRequest, you'll receive a new HttpSession object.

Demonstrating Session Lifecycle with Cookies

In order to familiarize you with the lifecycle of HttpSession objects, let's now consider a simple servlet that lets you examine certain session attributes, and invalidate existing sessions. Let's also examine the behavior of this servlet in the absence of cookies, and then discuss ways to generate web pages that work as desirable irrespective of whether the client browser accepts cookies or not.

Let's call this SessionLifeCycleServlet. When invoked, this servlet generates a page showing the session status, session ID, creation time, last accessed time, and maximum inactive interval. The servlet uses the methods in the HttpSession interface to print the above information. Apart from this, this servlet also provide links to reload the page, and to invalidate the current session.

Here is a sample screenshot of this servlet's response:

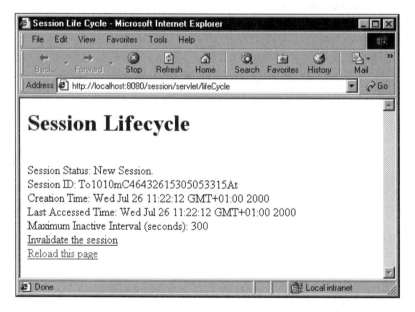

Notice that session is new, since this is the first access. In order to see how the above response is generated, consider the following source code. Enter this code in
c:\ProJavaServer\Chapter09\session\src\SessionLifeCycleServlet.java:

```
// Import Servlet packages
import javax.servlet.*;
import javax.servlet.http.*;
```

```
// Import Java packages
import java.io.*;
import java.util.Date;

public class SessionLifeCycleServlet extends HttpServlet {
  protected void doGet(HttpServletRequest request,
                       HttpServletResponse response)
           throws ServletException, IOException {
    String action = request.getParameter("action");

    if (action != null && action.equals("invalidate")) {
      HttpSession session = request.getSession();
      session.invalidate();
      response.setContentType("text/html");
      PrintWriter out = response.getWriter();

      out.println("<HTML>");
      out.println("<HEAD><TITLE>Session Lifecycle</TITLE></HEAD>");
      out.println("<BODY>");
      out.println("<P>Your session has been invalidated.</P>");
      String lifeCycleURL = "/session/servlet/lifeCycle";
      out.println("<A HREF=\"" + lifeCycleURL + "?action=newSession\">");
      out.println("Create new session</A>");
      out.println("</BODY></HTML>");
    } else {
      HttpSession session = request.getSession();
      response.setContentType("text/html");
      PrintWriter out = response.getWriter();

      out.println("<HTML>");
      out.println("<META HTTP-EQUIV=\"Pragma\" CONTENT=\"no-cache\">");
      out.println("<HEAD><TITLE>Session Lifecycle</TITLE></HEAD>");
      out.println("<BODY BGCOLOR=\"#FFFFFF\">");
      out.println("<H1>Session Lifecycle</CENTER></H1>");
      out.print("<BR>Session Status: ");
      if (session.isNew()) {
        out.println("New Session.");
      } else {
        out.println("Old Session.");
      }
      out.println("<BR>Session ID: ");
      out.println(session.getId());
      out.println("<BR>Creation Time: ");
      out.println(new Date(session.getCreationTime()));
      out.println("<BR>Last Accessed Time: ");
      out.println(new Date(session.getLastAccessedTime()));
      out.println("<BR>Maximum Inactive Interval (seconds): ");
      out.println(session.getMaxInactiveInterval());

      String lifeCycleURL = "/session/servlet/lifeCycle";
      out.print("<BR><A HREF=\"" + lifeCycleURL + "?action=invalidate\">");
      out.println("Invalidate the session</A></TD></TR>");
      out.print("<BR><A HREF=\"" + lifeCycleURL + "\">");
      out.println("Reload this page</A>");
      out.println("</BODY></HTML>");
      out.close();
    }
  }
}
```

401

Consider the highlighted parts of this source code. Let's look at the `else` block first. This block is executed when servlet is invoked without any parameters, and performs the following steps:

- Calls `getSession()` on the `HttpSession`, with `boolean true` as an argument.

- Calls `getId()` to get the session ID.

- Calls `getCreationTime()` to get the creation time of the session. Since this method returns the creation as milliseconds since January 1, 1970 00:00:00 GMT, we need to convert this into a `Date` object.

- Calls `getLastAccessedTime()` to get the session's last accessed time.

- Calls `getMaxInactiveInterval()` to get the current max-inactive-interval setting.

After printing the above, the servlet also generates two links: one to reload the page, and the other to invalidate the session. The first link simply points to the same page. The `no-cache` meta-tag in the generated HTML lets you reload the page by clicking on this link.

Note that the second link has a query string `action=invalidate` appended. When you click on this link, the `if` block of the `doGet()` method will be executed. In order to see this servlet in action, compile this servlet to create the class file at `c:\ProJavaServer\Chapter09\session\WEB-INF\classes`, and also create the following deployment descriptor as `c:\ProJavaServer\Chapter09\session\WEB-INF\web.xml`:

```xml
<?xml version="1.0" encoding="ISO-8859-1"?>
<!DOCTYPE web-app PUBLIC
    "-//Sun Microsystems, Inc.//DTD Web Application 2.2//EN"
    "http://java.sun.com/j2ee/dtds/web-app_2.2.dtd">

<web-app>
  <servlet>
    <servlet-name>lifeCycle</servlet-name>
    <servlet-class>SessionLifeCycleServlet</servlet-class>
  </servlet>

  <session-config>
    <session-timeout> <!-- In minutes -->
      5
    </session-timeout>
  </session-config>
</web-app>
```

Deploy the servlet by adding the following entry to `%TOMCAT_HOM%\conf\server.xml`:

```xml
<Context path="/session"
  docBase="c:/ProJavaServer/Chapter09/session">
</Context>
```

Start Tomcat, and enter the URL `http://localhost:8080/session/servlet/lifeCycle` in your browser. Make sure that cookies are enabled in your browser configuration. The browser output should be similar to that which was shown at the beginning of this example.

Now let's proceed to see what happens if the code in the `else` block is executed again. Click on the Reload this page link. Your browser output should be similar to that shown below:

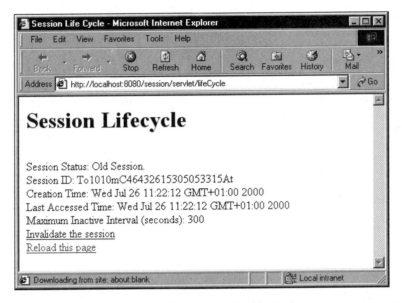

This time, you'll find that the session is old. The session ID and also the session creation time remain the same. Every time you click on the Reload this page link, what changes is the last accessed time.

This illustrates how simple it is to create and keep track of session. Let's now see what happens if you click on the Invalidate the session link. Since this URL has a query parameter `action=invalidate`, the `if` block of the `doGet()` method will be executed to generate the following output:

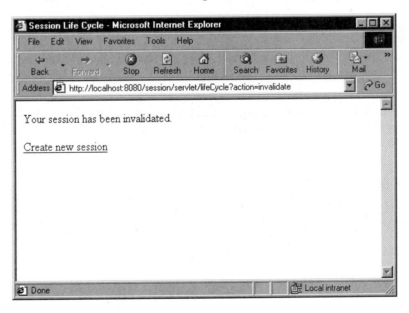

Now click on the **Create new session** link. The resulting page should be similar to the opening screen shot shown at the beginning of this example.

Now, examine the `if` block of the code. This part of the servlet gets the session from the request, calls the `invalidate()` method, and generates a new link back to the previous page.

Session Lifecycle Without Cookies

In order to see the behavior of the `SessionLifeCycleServlet` without cookies, disable cookies in your browser, and invoke the URL `http://localhost:8080/session/servlet/lifeCycle`. This time, when you attempt to reload the page, you'll notice that the session is always new, implying that the web container is not able to track the session.

As discussed previously, in cases where clients refuse to accept cookies, web containers can use the URL rewriting mechanism to track sessions. However, in order for this mechanism to work, all URLs in the page should be encoded using the `encodeURL()` method in the `HttpServletResponse` interface. This method appends a path string of the form `;jsessionid=123456789` to the input URL.

In the `SessionLifeCycleServlet`, replace both lines containing:

```
String lifeCycleURL = "/session/servlet/lifeCycle";
```

with:

```
String lifeCycleURL = response.encodeURL("/session/servlet/lifeCycle");
```

Recompile the servlet, and restart Tomcat. This time you'll notice that the web container is able to track sessions. When you reload the servlet, you'll find that the session is old, and that the URL shown by your browser is something like:

```
http://localhost:8080/session/servlet/lifeCycle;jsessionid=To1010mC8978836221982393At
```

With the help of the container (that is, the `encodeURL()` method on the `HttpServletResponse` interface), we're now able to implement URL rewriting.

> **Whether or not users of your web applications enable cookies in their browsers, it is good practice to always encode the URLs as shown above.**

Methods for Managing State

As we discussed at the beginning of this chapter, another important requirement for building web applications, as well as identifying the client, is for the server to be able to remember information related to previous requests/decisions. In simple terms, this means that once a request is received, and a business decision is made, you should be able to store that information for later use.

For example, based on the login information, your online banking application might determine that you cannot transfer funds across your accounts. If the application is capable of storing that information, it need not re-execute the logic for that decision-making process every time you request a fund transfer during the session. Similarly, consider an online registration form. If the registration process involves collecting a large amount of data (say, filling 4 or 5 forms), you might not wish to implement the entire process with a single HTML form. Instead, you should be able to implement this across multiple HTML pages (and requests). To do this, you should be able to validate and store information as soon as it is received from the client.

The HttpSession interface has facilities that meet this requirement. The setAttribute() and getAttribute() methods of the HttpSession interface allow you to store unique attributes within the HttpSession, and retrieve them any time before the session expires. An attribute is essentially a Java language object identified by an attribute name.

The getAttribute() Method

```
public Object getAttribute(String name)
```

Returns the attribute bound with the specified name in this session, or null if no object is bound under the name.

The getAttributeNames() Method

```
public Enumeration getAttributeNames(String name)
```

Returns an enumeration of the names of all attributes bound to the current session. You can use these names with the getAttribute() method to retrieve the objects.

The setAttribute() Method

```
public setAttribute(String name, Object attribute)
```

Binds (stores) an object in the session, with the given name. You can use the getAttribute() method to retrieve the object again. In the case of distributable containers (discussed below), this method may throw an InvalidArgumentException.

Since this method maintains only a reference to the attribute, you need to call this method whenever the object reference changes. For instance, when you add a Hashtable object as an attribute, the session holds only a reference to the Hashtable. Since adding elements to the Hashtable does not affect the reference to the Hashtable object, you need not call setAttribute() whenever you add/remove elements to the Hashtable. However, if you want to replace the Hashtable object with another Hashtable, you need to call the setAttribute() method again, passing the new Hashtable.

The removeAttribute() Method

```
public void removeAttribute(String name)
```

Unbinds and removes an object with the given name from the session.

Note that the above methods are not synchronized.

Multiple servlets executing requests can simultaneously access and modify the session attributes of a single session object at the same time. In case servlets in your application attempt to manipulate the same session attribute, you should make sure that such access is synchronized.

Also, as you'll see in the next chapter, web applications can be marked as distributable, in which case all session attributes must implement the java.lang.Serializable interface. Most of the commercial web containers, such as those listed in Chapter 7, provide facilities for distribution (also called clustering). When the container is distributable, the container runs in multiple JVMs (on multiple machines), and your applications will be deployed on each of these JVMs. The purpose of such a setup is to allow the container to distribute the processing load across these JVMs. In such cases, the web container is free to move the session objects from one JVM to another JVM, and send all client requests for that session to this JVM. However, for the container to be able to swap the sessions, the objects contained in the HttpSession should also be serializable.

Finally, even non-distributable containers may provide session persistence. Consider the case of a web application with a large number of simultaneous users (and sessions). Only some of these sessions may be active, while the rest are not active, yet not inactive enough to be invalidated (based on session timeout). In such cases, the container can choose to **passivate** some of least active sessions in a persistent storage such as the file system, so that the container can optimize the available memory. The container could later active such sessions based on user activity. In order to allow session passivation and activation, the attributes in the session should be serializable.

These constraints imply that you should consider avoiding storing non-serializable attributes, such as database connections input/output streams, in sessions.

Demonstrating State Management

Let's now build another simple servlet to demonstrate the methods for managing state in the HttpSession.

Enter the following source code in c:\ProJavaServer\Chapter09\session\src\AttributeServlet.java:

```java
// Import Servlet packages
import javax.servlet.*;
import javax.servlet.http.*;

// Import Java packages
import java.io.*;
import java.util.Enumeration;

public class AttributeServlet extends HttpServlet {

    protected void doGet(HttpServletRequest request,
                         HttpServletResponse response)
            throws ServletException, IOException {

        HttpSession session = request.getSession();

        String name = request.getParameter("attrib_name");
        String value = request.getParameter("attrib_value");
        String remove = request.getParameter("attrib_remove");
```

```
   if (remove != null && remove.equals("on")) {
     session.removeAttribute(name);
   } else {
     if (name != null && name.length() > 0 && (value != null)
            && value.length() > 0) {
       session.setAttribute(name, value);
     }
   }

   response.setContentType("text/html");
   PrintWriter out = response.getWriter();

   out.println("<HTML>");
   out.println("<META HTTP-EQUIV=\"Pragma\" CONTENT=\"no-cache\">");
   out.println("<HEAD><TITLE>Session Attributes</TITLE></HEAD>");
   out.println("<BODY>");
   out.println("<H1>Session Attributes</H1>");

   out.println("Enter name and value of an attribute");

   String url = response.encodeURL("/session/servlet/attributes");
   out.println("<FORM ACTION=\"" + url + "\" METHOD=\"GET\">");

   out.println("Name: ");
   out.println("<INPUT TYPE=\"text\" SIZE=\"10\" NAME=\"attrib_name\">");

   out.println("Value: ");
   out.println("<INPUT TYPE=\"text\" SIZE=\"10\" NAME=\"attrib_value\">");

   out.println("<BR><INPUT TYPE=\"checkbox\"
               NAME=\"attrib_remove\">Remove");
   out.println("<INPUT TYPE=\"submit\" NAME=\"update\" VALUE=\"Update\">");
   out.println("</FORM>");
   out.println("<HR>");
   out.println("Attributes in this Session");

   // Print all session attributes
   Enumeration e = session.getAttributeNames();
   while (e.hasMoreElements()) {
     String att_name = (String) e.nextElement();
     String att_value = (String) session.getAttribute(att_name);

     out.println("<BR><B>Name:</B> ");
     out.println(att_name);
     out.println("<B>Value: </B>");
     out.println(att_value);
   }
   out.println("</BODY></HTML>");
   out.close();
  }
}
```

This servlet lets you enter name-value pairs in a HTML form, and add this data to the session. This servlet also lets you remove attributes from session. Compile this servlet to create the class file at `c:\ProJavaServer\Chapter09\session\WEB-INF\classes`. Also add the following segment to `c:\ProJavaServer\Chapter09\session\WEB-INF\web.xml`:

```
...
<web-app>
  ...
  <servlet>
    <servlet-name>attributes</servlet-name>
    <servlet-class>AttributeServlet</servlet-class>
  </servlet>
  ...
</web-app>
```

Now restart Tomcat, and enter the URL `http://localhost:8080/session/servlet/attributes` in your browser. The browser will display a form to enter the name and value of an attribute and a check box to remove an attribute. Add any name-value pair and hit the Update button. You will find the list of current session attributes displayed below the form. Here is a typical output after entering a few attributes:

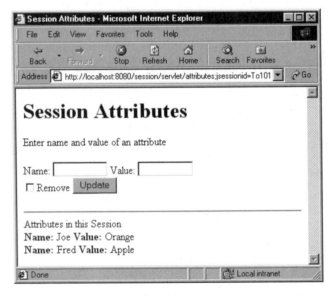

In order to remove any attribute from the session, enter the name of the attribute against the Name text box, check the Remove checkbox, and hit the Update button.

This very simple application illustrates how to store and retrieve attributes in the HttpSession object using the setAttribute(), getAttribute(), getAttributeNames(), and removeAttribute() methods.

Binding and Unbinding Objects to and from Sessions

Attribute objects can optionally implement the HttpSessionBindingListener interface, which allows the attribute objects to be notified when you add them to or remove them from the HttpSession. When the attribute implementing HttpSessionBindingListener is added to the HttpSession, the web container notifies the attribute that it is being bound to the session. Similarly, when the attribute is removed from the session, the web container notifies the attribute that it is being unbound from the session. The attribute can use the callback methods provided to initialize or clean up its state.

For instance, in a shopping cart application, consider the shopping cart attribute stored in the session. This object will be created when the customer first visits the site. Assume that the customer added items to the cart but, instead of proceeding to checkout, decided not to continue, and left the site. Later, when the user session expires, the container notifies the shopping cart attribute that it is being unbound from the session. The cart object can then save the shopping cart in a database.

When the same user revisits the site, the application binds the shopping cart attribute to the session again. This time, the shopping cart attribute can reload the saved shopping cart, and provide a seamless experience for the customer.

Note that, in order for the shopping cart attribute to implement such tasks, it may need access to the HttpSession to which it is associated. As you'll see below, the HttpSessionBindingEvent provides access to the HttpSession.

The HttpSessionBindingListener Interface

```
public interface HttpSessionBindingListener extends java.util.EventListener
```

This interface can be used to notify an object when it is being placed into the session (using the setAttribute() method), or removed from the session (via the removeAttribute() method).

The valueBound() Method

```
public void valueBound(HttpSessionBindingEvent event)
```

Notifies the object that it is being bound to a session.

The valueUnbound() Method

```
public void valueUnbound(HttpSessionBindingEvent event)
```

Notifies the object that it is being unbound from a session. The unbinding can happen either by explicitly removing it from the session, or during session invalidation.

The HttpSessionBindingEvent Class

```
public class HttpSessionBindingListener extends java.util.EventObject
```

This class represents session binding and unbinding events. An object of this type is passed to the valueBound() and valueUnbound() methods.

This class has the following methods:

The getName() Method

```
public String getName()
```

This method returns the name of the attribute that was used while binding/unbinding the attribute in the session.

The getSession() Method

```
public HttpSession getSession()
```

This method returns the HttpSession object to or from which the attribute is being bound/unbound.

A Simple Shopping Cart Using Sessions

In this section we will consider a simple shopping cart application, to illustrate various concepts associated with session tracking. Such applications typically allow a user to select items from a catalog and place them in a virtual shopping cart, before proceeding to the 'checkout' and paying for the items.

This shopping cart application has two servlets: one for generating a catalog, and the other for adding items to a cart and displaying the contents of the cart. In this application, we'll use the same set of `HttpSession` methods that we used in the `AttributeServlet`. However, the purpose of the shopping cart is to demonstrate how these methods can be combined to build real-life applications.

Here we will consider a bare-bones implementation without most of the features that you would expect in a fully functional shopping cart. I encourage you to add more functionality to this while exploring the Java Servlet API.

The Catalog Servlet

The catalog consists of two parts. The first part is a statement showing the current number of books selected in the shopping cart, and the second is an HTML form, with the list of books displayed within a group of check boxes.

The HTML form consists of a short list of items displayed in a table. Each item has a check box next to it for the user to select the item and add it to their shopping cart. In a typical shopping cart program, the catalog pages are generated from a database, but for our example, a static list is used for demonstrative purposes.

Enter the following source in `c:\ProJavaServer\Chapter09\cart\src\Catalog.java`:

```
// Import servlet packages
import javax.servlet.*;
import javax.servlet.http.*;

// Import Java IO package
import java.io.*;
import java.util.*;

public class Catalog extends HttpServlet {
  protected void doGet(HttpServletRequest req, HttpServletResponse res)
          throws ServletException, IOException {
    HttpSession session = req.getSession();

    int itemCount = 0;
    ArrayList cart = (ArrayList) session.getAttribute("cart");
    if (cart != null) {
      itemCount = cart.size();
    }

    res.setContentType("text/html");
    PrintWriter out = res.getWriter();

    out.println("<HTML><HEAD><TITLE>Simple Shopping Cart "
            + "Example</TITLE></HEAD>");
    out.println("<BODY><TABLE border=\"0\" width=\"100%\"><TR>");
```

```
           out.println("<TD VALIGN=\"top\"><IMG "
                   + "SRC=\"/cart/images/logo.gif\"></TD>");
           out.println("<TD align=\"left\" VALIGN=\"bottom\">");
           out.println("<H1>WROX Book Store</H1></TD></TR></TABLE><HR>");
           out.println("<P>You've " + itemCount + " items in your cart.</P>");
           out.print("<FORM ACTION=\"");
           out.println(res.encodeURL("/cart/servlet/cart"));
           out.println("\" METHOD=\"POST\">");
           out.println("<TABLE CELLSPACING=\"5\" CELLPADDING=\"5\"><TR>");
           out.println("<TD ALIGN=\"center\"><B>Add to Cart</B></TD>");
           out.println("<TD ALIGN=\"center\"></TD></TR><TR>");
           out.println("<TD ALIGN=\"center\">");
           out.println("<INPUT TYPE=\"Checkbox\" NAME=\"item\""
                   + " VALUE=\"Begining Java2 - JDK 1.3 Version\"></TD>");
           out.println("<TD ALIGN=\"left\">Item 1: "
                   + " Begining Java2 - JDK 1.3 Version</TD></TR><TR>");
           out.println("<TD ALIGN=\"center\">");
           out.println("<INPUT TYPE=\"Checkbox\" NAME=\"item\""
                   + " VALUE=\"Professional Java XML Programming with "
                   + "Servlets and JSP\"></TD>");
           out.println("<TD ALIGN=\"left\">Item 2: "
                   + " Professional Java XML Programming with Servlets "
                   + "and JSP</TD></TR><TR>");
           out.println("<TD ALIGN=\"center\">");
           out.println("<INPUT TYPE=\"Checkbox\" NAME=\"item\""
                   + " VALUE=\" Professional Java Server Programming\"></TD>");
           out.println("<TD ALIGN=\"left\">Item 3: Professional Java "
                   + "Server Programming</TD></TR>");
           out.println("</TABLE><HR>");
           out.println("<INPUT TYPE=\"Submit\" NAME=\"btn_submit\" "
                   + "VALUE=\"Add to Cart\">");
           out.println("</FORM></BODY></HTML>");

           out.close();
       }
   }
```

This servlet obtains the number of books from data stored in the HttpSession. It starts by using the getSession() method on the HttpServletRequest object to get the current session:

```
       HttpSession session = req.getSession();
```

This is the first step required for creating and tracking HTTP sessions. You'll also find a similar req.getSession() call in the ShoppingCart servlet.

It then uses a HttpSession attribute "cart" to find and display the number of books in the cart. As we'll see in a moment, the ShoppingCart servlet stores and updates this attribute when items are added to the cart, using an ArrayList object to store the list of selected books.

```
       ArrayList cart = (ArrayList) session.getAttribute("cart");
```

The rest of this servlet prepares the catalog. This generates a form with a POST action, which sends the list of selected books in the HTTP request.

The ShoppingCart Servlet

The ShoppingCart servlet is responsible for adding items to the cart. This servlet collects (from the POST request submitted by the Catalog servlet) the list of books selected, and updates the shopping cart. In this bare-bones implementation, the shopping cart is modeled as a java.util.ArrayList object holding the names of the items. This object is then stored as an attribute with name "cart" in the HttpSession.

Enter the following source in c:\ProJavaServer\Chapter09\cart\src\ShoppingCart.java:

```java
// Import servlet packages
import javax.servlet.*;
import javax.servlet.http.*;

// Import java packages.
import java.io.*;
import java.util.*;

public class ShoppingCart extends HttpServlet {

  public void doPost(HttpServletRequest req, HttpServletResponse res)
          throws ServletException, IOException {
    HttpSession session = req.getSession(true);

    ArrayList cart = (ArrayList) session.getAttribute("cart");

    if (cart == null) {
      cart = new ArrayList();
      session.setAttribute("cart", cart);
    }

    PrintWriter out = res.getWriter();
    res.setContentType("text/html");

    String[] itemsSelected;
    String itemName;
    itemsSelected = req.getParameterValues("item");

    if (itemsSelected != null) {

      for (int i = 0; i < itemsSelected.length; i++) {
        itemName = itemsSelected[i];
        cart.add(itemName);
      }
    }

    // Print Current Contents of Cart
    out.println("<HTML><HEAD><TITLE>");
    out.println("Shopping Cart Contents");
    out.println("</TITLE></HEAD>");
    out.println("<BODY>");
    out.println("<H1>Items currently in your cart</H1>");
    out.println("<HR>");
```

```
      Iterator iterator = cart.iterator();
      while (iterator.hasNext()) {
        out.println("<P>" + iterator.next() + "</P>");
      }

      out.print("<HR><P><A HREF=\"");
      out.print(res.encodeURL("/cart/servlet/catalog"));
      out.println("\">Back to the shop</A></P>");

      out.close();
    }
  }
```

Recall that when a form contains multiple check boxes with the same name, the parameter may have multiple values. Therefore, the getParameterValues() method is used to extract the selected books from the request.

Finally, we generate a page containing the current contents of the shopping cart, and a link back to the cart.

Compile these two Java files to generate the classes under c:\ProJavaServer\Chapter09\cart\WEB-INF\classes, and add the following deployment descriptor under c:\ProJavaServer\Chapter09\cart\WEB-INF\web.xml:

```xml
<?xml version="1.0" encoding="ISO-8859-1"?>
<!DOCTYPE web-app PUBLIC
   "-//Sun Microsystems, Inc.//DTD Web Application 2.2//EN"
   "http://java.sun.com/j2ee/dtds/web-app_2.2.dtd">

<web-app>

  <servlet>
    <servlet-name>catalog</servlet-name>
    <servlet-class>Catalog</servlet-class>
  </servlet>

  <servlet>
    <servlet-name>cart</servlet-name>
    <servlet-class>ShoppingCart</servlet-class>
  </servlet>

</web-app>
```

Deploy this application with Tomcat by adding the following entry to %TOMCAT_HOM%\conf\server.xml:

```xml
<Context path="/cart"
   docBase="c:/ProJavaServer/Chapter09/cart">
</Context>
```

Restart Tomcat to launch the shopping cart application. The URL for the cart is http://localhost:8080/cart/servlet/catalog.

The screenshots below show the catalog and shopping cart. The catalog has only three entries, and is generated using the Catalog servlet:

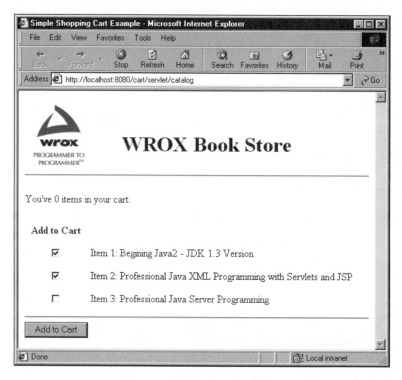

To add items to the cart, check the checkboxes against the item, and click the Add to Cart button. This will cause the ShoppingCart servlet to generate the shopping cart screen:

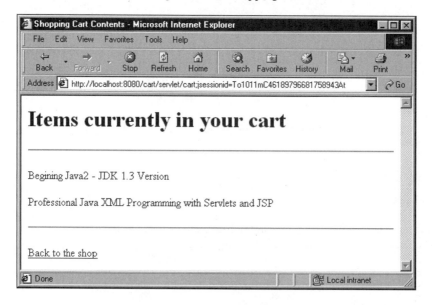

Servlet Context

In the Java Servlet API, the servlet context defines a servlet's view of the web application, and provides access to resources and facilities (such as logging) common to all servlets in the application. Unlike a session, which is specific to a client, the servlet context is specific to a particular web application running in a JVM. That is, each web application in a container will have a servlet context associated with it.

Servlet context is yet another useful concept provided by the servlet API. In the previous section, we saw how we could use `HttpSession` objects to maintain state relating to a single client on the server. The servlet context complements this facility by letting you maintain application-level state – that is, state information common to all servlets and clients in the application.

The Java Servlet API provides a `ServletContext` interface to represent a context: the resources shared by a group of servlets. In the 1.0 and 2.0 versions of the servlet API the `ServletContext` interface only provided access to information about the servlet's environment, such as the name of the server, MIME type mappings, etc., and a `log()` method for writing log messages to the server's log file. Most implementations provided one servlet context for all servlets within a host, or per virtual host.

Since version 2.1 of the API, the role of the `ServletContext` interface has been revised to represent the environment for each web application, and to act as a shared repository of attributes for all servlets in the application. The interface allows servlets in the same context to share information through context attributes, in a similar manner to the session attributes we have already seen.

In the current servlet specification (2.2), each servlet context is rooted at a specific path in the web server. In the examples for Tomcat in the previous chapters, you will have noticed that the deployment involves adding a `<Context>` tag, with the path to the application directory, to `server.xml`. For example, the `TechSupport` application of the previous chapter is associated with a context `/techSupport`. With the help of this notion, you can deploy multiple web applications under different context root names. All such applications can coexist as if they were deployed on different containers.

Let's take a look at the `ServletContext` interface.

The ServletContext Interface

```
public interface ServletContext
```

The `ServletContext` interface encapsulates the notion of a context for a web application. An object of this type can be obtained using the `getServletContext()` method of the `HttpServlet` object. `HttpServlet` in turn gets this object from the `ServletConfig` object that was passed to it during initialization.

The `ServletContext` interface specifies the following methods; web containers provide an implementation of the interface:

```
public String getMIMEType(String fileName)
public URL getResource(String path)
public InputStream getResourceAsStream(String path)
public RequestDispatcher getRequestDispatcher(String path)
public RequestDispatcher getNamedDispatcher(String name)
public String getRealPath(String path)
public ServletContext getContext(Sting uriPath)
```

```
public String getServerInfo()
public String getInitParameter(String name)
public Enumeration getInitParameterNames()
public Object getAttribute(String name)
public Enumeration getAttributeNames()
public void setAttribute(String name, Object attribute)
public void removeAttribute(String name)
public int getMajorVersion()
public int getMinorVersion()
public void log(String message)
public void log(String message, Throwable cause)
```

The getMimeType() Method

```
public String getMimeType(String filename)
```

This method returns the MIME type of a file by its extension. As we shall see in the next chapter, you can specify the MIME types that your application can handle in the deployment descriptor.

The getResource() Method

```
public URL getResource(String filename)
```

This method returns the URL to a resource at the specified path, and can be used to construct URL objects for files in the local file system.

The getResourceAsStream() Method

```
public InputStream getResourceAsStream(String filename)
```

This method is similar to getResource(), except that it returns an input stream associated with the URL.

The getRequestDispatcher() Method

```
public RequestDispatcher getRequestDispatcher(String path)
```

This method returns a RequestDispatcher object associated with the resource located at the current path. You can use the RequestDispatcher to delegate request/response processing to other resources within the application – we'll discuss RequestDispatcher in more detail later in this chapter.

The getNamedDispatcher() Method

```
public RequestDispatcher getNamedDispatcher(String path)
```

This method is similar to the getRequestDispatcher() method, except that this method accepts the alias names assigned to servlet classes in the deployment descriptor.

The getRealPath() Method

```
public String getRealPath(String path)
```

In a web application, resources are referred to by paths relative to the path pointing to the context, so this method lets you obtain the real path (on the server file system) from the path relative to the context.

The getContext() Method

```
public ServletContext getContext(String uripath)
```

This method returns a `ServletContext` object associated with the specified URL on the server. However, due to possible security limitations imposed by the web container, this method might return `null`, as this method otherwise lets you gain access to context objects that belong to other web applications.

The getServerInfo() Method

```
public java.lang.String getServerInfo()
```

This method returns the name and version of the servlet container on which the servlet is running. This information may be used for logging purposes.

The log() Methods

```
public void log(java.lang.String msg)
public void log(String message, Throwable throwable)
```

The `ServletContext` interface provides two methods for logging purposes. Of these, the second method can be used to log exceptions, while the first method can be used for general-purpose logging.

The getInitParameter and getInitParameterNames() Methods

```
public String getInitParameter(String name)
public Enumeration getInitParameterNames()
```

As with servlets themselves, we can specify initialization parameters for servlet contexts. These can be specified in the deployment descriptor using `<context-param>` tags. With the help of the above two methods, you can access these parameters.

The getAttribute(), getAttributeNames(), setAttribute(), and removeAttribute() Methods

```
public Object getAttribute(String name)
public Enumeration getAttributeNames()
public void setAttribute(String name, Object object)
public void removeAttribute(String name)
```

These four methods let you maintain the state of a web application. Any servlet can set an attribute, which can then be obtained by any other servlet within the same application, irrespective of whether these servlets are serving the same client or not. Using these methods, servlets can share information common to all servlets.

A Chat Application Using Context and Sessions

In this section, we shall build a chat application that involves both `ServletContext` and `HttpSession` objects. The chat application will allow users to:

❑ Create or delete chat rooms

❑ View a list of chat rooms, and join a chat room

❑ Group chat within a chat room

417

Before proceeding to build such an application, let's first look at certain modeling issues:

❑ The chat application consists of multiple chat rooms. Any user can leave a chat room and enter another chat room.

❑ In a given chat room, there will be more than one user exchanging messages.

In order to build such an application, we need to model certain classes:

❑ A ChatRoom class to represent a chat room. Since a ChatRoom is shared across multiple users (and therefore multiple sessions), the ServletContext is the right place to store a ChatRoom. However, since there can be more than one ChatRoom, we need to maintain a list of ChatRooms in the ServletContext.

❑ A ChatEntry to represent a chat message. In a chat room, multiple messages are exchanged between users. Since a ChatEntry is part of a ChatRoom, the ChatRoom class maintains a list of ChatEntry objects.

The diagram below gives an overview of relationships among these classes:

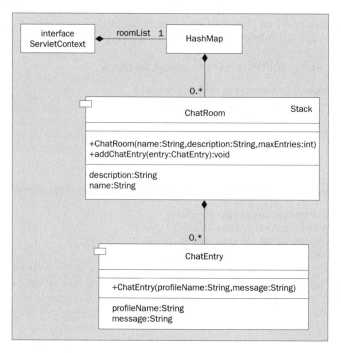

A java.util.HashMap class is used to hold a map of ChatRoom objects, and each ChatRoom contains a stack of ChatEntry objects. The HashMap object is the entry point to all the other objects, so a reference to the HashMap is stored as a ServletContext attribute under the name "roomList".

The HashMap, ChatRoom, and ChatEntry objects together represent the state of the chat application. There are also three servlets controlling the user interaction for the chat application:

❑ ChatAdminServlet handles creation and deletion of chat rooms.

❑   `ListRoomsServlet` lets the users browse through the list of chat rooms currently available.

❑   The `ChatRoomServlet` provides the user interface to a `ChatRoom`, allowing users to participate in the chat.

The ChatRoom Class

An instance of the `ChatRoom` class represents an individual chat room, and each instance maintains all the messages for a specific room. Save this source under `c:\ProJavaServer\Chapter09\chat\src\ChatRoom.java`:

```java
import java.util.*;

public class ChatRoom extends Stack {
  private String name;
  private String description;

  public ChatRoom(String name, String description, int maxEntries) {
    this.name = name;
    this.description = description;
    this.setSize(maxEntries);
  }

  public void addChatEntry(ChatEntry entry) {
    push(entry);
  }

  public int getChatEntriesSize() {
    return elementCount;
  }

  public Enumeration getChatEntries() {
    return elements();
  }

  public String getDescription() {
    return description;
  }

  public String getName() {
    return name;
  }
}
```

This class extends `java.util.Stack`. Each `ChatRoom` has a name, a description, and a maximum size that are passed as parameters to the constructor when the room is created. When a user enters a chat message, the `addChatEntry()` method is used to add the message to the room. The maximum size makes sure that when new messages are pushed, older messages beyond this size are popped out of the `ChatRoom`.

Though this class appears simple, there are certain reasons why we designed this class in the above manner. Firstly, multiple clients access a `ChatRoom` and add messages. In order to make sure that the `ChatRoom` is thread-safe, we need to synchronize access to methods that add/remove messages. However we're not doing so here, because the `java.util.Stack` class, which extends `java.util.Vector`, is synchronized. The methods that add and delete elements in a `Vector` are implemented in a thread-safe manner. Secondly, we're using a `Stack` to make sure that we maintain a finite number of messages in the `ChatRoom`. The `setSize()` method sets an upper limit in the number of elements in the `Stack`.

The ChatEntry Class

A `ChatEntry` object represents a message in a chat room. Save this source in
`c:\ProJavaServer\Chapter09\chat\src\ChatEntry.java`:

```java
import java.util.*;

public class ChatEntry
{
    private String profileName;
    private String message;

    public ChatEntry(String profileName, String message)
    {
        this.profileName = profileName;
        this.message = message;
    }

    public String getProfileName()
    {
        return profileName;
    }

    public String getMessage()
    {
        return message;
    }
}
```

A `ChatEntry` contains a chat message and the name of the user (`profileName`) who sent the message.

The Administration Servlet

`ChatAdminServlet` provides administration facilities for the chat application. This servlet implements
both the `doGet()` and `doPost()` methods. The `doGet()` method will be invoked when you directly
invoke the servlet, and the `doPost()` method when you delete or add chat rooms.

The response of this servlet when invoked for the first time is shown below; with this user interface, you
can add new chat rooms, or remove existing ones:

This servlet needs to implement:

❑ A doGet() method to generate a list of existing chat rooms (if any), followed by a form for creating a chat room.

❑ A doPost() method to process the response generated by the form submission. The processing involves creating a new chat room, or removing an existing room.

The complete source of the ChatAdminServlet is as follows; enter this source under c:\ProJavaServer\Chapter09\chat\src\ChatAdminServlet.java:

```java
import javax.servlet.*;
import javax.servlet.http.*;

import java.io.*;
import java.util.*;

public class ChatAdminServlet extends HttpServlet {

  String chatRoomPath;
  String listRoomsPath;
  String chatAdminPath;

  public void init() {
    ServletContext context = getServletContext();
    chatRoomPath = context.getInitParameter("CHATROOM_PATH");
    listRoomsPath = context.getInitParameter("LISTROOMS_PATH");
    chatAdminPath = context.getInitParameter("ADMIN_PATH");
  }

  public void doGet(HttpServletRequest req, HttpServletResponse res)
          throws IOException, ServletException {
    res.setContentType("text/html");
    PrintWriter out = res.getWriter();
    out.println("<HTML>");
    out.println("<HEAD><TITLE>Chat Room Administration</TITLE></HEAD>");
    out.println("<BODY>");
    out.println("<H1>Chat room administration</H1>");
    out.println("<FORM METHOD=\"POST\" ACTION=\""
                + res.encodeURL(chatAdminPath) + "\">");

    // Check for existing chat rooms
    HashMap roomList =
      (HashMap) getServletContext().getAttribute("roomList");
    if (roomList != null) {
      Iterator rooms = roomList.keySet().iterator();

      if (!rooms.hasNext()) {
        out.println("<P>There are no rooms</P>");
      } else {
        out.println("<P>Check the rooms you would like to remove,"
                  + "and press Update List.</P>");
```

```
      while (rooms.hasNext()) {
        String roomName = (String) rooms.next();
        ChatRoom room = (ChatRoom) roomList.get(roomName);
        out.println("<INPUT TYPE=CHECKBOX NAME=remove VALUE='"
                    + room.getName() + "'>" + room.getName() + "<BR>");
      }
    }
  }

  // Add fields for adding a room
  out.println("<P>Enter a new room and the description<P>");
  out.println("<TABLE>");
  out
    .println("<TR><TD>Name:</TD><TD><INPUT NAME=roomname
             SIZE=50></TD></TR>");
  out.println("<TR><TD>Description:</TD>");
  out.println("<TD><TEXTAREA NAME=roomdescr COLS=40 ROWS=5>");
  out.println("</TEXTAREA></TD></TR>");
  out.println("</TABLE>");

  // Add submit button
  out.println("<P><INPUT TYPE=SUBMIT VALUE='Update List'>");
  out.println("<P><A HREF=\"" + listRoomsPath + "\">Chat Now</A>");
  out.println("</FORM>");
  out.println("</BODY></HTML>");

  out.close();
}

public void doPost(HttpServletRequest req, HttpServletResponse res)
      throws IOException, ServletException {
  HashMap roomList = null;

  // Check for existing chat rooms
  synchronized (getServletContext()) {
    roomList = (HashMap) getServletContext().getAttribute("roomList");
    if (roomList == null) {
      roomList = new HashMap();
      getServletContext().setAttribute("roomList", roomList);
    }
  }

  // Update the room list
  String[] removeList = req.getParameterValues("remove");
  synchronized (roomList) {
    if (removeList != null) {
      for (int i = 0; i < removeList.length; i++) {
        roomList.remove(removeList[i]);
      }
    }
  }

  String roomName = req.getParameter("roomname");
  String roomDescr = req.getParameter("roomdescr");
```

```
    if (roomName != null && roomName.length() > 0) {
      synchronized (roomList) {
        roomList.put(roomName, new ChatRoom(roomName, roomDescr, 4));
      }
    }

    doGet(req, res);
  }

}
```

The key features of this class are:

❑   The doGet() method checks for a context attribute called "roomList". If there is none, it creates a new HashMap object and stores it in the context.

❑   If the HashMap is not empty, the doGet() method then prints a list of rooms (name of each room) and a checkbox as part of the form to submit a POST request to the same servlet.

❑   The doPost() method processes the POST request; this method can simultaneously remove existing rooms and add a new room. This method retrieves the HashMap from the context, and depending on the type of request, either deletes existing rooms (specified by request parameter "remove"), and/or adds a new room (specified by request parameters "roomname" and "roomdescr").

❑   After updating the HashMap, the doPost() method calls doGet(), to generate the list of rooms and the form.

Note that since the HashMap is stored in the context as an attribute, all servlets participating in this application can access the list of rooms.

We do not set the ServletContext "roomList" attribute after every update of the HashMap object. This attribute contains a reference to the HashMap object; we update the HashMap's data, but the *reference* is still the same, and we need not replace the HashMap object with another HashMap. Setting the attribute to the same object reference again would be redundant.

Servlets for Chatting

The ListRoomsServlet and ChatRoomServlet classes implement the end-user interface. They both access the context's state through the "roomList" attribute set by the ChatAdminServlet. Before we dive into the code, let's look at the overall design.

The ListRoomsServlet uses the HashMap object to get all ChatRoom objects, and sends a list of them to the client. The user can select the room to enter, causing the ChatRoomServlet to be invoked.

The ChatRoomServlet first uses the HashMap to get the ChatRoom selected by the user, and then gets all ChatEntry objects from the ChatRoom. It then sends a list of all the chat entries to the client. This servlet is also invoked when the user sends a new message to the room. In this case, it creates a new ChatEntry object and adds it to the selected ChatRoom.

The ListRoomsServlet Class

A user of this application first invokes the `ListRoomsServlet`, which lists all available rooms and allows the user to choose a name and enter a room. The screenshot below shows the response of the `ListsRoomServlet` after adding a couple of rooms:

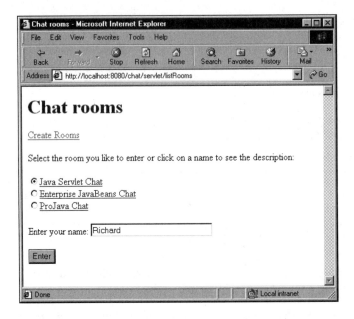

As shown above, the response of this servlet displays a list of chat rooms. When you click on a room, this servlet displays the description of the servlet. Alternatively, you can select a chat room (using the radio button next to the name of the room), enter a name (profile name), and click on Enter to enter the chat room.

Here is the complete source of the `ListRoomsServlet`: enter this source under `c:\ProJavaServer\Chapter09\chat\src\ListRoomsServlet.java`:

```
import javax.servlet.*;
import javax.servlet.http.*;

import java.io.*;
import java.util.*;
import java.net.URLEncoder;

public class ListRoomsServlet extends HttpServlet {

   String chatAdminPath;
   String listRoomsPath;
   String chatRoomPath;

   public void init() {
      ServletContext context = getServletContext();
      chatAdminPath = context.getInitParameter("ADMIN_PATH");
      listRoomsPath = context.getInitParameter("LISTROOMS_PATH");
      chatRoomPath = context.getInitParameter("CHATROOM_PATH");
   }
```

```
public void doGet(HttpServletRequest request,
                  HttpServletResponse response) throws IOException {
  response.setContentType("text/html");
  PrintWriter out = response.getWriter();

  String expand = request.getParameter("expand");
  HttpSession session = request.getSession();
  String profileName = (String) session.getAttribute("profileName");
  if (profileName == null) {
    profileName = "";
  }

  out.println("<HTML>");
  out.println("<HEAD><TITLE>Chat rooms</TITLE></HEAD>");
  out.println("<BODY>");
  out.println("<H1>Chat rooms</H1>");
  out.println("<FORM METHOD=POST ACTION=\"" + chatRoomPath + "\">");
  out.println("<P><A HREF=\"" + chatAdminPath
              + "\">Create Rooms</A></P>");

  // Get the list of rooms
  HashMap roomList =
    (HashMap) getServletContext().getAttribute("roomList");
  if (roomList == null) {
    out.println("<P>There are no rooms available right now.</P>");
  } else {

    // Add radio boxes for selecting a room
    out.println("Select the room you like to enter "
                + "or click on a name to see the description:<P>");

    Iterator rooms = roomList.keySet().iterator();
    boolean isFirst = true;
    while (rooms.hasNext()) {
      String roomName = (String) rooms.next();
      ChatRoom room = (ChatRoom) roomList.get(roomName);
      String listRoomsURL = listRoomsPath + "/?expand="
                            + URLEncoder.encode(roomName);
      listRoomsURL = response.encodeURL(listRoomsURL);

      out.println("<INPUT TYPE=RADIO NAME=roomName VALUE=\"" + roomName
                  + "\"" + (isFirst ? " CHECKED" : "") + ">"
                  + "<A HREF=\"" + listRoomsURL + "\">" + roomName
                  + "</A><BR>");
      isFirst = false;

      // Show description if requested
      if (expand != null && expand.equals(roomName)) {
        out.println("<BLOCKQUOTE>");
        if (room.getDescription().length() == 0) {
          out.println("No description available.");
        } else {
          out.println(room.getDescription());
        }
      }
```

```
        out.println("</BLOCKQUOTE><BR>");
      }
    }

    // Add a field for the profile name
    out.println("<P>Enter your name: ");
    out.println("<INPUT NAME=profileName VALUE='" + profileName
              + "' SIZE=30>");

    // Add submit button
    out.println("<P><INPUT TYPE=SUBMIT VALUE='Enter'>");
    out.println("</FORM>");
    }

    out.println("</BODY></HTML>");
    out.close();
  }
}
```

The HTTP GET method is used to invoke the servlet, so we use the doGet() method to generate an HTML page with a form containing the list of rooms, the user name field, and an Enter button.

To generate the list of chat rooms, this method calls the getAttribute() method on the ServletContext to obtain the list of chat rooms. The servlet also creates a session for each user. Note that, as discussed in the previous example, all URLs are encoded to make use of URL rewriting in case cookies are not being accepted by chat users.

The ChatRoomServlet Class

As seen above, the ListRoomsServlet generates a page with a <FORM> tag with the ACTION attribute set to the name of the ChatRoomServlet. The form contains a radio button control that holds the name of the selected room and a text field with the user's name, and uses the POST method to invoke the servlet again.

The ChatRoomServlet is given below; enter it in
c:\ProJavaServer\Chapter09\chat\src\ChatRoomServlet.java:

```
import javax.servlet.*;
import javax.servlet.http.*;

import java.io.*;
import java.net.*;
import java.util.*;

public class ChatRoomServlet extends HttpServlet {
  String chatRoomPath;
  String listRoomsPath;

  public void init() {
    ServletContext context = getServletContext();
    chatRoomPath = context.getInitParameter("CHATROOM_PATH");
    listRoomsPath = context.getInitParameter("LISTROOMS_PATH");
  }
```

```java
public void doGet(HttpServletRequest req, HttpServletResponse res)
        throws IOException, ServletException {

  res.setContentType("text/html");
  PrintWriter out = res.getWriter();

  ChatRoom room = getRoom(req, res);
  if (room == null) {
    return;    // This should not happen.
  }

  // Check if it's a request for a message list or a form
  String listPar = req.getParameter("list");
  if (listPar != null && listPar.equals("true")) {
    writeMessages(out, room, getProfileName(req));
  } else {
    out.println("<HTML>");
    out.println("<BODY>");
    out.println("<FORM METHOD=\"POST\" ACTION=\""
                + res.encodeURL(chatRoomPath) + "\" TARGET=\"_top\">");

    out.println("<P>Enter your message:</P>");
    out.println("<INPUT NAME=\"msg\" SIZE=\"30\">");

    // Add a Submit button
    out.println("<P><INPUT TYPE=SUBMIT VALUE='Send Message'>");

    // Add an Exit button
    out.println("</FORM>");
    out.println("<FORM ACTION=\"" + res.encodeURL(listRoomsPath)
                + "\" METHOD=\"GET\" TARGET=\"_top\">");
    out.println("<INPUT TYPE=SUBMIT VALUE=Exit>");
    out.println("</FORM>");

    out.println("</BODY></HTML>");
  }
  out.close();
}

public void doPost(HttpServletRequest req, HttpServletResponse res)
        throws IOException, ServletException {
  res.setContentType("text/html");

  ChatRoom room = getRoom(req, res);
  if (room == null) {
    return;
  }

  String profileName = getProfileName(req);

  // Save message if any
  String msg = req.getParameter("msg");
  if (msg != null && msg.length() != 0) {
    room.addChatEntry(new ChatEntry(profileName, msg));
  }
```

```
    writeFrame(res, room);
  }

  private String getProfileName(HttpServletRequest req) {
    HttpSession session = req.getSession(true);
    String profileName = (String) session.getAttribute("profileName");
    if (profileName == null) {

      // Entered a room for the first time?
      profileName = req.getParameter("profileName");
      if (profileName == null || profileName.length() == 0) {
        profileName = "A spineless spy";
      }
      session.setAttribute("profileName", profileName);
    } else {

      // Entered a new room with a new name?
      String newName = req.getParameter("profileName");
      if (newName != null && newName.length() > 0
            &&!newName.equals(profileName)) {
        profileName = newName;
        session.setAttribute("profileName", profileName);
      }
    }
    return profileName;
  }

  private ChatRoom getRoom(HttpServletRequest req,
                        HttpServletResponse res) throws IOException {
    HttpSession session = req.getSession(true);
    PrintWriter out = res.getWriter();

    String roomName = (String) session.getAttribute("roomName");
    if (roomName == null) {

      // Just entered?
      roomName = req.getParameter("roomName");
      if (roomName == null || roomName.length() == 0) {
        writeError(out, "Room not specified");
        return null;
      }
      session.setAttribute("roomName", roomName);
    } else {

      // Entered a new room?
      String newRoom = req.getParameter("roomName");
      if (newRoom != null && newRoom.length() > 0
            &&!newRoom.equals(roomName)) {
        roomName = newRoom;
        session.setAttribute("roomName", roomName);
      }
    }
```

```
    HashMap roomList =
      (HashMap) getServletContext().getAttribute("roomList");
    ChatRoom room = (ChatRoom) roomList.get(roomName);
    if (room == null) {
      writeError(out, "Room " + roomName + " not found");
      return null;
    }
    return room;
  }

  private void writeError(PrintWriter out, String msg) {
    out.println("<HTML>");
    out.println("<HEAD><TITLE>Error</TITLE></HEAD>");
    out.println("<BODY>");
    out.println("<H1>Error</H1>");
    out.println(msg);
    out.println("</BODY></HTML>");
  }

  private void writeFrame(HttpServletResponse res,
                          ChatRoom room) throws IOException {
    PrintWriter out = res.getWriter();

    out.println("<HTML>");
    out.println("<HEAD><TITLE>" + room.getName() + "</TITLE></HEAD>");
    out.println("<FRAMESET ROWS='50%,50%' BORDER=0 FRAMEBORDER=NO>");
    out.println("<FRAME SRC=\"" + res.encodeURL(chatRoomPath)
                + "?list=true\" NAME=\"list\" SCROLLING=\"AUTO\">");
    out.println("<FRAME SRC=\"" + res.encodeURL(chatRoomPath)
                + "?list=false\" NAME=\"form\" SCROLLING=\"AUTO\">");
    out.println("<NOFRAMES>");
    out.println("<BODY>");
    out.println("Viewing this page requires a browser capable of "
                + "displaying frames.");
    out.println("</BODY>");
    out.println("</NOFRAMES>");
    out.println("</FRAMESET>");
    out.println("</HTML>");
    out.close();
  }

  private void writeMessages(PrintWriter out, ChatRoom room,
                             String profileName) {
    StringBuffer sb = new StringBuffer();

    out.println("<HTML>");
    out.println("<HEAD><META http-equiv=\"refresh\" content=\"5\"></HEAD>");
    out.println("<BODY>");
    out.println("<B>Room: " + room.getName() + "</B><BR>" + "<B>Identity: "
                + profileName + "</B><BR>");

    // List all messages in the room
    if (room.size() == 0) {
      out.println("<FONT COLOR=RED>There are no messages in this room
                  yet</FONT>");
```

```
      } else {
        Iterator entries = room.iterator();
        while (entries.hasNext()) {
          ChatEntry entry = (ChatEntry) entries.next();
          if (entry == null) {
            continue;
          }
          String entryName = entry.getProfileName();
          if (entryName.equals(profileName)) {
            out.print("<FONT COLOR=BLUE>");
          }
          out.println(entryName + " : " + entry.getMessage() + "<BR>");
          if (entryName.equals(profileName)) {
            out.print("</FONT>");
          }
        }
      }
    }
    out.println("</BODY></HTML>");
  }
}
```

When compared to the rest of the classes in this application, this servlet seems complicated. The following screenshot shows you a chat session in progress:

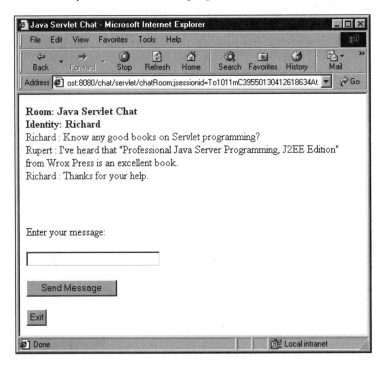

The following key points should help you navigate through this class:

❑ The screenshot above has two HTML frames in it. Of these, the top frame is used to display the messages posted in the room, while the bottom frame is used for the user to enter new chat messages. The HTML frameset is generated in the `writeFrame()` method, invoked in `doPost()`.

❑ The doGet() method plays the dual role of generating both the frames. In order to decide whether it should generate a list of messages, or a form for entering a new message, it uses the request parameter "list". If this parameter is "true" (when the GET request is generated by the top frame), doGet() generates the list of messages by calling the writeMessages() method. If this parameter is not present in the request (when the GET request is generated by the bottom frame), it simply generates the static form.

❑ The doPost() method is invoked when the user enters a new message. doPost() retrieves the current chat room using the getRoom() method, and the user name from the session. Using this data, it creates a new ChatEntry, and adds it to the chat room. It then calls writeFrame(), which forces two GET requests, one for each frame.

❑ Since new messages can be posted to the room almost continuously, we should refresh the top frame periodically. We use the refresh meta-tag to automatically reload this frame. See the writeMessages() method for the implementation of this.

Chat Setup

In order to set-up build, and deploy the chat room, perform the following steps:

A Welcome Page

Create an index.html page at c:\ProJavaServer\Chapter09\chat\index.html:

```
<HTML>
  <HEAD>
    <TITLE>Chat Application</TITLE>
    <BODY>
    <H1>Chat Application</H1>

    <P>Click <A HREF="/chat/servlet/chatAdmin">here</A> to
    administer chat rooms.</P>

    <P>Click <A HREF="/chat/servlet/listRooms">here</A> to view
    current chat rooms, and to join a chat room.</P>

  </BODY>
</HTML>
```

The purpose of this page is simply to provide links to the servlets in the application.

Compile the Classes

Compile the classes to create the class files in c:\ProJavaServer\Chapter09\WEB-INF\classes.

Deployment Descriptor

Create the following deployment descriptor at c:\ProJavaServer\Chapter09\WEB-INF\web.xml:

```
<?xml version="1.0" encoding="ISO-8859-1"?>

<!DOCTYPE web-app
  PUBLIC "-//Sun Microsystems, Inc.//DTD Web Application 2.2//EN"
  "http://java.sun.com/j2ee/dtds/web-app_2.2.dtd">
```

```
<web-app>
  <servlet>
    <servlet-name>chatAdmin</servlet-name>
    <servlet-class>ChatAdminServlet</servlet-class>
  </servlet>

  <servlet>
    <servlet-name>chatRoom</servlet-name>
    <servlet-class>ChatRoomServlet</servlet-class>
  </servlet>

  <servlet>
    <servlet-name>listRooms</servlet-name>
    <servlet-class>ListRoomsServlet</servlet-class>
  </servlet>

  <context-param>
    <param-name>ADMIN_PATH</param-name>
    <param-value>/chat/servlet/chatAdmin</param-value>
  </context-param>

  <context-param>
    <param-name>LISTROOMS_PATH</param-name>
    <param-value>/chat/servlet/listRooms</param-value>
  </context-param>

  <context-param>
    <param-name>CHATROOM_PATH</param-name>
    <param-value>/chat/servlet/chatRoom</param-value>
  </context-param>

</web-app>
```

As well as declaring the three servlet classes, this deployment descriptor also defines three additional context parameters. Each of these parameters defines a string that points to a servlet. Why are these required?

In this application, servlets generate content that points to other servlets. For instance, the content generated by the `ListRoomsServlet` has links to `ChatRoomServlet` and `ChatAdminServlet`. Instead of hard-coding these values in each of the servlets, we have used these context parameters to get the actual URLs of the servlets.

Deploy and Test

In order to deploy this application, add the following entry in `%TOMCAT_HOM%\conf\server.xml`:

```
<Context path="/chat"
  docBase="c:/ProJavaServer/Chapter09/chat">
</Context>
```

Restart Tomcat, and enter `http://localhost:8080/chat` in your browser to access the welcome file created above. Use the administration link to create chat rooms.

To view the list of chat rooms and to join a chat room, you can use the Chat Now button on the admin page, or enter the URL `http://localhost:8080/chat/servlet/listRooms` directly. Use the radio buttons to select a chat room, enter your name, and click on Enter to enter the chat room.

Servlet Collaboration

In the default servlet model, a servlet receives an HTTP request, executes some application logic, and prepares the response. This completes one request-response trip for the client. However, there are several scenarios in which this basic model is not adequate:

❑ A servlet receives an HTTP request from a client, processes application logic, and a JavaServer Page drives the response. In this case the servlet is not responsible for response generation. Instead, the JSP page is responsible for dynamic content.

❑ A servlet receives an HTTP request from a client, and processes application logic partially, then hands over the request to another servlet. The second servlet completes the application logic, and either prepares the response, or requests a JSP page to drive the response.

In both the scenarios, the servlet is not completely responsible for processing a request. Instead, it delegates the processing to another servlet (or a JSP page, which is equivalent to a servlet at run-time).

There are two types of solutions for addressing the above requirements:

❑ **Servlet chaining:** This was once a very widely used approach, and supported by some of the servlet engine vendors. Although this is not supported by the Java Servlet API specification, for the sake of completeness, you'll find a short description below.

❑ **Request Dispatching:** Request dispatching allows one servlet to dispatch the request to another resource (a servlet, a JSP page, or any other resource). Prior to version 2.2 of the servlet API, this approach used to be called 'inter-servlet communication'. The API for supporting inter-servlet communication has now been deprecated, and has been replaced by request dispatchers.

Servlet Chaining

Servlet chaining predates J2EE, and its component model. The idea of servlet chaining is very simple: you design a set of servlets, each of which does a single task. After developing these servlets, you configure your servlet engine to specify a chain of servlets for a given URL path alias. Once the servlet engine receives a request for this alias, the servlet engine invokes the servlets in the specified order. This is similar to piping on Unix, where output of one program becomes input for another program in the pipe.

Suppose you've servlets A, B, and C executing three parts of a request-response process for a single customer service. Let's assume that /custService is the alias given to this chain (/custSerice=A,B,C). Consider a browser sending a request to the URL path pointing to this alias. The servlet engine sends all requests for this alias to servlet A. After executing servlet A's service method, the servlet engine invokes servlet B's service method, followed by servlet C's service method. The final response is then sent to the client. Briefly, this is servlet chaining. Refer to the figure below for an overview of this approach:

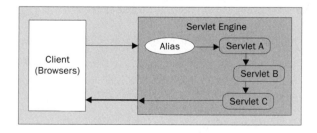

The key feature of servlet chaining is that you configure the servlet engine to do the chaining. During setup, you specify the order in which these servlets should be invoked.

Servlet chaining was initially introduced in the Java Web Server, but was never part of the servlet API specification. You'll still find some books talking about servlet chaining, but be advised that this non-standard feature is not supported by most of the web containers today. Instead, you should consider using the request dispatching approach.

Request Dispatching

Request dispatching allows a servlet or a JSP page to dispatch a request to another servlet, (or a JSP page, or even a plain HTML page), which will then be responsible for any further processing and for generating the response.

When the web container receives a request, it constructs `request` and `response` objects and invokes one of the servlet's service methods with the request and response objects. This is a process of the web container dispatching a request to a servlet. What if this servlet wants to dispatch the same request to another servlet after some preliminary processing? For this purpose, the first servlet should be able to obtain a reference to the second servlet. Using this reference, the first servlet can dispatch a request to the second servlet. In simple terms, this is **request dispatching**.

The Java Servlet API has a special interface called `javax.servlet.RequestDispatcher` for this purpose.

RequestDispatcher Interface

```
public Interface RequestDispatcher
```

This interface encapsulates a reference to another web resource at a specified path within the scope of the same servlet context. A `javax.servlet.RequestDispatcher` object can be used to dispatch requests to other servlets and JSP pages.

This interface has two methods, which allow you to delegate the request-response processing to another resource, after the calling servlet has finished any preliminary processing.

The forward() Method

```
public void forward(ServletRequest request, ServletResponse response)
        throws ServletException, java.io.IOException
```

This method lets you forward the request to another servlet or a JSP page, or an HTML file on the server; this resource then takes over responsibility for producing the response.

The include() Method

```
public void include(ServletRequest request, ServletResponse response)
        throws ServletException, java.io.IOException
```

This method lets you include the content produced by another resource in the calling servlet's response.

Obtaining a RequestDispatcher Object

There are three ways in which you can obtain a `RequestDispatcher` object for a resource:

❏ `javax.servlet.ServletContext` methods `getRequestDispatcher()` and `getNamedDispatcher()`:

`public RequestDispatcher getRequestDispatcher(String path)`
`public RequestDispatcher getNamedDispatcher(String name)`

❏ `javax.servlet.ServletRequest` method `getRequestDispatcher()`:

`public RequestDispatcher getRequestDispatcher(String path)`

Although these methods serve the same purpose, the usage depends on what information is available to you.

The two `getRequestDispatcher()` methods accept a URL path referring to the target resource. However, the `getRequestDispatcher()` method on `javax.servlet.ServletContext` requires the absolute path (that is, the path name should be begin with a `/`). For example, if you have a servlet `/myWebApp/servlet/servlet1`, and want to get the `RequestDispatcher` object for `/myWebApp/servlet/servlet2`, you should specify the complete path relative to the root context. Here the root context is `/myWebApp`, and the absolute path is `/servlet/servlet2`.

The same method on `javax.servlet.ServletRequest` accepts both absolute and relative paths. In the above example, you could now also `servlet2` as the path.

> A `javax.servlet.ServletRequest` is associated with a URL path, and the web container can use this to resolve relative paths into absolute paths.

The `getNamedDispatcher()` method is a convenience method that accepts a name associated with the servlet. This is the same name that you specify the deployment descriptor in the `<servlet-name>` element.

Note that the target resource (except for static resources) should implement the same type of HTTP request that the original servlet receives.

Tech Support Revisited

Let's now revisit and enhance the Tech Support application from the last chapter. Let's consider the following additional features:

❏ Instead of collecting customer data (such as first name, last name, and telephone number) every time, let's introduce a customer registration page.

❏ Using the customer's e-mail address, determine if a customer is a revisiting customer or a new customer. If the customer is new, direct the customer to the registration page.

❏ After registration, direct the customer to a response servlet.

❏ If the customer is a revisiting customer, direct the customer to the response servlet.

❏ Maintain separate database tables for support requests and customer data.

As you'll see shortly, these enhancements require extensive use of `RequestDispatchers`. The figure below shows the overall flow in this application:

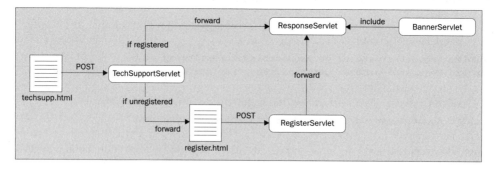

The flow shown above is very simple. The request from `techsupp.html` goes to the `TechSupportServlet`. If the customer is previously registered, the `TechSupportServlet` forwards the request to the `ResponseServlet`. Otherwise, the flow proceeds to the `register.html` page, to collect customer information. On submitting the form in this page, the request goes to `RegisterServlet`, which inserts the customer data in the database. After registration, the flow then proceeds to the `ResponseServlet`.

The `ResponseServlet` generates a page with a response message, and includes the output of `BannerServlet`. `BannerServlet` simply writes an HTML 'banner' without the HTML headers and footers (`<HTML>`, `<BODY>`, etc.).

Let's now consider the implementation.

The techsupp.html Page

This is the same as the page you created in the original Tech Support application, except that the customer's first name, last name, and telephone number are no longer included in the form. The form sends the request to `TechSupportServlet`.

Enter the following in `c:\ProJavaServer\Chapter09\techSupport\techsupp.html`:

```
<HTML>

<HEAD>
  <TITLE>XYZ Corporation, IT Department</TITLE>
</HEAD>
  <BODY>
    <H1>Technical Support Request</H1>
    <HR><BR>
    <CENTER>
      <FORM ACTION="/techSupport2/servlet/techSupport" METHOD="GET">
        <TABLE ALIGN="center" WIDTH="100%" CELLSPACING="2" CELLPADDING="2">
          <TR>
            <TD ALIGN="right">Email:</TD>
            <TD><INPUT TYPE="Text" NAME="email" ALIGN="LEFT"
                     SIZE="25"></TD>
          </TR>
          <TR>
            <TD ALIGN="right">Software:</TD>
```

```
      <TD>
        <SELECT NAME="software" SIZE="1">
          <OPTION VALUE="Word">Microsoft Word</OPTION>
          <OPTION VALUE="Excel">Microsoft Excel</OPTION>
          <OPTION VALUE="Access">Microsoft Access</OPTION>
        </SELECT>
      </TD>
      <TD ALIGN="right">Operating System:</TD>
      <TD>
        <SELECT NAME="os" size="1">
          <OPTION VALUE="95">Windows 95</OPTION>
          <OPTION VALUE="98">Windows 98</OPTION>
          <OPTION VALUE="NT">Windows NT</OPTION>
        </SELECT>
      </TD>
    </TR>
  </TABLE>

  <BR>Problem Description
  <BR>
  <TEXTAREA NAME="problem" COLS="50" ROWS="4"></TEXTAREA>

  <HR><BR>
  <INPUT TYPE="Submit" NAME="submit" VALUE="Submit Request">
    </FORM>
  </CENTER>
  </BODY>
</HTML>
```

This produces the form shown below:

TechSupportServlet

This is a revised version of the original `TechSupportServlet` class discussed in Chapter 8, which first inserts the customer service request in the database, and then checks the customer database to see if a customer exists with the given e-mail address. If one does, it uses a request dispatcher to redirect the customer

437

to `ResponseServlet`. If, however, the customer is unregistered, it forwards the request to `register.html`.

Enter the following in
`c:\ProJavaServer\Chapter09\techSupport\src\TechSupportServlet.java`:

```java
// Import Servlet packages
import javax.servlet.*;
import javax.servlet.http.*;

// Import other Java packages
import java.io.*;
import java.sql.*;

public class TechSupportServlet extends HttpServlet {
  String protocol;

  public void init() throws ServletException {
    String driver = getServletContext().getInitParameter("driver");
    protocol = getServletContext().getInitParameter("protocol");
    if (driver == null || protocol == null) {
      throw new UnavailableException("Driver not specified.");
    }

    try {
      Class.forName(driver);
    } catch (ClassNotFoundException cnfe) {
      throw new UnavailableException("Driver <" + driver
                              + "> not found in the classpath.");
    }
  }

  protected void doGet(HttpServletRequest request,
                       HttpServletResponse response)
          throws ServletException, IOException {
    HttpSession session = request.getSession();

    String email = request.getParameter("email");
    String software = request.getParameter("software");
    String os = request.getParameter("os");
    String problem = request.getParameter("problem");

    int requestId = 0;
    Connection connection = null;
    String insertStatementStr =
      "INSERT INTO SUPP_REQUESTS VALUES(?, ?, ?, ?, ?)";
    String selectCustomerStr =
      "SELECT CUSTOMERS.FNAME, CUSTOMERS.LNAME FROM CUSTOMERS WHERE "
      + CUSTOMERS.EMAIL = ?";

    try {
      connection = DriverManager.getConnection(protocol);

      PreparedStatement insertStatement =
        connection.prepareStatement(insertStatementStr);
      requestId = Sequencer.getNextNumber(protocol);

      insertStatement.setInt(1, requestId);
      insertStatement.setString(2, email);
```

```
      insertStatement.setString(3, software);
      insertStatement.setString(4, os);
      insertStatement.setString(5, problem);

      insertStatement.executeUpdate();

      // Now verify if the customer is registered or not.
      PreparedStatement selectStatement =
        connection.prepareStatement(selectCustomerStr);
      selectStatement.setString(1, email);

      ResultSet rs = selectStatement.executeQuery();

      if (rs.next()) {
        String firstName = rs.getString("FNAME");
        String lastName = rs.getString("LNAME");
        request.setAttribute("firstName", firstName);
        request.setAttribute("lastName", lastName);

        // Now invoke the Response servlet.
        RequestDispatcher rd =
          getServletContext().getNamedDispatcher("response");
        rd.forward(request, response);
      } else {

        // Customer is not registered.
        session.setAttribute("email", email);
        RequestDispatcher rd =
          request.getRequestDispatcher("/register.html");
        rd.forward(request, response);
      }
    } catch (SQLException sqle) {
      throw new ServletException("Database error", sqle);
    }
    finally {
      if (connection != null) {
        try {
          connection.close();
        } catch (SQLException sqle) {}
      }
    }
  }
}
```

The register.html Page

This page contains a form that collects customer registration information: the customer's first name, last name, and phone number. The form sends the request to `RegisterCustomerServlet`.

Enter the following in `c:\ProJavaServer\Chapter09\techSupport\register.html`:

```
<HTML>
  <HEAD>
    <TITLE>Customer Registration</TITLE>
  </HEAD>
  <BODY>
    <CENTER><H1>Customer Registration</H1></CENTER>
    <HR>
      Please register.
      <FORM ACTION="/techSupport2/servlet/register" METHOD="POST">
        <TABLE>
```

```
        <TR>
          <TD>First Name:</TD>
          <TD><INPUT TYPE="Text" NAME="txtFname" SIZE="30"></TD>
        </TR>
        <TR>
          <TD>Last Name:</TD>
          <TD><INPUT TYPE="Text" NAME="txtLname" SIZE="30"></TD>
        </TR>
        <TR>
          <TD>Phone Number:</TD>
          <TD><INPUT TYPE="Text" NAME="txtPhone" SIZE="30"></TD>
        </TR>
      </TABLE>
      <BR><INPUT TYPE="Submit" VALUE="Submit Request">
    </FORM>
  </BODY>
</HTML>
```

`register.html` produces the following form:

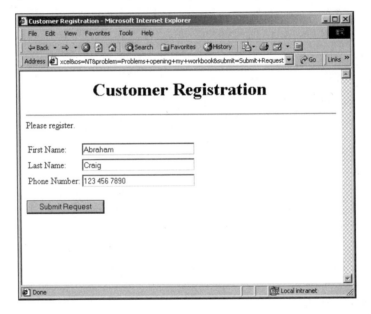

RegisterCustomerServlet

This servlet registers customer information. Upon registration, this servlet forwards the request to
`ResponseServlet`.

Enter the following in
`c:\ProJavaServer\Chapter09\techSupport\src\RegisterCustomerServlet.java`:

```
// Import servlet packages
import javax.servlet.*;
import javax.servlet.http.*;
```

```java
// Import Java packages
import java.util.*;
import java.sql.*;
import java.io.*;

public class RegisterCustomerServlet extends HttpServlet {
  String protocol;

  public void init() throws ServletException {
    String driver = getServletContext().getInitParameter("driver");
    protocol = getServletContext().getInitParameter("protocol");

    if (driver == null || protocol == null) {
      throw new UnavailableException("Driver not specified.");
    }

    try {
      Class.forName(driver);
    } catch (ClassNotFoundException cnfe) {
      throw new UnavailableException("Driver <" + driver
                                  + "> not found in the classpath.");
    }
  }

  public void doPost(HttpServletRequest request,
                     HttpServletResponse response)
         throws ServletException, IOException {

    HttpSession session = request.getSession();
    String fname = request.getParameter("txtFname");
    String lname = request.getParameter("txtLname");
    String email = (String) session.getAttribute("email");
    String phone = request.getParameter("txtPhone");

    Connection connection = null;
    String insertStatementStr = "INSERT INTO CUSTOMERS VALUES(?, ?, ?, ?)";
    try {
      connection = DriverManager.getConnection(protocol);

      PreparedStatement insertStatement =
        connection.prepareStatement(insertStatementStr);
      insertStatement.setString(1, email);
      insertStatement.setString(2, fname);
      insertStatement.setString(3, lname);
      insertStatement.setString(4, phone);

      insertStatement.executeUpdate();

    } catch (SQLException sqle) {
      throw new ServletException("Database error", sqle);
    }
    finally {
      if (connection != null) {
        try {
          connection.close();
        } catch (SQLException sqle) {}
      }
    }
```

```
    request.setAttribute("firstName", fname);
    request.setAttribute("lastName", lname);

    // Now invoke the Response servlet.
    RequestDispatcher rd =
      getServletContext().getNamedDispatcher("response");
    rd.forward(request, response);

  }
}
```

ResponseServlet

This servlet displays a confirmation message that the customer's request (and the profile, if entered) has been registered. This servlet 'includes' `BannerServlet` to include a banner in the content.

Enter the following in
`c:\ProJavaServer\Chapter09\techSupport\src\ResponseServlet.java`:

```
// Import Servlet Libraries
import javax.servlet.*;
import javax.servlet.http.*;

// Import Java Libraries
import java.io.*;
import java.util.*;

public class ResponseServlet extends HttpServlet {

  protected void doPost(HttpServletRequest request,
                        HttpServletResponse response)
          throws ServletException, IOException {
    doGet(request, response);
  }

  protected void doGet(HttpServletRequest request,
                       HttpServletResponse response)
          throws ServletException, IOException {

    response.setContentType("text/html");
    PrintWriter out = response.getWriter();

    // Send acknowledgment to the customer
    out.println("<HTML>");
    out.println("<HEAD><TITLE>Customer Service Response</TITLE></HEAD>");
    out.println("<BODY>");
    out.println("<H1>Customer Service Request Received</H1>");
    out.println("<p>Thank you for your request.");
    out.println("<p>Your request has been recorded and will be "
                + "responded to within three business days.");

    // Include a banner
    RequestDispatcher rd = request.getRequestDispatcher("/servlet/banner");
    rd.include(request, response);

    out.println("</BODY></HTML>");
    out.close();
  }
}
```

BannerServlet

This servlet generates very simple banner with the current user's name, followed by a standard footer. Note that this servlet does not set the response type, because it is included in the response being generated by the ResponseServlet.

Enter the following in c:\ProJavaServer\Chapter09\techSupport\src\BannerServlet.java:

```java
import java.io.*;
import javax.servlet.*;
import javax.servlet.http.*;


public class BannerServlet extends HttpServlet {

  protected void doPost(HttpServletRequest request,
                        HttpServletResponse response)
          throws ServletException, IOException {
    doGet(request, response);
  }

  protected void doGet(HttpServletRequest request,
                       HttpServletResponse response)
        throws ServletException, IOException {
    HttpSession session = request.getSession();

    String firstName = (String) request.getAttribute("firstName");
    String lastName = (String) request.getAttribute("lastName");

    PrintWriter out = response.getWriter();

    out.println("<HR>");
    out.println("Current User: " + firstName + " " + lastName);
    out.println("<HR>");
    out.println("XYZ Corporation, Customer Servoce.");
    out.println("<BR us at 1.800.xyz.corp.<BR>");
  }
}
```

ResponseServlet and BannerServlet together produce this output:

TechSupport Setup and Deployment

Compile all the Java source files in the `c:\ProJavaServer\Chapter09\techSupport\src` directory to generate class files in `c:\ProJavaServer\Chapter09\techSupport\WEB-INF\classes`. You will also need the `Sequencer` class from the earlier version of this application.

Then add the following deployment descriptor for this application, as `c:\ProJavaServer\Chapter09\techSupport\WEB-INF\web.xml`:

```xml
<?xml version="1.0" encoding="ISO-8859-1"?>

<!DOCTYPE web-app
    PUBLIC "-//Sun Microsystems, Inc.//DTD Web Application 2.2//EN"
    "http://java.sun.com/j2ee/dtds/web-app_2.2.dtd">

<web-app>

    <welcome-file-list>
      <welcome-file>techsupp.html</welcome-file>
    </welcome-file-list>

    <servlet>
      <servlet-name>techSupport</servlet-name>
      <servlet-class>TechSupportServlet</servlet-class>
    </servlet>

    <servlet>
      <servlet-name>response</servlet-name>
      <servlet-class>ResponseServlet</servlet-class>
    </servlet>

    <servlet>
      <servlet-name>banner</servlet-name>
      <servlet-class>BannerServlet</servlet-class>
    </servlet>

    <servlet>
      <servlet-name>register</servlet-name>
      <servlet-class>RegisterCustomerServlet</servlet-class>
    </servlet>

    <context-param>
      <param-name>driver</param-name>
      <param-value>COM.cloudscape.core.JDBCDriver</param-value>
    </context-param>

    <context-param>
      <param-name>protocol</param-name>
      <param-value>
jdbc:cloudscape:c:/ProJavaServer/Chapter09/techSupport/WEB-INF/db;autocommit=true
      </param-value>
    </context-param>
  </web-app>
```

Adjust the database driver and protocol name to suit your database configuration. If you're using CloudScape, use the following database schema and make sure you create the database tables in `c:\ProJavaServer\Chapter09\techSupport\WEB-INF\db`.

```
--
-- Table for storing the technical support requests
--
CREATE TABLE SUPP_REQUESTS(REQUEST_ID          INTEGER PRIMARY KEY,
                           EMAIL                VARCHAR(40),
                           SOFTWARE             VARCHAR(40),
                           OS                   VARCHAR(40),
                           PROBLEM              VARCHAR(256));


--
-- Sequencer table for generating sequence numbers for REQUEST_ID
--
CREATE TABLE SEQ_NO(NEXT_NO                     INTEGER);

INSERT INTO SEQ_NO VALUES(0);


--
-- Customer table
--
CREATE TABLE CUSTOMERS(EMAIL                    VARCHAR(40) PRIMARY KEY,
                       FNAME                    VARCHAR(15),
                       LNAME                    VARCHAR(15),
                       PHONE                    VARCHAR(12));
```

You're now ready to test this application. Open %TOMCAT_HOME%\conf\server.xml and add the following entry:

```
<Context path="/techSupport2"
    docBase="c:/ProJavaServer/Chapter09/techSupport">
</Context>
```

Then restart Tomcat.

To test the application, enter the URL http://localhost:8080/techSupport2. You should be able to navigate through the flow depicted at the beginning of this section.

Using RequestDispathers for Collaboration

In this application, we used the RequestDispatcher for the following purposes:

Forwarding the Request to ResponseServlet

The TechSupportServlet checks in the customer database whether the customer is already registered. If so, the request is forwarded to the ResponseServlet:

```
if(rs.next())
{
    String firstName = rs.getString("FNAME");
    String lastName = rs.getString("LNAME");
    request.setAttribute("firstName", firstName);
    request.setAttribute("lastName", lastName);

    // Now invoke the Response servlet.
    RequestDispatcher rd =
                getServletContext().getNamedDispatcher("response");
    rd.forward(request, response);
}
```

445

Since the ResponseServlet has an alias called "response" (specified in the deployment descriptor), we can use the getNamedDispatcher() method to get the RequestDispatcher object for the ResponseServlet. The same technique is used by the RegisterCustomerServlet to forward the request to the ResponseServlet.

Note that we're using the setAttribute() method on the request object to add the "firstName" and "lastName" attributes. Since the request is forwarded from either TechSupportServlet or RegisterServlet to the ResponseServlet, which then includes BannerServlet, BannerServlet can get these attributes from the request object while generating the banner content. Refer to the source of BannerServlet to see how the banner is generated.

Forwarding the Request to register.html

If the customer is not registered, the customer is directed to register.html:

```
RequestDispatcher rd =
    request.getRequestDispatcher("/register.html");
rd.forward(request, response);
```

We use the absolute path of register.html page to obtain a RequestDispatcher from the HttpServletRequest object, and call the forward() method to forward the request. Note that since register.html can only be invoked using a GET request, the form in techsupp.html had to use the GET method.

> Since the **forward()** method forwards the request to other resources, the calling servlet (**TechSupportServlet**) should not commit any output to the response.

For example, you should not call getWriter() to get a java.io.PrintWriter object and write content to it. However, if any content is written to the response, you should call the reset() method on the response object.

Including the Banner in ResponseServlet

ResponseServlet includes in its response a banner generated by BannerServlet. The purpose of this banner is to print the name of the current customer, and a static banner message. The doGet() method in ResponsServlet includes the following code:

```
RequestDispatcher rd = request.getRequestDispatcher("/servlet/banner");
rd.include(request, response);
```

Notice the difference between the forward() and include(). Whereas forward() makes the new servlet wholly responsible for generating the response, include() merely includes the called servlet's response into the response from the calling servlet. Using this approach, you can compose responses from multiple servlets.

Summary

In this chapter, we've covered the some of the important programming aspects of servlet based application development:

- ❏ Session tracking and associating state (attributes) with sessions: In all the examples in this chapter, we used the session object to maintain the state of a session.

- ❏ Servlet contexts: In the Chat application, we saw how the servlet context allows you to maintain application state. We've also used servlet context to access request dispatchers.

- ❏ Servlet collaboration: The revised Tech Support application illustrates how request dispatchers can be used to create conditional flow between servlets and static pages.

We have now covered the bulk of the servlet API. In the next chapter, we will consider deployment issues, including configuring deployment descriptors, implementing security, and packaging web applications.

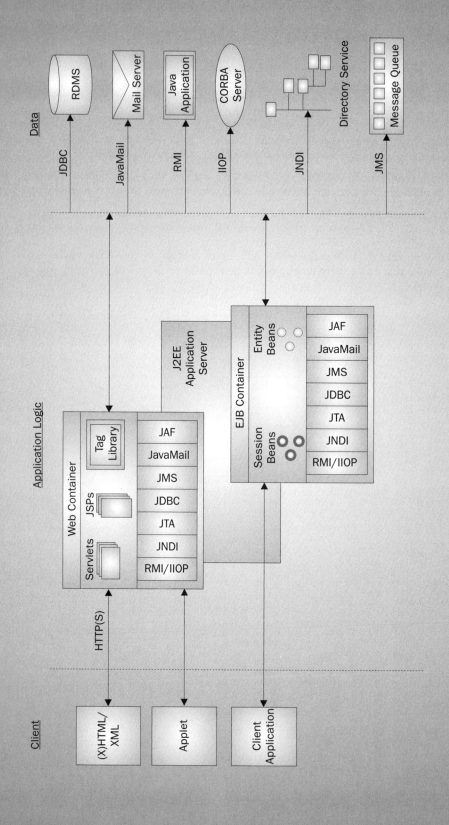

10

Web Deployment, Authentication, and Packaging

In J2EE, the design and development processes are clearly demarcated from deployment and packaging. While most of the high level and low level architectural issues can be addressed during design and development, the J2EE architecture encourages you to build application components in a loosely coupled manner, so that the components are reusable, the design and development process becomes modular, and runtime configuration is more flexible.

The focus of this chapter is on how to make use of the deployment and packaging facilities provided by the web container architecture, to introduce more flexibility into your applications. Specifically, we will address:

- ❏ The structure of a web application. We've seen the basic structure in previous chapters, and therefore we'll focus more on the rationale behind this structure.

- ❏ Mapping HTTP requests to different web application components.

- ❏ Implementing authentication for web applications. We'll discuss how different types of authentication models can be plugged into your web application without having to implement authentication at the application level.

- ❏ Using the deployment descriptor for configuring your web applications.

Structure of a Web Application

As we've seen in previous chapters, a web application is a collection of servlets, HTML pages, images, JSP pages, a deployment descriptor, other configuration files, etc. In this section we'll discuss the rationale behind the structure of web applications.

The notion of a **web application** was introduced for the first time in version 2.2 of the Java servlet specification; it closely follows the notion of EJB and J2EE applications defined in the J2EE standard. A web application is organized in a structured hierarchy of directories. Alternatively, as we shall see shortly, a web application can also be packaged into a **web application archive (WAR)** file.

Directory Structure

The directory structure of a web application consists of two parts:

❑ A private directory called WEB-INF containing resources that are not meant for client download

❑ A directory (including all its subdirectories, except the private WEB-INF directory) containing public resources

For example, a fictitious web application might have this structure:

```
myWebApp\
        index.html
        login.jsp
        404NotFound.html
        images\
                logo.gif
                banner.gif
        literature\
                Y2000AnnualReport.pdf
        WEB-INF\
                web.xml
                classes\
                        ShoppingCart.class
                        Catalog.class
                        CheckOut.class
                lib\
                    dbLibrary.jar
                    xmlTools.jar
```

The public resources of this application are the two HTML files and one JSP file directly under myWebApp, and the images and literature subdirectories. The other files, contained within the WEB-INF directory, are resources accessible only to the container.

A public resource is *any* file that is accessible to the users, including HTML, XML, and JSP documents, images, audio/video files, Java applets (classes as well as JAR files containing applets), word processor documents, etc. Except for JSP pages, which we will discuss in a moment, users can directly download these resources unchanged and render them in the client browser as per their MIME type.

For example, when an HTML page includes an <APPLET> tag referring to an applet in a JAR file, the web container faithfully delivers the JAR file *as is* to the client browser. Typically, the web container reads the static resource from the file system, and writes the contents directly to the network connection. Interpreting the content of these resources is the responsibility of the client browser. However, in order for the client to be able to correctly treat the content, the web container is required to set the MIME type correctly. As we shall see later, the container uses the MIME type settings from the deployment descriptor of the application.

However, there are other types of resource that should be protected from client browsers do
directly. These include:

- ❑ Servlets and JSP pages. These components include application logic, and possibly acc ...... .ω
  other resources such as databases, enterprise beans, etc.

- ❑ Resources that are meant for execution or use on the server side, such as Java class files and
  JAR files for classes used by your servlets, temporary files, deployment descriptors, other files
  that your servlets open directly, etc.

These are resources private to the web application and the container.

In order to accommodate private resources, the web container requires the WEB-INF directory to be
present in your application. This directory includes:

- ❑ A web.xml file, the deployment descriptor

- ❑ A classes subdirectory to include Java class files (including servlet class files), structured as
  per the usual Java packaging rules

- ❑ A lib subdirectory to contain any JAR files required by your applications

This structure has several advantages. The most significant is that several applications can coexist
without any conflict, under the same web container. This is akin to each application having its own sand
box; the public and private resources of an application are independent of any other application that
may be running on the container. While this model seems very intuitive in stand-alone applications, this
was not really so until the notion of web applications was introduced in J2EE.

In older versions of web containers (then called servlet 'engines'), you would typically keep all your
servlets under one /servlets directory, and keep all the public resources under the document root
of the web server. This is equivalent to having one large application combining all the servlets.
Grouping all the public resources under the web servers document root in this manner poses
maintenance constraints.

Secondly, the web container knows where to look for your classes. The class loader of the container
looks into the classes directory, and in the JAR files in the lib directory; you do not need to add
these classes and JAR files explicitly to the CLASSPATH. Note that, while deploying the sample
applications in the previous chapters, we did not change the CLASSPATH settings. The container could
load the servlet classes without CLASSPATH changes.

The above structure allows each web application to be managed independently of all other applications
that may be running in the container. For instance, in our examples in previous chapters, when adding a
new application to Tomcat we just added an extra <Context> tag to the server configuration file
(server.xml), without disturbing any of the other applications.

Notice that the public directory of a web application is similar to the document root directory structure
of conventional web servers. As when placing static content and other files in conventional web servers,
you maintain the public content in each web application under the application's root directory.

The difference is that each application now has its own document root.

Although JSP pages are included as public resources in each application, the web container does not send such files directly to clients. As you'll learn in Chapter 11, the container automatically compiles the JSP pages into servlets, and invokes the servlets for generating the response. However, since a JSP page is considered more equivalent to an HTML document than to a Java class, JSP pages are also included under public resources.

Web Archive Files

Web applications can be packaged into **web archive (WAR)** files; this process is similar to packaging Java class files into JAR files. The purpose of the packaging is the same – it is to provide simplified means of distributing Java class files and related resources together. WAR files can be created using the same `jar` command that you use for creating JAR files. Instead of deploying a web application as a directory structure, WAR files can be used as deployment units.

Let's consider the chat application developed in Chapter 9. We'll create a WAR file, and deploy the WAR file in the container instead of the web application directory.

We created the chat application under `c:\ProJavaServer\Chapter09\chat`. In order to create a WAR file, go to the `c:\ProJavaServer\Chapter09\chat` directory, and issue the following command:

```
jar -cf chat.war *
```

This command packs all the contents under this directory (including subdirectories) into an archive file called `chat.war`. This command has two command-line options: a `-c` option to create a new archive, and a `-f` option to specify the target archive file name. Note that we issued these two commands together as `-cf`. You can also monitor the included file with the `v` verbose option, which will echo the files to the screen.

Given a WAR file, you can use the following command to view its contents:

```
jar -tvf chat.war
```

This command lists the contents of the WAR file. Refer to your JDK documentation for other command-line options. You should find JAR documentation under `%JDK_HOME%\docs\tooldocs\win32\jar.html`, where `%JDK_HOME%` is your JDK installation directory. Instead of including all the contents, you may select individual files and subdirectories while creating WAR files. You can also use standard ZIP file manipulation tools such as WinZip to create and manipulate WAR files.

After creating a WAR file, any JSP 1.1 compliant server will automatically deploy the application, as long as the WAR file is placed in the appropriate directory. In Tomcat you should move this WAR file to the `%TOMCAT_HOME%\webapps` directory, and then restart Tomcat. This will automatically deploy the chat web application.

Tomcat uses the WAR file name (minus the extension) as the context, so that you can access the chat application at `http://localhost:8080/chat/servlet/chatAdmin`.

Although WAR files use the JAR format and can be created using the jar command, in terms of the basic purpose, WAR files differ significantly from JAR files. The purpose of JAR files is to package classes and related resources into compressed archive files. In the case of WAR files, a WAR file represents a web application, and not just a class archive.

When should you use WAR files? WAR files are not appropriate during the development stages, where you would compile your servlets several times. You may find it time consuming to recreate a WAR file each time you compile your servlet. During development stages, you should instead consider the auto-reloading features of web containers. Many web containers (including Tomcat) provide auto-reloading facilities for compiled servlet class files and JSP files. This is a very useful feature while you're rigorously changing and recompiling your servlets. With this feature, you need not restart the container. Instead, when this feature is enabled, the container will automatically reload the modified servlet classes. For instance, Tomcat specifies the following additional element in the <Context> tag to enable auto-reloading. Here is an example:

```
<Context path="/chat"
        docBase="c:/ProJavaServer/Chapter10/chat"
        reloadable="true">
</Context>
```

When you add the above <Context> tag in the server.xml under %TOMCAT_HOME%\conf, Tomcat automatically reloads Java class files and JAR files (under WEB-INF\classes, and WEB-INF\lib directories respectively) whenever these files change. This is a useful feature during debugging time. Note that auto-reloading requires the container to monitor the deployment directories (the docBase directories in the case of Tomcat) periodically, and this will degrade performance.

WAR files are more appropriate towards the end of application development phase, and after, where the number of code changes tends to come down, and you'll start to plan for packaging, and final production stages.

Mapping Requests to Applications and Servlets

In a web container, each web application is associated with a **context**, and all resources in a web application exist relative to that context. For example, in the greeting application in Chapter 7, the index.html file exists under the context /greeting/. You can access index.html at http://localhost:8080/greeting/index.html.

In addition, each context also has a ServletContext object associated with it. From the point of view of the web application, the ServletContext represents a view of the web container and allows servlets to access resources available to them. ServletContext is the virtual sandbox for all information sharing for servlets and other web components.

In the previous chapters, we've accessed servlets via the names specified for each servlet in the deployment descriptor. In this section, let's discuss how requests are mapped to servlets in a more generic and flexible fashion.

❑   An HTTP request always contains a Uniform Resource Identifier (URI) identifying the requested resource. The terms Uniform Resource Locator (URL) and Uniform Resource Identifier (URI) are often used inconsistently in books, specifications, and other documents. This is partly because the URL is the one of the most commonly used subsets of URIs for network protocols such as http, ftp, telnet, news, etc. Here I use the terms as they are used in the Servlet API specification, which is largely the same as their use in the HTTP specification:

❑ A URI is any string used to identify an Internet resource, in a name space. For instance, the address of any internet resource can be encoded in the form of a URI.

❑ A URL is such a string, in a format for a specific protocol such as http, ftp, telnet, news, etc. This format includes a scheme (such as, http), the domain name of the server, a path, and possibly query string parameters.

❑ Finally, a URL path is the part of the URL that identifies the resource within a specific server; in other words, just the part that denotes the path.

For instance, in the URI http://www.wrox.com/Consumer is a URL for the scheme http, located at the server www.wrox.com. The URL path of this resource is /Consumer.

Web containers use the same notion to identify web applications, and the resources within web applications. With the help of the URL path, web containers can identify the application (and the associated servlet context), and the resource within the application.

Therefore, each web application must be mapped to a unique URL path prefix, for instance /chat. This path prefix specifies an isolated namespace for all resources with the web application. The web container uses this prefix to map requests to resources within the web application.

In order to see how this mechanism works, consider a help.html file within the help subdirectory of an application, with its root deployed at a context path /catalog on a web container located at http://localhost:8080. This resource can be accessed as http://localhost:8080/catalog/help/help.html. This is similar to having a help.html file in the /catalog/help subdirectory under the document root of a web server located at http://localhost:8080. In this regard, the container behavior is similar to that of a web server, except that the container uses the context path name to identify the application.

The path name therefore serves as the document root for serving resources within the application. For instance, consider two applications deployed on Tomcat:

```
<Context path="/techSupport"
  docBase="c:/ProJavaServer/Chapter09/techSupport">
</Context>

<Context path="/chat"
  docBase="c:/ProJavaServer/Chapter10/chat">
</Context>
```

When the web container receives an HTTP request with a path starting with /chat the container can determine that the request should be handled by the Chat application, and similarly it can determine that all requests starting with /techSupport will be handled by the Tech Support application.

This mechanism can be extended to servlets within applications. In the same way as the context path is used to map a request to a web application, URL path mappings can be used to map requests to servlets.

There are two steps in this mapping process:

❑ **Defining alias names to servlets:**
Recollect that, in the chat application, we've defined three servlet classes in the deployment descriptor with alias names:

```
<servlet>
  <servlet-name>chatAdmin</servlet-name>
  <servlet-class>ChatAdminServlet</servlet-class>
</servlet>

<servlet>
  <servlet-name>chatRoom</servlet-name>
  <servlet-class>ChatRoomServlet</servlet-class>
</servlet>

<servlet>
  <servlet-name>listRooms</servlet-name>
  <servlet-class>ListRoomsServlet</servlet-class>
</servlet>
```

This is just a mapping of short alias names to servlet class names. The alias names allow you to refer to servlets more easily, and also to replace the implementation class for a servlet without modifying the references to the servlet within the application. This naming is a part of the process of defining a servlet in the deployment descriptor.

❑ **Mapping URL paths to servlet alias names:**
In all the previous examples, we've accessed servlets via a path such as `/context_name/servlet/servlet_name`. For example, the ChatAdminServlet is accessed as `http://localhost:8080/chat/servlet/chatAdmin`. However by mapping URL path requests to servlets instead, we will be able to provide more logical names to servlets.

Let's now study the second step in more detail. Consider the following rules for mapping URL paths to servlets:

URL path	Servlet Alias	URL
/admin	chatAdmin	http://localhost:8080/chat/admin
/start	listRooms	http://localhost:8080/chat/listRooms
/chat	chatRooms	http://localhost:8080/chat/chatRooms

The first two columns in this table list the URL path names that we intend to use for each servlet, while the third column shows the actual URLs that we can use to access these servlets.

In order to facilitate this mapping, you can use the `<servlet-mapping>` tags of the web application. Change the deployment descriptor of your chat application as shown below:

```
<?xml version="1.0" encoding="ISO-8859-1"?>

<!DOCTYPE web-app
```

```xml
     PUBLIC "-//Sun Microsystems, Inc.//DTD Web Application 2.2//EN"
     "http://java.sun.com/j2ee/dtds/web-app_2.2.dtd">

<web-app>

  <servlet>
    <servlet-name>chatAdmin</servlet-name>
    <servlet-class>ChatAdminServlet</servlet-class>
  </servlet>

  <servlet>
    <servlet-name>chatRoom</servlet-name>
    <servlet-class>ChatRoomServlet</servlet-class>
  </servlet>

  <servlet>
    <servlet-name>listRooms</servlet-name>
    <servlet-class>ListRoomsServlet</servlet-class>
  </servlet>

  <context-param>
    <param-name>ADMIN_PATH</param-name>
    <param-value>/chat/admin</param-value>
  </context-param>

  <context-param>
    <param-name>LISTROOMS_PATH</param-name>
    <param-value>/chat/</param-value>
  </context-param>

  <context-param>
    <param-name>CHATROOM_PATH</param-name>
    <param-value>/chat/chat</param-value>
  </context-param>

  <servlet-mapping>
    <servlet-name>chatAdmin</servlet-name>
    <url-pattern>/admin/*</url-pattern>
  </servlet-mapping>

  <servlet-mapping>
    <servlet-name>listRooms</servlet-name>
    <url-pattern>/start/*</url-pattern>
  </servlet-mapping>

  <servlet-mapping>
    <servlet-name>chatRoom</servlet-name>
    <url-pattern>/chat/*</url-pattern>
  </servlet-mapping>

  <servlet-mapping>
    <servlet-name>listRooms</servlet-name>
    <url-pattern>/</url-pattern>
  </servlet-mapping>
</web-app>
```

The above XML specifies that:

❑ All requests starting with /admin/ be routed to the chatAdmin servlet. For example, when you enter http://localhost:8080/chat/admin/, you will enter the administration page of the chat application

❑ All requests starting with /start/* be routed to the listRooms servlet

❑ All requests starting with /chat/* be routed to the chatRoom servlet

❑ All requests that do not match the above rules will be handled by the listRooms servlet

Also note the change in the values of ADMIN_PATH, LISTROOMS_PATH and CHATROOM_PATH. In the previous chapter, these values pointed to paths starting with /servlet. We no longer need these now.

Path mappings are relative to the context's URL path prefix. The container removes the context URI path prefix before evaluating URL pattern mapping rules. This means that a request for /chat/admin is first sent to the chat application context. The chat application context strips off the URI path prefix, and then compares the remainder of the path with the rules above, where it discovers that the request should be handled by the chatAdmin servlet. Requests that do not match any of the specific mapping rules will be matched with the default rule, /, and handled by the listRooms servlet.

A request with a URL that starts with something other than /chat is handed to a context with a matching URI path prefix, and the mapping rules specified for that web application are applied to figure out how to handle the request.

The figure below summarizes the path mapping for the chatAdmin servlet:

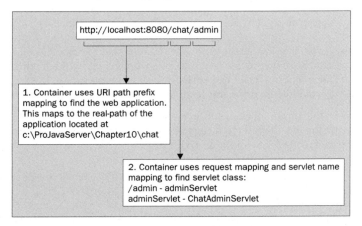

This diagram shows how the different parts of a URL identify a server (with a web container), a web application (and thereby a context), and finally a servlet to process the request. The server uses a URI path prefix map to locate the correct web application. The chat application context uses the remainder of the URI path, to find the name of the servlet to process the request, and finally a name-to-class map to locate the servlet class.

Since all URI paths within a context are relative to the context's root URI path, it's easy to move the application to a different place in the web container's name space. If we introduce a new version of the chat application and we want to use the /chat prefix for the new version, but still provide access to the old version at /oldchat, all we have to do is change the web container's context mappings, to map /chat to the new version and /oldchat to the old version.

Securing Web Applications

Implementing controlled access to web applications is a very common requirement. The most commonly used approach for web application security is to use login forms, and authenticate users based on their login names and passwords. This approach is usually combined with secure socket layer (SSL) with server-side digital certificates. Although more secure implementations are possible, and sometimes required, let's concentrate on how web containers and web applications can be configured to implement user authentication.

Before discussing details of how web containers can be set up to provide secure access, let's discuss the traditional approach that does not rely on the container. This is normally implemented according to the following steps:

❑ Program the application to have one or more entry points with login forms. For example, in the chat application, we can provide a login page, with a form to accept the login name and password of the chat administrator.

❑ Authenticate the user when they submit the login form, preferably over HTTPS. For this purpose, you should verify against a previously created user database or a file that contains user login names and passwords. For example, in the case of the chat admin servlet, we could maintain all users with administrative capabilities in a database. You'll require a new servlet, let's say, LoginServlet, to receive this request, connect to the database, and check if the user name and password match.

❑ Once the login is successful forward the user to the admin servlet.

But what prevents a user from directly accessing the admin servlet? There are two possibilities:

❑ The admin servlet should somehow be able to know that the user has already logged in. We can use a session attribute, let's say username, which is set by the login servlet when the login is successful. The admin servlet can verify if this attribute exists in the session, and if not, can send content explaining that the user cannot use the admin servlet.

❑ Alternatively, the admin servlet can force the user to a login servlet, and upon completion of login, instruct the login servlet to bring the user back to the admin servlet. Consider the following pseudocode for the admin servlet:

```
protected void doPost(HttpServletRequest req, HttpServletResponse res)
{
    HttpSession session = req.getSession();
    String userName = session.getAttribute("username");
    if(username == null || username.length() == 0)
    {
        session.setAttribute("referrer", "/servlet/adminServlet");
        RequestDispatcher rd = request.getRequestDispatcher(
                        "/servlet/loginServlet");
        rd.forward(request, response);
    }
    else
    {
        // Authenticated user. Proceed with chat adminstration
        ...
    }
}
```

The above code snippet tries to retrieve the username from the current user's session. (Note that the session exists whether or not the user has been authenticated.) If the username is not found in the session, the servlet sets a new attribute, referrer, in the session, with the URL path of the admin servlet as its value. The admin servlet then directs the users to the login servlet via the RequestDispatcher.

Now, let's consider the loginServlet:

```
protected void doPost(HttpServletRequest req, HttpServletResponse res)
{
    HttpSession session = req.getSession();
    String userName = req.getSession().getAttribute("username");
    if(username == null)
    {
        // Get the user name and password parameters from req.
        ...

        // Access the database and verify login and password
        ...
        // If successful
        if(...)
        {
            referrer = session.getAttribute("referrer");
            RequestDispatcher rd = request.getRequestDispatcher(referrer);
            rd.forward(request, response);
        }
        else
        {
            // Send content denoting login failure.
            ...
        }
    }
}
```

This servlet checks whether the user is valid, and if so, redirects the user back to the referrer; in our case, this is the admin servlet.

The above code snippets give one possible generic approach for implementing authentication. Note that you should include the first code snippet (shown for ChatAdminServlet) in all servers that require authenticated access.

In the J2EE parlance, this approach is called **programmatic security**. That is, the developer implements security by programming for it. If you want to implement security for a servlet (or for that matter a JSP page), you'll have to explicitly modify the servlet or JSP to verify whether the session belongs to an authenticated user and, if not, direct the user to the loginServlet. This approach is probably satisfactory for small applications where the security requirements and users do not change often.

The J2EE offers another approach, called **declarative security**. In this approach, you do not program for security, you declare that such and such a resource requires authenticated access and the user should have a specific role.

Compared to the above example, declarative security allows the web container, in effect, to implement the necessary code we showed in the admin servlet, and to completely implement the login servlet. If the container detects that there is no authenticated user associated with the session, it can direct the user to a login page, verify the login name and password, and if these are valid bring the user to the admin servlet. In order for the container to know that the admin servlet requires authenticated access, we simply need to instruct the container accordingly.

In simple terms, the above situation describes declarative security. In this approach, the container implements the mechanism for authentication. The only requirement for the web application developer is to make appropriate additions to the deployment descriptor to describe all resources that require authenticated access.

In J2EE, the authentication mechanism is based on **roles**. A role designates responsibilities and/or privileges of the user. For example, if two users Jack and Jill are designated as the administrators for the chat application, we can assign a role chatAdmin to both Jack and Jill. That is, although Jack and Jill are two different users, they both play the same role in the application.

The servlet API specification specifies four possible types of authentication:

- ❑   HTTP basic authentication
- ❑   HTTP digest authentication
- ❑   HTTPS client authentication
- ❑   Form-based authentication

Of these, conventional web servers such as Apache implement the basic and digest authentication approaches.

- ❑   **Basic authentication** is based on a user name and password. When a web page or a resource is designated with basic authentication, the web server requests the browser to send a user name and password. Based on this, the browser displays a dialog box to capture the user name and password, and sends these values to the web server. This approach can also be combined with SSL.

- ❑   **Digest authentication** is similar to basic authentication, except that the passwords are transmitted in an encrypted form. However, this mechanism is not so widely used as the basic authentication or the HTTPS client authentication.

- ❑   **HTTPS client authentication** requires the use of public key certificates and HTTPS (HTTP over SSL). This is a more secure approach, in that it requires a digital certificate that can be used to verify if the user is really who they claim to be.

- ❑   **Form-based authentication** is another type of authentication specified by the servlet specification. Using this approach, you can also define custom login and error pages for authentication.

Let's now look at the facilities provided by the servlet specification for programmatic and declarative security. In this chapter, we'll limit ourselves to the API for accessing user credentials, form-based login, and see how form-based authentication can implemented in Tomcat.

Programmatic Security

The `HttpServletRequest` interface provides the following methods to retrieve user/role information from the request:

The getAuthType() Method

```
public String getAuthType()
```

Returns the authentication type used to protect the servlet. Possible return values are `BASIC` to indicate basic authentication, `SSL` to indicate SSL based authentication, or `null` otherwise.

The getRemoteUser() Method

```
public String getRemoteUser()
```

Returns the login of the user making this request. The return value depends on the implementation of the container.

The getUserPrincipal() Method

```
public java.security.Principal getUserPrincipal()
```

Returns the `Principal` object associated with the current user session. A `Principal` object is used to represent an identity, such as the login or even a digital certificate, belonging to the requesting user.

The isUserInRole() Method

```
public boolean isUserInRole(String role)
```

Returns `true` if the current user has the role specified in the argument.

Note that these methods may or may not have been implemented in your web container. The purpose of this API is to allow more sophisticated implementations of authentication; these methods merely provide access to information that may have been gathered by the underlying web container implementation.

Form-Based Authentication

The form-based authentication approach is based on the web container invoking a login page automatically, based on the security constraints set on a page or resource in the web application. Let's consider implementing a form-based login feature for the chat application.

Let's designate Joe as the user designated to administer the chat rooms, with the login name `joe`. Joe can add to, delete from, and modify the list of chat rooms. We designate `chatAdmin` as Joe's role. Note that Joe can have other roles such as `sysadmin`. The objective is to allow only those users that have a role called `chatAdmin` access to invoke the chat admin servlet.

Let's first start with the deployment descriptor. Add the following to the `web.xml` file for the chat application, before the ending `</web-app>` tag:

```
<web-app>
  <!-- Insert servlet and context definitions -->

  <security-constraint>
   <web-resource-collection>
    <web-resource-name>chat</web-resource-name>
    <description>Chat administration pages</description>
    <url-pattern>/admin/*</url-pattern>
       <http-method>GET</http-method>
   </web-resource-collection>

   <auth-constraint>
    <description>Chat Administrator</description>
    <role-name>chatAdmin</role-name>
   </auth-constraint>

   <user-data-constraint>
    <transport-guarantee>NONE</transport-guarantee>
   </user-data-constraint>
  </security-constraint>

  <login-config>
   <auth-method>FORM</auth-method>
   <form-login-config>
    <form-login-page>/login.html</form-login-page>
    <form-error-page>/error.html</form-error-page>
   </form-login-config>
  </login-config>

  <security-role>
   <description>Registered customer</description>
   <role-name>chatAdmin</role-name>
  </security-role>
```

The above deployment description specifies a security constraint, and the authentication scheme.

The <security-constraint> tag includes definition of a resource collection, and the authorization requirement. The resource collection in the above includes all GET and POST requests with the url-pattern /admin/*. The <user-data-constraint> tag specifies how data should be transmitted across the wire. The possible values are NONE, INTEGRAL, and CONFIDENTIAL. The value NONE used here means that there is no transport requirement; a value of INTEGRAL would indicate the underlying data transmission should guarantee integrity of data, and a value of CONFIDENTIAL would require that the underlying transmission should prevent other entities from observing the data. Support for these values depends on both the clients and servers. For instance, SSL-enabled client browsers and web containers can participate in CONFIDENTIAL transmission.

The <security-constraint> element also includes an <auth-constraint> tag for the resource collection. In the example above, only users with role chatAdmin are allowed to access the resources.

The next step is to define a login configuration. The <login-config> tag specifies how authentication should be performed. In our example, we're using a form-based authentication, which requires us to specify a login page and an error page. Whenever login is required, the web container automatically sends the login page. Whenever a login fails, the web container automatically sends the error page. In our example, we're using login.html and error.html pages respectively to achieve this.

Here is the `login.html` page:

```
<HTML>
  <HEAD>
   <TITLE>Login Authentication</TITLE>
  </HEAD>

  <BODY>
   <H1>Please Login</H1>
   <FORM ACTION="j_security_check" METHOD="POST">
    <TABLE BORDER="0" WIDTH="30%" CELLSPACING="3" CELLPADDING="2">
      <TR>
       <TD><B>Login</B></TD>
       <TD><INPUT TYPE="text" SIZE="20" NAME="j_username"></TD>
      </TR>
      <TR>
       <TD><B>Password</B></TD>
       <TD><INPUT TYPE="password" SIZE="10" NAME="j_password"></TD>
      </TR>
      <TR>
       <TD><P><INPUT TYPE="submit" VALUE="Sign in"></TD>
      </TR>
    </TABLE>
   </FORM>
  </BODY>
</HTML>
```

The servlet specification requires that the form action parameter be `j_security_check`, the login input name `j_username`, and the password input name `j_password`. The j_security_check is a resource within the container that implements the authentication. There are no such constraints on the `error.html` page. Here is a sample file:

```
<HTML>
  <HEAD>
   <TITLE>Login Authentication</TITLE>
  </HEAD>
  <BODY BGCOLOR="#e0d0c0">
   <H1>Login now to create chat rooms</H1>
   <H3>Sorry, incorrect username/password. Try again</H3>
   <FORM ACTION="j_security_check" METHOD="POST">
    <TABLE BORDER="0" WIDTH="30%" CELLSPACING="3" CELLPADDING="2">
      <TR>
       <TD><B>Login</B></TD>
       <TD><INPUT TYPE="text" SIZE="20" NAME="j_username"></TD>
      </TR>
      <TR>
       <TD><B>Password</B></TD>
       <TD><INPUT TYPE="password" SIZE="10" NAME="j_password"></TD>
      </TR>
      <TR>
       <TD><INPUT TYPE="submit" VALUE="Sign in"></TD>
      </TR>
    </TABLE>
   </FORM>
  </BODY>
</HTML>
```

463

The above page includes the login form again with a message requesting for another attempt.

The next step is to add the user Joe. The exact procedure depends on the container vendor/provider. In the case of Tomcat, new users and roles can be added in the `%TOMCAT_HOME%\conf\tomcat-users.xml` file as shown below:

```
<tomcat-users>
  ...
    <user name="joe" password="joe" roles="chatAdmin" />
</tomcat-users>
```

However, at of writing this chapter, Tomcat (Version 3.1) does not completely support form-based authentication. Although Tomcat includes an experimentation version of form-based authentication, this is not suitable for demonstration purposes.

In order to test this application, let's instead consider the WebLogic Server from BEA. You may download an evaluation copy of this server from `http://www.bea.com`. In order to deploy and test the chat application, insert the following lines in the `%WEBLOGIC_HOME%\weblogic.properties` file, where `%WEBLOGIC_HOME%` is the installation directory. The `weblogic.properties` file is the server configuration file for WebLogic:

```
# Deploy the Chat application
weblogic.httpd.webApp.chat=c:/ProJavaServer/Chapter11/chat

# Chat user john
weblogic.password.john=john

# Add john to the chatAdmin group
weblogic.security.group.chatAdmin=john
```

Following the documentation, start the WebLogic server. Note that the WebLogic server runs at port 7001 by default. Enter `http://localhost:7001/chat/admin` in your browser. This should automatically display the `login.html` page. Enter `john` and `john` for the login and password. WebLogic verifies these values against those specified above, and then invokes the admin servlet. Once you login, the login is valid only for the current session. If you enter an incorrect login name or password, the container will send you the `error.html` page.

Note that this mechanism is very simple to implement, and requires no changes to your source code. All you have to do is to decide what roles each resource requires, and specify them in the deployment descriptor.

However, there is one limitation with this approach. At present, the servlet specification does not address support for custom login-password verification. It's up to the container vendor to decide how and where to store login and password data, and implement the verification. For instance, J2EE application servers such as Orion and WebLogic provide APIs that you can use to implement custom authentication. These servers provide you with APIs that the container will invoke during the authentication phase. All you have to do is to implement certain interfaces specified in the proprietary APIs. You can also use these APIs to build interfaces to create and manage users and their roles. Check with your server documentation before planning any security solution.

Deployment Configuration

In this section, we will discuss some of the important web application configurations that you can customize via the deployment descriptor. These are:

- ❑ **Context initialization parameters:** how to specify and access context initialization parameters.

- ❑ **Servlet initialization parameters:** how to specify and access servlet initialization parameters.

- ❑ **Servlet loading:** loading servlets on startup.

- ❑ **Session configuration:** how to specify the session timeout interval.

- ❑ **MIME mappings:** specifying MIME types for documents in the web application.

- ❑ **Welcome and error pages:** how to specify welcome and error pages. The welcome page is the page that the container invokes when the request URL maps to the root of the application. Error page configuration can be used to sending meaningful documents for standard HTTP errors and custom exceptions.

- ❑ **Distributable applications:** a brief discussion on distributable applications, and how you can enable distribution.

The Java Servlet specification v2.2 specifies the deployment descriptor in a DTD with the DOCTYPE declaration:

```
<!DOCTYPE web-app
    PUBLIC "-//Sun Microsystems, Inc.//DTD Web Application 2.2//EN"
    "http://java.sun.com/j2ee/dtds/web-app_2.2.dtd">
```

All web application deployment descriptors should include this DOCTYPE declaration.

The DTD of the deployment descriptor for web applications is available in Chapter 13 of the servlet specification. I strongly advise you to keep the DTD handy as you proceed with this section.

Context Initialization Parameters

Context parameters are attributes that are part of a servlet context; all servlets and JSP pages within a web application can get and set these attributes. The getInitParameter() and getInitParameterNames() methods discussed in Chapter 9 can be used to retrieve the context initialization parameters. In the examples of Chapter 9, we've used these context initialization parameters to specify database driver/protocol settings, and the URL paths of various servlets.

You can set context initialization parameters by using <context-param> elements in the deployment descriptor. The following deployment description adds an attribute name to the deployment descriptor:

```
<web-app>
  ...
  <context-param>
   <param-name>
    name
   </param-name>
```

```
        <param-value>
         Jack
        </param-value>
        <description>
         Name of Jack. Jack is Jill's brother.
        </description>
       </context-param>
     ...
   </web-app>
```

In the above, the <param-name> element refers to the name of the context parameter: this is the name you use while retrieving the parameter from the ServletContext using the getInitParameter() method. The <param-value> corresponds to the String value returned by getInitParameter(). You can optionally add a <description> element for each context parameter, to make the deployment descriptor more descriptive. Context initialization parameters are applicable to all servlets sharing the same context.

Servlet Initialization Parameters

Similar to setting parameters for the context, you can also specify initialization parameters for each servlet, using the <init-param> element. The following deployment description sets two initialization parameters:

```
<web-app>
...
  <servlet>
   <servlet-name>Jack</servlet-name>
   <servlet-class>mypackage.Jack</servlet-class>
   <init-param>
    <param-name>
      name
    </param-name>
    <param-value>
      Jill
    </param-value>
    <description>
      Name of Jill. Jill is Jack's brother.
    </description>
   </init-param>
  </servlet>
</web-app>
```

The description above specifies an initialization parameter called name for the mypackage.Jack servlet. Use the getInitParameter() method on the ServletConfig object to retrieve this initialization parameter.

Unlike context initialization parameters, servlet initialization parameters are specific for each servlet.

You can use initialization parameters to specify startup information for a servlet. Recollect that the freak servlet of Chapter 8 has an initialization parameter to specify an interval for servlet unavailability.

Loading Servlets on Startup

As discussed in Chapter 9, loading a servlet involves class loading from the deployment archive, servlet instantiation, and servlet initialization. By default, the web container does not guarantee any order in which servlets are loaded. The container may not even load a servlet until a request is received.

However, in certain cases, depending on your application design, you may like to specify that one or more of your servlets be loaded during the startup of the web application. Furthermore, you may like to impose a specific order in which these servlets should be loaded. The `<load-on-startup>` element lets you specify such a requirement:

```
<web-app>
  . . .
  <servlet>
   <servlet-name>Jack</servlet-name>
   <servlet-class>mypackage/Jack</servlet-class>
   <load-on-startup>10</load-on-startup>
  </servlet>
  <servlet>
   <servlet-name>Jill</servlet-name>
   <servlet-class>mypackage/Jill</servlet-class>
   <load-on-startup>20</load-on-startup>
  </servlet>
</web-app>
```

The `<load-on-startup>` element is optional. When this element is present for a servlet, the container loads it at the container startup. In order to enforce an order in which servlets are loaded, you should specify a positive integer for each servlet; the container loads servlets in the order specified by these integers. When this element is not specified, the load order is left to the container.

Session Timeout

`HttpSession` objects should not be allowed to live long after user inactivity, as these objects consume memory on the server side. Note that each user (as identified using the `HttpServletRequest` object) visiting the web application will have a unique `HttpSession` object associated. If your application has 10,000 active users, your container will have 10,000 `HttpSession` objects, each object potentially containing several attributes. In order to limit this, you should specify session timeout.

There are two ways in which you can specify a timeout:

❑ Programmatically by calling the `setMaxInactiveInterval()` method on the `HttpSession` object

❑ Using the `<session-timeout>` element in the deployment descriptor

The following deployment snippet illustrates the second approach:

```
<web-app>
  <!-- Servlet definitions -->

  <session-config>
```

```
        <session-timeout>120</session-timeout>
      </session-config>
    </web-app>
```

The timeout interval should be specified in minutes. The web container will automatically invalidate the session if the elapsed time between consecutive requests from a user is more than the specified timeout interval. The `getMaxInactiveInterval()` method on the `HttpSession` object returns the interval in seconds.

MIME Mappings

MIME, as you probably know by now, stands for **Multipurpose Internet Mail Extensions**. Although MIME was originally developed for transmission of non-textual e-mail messages, the HTTP protocol uses MIME types for describing content. Both web servers and web clients (browsers) use MIME types to indicate the type of content being exchanged. A MIME type is a string of the form `type/sub-type`. Examples of some of the common MIME types are `text/html`, `text/txt`, and `image/gif`.

When a web server sends a document to a client, the server should include a section in the response to indicate the type of the document. Web browsers use this information to render the document correctly. For example, if the web server sends a PostScript document without specifying the correct content type, the browser may not be able to identify that the request body contains a PostScript document and will render it incorrectly. However, most of the modern browsers try to identify the content type based on the extension specified in the request. Nonetheless, it's a good practice to specify MIME types for all types of content that the web server could possibly send.

In the case of dynamic content, the servlet generating the content should explicitly specify the MIME type using the `setContentType()` method on the `HttpServletResponse` object. However, how should we specify content types for all the documents in the public area of your web application? As we discussed at the beginning of this chapter, the web container serves such documents directly to the requesting clients. In order for the container to specify correct MIME types for all such documents, you should indicate the possible MIME types in the deployment descriptor of the application. If you're familiar with web server configurations, this is similar to configuring the `mime.types` (or equivalent) file. For example, if your web application contains Word documents, you should specify the following MIME type in the deployment descriptor:

```
<web-app>
  <!-- Servlet definitions -->

  <mime-mapping>
    <extension>doc</extension>
    <mime-type>application/msword</mime-type>
  </mime-mapping>
</web-app>
```

The container uses this information to correctly set the content type in the response header. Using this MIME type, the browsers will then be able to correctly identify how the content should be rendered. Note that, in general, web servers/containers as well as web browsers will be able to identify the MIME types based on the extension. If a standard MIME type for a specific content cannot be found for a given extension (or if the extension is non-standard), web containers as well as browsers use the default type, which is usually `text/plain`.

Welcome Files

Conventionally, the default welcome file for a web site is the `index.html` or the `index.htm` file. The same applies for a web application. When you type the URI path pointing to a web application (for example, `http://www.myserver.com/chat`), the container displays the welcome file associated with the `chat` application. The container also serves a welcome file when a request URL points to a directory, but cannot be resolved to a servlet.

However, you can specify any public resource such an HTML or JSP document as a welcome file using the `<welcome-file-list>` element in the deployment descriptor. For instance, the following snippet specifies a list of files as welcome files:

```
<web-app>
  <!-- Servlet definitions -->

  <welcome-file-list>
   <welcome-file>start.html</welcome-file>
   <welcome-file>go.html</welcome-file>
   <welcome-file>start.jsp</welcome-file>
  </welcome-file-list>
</web-app>
```

The web container uses the first file found as the welcome file. Note that the Java Servlet specification is unclear about how the container should treat these welcome files. The specification only specifies that an ordered list of welcome files can be specified. It does not specify any default order, or a default file. However, it is safe to assume (out of convention) that the first one of these welcome files will be loaded only when neither an `index.html` nor an `index.htm` file has been found. Refer to your container's documentation for additional information.

Error Pages

The deployment descriptor provides a very flexible mechanism for providing error pages based on various exceptions and HTTP error messages. We've briefly discussed error pages in Chapter 9. Before we go into more details of this mechanism, let's briefly discuss how standard HTTP errors are relevant in servlet programming.

There are two ways a servlet can indicate a failure. In both cases the actual logic for detecting an error is the responsibility of the servlet. The difference is the procedure for indicating an error to the web container.

Sending Errors

The first approach is to use the following methods of `HttpServletResponse`:

```
public void sendError(int statusCode) throws IOException
public void sendError(int statusCode, String message) throws IOException
```

Both of these methods will set the HTTP response status code and commit the response. The first of these methods accepts a status code, while the second one lets you add a user-defined message to further clarify the error to the client. No further output should be written after executing the `sendError()`

method. After sendError() is called, the web container sends an HTTP status code and HTTP status message in the response headers. If configured correctly (as we shall see below), the web container will send a special HTML or JSP document explaining the error, and usually logs the error. The client browser can extract the status code and status message from the response. If you're interested in how clients can extract this data, refer to the getResponseCode() and getResponseMessage() methods of the java.net.HttpURLConnection class.

The following table describes some of the more useful HTTP error codes you may encounter or wish to send. The error codes in this table are defined as constants in the HttpServletResponse interface:

HTTP Code	Error Code	Description
400	SC_BAD_REQUEST	The request was syntactically incorrect
401	SC_UNAUTHORIZED	Indicates that the request requires HTTP authentication
403	SC_FORBIDDEN	The server understood the request but refused to fulfill it
404	SC_NOT_FOUND	The requested resource is unavailable
500	SC_INTERNAL_SERVER_ERROR	An error within the HTTP server caused the request to fail
501	SC_NOT_IMPLEMENTED	The HTTP server does not support the functionality needed to fulfill this request
503	SC_SERVER_UNAVAILABLE	The HTTP server is overloaded and cannot service the request

Throwing ServletException

The second approach for indicating failures is to throw javax.servlet.ServletException or one of its subclasses. For instance, you might design a set of exception classes extending ServletException, and throw these from within your servlets.

Consider a servlet performing database access via the JDBC API. One common exception that your servlet might encounter is java.sql.SQLException. However, since the container cannot gracefully handle non-servlet exceptions such as the java.sql.SQLException, you cannot re-throw the same exception to the container. Therefore, your servlet must throw a subclass of javax.servlet.ServletException whenever it receives a java.sql.SQLException. For example, consider the following snippet in your servlet:

```
try {
  // Database access

  // Could not get a connection
}
catch(SQLException e) {
  throw new TryAgainException(e.getMessage, e);
}
```

The `TryAgainException` could be specified as follows:

```
public class TryAgainException extends ServletException {
  public TryAgainException(String message, Throwable cause) {
    super(message, cause);
  }
}
```

With the above code, the container receives a `TryAgainException` whenever your servlet encounters a `java.sql.SQLException`.

Now let's see how to make the container handle these exceptions.

Handling HTTP Errors and Exceptions

Using `<error-page>` elements in the deployment descriptor, you can program web applications to handle HTTP errors and exceptions gracefully. For each HTTP error or exception, you can designate the URL of a resource (a document); whenever the container receives the corresponding HTTP error or the exception, the container will send the specified resource in the response to the client.

For example, the deployment description below makes the container send the `/errors/TryAgain.html` file if either a `TryAgainException` or the `HttpServletResponse.SC_SERVER_UNAVAILABLE` error code occur:

```
<web-app>
  <!-- Servlet definitions -->

  <error-page>
   <exception-type>javax.servlet.TryAgainException</exception-type>
   <location>/errors/TryAgain.html</location>
  </error-page>

  <error-page>
   <errror-code>503</exception-type>
   <location>/errors/TryAgain.html</location>
  </error-page>
</web-app>
```

But how do we choose whether to throw exceptions or generate HTTP error codes? HTTP error codes can be used to specify common HTTP errors. However, you'll have to map your application errors to appropriate HTTP error codes, and this is not always easy: HTTP error codes have well-defined meaning and inappropriate error codes may change the meaning of the error. It is therefore more flexible to consider subclasses of `javax.sql.ServletException` to indicate application errors.

The `<location>` for an error page can also point to a servlet or a JSP. In such cases, the servlet throwing the exception can set the following details regarding the error using the `setAttribute()` method in the `HttpServletRequest` interface:

❑   Status Code for `javax.servlet.error.status_code`

❑   Exception Type for `javax.servlet.error.exception_type`

❑   Message for `javax.servlet.error.message`

The error handling servlet can access these attributes from the request object.

Distributable Applications

In version 2.2, the Java Servlet API specification introduced the notion of **distributable applications** and **distributable containers**. The purpose of these features is to address scalability and performance.

A distributable web container consists of a number of JVMs, running on one or more host machines. In this setup, you can deploy your web applications on each of these nodes in the container. A load-balancing strategy determines how the container routes incoming HTTP requests to one of these JVMs. The purpose of this mechanism is to make sure that the load is approximately equally distributed across all JVMs. A container vendor may use any load-balancing algorithm, from a very simple round-robin algorithm to more complex algorithms based on several parameters, such as the number of requests currently being handled by a JVM, average response time, custom priorities, and so on. Refer to your container's documentation for more details.

Irrespective of how the container implements distribution, and on the setup requirements of your distributable container, you can enable distribution using the deployment descriptor of your web application:

```
<web-app>
  ...
  <distributable />
  ...
</web-app>
```

As you see, it is very simple to specify that your web application is distribution-ready. However, as a developer of distributable web applications, your application should meet certain requirements.

This is because, in a distributable application, the same JVM may not receive all the requests from a particular client. That is, requests from a single client may be distributed across more than one node in the cluster. This requires that the HttpSession objects on each JVM should be consistent. In order to maintain this, the container may replicate the state of each session on all nodes in the cluster.

In order for this mechanism to work, all attributes that you set in the HttpSession should be Serializable. Otherwise, the container will not replicate such attributes in the cluster. You should also make sure that your application logic does not depend on any instance variables of your servlet classes. For instance, one example is maintaining an integer variable to count the number of requests. In a multi-JVM environment, the same servlet instance exists on multiple JVMs, and such variables across multiples instances could not be consistently updated.

Summary

In this chapter, we've seen how to package web applications, and how to use the deployment descriptor to configure web applications at deployment time. In the J2EE architecture, you will be using this mechanism throughout – from servlets, to messaging, to transactions, to enterprise beans. As you cover these topics in the rest of this book and start building production quality applications, you will see how powerful and flexible this mechanism is.

This chapter concludes our coverage of Java servlets. Before we move on to look at JavaServer Pages and other aspects of the Java 2 Enterprise Edition, note that J2EE has changed the way we do server-side programming. It's true that you still follow the basic Java programming tenets for building your applications. But as this technology becomes more and more sophisticated, the containers tend to impose more and more restrictions on, or to put it another way, define more exactly, what can be done and what cannot be. As long we recognize this, and try to stick to these restrictions in letter and spirit, our applications will be more robust.

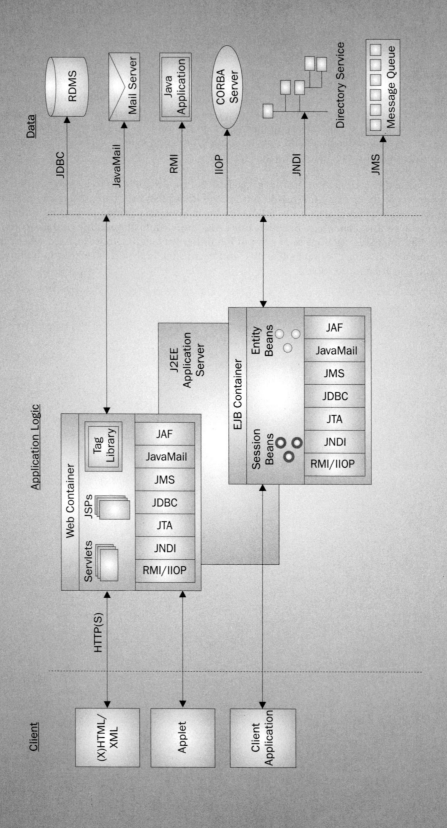

11

JSP Basics and Architecture

The goal of the **JavaServer Pages (JSP)** specification is to simplify the creation and management of dynamic web pages, by separating content and presentation. JSPs are basically files that combine standard HTML (or XML) and new scripting tags. JSPs therefore look somewhat like HTML, but they get translated into Java servlets the first time they are invoked by a client. The resulting servlet is a combination of the HTML from the JSP file and embedded dynamic content specified by the new tags. (This is not to say that JSPs *must* contain HTML: a JSP page might be composed only of Java code, or of custom tags that refer to externally compiled classes.)

In this chapter we will look at:

- ❏ The building blocks of JSP pages: directives, scripting elements, and the standard actions
- ❏ The implicit objects provided to allow JSPs to access their environment
- ❏ The important concept of scope
- ❏ Designing JSP-based applications
- ❏ An example application to bring the concepts together and demonstrate good design practices when using JSPs

Introducing JSP

JSP is not a product but, like other Java APIs, a specification provided by Sun Microsystems for vendors to implement; the JSP specification builds on the functionality provided by the servlet specification. So what differentiates JSPs from servlets?

- ❏ Servlets are Java's answer to CGIs. They execute on the server and intercept browser requests, acting as a sort of middle layer between clients and other applications. In doing so, servlets tend to mix the dynamic content into the static part to generate HTML.

❑ JSPs, on the other hand, are more in line with the J2EE model of separating static and dynamic content – separating presentation and logic – in a web application. That is the prime objective:

> **Simplifying the dynamic presentation layer in a multi-tiered architecture.**

Whereas servlets force you to mix the code with the static content, JSPs can use **beans** with a specified **scope** to separate the code out, or tag extensions, which are covered in Chapters 12 and 13.

> *Keep in mind, that even though JSPs contain special scripting tags, under the hood they are nothing but servlets.*

A simple JSP might look like this:

```
<%@page import="java.util.Date"%>
<html>
<body>
The current time is <%= new Date().toString() %>
</body>
</html>
```

For our examples in this chapter, create a `C:\ProJavaServer\Chapter11\JSPExamples` directory to hold our web application. Save the above code in a file called `simpleJSP.jsp`, and place it in the root of the web application (in other words, save it as `C:\ProJavaServer\Chapter11\JSPExamples\simpleJSP.jsp`).

Deploy the `JSPExamples` application in Tomcat by adding the following entry to `%TOMCAT_HOME%\conf\server.xml`:

```
<Context path="/JSPExamples"
         docBase="c:\ProJavaServer/Chapter11/JSPExamples">
</Context>
```

Start Tomcat and point your web browser to `http://localhost:8080/JSPExamples/simpleJSP.jsp`. You should see output similar to the following:

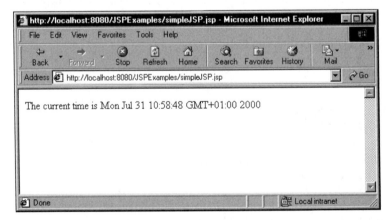

The first time the JSP engine intercepts a request for a JSP, it compiles this **translation unit** (the JSP page and any other dependent files), into a servlet. For example, Tomcat would compile the JSP above into a servlet that looks like:

```
import javax.servlet.*;
import javax.servlet.http.*;
import javax.servlet.jsp.*;
import javax.servlet.jsp.tagext.*;
import java.io.PrintWriter;
import java.io.IOException;
import java.io.FileInputStream;
import java.io.ObjectInputStream;
import java.util.Vector;
import org.apache.jasper.runtime.*;
import java.beans.*;
import org.apache.jasper.JasperException;
import java.util.Date;
```

```
public class _0002fsimpleJSP_0002ejspsimpleJSP_jsp_0 extends HttpJspBase {

  static {
  }
  public _0002fsimpleJSP_0002ejspsimpleJSP_jsp_0( ) {
  }

  private static boolean _jspx_inited = false;

  public final void _jspx_init() throws JasperException {
  }
```

```
  public void _jspService(HttpServletRequest request,
                          HttpServletResponse  response)
     throws IOException, ServletException {
```

```
    JspFactory _jspxFactory = null;
    PageContext pageContext = null;
    HttpSession session = null;
    ServletContext application = null;
    ServletConfig config = null;
    JspWriter out = null;
    Object page = this;
    String  _value = null;
    try {
      if (_jspx_inited == false) {
        _jspx_init();
        _jspx_inited = true;
      }
      _jspxFactory = JspFactory.getDefaultFactory();
      response.setContentType("text/html;charset=8859_1");
      pageContext = _jspxFactory.getPageContext(this, request,
                                                response,
                                                "", true, 8192, true);
```

```
        application = pageContext.getServletContext();
        config = pageContext.getServletConfig();
        session = pageContext.getSession();
        out = pageContext.getOut();

        // HTML // begin [file="C:\\simpleJSP.jsp";from=(0,33);to=(3,20)]
            out.write("\r\n<html>\r\n<body>\r\nThe current time is ");
        // end
        // begin [file="C:\\simpleJSP.jsp";from=(3,23);to=(3,46)]
            out.print( new Date().toString() );
        // end
        // HTML // begin [file="C:\\simpleJSP.jsp";from=(3,48);to=(7,0)]
            out.write("\r\n</body>\r\n</html>\r\n\r\n");
        // end

    } catch (Exception ex) {
        if (out.getBufferSize() != 0)
            out.clearBuffer();
            pageContext.handlePageException(ex);
    } finally {
        out.flush();
        _jspxFactory.releasePageContext(pageContext);
    }
  }
}
```

In other words, the first time a JSP is loaded by the **JSP container** (also called the **JSP engine**), the servlet code necessary to fulfill the JSP tags is automatically generated, compiled, and loaded into the servlet container. From then on, as long as the JSP source for the page is not modified, this compiled servlet processes any browser requests for that JSP page. If you modify the source code for the JSP, it is automatically recompiled and reloaded the next time that page is requested. (Of course, because of this you'll see a slow response for the first-time access to a JSP.)

The figure below summarizes this process:

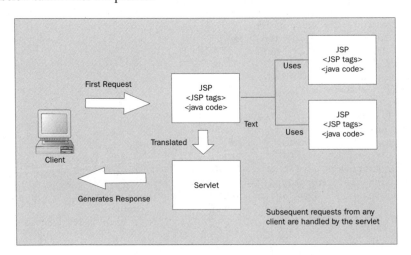

The figure also shows how a JSP can dynamically invoke other JSPs internally, while still giving the impression to the browser that it is doing all the work itself (using JSP's equivalent of the `RequestDispatcher` mechanism we used with servlets in Chapter 9).

The servlet class generated at the end of the translation process represents the well-defined relationship between a container and a JSP. According to the JSP specifications (which the containers implement) it must extend a superclass that is *either*:

❑ Specified by the JSP author via an `extends` attribute in the `page` directive,

or

❑ A JSP container specific implementation class that implements the `javax.servlet.jsp.JspPage` interface and provides some basic page-specific behavior. (Since most JSP pages use HTTP, their implementation classes must actually implement the `javax.servlet.jsp.HttpJspPage` interface, which itself extends `javax.servlet.jsp.JspPage`).

The `javax.servlet.jsp.JspPage` interface contains two methods:

```
public void jspInit()
```

This is invoked when the JSP is initialized, and is similar to the `init()` method in servlets. Page authors are free to provide initialization of the JSP by implementing this method in their JSPs.

```
public void jspDestroy()
```

This is invoked when the JSP is about to be destroyed by the container, and is similar to the `destroy()` method in servlets. Page authors are free to provide cleanup of the JSP by implementing this method in their JSPs.

The `javax.servlet.jsp.HttpJspPage` interface contains a single method:

```
public void _jspService(HttpServletRequest request,
                        HttpServletResponse response)
          throws ServletException, IOException
```

This method corresponds to the body of the JSP page and is used for threaded request processing, just like the `service()` method in servlets.

> **The implementation of this method is generated by the container and should never be provided by page authors.**

These three major life events methods work together in a JSP, as seen below:

479

- ❏ The page is first initialized by invoking the `jspInit()` method, which can be defined by the page author. This initializes the JSP in much the same way as servlets are initialized, when the first request is intercepted and just after translation.

- ❏ Every time a request comes to the JSP, the container generated `_jspService()` method is invoked, the request is processed, and the JSP generates the appropriate response. This response is taken by the container and passed back to the client.

- ❏ When the JSP is destroyed by the server (for example at shut down), the `jspDestroy()` method, which can be defined by the page author, is invoked to perform any cleanup.

> **It is worth noting that in most cases the `jspInit()` and `jspDestroy()` methods don't need to be provided by the JSP author, and can be omitted.**

The Nuts and Bolts

Let us jump head-on into writing JSPs. The structure of a JSP page is a cross between a servlet and an HTML page, with Java code enclosed between the constructs <% and %> and other XML-like tags interspersed.

JSP tags fall into three categories:

- ❏ **Directives:** These affect the overall structure of the servlet that results from translation

- ❏ Scripting elements: These let you insert Java code into the JSP page (and hence into the resulting servlet)

- ❏ Actions: These are special tags available to affect the runtime behavior of the JSP

- ❏ You can also write your own tags, as we shall see in Chapters 12 and 13.

Some general rules are applicable to JSP pages:

- ❏ JSP tags are case-sensitive.

- ❏ Directives and scripting elements have a syntax which is not based on XML, but an alternative XML-based syntax is also available.

- ❏ Tags based on XML syntax have either a start tag with optional attributes, an optional body, and a matching end tag; or they have an empty tag (possibly with attributes – see example below):

```
<somejsptag attributename="attribute value">
  body
</somejsptag>
```

or:

```
<somejsptag attributename="attribute value" />
```

- ❑ Attribute values in tags always appear quoted; either single or double quotes can be used. The special strings ' and " can be used (just as in HTML) if quotes are a part of the attribute value itself.

- ❑ Any whitespace within the body text of a document is not significant, but is preserved during translation into a servlet.

- ❑ The character \ (backslash) can be used as an escape character in a tag (for example, to use %, the sequence \% can be used).

- ❑ URLs used by JSPs follow servlet conventions, and a URL starting with a /, called a context-relative path, is interpreted with reference to the web application to which the JSP page belongs. (The ServletContext is available as an implicit object within JSP pages, as we will see later.)

- ❑ If the URL does not start with a / it is interpreted relative to the current JSP.

JSP Directives

JSP directives serve as messages sent to the JSP container from the JSP. They are used to set global values such as class declarations, methods to be implemented, output content type, etc., and do not produce any output to the client. Directives have scope for the entire JSP file; in other words, a directive affects the whole JSP file, but only that file. Directives start with <%@ and end with %>; the general syntax is:

```
<%@ directivename attribute="value" attribute="value" %>
```

There are three main directives that can be used in JSP:

- ❑ The page directive
- ❑ The include directive
- ❑ The taglib directive

The page Directive

The **page directive** is used to define and manipulate a number of important page-dependent attributes that affect the whole JSP (the entire compiled class file), and communicates these attributes to the JSP container. A page can contain any number of page directives, in any order, anywhere in the JSP. They are all assimilated during translation and applied together to the page. However, there can be only one occurrence of any attribute/value pair defined by the page directives in a given JSP. (An exception is the import attribute: there can be multiple imports.)

The general syntax of the page directive is:

```
<%@ page ATTRIBUTES %>
```

where the valid attributes are name value pairs as described overleaf:

Attribute	Description	Default value
language	Defines the scripting language to be used. For future use if JSP containers support multiple languages.	"Java"
extends	The value is a fully qualified class name of the superclass that the generated class (into which this JSP page is translated) must extend. This attribute should normally be avoided, and only used with extreme caution, because JSP engines usually provide specialized super-classes with a lot of functionality to be extended by the generated servlet classes. Use of the extends attribute restricts some of the decisions that a JSP container can make.	Omitted by default
import	Comma separated list of packages or classes, just like import statements in usual Java code.	Omitted by default
session	Specifies whether the page participates in an HTTP session. When "true" the implicit object named session (which refers to the javax.servlet.http.HttpSession) is available and can be used to access the current/new session for the page. If "false", the page does not participate in a session and the implicit session object is unavailable.	"true"
buffer	Specifies the buffering model for the output stream to the client. If the value is "none", then no buffering occurs and all output is written directly through to the ServletResponse by a PrintWriter. If a buffer size is specified (such as "24kb") then output is buffered with a buffer size not less than that value.	Implementation-dependent; at least 8kb
autoFlush	If "true", the output buffer to the client is flushed automatically when it is full. If "false", a runtime exception is raised to indicate buffer overflow.	"true"
isThreadSafe	Defines the level of thread safety implemented in the page. If the value is "true" the JSP engine may send multiple client requests to the page at the same time. If "false" then the JSP processor queues up client requests sent to the page for processing, and processes them one at a time, in the order they were received. This is the same as implementing the javax.servlet.SingleThreadModel interface in a servlet.	"true"

Attribute	Description	Default value
info	Defines an informative string that can subsequently be obtained from the page's implementation of the `Servlet.getServletInfo()` method.	Omitted by default
errorPage	Defines a URL to another JSP page, which is invoked if an unchecked runtime exception is thrown. The page implementation catches the instance of the `Throwable` object and passes it to the error page processing. See the `isErrorPage` attribute below.	Omitted by default
isErrorPage	Indicates if the current JSP page is intended to be another JSP page's error page. If `"true"`, then the implicit variable `exception` is available and refers to the instance of the `java.lang.Throwable` thrown at run-time by the JSP causing the error.	`"false"`
contentType	Defines the character encoding for the JSP and the MIME type for the response of the JSP page. This can have either the form `"MIMETYPE"` or `"MIMETYPE; charset=CHARSET"` with an optional whitespace after the ";". CHARSET, or character encoding, if specified, must be the IANA value for a character encoding.	The default value for the MIMETYPE is `text/html`; the default value for the CHARSET is `ISO-8859-1`.

Unrecognized attributes result in fatal translation errors.

Example

The following JSP, `pageDirective.jsp`, contains an attribute-rich page directive:

```
<%@ page language="Java" import="java.rmi.*,java.util.*"
    session="true" buffer="12kb" autoFlush="true"
    info="my page directive jsp" errorPage="error.jsp"
    isErrorPage="false" isThreadSafe="false"%>

<html>
  <head>
    <title>Page directive test page</title>
  </head>
  <body>
    <h1>Page directive test page</h1>

    This is a JSP to test the page directive.
  </body>
</html>
```

The include Directive

The **include directive** instructs the container to include the content of the resource in the current JSP, by inserting it, inline, in the JSP in place of the directive. Of course the file specified should be accessible and available to the JSP container.

It is important to note that the content of the included file is parsed by the JSP and this happens only at *translation time* (when the JSP page is compiled into a servlet).

The include action is used to include resources at runtime, as we will see later.

Most JSP containers *usually* keep track of the included file and recompile the JSP if it changes (they may choose not to recompile). The server may, however, choose whatever mechanism it prefers to read the included file. The syntax of the include directive is:

```
<%@ include file="Filename" %>
```

The only available attribute, `file`, specifies the filename of the file to include.

Example

The included file can be either a static file (such as an HTML file) or another JSP.

The example below, `includeDirective1.jsp`, requests the inclusion, during compilation, of a copyright file containing HTML legal disclaimers:

```
<html>
  <head>
    <title>Include directive test page 1</title>
  </head>
  <body>
    <h1>Include directive test page 1</h1>

    <%@ include file="/copyright.html" %>
  </body>
</html>
```

`copyright.html` contains the following:

```
<p>&copy; 2000 Wrox Press</p>
```

On placing both these files in the `C:\ProJavaServer\Chapter11\JSPExamples` directory and requesting `http://localhost:8080/JSPExamples/includeDirective1.jsp`, the resulting output is as follows:

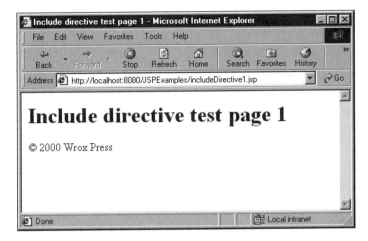

The next example shows how a JSP can be included. Consider the file `includeDirective2.jsp`:

```html
<html>
  <head>
    <title>Include directive test page 2</title>
  </head>
  <body>
    <h1>Include directive test page 2</h1>

    <%@ include file="included.jsp" %>
  </body>
</html>
```

The included JSP `included.jsp` is:

```
<%@ page import="java.util.Date" %>
<%= "Current date is " + new Date() %>
```

Again, save both these files to the `C:\ProJavaServer\Chapter11\JSPExamples` directory. The result on requesting `http://localhost:8080/JSPExamples/includeDirective2.jsp` is:

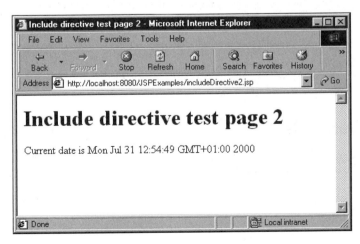

485

When `includeDirective2.jsp` is translated, the relevant portion of the resulting servlet code, stripped of comments, looks like this:

```
out.write("<html>\r\n  <head>\r\n    <title>Include directive test page
2</title>\r\n  </head>\r\n  <body>\r\n    <h1>Include directive test page
2</h1>\r\n\r\n     ");
out.write("\r\n");
out.print("Current date is " + new Date());
out.write("\r\n");
out.write("\r\n  </body>\r\n</html>\r\n");
```

You can see that the code from the included file has been inlined into the translated servlet.

The taglib Directive

The **taglib directive** allows the page to use **tag extensions (custom tags)** – see Chapters 12 and 13. It names the **tag library** that contains compiled Java code defining the tags to be used. The engine uses this tag library to find out what to do when it comes across the custom tags in the JSP. The syntax of the `taglib` directive is:

```
<%@ taglib uri="tagLibraryURI" prefix="tagPrefix" %>
```

and the available attributes are:

Attribute	Description	Default value
uri	A URI (Uniform Resource Identifier) that identified the tag library descriptor. A tag library descriptor is used to uniquely name the set of custom tags and tells the container what to do with the specified tags.	Not specifying a value causes a compilation error
tagPrefix	Defines the prefix string in `prefix:tagname` that is used to define the custom tag. The prefixes `jsp`, `jspx`, `java`, `javax`, `servlet`, `sun`, and `sunw` are reserved. For example if this value is `mytag` then when the container comes across any element that starts like `<mytag:tagname ... />` in the JSP, it references the tag library descriptor specified in the URI.	Not specifying a value causes a compilation error

Tag libraries are a very powerful, and often misunderstood, concept, and will be covered in detail in Chapters 12 and 13.

Scripting Elements

JSP scripting elements allow Java code – variable or method declarations, scriptlets (arbitrary Java code), and expressions – to be inserted into your JSP page.

Declarations

A **declaration** is a block of Java code in a JSP that is used to define class-wide variables and
generated servlet. Declarations are initialized when the JSP page is initialized, and have 'cla'
generated servlet, so that anything defined in a declaration is available throughout the JSP to other
declarations, expressions, and code. A declaration block is enclosed between `<%!` and `%>` and does not write
anything to the output stream. The syntax is:

```
<%! Java variable and method declaration(s) %>
```

Example

Consider the simple JSP below, `declaration.jsp`:

```
<%!
  int numTimes = 3;

  public String sayHello(String name) {
    return "Hello, " + name + "!";
  }
%>

<html>
  <head>
    <title>Declaration test page</title>
  </head>
  <body>
    <h1>Declaration test page</h1>

    <p>The value of numTimes is <%= numTimes %>.</p>
    <p>Saying hello to reader: "<%= sayHello("reader") %>".</p>
  </body>
</html>
```

This declares an `int` variable called `numTimes`, and a `sayHello()` method that greets the requested
person. Further down the page, expression elements (to be covered shortly) are used to return the value of
`numTimes` to the browser and to invoke the `sayHello()` method.

When `declaration.jsp` is saved to the `C:\ProJavaServer\Chapter11\JSPExamples` directory
and `http://localhost:8080/JSPExamples/declaration.jsp` is requested, the output is as follows:

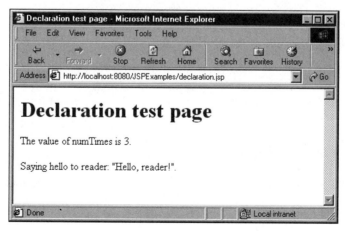

The generated servlet contains the declaration code:

```
import javax.servlet.*;
// ... more import statements

public class _0002fdeclaration_0002ejspdeclaration_jsp_1
        extends HttpJspBase {

  int numTimes = 3;

  public String sayHello(String name) {
    return "Hello, " + name + "!";
  }

  // ... More generated code
```

Scriptlets

A **scriptlet** is a block of Java code that is executed during the request-processing time, and is enclosed between <% and %> tags. What the scriptlet actually does depends on the code itself, and can include producing output for the client. Multiple scriptlets are combined in the generated servlet class in the order they appear in the JSP. Scriptlets, like any other Java code block or method, can modify objects inside them as a result of method invocations.

In Tomcat, all the code appearing between the <% and %> tags in the JSP gets put into the service() method of the servlet, as is, in the order in which it appeared. It is therefore processed for every request that the servlet receives. The syntax for scriptlets is:

```
<% Valid Java code statements %>
```

Example

In scriptlet.jsp below, a scriptlet executes a loop 10 times, printing out a message each time to the browser window (using the implicit object out) and to the System.out stream (in other words, to the console window within which Tomcat is running).

```
<html>
  <head>
    <title>Scriptlet test page</title>
  </head>
  <body>
    <h1>Scriptlet test page</h1>

    <%
      for(int i=0;i< 10;i++) {
        out.println("<b>Hello World. This is a scriptlet test " + i +
                "</b><br>");
        System.out.println("This goes to the System.out stream " + i);
      }
    %>

  </body>
</html>
```

Save `scriptlet.jsp` to the `C:\ProJavaServer\Chapter11\JSPExamples\` directory and request `http://localhost:8080/JSPExamples/scriptlet.jsp`. The output to the browser window should be:

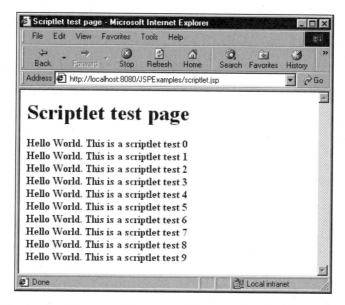

and the following should appear in the console window where Tomcat is running:

Expressions

An **expression** is a shorthand notation for a scriptlet that sends the value of a Java expression back to the client. The expression is evaluated at HTTP request processing time, and the result is converted to a `String` and displayed.

An expression is enclosed in the `<%=` and `%>` tags. If the result of the expression is an object, the conversion is done by using the object's `toString()` method. The syntax is:

```
<%= Java expression to be evaluated %>
```

Example

Consider the example JSP overleaf (`expression.jsp` – again, save it in `C:\ProJavaServer\Chapter11\JSPExamples`), which sets up a simple counter and shows declarations, scriptlets, and expressions working together:

```html
<html>
  <head>
    <title>Expression test page</title>
  </head>
  <body>
    <h1>Expression test page</h1>

    <%! int i=0 ; %>

    <%
      i++;
    %>

    Hello World!
    <%= "This JSP has been accessed " + i + " times" %>

  </body>
</html>
```

An `int` variable `i` is declared, and initially has the value `0`. Each time this instance of the generated servlet is called (when the browser requests `http://localhost:8080/JSPExamples/expression.jsp`) the variable is incremented by the scriptlet. Finally, an expression is used to print out the value of `i`, together with some surrounding text.

After this JSP has been requested a number of times, the browser will display:

Standard Actions

Standard actions are tags that affect the runtime behavior of the JSP and the response sent back to the client. They have to be provided by all containers, irrespective of the implementation.

Effectively, a standard action is a tag that can be embedded in a JSP page. During compilation into a servlet, the container comes across this tag and replaces it with Java code that corresponds to the required predefined task.

For example when it comes across the standard include action:

```
<jsp:include page="myjsp.jsp" flush="true" />
```

it takes the JSP `myjsp.jsp`, compiles it (if necessary), and includes the output produced by `myjsp.jsp` in the response, in place of the action tag. We will examine the semantics of this action in detail in a while.

The standard actions serve to provide page authors with basic functionality to exploit for common tasks. The standard action types are:

- ❏ `<jsp:useBean>`
- ❏ `<jsp:setProperty>`
- ❏ `<jsp:getProperty>`
- ❏ `<jsp:param>`
- ❏ `<jsp:include>`
- ❏ `<jsp:forward>`
- ❏ `<jsp:plugin>`

<jsp:useBean>

To separate code from presentation, it would be a good idea to encapsulate the code in a Java object (a **JavaBean**), and then instantiate and use this object within our JSP. The `<jsp:useBean>`, `<jsp:setProperty>`, and `<jsp:getProperty>` tags assist with this task.

The `<jsp:useBean>` action is used to instantiate a JavaBean, or locate an existing bean instance, and assign it to a variable name (or **id**). We can also specify the lifetime of the object by giving it a specific **scope** (we cover this later in detail). `<jsp:useBean>` ensures that the object is available, with the specified id, in the appropriate scope as specified in the tag. The object can then be referenced using its associated id from within the JSP, or even from other JSPs, depending on the scope.

The syntax for the `<jsp:useBean>` action is:

```
<jsp:useBean id="name" scope="scopeName" beandetails />
```

where and `beandetails` is one of:

- ❏ `class="className"`
- ❏ `class="className" type="typeName"`
- ❏ `beanName="beanName" type="typeName"`
- ❏ `type="typeName"`

The attributes available are:

Attribute	Description	Default value
id	The case sensitive name used to identify the object instance.	No default value
scope	The scope within which the reference is available. Possible values are "page", "request", "session", and "application". These values will be explained shortly.	"page"
class	The fully qualified class name.	No default value
beanName	The name of a bean, as you would supply to the instantiate() method in the java.beans.Beans class. This attribute can also be a request time expression. It is permissible to supply a type and a beanName, and omit the class attribute. The beanName follows the standard bean specification and can be of the form "a.b.c", where "a.b.c" is either a class, or the name of a serialized resource in which case it is resolved as "a/b/c.ser". (See the JavaBeans specification for more details.)	No default value
type	This optional attribute specifies the type of the scripting variable to be created, and follows standard Java casting rules. The type must be a superclass of the bean's class, an interface implemented by it, or the bean's class itself. Just like any casting operation, if the object is not of this type then java.lang.ClassCastException can be thrown at request time.	The value of the class attribute

Let us examine the underlying semantics that occur because of this tag in the order they occur:

❑ The container tries to locate an object that has this id, in the specified scope.

❑ If the object is found, and a type has been specified in the tag, the container tries to cast the found object to the specified type. A ClassCastException is thrown if the cast fails.

❑ If the object is not found in the specified scope, and no class or beanName is specified in the tag, an InstantiationException is thrown.

❑ If the object is not found in the specified scope, and the class can be instantiated, then this is done, and a reference to the object is associated with the given id, in the specified scope. If this fails then an InstantiationException is thrown.

❑ If the object is not found in the specified scope and a beanName is specified, then the instantiate() method of java.beans.Beans is invoked, with the beanName as an argument. If this method succeeds, the new object reference is associated with the given id, in the specified scope.

❑ If a new bean instance has been instantiated and the `<jsp:useBean>` element has a non-empty body, the body is processed; during this processing the new variable is initialized and available. Scriptlets or the `<jsp:setProperty>` standard action can be used to initialize the bean instance, if necessary.

The meanings of the possible values of the `scope` attribute will be covered in more detail shortly, but in brief:

❑ page scope means that the object is associated with this particular request to this page.

❑ request scope means that the object is associated with this particular client request. If the request is forwarded to another JSP using the `<jsp:forward>` action, or if another JSP is included using the `<jsp:include>` action, the object will be available.

❑ session scope means that the object will be available during any requests made by the same client within the current session.

❑ application scope means that the object will be available in any JSP page within the same web application.

The container looks for the Java class you specified in the CLASSPATH for that web application. If you are creating a bean of a class you have written yourself, place the compiled `.class` file either under the WEB-INF\classes directory in your web application, or in a JAR file in the WEB-INF\lib directory.

We will see an example of the `<jsp:useBean>` action once we have looked at `<jsp:setProperty>` and `<jsp:getProperty>`.

<jsp:setProperty>

The `<jsp:setProperty>` standard tag is used in conjunction with the `<jsp:useBean>` action described in the preceding section, to set the value of bean properties. Bean properties can be either simple or indexed.

The properties in a bean can be set either:

❑ At request time from parameters in the request object

❑ At request time from an evaluated expression

❑ From a specified string (or hard coded in the page)

When setting bean properties from the request object, the JSP can choose to set all properties in the bean via the standard action:

```
<jsp:setProperty name="help" property="*"/>
```

or a single property can be set explicitly by an action such as:

```
<jsp:setProperty name="help" property="word"/>
```

The `<jsp:setProperty>` action uses bean introspection to discover what properties are present, their names, whether they are simple or indexed, their type, and their accessor and mutator methods.

The syntax of the `<jsp:setProperty>` action is:

```
<jsp:setProperty name="beanName" propertydetails />
```

where `propertydetails` is one of:

- ❑ `property="*"`
- ❑ `property="propertyName"`
- ❑ `property="propertyName" param="parameterName"`
- ❑ `property="propertyName" value="propertyValue"`

and `propertyValue` is a string or a scriptlet. The attributes are:

Attribute	Description
name	The name of a bean instance, which must already have been defined by a `<jsp:useBean>` tag. Note that the name in `<jsp:setProperty>` and the one for `<jsp:useBean>` must be the same.
property	The name of the bean property whose value is being set.
	If the `property` attribute has the value `"*"`, the tag looks through all the parameters in the request object and tries to match the request parameter names and types to property names and types in the bean. The values in the request are assigned to each matching bean property, unless a request parameter has the value `" "`, in which case the bean property is left unaltered.
param	When setting bean properties from request parameters, it is not necessary for the bean have the same property names as the request parameters.
	This attribute is used to specify the name of the request parameter whose value you want to assign to a bean property. If the `param` value is not specified, it is assumed that the request parameter and the bean property have the same name.
	If there is no request parameter with this name, or if it has the value `" "`, the action has no effect on the bean.
value	The value to assign to the bean property. This can be a request-time attribute, or it can accept an expression as its value.
	(A tag cannot have both `param` and `value` attributes.)

When properties are assigned from `String` constants or request parameter values, conversion is applied using the standard Java conversion methods; for example, if a bean property is of type `double` or `Double` the `java.lang.Double.valueOf(String)` method is used. However, request-time expressions can be assigned to properties of any type, and the container performs no conversion. For indexed properties, the value must be an array.

<jsp:getProperty>

The `<jsp:getProperty>` action is complementary to the `<jsp:setProperty>` action, and is used to access the properties of a bean. It accesses the value of a property, converts it to a `String`, and prints it to the output stream to the client.

To convert the property to a `String`, the action:

❑ Invokes the `toString()` method on the property, if it is an object

❑ Converts the value directly to a `String`, if it is a primitive, using the `valueOf()` method of the corresponding wrapper class for the primitive type

This just like the behavior of Java's `System.out.println()` method.

The syntax is:

```
<jsp:getProperty name="name" property="propertyName" />
```

and the available attributes are:

Attribute	Description
name	The name of the bean instance from which the property is obtained.
property	Names the property to get; this is the instance variable in the bean. Of course, you must create a bean before using `<jsp:getProperty>`, by using `<jsp:useBean>` or by instantiating the object by a new operator.

Having seen the `<jsp:useBean>`, `<jsp:setProperty>`, and `<jsp:getProperty>` actions, let's build a simple example using all three. Our example will ask the user for their name and their favorite programming language, and then issue a verdict on their choice. The HTML form page, `beans.html`, is very simple:

```html
<html>
  <head>
    <title>useBean action test page</title>
  </head>
  <body>
    <h1>useBean action test page</h1>

    <form method="post" action="beans.jsp">
      <p>Please enter your username:
      <input type="text" name="name">
      <br>What is your favorite programming language?
      <select name="language">
        <option value="Java">Java
        <option value="C++">C++
        <option value="Perl">Perl
```

```
          </select>
          </p>

          <p><input type="submit" value="Submit information">
        </form>

    </body>
</html>
```

This sends a POST request to beans.jsp with two parameters: name and language. beans.jsp is also quite simple:

```
<jsp:useBean id="languageBean" scope="page" class="LanguageBean">
  <jsp:setProperty name="languageBean" property="*"/>
</jsp:useBean>

<html>
  <head>
    <title>useBean action test result</title>
  </head>
  <body>
    <h1>useBean action test result</h1>

    <p>Hello, <jsp:getProperty name="languageBean" property="name"/>.</p>

    <p>Your favorite language is
       <jsp:getProperty name="languageBean" property="language"/>.</p>

    <p>My comments on your language:</p>
    <p><jsp:getProperty name="languageBean" property="languageComments"/>
    </p>
  </body>
</html>
```

All the Java code has been removed to the LanguageBean class. beans.jsp creates an instance of LanguageBean with page scope, and uses the property="*" form of the <jsp:setProperty> action to set the bean's name and language properties. It can then use the <jsp:getProperty> action to retrieve the values of these properties, and also the languageComments property.

Finally, the source of LanguageBean is as follows:

```
public class LanguageBean {

  private String name;
  private String language;

  public LanguageBean() {}

  public void setName(String name) {
    this.name = name;
  }

  public String getName() {
    return name;
  }

  public void setLanguage(String language) {
    this.language = language;
```

```
   }

   public String getLanguage() {
      return language;
   }

   public String getLanguageComments() {
      if (language.equals("Java")) {
         return "The king of OO languages.";
      } else if (language.equals("C++")) {
         return "Rather too complex for some folks' liking.";
      } else if (language.equals("Perl")) {
         return "OK if you like incomprehensible code.";
      } else {
         return "Sorry, I've never heard of " + language + ".";
      }
   }
}
```

This is a nice, simple class with a no-argument constructor, set and get methods for the `name` and `language` properties, and also a `getLanguageComments()` method. This last method uses the value of the `language` property to issue some comments on the user's chosen language – this is invoked by the `<jsp:getProperty name="languageBean" property="languageComments"/>` action in `beans.jsp`.

Save `beans.jsp` and `beans.jsp` to `C:\ProJavaServer\Chapter11\JSPExamples`, and `LanguageBean.java` to `C:\ProJavaServer\Chapter11\JSPExamples\src`. Compile the bean into `C:\ProJavaServer\Chapter11\JSPExamples\WEB-INF\classes` (create this directory first) by running the command:

```
javac -d ..\WEB-INF\classes LanguageBean.java
```

from the `src` directory. Then point your browser at `http://localhost:8080/JSPExamples/beans.html`:

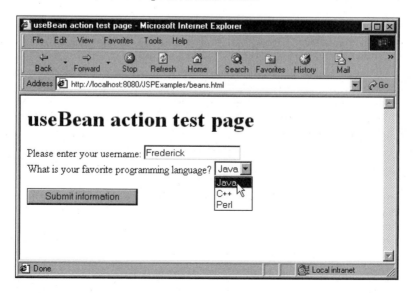

Enter your name and choose your favored language, then click the Submit information button:

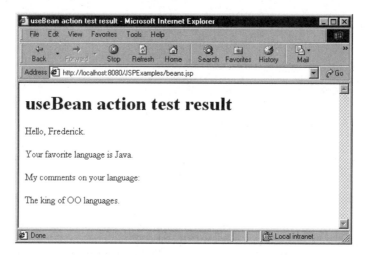

> The advantage of this approach over that used in previous examples (in which we freely mixed Java code and HTML) should be clear. Removing the logic to the `LanguageBean` class has made our JSP page much more readable, and more easily edited by someone who is a skilled web designer but does not undertstand the details of Java programming.

<jsp:param>

The `<jsp:param>` action is used to provide other tags with additional information in the form of name-value pairs. It is used in conjunction with the `<jsp:include>`, `<jsp:forward>`, and `<jsp:plugin>` actions, and its use is described in the relevant sections that follow. The syntax is:

```
<jsp:param name="paramname" value="paramvalue" />
```

and the available attributes are:

Attribute	Description
name	The key associated with the attribute. (Attributes are key-value pairs.)
value	The value of the attribute.

<jsp:include>

This action allows a static or dynamic resource, specified by a URL, to be included in the current JSP at request processing time. An included page has access to only the `JspWriter` object, and it cannot set headers or cookies. A request-time exception will be thrown if this is attempted. This constraint is equivalent to that imposed on `javax.servlet.RequestDispatcher`'s `include()` method, which is what servlets use if they want to do this type of inclusion.

If the page output is buffered then the buffer is flushed prior to the inclusion. The include action pays a small penalty in efficiency, and precludes the included page from containing general JSP code.

The syntax of the `<jsp:include>` action is:

```
<jsp:include page="URL" flush="true" />
```

or:

```
<jsp:include page="URL" flush="true">
  <jsp:param name="paramname" value="paramvalue" />
  ...
</jsp:include>
```

The attributes of the `<jsp:include>` action are:

Attribute	Description
filename	The resource to include. The URL format is the same as described earlier for the include directive.
flush	In JSP 1.1 this value must always be `"true"`, and `"false"` is not supported. If the value is `"true"`, the buffer in the output stream is flushed before the inclusion is performed.

A `<jsp:include>` action may have one or more `<jsp:param>` tags in its body, providing additional name-value pairs. The included page can access the original `request` object, which will contain both the original parameters, and the new parameters specified using the `<jsp:param>` tag. If the parameter names are the same, the old values are kept intact, but the new values take precedence over the existing values.

For example, if the request has a parameter param1=myvalue1, and a parameter param1=myvalue2 is specified in the `<jsp:param>` tag, the request received on the second JSP will have param1=myvalue2, myvalue1. The augmented attributes can be extracted from the request using the getParameter(String paramname) method in the javax.servlet.ServletRequest interface.

It is important to understand the difference between the include *directive* and this include *action*; the difference is summarized in the table below:

Include type	Syntax	Done when	Included content	Parsing
directive	`<%@ include file="filename" %>`	Compilation time	Static	Parsed by container
action	`<jsp:include page="filename" />`	Request processing time	Static or Dynamic	Not parsed but included in place

The include directive lets you include resources into multiple pages but requires you to update the modification date on the pages doing the include if the resource changes (in other words the container has to translate them again to reflect the changes). The include action includes files at request-processing time.

> **Use the include directive if your resource is not going to change frequently.**
> **Use the include action when the resource is frequently changing or is dynamic.**

Let's look at an example. The JSP below, includeAction.jsp, shows both the include types, for both a static and a dynamic resource:

```
<html>
  <head>
    <title>Include Action test page</title>
  </head>
  <body>
    <h1>Include Action test page</h1>

      <h2>Using the include directive</h2>

      <%@ include file="included2.html" %>
      <%@ include file="included2.jsp" %>

      <h2>Using the include action</h2>

      <jsp:include page="included2.html" flush="true" />
      <jsp:include page="included2.jsp" flush="true" />

  </body>
</html>
```

The two included files are included2.html:

```
<p>This is some static text in the html file</p>
```

and included2.jsp:

```
<%@ page import="java.util.Date" %>
<%= "Current date is " + new Date() %>
```

Saving these files in C:\ProJavaServer\Chapter11\JSPExamples and requesting http://localhost:8080/JSPExamples/includeAction.jsp, we get:

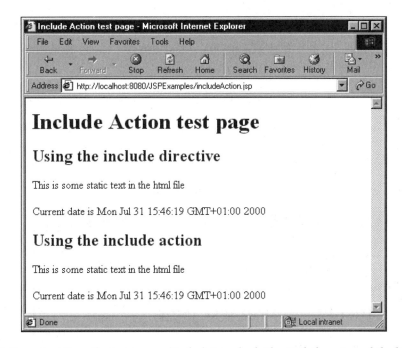

Even though the output from the two types of include may look identical, there is a subtle difference. Let us look at an excerpt from the generated servlet class, tidied up a little:

```
// ...

public void _jspService(HttpServletRequest request,
                        HttpServletResponse response)
        throws IOException, ServletException {
// ...

    out.write("<html>\r\n  <head>\r\n    <title>Include Action test
page</title>\r\n  </head>\r\n  <body>\r\n    <h1>Include Action test
page</h1>\r\n\r\n      <h2>Using the include directive</h2>\r\n\r\n          ");
    out.write("<h3>This is some static text in the html file</h3>");
    out.write("\r\n       ");
    out.write("\r\n");
    out.print( "Current date is " + new Date() );
    out.write("\r\n\r\n      <h2>Using the include action</h2>\r\n\r\n          ");
    {
      String _jspx_qStr = "";
      out.flush();
      pageContext.include("included2.html" + _jspx_qStr);
    }
    out.write("\r\n        ");
    {
      String _jspx_qStr = "";
      out.flush();
      pageContext.include("included2.jsp" + _jspx_qStr);
    }
    out.write("\r\n\r\n  </body>\r\n</html>\r\n");

// ...
}
```

The highlighted lines in the above code show how the container in-lines the resources for the include *directive*, and invokes them dynamically for the include *action*. To reiterate the difference, see what happens when the included resources are changed (without changing the parent JSP that includes them). Change `included2.html` so that it contains:

```
<p>This is some new text in the html file</p>
```

and change `included2.jsp` so that its contents are now:

```
<p>This is the new JSP</p>
```

When the page is requested again, the output now looks like this:

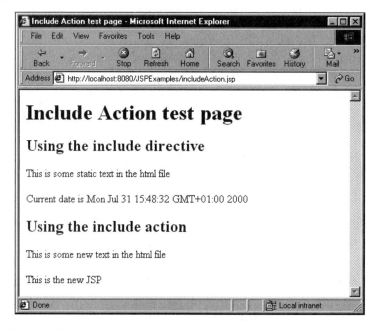

The parts included using the include *directive* are not altered, because the parent JSP (`includeAction.jsp`) has not changed and hence is not recompiled; however, the parts included using the include *action* are changed, because the include action performs the inclusion afresh each time the parent JSP is requested.

<jsp:forward>

The `<jsp:forward>` action allows the request to be forwarded to another JSP, to a servlet, or to a static resource. This is particularly useful when you want to separate the application into different views, depending on the intercepted request. We saw this design approach with servlets in Chapter 9, and will see more of it later in this chapter. The syntax is:

```
<jsp:forward page="URL" />
```

or:

```
<jsp:forward page="URL">
  <jsp:param name="paramname" value="paramvalue" />
  ...
</jsp:forward>
```

The resource to which the request is being forwarded must be in the same context as the JSP dispatching the request. Execution in the current JSP stops when it encounters a `<jsp:forward>` tag, the buffer is cleared, and the request is modified (this is a server-side redirect and the response buffer is cleared when it is processed) to assimilate any additionally specified parameters in the same way as described for the `<jsp:include>` action.

If the output stream was not buffered, and some output has been written to it, a `<jsp:forward>` action will throw a `java.lang.IllegalStateException`. The behavior of this action is exactly the same as the `forward()` method of the `javax.servlet.RequestDispatcher`.

Let's see a simple example of the `<jsp:forward>` action in use – a simple login form. The login form itself, in `forward.html`, is straightforward, sending a POST request to `forward.jsp`:

```html
<html>
  <head>
    <title>Forward action test page</title>
  </head>
  <body>
    <h1>Forward action test page</h1>

    <form method="post" action="forward.jsp">
      <p>Please enter your username:
      <input type="text" name="userName">
      <br>and password:
      <input type="password" name="password">
      </p>

      <p><input type="submit" value="Log in">
    </form>

  </body>
</html>
```

`forward.jsp` is the first JSP page we have seen that contains *no* HTML code:

```jsp
<%
  if ((request.getParameter("userName").equals("Richard")) &&
      (request.getParameter("password").equals("xyzzy"))) {
%>

<jsp:forward page="forward2.jsp" />

<% } else { %>

<%@ include file="forward.html" %>

<% } %>
```

This checks whether the username and password are acceptable to the system, and if so forwards the request to `forward2.jsp`; if the login attempt fails, it uses the include directive to present the login form to the user again.

> *In a real-world example the password-checking code would check against a database or a JNDI server, the Java code would be removed to a JavaBean or a tag extension, and the whole application would probably be secured using HTTPS.*

Finally, `forward2.jsp` presents the successfully logged-in user with a welcome page. Since the original request, including the form parameters, has been forwarded to this JSP, we can use the `request` object to display the user's name:

```html
<html>
  <head>
    <title>Forward action test: Login successful!</title>
  </head>
  <body>
    <h1>Forward action test: Login successful</h1>

    <p>Welcome, <%= request.getParameter("userName") %>

  </body>
</html>
```

Save all these files in `C:\ProJavaServer\Chapter11\JSPExamples` and request `http://localhost:8080/JSPExamples/forward.html`:

Entering the username Richard and the password xyzzy, we get to this page:

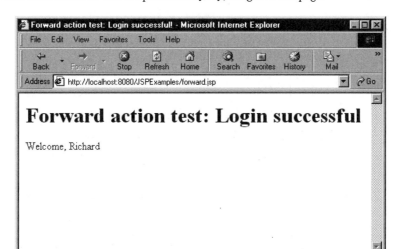

If any other username or password is entered, the login form is displayed again.

<jsp:plugin>

The <jsp:plugin> action is used in pages to generate client browser specific HTML tags (<OBJECT> or <EMBED>) that result in the download of the Java Plug-in software, if required, followed by the execution of the applet or JavaBeans component that is specified in the tag.

The <jsp:plugin> tag can optionally have two additional support tags:

❑   <jsp:params>, to pass additional parameters to the Applet or JavaBeans component.

❑   <jsp:fallback>, to specify the content to be displayed in the client browser if the plugin cannot be started because the generated tags are not supported. The <jsp:fallback> tag does what the HTML ALT attribute and <NOFRAMES> tag do.

The syntax of this action is:

```
<jsp:plugin type="bean|applet" code="objectCode" codebase="objectCodebase"
            align="alignment" archive="archiveList" height="height"
            hspace="hspace" jreversion="jreversion" name="componentName"
            vspace="vspace" width="width" nspluginurl="url"
            iepluginurl="url" >
  <jsp:params>
    <jsp:param name=" paramName" value=" paramValue" />
    <jsp:param name=" paramName" value=" paramValue" />
    ...
  </jsp:params>
  <jsp:fallback> Alternate text to display </jsp:fallback>
</jsp:plugin>
```

The available attributes for the `<jsp:plugin>` tag are:

Attribute	Details	Required
type	Identifies the type of the component: a Bean, or an Applet	Yes
code	Same as HTML syntax	Yes
codebase	Same as HTML syntax	No
align	Same as HTML syntax	No
archive	Same as HTML syntax	No
height	Same as HTML syntax	No, but some browsers do not allow an object of zero height due to security issues
hspace	Same as HTML syntax	No
jreversion	The Java runtime environment version needed to execute this object Default is `"1.1"`	No
name	Same as HTML syntax	No
vspace	Same as HTML syntax	No
title	Same as HTML syntax	No
width	Same as HTML syntax	No, but some browsers do not allow an object of zero width due to security issues
nspluginurl	URL where Java plugin can be downloaded for Netscape Navigator Default is implementation defined	No
iepluginurl	URL where Java plugin can be downloaded for Internet Explorer Default is implementation defined	No

Implicit Objects

The Servlet API includes interfaces that provide convenient abstractions to the developer, such as `HttpServletRequest`, `HttpServletResponse`, `HttpSession`, etc. These abstractions encapsulate the object's implementation; for example, the `HttpServletRequest` interface represents the HTTP data sent from the client along with headers, form parameters, etc., and provides convenient methods like `getParameter()`, and `getHeader()` that extract relevant data from the request.

JSP provides certain implicit objects, based on the servlet API. These objects are accessed using standard variables, and are automatically available for use in your JSP without writing any extra code. The implicit objects available in a JSP page are:

- ❑ request
- ❑ response
- ❑ pageContext
- ❑ session
- ❑ application
- ❑ out
- ❑ config
- ❑ page

The request Object

The request object represents the request that triggered the service() invocation. It is the HttpServletRequest that provides access to the incoming HTTP headers (for example, for cookies), request type (GET/POST), and request parameters, among other things. Strictly speaking, the object itself will be a protocol- and implementation-specific subclass of javax.servlet.ServletRequest, but few (if any) JSP containers currently support non-HTTP servlets. It has request scope.

The response Object

The response object is the HttpServletResponse instance that represents the server's response to the request. It is legal to set HTTP status codes and headers in the JSP page once output has been sent to the client (even though it is not permitted in servlets, since the output stream is buffered). Again, the object itself will, strictly speaking, be a protocol- and implementation-specific subclass of javax.servlet.ServletResponse. It has page scope.

The pageContext Object

The pageContext object provides a single point of access to many of the page attributes and is a convenient place to put shared data within the page. It is of type javax.servlet.jsp.PageContext, and has page scope.

The session Object

The session object represents the session created for the requesting client. Sessions are created automatically, and this variable is available even when there is no in-coming session (unless, of course, you have used a session="false" attribute in the page directive, in which case this variable will not be available). It is of type javax.servlet.http.HttpSession, and has session scope.

The application Object

The application object represents the servlet context, obtained from the servlet configuration object. It is of type javax.servlet.ServletContext and has application scope.

The out Object

The out object is the object that writes into the output stream to the client. To make the response object useful, this is a buffered version of the java.io.PrintWriter class, and is of type javax.servlet.jsp.JspWriter. The buffer size can be adjusted via the buffer attribute of the page directive.

The config Object

The config object is the ServletConfig for this JSP page, and has page scope. It is of type javax.servlet.ServletConfig.

The page Object

The page object is the instance of the page's implementation servlet class that is processing the current request. It is of type java.lang.Object, and has page scope. The page object can be thought of as a synonym to this within the page.

Scope

The scope of JSP objects – JavaBeans and implicit objects – is critical, as it defines the how long, and from which JSPs, the object will be available. For example, the session object has a scope which exceeds that of a page, as it may span several client requests and pages. The application object can provide services to a group of JSP pages that together represent a web application.

JSP scopes internally rely on contexts. A context provides an invisible container for resources, and an interface for them to communicate with the environment; for example, a servlet executes in a context (an instance of ServletContext, in fact). Everything that the servlet needs to know about its server can be extracted from this context, and everything the server wants to communicate to the servlet goes through the context. A rule of thumb:

> **Everything in JSP is associated with a context, and every context has a scope.**

What happens when a bean tag is compiled for the different values of scope can be seen below:

Page Scope

An object with page scope is bound to the javax.servlet.jsp.PageContext.

This is relatively simple – It means that the object is placed in the PageContext object, for as long as this page is responding to the current request. An object with this scope can be accessed by invoking the getAttribute() methods on the implicit pageContext object.

The object reference is discarded upon completion of the current Servlet.service() invocation (in other words, when the page is fully processed by the servlets generated from the JSP). When generating the servlet, the servlet engine creates an object in the service() method which follows the usual object scope convection in Java. This object is created and destroyed for each client request to the page.

This is the default scope for objects used with the <jsp:useBean> action.

Request Scope

`request` scope means that the object is bound to the `javax.servlet.ServletRequest`, and can be accessed by invoking the `getAttribute()` methods on the implicit `request` object.

The object reference is available as long as the `HttpRequest` object exists, even if the request is forwarded to different pages, or if the `<jsp:include>` action is used. The underlying, generated servlet relies on binding the object to the `HttpServletRequest` using the `setAttribute(String key, Object value)` method in the `HttpServletRequest`; this is transparent to the JSP author. The object is distinct for every client request (in other words it is created afresh and destroyed for each new request).

Session Scope

An object with `session` scope is bound to the `javax.servlet.jsp.PageContext`, and can be accessed by invoking the `getValue()` methods on the implicit `session` object.

In earlier implementations of the servlet API, a session always ran under a separate session context. (Though deprecated for security reasons, an implementation for the `HttpSessionContext` interface is still available on most servers. It allows you to get a list of sessions or a particular session by its ID – and that's not really that secure.) These days, the only session ID you can get at is the one that's part of the request from the client, passed to the `PageContext` and made available to the JSP.

The generated servlet relies on binding the object to the `HttpSession` using the `setAttribute(String key, Object value)` method. This too is transparent to the JSP author. The object is distinct for every client, and is available as long as the client's session is valid.

Application Scope

`application` scope means that the object is bound to the `javax.servlet.ServletContext`. An object with this scope can be accessed by invoking the `getAttribute()` methods on the implicit `application` object.

This is the most persistent scope. The generated servlet relies on binding the object to the `ServletContext` using the `setAttribute(String key, Object value)` method in the `ServletContext`. This is not unique to individual clients and, consequently, all clients access the same object as they all access the same `ServletContext`.

XML Equivalent Tags

The JSP 1.1 specification provides an equivalent XML-based syntax for JSP pages, replacing directives and scripting elements with XML-compliant alternatives. The syntax outlined up to this point is convenient for hand-authoring of JSP pages; however, an XML-based syntax may be more convenient in some contexts where it is useful to be able to manipulate a JSP page as an XML document.

DTD and Root Element

The DTD and root element for a JSP using the XML syntax are:

```
<! DOCTYPE root
    PUBLIC"-//Sun Microsystems Inc.//DTD JavaServer Pages Version 1.1//EN"
    "http://java.sun.com/products/jsp/dtd/jspcore_1_0.dtd">
```

```
<jsp:root xmlns:jsp="http://java.sun.com/products/jsp/dtd/jsp_1_0.dtd">

   remainder of JSP page

</jsp:root>
```

Directives

For a JSP directive of the form:

```
<%@ directiveName ATTRIBUTES %>
```

the equivalent XML-based syntax is:

```
<jsp:directive:directiveName ATTRIBUTES />
```

The exception is the `taglib` directive, which is represented by an `xmlns:` attribute within the JSP page's root element.

Scripting Elements

A JSP declaration of the form:

```
<%! declaration code %>
```

is represented in XML as:

```
<jsp:declaration> declaration code </jsp:declaration>
```

A scriptlet of the form:

```
<% scriptlet code %>
```

is represented by:

```
<jsp:scriptlet> scriptlet code </jsp:scriptlet>
```

Finally, an expression of the form:

```
<%= expression code %>
```

is represented by:

```
<jsp:expression> expression code </jsp:expression>
```

Actions

The JSP action syntax is already based on XML. The only changes necessary are due to quoting conventions, and to the syntax of any request-time attribute values.

JSP Design Basics

So far we have talked about how the JSPs execute within a container, and the nuts and bolts of JSP tags and directives. Let's now look at some of the design paradigms that can be used, together with what we have learnt so far, to develop complete applications. We will look at this in more detail in Chapter 14; here we present a brief overview.

Our aim in web application design must be to separate logic and presentation. There are two main approaches to JSP design:

- ❑ **Page-centric** or **client-server** designs. In these designs, requests are made directly to the JSP page that produces the response.

- ❑ **Dispatcher** or **n-tier** designs, in which the request is initially made to a JSP or a servlet that acts as a mediator or controller, dispatching requests to JSP pages and JavaBeans as appropriate.

Page-Centric or Client-Server Designs

In this approach, JSPs or servlets access the enterprise resources (a database, for example) directly, or through a JavaBean, and generate the response themselves. This approach is illustrated in the figure below:

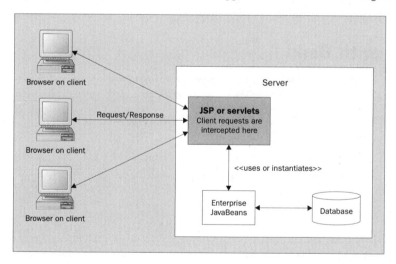

The advantage of such an approach is that it is simple to program, and allows the page author to generate dynamic content easily, based upon the request and the state of the resources.

However this architecture does not scale up well, and indiscriminate use of it usually leads to a significant amount of Java code embedded within the JSP page. This may not seem to be much of a problem for Java developers, but it is certainly an issue if the JSP pages are maintained by designers: the code tends to get in the designer's way, and you run the risk of your code becoming corrupted when others are tweaking the look and feel.

There are two main variants here: the **Page-View** and **Page-View with Bean** architectures.

Page-View

This basic architecture involves direct request invocations to a JSP page with embedded Java code, and markup tags that dynamically generate output for substitution within the HTML.

This approach has many benefits. It is very easy to get started, and is a low-overhead approach from a development standpoint. All of the Java code may be embedded within the HTML, so changes are confined to a limited area, reducing complexity. The figure below shows the architecture visually:

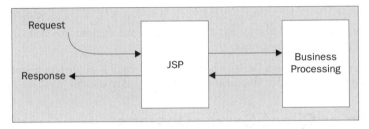

The big trade-off here is in the level of sophistication. As the scale of the system grows, some limitations of this approach surface, such as including too much business logic in the page. As we shall see, utilizing a mediating JSP or servlet and JavaBeans components allows us to separate developer roles more cleanly, and improves the potential for code reuse.

Page-View with Bean

This architecture is used when the Page-View architecture becomes too cluttered with business-related code and data access code. The architecture now evolves into a more sophisticated design, as shown in the figure below:

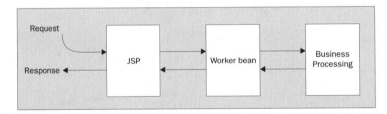

The Java code representing the business logic and simple data storage implementation has migrated from the JSP to the JavaBean worker. This refactoring leaves a much cleaner JSP with limited Java code, which can be comfortably owned by an individual in a web-production role, since it encapsulates mostly markup tags.

Additionally, a less technical individual could be provided with a property sheet for the JavaBean workers, providing a listing of properties that are made available to the JSP page by the particular worker bean, and the desired property may simply be plugged into the JSP `<jsp:getProperty>` action to obtain the attribute value.

Moreover, we have now created a bean that a software developer can own, so that its functionality may be refined and modified without the need for changes to the HTML or markup within the JSP source page. Another way to think about these changes is that we have created cleaner abstractions in our system by replacing implementation with intent.

The 'Dispatcher' Approach

We now move on to look at architectures based on the dispatcher or 'n-tiered' approach, where a JSP or servlet acts as a mediator or controller, delegating requests to JSP pages and JavaBeans. We will look at the **Mediator-View**, **Mediator-Composite View**, and **Service to Workers** architectures.

Mediator-View

Factoring common services, such as authentication, out to a mediating JSP or servlet allows us to remove potential duplication from our JSP pages. For example, we could have a servlet that checked that the user was authenticated, and forwarded the request once this was established.

In this architectural pattern that is emerging, the mediating JSP or servlet works with a 'presentation' JSP page and worker bean pair to fulfill a service request. This 'Mediator-View' architecture is shown below, illustrating how each service is partitioned. The mediating JSP or servlet initially handles the request, and delegates to a JSP/worker bean combination. The 'presentation' JSP populates bean properties from the request parameters and then uses the bean to prepare the data for presentation:

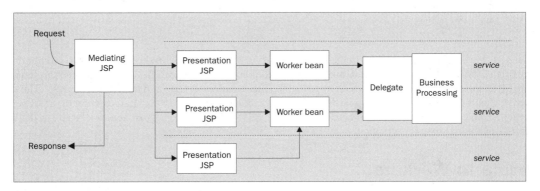

Mediator-Composite View

Sometimes we are building systems with dynamic template text as well as dynamic content. In other words, there is content being generated dynamically, and the template text that surrounds this data is also being constantly changed. Imagine that there are headers and footers in a page that are modified quite often, notifying individuals of status changes or information of special interest. It may not be desirable to recompile our JSP source each time this template text changes, since this involves a runtime delay and resource load. If we simply type our header and footer text directly into our JSP source, then we will need to modify that source each time we want to change the template text, and our modified source will need to be re-translated in order to service another request, causing this run time latency, and this scenario will repeat itself each and every time the text undergoes even slight modification.

Not only can we dynamically include resources, such as static HTML template fragments within our JSP source, but we can also include other JSPs, creating a multiple-level nesting of pages. In this case, the presentation is built from numerous static and dynamic resources, which together make up the page presented to the user. Each of these resources is potentially composed of additional nested pages. Although the HTML template text is considered a static resource, meaning it is not generated dynamically at run time, these template fragments are potentially a dynamic piece of the interface, since each can be modified continually with immediate updates occurring in the containing presentation. This 'Mediator-Composite View' architecture is shown visually overleaf:

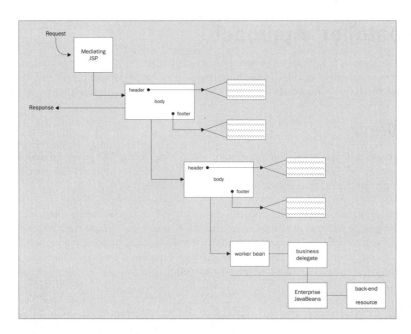

Each of these architectures builds on the previous ones in some way, and in this case we have modified the middle of the 'Mediator-View', while inheriting the front and back. As with the other dispatcher architectures, the mediator dispatches to a JSP, which imports the aforementioned static and dynamic resources. The figure above shows this nested server page including dynamic content generated via an invocation on a worker bean, which gets to the business processing through a delegate which once again acts as a façade to the back-end resource that may be 'wrapped' in an Enterprise JavaBeans component.

Service to Workers

The initial delegation point of the 'Service to Workers' architecture, shown visually below, is a worker bean that processes our business and data access code, once again via a client-side business abstraction. As with each of the dispatcher architectures, the mediating JSP or servlet handles the request from the client, providing the opportunity for the processing of common services. After the worker bean has completed its responsibility of populating the intermediate model for the JSP, the mediating component dispatches to the JSP to generate the presentation:

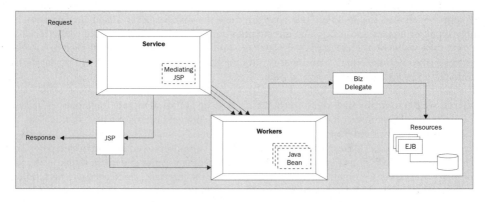

This architecture provides a cleaner separation between the view and the controller, since the JSP page is no longer making business calls, but simply accessing the state of the pre-populated worker bean. Depending on the workflow needs of the system, a decision will have to be made about the suitability of this architecture versus one where the initial delegation point is a JSP, such as the Mediator-View. The cleaner separation of view and controller is indeed an important factor in the decision as well, and often an overriding one. Certainly, if there is not a need for multiple business calls to generate the intermediate model, then this type of architecture is a good choice.

In some cases, though, we may only want portions of a model to be utilized in a display and we may not want to reuse this code across requests. If the granularity of the data access components necessitates multiple calls to retrieve the data, then the Mediator-View architecture may be better suited to handle this type of situation, since the JSP will make business calls on the beans as necessary.

JSP Technical Support

Finally, let's return to our Technical Support application from Chapter 9, and convert it to JSP-based operation. The application works in the same way as before. First, the user goes to the welcome page, and enters their e-mail address and details of their problem:

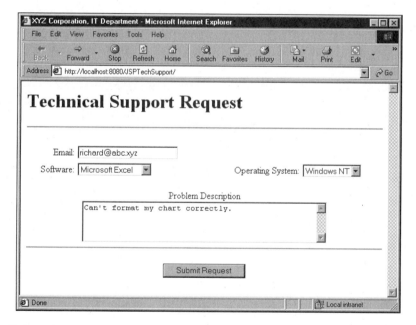

On clicking **Submit Request**, the application checks whether the user is known to the system (based on their e mail address), and if not forwards the request to the customer registration page:

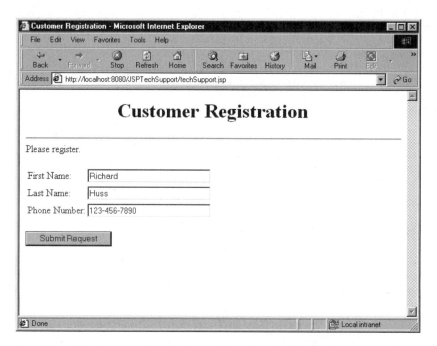

Once these details have been entered, the confirmation page is displayed:

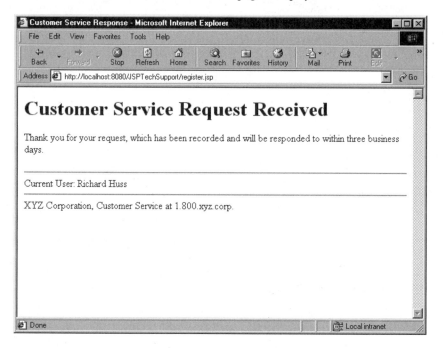

(If the user's e-mail address is already registered, the user will be taken straight to this page rather than to the registration form.)

Application Design

The broad structure of the application is roughly the same as before, except that the servlets are replaced by JSPs, with the logic removed to a JavaBean, `TechSupportBean`:

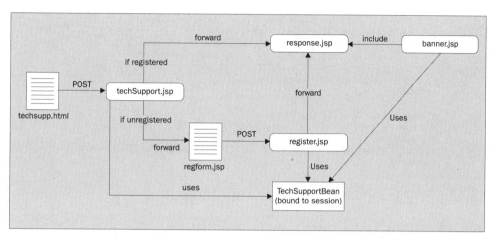

`TechSupportServlet` has been replaced by `techSupport.jsp`, `register.html` by `regform.jsp`, `RegisterCustomerServlet` by `register.jsp`, `ResponseServlet` by `response.jsp`, and `BannerServlet` by `banner.jsp`.

The `TechSupportBean` provides our 'model' of the application logic, and is used throughout the process of dealing with a support query: an instance is created in `techSupport.jsp` and bound to the session, and it is then reused in other JSPs in the application. The bean encapsulates the necessary database access code, and as information is gathered (from the forms and the database) it is stored in the bean's properties. By the time our user reaches `response.jsp`, the bean contains all the data about the support request, together with the user's details obtained either from an existing database entry or from the details supplied in the registration form. It can then be used in formulating the response to the user.

The Welcome Page

`techsupp.html` is the entry form to the system, and is virtually unchanged from the version in Chapter 9. The only difference is that we now use the POST method and send the request from the form to `techSupport.jsp`:

```
<html>

  <head>
    <title>XYZ Corporation, IT Department</title>
  </head>
  <body>
    <h1>Technical Support Request</h1>
    <hr><br>
    <center>
      <form action="/JSPTechSupport/techSupport.jsp" method="POST">
        <table align="center" width="100%" cellspacing="2" cellpadding="2">
          <tr><td align="right">Email:</td>
            <td><input type="text" name="email" align="left"
                       size="25"></td></tr>
```

```
        <tr><td align="right">Software:</td>
            <td><select name="software" size="1">
                <option value="Word">Microsoft Word</option>
                <option value="Excel">Microsoft Excel</option>
                <option value="Access">Microsoft Access</option>
            </select></td>
            <td align="right">Operating System:</td>
            <td><select name="os" size="1">
                <option value="95">Windows 95</option>
                <option value="98">Windows 98</option>
                <option value="NT">Windows NT</option>
            </select></td></tr>
    </table>

    <br>Problem Description<br>
    <textarea name="problem" cols="50" rows="4"></textarea>
    <hr><br>
    <input type="submit" name="submit" value="Submit Request">
    </form>
  </center>
 </body>
</html>
```

This page is designated as the application's welcome file in web.xml:

```
<?xml version="1.0" encoding="ISO-8859-1"?>

<!DOCTYPE web-app
    PUBLIC "-//Sun Microsystems, Inc.//DTD Web Application 2.2//EN"
    "http://java.sun.com/j2ee/dtds/web-app_2.2.dtd">

<web-app>
  <welcome-file-list>
    <welcome-file>techsupp.html</welcome-file>
  </welcome-file-list>
</web-app>
```

The Request-Processing JSP

When the user submits a technical support request, the information from their browser is sent to techSupport.jsp. This page contains no presentation details; it creates an instance of TechSupportBean bound to the session (if one does not already exist), and uses the <jsp:setProperty> action to set the bean's email, software, os, and problem properties to the values submitted by the user.

```
<%@ page errorPage="/error.jsp" %>

<jsp:useBean id="techSupportBean" scope="session" class="TechSupportBean" />
<jsp:setProperty name="techSupportBean" property="*"/>
```

It then uses a scriptlet to call the bean's registerSupportRequest() method, which stores the support request details in the database's SUPP_REQUESTS table and checks in the CUSTOMERS table to see whether this e-mail address is already registered:

```
<% techSupportBean.registerSupportRequest(); %>
```

Finally, we use the bean's `isRegistered()` method to retrieve details of whether or not the customer was recognized, and forward the request either directly to `response.jsp` if they were, or to `regform.jsp` otherwise:

```
<% if (techSupportBean.isRegistered()) { %>
    <jsp:forward page="response.jsp"/>
<% } else { %>
    <jsp:forward page="regform.jsp"/>
<% } %>
```

The TechSupportBean

So, how does `TechSupportBean` do all this work for `techSupport.jsp`? Let's start with the easy bit – the class declaration, member variables, and the property getter and setter methods:

```
import java.sql.*;

public class TechSupportBean {

  private String email;
  private String software;
  private String os;
  private String problem;
  private String firstName;
  private String lastName;
  private String phoneNumber;

  private String driver = "COM.cloudscape.core.JDBCDriver";
  private String protocol = "jdbc:cloudscape:c:/ProJavaServer/Chapter11/
                     JSPTechSupport/WEB-INF/db;autocommit=true";

  public TechSupportBean() {
    try {
      Class.forName(driver);
    } catch(ClassNotFoundException e) {}
  }

  public void setEmail(String email) {
    this.email = email;
  }

  // ... and similarly for the software, os problem, firstName, lastName,
  // and phoneNumber properties

  public String getEmail() {
    return email;
  }

  // ... and similarly for the software, os problem, firstName, lastName,
  // and phoneNumber properties


  // ... more properties and methods ...
}
```

Note that we have also provided a constructor in which we ensure that the JDBC driver class is loaded. In a production-quality application, the driver class name and the JDBC URL would probably be read from context parameters in the deployment descriptor.

We have also provided setter and getter methods for several properties we haven't dealt with yet: firstName, lastName, and phoneNumber. These details will either be retrieved from the database (if the user is already registered), or obtained in a moment from the registration form. Remember that this bean will be used throughout the user's session, not just from techSupport.jsp.

The real work happens in the registerSupport() method, and the actual code is very similar to that in Chapter 9. We reuse the Sequencer class unchanged. (This generates the unique support request numbers from the SEQ_NO table.) The main difference is that the registerSupportRequest() method does not actually forward the request itself – it simply sets a boolean property, registered, which is true if the user is registered, and which can be accessed from the controlling JSP. If the customer was registered, we additionally set the bean's firstName, lastName, and phoneNumber properties so they can subsequently be accessed from other JSPs:

```
private boolean registered;

public void registerSupportRequest() throws SQLException {

  int requestId = 0;
  Connection connection = null;
  String insertStatementStr =
    "INSERT INTO SUPP_REQUESTS VALUES(?, ?, ?, ?, ?)";
  String selectCustomerStr =
    "SELECT CUSTOMERS.FNAME, CUSTOMERS.LNAME, CUSTOMERS.PHONE FROM CUSTOMERS " +
    "WHERE CUSTOMERS.EMAIL = ?";

  try {
    connection = DriverManager.getConnection(protocol);

    PreparedStatement insertStatement =
      connection.prepareStatement(insertStatementStr);
    requestId = Sequencer.getNextNumber(protocol);

    insertStatement.setInt(1, requestId);
    insertStatement.setString(2, email);
    insertStatement.setString(3, software);
    insertStatement.setString(4, os);
    insertStatement.setString(5, problem);

    insertStatement.executeUpdate();

    // Now verify if the customer is registered or not.
    PreparedStatement selectStatement =
      connection.prepareStatement(selectCustomerStr);
    selectStatement.setString(1, email);

    ResultSet rs = selectStatement.executeQuery();
```

```
      if (rs.next()) {
        setFirstName(rs.getString("FNAME"));
        setLastName(rs.getString("LNAME"));
        setPhoneNumber(rs.getString("PHONE"));

        // The customer was registered -we can go straight to the
        // response page
        registered = true;
      } else {

        // Customer is not registered - need to go to the registration form
        registered = false;
      }
    }
    finally {
      if (connection != null) {
        try {
          connection.close();
        } catch (SQLException sqle) {}
      }
    }
  }


  public boolean isRegistered() {
    return registered;
  }
```

That's it for the moment in `TechSupportBean`, but we will need to come back and add one more method shortly.

The Registration Form

If the user was not registered, the request is forwarded to `regform.jsp`, where a registration form is displayed. In this version of the application, this page is a JSP simply so that a POST request can be forwarded to it, though we could of course add further personalization to the form using the details entered so far.

The code is very simple, and again is very similar to the corresponding page in the servlet version of the application:

```
<html>
  <head>
    <title>Customer Registration</title>
  </head>
  <body>
    <center><h1>Customer Registration</h1></center>
    <hr>
      Please register.
      <form action="/JSPTechSupport/register.jsp" method="POST">
        <table>
          <tr><td>First Name:</td>
<td><input type="text" name="firstName" size="30"></td></tr>
          <tr><td>Last Name:</td>
```

```
            <td><input type="text" name="lastName" size="30"></td></tr>
        <tr><td>Phone Number:</td>
            <td><input type="text" name="phoneNumber" size="30"></td></tr>
      </table>
      <br><input type="submit" value="Submit Request">
    </form>
  </body>
</html>
```

With the details entered, the user can submit their registration to `register.jsp`.

The Registration JSP

```
<%@ page errorPage="/error.jsp" %>

<jsp:useBean id="techSupportBean" scope="session" class="TechSupportBean" />
<jsp:setProperty name="techSupportBean" property="*"/>

<% techSupportBean.registerCustomer(); %>

<jsp:forward page="response.jsp"/>
```

This is very reminiscent of `techSupport.jsp`, but if anything even simpler. We set the bean's `firstName`, `lastName`, and `phoneNumber` properties from the details supplied in the form, and call the bean's `registerCustomer()` method to enter these details in the database:

```
// In TechSupportBean.java

public void registerCustomer() throws SQLException {

  Connection connection = null;
  String insertStatementStr = "INSERT INTO CUSTOMERS VALUES(?, ?, ?, ?)";
  try {
    connection = DriverManager.getConnection(protocol);

    PreparedStatement insertStatement =
      connection.prepareStatement(insertStatementStr);
    insertStatement.setString(1, email);
    insertStatement.setString(2, firstName);
    insertStatement.setString(3, lastName);
    insertStatement.setString(4, phoneNumber);

    insertStatement.executeUpdate();

  }
  finally {
    if (connection != null) {
      try {
        connection.close();
      } catch (SQLException sqle) {}
    }
  }
}
```

Finally, the request is forwarded to `response.jsp`.

The Response and Banner JSPs

By now, whether the user was registered or not, the request will have been forwarded to `response.jsp` and the `TechSupportBean`'s properties will be fully populated with details of the user and their support request. `response.jsp` prints out a simple message, using a static 'include' to incorporate the banner page footer, `banner.jsp`:

```
<%@ page errorPage="/error.jsp" %>
<html>
<head><title>Customer Service Response</title></head>
<body>
<h1>Customer Service Request Received</h1>

<p>Thank you for your request, which has been recorded and will be
responded to within three business days.</p>

<%@ include file="/banner.jsp" %>

</body></html>
```

`banner.jsp` itself simply accesses the bean once more to extract and print the user's name:

```
<jsp:useBean id="techSupportBean" scope="session" class="TechSupportBean" />

<hr>
Current User:
<jsp:getProperty name="techSupportBean" property="firstName" />
<jsp:getProperty name="techSupportBean" property="lastName" />
<hr>
XYZ Corporation, Customer Service at 1.800.xyz.corp.<br>
```

The Error Page

Finally, we provide a simple error page, `error.jsp`, which is referenced by all the JSPs which might fail during processing:

```
<%@ page isErrorPage="true" %>

<html>
<head>
  <title>XYZ Corporation, IT Department</title>
</head>
  <body>
    <h1>Technical Support</h1>

    <p>We're sorry, an error occurred processing your request.</p>

    <p>You got a <%= exception %>

  </body>
</html>
```

Deploying the Application

All that remains is to ensure that the necessary files are in the correct directories, and that the Java classes are compiled:

- ❑ The JSPs themselves simply go in `C:\ProJavaServer\Chapter11\JSPTechSupport`

- ❑ Place `web.xml`, as usual, in the `C:\ProJavaServer\Chapter11\JSPTechSupport\WEB-INF` directory

- ❑ The Java source files `TechSupportBean.java` and `Sequencer.java` go in `C:\ProJavaServer\Chapter11\JSPTechSupport\src`

- ❑ Compile the Java source files into the `C:\ProJavaServer\Chapter11\JSPTechSupport\WEB-INF\classes` directory by running the command

```
javac -d ..\WEB-INF\classes *.java
```

  from the `src` directory

- ❑ Set up the database: if you're using CloudScape, use the same database schema as before, but make sure you create the database tables in `c:\ProJavaServer\Chapter11\JSPTechSupport\WEB-INF\db` this time:

```
CREATE TABLE SUPP_REQUESTS(REQUEST_ID INTEGER PRIMARY KEY,
                           EMAIL VARCHAR(40),
                           SOFTWARE VARCHAR(40),
                           OS VARCHAR(40),
                           PROBLEM VARCHAR(256));

CREATE TABLE SEQ_NO(NEXT_NO INTEGER);

INSERT INTO SEQ_NO VALUES(0);

CREATE TABLE CUSTOMERS(EMAIL VARCHAR(40) PRIMARY KEY,
                       FNAME VARCHAR(15),
                       LNAME VARCHAR(15),
                       PHONE VARCHAR(12));
```

- ❑ Make sure you update `server.xml` to reference this application:

```
<Context path="/JSPTechSupport"
         docBase="c:\ProJavaServer/Chapter11/JSPTechSupport">
</Context>
```

- ❑ Finally, you can start Tomcat and request the appropriate URL, `http://localhost:8080/JSPTechSupport`.

So, how have we fared in converting the technical support application to JSP? The use of a JavaBean to encapsulate the database access and application logic has avoided a lot of the pitfalls into which we might otherwise have fallen. The JSPs divide cleanly into two groups:

❑   Those providing flow control and updating the application model, `techSupport.jsp` and `register.jsp`, which contain no HTML markup and do not create the response themselves

❑   Pages comprised largely of HTML, with only occasional action and expression tags: `regform.jsp`, `response.jsp`, `banner.jsp`, and `error.jsp`

This clean architecture will provide a good basis for any future enhancements to the application.

Summary

In this chapter we've talked about JSP syntax, constructs, semantics, and JSP design paradigms, and have seen a simple but clearly designed application. There is still a lot to cover , but with what has been covered in this chapter, and your own knowledge of HTML, you can start develop JSP-based dynamic web applications. The JSP syntax isn't really too complicated, so if you understand what was presented in this section you're ready to be productive with JSPs.

It is also worth keeping mind that writing JSPs can sometimes be painful, especially without an IDE. This is mainly because debugging a JSP page is not as easy as debugging a Java program with `jdb` or your favorite debugger. You would actually need to debug the generated servlet and relate it back to the JSP source; there are quite a few products now that allow you do this (for example, Enhydra and JBuilder).

In the next chapter, we will move on to look at a major new feature of the JSP 1.1 specification: **tag extensions**.

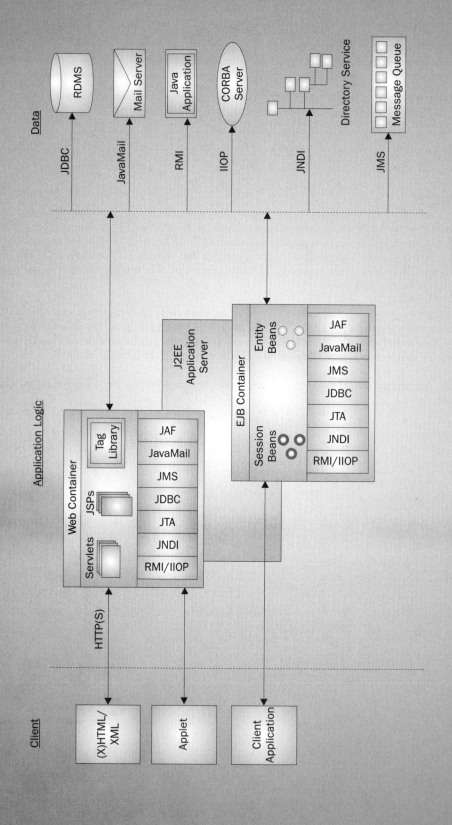

12

JSP Tag Extensions

From the point of view of the JSP developer, the only significant new feature of JSP 1.1 is support for **tag extensions** (often referred to as **custom tags**). However, this proves to be very significant indeed.

Tag extensions look like HTML (or rather, XML) tags embedded in a JSP page. They have a special meaning to a JSP engine at translation time, and enable application functionality to be invoked without the need to write Java code in JSP scriptlets. Well-designed tag extension libraries can enable application functionality to be invoked without the appearance of programming.

So in this chapter, we'll look at the basics of writing your own tags and then in the next chapter we'll look at some more advanced examples. So in this chapter we will cover:

- ❏ Tag extension basics
- ❏ The anatomy of a tag extension
- ❏ How to deploy a tag library
- ❏ How to write custom tag extensions

Let's get started then with what tag extensions are all about.

Tag Extension 101

Consider the `<jsp:forward>` action provided by the JSP specification. This tag dispatches the current request to another page in the current web application. It can be invoked with the following syntax:

```
<jsp:forward page="next.jsp" />
```

We can also to add additional parameters to the request before forwarding with an extended usage of `<jsp:forward>`, which nests one or more `<jsp:param>` tags within the `<jsp:forward>` tag:

```
<jsp:forward page="next.jsp" >
  <jsp:param name="image" value="house.gif" />
</jsp:forward>
```

Tag extensions allow a vast range of new functionality to be added to the JSP language and they can be invoked in a similarly intuitive way. For example, I could create a tag named `<wrox:forward>`, specify what attributes and subtags, if any, it requires, and implement it to perform a custom action before forwarding. Not only can this be added simply into the web page, it enforces separation of code and presentation, decouples the call from the class that implements the functionality associated with the tag, and can be simply incorporated into a design tool.

The key concepts in tag extensions are:

❑ **Tag name:**
A JSP tag is uniquely identifed by a combination of **prefix** (in this case jsp), and **suffix** (in this case forward), separated by a colon.

❑ **Attributes:**
Tags may have attributes, which use the XML syntax for attributes. The `<jsp:forward>` tag above has one attribute (page), while the `<jsp:param>` attribute has two (name and value). Attributes may be required or optional.

❑ **Nesting:**
Note how the `<jsp:param>` subtag is used in the second example above. Tag extensions can detect nested tags at runtime and cooperate. A tag directly enclosing another tag is called the *parent* of the tag it encloses: in the example above, the `<jsp:forward>` tag is the parent of the `<jsp:param>` tag.

❑ **Body content:**
This is anything between the start and end elements in a JSP tag, excluding subtags. A tag extension can access and manipulate its body content. Neither the `<jsp:forward>` nor `<jsp:param>` tags require body content. We will see later an example of a tag that can reverse its body content. It will be invoked like this (the body content is shown in bold):

```
<examples:reverse>
   Able was I ere I saw Elba
</examples:reverse>
```

The functionality associated with a tag is implemented by one or more Java classes. The tag handler (the class implementing the tag itself) is a JavaBean, with properties matching the tag's XML attributes. A Tag Library Descriptor (TLD) file is an XML document that describes a tag library, which contains one or more tag extensions. The JSP `taglib` directive must be used to import the tag library's tags in each JSP that wishes to use any of them.

Why, besides a clever syntax, might we choose to use tag extensions rather than JSP beans? Are tag extensions not simply another way of allowing JSP pages to parcel out work to Java classes?

Due to the richer interaction between the hosting JSP page and tag extensions, tag extensions can achieve directly what beans can only achieve in conjunction with scriptlets. Tag extensions may access the `PageContext`, write output to the output writer, redirect the response, and define scripting variables. As an indication of their power, *all* the standard JSP actions provided via tags of form `<jsp:XXXX>` could be implemented using tag extensions. The behavior of tag handlers is configured by their XML attributes and their body content (which can be the result of evaluating JSP expressions at runtime).

Typical uses of tag extensions are:

- ❑ To conceal the complexity of access to a data source or enterprise object from the page (possibly, the page author, who may not be experienced with enterprise data)

- ❑ To introduce new scripting variables into the page

- ❑ To filter or transform tag content, or even interpret it as another language

- ❑ To handle iteration without the need for scriptlets

Tag extensions can be used to deliver a range of functionality limited only by developers' imaginations and sensible programming practice.

Tag extensions differ from beans in that they are common building blocks, not tailored resources for a particular page or group of pages. Tags receive the attributes that control their behavior from the JSP pages using them, not the request to a particular JSP (as in the case of request-bean property mappings). A well-designed tag extension may be used in many JSP pages.

This reusability is particularly important. Since their implementation and interaction with the JSP engine is well defined in the JSP 1.1 specification, libraries of tag extensions can be developed and distributed, on a commercial or open source basis. Generic tags can be developed for particular industries or application types.

Tag extensions, although new to JSP, are a very old concept in dynamic page generation. Products such as Apple's WebObjects and BroadVision have delivered rich functionality through custom tags for years, although in a proprietary context. This experience in the use of custom tags can be valuable to JSP developers.

Tag extensions are a particularly welcome addition to the JSP developer's armory because they are easy to implement. The API surrounding them is relatively simple, and it is possible to use them to achieve results quickly. This is a reflection of the elegance of the design of the tag extension mechanism; in the true Java spirit it delivers rich functionality without excessive complexity.

> *The examples and most of the discussion in this chapter and the next assume that tag extensions will be used to generate HTML markup. While this is currently their most likely use, tag extensions can be used to generate any content type supported by JSP.*

A Simple Tag

Before we look at the API supporting tag extensions and the supporting infrastructure in detail, let's implement a simple tag. The simplest case is a tag without attributes or body content, which outputs some HTML. We'll add some dynamic content to prove that the tag is alive. Say we want to see the following output:

Hello world.
My name is <tag handler implementation class> and it is now <date and time>

We'll call our simple tag `hello`. Here's how we might use it in a JSP. I've named this simple example `hello.jsp`. The first line is a declaration used to import the tag library, which we will discuss in detail later:

```
<%@ taglib uri="/hello" prefix="examples" %>

<html>
  <head>
    <title>First custom tag</title>
  </head>
  <body>
    This is static output.
    <p />
    <i>
      <examples:hello></examples:hello>
    </i>
    This is static output again.
  </body>
</html>
```

All we need to do to implement the tag is to define a tag handler (a Java class implementing the tag's functionality), and provide the tag library descriptor. We can then import the tag library into any JSP that requires it.

The tag handler class must react to callbacks from the JSP engine when the tag is encountered in JSPs. The most important of these are `doStartTag()`, called when the opening of the tag is encountered, and `doEndTag()`, called when the closing tag is encountered. The implementation of `HelloTag` is quite simple, as most of the work of implementing the custom tag is done by the `TagSupport` superclass provided by the JSP 1.1 API. Don't worry if some of the details are puzzling: we'll look at this class, as well as the API it uses, in more detail in a moment. Note that the tag has access to the `PageContext` object of each JSP that uses it.

```
package tagext;

import java.io.IOException;
import java.util.Date;
import javax.servlet.jsp.*;
import javax.servlet.jsp.tagext.*;

// Implementation of a tag to generate a single piece of HTML
public class HelloTag extends TagSupport {
```

```
   // This method will be called when the JSP engine encounters the start
   // of a tag implemented by this class
   public int doStartTag() throws JspTagException {
     // This return value means that the JSP engine should evaluate
     // the contents and any child tags of this tag
     return EVAL_BODY_INCLUDE;
   }

   // This method will be called when the JSP engine encounters the end
   // of a tag implemented by this class
   public int doEndTag() throws JspTagException {
     String dateString = new Date().toString();
     try {
       pageContext.getOut().write("Hello world.<br/>");
       pageContext.getOut().write("My name is " + getClass().getName() +
                                  " and it's " + dateString + "<p/>");
     } catch (IOException ex) {
       throw new JspTagException
              ("Fatal error: hello tag could not write to JSP out");
     }

     // This return value means that the JSP engine should continue to
     // evaluate the rest of this page
     return EVAL_PAGE;
   }
} // class HelloTag
```

The tag library descriptor, which we'll name `hello.tld`, is required to map the tag to the tag handler class and defines the way JSPs may interact with the `HelloTag` class. The tag library descriptor is an XML document conforming to a DTD specified by Sun Microsystems:

```
<?xml version="1.0" encoding="ISO-8859-1" ?>
<!DOCTYPE taglib
        PUBLIC "-//Sun Microsystems, Inc.//DTD JSP Tag Library 1.1//EN"
        "http://java.sun.com/j2ee/dtds/web-jsptaglibrary_1_1.dtd">
<taglib>
  <tlibversion>1.0</tlibversion>
  <jspversion>1.1</jspversion>
  <shortname>examples</shortname>

  <info>Simple example library.</info>

  <tag>
    <name>hello</name>
    <tagclass>tagext.HelloTag</tagclass>
    <bodycontent>JSP</bodycontent>
    <info>Simple example</info>
  </tag>
</taglib>
```

The tag's suffix when used in JSPs must be `hello`, and its prefix is `examples`.

Note that as a tag library can include any number of tags, we'll add extra `<tag>` elements to this tag library descriptor for the remaining examples in this chapter.

Once everything is in the right place (see **Getting it running** below), `hello.jsp` should look like this in your browser:

You might wish to experiment to see what happens when you fail to close the tags, or try to access tags that are not found in your imported tag library. The resulting error messages are not specified in the JSP 1.1 specification, but most implementations should be reasonably informative and helpful.

Getting it Running

I'll discuss deployment options for tag libraries in more detail later, but in the meantime, let's look at how we can get this example running in Tomcat or any other server that supports the JSP 1.1 and Servlet 2.2 specifications.

If you have Tomcat, you can get started very quickly by copying `hello.war` (see instructions below) to the webapps directory in the Tomcat installation directory. Once you have done that, start Tomcat and type `http://localhost:8080/hello/hello.jsp` in your favorite browser. The output as above should come up. Below is included a somewhat more detailed explanation of how this works.

The best option is to package the tag library descriptor, the Java classes that implement the tags in the library, and the JSPs that use the tags in a single, self-contained, Web ARchive file, or WAR, as we have done here. This file can then be loaded into a JSP 1.1-compliant JSP engine and constitutes a self-contained **application**, with its own **context path** on the web server. (A context path is the directory under the server root at which the server publishes the top-level directory of the contents of the WAR. For example, the contents of the root directory of our WAR are published by the web server at `<server root>/tagext`, assuming that `tagext` is the name we give our application when we load it into the server. The WAR's internal directory structure will determine the published directory structure *under* the context root.)

Remember that a WAR is a JAR file, with special directories and a file named `web.xml` located in its `/WEB-INF` directory. The following shows the structure of the WAR file for this simple example; the source can be found under the folder `hello` in the code download:

```
hello.jsp
META-INF/
        MANIFEST.MF
WEB-INF/
        web.xml
        classes/
                tagext/
                        HelloTag.class
        tlds/
              hello.tld
```

There are a few WAR conventions specific to using tag libraries. We should place our tag library descriptor files in the `WEB-INF/tlds` directory. We need to use a special element in the `web.xml` file, `<taglib>`, to let the server know where to find the tag library's TLD within the WAR when JSPs in the WAR attempt to import it. The following is the `web.xml` file for the simple example:

```xml
<?xml version="1.0" encoding="UTF-8"?>

<!DOCTYPE web-app PUBLIC '-//Sun Microsystems, Inc.//DTD Web Application 2.2//EN'
'http://java.sun.com/j2ee/dtds/web-app_2.2.dtd'>

<web-app>
  <display-name>tagext</display-name>
  <description>Tag extensions examples</description>

  <session-config>
    <session-timeout>0</session-timeout>
  </session-config>

  <!-- Tag Library Descriptor -->
  <taglib>
    <taglib-uri>/hello</taglib-uri>
    <taglib-location>/WEB-INF/tlds/hello.tld</taglib-location>
  </taglib>

</web-app>
```

The easiest way to create the WAR is first to create the directory structure corresponding to the WAR's structure in your development environment. All we then need to do to build the WAR is to then issue the following command in the WAR's root directory. Note that we exclude the `.java` source files, which would unnecessarily inflate our WAR and may cause problems when we attempt to deploy it:

```
jar -cvf hello.war META-INF/MANIFEST.MF WEB-INF/classes/tagext/*.class WEB-
INF/tlds/hello.tld WEB-INF/web.xml *.jsp
```

As mentioned above, deploying this WAR on Tomcat 3.1 simply requires copying the WAR into the $TOMCAT_HOME/webapps directory. When Tomcat is started, it automatically unpacks the WAR and creates the application, with the application's name (and context path) being the name of the WAR. There is no need to make any changes to the system or server classpath. Each web application will be given its own classloader at runtime.

There is another way of deploying WARs in Tomcat, which is much more convenient during development. Tomcat lets us work on a WAR that exists not as a single file, but as an expanded directory structure. This makes development a lot easier. It's not necessary to restart Tomcat when changes are made to the JSPs, and it's not necessary to rebuild the archive every time you make a change, yet it's very easy to build the WAR when it is ready for release. To use this approach, add the following lines to the `server.xml` file, which is located in the `$TOMCAT_HOME/conf` directory. The `<Context>` element is a subelement of `<ContextManager>`.

```
<Context path="/tagext" docBase="<path to root of war>"
         defaultSessionTimeOut="30" isWARExpanded="true"
         isWARValidated="false" isInvokerEnabled="true"
         isWorkDirPersistent="false" />
```

`<path to root of war>` will be an absolute path following the directory convention of your operating system, and need not be under the Tomcat directory tree. I deployed this WAR on Windows NT, using `docBase="c:\ProJavaServer\Chapter12\hello"`. On a Unix system I might have used `docBase="/home/johnsonr/ProJavaServer/Chapter12/hello"`. (Note that Tomcat requires only single backslashes for Windows paths, unlike many Java programs, which require double backslashes.) Note the `isWARExpanded` attribute in the Tomcat `<Context>` element above.

Remember that WARs are portable. Other JSP engines will use different deployment conventions to those of Tomcat, but the WAR itself will not change. In JRun 3.0, the deployment process is as simple, and managed by a web interface. To deploy our application, log into the JRun Management Console (JMC), select the desired server from the tree in the left hand frame (the JRun Default Server is the correct choice for deployment in a new installation), and choose the WAR Deployment link. You will be prompted to select the path to the WAR, the application name – in this case, `tagext` – and the application URL (`/tagext`). Once the form is complete, press the Deploy button. When you see the message confirming successful deployment, restart JRun (also through the JMC), and your new web application will be available. If you used the default configuration, it will be published at `http://localhost:8100/tagext/`.

The following screenshot shows the JRun Management Console's WAR deployment form filled in with the values from my system for the examples in this chapter:

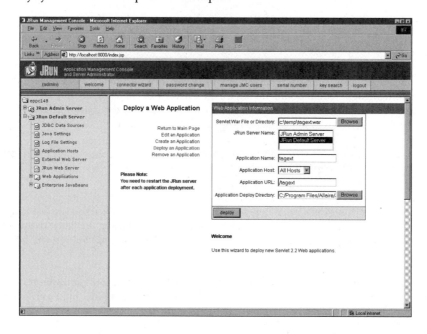

Anatomy of a Tag Extension

Before we return to our simple example, let's cover some basic theory of tag extensions.

A number of components are required to implement a tag extension. The minimal requirement is a tag handler and a tag library descriptor.

- ❏ A **tag handler** is a Java bean implementing one of two interfaces defined in the `javax.servlet.jsp.tagext` package, `Tag` or `BodyTag`. These interfaces define the lifecycle events relevant to a tag; most importantly, the calls the class implementing the tag will receive when the JSP engine encounters the tag's opening and closing tags.

- ❏ A **tag library descriptor**, as we have seen, is an XML document containing information about one or more tag extensions.

More complex tags will require an additional class extending the abstract class `javax.servlet.jsp.tagext.TagExtraInfo` to provide information about scripting variables that are made available to JSPs through the use of tags.

`TagExtraInfo` subclasses may also perform custom validation of tag attributes. Of course, the classes implementing a tag may require any number of helper classes, which will need to be packaged with the tag for it to be a complete deployable unit.

Before tags can be used in a JSP, the **taglib** directive must be used to import a tag library and associate the tags it contains with a prefix.

Let's look at each of these requirements in turn.

Tag Handlers

When the JSP engine encounters a tag extension in a JSP at translation time, it parses the tag library descriptor to find the required tag handler class, and generates code to obtain, and interact with, the tag handler. The `Tag` or `BodyTag` interfaces, one of which must be implemented by any tag handler, define callbacks that the servlet resulting from the JSP engine's code generation will make to the tag handler instance at runtime.

> *For performance reasons, JSP engines will not necessarily instantiate a new tag handler instance every time a tag is encountered in a JSP. Instead, they may maintain a pool of tag instances, reusing them where possible. When a tag is encountered in a JSP, the JSP engine will try to find a Tag instance that is not being used, initialize it, use it and release it (but not destroy it), making it available for further use. The programmer has no control over any pooling that may occur. The repeated use model is similar to a servlet lifecycle, but note one very important difference: tag handler implementations don't need to concern themselves with thread safety. The JSP engine will not use an instance of a tag handler to handle a tag unless it is free. This is good news: as with JSP authoring in general, developers need to worry about threading issues less often than when developing servlets.*

The javax.servlet.jsp.tagext.Tag Interface

The Tag interface defines a simple interaction between the JSP engine and the tag handler, sufficient for tags that don't need to manipulate their body content. Its core methods are the calls implementing classes will receive when the JSP engine encounters the tag's opening and closing tags, doStartTag() and doEndTag(). Before we look at the method contracts in more detail, a sequence diagram helps to visualize the calls made to the tag handler by the compiled servlet. Assume that the container already has a tag handler instance available, and in the default state:

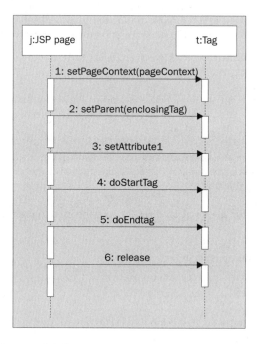

Let's look at the messages in more detail:

- ❑ The container initializes the tag handler by setting the tag handler's pageContext property, which the tag handler can use to access information available to the JSP currently using it.

- ❑ The container sets the tag handler's parent property. (Parent may be set to null, if the tag is not enclosed in another tag.)

- ❑ Any tag attributes defined by the developer will be set. This is a mapping from the XML attributes of the tag to the corresponding properties of the tag handler bean. For example, in the case of a tag invoked like this: <mytags:test name="John" age="43" />, the container will attempt to call the setName() and setAge() methods on the tag handler. The container will attempt to convert each attribute to the type of the corresponding bean property: for example, the String "43" will be converted to an int in this case. If the type conversion fails, an exception will be thrown and must be handled by the calling JSP page. (From a JSP's point of view, there is no difference between an exception thrown by a tag handler and one thrown by an expression of scriptlet in the page.)

❏ Next, the container calls the tag handler's doStartTag() method.

❏ The container calls the doEndTag() method.

❏ The container calls the release() method. This is not equivalent to a finalizer. Tag handlers differ from page beans in that their lifecycle is entirely independent of that of the JSPs that use them. Tag handlers must support repeated use before destruction, possibly in a number of JSPs. The implementation of the release() method must ensure that any state that may cause conflict in future uses is reset, and that any resources required during the tag's execution are freed.

Lets look at the doStartTag() and doEndTag() methods:

int doStartTag() throws JspException

Called after the tag has been initialized, when the JSP engine encounters the opening of a tag at run time. Its return value should be one of two constants defined in the Tag interface: EVAL_BODY_INCLUDE, which instructs the JSP engine to evaluate both the tag's body and any child tags it has, or SKIP_BODY, which instructs the JSP engine to ignore the body. This can throw a JspException, as will most of the methods in the tag handler API when an error condition is encountered; how it will be handled will depend on the JSP page using the tag. Most JSP pages will use an error page, so an exception thrown in a tag will abort the rendering of the page.

int doEndTag() throws JspException

doEndTag() is called when the JSP engine encounters the closing tag of an element at run time. Its return value can be EVAL_PAGE or SKIP_PAGE. EVAL_PAGE will cause the JSP engine to evaluate the rest of the page, SKIP_PAGE to terminate evaluation of the page. The SKIP_PAGE return value should be used only with very good reason; using tag handlers to terminate page evaluation is even worse than sprinkling random return statements in Java code, and may be confusing to the reader. A legitimate use might be to terminate page output if it is established that the user has insufficient privileges to view the whole of the page.

There are also a number of methods that relate to tag nesting, initialization, and reuse:

Tag getParent()
void setParent()

The specification also requires methods to expose the parent property. A tag's parent is the tag that directly encloses it in a JSP, or null if there is no enclosing tag. Tag implementations can query their parent at runtime, to obtain context information:

void setPageContext (PageContext pc)

setPageContext() is an initialization method, making the PageContext of the JSP available to the tag.

void release()

release() is a call to the tag handler to release any resources. Examples of this may be closing JDBC connections or open sockets that the handler requires for its function and to clear any state associated with it. The second is an often overlooked task in this context.

The javax.servlet.jsp.tagext.BodyTag Interface

BodyTag extends Tag, adding extra callbacks and other methods allowing the developer to work with the content of the tag.

A sequence diagram displays the interaction between calling JSP and tag handler in the case of a body tag; as you can see, it is somewhat more complex than that of the Tag interface:

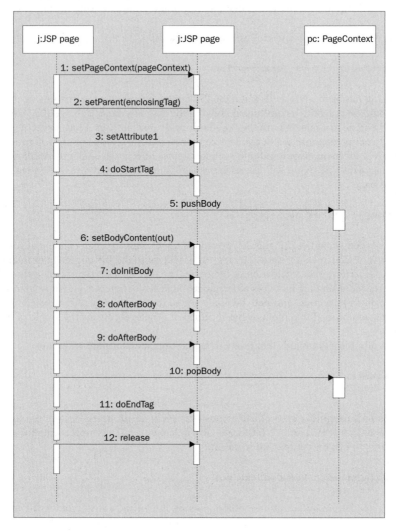

The extra steps involve the preservation of the JSP's JSPWriter (messages 5 and 10), and the possibility of repeated calls to the doAfterBody() method, which enables the BodyTag implementation to take control of the tag's execution at runtime.

The more significant methods of the `BodyTag` interface are listed below.

int doInitBody() throws JspException

Called after the tag has been initialized and `doStartTag()` has been called. Its return value should be `EVAL_BODY_TAG`, in which case the tag's body content and any child tags will be evaluated, or `SKIP_BODY`, in which case the body will be ignored. Watch out that you don't try to return `EVAL_BODY_INCLUDE` from a `BodyTag`'s `doInitBody()` or `doStartTag()` methods. The JSP engine will throw a `JspException` if it detects this.

int doAfterBody() throws JspException

`doAfterBody()` is called each time the tag's body has been processed. The return values are `EVAL_BODY_TAG` and `SKIP_BODY`. `EVAL_BODY_TAG` directs the JSP engine to evaluate the tag's body and any child tags *again* (resulting in at least one more call to this method), `SKIP_BODY`, causes processing of the body content to terminate. This can be used to conditionally loop through the tag content.

void setBodyContent(BodyContent bodyContent)

Initialization method to set the class used to manipulate body content.

The javax.servlet.jsp.tagext.BodyContent Class

The `BodyContent` class is the key to `BodyTag` functionality. `BodyContent` is a subclass of `JspWriter` that can be used to manipulate the body content of `BodyTag` implementations and store it for later retrieval. The `getBodyContent()` method of `BodyTagSupport` returns the `BodyContent` instance associated with a particular tag.

To understand the way in which the `BodyContent` class works, consider how `JspWriter` objects are handled in JSPs using `BodyTags`: messages 5 and 10 from the sequence diagram above. Before the `BodyTag` begins to evaluate its body content, the generated JSP implementation class includes the following line:

```
out = pageContext.pushBody();
```

After the `BodyTag`'s methods have been called, it includes a matching call:

```
out = pageContext.popBody();
```

What this means is that each `BodyTag` has a kind of play area, enabling it to manipulate its `BodyContent` without automatically affecting the `JspWriter` of the enclosing JSP page or tag. To generate output, the `BodyTag` needs to write the contents of its `BodyContent` into its enclosing writer explicitly (see below). This is the key difference between `BodyTags` and `Tags`: `Tag` implementations have no such flexibility, and therefore cannot modify or suppress their body content, although they can prevent it from being evaluated altogether by returning `SKIP_BODY` in their implementation of `doStartTag()`.

539

The most interesting methods in the `BodyContent` class are:

void clearBody()

Clears the body content. Useful if we want to manipulate the body content before writing it out.

JspWriter getEnclosingWriter()

Returns the enclosing `JspWriter`; this may be the writer of an enclosing tag, or the writer of a JSP itself. We normally use this method to get a JSP writer to which we can write the body content stored in a body tag when we have finished manipulating it. For example, we have used the following lines of code in the `doEndTag()` method of a number of `BodyTag` implementations in this chapter:

```
BodyContent bodyContent = getBodyContent();
if (bodyContent != null) {
  bodyContent.getEnclosingWriter().write(sbOut.toString());
}
```

This ensures that if there is any body content held in the body tag, it will be written to the enclosing JSP writer.

String getString()

This returns the content already held in the body content, as a `String`. This is useful if we need to examine what has been added to the body content with each iteration of a loop.

Convenience Classes

Some of the methods in `Tag` and `BodyTag` will be implemented the same way in most tags. So the `javax.servlet.jsp.tagext` package includes two convenience implementations of `Tag` and `BodyTag`: `TagSupport` and its subclass `BodyTagSupport`. Classes implementing tag extensions will normally be derived from one of these. The class diagram below shows the relationship between these classes and the `Tag` and `BodyTag` interfaces:

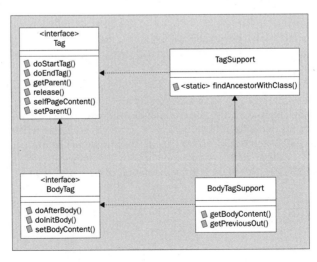

`TagSupport` and `BodyTagSupport` are concrete, not abstract classes, so they provide complete implementations of the corresponding interfaces, which do nothing except return the appropriate values to cause the JSP engine to continue rendering the page. So developers can safely omit methods that they are not interested in. Developers don't usually concern themselves with handling the `parent` property and `setPageContext()`. The `release()` method can also be omitted if it is not necessary to free resources or return the tag to its default state. The methods that a developer *will* normally want to override are `doStartTag()` and `doEndTag()` for all tags, and `doInitBody()` and `doAfterBody()` for `BodyTags` specifically.

`TagSupport` also makes an important convenience variable available to subclasses: `pageContext` (the saved `PageContext` which was set by the JSP engine when the tag was first used in a page). `BodyTagSupport` provides a `getBodyContent()` method, necessary to obtain a tag's `BodyContent` before manipulating it.

> *Like me, you might find the names* TagSupport *and* BodyTagSupport *confusing. These classes are standard implementations of the* Tag *and* BodyTag *interfaces. It should be pointed out that this naming is inconsistent with Sun's usual practice and Java convention; I think of them as* TagImpl *and* BodyTagImpl.

The javax.servlet.jsp.tagext.TagExtraInfo Class

Metadata classes extending the `TagExtraInfo` abstract class may be associated with tag handlers to provide extra information to a JSP engine. This optional association is specified in the tag library descriptor.

We will look at the implementation of a `TagExtraInfo` class in more detail later in this chapter, but the two methods you are most likely to override are:

```
VariableInfo[] getVariableInfo(TagData td)
```

This method is used to return information about scripting variables that the tag makes available to JSPs using it. It returns an array of `VariableInfo` objects, which contain information about the name of each scripting variable and its fully qualified class name. It describes whether or not the variable should be declared or whether the tag will merely overwrite the value of an existing variable, and the scope of the variable.

```
boolean isValid(TagData data)
```

This is sometimes used to validate the attributes passed to a tag at translation time. As an example, consider a tag with four attributes. Three may be optional, but if one of the optional attributes is specified the whole three must be present. There is no way to specify this behavior in a tag library descriptor. However, the `isValid()` method of the appropriate `TagExtraInfo` subclass could be implemented to return `false` if the parameters supplied at translation time are invalid. The default implementation of `isValid()` in `TagExtraInfo` always returns `true`. Note that *runtime* attribute validation is entirely different, and is the responsibility of the tag handler concerned.

Objects Available to Tag Handlers

All tag handlers have access to more context information than do most beans. This is available through the `PageContext` object they are passed on initialization. As you'll recall, `javax.servlet.jsp.PageContext` is a convenient holder for information about the runtime of a JSP page, including the `request` and `response` objects, and references to objects such as beans associated with the JSP.

This amount of access equals power. Note, though, that it is poor style to modify `request` and `response` directly from a tag handler. Custom tags should be thought of as generic building blocks intended for use in a wide variety of contexts. In practice tags should not be concerned with the parameters passed to the JSP page. Although a tag handler *can* access request parameters, relying on doing so will greatly reduce its reusability.

The Simple Example Revisited

To catch our breath after all this theory, let's look again at the Java implementation of the simple example we introduced earlier. We see that the tag handler extends `TagSupport`, and so gets most of its functionality for free. It has no state and accesses no file or other resources, so there is no need to override `release()`. We use `doEndTag()` to access the `PageContext`, obtain a `JspWriter`, and generate output:

```java
package tagext;

import java.io.IOException;
import java.util.Date;
import javax.servlet.jsp.*;
import javax.servlet.jsp.tagext.*;

//  Implementation of a tag to generate a single piece of HTML.
public class HelloTag extends TagSupport {

//  This method will be called when the JSP engine encounters the start
//  of a tag implemented by this class
  public int doStartTag() throws JspTagException {
    // This return value means that the JSP engine should evaluate
    // the contents and any child tags of this tag
    return EVAL_BODY_INCLUDE;
  }

//  This method will be called when the JSP engine encounters the end
//  of a tag implemented by this class
  public int doEndTag() throws JspTagException {
    String dateString = new Date().toString();
    try {
      pageContext.getOut().write("Hello world.<br/>");
      pageContext.getOut().write("My name is " + getClass().getName() +
                          " and it's " + dateString + "<p/>");
    }
    catch (IOException ex) {
      throw new JspTagException
              ("Fatal error: hello tag could not write to JSP out");
    }

    // This return value means that the JSP engine should continue to
    // evaluate the rest of this page
    return EVAL_PAGE;
  }
}  // class HelloTag
```

Note that we need to check for `IOExceptions` when generating output. Any exception encountered while processing the tag must be wrapped as a `JspException` if it is to be rethrown; it is good practice to use the `javax.servlet.jsp.JspTagException` subclass of `JspException`. (Note that, confusingly, this *isn't* in the same package as the other classes specific to tag handlers.)

We could actually have omitted the `doStartTag()` method. I include it for completeness, but in fact it does exactly what its superclass `TagSupport`'s `doStartTag()` method does: instruct the JSP engine to evaluate the tag's content and any subtags.

Tag Library Descriptors

Tag Library Descriptors or **TLD**s are XML documents with a `.tld` extension that describe one or more tag extensions. TLDs must conform to the Document Type Definition (DTD) included in the JSP 1.1 specification. Many of the elements are intended to provide support for JSP authoring tools, although such tools are yet to be widely available in the market.

The root element is `<taglib>`. It's defined in the DTD by:

```
<!ELEMENT taglib
  (tlibversion, jspversion?,
  shortname, uri?, info?,
  tag+) >
```

❏ `tlibversion` is the version of the tag library implementation. This is defined by the author of the tag library.

❏ `jspversion` is the version of JSP specification the tag library depends on. At the time of writing the value you should use is 1.1 (the default). The element is optional.

❏ `shortname` is a simple default name that could be used by a JSP authoring tool; the best value to use is the preferred prefix value: that is, a suggestion as to a prefix to use when importing the tag library. Although there is no way of enforcing this, hopefully developers using the library will follow this suggestion, and consistency will be achieved between all users of the tag library. The `shortname` should not contain whitespace, and should not start with a digit or underscore.

❏ `uri` is an optional URI uniquely identifying this tag library. If it is used, the value will normally be the URL of the definitive version of the tag library descriptor.

❏ `info` is an arbitrary text string describing the tag library. Think of it as the equivalent of a Javadoc comment relating to an entire class or package; the authoring tool may display it when the tag library is imported.

The `<tag>` element is the most important. It's defined in the DTD as:

```
<!ELEMENT tag
  (name, tagclass, teiclass?,
  bodycontent?, info?, attribute*) >
```

❏ `name` is the name that will identify this tag (after the tag library prefix).

❏ `tagclass` is the fully qualified name of the tag handler class that implements this tag. This class must implement the `javax.servlet.jsp.tagext.Tag` interface.

❏ `teiclass` stands for `TagExtraInfo` class, and defines the subclass of `javax.servlet.jsp.tagext.TagExtraInfo` that will provide extra information about this tag at runtime to the JSP. Not all tags require a `TagExtraInfo` class.

❑ `bodycontent` is an optional attribute specifying the type of body content the tag should have. Three values are legal: `tagdependent`, `JSP`, and `empty`. The default (and most useful) is `JSP`, which means that the tag's body content will be evaluated at run time like any other JSP content. `tagdependent` signifies that the JSP engine should *not* attempt to evaluate the content, but accept that while it may not understand it, it means something to the tag handler, and should therefore be passed unchanged. `empty` is useful when a tag should not have any body content. If this value is used, and the tag is not empty, JSP translation will fail.

`<attribute>` sub-elements describe each attribute accepted (or required) by the tag. The DTD definition is:

```
<!ELEMENT attribute
  (name, required?, rtexprvalue?) >
```

❑ `name` is the name of this attribute, as it will appear in JSPs using the tag.

❑ `required` specifies whether or not this attribute is mandatory. The valid values are `true` (the attribute is required), and `false` (the default, signifying an optional attribute). The attribute may have a default value.

❑ `rtexprvalue` specifies whether the attribute value can be the result of a JSP expression, or whether it has a fixed value at translation time when the tag is used in a JSP. Valid values are `true` and `false`. Again, the default is `false`, meaning that expressions are forbidden. If `rtexprvalue` is `true`, the following will be legal:

```
<examples:mytag attrib="<%=myObject.getValue()%>">
```

Allowing attributes to take expression values can be very useful. Setting attributes by the use of expressions allows their behavior to be determined at runtime. For example, very often tag attributes will be set to the value of properties of JSP beans. This relies on the use of a JSP expression.

The simple example's TLD was very straightforward. As this tag takes no attributes and has no associated `TagExtraInfo` class, only the bare minimum of elements is required:

```
<?xml version="1.0" encoding="ISO-8859-1" ?>
<!DOCTYPE taglib
        PUBLIC "-//Sun Microsystems, Inc.//DTD JSP Tag Library 1.1//EN"
        "http://java.sun.com/j2ee/dtds/web-jsptaglibrary_1_1.dtd">
<taglib>
  <tlibversion>1.0</tlibversion>
  <jspversion>1.1</jspversion>
  <shortname>examples</shortname>

  <info>Simple example library.</info>

  <tag>
    <name>hello</name>
    <tagclass>tagext.HelloTag</tagclass>
    <bodycontent>JSP</bodycontent>
    <info>Simple example</info>
  </tag>
</taglib>
```

> Although the XML structure is not complex, and at present TLDs will usually be written
> by hand, as JSP 1.1 becomes more widely supported tool support can be expected. This
> will synchronize TLDs and the relevant Java classes, avoiding time-wasting trivial errors.

Using Tag Extensions in JSP Pages

Unlike the standard actions such as `<jsp:forward>`, custom tags must be explicitly imported into JSP pages that wish to use them. The syntax for the `taglib` directive is shown below:

```
<%@ taglib uri="http://www.tagvendor.com/tags/tags.tld" prefix="examples" %>
```

The `uri` attribute tells the JSP engine where to find the TLD for the tag library. The `prefix` attribute tells the JSP engine what prefix will be given to tags from this library in the remainder of the JSP.

A JSP may import any number of tag libraries. The `taglib` directive will cause an exception at translation time if the tag library cannot be located; the first attempted access to any tag defined in the TLD will cause an exception at runtime if all the classes required to support the tag implementation cannot be loaded.

Once the tag library has been imported into the page, tags in a library can be called as follows:

```
<examples:someTag name="Rod">
...
</examples:someTag>
```

The way in which custom tags are used in JSPs is an example of Sun's efforts to introduce XML conventions into JSP syntax. Note that, unlike HTML attributes, the attributes of custom tag *must* be enclosed in double quotes, in accordance with the XML specification. (Of course it is good practice to write XML compliant HTML markup, but browsers do not currently enforce it.) Tag prefixes use the same syntax as XML namespaces.

When a tag requires no body content, it is best to use the XML shorthand to make this explicit:

```
<examples:hello name="Rod" />
```

> Tag prefixes are defined in JSPs, not, as one might expect, in tag libraries. Choice of prefix
> is a matter for developers, but consistency among JSP pages importing the same tag
> library is advisable. It is best to adopt the value of the **shortname** element in the tag
> library. The prefixes **jsp:**, **jspx:**, **java:**, **javax:**, **servlet:**, **sun:**, and **sunw:** are
> reserved. It's perhaps unfortunate that Sun has not defined a unique naming system such
> as the Java package naming system for tag library prefixes. Choosing a prefix unique to a
> company or organization is advisable: for example, instead of using the potentially
> clashing short name **tables**, it might be advisable to use **myCompany_tables**.

Deploying and Packaging Tag Libraries

There are three main ways of deploying and using tag libraries with a JSP engine. JSP developers must be familiar with all three, because each of them calls for slightly different syntax in the taglib directive. (This means that JSPs need to be modified slightly if they are to be deployed in a different way – surely an oversight in the JSP specification.)

No Packaging

The first and simplest means of deployment is simply placing the tag library descriptor under the server's document root, and the Java classes required to implement the tags in the server (or system) classpath. There is no attempt to package a tag library or an application. In this case, the taglib directive will look like this:

```
<%@ taglib uri="./hello.tld" prefix="examples" %>
```

The uri is simply a path on the host server, which may be relative (as in this example) or absolute. In this approach, the tag library desciptor (although not the classes implementing the tag handler) is always publicly available: anyone could view it by simply typing in its URL. This approach is easy to work with, but can create problems at deployment time: the JSP engine or system's classpath has to be hand edited to include the classes implementing the tag.

WAR

In a second approach to deployment, the tag library descriptor, the Java classes required to implement the tags, and the JSPs that use the tag library can be shipped together as a *web application*, in a Web ARchive file (better known a WAR file). This is the approach we've taken in this chapter. It is very attractive because it offers painless portability between servers and very easy deployment. In this case, the taglib directive will look like this:

```
<%@ taglib uri="/hello" prefix="examples" %>
```

Note that we don't specify the actual filename of the TLD, so there is no need to use the TLD extension. The server knows where to look in the current web application's WAR for a .tld file matching this URI because the mapping from URI to file location is specified in the web.xml file in a <taglib> element. The complete web.xml file for our simple example looked like this:

```
<?xml version="1.0" encoding="UTF-8"?>

<!DOCTYPE web-app PUBLIC '-//Sun Microsystems, Inc.//DTD Web Application 2.2//EN'
'http://java.sun.com/j2ee/dtds/web-app_2.2.dtd'>

<web-app>
  <display-name>tagext</display-name>
  <description>Tag extensions examples</description>

  <session-config>
    <session-timeout>0</session-timeout>
  </session-config>

  <taglib>
    <taglib-uri>/hello</taglib-uri>
```

```
        <taglib-location>/WEB-INF/tlds/hello.tld</taglib-location>
    </taglib>

</web-app>
```

The `<taglib>` element contains two subelements: `<taglib-uri>` specifies the URI that should be used in JSPs wishing to use the tag library; `<taglib-location>` specifies the path to the tag library descriptor relative to the `web.xml` file. Note that this path need not be publicly available to users of the web server: the server will not publish anything that is in the `WEB-INF` directory.

Remember the important directories in the WAR:

❑   `WEB-INF`:
    This contains the `web.xml` file, in which the TLD URI-location mapping must be specified.

❑   `WEB-INF/classes`:
    This contains Java classes required to implement tag libraries or otherwise support the functionality of the web application.

❑   `WEB-INF/lib`:
    This contains JAR files containing additional classes required to support the functionality of the web application.

❑   `WEB-INF/tlds`:
    By convention (although not mandated in any specification) this contains the tag library descriptors (but not tag handler classes) that will be made available to JSPs in the `web.xml` file. The TLDs could actually be placed anywhere in the WAR (so long as a mapping is included in the `web.xml` file), but adhering to this convention makes it easier to comprehend the WAR's structure.

Tag Library JAR

In a third approach to packaging and deployment, a tag library may be distributed in a JAR file whose `META-INF` subdirectory contains the tag library descriptor. The JAR file should also contain the classes required to implement the tags defined in the tag library, but *not* the JSPs that use the tag library. In this case, the `taglib` directive in JSP pages should refer to this JAR, which must be available to the JSP engine via a URL (or mapped URL). This enables custom tags to be supplied in self-contained units – a vital precondition for the successful distribution of third-party custom tags.

The `taglib` directive will look like this:

```
<%@ taglib uri="/tagext/hellotags.jar" prefix="examples" %>
```

The easiest way to JAR tag extension classes is to create a `META-INF` directory containing the tag library descriptor (renamed `taglib.tld` if necessary) under the root of your Java package hierarchy (that is, parallel to `com`). The `jar` tool can then be invoked easily from the root directory. The example below shows the process of creating a JAR file from the second group of examples in the next chapter, and the eventual contents of the file. The `viewJar` directory is the base of the Java package tree (here containing only the `jspstyle` package):

A recursive directory listing reveals the following files:

```
\viewJar\
        jspstyle\
                CellTag.class
                CellTagExtraInfo.class
                HeadingCloseTag.class
                HeadingOpenTag.class
                HeadingTag.class
                HeadingTagExtraInfo.class
                ListTag.class
                ListTagExtraInfo.class
                NameValueModel.class
                NameValueTag.class
                NameValueTagExtraInfo.class
                RowCloseTag.class
                RowOpenTag.class
                RowsTag.class
                RowsTagExtraInfo.class
                RowTagsExtraInfo.class
                StyledXMLTag.class
                TableTag.class
        META-INF\
                taglib.tld
```

The JAR file can be created running the command:

```
jar -cvf viewslib.jar jspstyle/*.class /META-INF
```

in the \viewJar directory.

The JAR's contents, shown by the command:

```
jar -tvf viewslib.jar
```

will be:

```
META-INF/
        MANIFEST.MF
        taglib.tld
jspstyle/
        CellTag.class
        CellTagExtraInfo.class
        HeadingCloseTag.class
        HeadingOpenTag.class
        HeadingTag.class
        HeadingTagExtraInfo.class
        ListTag.class
        ListTagExtraInfo.class
        NameValueModel.class
        NameValueTag.class
        NameValueTagExtraInfo.class
        RowCloseTag.class
```

```
RowOpenTag.class
RowsTag.class
RowsTagExtraInfo.class
RowTagsExtraInfo.class
StyledXMLTag.class
TableTag.class
```

Note that although I wrote this particular example using Windows NT, the `jar` tool (which is written in Java) uses identical syntax when running on other operating systems.

> *Warning: Tomcat 3.1 can produce translation errors if* `.java` *source files are included in tag library JARs.*

Combination of WAR and JAR

A combination of the second and third delivery methods is often useful. For example, consider a web application that uses a tag library that may also be of value in other web applications. The best approach is to package the tag library as a JAR, place this JAR in the `/META-INF/lib` directory of the web application's WAR, and create a mapping in the WAR's `web.xml` file to the tag library's TLD. This approach works well; the only issue is that the TLD must be extracted from the tag library JAR for it to be picked up by the `web.xml` file or JSPs in the WAR. Unfortunately the `<taglib>` element's mapping does not work directly to a JARed tag library. The tag library JAR can be directly imported into JSPs if it is publicly accessible, under the web application's root, but this is somewhat less elegant. It's seldom a good idea to publish more information than is strictly necessary.

This combination approach will be used later in the next chapter, as we'll need to reuse some of the tags to support the application developed in Chapter 14.

Writing Tag Extensions

Once the initial concepts are grasped, implementing tag extensions is surprisingly easy.

Processing Attributes

Our simple example is all very well, but it doesn't take advantage of the dynamic potential of custom tags. We *could* interrogate the `PageContext` to implement context-specific behavior, but there are far better alternatives.

> **The easiest way to parameterize tags is to pass in XML attributes.**

How do we make our tags handle attributes? The answer, not surprisingly, is that attributes in a TLD `tag` element map onto bean properties of the corresponding tag handlers. The mapping of attributes onto tag handler properties is, as we might expect, handled by the JSP engine using reflection and not only does it work with primitive types, we can pass *any* type to a tag handler. (Draft versions of the JSP 1.1 specification included a `type` subelement of the `attribute` TLD element; this has now been removed.)

Attributes can be either required or optional. This is specified in the TLD, as is whether attributes can take the value of JSP expressions at runtime, as we mentioned earlier.

Let's suppose we decide to pass a name as an attribute, and change our simple example to display the following:

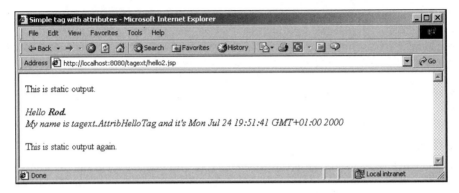

First, we need to write a tag handler with a name property. With this minor change, it's pretty much like HelloTag:

```java
package tagext;

import java.io.IOException;
import java.util.Date;
import javax.servlet.jsp.*;
import javax.servlet.jsp.tagext.*;

// Hello tag accepting a name attribute.
public class AttribHelloTag extends TagSupport
{
  private String  name;

  // Property getter for name
  public String getName() {
    return name;
  }

  // Property setter for name
  public void setName(String name) {
    this.name = name;
  }

  public int doEndTag() throws JspTagException {
    String dateString = new Date().toString();
    try {
      pageContext.getOut().write("Hello <b>" + name + "</b>.<br/>");
      pageContext.getOut().write("My name is " + getClass().getName() +
                                 " and it's " + dateString + "<p/>");
    }
    catch (IOException ex) {
      throw new JspTagException("Hello tag could not write to JSP out");
    }
    return EVAL_PAGE;
  }
}
```

You should save this in `WEB-INF/classes/tagext`. Don't be tempted to omit the property 'getter', which at first sight seems unnecessary. The JavaBeans specification requires both getter and setter for a bean property, and some JSP engines may rely on the presence of both methods at translation time. (JRun 3.0, unlike Tomcat, seems to rely on getters to determine property types.)

Now we must add a tag entry to our TLD describing the new tag, and specifying that it requires an attribute, `name`:

```
<tag>
  <name>helloAttrib</name>
  <tagclass>tagext.AttribHelloTag</tagclass>
  <bodycontent>JSP</bodycontent>
  <info>Simple example with attributes</info>
  <attribute>
    <name>name</name>
    <required>true</required>
    <rtexprvalue>true</rtexprvalue>
  </attribute>
</tag>
```

The JSP container will throw an exception if the required `name` attribute is not specified, and the attribute can be set with the runtime value of an expression, as well as with a static string (the value of `rtexprvalue` being `true`).

The calling JSP, `hello2.jsp`, is identical to `hello.jsp`, except for the way in which we invoke the tag itself:

```
<%@ taglib uri="/hello" prefix="examples" %>

<html>
  <head>
    <title>Simple tag with attributes</title>
  </head>
  <body>
    This is static output.
  <p />
  <i>
    <examples:helloAttrib name="Rod">
    </examples:helloAttrib>
  </i>

    This is static output again.
  </body>
</html>
```

Attributes are an excellent way of controlling tag behavior at runtime, and are especially valuable in ensuring that tags are generic and reusable.

Elegant as the attribute/property mechanism is, there is one annoying problem with passing `String` attributes to tags. Specifying some characters in attributes is messy. The double quote character, for example, is (for obvious reasons) illegal in an attribute, and we must use the entity reference `&quot;` if we want to include it. This rapidly becomes unreadable if the data includes multiple quotation marks. Attributes are also unsuited to handling lengthy values, for reasons of readability.

551

So there are limits to what can sensibly be achieved with attributes. Where complicated markup is concerned, consider the alternatives:

❑   Processing markup and expressions in the body of the tag, possibly repeatedly

❑   Defining a subtag that configures its ancestor. This is an advanced strategy, which we'll look at later in the following chapter

❑   Implementing the tag to read its markup from a template file or URL

The most elegant of these solutions, where feasible, is to manipulate the tag body. This will only be useful if the tag defines scripting variables that the tag body can use.

> *There is a curious and confusing inconsistency in JSP syntax when non-*`String`* tag attributes are the results of JSP expressions. Let's suppose we want to pass an object of class* `examples.Values` *(a kind of list) to a tag extension. The syntax:*
>
> ```
> <wrox:list values="<%=values%>"
> ```
>
> *is problematic, because we know from the JSP specification that an expression "is evaluated and the result is coerced to a* `String` *which is subsequently emitted into the current* `out` `JspWriter object`*". In the case of the custom tag above, however, the value of the expression is* not *coerced to a* `String`*, but passed to the tag handler as its original type.*

Body Content

So far we have used tags only to generate markup, we haven't considered what custom tags may do to their body content (anything found between their start and end tags).

Let's suppose we modify `hello.jsp` to add some code inside one of the tags, like this:

```
<examples:hello>
   This is tag content!
</examples:hello>
```

The result, shown by `tagcontent.jsp`, is that the content we have added is output in addition to any output generated by the tag. Whether the content appears before or after the tag's output depends on whether we chose to do tag output in the `doStartTag()` or `doEndTag()` methods. In the case of the `HelloTag`, the output will appear *before* the tag's own output, as shown in `tagcontent.jsp`:

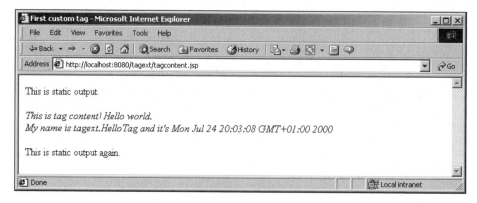

Tag content will be treated at run time as JSP (so long as the body content is set in the TLD to be JSP), so it may include expressions. Try modifying the last example like this:

```
<examples:hello>
This is tag content containing an expression: 37 * 16 = <%= 37 * 16 %>
</examples:hello>
```

Scriptlets are also legal, as is any other valid JSP content. The following will produce the same result:

```
<examples:hello>
<% int a = 37; %>
<% int b = 16; %>
This is tag content containing expressions and scriptlets:
       <%=a%> * <%=b%> = <%= a * b %>
</examples:hello>
```

The output in either case as shown in `tcexpr.jsp` is:

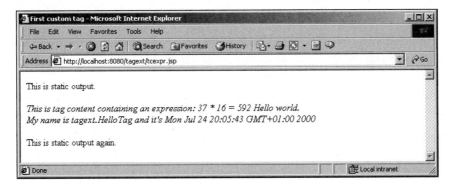

To do anything really useful with body content, however, we need to make our tags define scripting variables, or manipulate body content.

Tags Introducing Scripting Variables

We don't always want tags to produce output themselves. It's very useful for custom tags to introduce new scripting variables into the page, allowing calling JSPs to control the presentation without performing the processing involved in determining the content. Accordingly, there is a mechanism to allow tag extensions to define scripting variables.

Three steps are required to introduce scripting variables in a custom tag:

- ❑   Specify a `TagExtraInfo` class in the tag's entry in the TLD
- ❑   Implement the `TagExtraInfo` class to define the names and types of the variables
- ❑   Write code to add the variables to the `PageContext` in the tag handler itself

Let's look at these steps in turn.

Specifying a TagExtraInfo Class

As we have seen, a `TagExtraInfo` class can be associated with the tag by adding a `<teiclass>` element to the appropriate `<tag>` element in the TLD. It is good practice to follow the simple convention of naming your `TagExtraInfo` subclass for tag `xxxxTag` as `xxxxTagExtraInfo`. (Some developers prefer the shorter, but less self-documenting, form `xxxxTEI`.)

Implementing the TagExtraInfo Class

The implementation of the `TagExtraInfo` class is straightforward, once we understand the concepts involved. We will need to override the `getVariableInfo()` method for this:

```
VariableInfo[] getVariableInfo(TagData td)
```

The key to understanding how the scripting variable mechanism works is the `VariableInfo` class. We are only interested in the single constructor:

```
VariableInfo(String varName, String className, boolean declare, int scope);
```

Let us examine each parameter in turn:

- **Variable Name** (`varName`) is the name by which the scripting variable will be accessed in the JSP. It must be a legal Java identifier.

- **Class Name** (`className`) should be the fully qualified name of the variable's type. In practice, it will not be tested by the JSP engine at translation time, but used directly in code generation. For example, if `String` is specified for variable `name`, the JSP engine will generate a declaration such as `String name;` in the Java class representation of the JSP page.

- **Declare** (`declare`) is a `boolean` parameter that controls whether a *new* variable is to be created, or whether the tag will simply update the value of a variable already in the calling JSP page's `PageContext`. It is generally better practice to create new variables, although this may cause a translation-time error if the JSP has already used the variable name. Name conflicts can also arise if the same tag is nested, and descendants try to create new variables with the same name while an earlier one is still in scope. If the `declare` parameter is `true`, and a new variable is to be created, the JSP engine can generate Java code to declare a variable in the same way as a scriptlet may declare a variable: in the `_jspService()` method. In either case, the JSP will obtain the value for the variable set by the tag handler by looking in the `PageContext`.

- **Variable Scope** (`scope`). There are three types of scope defined for variables introduced within custom tags: `NESTED`, `AT_BEGIN`, and `AT_END`. If `NESTED` scope is specified, the variables are available to the calling JSP only within the body of the defining tag. (They will remain visible even if other tags are invoked within the defining tag.) If `AT_BEGIN` scope is specified, the variables will be available to the remainder of the calling JSP after the start of the defining tag. If `AT_END` scope is specified, the variables will be available to the remainder of the calling JSP after the end of the defining tag. Unless this is a strong reason for using the variables after the tag has been closed, the preferred scope is `NESTED`. In JSP pages, as in programming generally, additional variables introduce complexity.

Changes to the Tag Handler

We must not forget to modify the tag handler itself. Before they can be available to JSPs using the tag, variables must be added to the `PageContext` like this:

```
pageContext.setAttribute("variableName", myObject);
```

An Example

Suppose we've decided we'd like our `Hello` tag to be more configurable. Having "Hello" and other English text hard coded makes it little use in other language environments. Suppose we decide to use the tag to provide all the dynamic values we've seen it output (name, class name and date), but control the presentation entirely in the JSP.

First, we need to write a `TagExtraInfo` implementation to define the scripting variables; save this in the usual directory:

```
package tagext;

import javax.servlet.jsp.tagext.*;

// Class defining variables available to JSPs using VarHelloTag.
public class VarHelloTagExtraInfo extends TagExtraInfo {

  public VariableInfo[] getVariableInfo(TagData data) {
    return new VariableInfo[] {

      // The use of NESTED scope means that these scripting variables
      // will only be available inside the VarHelloTag.
      new VariableInfo("name", "java.lang.String", true, VariableInfo.NESTED),
      new VariableInfo("className", "java.lang.String", true,
                       VariableInfo.NESTED),
      new VariableInfo("date", "java.util.Date", true, VariableInfo.NESTED)
    };
  }
}
```

The tag handler itself is very simple, but differs from those we've seen so far in that it generates no markup. All it does is add values for the variables defined in the `TagExtraData` class to the `PageContext` in its `doStartTag()` method. (As these variables are only available within the tag, it would be useless to add them in the `doEndTag()` method.)

```
package tagext;

import java.io.IOException;
import java.util.Date;
import javax.servlet.jsp.*;
import javax.servlet.jsp.tagext.*;

// Simple tag handler with one attribute.
//   Generates no markup, but defines three scripting
// variables: name, className and date.
```

```
// @see VarHelloBodyTagExtraInfo
public class VarHelloTag extends TagSupport {
  private String  name;

  public String getName() {
    return name;
  }

  public void setName(String name) {
    this.name = name;
  }

  public int doStartTag() throws JspTagException {
    // Make the variables available to calling JSPs
    pageContext.setAttribute("name", name);
    pageContext.setAttribute("className", getClass().getName());
    pageContext.setAttribute("date", new Date());
    return EVAL_BODY_INCLUDE;
  }
}
```

The TLD entry is similar to those we have seen: only the addition of the `<teiclass>` element specifying the `TagExtraInfo` class associated with the tag handler is required to make the scripting variables available to calling pages:

```
<tag>
  <name>helloVars</name>
  <tagclass>tagext.VarHelloTag</tagclass>
  <teiclass>tagext.VarHelloTagExtraInfo</teiclass>
  <bodycontent>JSP</bodycontent>
  <info>Simple example defining scripting variables</info>
  <attribute>
    <name>name</name>
    <required>true</required>
    <rtexprvalue>true</rtexprvalue>
  </attribute>
</tag>
```

The calling JSP, `hello3.jsp`, can now do all the work of rendering the output:

```
<%@ taglib uri="/hello.tld" prefix="examples" %>

<html>
  <head>
    <title>Bonjour</title>
  </head>
  <body>

    HTML.
  <p/>

  <i>
```

```
    <examples:helloVars name="Isabelle">
      Bonjour <%=name%>. Je m'appelle <%=className%>.<br/>
      C'est <%=date%><p/>
    </examples:helloVars>
  </i>

    Plus de HTML.

  </body>
</html>
```

The screen output will be:

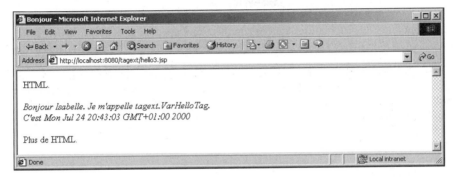

Note that we don't *need* to use the scripting variables we've created. The contents of the
`examples:helloVars` tag could be static, in which case they it would be output unchanged, or the tag
could be empty, in which case it would produce no HTML output at all.

> Note that because the scripting variables introduced by tags must be placed in the
> `PageContext` by the JSP engine, only object variables can be created. This is a minor
> annoyance when we would really like a primitive type. Also remember that, even if they
> are never accessed, the values of all the scripting variables must still be computed and
> placed in the `PageContext`.

Body Tags

What we've done so far with body content and scripting variables, using the `Tag` interface, is all very fine, but
it still doesn't help us to do anything really exciting with a tag's body content. What if we want to suppress the
content under some circumstances, filter it, or repeat it a number of times?

To do this, we need a richer API. Remember the `BodyTag` interface? The two methods we need are
`doInitBody()` and `doAfterBody()`. `doAfterBody()` is especially useful, as it enables us to decide after
each time the tag's body content has been processed whether to continue processing it, or move onto the end tag.

557

Body Tags and Iteration

One of the most common uses of body tags is to handle iteration. Control flow is handled much more cleanly in Java classes (such as tag handlers) than in JSPs, so placing iteration in custom tags can improve JSPs dramatically.

Let's modify our `VarHelloTag` to say hello to a number of people, using the `name` variable, and make the other scripting variables we've already used, `className` and `date`, available only *after* the looping of the tag has been completed.

We'll need to change the property passed in from a single `String` (name) to an indexed type. I've used `java.util.List`. We'll also need an instance variable to control our iteration over the list. (I could have obtained an `Iterator` from the `List`, but I also want to make the current position in the list available as a scripting variable.) I've added an `index` variable for this.

Handling the output of this tag requires a more complex implementation than we've seen before. I've used a `StringBuffer` to hold the output until we're ready to write it out, after list processing is complete.

The iteration is handled by the `doAfterBody()` method, which returns `EVAL_BODY_TAG` until the list has been exhausted. With each iteration, the value in the name variable is reset. At runtime, the body content of this tag will be evaluated for each element in the list, with the variable's value always up to date. The `doEndTag()` method is implemented to output the content we've built up in the `StringBuffer`:

```java
package tagext;

import java.io.IOException;
import java.util.*;
import javax.servlet.jsp.*;
import javax.servlet.jsp.tagext.*;

/**
 *  Body tag taking a list of names and iterating over its
 *  content for each name.
 *  No content will be generate for each iteration; however
 *  the scripting variable <i>name</i> will be set to each
 *  name in turn. After the close of this tag, scripting
 *  variables <i>className</i> and <i>date</i> will be available
 *  to JSPs using it.
 */
public class VarHelloBodyTag extends BodyTagSupport {
  // List of names passed in
  private List       names;

  // Where we're up to in iterating over the body content
  private int        index;

  // Output we're building up while iterating over the body content
  private StringBuffer  output = new StringBuffer();


  //  Getter for the names property/attribute
  public List getNames() {
    return names;
  }
```

```java
//  Setter for the names property/attribute
public void setNames(List names) {
  this.names = names;
}

  public int doStartTag() throws JspTagException {
  if (names.size() > 0 ) {
    setLoopVariables();
    return EVAL_BODY_TAG;

  }
  // If we get here, we have an empty list and this tag should
  // ignore any body content
  return SKIP_BODY;
  }

/**
 *  The JSP engine will call this method each time the body
 *  content of this tag has been processed. If it returns
 *  SKIP_BODY, the body content will have been processed for the
 *  last time. If it returns EVAL_BODY_TAG, the body will be processed
 *  and this method called at least once more.
 *  <p/>We store content in a StringBuffer, rather than write
 *  output directly.
 */
public int doAfterBody() throws JspTagException {
  BodyContent bodyContent = getBodyContent();
  if (bodyContent != null) {
    output.append(bodyContent.getString());
    try {
      bodyContent.clear();
    }
    catch (IOException ex) {
      throw new JspTagException("Fatal IO error");
    }
  }

  // If we still haven't got to the end of the list,
  // continue processing
  if (++index < names.size()) {
    setLoopVariables();
    return EVAL_BODY_TAG;

  }
  // If we get to here, we've finished processing the list
  return SKIP_BODY;
}

/**
 *  Called after processing of body content is complete.
 *  We use it to output the content we built up during processing
 *  of the body content.
 */
public int doEndTag() throws JspTagException {
  try {
    bodyContent.getEnclosingWriter().write(output.toString());
```

```
      }
      catch (IOException ex) {
        throw new JspTagException("Fatal IO error");
      }

      // We've finished processing.
      // Set variables for the rest of the page
      pageContext.setAttribute("className", getClass().getName());
      pageContext.setAttribute("date", new Date());

      // Process the rest of the page
      return EVAL_PAGE;
    }

    //  Make variable available for each iteration
    private void setLoopVariables() {
      pageContext.setAttribute("name", names.get(index).toString());
      pageContext.setAttribute("index", new Integer(index));
    }

  }
```

Note the call to `getBodyContent()`, to obtain the JSP content generated by each pass over the tag's body content.

This tag requires an associated `TagExtraInfo` class:

```
  package tagext;

  import javax.servlet.jsp.tagext.*;

  //  Variable information for the VarHelloBodyTag.
  public class VarHelloBodyTagExtraInfo extends TagExtraInfo {

    //  Return an array of variables set by the VarHelloBodyTag.
    public VariableInfo[] getVariableInfo(TagData data) {
      return new VariableInfo[] {
        new VariableInfo("name", "java.lang.String", true, VariableInfo.NESTED),
        new VariableInfo("index", "java.lang.Integer", true,
                         VariableInfo.NESTED),
        new VariableInfo("className", "java.lang.String", true,
                         VariableInfo.AT_END),
        new VariableInfo("date", "java.util.Date", true, VariableInfo.AT_END)
      };
    }

  }
```

Note the two scopes used, to distinguish between the loop variables and the variables to be made available after the tag has been processed.

The tag library entry is:

```
  <tag>
    <name>hellos</name>
    <tagclass>tagext.VarHelloBodyTag</tagclass>
    <teiclass>tagext.VarHelloBodyTagExtraInfo</teiclass>
    <bodycontent>JSP</bodycontent>
```

```
    <info>Simple iterative example</info>
    <attribute>
      <name>names</name>
      <required>true</required>
      <rtexprvalue>true</rtexprvalue>
    </attribute>
  </tag>
```

In the calling JSP page I've defined a `List` and added a few elements to give the tag something to display:

```
<%@ taglib uri="/hello" prefix="examples" %>

<%
  // Normally we don't declare variables, in JSPs,
  // but this example should be self-contained
  java.util.List names = new java.util.LinkedList();
  names.add("Rod");
  names.add("Isabelle");
  names.add("Bob");
%>

<html>
  <head>
    <title>Names tag</title>
  </head>
  <body>
    HTML.
    <p />

    <i>
      <examples:hellos names="<%=names%>">
        Hello <%=name%>. You're entry <%=index%> in my list.<br/>
      </examples:hellos>
      My name is <%=className%>.
      The time is <%=date%><p/>
    </i>

    More HTML.

  </body>
</html>
```

The output will be:

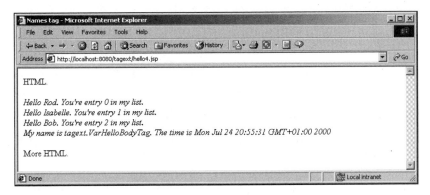

Although we developed it from our previous examples, this is close to a generic solution for list iteration, isn't it? It conceals the looping from the JSP and makes the successive list values and indices available. With minor changes, this class could take a `Collection`, or a Swing `ListModel`, and make it available to any JSP.

The main reason that this tag is so generic is that it doesn't generate markup. The more the JSP can control its output, the more useful a tag extension is.

Body Tags That Filter Their Content

Another idiomatic use of body tags is to perform filtering or other processing on their body content. This could be a simple text transformation, or could even interpret the tag's content as a custom language. The following simple example takes the tag's body content and writes it, reversed, into the calling JSP page.

Implementing the reversal is trivial; all we need to do is obtain the body content as a `String`, use it to initialize a `StringBuffer`, and call the `StringBuffer`'s `reverse()` method before writing out the resulting `String`:

```
package tagext;

import java.io.IOException;
import javax.servlet.jsp.*;
import javax.servlet.jsp.tagext.*;

// Simple body tag to reverse its content
public class ReverseTag extends BodyTagSupport {

  /*
   * Called after processing of body content is complete.
   * We use it to obtain the tag's body content and write
   * it out reversed.
   */
  public int doEndTag() throws JspTagException {
  BodyContent bodyContent = getBodyContent();
    // Do nothing if there was no body content
    if (bodyContent != null) {
      StringBuffer output = new StringBuffer(bodyContent.getString());
      output.reverse();
      try {
        bodyContent.getEnclosingWriter().write(output.toString());
      }
      catch (IOException ex) {
        throw new JspTagException("Fatal IO error");
      }
    }

    // Process the rest of the page
    return EVAL_PAGE;
  }
}
```

The tag library entry is also very simple. There are no variables requiring a `TagExtraInfo` class, and no attributes:

```
<tag>
  <name>reverse</name>
  <tagclass>tagext.ReverseTag</tagclass>
  <bodycontent>JSP</bodycontent>
  <info>Simple example</info>
</tag>
```

A simple test JSP, `reverse.jsp`:

```
<%@ taglib uri="/hello" prefix="examples" %>

<html>
  <head>
    <title>Reverse tag</title>
  </head>
  <body>
    <i>
      <examples:reverse>
        Don't try to put HTML markup in here:
        the results will be very interesting
        Hello world
      </examples:reverse>

      <p />

      <examples:reverse>
        Able was I ere I saw Elba
      </examples:reverse>
    </i>
  </body>
</html>
```

This should produce the following output:

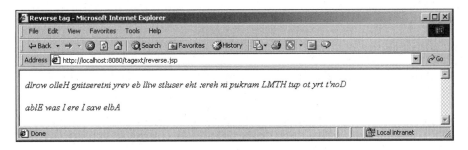

The result of placing HTML markup in the tag body will be unpredictable; hence I've used the tag twice so that I can introduce some formatting markup between the tag instances.

There are many useful applications for filtering body tags. One, which will be discussed in the next chapter, is performing an XSLT transform on XML content.

Tag Nesting

One might expect that specifying tag nesting of custom tags would be done in the TLD. However, TLDs don't allow for this, and nesting must be implemented by cooperating tag handler classes. Fortunately, the API helps us in this respect by providing methods on tag handlers we can use to obtain information about their parents and other ancestors. Although programmers of tag handlers must ensure that they enforce their desired tag nesting, the dynamic discovery of tag nesting at runtime allows for greater flexibility than would be possible if nesting were mandated in a static file. However, the absence of a formal grammar like a DTD or XML schema does place a responsibility on developers to ensure that any cooperation between tags is well documented.

Why might we use tag nesting? A common reason is to handle iteration (nested tags can simulate nested loops). Another is to let nested tags benefit from the context of the enclosing tag or tags.

Suppose we have additional information we want to display for the people named in our list, but that this information is expensive to retrieve from a database or legacy system. So we don't want the `hellos` tag to retrieve these additional fields with every iteration of the loop. (This need to retrieve regardless of usage is a disadvantage of using scripting variables.)

One solution is to use a descendant tag that draws its context from the enclosing tag and performs the additional lookups only when required: that is, only when the descendant tag is used. Let's implement a `NameTag` that requires no attributes, but retrieves additional information for the user its parent is currently processing. This information, nationality and city, will be exposed through scripting variables. Note that the child tag, like any body content, will be evaluated each time the parent iterates over its body content.

The JSP code invoking this functionality might look like this (using a scriptlet to define and display the extra information only when desired):

```
<examples:hellos names="<%=names%>" >
  Hello <%=name%>. You're entry <%=index%> in my list.
  <% if (condition) { %>
    <examples:nameInfo>
       <b>Nationality:</b> <%=nationality%> <b>City:</b> <%=city%>
    </examples:nameInfo>
  <% } %>
  <br/>
</examples:hellos>
```

To implement this, we'll first need to add a method to `VarHelloBodyTag` that exposes the necessary context, `String getName()`.

While we're at it, we'll create an interface `NameContext` that contains this new method. This way, we could make `VarHelloTag`, which already defines a `getName()` method, implement the interface and provide the necessary context for our new subtags.

> **With tag extensions, as always, remember to program to interfaces rather than concrete classes.**

The `NameContext` interface is trivial:

```
package tagext;

// Interface to provide context for nested tags
public interface NameContext {
  String getName();
}
```

So is the modification to `VarHelloBodyTag` (beyond making it implement `NameContext`) – simply the implementation of the new method:

```
//  Method from NameContext interface required to provide context to
// nested tags
public String getName() {
  return names.get(index).toString();
}
```

In a real application, we'd do some error checking here.

Now let's look at the new `NameTag` tag handler. Its main tasks are to obtain the context from an enclosing tag, and to retrieve the additional information. Note how it enforces correct nesting. There is a `getParent()` method in the `Tag` interface, but it is usually preferable to use `findAncestorWithClass()`. We don't want to limit the context in which we can use our tags. Can we guarantee that another tag or tags might not stand in the hierarchy between the two cooperating tags? If one or more do, and we have hard coded reliance on a particular parent tag class or interface, the nested tag will fail to find the ancestor it requires to provide its context.

For simplicity, I've hard coded the additional data in the class, in a hash table. For the sake of the example, imagine that this data is actually very expensive to retrieve. The extra information about people in the list will be their nationality, and the city they currently live in. My friends tend to travel quite a bit so these pieces of information may not be obviously related:

```
package tagext;

import java.io.IOException;
import java.util.*;
import javax.servlet.jsp.*;
import javax.servlet.jsp.tagext.*;

/**
 *  Tag nested within a tag implementing the NameContext interface
 *  to provide additional information about the relevant person.
 *  This information will be exposed through the <i>nationality</i>
 *  and <i>city</i> scripting variables.
 *  <br/>This tag requires no attribute, as it initializes itself from
 *  the appropriate ancestor tag.
 *  <p/>This tag produces no markup.
 */
public class NameTag extends TagSupport {
  // Data store
  private HashMap  infoHash = new HashMap();
```

```
//  Populate the data store. In a real application, this data would
//  be sourced from a database or another part of the application.
public NameTag() {
  infoHash.put("Rod", new PersonalInfo("Australian", "London"));
  infoHash.put("Isabelle", new PersonalInfo("French", "Gabon"));
  infoHash.put("Bob", new PersonalInfo("Australian", "Sydney"));
}

public int doStartTag() throws JspTagException {
  String nationality = "Unknown";
  String city = "Unknown";

  // Test whether this tag has an ancestor of the required type,
  // which we can use to obtain a name to lookup.
  // Note that using the findAncestorWithClass static method is more
  // flexible than using getParent(). getParent() will fail if
  // one or more tags separate this tag from the desired tag in
  // the runtime hierarchy of tag handlers.
  NameContext nameContextAncestor = (NameContext)
          TagSupport.findAncestorWithClass(this, NameContext.class);

  // The exception thrown here will be handled by the JSP engine as normal.
  // This will normally mean redirection to an error page.
  if (nameContextAncestor == null) {
    throw new JspTagException
            ("NameTag must only be used within a NameContext tag");
  }

  // If we get here, we have a valid ancestor from which we can obtain
  // a context.
  String name = nameContextAncestor.getName();
  PersonalInfo pi = (PersonalInfo) infoHash.get(name);
  if (pi != null) {
    nationality = pi.getNationality();
    city = pi.getCity();
  }
  pageContext.setAttribute("nationality", nationality);
  pageContext.setAttribute("city", city);
  return EVAL_BODY_INCLUDE;
}


// Inner class containing additional data retrieved for each name
private class PersonalInfo {
  private String  nationality;
  private String  city;

  public PersonalInfo(String nationality, String city) {
    this.nationality = nationality;
    this.city = city;
  }

  public String getNationality() {
    return nationality;
  }
```

```
      public String getCity() {
        return city;
      }
    }

  }
```

The `NameTag` class will require a simple `NameTagExtraInfo` class, which should contain no surprises. It simply publishes variables not published by the enclosing `VarHelloBodyTag`. Note that these scripting variables will only be available within the name tag itself, although those published by the enclosing tag will still be visible:

```
package tagext;

import javax.servlet.jsp.tagext.*;

//  Variable information for the NameTag.
//   @author  Rod Johnson
public class NameTagExtraInfo extends TagExtraInfo {

  //  Return an array of variables set by the VarHelloBodyTag.
  public VariableInfo[] getVariableInfo(TagData data) {
    return new VariableInfo[] {
      new VariableInfo("nationality", "java.lang.String", true,
                       VariableInfo.NESTED),
      new VariableInfo("city", "java.lang.String", true,
                       VariableInfo.NESTED),
    };
  }
}
```

We'll also need a new entry in our TLD file:

```
<tag>
  <name>nameInfo</name>
  <tagclass>tagext.NameTag</tagclass>
  <teiclass>tagext.NameTagExtraInfo</teiclass>
  <bodycontent>JSP</bodycontent>
  <info>Simple example of tag nesting</info>
</tag>
```

Let's now create a JSP to use the new tag, so that the additional lookup is performed part of the time. Of course normally application logic would determine this, but for the sake of the example we will simply decide this randomly.

The JSP, `hello5.jsp`, is very similar to the previous example:

```
<%@ taglib uri="/hello" prefix="examples" %>

<%
  // Normally we don't declare variables, in JSPs,
  // but this example should be self-contained
  java.util.List names = new java.util.LinkedList();
  names.add("Rod");
  names.add("Isabelle");
  names.add("Bob");
  names.add("Jens");
```

```
%>

<html>
  <head>
    <title>Nested tags</title>
  </head>
  <body>
    HTML.
    <p/>

    <i>
      <% java.util.Random rand = new java.util.Random(); %>
      <examples:hellos names="<%=names%>" >
        Hello <%=name%>. You're entry <%=index%> in my list.
        <% if (rand.nextInt(3) != 0) { %>
            <examples:nameInfo>
              <b>Nationality:</b> <%=nationality%> <b>City:</b> <%=city%>
            </examples:nameInfo>
        <% } %>
        <br/>
      </examples:hellos>
      My name is <%=className%>.
      The time is <%=date%><p/>
    </i>
      More HTML
  </body>
</html>
```

I've also added a new entry, Jens, to the list of names, to show what happens when no extra information is available. When I wrote the `NameTag` class I decided to handle this situation gracefully, as it didn't justify throwing an exception that would abort the rendering of any JSP using the tag. Instead, the placeholder value `"Unknown"` is placed in the `PageContext`. Note the use of a scriptlet inside the `<examples:hellos>` tag to perform the necessary conditional logic. This doesn't produce any output, and is evaluated each time the `<example:hellos>` tag processes its body content. Only if the condition is true – this is quasi-random in this example – will the subtag be evaluated, its variables calculated and added to the `PageContext` and its body content evaluated.

The output should look like this:

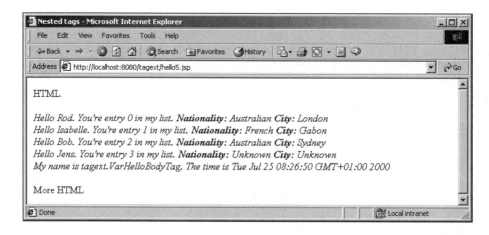

Try changing the example to move the `<examples:nameInfo>` tag outside the scope of a `<examples:hellos>` tag. Your JSP engine should provide a helpful error message, including the wording of the exception we made the `NameTag` throw in this case. The following is the page displayed by Tomcat 3.1:

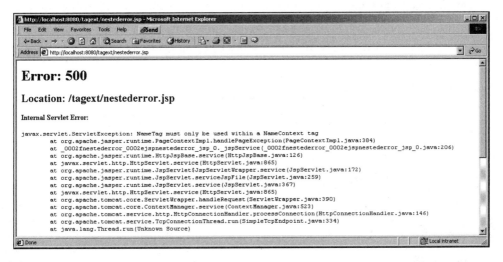

Once again we have seen the power of the ability to define scripting variables. Because the implementations of the tags don't contain any markup, we could easily use these tags to generate a content type other than HTML.

Handling Errors

What should tag handlers do if they encounter an error condition? The answer depends on whether the error is serious enough to invalidate the work of the calling JSP, and whether the tag is likely to be important enough to justify causing the calling page to redirect to an error page.

If the error is minor, the best solution is to output suitable error markup, or nothing at all, depending on the tag's purpose. An HTML comment may be added explaining the error in more detail. If the error is major, the best approach is to make the tag handler method that detects the problem throw a `JspTagException`. This will, in most cases, cause the calling page to redirect to an error page.

Tag Extension Idioms

In order to stress the mechanics of tag handlers themselves, I have deliberately used simple examples to this point. However, the range of functionality that can be delivered with tag extensions is very wide.

Some of the most important possibilities are:

❑ **Generating HTML output**
This is the simplest use of custom tags. It has some merit in that a standard building block is available, and can be changed simultaneously everywhere it occurs if necessary. However, in general, using Java code to generate HTML is clumsy and inflexible.

❑ **Using template content to generate HTML output**
A more sophisticated variant of the above, avoiding having messy markup generation in Java code and allowing modification of the generated markup without recompilation. Usually a mechanism will need to be designed and documented for controlling variable substitution and any other ways in which the template is made dynamic. An abstract class extending `TagSupport` or `BodyTagSupport` could provide standard template lookup and variable interpolation for use across a system. This is a common idiom, and can be very useful in real-world systems.

❑ **Defining scripting variables**
This is often a superior alternative to using tags to generate markup directly, especially when iteration is concerned. All computations and control flow is controlled by the tag handler classes, rather than the calling JSP, but the scripting variables are used within the JSP to allow markup generation to be changed easily. As a general rule, tags that define variables should not generate markup.

❑ **Transforming or interpreting tag body content**
This is an especially powerful use of tag extensions, with virtually unlimited potential. For example, a tag could establish a database connection and execute SQL contained in its body to display the results. A tag could implement an interpreter for a language, providing entirely new syntax and functionality within JSPs. (For example, it would be conceivable to design an `asp` tag that would interpret a subset of ASP for running legacy code.) In some of these cases, the `tagdependent` value should be used to describe the body content in the TLD.

Note that some of the possibilities of this idiom are not compatible with writing maintainable code. JSP is a standard, understood by a whole development community, whereas your tag content may not be, unless you choose some other standard such as SQL. It is also possible to create nested tags that interact in surprising ways; this also reduces readability.

❑ **A gatekeeper role**
A custom tag can check for login or some other condition, and redirect the response if the result is unsatisfactory.

❑ **Concealing access to enterprise objects or APIs that should not be visible from JSPs**
This is an easy way of providing a JSP interface to enterprise data. However, note that it is not consistent with good J2EE design to write tags that access databases via JDBC. Consider the alternative of a true n-tier architecture, in which the tag handlers access business objects such as session EJBs.

❑ **Exposing complex data**
Custom tags can be used to expose data (for example, in a list or table) that might otherwise require complicated JSP logic to display.

❑ **Handling iteration**
This is a simple and practical way of avoiding a profusion of scriptlets in JSPs. In this case it is especially important to make tags as generic as possible.

Remember that custom tags are building blocks, and will be most useful when they can be reused easily. The following principles help to make tag extensions reusable:

❑ Make tags as configurable as possible. This can be achieved through tag attributes and using nesting to provide context. Optional attributes can be used where default values can be supplied.

❑   Avoid generating HTML in your tag handler unless absolutely necessary.

❑   When tags handlers *must* generate HTML, ensure that the generated HTML can be used in a wide variety of contexts: try to avoid <html>, <form>, and other structural tags. Consider reading the HTML from a template file.

❑   Avoid making custom tags do unexpected things to the request and response. Just because tag handlers can access these objects through the PageContext does not mean it's a good idea. For example, how obvious will it be to a reader of a JSP using a custom tag that the tag may redirect the response? Unless the tag's documentation is scrupulous, figuring this out might require plunging into the tag's Java implementation. Consider another example: if a tag were to flush the JSP's output buffer, the JSP engine would be unable to redirect to an error page if anything went wrong in the rendering of the rest of the JSP. (The page would be in an illegal state, attempting redirection after it had written to the HTTP response.) This would limit the usefulness of the tag and, again, the behavior would be a challenge for a JSP developer to figure out.

When and how to use tag extensions is further discussed in Chapter 14, Writing Maintainable JSP Pages. Remember, however, that some caution is called for in using custom tags. Using too many tag extensions can make JSPs unreadable: the end result will be your own language, which may be the most efficient approach to solving a particular problem, but won't be intelligible to an outside observer, especially if your tags cooperate in complex ways.

Summary

JSP 1.1 tag extensions, or custom tags, are a powerful extension to the JSP model. Their use is limited only by the ingenuity of developers, and they will become an essential building block of well-engineered JSP interfaces.

Tag extensions can access the JSP PageContext. Their behavior can respond dynamically to the XML attributes they are invoked with, and their body content. They are implemented using:

❑   Java classes implementing tag behavior

❑   XML Tag Library Descriptor (TLD) files describing one or more tags, and the attributes they require

❑   Optional extra classes defining scripting variables introduced into the page by the custom tag

Tag extensions are a valuable way of separating presentation from content in JSP interfaces. Since they are a standard part of JSP 1.1, libraries of third party tags can be developed, and will become increasingly valuable building blocks in JSP development.

Importantly, tag extensions are very easy to develop, once the initial concepts are grasped. The tag extension mechanism achieves the goals expressed in the JSP 1.1 specification, that it should be portable, simple, expressive, and built upon existing concepts and machinery.

In the next chapter we will go on to look at some more complex examples of tag extensions.

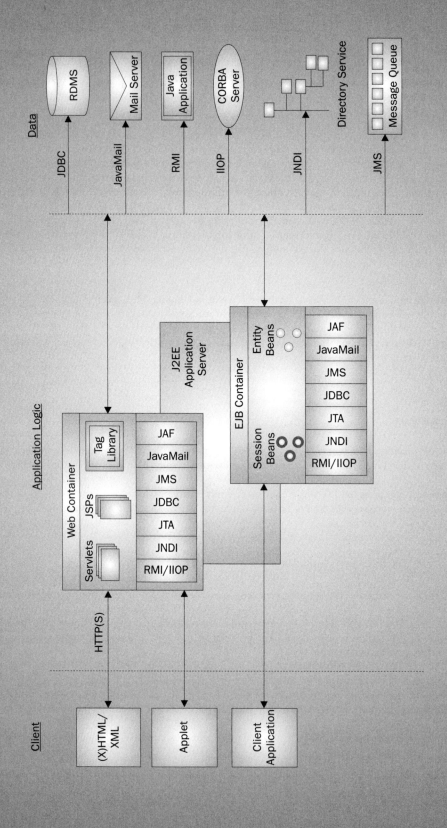

13

Advanced Custom JSP Tags

In the last chapter, we established the basics of writing tag extensions ourselves so now let's turn to some more practical examples of tag extension idioms in practice. In particular we will look at:

❑   XML transformations with an XSL tag

❑   Swing model tags for the ListModel and TableModel

❑   Tags in the Allaire tag library

The examples in this section are concerned with formatting data, so I've called the tag library for this section of the chapter the views library, and the code is available in the jspstyle directory. When you have loaded this into Tomcat the URL to the examples will begin something like http://localhost:8080/jspstyle.

An XSL Style Tag

Custom tags give us an elegant and concise way of including XML transforms in our JSPs. This is an example of the *transforming or interpreting tag body content* idiom described in Chapter 12. The following example shows how easy it is to use custom tags to place styled XML anywhere in your JSPs. (This section assumes some familiarity with XML and XSLT – see Chapter 5 for an introduction.)

To get this example running, you will need the IBM XML Parser for Java, and the Lotus XSL processor. (I used versions 2.0 and 0.18.5 respectively.) Both these are available from the IBM AlphaWorks site (http://alphaworks.ibm.com), along with good Javadocs and other documentation. The archives xml4j.jar and lotusxsl.jar must be on the CLASSPATH before starting the server. (If this example were to be packaged as a WAR, these archives could simply be placed in the WAR's /WEB-INF/lib directory. Note the commercial use licence.)

The following body tag makes one pass over its body content, which it considers to be an XML string, loads the XSL stylesheet specified in the `stylesheetURL` attribute, uses the Lotus XSL processor to transform the XML string into HTML or any other display format, and outputs the result. The usage will be as follows:

```
<views:xslt stylesheetURL="mystylesheet.xsl">
  <!-- xml content -->
</views:xslt>
```

This could potentially be a very useful tag. XML data is becoming more and more important, and XSL offers an attractive way to separate presentation from content.

Any exception encountered during the XML transformation, such as badly formed XML content or an invalid or missing stylesheet, will be wrapped as a `JspTagException` and rethrown. A production implementation would take more care to differentiate between the different exceptions it encountered and throw more informative exceptions:

```java
package jspstyle;

import java.io.IOException;
import javax.servlet.jsp.*;
import javax.servlet.jsp.tagext.*;

import com.lotus.xsl.*;
import org.xml.sax.SAXException;
import java.io.*;
import java.net.*;

/**
 * Tag to transform its XML body content using the XSL stylesheet
 * passed in as an attribute.
 * Note that this implementation is intended as an illustration only:
 * it makes no attempt at efficiency.
 */
public class StyledXMLTag extends BodyTagSupport {

    // URL (as a String) of the stylesheet we will use to transform XML content
    private String stylesheetURL;

    // Setter for the stylesheetURL attribute/property
    public void setStylesheetURL(String stylesheetURL) {
        this.stylesheetURL = stylesheetURL;
    }

    public int doEndTag() throws JspException {
        BodyContent bodyContent = getBodyContent();
        if (bodyContent != null) {
            String rawBody = bodyContent.getString();
            bodyContent.clearBody();
            try {
                bodyContent.getEnclosingWriter().write(xmlTransform(rawBody));
            } catch (Exception ex) {
                ex.printStackTrace();
```

```
            throw new JspTagException("Error: " + ex.getMessage());
        }
    }   // if bodyContent wasn't null

    return EVAL_PAGE;
}


/**
 * Implementation of XSLT transform.
 * This implementation requires the IBM XML parser and Lotus
 * XSL processor.
 * @param xmlin XML String to transform
 * @return transformed content: most likely HTML
 */
private String xmlTransform(String xmlin)
        throws MalformedURLException, FileNotFoundException, IOException,
            SAXException {
    InputStream styleSheetInputStream = null;
    try {

        // Refer to the Lotus XSL documentation for explanation of this code
        XSLProcessor processor = new XSLProcessor();
        XSLTInputSource xmlSource =
          new XSLTInputSource(new StringReader(xmlin));
        URL ssURL = new URL(stylesheetURL);
        styleSheetInputStream = ssURL.openStream();
        XSLTInputSource xslStylesheet =
          new XSLTInputSource(styleSheetInputStream);
        StringWriter transformationWriter = new StringWriter();
        XSLTResultTarget xmlOutput =
          new XSLTResultTarget(transformationWriter);
        processor.process(xmlSource, xslStylesheet, xmlOutput);
        return transformationWriter.toString();
    }
    finally {
        if (styleSheetInputStream != null) {
            styleSheetInputStream.close();
        }
    }
}   // xmlTransform
}
```

Don't try running this example on a live web site. A usable implementation would maintain a cache of stylesheets (most likely saving each stylesheet read by an instance of the tag in a hash table); this simple implementation reads a new stylesheet every time it renders content. This will prove extremely expensive.

The tag library <tag> element required is very simple. No TagExtraInfo class is required, as the tag defines no scripting variables:

```
<tag>
  <name>xslt</name>
  <tagclass>jspstyle.StyledXMLTag</tagclass>
  <bodycontent>JSP</bodycontent>
```

```
    <info>XSLT tag</info>
    <attribute>
      <name>stylesheetURL</name>
      <required>true</required>
      <rtexprvalue>true</rtexprvalue>
    </attribute>
  </tag>
```

A sample JSP, `xsl.jsp`, shows how flexible this approach is. The tag is used in three ways: to present XML hard coded into the JSP, XML from a static include, and XML sourced from a method call. In practice, the third mechanism is the most useful.

> **Note that it is not possible to source tag body content from a dynamic include in JSP 1.1, as flushing is illegal within a custom tag.**

As the `stylesheetURL` attribute can take a request-time value, the stylesheet used could be chosen dynamically based on user preferences or locale. If such dynamic styling were required, this would probably end up being a cleaner approach than performing all the conditional presentation in the JSPs themselves.

For reasons of simplicity and completeness I've included a `getXML()` method in a declaration in the JSP. In a real system, this XML would come from an external object, probably a page bean:

```
<%@ taglib uri="/views" prefix="views" %>

<html>
  <head>
    <title>XSLT example</title>
  </head>
  <body>
    This is styled XML from inline XML<br>

    <views:xslt stylesheetURL="http://localhost:8080/jspstyle/test.xsl">
      <content>
      <headline>Rover to survive as BMW sells</headline>
      <abstract>
        BMW today announced the sale of Rover cars to the Phoenix Group
      </abstract>
      <contentbody>
        There is widespread relief today in the West Midlands following
        BMW's agreement to sell Rover Cars to Phoenix Group. Although some
        job losses are expected...
      </contentbody>
      </content>
    </views:xslt>

  <p/>
    This is styled XML from included XML<br>

    <views:xslt stylesheetURL="http://localhost:8080/jspstyle/test.xsl">
      <%@ include file="test.xml" %>
    </views:xslt>
```

```
    <p/>
    This is styled XML from a method call:<br>
    <views:xslt stylesheetURL="http://localhost:8080/jspstyle/test.xsl">
      <%=getXML()%>
    </views:xslt>

  </body>
</html>

<%! String getXML() {
    return "<content><headline>Technology Markets Weaken</headline><abstract>Despite
a recent limited recovery, technology markets are still off the
boil</abstract><contentbody>Analysts in the City are pessimistic about the outlook
for a number of .com startups. This pessimism must be a contributing factor to the
present...</contentbody></content>";
}
%>
```

The XML content I've used is extremely simple, but of course the tag handler supports any complexity of XML and XSL. There are three data elements in the XML, corresponding to a simple publication article model. The contents of `test.xml` are:

```
<content>
  <headline>Germany Pushes for a Federal Europe</headline>
  <abstract>
    The German government remains committed to a Federal Europe.
  </abstract>
  <contentbody>
    Despite continued pressure on the Euro, the German government's commitment
    to an eventual European Federal System remains unshaken. Yesterday, the...
  </contentbody>
</content>
```

Again, in a real application, the XML would probably be valid, rather than merely well formed (that is, it would refer to a DTD), and the XSLT would be much more sophisticated.

The XSL stylesheet, `test.xsl`, contains a rule for each element of our simple XML structure. Please see the *XSLT Programmer's Reference* by Michael Kay (Wrox, 2000 ISBN 1861003129) for detailed coverage of XSLT. Simple changes to this stylesheet will produce very different output, without changing a line of JSP code:

```
<?xml version="1.0"?>
<xsl:stylesheet xmlns:xsl="http://www.w3.org/XSL/Transform/1.0">
  <xsl:template match="headline">
    <h2>
    <xsl:apply-templates/>
    </h2>
  </xsl:template>

  <xsl:template match="abstract">
    <font size="4"><i>
    <xsl:apply-templates/>
    </i></font>
```

```
      <p/>
    </xsl:template>

    <xsl:template match="contentbody">
      <font size="2">
      <xsl:apply-templates/>
      </font>
    </xsl:template>

  </xsl:stylesheet>
```

The output should look like this:

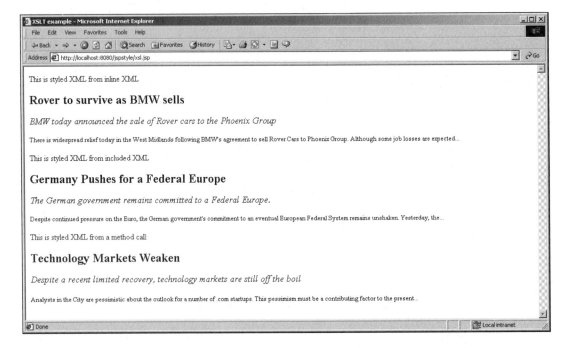

Allaire provide a commercial equivalent of this tag with the tag library bundled with JRun 3.0. We'll look at the Allaire tag library later in the chapter.

Swing Model Tags

Earlier, we mentioned the possiblity of using tag extensions to expose data models. Perhaps the most widely used models in Java are the Swing models. Implementing JSP tags to expose two of the most important models – `ListModel` and `TableModel` – is a very informative exercise, and very useful in practice.

Using the Swing ListModel

For example, consider an implementation of the Swing `ListModel`. The following tag handler takes a `ListModel` as an attribute, and iterates over its body content for each list entry. It produces no output, but defines two scripting variables, `index` and `value`, which can be used to produce output each time its body content is evaluated. This leaves JSPs using this tag with complete control of how the data will be formatted. The body content will build up as this tag performs the iteration, and is written out to the enclosing `JspWriter` in the `doEndTag()` method.

We have to be careful to handle an empty list correctly, if it should occur. We cannot attempt to access the model, as the private `setVariables()` method does, if the model is empty:

```java
package jspstyle;

import java.io.IOException;
import javax.servlet.jsp.*;
import javax.servlet.jsp.tagext.*;
import javax.swing.ListModel;

/**
 * A dynamic list iterator tag. Outputs no content, but provides scripting
 * variables to calling JSPs.
 * @see jspstyle.ListTagExtraInfo for variable definitions available
 * within this tag.
 * @author Rod Johnson
 */
public class ListTag extends BodyTagSupport {

  // ListModel we'll present data from
  private ListModel model;

  // Index of our current position in the list.
  // Incremented with each pass over our body content.
  private int index;

  // Setter for model attribute/property
  public void setModel(ListModel model) {
    this.model = model;
  }

  // Getter for model attribute/property
  public ListModel getModel() {
    return model;
  }

  // Make sure that variables are set before doAfterBody()
  // is called. We could use doInitBody() for the same purpose.
  public int doStartTag() throws JspException {
    if (model.getSize() > 0) {
      setVariables();
      return EVAL_BODY_TAG;
    }
    return SKIP_BODY;
  }

  // Convenience method to set variables before each loop iteration.
  private void setVariables() {
```

```
      pageContext.setAttribute("index", new Integer(index));
      pageContext.setAttribute("value", model.getElementAt(index));
    }

    // Check the index to see whether we need to make another pass
    // over our body content.
    // Ensure scripting variables are updated, but write no content.
    public int doAfterBody() throws JspException {
      if (++index < model.getSize()) {

        // We still have more list entries:
        // make at least one more pass overr body content
        setVariables();
        return EVAL_BODY_TAG;
      } else {

        // We've finished the list
        return SKIP_BODY;
      }
    }

    // Output the body content we have built up so far.
    public int doEndTag() throws JspException {
      try {
        if (bodyContent != null) {
          bodyContent.writeOut(bodyContent.getEnclosingWriter());
        }
      }
      catch (Exception ex) {
        throw new JspTagException("IO Error: " + ex.getMessage());
      }
      return EVAL_PAGE;
    }

}   // ListTag
```

We also need a `TagExtraInfo` class to define the scripting variables that will be available to the tag's body content, which will be evaluated for each list element:

```
package jspstyle;

import javax.servlet.jsp.tagext.*;

// Extra info defining variables for ListTag
// @author Rod Johnson
public class ListTagExtraInfo extends TagExtraInfo {

  public VariableInfo[] getVariableInfo(TagData data) {
    return new VariableInfo[] {
      new VariableInfo("value", "java.lang.Object", true,
                       VariableInfo.NESTED),
      new VariableInfo("index", "Integer", true, VariableInfo.NESTED)
    };
  }
}
```

The tag library entry must associate the tag with the `TagExtraInfo` class, and specify the mandatory `ListModel` parameter. (A complete TLD for the examples in this section will be included later.) To emphasize the correspondence to the Swing `JList`, I've named the tag `jspList`:

```
<tag>
  <name>jspList</name>
  <tagclass>jspstyle.ListTag</tagclass>
  <teiclass>jspstyle.ListTagExtraInfo</teiclass>
  <bodycontent>JSP</bodycontent>
  <info>Tag handler to expose a Swing ListModel</info>
  <attribute>
    <name>model</name>
    <required>true</required>
    <rtexprvalue>true</rtexprvalue>
  </attribute>
</tag>
```

Using this approach, it is very easy to present the same data in different ways, as the following JSP illustrates. It takes a short list and, with a minimal amount of code, presents it as an HTML list, in CSV format, and as a list of lines in increasing font size and changing in color:

```
<%@ taglib uri="views.tld" prefix="views" %>

<html>
  <head>
    <title>Swing model tag</title>
  </head>

<%
  // Define a simple list model. Of course this would come from
  // a page view bean in a real application.
  javax.swing.DefaultListModel listModel =
          new javax.swing.DefaultListModel();
  listModel.addElement("Rod");
  listModel.addElement("Gary");
  listModel.addElement("Paul");
  listModel.addElement("Jens");
  listModel.addElement("Portia");
%>
  <body>
    Simple use of the list model, using a static format for each element:
    <ul>
      <views:jspList model="<%=listModel%>" >
        <li><%=value%>
      </views:jspList>
    </ul>

    <p/>
    CSV representation of the list model, using a scriptlet to avoid having a
    separator after the last value<br/>
    <i>
      <views:jspList model="<%=listModel%>" >
        <%=value%>
        <% if (index.intValue() < listModel.getSize() - 1) { %>
          ,
        <% } %>
      </views:jspList>
    </i>
```

```
      <p/>
      <%! static String colours[] = { "green", "brown", "red", "magenta",
                                      "black" }; %>

      A more complex use of the list model, using a scriptlet to compute font
      size dynamically

      <views:jspList model="<%=listModel%>">
        <% int fontSize = 1 + index.intValue(); %>
        <br /><font color="<%=colours[index.intValue() % colours.length]%>"
                    size="<%=fontSize%>"><%=value%></font>
      </views:jspList>

    </body>
</html>
```

The output should look like this:

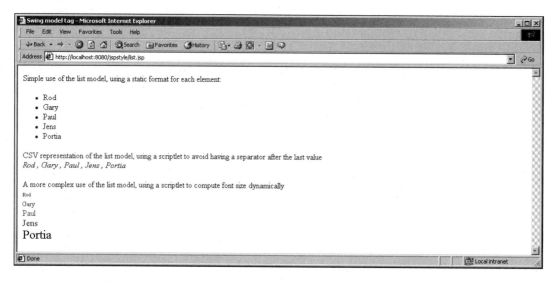

In a browser, the last list of names will vary in color and size.

Creating a Name-Value Mapping Model

While the Swing models are very useful in JSP authoring, there are some concepts useful in web interfaces that are not so common in windowing applications. One is a name-value mapping. This can be used in web interfaces in situations such as providing data for an HTML select control, mapping images to friendly names, and providing a set of hyperlinks.

This new requirement can, however, be addressed in a way that leverages a well-known Swing interface. (Never overlook the benefits of standardization.) We can start by defining a new model to support this concept, the NameValueModel, which extends the Swing ListModel. This maximizes the ways in which we can use data sources implementing it.

The `NameValueModel` has a single new method, `getName()`. `ListModel`'s `getElementAt()` method will provide the value corresponding to each name:

```
package jspstyle;

import javax.swing.ListModel;

/**
 * Extension of Swing ListModel interface to support
 * name-value mappings. The new getName() method will provide
 * the String name, while the ListModel getElementAt() method will
 * provide the object value.
 */
public interface NameValueModel extends ListModel {

  String getName(int i);

}
```

A slight variation on the concept of the `ListTag` enables us to implement the `NameValueTag`. All we need to do is set one extra variable:

```
package jspstyle;

import java.io.IOException;
import javax.servlet.jsp.*;
import javax.servlet.jsp.tagext.*;

/**
 * A dynamic NameValueModel iterator tag.
 * Outputs no content, but provides scripting
 * variables to calling JSPs.
 */
public class NameValueTag extends BodyTagSupport {

  // Model from which we'll obtain our content
  private NameValueModel model;

  // Our current index in the list
  private int index;


  // Required model attribute/property
  public void setModel(NameValueModel model) {
    this.model = model;
  }

  public NameValueModel getModel() {
    return model;
  }

  public int doStartTag() throws JspException {
    if (model.getSize() > 0) {
      setVariables();
```

```
      return EVAL_BODY_TAG;
    }

    // We'll only get here if the model is empty, and
    // we never want to evaluate this tag's body
    return SKIP_BODY;
  }

  private void setVariables() {
    pageContext.setAttribute("index", new Integer(index));
    pageContext.setAttribute("value", model.getElementAt(index));
    pageContext.setAttribute("name", model.getName(index));
  }

  // Iterate over elements in the model.
  // Ensure the variables are updated, but write no content.
  public int doAfterBody() throws JspException {
    if (++index < model.getSize()) {
      setVariables();
      return EVAL_BODY_TAG;
    } else {
      return SKIP_BODY;
    }
  }

  // Output the body content
  public int doEndTag() throws JspException {
    if (bodyContent != null) {
      try {
        bodyContent.writeOut(bodyContent.getEnclosingWriter());
      } catch (IOException ex) {
        throw new JspException("IO Error: " + ex.getMessage());
      }
    }
    return EVAL_PAGE;
  }

}    // NameValueTag
```

As in the NameValueModel there is a single extra value returned by the NameValueTagExtraInfo:

```
package jspstyle;

import javax.servlet.jsp.tagext.*;


public class NameValueTagExtraInfo extends TagExtraInfo {

  public VariableInfo[] getVariableInfo(TagData data) {
    return new VariableInfo[] {
      new VariableInfo("name", "java.lang.String", true,
                       VariableInfo.NESTED),
      new VariableInfo("value", "java.lang.Object", true,
                       VariableInfo.NESTED),
      new VariableInfo("index", "Integer", true, VariableInfo.NESTED)
    };
  }
}
```

Since we've chosen to make `NameValueModel` extend `ListModel`, we can extend the Swing `AbstractListModel` to implement it. This will provide useful support for listeners, which are especially important in Swing interfaces, which are not bound by the request-response pace of HTTP.

Purely to make the JSP self-contained, I've defined an inner class implementing the required model in a declaration. Don't be misled – there are few legitimate reasons to define inner classes in production JSPs:

```
<%@ taglib uri="/views" prefix="views" %>

<%!
  class TestNameValueModel
  extends javax.swing.AbstractListModel
   implements jspstyle.NameValueModel {

    private int entries;

    public TestNameValueModel() {
      java.util.Random rand = new java.util.Random();
      entries = rand.nextInt(20) + 3;
    }

    public int getSize() {
      return entries;
    }

    public Object getElementAt(int i) {
      return "value " + i;
    }

    public String getName(int i) {
      return "Name " + i;
    }
  }

  jspstyle.NameValueModel nvModel = new TestNameValueModel();
%>

<html>
  <head>
    <title>Swing model tags</title>
  </head>
  <body>

  <h2>Name value tags, using the jspNameValue tag</h2>
  This is not a Swing model, as no Swing model was suitable.<br />
  <select name="sel3">
    <views:jspNameValue model="<%=nvModel%>">
      <option value="<%=value%>"><%=name%>
    </views:jspNameValue>
  </select>

  <p>
    <select name="sel4" multiple>
      <views:jspNameValue model="<%=nvModel%>">
        <option value="<%=value%>"><%=name%>
      </views:jspNameValue>
    </select>
  </p>
  <p>Presented as hyperlinks: <br />
    <views:jspNameValue model="<%=nvModel%>">
      <a href="<%=value%>"><%=name%></a> |
```

```
      </views:jspNameValue>
    </p>
    <p>
      <i>Presented as a property list:</i>
      <br />
      <code>
        <views:jspNameValue model="<%=nvModel%>">
          <%=name%>=<%=value%><br>
        </views:jspNameValue>
      </code>
    </body>
  </html>
```

We add the appropriate entry in the tag library descriptor:

```
<tag>
  <name>jspNameValue</name>
  <tagclass>jspstyle.NameValueTag</tagclass>
  <teiclass>jspstyle.NameValueTagExtraInfo</teiclass>
  <bodycontent>JSP</bodycontent>
  <info>JSP Name-Value MVC tag</info>
  <attribute>
    <name>model</name>
    <required>true</required>
    <rtexprvalue>true</rtexprvalue>
  </attribute>
</tag>
```

We should get the following output. The screenshot shows the different ways in which the same data can be displayed using this tag:

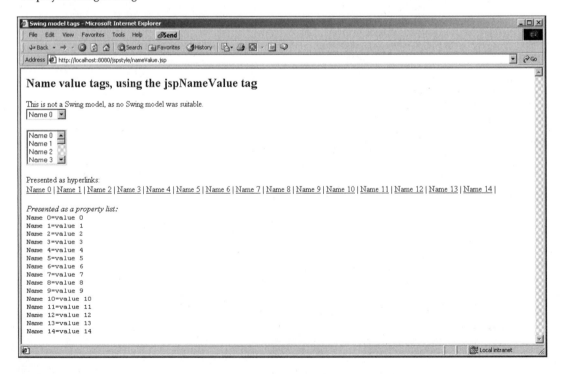

Using the Swing TableModel

The Swing `TableModel` is a particularly useful model to expose through custom tags. Tabular data is common, and using JSP scriptlets to present it calls for nested loops that may be confusing to page designers called upon to modify the page's output.

A similar approach can be used as for lists: using tags to handle iteration and design scripting variables, but to do as little of the HTML output as possible. However, designing a table tag is more challenging than designing a list tag. In the case of the list tag, it was easy to avoid having the tag handler generate HTML. This is not the case for the table tag. We could of course define a table tag that generated HTML `<table>`, `<tr>`, `<td>`, and other required markup values to make a complete HTML table with a minimum of JSP coding, but this would prove inflexible in practice. What if we wanted to make each row a different color? What if we wanted to generate a format other than HTML? What if we wanted to add extra columns containing content not sourced from the model?

Six values must be parameterized to design a reusable tag:

- ❏ The opening and closing of the table header

- ❏ The format of each header cell

- ❏ The opening and closing of each table row

- ❏ The format of each table cell

Simple HTML markup for each of these can still be used as a default value, meaning that a minimum of code will be required to use the table tag. We will need a cell tag that includes the required open and closing markup (`<td>` and `</td>` in the case of HTML).

The most obvious way to achieve this parameterization is to use tag attributes for these values. However, this doesn't work very well when we need to specify markup that is illegal in an attribute. At best the syntax will be cumbersome.

A slightly more complex, but much more effective, approach is to use nested tags to configure their ancestors. The complete structure will look like this:

```
<table>
  <views:jspTable model="<%=tableModel %>" >
    <views:headingOpen><tr bgcolor="black"></views:headingOpen>
    <views:headingClose></font></tr></views:headingClose>
    <views:headingCell><td><%=heading%></td></views:headingCell>
    <views:rows>
      <views:rowOpen><tr></views:rowOpen>
      <views:rowClose></tr></views:rowClose>
      <views:cell><td><%=value%></td></views:cell>
    </views:rows>
  </views:jspTable>
</table>
```

If we don't want a heading and are happy with the HTML default values we can do this, which merely provides all the elements requires to support iteration over the table's content:

```
<table>
  <views:jspTable model="<%=model%>">

  <views:rows><views:cell><td><%=value%></td></views:cell></views:rows>
  </views:jspTable>
</table>
```

Implementing the table tag calls for eight tag handler classes (one for each tag), but most of them aren't very complex. Let's look at the responsibility of each class before we move on to the details of implementation:

- ❑ TableTag – Saves the TableModel, making it available to subtags. Holds header open and header close properties.

- ❑ HeaderOpen – Configures the TableModel's header open property.

- ❑ HeaderClose – Configures the TableModel's header close property.

- ❑ HeaderTag – Corresponds to the <headerCell> tag. Handles iteration over the table headings, and outputs content including header open and close values. Defines heading (header value) and column (column index) variables.

- ❑ RowsTag – Handles iteration over the table's rows. Defines the row (row index) variable.

- ❑ RowOpenTag – Configures RowsTag's row open property.

- ❑ RowCloseTag – Configures RowsTag's row close property.

- ❑ CellTag – Implements the <cell> tag in the example; analogous to HeaderTag. Handles the iteration over a table row, including output of row open and close markup and each cell's value. Defines column (column index) and value (model value) variables.

We also need a number of TagExtraInfo classes to define scripting variables.

Tag cooperation will be implemented by having subtags check for ancestors with the required types: TableTag will provide context to all tags, and RowsTag will provide context to RowOpenTag, RowCloseTag, and CellTag.

As the TableTag doesn't perform any iteration itself, it doesn't need to implement BodyTag. Its purpose is purely to capture attributes and make them available to tags nested within it. It will define HTML default values for its two markup attributes, and provide getters and setters for them and for the TableModel. The doStartTag() method is also used to ensure that if the model is empty, the TableTag will not evaluate its subtags. The implementation is straightforward:

```
package jspstyle;

import java.io.IOException;
import javax.servlet.jsp.*;
import javax.servlet.jsp.tagext.*;
import javax.swing.table.TableModel;

/**
 * A dynamic table tag. This tag produces no output:
 * it's purpose is to expose the TableModel to subtags, and
 * store markup fragments for subtags.
```

```
 * The headerOpen and headerClose properties are meant for
 * subtags to use, although they can be set using attributes
 * of this tag.
 */
public class TableTag extends TagSupport {
  private static final String DEFAULT_HEADER_OPEN = "<tr>";
  private static final String DEFAULT_HEADER_CLOSE = "</tr>";

  private String headerOpen = DEFAULT_HEADER_OPEN;
  private String headerClose = DEFAULT_HEADER_CLOSE;

  private TableModel model;

  public void setModel(TableModel model) {
    this.model = model;
  }

  // Package-visible, for child tags
  TableModel getModel() {
    return model;
  }

  public String getHeaderOpen() {
    return headerOpen;
  }

  public void setHeaderOpen(String headerOpen) {
    this.headerOpen = headerOpen;
  }

  public String getHeaderClose() {
    return headerClose;
  }

  public void setHeaderClose(String headerClose) {
    this.headerClose = headerClose;
  }

  public int doStartTag() throws JspException {
    if (model == null) {
      throw new JspException("Model must not be null");
    }
    if (model.getRowCount() > 0) {

      // Only evaluate body if there's data in the model
      return EVAL_BODY_INCLUDE;
    } else {
      return SKIP_BODY;
    }
  }
}   // class TableTag
```

HeadingOpenTag and HeadingCloseTag will configure the corresponding property in the enclosing TableTag to the values in their body content. These values will later by used by the HeadingTag to write output. If either or both of these optional tags are omitted, the default values defined in TableTag will be used. We use `findAncestorWithClass()` to look for an enclosing `TableTag`, and throw an exception if none is found:

```
package jspstyle;

import javax.servlet.jsp.*;
import javax.servlet.jsp.tagext.*;

/**
 * Tag to set the headerOpen property of an enclosing
 * TableTag to its body content.
 */
public class HeadingOpenTag extends BodyTagSupport {
  private TableTag parent;

  public int doStartTag() throws JspException {
    parent = (TableTag) TagSupport.findAncestorWithClass(this,
             TableTag.class);
    if (parent == null) {
      throw new JspTagException("HeadingOpenTag must be enclosed in a "
                                + "TableTag");
    }
    return EVAL_BODY_TAG;
  }

  public int doEndTag() throws JspException {
    BodyContent bodyContent = getBodyContent();
    if (bodyContent != null) {
      parent.setHeaderOpen(bodyContent.getString());
    }
    return EVAL_PAGE;
  }
}
```

The `HeadingClose` tag is similar:

```
package jspstyle;

import javax.servlet.jsp.*;
import javax.servlet.jsp.tagext.*;

/**
 * Tag to set the headerClose property of an enclosing
 * TableTag to its body content.
 */
public class HeadingCloseTag extends BodyTagSupport {
  private TableTag parent;

  public int doStartTag() throws JspException {
    parent = (TableTag) TagSupport.findAncestorWithClass(this,
             TableTag.class);
    if (parent == null) {
      throw new JspTagException("HeadingCloseTag must be enclosed in a "
                                + "TableTag");
    }
```

```
      return EVAL_BODY_TAG;
  }

  public int doEndTag() throws JspException {
      BodyContent bodyContent = getBodyContent();
    if (bodyContent != null) {
      parent.setHeaderClose(bodyContent.getString());
    }
    return EVAL_PAGE;
  }
}
```

The job of iterating over every cell in the header row will be left to the HeadingTag. If this tag is omitted, the header will not appear. This tag will also output the opening and closing header values, as found in the TableTag ancestor. (Note that the headingOpen and headingClose tags should be used before the header tag itself.) We use a StringBuffer to build up the content we will output in the doEndTag() method:

```
package jspstyle;

import java.io.IOException;
import javax.servlet.jsp.*;
import javax.servlet.jsp.tagext.*;
import javax.swing.table.TableModel;

/**
 * Tag to iterate over headings.
 */
public class HeadingTag extends BodyTagSupport {
  private TableTag parent;
  private StringBuffer sbOut = new StringBuffer();

  private int col;

  public int doStartTag() throws JspException {
    parent = (TableTag) TagSupport.findAncestorWithClass(this,
            TableTag.class);
    if (parent == null) {
      throw new JspTagException
            ("HeadingTag must be enclosed in a TableTag");
    }
    sbOut.append(parent.getHeaderOpen());
    setVariables();
    return EVAL_BODY_TAG;
  }

  private void setVariables() {
    pageContext.setAttribute("heading",
                        parent.getModel().getColumnName(col));
    pageContext.setAttribute("column", new Integer(col));
  }
```

```
    public int doAfterBody() throws JspException {
      BodyContent bodyContent = getBodyContent();
      String bodyTag = bodyContent.getString();
      sbOut.append(bodyTag);
      bodyContent.clearBody();
      if (++col < parent.getModel().getColumnCount()) {
        setVariables();
        return EVAL_BODY_TAG;
      } else {
        return SKIP_BODY;
      }
    }

    public int doEndTag() throws JspException {
      try {
          BodyContent bodyContent = getBodyContent();
        if (bodyContent != null) {
          bodyContent.getEnclosingWriter().write(sbOut.toString());
          bodyContent.getEnclosingWriter().write(parent.getHeaderClose());
        }
      } catch (Exception ex) {
        throw new JspException("IO Error: " + ex.getMessage());
      }
      return EVAL_PAGE;
    }
}
```

The HeadingTag must set two scripting variables that will be accessible in its body. These must be defined in an associated TagExtraInfo class:

```
package jspstyle;

import javax.servlet.jsp.tagext.*;

public class HeadingTagExtraInfo extends TagExtraInfo {

  public VariableInfo[] getVariableInfo(TagData data) {
    return new VariableInfo[] {
      new VariableInfo("heading", "java.lang.String", true,
                    VariableInfo.NESTED),
      new VariableInfo("column", "Integer", true,
                    VariableInfo.NESTED)
    };
  }
}
```

The table body is generated by two iterating tags: one (the RowsTag) to iterate over the table's rows, and one (CellTag) to iterate over the cells in each row. The RowsTag must expose row opening and row closing properties in the same way as the TableTag does with its header properties. Unlike the TableTag, the RowsTag defines one scripting variable: the index of the row it is currently working on. This will be useful to expressions or scriptlets in subtags. The RowsTag must also expose a getRow() method, to let subtags establish the current row. Without this the CellTag could not access cells in the model:

```java
package jspstyle;

import java.io.IOException;
import javax.servlet.jsp.*;
import javax.servlet.jsp.tagext.*;
import javax.swing.table.TableModel;

/**
 * Tag to handle one row in a table. Iterates over its content
 * for each row in the table. Exposes rowOpen and rowClose properties
 * in the same way as TableTag exposes headerOpen and headerClose,
 * to allow subtags to communicate.
 */
public class RowsTag extends BodyTagSupport {
  private static final String DEFAULT_ROW_OPEN = "<tr>";
  private static final String DEFAULT_ROW_CLOSE = "</tr>";

  private TableModel model;
  private int row;
  private String rowOpen = DEFAULT_ROW_OPEN;
  private String rowClose = DEFAULT_ROW_CLOSE;

  public int doStartTag() throws JspException {
    TableTag parent = (TableTag) TagSupport.findAncestorWithClass(this,
            TableTag.class);
    if (parent == null) {
      throw new JspTagException("Rows tag must be enclosed in a Table tag");
    }
    model = parent.getModel();
    setVariables();
    return EVAL_BODY_TAG;
  }

  // Make the TableModel available to subtags in this package
  TableModel getModel() {
    return model;
  }

  String getRowOpen() {
    return rowOpen;
  }

  String getRowClose() {
    return rowClose;
  }

  void setRowOpen(String rowOpen) {
    this.rowOpen = rowOpen;
  }

  void setRowClose(String rowClose) {
    this.rowClose = rowClose;
  }
```

```
    private void setVariables() {
      pageContext.setAttribute("row", new Integer(row));
    }

    public int getRow() {
      return row;
    }

    /**
     * Iterate over this tag's body content and subtags for each
     * row in the TableModel.
     */
    public int doAfterBody() throws JspException {
      if (++row < model.getRowCount()) {
        setVariables();
        return EVAL_BODY_TAG;
      } else {
        return SKIP_BODY;
      }
    }

    public int doEndTag() throws JspException {
      try {
        BodyContent bodyContent = getBodyContent();
        if (bodyContent != null) {
          bodyContent.writeOut(bodyContent.getEnclosingWriter());
        }
      } catch (Exception ex) {
        throw new JspException("IO Error: " + ex.getMessage());
      }
      return EVAL_PAGE;
    }

}   // RowsTag
```

A `RowsTagExtraInfo` class is required to declare the `row` scripting variable:

```
package jspstyle;

import javax.servlet.jsp.tagext.*;

public class RowsTagExtraInfo extends TagExtraInfo {

  public VariableInfo[] getVariableInfo(TagData data) {
    return new VariableInfo[] {
      new VariableInfo("row", "Integer", true, VariableInfo.NESTED),
    };
  }
}
```

The `RowOpenTag` and `RowCloseTag` are analogous to the `HeadingOpenTag` and `HeadingCloseTags`; they configure the properties of their enclosing `RowsTag`:

```java
package jspstyle;

import javax.servlet.jsp.*;
import javax.servlet.jsp.tagext.*;

/**
 * Simple BodyTag to configure RowsTag parent.
 */
public class RowOpenTag extends BodyTagSupport {
  private RowsTag parent;

  public int doStartTag() throws JspException {
    parent = (RowsTag) findAncestorWithClass(this, RowsTag.class);
    if (parent == null) {
      throw new JspTagException("RowOpenTag must be enclosed in a RowsTag");
    }
    pageContext.setAttribute("row", new Integer(parent.getRow()));
    return EVAL_BODY_TAG;
  }

  public int doEndTag() throws JspException {
    if (bodyContent != null) {
      parent.setRowOpen(bodyContent.getString());
    }
    return EVAL_PAGE;
  }
}
```

RowCloseTag is very similar to RowOpenTag:

```java
package jspstyle;

import javax.servlet.jsp.*;
import javax.servlet.jsp.tagext.*;

/**
 * Simple BodyTag to configure RowsTag parent.
 */
public class RowCloseTag extends BodyTagSupport {
  private RowsTag parent;

  public int doStartTag() throws JspException {
    parent = (RowsTag) TagSupport.findAncestorWithClass(this,
          RowsTag.class);
    if (parent == null) {
      throw new JspTagException("RowOpenTag must be enclosed in a RowsTag");
    }
    return EVAL_BODY_TAG;
  }

  public int doEndTag() throws JspException {
    if (bodyContent != null) {
      parent.setRowClose(bodyContent.getString());
    }
    return EVAL_PAGE;
  }
}
```

The `CellTag` is more complex. It has the job of iterating over the content of each row, as well as outputting the row open and close values obtained from its `RowsTag` parent. It also obtains the row index from its parent; it needs this to access each cell in turn. It defines two scripting variables that will be updated with each iteration: `value` (the `Object` value of the value of each cell in turn); and `column` (the index of the current column in the model):

```java
package jspstyle;

import java.io.IOException;
import javax.servlet.jsp.*;
import javax.servlet.jsp.tagext.*;
import javax.swing.table.TableModel;

/**
 * Class to handle each cell in a table. Will be called
 * once for each row: must handle iteration for each column,
 * and output row open and row close values where necessary.
 * Mixes markup output (with values coming from parent tag)
 * with output from evaluating its body content, hence is
 * implemented using a StringBuffer to build up content.
 */
public class CellTag extends BodyTagSupport {

  // Current Column
  // We'll create a scripting variable for this.
  private int col;

  // Buffer in which we'll save up content
  private StringBuffer sbOut = new StringBuffer();

  // Enclosing tag
  private RowsTag parent;

  public int doStartTag() throws JspException {
    parent = (RowsTag) TagSupport.findAncestorWithClass(this,
            RowsTag.class);
    if (parent == null) {
      throw new JspTagException("CellTag must be enclosed in a RowsTag");
    }
    sbOut.append(parent.getRowOpen());
    setVariables();
    return EVAL_BODY_TAG;
  }

  private void setVariables() {
    Object valObj = parent.getModel().getValueAt(parent.getRow(), col);
    if (valObj == null) {

      // Http sessions are implemented using Hashtables rather
      // than the Java 2 HashMap. They don't take kindly to null values.
      valObj = "NULL";
    }
```

```
      pageContext.setAttribute("value", valObj);
      pageContext.setAttribute("column", new Integer(col));
    }

    public int doAfterBody() throws JspException {

      String bodyTag = bodyContent.getString();
      sbOut.append(bodyTag);
      bodyContent.clearBody();

      if (++col < parent.getModel().getColumnCount()) {
        setVariables();
        return EVAL_BODY_TAG;
      } else {

        // The column is finished
        sbOut.append(parent.getRowClose());
        return SKIP_BODY;
      }
    }

    // Output the content in our internal buffer
    public int doEndTag() throws JspException {
      try {
        if (bodyContent != null) {
          bodyContent.getEnclosingWriter().write(sbOut.toString());
        }
      } catch (IOException ex) {
        throw new JspException("IO Error: " + ex.getMessage());
      }
      return EVAL_PAGE;
    }
}    // class CellTag
```

Finally, we must not forget the `TagExtraInfo` class needed to tell JSPs about the scripting variables introduced by this tag:

```
package jspstyle;

import javax.servlet.jsp.tagext.*;

public class CellTagExtraInfo extends TagExtraInfo {

  public VariableInfo[] getVariableInfo(TagData data) {
    return new VariableInfo[] {
      new VariableInfo("value", "java.lang.Object", true,
                        VariableInfo.NESTED),
      new VariableInfo("column", "Integer", true,
                        VariableInfo.NESTED)
    };
  }
}
```

Here is the complete tag library descriptor for the examples in this section:

```xml
<?xml version="1.0" encoding="ISO-8859-1" ?>
<!DOCTYPE taglib
        PUBLIC "-//Sun Microsystems, Inc.//DTD JSP Tag Library 1.1//EN"
    "http://java.sun.com/j2ee/dtds/web-jsptaglibrary_1_1.dtd">
<taglib>
  <tlibversion>1.0</tlibversion>
  <jspversion>1.1</jspversion>
  <shortname>views</shortname>

  <info>MVC tag library. Author: Rod Johnson</info>

  <tag>
    <name>jspTable</name>
    <tagclass>jspstyle.TableTag</tagclass>
    <bodycontent>JSP</bodycontent>
    <info>JSP table view</info>
    <attribute>
      <name>model</name>
      <required>true</required>
      <rtexprvalue>true</rtexprvalue>
    </attribute>
    <attribute>
      <name>headerOpen</name>
      <required>false</required>
      <rtexprvalue>true</rtexprvalue>
    </attribute>
    <attribute>
      <name>headerClose</name>
      <required>false</required>
      <rtexprvalue>true</rtexprvalue>
    </attribute>
  </tag>

  <tag>
    <name>rows</name>
    <tagclass>jspstyle.RowsTag</tagclass>
    <teiclass>jspstyle.RowsTagExtraInfo</teiclass>
    <bodycontent>JSP</bodycontent>
    <info>JSP table tag</info>
  </tag>

  <tag>
    <name>headingCell</name>
    <tagclass>jspstyle.HeadingTag</tagclass>
    <teiclass>jspstyle.HeadingTagExtraInfo</teiclass>
    <bodycontent>JSP</bodycontent>
    <info>JSP table tag</info>
  </tag>

  <tag>
    <name>cell</name>
    <tagclass>jspstyle.CellTag</tagclass>
```

```
    <teiclass>jspstyle.CellTagExtraInfo</teiclass>
    <bodycontent>JSP</bodycontent>
    <info>JSP table tag</info>
</tag>

<tag>
  <name>rowOpen</name>
  <tagclass>jspstyle.RowOpenTag</tagclass>
  <bodycontent>JSP</bodycontent>
  <info>JSP table tag</info>
</tag>
<tag>
  <name>rowClose</name>
  <tagclass>jspstyle.RowCloseTag</tagclass>
  <bodycontent>JSP</bodycontent>
  <info>JSP table tag</info>
</tag>

<tag>
  <name>headingOpen</name>
  <tagclass>jspstyle.HeadingOpenTag</tagclass>
  <bodycontent>JSP</bodycontent>
  <info>JSP table tag</info>
</tag>
<tag>
  <name>headingClose</name>
  <tagclass>jspstyle.HeadingCloseTag</tagclass>
  <bodycontent>JSP</bodycontent>
  <info>JSP table tag</info>
</tag>

<!-- List tag -->
<tag>
  <name>jspList</name>
  <tagclass>jspstyle.ListTag</tagclass>
  <teiclass>jspstyle.ListTagExtraInfo</teiclass>
  <bodycontent>JSP</bodycontent>
  <info>JSP list MVC tag</info>
  <attribute>
    <name>model</name>
    <required>true</required>
    <rtexprvalue>true</rtexprvalue>
  </attribute>
</tag>

<!-- Name value tag -->
<tag>
  <name>jspNameValue</name>
  <tagclass>jspstyle.NameValueTag</tagclass>
  <teiclass>jspstyle.NameValueTagExtraInfo</teiclass>
  <bodycontent>JSP</bodycontent>
  <info>JSP Name-Value MVC tag</info>
  <attribute>
    <name>model</name>
    <required>true</required>
```

```
        <rtexprvalue>true</rtexprvalue>
      </attribute>
    </tag>

    <!-- Styled XML tag -->
    <tag>
      <name>xslt</name>
      <tagclass>jspstyle.StyledXMLTag</tagclass>
      <bodycontent>JSP</bodycontent>
      <info>XSLT tag</info>
      <attribute>
        <name>stylesheetURL</name>
        <required>true</required>
        <rtexprvalue>true</rtexprvalue>
      </attribute>
    </tag>
</taglib>
```

Before we move onto a JSP demonstrating these tags in use, we need an easy way of generating test data. The following class generates a randomly sized table containing cell values indicating row and column:

```java
package jspstyle;

import javax.swing.table.AbstractTableModel;

// Dummy table model to demonstrate jspTable tag extension.
public class TestTableModel extends AbstractTableModel {

    private int rows;
    private int cols;

    //  Create a random number of cells
    public TestTableModel() {
        java.util.Random rand = new java.util.Random();
        rows = rand.nextInt(20) + 3;
        cols = rand.nextInt(5) + 3;
    }

    public int getRowCount() {
        return rows;
    }

    public int getColumnCount() {
        return cols;
    }

    //  Return a String value showing the cell location
    public Object getValueAt(int row, int column) {
        return "[" + row + "," + column + "]";
    }

    public String getColumnName(int column) {
        return "Column " + column;
    }
}
```

A simple JSP example displays the most basic use of the table tags, relying on default (HTML markup) properties for the customisable attributes:

```
<%@ taglib uri="/views" prefix="views" %>
<%!
  jspstyle.TestTableModel model = new jspstyle.TestTableModel();
%>
<html>
  <head>
    <title>Swing model tags</title>
  </head>
  <body>
    <h2>Simple table tag, using the jspTable tag</h2>
    This example is a simple dynamic table sourced from a table model.<br>
    <br/>

    <table border="1">
      <views:jspTable model="<%=model%>">
        <views:rows><views:cell><td><%=value%></td></views:cell></views:rows>
      </views:jspTable>
    </table>
  </body>
</html>
```

The output should look like this:

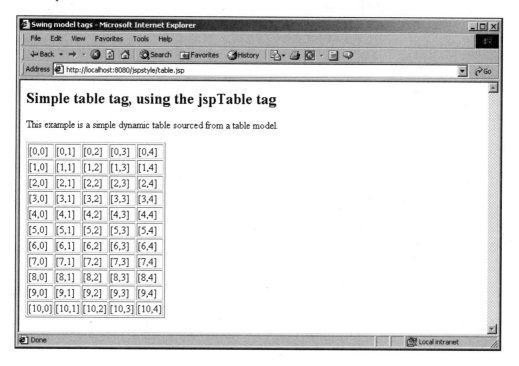

A more complex example JSP shows how flexible these tags are in practice, flexibility achieved largely because they were designed to allow all markup to be passed in by the JSPs that use them.

I've used several scriptlets to demonstrate how conditional logic and calculation can be based on the variables exposed by the model tags. As the data access and iteration is handled by the custom tags, it is possible to introduce short scriptlets without making the JSP hard to read. Here is the code for `table2.jsp`:

```
<%@ taglib uri="/views" prefix="views" %>
<%!
  jspstyle.TestTableModel model = new jspstyle.TestTableModel();
%>

<html>
  <head>
    <title>Swing model tags</title>
  </head>
  <body>
    <h2>Table tags, using the jspTable tag</h2>


This is a slightly more complex example, showing some computations and overriding
default behaviour
    <br/><br/>

    <table border="1" bgColor="cyan">
      <views:jspTable model="<%=model %>" >
        <views:headingCell><td><b><%=heading%></b> 10xcol=
          <%=column.intValue() * 10%></td>
        </views:headingCell>
        <views:rows>
          <views:cell>
            <td><%=value%> Multiple is <i>
              <%=column.intValue() * row.intValue()%></i></td>
          </views:cell>
        </views:rows>
        </views:jspTable>
    </table>


    <p />
    This is a slightly more complex example, showing conditional behaviour
    <br/><br/>
    <table border="1" bgColor="yellow" title="Fancier">
      <views:jspTable model="<%=model %>" >
        <views:headingCell><td><%=heading%></td></views:headingCell>
        <views:rows><views:cell>
          <% boolean isOdd = column.intValue() % 2 == 0; %>
          <%=isOdd ? "<td bgColor=red>" + value : "<td>" + value%>
        </views:cell></views:rows>
        </views:jspTable>
    </table>

  </body>
</html>
```

Here is one possible output of the model:

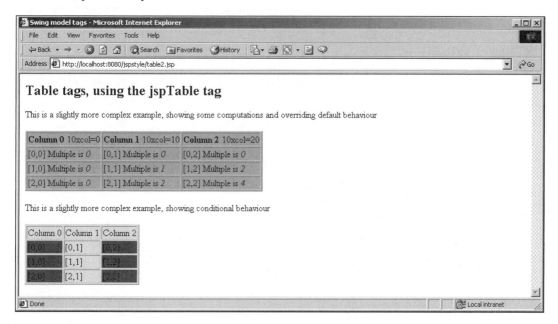

Delivery

We'll want to use the views library again in the next chapter. The best way to make it available as a unit is to package it as a JARed tag library. The following is a listing of the `viewslib.jar` file:

```
META-INF/
          MANIFEST.MF
          taglib.tld
jspstyle/
          CellTag.class
          CellTagExtraInfo.class
          HeadingCloseTag.class
          HeadingOpenTag.class
          HeadingTag.class
          HeadingTagExtraInfo.class
          ListTag.class
          ListTagExtraInfo.class
          NameValueModel.class
          NameValueTag.class
          NameValueTagExtraInfo.class
          RowCloseTag.class
          RowOpenTag.class
          RowsTag.class
          RowsTagExtraInfo.class
          RowTagsExtraInfo.class
          StyledXMLTag.class
          TableTag.class
```

When building the WAR for all the examples in this chapter, we need to place this JAR file in the /WEB-INF/lib directory, copy the taglib.tld file from the JAR and place it in our WAR somewhere outside the JAR, and create a mapping in the web.xml file telling the JSP engine where this TLD can be found:

```xml
<?xml version="1.0" encoding="UTF-8"?>

<!DOCTYPE web-app PUBLIC '-//Sun Microsystems, Inc.//DTD Web Application 2.2//EN'
'http://java.sun.com/j2ee/dtds/web-app_2.2.dtd'>

<web-app>
  <display-name>tagext</display-name>
  <description>Tag extensions examples</description>

  <session-config>
    <session-timeout>0</session-timeout>
  </session-config>

  <taglib>
    <taglib-uri>/hello</taglib-uri>
    <taglib-location>/WEB-INF/tlds/hello.tld</taglib-location>
  </taglib>

  <taglib>
    <taglib-uri>/views</taglib-uri>
    <taglib-location>/WEB-INF/lib/taglib.tld</taglib-location>
  </taglib>

</web-app>
```

Under the Hood

JSP developers are not normally too concerned with the code generated by the JSP engine for the JSP pages they write. However, it's always good to understand what is going on. The Java code generated at translation time for JSP pages using custom tags is quite simple, and helps us to understand the tag handler lifecycle.

Let's consider the example of our looping VarHelloBodyTag, which also defines several scripting variables.

This example shows code generated by Tomcat 3.1. Other JSP engines may generate different Java code, but the concepts and the results will be the same:

```java
import javax.servlet.*;
import javax.servlet.http.*;
import javax.servlet.jsp.*;
import javax.servlet.jsp.tagext.*;
import java.io.PrintWriter;
import java.io.IOException;
import java.io.FileInputStream;
import java.io.ObjectInputStream;
import java.util.Vector;
import org.apache.jasper.runtime.*;
import java.beans.*;
```

```
import org.apache.jasper.JasperException;

public class _0002fhello_00034_0002ejsphello4_jsp_2 extends HttpJspBase {

static {
  }

  public _0002fhello_00034_0002ejsphello4_jsp_2( ) {
  }

  private static boolean _jspx_inited = false;

  public final void _jspx_init() throws JasperException {
  }

  public void _jspService(HttpServletRequest request, HttpServletResponse
                          response)
    throws IOException, ServletException {

    JspFactory _jspxFactory = null;
    PageContext pageContext = null;
    HttpSession session = null;
    ServletContext application = null;
    ServletConfig config = null;
    JspWriter out = null;
    Object page = this;
    String  _value = null;
    try {

      if (_jspx_inited == false) {
        _jspx_init();
        _jspx_inited = true;
      }
      _jspxFactory = JspFactory.getDefaultFactory();
      response.setContentType("text/html;charset=8859_1");
      pageContext = _jspxFactory.getPageContext(this, request, response,
                                                "", true, 8192, true);

      application = pageContext.getServletContext();
      config = pageContext.getServletConfig();
      session = pageContext.getSession();
      out = pageContext.getOut();

      // HTML // begin [file="C:\\hello4.jsp";from=(0,44);to=(2,0)]
        out.write("\r\n\r\n");
      // end
      // begin [file="C:\\hello4.jsp";from=(2,2);to=(9,0)]

      // Normally we don't declare variables, in JSPs,
      // but this example should be self-contained
      java.util.List names = new java.util.LinkedList();
      names.add("Rod");
      names.add("Isabelle");
      names.add("Bob");
      // end
```

```
// HTML // begin [file="C:\\hello4.jsp";from=(9,2);to=(24,0)]
out.write("\r\n\r\n<html>\r\n<head>\r\n\t<title>Names
     tag</title>\r\n</head>\r\n\r\n\r\n<body>\r\n\r\nHTML.\r\n<p/>
     \r\n\r\n<i>\r\n\r\n");
// end
// begin [file="C:\\hello4.jsp";from=(24,0);to=(24,36)]

  /* ----  examples:hellos ---- */
tagext.VarHelloBodyTag _jspx_th_examples_hellos_5 =
        new tagext.VarHelloBodyTag();
 _jspx_th_examples_hellos_5.setPageContext(pageContext);
 _jspx_th_examples_hellos_5.setParent(null);
 _jspx_th_examples_hellos_5.setNames(names);
 try {
   int _jspx_eval_examples_hellos_5 =
                 _jspx_th_examples_hellos_5.doStartTag();
   if (_jspx_eval_examples_hellos_5 == Tag.EVAL_BODY_INCLUDE)
     throw new JspTagException("Since tag handler class
           tagext.VarHelloBodyTag implements BodyTag, it can't return
           Tag.EVAL_BODY_INCLUDE");
   if (_jspx_eval_examples_hellos_5 != Tag.SKIP_BODY) {
     try {
       if (_jspx_eval_examples_hellos_5 != Tag.EVAL_BODY_INCLUDE) {
         out = pageContext.pushBody();
         _jspx_th_examples_hellos_5.setBodyContent((BodyContent) out);
       }
       _jspx_th_examples_hellos_5.doInitBody();
       do {
         java.lang.String name = null;
         name = (java.lang.String) pageContext.getAttribute("name");
         java.lang.Integer index = null;
         index = (java.lang.Integer) pageContext.getAttribute("index");
       // HTML // begin [file="C:\\hello4.jsp";from=(24,36);to=(25,7)]
         out.write("\r\n\tHello ");
       // begin [file="C:\\hello4.jsp";from=(25,10);to=(25,14)]
         out.print(name);
       // HTML // begin [file="C:\\hello4.jsp";from=(25,16);to=(25,31)]
         out.write(". You're entry ");
       // begin [file="C:\\hello4.jsp";from=(25,34);to=(25,39)]
         out.print(index);
       // HTML // begin [file="C:\\hello4.jsp";from=(25,41);to=(26,0)]
         out.write(" in my list.<br/>\r\n");
       // begin [file="C:\\hello4.jsp";from=(26,0);to=(26,18)]
       } while (_jspx_th_examples_hellos_5.doAfterBody() ==
                 BodyTag.EVAL_BODY_TAG);
     } finally {
       if (_jspx_eval_examples_hellos_5 != Tag.EVAL_BODY_INCLUDE)
         out = pageContext.popBody();
     }
   }
   if (_jspx_th_examples_hellos_5.doEndTag() == Tag.SKIP_PAGE)
     return;
 } finally {
   _jspx_th_examples_hellos_5.release();
 }
```

```
                 java.lang.String className = null;
                 className = (java.lang.String) pageContext.getAttribute("className");
                 java.util.Date date = null;
                 date = (java.util.Date) pageContext.getAttribute("date");
             // HTML // begin [file="C:\\hello4.jsp";from=(26,18);to=(27,11)]
                 out.write("\r\nMy name is ");
             // begin [file="C:\\hello4.jsp";from=(27,14);to=(27,23)]
                 out.print(className);
             // HTML // begin [file="C:\\hello4.jsp";from=(27,25);to=(28,12)]
                 out.write(".\r\nThe time is ");
             // begin [file="C:\\hello4.jsp";from=(28,15);to=(28,19)]
                 out.print(date);
             // HTML // begin [file="C:\\hello4.jsp";from=(28,21);to=(34,7)]
                 out.write("<p/>\r\n</i>\r\n\r\nMore HTML.\r\n\r\n</body>\r\n</html>");

         } catch (Exception ex) {
             if (out.getBufferSize() != 0)
                 out.clearBuffer();
             pageContext.handlePageException(ex);
         } finally {
             out.flush();
             _jspxFactory.releasePageContext(pageContext);
         }
     }
 }
```

Notice how a do ... while loop is used to continue processing the tag's body until the tag handler's doAfterBody() method returns SKIP_BODY. Notice also how the PageContext pushBody() method is used to set the implicit variable out to a nested JspWriter. This variable can be manipulated inside the tag implementation without danger to the surrounding page output.

Notice how scripting variables are handled: although the variables are declared in the generated code (because the declares parameter was set to true in the VariableInfo objects), the JSP engine must still examine the PageContext to obtain values for them:

```
    java.lang.String name = null;
    name = (java.lang.String) pageContext.getAttribute("name");
```

This code isn't especially efficient. The JSP 1.1 specification outlines the possibility of tag handler reuse; Tomcat 3.1 makes no attempt at this. (Commercial JSP engines do tend to implement tag handler pooling: something to be aware of in case code that works in Tomcat breaks in another engine.) Also, contrary to good practice regarding beans, new is used to instantiate the tag handler classes. The JSP 1.1 specification is no doubt partly to blame here; only in the final release did it make it clear that tag handlers are beans, and it describes no mechanism for instantiating tag handlers from serialized files.

Tomcat is an open source project, run by the Apache group. This is most welcome, as it gives JSP developers control over the reference implementation of their technology. Unfortunately, Tomcat 3.1 also has a number of serious bugs that can frustrate developers. The nastiest for custom tag development is the way that Tomcat looks for the close of custom tags without allowing for possible whitespace. For example, if I try to close <mytag> using </mytag >, Tomcat will produce mysterious-sounding translation errors. It is actually looking for </mytag>, with no spaces within the angle brackets.

Third Party Custom Tags

The popularity of JSP and the existence of a well defined custom tag and tag library delivery mechanism will be likely create a substantial market for in custom tags. While the need for application-specific custom tags will always remain, there is real benefit in building libraries of industry- or architecture-specific tags. For example, all web search mechanisms tend to present their results in a similar manner. Generic custom tags could facilitate the formatting of results, whether from Google, Inktomi or any other service provider, so long as a consistent OO abstraction is used for results.

Visiting http://www.jsptags.com shows how far the development of standard tags has already progressed. Initiatives are well underway with custom tags available from major application server vendors such as Allaire (JRun) and BEA (WebLogic), as well as several open source projects.

Sun envisaged this kind of market in the JSP 1.1 specification, but they are also considering creating a standard library of tag extensions that will be available in all compliant JSP containers. JSR-000052 "A Standard Tag Library for JavaServer Pages" is endorsed by many industry partners, including Allaire, BEA, IBM, Netscape, Adobe and SilverStream.

We will take a brief look at several tags in the JRun Tag Library. All of the tags to be discussed can be found in a jruntags.jar file included with JRun Server 3.0, available for free download at http://commerce.allaire.com/download. The tags are pretty self-explanatory, so the focus will be on the design idioms involved, as well as to give some insight into the many possibilities for tag authoring. This particular tag library has been submitted to Sun for consideration as the standard tag library reference implementation. It has been tested on both Tomcat and JRun servers, and should work on any JSP 1.1 compliant server.

The tags are broadly categorized into three categories:

- ❑   Flow control.
- ❑   J2EE technologies.
- ❑   Client-side validation.

Flow Control

Tags that facilitate conditional and iterative presentation of body content data are excellent candidates for tag extensions. In the last chapter we wrote a body tag that performed the task of iterating over its body content. An alternative approach would have been to write a custom tag that determined the desired information (perhaps using information passed to tag through its attributes), and then introduced a scripting variable into the page that contained the results as a collection of objects. Finally, we could use some general-purpose iteration tag, such as the <foreach> tag to iterate through the collection.

An interesting tag in the JRun Tag Library is the <foreach> tag that simplifies the task of iterating through a collection of objects. The most common data types representing a collection of similar objects are:

- ❑   The ResultSet object.
- ❑   The Enumeration object.
- ❑   Any array of objects that subclass Object.
- ❑   A linked list of objects which subclass Object, used in combination with some Iterator object to traverse the linked list.

608

Each data type has a unique syntax required to iterate over the collection, for example, while(rs.next()) or while(e.hasMoreElements()) etc. A <foreach> tag has the same syntax regardless of the data type, and its tag handler determines the object's class and handles iteration accordingly. The following code fragment might be used to iterate over an Enumeration object that was added to the pageContext:

```
<%@ taglib uri="jruntags" prefix="jrun" %>
<%-- Asssume that these enumerations were added into the
page context by some other tag extension. --%>


<% java.util.Hashtable h = new java.util.Hashtable();
   h.put("No.1", "Dave");
   h.put("No.2", "Brian");
   h.put("No.3", "Paul");
   java.util.Enumeration employee_numbers = h.keys();
   java.util.Enumeration employee_names = h.elements();
%>

<table cellpadding="1">
  <tr>
    <td>
      <jrun:foreach item="name" type="java.lang.String"
                    group=<%= employee_numbers %>><%= name %>
        <br />
      </jrun:foreach>
    </td>
    <td>
      <jrun:foreach item="number" type="java.lang.String"
                    group="<%= employee_names %>"><%= number %>
        <br />
      </jrun:foreach>
    </td>
  </tr>
</table>
```

The output of this page is as follows:

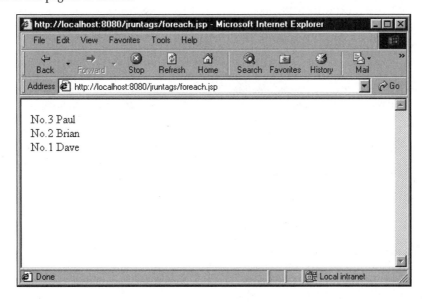

This design has numerous benefits including modularity and code reuse. It is easier to write a tag that introduces some scripting variable into the page context and then use a generalized <foreach> tag to handle iteration through the collection, than it is to write the iteration logic into every BodyTag class that needs to iterate over its body content. Furthermore, such a tag custom tag removes the need for scriptlet code within the JSP to control iteration.

Other possibilities include flow control such as <if>, <case> and <switch> statements. These tags have attributes that accept runtime expressions, which determine if the body content should be evaluated or skipped. A simple usage of tag-based flow control would be as follows:

```
<%@ taglib uri="jruntags" prefix="jrun" %>
<%-- "name" is a String variable that has somehow been placed into the page
     context. Here, for simplicitly, we just declare it manually: --%>

<%! String name = "Clement"; %>

<jrun:switch>

  <jrun:case expr='<%= name.equals("Clement") %>'>
     Hi Clement!
  </jrun:case>

  <jrun:case expr='<%= name.equals("Tom") %>'>
     Hi Tom!
  </jrun:case>

</jrun:switch>
```

The first string comparison (if any) to return true will have its body content evaluated. It is important to understand that the <if>, <case> and <swich> tag extensions don't offer anything that cannot be accomplished by using embedded JSP scriptlets that contain the flow control statements made available by the Java programming language. However, tag-based page-flow control offers a more natural look and feel when writing JSP pages, particularly for people who have little experience with java programming.

J2EE Technologies

Tag extensions can be written to provide a tag based abstraction of any API. Consider the following example, which performs a database-driven mass e-mailing. The code uses a <sql> tag that abstracts JDBC functionality, and then uses the <sendmail> tag that abstracts the JavaMail functionality:

```
<%@ page import="allaire.taglib.*" %>
<%@ taglib uri="jruntags" prefix="jrun" %>

<jrun:sql driver="com.jdbc.odbc.JdbcOdbcDriver" url="jdbc:odbc:Store"
          id="dbQuery">
  SELECT FirstName, Email
  FROM Customer
</jrun:sql>
<jrun:param id="dbQuery" type="QueryTable"/>

<jrun:foreach group="<%= dbQuery %>">
  <jrun:sendmail host="mail.company.com" sender="service@company.com"
    recipient='<%= dbQuery.get("Email") %>'
```

```
        subject="Thank you valued customer">
        Dear <%= dbQuery.get("FirstName") %>,
        We are excited to tell you about some new sales at our store.
    </jrun:sendmail>
  </jrun:foreach>
```

Here, we see that the `<sql>` tag performs a database query and returns to the page context. The `<sql>` tag is simply an abstraction of the JDBC API, and the tag handler uses the tag attributes to connect to a data source and create and execute the query specified within its body. Recall that the page context is a hashtable that provides access to all the namespaces associated with a JSP page and provides access to page attributes. An object placed in the page context isn't automatically available as a scripting variable for use in a scriptlet; to do this you would need to call the `PageContext.getAttribute()` method and perform the proper type casting.

The `<param>` tag does exactly that, fetching the `dbQuery` entry from the page context and casting it into a `QueryTable` object for use as a scripting variable. In this case, a `QueryTable` object is simply an object that implements the most common methods of the `java.sql.ResultSet` interface. The reason for this extra step is that we wouldn't want the execution of a tag that introduces an object into the page context to automatically make those variables available to your scriptlets by default. This is similar to the ability to ignore the return value of any Java method. By requiring this extra step there is a reduction in the risk of naming collisions or other undesired effects. Finally the `QueryTable` object is iterated through using a `<foreach>` tag, as discussed earlier. Next, a customized message is e-mailed for each customer in the database using a `<sendmail>` tag, which abstracts away the details of connecting to an SMTP mail transport and firing off a message contained within its body.

It should be noted that there is debate over what constitutes a 'good' tag. Java purists renounce such tag idioms because it is not model-2 architecture, and is against the spirit of J2EE - separating logic from presentation, essentially saying that just because you could, it doesn't mean that you should. Conversely an apathetic Java programmer would embrace such idioms, as it is remarkable what can be done in just a few lines of JSP. Finally there are Java moderates who understand the value of (say) the model-2 architectures, while accepting that not everybody knows how to architect such applications, or that other considerations such as time-to-market or ease-of-use are also valid, and thus make design decisions on a case-by-case basis.

Client-Side Validation

While tags that introduce text or simple markup into a page are less flexible, there is still scope for much functionality here. Take for example the task of validating form input using a client side scripting language like JavaScript. One could easily write different HTML input types that generate the JavaScript form validation functions, for example:

```
<%@ taglib uri="jruntags" prefix="jrun" %>

<jrun:form name="superform" action="someaction.jsp">

Required First Name: <jrun:input name="FirstName" type="text" required="true"/>
Credit Card: <jrun:input name="CreditCardNumber" type="creditcard"/>
Birthdate: <jrun:input name="BirthDate" type="date"/>
Number of Dependents: <jrun:input name="Dependents" type="integer"/>
Social Security Card: <jrun:input name="SSN" type="ssc"/>
Telephone Number: <jrun:input name="Telephone" type="phone" required="true"/>

<input type="submit" value="Submit"/>
```

These inputs are like regular HTML inputs, but have optional additional attributes that indicate if the input field is required, as well as new input types such as date, integer, phone, etc. By viewing the generated HTML page, we see the appropriate JavaScript input validation functions are automatically generated and in-lined into the page. For example, this is the JavaScript function that is generated to validate a 'required' input:

```
<script language="JAVASCRIPT" type="text/javascript">
<!--
function _allr_onError(form_obj, input_obj, obj_value, error_msg) {
    alert(error_msg);
    return false;
}

function _allr_hasValue(obj, obj_type) {
  if (obj_type.toUpperCase() == "TEXT" || obj_type.toUpperCase() == "PASSWORD") {
    if (obj.value.length == 0)
      return false;
    else
      return true;
  } else if (obj_type.toUpperCase() == "SELECT") {
    for (i=0; i < obj.length; i++) {
    if (obj.options[i].selected)
      return true;
    }
    return false;
  } else if (obj_type.toUpperCase() == "RADIO" ||
    obj_type.toUpperCase() == "CHECKBOX") {
    if (obj.checked) {
      return true;
    } else {
      for (i=0; i < obj.length; i++) {
      if (obj[i].checked)
        return true;
      }
      return false;
    }
  }
}

function _allr_checksuperform(_allr_this) {
  if (!_allr_hasValue(_allr_this.FirstName, "text" )) {
    if (!_allr_onError(_allr_this, _allr_this.FirstName,
                       _allr_this.FirstName.value,
                       "Error in FirstName. ")) {
    return false;
    }
  }
  return true;
}

<form ACTION="someaction.jsp" NAME="superform"
      onSubmit="return _allr_checksuperform(this)">
  Required First Name: <input type="text" NAME="FirstName">
  <input type="submit" VALUE="Submit" NAME="SendInfo">
</form>
```

In conclusion, the possibilities for tag extensions are limitless. The JRun tag library has tags that support distributed transactions, send/receive asynchronous messages, performs JNDI resource lookups, XSLT, servlet invocation, and there are many other tag libraries available. (Note that the EJB, JTA, and JMS tags won't work on Tomcat, as it does not support these technologies.) Third party tag libraries are good resources for code reuse and rapid application development, as well as seeing the various design idioms involved in tag programming.

Tools Support and Future Directions

The full potential of custom tags will not be realized until sophisticated JSP authoring and debugging tools that make it easy to work with custom tags and third party tag libraries are widely available. Clearly traditional Java IDEs, particularly the debuggers, are unable to handle the tag-based nature of JSP development. Currently, several vendors produce such tools including Macromedia's Dreamweaver UltraDev, IBM WebSphere Studio, and Allaire JRun Studio.

Finally, the JSP specifications are constantly being enhanced and future versions might include a standardized mechanism for customizing tag behavior at deployment time. Another interesting possibility is a mechanism for writing tag extensions in terms of JSP rather then using the Tag API, similar how a JSP generates a servlet. A 'Java Server Tag' (JST) would generate a tag handler class, thus doing the same thing with tag handlers that JSP did for servlets, notably improved separation of presentation from logic, as well as making things easier.

Overall, we have found it a pleasure to work with tag extensions. For a new technology, their usability is impressive. However, there are two enhancements we would love to see: allowing tag handlers to be instantiated from serialized files – after all, tag handlers are beans, and it should be possible to use property editors with them; and the ability to specify the default value of optional attributes in TLD files. This would enable tag behaviour to be modified easily at deployment time, without modifying Java code or properties files.

Summary

We have seen some further uses of JSP Tag Extensions in this chapter. This has shown how flexible the technology is, however tags should be designed carefully to maximize their re-use and ease-of-use. With some care we can build a suite of useful tags that can greatly enhance our sites.

We have seen how generation of dynamic content can be simplified by moving code from the HTML or JSP page and into class files including on the fly generation of tables. This makes our code more maintainable and should make the designers life easier too.

Third party tags can be a very useful resource, and are often a viable alternative to writing our own.

In the next chapter we will use the code we have generated, to see how we can write JSP files in such a way as to maximize on their maintainability.

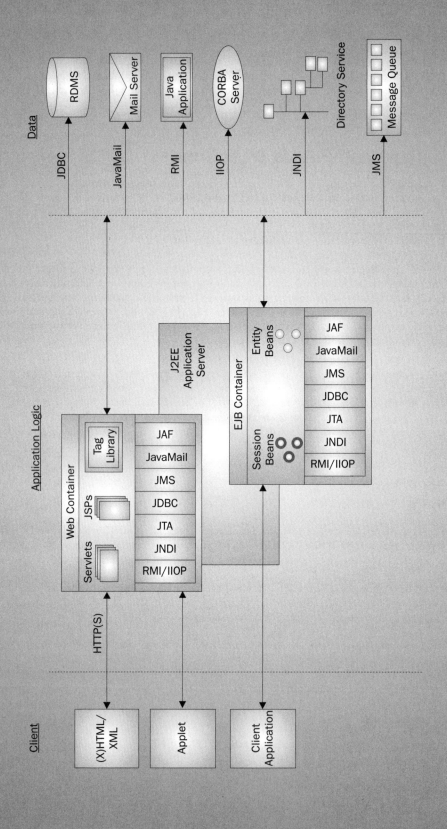

14

Writing Maintainable JSP Pages

Exciting as JSPs are, they do not solve all the problems of designing web interfaces. Presentation and content are not automatically cleanly separated, and there is often an impedance mismatch between OO middleware and HTML generation. The latter is not a problem unique to JSPs. The HTTP request-response punctuation of the work of web applications fits poorly with the need for an application's objects to cooperate. The problem of representing the state of Java objects as web pages and updating them using HTML forms is surprisingly awkward.

Many JSPs in production systems are hard to read and maintain. Too often they consist of a mish-mash of Java code in scriptlets and HTML markup, with jarring transitions between levels of abstraction that no experienced developer would tolerate in a Java application. Writing maintainable JSPs is not easy. While the Java language itself does a good job of helping developers to write maintainable code, JSP provides very little help and much temptation to do otherwise.

There is a scarcity of resources on writing good JSPs, as opposed to mastering JSP syntax. This is in marked contrast to the OO programming, where any good bookstore carries a shelf of books at every level from novice to expert.

This chapter is an effort to address this gap. We will:

- ❑ Describe approaches to JSP authoring that overcome the major pitfalls
- ❑ Discuss some of the practical challenges involved
- ❑ Present guidelines for good practice
- ❑ Discuss a sample application that accesses real-world data

In this chapter we assume that JSPs are being used primarily to generate HTML or XHTML. Of course this is not always the case. However, the concepts are generic enough to translate to any text based content generation. (If a binary or non human-readable format like PDF is to be generated, a servlet is the correct choice – see Chapter 12 for examples.)

The Goal

Most experienced JSP developers will share a basic rule:

A JSP should look like readable HTML page with a little dynamic content, rather than a Java program with embedded markup, or even a balance of scriptlets and markup.

There are many justifications for this rule. Two of the most important relate to the decision of when to use JSPs, and the division of roles in web development teams. Java servlets provide an excellent means of handling dynamic page generation in cases when it is logical to think of the page generator as a program. Equally importantly, the HTML on today's web sites can be very complex. Unless the page generation approach in use is understandable by page designers, it will be impossible for them to contribute their skills to maintaining and enhancing presentation on a site.

Two further rules follow from this basic premise. Together, they amount to *a clear separation of presentation and content*:

❑   **Ensure that business logic is where it belongs**
    This is emphatically not in a JSP. Not only do scriptlets (fragments of Java code embedded in JSPs) obscure the markup generation that is the main role of JSPs, but they are not reusable and do not fit into an OO model.

❑   **Ensure that presentation is centralized where it belongs**
    Presentation belongs in JSPs, assuming pages contain some dynamic content. (There is nothing wrong with pure HTML.) Don't generate HTML from Java code. Since the early days of servlets, developers have realized that Java code is poor at generating HTML markup. (The issues in escaping double quotes alone tend to make Java code generating raw HTML unreadable.) Having servlets read markup from properties files or templates is an improvement, or as an alternative we can use OO HTML generation libraries. The result, however, tends to be a web interface that is hard to understand. Each dynamic page is built from scattered building blocks that make little sense on their own. For example, tracking down a browser error that may be due to unbalanced or crossed tags is often difficult, as may be attempting to understand the behavior of JavaScript on a generated page.

Developers who have worked throughout the lifecycle of systems with JSP interfaces realize how important it is to create JSPs that can be manipulated by HTML designers. This usually amounts to ensuring that Java content (scriptlets) are limited, of easily manageable complexity, and clearly demarcated from HTML content.

The potential for JSPs to be refined by non-programmers is particularly important, as a clear division of roles between Java developers and HTML coders is crucial to the success of web development using

JSPs. Lack of such a division is one of the reasons JSP development tends to fall down a gap in development teams, without being subject to any real development process. There is much to be gained by empowering HTML specialists to work on JSPs; Java developers tend to lack design flair, and find HTML coding unrewarding. Developers should also consider the future of the JSPs they write. Are they likely to want to be interrupted while working on a new project to change the fonts and colours in a JSP-generated table? But can they expect anyone else to do it if their JSPs are really Java classes escaping into HTML to simplify the syntax of generating markup? The presentational requirements of real-world systems change with surprising frequency, and developers have a responsibility to create interfaces that permit rapid response to business needs.

These aims are surprisingly difficult to achieve in practice. To do so, we must visualize JSPs in the context of an n-tiered architecture, maximize our use of those features of JSP that enable the separation of presentation and content, and be aware of the pitfalls that must be avoided.

JSPs in a Multi-Tier Architecture

Unless we have a well-designed middleware layer exposing data at the appropriate level of abstraction, our JSPs will inevitably be complicated by business logic, which will soon become a nightmare to keep up to date. Before moving on to more practical coding issues, we must consider the place of a JSP layer in a well-designed J2EE system.

The J2EE model is based on the assumption that the presentation of data changes frequently, while the structure of the data being presented changes infrequently. (Note the distinction between change in data *values*, which occurs constantly in any system, and change in data *structure*. The latter will generally occur only with each major application rollout.) It is also important to remember that the J2EE model supports a variety of client types, not merely JSPs.

Multi-tier architectures are now a 'given' in large-scale web design. The diagram below tries to put more detail into the presentational tiers of a J2EE application:

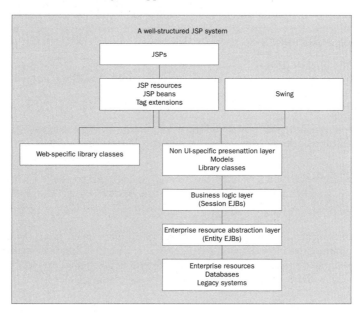

Although I have described this in terms of J2EE architecture, we are not required to use EJBs. There are applications where the robustness and scalability of an enterprise application server is not required, but in such cases the need for a clean JSP layer is unchanged. In such applications, a similar tiering can be implemented without using EJBs. Preserving the distinction between business logic layer and enterprise resource abstraction layer (implemented in EJB systems by session and entity beans respectively) is still advisable; if a system is separated into tiers with clearly defined interfaces, it will be easier to modify and maintain.

This is not the place for an in-depth look at J2EE architecture, but let us briefly consider each of these tiers in turn, from the bottom. The top four tiers will be of most interest to us. They are also the most often neglected in architectural discussions:

❑ **Enterprise resources**
Non-Java resources offering raw data without the business logic necessary for a particular application. Most commonly this tier will consist of one or more relational databases, but other possibilities are legacy systems and distributed resources accessed by JNDI.

❑ **Enterprise resource abstraction layer**
This is a relatively thin object abstraction layer wrapping the enterprise resources. In an EJB model, entity beans will be used to implement this layer.

❑ **Business logic layer**
This is not concerned with presentation, but will implement most of the application's workflow. This layer will provide the logic required to support the system's use cases. In an EJB architecture, it will be comprised of session beans. The design of this layer is crucial in underpinning a cleanly implemented JSP interface.

❑ **Non UI-specific presentation layer**
This layer is not always necessary, and often overlooked, but in more complex systems it will have an important role. The key question should be: *Is this presentation logic specific to a JSP interface, or would it be common to all interfaces?* I find it helpful to think of a Swing interface as an alternative. Swing models are a good example of non UI-specific presentation code: although they hook directly into Swing view components, they provide an abstraction that is usable by any kind of GUI.

❑ **Web-specific library classes**
These will perform any complex request parsing, cookie handling, encryption, or other functions specific to a web interface.

❑ **JSP resources**
This layer will include JSP beans and implementations of tag extensions. These classes will provide a bridge between JSPs and the enterprise objects they use.

❑ **JSPs**
A long way from the data and main business logic layer, aren't they? If we get this layering right, the JSPs will contain little, if any, Java code, but will be *views* of data provided by the supporting tiers of the application.

To get a more practical insight into how such architectures work in practice, imagine we are working on a new version of the user registration system on a large web site. Due to database changes, there are a number of rules that must be applied to logins: for example, some existing usernames are now illegal, and such users must be allowed to log in and then prompted to choose new usernames. Users from selected countries should be shown a special offer the first time they log in to the new version of the site. When users log in, cookie values must be generated to integrate with third party software. This cookie generation requires complex algorithms. Where should each piece of functionality required fit into a J2EE architecture?

- ❑ The new rules on usernames and the need to force some users to change their usernames should be implemented in the business logic layer. This is not specific to a JSP interface. It is not even specific to a graphical interface: the session EJBs implementing it could allow a remote CORBA client to support a command-line interface. The business logic layer will not only implement such special cases, but also provide an abstraction for all data access. UI code should not be tied to the schema of the database in use, but should only access (and be able to access) objects and methods helping to realize the use cases.

- ❑ The special offer is specific to presentation, but not to JSP. There might be a URL associated with the special offer, but a Swing client might present a link to this while still supporting the same login functionality. The implementation of this belongs in the non UI-specific presentation layer.

- ❑ The cookie generation requirement is, however, specific to HTTP. The classes involved in implementing the cookie generation algorithms would be of no interest to a remote CORBA client or a Swing applet. Their implementation should fit into the layer of web-specific library classes.

None of this functionality belongs in the JSPs themselves. The JSPs will be concerned with how the system *looks*, rather than how it works, and will use JSP beans, and tag extensions if necessary, to access the lower architectural layers.

Techniques for Writing Maintainable JSPs

Moving from the theoretical to the practical, let's consider some of the most important day-to-day issues in designing the JSP layer. It is assumed that the underlying middleware appropriately abstracts the business logic, and that we're not merely moving the deckchairs on the Titanic.

This discussion reflects a desire to leverage proven design patterns as far as possible within the HTTP request-response paradigm. Fortunately, we can still make effective use of what is perhaps the most successful of all architectural patterns: the model view controller pattern.

Request Controller Architecture

JSP design is often complicated by the need for JSPs both to perform request processing and to present content. These tasks are quite distinct for many pages, and request processing may be complicated. There are also other problems in designing JSP systems page-by-page. Some JSPs may need to manipulate session or application-wide resources or state. Others may need to examine request values to check whether to redirect the request. Simply mapping request properties onto a bean (see the discussion of JSP beans below) is not a universal solution, especially if redirection may be required.

There is an elegant solution to such problems, sometimes referred to as the "**JSP Model 2 Architecture**". I prefer to call it **request controller architecture**. It involves having one JSP or servlet as a single point of entry into an application or group of pages. The entry point produces no output itself but processes the request, optionally manipulates session and application state, and redirects requests to the appropriate JSP view. Complex applications may consist of a number of request controller page groups.

Request controller implementations usually include an `action` or similarly named parameter in each request. The value of this parameter is examined by the controller, which uses it to decide how to process the request.

Request controller architecture is one of the most useful approaches to building maintainable JSP systems. It is a true design pattern for JSPs. Systems built using it tend to be more flexible and extensible than those using a page-centric approach, and to achieve a better separation of presentation and content.

Request controller architecture promotes thinking of a web application as being in a well-defined state at any time. (This can easily be made explicit by holding a state variable in the request controller.) A state-oriented approach can be helpful in understanding and documenting web applications. (See the case study later in this chapter for an example of a state machine describing a web application.)

> *Request controller architecture is widely advocated (for example in Sun's J2EE Blueprint), and goes under a variety of names. IBM refers to it as "Structured Web Interactions" (see the excellent discussion at* `http://www-4.ibm.com/software/ebusiness/pm.html`*). IBM and a number of authors recommend using a servlet as the controller. In my view, whether or not to use a servlet is a matter of taste, so long as the logic of the controller is removed from the JSP itself. The examples in this chapter will use JSP controllers that use "request processor" classes to perform page flow decisions.*

Implementing Request Controller Architecture

The request controller pattern can be implemented in one JSP consisting of a long scriptlet and no HTML generation, but this is inelegant. Java classes, not JSPs, are the correct place for control logic. Compare, for example, the definition of methods in JSPs and Java classes. JSP declaration syntax is inelegant, and allows no opportunity to use Javadoc, or to expose methods to other objects. A better alternative is to make the JSP controller delegate control logic to a "request processor" class.

Assuming that page flow and other logic is to be placed in Java classes, but that we use JSP, rather than servlet, controllers, the minimal requirements to implement a request controller architecture are:

❑ **One controller JSP**
This will be a very simple JSP that will instantiate the request processor class and use it to find the appropriate view page for an incoming request. It will forward the request to this view. It's a good idea to use consistent naming conventions when implementing this pattern, to enable the application's structure to be grasped quickly. I give controllers names of the form `xxxxController.jsp`, where xxxx is the name of their role in the web application. (Controller JSPs will be of no interest to page designers, so consistent naming can help to clarify the division of responsibility within a team.)

❑ **One request processor class and a number of helper classes**
The request processor object will, as a minimum, decide on the appropriate view for each request. Before selecting a view, it will perform any processing required to handle each request (such as updating observers), unless the system is complex enough to warrant an **event mediator** (see below). The processing performed by a request processor instance may depend on the application's state, which the request processor must keep up to date. There will normally be one request processor object per user. It *is* possible to share these objects among all users of an application, but this is only advisable if the request processor is threadsafe. Again, consistent naming is beneficial. I give request processor classes names of the form `xxxxRequestProcessor` or `xxxxRequestController`.

❑ **Multiple view JSPs**

These will perform no request processing, but will generate all the system's pages. The request processor class will normally handle any complex session or request manipulation and the instantiation of objects backing the views. Many view JSPs will obtain the data they present from a page bean (see the discussion of JSP beans below).

The following is a typical example of a controller JSP. (We will look at it later as part of the case study.) It is merely an entry point into the application that leaves the page flow logic and state management to a Java class:

```
<%--
    JSP controller for the data explorer application.
    This page produces no output, but redirects each request
    to the appropriate JSP view.
    The logic required to make this choice
    is supplied by the RequestController session bean.
--%>

<%@page session="true" errorPage="systemError.jsp" %>

<%-- The controller object will be instantiated by a session's first
    call to this page --%>
<jsp:useBean id="controller" scope="session" class="ui.RequestController" />

<%--
    Each request to this page will be forwarded to the appropriate view,
    as determined by the controller and its helper classes. These classes
    will set the session state appropriately before returning the URL of
    a view, to which this page will forward the response.
--%>
<jsp:forward page="<%=controller.getNextPage(pageContext, request)%>"/>
```

The crucial method in the supporting class, `RequestController`, is

```
public String getNextPage(PageContext pageContext,
            HttpServletRequest request)
    throws BrowseException;
```

This returns the URL of the JSP view to which the response should be redirected after any necessary changes to session state. For example, this class contains code to instantiate a session bean used by the application, and make it available to JSPs:

```
BrowseSession session = (BrowseSession)
    pageContext.getAttribute(SESSION_BEAN_NAME, PageContext.SESSION_SCOPE);

if (session == null) {
  session = new BrowseSession();
  pageContext.setAttribute(SESSION_BEAN_NAME, session,
        PageContext.SESSION_SCOPE);
}
```

The `RequestController` needs to be passed parameters allowing it to access the request and, in some cases, the response. The `getNextPage()` method will probably begin by looking for an action or other well-known parameter in the request:

```
String action = request.getParameter("action");
// If no action was specified, the user must first log in
if (action == null || action.equals(""))
  return LOGIN_PAGE;
//... do something else, depending on the action
```

A sequence diagram helps to clarify the way in which the JSPs and Java classes collaborate to handle each incoming request:

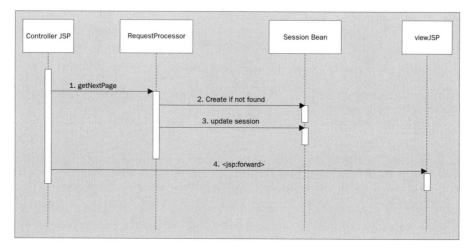

Some examples of the request controller pattern will also feature additional classes, which take over some of the responsibility of the request processor in complex systems:

❑ **Request to event translator class**
   This will translate requests into application-dependent event objects that can easily be passed to other classes.

❑ **Event mediator**
   This will take events and perform any updates to session or application state required.

A request processor using this approach might include code like this, invoking the request translator to convert the request into an event object that contains any required information, and passing the event object to the event mediator:

```
String action = request.getParameter("action");
// If no action was specified, the user must first log in
if (action == null || action.equals(""))
  return LOGIN_PAGE;
ApplicationEvent e = requestTranslator.requestToEvent(request);
eventMediator.processEvent(e);
```

The event mediator can then work with event objects, which it can pass to other application objects that are needed to handle an event, or which must be notified of it:

```
if (e.getEventType() == ApplicationEvent.UPGRADE) {
  upgradeHandler.handleUpgrade(e);
  logger.logEvent(e);
}
```

The request controller pattern is most useful in such cases, when processing requests to a system requires coordination between a number of objects. The class that provides this coordination implements the *mediator* design pattern; the use of an event class is an example of the *Command* design pattern.

> **Don't feel you need to use the <jsp:useBean> tag to instantiate all your JSP beans. There is a very useful form of this tag that does not specify an implementing class, and which throws an exception if no such object is defined in the HTTP session or request. Simply omit the class attribute of the useBean tag, and specify only the type, like this:**
>
> **<jsp:useBean id="browseSession" scope="session" type="ui.BrowseSession" />**
>
> **Beans used in such pages can be defined through a complete <jsp:useBean> tag elsewhere, or can be placed in the session by a controller.**

When Not to Use a Request Controller Architecture

Some web applications fit well with the notion of every page handling its own request parameters (probably using a bean). This approach can also work well for simple applications that maintain no session state – for example, relying on query strings for communication between pages. In such cases, a request controller architecture will deliver little benefit, and will probably not justify the complexity it introduces.

Using Includes in JSP

There is a real danger of code and markup duplication in JSP interfaces. Including common JSPs or JSP fragments where necessary can minimize this. This does not help to move code out of JSPs, or to achieve a true OO solution, but it can nevertheless significantly enhance system maintainability. It is analogous to procedural code reuse.

Two Types of Includes

JSP 1.1 supports two types of include: **static**, and **dynamic**. In a static include, the content of the included JSP fragment is inserted into the including JSP at translation time, and used along with that file's own content to build the Java source file that will be compiled. In a dynamic include, the request is passed to the specified URL, with its response being inserted into the page response. This means that the contents of a statically included file must be legal in the including file at the point at which it is included. Dynamic includes, however, need not even be JSPs; static HTML or other dynamically generated content such as ASP output can be included.

Static includes are performed using the include *directive*:

```
<%@ include file="_pickList.jsp" %>
```

Dynamic includes are performed using the include *action*:

```
<jsp:include page="include.jsp" flush="true" />
```

The `flush` parameter is optional (although Tomcat 3.1 wrongly insists on it). In JSP 1.1 the default, and only legal, value for the flush parameter is `true`. (We'll discuss this further shortly.) The `<jsp:param>` element can be used as a subtag of the `<jsp:include>` to pass data to the included page, as in the following JSP fragment:

```
<jsp:include page="include.jsp" flush="true" >
  <jsp:param name="newParam" value="extra" />
  <jsp:param name="existingParam" value="new value" />
</jsp:include>
```

The additional data will be available to the included page in the form of additional or overridden request parameters. In the example above, assume that the `newParam` parameter was not part of the request to the original page, while the `existingParam` parameter was. The included page will see the additional parameter, `newParam`, and the new value for `existingParam`. The scope of the new parameters will be the `<jsp:include>` call only; the new parameters will not be available after the include.

Because of limitations in the way dynamic includes work in JSP 1.1, static includes are the more useful of the two include types in practice. The main problem with dynamic includes is that the `<jsp:include>` action always causes a flush before the include. This means that dynamically included pages can't cause redirection to an error page on an uncaught exception – a very serious problem. (Sun are aware of the serious limitations in the usability of the JSP dynamic include mechanism. JSR 000053, for the development of the Servlet 2.3 and JSP 1.2 specifications, includes a call for "Proper support for inclusion of JSP pages without forcing flushing of buffers." See `http://java.sun.com/aboutJava/communityprocess/jsr/jsr_053_jspservlet.html` for further information.)

Dynamically included pages also have limited access to the response object; they cannot set headers (including cookies). Dynamic inclusion is also a performance overhead; static inclusion isn't really inclusion at all once the translation unit has been generated, so it has no performance penalty. Another serious drawback with dynamic includes is that the means of communication between including and included page cannot be enforced at translation time, except for primitive types for which we can use `<jsp:param>`. Objects can only be communicated using a mechanism like `setAttribute()`, meaning that if an include is used incorrectly, the problem will show up as a null pointer exception at runtime. Static includes don't have this problem. If an included JSP fragment accesses one or more variables, pages including it won't compile unless those variables are in scope at the time of the include.

Using Static Includes

Because communication between including and included pages is checked at translation time, it is useful and acceptable to parameterize static includes using scripting variables. The scripting variables required should be documented in a hidden header comment in the statically included JSP fragments, as should any dependencies on session beans. Static includes are unlikely to be reusable outside a particular application, so such dependencies are not usually problematic.

Static includes are not complete JSPs in their own right. This should be reflected through a naming convention such as prefixing the names of such fragments with an underscore. Such page building blocks may also be gathered in a special directory.

There is one drawback to using static includes that must be noted. JSP 1.1 defines no mechanism for letting pages know when static content they've included has changed. After translation, this content is compiled into self-contained implementation classes. So, when a statically included page fragment changes, remember to "touch" all the pages that include it (that is, update their last modification time), unless you are using a JSP engine that provides more sophisticated content management than the specification mandates.

> **Note also an irritating bug in Tomcat. Tomcat 3.1 won't compile a page with more than one include of the same static page, suggesting that this may be a recursive include.**

Using JSP Beans

The most obvious way to reduce the amount of Java code in a JSP is to use one or more JSP beans. This has been possible since the early days of JSP.

How best to use beans is not entirely clear-cut, and they are not the panacea one might at first think. There is some confusion in the way in which beans are supported in the JSP specification. A bean should really be a resource for the presentation of the page, but much emphasis has been given to mapping request parameters onto bean properties.

This can be done in two ways. Individual request parameters can be mapped onto a bean property using a `<jsp:setProperty>` action like this:

```
<jsp:setProperty name="bean" property="propertyName" param="paramName" />
```

Alternatively, all request properties can be mapped onto a bean in a single `<jsp:setProperty>` action like this:

```
<jsp:setProperty name="bean" property="*" />
```

In the latter case, remember that no exception will be thrown if there are request parameters that do not have matching bean properties. The bean will also need to check that all required attributes have been set by the mapping. Beans that process request parameters do not aspire to wide reusability, so tailoring them to handle a particular request structure using the `property="*"` syntax is generally best. Although the `<jsp:setProperty>` action is annoyingly ignorant of its context, and doesn't automatically act on the current bean if it is invoked within a `<jsp:useBean>` action, it is good practice to limit use of `<jsp:setProperty>` to `<jsp:useBean>` actions. (However, remember that the contents of a `<jsp:useBean>` action are only executed if the bean is instantiated. If the bean already existed in the JSP's PageContext, scriptlets or `<jsp:setProperty>` actions within the `<jsp:useBean>` action will be ignored.)

Beans in a well-engineered JSP interface usually fall into two types: **page beans**, which help in the presentation of a particular page and may process requests to it; and **session beans**, which provide common state across a user's session. These are entirely different in purpose, and should be considered separately.

There is a third bean type: **application beans**, which are shared between all users of a web application to maintain global state. These are less commonly used, but can produce significant efficiency gains if used appropriately.

Both page beans and session beans are necessary when implementing non-trivial systems. Most systems will use one session bean to hold state, and one page bean for each page that presents a view of complex data.

Page Beans

A page bean is a model, with the JSP being a view. Page beans are closely integrated with the JSPs that use them. They will only be used on multiple pages if the same content must be presented in different formats. (This is, however, a frequent requirement.) Typically, page beans will define 'getter' methods for each piece of dynamic content displayed by the corresponding JSP. These getters may return primitive types, or more complex object types, which the JSPs will be responsible for displaying (possibly through the use of custom tags). Page model beans may perform some request processing beyond the simple mapping of request parameters onto their attributes before exposing a model, but should not be used to handle complex page flow logic. (For example, they are not suited to handling redirection.)

Session Beans

Session beans belong to a user's session within an application, not a page. They are not tied to presentation, but help hold references to enterprise resources and other data allowing a user session to maintain and cache state. For example, a session bean might be used to hold a user's real name and email address through a session, and a reference to a session EJB that could be used to obtain more information. Session beans should never be used to process requests.

Developers new to J2EE often confuse JSP session beans with stateful session EJBs. These are different in purpose, although there may be a one-to-one correspondence between JSP session beans and stateful session EJBs in many systems. Although JSP session beans are not directly concerned with page production, they should be *views* of or proxies for enterprise middleware, not enterprise middleware themselves. Stateful session EJBs *are* part of the enterprise middleware, although they perform processing for a particular client.

Application Beans

Application beans are still wider in scope than session beans. They maintain state for all users of an application. They are used less often than session beans, but can be useful to minimize memory usage and enhance performance, especially when many users require access to some data that is expensive to retrieve or compute. Application beans are best used for read-only data. Using them to hold read-write data is a recipe for concurrency problems or synchronization bottlenecks. There is little need to use application beans to hold constant data for the application: this can be placed in the web.xml file of a web application and accessed using JNDI, or placed in .properties files following established Java convention.

> **Although the benefits of maintaining server-side state are well worthwhile, don't be tempted to cram large amounts of data into session objects. Any respectable application server or servlet engine will provide server clustering, and cluster-wide preservation of HTTP session state. This allows successive requests to be directed to different servers in the event of the failure of a particular server, or network congestion, without loss of session state. Implementing this will mean capturing the state of all session objects (probably using Java serialization) and constantly passing it over the wire to ensure synchronization. Thus session objects should only hold data that is modest in storage demands and constantly in use, together with references to enterprise objects or keys that can be used to retrieve other data as required.**

Bean Configuration

Remember that JSP beans *are* beans. One way to add flexibility to a running system is to write GUI property editors for JSP beans. This can empower the business owners of the system and free developers from the need to perform minor maintenance.

JSP beans can be instantiated from a serialized file by setting the `beanName` attribute of the `<jsp:useBean>` tag to a value supported by the `java.beans.Beans.instantiate()` method, such as the following, which tries to instantiate bean `mypackage.TestBean`:

```
<jsp:useBean id="test" scope="page" beanName="mypackage.TestBean" >
```

The `Beans` class will check for a serialized file of the form `mypackage/TestBean.ser`, and instantiate a bean from the `CLASSPATH` using new only if this fails.

For property editing to produce useful results, it is vital to make JSP beans as generic as possible. They should expose properties that control their behavior.

Dos and Don'ts

The most important rule with beans is that they shouldn't be used to generate HTML. Nor should they handle business logic that isn't specific to JSP presentation.

Because they get first shot at processing the values in the requests, page beans can be useful to provide data to custom tags. If request processing is really complicated, it is better centralized using the request controller pattern than handled by each JSP bean.

Using Tag Extensions

The tag extension mechanism is a powerful new feature of JSP 1.1 that greatly increases our ability to keep logic in Java, while most markup generation remains in JSPs.

Although tag extensions are also implemented by Java classes, they differ significantly from beans:

- ❑ Tag handlers can create scripting variables that can be accessed by JSPs that use the tags they implement

- ❑ Tag extensions are usually intended for use in multiple JSPs. They are standard building blocks, not resources for one or two JSPs

- ❑ Although they can access them, tag extensions should not normally be concerned with the parameters to the JSPs that call them. Tag extensions should have local context. Their behavior is controlled by the XML attributes they are given each time they appear, which may be dynamic. The following example shows three different uses of one tag, which implements simple search functionality. In the first case, all parameters to the tag are static, so it will always perform the same search (although, of course, the results of its search may change over time):

```
<wrox:search query="whale" format="html"  maxResults="5" firstResult="0" />
```

In the second case, the query is obtained from the request to the current JSP:

```
<wrox:search query="<%=request.getParameter("query")%>" format="html"
maxResults="5" firstResult="0" />
```

This approach is questionable, as no validation is performed on the request parameter before it is passed to the tag.

In the third case, the tag is configured by parameters obtained from two beans: a page bean that has processed the request to the current JSP, and a session bean holding the user's preferences:

```
<wrox:search
   query="<%=searchBean.getQuery()%>"
   format="<%=sessionBean.getFormat()%>"
   maxResults="<%=sessionBean.getMaxResults()%>"
   firstResult="<%=searchBean.getResultOffset()%>"
/>
```

The developer of the search tag may not have envisaged all these scenarios, but they all honor the contract between JSP and tag.

Tag extensions are discussed in detail in Chapters 12 and 13. The following discussion assumes familiarity with their use, so please refer back to those chapters, if necessary.

Categories of Tags

Tag extensions usually fall into two categories: **generic**, and **application-specific**.

The difference is significant, and relates to implementation as well as usage. In general, since tag handlers are Java classes, we prefer not to generate HTML within them. However, a blanket ban is inappropriate.

Generic tag extensions should be usable in a variety of contexts. Because markup generation tends to limit reusability, generic tag extensions should not normally generate HTML. The actual markup they are used to produce may differ widely. Generic tag extensions may increasingly come to be provided by specialists in tag extensions. Examples include tag extensions to access enterprise resources, such as databases, and tag extensions that interpret their body content as a language more appropriate to a particular problem than JSP code.

Application-specific tag extensions do not aspire to such wide reusability. They are the building blocks of one particular application. It may be appropriate for application-specific tag extensions to generate HTML. The benefits of having all your HTML in the one place, so that a number of pages will change after a change to a single tag, can outweigh the problems of markup generation in tag handlers. My experience has also shown that it is simply unrealistic to ban markup generation from application-specific tag handlers. Generating markup from within Java code remains inelegant; unless the markup is trivial, a better solution is to read in a template file and substitute variables into it. (An abstract superclass could make this behavior available in a consistent way to a number of application-specific tags.)

Examples of application-specific tags include application-wide headers and footers with some dynamic content specified using attributes, and the formatting of complex objects unique to the application. Application-specific tag extensions should still be made as generic as possible, through maximizing their potential for configuration at runtime.

Let's now look at some important uses of tag extensions.

Model Tags

Generic tag extensions are particularly well suited to making JSPs cleanly implement the model view controller pattern. This is an important and flexible use of tag extensions that justifies detailed discussion.

Typically, such view tags will obtain the models they require from page beans. They will use the model data to provide values and control flow to JSP views, concealing access to the model and iteration over the model's contents. The standard models defined in Swing are particularly useful, as they facilitate the sharing of UI code between Swing and JSP interfaces.

See Chapter 13 for implementations of JSP tags providing views for the Swing `ListModel` and `TableModel`. These are very useful, and they'll play a major role in the case study at the end of this chapter.

Translation Tags

Translation tags take their body content (the JSP or other content that appears between their start and end tags) and filter, translate, or interpret it. The variety of end results is almost limitless: typical examples are replacing the original content with a filtered version and writing it into the page output; or processing their body content multiple times.

Translation tags are usually generic tags. Chapter 12 provides a simple example: a tag that reverses its body content.

Another example of this type of tag suggested in the JSP 1.1 specification is a tag that executes SQL content and displays the results. This is a good indication of the power of translation tags, but it's not a good design approach. As we have seen, JSPs should be far removed from SQL in J2EE architecture.

Other examples include tags interpreting another language themselves (perhaps ASP, to incorporate fragments of a legacy system), and tags that might suppress their body content depending on context (for example, if a user had insufficient system privileges).

A particularly useful tag of this type is a tag to take XML body content and render it using an XSLT stylesheet specified as an attribute.

Tags as Application Building Blocks

These tags are application specific, and may generate HTML. Application-specific tags vary widely in character, and don't tend to fall easily into standard patterns.

Consider implementing personalization on a complex web site. One approach might be to use dynamic includes, and build up an interface using small, reusable JSPs. In practice this isn't very useful, due to the limitations of flushing in JSP 1.1 that we considered earlier. A more practical alternative is to use tag extensions as the building blocks of the interface. Communication with them, using attributes of any type, is a lot more sophisticated than communication between JSPs using dynamic includes, and the advantage of modularity remains.

Third Party Tag Libraries

Although tag extensions are a new feature of JSP, significant effort is already going into developing standard libraries. Leveraging standard code benefits everyone. Monitor the availability of standard tag libraries for your industry or application type. http://www.jsptags.com is a good starting point.

Dos and Don'ts

Elegant as tag extensions often are, they can still be abused. Using too many custom tags can produce JSPs that are incomprehensible to a reader first viewing a system, who may understand JSP, but not the ways in which a complex tag library works. This is justifiable only if it is demonstrably more effective than any alternative.

As we have seen, deciding whether or not it is appropriate for a particular tag to generate HTML (or XHTML) is a thorny issue. Avoid it if possible, but don't be rigid.

Tag handlers, like all objects, should be coded to be as generic as possible. A well-designed tag will provide a single solution for a requirement that appears in many JSPs. Experience shows that further uses are likely to suggest themselves once a tag is in use. By designing a tag to address too narrow an interpretation of the initial requirement and not carefully considering how to make it useful in as wide a variety of contexts as is reasonably possible, much of the tag's potential may be lost, and the effort put into developing it not fully leveraged.

Try to make tags configurable by attributes (which may be optional) and, possibly, by descendant tags that provide additional output depending on their context. When designing a tag, as when designing a library class, try to envisage all its likely uses and allow for them. If a number of tag handlers have significant commonality in their implementation, define an abstract base class implementing the common functionality.

Tag handlers can be made generic in four main ways:

- ❑ XML attributes.
- ❑ The way in which they process their body content.
- ❑ Tag nesting.
- ❑ Reading an HTML template.

Choosing between these mechanisms is the trickiest (and most rewarding) issue in designing reusable tags. Nesting can be very powerful, but can make your tags harder to use. If you use an HTML template, you will probably need to define a means of substituting variables. However, you can then get different behavior from the same tag without modifying its implementation by passing in the template reference as an attribute.

The abilities of tag handlers to play havoc with the host page's `request` and `response` objects (for example, to cause the response to be redirected), and to return values causing the JSP engine to skip evaluation of the remainder of the page, should be used with extreme caution. Will this behavior be obvious to readers of your JSPs? Although legitimate at times (for example in a tag handler that checks if users are logged in and redirects to a login page if they are not), it resembles the dreaded `goto`, exhibiting irrational behavior.

Handling Iteration

JSP pages often need to iterate over data. It is acceptable to use scriptlets to do this. However, if the iteration involves not merely access to multiple items of data to render the page, but other processing logic, one of the two following approaches may be preferable:

- ❑ Define a custom tag that handles the iteration, as in our list tag above. The tag handler will then perform the processing logic with each iteration, before processing its body content.

❑ Wrap the access to each element of the iteration in a bean, and make the bean perform the processing logic required before returning the result.

For example, consider the following code:

```
<% for (int i = 0; i < bean.getFields(); i++) {
  if (bean.isSpecialField(i)) {
    response.setCookie...
    LogHandler.Log(...
    // Several more lines of code setting application state
  } %>
  <input type="text" name="<%=bean.getName(i)%> value="<%=bean.getValue(i)%>" />
<% } %>
```

The handling of the special case is not concerned with presentation, but cookie generation and auditing. It doesn't belong in the JSP. A better solution is to modify the bean so that one of the methods takes any additional parameters required to handle the special case. I've modified the bean's getValue() method to take the JSP's response object as a parameter. Now the special case can be implemented by the bean, and is transparent to the JSP:

```
<% for (int i = 0; i < bean.getFields(); i++) { %>
    <input type="text" name="<%=bean.getName(i)%>
    value="<%=bean.getValue(i, response)%>" />
<% } %>
```

Handling Conditional Logic

The obvious way to handle conditional logic in JSPs is using scriptlets. For example, the following code will prepopulate a form field with a user's name if it is already held by the application, and distinguishes between unregistered users who arrived at this page by different routes:

```
<% String name = ""; %>
<% if (pageBean.getUserWasInvited ()) { %>
    Please enter your name as it appeared on your letter of invitation
<% } else if (pageBean.getUserIsRegistered()) { %>
    Please verify that your name appears correctly below
    <% name = pageBean.getName(); %>
<% } else { %>
    Please enter your name
<% } %>
<input type="text" name="name" value="<%=name%>" />
```

Sometimes, expressions can be used to handle simple conditionals, through use of the ternary operator. For example, the following expression is used in the case study later in this chapter to output commas only in between columns in a table, and not at the end of each row:

```
<%=(column < tableModel.getColumnCount() - 1) ? "," : "" %>
```

The ability of scriptlets and expressions to handle conditional logic is too useful to ignore. However, a mass of conditionals can quickly make a JSP verbose and hard to maintain. Even the simple if/else example above already requires a few seconds to comprehend. If the conditional statements are broken up by lengthy blocks of HTML (a common occurrence without careful design), or if there was a longer chain of if-else statements, it could quickly become unreadable.

If conditional logic is bloating scriptlets, consider the following alternative approaches:

❑   Use more JSPs. If a JSP produces two or more very different page structures, move the conditional logic out of the JSP and replace it with two or more simple JSPs.

❑   Handle the conditional logic in a page-view bean. The getters of the bean may return different values depending on the page's context.

❑   If the bodies of conditional statements are large, making the whole page hard to follow, consider replacing the bodies with static includes.

❑   Expose content as XML, using XSLT stylesheets determined by the conditional logic (see Using Styled XML below).

It can be easy to get results using these techniques. For example, consider code that performs the following logic for every form field, obtaining it from a session object if that object is non-null, otherwise assigning the field no value:

```
<% if (object != null && object.getFieldValue(fieldName) != null) %>
  <input type="text"
    name="<%=fieldName%>"
    value="<%=object.getFieldValue(fieldName)%>" />
<% } else { %>
  <input type="text" name="<%=fieldName%>" />
<% } %>
```

Although this looks relatively harmless, in a form with many fields it can pose a major problem to page maintainability. An easy and effective solution is to define a page bean that acts as a proxy for the object that may be null. The bean can then perform the test and return the appropriate value without the JSP performing any tests.

The necessary method in the bean will look like this:

```
public String getFieldValue(String fieldName) {
  if (object != null)
    return object.getFieldValue(fieldName);
  return "";
}
```

Every occurrence of the conditional expression in the JSP is now replaced by the following:

```
<input type="text"
  name="<%=fieldName%>"
  value="<%=bean.getFieldValue(fieldName)%>" />
```

This is both more readable and more maintainable. The conditional logic can be altered in one place without the need for repeated editing. This is, of course, a very simple example, but this pattern can be used in many contexts.

Using Styled XML

It's important to recognize when JSP is *not* the ideal means of rendering content. We have already considered the alternative of a servlet, which is preferable where the generated output is not human-readable. Another alternative is to present XML data as HTML using XSLT. This is a particularly good approach for rendering non-HTML content such as WML. A custom tag can perform the transform in an elegant way.

This use of islands of XML is a tradeoff between elegance and pragmatism. Despite its appeal, there are still performance issues in presenting *all* content as XML and performing server-side transforms on it. (The alternative of performing the transforms on the client presently works only in Internet Explorer, which is not fully compliant with XSLT standards.) XSLT is still difficult for non-programmers to write, and no satisfactory authoring tools are available as yet. Using XML and XSLT for those parts of the document that are most easily expressed as XML, however, can reduce, rather than increase, complexity, and will have little impact on performance.

> *See the XSLT Programmer's Reference by Michael Kay (Wrox ISBN 1-861-003-12-9) for detailed discussion of what can be achieved using XML and XSLT.*

When to Use Custom Superclasses for JSPs

JSPs have always had the ability to extend a class of their own choice, rather than the container's. This custom superclass can perform any kind of functionality behind the scenes.

Common uses of custom superclasses are to handle the request before the code in JSPs extending them is invoked, and to define additional implicit objects (although this is usually better done through tag extensions).

Imagine an implementation of data binding. Form fields with special names could be bound to properties of objects in the HTTP session. A custom superclass, `DataBoundHttpJspPage`, could look in the request for such fields and attempt to map them to the relevant objects using reflection. This would be transparent to JSPs extending it. They would sacrifice none of their functionality to use this feature.

Custom superclasses must fulfill the following requirements:

- ❑ They should implement the `HttpJspPage interface`.

- ❑ They should declare all of the methods in the `Servlet` interface to be `final`.

- ❑ They should invoke the `_jspService()` method in their `service()` method.

- ❑ Their `init(ServletConfig)` method should store the configuration, make it available via the `getServletConfig()` method, then invoke `jspInit()`. This enables JSPs to perform custom initialization if necessary.

- ❑ Their destroy method should invoke `jspDestroy()`. This enables JSPs to perform custom cleanup if necessary.

Custom superclasses should not be used if there is a simpler alternative. Using them can make the behavior of pages harder to understand and may interfere with the ability of the JSP engine to perform optimization. Remember that by telling the JSP engine that a particular JSP should be derived from your superclass, you deprive it of the power to derive the JSP from an optimized superclass of its own.

Standard Abstractions for Common Objects

The JSP expression mechanism is geared towards string content, and objects for which the `toString()` method will produce a desirable representation of their state, such as `Integer` objects.

Some objects are more complex, but nevertheless standard: consider hyperlinks. In fact, they're not even specific to JSP presentation; a Swing GUI could present a hyperlink in its interface.

Often it makes sense to define reusable objects for such common concepts. For example, if we define a `Link` object with `getTitle()` and `getURL()` methods, we can return it in a single call to a page view bean, and use it as a parameter to an object such as a tag handler.

Other candidate objects for such standard classes include images and checkboxes. The `NameValueModel` introduced in Chapter 13 is an example of a very general model that is useful in many situations.

Handling Exceptions

Perhaps the easiest way to complicate the code and confuse an HTML designer trying to manipulate a working JSP is to use JSPs to perform exception handling. Fortunately, this is seldom a good idea.

Of the many good features introduced in JSP 1.0, the error page mechanism was perhaps the most welcome. (This is the mechanism that allows an error page to be specified, to which the request will be redirected in the event of an uncaught exception.) There are two types of exceptions that JSP developers will be concerned with:

❑ Application exceptions that are possible in normal operation and do not cause a fatal error conditions.

❑ Unrecoverable exceptions reflecting an unexpected system failure such as inability to contact a database or a remote object such as an EJB.

Application exceptions should be concealed from JSPs through being handled in request controllers or JSP beans or tag handlers.

Unrecoverable exceptions can and should be ignored by JSP developers (so long as developers remember to declare error pages to handle them and display appropriate user-oriented information about the system failure). Suppose a session JSP bean cannot connect to an underlying session EJB. There is nothing the JSP can reasonably do to handle this situation: the best approach is to redirect the response to a page apologizing for an internal system error. This behavior can be achieved simply by declaring the affected methods in JSP beans and tag handlers to re-throw the underlying `RemoteException`.

Internationalization

Often companies have distinct web sites for each country in which they do business. However, in some cases, such as an online store, there may be no significant differences in interface. In this case, it is necessary to design a JSP interface that supports internationalization.

There are three obvious approaches:

- ❑ Write separate JSPs for each locale, which may leverage existing code by reusing beans and tag handlers.

- ❑ Use the Java resource bundle mechanism to source text from properties files.

- ❑ Concentrate language-specific content in environment entries set in the web.xml file of a WAR, which can be set at deployment time for each locale.

The second or third approaches are usually preferable, as maintaining parallel JSPs is error prone.

To use the second approach, we need a set of properties files for all the languages and, possibly, locales we wish to support, exactly as if we were writing a multilingual Java application. (The Java property manager will automatically load the correct property file for each locale, using a standard naming convention.). All text output in the JSPs will be replaced by calls to get formatted information from a bean. For example, code such as this, which displays text above a set of search results

```
<%=results.getCount()%> matches. Matches <%=results.getFirst()%> to
<%=results.getLast()%><br/>
```

will be replaced by code like:

```
<%=results.getFormattedStats()%><br/>
```

The appropriate page view bean will use the `java.text.MessageFormat` class to format content. This bean will need at least two additional methods to support this mechanism. One will conveniently return the dynamic values as an object array, ready for the `MessageFormat` class, and the other will return a formatted string:

```
/**
 * Return an array of statistics values
 */
public Object[] getStatsValues() {
  return new Object[] {
    new Integer(getCount()), new Integer(getFirst()),
    new Integer(getLast())
  };
}

/**
 * Return a String containing locale-specific presentation
 * for the statistics returned by this object
 */
public String getFormattedStats() {
  MessageFormat statsFormat = getPresentationFormat("results_stats");
  return statsFormat.format(getStatsValues());
}
```

The `getPresentationFormat()` method will probably be placed in another class, used by all page view beans. It will be responsible for instantiating `MessageFormat` objects based on the appropriate `ResourceBundle` for the current locale. The English resource bundle entry for these statistics would be:

```
results_stats={0} matches. Results {1} to {2}
```

The locale may simply be the locale of the web server, or it may be set programmatically for a particular session (for example, in response to a user choice at the home page).

This is a reasonably clean approach. The only real disadvantage is that it is often necessary to place markup in the properties file entries: for example, if the total number of matches was to appear in bold, <b> and </b> tags would need to be included in the message formats. This is not ideal, as spreading even small pieces of markup through multiple files makes it harder to track down errors such as unbalanced tags, and harder to comprehend how a complete page is constructed. However, given that structural markup such as table definitions and forms will remain in the single JSP, this is not a fatal drawback.

There is usually no necessity to implement such an internationalization mechanism before internationalization becomes a system requirement. If a JSP system is well designed, adding support in the beans and tag handlers and modifying the JSPs should not be a massive task.

Internationalization is covered in more detail in the Appendix D.

Documenting the JSP Layer

All experienced Java developers use Javadoc, and know just how helpful it is as projects grow in size and require collaboration among a significant number of developers. Unfortunately, JSPs offer no such built-in documentation support.

The first step to a well-documented JSP system is to place Java code in beans and tag handlers rather than JSPs. This will enable us to use Javadoc to generate documentation for most of our interface logic. However, we require strict documentation standards to fill the inevitable gaps.

Each of the components of a JSP interface requires a different type of documentation:

❑ **JSPs**
JSPs require code-level documentation in the form of hidden comments. These use the special syntax:

```
<%-- text of comment --%>
```

Unlike HTML comments (delimited by <!-- and -->), they will not be included in generated pages. A technical specification for the system should also discuss the parameters required by each JSP and page transitions. Any required parameters should be listed in a header in each JSP.

❑ **JSP beans**
JSP beans can be documented with Javadoc.

❑ **Tag extensions**
Tag extensions require several types of documentation, most of which will be outside the files that implement them:

❑ Javadoc for the tag handler classes.

- ❑ Documentation of any scripting variables they define.

- ❑ Documentation of any 'side effects' they may have. These include redirection of the response, and causing the remainder of the page to be skipped in some circumstances.

- ❑ Documentation of the attributes they require. XML tag library descriptors (TLDs) are too verbose for this purpose, and are not ideal reading matter for page designers.

- ❑ Example JSPs can be very useful in showing the potential of tag extensions.

Tool Support

Given the level of interest in JSP authoring, present authoring tools are disappointingly immature. A number of Java IDEs provide useful, but limited, assistance in writing JSPs. For example, Sun's free Forte for Java Community Edition 1.0 has a JSP editor that clearly delimits scriptlet content from markup, and can even compile JSP 1.0 code. This is very handy in avoiding frustrating syntax errors (such as failure to terminate a scriptlet). But integration with HTML editors and more sophisticated functionality is still lacking.

However, many vendors are working hard on the problem, and in the next generation of tools we can hope for major progress. Areas in which tool support could make JSP development easier and promote good practice include:

- ❑ Support for writing JSP beans in conjunctions with JSPs. Some vendors are already providing a rudimentary form of this.

- ❑ Support for request controller architectures.

- ❑ Sophisticated support for using custom tags.

Watch the major Java IDEs such as NetBeans, JBuilder, Visual Cafe, and Visual Age for further progress. Much better vertical integration for developing J2EE applications can also be expected from initiatives such as WebGain Studio (http://www.webgain.com/). This is a new product supported by BEA Systems, which is built on existing 'best of breed' tools such as DreamWeaver and Visual Cafe, and aims to provide a suite of tools to facilitate EJB and JSP development. Although it integrates most easily with the WebLogic application server, it is intended to support J2EE standards, rather than tie in to any one deployment environment.

Whether using sophisticated tools or not, it is usually a good idea to design and test the desired HTML code before beginning the final phase of JSP coding. It is *much* easier to resolve issues such as browser incompatibilities by editing static pages than by editing JSPs, however well designed they may be.

Coding Standards for Maintainable JSPs

This section attempts to take the techniques already discussed and distill them into a set of guidelines for JSP authoring. These guidelines do *not* aim to be hard and fast rules.

Design Principles and Coding Style

- ❑ The whole of the JSP/JSP bean presentation tier should be as thin and simple as possible. If it is impossible to achieve a thin JSP tier, it indicates shortcomings in the overall design. The business logic layer probably does not provide a consistent level of abstraction, or rich enough functionality.

637

❏ Remember that most JSPs should be read-only views, with a page bean providing the model. The way in which content is presented in a JSP may change as the desired HTML changes; the structure of the content itself changes more rarely, and it is acceptable for such changes to require updates to a bean.

❏ Think vertically. First identify the data that must be presented by a JSP, then design the appropriate bean to provide a model for the data. JSPs and JSP beans should be designed together.

❏ Business logic should be removed from JSPs as far as is reasonably possible. Business logic not specific to HTML presentation should live in the business logic layer or a non UI-specific presentation layer. Although such logic could easily be placed in JSP beans, this would be poor design as such business logic should be available to *all* clients, not merely JSPs. HTTP-specific logic (for example, cookie manipulation) belongs in beans or support classes, not JSPs.

❏ For non-trivial sets of pages, think and design in terms of *groups* of JSPs collaborating to provide a discrete piece of functionality, rather than treating each JSP as an individual piece of work. This will help in identifying session beans and whether the request controller design pattern may be appropriate.

❏ Try to place conditional logic in controllers rather than in views. For example, if a substantial part of a JSP varies according to a condition, the JSP is a candidate for refactoring, with a controller forwarding requests to two separate pages, each of which includes the common parts.

❏ Follow standard naming conventions for JSPs, included files, JSP beans, and classes implementing tag extensions. I use the following conventions:

    ❏ JSP controller: xxxxController.jsp

    ❏ Included JSPs: _descriptiveNameOfFragment.jsp

    ❏ JSP page model beans: <pagename>Bean

    ❏ JSP session beans: xxxxSessionBean

    ❏ Tag handlers and related classes: xxxxTag, xxxxTagExtraInfo

❏ Page import directives should be avoided in JSPs. The use of imports encourages the instantiation of classes other than JSP beans. The more verbose fully qualified syntax serves as a deterrent to this. Instead of issuing a directive like this:

```
<%@ page import="com.java.util.*" %>
```

refer to each class in the required package by its fully qualified name, for example:

```
<% java.util.List l = new java.util.LinkedList(); %>
```

❏ JSPs should not directly access request parameters. Request controllers or beans should perform such processing and expose processed model data. Accessing request parameters requires careful error checking; this is likely to be overlooked in JSPs, and will complicate them if it is not.

❏ JSPs should not access properties files, or use JNDI. JSP beans may access properties (for example, to support internationalization).

❑ If a JSP bean cannot have all its properties mapped from the page request, try to set properties within the `<jsp:useBean>` tag. This ensures that the bean will be appropriately initialized before it is used, and maximizes readability. Include also within the `<jsp:useBean>` tag any scriptlets required to initialize the bean.

❑ Avoid designing pages that both present a form and process its results. This tends to lead to confusing conditionals depending on the page's purpose in its context. Extra JSPs are cheap.

❑ Avoid code duplication in JSPs. The need for code duplication is an indication of poor design. Refactor the duplicated functionality into an included JSP, bean, or tag extension to make it reusable. Favor static includes over dynamic includes.

❑ JSP beans should never generate HTML. Java is not well suited to HTML generation, and JSP was designed to avoid this central drawback of servlets. Tag extension classes should not generate HTML without good reason.

❑ Using `out.println()` to generate page content should be avoided in JSPs. Using this syntax encourages thinking of JSPs as programs rather than web pages, and is likely to confuse an HTML designer editing a JSP.

❑ The JSP tier should *not* access data directly; this includes JDBC database access and EJB access. Beans used in the JSPs may access session EJBs or other objects in the business logic layer. However, even JSP beans should not access entity EJBs or use JDBC directly to access system data sources.

❑ Scriptlets should not exceed 5 lines in length. There are situations in which scriptlets cannot be avoided; accept these, but only after considering all genuine alternatives.

❑ JSPs should not instantiate complex read-write objects other than JSP beans. This risks giving JSPs the ability to perform inappropriate business logic.

❑ JSP session beans should not contain excessive amounts of data. This is a performance issue.

❑ If `<jsp:forward>` or `<jsp:include>` is used, and primitive values must be communicated to the external page, use one or more `<jsp:param>` subelements. If this is not possible, consider using a static include instead of communicating objects via `setAttribute()`, which risks unpleasant surprises at runtime.

❑ Custom tags should be used where appropriate to remove logic from JSPs.

❑ `<jsp:forward>` should be used with caution. It amounts to a JSP equivalent of a `goto`, and can make page behavior hard to comprehend. A controller page is an exception to this rule. Forwarding from pages other than controllers also violates the principle that a JSP is a view; if the JSP does not know how to respond to the request it was passed, there is probably an error in the design of the system.

❑ In general, declarations or scriptlets should *not* be used to create variables referred to throughout a JSP. State within a JSP should be held within beans. Custom tags may, however, legitimately declare scripting variables.

❑ Hidden comments should be used to prevent comments bloating HTML output. Document not only the handling of dynamic content, but any complex markup. This is likely to cause more confusion to readers than appropriately used expressions and custom tags.

❑ Avoid exception handling in JSPs.

❑   Each JSP should use an error page to handle exceptions that it cannot recover from. Exceptions should be caught in the JSP tier (but *not* the JSP itself) if it is still possible to produce a valid page. `RemoteExceptions` and other system errors are examples of exceptions that should simply propagate to an error page.

❑   In JSP error pages, use HTML comments to display a stack trace of the exception passed to the page. This is very helpful in debugging, and need not always be removed on a live system.

❑   `jspInit()` and `jspDestroy()` should only be used if they produce significant performance gains. Using these methods makes a JSP more like a servlet (a program) and less like a web page. Acquiring and relinquishing resources is the business of JSP beans and tag handlers, not JSPs, so there should be no need for cleanup. However, if necessary, it is possible to cordon off these methods so that they don't affect designers subsequently working on the JSP.

❑   Although it seems obvious, **hacking must be strictly avoided**. Hacking is bad enough in Java code, but quick hacks to JSPs are a maintenance nightmare, and quickly lead to an excessive amount of Java code in JSPs. The correct approach is to ensure that throughout the product life cycle, the architecture and the functionality evolve together. If changes are required to JSP beans (and even the business logic layer) to ensure this, this is preferable to a quick fix to JSPs that compromises the division between presentation and content and correct location of business logic.

❑   Methods and inner classes should not be defined in JSPs without very good reason. The kind of logic behind a method is better placed in a JSP bean.

Formatting JSP Pages

The most important rule is to think of JSP pages as HTML or XHTML documents. Follow the standards for markup formatting in use within your organization; these will probably include guidelines for indentation and overall layout (for example, using a blank line in the source file to mirror the use of a `<p/>` tag).

Format code with `<%` and `%>` on every line of scriptlets, except for lengthy scriptlets (say to perform initialization). This reduces the likelihood of frustrating errors with unbalanced escaping, avoids excessive white space, and helps reinforce the crucial point that JSPs are markup, not Java. This formatting style works best with Sun's recommended Java coding conventions, with the opening { of a compound statement on the same line as the conditional or other control flow expression that requires it.

The following looks verbose, and is hard to follow:

```
<%
if (condition)
{
%>
  Condition was true<br/>
<%
}
else
{
%>
  Condition was false<br/>
<%
}
%>
```

This is much more readable (and produces an identical compiled page):

```
<% if (condition) { %>
  Condition was true<br/>
<% } else { %>
  Condition was false<br/>
<% } %>
```

Note that the else keyword is on the same line as the close of the if compound statement:

```
<% } else { %>
```

You *must* use this condensed style for `if`/`else` statements and `try`/`catch` blocks. JSPs containing code like this will fail to compile:

```
<% try { %>
   . . .
<% } %>
<% catch (Exception ex) { %>
   . . .
<% } %>
```

If the catch statement and the close of the try block are consolidated like this, the code will compile:

```
<% } catch(Exception ex) { %>
```

The reason for this is that JSP engines will translate this JSP into a Java source file with an `out.println()` statement to preserve white space between the closing brace of the `try` block and the `catch` statement. This is a syntax error, as it means that the `try` and `catch` blocks are separated from each other. This affects all JSP engines I have seen. The following is the output from this code in JRun 3.0:

Fortunately, this error message almost makes sense: the output of many engines processing this page fragment will not.

Indent code within compound statements, as in the examples above. The following, without indentation, is hard to read:

```
<% if (condition) { %>
Condition was true
<% } else { %>
Condition was false
<% } %>
```

Using normal Java indentation (as in the earlier examples above) makes the code far more readable. Since JSPs should normally preserve HTML indentation, deeply nested Java indentation may create a conflict. The solution to this dilemma is to avoid using scriptlets to perform complex conditional logic and nested iteration.

Indent subelements of custom tags, and custom tag content if it would otherwise create a long line. Compare these two fragments. Which is the more readable?

```
<mytags:outer>
   <mytags:inner>
      This is inner content
   </mytags:inner>
</mytags:outer>
```

```
<mytags:outer>
<mytags:inner>
This is inner content
</mytags:inner>
</mytags:outer>
```

Finally, let's consider an integrated example of some of the issues we have covered.

The DBExplorer Application

The problem I have chosen is a database explorer: a JSP view of a relational database that enables the viewing of any table and the results of any query in a number of different formats.

Although this is a simple application, the challenge is to implement it to be both maintainable and extensible.

For this example, we used the example database `music1.mdb` file provided with j2sdkee1.2.1 with a DSN of `music`, however, any database with jdbc support will do.

Requirements

The requirement is for a web interface to allow users to browse the contents of relational databases. It will enable a user to connect to a database by specifying a JDBC driver and URL. The application will then allow users to see all the tables defined in the database, choose any table, and work with its data. It will also be possible for the user to enter SQL queries and see the tabular data they produce. It must be easy at any point during a user session for the user to disconnect from one database and connect to another.

Users will be allowed to choose the way in which they view data. Three views will be required in the first phase of development:

- ❏ A tabular view showing the table's content in a clear, read-only format
- ❏ A CSV view allowing data to be cut and pasted into a spreadsheet or text file
- ❏ An editable view, allowing any row to be updated

Initially, functionality will be more important than presentation, but it is essential that it is easy to improve the presentation of the JSP views without requiring heavy technical input.

It is likely that there will be future requirements for additional views: a number of XML views, and a Microsoft Excel format view which will enable users to download content without viewing it in their browsers. Each view page must allow the user to navigate to any other available view of the same data. Until a new view is selected, the current view will be the default during all browsing.

There may also be a requirement in the next phase of development for a Swing applet to allow a more responsive interface, so it is important that the data objects are not tied to JSP presentation.

The first phase of the system need not persist user preferences between sessions, although this will be a later requirement.

Another long-term requirement is support for data sources other than relational databases.

The following is a sample walk through of the required functionality.

On first accessing the application, the user will be asked to provide information about the required database connection:

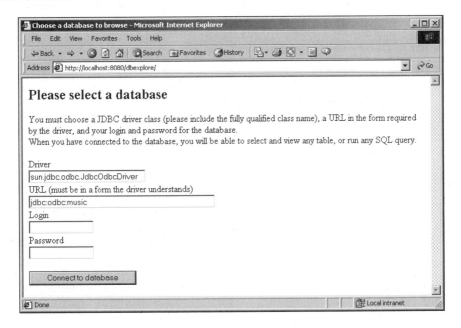

Once valid input is submitted, the user will be prompted to choose a table or enter an SQL query before viewing actual data:

After choosing a table, the user will be able to navigate between different views of data, with the ability to choose different tables or queries at any point. The following is a typical data view, and includes the navigation controls that will be available throughout the application:

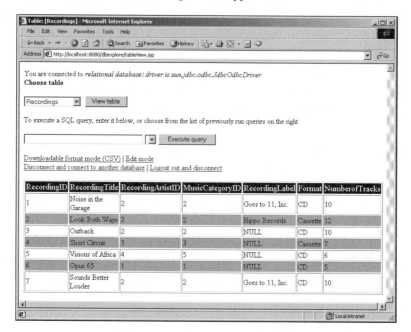

When users have finished browsing this or any other database they wish to connect to, they will be able to log out of the system, which will close any open resources and produce a confirmation page:

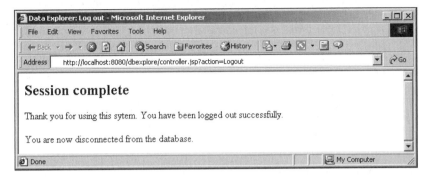

Design

The first step in the development cycle is for the JSP/Java developer to ask the business to produce a walkthrough of the pages: something similar but more detailed than these screenshots. This walkthrough will also define the required error handling. This will enable the developer to produce a proof of concept early in the project. Real world applications have risks. How difficult will it be to develop the most complex parts of their functionality? Will performance be satisfactory? Early proof of concept development enables these risks to be attacked and measured early in the project lifecycle, and is an important step in an iterative development process.

Complementing an understanding of page flow is the use of a state diagram, a very useful way of understanding and documenting the behavior of web applications. (Note that a state diagram is distinct from a page flow diagram. An application's state transitions may not correspond to the page flow of a user session.) The following state diagram shows the states the database explorer transitions through, and the legal transitions from each state:

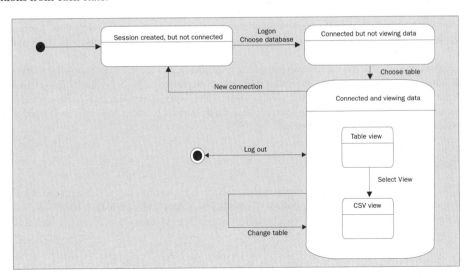

Working in parallel with the programmers, a web designer will produce HTML templates for the pages. Once the page flow is agreed and correctly implemented, these HTML templates will be made dynamic by the addition of the necessary JSP code. It is vital that the resulting JSPs contain a minimum of logic, so that they will be intelligible to page designers required to make ongoing changes to the rendering of the data. (The actual HTML I've written is very simple, as it is a side issue here. Imagine it's the output of the proof of concept phase.)

The first important technical design decision is to identify the application objects. (In a real project an architect, rather than a JSP developer, will probably take this decision.) We will need a data source object and one or more views that make it available to a GUI, and a number of JSPs to present the data. We will take the view that the JSPs are merely views of data exposed by middleware components; JSPs will not directly access the system data objects.

We must take a vertical view of the architecture and decide where each component belongs. The data source object clearly belongs in the enterprise resource abstraction layer. There is little workflow logic in this application beyond the required page flow, so the business logic layer doesn't have a major role. However, this is not to say that the JSPs will contain much of the application's logic. There is a clear need for a non UI-specific presentation layer. Remember that the requirements call for a Swing interface to be supported in the future, and some views of the data (such as the Excel view) that cannot be rendered by JSPs. This layer will not merely provide data for JSPs, but may service any GUI. It will consist of a number of models of the system's data.

We will use the *views* tag library introduced in Chapter 13 to enable us to use Swing data models where possible. This will enable us to generate markup dynamically without heavy use of scriptlets, and will ensure that as much of the system's implementation as possible is independent of JSP technology. Please refer to this chapter to see the implementation of this functionality.

User preferences will be held in a session bean. This will also hold a copy of the required data model for each user. Because the session bean can hold data models that change with the session state, there is (unusually) no requirement for page beans. This reflects the fact that all the application's views display the same data structure, which is therefore part of the application rather than unique to any page.

Due to the likelihood of additional views being added, using the request controller pattern maximizes flexibility. It means that when additional views are required, no page flow logic needs to be included in them.

The implementation of this case study will introduce a refinement of the request controller pattern in which the application's functionality can be extended without modifying the controller itself. This can be achieved by making the controller use the `action` parameter included with each request to choose which of a number of "request handler" objects will handle each request. Each request handler class can be loaded dynamically, using Java's ability to load a class by name.

Implementation

Because of the decoupling of presentation from data source, it is possible to consider presentation (JSP and supporting classes) and data sources separately. Once the interfaces are established, it will be possible for different developers (in a complex real-world application, different teams) to work in parallel on these two main divisions of the system.

Since we are primarily concerned with JSP here, let's start with the presentation code. This involves cooperating JSPs and Java classes, which we'll look at in turn as we follow a typical page flow through the application. We can assume that a `DataSource` interface will expose information about the current data source, including a `NameValueModel` (a type of `ListModel`) of available tables, and the ability to retrieve the data in any table as a Swing `TableModel`. Details specific to the implementation of the data source will not be available to the presentation objects.

Presentation Tier – The ui and ui.requesthandlers Packages

The core of the presentation tier is the request controller, `controller.jsp`. This is a very simple JSP that instantiates a `RequestController` session bean that implements page flow logic, and forwards the response to each request to the JSP view determined by the controller:

```jsp
<%--
    JSP controller for the data explorer application.
    This page produces no output, but redirects each request
    to the appropriate JSP view.
    The logic required to make this choice
    is supplied by the RequestController session bean.
--%>

<%@page session="true" errorPage="systemError.jsp" %>

<%-- The controller object will be instantiated by a session's first
     call to this page --%>
<jsp:useBean id="controller" scope="session" class="ui.RequestController" />

<%-- Each request to this page will be forwarded to the appropriate view,
     as determined by the controller and its helper classes. These classes
     will set the session state appropriately before returning the URL of
     a view, to which this page will forward the response. --%>
<jsp:forward page="<%=controller.getNextPage(pageContext, request)%>"/>
```

This JSP is the entry point for the application. (Later we will see how to specify this in the application's `web.xml` file.)

Logic

The `RequestController` class handles all page flow in the application, yet manages to avoid being limited to the page flow possibilities initially envisaged. To achieve this, it requires a number of `RequestHandler` objects to help it choose the required view. It loads the necessary class dynamically (by name), and instantiates an object of each type as required.

The task of the `RequestController` itself is to examine the `action` parameter, call the appropriate `RequestHandler` instance to determine the required JSP view, and return the URL of this view to `controller.jsp`. The `RequestController` determines the class of the required `RequestHandler` by a simple mapping from the action parameter value onto a value classname. For example, `DBConnect` (the first action required by the application) is mapped onto a Java class named `ui.requesthandlers.DBConnect`, which must implement the `RequestHandler` interface. For efficiency reasons, the `RequestController` class keeps instantiated request handlers in a hash table and uses them to handle future requests of the same type. This will ensure that the use of reflection does not degrade the application's performance.

If the action parameter is not passed to this page (for example at the time of the initial request to the application), the user is forwarded to the login page. Note the imports:

```
package ui;

import java.io.Serializable;
import javax.swing.*;
import javax.servlet.http.*;
import javax.servlet.jsp.*;

// Import the NameValueModel
import jspstyle.*;

import java.util.HashMap;
```

All requests go to the `RequestController` class; the class is responsible for instantiating the beans required by the system and uses reflection to instantiate request handlers as required. Notice that we specify a login page for users who don't have a connection:

```
public class RequestController implements Serializable {

  public static final String LOGIN_PAGE = "login.html";

  // Package from which to attempt to load RequestHandler objects
  private static final String REQUEST_HANDLER_PACKAGE ="ui.requesthandlers";

  // Name of the session bean used for this application.
  // This must be matched by the useBean actions in the JSPs.
  private static final String SESSION_BEAN_NAME = "browseSession";

  /**
   * Convenience method for RequestHandler implementations, allowing Java
   * classes to access the session bean easily. Unlike
   * checkSessionBeanIsAvailable(), this method will throw an exception if
   * the bean has not already been instantiated.
   * @return the session bean, which must have been instantiated already.
   */
  public static BrowseSession FindSessionBean(PageContext pageContext,
                                              RequestHandler rh)
  throws BrowseException {
    BrowseSession session = (BrowseSession)
      pageContext.getAttribute(RequestController.SESSION_BEAN_NAME,
                               PageContext.SESSION_SCOPE);

    if (session == null)
      throw new BrowseException(
        "Internal error: illegal state. Session bean shouldn't be" +
        "null handling action " + rh.getClass());
    return session;
  }

  // Hash table to hold instantiated classes for optimization
  private HashMap handlerHash = new HashMap();
```

`getNextPage()` is the method through which all requests to the application are sent. The method processes the request, updating the session and returning the URL of the resulting JSP view. This method will first check if the action parameter contains a value and if not will direct the user to the login page. Otherwise, if there is a value the method tries to instantiate the handler associated with the action, throwing a BrowseException if there is no handler associated with the action. Finally, we end by creating the session bean if it does not already exist through `checkSessionBeanIsAvailable()` method and return the URL of the view chosen by the handler:

```java
public String getNextPage(PageContext pageContext,
                          HttpServletRequest request)
                          throws BrowseException {
  String action = request.getParameter("action");

  // If no action was specified, the user must first log in
  if (action == null || action.equals(""))
    return LOGIN_PAGE;

  RequestHandler requestHandler = getHandlerInstance(action);

  // Create the session bean if it doesn't exist
  checkSessionBeanIsAvailable(pageContext);

  return requestHandler.handleRequest(pageContext, request);
}
```

As we have discussed, `getHandlerInstance()` stores instances of classes in a hash table so that after they are initially loaded (using `forName()`) they no longer need reloading, improving its speed and resource cost.

```java
private RequestHandler getHandlerInstance(String action)
        throws BrowseException {
  String handlerName = REQUEST_HANDLER_PACKAGE + "." + action;

  RequestHandler requestHandler =
                  (RequestHandler)handlerHash.get(handlerName);

  if (requestHandler == null) {
  // We don't have a handler instance associated with this action,
  // so we need to instantiate one and put it in our hash table

    try {
      System.out.println("Loading handler instance...");

      // Use reflection to load the class by name
      Class handlerClass = Class.forName(handlerName);

      // Check the class we obtained implements the RequestHandler interface
      if (!RequestHandler.class.isAssignableFrom(handlerClass))
        throw new BrowseException("Class " + handlerName + " does not " +
                           "implement the RequestHandler interface ");

      // Instantiate the request handler object
      requestHandler = (RequestHandler) handlerClass.newInstance();

      // Save the instance so we don't have to load it dynamically to
      // process further requests from this user
      handlerHash.put(handlerName, requestHandler);
    } catch (ClassNotFoundException ex) {
    throw new BrowseException("No handler for action [" +
                   handlerName + "]: class " + handlerName +
                   " could not be loaded. " + ex);
    } catch (InstantiationException ex) {
```

```
            // It probably doesn't have a no-argument constructor
            throw new BrowseException("Class "+ handlerName +
                        " could not be instantiated. " + " Is it a bean? " + ex);
        } catch (IllegalAccessException ex) {
            throw new BrowseException("Class " + handlerName +
                                " could not be instantiated. " +
                                "Does it have a public constructor? " + ex);
        }
    }

    // If we get to here, we have a valid RequestHandler instance,
    // whether it came from the hash table or from dynamical class loading
    return requestHandler;
}
```

`checkSessionIsAvailable()` checks for a session bean in the user session and returns it. If none can be found it will instantiate a new bean:

```
private void checkSessionBeanIsAvailable(PageContext pageContext) {
  BrowseSession session = (BrowseSession)
    pageContext.getAttribute(SESSION_BEAN_NAME, PageContext.SESSION_SCOPE);
    if (session == null) {
      System.out.println("RequestController: creating session object");
      session = new BrowseSession();

      // Place the session in the PageContext, so it will be accessible
      // to JSPs as a session bean
      pageContext.setAttribute(SESSION_BEAN_NAME, session,
                            PageContext.SESSION_SCOPE);
    }
  }
}
```

The `RequestHandler` interface, which each action class must implement, is very simple. It contains a single method, `handleRequest()`, which returns the URL of the required JSP view after performing any necessary updates to the session:

```
package ui;

import javax.servlet.http.*;
import javax.servlet.jsp.*;

// Interface to be implemented by objects that can process requests
public interface RequestHandler {

    /**
     *   Perform any processing requiring to support this request, and
     *   return the URL of the JSP view that should display the results
     *   of the request.
     *   @return the URL within the web application of the JSP view to which
     *   the controller should redirect the response
     */
    String handleRequest(PageContext pageContext,
                    HttpServletRequest request)
        throws BrowseException;
}
```

We can extend the application's functionality indefinitely without modifying the `RequestController` class by adding more action parameter values, corresponding `RequestHandler` parameters, and the necessary JSP views. To emphasize the decoupling between the framework of `RequestController` and `RequestHandler` interface (in the `ui` package) and the application's set of actions, we group installed request handlers in a separate package, `ui.requesthandlers`.

Before we look at the implementations of the `RequestHandler` interface, let's look at how they will communicate with the application's JSP views. This will be through the session bean, which will hold the current data source and information about the user's session (any current table selection, the history of user-typed SQL queries, and the current JSP view). Each JSP view will declare this session bean, which, however, will be instantiated in only one place, in the `RequestController` class. Although the session bean isn't concerned with presentation, it is slightly unusual in that it exposes models used by JSP views. This is normally the job of page beans:

```
package ui;

import java.io.Serializable;
import javax.servlet.http.*;
import javax.swing.AbstractListModel;
import javax.swing.table.TableModel;
import java.util.*;
import jspstyle.NameValueModel;

import datasources.*;
import datasources.db.DatabaseDataSource;

/**
 *  JSP session bean to contain information about user
 *  view preferences and models exposing user input history.
 *  Implements HttpSessionBindingListener interface to
 *  ensure that data source resources are freed
 *  when the session terminates.
 *  This bean allows the RequestHandler objects to communicate
 *  with the JSP views in the system.
 */

public class BrowseSession
        implements Serializable, HttpSessionBindingListener {

    // Current view page.
    private String viewPage = "tableView.jsp";

    // Current data source.
    // This object can change data source during the life of the application
    private DataSource      dataSource;

    // Index of the current table the user is viewing
    // -1 if they haven't selected a table
    private int             currentTableIndex;

    // Current table model.
    private TableModel      tableModel;
    private String          lastQuery;
```

```
    // List of SQL queries the user has typed in
    // This will back a NameValueModel of query history
    private List          queries = new LinkedList();

      private NameValueModel  queryModel = new QueryNameValueModel();

    //-----------------------------------------------------------------
    // Public methods
    //-----------------------------------------------------------------


    // @return the JSP view the user presently wants to use for viewing data
    public String getTableViewJSP() {
      return viewPage;
    }


    // Change the current view JSP
    public void setTableViewJSP(String viewPage) {
      this.viewPage = viewPage;
    }


    // Set the DataSource behind this session
    public void setDataSource(DataSource dataSource) {
      this.dataSource = dataSource;
    }


    public DataSource getDataSource()
      throws DataSourceException, BrowseException
    {
      if (dataSource == null)
        throw new BrowseException("No connection");

      return dataSource;
    }


    // Choose a table index in the DataSource
    public void setTableIndex(int index) {
      currentTableIndex = index;
      // Throw away any table model based on a query:
      // the user wants to see a table from the data source
      tableModel = null;
    }


    // Return the currently selected table index, -1 if no table index has
    // been selected
    public int getTableIndex() {
      return currentTableIndex;
    }


    // Return the name of the current table. If no table name is selected,
    // the user must have typed in a query: return the query
    public String getTableName()
      throws DataSourceException, BrowseException
    {
```

```java
    if (currentTableIndex < 0)
       return lastQuery;

    return getDataSource().getName(currentTableIndex);
}

// Return the current table model.
public TableModel getTableModel()
   throws DataSourceException, BrowseException
{
   // If we hold a table model in this class, the user typed in a query
   // and isn't looking at one of the tables in the data source
   if (tableModel != null)
     return tableModel;

   return getDataSource().getTableModel(currentTableIndex);
}

// Return current data source support for SQL?
public boolean getDataSourceSupportsSQL()
   throws DataSourceException, BrowseException
{
      return getDataSource() instanceof DatabaseDataSource;
   }

// If the current data source supports SQL queries, obtain and save a
// table model built from an SQL query
public TableModel getTableModelForSQL(String query)
    throws DataSourceException, BrowseException
{
   if (!getDataSourceSupportsSQL())
     throw new BrowseException("The current data source does not" +
                               " support SQL queries");
   lastQuery = query;
   // Save this query in the history list if it's new
   if (!queries.contains(query))
     queries.add(query);

   // The user isn't looking at a table in the data source, so
   // unset any table index value
   currentTableIndex = -1;
   tableModel =
         ((DatabaseDataSource)getDataSource()).getTableModelForSQL(query);

   return tableModel;
}

// Return a NameValueModel exposing this session's query history.
// This model is implemented by an inner class.
public NameValueModel getQueryModel() {
   return queryModel;
}
```

```
    public boolean isTableEditable()
        throws DataSourceException, BrowseException
    {
      return currentTableIndex >= 0 &&
                    getDataSource().isTableEditable(currentTableIndex);
    }
```

The last few methods make up the isXXX, getXXX and setXXX methods for the class. The remaining methods are the valueBound() and valueUnbound() methods and the inner class QueryNameValueModel that implements jspstyle.NameValueModel to expose the query history:

```
// Implemention of HttpSessionBindingListener
public void valueBound(HttpSessionBindingEvent event) {
  System.out.println("OperatorSession object bound to a session");
}

/**
 *    Use this callback from the JSP engine (issued when this object
 *    is being removed from the session when the session ends)
 *    to ensure that the data source cleans up after itself
 */
public void valueUnbound(HttpSessionBindingEvent event) {
  try {
    System.out.println("OperatorSession object unbound to a session:" +
                       " will cleanup data source");
    getDataSource().cleanup();
  } catch (Exception ex) {
    // It won't do anyone much good to throw this:
    // simply produce console output. In a real application,
    // this would go to a proper log
    ex.printStackTrace();
  }
}

private class QueryNameValueModel
    extends AbstractListModel
    implements NameValueModel
{
  public int getSize() {
    return queries.size();
  }

  public Object getElementAt(int i) {
    return queries.get(i);
  }

  public String getName(int i) {
    return queries.get(i).toString();
  }
}
```

Now let's start a walk through of the application. Let's return to the first page the user sees when entering the application, the login page. Like all external requests to the application, this goes to the controller JSP, which detects the absence of an action and forwards the response to the form:

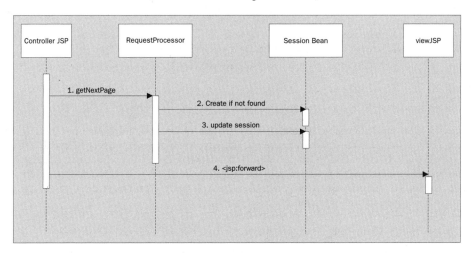

This page is `login.html`, and contains a form that, in addition to the driver name, url, login and password fields, contains a hidden `action` field with a value of `DBConnect`. This value will be used by the `RequestController` class to establish that the user should be directed to the `ui.requesthandlers.DBConnect RequestHandler` implementation:

```
<html>
  <head>
    <title>Choose a database to browse</title>
  </head>
  <body>

    <h2>Please select a database</h2>
    You must choose a JDBC driver class (please include the fully
    qualified class name), a URL
    in the form required by the driver, and your login and password for
    the database.
    <br/>
    When you have connected to the database, you will be able to select
    and view any table, or run any SQL query.
    <p/>

    <form method="post" action="controller.jsp">
      Driver<br/>
      <input type="text" name="driver" size="30"
             value="sun.jdbc.odbc.JdbcOdbcDriver" /> <br />
      URL (must be in a form the driver understands)<br/>
      <input type="text" name="url" size="50"
             value="jdbc:odbc:music" /><br />
      Login<br/>
      <input type="text" name="login" size="15" /><br />
```

```
      Password<br/>
      <input type="password" name="password"  size="15" /><br />
      <p/>

      <!-- Hidden field to provide correct action
          The value corresponds to a RequestHandler implementation -->
      <input type="hidden" name="action" value="DBConnect"/>
      <input type="submit" value="Connect to database" />
   </form>
  </body>
</html>
```

The DBConnect class must attempt to instantiate a data source object and, if the attempt succeeds, return the URL of another form that will allow the user to select a table to view or enter a query. (Note that the application could easily be extended to support non-JDBC data sources by the addition of another login form defining another action parameter leading to another RequestHandler that instantiated a different data source.) The DBConnect class instantiates a DatabaseDataSource. We'll meet the DataSource interface and this implementation of it later:

```java
package ui.requesthandlers;

import javax.servlet.http.*;
import javax.servlet.jsp.*;

import ui.*;

import datasources.*;
import datasources.db.*;

public class DBConnect implements RequestHandler {

    private static final String      TABLE_CHOICE_PAGE = "chooseTable.jsp";

    public String handleRequest(PageContext pageContext,
                                HttpServletRequest request)
      throws BrowseException
    {
      System.out.println(getClass() + ".handleRequest");
      String url = request.getParameter("url");
      String driver = request.getParameter("driver");

      if (url == null || driver == null || url.equals("") ||
          driver.equals(""))

        // Throw an exception that will land us on the system error page
        // with a link back to the login form to allow the user to try again
        throw new InvalidInputException("Both URL and driver must be supplied",
                                    RequestController.LOGIN_PAGE);

        // Some databases (like Access) allow null or empty authentication
        // information. Others, like Oracle, won't. We'll leave it to the driver
        // to throw an exception if necessary.
        String login = request.getParameter("login");
        String password = request.getParameter("password");
```

```
    BrowseSession session =
        RequestController.FindSessionBean(pageContext, this);

    try {
      DataSource dbDataSource =
                    new DatabaseDataSource(url, driver, login, password);
      session.setDataSource(dbDataSource);
    } catch (DataSourceException ex) {
      throw new BrowseException("Cannot connect to database: " +
                                ex.getMessage());
    }

    // If we get to here, everything is fine, and the session state is ready
    // to underpin the table choice view JSP
    return TABLE_CHOICE_PAGE;
  }
}
```

If the connection parameters were valid, the user will now see a page offering a choice of tables in the database:

This page is dynamic, implemented by `chooseTable.jsp`. Since we will need to offer a choice of table from every view in the application, we will factor out the actual form into an included JSP:

```
<%--
    JSP to allow the user to choose a table from
        the database. The user will be connected to a database
        and the session bean available before this view is invoked.
```

```
--%>

<%@page session="true" errorPage="systemError.jsp" %>

<%@ taglib uri="/views" prefix="views" %>

<%--
    The request controller will instantiate this bean
    This page will throw an exception here if the bean is not
    already in the PageContext
--%>
<jsp:useBean id="browseSession" scope="session" type="ui.BrowseSession" />

<html>
<head>
  <title>Choose a table</title>
</head>

  <body>
    <h2>Tables found</h2>

<%-- Parameter to _chooseTable.jsp: this value will ensure that
    the drop down is expanded on this page --%>
<% boolean multiSelect = true; %>

<%-- Include the actual form. We want to share this code
    with other pages --%>
<%@ include file="_chooseTable.jsp" %>

  </body>
</html>
```

The included JSP, _chooseTable.jsp, generates the form. It is parameterized by a boolean variable
(multiSelect) that must be defined in JSPs that include it, and which controls whether the table select will
be a dropdown, or a multi line select. The data comes from the data source added to the session object by the
DBConnect request handler. Data source objects expose a NameValueModel of the tables they contain,
and we can use the <views:jspNameValue> tag to display this data. This is a body tag, which iterates
over its body content based on the size and the content of the model it takes as an XML attribute. The JSP
content of the name value tag will be evaluated for every element in the model.

A second name value model will be exposed by the session bean to contain the history of any previous SQL
queries, if the data source is known by the session bean to support SQL. A separate form will be used to
display this model and allow the user to run a query:

```
<%--
    JSP fragment to allow the user to choose which table to view, and to
    allow SQL query input if we are connected to a relational database.
    There must be a valid connection before a JSP can include this fragment.
    Including JSPs must define a boolean variable named multiSelect. If this
    is true, the list of database tables will be expanded; otherwise it will
    appear as a drop down.
--%>

  You are connected to <i><%=browseSession.getDataSource()%></i>
  <br/>
  <b>Choose table</b><br/>
  <form method="post" action="controller.jsp">
    <select name="tableIndex"
```

```
    <% if (multiSelect) { %>
      size="15"
    <% } %>
  >

<%-- Use the NameValueModel exposed by the DataSource object
    to display the list of tables --%>
  <views:jspNameValue model="<%=browseSession.getDataSource()%>">
    <option value="<%=value%>"
      <% if (index.intValue() == browseSession.getTableIndex()) { %>
        selected="true"
      <% } %>
    >
    <%=name%>
    </option>
  </views:jspNameValue>
  </select>

<%-- Hidden parameter setting the actual action --%>
  <input type="hidden" name="action" value="ChooseTable"/>
    <% if (multiSelect) { %>
      <br />
      <p />
    <% } %>
    <input type="submit" value="View table" />
</form>

<%-- Only show the SQL query input form if we're connected to a relational
database --%>
  <% if (browseSession.getDataSourceSupportsSQL()) { %>
    To execute a SQL query, enter it below, or choose from the list
    of previously run queries on the right
    <form method="post" action="controller.jsp">
      <input type="hidden" name="action" value="RunQuery"/>
      <input type="text" name="query" size="40" />

<%-- The select box allows the user to choose from previously run queries --%>
      <select name="oldquery">
        <views:jspNameValue model="<%=browseSession.getQueryModel()%>">
          <option value="<%=value%>">
            <%=name%>
          </option>
        </views:jspNameValue>
      </select>
      <input type="submit" value="Execute query" />
    </form>
  <% } %>
```

The hidden action field of `ChooseTable` will cause the `RequestController` class to use the `ChooseTable` request handler class to process the request produced by submitting this form:

```
package ui.requesthandlers;

import javax.servlet.http.*;
import javax.servlet.jsp.*;

import ui.*;
```

```
/**
 *   Implementation of the RequestHandler interface to handle
 *   table choice. The user will have submitted a form
 *   selecting the index of the table the user would like to view
 *   before being directed to this RequestHandler. We need to update
 *   the user's session to record this selection, and forward to the
 *   table view JSP of the user's current view mode,
 */
public class ChooseTable implements RequestHandler {

    public String handleRequest(PageContext pageContext,
                                HttpServletRequest request)
      throws BrowseException {
  System.out.println(getClass() + ".handleRequest");
  String tableIndex = request.getParameter("tableIndex");
  if (tableIndex == null)
    // This shouldn't happen, but we'll check anyway
    throw new InvalidInputException("Please choose a table",
                                    "chooseTable.jsp");

    BrowseSession session =
                    RequestController.FindSessionBean(pageContext, this);

    session.setTableIndex(Integer.parseInt(tableIndex));

    // Using a method here rather than hard coding the page name
    // means that the user can continue in his or her current view mode.
    return session.getTableViewJSP();
    }
}
```

The user, having now chosen a table or entered an SQL query, will now see the default view of the tabular data. This is a simple HTML table, with a minimum of aesthetic refinement to make it readable by alternating the color of rows:

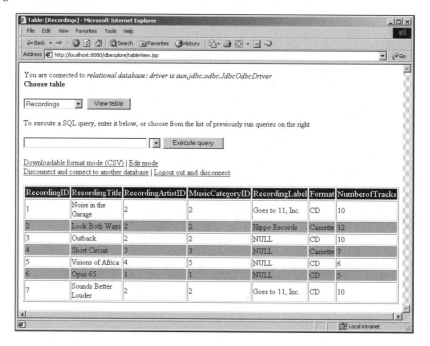

This page is produced by `tableView.jsp`. This JSP view finds what data should back the table by calling the session bean's `getTableModel()` method. The appropriate table model will have been set in the session bean by the `ChooseTable RequestHandler`'s call to the session bean's `setTableIndex()` method. The table choice and text input for SQL queries at the top of the page are produced by the same `_chooseTable.jsp` page fragment that we used in `chooseTable.jsp`.

As the requirement is for each view to remain the default until the user chooses to change it, this JSP calls the session bean's `setTableViewJSP()` method with its servlet path to ensure that it is now the default view.

The actual table is produced by the `<views:jspTable>` tag, which handles iteration over the table model it is passed as an XML attribute. This tag requires a number of descendant tags such as `<views:headingOpen>`, `<views:headingClose>` and `<views:rows>`, which make it possible to control all the generated markup:

```
<%-- Default table view of data. Read only. Uses some simple color banding.--%>

<%@page session="true" errorPage="systemError.jsp" %>

<%@ taglib uri="/views" prefix="views" %>

<%-- The request controller will instantiate this bean --%>
<jsp:useBean id="browseSession" scope="session" type="ui.BrowseSession" />

<%--    Make this the default view page until the user chooses another page --%>
<% browseSession.setTableViewJSP(request.getServletPath()); %>

<html>
  <head>
    <title>Table: [<%=browseSession.getTableName()%>]</title>
  </head>
  <body>

<%-- We only want a drop down, not an expanded list --%>
<% boolean multiSelect = false; %>
<%@ include file="_chooseTable.jsp" %>

<% javax.swing.table.TableModel tableModel = browseSession.getTableModel(); %>

<%@ include file="_chooseMode.jsp" %>

<% String color="white"; %>
<table border="1">
  <views:jspTable model="<%=tableModel %>" >
    <views:headingOpen>
      <tr bgcolor="black">
    </views:headingOpen>
    <views:headingCell>
        <td>
          <font size=4 color="white"><%=heading%></font>
        </td>
```

```
    </views:headingCell>
    <views:rows>
      <views:rowOpen>
          <%-- Use a scriptlet to achieve color banding for readability --%>
          <% color = (row.intValue() % 2 == 0) ? "white" : "cyan"; %>
        <tr bgColor="<%=color%>">
      </views:rowOpen>
      <views:rowClose></tr></views:rowClose>
      <views:cell><td><%=value%></td></views:cell>
    </views:rows>
  </views:jspTable>
</table>

  </body>
</html>
```

We need an additional page fragment to implement this page, _chooseMode.jsp. This provides the links to alternative views. It excludes the present view by checking the name of the page in which it is used. Note that additional links to new views can be added by modifying this single JSP fragment. These links are the only links within the application that do not pass through the controller JSP. This is legitimate because all views occur with the application in the same state, and render the same data:

```
<%--   JSP fragment to offer a choice of mode, depending on the user's
   location in the system.--%>

<% if (request.getServletPath().indexOf("tableView") == -1) { %>
  <a href="tableView.jsp">View mode</a> |
<% } %>

<% if (request.getServletPath().indexOf("csvView") == -1) { %>
  <a href="csvView.jsp">Downloadable format mode (CSV)</a> |
<% } %>

<% if (request.getServletPath().indexOf("editTable") == -1 &&
        browseSession.isTableEditable()) { %>
  <a href="editTable.jsp">Edit mode</a>
<% } %>

<br/>

<a href="controller.jsp?action=NewConnection">
  Disconnect and connect to another database
</a> |
<a href="controller.jsp?action=Logout">
  Logout out and disconnect
</a>
<p/>
```

Let's consider another view, the CSV view we were required to implement to allow users to cut and paste data into other applications. This looks quite different from the previous table, apart from sharing the common navigational controls at the top of the page:

This view also uses the `<views:jspTable>` tag. This is possible because this tag enables JSPs to control all aspects of the markup it produces, and so is not limited to generating HTML table code:

```
<%--  CSV table view of data. --%>

<%@page session="true" errorPage="systemError.jsp" %>
<%@ taglib uri="/views" prefix="views" %>

<%-- The request controller will instantiate this bean --%>
<jsp:useBean id="browseSession" scope="session" type="ui.BrowseSession" />

<%-- Make this the default view page --%>
<% browseSession.setTableViewJSP(request.getServletPath()); %>

<%
  javax.swing.table.TableModel tableModel = browseSession.getTableModel();
%>
<html>
  <head>
    <title>CSV View -- Table: [<%=browseSession.getTableName()%>]</title>
  </head>
  <body>

<% boolean multiSelect = false; %>
<%@ include file="_chooseTable.jsp" %>
<%@ include file="_chooseMode.jsp" %>
```

```
      Cut and paste the data below into any application
   </p>
   <code>
      <views:jspTable model="<%=tableModel %>" >
         <views:headingOpen></views:headingOpen>
         <views:headingClose><br/></views:headingClose>
   <%-- We use the ternary operator to ensure that we don't place a comma
      after the last entry on each line --%>
         <views:headingCell><%=heading%><%=(column.intValue()
         <tableModel.getColumnCount() - 1) ? "," : ""%></views:headingCell>
         <views:rows>
            <views:rowOpen></views:rowOpen>
            <views:rowClose><br/></views:rowClose>
            <views:cell><%=value%><%=(column.intValue()
            <tableModel.getColumnCount() - 1) ? "," : ""%></views:cell>
         </views:rows>
      </views:jspTable>
   </code>
   </body>
</html>
```

The third and final view we need to implement in the first phase of development is the edit view, allowing the user to update each row of the table. It will look like this:

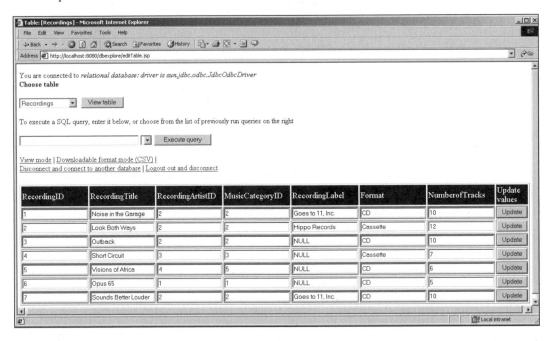

Again the `<jsp:table>` tag generates the required HTML, although the code is more complex. We further test the flexibility of the table tag by adding an additional header field (Update values) and column to the data values returned by the table model. Each row of the table is a form, with the usual hidden action value for the request controller (`UpdateTable`), and an additional hidden value containing the index of the row that the user wishes to update. The additional column will contain the submit button for each row.

Here is the listing for editTable.jsp:

```jsp
<%-- Editable table view. This will contain a form for each row of data.
--%>

<%@page session="true" errorPage="systemError.jsp" %>
<%@ taglib uri="/views" prefix="views" %>

<%-- The request controller will instantiate this bean --%>
<jsp:useBean id="browseSession" scope="session" type="ui.BrowseSession" />

<%-- Make this the default view page until the user chooses another page
--%>
<% browseSession.setTableViewJSP(request.getServletPath()); %>
<html>
  <head>
    <title>Table: [<%=browseSession.getTableName()%>]</title>
  </head>
  <body>
    <% boolean multiSelect = false; %>

<%@ include file="_chooseTable.jsp" %>
<%@ include file="_chooseMode.jsp" %>

<%
  javax.swing.table.TableModel tableModel = browseSession.getTableModel(); %>

<% String color="white"; %>
<table border="1">
  <views:jspTable model="<%=tableModel %>" >
    <views:headingOpen>
      <tr bgcolor="black"></views:headingOpen>
        <views:headingClose>
        <%-- We can use this to add an extra column --%>
        <td><font size=4 color="white">Update values</font></td>
      </tr>
    </views:headingClose>
    <views:headingCell>
        <td><font size=4 color="white"><%=heading%></font></td>
    </views:headingCell>
    <views:rows>
      <views:rowOpen>
        <%-- Each row of the table is a form --%>
        <form method="post" action="controller.jsp">

        <%-- As always, we need a hidden field containing the required
             RequestHandler's name --%>
        <input type="hidden" name="action" value="UpdateTable"/>
        <input type="hidden" name="row" value="<%=row.intValue()%>" />
        <%-- Use the ternary operator to implement color banding --%>
        <% color = (row.intValue() % 2 == 0) ? "gray" : "white"; %>
      <tr bgColor="<%=color%>">
      </views:rowOpen>
      <views:rowClose>
```

```
        <%--
          We need to provide the extra column we promised in the heading.
          We need to provide a variable containing the current alert's
          id for the included form
        --%>
        <td><input type="submit" value="Update" /></td>
      </form>
    </tr>
      </views:rowClose>
    <views:cell><td>

<% if (!tableModel.isCellEditable(row.intValue(), column.intValue())) { %>
 <%-- The primary key is not editable: don't use a form field --%>
   <b><%=value%></b>
 <% } else { %>
   <input type="text" name="<%=column.intValue()%>" value="<%=value%>" />
 <% } %>

      </td></views:cell>
    </views:rows>
  </views:jspTable>
</table>

  </body>
</html>
```

We need a confirmation page (`updateOK.jsp`) to let users know if their update request succeeded. The code for this is pleasingly simple:

```
<html>
  <head><title>Update succeeded!/title></head>
  <body>
    <a href="editTable.jsp">Continue editing table</a><br/>
    <a href="tableView.jsp">View table</a><br/>
  </body>
</html>
```

Before we look at the implementation of the `UpdateTable RequestHandler`, let's consider what would have happened if the update didn't succeed. Here, as anywhere else in the application if we encounter an error, we will be forwarded to the system error page, `systemError.jsp`. This page makes some attempt to tailor the error message depending on what we can learn from the exception passed to it, although a real application would need more sophisticated and user-friendly error handling. To support diagnostics, this page includes the exception's stack trace in an HTML comment:

```
<%@page isErrorPage="true" %>
<html>
  <head>
    <title>Data Browser: Error</title>
  </head>
  <body>
    <% if (exception instanceof ui.InvalidInputException) { %>
      <%-- Provide a link to allow the user to retry --%>
      Sorry. Your input was invalid.<br/>
```

```
      <i><%=exception.getMessage()%></i><br/>
      Please
      <a href="<%=((ui.InvalidInputException) exception).getRetryURL()%>">
        try again
      </a>.

   <% } else { %>
      Sorry. Your request could not be processed.<br/>
      <i><%=exception.getMessage()%></i><br/>
   <% } %>

<%-- Include the actual exception in a hidden comment --%>
<!--
   <% exception.printStackTrace(new java.io.PrintWriter(out)); %>
-->
   </body>
</html>
```

The following screenshot shows the output of the error page following an unsuccessful update, along with a source listing displaying the generated stack trace. (Since the simple implementation of JDBC data access behind this application doesn't support updates, attempts to update tables will always produce this result.)

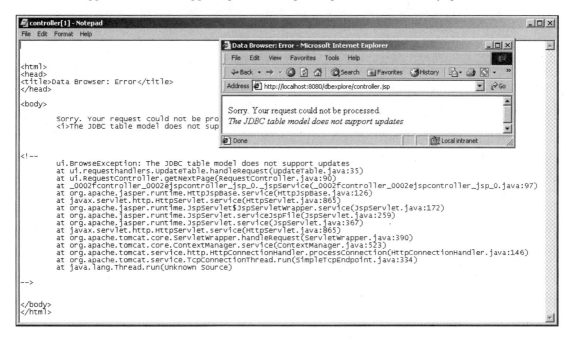

Now let's return to the RequestHandlers required to implement the remaining views. Remember the application's ability to run SQL queries, producing output like this:

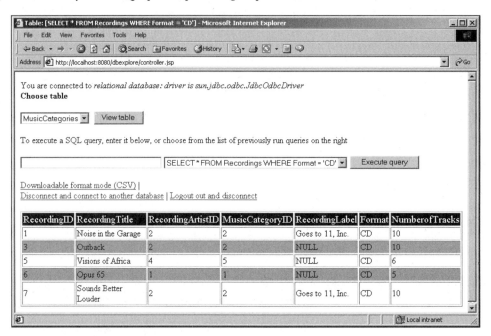

This functionality is implemented by the RunQuery RequestHandler. (However, the page may be rendered by any of the three view JSPs we have seen). RunQuery needs to check two parameters: query (which would have resulted from the user typing a new query), and oldquery, which may have resulted from the user choosing a previously run query from the drop down on the right of the query entry text field. If neither of these parameters contains data, the user's input was invalid, and this object should throw an exception causing the user to be sent to the error page, with a link back to a page allowing another try to enter a query:

```
package ui.requesthandlers;

import java.sql.SQLException;
import javax.servlet.http.*;
import javax.servlet.jsp.*;
import javax.swing.table.TableModel;

import datasources.*;
import ui.*;

public class RunQuery implements RequestHandler {

  public String handleRequest(PageContext pageContext, HttpServletRequest request)
      throws BrowseException {
    System.out.println(getClass() + ".handleRequest");
    String query = request.getParameter("query");
```

```
    if (query == null || "".equals(query))
    // We need to look at the value passed from the dropdown
      query = request.getParameter("oldquery");

    if (query == null || "".equals(query))
      throw new InvalidInputException("A query must be supplied",
                                      "chooseTable.jsp");
    System.out.println("RunQuery will execute query " + query);
    try {
      // Update the session bean appropriately
      BrowseSession session =
                  RequestController.FindSessionBean(pageContext, this);
      session.getTableModelForSQL(query);
      return session.getTableViewJSP();
    } catch (DataSourceException ex) {
      throw new BrowseException(ex.getMessage());
    }
  }
}
```

We also need to allow the user to return to the login page at any point and choose to connect to a new database. This is implemented by the NewConnection RequestHandler. To ensure that the data source cleans up after itself, we invalidate the current session. As the current BrowseSession object is unbound from the session, it will call the cleanup() method of its DataSource object. This is why the BrowseSession bean implements the HttpSessionBindingListener interface, meaning that the JSP engine will notify instances as they are bound to or unbound from a session. The next request to controller.jsp will result in the instantiation of a fresh session object.

```
package ui.requesthandlers;

import javax.servlet.http.*;
import javax.servlet.jsp.*;

import ui.*;

public class NewConnection implements RequestHandler {

  public String handleRequest(PageContext pageContext,
                              HttpServletRequest request) {
    // We can rely on the session object to clean up after itself:
    // all we need to do is invalidate the session
    pageContext.getSession().invalidate();
    return RequestController.LOGIN_PAGE;
  }
}
```

The logout RequestHandler is almost identical. It invalidates the session and forwards the response to a static page, logout.html:

```
package ui.requesthandlers;

import javax.servlet.http.*;
import javax.servlet.jsp.*;
```

```
import ui.*;

public class Logout implements RequestHandler {

  private static final String LOGOUT_PAGE = "logout.html";

  public String handleRequest(PageContext pageContext,
                              HttpServletRequest request) {
    // We can rely on the session object to clean up after itself:
    // all we need to do is invalidate the session
    pageContext.getSession().invalidate();
    return LOGOUT_PAGE;
  }
}
```

Making `logout.html` a static page helps avoid the temptation of trying to access session information: this has now been destroyed:

```
<html>
  <head>
    <title>Data Explorer: Log out</title>
  </head>

  <body>
    <h2>Session complete</h2>
      Thank you for using this system.
      You have been logged out successfully.
    <p/>
    You are now disconnected from the database.
  </body>
</html>
```

Finally, there is `UpdateTable`, the `RequestHandler` to handle the update action resulting from form submissions from `editTable.jsp`:

```
package ui.requesthandlers;

import java.sql.SQLException;
import javax.servlet.http.*;
import javax.servlet.jsp.*;
import javax.swing.table.TableModel;

import datasources.*;
import ui.*;

public class UpdateTable implements RequestHandler {

  public String handleRequest(PageContext pageContext,
                              HttpServletRequest request)
    throws BrowseException {
    System.out.println(getClass() + ".handleRequest");
    try {
```

```
            BrowseSession session =
                        RequestController.FindSessionBean(pageContext, this);
            TableModel model = session.getTableModel();
            String row = request.getParameter("row");
            if (row == null)
              throw new InvalidInputException("Invalid or missing table index",
                                              "login.html");

            for (int col = 0; col < model.getColumnCount(); col++) {
              // Look for parameter value for this column
              String colval = request.getParameter("" + col);
              if (colval != null) {
                 System.out.println("Value of " + col + " is " + colval);
                 model.setValueAt(colval, Integer.parseInt(row), col);
        // The following method will throw an exception if the last update failed
                 session.getDataSource().checkLastUpdate();
              }
            }
          } catch (DataSourceException ex) {
            throw new BrowseException(ex.getMessage());
          }

          return "/updateOK.jsp";
       }
    }
```

Two simple Java classes complete the support for the JSP interface. `BrowseException` is a subclass of `JSPException` that is thrown when `RequestHandlers` or the `RequestController` encounter errors. Having a custom exception hierarchy is useful in JSP systems as elsewhere: it enables us to include additional information with exceptions in more complex systems, and enables the applications to determine between types of error. (Little use is made of this capability in this application.):

```
package ui;

import javax.servlet.jsp.JspException;

public class BrowseException extends JspException {

    // Constructs a <code>BrowseException</code> with the specified detail
    // message.
    // @param msg the detail message.
    public BrowseException(String msg) {
      super(msg);
    }
}
```

A subclass of `BrowseException` is used for those cases when we know which page the user needs to return to correct invalid input. An `InvalidInputException` is thrown by `RequestHandlers` that detect that the user has submitted invalid data:

```
package ui;

// Extension of BrowseException to handle recoverable errors. This
// exception can tell the error page where the user can go to resubmit
// the invalid data.
public class InvalidInputException extends BrowseException {
  private String  retryURL;
```

```
    // Constructs an <code>InvalidInputException</code> with the specified
    // detail message.
    // @param msg the detail message.
    public InvalidInputException(String msg, String retryURL) {
      super(msg);
      this.retryURL = retryURL;
    }

    public String getRetryURL() {
      return retryURL;
    }
  }
```

Note that none of these classes or JSPs is closely tied to the data tier. This means that the application is not inextricably linked to relational database concepts. Even the support for SQL is a supplement to the application's basic functionality, not a fixed requirement. (If the BrowseSession bean detects that the current data source does not support SQL, the _chooseTable.jsp page fragment won't generate the form allowing SQL input.)

Data Tier – The datasources and datasources.db Packages

Remembering the likelihood that the interface may be used for data sources other than relational databases, let's begin by abstracting the common requirements of a data source into an interface. We'll consider a data source to be an object that consists of a number of tables, each with a name. A more sophisticated extension might have a getChildDataSources() method to allow hierarchical browsing of data sources. This functionality is not required in working with relational databases, but would be if we wished to expose JNDI directory contents.

A DataSource object exposes a NameValueModel of the tables it contains, and a method allowing the retrieval of a particular table:

```
package datasources;

import javax.swing.table.TableModel;

import jspstyle.NameValueModel;

public interface DataSource extends NameValueModel {

  TableModel getTableModel(int i) throws DataSourceException;
  boolean isTableEditable(int i) throws DataSourceException;

  // Ensure resources associated with the data source are freed
  void cleanup() throws DataSourceException;

  // check last update was successful
  // necessary as the TableModel, setValueAt() cannot be overridden
  public void checkLastUpdate() throws DataSourceException;

  // Additional methods could support hierarchical retrieval

}
```

We will also define an exception class that can be thrown by `DataSource` implementations, regardless of the data source-specific exceptions they may encounter:

```
package datasources;

public class DataSourceException extends Exception {

  // @param msg the detail message.
  public DataSourceException(String msg) {
    super(msg);
  }
}
```

The only implementation of `DataSource` we include in the sample application is `DatabaseDataSource`, which uses JDBC to access a database. It does not run queries itself (leaving this to `JDBCTableModel` objects), but obtains a connection to a database and retrieves database meta data to allow it to expose the list of tables as a `NameValueModel`. To emphasize the separation between common data source concepts and this particular implementation, we place `DatabaseDataSource` and the classes that support it in a separate package, `datasources.db`:

```
package datasources.db;

import datasources.*;
import java.sql.*;
import java.util.*;

import javax.swing.AbstractListModel;
import javax.swing.table.TableModel;

// Implementation of DatabaseDataSource exposing a relational database.
// Extends the Swing AbstractListModel for a partial implementation of
// the Swing ListModel, which NameValueModel extends.

public class DatabaseDataSource
      extends AbstractListModel
    implements DataSource, ConnectionFactory {

    // Connection parameters
    private String  url;
    private String  driverName;
    private String  user;
    private String  passwd;

    // List of tables found in the database
    private List    tableList;

    // The object that will perform the actual data retrieval
    JDBCTableModel  model;

  //constructor
  public DatabaseDataSource(String url, String driverName, String user,
                      String passwd) throws DataSourceException {
    this.url = url;
```

```
      this.driverName = driverName;
      this.user = user;
      this.passwd = passwd;

      try {
        //load the driver
        Class.forName(driverName);

        // Test the connection
        Connection connection = getConnection();
        loadMetaData(connection);
        connection.close();
        model = new JDBCTableModel(this);
      } catch (ClassNotFoundException ex) {
        throw new DataSourceException("Driver class " + driverName +
                                     " cannot be loaded");
      } catch (SQLException ex) {
        throw new DataSourceException("Unable to connect to database: " + ex);
      }
    }

    public String toString() {
        return "relational database: driver is " + driverName +
               " url is " + url;
    }


    // Methods from DataSource interface
    public boolean isTableEditable(int i) throws DataSourceException {
      return ((JDBCTableModel) getTableModel(i)).isEditable();
    }

    public TableModel getTableModel(int i) throws DataSourceException {
      String sql = "SELECT * FROM " + getName(i);
      return getTableModelForSQL(sql);
    }

    public TableModel getTableModelForSQL(String sql)
      throws DataSourceException {
      try {
        model.executeSQL(sql);
        return model;
      } catch (SQLException ex) {
        throw new DataSourceException("getTableModelForSQL with SQL=[" +
                                      sql + "] threw SQLException :" + ex);
      }
    }

    public void cleanup() throws DataSourceException {
      // The JDBCTableModel closes all resources,
      // So we don't need to do anything more
    }

    public void checkLastUpdate() throws DataSourceException {
      // Since our simple
```

```
doesn't implement the setValueAt()
    // method, we always tell the user the update failed
    throw new DataSourceException("The JDBC table model does not support" +
                                    "updates");
}

// Methods from NameValueModel interface

// Return the name of the ith table (indexed from 0)
public String getName(int i) {
  return tableList.get(i).toString();
}

// Return the number of tables we found
public int getSize() {
  return tableList.size();
}

// Return the index of the table:
// this will be a parameter to this class's getXXXX(int) methods
public Object getElementAt(int i) {
  return new Integer(i);
}

// Methods from ConnectionFactory interface that JDBCTableModel uses
public Connection getConnection() throws SQLException {
    // If this application were guaranteed to run in a J2EE-compliant
    // JSP engine, this connection could be obtained from a connection
    // pool specified in the application's web.xml file and accessed
    // via JNDI
    return DriverManager.getConnection(url, user, passwd);
}
```

The `loadMetaData()` method loads and stores information about the tables within the database. This information will be retrieved one during the life of the class. The information is returned by JDBC as a `ResultSet`. Each table description row has the following columns:

❑ String value giving the table catalog, `TABLE_CAT`. Value returned may be null.

❑ String value giving table schema, `TABLE_SCHEM`. Again value returned may be null.

❑ `TABLE_NAME` as a String.

❑ `TABLE_TYPE` as a String.

❑ `REMARKS` String => explanatory comment on the table.

Common types are `TABLE`, `VIEW` and `SYSTEM TABLE`. In this case we only want the table name and table type, columns 3 and 4:

```
private void loadMetaData(Connection connection) throws SQLException {
  DatabaseMetaData dbmd = connection.getMetaData();
```

```
  // Change the second parameter below to retrieve information
  // about a particular schema in the database
  ResultSet rs = dbmd.getTables(null, null, "%", null);

  tableList = new LinkedList();
  while (rs.next()) {
    String tableName = rs.getString(3);
    String tableType = rs.getString(4);

    // NB: this check may not work for all databases
    // With Oracle, it successfully excludes views and the many
    // strange system tables that would otherwise appear
    if (tableType.toUpperCase().equals("TABLE"))
      tableList.add(tableName);
    }
    // sort the table list by name
    Collections.sort(tableList);

  }
}
```

Note that DatabaseDataSource implements a simple interface, ConnectionFactory, unique to JDBC. This is used to enable DatabaseDataSource objects to communicate with the JDBCTableModel helper class without exposing their structure:

```
package datasources.db;

import java.sql.*;

public interface ConnectionFactory {
  Connection getConnection() throws SQLException;
}
```

The core of the JDBC functionality is contained in the JDBCTableModel class. This runs SQL queries and maintains an internal data structure built from the ResultSets:

```
package datasources.db;

import java.util.*;
import java.sql.*;
import javax.swing.table.*;

/**
 *    Class to present JDBC query results as Swing table models.
 *    Thanks to Gary Watson for the code on which this is based.
 */
class JDBCTableModel extends AbstractTableModel {

  /** Names of the current columns */
  private List columnNames;

  /** Types of the current columns (contains Class objects) */
  private List columnTypes;
```

```
/** Data in current table. Each entry is a List of cell value objects. */
private List rowList;

/** Object used to obtain JDBC connections */
private ConnectionFactory connectionFactory;

// Constructor using a DatabaseDataSource object to obtain connections to
// the database
public JDBCTableModel(ConnectionFactory connectionFactory) {
  this.connectionFactory = connectionFactory;
}

// Update the table's structure based on this query
public void executeSQL(String query) throws SQLException {
  // Clear any data already in the table
  rowList = new LinkedList();
  columnTypes = new LinkedList();
  columnNames = new LinkedList();

  Connection connection = null;
  Statement statement = null;

  try {
    System.out.println("** About to execute: " + query);
    connection = connectionFactory.getConnection();
    statement = connection.createStatement();
    ResultSet resultSet = statement.executeQuery(query);
    updateFromResultSet(resultSet);
    resultSet.close();
  }
  // We don't need to catch SQL exceptions: let this method throw them
  // We do need to ensure that we clean up, however
  finally {
    try {
      if (statement != null)
        statement.close();
    } catch (SQLException ex) {
      // Ignore this exception, but catch it so that we can
      // try to close the connection anyway
    }

    try {
      if (connection != null)
        connection.close();
    } catch (SQLException ex) {
      throw new SQLException("JDBCTableModel threw SQLException in" +
                             "cleanup:" + ex);
    }
  }
}

// This is a simple-minded implementation to check if table editable
public boolean isEditable() {
  return true;
```

```
    }

    // This is backed by the ResultSetMetaData our query generated
    public String getColumnName(int col) {
      String retVal;
      retVal = (String) columnNames.get(col);
      if(retVal == null) retVal = "";
      return retVal;
    }

    public Class getColumnClass(int col) {
      Class retVal;
      retVal = (Class) columnTypes.get(col);
      if(retVal == null) retVal = Object.class;
        return retVal;
    }

    public boolean isCellEditable(int row, int col) {
      // Should really check here whether the column is part of the primary
      // key. If it is, it shouldn't be editable
      return true;
    }

    public int getColumnCount() {
      return columnNames.size();
    }

    public int getRowCount() {
      return rowList.size();
    }

    public Object getValueAt(int row, int col) {
      // Find the object for the correct row and look in
      // it for the value
      List rowData = (List) rowList.get(row);
      return rowData.get(col);
    }

    //  Note that Swing models index from 0, JDBC ResultSets from 1
    public void setValueAt(Object value, int row, int col) {
      // Not implemented
      // This might be implemented by giving this class the ability to
      // execute an update, or by using a JDBC 2.0 updateable ResultSet
    }

    // Set the table's contents based on this ResultSet
    private void updateFromResultSet(ResultSet rs) throws SQLException {
      int curType;

      // We need the ResultSetMetaData to find out the number of
      // columns in this ResultSet and the column types and names
      ResultSetMetaData metaData = rs.getMetaData();
      int columns =  metaData.getColumnCount();
```

```
    for(int col = 0 ; col < columns; col++) {
      columnNames.add(metaData.getColumnLabel(col + 1));
      try {
        curType = metaData.getColumnType(col + 1);
      } catch (SQLException e) {
        // This will go to the default case in the switch below
        curType = -1;
      }

      switch(curType) {
        case Types.CHAR:
        case Types.VARCHAR:
        case Types.LONGVARCHAR:
          columnTypes.add(String.class);
        break;

        case Types.TINYINT:
        case Types.SMALLINT:
        case Types.INTEGER:
          columnTypes.add(Integer.class);
        break;

        case Types.BIGINT:
          columnTypes.add(Long.class);
        break;

        case Types.FLOAT:
        case Types.DOUBLE:
          columnTypes.add(Double.class);
        break;

        case Types.DATE:
          columnTypes.add(java.sql.Date.class);
        break;

        default:
          columnTypes.add(Object.class);
        break;
      }   // switch
    }   // for each column

      // Load the actual data
    while (rs.next()) {
      // We hold each row of data in a list
      List rowData = new LinkedList();
      for (int col = 0; col < columns; col++) {
        // Remember that ResultSet columns are indexed from 1!
        rowData.add(rs.getObject(col + 1));
      }
      rowList.add(rowData);
    }

  // Remember to let any listeners know the table has changed.
  // This table may be used to support Swing clients as well as
  // web applications
  fireTableChanged(null);
  }
}
```

A more complex implementation of JDBCTableModel would implement table update functionality, possibly through JDBC 2.0 updateable ResultSets. To retain focus on JSPs, I have left this task as an exercise for the reader.

Another interesting possibility would be to supplement the JDBCTableModel with an EntityBeanTableModel, and the DatabaseDataSource with an EntityDataSource. EntityDataSource could use JNDI to locate entity EJBs, and EntityBeanTableModel could return their state and allow it to be updated.

Reviewing the Application

Several things could be done to improve this sample application. The error handling could be more sophisticated. The HTML contained in the JSPs could be made more sophisticated, producing more attractive pages. The JDBCTableModel could be enhanced to support updates.

However, the soundness of its basic approach is proven by the ease with which some significant functional enhancements could be made.

The HTML contained in the existing JSP views could be improved easily by a page designer with a minimum of exposure to JSP concepts. No changes to these views could compromise the application's page flow, or produce a worse result than a JSP that temporarily wouldn't compile.

Consider adding the downloadable Excel data view. JSPs are not suited to generating such non-text formats, but a servlet could be added to the application to access the session state and generate this content. The servlet would obtain data from the same models as the JSP views. Adding additional HTML or XHTML views would be even easier: it would simply be necessary to write more JSP views. Each JSP view in this application is equivalent to an implementation of a single interface: the session bean will always expose the same data at the point when the controller forwards a request to a JSP view. (No such guarantee would be possible were the view pages to be public entry points for the application.)

Likewise, XML could be produced by the data tier or an additional view JSP, and transformed using an XSLT stylesheet tag. This could result in the addition of many views without further JSP coding, through the authoring of additional XSLT stylesheets.

Extending the application to handle JNDI directory data would require minimal changes to the front end: simply the implementation of additional DataSource implementations, perhaps in a datasources.jndi package.

Importantly, the interface design used for the data explorer is not predicated on using JSP. Most of the code could be reused in a Swing interface.

Deploying the Application

The last remaining file required to implement application is the WAR's web.xml file. This has two important jobs: it must let the JSP engine know where to locate the tag library descriptor required to describe the views tab library (see Chapter 13 for a description of the required syntax); and it must set the application's "welcome page" to be controller.jsp. The context for the application is set as dbexplore:

```
<?xml version="1.0" encoding="UTF-8"?>

<!DOCTYPE web-app PUBLIC '-//Sun Microsystems, Inc.//DTD Web Application 2.2//EN'
'http://java.sun.com/j2ee/dtds/web-app_2.2.dtd'>

<web-app>
  <display-name>dbexplore</display-name>
  <description>Database Explorer</description>

  <session-config>
    <session-timeout>100</session-timeout>
  </session-config>

  <welcome-file-list>
    <welcome-file>controller.jsp</welcome-file>
  </welcome-file-list>

  <taglib>
    <taglib-uri>/views</taglib-uri>
    <taglib-location>/WEB-INF/lib/taglib.tld</taglib-location>
  </taglib>

</web-app>
```

I developed this web application as an expanded WAR, testing it in both Tomcat 3.1 and JRun 3.0. My expanded WAR had the following directory structure:

```
dbexplore/
          controller.jsp
          systemError.jsp
          editTable.jsp
          login.html
          chooseTable.jsp
          tableView.jsp
          csvView.jsp
          _chooseTable.jsp
          updateOK.jsp
          _chooseMode.jsp
          logout.html
          WEB-INF/
                  web.xml
                  lib/
                      taglib.tld
                      viewsclasses.jar
                  classes/
                          ui/
                              InvalidInputException.class
                              RequestController.class
                              RequestHandler.class
                              BrowseSession$QueryNameValueModel.class
                              BrowseSession.class
                              BrowseException.class
                              requesthandlers/
```

```
                              NewConnection.class
                              RunQuery.class
                              DBConnect.class
                              ChooseTable.class
                              Logout.class
                              UpdateTable.class
          datasources/
                        DataSource.class
                        DataSourceException.class
                        db/
                           ConnectionFactory.class
                           DatabaseDataSource.class
                           JDBCTableModel.class
```

Note the inclusion of two files that include the implementation of the views tag library, both in the `WEB-INF/lib` directory: `taglib.tld` and `viewslib.jar`. The JSP engine automatically loads the classes in JARs placed in this directory, enabling the classes required to implement existing tag libraries to be packaged as a single distribution unit.

Before running the application, ensure that the JDBC drivers you wish to use are available to the JSP engine at runtime. The means of achieving this will differ between JSP engines. Although WARs are normally self-contained, it is impractical for this WAR to contain all the JDBC drivers it may be used with.

Summary

Writing maintainable JSPs is hard, but the effort involved is well worthwhile. Poorly designed JSP interfaces are costly to maintain and insufficiently responsive to business needs; well designed JSP interfaces cleanly separate presentation and content.

The first requirement in developing maintainable JSPs is a well-engineered J2EE solution, and an understanding of how a JSP layer fits into it. (I use the term JSP layer to refer to JSPs as well as the Java classes that immediately support them.) Considering using technologies such as XML/XSLT to complement JSPs if they are more appropriate to render your content.

Another key requirement is an understanding of how to leverage features of JSP that enable us to separate presentation and context: most importantly, JSP beans and tag handlers.

With this understanding, we are in a position to enforce strict coding standards. The key goal is to minimize the amount of Java code used in JSPs.

Finally, we must allow for the entire product lifecycle. Throughout the product lifecycle, the architecture and the functionality should remain in sync. If changes are required to JSP beans (and even session EJBs) to ensure this, this is preferable to a quick fix to JSPs that compromises the division between presentation and content and correct location of business logic.

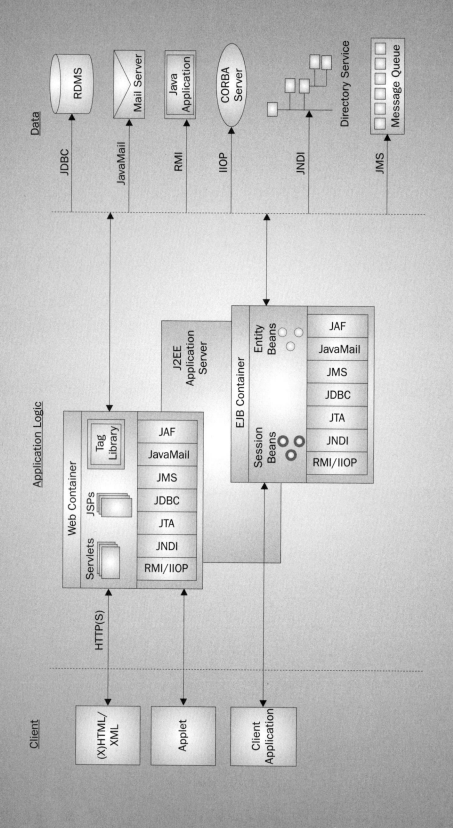

JSP and XML – Working Together

In this chapter, we'll investigate some ways in which XML and JSP can work together within a J2EE application. We'll see XML and JSP complementing each other, operating in the different components of the application - JSP presenting a surface that is populated with template material and dynamic information sources, while XML provides the channels along which information flows to the surface to be displayed in a dynamically constructed page.

In this chapter, we are going to be putting the knowledge we learned earlier in the book (Chapters 5 and 6) into practice by developing a XML-configured Newsletter JSP application. Over the course of this chapter we will see:

❑   How to use reflection to create classes and invoke methods by name

❑   How to use XML configuration files to define objects and methods to be invoked

❑   How to combine data from several different datasources

First, let's take a look at the overall application design.

JSP and XML

The following diagram shows where both JSP and XML fit into the picture:

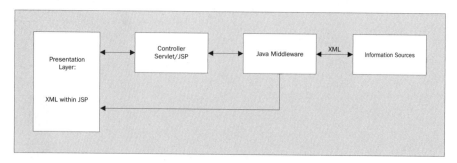

In terms of this diagram, JSP functions best in the Transformation and Presentation layer as template pages that can easily incorporate dynamic material from the Java classes of the application (usually JavaBeans). JSP can also function as the main entry point and controller of the application, the role frequently played by a servlet.

XML is best known as a standard for defining both presentation formats (languages) and formats for data representation and interchange. XML can also be used for dynamic configuration of J2EE applications. The tree structure of XML documents is well suited for describing many kinds of structured entities, including networks of Java objects that instantiate and use each other.

Our case study will be a Newsletter page that formats itself differently in response to the user profile and expressed preferences. Associated with each login is an XML configuration file that instantiates one of a number of possible applications. Each application is a different newsletter, on different subjects, perhaps formatted differently. Internally, each application is a different set of JavaBeans, instantiated from the XML configuration file. The JavaBeans query different information sources, including relational databases and XML files; they can also filter the obtained information through a variety of filters (implemented as SAX filters), before displaying it in HTML, XHTML or WML or, if desired, in other XML formats.

Modular Design and Modular Reading

Our case study application will consist of several large-scale components, such as Configuration or Database Access. Each large-scale component will, in turn, consist of several sub-components, such as Java classes, JSPs, or XML documents. (All of this will be shown in the diagram shortly.) We have structured our code so that each component has a precisely defined functionality, a kind of a contract with the rest of the application. This makes it easy to maintain the code: each component can be modified and extended individually, without affecting the rest of the application, as long as its contractual obligations are maintained.

> *It also affords you, the reader, the convenience of modular reading: after you have figured out the overall structure of the application and the role of each component, you can read component-specific sections in any order, leaving some of them for later which may never come. This way, you can be guided by your current interest and need rather then by the linear sequence of the chapter's text. We do believe that for maximal reading pleasure and educational impact you should read the entire chapter in order, but you don't have to.*

In outline, the chapter proceeds as follows:

- ❏ An overview of the application and its five major components
- ❏ Two utility classes
- ❏ Component 1: The Configuration component
- ❏ Component 2: The Database access component
- ❏ Component 3: The XML data access component
- ❏ Component 4: The Presentation component
- ❏ Component 5: The Control controller

The order in which the components are presented is not accidental: peripheral components that have to do with configuration and data access are more isolated and self-sufficient than the core presentation and control components that make use of the peripheral ones. However, we will define quite precisely each component's contract with the rest of the application, so as long as you read those "contract" subsections for each component you can jump straight into Presentation and Control.

A Profiled Newsletter – A Case Study

Consider a general situation in which there is an informational resource – a collection of relational databases and XML documents – used by many different users with somewhat different interests. The resource publishes a newsletter based on its data. Both the resource data and its subscribers have grown so diverse that it has become impractical to publish the same newsletter for everybody. Our task is to implement a user-customized newsletter that displays a user-selected view of the resource. The goal is to enable the user to specify the sources of information that the user is interested in by editing a user-specific XML configuration string. The sources of information, as we said, fall into two categories: XML documents and relational databases.

Caveats

Before we present the overall design, we should cover a couple of clarifications. Firstly, given the limitations of space and the intended audience of this chapter, our case study is more of a technology demo than a real application. If you use the configuration string that we provide, you will see exactly two information sources in your newsletter, one for each kind. However, you can easily configure a newsletter that returns query results from seventeen databases and thirty-three XML documents; it's just the matter of repetition.

Secondly, our information sources don't try to be exciting: no stock quotes, horse races, MP3 sound files or rock videos. One of us collected stamps as a boy, and so our resource started life as the catalog of a stamp collection. (For this reason, the newsletter is still called `StampPage`, and many code files have names that start with "sp", as in `spConfigure.jsp`.) One of the two information sources that we use is an XML document that is a catalog of stamps and other items; the other one is a relational database that contains weather information indexed by zip code. What's interesting here is not the content, but the technology. We're showing you how XML and JSP can help with feeding data into web pages where some of the data will be in XML files and some in databases, but we want to produce a unified presentation customized for each user.

The Main Design Features

The main features of the design are as follows:

❑ The user interacts with the program via JSP pages.

❑ Each user maintains an XML configuration document that the user can view and edit. For reasons mentioned – lack of space, intended audience – we will assume that the user can edit the document directly rather than through a friendly interface with drop-down menus of choices.

❑ Configuration documents are kept as text strings in a database table. Upon login, the user's configuration document is retrieved and passed on to the configuration component for processing. If the user chooses to change their configuration document, the changes take effect immediately.

❑ The content of the newsletter comes from relational databases and XML documents. In either case, the content is sent to the application as a stream of SAX events filtered through XSLT stylesheets. Stylesheets are cached upon first use, which dramatically improves performance.

An Overview of the Main Components

The application consists of five major components:

❑ Presentation

❑ Control

❑ Configuration

❑ Database Data Access

❑ XML Data Access

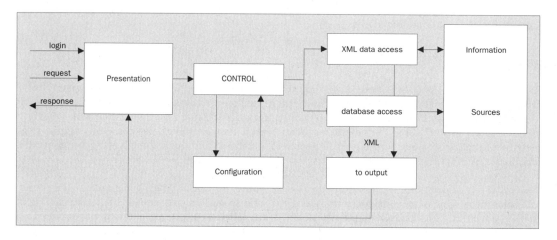

The **presentation component** consists of JSP pages:

- ❏   `top.jsp` is the login page that submits login data to `frames.jsp`
- ❏   `frames.jsp` is the main user interface page that consists of a control frame (`spControl.jsp`) and a data frame (`spQuery.jsp`)
- ❏   `errorpage.jsp` is for errors
- ❏   `spLogout.jsp` is for logout (invalidate session and say goodbye).

The main workhorse is `frames.jsp` that processes the request and sends back the response during a user session.

If the user chooses to revise his configuration, `frames.jsp` forwards the request to the **configuration component** that consists of **configuration control**, **default configuration data** and **the configuration class**.

Configuration control is executed by two JSPs:

- ❏   `spConfigure.jsp` is where the user can view and edit his configuration string
- ❏   `spSaveConfig.jsp` saves the `editedconfiguration` string to a database table and forwards to `frames.jsp`

If the user doesn't have a configuration string in the database, their `StampPage` is configured from default configuration data kept in `spStampPage.xml`. Whether the configuration data comes from the database or from the default configuration file, it is interpreted by the configuration class, `Config.java`. `Config` has a public static `Config()` method that is called by `StampPageFactory` to create an instance of `StampPage` on the basis of configuration data.

The **control component** consists of two Java beans: `StampPageFactory.java` and `StampPage.java`. A typical flow of control is for a JSP page to use a `StampPageFactory` to produce a `StampPage` bean for the session, configured according to the user's XML configuration string or default XML configuration file. The `StampPage` bean interacts with the database and XML information sources to produce the results for the `spQuery.jsp` page.

All interactions between the `StampPage` bean and information sources is executed by two data access components – one for relational databases, the other for XML text documents.

The **database access component** consists of:

- ❏   `DBConnector` interface and its default implementation, `DBConnectorImpl`
- ❏   `QueryHandler` that extends `DBConnectorImpl`
- ❏   `ResultSetParser` that converts a result set into a stream of SAX `DocumentHandler` calls

The **XML data access component** consists of:

- ❏   `DomSearch` that parses an XML document into a DOM tree and outputs the entire tree or a subtree satisfying certain search conditions
- ❏   `Dom2Sax` that "parses" a DOM node into a stream of SAX `DocumentHandler` calls

Note that both access components ultimately produce a stream of SAX events. That stream is consumed, in both cases, by a `Sax2Writer` class, that writes out the contents of the incoming XML document to a `java.io.Writer`. It uses a `JspWriter` to send the output to the appropriate JSP.

The diagram of the application can now be shown with more detail:

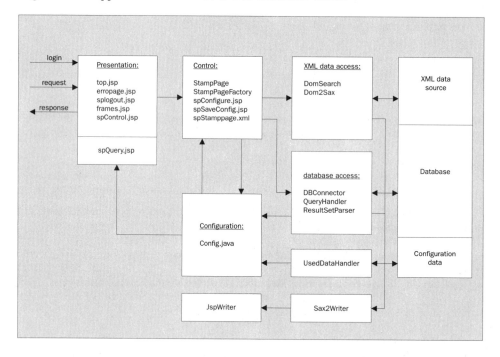

Not shown in this diagram are two utility classes, `PropDict` and `Logger`, which we use throughout this application and in most of our applications. The classes are described in complete detail in our chapter on XML parsing earlier in the book.

Try It Out

You can review the case study in action by following the execution of this use case:

❑   User connects to system, enters login.

❑   Since the user has no configuration string in the database, the stamps page is configured from the default XML file. It contains the results of the default database query and the default search of XML data.

❑   The user runs the search again, gets different XML data; the rest remains the same.

❑   The user views the default configuration data, changes the database query parameter and stores in the database. The contents of the data frame change to reflect the new configuration.

❑   The user logs out.

In order to run the case study you also need to configure a System DSN called `Weather` *to point to the* `Ch15Weather.mdb` *database included in the chapter's download.*

Also in the following screenshots we are using Mozilla. This is because the stylesheet uses Cascading Style Sheets 2 Constructs to style the output. It will work in IE 5 but it won't look quite so good.

The sequence of screen shots below illustrates the use case in progress. To start, connect to `top.jsp`. Upon connecting to `top.jsp`, you will see the following screen:

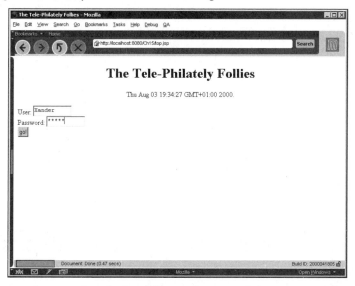

Fill in the user name and password, and submit. The resulting page below is generated in part by a `DomSearch` scan for a stamp from the user's (i.e. default) country-of-interest, and in part from a database query for weather from the user's (i.e. default) zip code. Controls for temporary change in the country or zip code are on the left:

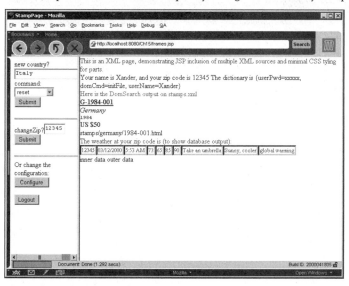

Click Submit under the reset combo box, you will get a different item retrieved from the XML data source; everything else remains the same:

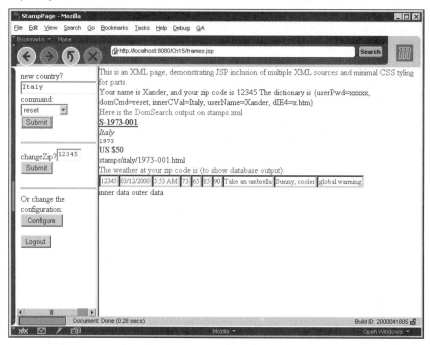

Now let's try changing the zip code to bring up a different weather report. Enter 13346 into the changeZip? box and hit the Submit button next to it:

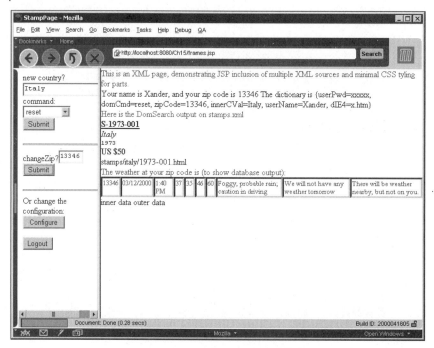

The next thing to try is changing the configuration data. Click Configure to load the data into a text area; then change the default zip code from 12345 to 11111:

Click Save, and you will see different database query results:

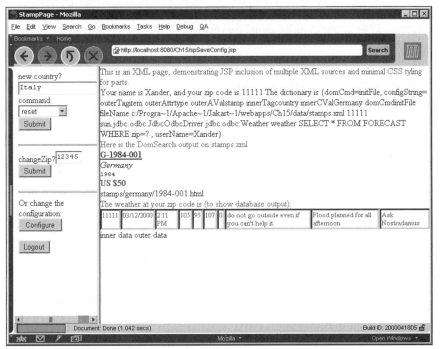

Click Logout to complete the use case and view the farewell message. The rest of the chapter explains how it all works.

The Configuration Component

This section is about configuring your applications dynamically from XML data. All configuring is done by the public static method Config(). This is the only "interface" exposed by the Config class to the application in which it is used.

The Config() method receives an XML description of the objects it needs to configure and operates on that description. There are three overloaded versions of Config(). The really important one takes a DOM node as an argument and works with it to configure an application. The other two receive an XML document (either as a file name or an org.xml.sax.InputSource), parse it into a DOM object and look for <top-config> element nodes in it. If found, they pass the first <top-config> to the version of Config() that expects a DOM node.

To configure an application means to instantiate and initialize its objects and their relationships. There are two kinds of relationships we need to consider:

❑ **Contain:**
Between a container (e.g. a Vector) and its elements

❑ **Own:**
Between an object and another object that it instantiates and initializes

In both cases in the process of instantiating and initializing a "parent" object we has to instantiate and initialize a "child" object that is one of the parent's variables or **fields**. For instance, if you are instantiating an object of class Employee that has a birthDay field of class Date, you also have to instantiate that field. This sounds and smells like recursion, and should indicate to you why XML is well suited as the syntax for configuration files.

Configuring from XML means configuring from Strings because XML documents contain only String values. Therefore, we have to be able to create an instance of a class *given its name*, or construct a field *given its name*, or call a method *given its name*. This is the subject matter of **reflection**, the ability of a class to say to itself, "Do I have a constructor with this signature? If so, call it!" or, "Do I have a field with this name? If so, call its constructor!" Most classes and methods that perform these services are in the Reflection package, java.lang.reflect. So, our first subsection here will briefly review a couple of classes from the Reflection package.

The configuration process consists of Java code operating on an XML document. After the review of Reflection, we will give an example of a configuration document and discuss the XML primitives (elements and attributes) that are used for configuration: what they mean and how they are processed. After that, we will be ready to go through the Java code of our Config class.

The Reflection Package

The overall package is well described in a number of books, and in online documentation, so in this section, we'll simply briefly present the features we'll actually use in this chapter.

As you know, Java has *classes* and objects; objects are created by *constructors*; they contain *members* that are either *fields* (variables) or *methods*. Correspondingly, the Reflection package has a `Member` interface that is implemented by `Constructor`, `Field` and `Method` classes. In addition, there is of course a `Class` class in the `java.lang` package that provides a default constructor as its `newInstance()` method. So, if you have a String variable `className`, you can create an instance of that class by calling `Class.forName(className).newInstance()`.

What if you want to call a constructor with arguments? Then you have to use the `Constructor` class.

The Constructor Class

Suppose you know that your class (whose name is `MyClass`) has a constructor that takes two arguments, an Integer and a String. (We do mean the Integer class rather than the primitive `int` type.) You also have two values, an Integer value and a String value that you want to use as arguments to construct an object of the `MyClass` class. You proceed in two steps:

❑   Obtain a `Constructor` object with the right signature; a signature is represented as an array of `Class` objects

❑   Call the `newInstance()` method of that `Constructor` object providing it with your arguments as an array of `Object` objects

Your code for the first step would be something like:

```
Class cl = Class.forName("MyClass");
Class [] signature = new Class[2];
signature[0] = Integer.class;
signature[1] = String.class;
Constructor cons = cl.getConstructor(signature);
```

It is common to create those signature arrays on the fly, compressing the last four lines into:

```
Constructor cons =
            cl.getConstructor(new Class [] {Integer.class, String.class});
```

Similarly, in calling the constructor, it is common to create an array of `Object` on the fly, out of the actual arguments to the constructor:

```
Object myObj = cons.newInstance(new Object[] {intArg, strArg});
```

This assumes that your argument values are in the `intArg` and `strArg` variables.

In the version of `Config` that is used in this chapter, we only use two kinds of constructors: the default and a constructor with a single String argument. However, you will see the same two steps and the same array arguments in finding and calling a method with a given signature.

Invoking Methods

To run a method, you go through the same two steps we just described; the only difference is that for methods you also have to specify the return type. A method that takes an Integer and a String and returns a String would be run as follows:

```
Class cl = Class.forName("MyClass");
Object myObj = cl.newInstance();
Method m = cl.getMethod(new Class[]{Integer.class, String.class});
String resultStr = (String) m.invoke(myObj, new Object[]{intVar, strVar});
```

A problem arises when we don't know what the signature of the method is, but instead try to find a method that matches a particular list of arguments. Suppose we have an array of Objects and we want to use it as a list of arguments for a method in class MyClass. We go to each Object in the array and ask "What is your class"? – they will tell us because every Object has a getClass() method. So suppose we get back an array of Class objects that contains java.lang.Integer and java.lang.String. We go to MyClass and we say "Get me a method that has this signature, String and Integer", and we fail because the actual method of MyClass expects a String and an int. Instead of the class of the second argument, we should have asked for its TYPE.

Another possible cause of failure is generic methods whose signatures are defined in terms of Objects. For instance, suppose that the hypothetical MyClass we've been talking about is java.util.Vector, and we are trying to run its set() method. Suppose even more specifically that we want to set its second element to the String value "Second". We have an Object array with two values, the integer 1 (the index of the second element) and the String "Second". Even if we are clever enough to figure out that the first Class object in the signature array should be int.TYPE, we'll still fail because the second Class object will be String.class, and the signature of Vector.set() is (int, Object).

A solution to this problem is to try all possible combinations of classes and TYPEs, and within classes, try not only the actual class of the given object but every ancestor of this class, up to and including Object. This would be very costly, even if done only once at configuration time (besides, the whole idea is to be able to configure another application in the middle of, e.g. an HTTP session). In this chapter, we'll use an intermediate solution: in case of failure, we try, in a single pass, replacing each class with TYPE, then with Object. You will see how it works when we get to the code of getMethod() of our Config class.

In general, you will see the Reflection package used extensively in Config, because its task is to instantiate objects and call their methods.

A Config File Example

For our first example, consider a file that configures an instance of a class called DomSearch. The class is used in the XML data access component and will be discussed in more detail there. For our example of how Config works, we only need to know these facts:

❑ The class has a PropDict field and we need to initialize it to a new PropDict object.

❑ The class has a setDef() method that simply calls the setDef() method of its internal PropDict. We need to call setDef() several times to populate its internal PropDict with the necessary properties. The properties in question are: fileName, outerTag, outerAttr, outerAVal, innerTag, innerCVal. The values for them come either from an HTML form over the web, from the command line, or from a .properties file.

❑ The class has an initFromDict() method that does further initialization from the newly populated PropDict. The last thing we need to do is call this method.

Here is the code that we want our `Config` to run:

```
DomSearch domSrch = new DSNextMatch();
 { PropDict propDict = new PropDict();
    domSrch.setDict(propDict);
    propDict.setDef("fileName",
        "c:/Progra~1/Apache~1/jakart~1/webapps/Ch15/data/stamps.xml");
    propDict.setDef("outerTag", "item");
    propDict.setDef("outerAttr", "type");
    propDict.setDef("outerAVal", "stamp");
    propDict.setDef("innerTag", "country");
    propDict.setDef("innerCVal", "Italy");
    propDict.setDef("domCmd", "initFile");
  }
  domSrch.initFromDict();
```

This is how that code is described for `Config` in our "XML configuration language". As you read through it, remember that element content is PCDATA, i.e., character strings that are not quoted. `Config` will know to make them into `java.lang.String` objects:

```
<top-config obClass="DomSearch">

  <!-- create and populate a PropDict object -->
  <set fieldName="dict" obClass=" PropDict">
    <apply name="setDef"><!-- call setDef() method with two arguments -->
      <ob>fileName</ob>
      <ob> c:/Progra~1/Apache~1/jakart~1/webapps/Ch15/data/stamps.xml</ob>
    </apply>
    <apply name="setDef">
      <ob>outerTag</ob>
      <ob>item</ob>
    </apply>
    <apply name="setDef">
      <ob>outerAttr</ob>
      <ob>type</ob>
    </apply>
    <apply name="setDef">
      <ob>outerAVal</ob>
      <ob>stamp</ob>
    </apply>
    <apply name="setDef">
      <ob>innerTag</ob>
      <ob>country</ob>
    </apply>
    <apply name="setDef">
      <ob>innerCVal</ob><ob>Italy</ob>
    </apply>
    <apply name="setDef">
      <ob>domCmd</ob>
      <ob>initFile</ob>
    </apply>
  </set>

  <!-- call initFromDict(), a method of no arguments -->
  <apply name="initFromDict" />
</top-config>
```

The next two sections explain the intended meaning of the tags and attributes of our configuration language.

The Meaning of Tags

We can summarize the meaning of our tags as follows (this is not a complete list but it includes some tags that have not yet been shown in action):

Tag	Description
top-config	The top-level object being created
add	Add an element to a container (e.g. to a Vector)
set	Set the value of a field
set-at	Set the value of a container element at specified index
apply	Invoke a method; arguments are children <ob> elements
app-node	Invoke a method; the argument is the value of <app-node> itself
ob	A dummy tag for bottom-level elements, a hook for future use

An example of using <set-at> would be to create a Vector:

```
<top-config obClass="java.util.Vector">
    <set fieldName="size" obClass="java.lang.Integer"
        cons="true" arg="4" />
    <set-at index="0">zero</set-at>
    <set-at index="1" obClass="java.util.Date" />
    <set-at index="2" obClass="java.lang.Double"
                        cons="true" arg="2.4" />
    <set-at index="3" obClass="java.util.Vector">
        <set fieldName="size" obClass="java.lang.Integer"
            cons="true" arg="2" />
        <set-at index="0">1</set-at>
        <set-at index="1">2</set-at>
    </set-at>
    ...
</top-config>
```

This example shows three different uses of <set-at> depending on the data type of the variable being set. Consider the values set at indices 0, 1 and 2:

❑   At index 0, we set a String variable, so <set-at> doesn't have an obClass attribute at all and the value is provided by the non-empty character content of <set-at>.

❑   At index 1, we set a Date variable, and we use the default no-argument constructor to provide its value. The <set-at> element is now empty, and the class of the variable is given as the value of the obClass attribute.

❑   Finally, at index 2, we set a Double variable and we use a non-default constructor. We indicate this by setting the value of cons attribute to "true" and providing a String argument to the constructor as the value of the arg attribute.

As we said, in this chapter we only use these two types of constructors: the default and the single-String-argument. It's surprising how much distance you can cover with just those two.

The Meaning of Attributes

More systematically, the following attributes are used in our `config` language:

Element	Attribute	Intended use
apply	name	Name of method to invoke
app-node	name	Name of method to invoke
set	fieldName	Name of field to set
	obClass	The class of value to create
	cons	Non-default constructor? (true/false)
	arg	String argument to non-default constructor
set-at	index	Index of element to set
	obClass	The class of value to create
	cons	Non-default constructor? (true/false)
	arg	String argument to non-default constructor
top-config	obClass	The class of value to create (+ cons and arg, as in set)

We do not have a DTD because we expect <top-config> elements to appear embedded in other XML documents, perhaps constructed dynamically from database queries or other sources. The language is so small that the two brief tables of elements and attributes, combined with a couple of examples, give enough information to be able to use it - especially after we work through the code that interprets it, Config.java.

The Java Code for XML Configuration

The material of this section is a bit involved. In effect, it introduces XML meta-programming: Config interprets XML documents as a description of Java code to be executed. As we said, it relies heavily on the Reflection package. There are, in effect, three layers of code:

- ❏ The control structure of Config that interprets XML data and identifies appropriate action, such as "construct an object" or "call a method"

- ❏ Those methods of Config that carry out those actions: construct object and invoke their methods

- ❏ The underlying classes and methods of java.lang.reflect that ultimately do the work

There are also three layers of data that are all mixed up together in the code but should be kept separate in your mind:

- ❏ XML elements and attributes

- ❏ DOM entities like Node and Element

- ❏ Java objects

So, for instance, there is a <set> element in the XML file whose meaning is, generally, "Set the value of a field". Ultimately, this is done by a setXXX() method of the object we are configuring: if the object has a field called size, it must have a setSize() method, and we have to invoke that method. This is how we get to it:

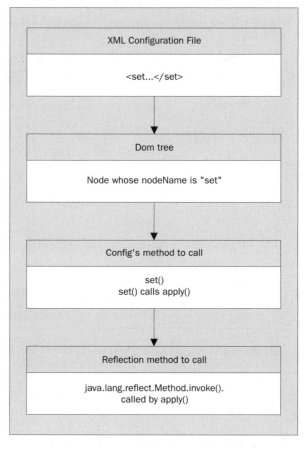

The <set> element becomes a DOM node of type Element whose name is "set", a Java String. The control structure of Config, having established that the name of the next element to process is "set", calls the set() method of Config. That method, in turn, calls apply() that eventually calls the invoke() method of java.lang.reflect.Method.

Yet another general pattern to observe is that Config() constructs objects and (through intermediaries) calls apply() that invokes methods of those objects. In the process of invoking those methods, apply() has to construct the values of their arguments, and in order to do that, apply() calls Config() that creates objects. Those who are familiar with Lisp may recognize a similarity with the eval-apply recursive pattern of that language.

Config Classified

The code of Config.java can be divided into parts as follows:

❑ Imports and declarations

❑ The Config() method and its helpers (this is the control structure)

❑ newObject() to construct objects

- ❑ Access methods: getField() and getMethod()
- ❑ Modification methods: add(), set() and setAt()
- ❑ Two versions of apply()
- ❑ Miscellaneous utilities

Instead of going through them in sequence, we are going to present them in a top-down way, starting with Config() and then working through all its 'children' calls. As you read through the code, keep the XML example in mind.

The Control Pattern of Config()

There are three Config() methods. The one that does the actual work of configuring takes a DOM Node as an argument and works with it to configure an application. The other two receive an XML document (either as a file name or an org.xml.sax.InputSource), parses it into a DOM object and look for <top-config> element nodes in it. If found, they pass the first <top-config> to the version of Config() that expects a DOM node.

> *Note that we allow for more than one <top-config> element. In other words, top-config is not the DOCTYPE of configuration documents, and configuration data can be embedded anywhere in an XML document that might serve other purposes as well. In this application, we look only at the first <top-config> ignoring the rest.*

The Config(String fileName) Constructor

To parse the XML file, we simply call the public static readFile() method of DomSearch that parses the file and returns a DOM Document:

```
import java.lang.reflect.Constructor;
import java.lang.reflect.Field;
import java.lang.reflect.Method;
import java.util.Vector;
import org.w3c.dom.*;
import org.xml.sax.*;

public class Config {

public static Object Config(String fileName) throws Exception
{
  Document doc = DomSearch.readFile(fileName);
  NodeList topConfigL = doc.getElementsByTagName("top-config");
  if(null == topConfigL || topConfigL.getLength() < 1)
    throw new Exception("No 'top-config' nodes in document " + fileName);

  return Config(topConfigL.item(0));
}
```

The Config(InputSource in) Constructor

This version is almost identical to the preceding one, except that instead of readFile() it calls readInputSource(); the InputSource is parsed into a DOM Document object:

```
public static Object Config(InputSource in) throws Exception
{
  Document doc = DomSearch.readInputSource(in);
  NodeList topConfigL=doc.getElementsByTagName("top-config");
  if(null == topConfigL || topConfigL.getLength() < 1)
    throw new Exception("No 'top-config' nodes in inputsource document");

  return Config(topConfigL.item(0));
}
```

The reason we want this version is that it enables us to save the configuration document as a text string in a data structure or a database table. Recall that an InputSource can be constructed from a character stream. So we can retrieve the "configuration string" from wherever it is stored and pass it to:

```
Config(new InputSource(new StringReader(configString)))
```

The config(Node node) Constructor

The final version of Config() is much longer. We will present it in pieces, together with some supporting code, before bringing it all together.

In summary, Config(Node node) analyzes the node it's given and takes appropriate action. If the node is not an element node (a text node, most likely), it returns its value as a nonNullString(). The definition of nonNullString() is:

```
public static String nonNullString(String S) {
  return S == null?"" : S;
}
```

If the node is an element node, we look for its obClass attribute. If there is no such attribute or its value is "string" then we again return the nonNullStringValue() of the element's contents. In our examples, this applies to <ob> elements that contain character data. This requires another version of nonNullString() to accept a node parameter:

```
public static String nonNullStringValue(Node node) {
  if(node.hasChildNodes()) // Usual case, a node with a #text child
    return nonNullString(node.getFirstChild().getNodeValue());
  return nonNullString(node.getNodeValue());
}
```

Finally, if it's an element node with an obClass attribute, we *construct an object* using either the default constructor or the single-String-argument constructor. To determine which constructor to use we look at the value of the cons attribute. Here's the corresponding part of Config():

```
Object ob;
if("".equals(elt.getAttribute("cons"))) {
  ob = newObject(obClassName);
}
else {
  ob = newObject(obClassName,elt.getAttribute("arg"));
}
```

The two versions of newObject() are as follows:

```
public static Object newObject(String className) throws Exception {
  return Class.forName(className).newInstance();
}

public static Object newObject(String className, String strVal)
      throws Exception {
  Class cl = Class.forName(className);
  Constructor cons = cl.getConstructor(new Class[]{java.lang.String.class});
  return cons.newInstance(new Object[]{strVal});
}
```

Once the object is created, we give it as the first argument to configChildren().
configChildren() goes out on a long recursive journey, processing the children nodes of the node
we have just processed to create our new object. When it returns, Config() exits also, returning the
created object. Here is the complete constructor:

```
public static Object Config(Node node)throws Exception {
  short nodeType = node.getNodeType();

  if(nodeType != Node.ELEMENT_NODE)
    return nonNullString(node.getNodeValue());

  Element elt = (Element)node;
  String obClassName = elt.getAttribute("obClass");

  if("".equals(obClassName) || "string".equals(obClassName))
    return nonNullStringValue(elt);
  Object ob;
  if("".equals(elt.getAttribute("cons"))) {
    ob = newObject(obClassName);
  }
  else {
    ob = newObject(obClassName,elt.getAttribute("arg"));
  }
  configChildren(ob, elt.getChildNodes());
  return ob;
}
```

The configChildren() method itself simply calls configChild() on each child, which will
recursively call Config():

```
public static void configChildren(Object ob, NodeList children)
      throws Exception {
  for(int i = 0; i < children.getLength(); i++)
    configChild(ob, children.item(i));
}
```

Where Are We?

Before we continue, let's take another look at the XML content, to see where we are in the configuration
process. Here is another small <top-config> that creates and populates a four-element Vector, then
adds another element to it:

703

```
<top-config obClass="java.util.Vector">
    <set fieldName="size"
         obClass="java.lang.Integer"
         cons="true"
         arg="4"
    />
    <set-at index="0">zero</set-at>
    <set-at index="1" obClass="java.util.Date" />
    <set-at index="2" obClass="java.util.Vector">
        <set fieldName="size" obClass="java.lang.Integer"
             cons="true" arg="2" />
        <set-at index="0">1</set-at>
        <set-at index="1">2</set-at>
    </set-at>
    <set-at index="3" obClass="PropDict">
        <apply name="setDef"><ob>dbName</ob>
            <ob>jdbc:odbc:Weather</ob>
        </apply>
    </set-at>
    <app-node name="add" obClass="java.util.Hashtable">
        <apply name="put"><ob>theDate</ob>
            <ob obClass="java.util.Date" />
        </apply>
    </app-node>
</top-config>
```

Let's assume this is the entire XML file (minus declarations), and we pass its name as an argument to `Config.Config()`:

❑   The file is parsed, and the `<top-config>` node is passed to the second call on `Config()`.

❑   The node is an element node, so we pass the first test in the code above.

❑   It has an `obClass` attribute, so we pass the second test.

❑   There is no `cons` attribute, so we call `newObject()` with just one argument, the value of the `obClass` attribute, which is "`java.util.Vector`".

❑   `newObject()` calls the default constructor.

❑   At this point, `Config()` calls `configChildren()`, with `<top-config>` as the current node.

❑   It has five children: one `<set>` and four `<set-at>`s. Each is given to `configChild()` to process, together with their parent, already processed into a new `Vector` object.

As you read through `configChild()`, think of it as working on the `<set>` element above, with a `Vector` object already constructed. `Vector`, as you recall, has a `size` field.

configChild() and Method Invocation

If `Config()` is for constructing objects, `configChild()` is for calling the methods of a newly-constructed object. The only way to get into `configChild()` is by calling `configChildren()` from inside `Config()` right after `Config()` has created an object. If `configChild()` needs to create an object as an argument to a method, it will recursively call `Config()`:

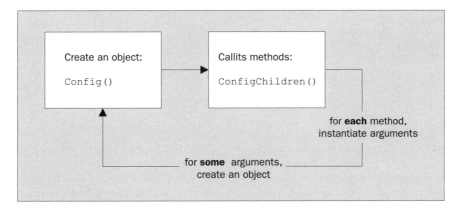

Another way to put this is to say that the node name of the child node can only be one of: 'set', 'set-at', 'add', 'apply' or 'app-node'. These are the methods of the Config class that call the methods of the object under construction using the invoke() method from the Reflection package. Only apply() calls invoke() directly; the rest call apply(), as shown in the table below:

XML tag	Config method
apply	apply
app-node	apply
set	set (calls apply)
set-at	setAt (calls apply)
add	add (calls apply)

The code of configChild() consists of conditional branches, one for each possible node name of the child. Within each branch, a public static method of Config is called that takes appropriate action. As a preview, here is the code of the entire conditional:

```
String name = elt.getNodeName();
...
if("set".equals(name))
  set(ob, elt.getAttribute("fieldName"), childOb);
else if("add".equals(name))
  add(ob, elt.getAttribute("fieldName"), childOb);
else if("set-at".equals(name))
  setAt(ob, elt.getAttribute("fieldName"),
        Integer.parseInt(elt.getAttribute("index")), childOb);
else if("app-node".equals(name))
  // Apply ob's method to this node's own value
  apply(ob, elt.getAttribute("name"), new Object[]{childOb});
else throw new Exception("node '" + name +
              "' should be 'set','set-at','apply' or 'app-node'");
```

We will look at some of those branches separately before bringing them all together. Let's start with the <set> branch because this is the next element in our XML file. The element looks like this:

```
<set fieldName="size"
     obClass="java.lang.Integer"
     cons="true"
     arg="4"
/>
```

The Java code of the corresponding conditional branch is like this:

```
if("set".equals(name))
  set(ob, elt.getAttribute("fieldName"), childOb);
```

Here ob is the "parent" object which is a Vector; it has a field called size and a method called setSize(). Config.set(), in summary, finds this method and invokes it with the value of childOb, which is the integer 4. How do we know it's the integer 4? Because we recursively called Config() on our <set> element, and its obClass is "java.lang.Integer", its cons attribute is "true" and its "arg" is the string "4". Accordingly, Config() called newObject() that called the constructor of the Integer class with a single argument, the string "4".

Here is the code for set(), add() and setAt():

```
public static void set(Object ob, String propName, Object val)
        throws Exception{
  apply(ob, makeSetterName(propName),new Object[]{val});
}

public static void add(Object ob, String propName, Object val)
        throws Exception {
  apply(ob, makeAdderName(propName),new Object[]{val});
}

public static void setAt(Object ob, String propName, int index, Object val)
      throws Exception {
  apply(ob, makeSetterName(propName),new Object[]{new Integer(index),val});
}
```

These require several utility methods, for example, makeSetterName() is a utility that combines "set" and "size" to come up with "setSize":

```
// String utils for getters, setters and adders
public static String makeSetterName(String propName) {
  return makePrefixName("set", propName);
}

public static String makeAdderName(String propName) {
  return makePrefixName("add", propName);
}

public static String makeGetterName(String propName) {
  return makePrefixName("get", propName);
}
public static String makePrefixName(String prefix, String propName) {
  StringBuffer buf = new StringBuffer(prefix.length() + propName.length());
```

```
      buf.append(prefix);
      if(propName.length() > 0) { // Empty for Vectors, &c get&set
        buf.append(Character.toUpperCase(propName.charAt(0)));
        buf.append(propName.substring(1));
        }
      return buf.toString();
  }
```

set(), add() and setAt() all call apply() to find and invoke the right method of the object. Before we tackle apply(), here is the complete code for configChild():

```
  public static void configChild(Object ob, Node child) throws Exception {
      short nodeType = child.getNodeType();
      if(nodeType != Node.ELEMENT_NODE) return;

      Element elt = (Element)child;
      String name = elt.getNodeName();
        // 'set', 'set-at', 'add', 'apply' or 'app-node'

      if("apply".equals(name)) {
      // Apply ob's method to values of grandchildren
        apply(ob, elt.getAttribute("name"), child.getChildNodes());
        return;
      }

      Object childOb = config(elt); // Produce val recursively; then use it
      if("set".equals(name))
        set(ob, elt.getAttribute("fieldName"), childOb);
      else if("add".equals(name))
        add(ob, elt.getAttribute("fieldName"), childOb);
      else if("set-at".equals(name))
        setAt(ob, elt.getAttribute("fieldName"),
              Integer.parseInt(elt.getAttribute("index")), childOb);
      else if("app-node".equals(name))
        // Apply ob's method to this node's own value
        apply(ob, elt.getAttribute("name"), new Object[]{childOb});
      else throw new Exception("node '" + name +
                  "' should be 'set','set-at','apply' or 'app-node'");
  }
```

We are almost done; the main remaining parts are apply() and getMethod(). This is where we cross over from the code of Config to the code of the java.lang.reflect package that ultimately instantiates objects and invokes their methods.

apply() and getMethod() – Invoking the Right Method

apply() invokes a method; while getMethod() provides it with a method to invoke. Remember that "a method to invoke" is an object of the class java.lang.reflect.Method. Once you have such an object, you can call its invoke() method.

apply() has three arguments. The first argument is the object whose method gets invoked. The second argument is the method's name. The third argument is the argument list for the method.

The argument list for the method can be given as a NodeList or as an array of Objects. The NodeList version goes through the list, converts each Node to the right kind of Object and calls the Object array version:

```
public static Object apply(Object ob, String name, NodeList children)
        throws Exception
{
  Vector argv = new Vector();

  for(int i = 0; i < children.getLength(); i ++) {
    Node child = children.item(i);
    if(child.getNodeType() == Node.ELEMENT_NODE)
      argv.add(config(child));
  }

  Object[]args = new Object[argv.size()];
  for(int i = 0; i <args.length; i++) args[i] = argv.get(i);
  return apply(ob, name, args);
}
```

The version of apply() that receives an Object array argument does the reflection. It has to proceed in two steps:

❑   First, on the basis of its array of Objects argument it must construct an array of Class objects that forms the signature of the method we want to invoke. We need such an array of Class objects in order to find the method – more precisely, to obtain the object of the class Method that corresponds to the method we need.

❑   Once the right object of class Method is constructed, we call it invoke() method:

```
public static Object apply(Object ob, String name, Object[] args)
        throws Exception
{

  // Given an Object array, construct the corresponding Class array
  // The Class array is the signature of the method we need
  Class[]classList = new Class[args.length];
  for(int i = 0; i < args.length; i++) {
    if(args[i] == null)
      classList[i] = java.lang.Object.class;
    else
      classList[i] = args[i].getClass();
  }

  // Find Method given the Class, the method's name, and the signature
  // The signature is specified as an array of Class objects
  Method method = getMethod(ob.getClass(), name, classList);

  // Invoke the method on object ob, with the arguments provided.
  // Result is usually Void and ignored
  return method.invoke(ob, args);
}
```

The most difficult part of this process is hidden in getMethod().

getMethod() and its Complexities

getMethod() has to deal with all the complexities of finding the right signature on the basis of a list of objects. The complexities, described in an earlier section on *Invoking Methods*, have to do with primitive types and inheritance: the same "Integer" object can correspond in the signature to Integer.class or Integer.TYPE or, indeed, Object, if it is the second argument of the setAt() method of the Vector class. (Remember that if a method expects an argument of a certain class, we can always give it an object of a derived class.)

This is how getMethod() deals with these complexities: it repeatedly tries each argument's class with either a primitive type (if possible) or Object.class, until a match is found or the range of possibilities is exhausted. To replace the observed class with a primitive type, getMethod() uses a primClass() utility that goes like this:

```
public static Class primClass(Class wrapper) {
   if(wrapper == java.lang.Integer.class) return Integer.TYPE;
   if(wrapper == java.lang.Character.class) return Character.TYPE;
   if(wrapper == java.lang.Boolean.class) return Boolean.TYPE;
   if(wrapper == java.lang.Byte.class) return Byte.TYPE;
   if(wrapper == java.lang.Short.class) return Short.TYPE;
   if(wrapper == java.lang.Long.class) return Long.TYPE;
   if(wrapper == java.lang.Float.class) return Float.TYPE;
   if(wrapper == java.lang.Double.class) return Double.TYPE;
   return wrapper;
}
```

The code for getMethod() follows:

```
public static Method getMethod(Class obClass, String name, Class[] valClass)
       throws Exception // We don't try all possible matches.
{
 String classList = "";

 try { return obClass.getMethod(name, valClass);
 // Value classes = declared classes
 } catch(Exception ex) {

    for(int i = 0; i < valClass.length; i++)
       try { // Check primitive wrappers: e.g. declare "int", use Integer
         valClass[i] = primClass(valClass[i]);
         return obClass.getMethod(name, valClass);
       } catch(Exception e) {}

    for(int i = 0; i < valClass.length; i++)
      classList += valClass[i].toString() + ",";

    for(int i = valClass.length-1; i >= 0; i--)
      try {  // Object declaration? e.g. Vector.set(int, Object)
        valClass[i] = java.lang.Object.class;
        return obClass.getMethod(name, valClass);
      } catch(Exception e) {}
   }
```

```
throw new Exception ("Cannot get method '" + name + "' for class '" +
                obClass.toString() + " for argtypes [" +
                classList + "]");
}
```

Even with an incomplete testing of all possibilities, this method is expensive. In the future, we will implement it using some form of caching, to improve performance.

JSPs and the Configuration File

This completes our discussion of `Config`, except we haven't shown you the actual configuration file for the case study. The reason is that it is mostly about configuring data access components, and it will make more sense to show it there. In both sections on data access components, we will show the corresponding portion of the XML configuration file, and we will show it all together in the Control component section, together with the code that works on it.

We proceed to data access components, beginning with the database.

The Database Component

We are going to move on to the component that interacts with the database. Its role in the application is to run database queries. It receives queries from the client via the control component, processes them, and returns the results as XML.

Also included in this section is the `UserDataHandler` class that manages user-profile strings stored in the database. Although it conceptually belongs with the Configuration component, its specific activities are those of the database component: it stores, retrieves and modifies database data.
The database consists of an interface and three classes, related as follows:

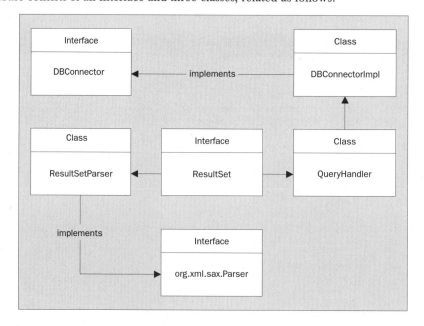

The individual items in this diagram can be described as follows:

- ❏ DBConnector declares the most general functionality of database interaction, including Connection management
- ❏ DBConnectorImpl is a do-nothing default implementation of DBConnector
- ❏ QueryHandler extends DBConnectorImpl to provide the functionality actually used in our case study
- ❏ ResultSetParser plays the same role in the database component as Dom2Sax plays in the XML components: it converts query results (ResultSet objects) produced by QueryHandler into a sequence of DocumentHandler calls

We'll go through them in the order they are listed.

DBConnector and Its Default Implementation

The DBConnector interface is designed to hide the details of connection pooling, or conceal its absence:

```java
import java.sql.*;

public interface DBConnector {

    // The first three methods have to do with connection management
    Connection getConnection() throws Exception;
    void freeConnection() throws SQLException;
    void close() throws SQLException;

    // The remaining four methods have to do with information
    // that is needed to open a connection
    void setDriver(String driverName);   // The name of the JDBC driver to use
    void setURL(String dbURL);           // The name of the "database URL"

    // The syntax varies from driver to driver
    void setUser(String user);           // User name for the database
    void setPwd(String pwd);             // Password

}
```

The default implementation does almost nothing, just the routine tasks:

```java
import java.sql.*;

public class DBConnectorImpl implements DBConnector {
    Connection conn = null;
    Driver driver = null;
    String dbDriver = "sun.jdbc.odbc.JdbcOdbcDriver";
    String dbName = "jdbc:odbc:PHONEBOOK";
    String dbUser = "";
    String dbPwd = "";
```

```
    public DBConnectorImpl(String driver, String name, String user,
                            String pwd) {
  setDriver(driver);
  setURL(name);
  setUser(user);
  setPwd(pwd);
}

public DBConnectorImpl() {}

public Connection getConnection() throws Exception {

  // Get an instance of DriverManager, call its getConnection() method
  if (conn != null) {
    return conn;
  }
  if (driver == null) {
    driver = (Driver) Class.forName(dbDriver).newInstance();
  }
  return conn = DriverManager.getConnection(dbName, dbUser, dbPwd);
}

public void freeConnection() throws SQLException {

  // Since there's no pool to return it to, do nothing at all.
}

public void close()
        throws SQLException {    // Could just return to pool
  if (conn != null) {
    conn.close();
  }
  conn = null;
}

public void setDriver(String driverName) {
  dbDriver = driverName;
}

public void setURL(String dbURL) {
  dbName = dbURL;
}
public void setUser(String user) {
  dbUser = user;
}
public void setPwd(String pwd) {
  dbPwd = pwd;
}
}
```

QueryHandler extends DBConnectorImpl in two ways: it overrides some of the method definitions, and it adds completely new functionality.

QueryHandler

QueryHandler contains an inner class that implements the "named query" abstraction. In QueryHandler, this is a protected inner class called DBQuery. A DBQuery object is, in effect, a query string for a PreparedStatement object, with a name given to it. QueryHandler contains two Hashtables of such DBQuery objects, indexed by their names: one Hashtable for SELECT queries, the other for UPDATE queries.

For instance, suppose you want to run queries like the one below, in which the actual zip code is entered by the user:

```
SELECT * FROM FORECAST WHERE zip=17171
```

You would proceed as follows:

- ❏ Create a query string with question marks for query parameters, in this case "SELECT * FROM FORECAST WHERE zip=?"

- ❏ Give the query a name, e.g. "weather"

- ❏ Add the query to the QueryHandler either by adding material to the XML initialization file, or directly by calling the addQuery() method of QueryHandler

- ❏ Use the query by running this line of code:

```
ResultSet rs = spBean.getQueryHandler().query("weather", "17171");
```

If you now go back to the configuration file and look at its QueryHandler section, you will see that its code calls on addQuery() with exactly those arguments:

```
<set fieldName="queryHandler" obClass="QueryHandler">
    <set fieldName="driver">sun.jdbc.odbc.JdbcOdbcDriver</set>
    <set fieldName="URL">jdbc:odbc:Weather</set>
    <set fieldName="user"></set>
    <set fieldName="pwd"></set>
    <apply name="addQuery"><ob>weather</ob>
      <ob>SELECT * FROM FORECAST WHERE zip=?</ob>
    </apply>
</set>
```

To run a query, the user would select that query by name (typically, from a SELECT element in an HTML form) and fill in the entry field with parameter values. This information would get to the QueryHandler via the Request object and the PropDict. The QueryHandler would retrieve the appropriate PreparedStatement object using the query name given, replace its question marks with the new parameter values, and run the query.

The rest of this section presents the code of QueryHandler. We divide the code in three parts: the main body of the main class, the inner DBQuery class, and some convenience functions.

The Main Class

The main class is largely a protective shell around `DBQueries`:

```java
import java.util.Hashtable;
import java.sql.*;

public class QueryHandler extends DBConnectorImpl {

  protected Hashtable queries = null, updates = null;

  public QueryHandler() {
    super();
    queries = new Hashtable();
    updates = new Hashtable();
  }
  public QueryHandler(String driver, String name, String user,
                      String pwd) {
    super(driver, name, user, pwd);
    queries = new Hashtable();
    updates = new Hashtable();
  }

  // addQuery, addUpdate add a Query object to Hashtable
  public void addQuery(String qName, String sqlStr) {
    queries.put(qName, new DBQuery(qName, sqlStr));
  }

  public void addUpdate(String qName, String sqlStr) {
    updates.put(qName, new DBQuery(qName, sqlStr));
  }

  public boolean hasQuery(String str) {
    return null != queries.get(str);
  }

  public boolean hasUpdate(String str) {
    return null != updates.get(str);
  }

  protected DBQuery getQuery(String name) throws Exception {
    DBQuery query = (DBQuery) queries.get(name);
    if (null == query) {
      throw new Exception("no such db query as " + name);
    }
    return query;
  }

  protected DBQuery getUpdate(String name) throws Exception {
    DBQuery update = (DBQuery) updates.get(name);
    if (null == update) {
      throw new Exception("no such db update as " + name);
    }
```

```
    return update;
  }

  // Given SELECT query name and parameters, run the query
  public ResultSet query(String name,
                         String[] params) throws Exception {
    return getQuery(name).query(params);
  }

  // Given UPDATE query name and parameters, run the query
  public int update(String name, String[] params) throws Exception {
    return getUpdate(name).update(params);
  }
```

As you can see, to run a query you retrieve the corresponding DBQuery object and tell it to run itself.

The DBQuery Class

It is DBQuery objects that actually run SQL queries using JDBC code. As you probably know (from more or less painful experience), SQL is not implemented uniformly across different database system. We felt that the most common denominator for our readers would be an ODBC Access database. For this reason, at two points in this section (in the code and comments to it), we refer to a specific limitation of the MS Access database system.

A Note on MS Access SQL

Instead of the standard LONGVARCHAR SQL type for long text strings, MS Access uses LONGTEXT, and it doesn't handle standard SQL in the expected way. Within the DBQuery class, we therefore have a setString() method which, instead of calling the built-in setString() method of PreparedStatement, uses an explicit cast:

```
preparedStatement.setObject(i, veryLongString, java.sql.Types.LONGVARCHAR);
```

This should do no harm with other databases, and it is needed for Access (which otherwise seems to truncate the String to 255 characters). After adding this code, we have a DBQuery class that can be used with Access or with other systems. In order to set up the data table for use with long strings, we also use:

```
CREATE TABLE UserData (UserName TEXT, ConfigString LONGTEXT)
```

Where standard SQL would use VARCHAR and LONGVARCHAR respectively. In this case, a reader who prefers, say, MySQL will probably have to replace TEXT with VARCHAR and compile.

The Code of the DBQuery Class

```
protected class DBQuery
{
  String name = null, queryStr = null;
  PreparedStatement pS = null;

  public DBQuery(String name, String qStr) {
    this.name = name;
    queryStr = qStr;
  }

  // Create PreparedStatement, run the query
  public ResultSet query(String[] params) throws Exception {
```

```
      if (pS == null) {    // Create PreparedStatement the first time it's run
        pS = getConnection().prepareStatement(queryStr);
      }
      for (int i = 0; i < params.length; i++) {
        setString(i + 1, params[i]);
      }
      return pS.executeQuery();
    }
    public int update(String[] params) throws Exception {
      if (pS == null) {
        pS = getConnection().prepareStatement(queryStr);
      }
      for (int i = 0; i < params.length; i++) {
        setString(i + 1, params[i]);
      }
      return pS.executeUpdate();
    }

    // The next method is needed only if you use MS Access
    // JDBC's setString() converts long strings to LONGVARCHAR
    // but Access insists on LONGTEXT
    public void setString(int i, String S) throws SQLException {
      if (S == null || S.length() < 256) {
        pS.setString(i, S);    // Default ok here
      } else {                 // Use setObject, with explicit type conversion
        pS.setObject(i, S, java.sql.Types.LONGVARCHAR);
      }
    }
    public void close() {
      if (pS == null) {
        return;
      }
      try {
        pS.close();
      } catch (Exception ex) {}
      pS = null;
    }
  }
```

Utilities

The rest of the methods in `QueryHandler` are utility methods, falling in two groups. The first group has methods that provide convenient syntax, e.g. `query(name,p1,p2)` instead of `query(name, [p1,p2])`. The second group has methods for closing everything up and releasing resources:

```
  // Provide convenient syntax for query() methods
  // Otherwise they require an array of String as second argument
  public ResultSet query(String name) throws Exception {
    return query(name, new String[]{});
  }

  public ResultSet query(String name, String p1) throws Exception {
    return query(name, new String[] {
      p1
    });
  }
```

```java
public ResultSet query(String name, String p1,
                       String p2) throws Exception {
  return query(name, new String[] {
    p1, p2
  });
}

public ResultSet query(String name, String p1, String p2,
                       String p3) throws Exception {
  return query(name, new String[] {
    p1, p2, p3
  });
}

public ResultSet query(String name, String p1, String p2,
                       String p3, String p4) throws Exception {
  return query(name, new String[] {
    p1, p2, p3, p4
  });
}

// Same for update() methods
public int update(String name) throws Exception {
  return update(name, new String[]{});
}

public int update(String name, String p1) throws Exception {
  return update(name, new String[] {
    p1
  });
}

public int update(String name, String p1,
                  String p2) throws Exception {
  return update(name, new String[] {
    p1, p2
  });
}

public int update(String name, String p1, String p2,
                  String p3) throws Exception {
  return update(name, new String[] {
    p1, p2, p3
  });
}

public int update(String name, String p1, String p2, String p3,
                  String p4) throws Exception {
  return update(name, new String[] {
    p1, p2, p3, p4
  });
}

// Close() methods
public void closeAll(Hashtable dbqueries) {
  java.util.Enumeration enum = dbqueries.keys();
  while (enum.hasMoreElements()) {
    ((DBQuery) dbqueries.get(enum.nextElement())).close();
  }
}
```

```
    public void close() throws SQLException {
      closeAll(queries);
      closeAll(updates);
      super.close();
    }

    public void freeConnection() throws SQLException {
      closeAll(queries);
      closeAll(updates);
      super.freeConnection();
    }
  }    // End of QueryHandler class
```

This completes the discussion of the `QueryHandler` class. This is a good moment to show you the portion of the XML configuration file that configures it for the application.

XML Configuration for QueryHandler

The XML configuration file for the application, `spStampPage.xml`, instantiates an object of the `StampPage` class. Its `<top-config>` element has three children, to configure three initial parameters of the application. One is a `DomSearch` object; we will show that part of the file in the section on XML data access. Another is a zip code `String`, to serve as a parameter for the initial database search. The third is `QueryHandler`. Here is the file:

```xml
<top-config obClass="StampPage">
  <!-- start configuring DSNextMatch, subclass of DomSearch -->
    ...
  <!-- end of configuring DSNextMatch, subclass of DomSearch -->

  <set fieldName="zipCode"><!-- initialize zipCode value -->
    12345
  </set>

  <!-- start configuring queryHandler -->
  <set fieldName="queryHandler" obClass="QueryHandler">
    <set fieldName="driver">sun.jdbc.odbc.JdbcOdbcDriver</set>
    <set fieldName="URL">jdbc:odbc:Weather</set>
    <set fieldName="user"></set>
    <set fieldName="pwd"></set>
    <apply name="addQuery">
      <ob>weather</ob>
      <ob>SELECT * FROM FORECAST WHERE zip=?</ob>
    </apply>
  </set>
  <!-- end configuring queryHandler -->
</top-config>
```

ResultSetParser

We now have all the bridges from string data submitted by the user from an HTML form – a query name and query parameters – to a `ResultSet` produced by the query. What we now have to do is convert a result set into a `DocumentHandler`. This is the job of `ResultSetParser`.

`ResultSetParser` has a diverse pedigree: it needs to know JDBC, SAX and DOM, as reflected in its imports:

```
import java.io.*;
import java.sql.*;
import org.xml.sax.*;
import org.xml.sax.helpers.AttributeListImpl;
import org.w3c.dom.*;
```

Most of `ResultSetParser` code provides basic support and is quite similar to Dom2Sax; you might want to review that class before proceeding further. The heart of `ResultSetParser` is its `parseLoop()` method that goes through a `ResultSet` and makes `DocumentHandler` calls. In doing so, it assumes that the "document" we are parsing has the following structure:

```
<table>
  <row>
    <field name='Zip'>13346</field>
    <field name='Day'>Saturday October 22,1953</field>
    <field name='RecTime'>13:40 PM </field>
    <field name='Temp'>37</field>
    <field name='DayLo'>35 </field>
    <field name='DayHi'>46 </field>
    <field name='Precip'>60</field>
    <field name='Warn'>Foggy, probable rain; caution in driving</field>
    <field name='Tomorrow'>We will not have any weather tomorrow</field>
    <field name='NextDay'>There will be weather nearby, but not on you.
    </field>
  </row>
  ...
</table>
```

Each row in such a document corresponds to a `ResultSet` record, each field corresponds to a field of that record, and the values of the name attribute would be the field names of the `ResultSet`. JDBC provides methods to retrieve these field names within its `ResultSetMetaData` interface.

With these preliminaries out of the way, we can look at the two key methods of `ResultSetParser`.

parse() and parseLoop()

There are several overloaded versions of `parse()` in this class, with various types of arguments, such as `String uri` and `InputSource in`. They have to be there because they are declared in the `Parse()` interface which `ResultSetParser` implements. However, these methods ignore their arguments and call the no-argument version because this particular parser doesn't want to parse anything; it just wants to walk through a `ResultSet` object that it has a reference to. Here is the version that actually does the work; it is very similar to the `parse()` method of Dom2Sax that takes a `Node` argument:

```
public void parse() throws IOException, SAXException {
    if (resultSet == null) {
        throw new SAXException("Can't parse empty result set");
    }
    parseOpen();
    parseLoop();
    parseClose();
}
```

719

parseOpen() and parseClose() call startDocument() and endDocument(), respectively. The parseLoop() method calls the other DocumentHandler methods as it loops through the ResultSet. By separating parseLoop() from the methods that open and close the document, we make it possible to produce parse() output without the XML headers as a component of a larger document. This is how it is used in our spQuery.jsp where parseLoop() is invoked directly:

```
The weather at your zip code is
<%
  QueryHandler qh = spBean.getQueryHandler();
  ResultSetParser rsp = new ResultSetParser();
  Sax2Writer s2w = new Sax2Writer(rsp, out); // Direct to JSPWriter
  rsp.setResultSet(qh.query("weather", spBean.getZipCode()));
  rsp.parseLoop(); // Don't generate xml headers
%>
```

Here is the code of parseLoop():

```
public void parseLoop() throws SAXException {
    try {

        String[] labels = resultSetLabels(resultSet);
        int columns = resultSetColumnCount(resultSet);
        String[] types = resultSetTypes(resultSet);

        // We are all set, can start the loop
        while (resultSet.next()) {
          documentHandler.startElement("row", new AttributeListImpl());
          for (int i = 1; i <= columns; i++) {
            String field = resultSet.getString(i);
            AttributeListImpl attrs = new AttributeListImpl();
            attrs.addAttribute("name", "CDATA", labels[i - 1]);
            documentHandler.startElement("field", attrs);
            documentHandler.characters(field.toCharArray(), 0,
                                       field.length());
            documentHandler.endElement("field");
          }
          documentHandler.endElement("row");
        }
        resultSet.close();
        resultSet = null;
    } catch (Exception e) {
        try {
          resultSet.close();
          resultSet = null;
        } catch (Exception ex) {}
        throw new SAXException(e);
    }
}    // End of parseLoop() method
```

The Rest of It

The rest of the code is completely straightforward; much of it is repeated unchanged or almost unchanged from Dom2Sax:

```java
import java.io.*;
import java.sql.*;
import org.xml.sax.*;
import org.xml.sax.helpers.AttributeListImpl;
import org.w3c.dom.*;

public class ResultSetParser implements Parser {

  DocumentHandler documentHandler;
  DTDHandler dTDHandler;
  EntityResolver entityResolver;
  ErrorHandler errorHandler;
  java.util.Locale locale;

  Logger lg;
  ResultSet resultSet;

  public ResultSetParser() {
    lg = new Logger();
  }

  public void parse(InputSource source)
          throws IOException, SAXException {
    parse();
  }

  public void parse(String fileName)
          throws IOException, SAXException {
    parse();
  }

  public static AttributeList toAttrList(NamedNodeMap nnm) {
    if (null == nnm) {
      return null;
    }
    AttributeListImpl attrs = new AttributeListImpl();
    for (int i = 0; i < nnm.getLength(); i++) {
      Node node = nnm.item(i);
      attrs.addAttribute(node.getNodeName(), "CDATA",
                         node.getNodeValue());
    }
    return attrs;
  }

  public void parse(ResultSet rs) throws IOException, SAXException {
    setResultSet(rs);
    parse();
  }

  public void setResultSet(ResultSet rs) {
    resultSet = rs;
  }
```

```java
public void parseOpen() throws IOException, SAXException {
  documentHandler.startDocument();
}

public void parseClose() throws IOException, SAXException {
  documentHandler.endDocument();
}

// parse() and parseLoop() go here

public void setDocumentHandler(DocumentHandler h) {
  documentHandler = h;
}

public void setDTDHandler(DTDHandler h) {
  dTDHandler = h;
}

public void setEntityResolver(EntityResolver r) {
  entityResolver = r;
}

public void setErrorHandler(ErrorHandler h) {
  errorHandler = h;
}

public void setLocale(java.util.Locale locale) {
  this.locale = locale;
}

public ResultSetParser(HandlerBase hB) {
  this();
  setHandlerBase(hB);
}

public void setHandlerBase(HandlerBase hB) {
  setDocumentHandler(hB);
  setDTDHandler(hB);
  setEntityResolver(hB);
  setErrorHandler(hB);
}

public static String [] resultSetLabels(ResultSet R)
       throws SQLException {
  ResultSetMetaData rsmd = R.getMetaData();
  String S []=new String[rsmd.getColumnCount()];
  for(int i = 0; i < S.length; i++) S[i] = rsmd.getColumnLabel(i + 1);
  return S;
}

public static int resultSetColumnCount(ResultSet R)
       throws SQLException {
  ResultSetMetaData rsmd = R.getMetaData();
  return rsmd.getColumnCount();
}
```

```
    public static String [] resultSetTypes(ResultSet R)
        throws SQLException {
      ResultSetMetaData rsmd = R.getMetaData();
      String S []=new String[rsmd.getColumnCount()];
      for(int i = 0; i < S.length; i++) S[i] = rsmd.getColumnTypeName(i + 1);
      return S;
    }
  }
```

This completes the material of `ResultSetParser` and the entire database component. However, we use the database not only for application data, but also to store and retrieve configuration strings. This is done by the `UserDataHandler` class that structurally belongs with the Configuration component but in terms of its functionality it is a database access class.

UserDataHandler

`UserDataHandler` is part of the configuration component. It sits between `StampPageFactory` and a database table that holds user names and corresponding XML configuration strings.

`UserDataHandler` is instantiated and used in two methods of `StampPageFactory`: `getUserData()` and `saveUserData()`:

```
  // Retrieve user data from database table
  public String getUserData() {
    if(userName == null)
      return null;
    if(null != configString)return configString;
    if(userDataHandler == null)
      userDataHandler=UserDataHandler.getInstance();
    configString=userDataHandler.getUserData(userName);
    return configString;
  }
  // Save user data in database table
  public void saveUserData() {
    if(userName == null)
      return;
    if(userDataHandler == null)
      userDataHandler = UserDataHandler.getInstance();
    userDataHandler.putUserData(userName, configString);
  }
```

Of these two, `getUserData()` is used every time a user logs in; it is invoked from `getStampPage()` that is invoked from `frames.jsp`. `saveUserData()` is invoked from `saveConfig.jsp` when the user edits the configuration string.

Imports, Declarations and Instantiation

`UserDataHandler` is a database-access class. It imports the JDBC package and owns an instance of `QueryHandler`:

```
  import Logger;
  import java.sql.*;
```

```
public class UserDataHandler {
  protected Logger lg;
  protected static UserDataHandler theInstance = null;
  protected QueryHandler qHandler=null;
  String dbDriver="sun.jdbc.odbc.JdbcOdbcDriver";
  String dbName="jdbc:odbc:Weather";
  String dbUser="";
  String dbPwd="";
```

In terms of software design patterns, UserDataHandler is a **Singleton class**: at any given time, there is only one instance of it. The reason is that we want to control access to the database of user data. (Database access methods are synchronized, too.) The standard way of implementing the Singleton pattern is to have a private constructor and a public static getInstance() method:

```
private UserDataHandler() {
  lg = new Logger();
}

public static synchronized UserDataHandler getInstance() {
  if (theInstance != null) {
    return theInstance;
  }
  return theInstance = new UserDataHandler();
}
```

The rest of the class makes sure there is a QueryHandler to use and uses it to initialize, save and retrieve user data. First, we set up a QueryHandler using the addQuery() and addUpdate() methods you have just seen in the database component. Since we don't know where the QueryHandler may be coming from, we declare setQueryHandler() to take an Object argument and cast it. As before, we use Access-specific LONGTEXT because LONGVARCHAR is not supported by Access:

```
public void setQueryHandler(Object ob) {
  qHandler = (QueryHandler) ob;

  // Provide defaults for queries
  if (!qHandler.hasUpdate("create")) {
    qHandler
      .addUpdate("create",
                "CREATE TABLE UserData (UserName TEXT, ConfigString
                LONGTEXT)");
  }
  if (!qHandler.hasUpdate("insert")) {
    qHandler
      .addUpdate("insert",
                "INSERT INTO UserData (UserName,ConfigString) VALUES(?,?)");
  }
  if (!qHandler.hasUpdate("replace")) {
    qHandler
      .addUpdate("replace",
                "UPDATE UserData SET ConfigString=? WHERE UserName=?");
  }
  if (!qHandler.hasQuery("userdata")) {
    qHandler
```

```
              .addQuery("userdata",
                      "SELECT ConfigString FROM UserData WHERE userName=?");
      }
    }
```

Now that we have a `QueryHandler` with all `DBQuery` objects in place, we can use it to initialize, save and retrieve:

```
    protected void initUserData() {
      try {
        if (null == qHandler) {
          setQueryHandler(new QueryHandler(dbDriver, dbName, dbUser,
                                           dbPwd));
        }
        qHandler.update("create");
      } catch (Exception ex) {
        lg.logIt("initUserData: ", ex);
      }
    }

    public synchronized String getUserData(String userName) {
      try {
        if (null == userName) {
          return null;
        }
        if (null == qHandler) {
          setQueryHandler(new QueryHandler(dbDriver, dbName, dbUser,
                                           dbPwd));
        }
        ResultSet resSet = qHandler.query("userdata", userName);
        if (resSet == null) {
          return null;
        }
        if (resSet.next()) {
          String cfg = resSet.getString(1);
          resSet.close();
          return cfg;
        }
        return null;
      } catch (Exception ex) {
        lg.logIt("getUserData(" + userName + ")", ex);
        return null;
      }
    }

    public synchronized int putUserData(String userName,
                                        String userData) {
      if (null == userName || null == userData) {
        return -1;
      }
      if (null == qHandler) {
        setQueryHandler(new QueryHandler(dbDriver, dbName, dbUser,
                                         dbPwd));
```

```
      }
      try {
        String prevVal = getUserData(userName);
        if (null == prevVal) {
          return qHandler.update("insert", userName, userData);
        } else {
          return qHandler.update("replace", userData, userName);
        }
      } catch (Exception ex) {
        lg.logIt("UserDataHandler.putUserData(" + userName + ",\n"
                 + userData + "\n)", ex);
        return -2;
      }
    }

    public void close() {
      if (null == qHandler) {
        return;
      }
      try {
        qHandler.close();
      } catch (Exception ex) {
        lg.logIt("UserDataHandler.close", ex);
      }
      qHandler = null;
    }
  }
```

This completes the main body of code for our case study. In conclusion, to show the system's flexibility, we develop four extensions to it, ranging from a very minor addition to a significant new component.

XML Data Access Component

For our XML data access component, we will reuse the `DomSearch` application of the XML Parsing chapter earlier in the book.

DomSearch Queries

The format of `DomSearch` queries is fairly specific: you can specify the following search parameters:

- ❏   outerTag: the name of an element
- ❏   outerAttr, outerAValue: the name and value of one of the its attributes
- ❏   innerTag: the name of one of its children elements
- ❏   innerCVal: a string that the character content of that children element must contain

For instance, given our XML data, you can search for subtrees of this form:

```
<item type="stamp" ...>

  <!-- maybe some children elements -->

  <country>Italy</country>

  <!-- maybe some more children elements -->

</item>
```

DomSearch vs. XSLT

A legitimate question to ask is, "Why use a Java class like DomSearch when XSLT provides a more general way of searching DOM trees for patterns specified by XPath expressions?" The answer is that, at least for now, integrating XSLT processors into applications is a non-trivial task. Even more importantly, an XSLT processor significantly increases the application's memory footprint and processing time. This may change, but for now, there is still a need for less general and more efficient alternatives.

DomSearch Output

The output of a DomSearch search is a DOM node that satisfies the conditions of the search. To make that node available to the rest of the application, we pass it through Dom2Sax, another class described in the XML Parsing chapter. Dom2Sax uses a SAX parser to traverse a DOM Node and output its contents as a sequence of SAX events. We call this process "virtual parsing" because there is no XML text involved; what gets parsed is a Java data structure.

Dom2Sax plays exactly the same role in the XML data access component that ResultSetParser plays in the database access component. In both cases, the contents of a Java data structure is "serialized" as a sequence of SAX events and sent to a Sax2Writer object. Sax2Writer, also defined and described in the XML Parsing chapter, writes out the contents of incoming events to a writer. In our case study, the writer in question is the JSPWriter associated with spQuery.jsp:

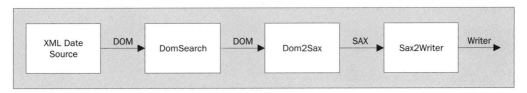

Instantiating DomSearch – DSNextMatch

A DomSearch object is created within this line of code in frames.jsp:

```
StampPage spBean = spBeanF.getStampPage();
```

As the Control component section explains in more detail, getStampPage() calls findStampPageByString() or findStampPageByFile(). Either of those methods calls Config.Config() to create a StampPage object and its possessions, including a DomSearch object. In the process, Config.Config() uses XML configuration data, coming either from the XML configuration string stored in the database or from an XML configuration file.

727

Before we look at that portion of the XML configuration file that configures DomSearch, we should explain that our DomSearch object in this application is really an object of a derived class called DSNextMatch. Its main difference from the parent is that it calls the nextMatch() method automatically every time after initFile() and reset(). This way, its output is always a single record (the next match), rather than the entire file, as in the parent class. (This didn't matter much for the command-line application of the earlier chapter.)

The code for DSNextMatch is as follows:

```
public class DSNextMatch extends DomSearch {

  // Same as DomSearch except nextMatch() is called after
  // initFile() within constructor, and after resetNode()
  protected String initFile() throws Exception {
    super.initFile();
    return nextMatch();
  }
  public String doCommand() { // Assumes values read in from dict
    try {
      if ("reset".equalsIgnoreCase(domCmd)) {
        resetNode();
        return nextMatch();
      } else {
        return super.doCommand();
      }
    } catch (Exception ex) {
      lg.logIt("DSNextMatch.doCommand: ", ex);
      return ("Error: DSNextMatch.doCommand " + ex);
    }
  }
}
```

Now that you know what DSNextMatch is, you can read the configuration data for DomSearch.

Configuration XML data for DomSearch

The portion of the default XML configuration file that configures DomSearch (really DSNextMatch) looks like this:

```
<top-config obClass="StampPage">
  <!-- start configuring DSNextMatch, subclass of DomSearch -->
  <set fieldName="domSearch" obClass=" DSNextMatch">
  <set fieldName="dict" obClass=" PropDict">
      <apply name="setDef"><!-- call setDef() method with two arguments -->
        <ob>fileName</ob>
        <ob>c:/Progra~1/Apache~1/jakart~1/webapps/Ch15/data/stamps.xml</ob>
      </apply>
      <apply name="setDef">
        <ob>outerTag</ob>
        <ob>item</ob>
      </apply>
      <apply name="setDef">
        <ob>outerAttr</ob>
```

```
                <ob>type</ob>
            </apply>
            <apply name="setDef">
                <ob>outerAVal</ob>
                <ob>stamp</ob>
            </apply>
            <apply name="setDef">
                <ob>innerTag</ob>
                <ob>country</ob>
            </apply>
            <apply name="setDef">
                <ob>innerCVal</ob><ob>Italy</ob>
            </apply>
            <apply name="setDef">
                <ob>domCmd</ob>
                <ob>initFile</ob>
            </apply>
        </set>
        <apply name="initFromDict" />
    </set>
    <!-- end of configuring DSNextMatch, subclass of DomSearch -->
    <!-- start configuring zipCode and queryHandler -->
    ...
    <!-- end configuring zipCode and queryHandler -->
</top-config>
```

As you can see (proceeding through the file from top down), we are configuring a DomSearch object. The first thing we do is create a PropDict object, set the dict field of DomSearch to that object and recursively configure it. Configuring the PropDict consists of setting a bunch of name-value pairs. You can recognize them as the default paramethers of a DomSearch query: fileName, outerTag, outerAttr, and so on. The last call on setDef() initializes domCmd to "initFile". This tells DomSearch to parse the XML file specified by the fileName property into a DOM tree.

After Config.Config() is done executing these configuration instructions, DomSearch is ready to receive queries.

Using DomSearch During a Session

During the session, the DomSearch object is retrieved from the StampPage bean by spQuery.jsp and used to run an XML query with the parameters of the current request:

```
<%
    StampPage spBean = spBeanF.getStampPage();
    PropDict dict = new PropDict(request);
    spBean.getDict().setDef(dict); // Adds new definitions from request.
    DomSearch domSrch = spBean.getDomSearch();
    domSrch.updateFromDict(dict);
    domSrch.doCommand();
%>
```

729

The last line runs the current domCmd with new settings obtained from the current request (if any).

The Presentation Component

The Presentation component consists of several JSPs, as shown earlier in the chapter.

The Login Page

The first thing the user sees is top.jsp, a barebones login page that forwards to frames.jsp:

```
<%@ page  errorPage="errorpage.jsp" %>
<html>
<head><title> The Tele-Philately Follies </title>
</head>

<body>
<center>
<h1> The Tele-Philately Follies </h1>
<p><%= new java.util.Date() %>. </p>
</center>

<form method="post" action="frames.jsp" >
    User: <input name="userName" type="text" size="10" /><br />
    Password: <input name="userPwd" type="password" size="10" /><br />
    <input type="submit" value="go!" />
</form>
</body>
</html>
```

frames.jsp, with its spControl.jsp and spQuery.jsp, is the main JSP page of the application, its front component.

The Main Frames Page and Initialization

The frames.jsp itself consists of a block of Java code and a barebones frameset template. The block of code consists of a login validation section and an initialization section. The validation section is just a placeholder where real validation can be included. The initialization section is real and discussed below:

```
<%@ page  errorPage="errorpage.jsp" %>
<jsp:useBean id="spBeanF"
   class="StampPageFactory" scope="session"/>
<%
// Validation section
  boolean userNameAndPasswordOkay = true; // Bean could check login data here
  if (!userNameAndPasswordOkay) {
%>
    <jsp:forward page="badLogin.jsp" />
<%
  }
// End validation section; start initialization section
// This code is best revisited after
```

```
        // Set up PropDict to hold request data,
        // for transfer to StampPageFactory and StampPage
        PropDict pDict = new PropDict(request);
        spBeanF.setUserName(pDict.getDef("userName"));

        // User name will be used to retrieve user profile
        String configFileName = "/data/spStampPage.xml";
        configFileName = application.getRealPath(configFileName);
        spBeanF.setConfigFile(configFileName);

        // Create a StampPage instance and transfer request data to it
        StampPage spBean = spBeanF.getStampPage();
        spBean.setDict(pDict);

        // Obtain instance of DomSearch to retrieve XML data
        // and get it ready for action
        DomSearch domSrch = spBean.getDomSearch();
        domSrch.updateFromDict(pDict);
        domSrch.doCommand("initFile");
    %>
    <html>
    <head><title> StampPage </title></head>
    <frameset cols="20%,80%">
      <frame name="ctlFrame" src="spControl.jsp">
      <frame name="dataFrame" src="spQuery.jsp">
    </frameset>
    </html>
```

The initialization process starts by transferring the user name from Request to StampPageFactory spBeanF via a PropDict. We also set the configFile property of spBeanF to provide default configuration in case there is no XML configuration string associated with the user name. With userName and configFile properties set, we call getStampPage() to obtain the StampPage bean for the session. With a StampPage in hand, we transfer Request data to it via a PropDict and obtain its DomSearch object. The DomSearch object is also initialized from Request data.

The initialization just described happens once per session, at login, when the action of the submitted form is frames.jsp. During the session, the forms submitted from spControl.jsp direct their action elsewhere.

Control and Data Frames

The control frame in this initial version offers the following choice of actions:

❑   Search an XML data source using DomSearch

❑   Change your XML configuration string

❑   Logout

There are three forms, one to run a query, another to change configuration, and a third to logout. Their action attributes are spQuery.jsp, spConfigure.jsp and spLogout.jsp, respectively. Here is spControl.jsp:

```
    <%@ page  errorPage="errorpage.jsp" %>
    <jsp:useBean id="spBeanF"
      class=" StampPageFactory" scope="session"/>
```

```
<!DOCTYPE HTML PUBLIC "-//W3C//DTD HTML 4.0 Transitional//EN">
<html><head><title>Frame control page for StampPage </title></head>
<body>

<form target="dataFrame" method="get"
      action="spQuery.jsp" >
  new country?<input type="text" name="innerCVal" value="Italy" />
  command:<select name="domCmd" size="1">
          <option value="nextMatch">nextMatch
          <option selected value="reset">reset
        </select>
  <input type="hidden" name="dIE4" value="x.htm" >
  <input type="submit" value="Submit">
</form>
<hr/>
<form target="dataFrame" method="get"
      action="spQuery.jsp" >
  changeZip?<input type="text" size="5" name="zipCode" value="12345" />
  <input type="hidden" name="dIE4" value="x.htm" >
  <input type="submit" value="Submit">
</form>
<hr/>
<form target="dataFrame" method="get"
      action="spConfigure.jsp" >
  Or change the configuration:
  <input type="submit" value="Configure" />
</form>

<form method="post" target="_parent" action="spLogout.jsp">
<input type="submit" value="Logout">
</form>
</body>
</html>
```

To remind you what this looks like, we repeat one of the initial sequence of screen shots. The code above shows in the control frame on the left:

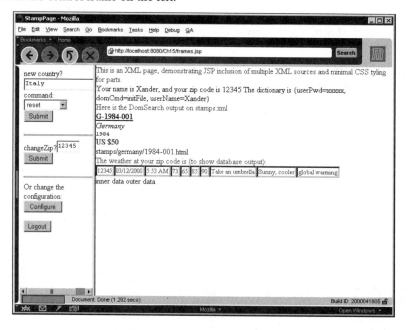

Let's take a look at the three possible actions, in reverse order of appearance.

The Logout Page – spLogout.jsp

The logout page is trivial: it invalidates the session, says goodbye and offers a link back to top.jsp. Note that its target is _parent, so it gets you out of the frameset:

```
<%@ page  errorPage="errorpage.jsp" %>
<jsp:useBean id="spBeanF"
    class="StampPageFactory" scope="session"/>
<!DOCTYPE HTML PUBLIC "-//W3C//DTD HTML 4.0 Transitional//EN">
<html><head><title>Logout page for StampPage </title></head>
<body>

<% session.invalidate(); %>
Goodbye, see you soon.
You can come back by clicking <a href="top.jsp">here</a>.
</body>
</html>
```

The Change-Configuration Page – spConfigure.jsp

In a real application, the change-configuration page would certainly have a friendlier interface, but for our purposes the current version simply offers a text area to view and edit the XML string:

```
<%@ page  errorPage="errorpage.jsp" %>
<jsp:useBean id="spBeanF"
    class="StampPageFactory" scope="session"/>
<!DOCTYPE HTML PUBLIC "-//W3C//DTD HTML 4.0 Transitional//EN">
<html><head><title>Configuration page for StampPage </title></head>
<body>
  <form target="_parent" method="post"
        action="spSaveConfig.jsp" >
    <input type="submit" value="Save" />
    <input name="userName" type="hidden"
           value="<%= spBeanF.getUserName() %>" />
    <textarea name="configString" rows="20" cols="50">
      <%=spBeanF.getConfigString()%>
    </textarea>
  </form>
</body>
</html>
```

If you click **Save**, the submitted string goes to spSaveConfig.jsp that invokes the methods of StampPageFactory to save the configuration data in the database for future sessions and also to use it in configuring the current StampPage:

```
<%@ page  errorPage="errorpage.jsp" %>
<jsp:useBean id="spBeanF"
    class="StampPageFactory" scope="session"/>
<%
  spBeanF.setConfigString(request.getParameter("configString"));
  spBeanF.saveUserData();          // For next time
  spBeanF.findStampPageByString(); // For this time.
%>
<jsp:forward page="frames.jsp" />
```

733

To save the string, `StampBeanFactory` interacts with the database via `UserDataHandler` that you have just seen. To configure the page for the current session, it uses the Configuration component. This is what happens in `findStampPageByString()`, which we are going to see momentarily, in the Control component.

The Query Results Page – spQuery.jsp

This is the actual newsletter demonstrating the merger of template material with the results of data retrieval from XML and database sources. This is a complex page, and we will present it in sections before bringing it all together.

JSP Directives and Actions

We start, as always, with a page directive and a `useBean` action. We then clear the output stream so they don't generate empty lines, and place the XML declaration on the same line (nothing should precede the XML declaration on output, not even a blank line):

```
<%@ page errorPage="errorpage.jsp"
    contentType="application/xml" %>
<jsp:useBean id="spBeanF"
    class="StampPageFactory" scope="session"/>
<%
    out.clear(); // don't send the empty lines from directives above
%><?xml version="1.0" ?>
```

Template XML Content – The Stylesheet Instruction

Next, we output the `Processing Instruction` for a stylesheet to go with our XML output:

```
<?xml-stylesheet
  href="http://localhost:8080/Ch15/styles/stamps.css"
  type="text/css"
?>
```

A CSS stylesheet is, of course, limited in what it can do with an XML file. A possible extension would be to use XSLT stylesheets within this system producing XHTML output (that can be further styled using CSS).

Here is the style sheet:

```
collection {
  display: block;
}

item {
  display: list-item;
  float: none;
  border: none;
  background: inherit;
}

num {
  display: block;
  font-weight: bold;
```

```
    color: blue;
    text-decoration: underline;
    cursor: pointer;
}

country {
  display: block;
  font-style: italic;
}

year {
  display: block;
  font-family: monospace;
  font-size: 8pt;
}

price {
  display: none;
}

purchase-price {
  display: block;
  color: rgb(20,100,0);
  font-weight: bold;
  text-align:left;
}

field {
  display: list-item;
  color: blue;
}

table {
  display:table;
  font-style: normal;
  color:blue;
}

row { display:table-row; }
tr { display:table-row; }

tr td {display:table-cell; border-style:inset;}
tr th {display:table-cell; border-style:inset; color:red; }
row field {
  display:table-cell; padding:1px; font-size:10pt; border-style:inset;
}
```

Process Request Data

Next we start running the application. Our first task is to transfer request data to the `StampPage` bean:

```
<%
    StampPage spBean = spBeanF.getStampPage();
    PropDict dict = new PropDict(request);
    spBean.getDict().setDef(dict); // Adds new definitions from request
    String zipCode = dict.getDef("zipCode"); // Update zip code
    if(zipCode.length() > 0)
      spBean.setZipCode(zipCode);
    spBean.getDomSearch().updateFromDict(dict); // Update DomSearch
```

```
         String domCmd=  dict.getDef("domCmd"); // Get new domCmd for DomSearch
         if(domCmd.length() > 0) // Run the command with new settings from request
            spBean.getDomSearch().doCommand(domCmd);
      %>
```

Combine Dynamic Output with Template Content

Now we can produce output, combining template data with dynamic content produced by the bean:

```
<toptag>
  <field>
This is an XML page, demonstrating JSP inclusion of multiple XML sources and
minimal CSS styling for parts.
  </field>

<name> Your name is <%= spBeanF.getUserName() %></name>, and
<zipcode>  your zip code is <%= spBean.getZipCode() %>  </zipcode>
<dict> The dictionary is <%= spBean.getDict() %> </dict>
```

Next, we obtain a `DomSearch`, reset it, and have it produce output from `stamps.xml` styled by our stylesheet `stamps.css`:

```
<%
DomSearch domSrch = spBean.getDomSearch();
domSrch.doCommand("reset");
domSrch.setWriter(out);
domSrch.writeData() ;
%>
```

The next block of code produces database output from the `Ch15Weather` database (available in the sourcecode for this chapter). Three objects are involved: a `QueryHandler` that runs queries, a `ResultSetParser` that converts `ResultSets` into a sequence of `DocumentHandler` calls, and the familiar `Sax2Writer` that writes out such a sequence to a character stream, which in this case is the `JSPWriter`:

```
The weather at your zip code is (to show database output)
<%
QueryHandler qh = spBean.getQueryHandler();
ResultSetParser rsp = new ResultSetParser();
Sax2Writer s2w = new Sax2Writer(rsp, out); // Send output to JspWriter out
rsp.setResultSet(qh.query("weather", spBean.getZipCode()));
rsp.parseLoop(); // Don't generate xml headers
%>
```

Finally, just to show that the JSP can do easy things as well as fairly difficult things, we produce some static XML material and quit:

```
<xmltag>
  <nestedTag>
    inner data
  </nestedTag>
  outer data
</xmltag>
</toptag>
```

Finally, we just need our ubiquitous error page:

```
<html><head><title>ErrorPage</title></head>
<body>

<%@ page isErrorPage="true" %>
Problem:
<%
  Logger lg = new Logger();
  lg.logIt("Newsletter jsps error", exception);
%>
<h1> <%= exception.getMessage() %> </h1>

<% exception.printStackTrace(new PrintWriter(out)); %>
<br>
Something went wrong. We're very sorry.
</body>
</html>
```

This completes our discussion of the JSP pages of the application. As you have seen, a typical flow of control is for a JSP to use a StampPageFactory that produces a StampPage bean for the session, configured according to the user's XML configuration string or default XML configuration file. The StampPage bean interacts with the database and XML information sources and, through intermediaries, produces the results to the spQuery.jsp page. The intermediaries fall into two groups, one for the database, the other for XML; both ultimately use Sax2Writer, with a JspWriter as the output stream.

We can now work through the two JavaBeans of the Control component, StampPage and StampPageFactory.

The Control Component

We are going to review this code in action, as it gets engaged in our use cases. The factory bean goes first.

The StampPageFactory Bean

The factory bean is first used in frames.jsp to initialize a session. We repeat the code here for convenience:

```
<%
    // Login validation section; if ok then...
    PropDict pDict = new PropDict(request);
    spBeanF.setUserName(pDict.getDef("userName"));
    String configFileName="/data/spStampPage.xml";
    configFileName=application.getRealPath(configFileName);
    spBeanF.setConfigFile(configFileName);

    StampPage spBean = spBeanF.getStampPage();
    ...
```

The first five lines of this code don't need explaining: they simply set two properties of the factory bean. The last line produces an instance of StampPage. Here is the code of getStampPage():

```
import org.w3c.dom.*;
import org.xml.sax.*;

public class StampPageFactory {
  protected Logger lg;
  protected StampPage stampPage = n ull;
  protected String configString = null, username = null, configFile = null;
  protected UserDataHandler userDataHandler=null;

  public StampPage getStampPage() {
    if (null != stampPage) {              // Not the beginning of session
      return stampPage;
    } else if (null != configString) {    // configString already set
      return findStampPageByString();
    } else if (null
              != getUserData()) {         // Get configString from database
      return findStampPageByString();
    } else {
      return findStampPageByFile();       // No configString; use default
    }
  }
}
```

getUserData() uses the methods of UserDataHandler to retrieve the configuration string:

```
public String getUserData() {
  if (userName == null) {
    return null;
  }
  if (null != configString) {
    return configString;
  }
  if (userDataHandler == null) {
    userDataHandler = UserDataHandler.getInstance();
  }
  configString = userDataHandler.getUserData(userName);
  return configString;
}
```

One way or another, from a string or from a file, getStampPage() configures a StampPage using XML configuration data. This is where the Control component connects to the Configuration component, and we finally get to see the XML configuration file for the application. Let's proceed to configuration methods of the factory bean: findStampPageByString() and findStampPageByFile().

The Configuration Methods and the Configuration File

This section will be very brief because most of the work is done by the `Config` class from an earlier section. Otherwise, it's just the matter of calling `Config()` the right way:

```
public StampPage findStampPageByString() {
  try {
    // Create an InputSource from String, give it to Config.Config()
    InputSource in =
      new InputSource(new java.io.StringReader(configString));
    stampPage = (StampPage) Config.Config(in);
  } catch (Exception ex) {
    lg.logIt("findStampPageByString [\n" + configString + "]", ex);
    return null;
  }
  return stampPage;
}

public StampPage findStampPageByFile() {
  try {
    return stampPage = (StampPage) Config.Config(configFile);
  } catch (Exception ex) {
    lg.logIt("findStampPageByFile [\n" + configFile + "]", ex);
    return null;
  }
}
```

At this point, we will take a final look at the XML config file to remind ourselves what this code actually does. Here's `spStampPage.xml` in full:

```
<top-config obClass="StampPage">
  <!-- Configure DSNextMatch, subclass of DomSearch -->
  <set fieldName="domSearch" obClass="DSNextMatch">
    <set fieldName="dict" obClass="PropDict">
    <apply name="setDef"><ob>outerTag</ob><ob>item</ob></apply>
    <apply name="setDef"><ob>outerAttr</ob><ob>type</ob></apply>
    <apply name="setDef"><ob>outerAVal</ob><ob>stamp</ob></apply>
    <apply name="setDef"><ob>innerTag</ob><ob>country</ob></apply>
    <apply name="setDef"><ob>innerCVal</ob><ob>Germany</ob></apply>
    <apply name="setDef"><ob>domCmd</ob><ob>initFile</ob></apply>
    <apply name="setDef">
      <ob>fileName</ob>
      <ob> c:/Progra~1/Apache~1/jakart~1/webapps/Ch15/data/stamps.xml</ob>
    </apply>
    </set>
    <apply name="initFromDict" />
  </set>
  <!-- End of configuring DSNextMatch -->

  <set fieldName="zipCode">12345</set> <!-- configure zipCode -->

  <!-- Configure QueryHandler -->
  <set fieldName="queryHandler" obClass="QueryHandler">
    <set fieldName="driver">sun.jdbc.odbc.JdbcOdbcDriver</set>
    <set fieldName="URL">jdbc:odbc:Weather</set>
    <set fieldName="user"></set>
    <set fieldName="pwd"></set>
    <apply name="addQuery">
      <ob>weather</ob>
```

```
            <ob>SELECT * FROM FORECAST WHERE zip=?</ob>
          </apply>
        </set>
      </top-config>
```

As you can see, we configure three fields, a zip code, a DomSearch and a QueryHandler. (Since DomSearch and QueryHandler are objects that have fields of their own, they are configured recursively, from a recursive XML structure.) In the case of DomSearch, we actually configure a subclass of DomSearch called DSNextMatch.

Whichever way we configure, the StampPage comes equipped with those three fields. Before we look inside it, let's review the remaining lines of code from frames.jsp, after it has obtained an instance of StampPage:

```
        spBean.setDict(pDict);                       // Update from request data
        DomSearch domSrch = spBean.getDomSearch();   // Obtain a DomSearch,
                                                     // Actually a DSNextSearch
        domSrch.updateFromDict(pDict);               // Update from request data
        domSrch.doCommand("initFile");
      %>
```

The Rest of It

Here are the remaining methods of StampBeanFactory:

```
      public StampPageFactory() {
        lg = new Logger();
      }

      public StampPageFactory(String defaultFile) {
        this();
        setConfigFile(defaultFile);
      }

      public void saveUserData() {
        if (userName == null) {
          return;
        }
        if (userDataHandler == null) {
          userDataHandler = UserDataHandler.getInstance();
        }
        userDataHandler.putUserData(userName, configString);
      }

      public void setUserName(String S) {
        userName = S;
      }

      public void setConfigString(String S) {
        configString = S;
      }
```

```
    public void setConfigFile(String S) {
      configFile = S;
    }

    public String getConfigString() {
      if (null == configString) {
        configString = fileToStringBuffer(configFile).toString();
      }
      return configString;
    }

    public static StringBuffer fileToStringBuffer(String fName) {
      StringBuffer sBuff = new StringBuffer();
      InputStreamReader inStr = null;
      try {
        inStr = new InputStreamReader(new FileInputStream(fName));
        char[] cBuff = new char[4096];
        int charsRead;
        while (-1 != (charsRead = inStr.read(cBuff))) {
          sBuff.append(cBuff, 0, charsRead);
        }
      } catch (Exception ex) {
        ex.printStackTrace();
        return null;
      }
      finally {
        try {
          inStr.close();
        } catch (Exception ex) {}
      }
      return sBuff;
    }

    public void setUserDataHandler(Object ob) {
      userDataHandler = (UserDataHandler) ob;
    }

    public String getUserName() {
      return userName;
    }
  }
}
```

The StampPage Bean

This is an empty shell of a class, like a holding company: all the work is done by the objects it owns. It has four protected fields and get/set methods for all of them. In addition, it has two "syntactic sugar" methods for setting and getting the values of its PropDict. Otherwise, it does nothing: all the interesting action is in the data access components, DomSearch and QueryHandler , configured according to user preferences, as described in their respective sections:

```
import java.io.*;
import java.util.Properties;
public class StampPage {
```

```
    protected PropDict dict;
    protected DomSearch domSearch;
    protected String zipCode;
    protected QueryHandler qHandler;

    Logger lg;

    // This class handles a session's data, customized to a user;
    // all will be initialized from a single xml file, in nested structure

    public StampPage() {
      lg = new Logger();
    }

    // Set and get methods
    public void setDict(PropDict defs) {
      dict = defs;
    }
    public void setDomSearch(Object ds) {
      domSearch = (DomSearch) ds;
    }
    public void setZipCode(String zip) {
      zipCode = zip;
    }
    public void setQueryHandler(Object qh) {
      qHandler = (QueryHandler) qh;
    }

    public PropDict getDict() {
      return dict;
    }
    public DomSearch getDomSearch() {
      return domSearch;
    }
    public String getZipCode() {
      return zipCode;
    }
    public QueryHandler getQueryHandler() {
      return qHandler;
    }

    // To provide access to PropDict
    public void setDef(String name, String val) {
      if (null == dict) {
        dict = new PropDict();
      }
      dict.setDef(name, val);
    }
    public String getDef(String name) {
      if (null == dict) {
        dict = new PropDict();
      }
      return dict.getDef(name);
    }
  }   // End of StampPage class
```

This completes the minimalist implementation of the configurable newsletter.

Your case studies files should look something like this:

```
Chapter15\
        Data\
                Ch15Weather.mdb
                SpStampPage.xml
                Stamps.xml
        Styles\
                Stamps.css
        WEB_INF\
                Classes\
                        Config.class
                        DBConnector.class
                        DBConnector.class
                        Dom2Sax.class
                        DomSearch.class
                        DSNextMatch.class
                        Logger.class
                        PropDictv.class
                        QueryHandler$DBQuery.class
                        QueryHandler.class
                        ResultSetParser.class
                        Sax2Writer.class
                        StampPage.class
                        StampPageFactory.class
                        UserDataHandler.class
        errorpage.jsp
        frames.jsp
        spConfigure.jsp
        spControl.jsp
        spQuery.jsp
        spSaveConfig.jsp
        top.jsp
```

Extensions to the Basic Functionality

There are plenty of extensions that you can make to this case study. We don't have room to go into them here, but if you download the sourcecode for this chapter you will find an additional MS Word document that provides instructions on how to add the following extensions:

❑   Changing the exiting database query

❑   Adding a new database query

❑   Adding another database

❑   An XSLT subsystem for XML output

Summary

In this chapter, we have shown several ways in which XML can be used in a web application with a JSP presentation component.

- ❑ We have XML in files as an information resource
- ❑ We use XML in the browser as a markup language, styled with CSS
- ❑ We use XML as a "configuration language", to dynamically configure complex networks of objects, including objects like `Vector` which themselves know nothing about XML
- ❑ We use XML for data interchange between components of the application, including database components

The main idea of the chapter is quite general. We develop a "configuration language" that makes it possible to describe the state of a network of Java classes, and a `Config` class that interprets such XML descriptions and instantiates the classes. A JSP uses the `Config` class and an XML configuration file to configure an application.

In this particular case study, the instantiated classes form data access components that know how to access data sources (XML data and databases), query them, and output query results as XML. The JSP pages combine those results and template data into a single page (XML or HTML), complete with a CSS stylesheet. To change the contents of the page, you only have to change the XML configuration page and the JSP.

In the next chapter, we will look at another example of how to use XML as configuration information, but this time within a JDBC XML Connector servlet.

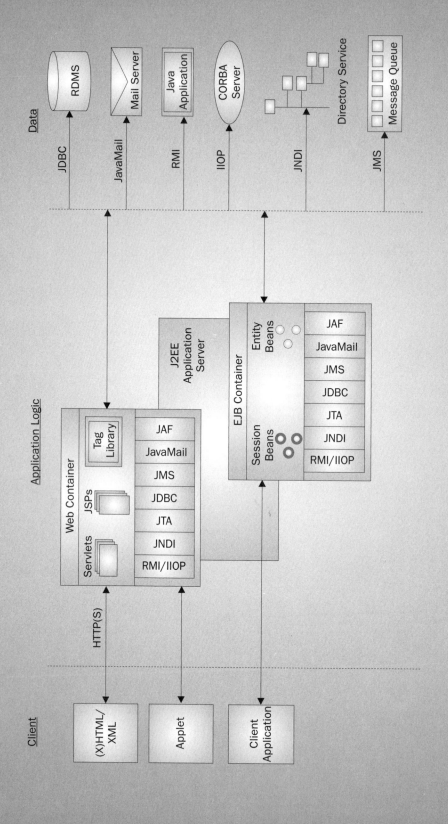

16

An XML-Based JDBC Connector Servlet Framework

In August 1999, I embarked on a project to create a 'DBBean' that encapsulated the boilerplate JDBC code used to execute simple queries and transactions. My intent was to create a component that could be reused in both servlets and JSPs to avoid having to write the same JDBC code over and over again.

The more I thought about it, though, the more I realized that a mere JavaBean was not a sufficient layer of abstraction for the problem I was trying to solve. While a JavaBean provides good reuse, it has the disadvantage of requiring a certain degree of Java knowledge on the part of the developer using it. What I really wanted was a reusable component that would allow your typical web developer (who may or may not know Java) to access relational database systems via JDBC from servlet-capable web sites, without writing a line of Java code. I also wanted a framework that would allow the rapid creation of XML data servers, which would transparently serve XML data structures via HTTP to other applications. Hence, the JDBC Connector Servlet idea was born.

The **JDBC Connector Servlet (JCS)** is a Java servlet that provides an XML-based scripting interface to JDBC data sources. This servlet allows web developers who do not know Java to programmatically access data sources via any JDBC driver. It also allows JSP and servlet developers to achieve a clean separation between their server-side presentation logic and their data access (SQL) logic. As part of this framework, I also implemented a JSP custom tag that simplifies integration between JSPs and the JCS engine in JSP 1.1 compatible containers. This framework is an excellent example of how you can use Java to create reusable components and frameworks that can be leveraged by less technical developers and power users. It also illustrates the following advanced Java programming concepts:

- ❏ Implementing parser functionality
- ❏ XML object serialization
- ❏ Using the JDBC API

❑   Using the Servlet API

❑   Implementing a JSP 1.1 custom tag

❑   Designing a device-independent content delivery architecture using XSLT and JCS

This case study is broken down into two major sections. The first section, entitled *Implementing the JDBC Connector Servlet*, will walk you through the steps I took in designing and developing this tool, including a detailed analysis of the Java code. The second section, entitled *Using the JDBC Connector Servlet*, will show you how to develop database-driven web applications using this tool by walking you through the construction of a Guestbook application and a SQL Server database browser.

Implementing the JDBC Connector Servlet

The process I used in designing and developing this framework was as follows:

❑   Determine the framework's functional requirements

❑   Design a high-level architecture

❑   Design the tool's scripting framework

❑   Design and develop the Java classes that implement the scripting framework

❑   Design and develop the other artifacts needed to deploy the framework to J2EE containers, such as the JSP custom tag library descriptor and the web application deployment descriptor

❑   Package the framework's binaries for deployment to servlet engines and application servers that support J2EE

❑   Deploy JCS to a J2EE web container

The Framework's Functional Requirements

In order to be useful in supporting RAD (rapid application development) for Java developers and web developers alike, as well as providing maximum flexibility and extensibility, I decided that JCS queries would be authored as XML documents. To keep it simple initially, I decided to use a 'DTDless' XML document instead of requiring validation against a DTD. This would give me maximum flexibility to grow the idea, with the ultimate goal of formalizing a query specification using the emerging XML Schema standard once the concept was validated with real-world use and feedback from the community.

> *In case you are interested in the current status of the XML Schema specification, it has left 'last call' at the W3C as of July 5, 2000, and will soon go to Candidate Recommendation status. See* `http://www.w3.org/XML/Schema.html` *for more details.*

Additionally, there were some obvious web database development 'best practices' that JCS would have to implement to be useful to the typical web developer. Therefore, I determined that the JCS would have to provide the following specific functionality:

❑ First and foremost, JCS must provide a mechanism by which a developer can query a database, and return the resultset back to the browser as HTML. Therefore, the first requirement for JCS is to be able to perform a SELECT statement against a JDBC data source and merge the output with a pre-defined HTML template. If for some reason the developer chooses not to define a template, then there has to be some kind of default output. In this case, I decided that JCS would send the data back to the client as an XML document.

❑ Then I asked myself, "Why limit the developer to just HTML?" For example, a wireless application developer might want to use JCS to query a database, serialize the resultset as WML (wireless markup language), and send it to a WAP device using MIME type text/vnd.wap.wml. This led me to the second requirement: JCS must be able to send content of various different MIME types back to the requesting device.

❑ The third requirement is fairly obvious: JCS must be able to execute INSERT, UPDATE, and DELETE statements against a JDBC data source. Any good database-scripting framework allows the authoring of scripts that modify data. Since INSERT, UPDATE, and DELETE statements do not return resultsets, JCS would have to redirect the browser to another URL upon successful execution of the SQL operation.

❑ The fourth requirement is also fairly obvious: JCS must allow use of HTML form, CGI, system and custom variables in JCS query files. That way, web developers can pass parameters from an HTML form to a JCS query via HTTP GET or POST. They can also query the HTTP environment (via CGI variables) and access system functionality (such as date/time). Finally, via custom variables, they have a mechanism that allows them to create their own variables, if needed, for use in a JCS query.

❑ Server-side includes (SSIs) are also to be supported. SSIs allow you to reuse 'library' files throughout a web site. For example, if you have a navigation bar that must appear on every page, you create an include directive in every page to point to your navigation bar file, rather than paste the navigation bar HTML in every file. That way, if the navigation bar changes, you make the change in only one place.

❑ A further requirement is to allow the developer to optionally specify a maximum number of rows to be returned by a given query. Otherwise, the developer might inadvertently execute a SELECT statement that returns a ridiculously large number of rows, which is obviously not ideal.

❑ What happens if a SELECT statement returns zero records? Most web developers want a mechanism that allows them to display default content in that event. For example, you might want to display a message that says, "We were unable to find any data that matched your search, please try again." To accommodate this, JCS must allow the developer to specify default content to be sent to the browser in the event that a SELECT statement returns an empty resultset.

❑ When non-technical content authors enter content into a web-based database front-end, they frequently hit the *Enter* key to start a new line. This translates to a CR/LF combination. This causes a problem when web developers want to display this text as HTML. The browser essentially ignores the CR/LF character, causing the formatting to look messy to the end user. Therefore, JCS must provide developers with a mechanism to optionally replace CR/LF characters with HTML line breaks at runtime. This will allow the proper display of multi-paragraph data on dynamic, database-driven web pages with minimal coding.

❑ Suppose an exception occurs – for example, the database server might be down at 2:00 AM for maintenance. It wouldn't be good for the end user to get a page saying, "HTTP 500 error, a Java exception occurred..." A better message would be, "We're sorry, but our site is temporarily unavailable. Please try again later. For more assistance, please call 800-HELP-ME." Therefore, JCS must provide web developers with a way to redirect the browser to a custom error page when an exception occurs.

❑ Another requirement is targeted mainly at Java developers who might find utility in using JCS to speed up their own development cycles: it should be possible to use JCS queries within JSP applications, by providing both a bean interface and a custom tag. Even though my original target audience for this framework was web developers who don't know Java, I realized that experienced Java developers would find great utility in using this tool within their JSP and servlet applications, especially in their endeavor to separate SQL logic from application logic.

❑ Most developers of data-driven web sites appreciate the ability to generate a unique ID within their scripts. This allows them to populate primary key fields when inserting records into tables. Therefore, JCS must provide a tag for generating unique IDs.

❑ Finally, JCS must allow the developer to optionally encode SQL statements by doubling up single quote characters where appropriate. This would allow the transparent handling of SQL statements such as this:

```
INSERT INTO tablename ("fieldname") VALUES ('This contains a 'single' quote')
```

Apart from the functional requirements, there were some technical requirements I considered. First, I wanted to limit the framework's dependencies to the core API and the relevant javax packages only. I didn't want to get into a situation where I'd have to tell end users, "It will only run on this app server because it relies on functionality in package such-and-such". Second, for maximum reach, I wanted to target JDK 1.1.x as opposed to using JDK 1.2 functionality, such as the collections API. I also wanted to, within reason, provide code that would run in most commercially available servlet engines.

While 'officially' JCS requires version 2.2 of the servlet API and version 1.1 of the JSP specification, I have tested it in servlet engines that support the servlet API version 2.1, and the JSP specification version 1.0, and it runs fine (minus the JSP custom tag, of course).

The JCS Architecture

With the JDBC Connector Servlet, web developers author their database operations as XML documents. When a remote web browser requests the URL for one of these XML-based queries, the servlet engine will dispatch the request to the JDBC Connector Servlet for handling. The JDBC Connector Servlet will instantiate the JCS engine, which will parse the query file and execute the specified SQL statement against the database. It will then merge the resultset with the output template defined by the query, and send the resulting output to the requesting user agent using the MIME type specified in the JCS query file. If an output template is not defined, the JCS engine will simply serialize the resultset as an XML document, and return it to the calling client as MIME type text/xml.

The package also comes with a bean interface, and a JSP 1.1 custom tag interface, to allow JSP developers to use it within a JSP page. In essence, the package implements a simple XML-based database-scripting framework for servlet and JSP-enabled web servers. This diagram visually depicts JCS' logical architecture:

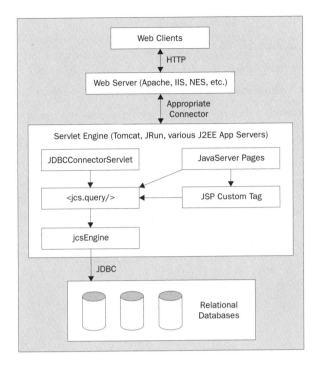

The JCS Scripting Framework

JCS provides a simple, XML-based scripting framework that developers can use to author web-based JDBC queries. JCS queries are simply XML documents containing special tags that define database connection parameters, SQL code, and output. As XML documents, they can be authored using any one of a number of XML authoring tools on the market today. (You can view a list of XML editors at `http://www.xml.com/pub/Guide/XML_Editors`.) They can also be authored using an ASCII text editor, such as Notepad or the vi editor. Since they are text files, they can be updated rapidly without needing to recompile a binary executable file. As we all know, this saves a great deal of time.

When designing the JCS query's XML schema, I followed several different principles:

❑   First, I decided to create a `jcs` namespace, to avoid potential node name collisions in the future, given the possibility that a future XML application developer might write code that merges a JCS query with another XML document that contains a node name the same as one of the JCS node names.

❑   Secondly, as a convenience to developers, I decided to limit JCS' XML taxonomy to two tiers only. Since I anticipated that most developers would use ASCII text editors to code JCS queries by hand (at least initially, while waiting for the XML authoring tool market to mature), I didn't want them to have to worry about properly nesting multiple layers of XML tags.

As you'll recall, one of the requirements of JCS is to support several different categories of variables, to allow developers to insert dynamic data into their JCS queries at runtime. This data can come from a variety of different places:

- ❑ The HTTP GET or POST key-value pairs
- ❑ The HTTP environment
- ❑ A resultset row's field values
- ❑ System related dynamic data (such as the current date)
- ❑ Custom properties passed from either the servlet container's configuration properties or a JSP

I'll cover these in more detail later. As a convention, I decided that variables would be referenced in a JCS query using the format #variablecategory.variablename#.

The root node of the JCS Query XML document is the `<jcs:query>` node. This node has a number of child nodes that define the parameters of the JDBC operation, as well as what output should be sent back to the requesting client upon completion of the operation. Here's a snapshot of what a JCS query looks like:

```
<?xml version="1.0"?>
<jcs:query xmlns:jcs="http://www.jresources.com/xml/jcs/1.0">

    <jcs:mime_type>
        <!--Your output's MIME Type -->
    </jcs:mime_type>

    <jcs:jdbc_url>
        <!-- The URL of the JDBC data source-->
    </jcs:jdbc_url>
    <jcs:jdbc_uid>
        <!-- Your userid-->
    </jcs:jdbc_uid>
    <jcs:jdbc_pwd>
        <!-- Your password-->
    </jcs:jdbc_pwd>
    <jcs:jdbc_driver>
        <!-- Your JDBC driver-->
    </jcs:jdbc_driver>

    <jcs:sql>
        <!-- Your SQL statement. Here's an example:-->
        SELECT * FROM guestbook WHERE ID = '#form.ID#'
    </jcs:sql>

    <jcs:error_page>
        <!--The page to redirect to in the event an exception is thrown -->
    </jcs:error_page>

    <jcs:redirect_url>
        <!--The page to redirect to after successfully executing an INSERT,
            UPDATE, or DELETE statement-->
    </jcs:redirect_url>

    <jcs:maxrows>
        <!--the maximum number of rows to be returned in the query-->
```

```
      </jcs:maxrows>

      <jcs:template>
        <!-- This is your output template-->
        <![CDATA[
          <jcs:include>
            <!-- Include file reference goes here-->
          </jcs:include>
          <!-- HTML markup goes here-->
          <jcs:resultset>
            <!-- HTML markup goes here-->
            Use #FIELD_NAME# to insert the contents of a particular field
            <!-- HTML markup goes here-->
          </jcs:resultset>
          <!-- HTML markup goes here-->
        ]]>
      </jcs:template>

      <jcs:empty_resultset_output>
        <!--The default output returned in place of the resultset enumeration
            if the resultset is empty-->
        <![CDATA[
          <!-- HTML markup goes here-->
        ]]>
      </jcs:empty_resultset_output>

      <jcs:line_break_character>
        HTML
      </jcs:line_break_character>
    </jcs:query>
```

Notice in particular the `<jcs:template>` tag, which provides a 'template' with which the query data is merged to produce the desired output. The `<jcs:resultset>` tag is used within this to iterate over the rows of the data returned from the query, with resultset field variables to insert the values of particular fields within each row.

JCS Query Tags

JCS query tags fall into five general categories:

❑   Database connectivity parameter tags

❑   The SQL tag

❑   Output definition tags

❑   Special function tags

❑   Template-specific tags

Database Connectivity Parameter Tags

The first category of tags contains those that define connectivity parameters, specifically what database to connect to, which JDBC driver to use, and the credentials you should present to the database for authentication. The tags are:

753

Tag Name	Default Value	Description
jcs:jdbc_driver	sun.jdbc.odbc.JdbcOdbcDriver	Defines the JDBC driver the JCS engine should use
jcs:jdbc_url	None – This is a mandatory entry	Defines the JDBC data source the JCS engine should query
jcs:jdbc_uid	Zero-length string	The user ID with which to log onto the JDBC data source
Jcs:jdbc_pwd	Zero-length string	The password with which to log onto the JDBC data source

The SQL Tag

The second category contains the <jcs:sql> tag, which defines the actual SQL statement that you will execute against the database.

Output Definition Tags

The third category is tags that define the output. These include tags that allow you to define the MIME type, a redirect URL, an output template, default output for empty resultsets, an error page, and the maximum number of rows to return in the resultset:

Tag Name	Default Value	Description
jcs:mime_type	text/html	Defines the MIME type JCS should send back to the browser.
jcs:redirect_url	None	If present, JCS will send a 302 redirect message specifying this URL back to the browser after executing the specified query. This tag is normally used with INSERT, UPDATE, and DELETE queries only.
jcs:template	None	A CDATA section describing the template with which to merge the returned resultset. This is normally used with SELECT statements. Templates can contain additional JCS tags for enhanced functionality. If a template is not defined, the JCS engine will simply serialize the resultset as an XML document, and return it to the calling client as MIME-type text/xml. Since it is a CDATA section, it can contain characters that are not legal XML grammar, including <, >, and &.

Tag Name	Default Value	Description
jcs:empty_resultset_output	Zero-length string	A CDATA section describing the default output returned in place of the resultset enumeration if the resultset is empty. This is normally used with SELECT statements. If the jcs:template tag is not present, then this tag is ignored. Since it is a CDATA section, it can contain characters that are not legal XML grammar.
jcs:error_page	None	If present, JCS will send a 302 redirect message specifying this URL back to the browser upon receipt of an exception. If not present, the JCS Engine will simply throw the exception to its host environment (e.g. servlet, JSP, etc.)
jcs:maxrows	NA	If present, this tag identifies the maximum number of rows to be returned in the query.

Special function tags

The fourth category includes tags that perform a specific function. These tags are:

Tag Name	Default Value	Description
jcs:encode_sql	N/A	This tag doubles up single quote characters for its text. In other words, it will replace a single quote character with two consecutive single quote characters. This is necessary for some SQL statements.
jcs:line_break_character	\r\n	Defines how to handle carriage return and line feed characters in data retrieved from the database. Currently supports 'HTML' only. If this is used, then the JCS engine will replace CR/LF combinations with the HTML character. If not present, it takes no action on CR/LF combinations. A useful future enhancement would be an 'XHTML' option to replace CR/LF combinations with the tag.

Template-specific tags

The final category defines two additional tags that can be used within the `<jcs:template>` CDATA section only: the `<jcs:resultset>` and the `<jcs:include>` tags.

Tag Name	Description
jcs:include	Creates a server-side include reference within a JCS output template. Currently, the JCS engine can recursively handle up to 15 SSIs, since each SSI involves a disk I/O hit. Note that this SSI path is relative to the location of the calling JCS query.
jcs:resultset	Enumerates through the resultset returned by the calling JCS query

While expedient, hard-coding a maximum SSI limit is not the best strategy from a design standpoint. Ideally, this parameter would exist in a properties file, thereby allowing the administrator to configure it. Implementing this is left as an exercise for the reader.

Variable Types

To provide a mechanism whereby the JCS query developer can access dynamic data, the JDBC Connector Servlet supports several different variable types. These variable types include form variables, resultset field variables, CGI variables, and system variables. In each case, variable names are case sensitive.

Form Variables

Form variables are variables passed to the server by the client via either the HTTP POST request body key-value pair, or the HTTP GET query string. Essentially, each form variable maps to a key in the `javax.servlet.http.HttpServletRequest` implementation that is passed to the JCS engine through either the JDBC Connector Servlet or a JSP (more on that later).

In JCS queries or templates, form variables take the form `#form.variablename#`. For example, given the following HTML form:

```
<FORM METHOD="POST" ACTION="guestbook_add.jcs">
  <P>Your first name: <INPUT TYPE="text" NAME="fname" SIZE="20"></P>
  <P>Your last name:  <INPUT TYPE="text" NAME="lname" SIZE="20"></P>
  <P>Your comments:  <TEXTAREA ROWS="5" NAME="comments"
     cols="30"></TEXTAREA></P>
  <P><INPUT TYPE="submit" VALUE="Submit" NAME="B1">
     <INPUT TYPE="reset" value="Reset"
  NAME="B2"></P>
</FORM>
```

The JCS query form handler, entitled `guestbook_add.jcs`, could look like this:

```
<?xml version="1.0"?>
<jcs:query xmlns:jcs="http://www.jresources.com/xml/jcs/1.0">
  <jcs:jdbc_url>jdbc:odbc:guestbook</jcs:jdbc_url>
  <jcs:sql>
    INSERT INTO guestbook ("ID", "fname", "lname", "comments", "host", "date")
VALUES ('#system.UID#','#form.fname#','#form.lname#', '#form.comments#',
'#CGI.REMOTE_ADDR#', Now())
  </jcs:sql>
  <jcs:redirect_url>guestbook.jcs</jcs:redirect_url>
  <jcs:error_page>error_page.htm</jcs:error_page>
</jcs:query>
```

This inserts a row into the `guestbook` table containing (among other data) the contents of the three form fields, using the `#form.fname#`, `#form.lname#`, and `#form.comments#` variables. (It also uses a system variable and a CGI variable, which will be explained in a moment.)

Resultset Field Variables

Resultset field variables are used in output templates to allow you to reference the values of a given record's fields as you enumerate through the resultset. It takes the form `#fieldname#`. Here's an example:

```
<jcs:include>
templates\header.inc
</jcs:include>

<jcs:resultset>
  <p><b>#fname# #lname#'s Guestbook Entry</b></p>
  <p><b>Comments: </b>#comments#</p>

  <p><b>Date entered: </b>#date#</p>

  <p><b>Originating Host: </b>#host#</p><br>
  <p><a href="guestbook_delete.jcs?ID=#ID#">Delete this entry</a></p>
</jcs:resultset>

<jcs:include>
templates\footer.inc
</jcs:include>
```

This extract from the `<jcs:template>` element outputs each row of the resultset in turn, printing out the contents of the fname, lname, comments, data, and host fields using the corresponding resultset field variables `#fname#`, `#lname#`, etc.

CGI Variables

No web application scripting framework would be complete without the ability to access CGI variables from within scripts, and JCS is no exception. With JCS, you can access commonly used CGI variables from within a JCS query using the form `#CGI.variablename#`. This supported variables are:

Variable Name	Description
`#CGI.REMOTE_ADDR#`	The IP address of the requesting client
`#CGI.SERVER_PROTOCOL#`	The protocol and version used (e.g. HTTP/1.1)
`#CGI.QUERY_STRING#`	The HTTP GET query string (that is, everything in the URL after the question mark)
`#CGI.REMOTE_USER#`	The User ID of the remote user, if applicable
`#CGI.SCRIPT_NAME#`	The script name environment variable
`#CGI.SERVER_NAME#`	The server's host name
`#CGI.SERVER_PORT#`	The port on which the HTTP server is running
`#CGI.REMOTE_HOST#`	The host name or IP address of the requesting client

System Variables

System variables are variables that provide system-specific functionality. They are referenced in JCS queries using the format #system.variablename#. JCS currently supports only two system variables, which are described in the table below:

Variable Name	Description
#system.date#	The server's current date
#system.UID#	Generates a unique ID by concatenating the server's current system time (to millisecond precision) with a string and a statically incremented counter

Custom Variables

Custom JCS variables are variables that are referenced in JCS queries using the #jcs.variablename# moniker. They are essentially an arbitrary list of key-value pairs passed to the JCS engine as an instance of the java.util.Properties class. We will get into greater detail on how this is done in the next section.

The Java Classes that Implement JCS

When it came time to design my object model, my goal was to design it in as modular a manner as possible. This meant that I would break my Java classes into three general categories:

❑   **Classes that provided functionality that I could reuse in other applications**
For this first category, I wrote two classes. The FunctionLib class contains a variety of general-purpose static methods that can be used by a variety of different Java applications. Accordingly, I put it in the com.jresources.util package. The XMLSerializableResultset class serializes a JDBC resultset as a well-formed XML document. Since this, too, can be used by a variety of different applications, I placed it in the com.jresources.jdbc package.

❑   **Classes that implemented the core JCS functionality described in the sections above**
The second category consists of four classes. The jcsRuntimeException class encapsulates a JCS exception. The jcsQuery class parses and encapsulates a JCS query file. The jcsTemplateParser class tokenizes a string using the opening and closing tags of an XML node as delimiters. The jcsEngine class, the heart of the JCS framework, processes a JCS request. All four of these classes are in the com.jresources.jcs package.

❑   **Classes that provide the server-side presentation services for the JCS framework**
There are three classes in this third category. The jcsCustomTag class implements a JSP 1.1 custom tag that executes a specified JCS query using an instance of jcsEngine, and reads the output into a variable that can then be referenced in the parent JSP. The jcsCustomTagOutput class provides an interface to allow the parent JSP to access the contents of the specified output variable. I put these two classes in the com.jresources.jcs package. The JDBCConnectorServlet class is a servlet that processes incoming HTTP requests on JCS queries. It translates the URL of the JCS query file to a real path, instantiates the jcsEngine class, passes it the JCS query file path, and places the query results into the HTTP response stream. I put this class in the com.jresources.servlets package.

The diagram below illustrates these classes and packages:

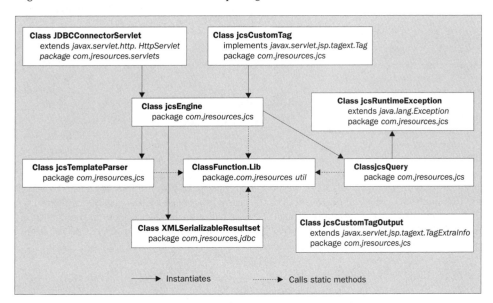

The com.jresources.util Package

The com.jresources.util package contains the FunctionLib class. This class contains a variety of general-purpose static methods that can be used by a variety of different Java applications:

Class FunctionLib

This class provides a variety of interesting functionality for the remainder of the JCS classes. This functionality includes unique ID generation, search-and-replace operations, XML parsing, and file I/O, among others.

The generateUID() method generates a unique ID by concatenating the current system time (to millisecond precision) with a string and a statically incremented counter. This method essentially implements the #system.UID# variable described above. Since this method will be accessed by multiple threads, and it increments the `UIDCounter` class variable, we will modify the method declaration with the `synchronized` keyword to eliminate the possibility of a race condition occurring:

```
package com.jresources.util;

import java.io.*;

public class FunctionLib {
  private static long UIDCounter = System.currentTimeMillis();
  public static synchronized String generateUID() {
    FunctionLib.UIDCounter++;
    return System.currentTimeMillis() + "JCS" + UIDCounter;
  }
}
```

As a companion to the `generateUID()` method, `FunctionLib` also implements a `ReplaceUID()` method. This method replaces all occurrences of the string referenced by the variable `oldWord` with a UID in the string referenced by the variable `content`. As we will see when we talk about the `jcsEngine` class later, this method will be used to generate new UIDs for multiple references to `#system.UID#` in a given JCS query:

```
public static String ReplaceUID(String content, String oldWord) {
  String tempString = new String(content);
  int position = tempString.indexOf(oldWord);
  while (position > -1) {
    String newWord = FunctionLib.generateUID();
    tempString = tempString.substring(0, position) + newWord
                 + tempString.substring(position + oldWord.length());
    position = tempString.indexOf(oldWord, position + newWord.length());
  }
  return tempString;
}
```

The `OpenFile()` method opens the specified file and returns its contents as an instance of `java.lang.String`. This method is used by the JCS engine to open JCS query files. It is also used to open files referenced by server-side include directives:

```
public static String OpenFile(String filename) throws Exception {
  String results = "";
  String line;

  // Create an instance of the File class
  File in_file = new File(filename);
  byte[] bFileContents = new byte[(int) in_file.length()];
  try {
    FileInputStream fis = new FileInputStream(in_file);
    int intResults = fis.read(bFileContents);
    if (intResults != in_file.length()) {
      throw new IOException("The entire file was not read...error: "
                            + filename);
    }
    results = new String(bFileContents);
    fis.close();
  }
```

```
      // Handle various error conditions
      catch (FileNotFoundException fnfe) {
        throw new Exception("Unable to find the file " + filename);
      } catch (IOException ioe) {
        throw new Exception("General Input/Output Error");
      } catch (Exception e) {
        throw new Exception("An Unknown Error Occurred.");
      }
      return results;
   }
```

The `Replace()` method replaces all occurrences of the string referenced by the variable `oldWord` with the string referenced by the variable `newWord` in the string referenced by the variable `content`. It is used throughout the application by virtually every class:

```
  public static String Replace(String content, String oldWord,
                               String newWord) {
    String tempString = new String(content);
    int position = tempString.indexOf(oldWord);
    while (position > -1) {
      tempString = tempString.substring(0, position) + newWord
                 + tempString.substring(position + oldWord.length());
      position = tempString.indexOf(oldWord, position + newWord.length());
    }
    return tempString;
  }
```

The next couple of methods implement some simple XML parser functionality. When I first wrote JCS, it was difficult to find a production-quality Java DOM or SAX parser. Moreover, I wanted to reduce the amount of overhead in the application for performance reasons. I also wanted to reduce the dependency of the JCS framework on external code that could, down the road, require expensive licensing fees and other hassles. Hence, I decided to implement some of my own simple parser functionality. As time goes on, it is definitely my intent to modify the `jcsQuery` class (sooner rather than later) to use one of the various DOM and SAX parsers that are now freely available. This will enhance functionality, and improve standardization.

The first method, `getInnerXML()`, returns the inner XML of the first occurrence of the specified tag in the specified XML markup fragment. Once it has parsed out the inner XML, it 'trims' it to remove any leading and trailing white space. If it cannot find the XML node in question, it simply returns the value of `defaultValue`:

```
  public static String getInnerXML(String rawXML, String tagname,
                                   String defaultValue) {
    String tempString = new String(rawXML);
    int position = tempString.indexOf("<" + tagname);
    if (position > -1) {
      tempString = tempString.substring(position + tagname.length());
      position = tempString.indexOf(">");
      if (position > -1) {
        tempString = tempString.substring(position + 1);
        position = tempString.indexOf("</" + tagname);
        if (position > -1) {
```

```
        tempString = tempString.substring(0, position);
      } else {
        tempString = defaultValue;
      }
    } else {
      tempString = defaultValue;
    }
  } else {
    tempString = defaultValue;
  }
  return tempString.trim();
}
```

The next method returns the inner text of a CDATA section. This is used by the `jcsQuery` class to parse the `<jcs:template>` and `<jcs:empty_resultset_output>` tags, which are CDATA sections. If it cannot find the CDATA section in question, it simply returns the value of `defaultValue`:

```
public static String getCDATASection(String rawXML, String tagname,
                                     String defaultValue) {
  try {
    String innerXML = getInnerXML(rawXML, tagname, defaultValue);
    String cDataStart = "<![CDATA[";
    String cDataEnd = "]]>";
    String innerXMLStart = innerXML.substring(0, cDataStart.length());
    String innerXMLEnd = innerXML.substring(innerXML.length() -
                        cDataEnd.length());
    if((innerXMLStart.equals(cDataStart))&&
          (innerXMLEnd.equals(cDataEnd))){
      return innerXML.substring(cDataStart.length(),
            innerXML.length() - cDataEnd.length()).trim();
    } else {
      return innerXML;
    }
  } catch (Exception e) {
    return defaultValue;
  }
}
```

The `EncodeSpecialCharacters()` method applies XML encoding rules to special characters. XML grammar rules reserve the &, <, >, and " characters, so data stored within an XML node or attribute cannot contain these characters; they must be encoded using `&amp;`, `&lt;`, `&gt;`, and `&quot;`, respectively. The `XMLSerializableResultset` class will use this method to ensure that field contents are converted to parse-able XML:

```
public static String EncodeSpecialCharacters(String sData) {
  if (sData != null) {
    sData = FunctionLib.Replace(sData, "&", "#amp;");
    sData = FunctionLib.Replace(sData, "#amp;", "&amp;");
    sData = FunctionLib.Replace(sData, "<", "&lt;");
    sData = FunctionLib.Replace(sData, ">", "&gt;");
    sData = FunctionLib.Replace(sData, "\"", "&quot;");
  } else {
    sData = "";
```

```
    }
    return sData;
}
```

The `stripComments()` method strips all XML comments from the specified XML markup fragment. The `jcsQuery` class will use this method to pre-process the JCS query file:

```
public static String stripComments(String content) throws Exception {
  int start;
  int end;
  start = content.indexOf("<!--");
  while (start > -1) {

    // get the ending content tag
    end = content.indexOf("-->", start);
    if (end == -1) {
      throw new Exception("XML comment is missing a closing tag");
    }
    String tempString = content.substring(start, end + 3);
    content = Replace(content, tempString, "");
    start = content.indexOf("<!--");
  }
  return content;
}
```

The `SQLEncode()` method encodes SQL statements by doubling up single quote characters where appropriate. This allows the transparent execution of SQL statements that contain nested single quotes. For example, the following SQL statement will cause an error when you try to execute it:

```
INSERT INTO tablename ("fieldname") VALUES ('This contains a 'single' quote')
```

To make it legal, you have to double-up the single quotes around the word "single, like this:

```
INSERT INTO tablename ("fieldname") VALUES ('This contains a ''single'' quote')
```

This method implements this functionality:

```
public static String SQLEncode(String content) {
  return FunctionLib.Replace(content, "\'", "\'\'");
}
```

The `HTMLLineBreak()` method replaces a carriage return character with an HTML <BR> tag. The `jcsEngine` class uses this method to ensure that multi-paragraph resultset data is displayed properly when the web browser renders the HTML:

```
public static String HTMLLineBreak(String content) {
  content = FunctionLib.Replace(content, "\r", "<br>");
  return content;
}
```

Last, but certainly not least, we have the `StringToInt()` method. This method converts the string representation of an integer to an `int`. If the string is not convertible to an `int`, it returns a `-1`:

```
public static int StringToInt(String sNum) {
  try {
    return Integer.parseInt(sNum);
  } catch (Exception e) {
    return -1;
  }
}
```

The com.jresources.jdbc Package

The `com.jresources.jdbc` package contains one class – the `XMLSerializableResultset` class:

```
                 XMLSerializableResultset
  -XMLResultset:String
  +XMLSerializableResultset
  +XMLSerializableResultset
  +toString:String
  -ResultSet2XML:String
  -EncodeSpecialCharacters:String
   resultset:Resultset
   XML:String
```

Class XMLSerializableResultset

This class serializes a JDBC resultset as a well-formed XML document. The outputted XML document will conform to this structure:

```
<?xml version="1.0" encoding="ISO-8859-1"?>
<resultset>
  <record>
    <fieldname>fieldvalue</fieldname>
  </record>
</resultset>
```

This class is used by the `jcsEngine` class to serialize the JDBC resultset returned by a SELECT statement when the JCS query has not specified an output template. If you use the default constructor to instantiate the class, then you need to call `setResultset()` (discussed below) to specify the resultset that you want to serialize into XML:

```
package com.jresources.jdbc;

import java.sql.*;
import java.util.*;
import com.jresources.util.FunctionLib;

public class XMLSerializableResultset {
  private String XMLResultset = "";
  public XMLSerializableResultset() {}
```

This constructor creates an instance of the class using the specified `Resultset`. It calls `ResultSet2XML()` method covered below to serialize the resultset as an XML document, and store it in the `XMLResultset` instance variable. The `setResultset()` mutator method does the same thing:

```
public XMLSerializableResultset(ResultSet rs) {
   XMLResultset = this.ResultSet2XML(rs);
}

public void setResultset(ResultSet rs) {
   XMLResultset = this.ResultSet2XML(rs);
}
```

The `getXML()` accessor method returns the specified resultset as XML by simply returning the value of the `XMLResultset` instance variable. The `toString()` method (which overrides `toString()` in `java.lang.Object`) performs the same function:

```
public String getXML() {
   return XMLResultset;
}

public String toString() {
   return XMLResultset;
}
```

The `ResultSet2XML()` method does the heavy lifting for the `XMLSerializableResultset` class. As it enumerates through the specified resultset, it creates `record` nodes by appending the appropriate XML markup to a `StringBuffer` class instance that contains the `<?xml?>` processing instruction and the `<resultset>` root node. Field names obtained from the resultset's meta-data become child nodes of each `<record>` node, and field values, pre-processed with the `FunctionLib` class's `EncodeSpecialCharacters()` method, become the field nodes' values. Once we have looped through the entire resultset, we terminate the resultset node, and return the XML data structure as a string:

```
private String ResultSet2XML(ResultSet rs) {
   StringBuffer strResults =
      new StringBuffer("<?xml version=\"1.0\" encoding=\"ISO-8859-
1\"?>\r\n<resultset>\r\n");
   try {

      ResultSetMetaData rsMetadata = rs.getMetaData();
      int intFields = rsMetadata.getColumnCount();
      while (rs.next()) {
        strResults.append("<record>\r\n");
        for (int i = 1; i <= intFields; i++) {
          strResults.append("<" + rsMetadata.getColumnName(i).toLowerCase()
                        + ">"
                        + EncodeSpecialCharacters(rs.getString(i))
                        + "</"
                        + rsMetadata.getColumnName(i).toLowerCase()
                        + ">\r\n");
        }
        strResults.append("</record>\r\n");
      }
```

```
      } catch (Exception e) {}
      strResults.append("</resultset>");
      return strResults.toString();
   }
   private String EncodeSpecialCharacters(String sData) {
     return FunctionLib.EncodeSpecialCharacters(sData);
   }
}
```

The com.jresources.jcs Package

The com.jresources.jcs package contains classes that provide the bulk of the functionality of the JCS framework. It contains the following classes:

- ❑ The jcsRuntimeException class encapsulates a JCS exception
- ❑ The jcsQuery class parses and encapsulates a JCS query file
- ❑ The jcsTemplateParser class tokenizes a string using the opening and closing tags of an XML node as delimiters
- ❑ The jcsEngine class, the heart of the JCS framework, processes a JCS request
- ❑ The jcsCustomTag class implements custom JSP tag interface to the jcsEngine
- ❑ The jcsCustomTagOutput class provides an interface to allow the host JSP to access jcsCustomTag's output

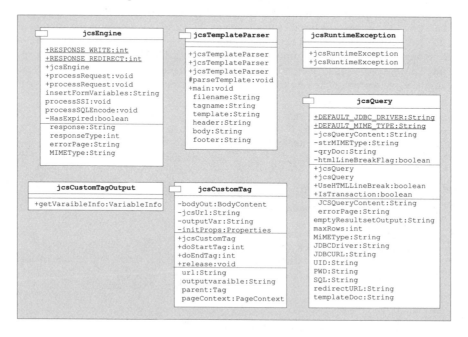

Class jcsRuntimeException

The `jcsRuntimeException` class encapsulates a JCS run time exception. It extends `java.lang.Exception`, and is used to create a 'branded' exception for JCS. Several of the classes in the `com.jresources.jcs` package contain methods that explicitly throw `jcsRuntimeException`:

```
package com.jresources.jcs;

public class jcsRuntimeException extends Exception {
  public jcsRuntimeException() {
    super();
  }
  public jcsRuntimeException(String msg) {
    super(msg);
  }
}
```

Class jcsQuery

The `jcsQuery` class parses a JCS query file using the simple XML parsing methods we created in the `FunctionLib` class. Initially, we will declare our instance variables, as well as a few constants for default values. These constants include `DEFAULT_JDBC_DRIVER` (which is initialized to the value of Sun's ODBC-JDBC bridge), and `DEFAULT_MIME_TYPE` (which is set to `text/html`). Another important note, if you instantiate this class using the default constructor, you should call `setJCSQueryContent()` (covered below) to parse the JCS query and initialize the instance variables:

```
package com.jresources.jcs;

import com.jresources.util.FunctionLib;

public class jcsQuery {

  // constants
  public static final String DEFAULT_JDBC_DRIVER =
    "sun.jdbc.odbc.JdbcOdbcDriver";
  public static final String DEFAULT_MIME_TYPE = "text/html";

  // the JCS Query raw XML
  private String jcsQueryContent;

  // "Read-only" instance variables
  private String strMIMEType = this.DEFAULT_MIME_TYPE;
  private String JDBCDriver = this.DEFAULT_JDBC_DRIVER;
  private String JDBCURL;
  private String UID;
  private String PWD;
  private String SQL;
  private String qryDoc;
  private String templateDoc;
  private String redirectURL;
  private String errorPage;
  private String emptyResultsetOutput;
  private int maxRows = -1;
  private boolean htmlLineBreakFlag = false;
```

The `jcsQuery` class contains two constructors: the default constructor, and a constructor that takes an instance of `java.lang.String` as an argument. The `jcsQuery(String qryContent)` constructor takes the raw XML of a JCS query, parses it, and initializes the instance variables by calling the `setJCSQueryContent()` method. The `getJCSQueryContent()` method is an accessor method that returns the raw XML of the query:

```
public jcsQuery() {}
public jcsQuery(String qryContent) throws jcsRuntimeException {
  this.setJCSQueryContent(qryContent);
}

public String getJCSQueryContent() {
  return this.jcsQueryContent;
}
```

The `setJCSQueryContent()` method is the `jcsQuery` class's work horse. It sets the raw XML of a JCS query, parses it, and initializes the instance variables. The first operation it performs is to assign the raw XML to the `jcsQueryContent` instance variable:

```
public void setJCSQueryContent(String qryContent) throws jcsRuntimeException {
  this.jcsQueryContent = qryContent;
```

Next, the method gets the value of the XML document's root node and strips out any comments:

```
try {
  qryContent =
    FunctionLib.stripComments(FunctionLib.getInnerXML(qryContent,
                                        "jcs:query", ""));
} catch (Exception e) {
  throw new jcsRuntimeException(e.getMessage());
}
```

Next, it gets the values of the rest of the nodes using the static `getInnerXML()` method of the `FunctionLib` class. In each case, it specifies the appropriate default value (see the JCS query reference section above for default values for each JCS query tag). Since the `<jcs:template>` and `<jcs:empty_resultset_output>` tags are CDATA sections, we'll use the `getCDATASection()` method to retrieve those:

```
strMIMEType = FunctionLib.getInnerXML(qryContent, "jcs:mime_type",
                                this.DEFAULT_MIME_TYPE);
JDBCDriver = FunctionLib.getInnerXML(qryContent, "jcs:jdbc_driver",
                                this.DEFAULT_JDBC_DRIVER);
JDBCURL = FunctionLib.getInnerXML(qryContent, "jcs:jdbc_url", "");
UID = FunctionLib.getInnerXML(qryContent, "jcs:jdbc_uid", "");
PWD = FunctionLib.getInnerXML(qryContent, "jcs:jdbc_pwd", "");
SQL = FunctionLib.getInnerXML(qryContent, "jcs:sql", "");
redirectURL = FunctionLib.getInnerXML(qryContent, "jcs:redirect_url",
                                "");
templateDoc = FunctionLib.getCDATASection(qryContent, "jcs:template",
                                "");
emptyResultsetOutput = FunctionLib.getCDATASection(qryContent,
                "jcs:empty_resultset_output", "");
errorPage = FunctionLib.getInnerXML(qryContent, "jcs:error_page", "");
```

To determine whether to convert carriage return combinations in resultset field values to the HTML `<BR>` tag, we will check the value of the `<jcs:line_break_character>` node, if it exists. After converting it to lower case, we will use the ternary operator to check equality with `"html"`, and assign the results of this operation to the `htmlLineBreakFlag` boolean instance variable:

```
    htmlLineBreakFlag =
      FunctionLib.getInnerXML(qryContent, "jcs:line_break_character", "")
      .toLowerCase().equals("html") ? true : false;
    maxRows = FunctionLib.StringToInt(FunctionLib.getInnerXML(qryContent,
          "jcs:maxrows", "-1"));
  }
```

The rest of the methods are accessor methods to encapsulate the `jcsQuery` class's instance variables:

```
    /**Returns the query's error page*/
    public String getErrorPage() {
      return this.errorPage;
    }

    /**
     * Returns the query's empty resultset
     * output (the default output if the
     * resultset returns no rows
     */
    public String getEmptyResultsetOutput() {
      return this.emptyResultsetOutput;
    }

    /**
     * Returns the maxrows flag
     */
    public int getMaxRows() {
      return this.maxRows;
    }

    /**
     * Indicates whether or not to use the <BR> character to signify line breaks
     */
    public boolean UseHTMLLineBreak() {
      return this.htmlLineBreakFlag;
    }

    /**
     * Returns the MIME Type of the query's result set
     */
    public String getMIMEType() {
      return this.strMIMEType;
    }

    /**
     * Returns the query's JDBC driver
     */
```

```java
public String getJDBCDriver() {
  return this.JDBCDriver;
}

/**
 * Returns the query's JDBC URL
 */
public String getJDBCURL() {
  return this.JDBCURL;
}

/**
 * Returns the UserID needed to log onto the database
 */
public String getUID() {
  return this.UID;
}

/**
 * Returns the password needed to log onto the database
 */
public String getPWD() {
  return this.PWD;
}

/**
 * Returns the query's SQL statement
 */
public String getSQL() {
  return this.SQL;
}

/**
 * Returns the query's redirect URL
 * (applicable to update-insert-delete queries only)
 */
public String getRedirectURL() {
  return this.redirectURL;
}

/**
 * Returns the query's output template
 */
public String getTemplateDoc() {
  return this.templateDoc;
}
public boolean IsTransaction() {
  String sql = SQL.toLowerCase();
  if (sql.indexOf("select") > -1) {
    return false;
  } else {
    return true;
  }
}

}
```

Class jcsTemplateParser

The `jcsTemplateParser` class parses a JCS template; the template can be read either from a file or an instance of `java.lang.String`. It breaks the template down into three pieces using a given XML tag as a delimiter (the delimiter is not included in the three pieces). This class is used by the `jcsEngine` class to tokenize HTML and XML markup fragments (break them up into individual 'tokens') to facilitate the insertion of dynamic data into the fragment. The specific use is to process `<jcs:resultset>` enumeration, as well as recursive processing of server-side includes using the `<jcs:include>` tag, and recursive processing of the `<jcs:encode_sql>` directive (more on this later). If you use the default constructor to instantiate the class, you must remember to set the custom tag (if applicable), and the raw template text using mutator methods discussed below:

```
package com.jresources.jcs;

import com.jresources.util.FunctionLib;

public class jcsTemplateParser {
  private String filename;
  private String template = "";
  private String header = "";
  private String body = "";
  private String footer = "";
  private String tagname = "jcs:resultset";

  public jcsTemplateParser() {}
```

The `jcsTemplateParser` class has two other constructors. The first constructor takes an absolute file name and parses it using the default tag (`<jcs:resultset>`). Use this constructor only if you want to use the default tag. The second constructor takes an absolute file name and parses it using the specified tag. Use this constructor if you are parsing a file with a custom tag:

```
public jcsTemplateParser(String sfilename) throws Exception {
  this();
  filename = sfilename;
  this.setTemplate(FunctionLib.OpenFile(filename));
}

public jcsTemplateParser(String sfilename,
                         String sTagname) throws Exception {
  this();
  filename = sfilename;
  tagname = sTagname;
  this.setTemplate(FunctionLib.OpenFile(filename));
}
```

The `parseTemplate()` method does most of the heavy lifting for the `jcsTemplateParser` class. This method parses the current template (the value of the `template` instance variable) using the tag name stored in the `tagname` instance variable. It first reads the fragment up to the first occurrence of '`<tagname`', and stores this chunk in the `header` instance variable. Then, it reads to the first occurrence of '`>`'. From there, it reads to the first occurrence of '`</tagname`', and stores this chunk into the `body` instance variable. Then, it reads to the next occurrence of '`>`'. The remainder of the markup fragment is placed in the `footer` instance variable:

```
protected void parseTemplate() {
  String tempString = this.template;
  int position = tempString.indexOf("<" + tagname);
  if (position > -1) {
    this.header = tempString.substring(0, position);
    tempString = tempString.substring(position + tagname.length());
    position = tempString.indexOf(">");
    if (position > -1) {
      tempString = tempString.substring(position + 1);
      position = tempString.indexOf("</" + tagname);
      if (position > -1) {
        this.body = tempString.substring(0, position);
        tempString = tempString.substring(position + tagname.length());
        position = tempString.indexOf(">");
        if (position > -1) {
          this.footer = tempString.substring(position + 1);
        }
      }
    }
  }
}
```

The next three methods are mutator methods that control access to various private instance variables. The setFilename() method sets a new filename, opens it, and parses it by passing the file contents to the setTemplate() method. The setTagname() method sets a new tagname and re-parses the template by calling the parseTemplate() method. The setTemplate() method sets and parses a new template by calling the parseTemplate() method:

```
public void setFilename(String sfilename) throws Exception {
  filename = sfilename;
  this.setTemplate(FunctionLib.OpenFile(filename));
}

public void setTagname(String tag) {
  tagname = tag;
  this.parseTemplate();
}

public void setTemplate(String tag) {
  template = tag;
  this.parseTemplate();
}
```

The rest of the methods are accessor methods to encapsulate the jcsTemplateParser class's instance variables:

```
/**
 * This method returns the current tag
 */
public String getTagname() {
  return tagname;
}
```

```
/**
 * This method returns the current filename
 */
public String getFilename() {
  return filename;
}

/**
 * This method returns the current template's entire text
 */
public String getTemplate() {
  return template;
}

/**
 * This method returns the current template's header text
 */
public String getHeader() {
  return header;
}

/**
 * This method returns the current template's body text
 */
public String getBody() {
  return body;
}

/**
 * This method returns the current template's footer text
 */
public String getFooter() {
  return footer;
}
}
```

Class jcsEngine

The `jcsEngine` class is the heart of the JCS framework. This is the class that actually processes a JCS request. It can be used by a servlet, a JSP page, or a JSP custom tag. The calling client uses `jcsEngine` by instantiating it and calling one of the `processRequest()` overloaded methods, passing in the `HTTPServletRequest` object, the path to the JCS query file, and optionally an instance of `java.util.Properties` to provide custom JCS variable support. Once `processRequest()` has been called, the calling client queries the response type using the `getResponseType()` accessor method. If the response type is `jcsEngine.RESPONSE_WRITE`, it sends the value returned by the `getResponse()` accessor method to the browser using the MIME type specified by the `getMIMEType()` accessor method. If it is `jcsEngine.RESPONSE_REDIRECT`, it redirects the browser to the URL derived from the value returned by the `getResponse()` accessor method. If an exception occurs, the calling servlet or JSP page can query the `getErrorPage()` accessor method for an error page to which to redirect the browser:

```
package com.jresources.jcs;

import javax.servlet.http.*;
import java.io.*;
```

```
import java.sql.*;
import com.jresources.util.FunctionLib;
import java.util.Enumeration;
import java.util.Calendar;
import java.util.Properties;
import com.jresources.jdbc.XMLSerializableResultset;

public class jcsEngine {
  private String response;
  private int responseType;
  private String errorPage = "";
  private String MIMEType;
  public static final int MAX_SSI = 15;
  public static final int RESPONSE_WRITE = 0;
  public static final int RESPONSE_REDIRECT = 1;
  public jcsEngine() {}

  public String getResponse() {
    return this.response;
  }

  public int getResponseType() {
    return this.responseType;
  }

  public String getErrorPage() {
    return this.errorPage;
  }

  public String getMIMEType() {
    return this.MIMEType;
  }

  public void processRequest(HttpServletRequest request,
                             String qryDoc) throws Exception {
    this.processRequest(request, null, qryDoc);
  }
```

The `jcsEngine` class contains a variety of methods that are called by `processRequest()` to pre- or post-process JCS query files. The first of these methods is `insertFormVariables()`. This method replaces JCS form variables with the values of the corresponding HTML form variables passed in via the `HTTPServletRequest` object. It also inserts the values of various CGI variables where corresponding JCS CGI variables exist in the JCS file:

```
String insertFormVariables(String content, HttpServletRequest request) {
    Enumeration e = request.getParameterNames();
    while (e.hasMoreElements()) {
      String keyname = (String) e.nextElement();
      content = FunctionLib.Replace(content, "#form." + keyname + "#",
                                    request.getParameter(keyname));
    }
    content = FunctionLib.Replace(content, "#CGI.REMOTE_ADDR#",
                                  request.getRemoteAddr() == null ? ""
                                  : request.getRemoteAddr());
```

```
        content = FunctionLib.Replace(content, "#CGI.SERVER_PROTOCOL#",
                        request.getProtocol() == null ? ""
                        : request.getProtocol());
        content = FunctionLib.Replace(content, "#CGI.QUERY_STRING#",
                        request.getQueryString() == null ? ""
                        : request.getQueryString());
        content = FunctionLib.Replace(content, "#CGI.REMOTE_USER#",
                        request.getRemoteUser() == null ? ""
                        : request.getRemoteUser());
        content = FunctionLib.Replace(content, "#CGI.SCRIPT_NAME#",
                        request.getServletPath() == null ? ""
                        : request.getServletPath());
        content = FunctionLib.Replace(content, "#CGI.SERVER_NAME#",
                        request.getServerName() == null ? ""
                        : request.getServerName());
        content =       FunctionLib.Replace(content, "#CGI.SERVER_PORT#",
                        new Integer(request.getServerPort()).toString());
        content = FunctionLib.Replace(content, "#CGI.REMOTE_HOST#",
                        request.getRemoteHost() == null ? ""
                        : request.getRemoteHost());
        content = FunctionLib.Replace(content, "#system.date#",
                        new java.util.Date().toString());
        content = FunctionLib.ReplaceUID(content, "#system.UID#");
        return content;
    }
```

The `insertJCSVariables()` method replaces the appropriate custom JCS variables in the JCS query with the values contained in the `java.util.Properties` class instance passed into the method:

```
String insertJCSVariables(String content, Properties request) {
    Enumeration e = request.keys();
    while (e.hasMoreElements()) {
        String keyname = (String) e.nextElement();
        content = FunctionLib.Replace(content, "#jcs." + keyname + "#",
                            request.getProperty(keyname));
    }
    return content;
}
```

The `processSSI()` method recursively processes up to 15 server-side includes. First, it uses an instance of the `jcsTemplateParser` class to parse the template (passed in as the zero index of a `String` array so it can be updated from within the method). After appending the template's header to the passed-in `StringBuffer`, it opens the specified include file (which is the value of the template's body), and appends the contents of the file. Next, it appends the template's footer to the `StringBuffer`, assigns the string representation of the `StringBuffer` to the template `String` array's zero index, and makes a recursive call to itself to process any additional server-side includes:

```
void processSSI(String[] template, StringBuffer results,
                String rootScript, int safetyCounter) {
    int position = template[0].indexOf("<jcs:include");
    if (position > -1 && safetyCounter < MAX_SSI) {
        jcsTemplateParser parser = new jcsTemplateParser();
        parser.setTagname("jcs:include");
```

```
    parser.setTemplate(template[0]);
    results.append(parser.getHeader());
    String SSIFilename =
      new File(new File(rootScript).getParent(),
               parser.getBody().trim()).getAbsolutePath();
    try {
      results.append(FunctionLib.OpenFile(SSIFilename));
    } catch (Exception e) {
      results.append("Unable to find the include file " + SSIFilename);
    }
    results.append(parser.getFooter());
    template[0] = results.toString();
    safetyCounter++;
    processSSI(template, new StringBuffer(), rootScript, safetyCounter);
  }
}
```

The processSQLEncode() method recursively processes any <jcs:encode_sql> tags in the specified JCS query. Its methodology is similar to the processSSI() method above; it uses the jcsTemplateParser class to parse the query, processes the template's body with the FunctionLib class's SQLEncode() method, and then makes a recursive call to itself to process any other <jcs:encode_sql> directives in the query:

```
void processSQLEncode(String[] template, StringBuffer results) {
  int position = template[0].indexOf("<jcs:encode_sql");
  if (position > -1) {
    jcsTemplateParser parser = new jcsTemplateParser();
    parser.setTagname("jcs:encode_sql");
    parser.setTemplate(template[0]);
    results.append(parser.getHeader());
    results.append(FunctionLib.SQLEncode(parser.getBody()));
    results.append(parser.getFooter());
    template[0] = results.toString();
    processSQLEncode(template, new StringBuffer());
  }
}
```

The processRequest() method does most of the heavy lifting for the JCS engine:

❑ First, it creates a StringBuffer that is used to keep a running tally of the response

❑ Next, it opens the JCS query file, and pre-processes it with the insertFormVariables() method to apply the HTML form variables passed in with the HTTPServletRequest object

❑ Next, it pre-processes the JCS query using the insertJCSVariables() method if the java.util.Properties custom variable property bag is not null

❑ Next, it processes any <jcs:encode_sql> directives with the processSQLEncode() method.

❑ Once all of the pre-processing is done, it parses the JCS query by creating an instance of the jcsQuery class

```
public void processRequest(HttpServletRequest request,
                           Properties customProps,
                           String qryDoc) throws Exception {
    StringBuffer strResults = new StringBuffer("");
    String qryContent = FunctionLib.OpenFile(qryDoc);
    qryContent = this.insertFormVariables(qryContent, request);
    if (customProps != null) {
        qryContent = this.insertJCSVariables(qryContent, customProps);
    }
    String[] workingQuery = new String[1];
    workingQuery[0] = qryContent;
    this.processSQLEncode(workingQuery, new StringBuffer());
    qryContent = workingQuery[0];
    jcsQuery objQuery = new jcsQuery(qryContent);
```

Once the query is parsed, we set the JCS engine's `errorPage` instance variable from the JCS Query object. We do this to ensure that it is initialized in the event an exception is thrown. Next, we must process any server-side includes that we have in the query's template, if one exists:

```
    errorPage = objQuery.getErrorPage();
    String[] workingTemplate = new String[1];
    if (objQuery.getTemplateDoc() != "") {
        workingTemplate[0] = objQuery.getTemplateDoc();
        this.processSSI(workingTemplate, new StringBuffer(), qryDoc, 0);
    }
```

Now we are ready to start doing some database access. First, we instantiate and register the JDBC driver. Next, we connect to the database and create a `Statement` object:

```
    Class.forName(objQuery.getJDBCDriver());
    Connection conn = DriverManager.getConnection(objQuery.getJDBCURL(),
            objQuery.getUID(), objQuery.getPWD());
    Statement s = conn.createStatement();
```

If our SQL statement is a 'write' query, we don't want a resultset back. Therefore, we will execute it using the `executeUpdate()` method of the `Statement` object. Upon successful completion, we will set the `response` instance variable to our query's redirect URL, the response type to `jcsEngine.RESPONSE_REDIRECT`, and return from the method. If there is no redirect URL to go to, we will simply append the JCS template, if one exists, 'as is' to the `results StringBuffer`.

If the SQL statement is a SELECT statement, we will call our `Statement` object's `executeQuery()` method. This will return a `Resultset`. If the query does not contain a template, we will serialize the resultset as an XML document using the `XMLSerializableResultset` class. Then, we will set the `response` instance variable to the resulting XML document, set the `MIMEType` instance variable to `text/xml`, set the response type to `jcsEngine.RESPONSE_WRITE`, and return from the method:

```
    if (objQuery.IsTransaction()) {
        s.executeUpdate(objQuery.getSQL());
        if (objQuery.getRedirectURL() != "") {
            conn.close();   // clean up the db connection
            this.response = objQuery.getRedirectURL();
```

```
            this.responseType = jcsEngine.RESPONSE_REDIRECT;
            return;
        } else {
            strResults.append(workingTemplate[0]);
        }
    } else {
        if (objQuery.getMaxRows() > -1) {
            s.setMaxRows(objQuery.getMaxRows());
        }
        ResultSet rs = s.executeQuery(objQuery.getSQL());
        if (objQuery.getTemplateDoc().equals("")) {
            XMLSerializableResultset xrs = new XMLSerializableResultset(rs);
            this.response = xrs.getXML();
            this.MIMEType = "text/xml";
            this.responseType = jcsEngine.RESPONSE_WRITE;
            rs.close();
            conn.close();
            return;
```

Otherwise, we will use the `jcsTemplateParser` class to tokenize the header, body and footer of the template using the `<jcs:resultset>` beginning and ending pairs as tokens. We will append the header to the output `StringBuffer`, and enumerate through the resultset. For each record, we will replace each instance of `#fieldname#` in the template's body with that field name's value. (If the field specified is not found in the resultset, the string `#fieldname#` will be sent back to the browser unchanged.) We will then append this chunk to the output `StringBuffer`.

If the resultset has no records, we will append the `EmptyResultsetOutput` chunk to the output `StringBuffer`. Once we are done with the resultset, we will append the template footer to the output `StringBuffer`, set the correct MIME type from the query object, and clean up the resultset and database connection. Finally, we will once again make sure we fill out any remaining form, CGI, or custom variables in the template. Once we are done, we will assign our output to the `response` instance variable, and return from the method:

```
        } else {
            jcsTemplateParser template = new jcsTemplateParser();
            template.setTemplate(workingTemplate[0]);
            strResults.append(template.getHeader());
            ResultSetMetaData rsMetadata = rs.getMetaData();
            int intFields = rsMetadata.getColumnCount();
            String recordOutput;
            String currFieldValue;
            String AdjFieldValue;
            int recordCount = 0;
            while (rs.next()) {
                recordOutput = template.getBody();
                for (int i = 1; i <= intFields; i++) {
                    currFieldValue =
                        FunctionLib.EncodeSpecialCharacters(rs.getString(i));
                    AdjFieldValue = objQuery.UseHTMLLineBreak()
                                ? FunctionLib.HTMLLineBreak(currFieldValue)
                                : currFieldValue;
                    recordOutput = FunctionLib.Replace(recordOutput,
                                                "#"
```

```
                                            + rsMetadata.getColumnName(i)
                                            + "#", AdjFieldValue);
            }
          strResults.append(recordOutput);
          recordCount++;
        }
        if (recordCount == 0) {
          strResults.append(objQuery.getEmptyResultsetOutput());
        }
        strResults.append(template.getFooter());
      }
      rs.close();

    }
    conn.close();
    this.MIMEType = objQuery.getMIMEType();
    this.responseType = jcsEngine.RESPONSE_WRITE;
    String tmpResponse = insertFormVariables(strResults.toString(),
                                              request);
    if (customProps != null) {
      tmpResponse = this.insertJCSVariables(tmpResponse, customProps);
    }
    this.response = tmpResponse;
    return;
  }
}
```

Class jcsCustomTag

The jcsCustomTag class provides functionality for the <jcs:query_object> custom JSP tag. This tag is a wrapper around the jcsEngine class that allows pages written to the JSP 1.1 specification to execute JCS queries. The tag has two attributes:

- url, which specifies the virtual URL of the JCS query file to be executed
- outputvariable, the name of a variable in which the query's output will be placed

As with any other custom tag, jcsCustomTag implements the javax.servlet.jsp.tagext.Tag interface, and provides functionality for the setParent(), setPageContext(), getParent(), doStartTag(), doEndTag(), and release() methods. It also provides mutator methods for the tag's two attributes.

```
package com.jresources.jcs;

import javax.servlet.jsp.*;
import javax.servlet.jsp.tagext.*;
import javax.servlet.*;
import javax.servlet.http.*;
import java.io.*;
import java.util.Properties;
import java.util.Enumeration;

public class jcsCustomTag implements Tag {
  private BodyContent bodyOut;
```

```
    private PageContext pageContext;
    private Tag parent;
    private String jcsUrl = "";
    private String outputVar;
    private Properties initProps = new Properties();
    public jcsCustomTag() {
      super();
    }
    public void setUrl(String value) {
      this.jcsUrl = value;
    }
    public void setOutputvariable(String value) {
      this.outputVar = value;
    }
    public void setParent(Tag parent) {
      this.parent = parent;
    }
    public Tag getParent() {
      return this.parent;
    }
```

The setPageContext() method implementation reads the web application's initialization parameters from the PageContext object into the instance of java.util.Properties represented by the initProps instance variable. This allows the JSP developer to create custom, configurable, application-scope properties that can be used by all instances of the <jcs:query_object> tag. For example, a developer might want to create a default JDBC database URL property that would be used throughout the entire application to keep from having to type it individually into all of the JCS query files. This Properties object will be used later to initialize the JCS custom variables.

```
    public void setPageContext(PageContext pageContext) {
      this.pageContext = pageContext;
      Enumeration e =
        this.pageContext.getServletContext().getInitParameterNames();
      while (e.hasMoreElements()) {
        String currParam = (String) e.nextElement();
        InitProps put(currParam,
               pageContext.getServletContext().getInitParameter(currParam));
      }
    }
```

Since our <jcs:query_object> custom tag does not have a body, we will simply inform the calling environment to skip the body processing in the doStartTag() method implementation:

```
    public int doStartTag() throws JspException {
      return Tag.SKIP_BODY;
    }
```

The doEndTag() method implementation contains the bulk of the jcsCustomTag class's logic. First, we create an instance of the jcsEngine class. Next, we call processRequest(), passing in the HTTP Request object obtained from the page context, our initProps instance variable, and the real path to our JCS query URL. We then query the JCS engine's response type. If it calls for a redirect, we redirect the browser to the redirect page, and inform the calling JSP to skip the rest of the page. Otherwise, we set our JCS query output to the outputVar instance variable, and evaluate the remainder of the JSP:

```
public int doEndTag() throws JspException {
  try {
    jcsEngine jcs = new jcsEngine();
    jcs
      .processRequest((HttpServletRequest) pageContext.getRequest(),
                      initProps,
                      pageContext.getServletConfig().getServletContext()
                        .getRealPath(this.jcsUrl));
    HttpServletResponse response =
      (HttpServletResponse) pageContext.getResponse();
    if (jcs.getResponseType() == jcsEngine.RESPONSE_REDIRECT) {
      response.sendRedirect(jcs.getResponse());
      return Tag.SKIP_PAGE;
    } else {
      pageContext.setAttribute(outputVar, jcs.getResponse());
      return Tag.EVAL_PAGE;
    }
  } catch (Exception e) {
    throw new JspTagException(e.toString());
  }
}
```

Finally, in the `release()` method implementation we free up our resources:

```
public void release() {
  bodyOut = null;
  pageContext = null;
  parent = null;
}
```

Class jcsCustomTagOutput

The `jcsCustomTagOutput` class provides an interface to allow the host JSP page to access the contents of the specified output variable. It subclasses `javax.servlet.jsp.tagext.TagExtraInfo`, and overrides the `getVariableInfo()` method. This method returns a `javax.servlet.jsp.tagext.VariableInfo` class instance that identifies the variable named in the `<jcs:query_object>` tag's `outputvariable` attribute as an instance of `java.lang.String`, available for scripting after the end tag is executed:

```
package com.jresources.jcs;

import javax.servlet.jsp.tagext.*;

public class jcsCustomTagOutput extends TagExtraInfo {
  public VariableInfo[] getVariableInfo(TagData data) {
    return new VariableInfo[] {
      new VariableInfo(data.getAttributeString("outputvariable"), "String",
                       true, VariableInfo.AT_END)
    };
  }
}
```

The com.jresources.servlets Package

The com.jresources.servlets package contains the JDBCConnectorServlet class:

Class JDBCConnectorServlet

The JDBCConnectorServlet class is the actual JDBC Connector Servlet. Like any other servlet, it subclasses javax.servlet.http.HttpServlet, and overrides the init(), doPost(), and doGet() methods. The init() method gets custom properties on startup from the servlet engine's environment, and stores them in an instance of java.util.Properties. This will be passed to the JCS engine for JCS custom variable processing:

```
package com.jresources.servlets;

import javax.servlet.*;
import javax.servlet.http.*;
import java.io.*;
import com.jresources.jcs.*;
import java.util.Enumeration;
import java.util.Properties;

public class JDBCConnectorServlet extends HttpServlet {
  private java.util.Properties initProps = new Properties();
  public void init(ServletConfig config) throws ServletException {
    super.init(config);
    Enumeration e = config.getInitParameterNames();
    while (e.hasMoreElements()) {
      String currParam = (String) e.nextElement();
      initProps.put(currParam, config.getInitParameter(currParam));
    }
  }
```

Since JCS was designed to handle HTTP GET's and POST's identically, the doPost() method simply calls doGet(), passing in the request and response object received from the service() method:

```
public void doPost(HttpServletRequest request,
                   HttpServletResponse response) throws IOException,
                   ServletException {
  doGet(request, response);
  }
}
```

The servlet's doGet() method contains the servlet's main logic. After creating an instance of the jcsEngine class, the method attempts to determine the real path of JCS query file so it can be opened by the jcsEngine.

It first checks the PATH_INFO environment variable:

❑   If it is null, the servlet assumes that it was invoked as a result of a URL request for a JCS file (e.g. http://hostname/dir/myQuery.jcs), and obtains the JCS query file's real path by passing the SCRIPT_NAME environment variable to the servlet context's getRealPath() implementation.

❑   Otherwise, it uses the path info (for example, the path info for http://hostname/servlet/JCS/dir/myQuery.jcs is /dir/myQuery.jcs), and gets the path info's real path via the request object's getPathTranslated() method.

```
public void doGet(HttpServletRequest request,
                  HttpServletResponse response) throws IOException,
                  ServletException {
  jcsEngine mainMod = new jcsEngine();
  try {
    String qryDoc;

    // determine the location of the jcs query
    // first priority is the path info...second is the servletPath
    if (request.getPathInfo() == null) {
      qryDoc =
        getServletConfig().getServletContext()
          .getRealPath(request.getServletPath());
    } else {
      qryDoc = request.getPathTranslated();
    }
```

The next step is to execute the JCS query by calling the processRequest() method of the jcsEngine class instance. Upon completion, we query the response type to determine whether to send a 302 redirect header back to the user agent, or simply put the query's output into the HTTP response stream:

```
      mainMod.processRequest(request, this.initProps, qryDoc);
      if (mainMod.getResponseType() == jcsEngine.RESPONSE_REDIRECT) {
        response.sendRedirect(mainMod.getResponse());
      } else {
        PrintWriter out = response.getWriter();
        response.setContentType(mainMod.getMIMEType());
        out.println(mainMod.getResponse());
      }
    } catch (Exception e) {
      String errorMsg = "An error occurred while executing the query "
                        + request.getServletPath()
                        + " with the JCS servlet: " + e.toString();
      this.getServletContext().log(errorMsg, e);
      if (mainMod.getErrorPage() == "") {
        throw new ServletException(errorMsg, e);
      } else {
        response.sendRedirect(mainMod.getErrorPage());
      }
    }
  }
}
```

Other Artifacts

To deploy JCS as a servlet 2.2 web application, there are a couple of more files we must prepare: the JSP custom tag library descriptor, and the web application deployment descriptor.

The JSP Custom Tag Library Descriptor (jcs_taglib.tld)

The JSP custom tag library descriptor is an XML document that provides the JSP engine with metadata about a collection of related JSP custom tags. In our case, we will include information about our `<jcs:query_object>` custom tag, including version information and a short description of the tag library. We must also provide the fully qualified class names of the `javax.servlet.jsp.tagext.Tag` implementation and `javax.servlet.jsp.tagext.TagExtraInfo` subclass, and all legal attributes for the custom tag:

```xml
<?xml version="1.0" encoding="ISO-8859-1" ?>
<!DOCTYPE taglib
        PUBLIC "-//Sun Microsystems, Inc.//DTD JSP Tag Library 1.1//EN"
        "http://java.sun.com/j2ee/dtds/web-jsptaglibrary_1_1.dtd">
<taglib>
  <tlibversion>1.0</tlibversion>
  <jspversion>1.1</jspversion>
  <shortname>jcs</shortname>
  <uri></uri>
  <info>
    A custom JSP tag implementation of the JResources.com JDBC connector servlet
  </info>
  <tag>
    <name>query_object</name>
    <tagclass>com.jresources.jcs.jcsCustomTag</tagclass>
    <teiclass>com.jresources.jcs.jcsCustomTagOutput</teiclass>
    <info>A custom JSP tag implementation of the JResources.com JDBC
      connector servlet</info>
    <attribute>
      <name>url</name>
      <required>true</required>
    </attribute>
    <attribute>
      <name>outputvariable</name>
      <required>true</required>
    </attribute>
  </tag>
</taglib>
```

The Web Application Deployment Descriptor (web.xml)

The web application deployment descriptor is used to set up the web application's container. It includes descriptive meta-data about the web application, as well as application-scope parameters and various servlet registration parameters:

```xml
<?xml version="1.0" encoding="ISO-8859-1"?>
<!DOCTYPE web-app
    PUBLIC "-//Sun Microsystems, Inc.//DTD Web Application 2.2//EN"
    "http://java.sun.com/j2ee/dtds/web-app_2.2.dtd">
```

```
<web-app>
  <display-name>JResources.com JDBC Connector Servlet</display-name>
  <description>
    The JResources.com JDBC Connector Servlet is a Java
    servlet that provides an XML-based interface to JDBC data
    sources. With the JResources.com JDBC connector servlet,
    web developers now have an easy way to query and modify
    JDBC databases without writing a line of Java code.
  </description>
```

For JCS, we will set up a couple of application-scope parameters that will facilitate development of our sample guestbook application, to be discussed in the next section. These include the default JDBC URL of the guestbook application's ODBC system DSN, as well as a sample output message. These parameters are read into an instance of `java.util.Properties` by the `com.jresources.jcs.jcsCustomTag` class to allow it to be passed to the `jcsEngine`, where the key-value pairs can be read into custom JCS variables:

```
<context-param>
  <param-name>jdbc_url</param-name>
  <param-value>jdbc:odbc:guestbook</param-value>
  <description>
    The default URL for the guestbook app's database
  </description>
</context-param>
<context-param>
  <param-name>output</param-name>
  <param-value>
    This is an example of using JCS from a JSP with custom
    properties read from the web application's context parameters.
    In Tomcat, these are set up in the WEB-INF/web.xml file
  </param-value>
  <description>
    Sample output for the guestbook app
  </description>
</context-param>
```

Next, we need to register the `JDBCConnectorServlet`. We'll give it the alias `JCS`, and some parameters. As we discussed, the `JDBCConnectorServlet` can handle an arbitrary list of initialization parameters, which it reads into an instance of `java.util.Properties` for consumption by the JCS engine as custom JCS variables. We'll also map the JCS servlet to files with an extension of `*.jcs`. This will cause the servlet engine to dispatch all URL requests for JCS files to the `JDBCConnectorServlet` for handling:

```
<servlet>
  <servlet-name>
    JCS
  </servlet-name>
  <servlet-class>
    com.jresources.servlets.JDBCConnectorServlet
  </servlet-class>
  <init-param>
    <param-name>
      defaultDriver
    </param-name>
    <param-value>
```

```
            sun.jdbc.odbc.JdbcOdbcDriver
        </param-value>
      </init-param>
   </servlet>
   <servlet-mapping>
     <servlet-name>
       JCS
     </servlet-name>
     <url-pattern>
       *.jcs
     </url-pattern>
   </servlet-mapping>
```

Finally, we must register our custom tag library descriptor and specify its location in the web application's file structure. Per the directory structure recommended in the servlet 2.2 specification, we will place the tag library descriptor in the web application's WEB-INF directory:

```
   <taglib>
     <taglib-uri>
        http://www.jresources.com/jcs/jcs_taglib.tld
     </taglib-uri>
     <taglib-location>
        /WEB-INF/jcs_taglib.tld
     </taglib-location>
   </taglib>
 </web-app>
```

Packaging the Framework for J2EE Deployment

We are now ready to compile our Java classes, build a JAR archive, generate javadoc, and package the whole ball of wax into a web application archive for easy deployment, distribution, and installation on J2EE web containers. The JDBC Connector Servlet should work in any servlet engine that supports the Java Servlet API version 2.2 or higher, and the JSP specification 1.1 or higher. However, it was developed and extensively tested using Tomcat 3.1, the open-source servlet and JSP reference implementation developed by the Apache Group. Consequently, we will use Tomcat to run all of the examples we go through in the remainder of the chapter.

The code in this chapter is contained within the C:\ProJavaServer\Chapter16\ directory, within which are the directories:

❑ jcs
  The root directory, which contains the index.html home page

❑ jcs\bin
  Contains the build.bat batch file used to build the JCS web application

❑ jcs\doc
  The javadoc API documentation for the JCS framework

❑ jcs\samples
  Files for the Guestbook and SQL Server database browser sample applications

❑ jcs\src
  The JCS Java source code

- ❑ jcs\WEB-INF
  Java class files, web.xml, tag library descriptor, etc.

- ❑ tomcat
  The WAR file generated by the build.bat script

The first step is to perform the build process. To accomplish this in the most efficient manner, we use a Windows batch file, called build.bat. This process includes:

- ❑ Compiling the Java source

- ❑ Packaging the bytecode into a JAR

- ❑ Generating API documentation using javadoc

- ❑ Packaging our entire application into a WAR (web application archive) using the jar tool

Compile the Java Classes

First, we'll compile our classes using javac. Since our classes import classes from the servlet API packages, we must ensure that Tomcat's servlet.jar is in the CLASSPATH. The resulting bytecode goes into the web application's WEB-INF/classes directory:

```
@echo off
REM These are the variables that javac needs
set myClasspath=..\WEB-INF\classes
set basepath=..\src
set TOMCAT_HOME=c:\jakarta-tomcat
set CLASSPATH=%TOMCAT_HOME%\lib\servlet.jar;
REM Compile the code...
javac -d %myClasspath% -classpath %CLASSPATH% %basepath%\*.java
```

Package the Bytecode into a JAR

Next, we'll build the JAR archive. This goes into the web application's /WEB-INF/lib/ directory:

```
REM Set the directory where the JAR should be built
set jarpath=..\WEB-INF\lib
REM Build the JAR...
jar cvf %jarpath%\jcs1.0.jar -C %myClasspath%\ .
```

Generate the Javadoc Documentation

Thirdly, we'll generate our javadoc API documentation. This will go into the web application's doc/ subdirectory. Once again, we need to ensure that servlet.jar is placed into the CLASSPATH:

```
REM Set the directory where the javadoc files should be built
set docpath=..\doc
REM Build the javadoc...
javadoc -d %docpath% -classpath %CLASSPATH% %basepath%\*.java
```

Package the Application into a WAR

Finally, we'll use the jar tool to package the entire application into a WAR file. Once this is built, we can distribute the application to our end users:

```
REM Set the directory where the completed WAR should be built (warpath), and the
directory to be recursively archived (apppath)
set warpath=..\..\tomcat
set apppath=..\..\jcs
REM Build the WAR...
jar cvf %warpath%\jcs.war -C %apppath%\ .
```

Deploying JCS to a J2EE Servlet Container

Once the JCS WAR file is built, we can now deploy it to a J2EE servlet container. Once again, we will use Tomcat 3.1:

❑   If Tomcat is already running, stop it using the shutdown.bat batch file (or the shutdown.sh shell script for UNIX users) in the \jakarta-tomcat\bin directory.

❑   Locate the \ProJavaServer\Chapter16\code\tomcat\jcs.war web application archive, and place it in the \jakarta-tomcat\webapps directory. If there is an unpacked, older version of JCS in the webapps directory, delete it. (This would happen if you are redeploying the WAR file after tweaking the source code and re-running the build.bat batch file.)

❑   Start Tomcat by running the startup.bat (or startup.sh for UNIX users) shell script.

❑   Point your browser to http://localhost:8080/jcs/index.html. This file is located in the jcs.war archive's file system root. Tomcat will automatically unpack the archive at the first access. You should see this page:

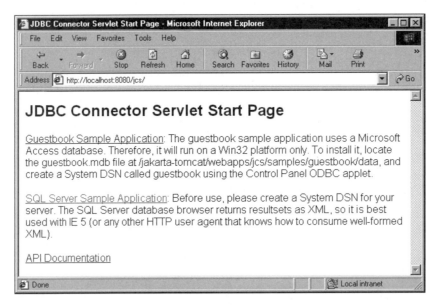

If you are using another servlet runner, installation will vary. If it supports the servlet 2.2 specification, it should be able to consume the jcs.war file in a manner similar to Tomcat. JCS can also be used in older servlet runners that conform to the servlet version 2.1 and the JSP 1.0 specifications (minus the

JSP custom tag, which requires JSP 1.1 support). For these servlet runners, you must, as a general rule, perform the following steps:

- ❑ Unpack the `jcs.war` file using any zip compression tool (such as Winzip or PKZip) or `jar`.
- ❑ Place the `jcs1.0.jar` file in your VM's CLASSPATH.
- ❑ Create an alias called JCS for the `com.jresources.servlets.JDBCConnectorServlet` class.
- ❑ Create a mapping between JCS and the `*.jcs` file mask.

Once you have installed JCS, you can invoke the servlet one of the following ways:

- ❑ `http://hostname/dir/YourQueryName.jcs`.
- ❑ `http://hostname/servlet/JCS/dir/YourQueryName.jcs`.
- ❑ `http://hostname/webappname/servlet/JCS/dir/YourQueryName.jcs`.

Using the JDBC Connector Servlet

Now that we have built JCS, we can start using it to develop applications. This section will get you started using JCS to develop database-driven web applications. We will cover two applications:

- ❑ The Guestbook application.
- ❑ The SQL Server database browser.

The code for both of these sample applications can be downloaded from our web site. After you have downloaded the sample code archive, unpack it and look in the `\ProJavaServer\Chapter18\code\jcs\samples` directory.

The Guestbook Sample Application

The Guestbook application is a simple, yet comprehensive, example of the types of applications you can develop using JCS. This application allows you to:

- ❑ View a guestbook using both a web browser and a WAP (wireless access protocol) device.
- ❑ Consume guestbook data using any device that can parse well-formed XML (such as another application).
- ❑ Add and delete an entry.

The application shows various levels of JSP integration, and helps bring everything together by illustrating the following JCS concepts:

- ❑ Creating a SELECT query.
- ❑ Adding and modifying data using INSERT and DELETE SQL statements.
- ❑ Generating XML output from query results.

❑ Using JCS from within a JSP.

❑ Using server-side XSLT with JCS. This technique allows you to get a clean separation of database content and presentation by authoring JCS queries that return XML, XSL stylesheets that define presentation, and using the Xalan XSLT processor within a JSP to transform the XML data into HTML and WML in a device-independent manner.

The chart below shows the high level architecture of the Guestbook application. The application contains three general categories of files:

❑ **JCS files that implement database operations**
These include viewing the entire guestbook in HTML and XML formats, viewing a particular guestbook entry, and adding and deleting a guestbook entry.

❑ **JSP files that demonstrate JCS/JSP integration**
These use both the bean interface and the JSP custom tag. Most of the JSPs duplicate functionality implemented in the aforementioned JCS files, although there are two examples that show server side XSLT from JCS-generated XML resultsets. The JSPs target both web browsers and WAP devices.

❑ **Library files that are reused by the JCS and JSP files**
Most of these files are server-side include files that contain common look-and-feel and navigation, as well as useful client-side JavaScript functions.

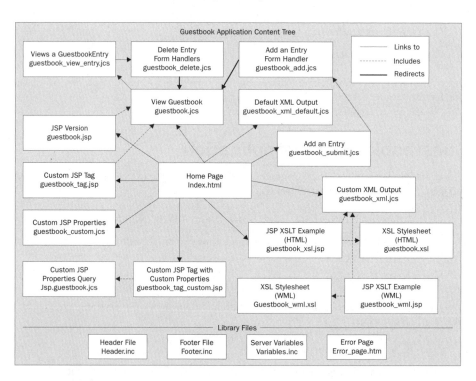

In the next couple of sections, we will walk through how to build this application using JCS:

Once you have placed the `jcs.war` application archive in the `jakarta-tomcat\webapps` directory and started Tomcat, you will find the Guestbook sample application at `http://localhost:8080/jcs/samples/guestbook/index.html`. When you open this URL, you should see a page that looks like this:

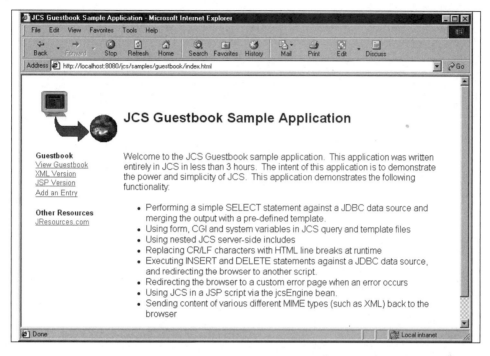

Since it uses a Microsoft Access database, it will run unmodified on a Win32 platform only. To ensure that the database is installed correctly, locate the `guestbook.mdb` file in `/jakarta-tomcat/webapps/jcs/samples/guestbook/data`, and create a System DSN called **Guestbook** that points to this MDB file using the **Control Panel ODBC** applet.

Creating a SELECT query

The first query that we will discuss is `guestbook.jcs`, which enumerates through all of the guestbook entries, sorted by date in ascending order. In the first part of the query, we will define the URL of the JDBC data source (the Guestbook system DSN we created above), and the SQL statement. Please note that since we have not specified a JDBC driver; we will use the default driver, which is the Sun ODBC-JDBC bridge (`sun.jdbc.odbc.JdbcOdbcDriver`). We are also omitting the `<jcs:jdbc_uid>` and `<jcs:jdbc_pwd>` tags. Our Microsoft Access database is unsecured, so a User ID and password are not needed:

```xml
<?xml version="1.0"?>
<jcs:query xmlns:jcs="http://www.jresources.com/xml/jcs/1.0">
  <jcs:jdbc_url>jdbc:odbc:guestbook</jcs:jdbc_url>
  <jcs:sql>SELECT * FROM guestbook ORDER BY date</jcs:sql>
```

The next step is to define the output template for the resultset returned by our query. This template contains two server-side includes (a header and footer file). It also contains the `<jcs:resultset>` enumeration tag, as well as field variables interspersed with HTML markup. To 'time stamp' the output, we will use the `#system.date#` JCS variable:

```
<jcs:template>
  <![CDATA[
    <jcs:include>
      templates\header.inc
    </jcs:include>
      <p><b>Guestbook Entries</b> (as of #system.date#)</p>
      <table>
        <tr>
          <td>
            <b>Visitor</b>
          </td>
          <td>
            <b>Date</b>
          </td>
        </tr>
        <jcs:resultset>
          <tr>
            <td>
              <a href="guestbook_view_entry.jcs?ID=#ID#">#fname# #lname#</a>
            </td>
            <td>
              <i>#date#</i>
            </td>
          </tr>
        </jcs:resultset>
      </table>
    <jcs:include>
      templates\footer.inc
    </jcs:include>
  ]]>
</jcs:template>
```

What happens if there are no records in the guestbook data table? If that is the case, we want to return a custom message informing the user of this. To do this, we will use the `<jcs:empty_resultset_output>` tag. If the query returns an empty result set, the contents of this CDATA section will be inserted into the output stream in lieu of the `<jcs:resultset>` tag's output:

```
<jcs:empty_resultset_output>
  <![CDATA[
  <tr>
  <td colspan="2">
  <font color="red">There are no entries in the guestbook.</font>
  </td>
  </tr>
  ]]>
</jcs:empty_resultset_output>

<jcs:line_break_character>HTML</jcs:line_break_character>
</jcs:query>
```

When we request `guestbook.jcs`, the output looks like this:

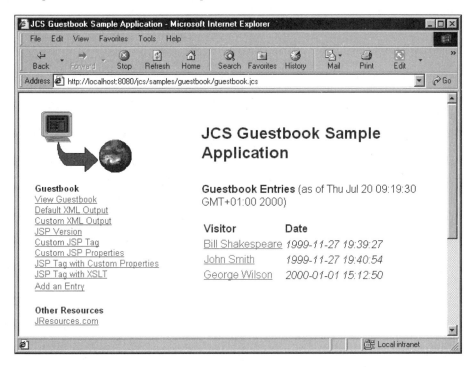

Creating an INSERT Query

Our next step is to create a JCS INSERT query. This will allow users to add entries to the guestbook. We will name this query `guestbook_add.jcs`. This query will be the HTTP POST action handler for the following HTML form:

```
<form method="POST" action="guestbook_add.jcs">
  <p>Your first name: <input type="text" name="fname" size="20"></p>
  <p>Your last name:  <input type="text" name="lname" size="20"></p>
  <p>Your comments:  <textarea rows="5" name="comments"
    cols="30"></textarea></p>
  <p><input type="submit" value="Submit" name="B1"><input type="reset"
    value="Reset" name="B2"></p>
</form>
```

The SQL statement contains several different JCS variables and tags to allow the insertion of dynamic data into the guestbook database. It uses the `#system.UID#` variable to generate a unique ID for the guestbook data table's primary key field. It uses various form variables that map to the key names of the input objects on the aforementioned HTML form. Note how the form variables are encapsulated by the `<jcs:encode_sql>` tag. This directive allows users to use single quotes within their guestbook entries. To enter the IP address of the requesting host into the guestbook table's host field, we will use the `#CGI.REMOTE_ADDR#` variable:

```
<?xml version="1.0"?>
<jcs:query xmlns:jcs="http://www.jresources.com/xml/jcs/1.0">
   <jcs:jdbc_url>jdbc:odbc:guestbook</jcs:jdbc_url>
   <jcs:sql>
INSERT INTO guestbook ("ID", "fname", "lname", "comments", "host", "date") VALUES
('#system.UID#','<jcs:encode_sql>#form.fname#</jcs:encode_sql>','<jcs:encode_sql>#
form.lname#</jcs:encode_sql>', '<jcs:encode_sql>#form.comments#</jcs:encode_sql>',
'#CGI.REMOTE_ADDR#', Now())
   </jcs:sql>
```

Since `guestbook_add.jcs` is an INSERT query, it will not return a resultset. Consequently, we will not include the `<jcs:template>` and `<jcs:empty_resultset_output>` tags. Instead, we will use the `<jcs_redirect_url>` tag to redirect the requesting user agent to `guestbook.jcs` upon successful completion of the transaction. If an exception occurs, we will redirect the browser to a custom error page (`error_page.htm`) using the `<jcs:error_page>` tag:

```
   <jcs:redirect_url>guestbook.jcs</jcs:redirect_url>
   <jcs:error_page>error_page.htm</jcs:error_page>
</jcs:query>
```

Creating a DELETE Query

Our next step is to create a JCS DELETE query. This will allow authorized users to delete guestbook entries. We will call this query `guestbook_delete.jcs`. To identify which guestbook entry ID to delete, we'll read that from the ID key of the query string:

```
<?xml version="1.0"?>
<jcs:query xmlns:jcs="http://www.jresources.com/xml/jcs/1.0">
   <jcs:jdbc_url>jdbc:odbc:guestbook</jcs:jdbc_url>
   <jcs:sql>
     delete from guestbook where ID = '#form.ID#'
   </jcs:sql>
   <jcs:redirect_url>guestbook.jcs</jcs:redirect_url>
   <jcs:error_page>error_page.htm</jcs:error_page>
</jcs:query>
```

Generating Default XML Output (JDBC Resultset Serialized as XML)

With JCS, you can support different MIME types. For example, you can serialize a resultset as an XML document, thereby allowing virtually any type of client to consume the results of your query using the XML DOM. By default, the JDBC Connector Servlet serializes the resultset as an XML document if no `<jcs:template>` tag is provided in the query. This serialized XML resultset is returned to the HTTP user agent as MIME type `text/xml`. For example, we will create a query called `guestbook_xml_default.jcs`. Here's the source code listing for this file:

```
<?xml version="1.0"?>
<jcs:query xmlns:jcs="http://www.jresources.com/xml/jcs/1.0">
   <jcs:jdbc_url>jdbc:odbc:guestbook</jcs:jdbc_url>
   <jcs:sql>select * from guestbook order by date</jcs:sql>
</jcs:query>
```

The output returned to the browser will look like this, assuming you are using Microsoft Internet Explorer 5.0 (if you are using an older browser, it will prompt you to save it to a file):

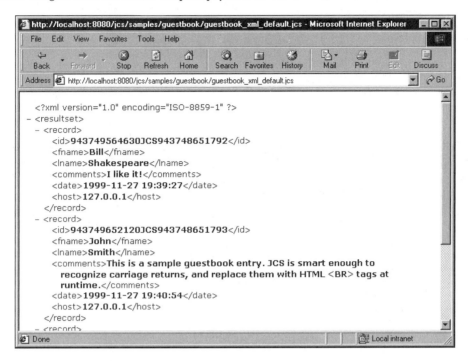

Generating Custom XML Output

However, what if you want to stream your data to the calling client using a custom XML structure? You can do this easily by creating a query that specifies a MIME type of text/xml, and authoring a template that dynamically creates your XML document. Here's how you do it:

Create your query, using the `<jcs:mime_type>` tag to specify the MIME type of your output (in this case, text/xml). This query is located in `\wrox\ProJavaServer\Chapter16\code\jcs\samples\guestbook\guestbook_xml.jcs`:

```
<?xml version="1.0"?>
<jcs:query xmlns:jcs="http://www.jresources.com/xml/jcs/1.0">
  <jcs:mime_type>text/xml</jcs:mime_type>
  <jcs:jdbc_url>jdbc:odbc:guestbook</jcs:jdbc_url>
  <jcs:sql>select * from guestbook order by date</jcs:sql>
  <jcs:template>
    <![CDATA[
    <?xml version="1.0"?>
    <guestbook date="#system.date#">
    <jcs:resultset>
    <entry id="#ID#">
    <visitor fname="#fname#" lname="#lname#"/>
    <comments>
    #comments#
```

```
            </comments>
            <date>#date#</date>
            <host>#host#</host>
            </entry>
            </jcs:resultset>
            </guestbook>
            ]]>
        </jcs:template>
    </jcs:query>
```

Now run your query. This is what your output will look like in Microsoft Internet Explorer 5.0:

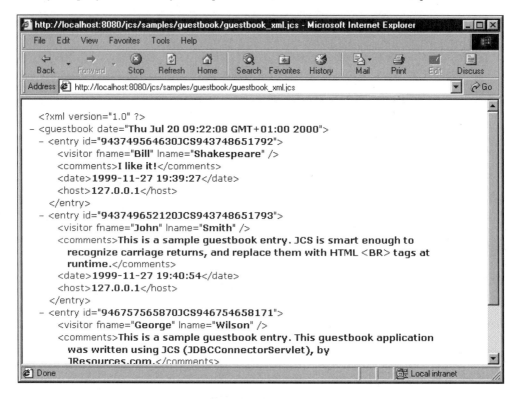

Using the jcsEngine Bean in a JSP Page

Suppose you want to integrate JCS queries with an existing JSP? It's easy: the JCS engine provides a bean interface for integration with JSPs (or custom servlets, for that matter). To do so, create a JSP that creates an instance of the jcsEngine class, calls the processRequest() method, and queries the response type to determine whether to put the response in the HTTP output stream, or redirect the client to the URL specified in the response. We'll call this file guestbook.jsp. When executed, this JSP will produce output exactly like the output of guestbook.jcs, shown in an earlier screen shot:

```
<jsp:useBean id="jcs" scope="request" class="com.jresources.jcs.jcsEngine" />
<%
try {
  jcs.processRequest(request, getServletConfig().getServletContext().
                             getRealPath("/samples/guestbook/guestbook.jcs"));
}
catch (Exception e) {}
if (jcs.getResponseType() == com.jresources.jcs.jcsEngine.RESPONSE_REDIRECT) {
  response.sendRedirect(jcs.getResponse());
} else {
%>
<%=jcs.getResponse()%>
<%
}
%>
```

If you need to send custom properties to the JCS engine, the engine provides an interface to do this using the java.util.Properties class. You can reference these properties in a JCS query using the #jcs.propname# variable convention mentioned earlier in this chapter. In this example, our JSP, called guestbook_custom.jsp, creates a Properties object, and stores two keys in it: a JDBC URL in the jdbc_url key, and a little message in a key named output:

```
<jsp:useBean id="jcs" scope="request" class="com.jresources.jcs.jcsEngine" />
<%
java.util.Properties prop = new java.util.Properties();
prop.put("jdbc_url", "jdbc:odbc:guestbook");
prop.put("output", "This is an example of using JCS from a JSP with custom
properties passed from the JSP script to the JCS engine");
try{
  jcs.processRequest(request, prop,
                     getServletConfig().getServletContext().
                         getRealPath("/samples/guestbook/jsp.guestbook.jcs"));
} catch (Exception e) {}
if (jcs.getResponseType() == com.jresources.jcs.jcsEngine.RESPONSE_REDIRECT) {
  response.sendRedirect(jcs.getResponse());
} else {
%>
<%=jcs.getResponse()%>
<%
}
%>
```

Now let's look at the jsp.guestbook.jcs query. You'll notice that the <jcs:jdbc_url> node references the #jcs.jdbc_url# custom variable, and the <jcs:template> tag puts the value of the #jcs.output# variable into the HTTP response stream:

```
<?xml version="1.0"?>
<jcs:query xmlns:jcs="http://www.jresources.com/xml/jcs/1.0">
  <jcs:jdbc_url>#jcs.jdbc_url#</jcs:jdbc_url>
  <jcs:sql>select * from guestbook order by date</jcs:sql>
  <jcs:template>
    <![CDATA[
    <jcs:include>
```

```
      templates/header.inc
    </jcs:include>
    <p><b>Guestbook Entries</b> (as of #system.date#)</p>
    <table>
      <tr>
        <td>
          <b>Visitor</b>
        </td>
        <td>
          <b>Date</b>
        </td>
      </tr>
      <jcs:resultset>
      <tr>
        <td>
          <a href="guestbook_view_entry.jcs?ID=#ID#">#fname# #lname#</a>
        </td>
        <td>
          <i>#date#</i>
        </td>
      </tr>
      </jcs:resultset>
    </table>
    <p><b>#jcs.output#</b></p>
    <jcs:include>
      templates/footer.inc
    </jcs:include>
    ]]>
  </jcs:template>
  <jcs:line_break_character>HTML</jcs:line_break_character>
</jcs:query>
```

This is what the query looks like when it is run. Notice the text that is displayed at the bottom of the right-hand portion of the page:

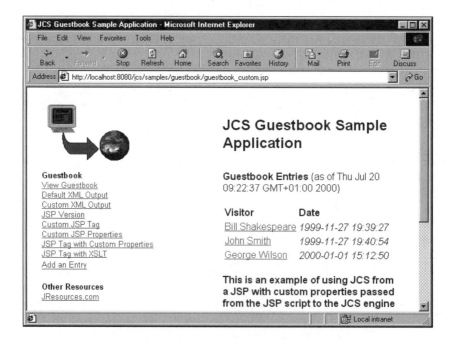

Using the <jcs:query_object> Custom Tag in a JSP Page

JCS also provides a custom tag interface for integration with JSP. This <jcs:query_object> tag implemented by the com.jresources.jcs.jcsCustomTag class discussed above. The <jcs:query_object> tag has two attributes:

❑ url, used to assign your JCS query's virtual path.

❑ outputvariable. The <jcs:query_object> tag assigns the jcsEngine output to a String variable that has the same name as the value of this attribute. From there, the JSP can reference the JCS engine's output through this variable.

Here's an example. This file is entitled guestbook_tag.jsp, and is located in the sample application:

```
<%@ taglib uri="http://www.jresources.com/jcs/jcs_taglib.tld" prefix="jcs" %>

<jcs:query_object url="/samples/guestbook/guestbook.jcs"
 outputvariable="guestbook" />

<%=guestbook%>
```

The example works as follows:

❑ The tag library is referenced using the taglib directive.

❑ The <jcs:query_object> tag is used to reference the guestbook.jcs query and assign the query results to the guestbook scripting variable.

❑ The contents of the guestbook variable are output to the browser.

Using XSLT with JCS

The examples we walked through in the previous sections involved sending the output of a JCS query directly to the calling client. But suppose you want to author JCS queries in a manner that is independent from how the data will be ultimately displayed on a device? For example, you might want to author a query that will be displayed by a web browser as HTML and a WAP client as WML. Additionally, you want other applications to be able to consume the XML output from this query using a DOM or SAX parser.

You can implement this 'device-independent content delivery architecture' using XSLT. To do this, you author a JCS query that returns your resultset as XML, as we discussed in previous sections. For each content type, you author an XSL stylesheet that algorithmically transforms your XML output to another XML format, such as 'well-formed' HTML, or WML. Then you use an XSLT processor, such as Xalan 1.1, to perform your XSLT operations. This architecture is illustrated in the figure over:

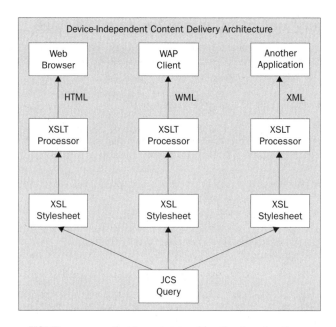

Xalan is an open-source XSLT processor that is maintained by the Apache Group; you can download version 1.1 from `http://xml.apache.org`. To use it in Tomcat applications, ensure that the `xalan.jar` and `xerces.jar` (the Xerces XML parser) archives are in Tomcat's `CLASSPATH`. If you don't want to use Xalan, or you would like to try another XSLT processor, there are several quality XSLT processors implemented in Java. Examples include:

❏ IBM LotusXSL (`http://alphaworks.ibm.com/tech/LotusXSL`)

❏ James Clark's XT package (`http://www.jclark.com/xml/xt.html`)

To give you an example, we will first create a XSL stylesheet that transforms our custom Guestbook XML document discussed earlier to HTML. We'll call this file `guestbook.xsl`. This stylesheet reproduces the 'look-and-feel' of the Guestbook application's main page, shown above. The stylesheet looks like this:

```
<?xml version='1.0'?>
<xsl:stylesheet xmlns:xsl="http://www.w3.org/1999/XSL/Transform" version="1.0">
  <xsl:template match="/">
  <xsl:apply-templates/>
  </xsl:template>
  <xsl:template match="guestbook">

    (Additional mark-up removed for brevity)

    <p><b>Guestbook Entries</b> (as of <xsl:value-of select="@date"/>)</p>

    (Additional mark-up removed for brevity)

    <xsl:apply-templates/>

    (Additional mark-up removed for brevity)
```

```
      </xsl:template>
      <xsl:template match="entry">
        <tr>
          <td>
            <a>
              <xsl:attribute name="href">
                guestbook_view_entry.jcs?ID=<xsl:value-of select="@id"/>
              </xsl:attribute>
              <xsl:value-of select="visitor/@fname"/>
              <xsl:text> </xsl:text>
              <xsl:value-of select="visitor/@lname"/>
            </a>
          </td>
          <td>
            <i><xsl:value-of select="date"/></i>
          </td>
        </tr>
      </xsl:template>
    </xsl:stylesheet>
```

Next, we will create a JSP that will encapsulate both the JCS query execution and the XSLT operation. The Xalan XSLT processor will perform the transformation using the results of the JCS query and the XSL stylesheet file, and place the resulting HTML in the HTTP response stream. This file is called guestbook_xsl.jsp, and is located in the sample application:

```
<%@ page
import="org.xml.sax.SAXException,org.apache.xalan.xslt.XSLTProcessorFactory,org.ap
ache.xalan.xslt.XSLTInputSource,org.apache.xalan.xslt.XSLTResultTarget,org.apache.
xalan.xslt.XSLTProcessor" %>
<%@ taglib uri="http://www.jresources.com/jcs/jcs_taglib.tld" prefix="jcs" %>
<jcs:query_object url="/samples/guestbook/guestbook_xml.jcs"
outputvariable="guestbook" />
<%
try {
  XSLTProcessor processor = XSLTProcessorFactory.getProcessor();
  processor.process(new XSLTInputSource(
                      new java.io.StringReader(guestbook.toString())),
                      new XSLTInputSource("file:///" +
                      getServletConfig().getServletContext()
                        .getRealPath("/samples/guestbook/guestbook.xsl")),
                    new XSLTResultTarget(out));
} catch(Exception e) {
%>
An error occurred processing your operation
<%
}
%>
```

If we want to extend this application to wireless devices such as web phones, we can simply create a new XSL stylesheet that transforms our custom Guestbook XML document discussed earlier to WML (wireless markup language). We'll call this file guestbook_wml.xsl. This stylesheet presents the data contained in our guestbook in a manner that is appropriate for small screen wireless devices:

```
<?xml version='1.0'?>
<xsl:stylesheet xmlns:xsl="http://www.w3.org/1999/XSL/Transform" version="1.0">
  <xsl:template match="/">
    <xsl:apply-templates/>
  </xsl:template>
  <xsl:template match="guestbook">
    <wml>
      <head>
        <meta http-equiv="Cache-Control" content="max-age=0"/>
      </head>
      <card id="i1">
        <p>
          <xsl:apply-templates/>
        </p>
      </card>
    </wml>
  </xsl:template>
  <xsl:template match="entry">
    <b>
      <xsl:value-of select="visitor/@lname"/>
      ,
      <xsl:value-of select="visitor/@fname"/>
    </b>
    <br/>
    <xsl:value-of select="date"/>
    <br/>
    <xsl:value-of select="comments"/>
    <br/>
  </xsl:template>
</xsl:stylesheet>
```

Of course, we must modify the JSP to account for the different stylesheet file name, as well as the different MIME type required for WAP devices (text/vnd.wap.wml). We'll call this file guestbook_wml.jsp:

```
<%@ page
import="org.xml.sax.SAXException,org.apache.xalan.xslt.XSLTProcessorFactory,org.ap
ache.xalan.xslt.XSLTInputSource,org.apache.xalan.xslt.XSLTResultTarget,org.apache.
xalan.xslt.XSLTProcessor" %>
<%@ taglib uri="http://www.jresources.com/jcs/jcs_taglib.tld" prefix="jcs" %>
<jcs:query_object url="/samples/guestbook/guestbook_xml.jcs"
outputvariable="guestbook" />
<%
//set the correct MIME type for WAP
response.setContentType("text/vnd.wap.wml");

/* This sample uses Xalan 1.0.1. Download it from http://xml.apache.org. Ensure
   that xalan.jar and xerces.jar are in Tomcat's classpath. */

try {
  XSLTProcessor processor = XSLTProcessorFactory.getProcessor();
  processor.process(new XSLTInputSource(
                      new java.io.StringReader(guestbook.toString())),
                  new XSLTInputSource("file:///" +
                    getServletConfig().getServletContext()
```

```
                            .getRealPath("/samples/guestbook/guestbook_wml.xsl")),
                    new XSLTResultTarget(out));
} catch(Exception e) {
%>
An error occurred processing your operation
<%
}
%>
```

When a web phone user points his device to `guestbook_wml.jsp` URL, the phone will forward it through the wireless service provider's WAP gateway to the web server. The web server will send the HTTP response back to the WAP gateway, which will send it back to the phone. The resulting output will look like this:

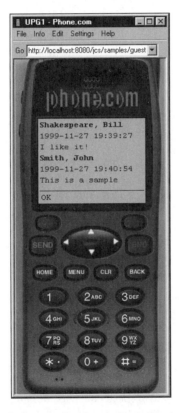

As you can see from walking through the guestbook sample application, JCS is a simple yet powerful framework for developing device-independent, data-driven web applications. In the next section, we will continue to build on this framework by developing an SQL Server database browser using JCS.

The SQL Server Database Browser Application

The SQL Server database browser application shows you how to use JCS to create a simple web-based interface to SQL Server databases with only 49 lines of XML mark-up. Since most of the data is streamed back to the calling client as XML, this application could also be used as a simple HTTP and XML-based data

server for Internet applications. It is located at
`http://localhost:8080/jcs/samples/sqlserver/default.htm`. Before use, create a System DSN to your SQL Server database. The database browser returns resultsets as XML, so it is best used with Microsoft Internet Explorer 5.0 or higher (or any other HTTP user agent that knows how to consume well-formed XML). This chart shows the architecture of the database browser application:

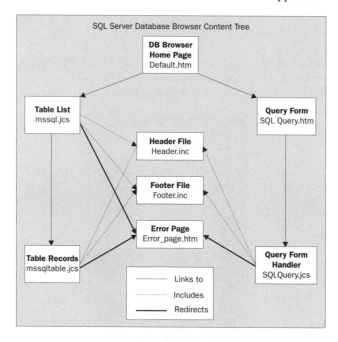

The database browser application can easily be modified to access an Oracle database instead of SQL Server – the relevant code is included in the download for this chapter and can be accessed at `http://localhost:8080/jcs/samples/oracle/default.htm`. You will need to download the Oracle JDBC thin driver package from `http://www.oracle.com` and place it in your CLASSPATH.

Enumerating Through SQL Server Tables

The SQL Server database browser's home page contains an HTML form that provides the user with an interface to enter database connection information. This information includes the System DSN name, user ID, and password. It also contains a field to specify the maximum number of records to return. The default value of this field is 500 records. This allows the user to 'throttle' the output to prevent JCS from returning all of the records of a huge table.

As an aside, when I first developed the database browser application, I did not have this functionality built in. Consequently, the first query I ran returned all of the rows of a 10,000 record table. As verbose as XML is, the document sent back was probably between 5-10 megabytes. The JCS servlet on the remote web server handled it without a problem; unfortunately, when my local copy of IE 5.0 tried to render the entire document, the NT workstation I was working on ran out of virtual memory, and subsequently 'blue-screened'.

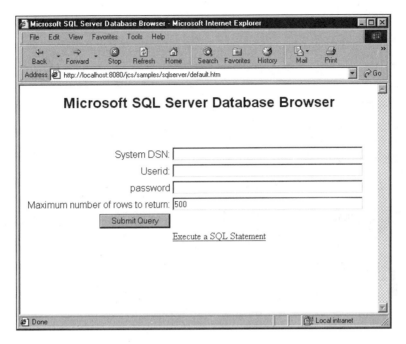

When the user submits this form, it posts to a JCS query called `mssql.jcs`. This query uses the form input to dynamically construct the JDBC URL, using the JDBC-ODBC Bridge. The SQL statement returns the names of all of the tables the user is authorized to view:

```
<?xml version="1.0"?>
<jcs:query xmlns:jcs="http://www.jresources.com/xml/jcs/1.0">
  <jcs:mime_type>text/html</jcs:mime_type>
  <jcs:jdbc_url>jdbc:odbc:#form.dbname#</jcs:jdbc_url>
  <jcs:jdbc_uid>#form.uid#</jcs:jdbc_uid>
  <jcs:jdbc_pwd>#form.pwd#</jcs:jdbc_pwd>

  <jcs:sql>select name from sysobjects where type = 'U'</jcs:sql>
```

As we enumerate through all of the table names in the resultset, we create a hyperlink for each table. For the hyperlink's target, we dynamically construct a query string from the form input. This will ensure that database connect information is passed to the follow-on query, `mssqltable.jcs` (more on this later). If the JCS engine throws an exception, we will redirect the user to an error page:

```
<jcs:template>
  <![CDATA[
  <jcs:include>
    header.inc
  </jcs:include>
  <p align="center"><font size="5" face="Arial"><strong>SQL Server
  Database Tables for #form.dbname#</strong></font></p>

  <p><font face="Arial"></font> </p>
  <jcs:resultset>
```

```
<a href="mssqltable.jcs?tablename=#name#&uid=#form.uid#&pwd=#form.pwd#&dbname=#for
m.dbname#&maxrows=#form.maxrows#">#name#</a>
<br>
    </jcs:resultset>
    <jcs:include>
       footer.inc
    </jcs:include>
    ]]>
   </jcs:template>
   <jcs:error_page>error_page.htm</jcs:error_page>
</jcs:query>
```

When we run this query, the output will look like this:

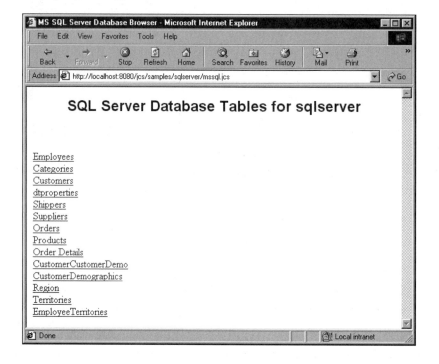

Note that we are using the Microsoft's Northwind sample database here.

Serializing a SQL Server Table as an XML Document

When the user clicks on one of the hyperlinks created by `mssql.jcs`, the browser sends an HTTP GET request to `mssqltable.jcs`. In this case, the JCS form variables are read from the key-value pairs sent in the query string. `mssqltable.jcs` will simply select all rows from the specified table, using the `maxrows` parameter to limit the size of the resultset. Since we have not included an output template, JCS will simply serialize the resultset as an XML document using the `XMLSerializableResultset` class, and send it back as MIME type `text/xml`:

```xml
<?xml version="1.0"?>
<jcs:query xmlns:jcs="http://www.jresources.com/xml/jcs/1.0">
  <jcs:mime_type>text/xml</jcs:mime_type>
  <jcs:jdbc_url>jdbc:odbc:#form.dbname#</jcs:jdbc_url>
  <jcs:jdbc_uid>#form.uid#</jcs:jdbc_uid>
  <jcs:jdbc_pwd>#form.pwd#</jcs:jdbc_pwd>

  <jcs:sql>select * from [#form.tablename#]</jcs:sql>
  <jcs:error_page>error_page.htm</jcs:error_page>
  <jcs:maxrows>#form.maxrows#</jcs:maxrows>
</jcs:query>
```

This is what the output looks like when the query is executed:

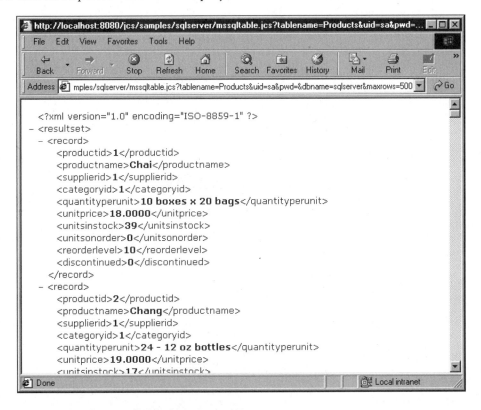

Executing an Arbitrary SQL Statement

In the previous examples, we learned how to create JCS queries that allowed simple browsing through SQL Server tables. But what if you want to execute an arbitrary SQL statement against a SQL Server database? To do that, you would simply add a `textarea` to the HTML form that allows the user to enter a valid SQL statement. If the user enters an invalid SQL statement, the error handling described below will catch it. We'll assign this `textarea` the name `sql`:

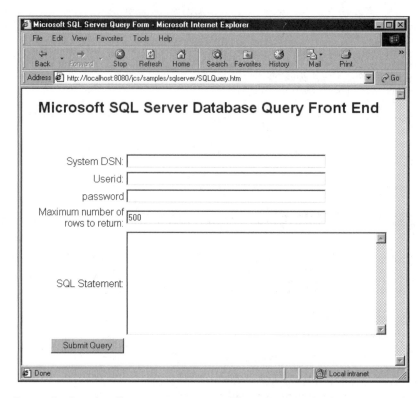

Next, we will write the form handler, SQLQuery.jcs. This query uses the form input to dynamically construct the JDBC URL. The SQL statement is read from the HTML form's sql key, and the Resultset is returned to the browser as XML using XMLSerializableResultset. If an error occurs, JCS will redirect the browser to a custom error page:

```
<?xml version="1.0"?>
<jcs:query xmlns:jcs="http://www.jresources.com/xml/jcs/1.0">
  <jcs:mime_type>text/xml</jcs:mime_type>
  <jcs:jdbc_url>jdbc:odbc:#form.dbname#</jcs:jdbc_url>
  <jcs:jdbc_uid>#form.uid#</jcs:jdbc_uid>
  <jcs:jdbc_pwd>#form.pwd#</jcs:jdbc_pwd>

  <jcs:sql>#form.sql#</jcs:sql>
  <jcs:error_page>error_page.htm</jcs:error_page>
  <jcs:maxrows>#form.maxrows#</jcs:maxrows>
</jcs:query>
```

That's all there is to it: a simple, yet eminently useful browser-based interface to your SQL Server database servers, created using JCS.

Summary

This case study has been a quick overview of how to use the power of Java to create JCS, an XML-based scripting interface to the JDBC API that can be used in applications by web developers who are not familiar with Java. If you haven't done so already, you should download the code from our web site and play around with the guestbook and SQL Server database browser sample applications. You should also start writing some of your own JCS applications. And, if you are so inclined, you should start digging into the Java source to improve the framework. Recommended improvements include:

❑   Implementing additional JDBC functionality (e.g. prepared statements, callable statements, and transactions).

❑   Modifying the `jcsQuery` class to use one of the various DOM and SAX parsers available instead of the simple XML parsing functionality it currently uses.

❑   Adding JDBC connection pooling functionality.

❑   Defining an XML-SQL meta-language. This would allow web developers to author queries without worrying about writing SQL code. It would also make it easier to develop 'smart' query builders for JCS query authoring.

❑   Adding in-memory JCS query and SSI caching to improve performance.

In the next chapter, we'll complete our look at J2EE web components by looking at how to add e-mail support through the JavaMail API.

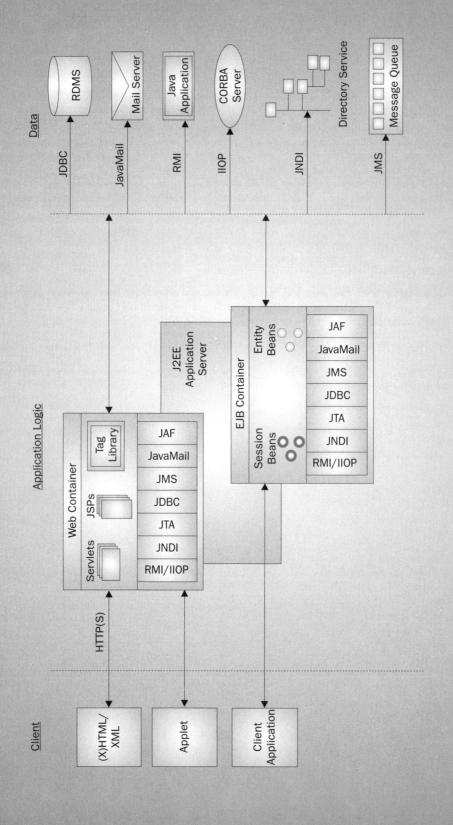

17

JavaMail

Despite the immense popularity of the World Wide Web, the Internet's most used service is still, by far, electronic mail. The ability to send messages to colleagues, friends, and loved ones is practically, by definition, fundamental to being 'on the Net'. However, the details necessary for packaging, sending, and receiving messages are complex and involve a myriad of different protocols. It seems easy from within the typical e-mail client but making the same functionality available programmatically would require learning multiple APIs and permanently coupling your application to the particular protocols those APIs exposed.

The **JavaMail** specification, however, provides a collection of abstract classes that define the common objects and their interfaces for any general mail system. By defining the interfaces for mail sessions, messages, transports, and stores, Sun has given Java programmers an easy and extensible object-oriented view of the many existing protocols currently in use.

While the interfaces and abstract classes themselves are not directly usable, it's the JavaMail providers that implement the API that provide the concrete functionality needed to communicate using specific protocols. Sun's reference JavaMail implementation includes providers for some of the most essential protocols and specifications on the Internet today. These include the **Simple Mail Transfer Protocol (SMTP)**, the **Internet Message Access Protocol (IMAP)**, and the **Multipurpose Internet Mail Extensions (MIME)**. A provider for the **Post Office Protocol 3 (POP3)** is available from Sun as well. Various other third-party providers can be obtained or you may implement these yourself.

There are basically two different types of protocols that providers can implement. A **Transport** is Sun's term for a service that has the capability to send messages to their destination. The most commonly used transport type is the ubiquitous SMTP transport. A **Store**, on the other hand, is a service you would connect to in order to retrieve messages that have been delivered to your mailbox. Most users should be familiar with the POP3 store although IMAP stores are becoming increasingly popular.

Since both the POP3 and IMAP providers implement the same interface, any JavaMail enabled application can access a POP3 store in the same manner as an IMAP store, as well as access other stores for which a provider exists (such as NNTP, P7, mbox, etc.). Specific message transports such as SMTP and X.400, for example, can also be used interchangeably.

Being able to interact with potentially any messaging system through a single API is JavaMail's greatest strength. By the end of the chapter, you should have enough of a grasp of the JavaMail API to develop enterprise components capable of taking advantage of the many existing Internet messaging protocols, and all this without having to know any of their low-level details.

Setup Instructions

Note that both the JavaMail API and Java Activation Framework are included in the Enterprise Edition of the Java 2 Platform so no separate download is necessary.

As of this writing, the current version of the JavaMail API is 1.1.3. It is not included in the current Java 2 Standard Edition distribution. You'll need to download the reference implementation from Sun's JavaMail site at `http://java.sun.com/products/javamail/`, extract the archive's contents, and ensure the included `mail.jar` file is available to the Java Virtual Machine. This is usually accomplished by adding its path to the CLASSPATH environmental variable or by specifying it on the command line using the -classpath option when invoking the interpreter.

Note that the reference implementation does include providers for SMTP and IMAP but Sun's POP3 provider will need to be downloaded separately from the same site and installed in a similar manner. Other POP3 providers by third parties do exist and Sun does maintain a list of third-party providers at their JavaMail site if you choose to use another. Some of the examples in this chapter assume that a POP3 provider is installed.

JavaMail is dependant on the Java Activation Framework being installed. You can retrieve the reference implementation from `http://java.sun.com/beans/glasgow/jaf.html`. Download, extract, and ensure the `activation.jar` file is in your CLASSPATH.

The Provider Registry

JavaMail was designed to be extensible so that when new protocols were developed, providers for those protocols could be added to a system and be immediately usable by any of the pre-existing JavaMail enabled applications with little change. The way in which these applications detect which providers are available to them is done through the **Provider Registry**.

The registry is simply a single file named `javamail.providers` which should be located in %JAVA_HOME%/lib. If that file is missing, JavaMail will look in the META-INF directory under each directory or JAR in your CLASSPATH. Once it finds that file, it stops looking and then proceeds to look for a file named `javamail.default.providers` in the same manner and add its entries to the previously found file, if any. The providers that came with Sun's JavaMail implementation are listed here. What this means to you is that you can add a single package containing any number of providers (as long as it includes a `javamail.providers` file in its META-INF directory – it should) without needing to create the 'official' registry yourself. Adding another package could possibly cause your previous providers to 'disappear', depending on what order they appear in your classpath. For our examples, we'll only be using the default providers along with Sun's POP3 provider so we shouldn't need to worry about it.

Here's a program that can list the available providers on your system:

```
import javax.mail.*;

class ListProviders
{
  public static void main(String[] args)
  {
    Session session =
      Session.getInstance(System.getProperties(), null);

    Provider[] providers = session.getProviders();

    for (int i = 0; i < providers.length; ++i)
    {
      System.out.println(providers[i]);
    }
  }
}
```

The JavaMail API

The JavaMail API is one of the larger packages in the J2EE distribution. It isn't because it is overly complex – it is, in fact, fairly simple to use and understand once you've been given a gentle introduction.

This chapter should serve as a roadmap for those who need pointed in the right direction and not as a replacement for the JavaMail documentation. It's certainly not as detailed as the generated documentation but the classes and methods are grouped in a somewhat logical and concise manner and the chapter is intended to be read from beginning-to-end to give the reader a fairly comprehensive overview of the packages.

By the end of this chapter, we will be able to:

❑   Start a JavaMail session

❑   Construct messages (with attachments)

❑   Send messages using a transport

❑   Retrieve messages from remote stores

❑   Navigate and search through the folders on remote stores

This chapter will not go into much, if any, of the details of the protocols and specifications that the JavaMail API handles for us. From time to time, we'll mention an RFC (Request For Comments) document that contains all the gory details on a particular subject that JavaMail tries to hide. For those who are interested, you can find these documents at http://ietf/org/rfc.html.

Most of the methods documented in this chapter are declared as throwing a `MessagingException`. This is the base class for all of the exceptions defined in the JavaMail API. Where appropriate, there is a mention of the specific exceptions that developers may want to handle separately.

javax.mail.Session

`javax.mail.Session` acts as a factory for the installed `Transport` and `Store` implementations. It's also responsible for managing a user's mail configuration settings and handling authentication for the individual services used during the session. Not to be confused with a `javax.servlet.http.HttpSession` object, the JavaMail `Session` is simply a way to associate providers with a particular set of user properties and an authentication mechanism. No state information (in the servlet sense) is maintained in this type of session. JavaMail sessions are usually constructed on a per user basis. So, in all likelihood, you will be storing your JavaMail session as an object in your servlet's session so that the appropriate relationship can be maintained. Your application will be retrieving the correct `Transport` and `Store` objects based on the current user's settings by interacting with the `Session`. Those transports and stores will retrieve any credentials needed to actually authenticate the user by asking the `Authenticator` object associated with the session, if needed. Note, though, that applications are in no way restricted to using a single session. In fact, server-side applications will likely be creating a session for each connected client.

Constructing a Session

Unlike most typical classes, the JavaMail `Session` class does not implement any public constructors. This might seem to hamper its usability from outside the class. Instead, potential clients are expected to use the one of the following public static methods to acquire session references:

```
static Session getInstance(Properties props, Authenticator
    authenticator)
```

The `getInstance()` method constructs and returns a new unshared `Session` instance with the specified `Properties` and `Authenticator`.

```
static Session getDefaultInstance (Properties props,
    Authenticator authenticator)
```

Returns the default (shared) `Session` instance. The first time this method is called in a VM, a new instance is constructed with the specified `Properties` and `Authenticator` and established as the default instance for that VM. Subsequent calls will ignore the properties parameter and only return the default instance if the authenticator instance is identical to the instance used when first constructing the default session. A `SecurityException` is thrown if this is not the case.

The `getInstance()` method returns a new instance with each invocation. `getDefaultInstance()`, on the other hand, repeatedly returns the same instance (as long as the specified `Authenticator` is a reference to the same instance passed in when the default session was initially created). Sessions can potentially contain security sensitive user information and so `getDefaultInstance()` checks the specified `Authenticator` to ensure it's the same instance passed in to the initial `getDefaultInstance()` call.

A session's default instance is most useful when developing single-user applications. Even then, it's not that much more cumbersome to use `getInstance()` and maintain a reference to that same instance for the lifetime of that application run. The potential security hazards associated with `getDefaultInstance()`, in my mind, outweigh any perceived benefits.

The `java.util.Properties` object that's passed into both of these methods is usually obtained by invoking the `System.getProperties()` method. JavaMail-specific properties can then be added:

```
Properties props = System.getProperties();
props.put("mail.transport.protocol", "smtp");
props.put("mail.smtp.host", "mail.foo.com");
Session session = Session.getInstance(props, null);
```

Session Properties

Property	Description	Default Value
mail.transport.protocol	The default Transport protocol. The Transport class returned from `Session.getTransport()` will implement this protocol.	The first appropriate configured protocol.
mail.store.protocol	The default Store protocol. The Store class returned from `Session.getStore()` will implement this protocol.	The first appropriate configured protocol.
mail.host	The default host for both Store and Transport protocols without their own host property.	The local machine.
mail.user	The default user name for both Store and Transport protocols without their own user property.	user.name
mail.from	The user's return e-mail address.	username@host
mail.*protocol*.host	The host specific to a particular protocol.	mail.host
mail.*protocol*.user	The default user name specific to a particular protocol.	mail.user
mail.debug	The default debug setting for sessions. This can be overridden with `setDebug(boolean)`.	false

Properties getProperties()

`getProperties()` Return the properties collection specified when constructing the session.

String getProperty(String name)

This method returns the value of the specified property or null if it doesn't exist.

```
void setDebug(boolean debug)
```

Set the debug setting for this session. This setting can be initialized to true by setting the `mail.debug` property to true in the `Properties` instance passed in to `getInstance()` or `getDefaultInstance`. Setting this to true results in debug messages being output to the console by both the session and its providers.

```
boolean getDebug()
```

Return the debug setting for this session. Providers can use this method to determine whether or not they should output debug messages.

There are quite a few more methods found in the `Session` class. As stated earlier, a JavaMail `Session` is mainly used as a factory for `Transport` and `Store` providers. We'll see how to use those factory methods later in our coverage of both transports and stores.

javax.mail.Authenticator and PasswordAuthentication

The other parameter passed into the `Session.getInstance()` and `getDefaultInstance()` methods is some concrete subclass of `Authenticator`. The only method that requires a non-default implementation is `getPasswordAuthentication()`. This is an application-specific function. Some implementations may prompt the user using a Swing dialog. Another may retrieve the necessary information from a database. Any number of implementations is possible as long as a `PasswordAuthentication` instance is returned:

```
javax.mail.PasswordAuthentication getPasswordAuthentication()
```

Invoked by a `Session` when password authentication is needed. Implemented by `Session` clients in an application-defined manner. Returning a `PasswordAuthentication` instance is simple a matter of invoking its lone constructor as shown below:

```
PasswordAuthentication(String userName, String password)
```

The only public constructor for `PasswordAuthentication` instances. This should be constructed and returned in the client's implementation of `getPasswordAuthentication`. The `Authenticator` class also includes several protected methods that provide access to the typical properties that would enable building a reasonably explicit prompt for the user.

```
protected String getRequestingProtocol()
protected int getRequestingPort()
protected InetAddress getRequestingSite()
```

The methods above return a string describing the protocol requesting authentication, and the port and site address the provider is attempting to connect to respectively. There are several more methods concerned with authentication, namely:

```
protected String getRequestingPrompt()
protected String getDefaultUserName()
```

getRequestingPrompt() returns the provider specified prompt to be displayed to the interactive user, getDefaultUser() gets the default user name for this connection. The authenticator should allow users to override this suggestion, if necessary.

This following is a fully functional (albeit utterly unacceptable) Authenticator:

```java
import javax.mail.*;
import javax.swing.*;

public class MyAuthenticator extends Authenticator
{
  public PasswordAuthentication getPasswordAuthentication()
  {
  String password = JOptionPane.showInputDialog(
                    "Connecting to " + getRequestingProtocol() +
                    " mail service on host " + getRequestingSite() +
                    ", port " + getRequestingPort() +
                    " as user " + getDefaultUserName() +
                    ".\n" + getRequestingPrompt());

  if (password == null)
    return null;
  else
    return new PasswordAuthentication(getDefaultUserName(), password);
  }
}
```

In case you're curious about exactly how Authenticator derivatives manage to somehow obtain the requesting protocol, requesting site, etc, without a non-default constructor or setters for those properties, here is the explanation. There's a package private method that's invoked by the Session that takes as parameters all of the necessary information. This method, in turn, invokes getPasswordAuthentication() after setting its private member fields. While this enables the getters to work as expected, it restricts the usage of Authenticator so that the only means of obtaining a PasswordAuthentication is via the Session's requestPasswordAuthentication() method.

javax.mail.Message

Messages are the focal point of the JavaMail API, naturally enough. The abstract class javax.mail.Message and its implemented interface javax.mail.Part define the general properties and content for mail messages. Subclasses of Message implement the concrete functionality needed for specific messaging systems. Sun's JavaMail implementation includes the javax.mail.internet.MimeMessage class that implements both the standard for Internet messages (as defined by RFC 822) and the Multipurpose Internet Mail Extensions (RFC 2045-2049).

Actual Message implementations are accessed through a small number of interfaces and abstract class definitions. The reason for the somewhat convoluted hierarchy is the requirement that messages be able to encapsulate multiple parts of differing content type. The Part interface provides most of the functionality we'll be using whether on the actual message or one part of a larger message:

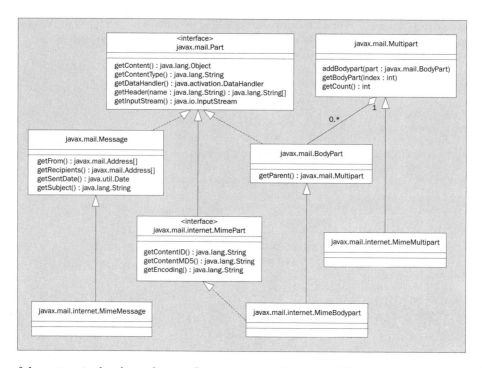

Most of the getters in the above diagram have corresponding setters. There are many more methods that aren't listed in the above diagram.

Constructing a Message

The two most common ways for a `Message` implementation to be constructed is using the `MimeMessage(Session)` constructor or the `reply(boolean)` method.

> **`MimeMessage(Session session)`**

Constructs a new and empty (of headers, content, and flags) `MimeMessage` in the specified `Session`. We'll learn more about the `MimeMessage` subclass later.

> **`Message reply(boolean replyToAll)`**

`reply()` returns a new `Message` with headers suitable to be used as a reply to this message. The subject is automatically prefixed with the string "Re: " (unless it already does so).

Message Headers

Let's take a look at the source for an Internet Message for a moment:

```
Message-ID: <4330645.959625642681.JavaMail.Administrator@injektilo>
Date: Mon, 29 May 2000 11:40:41 -0700 (PDT)
From: jason@injektilo.org
To: craigb@wrox.com
Subject: NO MAIL AT ALL
```

```
Mime-Version: 1.0
Content-Type: text/plain; charset=us-ascii
Content-Transfer-Encoding: 7bit

I have severed contact with the outside world
I have food so don't worry
```

If this is familiar to you, bear with me for a moment. Let us examine how this message is made up. The message is divided into two sections: the **header** and the **content**, which are separated by a double return. Each header is on a line and is identified by a header name, followed by a colon, and then by its value. The remainder of the message is the content.

Originally, messages could only contain 7-bit, US-ASCII characters with each line limited to 1000 characters in length in accordance with the SMTP line limit imposed in RFC 821. This made sending arbitrarily sized binary attachments rather problematic—a problem that wasn't officially addressed until the advent of the MIME extensions. The MIME authors were able to extend the capabilities of Internet messages while maintaining compatibility with the previous standard. This did, however, complicate the task of encoding and decoding messages. The JavaMail API, thankfully, exposes the headers as standard getters and setters.

Note that these headers are specific to RFC 822 and the MIME extensions (RFC 2045-2049). Since those are, by far, the most prevalent message formats, the documentation for the following `Message` methods will often refer to the headers that are set or retrieved by its most common subclass, `MimeMessage`. The `Message` class was, however, designed as an abstract interface to any possible implementation so keep this in mind as you read the next several sections.

Note that modifying a message's properties is subject to the underlying implementation and may throw an `IllegalWriteException` (a `MessagingException` derivative).

As an example of when this may happen imagine that we are attempting to modify a message we have retrieved. Messages in stores are organized into folders. Before a message can be retrieved, the folder needs to be opened. When opening a folder, we can specify a permission modifier, such as READ_ONLY etc. Attempting to modify a message retrieved from a folder that was opened in READ_ONLY mode will result in an unchecked runtime `IllegalStateException` being thrown.

The From: Header

All messages originate from some sender(s). The `Message` class provides several means, including a convenient default using `Session` properties, by which the standard `From` header can be set. The `setFrom()` method can be used in one of two way. The no parameter form sets the `From` header to the address specified in the `Session`'s `mail.user` property or if not present, `user.name`. Alternatively we can set the `From` header to the specified address by passing an `Address` object.

```
void setFrom()
void setFrom(Address address)
```

If the message `From` header should contain multiple addresses, the `addFrom()` method allows us to pass an array of type `Address`:

```
void addFrom(Address[] addresses)
```

And these methods are complemented by a getter, which returns an array of the Addresses in the From header:

Address[] getFrom()

Address is the abstract superclass for any number of possible implementations. The JavaMail API was not designed solely for use with the standard Internet protocols. Since the Internet is the dominant platform for the exchange of electronic mail, however, Sun included the javax.mail.internet.InternetAddress class as part of the standard JavaMail distribution.

Besides the standard constructor, the InternetAddress class includes a convenient factory method that makes it easy to parse a comma-separated list of addresses into an array:

```
message.setFrom(new InternetAddress("jason@injektilo.org"));
message.addFrom(InternetAddress.parse("moz@injektilo.org, tom@injektilo.org"));
```

The Reply-To: Header

In addition we can set and get the address to where replies for the message will go.

void setReplyTo(Address[] addresses)

Set the Reply-To header to the specified addresses. These addresses are automatically set as recipients when constructing a message using the reply() method.

Address[] getReplyTo ()

Get an array of addresses that replies should be sent to or null it this can't be determined. The default implementation invokes getFrom(). The MimeMessage implementation checks for the existence of a Reply-To header first.

The To:, cc: and Bcc: Headers

The recipients of a Message come in three or more flavours. 'Normal' recipients are denoted by the (possibly multiple) To headers. Carbon copied recipients (specified with Cc headers) are publicly acknowledged as being sent a copy of the message. Blind carbon copied recipients (Bcc), on the other hand, are not included in the list of recipients sent to the primary and secondary recipients.

The Message class defines the inner 'typesafe enum' class, RecipientType, to specify which flavour of recipients being addressed in the following group of methods. It should be no surprise that the possible values for this enum are TO, CC, and BCC. The MimeMessage subclass also defined a fourth RecipientType, NEWSGROUPS, for use with NNTP providers.

```
void setRecipient(Message.RecipientType type, Address address)
void setRecipients(Message.RecipientType type, Address[] addresses)
```

Set the To, Cc, or Bcc header to the specified Address(es).

```
void addRecipient(Message.RecipientType type, Address address)
void addRecipients(Message.RecipientType type, Address[]
  addresses)
```

Add the specified `Address(es)` to any of the existing To, Cc, or Bcc headers.

```
Address[] getRecipients(Message.RecipientType type)
Address[] getAllRecipients()
```

Return the addresses of the recipients, of the specified type or regardless of type, respectively.

The Subject: Header

Most messages minimally include a subject and date. The message class includes setters and getters for both those values.

```
void setSubject(String subject)
String getSubject()
```

`getSubject()` returns null if there is no subject.

The Date: Header

```
void setSentDate(Date date)
Date getSentDate()
```

Set or return the sent date for the message. This sets the standard Date header. `getSentDate()` returns null if the date is not known.

Received Date

The `Store` provider should set a message's received date when it's delivered to the user's INBOX but the current `MimeMessage` implementation consistently returns null. There is no standard RFC 822 or otherwise header that indicates when a message was received making a default implementation rather difficult. Without a standard header, there's no consistent way in which a message could reliably extract this information. It's possible that other `Message` implementations may provide the appropriate functionality with this method:

```
Date getReceivedDate()
```

Return the date this message was received by the recipient.

Folder and Message Number

Messages that are persisted in some `Store` are organized into `Folders`. Each message within a folder is temporarily assigned a unique (within that `Folder`) number to help identify it to the `Store` provider. This is a `Store` implementation detail that probably didn't need to be exposed to clients so most applications should operate directly on the message and disregard the message number.

```
Folder getFolder()
```

Get the `Folder` that contains this `Message` or null if this is either a new or nested `Message`.

```
int getMessageNumber()
```

Return the message number corresponding to this `Message` or 0 if this is either a new or nested `Message` (i.e., does not belong to a folder). This number *can* change if other messages are removed from the `Folder`.

821

Message Flags

As messages are received, read, replied to, and deleted, among other things, flags can be set on the message to make it possible for user agents to give visual cues to the user regarding each message's status. The flags themselves do not provide these cues, of course. It's their interpretation by the client that can determine how they're displayed, if at all.

Not all providers support flagging messages but there is a mechanism by which a client can determine what flags, if any, can be set. In addition, some advanced implementations make it possible to set user-defined flags on a message. These user-defined flags are usually represented as arbitrary strings of the user or user agent's choosing. As an example, some clients make it possible to flag a message for follow up. By explicitly flagging a message, not only is it possible to provide some sort of cue for messages with a particular flag, a client could filter the message list so that it only displays messages that need to be followed up. The JavaMail API's search package contains the FlagTerm class enabling developers to quickly implement this sort of filtering mechanism.

In order to support both the typical flagging of messages using the typical static final constants and the user defined flagging using strings, the JavaMail designers came up with a fairly clever approach that centers on the Flags class. An inner 'typesafe enum' class, called Flag, defines several static instances of itself to represent the standard set of flags. The outer Flags object acts like a container for these Flag instances as well as for arbitrary String instances. This is achieved by overloading the add, remove, and contains methods in the Flags class.

Method	Description
void add(Flags.Flag flag)	Add the specified system flag.
void add(String flag)	Add the specified user flag.
void add(Flags flags)	Add all of the flags (system and user) contained in the specified flags collection.
boolean contains(Flags.Flag flag)	Test for the specified system flag.
boolean contains(String flag)	Test for the specified user flag.
boolean contains(Flags flags)	Test for the all of the flags (system and user) in the specified flags collection.
void remove(Flags.Flag flag)	Remove the specified system flag.
void remove(String flag)	Remove the specified user flag.
void remove(Flags flags)	Remove all of the flags (system and user) in the specified flags collection.
Flags.Flag[] getSystemFlags()	Return all of the system flags contained in this flags collection.
String[] getUserFlags()	Return all of the user flags contained in this flags collection.

The available system flags are listed in the following table:

Flag	Description
ANSWERED	The message has been replied to. Clients can alter this flag on a message.
DELETED	The message is marked for deletion and will be removed from the folder when the expunge method is invoked. Clients can alter this flag on a message.
DRAFT	The message is an unsent, draft.
FLAGGED	The message is flagged. Usage of this flag is application dependant. Clients can alter this flag on a message.
RECENT	The message arrived in the folder since the previous opening by the user. Clients cannot alter this flag on a message.
SEEN	The message's content has been 'viewed' by the user. This flag is set when getInputStream or getContent is invoked on the Message. Clients can alter this flag on a message.
USER	The folder this message contains supports user-defined flags. Clients cannot alter this flag on a message.

Getting back to the Message class, the following methods are available for manipulating a message's flags:

Method	Description
void setFlag(Flags.Flag flag, boolean set)	Set or clear the specified individual Flag for this message.
void setFlags(Flags flag, boolean set)	Set or clear all of the individual flags in the specified Flag object. Flags currently set in the message but not in the parameter are ignored.
Flags getFlags()	Return a clone of the Flag object for this method. Modifying this clone will have no affect on the message.
boolean isSet(Flags.Flag flag)	Test for a specific flag's existence within the message's flags.
boolean isExpunged()	Return true if this message has been marked as deleted and subsequently expunged from the folder. The only other method that can be invoked on an expunged method is getMessageNumber.

Some store and folder implementations allow messages to be altered. Modifications to messages need to be confirmed by invoking the saveChanges() method. The static Transport.send() methods invoke saveChanges() on a message before attempting to send it.

```
void saveChanges()
```

Save any modifications made to the message since it was last saved. For messages that exist in `Folders`, the folder must not have been opened in READ_ONLY mode.

The JavaMail API includes surprisingly comprehensive search capabilities. It's possible to build some rather complex search terms to determine if a given message meets the specified criteria. We'll see more of this in our coverage of the `javax.mail.search` package.

```
boolean match(SearchTerm term)
```

Apply the specified search term to the message and return the result.

We'll learn more about search terms in our coverage of the search package later in the chapter.

javax.mail.Part

Our overview of the `Message` class may seem to have left out the most crucial component of a message: its content. All messages implement the `Part` interface. This defines the methods used for storing and retrieving the content of a message or part of one, as we'll see later in our coverage of the `Multipart` and `MimeMultipart` classes. The `Part` interface also defines the standard properties that both whole messages and body parts have in common.

Activation

Before we can actually set or retrieve a part's content, we need to learn about the JavaBeans Activation Framework (JAF), a little-known API also included in the Java 2 Enterprise Edition or available as a separate extension. The JavaMail API is one of the few products that make use of the JAF. Its main purpose is to be able to identify arbitrary types of data, provide a consistent interface for obtaining actual instances of the appropriate classes for those types, and, optionally, to expose the operations that are performable on those types via an appropriate JavaBean.

After the advent of the MIME extensions, Internet messages were suddenly capable of containing a virtually unlimited number of content types. JavaMail leverages the functionality provided by the JAF in order to provide a simple and consistent interface to any number of disparate data sources. The `javax.activation.DataHandler` class provides this interface. It's simply a convenient wrapper around some implementation of the `javax.activation.DataSource` interface. Two useful such implementations, `javax.activation.FileDataSource` and `URLDataSource`, are provided by Sun as part of the JAF. We'll be using the `FileDataSource` later in the chapter to 'attach' files to a message.

The `DataSource` (and its encapsulating `DataHandler`) can provide access to the raw bytes of a data type with their `getInputStream()` and `getOutputStream()` methods. The `DataSource` is responsible for providing these streams. `FileDataSource` objects simply return either a `java.io.FileInputStream` or `FileOutputStream`. The `Message` implementation uses these streams to transmit and retrieve a part's content, regardless of what type it really is.

At a higher and more useful level of abstraction, `DataHandler` exposes the `getContent()` method. This returns an actual Java instance that can be immediately downcast to the appropriate Java class and used directly by programmers by invoking whatever methods are made available in that class. This usually returns an instance of `java.lang.String` but could just as easily be a `java.awt.Image`. If the MIME type for the content has a registered `javax.activation.DataContentHandler` implementation, an object specific to that type will be returned. Otherwise, an `InputStream` is returned to the caller. Sun has provides handlers for `text/plain`, `text/html`, `multipart/mixed`, and `message/rfc822` MIME types in their JavaMail implementation.

Practically speaking, if a part's content type is set to `text/plain`, invoking `getContent()` on the part will return an instance of `java.lang.String` as will a part with a content type of `text/html`. Instances of `MimeMultipart` and `MimeMessage` are returned for parts with content types `multipart/mixed` and `message/rfc822`, respectively. This should be adequate for most purposes. Other content types can be accessed directly via its `InputStream` or written to disk or some other medium with Message's `writeTo()` method. We'll see examples of these later in the chapter.

As daunting as this might sound at first, you'll soon see that the JavaMail API exposes some convenience methods that handle most of the work for us. For those cases that don't, the example code should make the necessary steps clear.

Content

At its lowest level, the `Part` interface lets you set and retrieve content by directly manipulating `DataHandlers`:

void setDataHandler(javax.activation.DataHandler dh)

Set the part's content to the specified `DataHandler`.

javax.activation.DataHandler getDataHandler()

Return the `DataHandler` for the content.

If you'd rather not handle the `DataHandler` yourself, all `Part` implementations are required to implement the following convenience methods:

void setContent(java.lang.Object object, String type)

Set the content for this part based on the specified type. The object is wrapped by the `Part` implementation in a `DataHandler` using the registered `DataContentHandler` for this type.

void setText(String text)

Set the content for this part to the specified string with a content type of 'text/plain'.

void setContent(Multipart mp)

Set the content for this part to be the specified `Multipart` object. The content type will be set to `multipart/mixed`.

java.lang.Object getContent()

Return the content for this part, which can be downcast to an appropriate object based on the content type or an `InputStream` if the content type does not have a registered `DataContentHandler`.

The typical task of setting a part's content to some plain text can be achieved with any of the following three method invocations:

```
part.setDataHandler(new DataHandler(text, "text/plain"));
part.setContent(text, "text/plain");
part.setText(text);
```

Retrieving a part's content always uses the getContent() method. The plain text that we set in the part in the above example can be retrieved back as a String object like this:

```
String text = (String)part.getContent();
```

If the part's type were not a registered content type, the resulting object would have been an InputStream that can be used to retrieve the raw bytes of the content. As an example, the following code can be used to save unregistered content to disk so that the user can use a separate application to process the data:

```
Object content = part.getContent();

if(content instanceof InputStream)
{
  InputStream is = (InputStream)content;
  OutputStream os = new FileOutputStream("content");
  int n;
  byte buffer[] = new byte[1024];

  while ((n = is.read(buffer)) > 0) {
    os.write(buffer, 0, n);
  }
  is.close();
}
```

Of course, it's even easier to get the part's data handler and use the writeTo() method:

```
DataHandler dh = message.getDataHandler();
OutputStream os = new FileOutputStream("content");

dh.writeTo(os);
```

The MIME specification allows for content types to be modified by parameters. For example, the sample message source we saw earlier had a content type of 'text/plain; charset=us-ascii'. The charset parameter does not affect the nature of the content so comparing types should ignore any and all parameters.

String getContentType()

Return the content type of this part or null if unknown.

boolean isMimeType(String mimeType)

Return true if the specified content type matches the content type of the part–ignoring any parameters. The parameter's subtype can contain the wildcard character '*' to ignore the part's subtype. Since it would be impossible for any system to have registered `DataContentHandlers` for every possible content type, access to the raw bytes of a part's content is provided via the following method:

```
java.io.InputStream getInputStream()
```

Return an `InputStream` that decodes the content transfer encoding before returning the content's bytes.

Part Headers

The headers available for programmatic access via the `Message` class are by no means the only possible attributes that can appear on a message. Internet messages were designed to be extensible. New headers can and have come into existence long after RFC 822 was initially published. The `Part` interface exposes the necessary functionality for setting and retrieving any imaginable header's value. These methods were most likely included as insurance that new types of headers would not make the use of the JavaMail API obsolete. Most applications, however, will only find themselves using the standard getters and setters as that should cover most, if not all, your needs.

Like the `Message` class, if the part is not in a modifiable state (for example, the provider which returned the part does not support modification or the folder the message was retrieved from was opened in `READ_ONLY` mode) then the following methods that modify (add, set, remove) headers will throw either an `IllegalWriteException` or an `IllegalStateException`.

Method	Description
void addHeader (String headerName, String headerValue)	Add a header with the specified name and value to the part. This does not replace or remove any existing headers with the same name.
void setHeader (String headerName, String headerValue)	Removing all matching headers but the first and set its value to that specified.
void removeHeader (String headerName)	Remove any headers matching the specified name.
String[] getHeader String headerName)	Return all the values for headers that match the specified name as an array of String objects.
java.util.Enumeration getAllHeaders()	Return an enumeration that can be used to iterate over the existing headers in the part. The Object returned from the enumeration's nextElement() method can be downcast to javax.mail.Header which contains the following two public methods: String getName() and String getValue().
java.util.Enumeration getMatchingHeaders (String[] headerNames)	Return an enumeration of Headers matching any of the names in the specified String array.
java.util.Enumeration getNonMatchingHeaders(String[] headerNames)	Return an enumeration of Headers not matching any of the names in the specified String array.

The MIME specification allows for some optional headers that a user agent can take advantage of, if present. A `Part`'s description, disposition, and file name can be specified using the following methods.

The term disposition is defined as indicating whether it should be displayed inline or saved separately as an attachment. It can also include a number of parameters but filename is the only one that is programmatically accessible. See RFC 2183 for more details on the Content-Disposition header and its intended uses.

Method	Description
`void setDescription (String description)`	Set the description for this part.
`String getDescription()`	Return the description for this part or null if none is available.
`void setDisposition (String disposition)`	Set this part's disposition. Users should use either one of the `Part` interface constants, `ATTACHMENT` or `INLINE`. A suitable default will be chosen for the part if this attribute is not explicitly set.
`String getDisposition()`	Return the disposition for this part without any parameters or null if no disposition was provided. The resulting string should be compared with the `Part` interface constants, `ATTACHMENT` or `INLINE`.
`void setFileName (String fileName)`	Set the suggested file name for this part. The file name should not contain any directory path information. This method will set the filename parameter on the `Content-Disposition` header as well as the non-standard name parameter on the `Content-Type` header.
`String getFileName()`	Return the suggested file name for this part or null if none is available. This checks both the `Content-Disposition` header as well as the `Content-Type` for their filename and name parameters, respectively.

In this modern age of spam, users with low-bandwidth connections might prefer to limit the amount of time they spend retrieving messages from remote stores. A fully featured user agent might indicate an approximation of a message's size with the following two methods:

```
int getLineCount()
```

Return the number of lines this part's content contains or −1 if this can't be determined.

```
int getSize()
```

Return the size of this part's content in bytes or −1 if this can't be determined.

There's one last utility method available in the `part` interface:

```
void writeTo(OutputStream os)
```

Write the part, appropriately encoded, to the specified output stream. This is usually used by transport implementations in order to serialize the message for transmission but we can use it to get a dump of the message source, as we'll see later.

javax.mail.Multipart and BodyPart

Multipart messages are composed of one or more body parts. The abstract Multipart class defines the methods necessary for collecting these body parts. Its primary type is always 'multipart'. Each component in a multipart message, according to the MIME specification, needs it's own set of headers and content. The BodyPart class, therefore, needs the functionality exposed by the Part interface. Body parts, however, share several attributes with the other parts in the message. To, From, Date, Subject, etc, are specified at the message level—not on a part-by-part basis. If you've been wondering why the Part interface needed to be separated from the Message class, this is it.

Method	Description
void addBodyPart(BodyPart part)	Add a body part to the end of this multipart's list of body parts.
void addBodyPart (BodyPart part, int index)	Insert the body part into the specified index in this multipart's list of body parts.
boolean removeBodyPart (BodyPart part)	Remove the specified body part from this multipart and return true if successful, otherwise false if the body part was not found.
void removeBodyPart (int index)	Remove the body part found at the specified index.
int getCount()	Return the number of body parts comprising this multipart.
BodyPart getBodyPart (int index)	Return the body part found at the specified index.
String getContentType()	Return the type of this multipart. The typical result would be 'multipart/mixed' but MIME defines several other subtypes including: 'alternative', 'parallel', 'related', 'signed'. There are no standard implementations for these subtypes, however.
void setParent(Part parent)	Set the parent part for this multipart. This is normally called by the implementation of Part's setContent(Multipart) method.
Part getParent()	Return the part that contains this multipart or null if unknown.

The BodyPart class extends the Part interface with a single method:

```
Multipart getParent()
```

Return the multipart parent for this body part.

javax.mail.internet.MimePart

The MimePart interface extends Part with several MIME-specific methods including some that provide lower-level access to the message headers. This gives developers a high degree of control over what actually appears in the message source, as needed. Most of the additional properties are optional for most parts and messages but it's worth noting that they are available.

Method	Description
void setText(String text, String charset)	Set the content for this part to the specified text and encoded using the specified charset. The Content-Type header is set to text/plain and given the charset string as a parameter.
String getEncoding()	Return the value of the Content-Transfer-Encoding header. This header is appropriately set when saveChanges() is invoked on a message containing this part. For example, a part with content consisting of mostly 8-bit binary data will be encoded using the base64 algorithm as described in RFC 2045.
String getContentID()	Return the value of the Content-ID header or null if none is present. The content ID is used to uniquely identify a part that may be referred to from other parts. It's unclear why there is no corresponding setContentID() method here in the MimePart interface but it does appear in the MimeMessage class.
void setContentLanguage (String[] languages)	Set the Content-Language header for this part. The specified strings will be concatenated in a single comma-separated list. See RFC 1766 for more details.
String[] getContentLanguage()	Return an array of languages required by a reader in order to comprehend this part's content.
void setContentMD5 (String md5)	Set the Content-MD5 header for this part. This is used to ensure that a part's content has not been altered during transit. This optional header is documented in RFC 1864.
String getContentMD5()	Return the Content-MD5 string for this part or null if not found.

As we've seen so far, several MIME headers, including but certainly not limited to Content-Type and Content-Disposition, can be parameterized. The raw access to header lines provided by the MimePart interface ensures that developers have the capability to construct any new headers that come into existence that are not just simple name/value pairs.

```
String getHeader(String headerName, String delimiter)
```

Return all the values for a given header in a single string separated by the specified delimiter. If delimiter is null, only the first value is returned.

```
void addHeaderLine(String line)
```

Add a raw RFC 822 conformant header line to the part.

```
Enumeration getAllHeaderLines()
```

Return an enumeration of the raw header lines in the part.

```
Enumeration getMatchingHeaderLines(String[] names)
```

Return an enumeration of raw header lines matching the specified names.

```
Enumeration getNonMatchingHeaderLines(String[] names)
```

Return an enumerator of raw header lines not matching the specified names.

javax.mail.internet.MimeMessage

We've already mentioned the MimeMessage class as the only Sun-provided concrete implementation of Message. In your dealings with the JavaMail API, the MimeMessage class will probably be the only Message implementation that you'll need to make use of. Like all good object-oriented applications, though, you should not rely on this sort of implementation detail. It's always possible for a store to use some entirely different implementation although in all likelihood it will be MimeMessage or some subclass of it.

The MimeMessage class implements all of the abstract methods defined in Message as wells as those defined in both Part and MimePart that we've been studying so far. The following example is a complete application that opens a session, constructs a message, and outputs it to the screen:

```java
import java.io.*;
import javax.activation.*;
import javax.mail.*;
import javax.mail.internet.*;

public class MimeMessageExample
{
  public static void main(String[] args)
      throws Exception
  {
  Session session = Session.getInstance(System.getProperties(), null);

  MimeMessage message = new MimeMessage(session);

  message.setFrom(new InternetAddress("jason@injektilo.org"));
  message.setRecipient(Message.RecipientType.TO,
              new InternetAddress("craigb@wrox.com"));
```

```
    message.setSubject("NO MAIL AT ALL");

    String text = "I have severed contact with the outside world\r\n" +
            "I have food so don't worry\r\n";

    // The folowing three methods are equivalent:
    message.setText(text);
    // message.setContent(text, "text/plain");
    // message.setDataHandler(new DataHandler(text, "text/plain"));

    message.saveChanges();
    message.writeTo(System.out);
    }
}
```

In the following sections, we'll see how we can send this message to its recipients using a `Transport`. Until then, here are the few new methods introduced in the `MimeMessage` class:

void setSubject(String subject, String charset)

Set the subject for this message, encoding it in the specified `charset`. Historically, headers were limited to US-ASCII `charset` but RFC 2047 describes a standard way in which other `charsets` could be used.

void setContentID(String contentID)
String getMessageID()

Not that there is no analogous `setMessageID()` method. A unique ID is generated when the `saveChanges()` method is invoked on the message.

void writeTo(OutputStream os, String[] ignoredHeaders)

Write the message to the specified output stream but omitting the specified headers.

javax.mail.internet.MimeMultipart and MimeBodyPart

Like `MimeMessage`, `MimeMultipart` and `MimeBodyPart` are the concrete implementations that most clients will be using when constructing multipart messages.

`MimeMultipart` introduces the following methods:

void setSubType(String subtype)

Set the subtype of this multipart to the specified string. This defaults to 'mixed'. Alternative subtypes include 'alternative', 'parallel', 'related', and 'signed'. See RFC 2046 for more details on the different meanings of these subtypes. The default should be appropriate for most applications.

BodyPart getBodyPart(String contentID)

Return the body part with the specified content ID or null if not found.

The following example shows how a MimeMultipart is constructed and given two MimeBodyParts. This is analogous to 'attaching' a file to a message:

```java
import java.io.*;
import javax.activation.*;
import javax.mail.*;
import javax.mail.internet.*;

public class MimeMultipartExample
{
  public static void main(String[] args)
    throws Exception
  {
    if (args.length < 1) {
      System.out.println("Usage: java MimeMultipartExample fileName");
      System.exit(1);
    }

    String fileName = args[0];

    Session session =  Session.getInstance(System.getProperties(), null);
    Message message = new MimeMessage(session);

    message.setFrom(new InternetAddress("jason@injektilo.org"));
    message.setRecipient(Message.RecipientType.TO,
                                    new InternetAddress("craigb@wrox.com"));

    message.setSubject(fileName);

    // Text part
    BodyPart bodyPart1 = new MimeBodyPart();
    bodyPart1.setText("i sat in the cupboard and wrote it down neat\r\n");

    // File part
    BodyPart bodyPart2 = new MimeBodyPart();
    FileDataSource fileDataSource = new FileDataSource(fileName);
    bodyPart2.setDataHandler(new DataHandler(fileDataSource));
    bodyPart2.setFileName(fileDataSource.getName());

    Multipart multipart = new MimeMultipart();
    multipart.addBodyPart(bodyPart1);
    multipart.addBodyPart(bodyPart2);

    message.setContent(multipart);

    message.saveChanges();
    message.writeTo(System.out);
  }
}
```

javax.mail.Service

The JavaMail API provides an abstraction for two types of services that sessions can create, `Transports` and `Stores`. The behavior common to both was extracted out into an even higher abstraction, the `Service`.

Both types of services require that a connection be established before messages can be sent or retrieved. Establishing the connection requires a host and port. The `Session` properties can be used as defaults (using the parameter-less connect method) or they can be explicitly specified (using one of the other connect methods). Both types of services also support some optional authentication mechanism. In practice, transports usually don't require this but stores universally do as they contain messages with potentially sensitive information intended solely for the listed recipients. Some ISPs, though, are starting to require usernames and passwords in order to use their transports to prevent unauthorized spammers from abusing their services.

Services (and some components of services like folders) can optionally be identified by a `URLName`. This is a simple textual representation of a transport, store, or folder. Minimally, it includes the protocol in the typical scheme part (before the colon) and can include the username, password, host, and port.

For example, a `URLName` designating a user's POP3 account may look something like this: `pop3://username:password@hostname:port`.

The `URLName` class represents a string that includes whatever information is necessary in order to make a connection to some server. Connecting with a `URLName` is just one of the means by which a connection can be made. It should not be confused with the `java.net.URL` class, which represents an actual connection. `URLNames` can be constructed by specifying each of those components that are parsing a string representation of that `URLName`. A `getURL()` method is available to return the traditional Java URL object although this has limited use for our current discussion. The class also includes getters for its various components. Whether or not you choose to use `URLNames` in your application is up to you because, as we'll soon see, there are multiple ways in which a connection can be established to the services we're interested in.

Method	Description
`URLName getURLName()`	Return a URL name corresponding to this service. This URL name never includes the password used to connect to the service.
`void connect()`	Connect to the service using any suitably available default values for the host, port, and user. If the password is null, the service will attempt to query the session for the appropriate password authentication, which may involve prompting the user if an authenticator was established with the session.
`void connect(String host, String user, String password)`	Connect to the specified host using the specified user and password for authentication. The default port is protocol-specific. For example, the SMTP protocol's default port is 25.

Method	Description
`void connect(String host, int port, String user, String password)`	Connect to the specified host and port using the specified user and password for authentication.
`boolean isConnected()`	Return true if this service is still connected to the remote host.
`void close()`	Close the connection to this service.

javax.mail.Transport

Sending a message is achieved using a Transport. Sun's JavaMail implementation comes with a fully functional SMTP transport that might very well be the only transport provider you will ever need.

As a convenience to those developers who just want to fire off a quick message, the `Transport` class contains two static methods that make this a simple task.

> `static Transport.send(Message message)`

Send the message using an appropriate transport for each of the message's recipient's address type. The transports will be retrieved from the message's session and a connection established with the parameterless connect method. This method invokes `saveChanges` on the message before attempting to send it.

> `static Transport.send(Message message, Address[] recipients)`

Send the specified message similarly to above but ignoring the message's recipients and instead sending it to the specified recipients. This method invokes `saveChanges` on the message before attempting to send it.

Here is our first example capable of sending a message to any user on the Internet:

```
import java.util.*;
import javax.mail.*;
import javax.mail.internet.*;

public class TransportSendExample
{
  public static void main(String[] args)
    throws MessagingException
  {
    if (args.length < 3) {
      System.out.println(
        "Usage: java TransportSendExample "
        + "smtpHost fromAddress toAddress");
      System.exit(1);
    }

    String smtpHost = args[0];
```

```
        String fromAddress = args[1];
        String toAddress = args[2];

        Properties properties = System.getProperties();
        properties.put("mail.smtp.host", smtpHost);
        Session session = Session.getInstance(properties, null);

        MimeMessage message = new MimeMessage(session);

        message.setFrom(new InternetAddress(fromAddress));
        message.setRecipient(Message.RecipientType.TO,
          new InternetAddress(toAddress));

        message.setSubject("JavaMail example");

        message.setText("Did it work?");

        Transport.send(message);
    }
}
```

As convenient as the static send methods are, we often find that finer control is needed. We mentioned earlier that the session acts as a factory for both transports and stores. There are actually five different means by which the correct transport can be constructed and returned to the user.

Method	Description
Transport getTransport()	Return a transport that implements the protocol specified in the session's `mail.transport` protocol property.
Transport getTransport (String protocol)	Return a transport that implements the specified protocol.
Transport getTransport (Address address)	Return a transport capable of sending a message to the specified address type. A configurable address map determines the chosen provider. Since most of the messages we'll be sending are Internet-specific, we can ignore the details of how this address map is configured for now.
Transport getTransport (URLName url)	Return a transport that implements the protocol as found in the 'scheme' part of the specified URL name. Any host, port, user, and password found in the URL name will be used as defaults when connecting to the transport.
Transport getTransport (Provider provider)	Return a transport implemented by the specified provider.
	Once an actual instance of a transport has been obtained and a connection established, the only useful method that can be invoked is `sendMessage()`.
SendMessage (Message msg, Address[] recipients)	Send the specified message to the specified recipients using this transport. This method does not invoke `saveChanges()` on the message before attempting to send it.

Retrieving our own instance of a transport and sending the message could be done using the following code:

```
Transport transport = session.getTransport("smtp");
transport.connect();

transport.sendMessage(message, message.getAllRecipients());

transport.close();
```

Note that both the static send messages as well as the non-static `sendMessage()` method are documented as possibly throwing a `SendFailedException`. Exceptions thrown while sending a message indicate that at least one invalid address was included in the recipients list. The message could still have been sent to any valid addresses. The `SendFailedException` class includes methods to determine which addresses may actually receive the message.

Address[] getInvalidAddresses()

Return an array of invalid addresses.

Address[] getValidSentAddresses()

Return an array of valid addresses for which transmission was successful.

Address[] getValidUnsentAddresses()

Return an array of valid addresses for which transmission was not successful.

A successfully sent message may still never reach its destination. Once delivered to the transport, the transport may be unable to deliver the message for any number of reasons. A user account may no longer exist at the recipient's host. The recipient's mail server could be down. The message may be rejected for being too large. These types of failures are usually reported by returning the letter to the sender. A truly robust implementation would keep a log of messages sent and periodically check the sender's store for bounced messages.

javax.mail.Store

Like transports, there are five different ways of retrieving a `Store` (or `Folder`) object via the `Session`.

Method	Description
Store getStore()	Return a store that implements the protocol specified in the session's `mail.store.protocol` property.
Store getStore (String protocol)	Return a store that implements the specified protocol.
Store getStore (URLName url)	Return a store that implements the protocol as found in the 'scheme' part of the specified URL name. Any host, port, user, and password found in the URL name will be used as defaults when connecting to the store.

Table continued on following page

Method	Description
`Store getStore (Provider provider)`	Return a transport implemented by the specified provider.
`Folder getFolder (URLName url)`	Return an un-opened folder from the store specified in the URL name. This will connect to the store and invoke the store's `getFolder(URLName)` method.

Like your typical file system, stores organize messages in folders. Every `Store` is required to have at least one folder, the default folder. This is typically the root of the hierarchy even when it doesn't need to be. POP3, for example, has no concept of folders but in order to ensure that the JavaMail API remained suitable for both the more advanced IMAP protocol as well as the various legacy protocols, this default folder needs to be 'supported' by all store providers. In the POP3 case, the default folder is used simply as a container for the one and only "real" folder supported by the store, the INBOX folder.

INBOX is a reserved folder name that represents the primary folder for this user on this server. POP3 and IMAP stores will provide an INBOX folder but others such as NNTP may not.

`Folder getDefaultFolder()`

Return the default folder for this store.

`Folder getFolder(String name)`

Return an un-opened folder with the specified name. The folder does not have to be a currently existing folder in the store. Some `Store` implementations allow path information to be included in the name.

`Folder getFolder(URLName url)`

Return an un-opened folder for as designated by the specified URL name.

Once a store is retrieved from the session, the INBOX is only a single line of code away:

```
Store store = session.getStore();
Folder inbox = store.getDefaultFolder().getFolder("INBOX");
```

Most of a `store`'s functionality is provided by the `Folder` class, which we'll discuss next.

javax.mail.Folder

Except for the default and INBOX folders mentioned above, folders can be created and named as the user sees fit as long as the underlying provider implementation supports additional folders. IMAP stores, for example, do support this functionality but POP3 stores do not.

Method	Desciption
`Store getStore()`	Return the store this folder resides in.
`String getName()`	Return the name of this folder.
`String getFullName()`	Return the full name of this folder using the character returned from `getSeparator()` as a delimiter.
`char getSeparator()`	Return the delimiter used to separate the different levels in a folder's path.
`URLName getURLName()`	Return a URL name designating this folder. This URL name never includes the password used to connect to the store.

Some store implementations, notably IMAP and NNTP, may support folder subscriptions. These are folders that are marked by the user as 'subscribed' or 'active'.

`void setSubscribed(boolean subscribed)`

Subscribe or unsubscribe to this folder as specified by the subscribed parameter.

`boolean isSubscribed()`

Return true if this folder is set as subscribed by the user.

Navigating through a store's hierarchy of folders can be accomplished using the following methods. Note that stores do not cache `Folder` objects so each folder returned is a new, distinct instance.

Method	Description
`Folder getParent()`	Return the parent folder to this folder or null if this is the root of the folder hierarchy.
`Folder getFolder (String name)`	Return the folder corresponding to the specified name. This does not have to be a currently existing folder. The new folder is relative to this folder unless an absolute path was given.
`Folder[] list (String pattern)`	Return a list of folders matching the specified pattern. The allowed wildcard characters include '*' which matches any number of characters and '%' which matches any number of characters except the character returned by `getSeparator`.
`Folder[] list()`	Return the list of folders found under this folder. This simply invokes `list("%")`.
`Folder[] listSubscribed (String pattern)`	Return a list of subscribed folders matching the specified pattern.
`Folder[] listSubscribed()`	Return the list of subscribed folders found under this folder. This simply invokes `listSubscribed("%")`.

The `Folder` instances returned from the above methods are not only un-opened but don't necessarily actually have to exist in the store. Creating, opening, and otherwise manipulating the folders is done using the following methods:

Method	Description
`boolean exists()`	Return true if the folder physically exists in the store.
`boolean create (int type)`	Create the folder in the store. The folder's name was already specified when retrieving the folder with the `getFolder()` method. The type parameter can be `Folder.HOLDS_FOLDERS`, `Folder.HOLDS_MESSAGES`, or both logically.
`int getType()`	Return the type of this folder. This is the bit pattern passed in to the `create()` method.
`void open(int mode)`	Open this folder in the specified mode. The mode can be `Folder.READ_ONLY` or `Folder.READ_WRITE`.
`boolean isOpen()`	Return true if the folder is currently open.
`int getMode()`	Return the mode this folder was opened in.
`Message[] expunge()`	Permanently delete all messages in the folder marked with `Flags.Flag.DELETED`. The expunged messages are returned to the caller. Note that previously retrieved messages' message numbers may change after invoking this method.
`void close (boolean expunge)`	Close this folder. The expunge parameter specifies whether messages marked with `Flags.Flag.DELETED` should be permanently removed from the folder.
`boolean renameTo (Folder folder)`	Rename this folder using the name from the specified folder. This will only succeed when invoked on an un-opened folder. The boolean return value indicates whether the renaming was successful or not.
`boolean delete (boolean recurse)`	Delete this folder. This can only succeed when invoked on an un-opened folder. If the folder contains subfolders and the recurse parameter was specified as false, this folder will not be deleted but any messages found in the folder may or may not be deleted depending on the implementation. The boolean return value indicates whether the deletion was successful or not.

Many of the `Folder` methods can be invoked even if the folder hasn't yet been opened. Those that do require the folder to be either opened or closed are documented as throwing either an unchecked runtime `IllegalStateException` or the checked `FolderClosedException`. Operations that require a folder to have been opened in `READ_WRITE` mode will also throw an `IllegalStateException`. Operations performed on a folder that does not exist throw `FolderNotFoundException`. Since these are mostly `MessagingException` derivatives, it should be fairly easy to perform rudimentary error handling.

Since store implementations have different capablities to set certain flags, the `Folder` class provides the ability to query the implementation for the set of flags that it does support. It also includes some convenience methods for quickly setting or unsetting the flags on a set of messages. It's possible for implementations to optimize the setting of flags for multiple messages at once so these convenience methods might actually offer a performance improvement over invoking `setFlags` on each individual message.

```
Flags getPermanentFlags()
```

Return a `Flags` object indicating what flags are supported by this implementation.

```
void setFlags(Message[] messages, Flags flags, boolean set)
```

Set or clear all of the individual flags in the specified `flags` object for the specified messages. Flags currently set in the message but not in the parameter are ignored.

```
void setFlags(int start, int end, Flags flags, boolean set)
```

Set or clear all of the individual flags in the specified `flags` object for the specified range of messages.

```
void setFlags(int[] msgnums, Flag flags, boolean set)
```

Set or clear all of the individual flags in the specified `flags` object for the specified message numbers.

Retrieving messages from within a folder is just as easy as retrieving folders from the store. Unlike folders, however, the provider caches messages. Repeatedly invoking `getMessages()` will not repeatedly return the same instances. There is some precise optimization reasoning behind this somewhat contradictory design. JavaMail requires instances of any specific Message subclass to be 'lightweight.' A lightweight message object guarantees that it will only transfer the actual information from the store to the local machine when it is actually needed. The advantages to enforcing this can be seen when a message with an attachment several gigabytes in size is being stored on the server. Forcing an application to download the entire message just to display whom the message is from and the subject would be a waste of time, space, bandwidth and money. Retrieving part of a message's data is easy accomplished with IMAP implementations but the ability to download only the attributes of a message and not the content is an optional command in POP3. Thankfully, most servers do implement this option letting Sun's provider take advantage of it.

Method	Description
`int getMessageCount()`	Return the number of messages found in this folder or −1 if this can't be determined in the folder's current state.
`boolean hasNewMessages()`	Return true if this folder contains messages that arrived since the last time this folder was opened.
`int getNewMessageCount()`	Return the number of new messages found in this folder or −1 if this can't be determined in the folder's current state.

Table continued on following page

Method	Description
`int getUnreadMessageCount()`	Return the number of unread messages found in this folder or −1 if this can't be determined in the folder's current state.
`Message getMessage (int number)`	Return the message corresponding to the specified number.
`Message[] getMessages()`	Return all the messages currently found in the folder.
`Message[] getMessages (int start, int end)`	Return an array of messages corresponding to the specified range of numbers.
`Message[] getMessages (int[] msgnums)`	Return an array of messages corresponding to the specified message numbers.

The following command line application will connect to a POP3 store and retrieve the specified message:

```
import javax.mail.*;

public class Pop3StoreExample
{
  public static void main(String[] args)
    throws Exception
  {
    if (args.length < 4)
    {
      System.out.println("Usage: java Pop3StoreExample "
        + "host username password messageNumber");
      System.exit(1);
    }

    String host = args[0];
    String username = args[1];
    String password = args[2];
    int messageNumber = Integer.parseInt(args[3]);

    Session session = Session.getInstance(System.getProperties(), null);

    Store store = session.getStore("pop3");
    store.connect(host, username, password);

    Folder inbox = store.getDefaultFolder().getFolder("INBOX");
    inbox.open(Folder.READ_ONLY);

    if(inbox.getMessageCount() >= messageNumber)
    {
      Message message = inbox.getMessage(messageNumber);
      message.writeTo(System.out);
    } else {
      System.out.println("Invalid message number.");
    }

    inbox.close(false);
    store.close();
  }
}
```

With JavaMail's lightweight messaging scheme, data isn't requested from the remote store until explicitly requested. Some stores, notably those implementing the IMAP protocol, support fetching data for a range of messages in a more efficient manner. The JavaMail API exposes this capability using the fetch method. The `FetchProfile` class is used to indicate what data needs to be pre-fetched. Individual headers can be requested using the `add(String)` method as well as groups of pre-defined headers using the add(FetchProfile.Item) method.

void fetch(Message[] messages, FetchProfile profile)

Pre-fetch the requested data for the specified messages.

The following example pre-fetches the ENVELOPE headers (From, To, Cc, Bcc, ReplyTo, Subject, Date) and the Message-ID header for all of the messages in a folder:

```
FetchProfile profile = new FetchProfile();
profile.add(FetchProfile.Item.ENVELOPE);
profile.add("Message-ID");
folder.fetch(folder.getMessages(), profile);
```

Some store implementations allow you to move messages from one folder to the other. For those that do, the following two methods are available:

void appendMessages(Message[] messages)

Append the specified messages to this folder.

void copyMessages(Message[] messages, Folder folder)

Copy the specified messages (which must belong to the current folder) to the specified folder. The destination folder does not need to be opened.

By utilizing the Message class' match() method, the following two convenience methods are available in the Folder class. Note that it's possible for IMAP store folders to provide very efficient server-side searching in contrast to the brute force method that would occur if each message was matched individually by the client.

Message[] search(SearchTerm term)

Return an array of messages that match the specified search term.

Message[] search(SearchTerm term, Message[] messages)

Search the given messages for matches against the specified search term. The messages must belong to this folder.

javax.mail.search.*

The root class for all search terms is, appropriately enough, the SearchTerm class. It contains the single match method taking in a Message as a parameter and returning a boolean result.

Here's an alphabetical list of the concrete SearchTerm derivatives and their constructor's parameters:

Method	Description
AndTerm(SearchTerm term1, SearchTerm term2)	This term results in a successful match when both terms match.
AndTerm(SearchTerm[] terms)	Matches when all of the specified terms match.
BodyTerm(String pattern)	Searches a message's body for the specified pattern only if the message's primary type is 'text' or if the message contains multipart content and the first body part's primary type is 'text'.
FlagTerm (Flags flags, boolean set)	Matches if a message's specified flags are set or not.
FromStringTerm (String pattern)	Performs a case-insensitive string comparison on the From header.
FromTerm (Address address)	Matches if a message is from the specified address.
HeaderTerm(String headerName, String pattern)	Performs a case-insensitive string comparison on the specified header name.
MessageIDTerm (String messageID)	Matches the Message-ID header in a message.
MessageNumberTerm (int messageNumber)	Matches a message base on message number. The usefulness of this term eludes me.
NotTerm(SearchTerm term)	Results in a successful match only if the specified term returned an unsuccessful match.
OrTerm(SearchTerm term1, SearchTerm term2)	Matches if either of the specified terms successfully matches.
OrTerm(SearchTerm[] terms)	Matches if any of the specified terms successfully matches.
ReceivedDateTerm (int comparison, Date date)	Compares the specified date to the message's received date using the given comparison type (see below).
RecipientStringTerm(Message .RecipientType type, String pattern)	Performs a case-insensitive string comparison on the To addresses of the specified type.
RecipientTerm(Message. RecipientType type, Address address)	Matches if the specified address is one of the recipient addresses of the given type.

Method	Description
SentDateTerm(int comparison, Date date)	Compares the specified date to the message's sent date using the given comparison type.
SizeTerm(int comparison, int size)	Compares the message's size to the specified size.
SubjectTerm(String pattern)	Performs a case-insensitive search of a message's subject header.

The abstract ComparisonTerm class defines the following self-explanatory constants to be used by its derivatives for performing comparisons: EQ (equal to), GE (greater than or equal to), GT (greater than), LE (less than or equal to), LT (less than), NE (not equal to).

Thanks to the logical AndTerm, OrTerm, and NotTerm classes, it's possible to combine search terms into some fairly complex predicates. For example, here's some code my editor found rather useful these last few months:

```
if(message.match (new AndTerm(
  new FromTerm(new InternetAddress("jason@injektilo.org")),
    new AndTerm(
      new SubjectTerm("chapter"),
      new BodyTerm("late")))))
{
  Message reply = message.reply();
  reply.setText("Resistance is futile!");
  Transport.send(reply);
}
```

Working Example

These days it seems that the majority of e-mail accounts are hosted by purely web-based offerings such as Hotmail or mailto:Net@ddress. The convenience of being able to read and reply to your own personal e-mail from virtually anywhere in the world without any sort of configuration or synchronization hassle is hard to beat. There still remains, however, a significant amount of e-mail accounts that are accessible only via specific protocols such as POP3 and IMAP. Those accounts are the ones that the JavaMail API was designed to provide convenient programmatic access to.

By utilizing the JavaServer Pages technology also available in the Java 2 Enterprise Edition, we've created a web application that uses the JavaMail API to retrieve messages from a user's POP3, IMAP, or other store. Quite a bit of the functionality you'd expect to find in a real e-mail client is available including reading, replying, deleting, and even copying/moving messages to any of the available folders.

Like in all good web applications, keeping a strict separation between the presentation and the implementation was one of our primary goals. The little code that appears in the JSPs is mostly to perform if conditions and looping constructs. Even these could have been removed with a custom tag library. The important functionality is entirely encapsulated in our WebMailBean class. As a result, the JSPs had no need to import any of the JavaMail packages. This removes most of the "clutter" from the

JSP – leaving a blank canvas for the web designer to work his magic on. Conversely, not a single `out.print` statement appears in the bean. The Java developer, then, is free to focus on the JavaMail-specific functionality. Both teams are capable of working independently without stepping on each other's toes. And, as you'll soon see, this is merely a simple prototype – both teams still have quite a bit of work to do.

> *This example is available for download as a ready-to-run WAR and as a JAR containing the pages and bean in source form. Both archives include the JavaMail and activation JARs to facilitate installation for those of you who might not be using the Java 2 Enterprise Edition that includes them.*

The following listing (`mail.jsp`) is the application's central point of control. It vaguely models the Mediator pattern, dispatching to the appropriate JSP (to login, for example) or forwarding requests for specific commands to the session's bean. Ensuring a user is logged in is a simple boolean check that forwards to the user to the `login.jsp`, if necessary.

Mail-related commands, such as "Send", "Delete", "Copy", and "Move" are indicated by the presence of a "command" parameter in the request object. If any command exists, the entire request is passed to the bean's `doCommand` method as the commands each have their own set of parameters that are needed in order to perform their task. Coding this dispatcher as a servlet that extracts the command and parameters, passes them to the bean for execution, and then forwards the user to the correct JSP would have resulted in a cleaner and less coupled design but it would have also resulted in extra code that is not very relevant to this example:

```
<%@ page language='java' %>

<jsp:useBean id='webMail' class='WebMailBean' scope='session'/>

<jsp:setProperty name='webMail' property='protocol'/>
<jsp:setProperty name='webMail' property='host'/>
<jsp:setProperty name='webMail' property='port'/>
<jsp:setProperty name='webMail' property='user'/>
<jsp:setProperty name='webMail' property='password'/>

<%-- Is the user logged in to the store? --%>

<% if(!webMail.isConnected()) { %>

  <jsp:forward page='login.jsp'/>

<% } %>

<html>
  <head><title>WebMail</title></head>
<body>

<%-- Does a command need to be executed? --%>
<%
  if(request.getParameter("command") != null) {
    webMail.doCommand(request);
  }
%>

<%-- Change the current folder, if necessary. --%>
```

```
<jsp:setProperty name='webMail' property='folder'/>

<%-- Display the messages in this folder. --%>
<h2><jsp:getProperty name='webMail' property='folderName'/></h2>

<a href='write.jsp?to=&subject='>Compose</a> |
<a href='logout.jsp'>Logout</a>

<form method='post' action='<%= request.getRequestURI() %>'>

  Folder:
  <select name='folder'>
    <% String[] folderNames = webMail.getFolderNames();
    for(int i = 0; i < folderNames.length; ++i) { %>
      <option><%= folderNames[i] %></option>
    <% } %>
  </select>

  <input type='submit' value='Go'>

</form>

<% int messageCount = webMail.getMessageCount();

if(messageCount == 0) { %>

<h1>No messages</h1>

<% } else { %>

  <form method='post' action='mail.jsp'>

  <table border='1'>

  <tr>
    <td>Check</td>
    <td>Date</td>
    <td>From</td>
    <td>Subject</td>
    <td>Size</td>
  </tr>

  <% webMail.setMessage(0); %>
    <% for(int i = 1; webMail.getNextMessage(); ++i) { %>

  <tr>
    <td><input type='checkbox' name='number'
      value='<%= webMail.getMessageNumber() %>'></td>
    <td><jsp:getProperty name='webMail'
      property='messageSentDate'/></td>
    <td><jsp:getProperty name='webMail'
      property='messageFrom'/></td>
    <td>
      <a href='<%= "read.jsp?message=" +
        webMail.getMessageNumber() %>'>
        <jsp:getProperty name='webMail'
          property='messageSubject'/>
      </a>
    </td>
    <td><jsp:getProperty name='webMail'
```

```
          property='messageSize'/></td>
      </tr>

      <% } %>
      </table>

      <input type='submit' name='command' value='Delete'>
      <input type='submit' name='command' value='Copy'>
      <input type='submit' name='command' value='Move'>

      <select name='to'>

        <option value=''>Selected Messages To:</option>
          <% String[] otherFolders = webMail.getOtherFolderNames();
          for(int i = 0; i < otherFolders.length; ++i) { %>

          <option><%= otherFolders[i] %></option>
        <% } %>
      </select>
      </form>

  <% } %>

  </body>
  </html>
```

The user is asked for their log-in details:

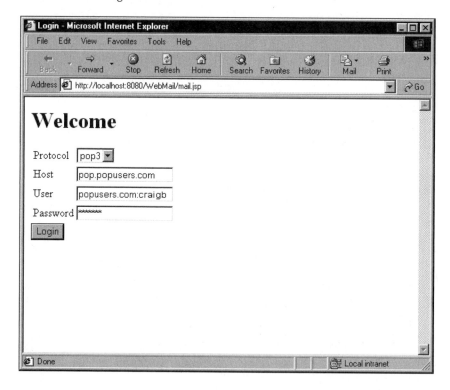

They can now see any e-mails, and delete, copy or move them:

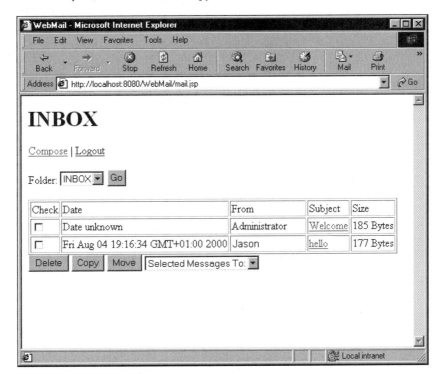

As you can see from the screen shot, `mail.jsp` also displays any messages in the session's current folder. It uses the – familiar to most web users – checkbox interface to allow multiple selections of messages. The selected messages can be deleted, copied, or moved en masse. Folders are selected via select elements for both the current view and the target of both the move and copy operations. Switching folders and performing commands simply sets the appropriate parameters and reloads the current URI.

In order to keep the amount of code that appears in the JSP to an absolute minimum, the `WebMailBean` exposes some unusual (in the traditional JavaBean sense but not so for web application developers) properties. The `setMessage` property is initially set to 0 to prepare for a succession of `getNextMessage()` property invocations. After each call to `getNextMessage()`, there is a family of `getMessageXxx()` properties that allows the JSP to retrieve properties for the current message as strings so that they are immediately presentable to the user. The `setMessage()` and `getMessageXxx()` properties are also used by `read.jsp` (available from Wrox's website) when displaying a single message and its content.

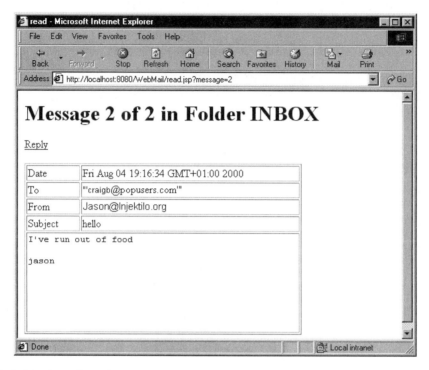

Also included in the web application are `write.jsp`, `login.jsp`, and `logout.jsp`. Their implementations mostly consist of simple HTML forms and are available for download.

The `WebMailBean` itself is the workhorse for this application. It, in turn, delegates virtually everything to some component of the JavaMail API. The bean simply acts as an intermediary between the JSP page designer and the pure Java code that's necessary to use the API.

You may notice that each of the methods is marked as throwing `MessagingExceptions`. There is next to no error checking being performed in this example, as it would have resulted in the usual amount of try/catch clauses that would only detract from our intended goal of showing the JavaMail API being used in action. Of course, no application should actually be put into action without the necessary error checking so this is left as an exercise to the reader.

The bean's constructor assumes that you'll be using the SMTP transport as your default mechanism for sending messages. This is most likely true for most users but the default host for that transport is currently hard-coded to a bogus value (no, you can't use mine). This should have been an initialization parameter. As it is, you'll need to recompile before you can send messages:

```
import java.io.*;
import java.util.*;
import javax.mail.*;
import javax.mail.internet.*;
import javax.servlet.*;
import javax.servlet.http.*;

public class WebMailBean implements HttpSessionBindingListener {
  Session session = null;
```

```
String protocol = null;
String host = null;
int port = -1;
String user = null;
String defaultFrom = null;
Store store = null;
Folder[] folders = null;
String[] folderNames = null;
Folder currentFolder = null;
int currentMessageNumber = 0;
Message currentMessage = null;

// Replace "mail.yourisp.com" with an actual
// SMTP server you have permission to use.
public WebMailBean() {
  Properties properties = System.getProperties();
  properties.put("mail.transport.protocol", "smtp");
  properties.put("mail.smtp.host", "mail.your-isp.com");
  session = Session.getInstance(properties, null);

  // session.setDebug(true);
}

// Return an array of installed store protocols.

public String[] getProtocols() {
  Provider[] providers = session.getProviders();

  List storeProtocols = new ArrayList();

  for (int i = 0; i < providers.length; ++i) {
    if (providers[i].getType() == Provider.Type.STORE) {
      storeProtocols.add(providers[i].getProtocol());
    }
  }

  return (String[]) storeProtocols.toArray(new String[0]);
}

// The following property setters (protocol,
// host, port, user, password) are used
// by JSPs in lieu of a constructor. The
// password property needs to be the last
// one set.

public void setProtocol(String protocol) {
  if (this.protocol == null) {
    this.protocol = protocol;
  }
}

public String getProtocol() {
  return this.protocol;
}

public void setHost(String host) {
  if (this.host == null) {
    this.host = host;
  }
}
```

```java
public String getHost() {
  return this.host;
}

public void setPort(int port) {
  if (this.port == -1) {
    this.port = port;
  }
}

public int getPort() {
  return this.port;
}

public void setUser(String user) {
  if (this.user == null) {
    this.user = user;
  }
}

public String getUser() {
  return this.user;
}

// Setting the password initiates a connection.

public void setPassword(String password) throws MessagingException {
  connect(password);
}

// The default from address is initially
// generated using the user and host
// properties.

public String getFrom() {
  if (defaultFrom == null) {
    defaultFrom = user + "@" + host;

  }
  return defaultFrom;
}

// For internal use only.

void connect(String password) throws MessagingException {
  if (store == null) {
    store = session.getStore(protocol);
    store.connect(host, port, user, password);
    cacheFolders();
    setFolder("INBOX");
  }
}

// This can be used by JSPs to determine
// whether the user needs to login.

public boolean isConnected() {
  if (store != null) {
    return store.isConnected();

  }
```

```
      return false;
   }

   // For internal use only.

   void close() {
     if (isConnected()) {
       try {

         // Close all open folders.

         if (folders != null) {
           for (int i = 0; i < folders.length; ++i) {
             if (folders[i].isOpen()) {
               folders[i].close(true);
             }
           }
         }

         if (store != null) {
           store.close();
         }

       } catch (MessagingException e) {

         // Not much we can do here.
       }
     }
   }

   // Cache all of the folders underneath the default
   // folder. This will keep us from constantly
   // opening and closing the same folders.

   void cacheFolders() throws MessagingException {
     Folder defaultFolder = store.getDefaultFolder();
     Folder[] childFolders = defaultFolder.list();

     List availableFolders = new ArrayList();

     for (int i = 0; i < childFolders.length; ++i) {
       String folderName = childFolders[i].getName();

       // Ignore "hidden" folders and INBOX.
       // We want to add INBOX to the head of the list.

       if (!folderName.startsWith(".")
             && !folderName.equalsIgnoreCase("INBOX")) {
         availableFolders.add(childFolders[i]);
       }
     }

     // Sort the folders by name.

     Collections.sort(availableFolders, new Comparator() {
       public int compare(Object o1, Object o2) {
         return ((Folder) o1).getName()
           .compareToIgnoreCase(((Folder) o2).getName());
       }
     });
```

```
    // Add INBOX as the first folder in the list.
    Folder inbox = defaultFolder.getFolder("INBOX");

    if (inbox.exists()) {
      availableFolders.add(0, inbox);

    }
    folders = (Folder[]) availableFolders.toArray(new Folder[0]);
  }

  // Finds a folder based on name out of our
  // cached array of folders.
  // For internal use only.

  Folder findFolder(String folderName) {
    for (int i = 0; i < folders.length; ++i) {
      if (folders[i].getName().equals(folderName)) {
        return folders[i];
      }
    }

    return null;
  }

  // Only folders underneath the store's default folder
  // can currently be set.

  public void setFolder(String folderName) throws MessagingException {
    currentFolder = findFolder(folderName);

    if ((!currentFolder.isOpen()) && (currentFolder.exists())
          && ((currentFolder.getType() & Folder.HOLDS_MESSAGES)
              != 0)) {
      currentFolder.open(Folder.READ_WRITE);
    }

    currentMessageNumber = 0;
    currentMessage = null;
  }

  // Get the current folder's name.
  public String getFolderName() {
    return currentFolder.getName();
  }

  // Get the names of all the cached folders.
  public String[] getFolderNames() {
    String[] folderNames = new String[folders.length];

    for (int i = 0; i < folders.length; ++i) {
      folderNames[i] = folders[i].getName();
    }

    return folderNames;
  }

  // Get the names of all the folders except for the
  // current one. This is useful for operations that
  // move messages from one folder to any of the other
  // available folders.
```

```
public String[] getOtherFolderNames() {
  String[] folderNames = new String[folders.length - 1];

  for (int i = 0, j = 0; i < folders.length; ++i) {
    if (folders[i] != currentFolder) {
      folderNames[j++] = folders[i].getName();
    }
  }

  return folderNames;
}

// Return the number of messages in the current folder.
public int getMessageCount() throws MessagingException {
  return currentFolder.getMessageCount();
}

// Use this to loop over the non-deleted
// messages in the current folder.
public boolean getNextMessage() throws MessagingException {
  int messageCount = currentFolder.getMessageCount();

  for (int i = currentMessageNumber + 1; i <= messageCount; ++i) {
    Message nextMessage = currentFolder.getMessage(i);

    if (!nextMessage.isSet(Flags.Flag.DELETED)) {
      currentMessageNumber = i;
      currentMessage = nextMessage;

      return true;
    }
  }

  return false;
}

// Set the bean's current message to the specified number.
// Pass in 0 to reset the current message pointer.
public void setMessage(int messageNumber)
        throws MessagingException {
  if (messageNumber == 0) {
    currentMessageNumber = messageNumber;
    currentMessage = null;

  } else {
    currentMessageNumber = messageNumber - 1;
    getNextMessage();
  }
}

// Get the current message's number.
public int getMessageNumber() {
  return currentMessage.getMessageNumber();
}

// Get the current message's sent date as a string.
public String getMessageSentDate() throws MessagingException {
  Date sentDate = currentMessage.getSentDate();

  if (sentDate != null) {
    return sentDate.toString();
```

```
      } else {
        return "Date unknown";
      }
    }

    // Get the current message's first from address or
    // reply-to address as a string.
    public String getMessageFrom() throws MessagingException {
      Address[] addresses = currentMessage.getFrom();

      if (addresses == null) {
        addresses = currentMessage.getReplyTo();

      }
      if (addresses.length > 0) {
        return addresses[0].toString();

      }
      return "";
    }

    // Get the current message's first reply-to address
    // as a string.
    public String getMessageReplyTo() throws MessagingException {
      Address[] addresses = currentMessage.getReplyTo();

      if (addresses.length > 0) {
        return addresses[0].toString();

      }
      return "";
    }

    // Get the current message's first to address as a string.

    public String getMessageTo() throws MessagingException {
      Address[] addresses =
        currentMessage.getRecipients(Message.RecipientType.TO);

      if (addresses != null && addresses.length > 0) {
        return addresses[0].toString();

      }
      return "";
    }

    // Get the current message's subject.

    public String getMessageSubject() throws MessagingException {
      String subject = currentMessage.getSubject();

      if (subject == null) {
        subject = "";

      }
      return subject;
    }

    // Get the current message's size as an
    // abbreviated string.
```

```
public String getMessageSize() throws MessagingException {
  String size = "?";

  int bSize = currentMessage.getSize();

  if (bSize != -1) {
    if (bSize >= 1024 * 1024) {
      int mbSize = bSize / (1024 * 1024);
      size = mbSize + " MB";

    } else if (bSize >= 1024) {
      int kbSize = bSize / 1024;
      size = kbSize + " KB";

    } else {
      size = bSize + " Bytes";
    }
  }

  return size;
}

// Get the text for this message. This only works
// if the message's primary type is "text"
// or if it's "multipart" and the first body
// part's primary type is text.
public String getMessageText()
        throws IOException, MessagingException {
  String text = currentMessage.getContentType();

  if (currentMessage.isMimeType("text/*")) {
    text = (String) currentMessage.getContent();
  } else if (currentMessage.isMimeType("multipart/*")) {
    Multipart multipart = (Multipart) currentMessage.getContent();
    BodyPart firstPart = multipart.getBodyPart(0);

    if (firstPart.isMimeType("text/*")) {
      text = (String) firstPart.getContent();
    }
  }

  return text;
}

// Turn an array of message numbers as strings
// into an array of messages from the current
// folder. This can be used for commands that
// act on multiple messages like delete, copy,
// and move.
// For internal use only.

Message[] findMessages(String[] messageNumbers)
        throws MessagingException {
  if (messageNumbers != null) {
    List messageList = new ArrayList();

    for (int i = 0; i < messageNumbers.length; ++i) {
      int messageNumber = 0;

      try {
        messageNumber = Integer.parseInt(messageNumbers[i]);
```

```
        } catch (NumberFormatException e) {
          messageNumber = 0;
        }

        if (messageNumber > 0) {
          messageList.add(currentFolder.getMessage(messageNumber));
        }
      }

      return (Message[]) messageList.toArray(new Message[0]);
    }

    return new Message[0];
  }

  // Perform a specialized command. The request's parameters
  // should contain a value named "command" and an array of
  // message numbers called "number".
  // The copy and move commands need a folder name in
  // the "to" parameter.
  // The send command needs from, to, cc, bcc, subject,
  // and text parameters. It can also have a reply parameter
  // that indicates the message should be a reply to
  // an existing message in the current folder.
  // This isn't very elegant but it's better than
  // putting the code in a JSP.

  public void doCommand(HttpServletRequest request)
          throws MessagingException {
    String command = request.getParameter("command");
    String[] messageNumbers = request.getParameterValues("number");
    String toFolderName = request.getParameter("to");

    Folder toFolder = findFolder(toFolderName);

    if ("Copy".equalsIgnoreCase(command)) {
      if (toFolder != null) {
        Message[] messages = findMessages(messageNumbers);
        currentFolder.copyMessages(messages, toFolder);
      }
    } else if ("Move".equalsIgnoreCase(command)) {

      if (toFolder != null) {
        Message[] messages = findMessages(messageNumbers);
        currentFolder.copyMessages(messages, toFolder);
        currentFolder.setFlags(messages,
                          new Flags(Flags.Flag.DELETED), true);
      }
    } else if ("Delete".equalsIgnoreCase(command)) {

      Message[] messages = findMessages(messageNumbers);
      currentFolder.setFlags(messages, new Flags(Flags.Flag.DELETED),
                        true);

    } else if ("Send".equalsIgnoreCase(command)) {

      defaultFrom = request.getParameter("from");
      String to = request.getParameter("to");
      String cc = request.getParameter("cc");
      String bcc = request.getParameter("bcc");
      String subject = request.getParameter("subject");
```

```
      String text = request.getParameter("text");

      String reply = request.getParameter("reply");

      Message message = null;
      int replyNumber = 0;

      try {
        replyNumber = Integer.parseInt(reply);

      } catch (NumberFormatException e) {}

      if (replyNumber > 0) {
        message = currentFolder.getMessage(replyNumber).reply(false);
      } else {
        message = new MimeMessage(session);
      }

      message.setFrom(new InternetAddress(defaultFrom));

      if (to != null) {
        message.setRecipients(Message.RecipientType.TO,
                        InternetAddress.parse(to));

      }
      if (cc != null) {
        message.setRecipients(Message.RecipientType.CC,
                        InternetAddress.parse(cc));

      }
      if (bcc != null) {
        message.setRecipients(Message.RecipientType.BCC,
                        InternetAddress.parse(bcc));

      }
      message.setSubject(subject);
      message.setText(text);

      Transport.send(message);
    }
  }

  // HttpSessionBindingListener methods

  public void valueBound(HttpSessionBindingEvent event) {}

  // Close the store when the session ends.

  public void valueUnbound(HttpSessionBindingEvent event) {
    close();
  }
}
```

As mentioned earlier, a servlet could have been used to dispatch commands to the bean. This could decouple the bean from having to depend on the names of the HTTP request parameters. It would then be usable in applications other than this one.

Other enhancements, besides a general increase in robustness, could include better handling for multipart messages. Actually listing the parts and their content types would be a good start. Then allowing users to download those parts to their local disk would be even better. Some content types such as image/gif and image/jpeg could actually be displayed to the user instead of requiring them to be downloaded and loaded in a separate application.

JavaMail's rich search capabilities could be put to good use in this application as well. Allowing the user to navigate to folders other than those contained by the default folder would also be a worthwhile improvement. Of course, this would complicate copying and moving messages (the main reason why we decided against sub-subfolders in this example).

Given these improvements to the code, some additional functionality to access some sort of online address book, and an IMAP server, the services provided by the likes of Hotmail could easily be made available to your company's employees or even just your friends and family on the Web.

Summary

The JavaMail API provides an easy, extensible OO way of incorporating mail functionality into our application. JavaMail allows access to Internet mail in differing protocols in a consistent way thus simplifying programming requirements.

As e-mail remains the single most used service on the Internet, the killer app or killer apps, many applications will require it, however, with the addition of the JavaMail API, our task as developer easier as we can be free to concentrate on the business logic and can stay away from dealing directly with the various protocols and their associated problems.

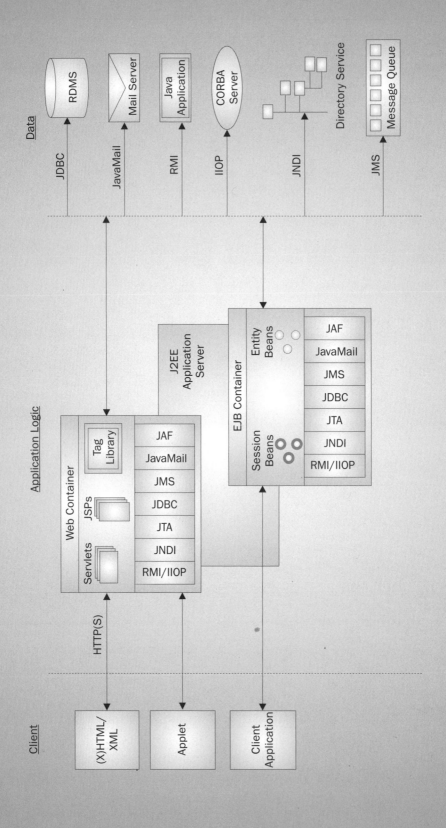

18

EJB Architecture and Design

Previous chapters have talked about the Java APIs that can help you build server applications. Some of those APIs – such as JDBC and JNDI – provide access to low-level services that any application can use. Other APIs, such as servlets and JSP, allow you to write components that execute in a structured environment (known as a container) that provides higher-level services. This chapter introduces an API for a new type of component – **Enterprise JavaBeans (EJB)**.

EJB components are designed to encapsulate business logic, and to protect the application developer from having to worry about system level issues. Those issues include transactions, security, scalability, concurrency, communication, resource management, persistence, error handling, operating environment independence, and more.

There are two versions of the Enterprise JavaBeans technology specification that I used in writing this part of the book. The first is the 1.1 version, which was the highest officially released version at the time of this writing. The second is the 2.0 version, which was available in a public draft form. For the most part, Chapters 18 to 22 are based on the 1.1 version but apply to either version. Chapter 23 discusses the new additions in the 2.0 version of the specification. Both these specifications are available from the Sun web site at www.javasoft.com/products/ejb/. Before you download them and start reading, you should understand that the intended audience is container developers, not component developers.

There are six chapters in this book that concern themselves with Enterprise JavaBeans technology. In this chapter, we will take a general look at why, when, where, and how we would develop EJB components in your applications. In particular, we'll look at the following issues:

- ❑ The services that an Enterprise JavaBeans container can provide

- ❑ The circumstances in which it makes sense to use EJB components in your design

- ❑ What an EJB component looks like

❑ How a client programmer (who might be developing server-side web components) sees an EJB

❑ The view of an EJB component by an EJB developer

❑ The mechanisms by which the EJB container provides its services

❑ The rules that an EJB developer must follow

❑ How to use EJBs in a web architecture

After we have discussed this background information, we'll talk about the design process for an architecture that will use EJB components. Once we get some theory out of the way, we'll look at a practical example that will be carried forward to subsequent chapters.

The following two chapters, Chapter 19 and Chapter 20, will discuss in detail the two main types of EJB components: session beans and entity beans. (Chapter 23 adds a third type: the message-driven bean.) Each type has two main sub-types: session beans can be stateful or stateless; and entity beans can have bean-managed or container-managed persistence. We'll look at the trade-offs and design uses for each type and sub-type of bean by developing alternate versions of simple EJB components. Also, we'll implement the example whose design we explore in this chapter.

Chapter 21 examines in detail four of the services that an EJB container will provide: transactions, security, exception handling, and remote communication. Some of this material is a little complicated, but you'll need to understand it if you plan to use EJB components in a real-world high volume environment.

Chapter 22 looks at EJB components from the perspective of the development process. We'll examine the roles that are explicitly defined in the EJB specification, and the activities that are necessary for each role. Also, we'll extend the sample application from Chapters 19 to 21 to include a web interface. Besides providing an example of a web architecture with EJB components, this gives us a chance to consider how we should set up our environment for an application with both web and EJB components.

Finally, Chapter 23 looks at the draft EJB 2.0 specification. Important new additions were made, especially in the area of persistence services and integration with JMS. Among other topics, we'll look at what we need to do to convert our sample entity beans from EJB 1.1 persistence to EJB 2.0 persistence.

Enterprise JavaBeans vs. JavaBeans

The choice of name for this type of component is perhaps unfortunate, because the Enterprise JavaBeans API – also known as a component architecture – has little in common with the similarly named JavaBeans component architecture. JavaBeans and Enterprise JavaBeans have very different goals:

> **The JavaBeans architecture is meant to provide a format for general-purpose components, whereas the Enterprise JavaBeans architecture provides a format for highly specialized business logic components.**

EJB components, servlet components, and JSP components have more similarities with each other, than any of them have with JavaBeans.

The following chart may help you to understand the place of Enterprise JavaBeans technology next to Java's other component technologies:

	JavaBeans	Servlets	JavaServer Pages	Enterprise JavaBeans
Purpose of component	General purpose component architecture	Implements a request-response paradigm, especially for web protocols	Provides for the generation of dynamic content, especially for web environments	Provides for the encapsulation and management of business logic
Tier of execution	Any: client (e.g. Swing component) or server (e.g. used by a JSP page)	Server (specifically web tier)	Server (specifically web tier)	Server (specifically business logic tier)
Some typical services provided by the runtime execution environment	Java libraries. Other services vary greatly with the container (e.g. Microsoft Word document, Java application).	Lifecycle services, network services, request decoding, response formatting.	All servlet services, scripting, tag extensions, response buffering.	Persistence, declarative transactions and security, connection pooling, lifecycle services.

What Are EJBs?

Although we have talked about EJBs in fairly theoretical terms until this point, we have not addressed the issue of what an EJB component looks like.

> **An EJB is just a collection of Java classes and an XML file, bundled into a single unit. The Java classes must follow certain rules and provide certain callback methods.**

From the bean programmer's point of view, that's all there is to it. The EJB will run in an EJB container in an application server. The container takes responsibility for the system level issues. This division of labor between the bean programmer and the container is the central idea of Enterprise JavaBeans technology.

As Enterprise JavaBeans is a member of the Java technology family, it should come as no surprise that EJBs are not limited to any particular operating system. Developers can write an Enterprise JavaBean on Windows NT, for example, and deploy it on Linux, Solaris, or the AS/400. This becomes significant when you consider that the only roughly comparable alternative to the EJB model, Microsoft's MTS/COM+, is available exclusively for Microsoft platforms.

The CORBA component model, part of the OMG's 3.0 specification, is essentially a multi-language superset of the Enterprise JavaBeans specification. It is possible that, in time, these language-neutral components will play an important role in many application architectures. However, as far as I know no one has even released an implementation of a CCM container.

EJBs are also not limited to any particular company, server implementation, middleware, or communication protocol. Enterprise JavaBeans are just a *specification* that any company can implement in any number of different ways. Your EJB, if it doesn't take advantage of any proprietary extensions, can be moved from server implementation-to-server implementation as your requirements change. You might develop on a free, open-source server (there are at least three under active development), and deploy on a high-end container that provides features such as load balancing and fail-over. My understanding of the basic principals of economics brings me to believe that the fierce competition in this market means you will pay less for more features, better reliability, and better management as time goes on. As this happens, because of the portability of EJB components, you will benefit without needing to change your code.

As mentioned above, EJBs are reusable components. Component-based development has proved its worth in developing client applications. No one would consider building a GUI without using pre-built components, be they called widgets, beans, or ActiveX controls. It's a gross oversimplification to call Enterprise JavaBeans the server-side equivalent of a combo box, but the intent is roughly the same. An EJB is intended to be a reusable bundle of business logic. You might not sell your EJBs for reuse by other companies, but you will be likely to reuse its business logic in multiple contexts within your company.

EJBs can work with any type of client:

❑   You can use servlets and JSPs to provide access for web clients

❑   You can access EJBs directly from Java clients using RMI

❑   You can use CORBA to access a server that supports RMI/IIOP

❑   You can use XML through a servlet to provide access for any type of client that supports XML

And this doesn't exhaust the possibilities.

EJBs can boost developer productivity for the small, workgroup application. They can help structure the model behind your company's interactive web site. They can even be made to scale to the largest e-commerce application.

Varieties of Beans

The primary goal of Enterprise JavaBeans technology is to be a standard component architecture for building distributed object-oriented business systems. This is an ambitious goal that could not be met with a single model for a component. The Enterprise JavaBeans 1.1 specification provides two different models for callback methods and runtime lifecycles. Beans are called either **entity beans** or **session beans**, depending on the model to which they are written.

> *The Enterprise JavaBeans 2.0 specification introduces a third model for a new type of bean called the **message-driven bean** – See Chapter 23 for more information on message-driven beans.*

Entity beans and session beans are quite different, and each has a chapter in this book to explaining its callback methods and the details for its use (Chapter 19 for session beans, and Chapter 20 for entity beans). However, as this distinction is so fundamental, we'll quickly review the key differences here.

A session bean is intended for the use of a single client. You can think of it as an extension of the client on the server. It may provide business logic, such as calculating the rate of return for an investment, or it may save state, such as a shopping cart for a web client. A session bean's lifespan should be no longer than that of its client. When the client leaves the web site or the application is shut down, the session bean disappears.

You can think of an entity bean as an object-oriented representation of data in a database. Like a database, multiple clients can safely access it simultaneously. An entity bean might represent a customer, a product, or an account. The lifespan of an entity bean is exactly as long as that of the data it represents in the database.

Each type of bean has two important sub-types. A session-bean can be either **stateful** or **stateless**. A stateful bean can keep information on behalf of its client across method calls (like a shopping-cart bean would). A stateless bean cannot (nor would need to, for example a calculator bean). This is an important distinction (for reasons that we will discuss), and in practice, you will use stateful and stateless session beans for very different purposes.

An entity bean can have its relationship to the data in the database managed by the programmer (**bean-managed persistence**) or the container (**container-managed persistence**). This distinction will often be important from the perspectives of productivity or performance. However, you can use either type of bean interchangeably in your design.

How many different "types" of beans must you decide between? From the standpoint of callback methods and the base interfaces that the beans must implement, there are two: session beans and entity beans. From the standpoint of your architecture, there are three: stateful session beans, stateless session beans, and entity beans. From the standpoint of your implementation, there are four: stateful session beans, stateless session beans, entity beans with container-managed persistence, and entity beans with bean-managed persistence. By the time you have finished reading this chapter and the next five, you will understand the issues and trade-offs among each type of bean quite well.

Why Use EJBs In Your Design?

A designer of a server-side Java application needs to understand how servlets, JSP pages, and Enterprise JavaBeans work together, and which are appropriate in different circumstances. Why, specifically, is the Enterprise JavaBeans API necessary? Countless web sites have demonstrated that it is possible to provide dynamic content using servlets or JSPs alone. It might seem that this new API adds unnecessary complexity to the development process.

It is important to understand that every API has circumstances where its use is appropriate, and circumstances where it should not be used. The Enterprise JavaBeans specification is intended to provide enterprise-level services, i.e. to provide software services that are fundamental to an organization's purpose, and regardless of the scale of those services Therefore, the EJB specification has some complexity in its administration and programming model. A dynamic application with modest business-logic requirements will probably be best served by avoiding this complexity and using a strictly JSP/servlet implementation (which would use JavaBeans components for business logic and data access). To take it a step further, a simple web site with no dynamic requirements at all should probably skip server-side Java altogether, and be written in HTML.

The Enterprise JavaBeans API was designed to keep the application programmer from having to provide systems-level services, so that they are free to concentrate on business logic. A web site that simply needs to provide dynamic content to its users probably doesn't require those systems-level services in the first place. However, many applications do require those services, and the Enterprise JavaBeans technology fulfills this need.

Sun's documentation for the Java 2 Enterprise Edition platform includes a publication discussing how various J2EE technologies fit together (*Designing Enterprise Applications with the Java 2 Platform, Enterprise Edition,* also known as the *J2EE Blueprints*). This document lists four basic architectures for web applications:

❑   Basic HTML

❑   HTML with JSP pages and servlets

❑   Servlets and JSP pages that access modular JavaBeans components

❑   Servlets, JSP pages, JavaBeans components, and Enterprise JavaBeans

Each of these architectures is increasingly complex, but also increasingly robust. As seen earlier in this book, it's very simple to write a JSP page or servlet that provides dynamic content. It's possible to embed scripting and dynamic data access right in the presentation logic for rapid application development. However, the result will be code that is difficult to extend and maintain, and an application development process in which it is difficult to separate the roles of web designer and business logic developer.

An application of any complexity will benefit from a more modular approach. Earlier in this book, we saw how JavaBeans could be used together with JSPs to separate data processing from presentation logic and provide for reuse. Although additional work may be required up-front, all but the simplest web applications will be better for this investment.

In one sense, adding Enterprise JavaBeans technology is simply extending this modularity one more level. As the requirements of the application increase in complexity, access to the enterprise's business logic and data is moved to EJB components. However, the decision to use EJBs should not be based on application complexity alone. A requirement for any of the services provided by an EJB container can also indicate whether Enterprise JavaBeans technology is appropriate (such as transactions, scalability, persistence, security, future growth possibilities, and access from other types of clients.)

Are you still not sure if you should use EJB technology in your project? One way to look at EJBs is that they are the *business objects* of your application. That means that they are the object representations of your enterprise's rules about what it owns, what it owes, how it operates, who works there, who can get credit, what's for sale, how much to charge, etc. If you need to access these rules, you should do it through the business-object representation. If the application you are building needs to capture the complexity of a process – if it needs to read, validate, transform, and write data in consistent units; if it needs to be kept secure; if it needs to be reused in different contexts – then it makes sense to take advantage of the services that an Enterprise JavaBeans container can provide.

Everything about the EJB specification is designed for this task of representing business objects without making the business-logic programmer provide system level services. EJB technology is not suited to be used as a reporting system, for analytical processing, or to serve files to the web. But if you need to access business logic of any complexity, you will find that writing your business logic as EJB components will open up new possibilities in developer productivity, application deployment, performance, reliability, reusability, and more.

The EJB Container and Its Services

A container is an execution environment for a component. The component lives in the container; the container provides services for the component. Similarly, a container often lives in an application server, which provides an execution environment for it and other containers:

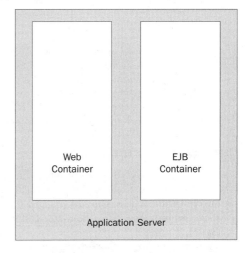

Web Container

EJB Container

Application Server

Technically, a component interacts only with its container and the resources the container provides. As the interface between the container and an application server isn't well defined, a single vendor will almost always provide both and the distinction is often meaningless. If an API between a container and an application server is ever standardized, at that time the distinction will become more important.

The primary reason that you would write an Enterprise JavaBeans component is to take advantage of the services that the container (i.e. the execution environment) provides. Understanding what these services comprise will help you understand when you should make the decision to use EJB components in your design, and what role they should play. Here are some of the services you can expect from an EJB container.

Persistence

Of course, you can read and write to a database using the JDBC API directly. This may be appropriate if you simply need to read some data to generate a dynamic web page, or update some simple information. If you have more complex needs, EJBs provide various persistence services. These services range from simple connection pooling all the way to managing the persistence automatically, and keeping the application developer from ever having to write SQL code.

Writing data-access code is error prone and time consuming unless you use a tool such as an object/relational mapping framework. The EJB specification recognizes this fact when it says of EJBs that do not take advantage of automatic persistence, "We expect that most enterprise beans will be created by application development tools which will encapsulate data access in components".

Consider some of the issues if you write data access code yourself:

❑ How do you generate updates to the database tuned to the data that has changed?

❑ How do you sufficiently test these dynamically generated updates?

❑ How do you handle the situation where complicated graphs of objects must be synchronized with the database?

❑ How do you handle mappings of datatypes to different databases?

❑ How do you map relationships between Java objects to relationships between database tables?

❑ And so on.

None of these tasks are impossible, or even difficult for a qualified programmer. But do they add value to your product, or are they simply an unnecessary cost? A vendor of a well-known object-relational tool makes the claim that it can save a developer 40 hours per EJB. I won't pass judgment on this claim, which if true, certainly includes time spent testing and debugging. However, I will say this, the persistence services provided by an EJB execution environment can make the difference between success and failure in a real-world project with time, budget, and personnel constraints.

Declarative Transactions

It's true that the JDBC API provides functionality to manage a transaction, and this could conceivably be done from a servlet or JSP. However, transaction management can be complex, particularly if multiple data-access components and/or multiple data sources are involved. Complex transactions with EJBs can be managed without any coding.

Transactions are explained in greater detail in Chapter 21. You may have heard of the two Java APIs related to transaction management. JTA, or the Java Transaction API, provides a standard interface between a transaction manager, an application server, a resource manager, and an application or application component. Almost none of this API, with the exception of the `UserTransaction` interface, is intended for an application programmer – and you probably shouldn't even use the `UserTransaction` interface (more on this later). Even less likely to be directly useful to an application programmer is JTS, or the Java Transaction Service. This is a specification intended for vendors who need to map a JTA implementation to the CORBA Object Transaction Service 1.1 specification. Now that I've introduced you to these APIs, you can safely forget all about them, unless you're a systems vendor.

Data Caching

Under certain circumstances, EJB data caching can provide a significant improvement in both performance and scalability of an application without any coding on the part of the application developer.

Declarative Security

In every real-world application, access to data and business logic functionality must be secure. It is possible for the developer to provide security using servlets or JSP pages, but this can be a complex and error-prone task. This is especially true if multiple servlets or JSP pages use classes with common business logic; a custom security framework would need to be provided by the application. Access to EJB components can be regulated without any coding.

Error Handling

Few applications of any size will be successful without a clear and consistent error-handling framework. The EJB specification clearly defines how errors affect transactions, client results, server logging, and component recovery.

Component Framework for Business Logic

Developing software that represents complex business logic requires a large investment in an enterprise's resources. Realizing this, software developers have for decades been pursuing the goal of software reuse. Component reuse has been one of the most successful strategies. EJBs are server-side components that can be used simultaneously by many different clients – web server-side presentation logic represented by servlets and JSPs, as well as a multitude of others (such as Swing GUI clients, Visual Basic programs, Excel spreadsheets, and Palm Pilots, to name a few). If the business logic embodied in your application requires a large development investment, this is an ideal way to enable maximum returns.

Scalability and Fail-Over

The Enterprise JavaBeans specification requires the application developer to follow certain rules in coding their business logic components. These rules are designed to enable the application server to manage large numbers of simultaneous clients making significant demands on business logic components and data access components. They are also designed to enable the application server to work in a cluster (across multiple machines) and to recover from the failure of any clustered node. Although web servers can be made to scale as well, web containers are not designed specifically to scale components with business logic and data access code, like EJB containers are. (For instance, Chapter 19 discusses how many users can share instances of a service session bean ("pooled"), conserving system resources.) The equivalent service component on the web tier, a JavaBean, will not be pooled without custom programming. As another example, Chapter 20 discusses how an EJB container can use various strategies to cache entity data. There is no such mechanism available for servlets or JSPs.).

Portability

Although the application developer can provide some of the same services as an Enterprise JavaBeans container, each of those services must be developed and integrated separately. If a changing business environment imposes new requirements on an application, those new requirements must be met with custom code (or at least purchased technology that must be integrated by hand). Since Enterprise JavaBeans are written to an industry-standard API, they can often be run unmodified in a new application server that provides increased functionality.

Manageability

The basic problem with managing web components that contain business logic and perform data access is that they are not visible to management tools. For instance, consider the problem of controlling who can change a customer's credit line. To secure this functionality with Enterprise JavaBeans, you simply use the declarative access control that the Enterprise JavaBeans container provides. To manage access, add or remove users from the appropriate role. To secure the equivalent application developed exclusively with web components, you must secure access to each and every user interface (i.e. web view) that provides this functionality.

How the Container Provides Services

Without getting too involved with details, it may help you to have some idea of the mechanisms by which the EJB container provides its various services to EJB components. There are three basic ideas. First, there are clearly defined responsibilities between the various parts of an application using Enterprise JavaBeans components – the client, the EJB container, the EJB component (and in EJB 2.0 the persistence manager). The definition of these responsibilities is formally known as a **contract**.

Second, the services that the container provides are defined in such a way that they are **orthogonal** to the component. In other words, security, persistence, transactions, and other services are separate from the Java files that implement the business logic of the component.

Third, the container **interposes** on each and every call to an EJB component so that it can provides its services. In other words, the container puts itself between the client and the component on every single business method call. The rest of this section explains these concepts in more detail.

Contracts

A contract in this context is simply a statement of responsibilities between different layers of the software. If each layer of the software follows the rules of its respective contract, it can work effectively with the layer above and the layer below, *without knowing anything else about that layer*.

This means, in general, that you can mix and match layers without rewriting your code, as long as you stick to the contract, and nothing but the contract. There are three well-defined layers in the EJB 1.1 specification: client, bean, and container (with another, the persistence manager, being added in EJB 2.0). As a result of the contracts between these layers, your bean can run in different containers, unmodified. Your client can access different beans, unmodified:

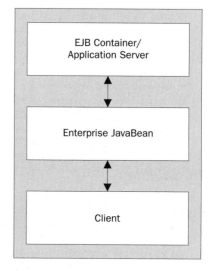

Of course, the contracts are written with more than portability in mind. The rules are carefully crafted to make it possible for server vendors to build their servers on many different technologies, with many different capabilities. The bean programmer can follow these relatively simple rules and patterns to take advantage of the services and capabilities of any of these application servers.

What kinds of rules are there for the bean programmer? We'll cover them later in the book, but the main ones (with more information to come) are:

❑ The developer of an EJB component (a.k.a. the 'bean provider') must implement the business methods (any method that provides access to the logic of the application) in the implementation class

❑ The bean provider must implement the `ejbCreate()`, `ejbPostCreate()`, and `ejbRemove()` methods, and the `ejbFind<METHOD>()` methods if the bean is an entity with bean-managed persistence

❑ The bean provider must define the enterprise bean's home and remote interfaces

❑ For session beans, the bean provider must implement the container callbacks defined in the `javax.ejb.SessionBean` interface

❑ For entity beans, the bean provider must implement the container callbacks defined in the `javax.ejb.EntityBean` interface

❑ The bean provider must not use programming practices that would interfere with the container's runtime management of the enterprise bean instances

Services

The EJB container exists to provide the bean programmer with services. For the most part, the bean programmer just needs to follow the rules to automatically take advantage of these services. They can simply tell the container the details of what should be provided. This "telling the container" is known as **declarative semantics**, and is one of EJB's best features. Declarative information is specified in an XML file known as the deployment descriptor. For many features, even this declarative information is not necessary, and the container will provide the feature without any work on the bean programmer's part at all.

One of the services available in every application server with an EJB container is transaction management. Transactions are how a system keeps its data consistent in the face of conflict or failure. The container will let an application developer indicate – without any programming – how changes to the enterprise's data by the client must be treated to ensure consistency.

Another important service provided by EJB containers is automatic persistence. This is an optional feature for the bean developer, but it offers many projects a valuable alternative to writing thousands of lines of data access code.

There are many other services that every container will provide. Declarative security protects EJB resources from unauthorized access. Resource management (such as connection pooling) and concurrency control make access from multiple users easier. Error handling makes it easier for the application developer to be productive. Communication services make remote access easier.

Some containers will provide optional services. An important option for large projects is clustering for fail-over and scalability. Management tools are not part of the EJB specification, but are provided as an optional component by server vendors, and can be important to the success or failure of any project. The optional services that are available are limited only by a vendor's imagination. As the Java APIs expand to envelop the world, some of these additional services may become standardized. One example is the soon-to-be-released management API (JMX) that may provide a lowest-common-denominator for management implementations.

The important point to understand about all these services is that they are implemented by the container developer, not by the business-logic programmer. This is possible, even though the container developer knows nothing about the business logic, because the business logic components – the Enterprise JavaBeans – follow the contract defined in the specification.

Interposition

An application developer follows the rules of the bean-development contract, and the container is then able to provide system-level services. But how, exactly, is this possible? There is a lot to it. Writing a quality EJB container is a difficult task. But there is one central concept that makes it easier for the bean developer to understand what is happening, **interposition**.

Think back to the Chapter 2, on RMI. Remember the discussions about stubs, and how they serve as proxies for a remote object? The stub *interposes* between the client interface and the remote object to provide marshalling and network transport. In the same way, the EJB container interposes between the client business interface and the EJB's business logic to provide services such as transactions, security, error handling, and persistence management.

So let's follow a typical method call to an Enterprise JavaBean from a remote client:

❑   First, the client makes a call on an RMI stub

❑ This RMI stub interposes on the method call in order to marshal parameters and send the information across the network

❑ A skeleton on the server side unmarshals the parameters and delivers them to the EJB container

But the method call hasn't reached the business logic yet. Now there is a second interposition (some of the following steps may be optimized away, but logically the interposition will always happen as follows):

❑ The container will examine the security credentials of the caller of that method

❑ It will start or join with any required transactions

❑ It will make any necessary calls to persistence functions

❑ It will trigger various callbacks to allow the EJB component to acquire resources

❑ Only after all of this is done will the actual business method be called

❑ Once it is called, the container will do some more work with transactions, persistence, callbacks, and so on

❑ Finally, the results of the business method, be it returned data or an exception, will be sent back to the remote client

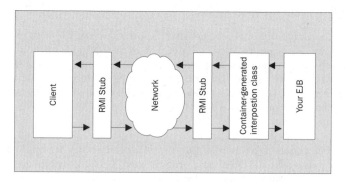

This explains the reason behind one of the less intuitive parts of Enterprise JavaBeans technology. The application developer will write an interface that declares their business logic functions (represented by the "RMI Stub" in the above diagram), and they will write a class that implements those functions. But as mentioned above, the class isn't required to implement the interface. In fact, the programmer is strongly discouraged from implementing that interface in their business logic class. How is it possible, then, for the remote call to a function in the interface to eventually reach the corresponding business logic implementation? Basically, interface implementation has been replaced with a naming convention. The container will use Java introspection – either when you deploy your EJB or at runtime – to match methods in the interface with methods in the implementation.

Working with EJBs

The Enterprise JavaBeans specification is written for three audiences:

❑ The client developer

❏ The EJB developer

❏ The EJB container developer

This book is written for the Java server-side programmer, who may have to write and use EJBs; it does not address the technical requirements of the specification from the container developer's point of view.

The Client Developer's View

A client is any user of an Enterprise JavaBean, and could be a Java client-side application, a CORBA app, a servlet, or another EJB. A server-side programmer who is designing a web application, or using a servlet to mediate communication with an EJB, needs to understand how EJBs are accessed and used. In large projects, it is quite likely that the web programmer and the EJB programmer are different people.

The client programmer has a smaller set of concerns than a bean developer with regard to using EJBs. Basically, they need to know how to find or create the bean, how to use its methods, and how to release its resources. A client always uses the same procedure for object creation, lookup, method invocation, and removal, regardless of how an EJB is implemented or what function it provides to the client. The client does not need to worry about the implementation of the EJB, callbacks that the EJB container will make on the EJB, or nature of the services provided to the EJB.

Every Enterprise JavaBean has two interfaces:

❏ The **home interface** is primarily for lifecycle operations: creating, finding, and removing EJBs. The home interface isn't associated with a particular bean, just with a type of bean.

❏ The **remote interface** is for business methods. Logically, it represents a particular bean on the server. The remote interface also provides some infrastructure methods associated with a bean instance, rather than a bean type.

A client programmer will acquire an EJB's home interface through JNDI, which is explained in Chapter 4. They can use this home interface to:

❏ Create or find an instance of a bean, which will be represented to the client as a remote interface

❏ Execute business methods on that instance of the bean

❏ Get a serializable reference to the bean, known as a **handle**

❏ Remove the bean

The removal of a bean can mean radically different things, depending on the type of bean. In the case of a stateful session bean, it means the developer has finished using it. The server can then release the resources associated with that bean. In the case of a stateless session bean, it means basically the same thing – although the server probably wasn't consuming any resources for the bean, because it lacked state to begin with. In the case of an entity bean, removing the bean means removing its representation in the persistent data store – in other words, deleting it from the database. Obviously, you will want to be clear on these differences.

Let's work through the process step-by-step, using an example of a client application that wants to call a `placeOrder()` method on an `OrderManagement` stateless session bean. (We'll look at how to construct this `OrderManagement` stateless session bean in the very next section. These examples are meant only to give you an idea of the code you will be writing as a component developer – they really don't do much. However, at the end of that section, you will be able to deploy the bean in an application server and run this client if you so choose.)

First, the client will need to be authenticated in some server-specific way. If the client is a web application, for example, the authentication may take place using SSL.

Second, the client will need to get a properly initialized `InitialContext` as the starting point for the JNDI lookup. If the client is an EJB executing in a container, and the EJB it would like to reference is declared as a resource in the XML deployment descriptor, the `InitialContext` will be ready to use as soon as it is instantiated:

```
Context ctx = new InitialContext();
```

If the client is executing outside of a container, the `InitialContext` will require certain server-dependent properties. These can be provided in code or using a resource file. The initialization of the context will be specific to your application server or JNDI provider. As an example, I'll do it programmatically using values appropriate for the 2.0 version of the open-source server jBoss, available from www.jboss.org:

```
package orderMgmt;

import java.util.Properties;
import javax.naming.Context;
import javax.naming.InitialContext;

public class Client
{
  public static void main(String[] args)
  {
    try
    {
      Properties prop = new Properties();
      prop.put(Context.INITIAL_CONTEXT_FACTORY,
               "org.jnp.interfaces.NamingContextFactory");
      prop.put(Context.PROVIDER_URL, "localhost:1099");

      Context ctx = new InitialContext(prop);
```

Now, let's find the home interface for the `OrderManagement` bean. The first step is to look it up using the initial context we have just set up. The name we use to look up the bean depends on the type of client. If the client is an EJB executing in a container, and the EJB it would like to reference is declared as a resource in the XML deployment descriptor, then the name will be a sub-context of the name `java:comp/env/`. Furthermore, the specification recommends, but does not require, that names of EJBs be bound in the subcontext `ejb`. So we might look the home interface up like this:

```
Object objref = ctx.lookup("java:comp/env/ejb/OrderManagement");
```

From the perspective of a client executing outside of a container, the bean can be bound to any name in the JNDI namespace. For a Swing GUI client, we might look the home interface up like this (and this is the code that you should add to the `Client.java` file if you're scoring at home):

```
Object objref = ctx.lookup("OrderManagement");
```

The client JNDI namespace may include the home interfaces of EJBs from multiple application servers located anywhere on a network. In general, the client doesn't need to know the location of the EJB or the identity of its server; it doesn't need to know anything but the name to which the bean's home interface is bound.

Next, we want to cast this home interface reference to the `OrderManagementHome` class. This isn't quite as simple as a Java language cast. To ensure your client works with any underlying communication protocol, the specification recommends that the client use `javax.rmi.PortableRemoteObject`'s `narrow()` method. IIOP in particular does not support simple casting. So the code would look like this (you should add this to the `Client.java` file):

```
OrderManagementHome home =
                (OrderManagementHome)javax.rmi.
                PortableRemoteObject.narrow(objref,
                                OrderManagementHome.class);
```

We use the home interface to create an instance of the `OrderManagement` class. It's important to understand that this instance is created on the server. All we have on the client is a remote reference to it (in other words, the client has a stub). The code would look like this (add to `Client.java`):

```
OrderManagement orderManagement = home.create();
```

Now, we can use the business methods defined in the `OrderManagement` bean. In this case, we want to call the `placeOrder()` method. Let's assume that it takes three parameters: customer name, product name, and quantity. The code might look like this (add to `Client.java`):

```
orderManagement.placeOrder("Dan OConnor",
                        "Wrox books on programming", 1000);
```

Finally, we can signal to the server that we are done using this instance of the `OrderManagement` bean. We could do this using the life cycle home interface, but it is actually more convenient to call a utility `remove()` method defined in every EJB remote interface. The code would look like this:

```
        orderManagement.remove();
        System.out.println("Order successfully placed.");
    }
    catch (Exception e)
    {
        e.printStackTrace();
    }
  }
}
```

Using Enterprise JavaBeans technology from the client can be this simple. Writing a client that uses distributed functionality is only moderately more difficult than writing a local client using EJBs.

The Bean Programmer's View

The bean programmer's main responsibility is to write business logic. As much as possible, the Enterprise JavaBeans specification tries to relieve us of any system-level tasks. In exchange, the bean programmer must structure their code in a particular way. Let's talk about that structure.

No matter what type of EJB the programmer is writing – stateless session, stateful session, or entity – there are three primary Java files and one XML file that they must create. Two of these Java files are the interfaces discussed in the previous section: the home interface and the remote interface. The third is the class that contains the actual business logic, as well as some required callbacks. The XML file, called the deployment descriptor, contains the structural information about the bean, declares the bean's external dependencies, and specifies certain information about how services such as transactions and security should work. There will probably be additional Java classes that support the operation of the bean, such as helper classes that implement business logic, or, in the case of an entity bean with a compound primary key, a class that represents that key.

All these files get packaged up into a JAR – the standard Java deployment unit that is essentially a zip file. There can be many beans in a single JAR file, but there will be only one XML descriptor for each JAR file. That XML deployment descriptor must be named `ejb-jar.xml`, and must go into a specific directory (so the EJB container will know where to look for it). That directory is `META-INF`, which must be in all capital letters.

> *A common source of frustration for beginning EJB component developers is to put their deployment descriptor in `Meta-inf` or `meta-inf`.*

The rest of the files go in directories appropriate to their packages. For the `OrderManagement` example bean on which we are currently working, the structure of our JAR file will be as follows:

```
META-INF\
         ejb-jar.xml

orderMgmt\
         OrderManagement.class
         OrderManagementHome.class
         OrderManagementBean.class
```

There are many ways to create this JAR file, ranging from specialized tools, to zip-file utilities, to the standard JAR packaging tool in the Java SDK. Use whatever method you like; the result will be the same.

Additionally, there will be server-dependent information that needs to be specified when the bean is deployed. For instance, logical resource names and security roles will need to be mapped to actual entities in a specific operating environment. Fields in entity beans using container-managed persistence may need to be mapped to specific database table columns. Exactly what additional information needs to be specified will vary, but the specification is written such that EJBs can be developed without taking this into account.

Most likely, an EJB developer will be working from a design that includes the business logic interface they should provide. This interface is a good starting point from which to build an Enterprise JavaBean. The methods in that interface will probably correspond to the methods in the EJB remote interface, with one difference: because EJBs can be accessed remotely, every method in the remote interface (and the home interface) must be declared to throw `java.rmi.RemoteException`. Since `RemoteException` is a checked exception, this ensures that the client will be aware of issues such as the potential for network failure.

The remote interface in EJB must extend `javax.ejb.EJBObject`, which extends `java.rmi.Remote`. `EJBObject` declares some common methods that relate to any instance of an EJB:

```
package javax.ejb;

public interface javax.ejb.EJBObject extends java.rmi.Remote {

    EJBHome getEJBHome()
            throws java.rmi.RemoteException;

    Handle getHandle()
            throws java.rmi.RemoteException;

    Object getPrimaryKey
            throws java.rmi.RemoteException;

    boolean isIdentical(EJBObject obj)
            throws java.rmi.RemoteException;

    void remove()
            throws java.rmi.RemoteException, javax.ejb.RemoveException;

}
```

The EJB developer, in general, doesn't need to write code to support these methods: they are available to the client developer for free, in every bean that they use. (Some won't make sense in certain contexts, in which case calling them results in an exception.)

Here is a class diagram of the relationship between the three classes, using our `OrderManagement` interface for the business interface. Note that `java.rmi.Remote` is a tagging interface with no methods:

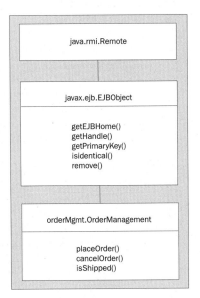

Let's continue with the example the order management bean that the previous section referenced as a client. We already know that there is a `placeOrder()` method. Let's also develop `cancelOrder()` and `isShipped()` methods. (In this interface I have made the simplifying, but unrealistic, assumption that a customer could identify an order by indicating the product ordered. The manufacturing example in the following chapters uses an order number and sales division to identify the customer's order.) The EJB's remote interface would look like this:

```
package orderMgmt;

public interface OrderManagement extends javax.ejb.EJBObject
{
    void placeOrder(String custName, String prodName, int quantity)
        throws java.rmi.RemoteException;

    void cancelOrder(String custName, String prodName)
        throws java.rmi.RemoteException;

    boolean isShipped(String custName, String prodName)
        throws java.rmi.RemoteException;
}
```

Notice that the application developer *never implements this interface.* The curious reader may wonder who does implement it; the answer is that the EJB container does. There are several ways that a container may implement this interface, but you may think of it generating and compiling Java code in the background when you deploy your bean. The code that it generates is where the container provides services such as transaction management and security. This code is where the 'interposition' discussed earlier actually happens.

Of course, the application developer "implements" the interface in the sense that they must provide the business logic in an implementation class. But they need not ever write `OrderManagementBean` **implements** `OrderManagement`, and in fact, is strongly discouraged from doing so. This is the container's privilege.

> *How the home or remote interface is actually implemented is an implementation detail that the bean programmer never needs to consider. If you are curious, I can tell you that the open source server jBoss has used three techniques. First, it has simply generated Java code based on a template and compiled this code automatically. Second, it has dynamically constructed Java bytecode in memory. Third, it has used the `java.lang.reflect.Proxy` class available as of JDK 1.3. Technically, there is no requirement that the interface be implemented at all. I can easily imagine writing C++ code to perform this role – although I can't easily imagine why.*

The next task in writing the order management bean is to write the home interface, which must extend `javax.ejb.EJBHome`. `EJBHome` looks like this:

```
package javax.ejb;

public interface EJBHome extends java.rmi.Remote {

    EJBMetaData getEJBMetaData()
            throws java.rmi.RemoteException;
```

```
HomeHandle getHomeHandle()
        throws java.rmi.RemoteException;

void remove(Handle handle)
        throws java.rmi.RemoteException, javax.ejb.RemoveException;

void remove(Object primaryKey)
        throws java.rmi.RemoteException, javax.ejb.RemoveException;
}
```

These methods are available to the client programmer, without any additional work by the EJB developer. The programmer will write a home interface, derived from this interface, which adds one or more methods depending on the type of bean. A stateful session bean will add one or more `create()` methods. An entity bean will add zero or more `create()` methods, and one or more `finder()` methods (these are explained in the chapter on entity beans). A stateless session bean, such as our order management bean, must define exactly one, parameterless, `create()` method.

Our `OrderManagement` EJB's home interface would look like this:

```
package orderMgmt;

public interface OrderManagementHome extends javax.ejb.EJBHome
{
  OrderManagement create()
    throws java.rmi.RemoteException, javax.ejb.CreateException;
}
```

Most of the work in writing an Enterprise JavaBean will be in developing the actual business logic. One class, often called the 'bean' class or 'implementation' class, is the central point for development of this business logic. Of course, like any Java class, this bean class may defer processing to other helper classes.

The specific structure of the bean class is dependent on the type of EJB. An entity bean must be derived from `javax.ejb.EntityBean`, whereas a session bean must be derived from `javax.ejb.SessionBean`. The bean class must implement the callbacks defined in its respective interface – although those callback methods may often be left blank.

The bean class must have a `public` method named `ejbCreate()` (with matching arguments) corresponding to every `create()` method declared in the home interface. For a session bean, the return type will be `void`. For an entity bean, the return type will be the class of the primary key – more about this later. An entity bean must also implement a corresponding `ejbPostCreate()` method. For an entity bean with bean-managed persistence, methods must be implemented that correspond to the finder methods declared in the bean's home interface. Again, more on all these callbacks later. (We are implementing a session bean here, and so we will use the session bean callbacks.)

Finally, the bean class must have business logic methods corresponding to those that were declared in the bean's remote interface. These methods are the *raison d'etre* for the whole of Enterprise JavaBeans technology.

881

The structure of our order management bean class might look like this:

```
package orderMgmt;

import javax.ejb.SessionContext;

public class OrderManagementBean implements javax.ejb.SessionBean
{

  public void placeOrder(String custName, String prodName, int quantity)
  {
    // ... Business logic ...
  }

  public void cancelOrder(String custName, String prodName)
  {
    // ... Business logic ...
  }

  public boolean isShipped(String custName, String prodName)
  {
    // ... Business logic ...
    return true;
  }

  public void ejbCreate()
  {
    // Can be empty
  }

  public void ejbRemove()
  {
    // Can be empty
  }

  public void ejbActivate()
  {
    // Can be empty
  }

  public void ejbPassivate()
  {
    // Can be empty
  }

  public void setSessionContext( SessionContext ctx )
  {
    // Can be empty
  }
}
```

The only part of our bean that we haven't yet discussed is the deployment descriptor. As it is in XML format, it can easily be read and edited by human beings. In general, however, you will produce this file using a tool, probably one that comes with your chosen application server or IDE. There is also at least one very good open-source deployment descriptor editor, EJX, available at http://www.dreambean.com. EJX has plug-ins for editing various EJB-related XML files, including the deployment descriptor and the jBoss open-source application-server specific files:

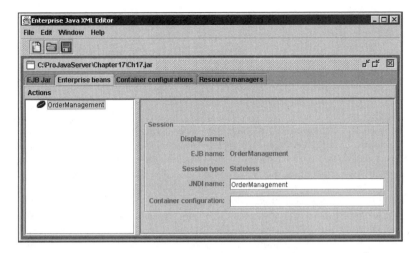

Various elements of the deployment descriptor are discussed in detail in the following chapters. Here, without further explanation, is the XML deployment descriptor for our very simple OrderManagement example:

```xml
<?xml version="1.0"?>

<ejb-jar>
  <enterprise-beans>
    <session>
        <ejb-name>OrderManagement</ejb-name>
        <home>orderMgmt.OrderManagementHome</home>
        <remote>orderMgmt.OrderManagement</remote>
        <ejb-class>orderMgmt.OrderManagementBean</ejb-class>
        <session-type>Stateless</session-type>
        <transaction-type>Container</transaction-type>
    </session>
  </enterprise-beans>

  <assembly-descriptor>
    <container-transaction>
      <method>
          <ejb-name>OrderManagement</ejb-name>
          <method-name>*</method-name>
      </method>
      <trans-attribute>Required</trans-attribute>
    </container-transaction>
  </assembly-descriptor>
</ejb-jar>
```

I developed and tested this simple bean on the jBoss application server. To run this "do-nothing" bean on that application server is very easy. Type in the four Java files discussed above (or download them from the Wrox web site): OrderManagement.java, OrderManagementBean.java, OrderManagementHome.java, and Client.java. Type in the XML deployment descriptor, and save it as ejb-jar.xml (remember, this name is mandatory). Compile the class files (you will need to include a path to the javax.ejb package in the CLASSPATH), and place them in a JAR file with the following structure:

```
META-INF\
        ejb-jar.xml

orderMgmt\
        OrderManagement.class
        OrderManagementHome.class
        OrderManagementBean.class
```

After you have developed a component, the next step is deploying it on your application server. Typically this means that you must map references in your code (to resources, other beans, security roles, etc.) to actual equivalents in your organizations environment (your Oracle database, your JNDI namespace, your security system, etc.) Consult your application server documentation if you need help with this.

If you are running this example with jBoss, you can take advantage of the "intelligent defaults" mode and just drop your JAR file in the "deploy" directory of your jBoss distribution. That's the whole deployment process. Like magic, your bean will be deployed and you can access it from the client we've written. (You won't always be able to do this: for example, you might need to use security for your bean; or you might have beans that access more than one database, making it impossible for jBoss to guess which one it should use. But we're hardly taxing the system with our lowly OrderManagement bean.)

When you run your client, make sure that you have all the JAR files in the jBoss "client" directory on your path. These are the infrastructure files that jBoss needs to run. (Well... they can be downloaded dynamically instead, but it's easier this way.) Remember that we hard-coded "localhost" when we set up the properties file for JNDI, so run the client and the jBoss server on the same machine. Run your client, and if you've typed in everything correctly, you'll see the meaningless "Order successfully placed" message appear:

What You Can't Do in an EJB Component

I've talked at length about the benefits of programming to the Enterprise JavaBeans specification if you are developing a transactional system. As an application developer, you are relieved of system-level programming tasks. This is a great advantage for programmer productivity, application capability, and system reliability. But to benefit, you must agree to work within the framework of EJB technology, and this means there are certain things you cannot do.

Certain EJB containers will allow you to do some of these things so you must balance the trade-off between portability and capability.

Some of these things you are unlikely to want to do anyway. You can't use the Reflection API to access information otherwise inaccessible to you. You can't create a class loader or replace a security manager. You can't set the socket factory used by ServerSocket or Socket. You can't use the object substitution features of the serialization protocol. It's unlikely that the typical application developer will run into these restrictions.

Some other, more common programming techniques are also restricted. A typical application developer may well run into these restrictions, and will want to know the reason for the restrictions, and how their goal can be otherwise accomplished.

You Can't Use Threads or the Threading API

This means you can't use the `synchronized` keyword in any of your bean class methods. Synchronizing the accesses of multiple beans could lead to deadlock. (You can still use utility classes with synchronized methods, such as `Vector`.) You can't start, stop, suspend, or resume a thread.

According to the specification, allowing the bean to manage threads would decrease the EJB container's ability to properly manage the runtime environment. Some implementations associate transaction or security contexts with the thread; if the bean were to create additional threads, this mechanism might not work. Or consider the case where an application service provider wants to host beans from multiple customers on a few big Unix boxes. This ASP needs to monitor and control resource usage of each application, so that it can meet its quality of service guarantees. One such resource is thread usage. If a bean were allowed to create additional threads, this would be harder to manage and control.

The truth is that it would be possible in some future version of the specification to provide a special threading API. This API could allow the EJB component to retrieve threads from a container-managed pool of threads, subject to whatever limitations and management the container and the system administrator desired. There are no fundamental technical problems with this approach. This API does not exist today, in either the EJB 1.1 specification or the EJB 2.0 specification.

In general, the application developer can trust the container to manage threads efficiently for them. Typically, there will be a pool of threads that are managed by the server. When a client request arrives, one of those pooled threads would be assigned to process that particular request. Explicit thread management shouldn't be necessary in most cases, and is unlikely to be possible in any case.

What about when the business logic for a single request requires parallel processing of several independent paths for efficient operation? For example, let's say that before I return an answer from my business method, I need to get information from an ERP system, a legacy sales management system, and a Lotus Notes server. Each of these systems takes ten seconds to process my request, and none of them depends on data from any of the others. Calling them in parallel might take around ten seconds. Calling them in series will require at least thirty. Unfortunately, there is no good answer for this situation in the current version of the specification.

You Can't Use the AWT

EJBs cannot use the AWT to display information or to input information from a keyboard.

It's very unlikely that your application server would allow direct interaction between your EJB and the keyboard or monitor. An application developer who wanted to do this should reconsider their understanding of the separation between the GUI and the business logic layers.

You Can't Act as a Network Server

This means you can't listen, accept, or multicast on a socket. It doesn't mean you can't use sockets at all, a common misconception: you can use a socket as a client. If the EJB were to act as a network server, it would interfere with the container's ability to use it as a business logic component. If you need to serve files, use an appropriate environment, such as a servlet container.

You Can't Use Read/Write Static Fields

This is a hard one for many programmers to let go of. But there are at least two problems with using writable static fields. First, you would need to protect them against concurrent accesses, which would violate the rule about thread synchronization. Second, static fields are only visible in one Java Virtual Machine. But many EJB containers will utilize multiple virtual machines for reasons of performance or reliability, and sometimes those virtual machines will be on multiple physical machines. There is no mechanism to propagate the update of a static field. This doesn't mean you can't use static fields at all: they just need to be read-only. You should probably declare any static field as `final` to enforce this requirement. Instead of writable static fields, you should use an appropriate shared resource, like a database.

You Can't Use the java.io Package

The specification says, "The file system APIs are not well-suited for business components to access data. Business components should use a resource manager API, such as JDBC API, to store data." This is certainly true. Files systems do not provide support for transactions, for instance. Another problem is that you cannot portably depend on a specific file-system structure – or even the existence of a file system at all. (What if the EJB container is embedded in a database?) If you want to load a resource, use the Java API method `java.lang.Class.getResourceAsStream()`. If you want to load or store data, use a database or the equivalent.

You Can't Load a Native Library

According to the specification, this is for security reasons. Any time you load a native library, you have portability concerns as well.

What if you absolutely need native code for some reason? Actually, how to develop any type of resource for your EJBs to access is currently underspecified. Look for a solution to this problem in something called the Connector API, which is currently part of the Java Community Process.

You Can't Use "this" as an Argument or Return Value

This restriction could actually use some clarification. You can't return the `this` reference of your 'bean' class to the client, or pass it as a parameter to a method call to another bean. The reason is that all interactions with the bean must pass through the 'interposition' class that we discussed earlier. This doesn't mean that you can't pass the reference to the bean instance reference to a helper class; you can and probably will. The helper class is considered part of the bean class, and doesn't need to go through the interposition class.

By the way, this is one of two reasons that you shouldn't implement the remote interface in your bean class. If it doesn't implement the interface, it can't be accidentally passed as a parameter or return value for a method expecting that remote interface. (The other reason not to implement the remote interface is because it's bad form to have to provide useless, empty implementations of the methods in `javax.ejb.EJBObject`.)

Instead of passing the `this` reference, pass the result of `SessionContext.getEJBObject()` or `EntityContext.getEJBObject()`.

You Can't/Shouldn't Use Loopback Calls

You can't, in the case of session beans, and you probably shouldn't, in the case of entity beans. Loopback calls are situations where EJB A calls EJB B, and EJB B then calls EJB A. Session beans are designed to be non-reentrant. Any time a call comes to them while they are processing another call, an exception is thrown.

If you think about it, this isn't such a serious limitation on session beans. A stateless session bean will never be involved in a loopback, because a new instance will be used for every method call. A stateful session bean shouldn't be referred to by any other EJB, but only by the client. A re-entrant call means that the client called it simultaneously from two different threads in the same transaction. Entity beans should not be designed to use loopback calls if possible, because:

❑   The entity bean programmer must design the entity bean with this possibility in mind

❑   The container cannot distinguish a legal loopback from an illegal concurrent call in the same transaction context.

You can probably get whatever effect you are looking for without requiring loopback calls.

EJB Components on the Web

The decision to use Enterprise JavaBeans technology in a web application may be made based on the requirements of the application for transactions, persistence, security, scalability, and so on. But deciding on technology is only the first step. How should such a web application be structured? A web application can maximize its flexibility and modularity by using EJBs as part of a classic **model-view-controller (MVC)** design. This pattern for building user interfaces originated in the Smalltalk world, and has found widespread applicability in the design of countless projects.

A design pattern is an arrangement of classes, their responsibilities, and their relationships, that serves as a re-usable solution to a particular design problem. There is a wealth of information on MVC and other design patterns, available on the Internet and in books such as the classic, "Design Patterns: Elements of Reusable Object-Oriented Software," by the so called 'gang of four' Gamma, Helm, Johnson, and Vlissides, from Addison-Wesley, ISBN 0-201633-61-2.

There are three classes of objects in the MVC architecture:

❑   **The model:**
    This is the data and business-logic component (sometimes known as the application object or business object, depending on the context). A model can serve multiple views.

❑   **The view:**
    This is the presentation component, also known as the user-interface component. There might be many views providing different presentations of a single model.

❑   **The controller:**
    This is the component that responds to user input. The controller translates user-interface events into changes to the model, and then defines the way the user-interface reacts to those events. In some versions of MVC, the view and the controller are collapsed into a single entity.

These three classes of objects are not components in the sense that EJBs are components: they are **logical divisions of functionality**. The aim of using these divisions to design your web application is to decouple the business logic, the presentation logic, and the web site design. There are at least four advantages to this:

❑   The application will be more resilient in the face of change. A web page's design can be changed without knowledge of business logic or site structure. Business logic or the data model can be changed without knowledge of web page design or site structure. Site structure can change without affecting business logic or the data model. A new type of interface, such as a wireless application, can be added simply by replacing the view.

❑ Business logic programmers, web site designers, and graphic artists can work independently. A likely point-of-failure in any large programming project is miscommunication among team members. If the elements of the project are decoupled, less communication is necessary and the project's people can work on what they do best.

❑ The separation of business logic, presentation logic, and web site design encourages the development of specifications and clear documentation of the code.

❑ The most expensive resources, such as experienced technical developers, are free to concentrate on the most complex part of the application.

In this architecture, the model component should often be implemented using Enterprise JavaBeans components. The motivation for this is that EJBs execute in a container that provides system-level services to the application developer. These services are not available outside the container, so model functionality – data access and business logic – that occurs in a servlet, JSP, or JavaBean component would not be able to take advantage of these services.

The view component can be implemented using JSPs. The technique of using JSPs to separate business logic and presentation logic (with JavaBeans and tag libraries) was discussed earlier in this book. In a highly structured application, these JSPs will relate only to the display of model data.

The controller component is implemented using a combination of a servlet or JSP page, possibly an EJB, and some helper classes. Using a controller in web application design is a valuable concept that overcomes many of the problems inherent in developing web applications. The controller component's servlet or JSP receives all requests for application URLs. This first part of the controller, sometimes called a 'front component', can ensure that security is uniformly applied, application state is initialized, and important workflow isn't bypassed. Using this application design, it's easy to prevent someone reaching a page out of sequence.

The next phase of the controller component translates the web request into generic application 'events'. This is important to remove from other application components any dependency on the specifics of web protocols (HTTP). It would be possible to skip this step, but this would prevent subsequent components from being reused in different contexts.

The final phase of the controller component is a JavaBean proxy (not an EJB), which may forward the generic application events to the Enterprise JavaBean controller. This controller is responsible for any update to the application's transactional data, accessed through EJB components. This EJB controller returns a notification of any changes in the model to the JavaBean proxy. This proxy can then notify the relevant JSP views that the model has been updated.

Since the view component is decoupled from the model and the controller components, it can be replaced for different clients. For instance, one client may require an HTML document be returned to it, while another client may require an XML document. JSPs that generate HTML or XML may be dynamically chosen in this architecture.

The following diagram describes a basic implementation of a model-view-controller implementation for a web site:

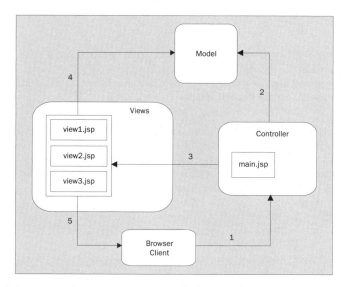

The browser client makes an HTTP request (GET or POST) [1]. All such requests go to the 'front component,' which in this case is a JSP page called main. The controller implementation (which can be a JavaBean, an EJB, or a combination) updates the model if necessary by forwarding the user-interface event, possibly in a transformed or normalized form [2]. The controller selects a view for display [3], which then updates itself against the model [4]. The view's output is returned to the client [5].

I provide an example of this model-view-controller architecture in Chapter 22, when I provide a web interface for the manufacturing example that we begin to develop in the next chapter.

> *Sun also provides an example of this architecture in its J2EE Blueprints document, in the form of an e-commerce site that sells pets on the web. Sun's version adds two additional layers of abstraction, by introducing a layer that translates web events into application events, and by providing an event notification architecture between the model and the views (which cache some model data). If you are interested in exploring this topic beyond what is presented in this book, you can download the Blueprints document from Sun's web site at*
> `www.javasoft.com/j2ee/blueprints/`.

Client-Tier Access to EJBs

Sometimes the presentation logic and workflow are handled on the client tier, as in the case of a Visual Basic application. Such an application might still implement the model-view-controller pattern on the client side, but there would not necessarily be a need to provide this level of structure on the server. There might still be a need to take advantage of services that an EJB container can provide. In the cases where web services are not needed, a client application will probably access EJBs directly.

In the simplest case, a client can access an Enterprise JavaBean remotely using RMI. This is certainly the case for Java GUI clients. A client written in a language other than Java can also access an EJB directly using IIOP (or Internet Inter-ORB Protocol, which is a standard protocol that allows CORBA ORBs to interoperate)

Yes, for this to happen the application server must also function as a CORBA ORB. One of the explicit goals of the EJB 1.1 specification is compatibility with CORBA protocols. IIOP communication transport is made mandatory in the EJB 2.0 draft specification, and all compliant application servers will have ORB functionality.

There is a third possibility that provides maximum flexibility in terms of client access: a model EJB whose data is transformed by a 'view' servlet. The Servlet API provides for servlets that are capable of sending and receiving arbitrary data in a 'request/response' format. A client that requires that a particular format be used to communicate with the server can use such a servlet to mediate communications with the Enterprise JavaBeans needed by that client:

When would this direct access architecture be appropriate (with or without a mediating 'view' object)? This is the design that would be used to implement a client/server application. Choosing between direct access to EJBs and web access to EJBs is often the same as choosing between a "thin-client" web app and a "fat-client" (but still three-tier) client server app. Many factors will influence this decision, such as client-interface requirements and application distribution issues.

One rule of thumb is that Internet access (or any distributed access) by a large group of users will typically indicate that a web application is required, and access to enterprise data should be mediated by a view component and a controller component on the web tier. Another rule of thumb is that users on a local network will frequently expect a level of client services that may require a stand-alone GUI client, rather than a web browser; this stand-alone GUI can access the Enterprise JavaBeans tier directly. Java applets are the wildcard, combining the distribution advantages of a web application with the presentation abilities of a stand-alone GUI. Rather than call a method on an EJB directly using RMI, they will sometimes access Enterprise JavaBeans through a servlet using HTTP to bypass corporate firewalls.

Of course, there's nothing to stop you from directly accessing an EJB from a servlet to provide a simple web page, rather than use the model-view-controller architecture discussed above. If you have a web application of limited scope, and an existing EJB that you want to reuse, this approach can be appropriate. Also, if you have a web application with limited presentation and navigation needs, but heavy business logic and data access requirements, you might find yourself directly accessing an EJB from a servlet or a JSP page's helper class. Before you take this approach in your web app, consider carefully if there is any chance for the scope of your project to increase – now or in the future.

Design of the EJB Tier

Up until this point, the discussion about design of applications using Enterprise JavaBeans has ignored the design of the EJB tier itself. In developing the EJB components for your application, you are implementing a model of your enterprise. To a large extent, the design of this tier should be independent of the design of the web tier or the client tier. This independence promotes reusability of business logic and data access components, which in many systems are the most difficult and expensive to develop. It also allows for presentation logic to change independently of your business logic. This is an important design goal for most systems, because presentation logic tends to be more volatile than business logic.

UML Use Cases

UML is the Unified Modeling Language, the standard language for expressing the model of the software system that you intend to build. **Use cases** are the subset of UML that express the functionality the software should deliver, as perceived by external actors. A single use case specifies one complete function, such as 'place an order' or 'submit an employee evaluation'. Use cases describe what to do, and not how to do it. How they are actually implemented by the software is unimportant to this stage of the design process.

> *There is not currently any direct support for Enterprise JavaBeans components in the UML. However, a UML "profile" for Enterprise JavaBeans is currently being developed under the Sun Community Process. This profile is a set of extensions that would allow UML to directly express (in a standard way) the structure and semantics specific to EJBs. This would ensure that these models were portable across tools from different vendors*

The EJB developer must be able to translate a use case into an implementation of the described functionality. The functionality of a use case begins when an **actor** (something outside the software, such as a person or another software system) makes a request of the system. It doesn't end until the software has accomplished the purpose embodied by that request. Considering how much code might be needed to implement a use case, it should be obvious that the correspondence between use cases and EJBs is not one-to-one. In fact, multiple EJBs will be used to implement most use cases, and both session beans and entity beans will be used in the most common scenarios.

Analysis Objects

In UML, a use case model is realized by modeling classes that implement that use case, along with their relationships and interactions. The exact procedure for modeling a use case – the process, the diagrams – is unimportant to understanding how to represent a use case by EJBs. What is helpful is to consider three types of **analysis objects** that the inventor of use cases, Ivar Jacobson, described from his experiences in building large, maintainable software systems ("Object-Oriented Software Engineering, A Use Case Driven Approach," by Jacobson, Christerson, Jonsson, and Overgaard) – and how these types of objects can be expressed using EJBs.

Interface Objects

The interface object (also known as a **boundary object**) is responsible for controlling access to the Enterprise JavaBeans tier from any client. This includes other server-side components, such as servlets and JSP pages. An excellent example of an interface object is the controller servlet for the web application's model-view-controller architecture. Note that we are using the word "interface" generically, and not in the sense of the Java language interface keyword.

> **An interface object should always be represented by a session bean in the implementation.**

Capabilities of the client and requirements of the specific application will determine whether the session bean should be stateful or stateless.

Control Objects

Control objects provide services to the application. They model functionality that is not naturally associated with a particular entity or interface. Often, this is because more than one entity needs to be operated on at one time; an example might be determining if there is sufficient inventory to manufacture a product. Other times, it may be because a relevant entity was not identified in the model; an example might be charging someone's credit card.

> **Control objects should be represented by session beans in the implementation. (The EJB 2.0 specification introduces home interface business methods that can also be used to implement control objects.)**

As they can be called from other EJBs, they should always be stateless. Conversational state in the EJB tier, if it exists at all, should always be maintained in an interface object, to avoid complexity and improve scalability.

Entity Objects

Entity objects model those business objects that should maintain their state after the use case completes. Typically, this means that they represent data from the database. Some examples are a customer, a product, an order, a personnel evaluation, a network event, or a deadline for a project.

> **Entity objects are often, but not always, represented by entity beans in the implementation model. Sometimes they are represented by dependent objects inside an entity bean, and sometimes they are implemented without any object representation at all (e.g. by JDBC code in a session bean).**

Of course, there are endless classification schemes by which you can organize your object model. Jacobson chose these three classifications because he believed the most stable systems were designed so that changes to that system could be kept as isolated as possible. Notice that this is also a motivation for the more general principle of separating design logic from business logic.

How do these three types of objects help to ensure that changes to the system remain local to a small portion of the implementation? There are two primary differences from a naïve object model that only represents entities (such as products, customers, employees, or contracts):

❑ Interface objects protect the other object types from the volatility of other tiers of the architecture. As a general rule, the further you travel from the data model to the client, the more likely the implementation will need to change. Business logic in the Enterprise JavaBeans tier will change gradually as the policies they represent change. The design of a web application may find itself undergoing continuous revision as the users discover new opportunities for improving their productivity and convenience. Changes to the interface should only affect the interface object.

❑ Control objects preserve the locality of functions that cut across multiple real-life entities. It is, of course, possible to break this functionality apart and assign it to the entities that are affected, since entities model behavior as well as representing data. However, when the time comes that this functionality needs to be modified, it's easiest if it can be changed in one place.

Analysis models of use cases are not developed in isolation. The appropriate analysis objects are often determined in an iterative process that involves consideration of multiple use cases. As a rule of thumb, an interface object will represent access to a set of related use cases for a particular class of users via a particular method (which could be via a web application, a GUI client, a business-to-business XML protocol, an ERP system, or almost anything else). A control object will often represent the activities associated with a single use case.

Analysis vs. Implementation

Just as there is not a one-to-one correspondence between use cases and Enterprise JavaBeans, there is also not a one-to-one correspondence between analysis objects (interface, control, and entity) and EJB components. Those analysis objects are logical creations that must then be mapped to actual implementation classes. We have already seen one example of this lack of one-to-one correspondence in the model-view-controller web application design, where the interface object spans two tiers: the controller session bean (EJB tier) and the proxy JavaBean (web tier).

Why do an analysis that does not result in an object model that we can directly implement using Enterprise JavaBeans? The goals of the analysis phase are to provide a resilient structure for our application and to understand how the functionality should be divided between component roles (interface, entity, or control). Once this structure has been established, we can then consider the effects on our design of our implementation tools and component architecture. In this particular case, of course, we must consider the capabilities and limitations of the Enterprise JavaBeans implementation environment.

> *Sometimes a design model, whose purpose it is to refine and formalize the analysis model, will come before the implementation environment is taken into account. The exact process is unimportant to understanding the effects of using EJB technology in the design of your application.*

The most important limitation, and the one that will probably drive your implementation model from an architectural standpoint, is that EJBs are **heavyweight components**. This means that there is a cost to implementing an object as an EJB, which you must take into account. This cost exists for two reasons:

❏　They are intended to be accessible by remote clients. Any communication across a network is going to have associated costs.

❏　The services provided by the EJB container have what you can think of as setup costs. As the container must take action to provide each access of a component's business logic with protection from unauthorized access, support for transactional use, controlled transfer of enterprise data, and more, access to an EJB component can be thought of as relatively expensive.

As a consequence of being heavy weight components, EJBs are often used to represent an aggregation of objects that exist in the analysis model. Those other objects may have a correspondence in the implementation, but they may be simple lightweight Java objects (such as JavaBeans components), rather than Enterprise JavaBeans. Furthermore, functionality that might be represented by multiple operations on the analysis objects should be transformed into a single operation on an object in the implementation. Let's consider how this aggregation of objects or functionality would apply to the three types of objects in the analysis model:

❏　Interface objects will typically be represented by a single object per outside user in the analysis model, and a single session bean in the design. However, operations available to the user interface will probably need to be aggregated in the implementation. A good example is model attribute access. Getter and setter methods are usually not appropriate on remote objects, because each call to get or set data means another round-trip across the network. Therefore, the interface object will need to accept and return some sort of collection in response to data updates and retrieval. Depending on the situation and the capabilities of the client, it may be possible to reference a control object directly. If no interface-specific functionality is required, no interface session bean should be developed.

❑ Control objects in the analysis model often correspond to a single use case. This analysis-model object contains the business logic necessary to perform a sequence of operations, modify and retrieve data from the relevant entity objects, and validate the results. In the implementation, a use case will typically have a representation in a single method of the interface session EJB. For example, the 'place an order' use case might have a corresponding method in the interface session EJB `placeOrder(CustomerInfo, ShoppingCart)`. Control functionality specific to the type of user will probably be implemented right in that interface object, either directly or as a helper object, depending on its complexity. However, in many cases control object functionality will be common to multiple use cases. For instance, multiple use cases may require order-placement functionality. Control functionality that is common to multiple use cases should be moved into a session bean or multiple session beans that provide reusable services. In this common case, the role of the implementation's interface session bean will be to translate the request into a generic form, to ensure that workflow rules aren't violated, and to call the appropriate service-layer beans. Service-layer beans will be implemented as stateless session beans. The combination of interface session bean plus service-layer session beans will comprise the control object.

❑ Entity objects have the most variation in their deviation from the analysis model. Even while doing analysis, it is sometimes difficult to identify what should be modeled as an attribute (i.e. a "member variable") and what should be a domain object (i.e. a "class"). This is made even more difficult in the implementation, because entity objects are often the most heavyweight of all the Enterprise JavaBean types. This is because they are accessed in greater numbers: in a particular use case, there may be one interface session bean, three or four session beans providing control functionality, and potentially hundreds (or even thousands) of participating entity beans. Also, entity beans need to load their state from the database, which is a relatively expensive operation for most environments. It's not unusual for first-class entities in the analysis model to be represented by attributes in the implementation, modeled as JavaBeans or similar Java classes. It is even possible to implement entity objects as data-access classes used by session beans, and to exclude entity beans from your implementation altogether. (Since entity beans provide important persistent services, this is not usually recommended. See Chapters 19 and 20 on session and entity beans for more detail about their use and design.)

Your choice of technology will probably also have an affect on your final design. One of the most important factors will be the object/relational mapping capabilities of the products you choose. Some application servers with EJB support, even some of the more popular ones, have only limited support for automatically persisting complex entity objects to underlying relational tables. If this is the case with your application server, you have several choices. Sometimes you can purchase add-on products that will provide container-managed persistence in cooperation with your application server. You may choose an object/relational mapping tool that is not directly supported by your container. In this case, you have the option of using entity objects with bean-managed persistence, or session beans that update the database directly.

An important rule to remember is that session beans are not designed to represent transactional data. A session bean may update the database, but it must not model data directly. This is because it does not have the container callbacks and management that entity beans do to allow them to intelligently participate in transactions, synchronize concurrent accesses, respond to errors, and so on. (This will be explained in more detail at the beginning of Chapter 20, in the section about trying to construct an entity-equivalent out of a session bean.) Finally, you might choose to model dependent objects as entity beans. This is not an ideal situation, but support for the correct database mappings with this approach is practically guaranteed with any EJB container.

Your scalability requirements may affect your choice of component type when implementing an interface object. It is more expensive to maintain conversational state on the server than on the client. The choice of stateful or stateless session bean for the interface component will often be made based on the volume of use planned for the application. Obviously, storing state in different tiers can result in significantly different implementations.

The Role of State in the Interface Object

The Enterprise JavaBeans specification provides for two types of session beans: stateful and stateless. Stateless session beans are always used for the services layer. Choosing a type of session bean for the interface object is more difficult. Allowing the interface object to have state may simplify application design. For instance, the client may not be able to manage state as effectively, such as with a web browser. However, in reality, it is almost always possible to keep state in a tier closer to the client.

One of the main advantages to keeping conversational state in an interface object session bean is to enforce the workflow of a use case or set of use cases. Consider the not-uncommon situation where prior to making a purchase a web visitor must either sign in, which allows the application to retrieve the relevant customer information, or create a customer record, with shipping information, contact information, optional e-mail and site preferences, etc. A stateful session bean interface object could enforce this requirement. A stateless session bean would need to depend on the user interface to do so, because it could not remember the customer's actions between method calls.

An Example of EJB Design

Over the course of the next five chapters, we will be building a small sample application. By this time, most programmers know that you can build an e-commerce application using Enterprise JavaBeans technology. It's understandable that this application space is referenced so often; many of the people who are interested in server-side Java programming want to write an application to support commerce on the web. However, the basic techniques are broadly applicable to almost any Java server-side solution, so for a change, I thought we'd use an example that included some manufacturing. In this chapter, we'll consider its design.

Consider the case of a company that develops products, takes orders for those products, and then manufactures them and ships them. I've created some simple requirements, as follows:

❏ The engineering department needs to be able to define a product as a series of steps that the manufacturing facility will follow to build it.

❏ We need to be able to take orders over the web, and by phone using operators who are recording orders from our salesmen. We need to be able to notify the manufacturing department that an order for a particular product, to be delivered on a particular date, has been placed. The identifier for this order is unique within a particular sales division, but each sales division has its own numbering scheme for orders and duplicate order numbers may exist between sales divisions.

❑   We need to be able to cancel an order on which manufacturing has not yet started. We need to be able to prevent the cancellation of an order on which work has already started.

❑   The manufacturing department needs to be able to select an appropriate order for manufacture, based on the time required to build a product and the maximum time that the company will hold a product in inventory.

❑   Management must be able to retrieve a list of overdue orders.

❑   The manufacturing department must be able to notify the shipping department that a product is ready for shipment. It must be able to indicate the carrier that is appropriate for the size and weight of the product as manufactured, and the loading dock to which the product has been sent. It must be able to identity itself in case there is a quality problem with the product, and must be able to record the date completed in order to respond to customer inquiries.

For this hypothetical company, we can identify six actors:

❑   An engineer

❑   A web customer

❑   A phone operator who takes orders from a catalog

❑   A floor manager who manages the manufacturing process

❑   A crew member that actually builds the product ordered

❑   A manager who tracks overdue orders

There will also be seven use cases:

❑   Create a Product

❑   Place an Order

❑   Cancel an Order

❑   Select an Order for Manufacture

❑   Build a Product

❑   Ship an Order

❑   List Overdue Orders

Here is a use case diagram that might result from our analysis:

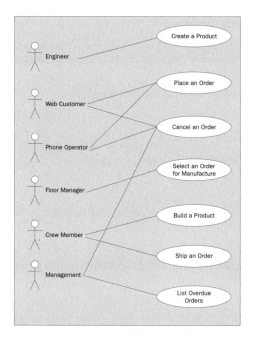

Here are the details about what must be done to accomplish the purpose of each use case. I have emphasized the steps of each use case that we will actually implement.

Create a Product

- ❏ **Select a product identification tag and a descriptive product name**
- ❏ **Add the routing steps to be followed during the manufacture of the product**
- ❏ Create the inventory records necessary managing the manufacturing process of this product
- ❏ Set the price

Place an Order

- ❏ Calculate the total price of the order
- ❏ Validate the payment method
- ❏ **Record the order**
- ❏ Return order tracking information to the customer
- ❏ E-mail confirmation of the order

Cancel an Order

- ❏ **Make sure that the order is not already being manufactured**
- ❏ **Change the order status to cancelled**
- ❏ Credit the customer account or credit card
- ❏ E-mail confirmation of the cancellation

Select an Order for Manufacture

- ❑ **List the eligible orders, defined as those where the status is open, and today's date is greater than the due date of the order minus the time it takes to build it, minus the time that we're willing to have it sit in inventory**

- ❑ **Choose one of them to build the corresponding product**

- ❑ Ensure that sufficient inventory exists

- ❑ Decrement the inventory

- ❑ Check minimum inventory levels; contact supplier if necessary

Build a Product

- ❑ **Iterate through the routing steps defined for that product, following the instructions**

Ship an Order

- ❑ **Indicate the carrier chosen and the loading dock to which the finished product will be moved**

List Overdue Orders

- ❑ **List the overdue orders, defined as those where the status is open and today's date plus the lead-time required for manufacture is greater than the due date, or those where the status is in-process, and today's date is greater than the due date**

In practice, I'll be implementing two sets of interfaces to this application: a set of stand-alone Java clients and a web application. For the purposes of this analysis, let's use our imaginations and imagine that there are several other clients: a Swing GUI that the phone operator uses; a Visual Basic application that the guys in engineering use; and a Palm Pilot interface that the manufacturing crews use. (The rest use web interfaces.) For each client application, there is an interface object in our analysis model.

UML has an extension method, called a **stereotype**, which "specializes" an element defined in the modeling language. A stereotype can be represented by text surrounded by brackets (<<interface>>) or by an icon. Interface objects, control objects, and entity objects have standard stereotypes, with icon representations. The stereotype icon for an interface object in UML looks something like this:

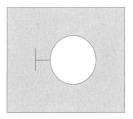

By inspecting the use cases, I can identify the following entity objects in the analysis model (the ones we actually use in our simplified implementation are emphasized):

- ❑ **Product**

- ❑ **Order**

- ❑ **Routing step**

- ❑ **Shipment**

- ❑ Account

❑   Supplier

❑   **Shipping company**

❑   Customer

The stereotype for an entity object in UML looks like this:

Typically, there is a one-to-one correspondence between use cases and control objects. The control objects here would be:

❑   Create a Product

❑   Place an Order

❑   Cancel an Order

❑   Select an Order for Manufacture

❑   Build a Product

❑   Ship an Order

❑   List Overdue Orders

The stereotype for a control object in UML looks like this:

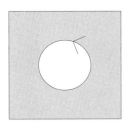

I'll present three views of a possible analysis model. The first view shows the use case actors and their respective interface objects:

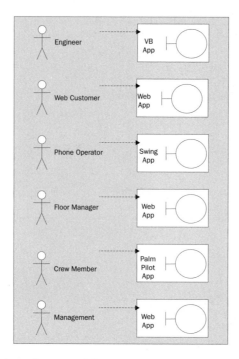

The second shows the interface objects and the control objects with which they interact:

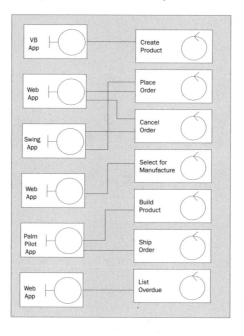

And the last shows how the control objects interact with entity objects. You will notice how the object model, even for what amounts to a toy problem, is complicated enough that it is probably better viewed in segments with a modeling tool, than drawn all at once:

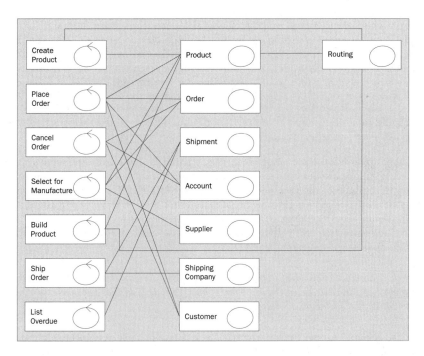

Fortunately, this complexity is hidden from any user interface by the interface objects. Notice, too, that functionality such as 'place order' could have been located across the order, product, account, and customer objects. However, this would have increased the surface area of our design.

The analysis model now needs to be translated into an implementation appropriate for our environment. As I said before, this will not be a simple one-to-one translation from analysis object to EJB component. Let's start by considering the interface objects:

Actor	User Interface Type	Interface Object Implementation
Engineer	Visual Basic	Session Bean (RMI/IIOP)
Web customer	Web Application / JSPs	JavaBean proxy / Session Bean
Phone operator	Swing GUI	Session Bean
Floor manager	Web Application / JSPs	JavaBean proxy / Session Bean
Crew member	Palm Pilot XHTML	Servlet to Session Bean
Management	Web Application / JSPs	JavaBean proxy / Session Bean

Notice that in four of the six cases, the interface object from the analysis model could translate into multiple components on multiple tiers.

One detail that isn't evident from this chart is that there aren't necessarily six different session beans. The phone operator, web customer, and business-to-business customer may be able to share a single session bean interface. Recall the earlier discussion about the model-view-controller architecture. Remember that there was a class in the controller component responsible for translating web requests into generic application events? It is this translation that makes it possible to consider reusing the interface session bean for more than one interface. Of course, it may also be that the requirements of the different applications necessitate providing custom functionality. In this case, different interface objects would be used. For instance, in the real world web customers and our salesmen's customers may get different pricing, different credit approval processes, different limits on orders, drop-ship orders rather than deliveries from inventory, and so on, depending on the different profiles of those customers.

Let's consider the entity objects next. Assume that we have an application server with adequate object-relational mapping capabilities. Furthermore, assume that we are going to use entity beans where appropriate, so that we can take advantage of our container's persistence services.

In this case, there are at least two changes that we are going to make from the analysis model to the implementation. First, we are going to demote routing steps from a first class business object (i.e. a component) to an attribute of the product (i.e. a member variable). This is done in recognition of the fact that entity beans are heavyweight objects, and we don't want to have every use of a line item pass through the container's services layer. A common rule of thumb is that objects whose lifecycle (creation and destruction) is completely controlled by another object should be attributes of that EJB entity, even if they were first-class objects in the analysis.

> Note that there are a lot of opportunities for an EJB container to optimize these 'heavyweight' calls between components that are executing in the same Java Virtual Machine. The extent to which a container will do this varies greatly between vendors.

Secondly, we are going to model the shipments as a session bean service, rather than an entity. My reason for this approach was development simplicity. The manufacturing application doesn't need to access the shipment information once it is added to the database. Having a single business method that uses SQL might be marginally better than writing an entity bean whose only purpose was to be created, in terms of development cost.

Finally, let's consider the control objects. In the analysis model there were six: Create a Product, Place an Order, Cancel an Order, Select an Order for Manufacture, Build a Product, Ship an Order, and List Overdue Orders. We could make six session beans to represent these control objects. But besides being heavyweight objects at execution time, EJBs have a certain amount of weight in the development process too. Each EJB must have at least three Java files and some configuration information. All other things being equal, one EJB is better than three. Placing, canceling, and listing orders seem cohesive enough to put into a single service bean ("Manage Orders"). Likewise, selecting an order for manufacture, building the product, and shipping the order all take place on the factory floor ("Manufacture"). The "Create a Product" control object should probably have a session bean of its own.

One issue we will have to consider is whether we can combine any control objects and interface objects into a single session bean. The answer will depend on the complexity of our system and the requirements we will have for component reuse. You can reuse a session bean implementation of a control object more easily than a session bean implementing both interface and control logic. Those reasons are the same as we gave earlier for differentiating between interface and control logic in the analysis model: localization of changes. Additionally, if your interface object has state, it cannot be reused by other EJB components at all, because that state must belong to a single client.

Can we stop here? Actually, we have to consider one last issue: to what extent should we factor additional functionality into its own stateless session service EJBs? If this were a description of our enterprise's entire software implementation, we could probably stop here. Certain aspects of the control objects' functionality would probably be implemented as JavaBean helper classes, but this would be an implementation detail irrelevant to the Enterprise JavaBeans framework. However, it is more likely the case that we would need to consider which services might be used by other control objects in parts of the software that haven't been described here. For example, it is quite likely that checking inventory levels will be done by accounting software, management software, and more. So the functionality to check inventory levels should be promoted to a stateless session bean that provides methods related to inventory. Another example is the e-mail that we sent in several of the use cases. It is quite likely that there will be enterprise-wide policies on the form that e-mail to customers should take. So there should be a session bean with the responsibility to send e-mail to customers.

It's sometimes difficult to determine what should be implemented as a stateless session bean and what should be a helper class or function. There is a basic trade-off between implementation efficiency and ease of coding on the one hand (for helper classes), and reusability and manageability on the other hand (for stateless session bean services). One thing that favors stateless session beans is that, even though there are still costs associated with calling them compared to generic Java code, they are the least costly of the three types of beans. They can be pooled and reused efficiently, unlike stateful session beans, and do not have persistence requirements, unlike entity beans. In general, if some piece of functionality would be useful on its own to multiple clients, it should at least be considered for promotion to a reusable service. However, the largest grouping of functionality possible should be chosen for promotion.

Summary

This chapter introduced Enterprise JavaBeans, or EJBs for short. EJBs are designed to encapsulate business logic, and to protect the application developer from having to worry about system level issues.

We learned the following about EJBs:

❑   They are intended for transactional systems

❑   They are portable, reusable server-side components that execute in a container

❑   They assist developer productivity, extend application capability, and improve system stability

❑   They are accessible from many different types of clients

❑   There are three types of beans: stateful session, stateless session, and entity

❑   There are four major parts to every bean: the home interface, the remote interface, the implementation class, and the XML deployment descriptor

❑   The enterprise bean developer must follow certain rules to get the benefits of Enterprise JavaBeans technology

❑   The roles of EJBs can be understood by analyzing a model of your enterprise in terms of interface objects, control objects, and entity objects

In the next chapter, we'll look at session beans more closely. First, we'll consider the role that they play in representing business logic and workflow. Next, we'll consider the issue of stateful vs. stateless session beans, and where conversational state should be kept in your application. To write a session bean, you need to understand the callbacks that the EJB container will make into your code; we'll examine these methods and what your responsibilities are in implementing them. Finally, we'll begin to implement a version of the application that we analyzed in this chapter.

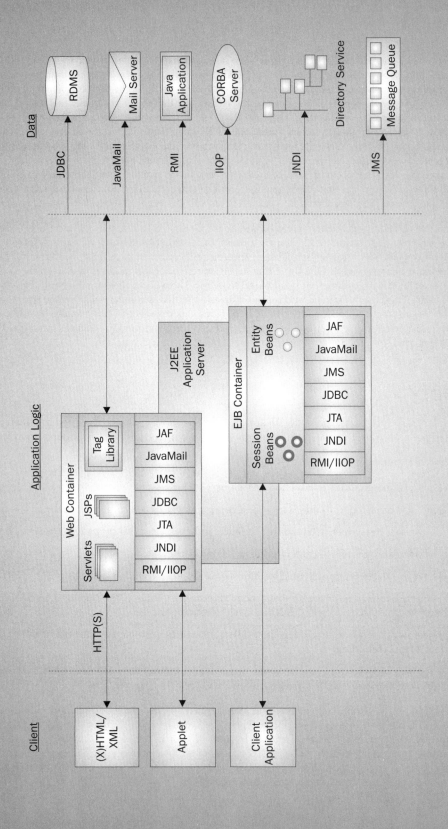

19

Session Beans and Business Logic

The Enterprise JavaBeans 1.1 specification provides two different models for callback methods and runtime lifecycles. Beans are called entity beans or session beans, depending on the model to which they are written. This chapter discusses **session beans**, which are the type of EJB component you will use for any component that does not directly represent an entity. (The next chapter will discuss entity beans, and Chapter 23 will describe the message-driven bean introduced in the EJB 2.0 specification.) You use a session bean to represent workflow, business logic, and private application state.

The following topics are covered in detail:

- ❑ The differences between stateful and stateless session beans
- ❑ The role of session beans in implementing business logic
- ❑ The use of session beans as a façade
- ❑ The trade-offs to consider for storing state on various tiers of your design
- ❑ The use of session beans to access persistent storage
- ❑ The callbacks and lifecycle of a session bean
- ❑ How to use a JDBC connection in your code
- ❑ How to access environment variables

As we discuss the callbacks and lifecycle of a session bean, we'll develop two simple beans: a stateless session bean and a stateful session bean. You'll be able to run these beans in this chapter. In addition, we'll continue developing the manufacturing example for which we did some design in the last chapter. In the context of this application, we'll talk about some basic implementation techniques, such as returning view objects to the client. However, this application makes use of several entity beans, so you'll have to wait until Chapter 20 before you can actually compile, deploy, and run these beans.

Session Beans and State

There are two types of session beans: **stateful** and **stateless**. Those two types have much in common:

❑   Both implement the `javax.ejb.SessionBean` interface, and therefore have the same container callbacks

❑   Both represent a private resource for the client that created them

❑   Both are intended to model a process or a task

❑   Both can update shared data, but do not represent that shared data in the way that an entity bean does

In fact, the only way that an EJB container can distinguish a stateless session bean from a stateful session bean is to look in the XML descriptor file to see which type the programmer intended.

The primary difference between the two types of beans – as is obvious from their names – is how they treat **object state** (in other words, their variables).

> **A stateful session bean can keep data between client accesses. A stateless session bean must not.**

This simple but important difference has complex ramifications for the design of your system. We'll talk about this later in the chapter, but a basic rule to keep in mind is that stateful session beans should only be used at the *boundary* of the object model.

Recall the simple division of functionality for objects in the analysis model that we described in the last chapter. There are three basic types: **interface objects**, **control objects**, and **entity objects**. An EJB component that implements an interface object may be implemented as a stateless or stateful session bean. An EJB component implementing a control object that is called from an EJB component implementing an interface object must be a stateless session bean. Entity objects in the analysis model do not always have a corresponding component in the implementation. When they do, that component must be an entity bean. Although a session bean can update shared data, it cannot represent that data in the way that an entity bean can. (You can read more about this in Chapter 20 on entity beans.)

Representing Business Logic

Both entity beans and session beans have business logic. However, the business logic in an entity bean should typically be limited to validation and transformation logic for the data that the entity represents. Everything else – all information about an enterprise's workflow or processes – belongs in session beans.

A good architecture for many purposes is to arrange these session beans into two layers. The lower layer provides generic, reusable services, such as 'release work-order' or 'validate credit card' (I'll refer to this as the **services layer**). This is where the control objects in the analysis model are implemented. The higher layer provides controlled access to these services from clients such as an MRP system (manufacturing resource planning) or a shopping-cart servlet (I'll refer to this as the **access control layer**). This is where the interface objects in the analysis model are implemented.

In the previous chapter, we discussed the reason for differences between your analysis model and the actual implementation of your application. You might combine control-related activities, such as notifying a manager that a customer is approaching his credit limit, with interface-related activities, such as providing an interface to e-commerce functionality for JSP pages. Obviously the division of labor between these two layers will not be clear-cut. In general, I would err on the side of separating reusable components out of your initial design.

There is one thing of which you will want to be aware, if you do use this architecture. **Conversational state** should *never* be maintained in the services layer. It must *always* be kept in the access control layer, if it is saved in an EJB at all. In other words, a control object should never depend on keeping state between business method calls. A control object implementation can be part of a stateful session bean if the programmer has combined a control object with an interface object to simplify things, but the control object should not depend on this state. One reason is that it reduces the reusability of the control object in different contexts. There is, however, a more general formulation of this rule prohibiting service-layer state, based on EJB-specific criteria.

> If you are using stateful session beans, *they should never be chained together* through mutual business method calls.

The EJB container has the option of discarding state after a configurable time-out period. In other words, it can destroy your stateful session bean and throw an exception the next time you try to call it. Managing state with multiple expirations introduces unnecessary complication into your design.

Perhaps the most important design pattern to emerge so far in systems using Enterprise JavaBeans technology is to use the session bean to provide a **façade** to a client.

> A façade is a higher-level interface to a set of interfaces in a subsystem, and can be considered a more general case of the analysis-model interface object discussed earlier.

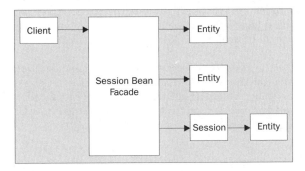

There are several generally applicable reasons to use the façade pattern, such as reducing complexity and minimizing dependencies between subsystems. These reasons were discussed in the previous chapter, and all these reasons apply to the case of EJBs. But there are several additional reasons to provide a client a façade that are specific to distributed systems and Enterprise JavaBeans technology.

A typical client will need to access the business logic in multiple session beans and the validation logic in multiple entity beans. Consider the following four advantages to using a façade, rather than accessing those session and entity beans directly from the client:

- ❏ **Decreased network traffic**
  Network traffic has always been a limitation on the performance of distributed object systems. Object oriented programming typically involves numerous calls to methods that implement discrete and limited functionality. The classic examples are get and set methods. If these method calls are occurring remotely, all the parameters and return values must be sent across the network. For instance, assume that a client wants to sum the results of calling getPrice() on a collection of 100 entity beans. If the client called the entity beans directly, every single invocation and every single response would travel across the network. If the client called a session bean façade that did the addition for it, only one invocation and one response need travel across the network. By invoking the entity beans locally, the session bean façade in our example reduced network traffic by two orders of magnitude. (Of course, this assumes that the façade is on the same machine – or on an isolated network link – with the other beans that it accesses.)

- ❏ **Declarative transactional control**
  In a typical business system, the results of multiple operations must be applied as a single unit. The classic, oft-repeated example is of an account transfer in a banking system. The transfer involves two operations: deleting money from one account and adding money to the other. If one operation should fail and the other succeed, either the bank or the customer is out some money. If a session bean façade makes both calls, the EJB container can manage the process automatically based on declarative information provided by the developer. If the client makes both calls, the client is responsible for ensuring that the operations are atomic – both must succeed or both must fail.

- ❏ **Fewer unnecessary interpositions**
  To provide its services to EJBs, the container adds a layer of indirection between the client and the bean. This layer will inevitably consume some resources on the server, such as processor time and memory space. If an EJB is calling another EJB in the same container, some of this work can be optimized away, and server resources can be saved for business logic. For instance, the server may avoid some security checks after the first one has succeeded.

- ❏ **Business logic on the correct tier**
  If multiple calls to multiple beans are necessary to provide a business function, there will usually be some order and relationship to these calls. Along with tightly coupling the client layer to the business logic layer's implementation, making these calls from the client means that a certain amount of workflow is located on the client tier.

In general, all your accesses to EJBs from client applications should be through a small number of session bean façades. Obviously this rule does not apply to EJBs themselves, which can have non-façade session or entity beans as clients; otherwise the façade would need a façade, ad infinitum. There will be circumstances that create additional exceptions to this or any design rule. Consider the disadvantages carefully before deciding that you have one of those exceptions.

The Difficult Problem of Conversational State

State can be divided into two types: **transactional** and **conversational**.

❑ Roughly speaking, transactional state is the data you store in the persistent store. Multiple clients can read and modify this data without conflict. If the application server crashes or is restarted, the data is still available in the data store. An example would be an order that a customer has placed.

❑ Conversational state is the data cached in application variables, either on the client or the server. This is private data that isn't accessible by other clients. An example of this is the ubiquitous web site shopping cart. If the conversational state isn't turned into transactional state, it can disappear when a component of the application (on the client or server) disappears

This section refers exclusively to conversational state. Conversational state does not include implementation artifacts such as a connection to a database or a socket that is maintained throughout the life of the component, regardless of the actions of the client.

> *Keeping transactional data consistent is a difficult problem too. Fortunately, it is one that the computer industry has a lot of experience at solving. Relational databases are a mature technology and the techniques for using them effectively are well known. Meanwhile the problem of where to store conversational state, while perhaps objectively easier, is also a newer problem (at least in terms of modern multi-tiered designs) and more likely to provoke a lively discussion among experienced application designers.*

Any non-trivial application will have conversational state. Depending on the client, this state can be stored in different ways. A Swing GUI can obviously store state in Java objects. A web browser can store state on the client (cookies, hidden fields, URL rewriting, etc.) or on the server (HTTP session). State that is logically conversational may actually be stored in a transactional database, or it may simply be stored in memory.

Session beans offer another place in which state can be stored. Under certain circumstances, this can make application development easier. State can be stored in a unified way for multiple types of clients: a web client, a Swing GUI client, and a Palm Pilot, for instance. The alternative would be maintaining state by three different methods, which may not allow the same capabilities present with your application server.

But the potential advantages in application development must be balanced against the cost in application scalability and performance. To understand the trade-off, it helps to understand a little about what is happening behind the scenes with the EJB container.

Logically, all session beans are mapped one-to-one with a particular client reference, as shown in the following diagram. The EJB is created when the client calls `create()` and destroyed when the client calls `remove()`:

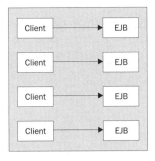

If there are five thousand web clients using your application, there will be five thousand session beans on the server. With a stateless session bean, however, the container has the opportunity for a tremendous optimization by **pooling** beans. Since they don't have state, there is no effect on the bean from any client's call – so one bean can be reused for multiple clients:

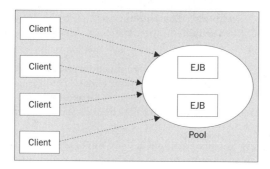

This has a great effect on the available resources. Rather than five thousand stateless session beans, a container might have a pool of just fifty. Of course, the pool could be dynamically adjusted to meet an arbitrary number of concurrent requests for service.

> *A "pool" is simply a collection of instances that are available to service requests. A particular server might pool components, threads, database connections, socket connections, and many other resources. This pooling is invisible to the component developer, although the administrator of the server may be able to change its behavior.*

If stateless session beans don't have state, why do they have variables? Stateless session beans can have permanent state that is not associated with a particular client. For instance, a bean might have an open socket to a resource used by every client. Why can't they be multi-threaded? This is by design, to simplify the development model for EJB components. As EJBs are never accessed by more than one thread at a time, the bean programmer doesn't need to worry about synchronizing access to this permanent state. Also, stateless session beans can have temporary state associated with a client within a particular method call. They just can't maintain this state across method calls. For instance, imagine that the client has called the EJB method calculateDemand(Product product). This method calls ten helper methods. As a convenience, the programmer might set a product variable, rather than passing the product to all ten helper methods. However, the next time the session bean is called, nothing can be assumed about the value of that product variable.

> *Personally, I don't think you can do this and have well-structured code. Those state variables seem too much like global variables to me, which by consensus the software development industry has been against since the 1970s.*

To help the EJB container manage a large number of stateful session beans, callbacks and rules were included in the specification to give the container the ability to move a stateful session bean to temporary storage, and restore it from that storage, between transactions. The algorithm the container uses to decide when to store a bean is specific to a particular EJB container. Storing a bean is called **passivation**, and reactivating it is called **activation**.

Activation and passivation are effective methods to deal with the problem of limited server resources. However, they only work to a point – although this point is always moving forward with better – designed servers and more capable computers. Still, if it is important for your application to scale, the best practice is to keep state on the client and pass it back to the server with each invocation. In the case of a Java client, this may actually be easier than using a stateful session bean. In the case of a thin web client, state storage on the client can be difficult, largely because of the variations of environments and permissions in which your client application may be run. You will have to carefully analyze the trade-offs of performance, security, and development productivity.

Session Beans and Persistent Storage

The end result of business logic is often the modification or addition of data to your enterprise's persistent store. The Enterprise JavaBeans specification provides for entity beans to represent this data and to provide persistent services.

However, it is possible to bypass entity beans and access a persistent store (such as a database) directly from your session beans. In other words, your session beans will become responsible for the functionality represented by entity objects in your analysis model. As you are bypassing many of the container's persistent services, this will usually introduce additional complexity into your development effort. If you are using an object database or an object-relational mapping tool, this does not apply and a pure session-bean approach may be the way to go. Under certain circumstances, you can also increase your performance by coding direct data access instead of using entity beans.

> *Under other circumstances, a pure session-bean approach will have a detrimental effect on performance. Determining which is the case in your situation will involve consideration of database locking strategies, data-access patterns in your application, your EJB container's implementation, and isolation-level requirements. Before you go profiling different architectures, ask yourself how much you really need to scale. Most of us don't work for an airline or the IRS. The most common situations will call for using entity beans with container-managed persistence for operations on single entities and small groups. Session beans will be an appropriate vehicle for operations on a set of data (e.g. a count, sum, or list).*

If you build your system using nothing but stateless session beans, you will be using one of the oldest architectures for large systems. The biggest systems were once built using Transaction Processing monitors. These TP monitors played the same role that an EJB container does today. Rather than a bean method, the application programmer would write a program that could take start-up parameters. The client program would make a call to the TP monitor, which would run the program with the client's parameters. All state would be maintained in the database. This architecture can be made to work for very large transactional systems that don't have caching requirements beyond that provided by the database.

The Enterprise JavaBeans 1.0 specification made entity beans optional; the expectation was that developers using a container without support for entity beans would code direct access to the database in session beans, probably through a tool of some sort. Even though version 1.1 made support for entities mandatory, it still remains a valid choice to depend on session beans exclusively.

The Financial Aid Calculator Bean

EJB components have callback methods by which the container provides them with notifications about their lifecycle (i.e. when they are about to be created, destroyed, saved to a persistent store, or retrieved from a persistent store). These callback methods for each type of bean (session, entity, and in EJB 2.0, message-driven) are defined in interfaces in the `javax.ejb` package. Stateful and stateless session beans both have the same callback methods, because they both must implement `javax.ejb.SessionBean`. However, these callback methods are used in different ways, because stateful and stateless session beans have different lifecycles within the container.

We're going to look at the use and lifecycle differences of stateful session beans and stateless session beans by implementing the same functionality twice. Then we'll implement it a third time, showing how stateful and stateless session beans can cooperate (one in the access control layer and one in the services layer.)

> *By the way, I developed and tested these examples on the jBoss open-source application server. As in Chapter 18, the client JNDI properties are hard-coded for jBoss. You can change these to values appropriate for a different application server (or even externalize them and remove any dependencies that the client has on an application server). You can deploy these examples by dropping a properly-configured JAR file into the `deploy` directory of jBoss, and you can run the clients by making sure that the appropriate files (all those in jBoss' `client` directory) are on the CLASSPATH. At the appropriate time, I'll remind you what your JAR file should contain.*

The application we're going to write will calculate the financial aid that a student will require to attend a university, by applying a formula that takes into account university costs and family resources.

> *If you happen to be a university administrator rather than a Java programmer, you should know that I made this formula up and you should not subject your students to it.*

First, let me describe the formula I'll be using. Our final calculation will be that the student's need equals the cost of university minus the sum of their parent's contribution and their summer earnings. Our client application will print this out, along with the applicant's name (so that they don't feel quite as unhappy with a bad result).

The formula has several intermediate steps. The cost of university is calculated as the sum of three numbers: tuition and fees; room and board; and books and supplies. The parent's contribution is calculated as the sum of three numbers: a percentage of parent 1's income; a percentage of parent 2's income; and a percentage of their assets. The percentage of assets available is also calculated using three numbers: the value of their liquid assets; the value of their primary home; and the value of their other assets. Of course someone who was good at math could roll all these steps into one formula. I'm using them as a proxy for workflow steps that could not be so combined.

The Stateless Financial Calculator Bean

Let's begin with the stateless session bean version. Remember, there are four basic parts to an EJB component: its remote interface, its home interface, its implementation class, and its deployment descriptor. First, we'll define our remote interface. This provides the client access to the EJB's business functionality. Like every remote interface in Java, every method must declare that it throws `java.rmi.RemoteException`. As described in the previous chapter, this interface must extend `EJBObject`:

```
package finCalc.stateless;

import javax.ejb.EJBObject;

public interface FinancialNeedCalculator extends EJBObject {

  public double calculateNeed(double attendanceCost,
                              double parentsContribution,
                              double studentSummerWork)
        throws java.rmi.RemoteException;

  public double calculateAttendanceCost(double tuitionAndFees,
                                        double booksAndSupplies,
                                        double roomAndBoard)
        throws java.rmi.RemoteException;

  public double calculateParentsContribution(double parent1Contribution,
                                             double parent2Contribution,
                                             double groupContribution)
        throws java.rmi.RemoteException;

  public double calculateParentContribution(double income)
        throws java.rmi.RemoteException;

  public double calculateGroupContribution(double liquidAssets,
                                           double primaryHomeValue,
                                           double otherAssets)
        throws java.rmi.RemoteException;

  public String getMessage(String applicant, double need)
        throws java.rmi.RemoteException;
}
```

Since our session bean is stateless, we must pass application state data back and forth from the client to the server. The result of every intermediate calculation must be returned to the client from the server, and then handed back to the server from the client when it's needed for a later step. To illustrate this point, here's the client that we will use:

```
package finCalc.stateless;

import java.util.Properties;
import javax.naming.Context;
import javax.naming.InitialContext;

public class TestClient {

  // Test data

  public static void main(String[] args) {

    try {
      Properties prop = new Properties();
      prop.put(Context.INITIAL_CONTEXT_FACTORY,
               "org.jnp.interfaces.NamingContextFactory");
```

```
        prop.put(Context.PROVIDER_URL, "localhost:1099");

        Context ctx = new InitialContext(prop);

        Object objref = ctx.lookup("StatelessFinancialNeedCalculator");

        FinancialNeedCalculatorHome home =
          (FinancialNeedCalculatorHome) javax.rmi.PortableRemoteObject
            .narrow(objref, FinancialNeedCalculatorHome.class);

        FinancialNeedCalculator calculator = home.create();

        double attendanceCost =
          calculator.calculateAttendanceCost(30000.0, 500.0, 2000.0);

        double parent1 =
          calculator.calculateParentContribution(55000.0);

        double parent2 =
          calculator.calculateParentContribution(35000.0);

        double group = calculator.calculateGroupContribution(10000.0,
              150000.0, 6000.0);

        double parentsContribution =
          calculator.calculateParentsContribution(parent1, parent2,
                                          group);

        double need = calculator.calculateNeed(attendanceCost,
                                          parentsContribution,
                                          2500.0);

        System.out.println(calculator.getMessage("Daniel", need));

        calculator.remove();

    } catch (Exception e) {
        e.printStackTrace();
    }
  }
}
```

You can see that the client must save the results of intermediate steps like
calculateParentContribution for use in later steps such as calculateParentsContribution.

The home interface is the second basic part to an EJB component. This interface gives the programmer access to lifecycle functionality such as the creation and destruction of the component. You can see its use in the sample client, above. The programmer creating a session bean need only worry about declaring "create" methods in the home interface. For the writer of a stateless session bean, there can only be one create() method with no parameters. The reason for this should be obvious – if the EJB doesn't have state, what will it matter if you give it a parameter when you create it? It will have "forgotten" it by the first business method call. The home interface for a stateless session bean is the most boring piece of code in the world, because it will always take this form (just change the package name, the interface name, and the return value from the create() method):

```
package finCalc.stateless;

import javax.ejb.EJBHome;

public interface FinancialNeedCalculatorHome extends EJBHome
{
  FinancialNeedCalculator create()
    throws java.rmi.RemoteException, javax.ejb.CreateException;
}
```

The implementation class is the third basic part to an EJB component. It has both container callback methods and business logic implementation methods. For a session bean, it must implement the javax.ejb.SessionBean interface, which provides it with a template of callback methods that the container requires. In addition, the EJB developer must add an ejbCreate() method for each create() method in the home interface, with matching parameters and a return type of void. Of course, for a stateless session bean there will be exactly one of these with no parameters. Here is the class for our financial need calculator bean:

```
package finCalc.stateless;

import javax.ejb.SessionBean;
import javax.ejb.SessionContext;

public class FinancialNeedCalculatorEJB implements SessionBean {

  public void ejbActivate() {}

  public void ejbPassivate() {}

  public void ejbRemove() {}

  public void ejbCreate() {}

  public void setSessionContext(SessionContext ctx) {}

  public double calculateNeed(double attendanceCost,
                              double parentsContribution,
                              double studentSummerWork) {
    double need = attendanceCost - (parentsContribution
                + studentSummerWork);
    return (need < 0.0) ? 0.0 : need;
  }

  public double calculateAttendanceCost(double tuitionAndFees,
                                        double booksAndSupplies,
                                        double roomAndBoard) {
    return tuitionAndFees + booksAndSupplies + roomAndBoard;
  }

  public double calculateParentsContribution(double parent1Contribution,
                                             double parent2Contribution,
                                             double groupContribution) {
    return parent1Contribution + parent2Contribution
         + groupContribution;
```

```
    }

    public double calculateParentContribution(double income) {
      return (income * 0.2);
    }

    public double calculateGroupContribution(double liquidAssets,
                                     double primaryHomeValue,
                                     double otherAssets) {
      return (liquidAssets * 0.3) + (primaryHomeValue * 0.05)
             + (otherAssets * 0.075);
    }

    public String getMessage(String applicant, double need) {
      return "Dear " + applicant
             + ", your need has been calculated at " + need + ".";
    }
  }
```

The first thing you'll notice about the lifecycle and framework methods is that they're all empty. The business logic programmer, in the default case, doesn't need to do anything. The container will do all the heavy lifting. Let's look at them individually.

public void ejbCreate()

In a stateless session bean, the `ejbCreate()` method will not necessarily be called in correspondence with a call to the bean's home interface `create()` method by the client. You should think of `ejbCreate()` as a constructor, to initialize the bean with resources that can be used by any client. (Client-specific resources aren't relevant to a stateless session bean.)

You can define a no-argument constructor, if you want. However, in that constructor you can't access any of the following:

❑　`SessionContext` methods: `getEJBHome()`, `getCallerPrincipal()`, `isCallerInRole()`, `getEJBObject()`

❑　JNDI to `java:comp/env`

❑　Resource managers (e.g. a JDBC connection)

❑　Other EJBs

> *You shouldn't define a constructor with arguments. If you do, it will never get called. Your EJB's lifecycle is controlled by the container and it will always use the no-arguments constructor. If you, out of sheer obstinacy, do define a constructor with arguments, you must also define one without arguments. Otherwise, the container won't be able to instantiate your bean. The specification mandates this behavior, because initialization should be done in one of the lifecycle methods and so there's no reason to add complexity to the configuration process to allow a different constructor to be called.*

public void ejbActivate()
public void ejbPassivate()

The container never passivates (and therefore never activates) a stateless session bean, and these two callback methods will therefore never be called. They need to be implemented because they are used for stateful session beans, and so are declared in the SessionBean interface.

public void ejbRemove()

The method ejbRemove() is called by the container before it removes its references to the component and allows its memory to be reclaimed. Any resources that were allocated in ejbCreate() should be deallocated here.

> Note that the EJB programmer must not define a finalize() method to deallocate any resources. In addition to being a bad programming practice in general (there are no guarantees about when, or if, finalize() will be called), it is also specifically prohibited by the Enterprise JavaBeans specification.

public void setSessionContext(SessionContext ctx)

If the programmer wants to use the SessionContext in any business method, they must save a reference to it when the container calls setSessionContext(). The container will call this method right before ejbCreate(), so the programmer can access it in the ejbCreate() method if desired.

The session context provides the following to the bean programmer:

❏ The getEJBObject() method returns the session bean's remote interface

❏ The getEJBHome() method returns the session bean's home interface

❏ The getCallerPrincipal() method returns the java.security.Principal that identifies the invoker of the bean instance's EJB object

❏ The isCallerInRole() method tests if the session bean instance's caller has a particular role

❏ The setRollbackOnly() method allows the instance to mark the current transaction such that the outcome of the transaction must be a rollback. Only instances of a session bean with container-managed transaction demarcation can use this method. (This is the normal case.)

❏ The getRollbackOnly() method allows the instance to test if the current transaction has been marked for rollback. Only instances of a session bean with container-managed transaction demarcation can use this method. (This is the normal case.)

❏ The getUserTransaction() method returns the javax.transaction.UserTransaction interface. The instance can use this interface to demarcate transactions and to obtain transaction status. Only instances of a session bean with bean-managed transaction demarcation can use this method. In general, you should let the container manage your transactions.

If the programmer wanted access to any of this functionality, they would write code that looked something like this:

```
public class FinancialNeedCalculatorEJB implements SessionBean {
```

```
    SessionContext ctx;

    // ...

    public void setSessionContext(SessionContext ctx) {
      this.ctx = ctx;
    }

  }
```

Note that the session context must not be stored in a transient variable. This is so that the reference won't be lost during passivation. (The rule should probably be followed with stateless session beans, even though they won't be passivated.)

These callback methods are used by the container at well-defined points in the session bean's lifecycle. The following diagram may help you to conceptualize the process:

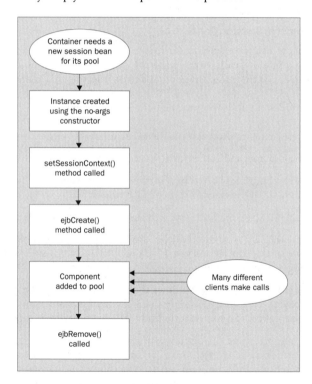

Note that the `ejbCreate()` and `setSessionContext()` methods are not correlated with any particular client's use of the component. The container decides when it needs a new instance. This may or may not be prompted by a client's business method call. If the container wants to decrease the size of the pool, it will call `ejbRemove()` on one of the instances and then remove it from the active pool. Formally, this is called **transitioning** from the *method-ready* state to the *does-not-exist* state.

The last basic part of an EJB component is its deployment descriptor. You will typically create this with a tool (although modifying it by hand isn't that hard). Here is the deployment descriptor for our financial need calculator (this is pretty much its minimal form):

```xml
<?xml version="1.0"?>

<ejb-jar>
 <enterprise-beans>
   <session>
      <ejb-name>StatelessFinancialNeedCalculator</ejb-name>
      <home>finCalc.stateless.FinancialNeedCalculatorHome</home>
      <remote>finCalc.stateless.FinancialNeedCalculator</remote>
      <ejb-class>finCalc.stateless.FinancialNeedCalculatorEJB</ejb-class>
      <session-type>Stateless</session-type>
      <transaction-type>Container</transaction-type>
   </session>
 </enterprise-beans>

 <assembly-descriptor>
   <container-transaction>
     <method>
        <ejb-name>StatelessFinancialNeedCalculator</ejb-name>
        <method-name>*</method-name>
     </method>
     <trans-attribute>Supports</trans-attribute>
   </container-transaction>
 </assembly-descriptor>
</ejb-jar>
```

The correspondence between the `<ejb-name>` in the deployment descriptor and the name by which we look up the bean isn't required. You can deploy a bean into the JNDI namespace under a different name. I used the same name because it saves a configuration step under some application servers that will just assume they are the same in the absence of information to the contrary (such as jBoss and Orion). For more information about deployment and deployment descriptors, see Chapter 22.

You can now run this example. You should create a JAR file with your class files and deployment descriptor in the following directories:

```
META-INF/
          ejb-jar.xml
finCalc/
        stateless/
                  FinancialNeedCalculator.class
                  FinancialNeedCalculatorHome.class
                  FinancialNeedCalculatorEJB.class
```

Deploy this JAR in your application server. If you're using jBoss, simply drop it in the `deploy` directory. Set up your client's CLASSPATH according to your application server's requirements. If you're using jBoss, make sure that the JARs in the `client` directory are on the CLASSPATH. If your client is working, it should provide the following result:

The Stateful Financial Calculator Bean

Now let's develop another version of this EJB component, as a **stateful** session bean. The main difference between stateful and stateless session beans is that a stateful session bean can store application state between method calls, whereas a stateless bean cannot. In our new version of the bean, we'll take advantage of this capability by storing all the input parameters between method calls, and then calculating the result all at once. Here is the new remote interface:

```
package finCalc.stateful;

import javax.ejb.EJBObject;

public interface FinancialNeedCalculator extends EJBObject {
  public void setStudentSummerWork(double studentSummerWork)
        throws java.rmi.RemoteException;

  public void setAttendanceCosts(double tuitionAndFees,
                                 double booksAndSupplies,
                                 double roomAndBoard)
        throws java.rmi.RemoteException;

  public void setParentIncome(double income)
        throws java.rmi.RemoteException, TooManyParentsException;

  public void setGroupAssets(double liquidAssets,
                             double primaryHomeValue,
                             double otherAssets)
        throws java.rmi.RemoteException;

  public String getMessage() throws java.rmi.RemoteException;
}
```

The setParentIncome() method can be called twice. I've introduced a new class to this example – TooManyParentsException – to be used in the event that the setParentIncome method is called a third time:

```
package finCalc.stateful;

public class TooManyParentsException extends Exception {
  public TooManyParentsException() {}
}
```

A stateful session bean's home interface can be slightly more interesting than a stateless session bean's home interface, because there can be multiple create() methods with various signatures. It makes sense to be able to pass information to a stateful session bean's create() methods, because that stateful session bean can "remember" what the client told it during subsequent business method calls. Here is the calculator's home interface, which takes the applicant's name as a parameter (which will be used in formatting the message):

```
package finCalc.stateful;

import javax.ejb.EJBHome;
```

```
public interface FinancialNeedCalculatorHome extends EJBHome {
  FinancialNeedCalculator create(String applicant)
          throws java.rmi.RemoteException, javax.ejb.CreateException;
}
```

Notice how the stateful session bean's implementation class has taken on the "workflow" that was located in the client in the stateless session bean example. The getMessage() method looks almost identical to the client:

```
package finCalc.stateful;

import javax.ejb.SessionBean;
import javax.ejb.SessionContext;

public class FinancialNeedCalculatorEJB implements SessionBean {

    String applicant;
    double studentSummerWork;
    double tuitionAndFees;
    double booksAndSupplies;
    double roomAndBoard;
    double parent1Income;
    boolean parent1Set;
    double parent2Income;
    boolean parent2Set;
    double liquidAssets;
    double primaryHomeValue;
    double otherAssets;

    public void ejbActivate() {}

    public void ejbPassivate() {}

    public void ejbRemove() {}

    public void ejbCreate(String applicant) {
      this.applicant = applicant;
      parent1Set = false;
      parent2Set = false;
    }

    public void setStudentSummerWork(double studentSummerWork) {
      this.studentSummerWork = studentSummerWork;
    }

    public void setAttendanceCosts(double tuitionAndFees,
                                   double booksAndSupplies,
                                   double roomAndBoard) {
      this.tuitionAndFees = tuitionAndFees;
      this.booksAndSupplies = booksAndSupplies;
      this.roomAndBoard = roomAndBoard;
    }
```

```
    public void setParentIncome(double income)
          throws TooManyParentsException {
      if (parent2Set) {
        throw new TooManyParentsException();
      } else if (parent1Set) {
        this.parent2Income = income;
        this.parent2Set = true;
      } else {
        this.parent1Income = income;
        this.parent1Set = true;
      }
    }

    public void setGroupAssets(double liquidAssets,
                              double primaryHomeValue,
                              double otherAssets) {
      this.liquidAssets = liquidAssets;
      this.primaryHomeValue = primaryHomeValue;
      this.otherAssets = otherAssets;
    }

    public String getMessage() {
      double attendanceCost =
        this.calculateAttendanceCost(tuitionAndFees, booksAndSupplies,
                                    roomAndBoard);

      double parent1 = this.calculateParentContribution(parent1Income);

      double parent2 = this.calculateParentContribution(parent2Income);

      double group = this.caculateGroupContribution(liquidAssets,
              primaryHomeValue, otherAssets);

      double parentsContribution =
        this.calculateParentsContribution(parent1, parent2, group);

      double need = this.calculateNeed(attendanceCost,
                                      parentsContribution,
                                      studentSummerWork);

      return this.getMessage(applicant, need);
    }

    public void setSessionContext(SessionContext ctx)
          throws javax.ejb.EJBException, java.rmi.RemoteException {}

    private double calculateNeed(double attendanceCost,
                                double parentsContribution,
                                double studentSummerWork) {
      double need = attendanceCost - (parentsContribution
                    + studentSummerWork);
      return (need < 0.0) ? 0.0 : need;

    }
```

```
      private double calculateAttendanceCost(double tuitionAndFees,
                                             double booksAndSupplies,
                                             double roomAndBoard) {
        return tuitionAndFees + booksAndSupplies + roomAndBoard;
      }

      private double calculateParentsContribution(double parent1Contribution,
                                                  double parent2Contribution,
                                                  double groupContribution) {
        return parent1Contribution + parent2Contribution
              + groupContribution;
      }

      private double calculateParentContribution(double income) {
        return (income * 0.2);
      }

      private double caculateGroupContribution(double liquidAssets,
                                               double primaryHomeValue,
                                               double otherAssets) {
        return (liquidAssets * 0.3) + (primaryHomeValue * 0.05)
              + (otherAssets * 0.075);
      }

      private String getMessage(String applicant, double need) {
        return "Dear " + applicant
              + ", your need has been calculated at " + need + ".";
      }
    }
```

Except for the `create()` method discussed earlier, the life cycle methods (`ejbActivate()`, `ejbPassivate()`, `ejbRemove()`, and `setSessionContext()`) in this bean are empty, just like they were for the stateless session bean. The main difference is that `ejbActivate()` and `ejbPassivate()` may actually be called, depending on the container configuration and resource utilization. Before a bean is swapped out to temporary storage the container will call `ejbPassivate()`. Before the bean is recreated from that storage, the container will call `ejbActivate()`.

Why are these callback methods important? If the bean programmer had acquired and saved a resource that couldn't be passivated (e.g. a database or socket connection), they would need to release it in `ejbPassivate()` and reacquire it in `ejbActivate()`. More formally, the bean developer must ensure two things are true after `ejbPassivate()` returns:

❑ The objects that are assigned to the bean's non-transient fields must be ready for serialization. They must be `null`, a serializable object, or an EJB-related object that the container will handle. These special EJB-related objects include remote interfaces, home interfaces, `SessionContext` objects, a reference to the environment naming context or any of its subcontexts, or a reference to a `UserTransaction` object. Often, this will be true without any action in `ejbPassivate()`.

❑ The bean developer must close any open resources, such as open sockets and open database cursors. Typically, a bean will not maintain open resources; rather, it will acquire them from the container as needed. The bottom line? Typically, `ejbPassivate()` will be left empty and the container will handle the details.

The same is true of the `ejbActivate()` callback. It exists to give the developer a chance to reacquire any resources that it closed during `ejbPassivate()`. Typically, this method will be left empty. One word of warning: if you have state that the container can't manage during passivation and activation (such as a non-serializable object stored in a non-transient variable), the container is free to discard your EJB instead.

Compare this diagram to the earlier one for a stateless session bean:

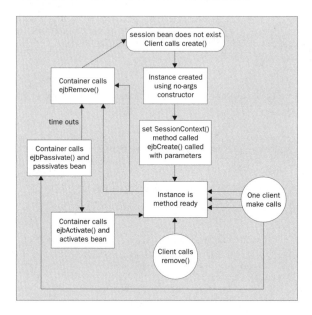

The additional complexity is from the container's need to effectively manage per-client state: `ejbActivate()`, `ejbPassivate()`, time outs, and the client's requirement to control the creation and destruction of instances.

Here is the new client. Unlike the previous version, there is no dependency in the order in which the methods are called. The stateful session bean has taken responsibility to perform the calculations in the correct order at the end of the workflow. Alternatively, it could process the information as it is received, and enforce the workflow by throwing an exception if one of its methods were called out of the correct order:

```
package finCalc.stateful;

import java.util.Properties;
import javax.naming.Context;
import javax.naming.InitialContext;

public class TestClient {

  // Test data

  public static void main(String[] args) {
    try {
      Properties prop = new Properties();
      prop.put(Context.INITIAL_CONTEXT_FACTORY,
```

```
                     "org.jnp.interfaces.NamingContextFactory");
        prop.put(Context.PROVIDER_URL, "localhost:1099");

        Context ctx = new InitialContext(prop);

        Object objref = ctx.lookup("StatefulFinancialNeedCalculator");

        FinancialNeedCalculatorHome home =
          (FinancialNeedCalculatorHome) javax.rmi.PortableRemoteObject
            .narrow(objref, FinancialNeedCalculatorHome.class);

        FinancialNeedCalculator calculator = home.create("Daniel");

        calculator.setParentIncome(55000.0);
        calculator.setParentIncome(35000.0);
        calculator.setGroupAssets(10000.0, 150000.0, 6000.0);
        calculator.setAttendanceCosts(30000.0, 500.0, 2000.0);
        calculator.setStudentSummerWork(2500.0);

        System.out.println(calculator.getMessage());

        calculator.remove();

    } catch (Exception e) {
      e.printStackTrace();
    }
  }
}
```

Here is the new deployment descriptor, indicating that this is a stateful session bean:

```xml
<?xml version="1.0"?>

<ejb-jar>
 <enterprise-beans>
   <session>
     <ejb-name>StatefulFinancialNeedCalculator</ejb-name>
     <home>finCalc.stateful.FinancialNeedCalculatorHome</home>
     <remote>finCalc.stateful.FinancialNeedCalculator</remote>
     <ejb-class>finCalc.stateful.FinancialNeedCalculatorEJB</ejb-class>
     <session-type>Stateful</session-type>
     <transaction-type>Container</transaction-type>
   </session>
 </enterprise-beans>

<assembly-descriptor>
   <container-transaction>
     <method>
        <ejb-name>StatefulFinancialNeedCalculator</ejb-name>
        <method-name>*</method-name>
     </method>
     <trans-attribute>Supports</trans-attribute>
   </container-transaction>
 </assembly-descriptor>
</ejb-jar>
```

You can now run this example. You should create a JAR file with your class files and deployment descriptor in the following directories:

```
META-INF/
            ejb-jar.xml
finCalc/
        stateful/
                    FinancialNeedCalculator.class
                    FinancialNeedCalculatorHome.class
                    FinancialNeedCalculatorEJB.class
                    TooManyParentsException.class
```

Deploy this JAR in your application server. If you're using jBoss, simply drop it in the `deploy` directory. Set up your client's `CLASSPATH` according to your application server's requirements. If you're using jBoss, make sure that the JARs in the `client` directory are on the `CLASSPATH`. If your client is working, it should provide the same result as the previous example:

I have a second client that demonstrates how three parents are unacceptable to our somewhat conservative EJB component and will throw an exception:

```java
package finCalc.stateful;

import java.util.Properties;
import javax.naming.Context;
import javax.naming.InitialContext;

public class TestClient2 {
  public static void main(String[] args) {
    try {
      Properties prop = new Properties();
      prop.put(Context.INITIAL_CONTEXT_FACTORY,
              "org.jnp.interfaces.NamingContextFactory");
      prop.put(Context.PROVIDER_URL, "localhost:1099");

      Context ctx = new InitialContext(prop);

      Object objref = ctx.lookup("StatefulFinancialNeedCalculator");

      FinancialNeedCalculatorHome home =
        (FinancialNeedCalculatorHome) javax.rmi.PortableRemoteObject
          .narrow(objref, FinancialNeedCalculatorHome.class);

      FinancialNeedCalculator calculator = home.create("Daniel");
```

```
        calculator.setParentIncome(55000.0);
        calculator.setParentIncome(35000.0);
        calculator.setParentIncome(65000.0);
        calculator.setGroupAssets(10000.0, 150000.0, 6000.0);
        calculator.setAttendanceCosts(30000.0, 500.0, 2000.0);
        calculator.setStudentSummerWork(2500.0);

        System.out.println(calculator.getMessage());

        calculator.remove();

    } catch (Exception e) {
        e.printStackTrace();
    }
  }
}
```

When you run this client, you should get a stack trace that looks something like this (results will vary with your environment):

Of course, a more sophisticated client would have caught the exception and handled it gracefully.

Combining Stateful and Stateless Beans

Let's develop one final version of this application, where we have two EJB components: one in the **access control layer** and one in the **services layer**. This will make some of the design principles that I've been talking about more explicit. We already have our services layer EJB component done – it's just the stateless version that we've already looked at. The next step is to gut the stateful session bean of all its calculations and have it call that session bean instead.

We start with the same home and remote interfaces and the same exception class as our stateful session bean example (exception for the packages; I'm using `finCalc.both`). The client is also in a different package, and has one other slight difference, because it's looking up a different component:

```
    Object objref = ctx.lookup("FinancialNeedCalculatorInterface");
```

Apart from changing the lookup the client is unchanged from the stateful example.

The implementation class is quite different, because rather than having a bunch of private implementation methods (like our last example), it calls on the stateless session bean to provide it with results. The Enterprise JavaBeans specification allows EJB components in a single application to reference each other by a logical name, typically (as per the spec's recommendation) in the format `java:comp/env/ejb/bean-name`. This link must be declared in the deployment descriptor. At application deployment time, the deployer binds the references of the actual referenced beans into the namespace of the referring bean using application-server specific tools.

The "namespace" of an EJB is just the arrangement of objects that are accessible to it through JNDI.

The developer of the EJB component can indicate the specific deployed bean to which he or she would like the reference to refer, by adding an `<ejb-link>` element in the deployment descriptor. The code with which we do this lookup bears examination:

```
InitialContext initial = new InitialContext();
        finCalc.stateless.FinancialNeedCalculatorHome home =
            (finCalc.stateless.FinancialNeedCalculatorHome)
              javax.rmi.PortableRemoteObject.narrow(
                initial.lookup("java:comp/env/ejb/CalculatorService"),
                finCalc.stateless.FinancialNeedCalculatorHome.class);
```

Unlike a stand-alone client, an EJB does not need to configure the `InitialContext` properties before accessing other application objects through JNDI. The container will handle the configuration. Otherwise, this is the same code we've been seeing in our clients all along. (I'm using the full package names of the service bean class because it otherwise has the exact same name as our access control bean.)

Here is the entire class:

```
package finCalc.both;

import javax.ejb.SessionBean;
import javax.ejb.SessionContext;
import javax.naming.InitialContext;

public class FinancialNeedCalculatorEJB implements SessionBean {

  String applicant;
  double studentSummerWork;
  double tuitionAndFees;
  double booksAndSupplies;
  double roomAndBoard;
  double parent1Income;
  boolean parent1Set;
  double parent2Income;
  boolean parent2Set;
  double liquidAssets;
  double primaryHomeValue;
  double otherAssets;

  public void ejbActivate() {}

  public void ejbPassivate() {}

  public void ejbRemove() {}

  public void ejbCreate(String applicant) {
    this.applicant = applicant;
    parent1Set = false;
    parent2Set = false;
  }
```

```
public void setStudentSummerWork(double studentSummerWork) {
  this.studentSummerWork = studentSummerWork;
}

public void setAttendanceCosts(double tuitionAndFees,
                               double booksAndSupplies,
                               double roomAndBoard) {
  this.tuitionAndFees = tuitionAndFees;
  this.booksAndSupplies = booksAndSupplies;
  this.roomAndBoard = roomAndBoard;
}

public void setParentIncome(double income)
       throws TooManyParentsException {
  if (parent2Set) {
    throw new TooManyParentsException();
  } else if (parent1Set) {
    this.parent2Income = income;
    this.parent2Set = true;
  } else {
    this.parent1Income = income;
    this.parent1Set = true;
  }
}

public void setGroupAssets(double liquidAssets,
                           double primaryHomeValue,
                           double otherAssets) {
  this.liquidAssets = liquidAssets;
  this.primaryHomeValue = primaryHomeValue;
  this.otherAssets = otherAssets;
}

public String getMessage() {
  try {
    InitialContext initial = new InitialContext();
    finCalc.stateless
      .FinancialNeedCalculatorHome home =
        (finCalc.stateless
          .FinancialNeedCalculatorHome) javax.rmi
            .PortableRemoteObject
              .narrow(initial
                .lookup("java:comp/env/ejb/CalculatorService"), finCalc
                  .stateless.FinancialNeedCalculatorHome.class);

    finCalc.stateless.FinancialNeedCalculator calculator =
      home.create();

    double attendanceCost =
      calculator.calculateAttendanceCost(tuitionAndFees,
                                         booksAndSupplies,
                                         roomAndBoard);
```

929

```
        double parent1 =
          calculator.calculateParentContribution(parent1Income);

        double parent2 =
          calculator.calculateParentContribution(parent2Income);

        double group =
          calculator.calculateGroupContribution(liquidAssets,
                                        primaryHomeValue,
                                        otherAssets);

        double parentsContribution =
          calculator.calculateParentsContribution(parent1, parent2,
                                        group);

        double need = calculator.calculateNeed(attendanceCost,
                                        parentsContribution,
                                        studentSummerWork);

        return calculator.getMessage(applicant, need);
      } catch (javax.ejb.CreateException ce) {
        throw new javax.ejb.EJBException(ce);
      } catch (javax.naming.NamingException ne) {
        throw new javax.ejb.EJBException(ne);
      } catch (java.rmi.RemoteException re) {
        throw new javax.ejb.EJBException(re);
      }
    }

  public void setSessionContext(SessionContext ctx)
          throws javax.ejb.EJBException, java.rmi.RemoteException {}

}
```

The deployment descriptor provides information to the container about both beans. It also sets up the reference from our stateful session bean to the stateless one:

```xml
<?xml version="1.0"?>

<ejb-jar>
  <enterprise-beans>
    <session>
      <ejb-name>FinancialNeedCalculatorInterface</ejb-name>
      <home>finCalc.both.FinancialNeedCalculatorHome</home>
      <remote>finCalc.both.FinancialNeedCalculator</remote>
      <ejb-class>finCalc.both.FinancialNeedCalculatorEJB</ejb-class>
      <session-type>Stateful</session-type>
      <transaction-type>Container</transaction-type>
      <ejb-ref>
        <ejb-ref-name>ejb/CalculatorService</ejb-ref-name>
        <ejb-ref-type>Session</ejb-ref-type>
        <home>finCalc.stateless.OrderHome</home>
```

```
            <remote>finCalc.stateless.Order</remote>
            <ejb-link>FinancialNeedCalculatorService</ejb-link>
          </ejb-ref>
        </session>
        <session>
          <ejb-name>FinancialNeedCalculatorService</ejb-name>
          <home>finCalc.stateless.FinancialNeedCalculatorHome</home>
          <remote>finCalc.stateless.FinancialNeedCalculator</remote>
          <ejb-class>finCalc.stateless.FinancialNeedCalculatorEJB</ejb-class>
          <session-type>Stateless</session-type>
          <transaction-type>Container</transaction-type>
        </session>
      </enterprise-beans>

      <assembly-descriptor>
        <container-transaction>
          <method>
            <ejb-name>FinancialNeedCalculatorInterface</ejb-name>
            <method-name>*</method-name>
          </method>
          <trans-attribute>Supports</trans-attribute>
        </container-transaction>
        <container-transaction>
          <method>
            <ejb-name>FinancialNeedCalculatorService</ejb-name>
            <method-name>*</method-name>
          </method>
          <trans-attribute>Supports</trans-attribute>
        </container-transaction>
      </assembly-descriptor>
    </ejb-jar>
```

You can now run this example. You should create a JAR file with your class files and deployment descriptor in the following directories:

```
META-INF/
          ejb-jar.xml
finCalc/
        both/
              FinancialNeedCalculator.class
              FinancialNeedCalculatorHome.class
              FinancialNeedCalculatorEJB.class
              TooManyParentsException.class
        stateless/
                  FinancialNeedCalculator.class
                  FinancialNeedCalculatorHome.class
                  FinancialNeedCalculatorEJB.class
```

Deploy this JAR in your application server. If you're using jBoss, simply drop it in the `deploy` directory. Set up your client's `CLASSPATH` according to your application server's requirements. If you're using jBoss, make sure that the JARs in the `client` directory are on the `CLASSPATH`. If your client is working, it should once again provide the following result:

```
C:\WINNT\System32\cmd.exe                                    _ □ X

C:\ProJavaServer\Chapter19\Both>java -cp c:\jboss2_pr3\lib\ext\jboss.jar;c:\jboss2_pr3\lib\ext\ejb.j
ar;c:\jboss2_pr3\lib\ext\jnpserver.jar;c:\jboss2_pr3\lib\ext\jta-spec1_0_1.jar;. finCalc.both.TestCl
ient
Dear Daniel, your need has been calculated at 1050.0.

C:\ProJavaServer\Chapter19\Both>_
```

Implementing Our Manufacturing Application

It's time to begin implementing the sample application for which we performed some analysis in the previous chapter. Now, how do we translate this analysis into an actual implementation? Any software implementation will be influenced by a variety of factors, including development costs, performance and scalability requirements, user expectations, personnel, etc. In this case, I will assume that these factors motivate me to keep the implementation simple, largely because that's best for the pedagogical purpose of explaining how EJBs are used.

The slice of the analysis model that I've chosen to implement has four entity objects: product, routing instructions, orders, and shipments.

❑   A product will consist of an identifier, a human-readable name, and an ordered list of routing instruction entities to control the manufacturing process.

❑   An order will consist of the product ordered, a due date, an identifying key (order number plus sales division), and a status (open, canceled, manufacture in-process, and completed).

❑   The shipment information will consist of an order key, a loading dock, a manufactured-by field, and a date completed.

❑   A routing instruction has a sequence (an integer) and an instruction (a String).

The entity objects in your analysis model will usually translate into entity beans, or attributes of entity beans, in your implementation. In this case, I will have two entity beans:

❑   An order

❑   A product, with routing instructions as a simple attribute

Note that in other circumstances, routing instructions might need to be a first class entity. I once worked on an ERP system where this would have been the case, because routing instructions were shared by multiple products. Here their lifecycle depends completely on their parent product, which always makes an entity a strong candidate for being implemented as an attribute.

As mentioned in the last chapter, it might make sense to update shipment information directly from a session bean. Note that this session bean can manipulate the database directly, but does not represent a 'shipment entity'. My reason for this approach is development simplicity. Also, by updating the database directly, I am demonstrating a valid alternative choice of which you should be aware.

My code is quite simple, so I decided on having only two session beans that are responsible for implementing all the control and interface objects:

❑   A stateless session bean used to manage orders, which also has a utility function to create sample products

❑   A stateful session bean used to control the manufacturing process

Even with the simplicity of my requirements, I'm cheating a little; it doesn't make sense to have the product creation mixed in with order management. Once you start modeling the complexity of a real-world organization, you will want to start dividing your functionality into more cohesive access control and service level components.

Let's consider the roles that these two session beans play. First, each serves as an interface object to some of the clients in this application. The EJB that controls the manufacturing process manages conversational state for its manufacturing clients. It can use this state directly to ensure that the rules of the workflow (such as a product must be selected before its routing can be displayed) are followed. However, you should keep in mind that two distinct roles are involved in this: interface object implementation and control object implementation. An application's state must be contained in the client or an 'interface' object. Actually using this state is really the job of a service object, if we were to match EJB components up to their analysis roles perfectly.

The stateless session EJB that manages orders acts as an interface object for some clients, but it also acts as a pure control object for the manufacturing EJB. As the business methods in EJBs tend to have coarse-grained functionality, it's not unusual that a client with a similar 'theme' as a particular service-layer session bean can use that bean directly as its interface. However, if reusability and maintainability are important concerns, you should avoid specializing this session bean for particular clients. Instead, introduce a component that separately implements the interface functionality if necessary.

Note that creating lists of entities is a function of control objects in the analysis model, but the situation is more complicated in an implementation using Enterprise JavaBeans technology. Collections of entities can be produced using a factory method on an entity bean's home interface; these factory methods are known as **finder methods**. These finder methods will be explained in Chapter 20, but basically they return an EJB remote interface or collection of remote interfaces that meet application-defined criteria. However, returning a collection of entities to the client violates the guideline that the implementation of the analysis model should be hidden behind a façade, and can also have negative consequences for performance. In the session-bean implementation of the control logic, we apply any additional transformations required by our business rules to the collection, and then we return a view on the entity beans that contains only the information relevant to the client, rather than entity bean references.

The clients are complete abstractions. In the real world, they probably would be web applications or Swing GUI clients, and the functionality would be more clearly divided and flexible. (In Chapter 22, we actually develop a simple web front-end to this application.) Here they exist only to test the server-side code and demonstrate how EJBs can be used. There are four clients, although one of those clients is spread out over two executable classes. Note that all client access is to one of the session beans. In keeping with the façade pattern, no non-bean client accesses an entity bean:

❑   The `CreateProducts` class calls a utility function to create sample products for use in the other examples. I won't discuss it further.

❑   The `PlaceSampleOrders` class places six orders that are due for delivery at various times. Two of the orders are needed so far in the future that they shouldn't yet be scheduled for manufacture; two orders are ready to be manufactured, and can be finished on time; and two are overdue if lead time is taken into account.

❑ ManageSampleOrders prints out the overdue orders to System.out. It then cancels the first overdue order.

❑ The final client is contained in two classes, BeginManufacture and CompleteManufacture; these are two different executable classes. The BeginManufacture class creates a stateful session bean, which it uses to print out the orders that are eligible for manufacture. It then selects the first order available, serializes a handle to that EJB for use by the next application, and exits. The CompleteManufacture class prints out the product routings in order, ships the product, and calls remove() on the session bean.

This sample application is much simpler than a real-world application would ever be. However, the techniques demonstrated here could be valuable to your development efforts using Enterprise JavaBeans technology. The complete code for these examples can be downloaded from the Wrox web site at http://www.wrox.com.

Clients and the Business Logic Interfaces

In this section, we'll look at the implementation of the home and remote interfaces of the session beans, and the clients that use them. In the development process, the business interfaces provide a contract to the clients, which should not need to know about the details of the implementation. We won't actually look at the implementation classes until the next section – and we won't see the deployment descriptor until the next chapter, because it describes the entity beans as well as the session beans. If you're very curious you can peek ahead a few pages.

Here is a quick rundown on the classes we'll look at in this section. First, in the factory.manage_orders package:

❑ ManageOrders (remote interface)

❑ ManageOrdersHome (home interface)

❑ DuplicateOrderException

❑ NoSuchOrderException

❑ NoSuchProductException

❑ OpenOrderView

❑ OverdueOrderView

In the factory.manufacture package:

❑ Manufacture (remote interface)

❑ ManufactureHome (home interface)

Finally, in the factory.client package:

❑ ContextPropertiesFactory

❑ BeginManufacture

❑ CompleteManufacture

- ❏ PlaceSampleOrders
- ❏ ManageSampleOrders
- ❏ CreateProdcuts

Mixed in with this code, there are two new discussions of EJB technique. The first is **handle serialization**, and the second is how to handle **listing behavior**.

The remote interfaces of the two session beans, `factory.manage_orders.ManageOrders` and `factory.manufacture.Manufacture`, represent all the business logic available to the four clients.

`ManageOrders` is the stateless session bean. Its remote interface looks like this:

```
package factory.manage_orders;

import javax.ejb.*;
import java.util.Date;
import java.rmi.RemoteException;
import factory.order.OrderNotCancelableException;

public interface ManageOrders extends EJBObject {
  void placeOrder(int salesDivision, int orderNumber, String product,
                  Date dateDue) throws RemoteException,
                                    NoSuchProductException,
                                    DuplicateOrderException;

  void cancelOrder(int salesDivision, int orderNumber)
       throws RemoteException, NoSuchOrderException,
            OrderNotCancelableException;

  OverdueOrderView[] getOverdueOrders() throws RemoteException;

  OpenOrderView[] getSchedulableOrders() throws RemoteException;

  void createSampleProducts() throws RemoteException;

  void createProduct(String id, String name) throws RemoteException;

  void addRoutingInstruction(String id, int sequence,
                             String instruction) throws RemoteException;
}
```

An order has a key consisting of a sales division plus an order number. The method to place an order provides a unique combination of division and order number. The method to cancel an order must reference an existing division and order number combination. The product to be manufactured is identified by an existing string key. If any of these expectations are violated, an exception (`NoSuchProductException`, `DuplicateOrderException`, or `OrderNotCancelableException`) is thrown. Here are those (unremarkable) classes:

```
package factory.manage_orders;

public class DuplicateOrderException extends Exception {
```

```
   public DuplicateOrderException() {}
}
```

```
package factory.manage_orders;

public class NoSuchOrderException extends Exception {

  public NoSuchOrderException() {}
}
```

```
package factory.manage_orders;

public class NoSuchProductException extends Exception {

  public NoSuchProductException() {}
}
```

The two methods to retrieve lists of orders (getOverdueOrders() and getSchedulableOrders()) return arrays of 'view objects'. This is one strategy of several to provide lists of information. Another possible strategy is to return a class that implements the java.sql.ResultSet interface or the new javax.sql.Rowset interface (see Chapter 3), with the information provided in rows and columns.

The reader with experience in building business systems will notice that, in terms of listing behavior, I've given myself an easy task here. I can assume there will be a manageable number of open or overdue orders to return from these methods. However, it's easy to think of cases where the result set will not be manageable.

For instance, consider a "search" or "open" interface in a client application where the user can set arbitrary criteria on the search. If the client doesn't set useful criteria on their search, some applications could try to return millions of rows of data.

The correct solution to this problem will depend on the specifics of your application. Perhaps you can return a chunk of rows, tell the user there is more data, and make them refine the search. Maybe you can have the client pass a marker to the server with each request, so that all the data can be returned in discrete chunks. (Since the application server is almost certainly pooling connections to the database that have already been opened, the client will not have to wait for the process of opening and closing connections that some programmers may be familiar with from other environments.)

Another closely related issue not demonstrated by this sample application is how to transfer data about a single entity from the server to a client application. This is a common requirement. Many applications will present screens designed to edit the data associated with an entity such as a customer, a product, or a company. The same issues that motivate the use of the façade pattern prevent individual calls to the server to retrieve or set data. (That means you shouldn't use a sequence of calls like getFirstName(), getMiddleName(), getLastName(), getAddr1(), getAddr2(), etc.) The data needs to be transferred in a collection of some kind (your method might be getSimpleCustomerData()).

What should this collection look like? The two basic strategies mirror those for returning simple lists of information. The first is to return a view object, which should be a simple serializable collection of data, like OverdueOrderView or OpenOrderView. Here is the code for OpenOrderView; notice it is just structured data with no functionality:

```
package factory.manage_orders;

import java.io.Serializable;
import java.util.Date;

public class OpenOrderView implements Serializable {
  public final int salesDivision;
  public final int orderNumber;
  public final String product;
  public final Date dateDue;

  public OpenOrderView(int salesDivision, int orderNumber,
                       String product, Date dateDue) {
    this.salesDivision = salesDivision;
    this.orderNumber = orderNumber;
    this.product = product;
    this.dateDue = dateDue;
  }
}
```

And here is the code for OverdueOrderView:

```
package factory.manage_orders;

import java.io.Serializable;
import java.util.Date;

public class OverdueOrderView implements Serializable {
  public final int salesDivision;
  public final int orderNumber;
  public final String product;
  public final String status;
  public final Date dateDue;

  public OverdueOrderView(int salesDivision, int orderNumber,
                          String product, String status,
                          Date dateDue) {
    this.salesDivision = salesDivision;
    this.orderNumber = orderNumber;
    this.product = product;
    this.status = status;
    this.dateDue = dateDue;
  }
}
```

The benefit of this approach is that it is simple to program and to understand the code; the disadvantage is that the view object is specific to a particular client or type of client, introducing coupling between the client and server.

The second strategy is to use a generic class with self-describing data. When talking about listing behavior, I mentioned implementing java.sql.ResultSet. As we are sending information about a single entity, and because that information might have non-tabular data (e.g. tree data or subordinate grid data), ResultSet isn't the ideal interface in this case. A good alternative is to return a java.util.Map, with key-value pairs representing a description of the data (perhaps an identifying Integer) and the data itself. The client could request just the data it needed, and the server could send this data with no foreknowledge of the request.

By the way, here is the home interface. As is the case with all stateless session beans, it is unremarkable:

```
package factory.manage_orders;

import javax.ejb.*;

public interface ManageOrdersHome extends EJBHome {
  ManageOrders create()
          throws java.rmi.RemoteException, javax.ejb.CreateException;
}
```

Manufacture is the stateful session bean; its remote interface looks like this:

```
package factory.manufacture;

import javax.ejb.*;
import java.rmi.RemoteException;
import factory.manage_orders.OpenOrderView;
import factory.manage_orders.NoSuchOrderException;

public interface Manufacture extends EJBObject {
  OpenOrderView[] getOpenOrders() throws RemoteException;

  void selectForManufacture(int salesDivision, int order_number)
          throws RemoteException, NoSuchOrderException,
                  BadStatusException;

  boolean hasNextRouting()
          throws RemoteException, NoSelectionException;

  String getNextRouting()
          throws RemoteException, NoSelectionException;

  void ship(String carrier, int loading_dock)
          throws RemoteException, NoSelectionException;
}
```

Note that, unlike with the ManageOrders bean, there is an implied order to these method calls. You must first select an order for manufacture. You then work through the routings (presumably building the product as you go). Finally, you ship the product. If you neglect to select the order before trying to read the routings for it, or before shipping it, a NoSelectionException will be thrown. This is easy to program with a stateful session bean. If we had made this a stateless session bean, we would have needed to pass the selected order as a parameter to every method call. We would also have needed to pass a cursor of some sort to the hasNextRouting() and getNextRouting() methods, because the bean, having no state, couldn't track this for us.

Also unlike the `ManageOrders` bean, there is something interesting in the home interface: a `create()` method with a parameter. This parameter identifies the 'cell' that is manufacturing the product. When the product is shipped, this information will automatically be added to the shipments table. Here is that home interface:

```
package factory.manufacture;

import javax.ejb.*;
import java.rmi.RemoteException;

public interface ManufactureHome extends EJBHome {
    Manufacture create(String manufactureCellID)
            throws RemoteException, CreateException;
}
```

As a reminder, a stateless session bean can't have any parameters in its `create()` method, nor is there any reason to want them to have any. Since a stateless session bean doesn't save information on behalf of a client, any information you provided in a `create()` method would be gone by the time you made the first business method call. Bottom line: if you've seen one home interface for a stateless session bean, you've seen them all.

The clients reference the server entirely through the two session bean interfaces. To keep things simple, all the clients are classes with only a static `main()` function. (To see web clients for these EJB components, look in Chapter 22.) They all follow a simple two-step pattern:

❑ Acquire a reference to a session bean

❑ Use that reference to accomplish some business purpose

Acquiring a reference to a session bean is done in these examples in one of two ways. First, there is the get-the-home-interface-from-JNDI/create-a-session-bean route. That code looks like this, for the stateless session bean:

```
ContextPropertiesFactory factory = new ContextPropertiesFactory();
Properties prop = factory.getInitialContextProperties();
InitialContext initial = new InitialContext(prop);

Object homeObject = initial.lookup("ManageOrders");

ManageOrdersHome home = (ManageOrdersHome)
        PortableRemoteObject.narrow(homeObject, ManageOrdersHome.class);

ManageOrders manageOrders = home.create();
```

Or this, for the stateful session bean (the only real difference being the parameter to the `create()` method)):

```
ContextPropertiesFactory factory = new ContextPropertiesFactory();
Properties prop = factory.getInitialContextProperties();
InitialContext initial = new InitialContext(prop);
```

```
Object homeObject = initial.lookup("Manufacture");

ManufactureHome home = (ManufactureHome)
            PortableRemoteObject.narrow(homeObject, ManufactureHome.class);

Manufacture manufacture = home.create(MANUFACTURE_CELL);
```

ContextPropertiesFactory is my own class. There are many ways to set up the properties for InitialContext; the best two are probably to put a jndi.properties file on the CLASSPATH, or to load an application-specific properties resource file using getResourceAsStream(). To make it clearer what is happening, I have removed this level of indirection from the sample clients. Here is ContextPropertiesFactory hard-coded for the Orion application server, on which I developed this example:

```
package factory.clients;

import javax.naming.Context;
import java.util.Properties;

public class ContextPropertiesFactory {

  public Properties getInitialContextProperties() {
    Properties prop = new Properties();
    prop
      .setProperty(Context.INITIAL_CONTEXT_FACTORY,
       "com.evermind.server.ApplicationClientInitialContextFactory");
    prop.setProperty(Context.PROVIDER_URL,
                     "ormi://localhost/factory");
    prop.setProperty(Context.SECURITY_PRINCIPAL, "admin");
    prop.setProperty(Context.SECURITY_CREDENTIALS, "123");
    return prop;
  }

  public void makePropertiesDefault() {
    System.setProperties(getInitialContextProperties());
  }
}
```

In general, you can pass these properties to the InitialContext in its constructor. If your EJB container's vendor requires these properties to be set when you are restoring an EJB reference from a handle, you will need to set the system properties with these values, like I do in makePropertiesDefault().

The second way that I acquire a reference to a session bean in these examples is to get it from a handle that has been serialized to disk. At the end of the 'begin manufacture' client app, the handle is serialized as follows:

```
Handle handle = manufacture.getHandle();
FileOutputStream file_out = new FileOutputStream(FILE_NAME);
ObjectOutputStream out = new ObjectOutputStream(file_out);
```

```
out.writeObject(handle);
System.out.println("Written object for next stage.");
```

At the beginning of the 'complete manufacture' client app, the reference to the stateless session bean is restored as follows:

```
FileInputStream inStream = new FileInputStream(FILE_NAME);
ObjectInputStream in = new ObjectInputStream(inStream);
Handle handle = (Handle)in.readObject();
Manufacture manufacture = (Manufacture)
    PortableRemoteObject.narrow(handle.getEJBObject(), Manufacture.class);
```

Both home references and remote references have handles that can be serialized, and which can be transferred between programs using such methods as files, sockets, or RMI. They can be saved in a servlet's session, and can even be e-mailed (or more practically, moved around with messaging middleware). But remember that references to remote objects in EJB are single-threaded. Simultaneous access from multiple clients or multiple threads is an error and will result in an exception being thrown.

Here are those two clients in their entirety. First, `BeginManufacture`:

```
package factory.clients;

import java.rmi.RemoteException;
import javax.ejb.*;
import javax.naming.*;
import javax.rmi.PortableRemoteObject;
import java.util.Properties;
import java.io.*;

import factory.manufacture.Manufacture;
import factory.manufacture.ManufactureHome;
import factory.manage_orders.OpenOrderView;

public class BeginManufacture {

  private static final String MANUFACTURE_CELL = "Station1";
  private static final String FILE_NAME = "C:/current_product.ser";

  public static void main(String[] args) {

    try {
      ContextPropertiesFactory factory =
        new ContextPropertiesFactory();
      Properties prop = factory.getInitialContextProperties();
      InitialContext initial = new InitialContext(prop);

      Object homeObject = initial.lookup("Manufacture");

      ManufactureHome home =
        (ManufactureHome) PortableRemoteObject.narrow(homeObject,
            ManufactureHome.class);

      Manufacture manufacture = home.create(MANUFACTURE_CELL);
```

```
        OpenOrderView[] openOrders = manufacture.getOpenOrders();

        if (openOrders.length == 0) {
          System.out.println("Nothing to make; go home.");
          return;
        }

        System.out.println("Selecting from the following open orders:");
        for (int iter = 0; iter < openOrders.length; iter++) {
          OpenOrderView openOrder = openOrders[iter];

          System.out.println("Sales Division: "
                          + openOrder.salesDivision + "; Order #: "
                          + openOrder.orderNumber + "; Product: "
                          + openOrder.product + "Date due: "
                          + openOrder.dateDue);
        }

        // Get the first open order
        for (int iterFind = 0; iterFind < openOrders.length;
            iterFind++) {
          try {
            OpenOrderView openOrder = openOrders[iterFind];
            manufacture.selectForManufacture(openOrder.salesDivision,
                                      openOrder.orderNumber);
            Handle handle = manufacture.getHandle();
            FileOutputStream file_out = new FileOutputStream(FILE_NAME);
            ObjectOutputStream out = new ObjectOutputStream(file_out);
            out.writeObject(handle);
            System.out.println("Written object for next stage.");
            break;
          } catch (factory.manufacture.BadStatusException bse) {

            // Someone grabbed it before we did
            bse.printStackTrace();
          }
        }

    } catch (FileNotFoundException fnfe) {
      fnfe.printStackTrace();
    } catch (RemoteException re) {
      re.printStackTrace();
    } catch (IOException ioe) {
      ioe.printStackTrace();
    } catch (factory.manage_orders.NoSuchOrderException nsoe) {
      nsoe.printStackTrace();
    } catch (NamingException ne) {
      ne.printStackTrace();
    } catch (CreateException ce) {
      ce.printStackTrace();
    }

  }
}
```

The 'begin manufacture' client prints out a list of the open orders that are eligible for manufacture. The client doesn't need to worry about these eligibility requirements; this is a business rule that is implemented on the server. Next, the client selects one of these items for manufacture:

This code is slightly more complicated than any of the other client-side code we will encounter. We have a list of open orders. Why do we need to catch an exception that would only be thrown if we tried to manufacture an order that wasn't open?

Between the time when we got the list of open orders and the time we tried to select one of those orders for manufacture, some other manufacturing cell could have already started work on that same order. The problem is that we could be working with stale data. Within a single transaction (and depending on isolation levels), we could be sure that our list of open orders would remain open until we selected one for manufacture. But we cached data on the client (in the form of the openOrders array), and now we must deal with the possibility that our cached data is stale, hence the loop.

Note that my loop, although it has the virtue of simplicity, is not a perfect solution to this problem. We could go through the entire original list of open orders without finding one that was still opened, in which case we would exit the program without doing any more work. But in the meantime, new orders could have been placed. With the current solution, we need to run the program again if that happens.

This is a special case of a more general problem that will be discussed in Chapter 21 on transactions.

And next, CompleteManufacture:

```java
package factory.clients;

import java.rmi.RemoteException;
import javax.ejb.*;
import javax.naming.*;
import javax.rmi.PortableRemoteObject;
import java.util.Properties;
import java.io.*;

import factory.manufacture.Manufacture;
import factory.manufacture.ManufactureHome;
import factory.manage_orders.OpenOrderView;

public class CompleteManufacture {

  private static final String FILE_NAME = "C:/current_product.ser";
  private static final String CARRIER = "State Express";
  private static final int LOADING_DOCK = 1;

  public static void main(String[] args) {

    try {
      ContextPropertiesFactory factory =
        new ContextPropertiesFactory();
      factory.makePropertiesDefault();

      FileInputStream inStream = new FileInputStream(FILE_NAME);
      ObjectInputStream in = new ObjectInputStream(inStream);
      Handle handle = (Handle) in.readObject();
```

```
            Manufacture manufacture =
               (Manufacture) PortableRemoteObject
                 .narrow(handle.getEJBObject(), Manufacture.class);
            System.out.println("Product routings:");

            while (manufacture.hasNextRouting()) {
               String routing = manufacture.getNextRouting();
               System.out.println(routing);
            }

            System.out.println("Product finished; shipping...");
            manufacture.ship(CARRIER, LOADING_DOCK);
            manufacture.remove();

         } catch (Exception e) {
            e.printStackTrace();
         } catch (Throwable t) {
            t.printStackTrace();
         }
      }
   }
```

This 'complete manufacture' client picks up where the 'begin manufacture' client left off.

Notice that we take care to remove the stateful session bean from the server. This isn't important with stateless session beans because they aren't consuming any resources on the server to begin with; `remove()` is typically a no-op. But if we fail to remove a stateful session bean when we're finished with it, it will live on, clogging up the memory (or at least the passivation store) of the server until it times out.

The 'place sample orders' client creates six orders. I have chosen due dates for the orders so that two orders will be overdue, two orders will be schedulable and not overdue, and two orders will be due far enough in the future that they should not be scheduled. This will exercise all of our business logic. Here is the code:

```
package factory.clients;

import java.rmi.RemoteException;
import javax.ejb.*;
import javax.naming.*;
import javax.rmi.PortableRemoteObject;
import java.util.Properties;
import java.util.Calendar;
import java.util.Date;

import factory.manage_orders.ManageOrders;
import factory.manage_orders.ManageOrdersHome;

public class PlaceSampleOrders {

   private static final int SALES_DIVISION_1 = 1;
   private static final int SALES_DIVISION_2 = 2;
   private static final int SALES_DIVISION_3 = 3;
```

```
    private static final int ORDER_1 = 1;
    private static final int ORDER_2 = 2;
    private static final int ORDER_3 = 3;
    private static final int ORDER_4 = 4;
    private static final int ORDER_5 = 5;

    private static final String PRODUCT_1 = "DESK01";
    private static final String PRODUCT_2 = "CHAIR01";
    private static final String PRODUCT_3 = "LAMP01";

    public static void main(String[] args) {

      try {
        ContextPropertiesFactory factory =
          new ContextPropertiesFactory();
        Properties prop = factory.getInitialContextProperties();
        InitialContext initial = new InitialContext(prop);

        Object homeObject = initial.lookup("ManageOrders");

        ManageOrdersHome home =
          (ManageOrdersHome) PortableRemoteObject.narrow(homeObject,
              ManageOrdersHome.class);

        ManageOrders manageOrders = home.create();

        Calendar calendarNotSchedulable = Calendar.getInstance();
        calendarNotSchedulable.add(Calendar.DAY_OF_YEAR, 14);

        Calendar calendarSchedulable = Calendar.getInstance();
        calendarSchedulable.add(Calendar.DAY_OF_YEAR, 5);

        Calendar calendarOverdue = Calendar.getInstance();

        manageOrders.placeOrder(SALES_DIVISION_1, ORDER_1, PRODUCT_1,
                          calendarNotSchedulable.getTime());

        manageOrders.placeOrder(SALES_DIVISION_2, ORDER_1, PRODUCT_2,
                          calendarNotSchedulable.getTime());

        manageOrders.placeOrder(SALES_DIVISION_1, ORDER_2, PRODUCT_3,
                          calendarSchedulable.getTime());

        manageOrders.placeOrder(SALES_DIVISION_2, ORDER_2, PRODUCT_1,
                          calendarSchedulable.getTime());

        manageOrders.placeOrder(SALES_DIVISION_1, ORDER_3, PRODUCT_2,
                          calendarOverdue.getTime());

        manageOrders.placeOrder(SALES_DIVISION_2, ORDER_3, PRODUCT_3,
                          calendarOverdue.getTime());

      } catch (Exception e) {
        e.printStackTrace();
      }

    }
}
```

945

The 'manage orders' client lists the orders that are overdue, and then cancels the first overdue order:

```java
package factory.clients;

import java.rmi.RemoteException;
import javax.ejb.*;
import javax.naming.*;
import javax.rmi.PortableRemoteObject;
import java.util.Properties;

import factory.manage_orders.ManageOrders;
import factory.manage_orders.ManageOrdersHome;
import factory.manage_orders.OverdueOrderView;
import factory.manage_orders.OpenOrderView;

public class ManageSampleOrders {

  public static void main(String[] args) {

    try {
      ContextPropertiesFactory factory =
        new ContextPropertiesFactory();
      Properties prop = factory.getInitialContextProperties();
      InitialContext initial = new InitialContext(prop);

      Object homeObject = initial.lookup("ManageOrders");

      ManageOrdersHome home =
        (ManageOrdersHome) PortableRemoteObject.narrow(homeObject,
            ManageOrdersHome.class);

      ManageOrders manageOrders = home.create();

      // List overdue orders
      OverdueOrderView[] overdueOrders =
        manageOrders.getOverdueOrders();
      for (int iter = 0; iter < overdueOrders.length; iter++) {
        OverdueOrderView overdueOrder = overdueOrders[iter];
        System.out.println("Product " + overdueOrder.product
                    + " is due on " + overdueOrder.dateDue
                    + ".  It's status is "
                    + overdueOrder.status + ".");
      }

      // Cancel first overdue order
      if (overdueOrders.length > 0) {
        OverdueOrderView overdueOrder = overdueOrders[0];
        System.out.println("About to cancel an order...");
        try {
          manageOrders.cancelOrder(overdueOrder.salesDivision,
                        overdueOrder.orderNumber);
          System.out.println("Canceled order for "
                      + overdueOrder.product.trim() + ".");
        } catch (factory.manage_orders.NoSuchOrderException nsoe) {
```

```
            System.out.println("Failed to find order.");
          } catch (factory.order.OrderNotCancelableException once) {
            System.out.println("Cannot cancel an order in production.");
          }
        }

      } catch (RemoteException re) {
        re.printStackTrace();
      } catch (NamingException ne) {
        ne.printStackTrace();
      } catch (CreateException ce) {
        ce.printStackTrace();
      }
    }
  }
}
```

This code is pretty simple to understand. Notice the OrderNotCancelableException. This is the client-side expression of a business rule on the server that does not allow orders to be cancelled once production has started. The exception that you throw in your business logic is automatically forwarded to the client, unless it is a RuntimeException or error. For more information about exception handling in EJBs, see Chapter 21.

Ideally, your client should indicate whether an operation would succeed before it is attempted. For instance, the button or menu-item could be grayed-out. Obviously, a more creative approach will be required for a web browser or WAP clients. In any case, this exception will indicate which business rule was violated and allow feedback to the client.

Finally, the client that creates some sample products:

```
package factory.clients;

import java.rmi.RemoteException;
import javax.ejb.*;
import javax.naming.*;
import javax.rmi.PortableRemoteObject;
import java.util.Properties;

import factory.manage_orders.ManageOrders;
import factory.manage_orders.ManageOrdersHome;

public class CreateProducts {

  public static void main(String[] args) {

    try {
      ContextPropertiesFactory factory =
        new ContextPropertiesFactory();
      Properties prop = factory.getInitialContextProperties();
      InitialContext initial = new InitialContext(prop);

      Object homeObject = initial.lookup("ManageOrders");
```

```
        ManageOrdersHome home =
          (ManageOrdersHome) PortableRemoteObject.narrow(homeObject,
              ManageOrdersHome.class);

        ManageOrders manageOrders = home.create();

        manageOrders.createSampleProducts();

      } catch (RemoteException re) {
        re.printStackTrace();
      } catch (NamingException ne) {
        ne.printStackTrace();
      } catch (CreateException ce) {
        ce.printStackTrace();
      }

    }
  }
```

Stateless Session Bean Implementation

Our sample application's stateless session bean, `ManageOrders`, has the main implementation class `factory.manage_orders.ManageOrdersEJB`. I have divided this class into sections:

❑ Business methods

❑ Implementation helper methods

❑ Lifecycle and framework methods

In addition, we will see the code for another class in this section: `ProductCreationHelper`. This is a regular Java class that assists us with our implementation.

Business Methods

The business methods implemented in this class correspond to the business methods declared in the bean's remote interface. They match up based on a convention: they have the same name and method signature. Note that I don't throw `java.rmi.RemoteException` from any implementation method. Throwing it is allowed, but is deprecated behavior. In general, the bean developer should throw an application exception to indicate a business logic error, and an `EJBException` to indicate a system error of some sort.

Let's look first at the business methods:

```
package factory.manage_orders;

import javax.ejb.*;
import javax.naming.*;
import javax.rmi.PortableRemoteObject;
import java.rmi.RemoteException;
import java.util.Date;
import java.util.Collection;
```

```
import java.util.Iterator;
import java.util.LinkedList;
import factory.order.OrderHome;
import factory.order.Order;
import factory.order.OrderPK;
import factory.order.StatusStrings;
import factory.product.Product;
import factory.product.ProductHome;
import factory.product.RoutingInstruction;
import factory.order.OrderNotCancelableException;

public class ManageOrdersEJB implements SessionBean {

  private static final int MILLIS_IN_DAYS = 86400000;
```

The placeOrder() method makes use of both our sample's entity beans, Order and Product, which will be covered in more detail in Chapter 20. This method calls two helper methods, getProductHome() and getOrderHome(). These encapsulate JNDI access to the home interfaces, and will be looked at briefly in the next section:

```
// Business methods
  public void placeOrder(int salesDivision, int orderNumber,
                         String productName,
                         Date dateDue) throws NoSuchProductException,
                                                 DuplicateOrderException {

    try {

      // Find the product
      ProductHome productHome = getProductHome();
      Product product = productHome.findByPrimaryKey(productName);

      // create the order
      OrderHome orderHome = getOrderHome();
      orderHome.create(salesDivision, orderNumber, product, dateDue);

    } catch (NamingException ne) {
      throw new EJBException(ne);
    } catch (RemoteException re) {
      throw new EJBException(re);
    } catch (FinderException fe) {
      if (fe instanceof ObjectNotFoundException) {
        throw new NoSuchProductException();
      } else {
        throw new EJBException(fe);
      }
    } catch (CreateException ce) {
      if (orderExists(salesDivision, orderNumber)) {
        throw new DuplicateOrderException();
      } else {
        throw new EJBException(ce);
      }
    }
  }
```

It's worth considering how business logic concerns dictate responses to the handling of FinderException and the CreateException. If the finder exception is a result of the product not being found in the database, a checked exception, NoSuchProductException, is sent to the client. If the finder exception is because of some other, indeterminate cause, the unchecked EJBException is thrown instead. (The client will receive a RemoteException.) A similar pattern exists with the CreateException, although we need to use the orderExists() helper function to determine the cause of the CreateException.

The business method cancelOrder() doesn't introduce anything new. The OrderNotCancelableException is thrown by the order's corresponding business method cancelOrder():

```
public void cancelOrder(int salesDivision, int orderNumber)
        throws NoSuchOrderException, OrderNotCancelableException {

    try {

        // Find the order
        OrderHome orderHome = getOrderHome();
        OrderPK orderPK = new OrderPK(salesDivision, orderNumber);

        // Cancel it
        Order order = orderHome.findByPrimaryKey(orderPK);
        order.cancelOrder();

    } catch (NamingException ne) {
        throw new EJBException(ne);
    } catch (RemoteException re) {
        throw new EJBException(re);
    } catch (FinderException fe) {
        if (fe instanceof ObjectNotFoundException) {
            throw new NoSuchOrderException();
        } else {
            throw new EJBException(fe);
        }
    }
}
```

The business methods getOverdueOrders() and getSchedulableOrders() build on the functionality offered by the Order entity bean's home methods, findUncompletedOrders() and findOpenOrders(). The business methods then apply additional business rules to screen the collections returned from the finder methods. Several parameters (lead time and maximum inventory time) come from helper methods that will be explained in the next section:

```
public OverdueOrderView[] getOverdueOrders() {

    try {
        LinkedList overdueOrders = new LinkedList();
        Date today = new Date();
        long todayMillis = today.getTime();
        long leadTimeMillis = getLeadTimeDays() * MILLIS_IN_DAYS;
        OrderHome orderHome = getOrderHome();
```

```
            Collection uncompletedOrders =
              orderHome.findUncompletedOrders();
            Iterator iterUncompletedOrders = uncompletedOrders.iterator();

            while (iterUncompletedOrders.hasNext()) {
              Order uncompletedOrder =
                (Order) PortableRemoteObject
                  .narrow(iterUncompletedOrders.next(), Order.class);
              Date dateDue = uncompletedOrder.getDateDue();
              String status = uncompletedOrder.getStatus();
              long dueDateMillis = dateDue.getTime();
              if ((status.equals(StatusStrings.OPEN)
                        && (todayMillis + leadTimeMillis > dueDateMillis))
                  || (status.equals(StatusStrings.IN_PROCESS)
                        && (todayMillis > dueDateMillis))) {
                OverdueOrderView view =
                  new OverdueOrderView(uncompletedOrder
                    .getSalesDivision(), uncompletedOrder
                    .getOrderNumber(), uncompletedOrder
                      .getProductOrdered().getName(), status, dateDue);
                overdueOrders.add(view);
              }
            }

            OverdueOrderView[] overdue =
              new OverdueOrderView[overdueOrders.size()];
            return (OverdueOrderView[]) overdueOrders.toArray(overdue);

          } catch (NamingException ne) {
            throw new EJBException(ne);
          } catch (RemoteException re) {
            throw new EJBException(re);
          } catch (FinderException fe) {
            throw new EJBException(fe);
          }
        }

        public OpenOrderView[] getSchedulableOrders() {

          try {
            LinkedList schedulableOrders = new LinkedList();
            Date today = new Date();
            long todayMillis = today.getTime();
            long maxInventoryTimeMillis = getMaxInventoryTimeDays()
                                  * MILLIS_IN_DAYS;
            long leadTimeMillis = getLeadTimeDays() * MILLIS_IN_DAYS;
            OrderHome orderHome = getOrderHome();
            Collection openOrders = orderHome.findOpenOrders();
            Iterator iterOpenOrders = openOrders.iterator();

            while (iterOpenOrders.hasNext()) {
              Order openOrder =
                (Order) PortableRemoteObject.narrow(iterOpenOrders.next(),
                                            Order.class);
```

```
          Date dateDue = openOrder.getDateDue();
          long dueDateMillis = dateDue.getTime();
          if (todayMillis
                >= dueDateMillis - leadTimeMillis
                  - maxInventoryTimeMillis) {
            OpenOrderView view =
              new OpenOrderView(openOrder.getSalesDivision(),
                                openOrder.getOrderNumber(),
                                openOrder.getProductOrdered().getName(),
                                dateDue);
            schedulableOrders.add(view);
          }
        }

        OpenOrderView[] schedulable =
          new OpenOrderView[schedulableOrders.size()];
        return (OpenOrderView[]) schedulableOrders.toArray(schedulable);

      } catch (NamingException ne) {
        throw new EJBException(ne);
      } catch (RemoteException re) {
        throw new EJBException(re);
      } catch (FinderException fe) {
        throw new EJBException(fe);
      }
    }
```

The business methods createProduct() and addRoutingInstruction() are for use by the web interface we will develop in Chapter 22. They both make use of entity beans, which we will be examining more closely in the next chapter. The createProduct() method takes the id and name of the product as parameters, using these to create a product entity bean with an empty routing instruction list. The product entity bean will insert a corresponding record in the database. After the product has been created, the addRoutingInstruction() method can be used to add corresponding routing instructions, one at a time:

```
    public void createProduct(String id, String name) {

      try {
        ProductHome productHome = getProductHome();
        productHome.create(id, name, new RoutingInstruction[]{});

      } catch (NamingException ne) {
        throw new EJBException(ne);
      } catch (CreateException ce) {
        throw new EJBException(ce);
      } catch (RemoteException re) {
        throw new EJBException(re);
      }

    }

    public void addRoutingInstruction(String id, int sequence,
                                      String instruction) {
```

```
        try {
          ProductHome productHome = getProductHome();
          Product product = productHome.findByPrimaryKey(id);
          product.addRoutingInstruction(sequence, instruction);

        } catch (FinderException fe) {
          throw new EJBException(fe);
        } catch (NamingException ne) {
          throw new EJBException(ne);
        } catch (RemoteException re) {
          throw new EJBException(re);
        }

      }
```

The `createSampleProducts()` business method exists only to kick-start the sample application, but one feature is worth discussing: its implementation is in a helper class:

```
    public void createSampleProducts() {

      try {
        ProductHome productHome = getProductHome();

        // Create three sample products
        ProductCreationHelper pch =
          new ProductCreationHelper(productHome);
        pch.createAll();

      } catch (NamingException ne) {
        throw new EJBException(ne);
      }
    }
```

In general, this helper class is identical to the main implementation class from the specification's point of view, as far as the limitations and privileges of EJBs go. You still can't create threads, access the file system, etc. That's the case with `ProductCreationHelper`, which takes actions that could just as easily have been in-line:

```
    package factory.manage_orders;

    import javax.ejb.EJBException;
    import factory.product.Product;
    import factory.product.ProductHome;
    import factory.product.RoutingInstruction;
    import factory.product.NoSuchRoutingInstruction;

    public class ProductCreationHelper {

      ProductHome productHome;

      public ProductCreationHelper(ProductHome productHome) {
```

```
      this.productHome = productHome;
    }

  public void createAll() {

    try {
      createDesk();
      createChair();
      createLamp();

    } catch (Exception e) {
      e.printStackTrace();
      throw new EJBException(e);
    }
  }

  public void createDesk() throws Exception {

    RoutingInstruction compress = new RoutingInstruction(5,
          "Compress the wood.");
    RoutingInstruction stain = new RoutingInstruction(10,
          "Stain the wood.");
    RoutingInstruction assemble = new RoutingInstruction(15,
          "Assemble the desk.");
    RoutingInstruction[] routings = new RoutingInstruction[] {
      compress, stain, assemble
    };

    productHome.create("DESK01", "Compressed Wood Desk", routings);
  }

  public void createChair() throws Exception {

    RoutingInstruction extrude = new RoutingInstruction(5,
          "Extrude plastic.");
    RoutingInstruction glue = new RoutingInstruction(10,
          "Glue together.");
    RoutingInstruction paint = new RoutingInstruction(15,
          "Spraypaint.");
    RoutingInstruction[] routings = new RoutingInstruction[] {
      extrude, glue, paint
    };

    productHome.create("CHAIR01", "Quality Plastic Chair", routings);
  }

  public void createLamp() throws Exception {

    RoutingInstruction getBulb = new RoutingInstruction(5,
          "Get bulb from inventory.");
    RoutingInstruction getLamp = new RoutingInstruction(10,
          "Get lamp from inventory.");
    RoutingInstruction screwTogether = new RoutingInstruction(15,
          "Screw together.");
    RoutingInstruction frayCord = new RoutingInstruction(20,
```

```
                "Pre-fray the cord");
    RoutingInstruction[] routings = new RoutingInstruction[] {
        getBulb, getLamp, screwTogether, frayCord
    };

    Product lamp = productHome.create("LAMP01", "Custom Made Lamp",
                                       routings);
    try {
        lamp.deleteRoutingInstruction(21);
    } catch (NoSuchRoutingInstruction nsri) {
        lamp.deleteRoutingInstruction(20);
    }

    }

}
```

However, let's consider an exceptional case. Assume you have decided that your EJBs need to perform an action that is prohibited by the specification, and your current application server will support this behavior. If your application server enforces the restrictions of EJB, it will do this by using Java's security model. You may need to bypass the Java security limitations under which your bean executes, and which are intended to protect the server from insecure or potentially damaging operations. (This does not mean you are bypassing the access controls on EJBs, which is an entirely different system.) You will need to use a helper class to do this, along with a `doPrivileged()` call.

Java security is tied to the class loader. With most application servers, your EJBs will be loaded by one (or more) class loader(s), and the application server will have a different class loader that it uses for the classes on its CLASSPATH. To bypass security and perform the non-portable operation, you would put your helper class on the CLASSPATH and make the privileged call. Java security and its relationship to the class loader and the `doPrivileged()` call is a standard (if somewhat esoteric) Java language feature. Consult a language reference if you need more information.

As a rule, unless you have a very good reason, don't do this. You will affect the portability of the components you write.

Implementation Helper Methods

Continuing with our implementation of `ManageOrdersEJB`, add this code to the code above:

```
// Implementation helpers

private boolean orderExists(int salesDivision, int orderNumber) {

    try {
        OrderHome orderHome = getOrderHome();
        OrderPK orderPK = new OrderPK(salesDivision, orderNumber);
        Order order = orderHome.findByPrimaryKey(orderPK);
        return true;

    } catch (Exception e) {
        return false;
    }
}
```

```
private int getLeadTimeDays() throws NamingException {
  InitialContext initial = new InitialContext();
  Integer leadTimeDays =
    (Integer) initial.lookup("java:comp/env/lead_time");

  // A null pointer will roll back the transaction
  return leadTimeDays.intValue();
}

private int getMaxInventoryTimeDays() throws NamingException {
  InitialContext initial = new InitialContext();
  Integer inventoryTimeDays =
    (Integer) initial.lookup("java:comp/env/max_inventory_time");

  // A null pointer will roll back the transaction
  return inventoryTimeDays.intValue();
}

private ProductHome getProductHome() throws NamingException {
  InitialContext initial = new InitialContext();
  ProductHome home =
    (ProductHome) javax.rmi.PortableRemoteObject
      .narrow(initial.lookup("java:comp/env/ejb/Product"),
              ProductHome.class);
  return home;
}

private OrderHome getOrderHome() throws NamingException {
  InitialContext initial = new InitialContext();
  OrderHome home =
    (OrderHome) javax.rmi.PortableRemoteObject
      .narrow(initial.lookup("java:comp/env/ejb/Order"),
              OrderHome.class);
  return home;
}
```

Notice that while business methods accessible through the remote interface must all be public, these implementation methods can be declared as `private`. The first method, `orderExists()`, was referenced above and is pretty self-explanatory. The order entity bean's home interface is used to try to find a pre-existing order with the same key. If one is found, `true` is returned, otherwise `false` is returned.

The next two implementation helper methods retrieve the lead-time and maximum-inventory-time parameters from the bean's JNDI environment. This read-only information is specified in the bean's deployment descriptor. This is less flexible than storing the information in the database, of course (which in a real manufacturing application it would be stored). To change the information the bean reads from the deployment descriptor, you would need to redeploy the bean on your application server. However, storing the information in the deployment descriptor is more flexible than hard-coding values in code. To change the information in code, you would need to rebuild the bean *and* redeploy.

In general, the type of information that belongs in the bean's environment is customization information that is unlikely to be volatile for a particular deployment. Good candidates might be the company's name, SQL statements for direct database access, or an IP address of an ERP application's server. A very bad candidate would be the exchange rate between the Euro and the Dollar.

Environment entries can be any of the following types: String, Boolean, Byte, Short, Integer, Long, Float, and Double. These entries are typically specified using a tool provided by your application server vendor. The format in the XML deployment descriptor can be edited by hand, if you desire. The sample application's environment entries for the 'manage orders' bean looks like this:

```
<env-entry>
   <env-entry-name>lead_time</env-entry-name>
   <env-entry-type>java.lang.Integer</env-entry-type>
   <env-entry-value>3</env-entry-value>
</env-entry>
<env-entry>
   <env-entry-name>max_inventory_time</env-entry-name>
   <env-entry-type>java.lang.Integer</env-entry-type>
   <env-entry-value>10</env-entry-value>
</env-entry>
```

The names that you specify for your environment variables (with the <env-entry-name> element) will be available to your bean in the "java:comp/env/" context. See the code for an example of this mapping.

The next two implementation helper methods retrieve the home interfaces of the two entity EJBs that are referenced by this EJB (Order and Product). The bean developer declares the logical names of the beans that they references in the deployment descriptor, as described above. Here are the declarations for the 'manage orders' EJB from the sample application:

```
<ejb-ref>
   <ejb-ref-name>ejb/Order</ejb-ref-name>
   <ejb-ref-type>Entity</ejb-ref-type>
   <home>factory.order.OrderHome</home>
   <remote>factory.order.Order</remote>
   <ejb-link>Orders</ejb-link>
</ejb-ref>
<ejb-ref>
   <ejb-ref-name>ejb/Product</ejb-ref-name>
   <ejb-ref-type>Entity</ejb-ref-type>
   <home>factory.product.ProductHome</home>
   <remote>factory.product.Product</remote>
   <ejb-link>Product</ejb-link>
</ejb-ref>
```

As mentioned above, the ejb-link entry is an optional entry that the bean developer can use to make sure that the deployer keeps the namespace consistent. In this case it says, "Whatever name you give to my Product or Order bean in the JNDI namespace, you need to use that same name to link to the ejb/Product or ejb/Order reference".

Lifecycle and Framework Methods

The lifecycle methods are all empty. For more information on their purpose, see the explanation earlier in this chapter:

```
// Framework & lifecycle methods

public void ejbCreate() {}
```

```
    public void ejbActivate() {}

    public void ejbPassivate() {}

    public void ejbRemove() {}

    public void setSessionContext(SessionContext ctx) {}
}
```

Stateful Session Bean Implementation

Our sample application's stateful session bean, `Manufacture`, has the main implementation class `factory.manufacture.ManufactureEJB`. This is the only class that you'll be creating in this section. There are two new ideas that we will look at in this code: **how to use database connections** and **how to retrieve environment variables**. Unlike the stateless session bean discussed earlier, the `Manufacture` bean maintains state:

```
    package factory.manufacture;

import javax.ejb.*;
import javax.naming.*;
import java.rmi.RemoteException;
import java.sql.Connection;
import java.sql.SQLException;
import java.sql.PreparedStatement;
import javax.sql.DataSource;
import java.util.Arrays;
import java.util.List;
import java.util.Collections;
import java.util.Iterator;
import java.util.Date;
import factory.product.Product;
import factory.product.ProductHome;
import factory.order.Order;
import factory.order.OrderHome;
import factory.order.OrderPK;
import factory.order.StatusStrings;
import factory.manage_orders.OpenOrderView;
import factory.manage_orders.ManageOrders;
import factory.manage_orders.ManageOrdersHome;
import factory.manage_orders.NoSuchOrderException;
import factory.product.RoutingInstruction;

public class ManufactureEJB implements SessionBean {

    // Properties
    public String manufactureCellID;
    public List routingInstructions;
    public int currentPosition;
    public int lastPosition;

    public boolean orderSelected;
    public int selectedSalesDivision;
    public int selectedOrderNumber;
```

The `manufactureCellID` variable is set in the `ejbCreate()` call. Unlike the stateless session bean's `ejbCreate()` call, this has a one-to-one correspondence with a matching `create()` call by the client on the bean's home interface. Notice that I also use `ejbCreate()` like a constructor to initialize `orderSelected`. We'll look at this method next, along with the other (empty) lifecycle methods:

```
// Framework & lifecycle methods

public void ejbCreate(String manufactureCellID) {
  this.manufactureCellID = manufactureCellID;
  orderSelected = false;
}

public void ejbActivate() {}

public void ejbPassivate() {}

public void ejbRemove() {}

public void setSessionContext(SessionContext ctx) {}
```

Next, the business methods:

```
// Business methods

public OpenOrderView[] getOpenOrders() {

  try {
    ManageOrdersHome homeManageOrders = getManageOrdersHome();
    ManageOrders manageOrders = homeManageOrders.create();
    return manageOrders.getSchedulableOrders();

  } catch (NamingException ne) {
    throw new EJBException(ne);
  } catch (RemoteException re) {
    throw new EJBException(re);
  } catch (CreateException ce) {
    throw new EJBException(ce);
  }
}

public void selectForManufacture(int salesDivision, int order_number)
        throws NoSuchOrderException, BadStatusException {

  try {
    OrderHome homeOrder = getOrderHome();
    OrderPK orderPK = new OrderPK(salesDivision, order_number);
    Order order = homeOrder.findByPrimaryKey(orderPK);
    String orderStatus = order.getStatus();
    if (!orderStatus.equals(StatusStrings.OPEN)) {
      throw new BadStatusException(orderStatus);
    }
    order.beginManufacture();
    Product product = order.getProductOrdered();
    RoutingInstruction[] productRouting =
```

```
          product.getRoutingInstructions();
        routingInstructions = Arrays.asList(productRouting);
        Collections.sort(routingInstructions);
        currentPosition = 0;
        lastPosition = routingInstructions.size() - 1;
        selectedSalesDivision = salesDivision;
        selectedOrderNumber = order_number;
        orderSelected = true;

    } catch (NamingException ne) {
      ne.printStackTrace();
      throw new EJBException(ne);
    } catch (RemoteException re) {
      re.printStackTrace();
      throw new EJBException(re);
    } catch (FinderException fe) {
      fe.printStackTrace();
      if (fe instanceof ObjectNotFoundException) {
        throw new NoSuchOrderException();
      } else {
        throw new EJBException(fe);
      }
    }
  }
}

public boolean hasNextRouting() throws NoSelectionException {
  if (!orderSelected) {
    throw new NoSelectionException();
  }
  return (currentPosition <= lastPosition);
}

public String getNextRouting() throws NoSelectionException {
  if (!orderSelected) {
    throw new NoSelectionException();

  }
  RoutingInstruction ri =
    (RoutingInstruction) routingInstructions.get(currentPosition++);
  return ri.instruction;
}

public void ship(String carrier,
                 int loading_dock) throws NoSelectionException {

  // Sales division, order number, carrier,
  // loading dock, date completed, manufactured by

  if (!orderSelected) {
    throw new NoSelectionException();

  }
  Connection con = null;
```

```
    try {
      con = getConnection();
      PreparedStatement statement =
        con.prepareStatement(getShipmentSQLString());
      statement.setInt(1, selectedSalesDivision);
      statement.setInt(2, selectedOrderNumber);
      statement.setString(3, carrier);
      statement.setInt(4, loading_dock);
      statement.setDate(5, new java.sql.Date((new Date()).getTime()));
      statement.setString(6, manufactureCellID);
      statement.executeUpdate();
      statement.close();
      con.close();
      orderSelected = false;

      OrderHome homeOrder = getOrderHome();
      OrderPK orderPK = new OrderPK(selectedSalesDivision,
                                    selectedOrderNumber);
      Order order = homeOrder.findByPrimaryKey(orderPK);
      order.completeManufacture();

    } catch (NamingException ne) {
      ne.printStackTrace();
      throw new EJBException(ne);
    } catch (SQLException sqle) {
      try {
        if (con != null) {
          con.close();
        }
      } catch (Exception e) {}
      sqle.printStackTrace();
      throw new EJBException(sqle);
    } catch (RemoteException re) {
      throw new EJBException(re);
    } catch (FinderException fe) {
      throw new EJBException(fe);
    }
  }
```

The 'selected order' is indicated by two variables that represent the order's key, selectedSalesDivision and selectedOrderNumber. They are set in the business method selectForManufacture(). This business method performs the following additional steps:

❑ Verifies that the order exists and is eligible for manufacture

❑ Sets the status of the order so that other manufacturing cells will realize that the order is being built

❑ Retrieves the routing instructions for the ordered product, sorts them, and caches them in a variable

❑ Sets the orderSelected variable to true so that subsequent method calls in the workflow will be able to proceed

The first step in the workflow that the Manufacture bean embodies (even before selecting an order for manufacture) is to get a list of open orders. The implementation of this business method is simple, because it delegates all its work to the stateless session ManageOrders EJB discussed in the last section. This is a simple example of a 'services layer' architecture. Notice that the stateful session bean calls the stateless session bean – but not the other way around.

Following order selection, the next step in the workflow is to iterate through the product routings while we are building the product. Again, this is quite simple. We are simply iterating through the collection set up in the `selectForManufacture()` method. Notice that we make sure the workflow has been followed, by checking the `orderSelected()` variable. If it hasn't been, we throw a business exception to the client to give it the opportunity to correct the error. Notice also that we are iterating through stale data. The product design could have changed during the manufacturing process, and it won't be reflected in the iteration. This is OK with us, though: we don't want to change to a new routing list halfway through building the product.

The last business method, `ship()`, changes the order status to indicate that manufacturing is completed. It does this using the `Order` entity bean, and also inserts a shipment record in the database. This is included as an example of accessing a database directly from a session bean.

First, notice where the SQL text came from: the bean's environment. The implementation helper method `getShipmentSQLString()` (shown below) retrieves the SQL from the XML deployment descriptor. This partially decouples the EJB's Java code from the specifics of the database. If we want to use the same business logic with a different database structure, we can, without rewriting the bean. This is an ideal case for storing information in the deployment descriptor:

```
private String getShipmentSQLString() throws NamingException {

    InitialContext initial = new InitialContext();
    String sql = (String) initial.lookup("java:comp/env/shipmentSQL");
    return sql;
}
```

The deployment descriptor environment entry looks as follows:

```
<env-entry>
  <env-entry-name>shipmentSQL</env-entry-name>
  <env-entry-type>java.lang.String</env-entry-type>
  <env-entry-value>insert into shipments (division, order_number, carrier,
                   loading_dock, date_completed, manufactured_by) values
                   (?, ?, ?, ?, ?, ?)
  </env-entry-value>
</env-entry>
```

On the database that I use for development, the table might be defined like this:

```
CREATE TABLE SHIPMENTS (DIVISION INTEGER NOT NULL,
                        ORDER_NUMBER INTEGER NOT NULL,
                        CARRIER CHAR(50),
                        LOADING_DOCK INTEGER,
                        DATE_COMPLETED DATE,
                        MANUFACTURED_BY CHAR(50),
                        PRIMARY KEY (DIVISION, ORDER_NUMBER));
```

The connection to the database must be retrieved under controlled circumstances. The bean programmer can't simply go get one using JDBC's `DriverManager`. The EJB container needs to manage the process, to implement features such as transaction management and connection pooling. So the programmer must acquire a `DataSource` from the JNDI namespace (which is a "factory class" for

JDBC connections), and use this to produce the connection. You can see an example of this in the helper method below. (Also, while an EJB is in a transaction, the bean programmer isn't allowed to interfere with the container by calling `commit()` or `rollback()` on the connection.)

The bean programmer must declare in the XML deployment descriptor that they are going to use a resource such as a JDBC connection. (Other possible resources include JMS or JavaMail connections.) Note that this reference to a JDBC connection is a logical reference that will be mapped by the container into the JNDI namespace. An actual corresponding JDBC connection will be specified when the bean is deployed. The XML for our sample looks like this:

```
<resource-ref>
  <res-ref-name>jdbc/shipDB</res-ref-name>
  <res-type>javax.sql.DataSource</res-type>
  <res-auth>Container</res-auth>
</resource-ref>
```

The EJB can give a username and password itself, but hard-coding this in the bean code is usually a bad idea. In this sample, I depend on the container to authenticate the bean to the database. When I deploy the application, I can specify a username and password dynamically. (Exactly how to do this is specific to your application server.)

Finally, here are the helper methods:

```
// Implementation helper
private OrderHome getOrderHome() throws NamingException {
  InitialContext initial = new InitialContext();
  OrderHome home =
    (OrderHome) javax.rmi.PortableRemoteObject
      .narrow(initial.lookup("java:comp/env/ejb/Order"),
          OrderHome.class);
  return home;
}

private ManageOrdersHome getManageOrdersHome()
      throws NamingException {
  InitialContext initial = new InitialContext();
  ManageOrdersHome home =
    (ManageOrdersHome) javax.rmi.PortableRemoteObject
      .narrow(initial.lookup("java:comp/env/ejb/ManageOrders"),
          ManageOrdersHome.class);
  return home;
}

private Connection getConnection()
      throws SQLException, NamingException {
  Context initial = new InitialContext();
  DataSource dataSource =
    (DataSource) initial.lookup("java:comp/env/jdbc/shipDB");
  return dataSource.getConnection();
}
```

```
    private String getShipmentSQLString() throws NamingException {
      InitialContext initial = new InitialContext();
      String sql = (String) initial.lookup("java:comp/env/shipmentSQL");
      return sql;
    }
  }
```

The `getConnection()` helper method finds the connection factory class `javax.sql.DataSource` from the environment, in much the same way that we retrieve configuration parameters. From the connection factory, we retrieve and return a connection.

It's important to understand that this isn't your ordinary, garden-variety database connection. The container will almost certainly have wrapped this connection in an enclosing class that also implements the `Connection` interface. You can use the wrapper just like you would the underlying connection, but when you close the connection, it doesn't really close. It sticks around, ready to complete this transaction or return to the connection pool.

Most programmers learn very quickly that connections to a database are expensive to open and close, and doing so should be avoided where possible. They learn to keep connections around, reusing them in their code. Programming with an application server turns that rule on its head. Opening and closing connections is cheap, because the connections don't really get opened or closed. With an application server, the expensive thing is to keep a connection around – because then it can't be pooled for use by multiple beans. It's possible to tuck a connection away in your bean to reuse in multiple transactions, but in general you shouldn't do this. Acquire a resource, use that resource, and let the resource go. It's worth repeating: acquire a resource, use that resource, and let the resource go:

```
con = getConnection();
PreparedStatement statement = con.prepareStatement(getShipmentSQLString());
statement.setInt(1, selectedSalesDivision);
statement.setInt(2, selectedOrderNumber);
statement.setString(3, carrier);
statement.setInt(4, loading_dock);
statement.setDate(5, new java.sql.Date((new Date()).getTime()));
statement.setString(6, manufactureCellID);
statement.executeUpdate();
statement.close();
con.close();
```

I closed the connection, but it didn't really close. The wrapper class intercepted this. I said close, but the application server heard re-use.

Finally, here are a couple of exception classes that we need:

```
package factory.manufacture;

public class NoSelectionException extends Exception {

  public NoSelectionException() {}
}
```

```
package factory.manufacture;
```

```
public class BadStatusException extends Exception {
  private String status;

  public BadStatusException(String status) {
    this.status = status;
  }

  public String getStatus() {
    return status;
  }
}
```

At this point, you cannot deploy and run the sample application. You need to proceed to the next chapter, where we will add the entity beans.

Summary

This chapter discussed session beans in depth. Here is a review of some of the main points:

- ❑ Session beans represent a process, task, or workflow

- ❑ There are two types of session beans: stateful and stateless

- ❑ Stateful session beans may ease application development at the cost of scalability

- ❑ Stateless session beans can provide services to clients or to other beans

- ❑ The client view of server functionality should be through a session bean façade

- ❑ Environment entries and external resources can be declared in the deployment descriptor and accessed through the JNDI namespace

In the next chapter, we'll look at entity beans more closely. First, we'll show why session beans can't perform the same function in your application as entity beans. Then we'll consider some of the advantages of using entity beans, especially with regard to performance. Next, we'll look at two variations of entity beans: those with container-managed persistence and those with bean-managed persistence. We'll look at the advantages and disadvantages of each, while developing two versions of a single bean (much as we did in this chapter.) We'll also look at the lifecycle and container callbacks of an entity bean, along with some entity-specific things like primary keys, finder methods, and caching. Finally, we'll complete and run our sample application.

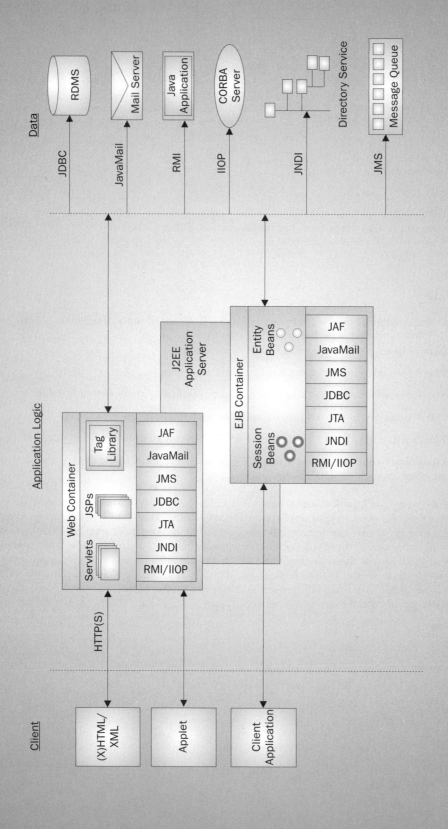

20

Entity Beans and Persistence

Entity Enterprise JavaBeans represent the entity objects in your analysis model. They can correspond to real-world concepts, such as customers or products, or they can correspond to abstractions, such as manufacturing processes, company policies, or customer purchases.

This notion of **representation** is important to understand. After all, a session bean can access any data that an entity bean can. But although a session bean can access data, it can't provide an object-oriented *representation* of that data. How does an entity bean differ? Why can't you have a 'customer' session bean or a 'product' session bean, like you can with entity beans?

The basic explanation is simple, even if the details are complicated. The state that entity beans represent is **shared, transactional** state. In contrast, if a session bean has state, it must be **private** and **conversational**. So the fundamental problem in representing an object with a session bean is in how that state is made available to clients of that bean. An entity bean is (logically, anyway) a single point of access for that data: any client that accesses the data will go through that entity bean. A session bean, on the other hand, is only accessible to a single client. If there are multiple clients, there will be multiple session beans.

In this chapter we will:

- ❑ Compare and contrast using an entity bean compared to session beans
- ❑ Compare and contrast entity beans whose persistence mechanism is container managed and those whose persistence mechanism is managed by the bean developer
- ❑ How to develop entity beans (both container- and bean-managed persistent versions)
- ❑ Complete our manufacturing application from the last chapter

Why Not Use Session Beans?

To understand the difference between entity beans and session beans, let's consider how we might try to make session beans play the same role that entity beans do in representing an object such as a customer. We'll try to build an entity bean out of session bean parts, and then consider the limitations of what we have done.

Using a Stateful Session bean

First, let's try to use a stateful session bean. For a customer, we could write a bean class that looked something like this:

```
public class Customer implements SessionBean {
  public int customerID;
  public String customerName;
  public String customerAddr;
  public String city;
  public String state;
  public String postalCode;

  public void ejbCreate(String customerID) {
    this.customerID = customerID;
  }

  public void setCustomerName(String customerName) {
    this.customerName = customerName;
  }

  public String getCustomerName() {
    return customerName;
  }

  // ... Similar methods ...

  public void saveStateToDatabase() {

    // ... SQL code ...
  }

  public void loadStateFromDatabase() {

    // ... SQL code ...
  }

  // ... Lifecycle methods ...

}
```

This session bean's state is the customer data for a particular customer: name, address, and so on. The state is loaded from the database by one method (`loadStateFromDatabase()`), and saved to the database by another (`saveStateToDatabase()`). This bean is intended to provide an object-oriented representation of a particular customer; data is accessed as properties of the Customer object.

When do our methods to load and save the state to the database get called? You might be envisioning client code cluttered with calls to these methods, sitting around the business logic like a pair of bookends. This would be a disadvantage of session beans compared to entity beans, which have special callbacks that help the container manage their state automatically.

However, a session bean can duplicate these special container-managed-state callbacks by implementing the `javax.ejb.SessionSynchronization` interface. This provides stateful session beans with optional callbacks that the container will use to notify the bean of when a transaction begins and when that transaction is about to end. Transaction boundaries are excellent points at which to synchronize object state with the database.

> *A transaction is a set of operations that must be processed as a single unit. To be considered transactional, the set of operations comprising this single unit of work must exhibit certain well-defined characteristics, often referred to by their mnemonic acronym A.C.I.D, which stands for **atomic**, **consistent**, **isolated**, and **durable**. For more information about transactions and their use in Enterprise JavaBeans technology, please see Chapter 21.*

When the bean is notified that the transaction has begun, it can call a `loadStateFromDatabase()` method or the equivalent. When the container notifies the bean that the transaction is about to end successfully, the session bean can save its data to the database at that time, by calling `saveStateToDatabase()` or the equivalent. Here is the code we would need to add to the customer session bean to get it to synchronize on transaction boundaries:

```
public class Customer implements SessionBean, SessionSynchronization {

    // ...

    public void afterBegin() {
        loadStateFromDatabase();
    }

    public void afterCompletion(boolean commit) {

        /*
         * This could be used to restore the state
         * to what it was before the transaction began,
         * if commit were to be false (indicating a
         * rollback)
         */

        // Empty
    }

    public void beforeCompletion() {

        /*
         * this method will only be called
         * if the transaction has not been rolled back
         */
        ;
        saveStateToDatabase();
    }
}
```

It seems at first glance that we now have a perfectly adequate representation of a customer entity, using only a stateful session bean. However, remember that this session bean represents the state of the customer for a *single* client only. To understand the limitation of using private, conversational state to represent shared data, consider the case where we have two session beans within one transaction that need to access customer data.

Imagine that we're processing an order. As part of this order, we need to change the customer's ship-to address, and also change the customer's available credit. These activities are performed by the 'manage preferences' and 'manage accounts' stateless session beans, respectively. As part of their work, both of those session beans need to alter data managed by the Customer object. Each will create a stateful session bean to represent the customer, using the `create()` method to associate the customer ID with the bean. Each will then invoke the appropriate business method on their respective session bean. Let's say those methods are `setCustomerPreferences(CustomerPreferencesView preferences)` and `setAvailableCredit(double availableCredit)`.

As the business methods are invoked, each Customer bean (the one in 'manage preferences' and the one in 'manage accounts') is enlisted into the transaction. When this happens, `afterBegin()` is called on each bean, and the state data is loaded. Notice that we have two copies of the same state data. Each copy is accessible only by its client.

Now we face our first dilemma. The 'manage preferences' and 'manage accounts' session beans provide a service, but they do not maintain state associated with a particular client, transaction, or method. This would include any reference to the customer beans that they are using. What, then, do we do with the Customer beans? Remember, they have state and are consuming server resources.

We have two choices, one of them illegal and one of them bad:

- ❑ We could try to remove the bean. But this is illegal; a stateful session bean can't be removed while it is in the middle of a transaction. (Even if it could be removed, we'd have to call the `saveStateToDatabase()` method manually, because the bean wouldn't be around at the end of the transaction for it to be called automatically. But don't even think about calling `remove()` on the bean – it just won't work. It's illegal under the specification.)

- ❑ Alternatively, we could let the beans time-out automatically and be removed by the application server. But this is messy, and can lead to performance problems. The EJB container will be managing our state, and references to the EJBs, even though they will never be accessed again.

Contrast this to the case of entity beans. They are shared objects, and the instantiation and destruction of the EJBs is managed directly by the container. In the example we are considering, the 'manage preferences' and 'manage accounts' session beans can use their entity bean references and forget about them. As the entity beans don't belong to any one client, the client isn't responsible for removing them from the container. Remember that the lifecycle methods for the creation and removal of session beans **refer to the EJB in the container**, but the lifecycle methods for creation and removal of entity beans **refer to the underlying storage mechanism**, such as a database.

This dilemma isn't the only one that we face in using this stateful session bean to represent a Customer object. We saw in the example above that there may be multiple copies of the same data, because a session bean represents private, conversational data, and not shared, transactional data. When there are multiple copies, those copies can become unsynchronized. In one or both of the copies, the data can be **stale**.

In our example, there are two copies of the customer stateful session bean participating in the transaction. One is owned by the 'manage preferences' bean, and has a new ship-to address; and one is owned by the 'manage accounts' bean, and has a new available-credit value. When the transaction is about to commit, the container will call `beforeCompletion()` sequentially on the two customer beans (in an undefined order). The first bean will update the information in the database when its `beforeCompletion()` method is called. When the second bean's `beforeCompletion()` method is called, it will write over the information in the database put there by the first bean. The data in the database will be left in an *inconsistent* state.

Contrast this to the case of entity beans. As they are shared objects, the changes from one client in a transaction (e.g. the 'manage preferences' bean) will be reflected in an access by a different client (e.g. the 'manage accounts' bean). As far as the clients are concerned, there is only one bean, which they both are accessing. The bean's data, because it is shared data, will be kept in a consistent state. (One way to think of this is that the entity bean is a proxy for the database data.)

Using a Stateless Session Bean

So we can't use state in a stateful session bean as a mechanism to represent an entity object. Let's consider how we might try to represent an entity object using a stateless session bean. There are two consequences to our lack of state:

- ❏ The stateless session bean being referenced by the client cannot be associated with an identity (i.e. with a primary key of a database row), because it could not remember that identity from method call-to-method call. (This is the same as the reason why a stateless session bean will never have a `create()` method with parameters.) So we'll have to pass the identity in to each method call.

- ❏ The stateless session bean cannot cache any information associated with the entity. So any information needed to process a business method must be read during that method, and any updates to information must be immediately written to the data store. This means that every method that accesses state is going to have some data-reading code at the start, and every method that modifies state is going to have some data-writing code at its close.

Our sample Customer bean might look like this:

```
public class Customer implements SessionBean {

  public void setCustomerName(String customerID, String customerName) {
    Connection con = null;
    try {
      con = getConnection();
      PreparedStatement statement =
        con.prepareStatement("UPDATE Customer SET Name=? WHERE id=?");
      statement.setString(1, customerName);
      statement.setString(2, customerID);
      int updated = statement.executeUpdate();
      if (updated != 1) {
        throw new EJBException("Customer not found.");
      }
    } catch (SQLException sqle) {
      throw new EJBException(sqle);
```

```
      }
    finally {
      try {
        if (con != null) {
          con.close();
        }
      } catch (Exception e) {}
    }
  }

  public String getCustomerName(String customerID) {
    Connection con = null;
    try {
      con = getConnection();
      PreparedStatement statement =
        con.prepareStatement("SELECT Name FROM Customer WHERE id=?");
      statement.setString(1, customerID);
      ResultSet resultSet = statement.executeQuery();
      if (!resultSet.next()) {
        throw new EJBException("Customer not found.");
      }
      return resultSet.getString(1);
    } catch (SQLException sqle) {
      throw new EJBException(sqle);
    }
    finally {
      try {
        if (con != null) {
          con.close();
        }
      } catch (Exception e) {}
    }
  }

  // ...

}
```

This code suffers from none of the fatal flaws that were present in the stateful version of our customer session bean. First, the client need not worry about the removal of the session bean. Since each operation on a stateless session bean is atomic (i.e. changes in state will not be visible on subsequent calls), calling remove() on one during a transaction is not an error. Even if you don't call remove() at all, there probably will not be any negative consequences, because there are no server resources associated with this session bean's identity.

Second, there are no private caches of state that can become unsynchronized and inconsistent. All the state is kept in the database (or other data store), and any database that you use for enterprise data will be multi-user and transactional. This means that the database will manage concurrent accesses and ensure that your data remains consistent.

That doesn't mean that this approach renders entity beans obsolete. The first thing to notice about this code is that it will be somewhat painful to write, unless some kind of tool is used to generate data access classes. Embedding SQL directly in your Java is a tedious and error-prone task. The second thing to notice is that the customer stateless session bean is not providing an object-oriented view of your data. Instead, it is providing a function library of the sort that is popular with C programming. There is nothing wrong with this approach from a code-correctness standpoint. But the task we set ourselves was to provide an object-oriented representation of a customer: functionality *plus* data. The stateless session 'customer' bean has only functionality; it does not have data, nor does it have identity.

As I mentioned in Chapter 19 on session beans, implementing your business model without entity beans is a valid choice. However, you will have to limit yourself to the 'function library' approach of direct-database access, rather than the more object-oriented approach allowed by entity beans.

Benefits of Entity Beans

Entity beans provide benefits beyond simply allowing you to represent shared, transactional state in your object model. In keeping with the general philosophy of Enterprise JavaBeans technology, the EJB container will provide the EJB developer with a number of system-level persistence services in order to free them to concentrate on business logic programming. Four major ones are:

❏ **Container callbacks to manage caching within a transaction**
These callbacks play the same role as our homemade afterBegin(), loadStateFromDatabase(), beforeCompletion(), and saveStateToDatabase() methods did when we tried to construct an entity bean from a stateful session bean.

❏ **Support for concurrent access**
The container has several strategies that it can employ to accomplish this. One is simply to defer concurrency control to the database, like we did with the customer stateless session bean in the above code. Another strategy, appropriate in certain circumstances, is to synchronize access to a single entity bean with a particular identity. EJB containers can also use a combination of these methods.

❏ **Maintaining a cache between transactions**
Depending on the application and the database access patterns, this can significantly improve performance.

❏ **Providing all the persistence management code**
Every EJB 1.1-compliant container will take care of saving your entity beans for you, if you choose, and this can be a tremendous productivity booster. Many developers would tell you that this is the main advantage of entity beans, if not Enterprise JavaBeans technology in general. Not only can container-managed persistence free the developer from writing data access code (usually SQL), but it can also provide optimizations such as carefully tuned updates of only the relevant data.

Container- vs. Bean-Managed Persistence

The EJB container can manage the process of saving and restoring the state of your entity beans; this is known as **container-managed persistence**, or **CMP**. Alternatively, bean developers can take control of the bean's persistence themselves; this is known as **bean-managed persistence**, or **BMP**.

One of the most important implementation decisions in any project that uses Enterprise JavaBeans technology is which form of persistence management the entity beans will use. There is no question that persistence is one of those system-level services that are not the appropriate domain of business logic programmers. The most common manifestation of persistence code is SQL. Writing SQL code that moves the state of a Java object back-and-forth from a database is a tedious, time-consuming, error-prone process, especially if the data model exhibits any complexity. The Enterprise JavaBeans framework was written largely to move these system-level issues to the EJB container. For many projects, it will make sense to take advantage of the ability of the container to manage your bean's persistence, as this leaves the task of synchronization to the container.

However, bean-managed persistence is an important choice in some circumstances. The basic problem is that, although every EJB-1.1 compliant container must provide support for container-managed persistence, the specification does not indicate *how* this support must be provided. In fact, a container need not necessarily provide any CMP support for mapping your entity bean's state to columns in a database. It could use Java serialization to write the whole bean to one column and still be compliant. This would rarely be adequate for a project, and might necessitate the use of bean-managed persistence if your EJB container used serialization.

On the other hand, this extreme case doesn't exist in real life. Every single application server with EJB support of which I am aware, including the open-source ones, has some support for mapping your objects to the fields in a relational database.

The trick is determining whether your EJB container has the level of support for container-managed persistence that you require. If it does, take advantage of this support to free your business logic programmers from writing persistence logic. The boost in productivity is potentially very large, and depending on the EJB container, the boost in application performance may be large, too.

> *The situation with containers that implement the EJB 2.0 specification is likely to be much better. Component developers can depend on the EJB 2.0 container to manage mappings between multiple tables and entity relationships. It is even possible that the portion of the container responsible for performing these mappings (the persistence manager) will be portable across EJB 2.0 containers.*

If your target data store is an ERP system or some other existing application, you will probably need to use bean-managed persistence. Rather than writing SQL code you will probably be using vendor-specific protocols, which would not be supported by a generic EJB container. If your target data store is a relational database, and your EJB container does not have adequate CMP support for your project, you have four choices:

❑   **Find another EJB container**
This is not possible for everyone – perhaps you are writing components for resale, and don't want to limit your market, or perhaps you are an application developer constrained by the choice someone else made. However, there are capable application servers with sophisticated object/relational mapping capabilities on the market. Due to the tremendous productivity advantages of using container-managed persistence, the capabilities of the application server in this regard should be considered when making a technology decision. As more EJB containers implement the EJB 2.0 specification, this will become less of an issue.

❑   **Use a third-party object/relational mapping tool**
You can use a third-party object/relational mapping tool either with entity beans and bean-managed persistence, or using session beans exclusively. This is a good choice, although it has two major disadvantages: cost (many of these object/relational mapping tools are expensive,

although there is at least one major open-source project to develop such a tool), and secondly you have tied your application to a proprietary third-party framework.

Some EJB containers are able to integrate third-party object/relational mapping tools so that their functionality is accessible by beans using container-managed persistence. This makes entity beans easier to develop, keeps the developer from being tied to the product, and allows the third-party tool to take advantage of some additional optimizations.

❑ **Change your design**
You can change your design to reflect the limitations of your chosen tool, and use container-managed persistence. (Depending on what those limitations are, and what your needs are, this may not be possible.) For instance, your EJB container may not have support for mapping dependent objects into their own tables with a foreign-key relationship to the main table. If your container had better support for modeling relationships between entity beans, you could promote those dependent objects into first class entity beans to preserve a normalized database design. There are two disadvantages to this approach: performance (as in the dependent-object example, your new design may result in a heavier-weight object model implementation), and your altered design may be more difficult to implement, maintain, and understand.

❑ **Write your own data-access code**
It is a large commitment to decide to have your developers take responsibility for writing the persistence code that your application requires. If you do decide to do this, you should encapsulate the persistence code in data-access helper components of your entity beans. If you find that a significant portion of your development efforts are being spent on writing SQL statements inside of callback methods in entity beans, stop and reconsider. The expectation of the EJB specification writers was that most EJBs that used bean-managed persistence would be created using a tool. Section 9.1.3.2 of the EJB specification states:

"We expect that most enterprise beans will be created by application development tools which will encapsulate data access in components. These data access components will probably not be the same for all tools. This EJB specification does not define the architecture for data access objects or strategies."

As the capabilities of EJB containers continue to improve in the face of the fierce competition that has developed between implementers of this API, and given the changes to the persistence model in the EJB 2.0 specification (see Chapter 23 for details), sophisticated object/relational mapping capabilities are bound to become ubiquitous – the application server vendors will add these capabilities to their products, and because interfaces will develop to allow third party object/relational tools to be integrated with EJB containers. One of the open-source application servers, jBoss, has the capability today to 'plug in' any third party's object relational mapping tool after a certain amount of glue code has been written. As time goes on, it will make no more sense for business logic programmers to be writing object/relational mapping code than it would for them to be writing relational databases. That day has not quite arrived, but a careful evaluation of the requirements of the application and the capabilities of the tools is necessary before making a decision to write entity beans that manage their own persistence. (Chapter 22 considers some of the criteria you should consider in selecting an application server.)

The SportBean Laboratory

The responsibility for implementing an entity bean's persistence services lies with:

❑ The developer for a bean with bean-managed persistence

❑ The EJB container for a bean with container-managed persistence

As we discuss the different aspects of an entity bean, we'll be building two different versions of a single entity bean that represents a sport team: one using bean-managed persistence, and one using container-managed persistence. You'll be able to compare the steps necessary to implement the two types of beans, to see the advantages, disadvantages, and differences of each.

There will be significant differences between the implementations of a CMP entity bean and a BMP entity bean, because of the differing responsibilities. Most of those differences will be in the container's persistence callbacks, the factory methods, and the primary key class, which we are going to examine as we code the two versions of these beans.

Our sample sports team bean is quite simple. A sports team is identified by a sport (e.g. football or basketball) and a nickname (such as Packers or Knicks). In addition, it has an owner name and a single 'franchise player' who is the best player on that team. For our purposes, the business logic isn't relevant here; I've included some setter and getter methods for our testing. Business methods can be coded the same, regardless of the type of persistence.

> *I developed these examples on the Orion Application server, available free for development from*
> *www.orionserver.com. After we complete the components, I'll give some hints about deploying the*
> *sample on this server.*

Primary Keys

Every entity bean has a **primary key** that represents a unique identity. This primary key must be represented by a primary key class that the bean developer defines or specifies. In other words, this class contains the information necessary to find that entity in the persistent store. It is used internally by the EJB container, and also by the client to find a particular instance of the entity. This class must follow certain rules.

For bean-managed persistence, the rules are exceedingly simple. The format of the class is pretty much left up to the bean developer, since the bean developer and not the EJB container is the one who is going to be using it:

❑ The primary key can be any legal value type in RMI/IIOP (which implies that it must be serializable)

❑ It must also provide suitable implementations of the hashCode() and equals() methods

❑ It must have a unique value within the set of all beans of a particular type

Those are the only formal rules. Obviously in practice, the primary key class will have state fields that correspond to the values of the entity bean's primary key. For instance, a Customer entity bean may have a primary key that has a customerID field of type int. Alternatively, the Customer entity in this example may use the type java.lang.Integer, which meets all the requirements.

There are a few extra rules for a bean with container-managed persistence. The basic problem is that the container is responsible for managing the entity's creation, finding, loading, saving, and deletion. To do all these things, the container needs to be able to create a primary key, so the key class must have a no-arguments public constructor.

The container also needs to be able to map the bean's state to the state of the primary key class, and vice versa. So there are a few rules that are designed to make this possible. The specification provides two different methods for providing key classes for beans using CMP. One is a general case, good for primary keys with any number of fields; the other is a special case, for convenience in dealing with a primary key with one field.

The general case accomplishes the mapping using a naming convention: the public fields in the primary key class correspond to the equivalent public fields in the bean class. For example, we will define a primary key class named `SportTeamPK` for our `SportTeam` entity bean that has two fields that form its primary key: `sport` and `nickName`. `SportTeamPK` would need corresponding fields of the same type and name. The class will look like this (change the package name, depending on whether you are typing in the CMP or BMP version:

```java
package sportBean.cmp;

import java.io.Serializable;

public class SportTeamPK implements Serializable {
  public String sport;
  public String nickName;

  public SportTeamPK() {}

  public SportTeamPK(String sport, String nickName) {
    this.sport = sport;
    this.nickName = nickName;
  }

  public String getSport() {
    return sport;
  }

  public String getNickName() {
    return nickName;
  }

  public int hashCode() {
    // Assumes key cannot be null
    return (sport + nickName).hashCode();
  }

  public boolean equals(Object other) {
    if ((other == null) || !(other instanceof SportTeamPK))
      return false;

    SportTeamPK otherPK = (SportTeamPK) other;

    return sport.equals( otherPK.sport) &&
      nickName.equals(otherPK.nickName);
  }
}
```

This same class can be used for the BMP and CMP versions of our sports team bean, though we could have more flexibility in the BMP version, if we wanted to use it. For instance, we could name the fields differently, or make them private and provide accessor methods. In this case, we'll use the same class to keep things simple.

The special case accomplishes the mapping by indicating the relevant entity bean field in the deployment descriptor, and is provided for convenience in using types such as `Long`, `Integer`, and `String` as the primary key, where a mapping based on a naming convention is clearly not possible. For instance, a sports team bean that had a single string key such as "Football Cardinals" or "Baseball Cardinals" could take advantage of this special case and not define a separate primary key class.

The fully qualified class of the primary key is always specified in the deployment descriptor for entity beans with bean-managed persistence. It is almost always specified for beans with container-managed persistence as well, except for a special case where the type isn't known until deployment. Here are some possible examples. The first example is for both versions (BMP and CMP) of our sports team bean:

```
<prim-key-class>com.somecompany.sportstrack.SportTeamPK</prim-key-class>
```

The second case would be used if the identifying key for the sports team bean had only a single field as the key:

```
<prim-key-class>java.lang.String</prim-key-class>
```

In the case of an entity bean with container-managed persistence that uses a simple type as its primary key, the bean developer specifies in the deployment descriptor the container-managed field of the entity bean that contains the primary key. The field's type must be the same as the primary key type. Here are some possible examples:

```
<primkey-field>sportsTeamID<primkey-field>
```

or:

```
<primkey-field>socialSecurity<primkey-field>
```

The EJB developer may wish to use a synthetic key, such as an auto-incrementing key, as the primary key of their entity bean. There are two possible strategies. The first is to generate the key using a session bean. This session bean might retrieve a block of keys from the database, and distribute keys sequentially from this block to requesting entity beans. The second strategy is to depend on the database to automatically create the synthetic keys when the entity bean's state is inserted. If the entity bean uses container-managed persistence, the EJB container's object/relational mapping tools must support this functionality for the target database.

The C.R.U.D. Callbacks

C.R.U.D. is an acronym that defines the four types of activities comprising persistence:

- ❏ Create
- ❏ Read
- ❏ Update
- ❏ Delete

There is one callback type defined for each of these activities in entity beans: the `ejbCreate()` and `ejbPostCreate()` methods; `ejbLoad()`; `ejbStore()`; and `ejbRemove()`, respectively. The signatures of these callback methods are the same whether container-managed or bean-managed persistence is used. However, the code that the bean programmer writes will be very different based on the type of persistence.

Create

When a client calls `create()` for an entity bean, state data is inserted into the corresponding data store (such as a relational database). This is transactional data that is accessible from multiple clients. In contrast, when a client calls `create()` for a stateful session bean, the EJB container creates a private, non-transactional store of data in the application server's temporary storage. This difference is important to understand.

> When you call **create()** on a session bean's home interface, you are creating an instance of that session bean, whereas when you call **create()** on an entity bean's home interface, you are actually inserting a record in the database.

There can be multiple forms of the `create()` method defined in the bean's home interface, and these `create()` methods may take different parameters, which correspond to the bean's state at the time of creation. The parameters must have enough information to at least initialize the primary key of the entity. All the `create()` methods must return the bean's remote interface, so that when the client programmer calls `create()` on the home interface, they will have a reference to that bean on which business methods may be called.

All the `create()` methods must throw `java.rmi.RemoteException`, because they can be remote methods. They must also throw `javax.ejb.CreateException`, which is used to indicate an application-level problem during the attempt at creation. (They may also throw user-defined exceptions.) An example of an application-level problem would be illegal parameters passed to `create()`.

The `create()` methods for our sports team EJB (note that these are the same for the BMP version and the CMP version; just change the package name) are:

```
package sportBean.cmp;

import javax.ejb.*;
import java.rmi.RemoteException;
import java.util.Collection;

public interface SportTeamHome extends EJBHome {

  SportTeam create(String sport, String nickName)
                throws RemoteException, CreateException;

  SportTeam create(String sport, String nickName, String ownerName,
              String franchisePlayer) throws RemoteException,
              CreateException;
```

Each one of these forms of the create() method that the bean programmer has defined in the bean's home interface must have two matching methods in the bean's implementation class. So in our case, there will be four creation-related methods in our implementation class.

The two methods for each create() in the home interface must be named ejbCreate() and ejbPostCreate(), and must have the same parameters in the same order as the create() method. The methods must be declared public, and must not be final or static. The return type of ejbCreate() is the primary key class of the entity bean, and the return type of ejbPostCreate() is void. (We will finish the definition of this interface when we add the finder methods, below.)

One point of confusion for many programmers is why an ejbCreate() and an ejbPostCreate() are both necessary. As a general rule, the bean programmer – for either bean-managed persistence or container-managed persistence – will do all their work in ejbCreate(), leaving ejbPostCreate() empty. The fundamental reason that the ejbPostCreate method exists is because the programmer is never allowed to pass "this" as a parameter to a remote method; they must always use the remote interface instead. However, the remote interface for the bean is not available until ejbCreate() returns. If they need the remote interface *during* the creation of the EJB component, there would be no way to proceed. Rather than leave this hole in the spec, an "after create" method was developed in which the remote interface would be available. This method is ejbPostCreate(). The same situation exists with the primary key in container-managed persistence, because the container creates the key. If the primary key is needed for some reason, that work also needs to be done in ejbPostCreate(). Why would you need to pass the EJB's remote reference or primary key to another EJB during its creation? The only good reason I've seen is to set up relationships, e.g. when you create the employee you want the boss to have a reference.

In a container-managed bean, the parameters that are passed in by the client will be used to initialize the entity bean's state. Although the return type of the ejbCreate() method is the same as the primary key, the bean developer should just return null. The container will ignore the returned value, regardless. In a bean-managed bean, the bean must insert its state into the underlying data store – for a relational database, this means that the developer will write an INSERT statement in SQL. The bean developer should use the data to initialize the state variables of the bean, except in the very unusual case that the BMP entity bean is storing its state directly in the database without using any instance variable intermediaries. (This would be like our stateless session bean implementation of customer, only with implicit identity.) Finally, the bean developer should construct an instance of its primary key and return it.

Here is the CMP version of our sports team entity bean's creation callbacks (we'll be adding to this class as we discuss various callbacks):

```java
package sportBean.cmp;

import javax.ejb.*;
import javax.naming.*;
import java.rmi.RemoteException;
import java.sql.Connection;
import java.sql.SQLException;
import java.sql.PreparedStatement;
import java.sql.ResultSet;
import javax.sql.DataSource;
import java.util.*;

public class SportTeamEJB implements EntityBean {
```

```
      public String sport;
      public String nickName;
      public String ownerName;
      public String franchisePlayer;

      public SportTeamPK ejbCreate(String sport,
                                   String nickName) throws CreateException {
        this.sport = sport;
        this.nickName = nickName;
        ownerName = null;
        franchisePlayer = null;
        return null;
      }

      public void ejbPostCreate(String key, String relatedData) {}

      public SportTeamPK ejbCreate(String sport, String nickName,
                                   String ownerName,
                                   String franchisePlayer)
            throws javax.ejb.CreateException {
        this.sport = sport;
        this.nickName = nickName;
        this.ownerName = ownerName;
        this.franchisePlayer = franchisePlayer;
        return null;
      }

      public void ejbPostCreate(String sport, String nickName,
                                String ownerName, String franchisePlayer) {}
```

Here is the same sports team entity bean with bean-managed persistence. (Again, we'll be adding to this class.) Notice that there are two basic differences:

❑ The ejbCreate() methods have JDBC and SQL code to insert a record into the database

❑ The method returns an instance of a primary key, rather than null

```
package sportBean.bmp;

import javax.ejb.*;
import javax.naming.*;
import java.rmi.RemoteException;
import java.sql.Connection;
import java.sql.SQLException;
import java.sql.PreparedStatement;
import java.sql.ResultSet;
import javax.sql.DataSource;
import java.util.*;

public class SportTeamEJB implements EntityBean
{
  public String sport;
  public String nickName;
```

```java
    public String ownerName;
    public String franchisePlayer;

    EntityContext ctx;

    public SportTeamPK ejbCreate(String sport,
                                 String nickName) throws CreateException {
      this.sport = sport;
      this.nickName = nickName;
      ownerName = null;
      franchisePlayer = null;

      Connection con = null;
      try {
        con = getConnection();
        PreparedStatement statement =
          con.prepareStatement("INSERT INTO SPORTSTEAMS (SPORT, NICKNAME) "
                                + "VALUES (?, ?)");
        statement.setString(1, sport);
        statement.setString(2, nickName);
        if (statement.executeUpdate() != 1) {
          throw new CreateException("Failed to create sports team.");
        }
      } catch (SQLException sqle) {
        throw new EJBException(sqle);
      }
      finally {
        try {
          if (con != null) {
            con.close();
          }
        } catch (SQLException sqle) {}
      }

      return new SportTeamPK(sport, nickName);
    }

  public void ejbPostCreate(String key, String relatedData) {}

    public SportTeamPK ejbCreate(String sport, String nickName,
                                 String ownerName,
                                 String franchisePlayer)
           throws javax.ejb.CreateException {
      this.sport = sport;
      this.nickName = nickName;
      this.ownerName = ownerName;
      this.franchisePlayer = franchisePlayer;

      Connection con = null;
      try {
        con = getConnection();
        PreparedStatement statement =
          con.prepareStatement("INSERT INTO SPORTSTEAMS (SPORT, NICKNAME, "
                                + "OWNERNAME, FRANCHISEPLAYER ) VALUES
                                (?, ?, ?, ?)");
```

```
          statement.setString(1, sport);
          statement.setString(2, nickName);
          statement.setString(3, ownerName);
          statement.setString(4, franchisePlayer);
          if (statement.executeUpdate() != 1) {
            throw new CreateException("Failed to create sports team.");
          }
        } catch (SQLException sqle) {
          throw new EJBException(sqle);
        }
        finally {
          try {
            if (con != null) {
              con.close();
            }
          } catch (SQLException sqle) {}
        }

        return new SportTeamPK(sport, nickName);
      }

      public void ejbPostCreate(String sport, String nickName,
                                String ownerName, String franchisePlayer) {}
```

It is possible and sometimes appropriate to have an entity bean with no create() methods. An entity bean is just an object-oriented view on transactional, shared data. In an environment with non-EJB applications, this data – and therefore, these entity beans – may exist without create() ever being called. If this data should be created *only* by these non-EJB applications, then the entity beans can be written without any create() methods. For instance, our sports team database records might be created exclusively by someone with a Star Office spreadsheet linked to our database, with our EJB application being Used to keep the information about owners and franchise players up-to-date. No create() methods would be required in this case.

Read

The ejbLoad() callback method corresponds roughly to the 'read' functionality of entity beans. A simple way to look at it is that the entity will load the data from the database in correspondence to the container's ejbLoad() call. With container-managed persistence, the EJB container will take care of transferring the entity's state from the database to the entity's instance variables. In this case, the bean programmer will often leave the ejbLoad() method blank, but may choose to do some post-processing of the loaded data. With bean-managed persistence, the bean programmer will write their data-access code (probably JDBC and SQL code) in ejbLoad() to transfer the entity's state to instance variables.

This description is a good way to understand the process, but it is not the whole story. Technically, ejbLoad() doesn't tell the bean that it must actually load data: it just tells the bean that it must *re-synchronize* its state with the underlying data store. This is a subtle but potentially important difference.

> **The bean's persistence implementation may choose to defer loading the state until that state is actually used.**

Let's consider an example. An Order entity bean may have an order number, a customer name, and a list of line items. When `ejbLoad()` is called for an entity bean that represents a particular order, the state of that order – the number, name, and line items – must be synchronized with the database. In this example, the persistence logic may choose to update the name and number immediately from the database. But retrieving the list of related line items is a potentially expensive operation, so a 'dirty' flag is set instead. If the only method that is called on this order bean is `getCustomerName()`, the line items will never need to be loaded. Any method that must access the list, such as `totalLineItems()` for example, will need to check the dirty flag and load the list from the database if it is set.

> *It's possible, even likely, that your container's automatic persistence loads the entire bean when* `ejbLoad()` *is called. (This is known as 'eager loading of state'.) This can affect both your application design and your choice of bean-managed persistence or container-managed persistence. In EJB 2.0's persistence model, it is much easier for the container to provide dynamic loading of state information.*

The role of `ejbLoad()` in container-managed persistence is to process the data after it has been loaded from the database. Often, the data will not need processing at all, and your `ejbLoad()` method will be empty. Sometimes, however, changes will be necessary. A practical example is that you may store your String data in `char` database fields of a certain size, and the database may append blanks to your strings to pad them to the correct length. Although this may be more efficient than using a `varchar` data type, those trailing blanks can be annoying. You could use `ejbLoad()` to trim those trailing blanks. Here is the `ejbLoad()` callback in the CMP version of our sports bean example (add this to the file `SportsTeamEJB.java`):

```java
public void ejbLoad() {
   if (sport != null) {
      sport.trim();
   }
   if (nickName != null) {
      nickName.trim();
   }
   if (ownerName != null) {
      ownerName.trim();
   }
   if (franchisePlayer != null) {
      franchisePlayer.trim();
   }
}
```

The role of `ejbLoad()` in bean-managed persistence is to notify the bean that it must invalidate the current cached state and to prepare for business method invocations. In practical terms, this usually means replacing the state by loading it from the database.

To find the entity bean's data in the database, you will need the primary key. By the time that `ejbLoad()` is called, the primary key has been associated with the entity and is available from its context. This entity context is associated with the bean by a callback method, just like the session context is associated with a session bean. The interface of the `EntityContext` (excluding the methods it inherits from `EJBContext`) is:

```java
public EJBObject getEJBObject() throws IllegalStateException;

public Object getPrimaryKey() throws IllegalStateException;
```

A bean that uses bean-managed persistence would need to use the entity context to retrieve its associated primary key in the implementation of `ejbLoad()`, using the `setEntityContext()` / `unsetEntityContext()` pair of callbacks to save the entity context for use. Add the following methods (to the bean-managed persistence version only) of the sports team entity bean:

```
public void setEntityContext(EntityContext ctx) {
  this.ctx = ctx;
}

public void unsetEntityContext() {
  ctx = null;
}
```

The implementation for these methods may be empty for the container-managed persistence version:

```
public void setEntityContext(EntityContext ctx) {}

public void unsetEntityContext() {}
```

Here is the BMP version of `ejbLoad()` for the sports team bean. Notice how we use the saved `EntityContext` to retrieve the primary key:

```
public void ejbLoad() {
    SportTeamPK primaryKey = (SportTeamPK) ctx.getPrimaryKey();

    Connection con = null;
    try {
      con = getConnection();
      PreparedStatement statement =
        con
          .prepareStatement("SELECT OWNERNAME, FRANCHISEPLAYER "
                          + "FROM SPORTSTEAMS WHERE SPORT = ?
                          AND NICKNAME = ? ");
      statement.setString(1, primaryKey.getSport());
      statement.setString(2, primaryKey.getNickName());

      ResultSet resultSet = statement.executeQuery();
      if (!resultSet.next()) {
        throw new EJBException("Object not found.");
      }
      sport = primaryKey.getSport();
      nickName = primaryKey.getNickName();
      ownerName = resultSet.getString(1);
      franchisePlayer = resultSet.getString(2);
      resultSet.close();
      statement.close();
    } catch (SQLException sqle) {
      throw new EJBException(sqle);
    }
    finally {
      try {
        if (con != null) {
```

```
        con.close();
      }
    } catch (SQLException sqle) {}
  }
}
```

Update

The `ejbStore()` callback method corresponds roughly to the 'update' functionality of entity beans. Of course, the actual modification of the entity bean's cached state will be done through calls to business methods, such as `setShipmentAddress()` or `calculateSalesTax()`. The container will call the `ejbStore()` method to notify the bean that it must synchronize its state with the database. For a bean with container-managed persistence, this method will be called directly before the container writes the altered bean state to the database, and the programmer of a CMP bean may use this opportunity to pre-process the bean's data to ensure that it is in an appropriate state for persistent storage. Typically, however, this method will be left empty. For a bean with bean-managed persistence, the programmer is responsible for providing in this method the logic that will transfer the bean's state to the underlying data store. For a relational database, this will typically mean that the bean programmer will write JDBC code and SQL update statements.

> With `ejbLoad()`, the bean had the option to defer the actual loading of state until it was used. There is no such option with `ejbStore()`. Any modifications to the object's state must be written to the data store immediately. The equivalent optimization is probably something called 'tuned updates'. In other words, only the modified state need be written to the data store; if something hasn't changed, you can leave it alone.

Here is `ejbStore()` for the sports team entity bean with bean-managed persistence. Note that we do not need to retrieve the primary key from the entity context (although we could), because the information is available to us in the instance variables of this class:

```
public void ejbStore() {
  Connection con = null;
  try {
    con = getConnection();
    PreparedStatement statement =
      con.prepareStatement("UPDATE SPORTSTEAMS SET OWNERNAME=?,
                            FRANCHISEPLAYER=? " + "WHERE SPORT = ?
                            AND NICKNAME = ? ");
    statement.setString(1, ownerName);
    statement.setString(2, franchisePlayer);
    statement.setString(3, sport);
    statement.setString(4, nickName);

    if (statement.executeUpdate() != 1) {
      throw new EJBException("Failed to save object state.");
    }
    statement.close();
  } catch (SQLException sqle) {
    throw new EJBException(sqle);
  }
  finally {
    try {
```

```
        if (con != null) {
          con.close();
        }
      } catch (SQLException sqle) {}
    }
  }
```

The equivalent version for the CMP version of the sports team bean is empty:

```
public void ejbStore() {}
```

Delete

When a client calls `remove()` on an entity bean, data is deleted from the corresponding data store. In contrast, when a client calls `remove()` for a stateful session bean, the EJB container discards the session bean instance in the application server's temporary storage. It is important to understand this difference. You should always call `remove()` when you are done using a stateful session bean; otherwise, the EJB container will waste resources managing this instance.

> You should not call **remove()** on an entity bean unless you want to delete that record.
> The EJB container will manage the entity bean's instance in the container.

For an entity bean with container-managed persistence, the `ejbRemove()` method can usually be left empty, and the container will handle the deletion of the instance from the underlying data store. The programmer of an entity bean with container-managed persistence may use this method to implement any actions that must be done (such as updating related data or notifying other systems) before the entity object's representation is removed from the database. Here is the method for our sports team bean with container-managed persistence:

```
public void ejbRemove() {}
```

For an entity bean with bean-managed persistence, the programmer is responsible for providing the logic that will remove the object from the underlying resource. For a relational database, this will typically mean that the bean programmer will write JDBC code and SQL delete statements.

Note that, as with any business method, the data will be loaded by the container (by calling `ejbLoad()`) before `ejbRemove()` is called. This allows the programmer to perform validation of the remove request, and to update related data or systems, without loading the data independently of the EJB container callback.

Here is the version with bean-managed persistence:

```
public void ejbRemove() throws javax.ejb.RemoveException {
  Connection con = null;
  try {
    con = getConnection();
    PreparedStatement statement =
      con.prepareStatement("DELETE FROM SPORTSTEAMS "
```

987

```
                                + "WHERE SPORT = ? AND NICKNAME = ? ");
          statement.setString(1, sport);
          statement.setString(2, nickName);

          if (statement.executeUpdate() != 1) {
            throw new EJBException("Failed to remove object.");

          }
          statement.close();
       } catch (SQLException sqle) {
          throw new EJBException(sqle);
       }
       finally {
         try {
           if (con != null) {
             con.close();
           }
         } catch (SQLException sqle) {}
       }
     }
```

BMP Callbacks vs. CMP Callbacks

The signatures of the create, read, update, and delete callbacks are the same for bean-managed persistence and container-managed persistence. The implementations are very different, however:

❑ For entity beans with bean-managed persistence, these callbacks are responsible for solving the entire problem of synchronizing state with the underlying data store for creates, reads, updates, and deletes

❑ For entity beans with container-managed persistence, these callbacks (with the exception of ejbCreate() methods) are just used for 'fine-tuning' the container's operations

Just to make the difference clear, here is a typical implementation of these callbacks for a container-managed entity bean:

```
public String ejbCreate(String key, String relatedData) {
  this.key = key;
  this.relatedData = relatedData;
}

public void ejbPostCreate(String key, String relatedData) {}

public void ejbLoad() {}

public void ejbRemove() {}

public void ejbStore() {}
```

Notice that there is very little development cost, very little maintenance cost, and very little room for error in the implementation of any of these methods. That is part of what container-managed persistence buys you.

The Deployment Descriptor

The type of persistence – bean managed or container managed – is specified in the XML deployment descriptor for the EJB. The `<persistence-type>` element of the deployment descriptor will be one of the following:

```
<persistence-type>Bean</persistence-type>
```

or:

```
<persistence-type>Container</persistence-type>
```

If the bean's persistence is container-managed, the fields that are persisted must also be specified in the deployment descriptor. Each entry in the deployment descriptor has the name of the field in the class, and may also have a description. Here is an example of two fields from the CMP version of our sports team entity bean (with an optional description thrown in):

```
<cmp-field>
  <field-name>sport</field-name>
  <description>Like basketball or cricket.</description>
</cmp-field>
<cmp-field>
  <field-name>nickName</field-name>
</cmp-field>
```

All the container-managed fields listed in the deployment descriptor must be declared public and must not be transient in the bean class. They must be serializable, primitive types, or references to other EJBs. In a bean with container-managed persistence, all the persistence code must be left to the container.

Here is the complete deployment descriptor for the CMP version of our bean:

```
<?xml version="1.0"?>

<ejb-jar>
 <enterprise-beans>
    <entity>
         <ejb-name>CMPSportsBean</ejb-name>
         <home>sportBean.cmp.SportTeamHome</home>
         <remote>sportBean.cmp.SportTeam</remote>
         <ejb-class>sportBean.cmp.SportTeamEJB</ejb-class>
         <prim-key-class>sportBean.cmp.SportTeamPK</prim-key-class>
         <reentrant>False</reentrant>
         <persistence-type>Container</persistence-type>
         <cmp-field><field-name>sport</field-name></cmp-field>
         <cmp-field><field-name>nickName</field-name></cmp-field>
         <cmp-field><field-name>ownerName</field-name></cmp-field>
         <cmp-field><field-name>franchisePlayer</field-name></cmp-field>
    </entity>
 </enterprise-beans>
```

989

```
<assembly-descriptor>
  <container-transaction>
    <method>
        <ejb-name>CMPSportsBean</ejb-name>
        <method-name>*</method-name>
    </method>
    <trans-attribute>Required</trans-attribute>
  </container-transaction>
</assembly-descriptor>
</ejb-jar>
```

Here is the version of the deployment descriptor for the version with bean-managed persistence. It doesn't have `<cmp-field>` elements, but does declare that we use a resource (the JDBC connection):

```
<?xml version="1.0"?>

<ejb-jar>
 <enterprise-beans>
    <entity>
        <ejb-name>BMPSportsBean</ejb-name>
        <home>sportBean.bmp.SportTeamHome</home>
        <remote>sportBean.bmp.SportTeam</remote>
        <ejb-class>sportBean.bmp.SportTeamEJB</ejb-class>
        <prim-key-class>sportBean.bmp.SportTeamPK</prim-key-class>
        <reentrant>False</reentrant>
        <persistence-type>Bean</persistence-type>
        <resource-ref>
            <res-ref-name>jdbc/sportsJDBC</res-ref-name>
            <res-type>javax.sql.DataSource</res-type>
            <res-auth>Container</res-auth>
        </resource-ref>
    </entity>
 </enterprise-beans>

 <assembly-descriptor>
   <container-transaction>
     <method>
        <ejb-name>BMPSportsBean</ejb-name>
        <method-name>*</method-name>
     </method>
     <trans-attribute>Required</trans-attribute>
   </container-transaction>
 </assembly-descriptor>
</ejb-jar>
```

Caching

A **cache** is a secondary copy of data that is typically made for reasons of performance or convenience. The instance variables in your entity bean that represent the object's persistent state are actually a cache of the data whose permanent storage location is in your database. For instance, in your Customer entity bean you may have three strings for the customer's first name, middle name, and last name. These three variables might be secondary copies of the data from three columns in a relational database table named `customer`: fname, mname, and lname. Here is a simple table to make this example clearer:

Data	Primary Copy	Cached Copy
Customer's first name	Database column `fname`	Entity bean field `fname`
Customer's middle name	Database column `mname`	Entity bean field `mname`
Customer's last name	Database column `lname`	Entity bean field `lname`

The cache consisting of your entity bean instance variables suffers from the same potential problem that any cache does: it may get out of synch with the primary copy of the data. To continue with our simple customer example, the record in the database may have an `lname` of 'Smith' after an update by a customer management system, but the corresponding entity bean field may still have the former name of 'Jones'. With both bean-managed persistence and container-managed persistence, it is the combined responsibility of the EJB container and the underlying data store to manage the synchronization of an entity's cache. The topic of caching is closely related to the C.R.U.D. callbacks and the transfer of an entity object's state to and from the persistent data store. The EJB container will call `ejbLoad()` and `ejbStore()` at the times that it feels is necessary to keep the local cache in synch with the primary copy of the data.

As a bean programmer, you do not need to concern yourself with exactly when the container will call `ejbLoad()` and `ejbStore()`. You must be prepared for either method call to happen at any time between business logic methods, even within a single transaction. (They would not be called in the middle of a business method, though. Remember that all access to an EJB is single-threaded.) Still, it's nice to understand the common strategies that EJB containers will employ in various situations, so you can make informed decisions about application servers, deployment, and so on.

Let's say that a client wants to use a copy of our three-field customer bean. They want to call two methods on the bean: `setFirstName()` and `setMiddleName()`. There are two distinct cases we must consider, depending on whether or not these methods are called in the same transaction:

❑ In the first case, these two methods are called in the same transaction.
Before the first business logic method is called, the container or the bean (depending on CMP vs. BMP) will load the state from the database corresponding with a call to `ejbLoad()`. Now the `setFirstName()` business method is called. At this point, the container has the option of calling `ejbStore()` and `ejbLoad()` again, before calling `setMiddleName()`. It might do this if it were part of an application server cluster, and it could not guarantee that the same entity bean instance would be used for both business methods. However, in the most common case, it will simply go ahead and call the `setMiddleName()` method right away. It can do this because both methods are part of the same transaction, and transactions are designed to ensure that modifications to a data store are isolated from other activities against that data. In other words, `ejbLoad()` and `ejbStore()` will be called for entity objects on transaction boundaries. (Note that this is not mandated by the specification; it is simply a common implementation strategy.)

❑ In the second case, these two methods are called in different transactions.
Again, before the first business logic method is called the container or the bean will load the state from the database corresponding with a call to `ejbLoad()`. Once `setFirstName()` has been called, the transaction completes and `ejbStore()` is called to update the datastore. Now `setMiddleName()` is called. In the general case, the EJB container will simply repeat the process, calling `ejbLoad()` and `ejbStore()` around the invocation of `setMiddleName()`. The cache must be resynchronized with `ejbLoad()` because, in between the two transactions, some other process or application could have modified the data.

991

There are, however, two special cases that may allow the EJB container to avoid calling `ejbLoad()` on the entity instance at the start of transactions subsequent to the first:

❑ The first is that all accesses to the data go through the EJB container and that entity bean. If this were the case, then the container knows that the cache in the entity bean and the data in the persistent data store are in synch. Every change to the data will happen in the cache before it is reflected in the data store, if all accesses are through the bean. However, if any non-EJB technology is used to modify the data (e.g. an ERP system), then this approach cannot be used.

❑ The second case is when the particular application does not absolutely need the freshest data. Obviously this will not apply in the case of a banking system that must keep account information in synch. However, it will be the case for a surprising number of systems – an e-commerce system, perhaps. The cached data could be set to expire after a certain amount of time, and would be refreshed after that period. If the prices for products were changed by some non-EJB demand-management software, this change would not be reflected in the e-commerce application immediately. But after the cached data expired (say in five minutes) it would be. The benefit might be far fewer database accesses, and much better application performance. The consequences – a five minute delay in changed prices – would probably be negligible.

If your application server provides this optimization of data caching between transactions, you would set this with an application server-specific configuration tool. Typically, the optimization is available if you indicate that the EJB container has 'exclusive access to the database', or similar.

Although the EJB container can optimize away calls to `ejbLoad()` at the beginning of a transaction, it can never do this for `ejbStore()` at the completion of the transaction. The Enterprise JavaBeans 1.1 specification absolutely requires that `ejbStore()` be called when a transaction in which the entity bean is participating completes. This is because one of the guarantees that a transactional system makes is that a transaction is *durable*. If the modified data is held in a temporary cache in the entity bean, and the entity bean is subsequently destroyed before it gets the chance to finally write its data to permanent storage, the 'durable' part of the transactional guarantee has been violated. This could happen because a subsequent call to the bean resulted in a non-application exception, or even because the application server crashed.

What about the case where no data has changed? Judging by e-mail to Internet newsgroups that I have seen, novice EJB programmers are sometimes appalled to see all their entity data being re-written to the database after they call an innocuous method like `getName()`. Sometimes, they consider it to be a bug in their application server. In reality, the EJB container is required to call this callback method at the completion of a transaction, as part of its contract with the bean programmer. But that doesn't mean that your unmodified data needs to be written to the database after every use of an entity bean.

A bean that uses bean-managed persistence should implement a strategy to determine whether the data has changed. One possibility is to simply maintain a 'modified' flag, which is checked in the `ejbStore()` method to see if any action needs to be taken. Another possibility is to keep 'before' and 'after' copies of the data, to compare them to build an UPDATE statement that affects only the data that has changed.

A bean that uses container-managed persistence must rely on the container to manage the updates effectively. The strategy that an EJB container would use to accomplish this is specific to that container. If your application server writes the entire state of your bean to the database after every use, regardless of whether the data has been modified, there is a simple step you can take to correct the problem. Get a different application server.

Finder Methods

Entity beans represent shared data. If this data is shared, there must be some mechanism for clients to get access to a particular entity bean. Notice that this problem doesn't come up for session beans; the client gets access to the bean when it creates it, and no one else ever uses it. But the entity bean may be created by one client and used by any number of completely different clients. Each of these clients must be able to find the bean for which they are looking.

As a solution for this problem, the Enterprise JavaBeans specification defines a mechanism called **finder methods**. One or more of these 'finder' methods are declared in the entity bean's home interface, one for each way to find that entity object or a collection of that type of entity object. These finder methods follow a certain naming convention: they all start with the prefix **find**. Some examples are findOpenAccounts(), findOrdersByDate(), or findManagerForEmployee(). They can take any parameters that are necessary to specify the details of the search, as long as those parameters follow the normal rules for RMI/IIOP (the main rule, as mentioned before, is that they need to implement java.io.Serializable, be a primitive type, or be a remote interface).

Finder methods that will have at most one result will have a return type of the remote interface for that entity bean. For instance, the findManagerForEmployee() method defined on a com.somecompany.personnel.ManagerHome class might have a return type of com.somecompany.personnel.Manager (and, of course, a parameter of type Employee). (The findByPrimaryKey() method in any entity bean is an example of this type of finder.) Finder methods that can have zero or more results will have a return type of either java.util.Enumeration or java.util.Collection. (The findByOwnerName() method is an example from the SportTeamHome interface.) If compatibility with 1.1 JDKs is required, Enumeration must be chosen. Otherwise, it is probably better to return a Collection, which provides a more flexible interface to the results.

In addition to the java.rmi.RemoteException thrown by all remote methods, every finder method must also declare that it throws the javax.ejb.FinderException. If a finder of the type that has at most one result does not find any matching entity, the method will throw a subclass of the FinderException class: an instance of the javax.ejb.ObjectNotFoundException. If a finder of the type that has zero or more results does not find any matching entities, the method will simply return an empty collection or an enumeration with zero elements.

Every entity bean must declare a certain 'well known' finder named findByPrimaryKey(), that takes a single parameter of the same type as the entity's primary key class. This finder will either return the instance of the entity bean with that primary key, or will throw an ObjectNotFoundException. Additional finders beyond findByPrimaryKey() are optional. Some entities will have no other finders; others may have several.

The implementation of the 'finding' logic will be provided by the EJB container for beans with container-managed persistence, and the bean developer need not write supporting Java code of any sort. However, there is obviously not enough information in the finder method's signature for the container to figure out the finder's intent and implement the logic. How would a container know how to implement findMostAppropriateWarehouse(Product product, Date dateNeeded)? When the EJB is actually deployed, additional information needs to be specified in what is currently an application-server-specific format, about how the finder method should behave.

For entity beans with bean-managed persistence, the EJB developer must provide a Java implementation of each finder's logic in the bean's implementation class. This method will have identical parameters, and will have a matching name of the following convention: if the finder method is findXXX(), the implementation of that finder method will be named ejbFindXXX(). The return type for a finder method that has at most one result will be an instance of the primary key class for that entity, and the return type for a finder method implementation that has zero or more results will be either a concrete implementation of Collection, or an Enumeration, depending on the return type of the corresponding finder method in the home interface. The items contained in the collection or returned by the enumeration will be instances of the primary key classes for the corresponding entities. Notice that the implementation of findByPrimaryKey() will take a primary key as a parameter, check to make sure the database record actually exists, and return that same primary key as the result if it does. Although the EJB container already has the primary key for this particular finder method, the EJB developer is asked to return it anyway so that its use is consistent with other finders that return zero or one results.

You do not have any meaningful access to the state-related instance variables in the implementation of a finder method, nor any other identity-specific information. An entity bean that is used for a finder method will not be associated with a particular instance of state in the database. This is different from most other entity bean methods, such as the lifecycle methods and the business-logic methods. The finder method must stand alone in the entity bean implementation class. Although it must not be declared as static, you can think of it as having the same role as a static factory method might in a non-EJB Java class.

Continuing with our sports team example, here is an example of a findByPrimaryKey() implementation for the version with bean-managed persistence (remember that there is no equivalent for the version with container-managed persistence; add these methods to the BMP version of SportTeamEJB.java):

```java
public SportTeamPK ejbFindByPrimaryKey(SportTeamPK primaryKey)
        throws FinderException {
  Connection con = null;
  try {
    con = getConnection();
    PreparedStatement statement =
      con.prepareStatement("SELECT SPORT "    // Doesn't matter
                           + "FROM SPORTSTEAMS WHERE SPORT = ?
                           AND NICKNAME = ? ");
    statement.setString(1, primaryKey.getSport());
    statement.setString(2, primaryKey.getNickName());

    ResultSet resultSet = statement.executeQuery();
    if (!resultSet.next()) {
      throw new ObjectNotFoundException();
    }
    resultSet.close();
    statement.close();
    return primaryKey;
  } catch (SQLException sqle) {
    throw new EJBException(sqle);
  }
  finally {
    try {
      if (con != null) {
        con.close();
      }
    } catch (SQLException sqle) {}
  }
}
```

Here is an example of a finder implementation that has zero or more results and returns a collection:

```
public Collection ejbFindByOwnerName(String ownerName)
        throws FinderException {
  Connection con = null;
  try {
    con = getConnection();
    PreparedStatement statement =
      con.prepareStatement("SELECT SPORT, NICKNAME " // Primary key info
                            + "FROM SPORTSTEAMS WHERE OWNERNAME = ? ");
    statement.setString(1, ownerName);
    ResultSet resultSet = statement.executeQuery();

    LinkedList queryMatches = new LinkedList();
    while (resultSet.next()) {
      SportTeamPK pk = new SportTeamPK(resultSet.getString(1),
                                       resultSet.getString(2));
      queryMatches.add(pk);
    }

    resultSet.close();
    statement.close();
    return queryMatches;
  } catch (SQLException sqle) {
    throw new EJBException(sqle);
  }
  finally {
    try {
      if (con != null) {
        con.close();
      }
    } catch (SQLException sqle) {}
  }
}
```

For both the CMP version and the BMP version of our sports team bean, you should complete the home interface as follows:

```
SportTeam findByPrimaryKey(SportTeamPK sportTeam)
        throws RemoteException, FinderException;

Collection findByOwnerName(String ownerName)
        throws RemoteException, FinderException;
}
```

Note that for the CMP version, you will need to provide information in an application-server-specific format so that the EJB container will know how to implement the finder methods for you.

Activation and Passivation

Two of the callbacks for entity beans are `ejbActivate()` and `ejbPassivate()`. Session beans had these same callbacks, but they served different purposes. Actually, for stateless session beans, they serve no purpose at all; they are there so that stateless and stateful session beans can implement the same interface. For stateful session beans, they indicate to the bean that it is about to be saved to or restored from secondary storage, to help the EJB container manage its working set. Entity beans have no need to be saved to secondary storage: by definition, they already exist in persistent storage. If the container isn't using an entity bean, it doesn't need to worry about preserving its state before freeing its resources.

For entity beans, `ejbActivate()` provides a notification that the entity bean instance has been associated with an identity (i.e. a primary key) and it is now ready for `ejbLoad()` to be called prior to business method invocation. A matching `ejbPassivate()` method will be called to notify the entity bean that it is being disassociated with a particular identity prior to reuse (with another identity or for finder methods), or perhaps prior to being dereferenced and made eligible for garbage collection.

The only case where the entity bean would care about the information provided by `ejbActivate()` and `ejbPassivate()` is if it were managing some resource that depended on a bean's identity. Outside of this case, the implementation of these methods can be left empty. An example of where the entity bean might need a resource associated with a particular identity is if it had a remote reference to a non-Java object whose state needed to be synchronized with the state of the entity bean, such as a business object in a proprietary application server belonging to a vendor of ERP systems.

If the resource needs to be associated with a particular identity, you must actually provide for initialization of that resource in both `ejbPostCreate()` and `ejbActivate()`, because the entity can become associated with an identity through either of these paths. (Note that you need `ejbPostCreate()` rather than `ejbCreate()`, because `ejbPostCreate()` is where the identity becomes available.) Similarly, you must use both `ejbPassivate()` and `ejbRemove()` for resource release.

It's also possible that the resource doesn't need to be associated with a particular identity, but just needs to be generally available to any identity. For instance, you may have a connection to a legacy ERP system that you can use to synchronize data for any object. You can use the `setEntityContext()` and `unsetEntityContext()` callback methods to allocate and deallocate the resource in this case.

Here are the methods for both versions of our sports bean implementation (these go in the `SportTeamEJB` files for BMP and CMP):

```
public void ejbActivate() {}

public void ejbPassivate() {}
```

The Complete Lifecycle

This diagram summarizes the information about container callbacks for entity beans. In the **pooled state**, an entity instance is initialized but it is not associated with a particular identity. In other words, it doesn't have a particular primary key, nor does it represent the state of any particular row in the database. In this state, it can only be used for finder methods (which apply to entity beans in the aggregate) – or in EJB 2.0, for home business methods. (See Chapter 23 for more information on EJB 2.0.) In the **ready state**, the instance is associated with a particular identity and can be used for business methods. The EJB container can create an instance of an entity bean and move it to the pooled or ready state at its discretion, calling `ejbLoad()` and `ejbStore()` according to the rules described earlier in this chapter. In practice, an EJB container will only move an entity to the ready state when a client wants to use it, and it will leave that entity in the ready state, move it to the pooled state, or destroy the bean depending on the caching strategy in place. Here is the diagram:

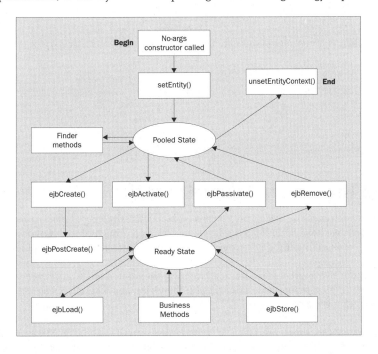

Reentrancy

Unlike session beans, which are never reentrant, an entity bean can be specified as reentrant or non-reentrant. A reentrant bean is one that allows a 'loopback' – for example, an Order entity bean calls a Lineitem entity bean, which then calls the Order bean. The initial call to the Lineitem 'looped back' to the Order.

If the Order bean in this example were specified as reentrant, the call would be allowed. If the Order bean were specified as not being reentrant, the EJB container would disallow the call and throw a `java.rmi.RemoteException`.

Many programmers are used to a style of programming where child items (such as a line item) have a reference to their containing parent (such as an order). This is admittedly useful in a variety of situations, and is allowed. However, making entity beans reentrant is discouraged (not forbidden) by the specification. This is because it makes it impossible for the container to prevent a certain class of error.

If a bean is coded as reentrant, the EJB container cannot prevent a multi-threaded client operating within a single transaction from making multiple calls to the entity bean. Although entity beans are designed to be single-threaded, this could lead to a situation where two (or more) threads of control were operating on a single instance of an entity bean simultaneously. This is the type of system error that Enterprise JavaBeans technology was designed to free the business logic programmer from worrying about, which is partly why the specification suggests that bean programmers avoid reentrant beans.

Just as an aside, it seems to me that you would have to bend over backwards to create a situation where an entity bean was accessed by multiple threads of control in the same transaction. For instance, since session beans can't have multiple threads, you couldn't do it if you accessed your entity beans through a session bean façade. In any case, I won't contradict the specification, which advises caution if you write reentrant beans. In my experience, caution while programming is never wasted.

Whether or not a bean is reentrant is indicated in the XML deployment descriptor, and looks like one of the following:

```
<reentrant>True</reentrant>
```

or:

```
<reentrant>False</reentrant>
```

Completing the Sports Team Example

In considering the differences between entity beans with container-managed persistence and those with bean-managed persistence, we have completed the home interface and much of the implementation class for the sports team example. In addition, I have provided the complete deployment descriptors for both examples.

In order to try out our two sports beans, we need to finish the implementation classes and provide a remote interface and a client. I developed these examples on the Orion application server, so I'll also tell you what you need to do to deploy the beans there.

Let's start by looking at the remote interface. It is the same for both versions (CMP and BMP), except for the package name. The client need never care about the persistence mechanism used by the EJB:

```
package sportBean.bmp;

import javax.ejb.*;

public interface SportTeam extends EJBObject {

  public void setOwner(String ownerName)
          throws java.rmi.RemoteException;

  public String getOwner() throws java.rmi.RemoteException;

  public void setFranchisePlayer(String playerName)
          throws java.rmi.RemoteException;

  public String getFranchisePlayer() throws java.rmi.RemoteException;

}
```

Of course, we need to provide corresponding methods in our implementation class. These are also the same for both versions of persistence – in other words, your business logic also need not care about the persistence mechanism:

```
public void setOwner(String ownerName) {
  this.ownerName = ownerName;
}

public String getOwner() {
  return ownerName;
}

public void setFranchisePlayer(String playerName) {
  this.franchisePlayer = playerName;
}

public String getFranchisePlayer() {
  return franchisePlayer;
}
```

With the addition of these methods, the CMP version of the implementation class is complete. The BMP version uses a utility method to retrieve the connection:

```
private Connection getConnection() {
  try {
    Context initial = new InitialContext();
    DataSource dataSource =
      (DataSource) initial.lookup("java:comp/env/jdbc/sportsJDBC");
    return dataSource.getConnection();
  } catch (javax.naming.NamingException ne) {
    ne.printStackTrace();
    throw new EJBException(ne);
  } catch (java.sql.SQLException sqle) {
    sqle.printStackTrace();
    throw new EJBException(sqle);
  }
}
```

Now it, too, is complete. Finally, let's provide a simple client for testing our beans. The only differences in the clients will be the package names (of course even this isn't necessary), the properties for initializing the JNDI context, and the lookup of the home interface. Here is the version for CMP:

```
package sportBean.cmp;

import java.rmi.RemoteException;
import javax.ejb.*;
import javax.naming.*;
import javax.rmi.PortableRemoteObject;
import java.util.Properties;
import java.util.Collection;
import java.util.Iterator;

public class TestClient {

  public static void main(String[] args) {
    try {
      Properties prop = new Properties();
```

```
      prop
        .setProperty(Context.INITIAL_CONTEXT_FACTORY,
          "com.evermind.server.ApplicationClientInitialContextFactory");
      prop.setProperty(Context.PROVIDER_URL,
                      "ormi://localhost/CMPSportsApp");
      prop.setProperty(Context.SECURITY_PRINCIPAL, "admin");
      prop.setProperty(Context.SECURITY_CREDENTIALS, "123");

      InitialContext initial = new InitialContext(prop);

      Object homeObject = initial.lookup("CMPSportsBean");

      SportTeamHome home =
        (SportTeamHome) PortableRemoteObject.narrow(homeObject,
              SportTeamHome.class);

      SportTeam team = home.create("basketball", "Kings",
                                   "Joe Maloof", "Jason Williams");

      System.out.println("Current franchise player: "
                        + team.getFranchisePlayer());

      team.setFranchisePlayer("Dan OConnor");

      System.out.println("New franchise player: "
                        + team.getFranchisePlayer());

      Collection collection = home.findByOwnerName("Joe Maloof");
      Iterator iter = collection.iterator();
      if (!iter.hasNext()) {
        System.out.println("Found no such owner.");
      } else {
        Object objRef2 = iter.next();
        SportTeam teamRef2 =
          (SportTeam) PortableRemoteObject.narrow(objRef2,
                                                SportTeam.class);

        System.out.println("Owner name: " + teamRef2.getOwner());
      }

      team.remove();
    } catch (RemoteException re) {
      re.printStackTrace();
    } catch (NamingException ne) {
      ne.printStackTrace();
    } catch (CreateException ce) {
      ce.printStackTrace();
    } catch (javax.ejb.RemoveException re) {
      re.printStackTrace();
    } catch (javax.ejb.FinderException fe) {
      fe.printStackTrace();
    }
  }
}
```

The version for BMP is quite similar. The differences are indicated here:

```
package sportBean.bmp;

import java.rmi.RemoteException;
import javax.ejb.*;
import javax.naming.*;
import javax.rmi.PortableRemoteObject;
import java.util.Properties;
import java.util.Collection;
import java.util.Iterator;

public class TestClient {

  public static void main(String[] args) {
    try {
      Properties prop = new Properties();
      prop
        .setProperty(Context.INITIAL_CONTEXT_FACTORY,
          "com.evermind.server.ApplicationClientInitialContextFactory");
      prop.setProperty( Context.PROVIDER_URL,
          "ormi://localhost/BMPSportsApp" );
      prop.setProperty( Context.SECURITY_PRINCIPAL, "admin" );
      prop.setProperty( Context.SECURITY_CREDENTIALS, "123" );

      InitialContext initial = new InitialContext(prop);

      Object homeObject = initial.lookup("BMPSportsBean");

      SportTeamHome home =
        (SportTeamHome) PortableRemoteObject.narrow(homeObject,
            SportTeamHome.class);
```

To review, the CMP EJB consists of the following files:

```
sportBean/
          cmp/
                SportTeam.class
                SportTeamEJB.class
                SportTeamHome.class
                SportTeamPK.class
META-INF/
          ejb-jar.xml
```

Similarly, the BMP EJB consists of the following files:

```
sportBean/
          bmp/
                SportTeam.class
                SportTeamEJB.class
                SportTeamHome.class
                SportTeamPK.class
META-INF/
          ejb-jar.xml
```

Make sure that the correct deployment descriptor (`ejb-jar.xml`) is included for each component.

The BMP example must also have an existing table in your database. You can define that table with the following SQL:

```
CREATE TABLE SPORTSTEAMS (SPORT CHAR(25) NOT NULL,
              NICKNAME CHAR(25) NOT NULL,
              OWNERNAME CHAR(25),
              FRANCHISEPLAYER CHAR(25),
              PRIMARY KEY (SPORT, NICKNAME));
```

The table for the CMP example could look the same. Most EJB containers (commercial and open-source) would be able to map the bean to this table without trouble. Many EJB containers (such as Orion and jBoss) will also create an appropriate table automatically on deployment if you desire.

I developed and tested these two components on the Orion application server, which is free for development and can be downloaded from `www.orionserver.com`. I'll provide a brief description of how you can test these beans on Orion as well. (You should refer to the Orion documentation as the definitive source on how to configure the server and deploy your EJBs, and for a detailed explanation of the configuration files.)

First, both these entity beans store their state data in a database. You should **configure Orion to work with your database of choice**. (There must be a table in this database for the BMP example. We'll let Orion create an appropriate table for the CMP table – although you could use an existing table here as well.)

> *In this example I am using HypersonicSQL, You will find an in-process version is installed with Orion (there is `hsql.jar` file in Orion's `lib` directory. Alternative, you can download the latest version from* `http://hsql.oron.ch.`

In the `config` directory under the main installation directory, there will be a file called `data-sources.xml`. You want to have one entry that looks something like this, with the username, password, database url, connection driver, and schema set to correct values for your environment. (The schema refers to an XML file located in a sub-directory that tracks database idiosyncrasies. Versions are included for several major databases, and it's easy to adapt them to your own if necessary):

```
<?xml version="1.0"?>
<!DOCTYPE data-sources PUBLIC "Orion data-sources"
"http://www.orionserver.com/dtds/data-sources.dtd">

<data-sources>
    <!--
        An example DataSource that uses an ordinary JDBC-driver to create
        the connections, to install; set the proper URL to the db, specify
        the db-driver name and unrem the below section. This creates all the
        needed kinds of data-sources, transactional, pooled and EJB-aware
        sources.
    -->
    <data-source
        name="Default data-source"
        class="com.evermind.sql.ConnectionDataSource"
        location="jdbc/DefaultDS"
        pooled-location="jdbc/DefaultPooledDS"
        xa-location="jdbc/xa/DefaultXADS"
        ejb-location="jdbc/DefaultEJBDS"
        url="jdbc:HypersonicSQL:c:/orion/database/sportsDB"
```

```
            connection-driver="org.hsql.jdbcDriver"
            username="sa"
            password=""
            schema="database-schemas/hypersonic.xml"
        />
</data-sources>
```

In order to use the default admin user you will need to open the `principals.xml` *file and remove the* `deactivated=true` *parameter for this user.*

Second, prepare your bean for deployment by **setting up an appropriate directory structure**. There are two important points to be made here relating to Orion server. The first point is that its unit of deployment is a J2EE-standard **enterprise archive file** (`.ear` file). This isn't anything complicated; it's just a JAR file that contains other JAR files (such as one or more EJB jars) and a deployment descriptor for the application in a `META-INF` sub-directory, which must be named `application.xml`. (This deployment descriptor shouldn't be confused with an EJB deployment descriptor. Although both are XML files located in the `META-INF` directory of their respective archives, they have different format and purposes.)

Why do we need the enterprise archive format? We want to be able to combine multiple EJB JARs, along with web archive files (WARs), into a single application unit. You are still preparing your EJB JAR, even if your target application server supports the EAR format. You just need to wrap it in one more archive (i.e. zip file). We'll see an example of combining an EJB JAR with a web archive (WAR) in Chapter 22, when we add a web interface to our sample manufacturing application.

What is the purpose of the application deployment descriptor? First, it declares the modules contained in the EAR file. Second, it can declare security roles that will be global to any contained modules (whether they be EJB JARs or servlet/JSP WARs). The application deployment descriptor for the CMP version of our sports bean looks like this (the module is just the name of the EJB JAR):

```
<?xml version="1.0"?>
<!DOCTYPE application PUBLIC "-//Sun Microsystems, Inc.//DTD J2EE Application
1.2//EN" "http://java.sun.com/j2ee/dtds/application_1_2.dtd">

<application>
    <display-name>CMPSports sample</display-name>
    <module>
        <ejb>ejbs</ejb>
    </module>
</application>
```

The application deployment descriptor for the BMP version of our sports bean looks like this:

```
<?xml version="1.0"?>
<!DOCTYPE application PUBLIC "-//Sun Microsystems, Inc.//DTD J2EE Application
1.2//EN" "http://java.sun.com/j2ee/dtds/application_1_2.dtd">

<application>
    <display-name>BMPSports sample</display-name>
    <module>
        <ejb>ejbs</ejb>
    </module>
</application>
```

The second point to consider about the Orion server relevant to setting up an appropriate directory structure is that, as a convenience to developers, it does not actually make you package up your files in archives. Instead, you can leave them 'unzipped' in a directory structure and Orion will work with those unarchived files. This removes one step in the develop-deploy-test cycle and can be a real convenience. (Of course, you can work with archived files if you choose.)

These directions assume that you are going to work with the unarchived files directly. To create an appropriate directory structure for the BMP example, add a directory named bmpsportsapp (this name is arbitrary) to the existing applications subdirectory of the Orion installation directory. The files beneath the bmpsportsapp directory should be as follows:

```
bmpsportsapp/
          META-INF/
                    application.xml
          ejbs/
              sportBean/
                        bmp/
                              SportTeam.class
                              SportTeamEJB.class
                              SportTeamHome.class
                              SportTeamPK.class
                  META-INF/
                          ejb-jar.xml
```

To create an appropriate directory structure for the CMP example, add a directory named cmpsportsapp to the existing applications subdirectory of the Orion installation. The files beneath the cmpsportsapp directory should be as follows:

```
cmpsportsapp/
          META-INF/
                    application.xml
          ejbs/
              sportBean/
                        cmp/
                              SportTeam.class
                              SportTeamEJB.class
                              SportTeamHome.class
                              SportTeamPK.class
                  META-INF/
                          ejb-jar.xml
```

The third step in running the examples on Orion is to **add that application** to Orion's server configuration file. This is an XML file located in the config directory beneath the Orion installation directory, called server.xml. (This file can also be used to specify many other server-related settings, such as the library path, the maximum number of HTTP connections allowed, and the transaction timeout. The default settings are fine to run any example in this book.) You need to add two <application> elements; one for each example (the BMP app and the CMP app). Your server.xml file should look something like this (please refer to the Orion documentation for more information):

```
<?xml version="1.0"?>
<!DOCTYPE application-server PUBLIC "Orion Application Server Config"
"http://www.orionserver.com/dtds/application-server.dtd">
```

```
<application-server
    application-directory="../applications"
    deployment-directory="../application-deployments"
>
    <!-- Path to the libraries that are installed on this server. These will
         be accesable for the servlets etc -->
    <library path="../lib" />
    <rmi-config path="./rmi.xml" />
    <!-- JMS-server config link, uncomment to activate the JMS service -->
    <!-- <jms-config path="./jms.xml" /> -->
    <principals path="./principals.xml" />
    <log>
        <file path="../log/server.log" />
    </log>

    <global-application name="default" path="application.xml" />

    <global-web-app-config path="global-web-application.xml" />
    <web-site path="./default-web-site.xml" />

    <application name="BMPSportsApp" path="../applications/bmpsportsapp" />
    <application name="CMPSportsApp" path="../applications/cmpsportsapp" />
    <!-- Compiler, activate this to specify an alternative compiler such
         as jikes for EJB/JSP compiling. -->
    <!-- <compiler executable="jikes" classpath="/myjdkdir/jre/lib/rt.jar"
         /> -->
</application-server>
```

The application name is arbitrary, but the client must use that application name to lookup the EJB home interface reference in the JNDI namespace. If you decide to change either application name, make the corresponding change in the test client.

At this point, our application will be deployed when Orion is started. Notice that we were able to skip many steps in the deployment process, such as mapping datasource references to actual datasource. Like jBoss, Orion will make guesses in order to get your application up and running using intelligent defaults. Except for specifying finder methods, this will be sufficient to run any application in this book. Consult the Orion documentation for more information about deployment.

Once the application has been deployed, we have to **configure the finder method for the CMP example**. Remember that, except for findByPrimaryKey(), the finder method for EJB 1.1 CMP entity beans must be specified in an application-server specific format. After the initial deployment, this finder method is specified using a syntax specified in the Orion documentation, in the generated file orion-ejb-jar.xml, which will be found in a subdirectory of the application-deployments directory. For this example, Orion once again uses "intelligent defaults" that allows us to skip a step. It made a guess about what we wanted from our finder method, based on the correspondence between the member variable ownerName and the finder method name findBy**OwnerName**. Based on this, it generated the definition of the finder method for us – a definition that happens to be correct. In other words, for this example, you can skip this (often necessary) step.

Now start up the Orion server:

```
java -jar orion.jar
```

You should see the database being created:

The final step is to **run the client**. Orion is a complete implementation of a J2EE application server, which includes the concept of a 'client container'. This client container provides a managed environment, just like an EJB container does for an EJB or a web container does for a servlet. The managed environment is much less extensive than the equivalent for those components. In practice, what this means is that there is an XML deployment descriptor for your Orion client, in which you declare environment entries, EJB references, and resource references – much like you would do for an EJB in its deployment descriptor. This XML deployment descriptor must be `named application-client.xml`, and it must be located in a directory named `META-INF` somewhere on the client's `CLASSPATH`.

Here is the application client deployment descriptor for the BMP example (the display name is arbitrary, and is basically used for organizing the display of this information in GUI tools):

```xml
<?xml version="1.0"?>
<!DOCTYPE application-client PUBLIC "-//Sun Microsystems, Inc.//DTD J2EE
Application Client 1.2//EN" "http://java.sun.com/j2ee/dtds/application-
client_1_2.dtd">

<application-client>
    <display-name>wrox</display-name>
    <ejb-ref>
            <ejb-ref-name>BMPSportsBean</ejb-ref-name>
            <ejb-ref-type>Entity</ejb-ref-type>
            <home>sportBean.bmp.SportTeamHome</home>
            <remote>sportBean.bmp.SportTeam</remote>
    </ejb-ref>
</application-client>
```

And here is the application client deployment descriptor for the CMP example:

```xml
<?xml version="1.0"?>
<!DOCTYPE application-client PUBLIC "-//Sun Microsystems, Inc.//DTD J2EE
Application Client 1.2//EN" "http://java.sun.com/j2ee/dtds/application-
client_1_2.dtd">

<application-client>
```

```
        <display-name>wrox</display-name>
        <ejb-ref>
                <ejb-ref-name>CMPSportsBean</ejb-ref-name>
                <ejb-ref-type>Entity</ejb-ref-type>
                <home>sportBean.cmp.SportTeamHome</home>
                <remote>sportBean.cmp.SportTeam</remote>
        </ejb-ref>
</application-client>
```

When you run the client, regardless of which version of persistence, you should get the following output:

Relationships

One of the most common questions asked about entity beans is how to implement relationships between them. The EJB 1.1 specification is largely silent on this question. Of course, for beans with bean-managed persistence, the business-logic programmer must code the mapping between beans manually. Ideally, they will store the primary keys of related entities in tables while following good relational design principles. Exactly how to implement an object/relational mapping framework for bean-managed persistence is well beyond the scope of this book.

> *A Java standard for object relational mapping has just entered the public review stage of the Java Community Process. This standard is known as Java Data Objects, or JDO. A good source of additional information about object/relational mapping is* www.cetus-links.org.

For beans with container-managed persistence, the specification mandates that the container be able to store references to other entity beans, so this means the case of one-to-one relationships must get some rudimentary handling at least. Furthermore, because the specification also mandates that the container be able to store references to any serializable object, it is possible to have a serializable collection of references to other entity beans. This means that the case of one-to-many relationships must get some basic handling by the container as well.

Unfortunately, a requirement of most real-word projects is that the data be stored in a form that is generally accessible. Although unfortunate, it is not uncommon to find that (especially in the case of one-to-many relationships or even more complicated situations) your EJB 1.1 container will need to resort to dumping the data into a binary large object field in the database. Even if your EJB container provides support for foreign-key references in related tables (the preferred solution), whatever technique you use to achieve this will not be portable, because there is no standard way defined of handling relationships.

> *The situation improves dramatically with EJB 2.0 container-managed persistence. Turn to Chapter 23 for more information on how relationships are handled in the new version of the EJB specification.*

One technique that can be helpful is to manage the relationship in reverse. Rather than storing references to related entity beans in the 'contains' or 'refers to' bean, you can define a finder method in the 'contained-in' or 'referenced' bean that takes the primary key of the first bean and returns a collection of the related beans. This is a portable solution, although less simple than the collection-of-references technique would be.

Completing Our Manufacturing Application

We began modeling a manufacturing facility in the last chapter. We referenced two entity beans in that chapter's code, while deferring a complete treatment on those two beans, `Order` and `Product`, until this chapter. As I chose container-managed persistence, the implementation of these two classes is quite simple.

Please note that the exact mapping of these classes to database tables will depend on the implementation of your EJB container's object/relational mapping for container-managed persistence. In the best case scenario, you will have great flexibility, enough to match your beans to pre-existing tables used for other systems. For an adequate container, the worst-case scenario is probably that the product's dependent objects get serialized into a single table column. (Most containers will handle the one-to-one relationship between order and product by storing the product's key in a column of the order table. This is the behavior you probably want.)

One optional feature that your container may have is to automatically create the tables that it will use for the CMP persistence of an entity bean. If you take advantage of this feature, you will automatically get a database structure appropriate for your container's capabilities. You will also save yourself the trouble of configuring the object/relational mapping. Of course, this feature would not be useful if you are working with an existing relational database design.

The Order Bean

The Order bean has five state properties. One of these is a reference to another entity bean (the product). This relationship is pretty intuitive: an order is for a product. Of course, in a real-world application, an order would probably have a list of line items; each of those line items would probably have a product and a quantity, as well as other information. But this is enough to get the idea:

```
package factory.order;

import javax.ejb.*;
import javax.naming.*;
import java.rmi.RemoteException;
import factory.product.Product;
import factory.product.ProductHome;
import java.util.Date;

public class OrderEJB implements EntityBean
{
  // Properties
  private static final String OPEN_STATUS = "o";
  private static final String DEFAULT_STATUS = OPEN_STATUS;
  private static final String CANCELED_STATUS = "c";
  private static final String IN_PROCESS_STATUS = "m";
  private static final String COMPLETED_STATUS = "f";

  public int salesDivision;
  public int orderNumber;
  public Product productOrdered;
  public String status;
  public Date dateDue;
```

Notice that I have defined five private static variables for use in the implementation. The specification allows for static variables in EJBs, but they must be read-only. To enforce this, I have declared them `final`.

The key for the order is a combination of the sales division and the order number, because every sales division has its own system for assigning order numbers, and the two systems would assign conflicting orders. Remember that every primary key must be unique. Here is the primary key for the Order bean:

```java
package factory.order;

import java.io.Serializable;

public class OrderPK implements Serializable {

    public int salesDivision;
    public int orderNumber;

    // Mandatory empty constructor
    public OrderPK() {}

    // Convenience constructor
    public OrderPK(int salesDivision, int orderNumber) {
        this.salesDivision = salesDivision;
        this.orderNumber = orderNumber;
    }

    public int hashCode() {
        return (salesDivision << 8 ) + orderNumber;
    }

    public boolean equals(Object other) {
        if ((other == null) || !(other instanceof OrderPK))
            return false;

        OrderPK otherPK = (OrderPK) other;

        return (salesDivision == otherPK.salesDivision) &&
            (orderNumber == otherPK.orderNumber);
    }
}
```

The public state fields (`salesDivision` and `orderNumber`) must be named exactly the same and have the same type as the corresponding fields in the bean.

Here are the business methods for the order in the remote interface. They are pretty much self-explanatory:

```java
package factory.order;

import javax.ejb.*;
import java.rmi.RemoteException;
import java.util.Date;
import factory.product.Product;

public interface Order extends EJBObject {
```

1009

```
    public int getSalesDivision() throws RemoteException;

    public int getOrderNumber() throws RemoteException;

    public Product getProductOrdered() throws RemoteException;

    public String getStatus() throws RemoteException;

    public void cancelOrder()
            throws RemoteException, OrderNotCancelableException;

    public void beginManufacture() throws RemoteException;

    public void completeManufacture() throws RemoteException;

    public Date getDateDue() throws RemoteException;
}
```

And here is the implementation of those methods, which should be added to the `OrderEJB` class:

```
// Business methods

public int getSalesDivision() {
    return salesDivision;
}

public int getOrderNumber() {
    return orderNumber;
}

public Product getProductOrdered() {
    return productOrdered;
}

public String getStatus() {
    if (status.equals(OPEN_STATUS)) {
        return StatusStrings.OPEN;
    } else if (status.equals(CANCELED_STATUS)) {
        return StatusStrings.CANCELED;
    } else if (status.equals(IN_PROCESS_STATUS)) {
        return StatusStrings.IN_PROCESS;
    } else if (status.equals(COMPLETED_STATUS)) {
        return StatusStrings.COMPLETED;
    }
    throw new EJBException("Unknown status");
}

public void cancelOrder() throws OrderNotCancelableException {
    if (status.equals(IN_PROCESS_STATUS)
            || status.equals(COMPLETED_STATUS)) {
        throw new OrderNotCancelableException();
    }
```

```
    status = CANCELED_STATUS;
  }

  public void beginManufacture() {
    status = IN_PROCESS_STATUS;
  }

  public void completeManufacture() {
    status = COMPLETED_STATUS;
  }

  public Date getDateDue() {
    return dateDue;
  }
```

One thing to note is that the order status is stored as a single letter in the database and in the cached state of the Order bean. However, the client expects to get a human-readable string when it asks about the status. I have defined these strings in an outside class for simplicity, although the best approach is probably to load them from a resource (to support internationalization, for example):

```
package factory.order;

public class StatusStrings {
  public static final String OPEN = "open";
  public static final String CANCELED = "canceled";
  public static final String IN_PROCESS = "in process";
  public static final String COMPLETED = "completed";
}
```

We translate them when the client asks for them in the getStatus() method. We could have cached the status in human-readable form in a transient variable (and worked with it in the business logic in that form) by adding logic in ejbLoad() to translate it from its database format. Then in ejbStore() we could retranslate it into database form and save it in a container-managed non-transient field. This seemed like a lot of work for little value. In some other, more complicated, cases, this might be the way to go.

The OrderNotCancelableException thrown from the cancelOrder() method is an unremarkable class already discussed briefly in the last chapter. It is defined as follows:

```
package factory.order;

public class OrderNotCancelableException extends Exception {

  public OrderNotCancelableException() {}
}
```

Except for a little post-processing in ejbLoad(), most of the callback functions in OrderEJB are empty. We can leave everything to the container:

```
public void ejbLoad() {
  status = status.trim();
}
```

```
    public void ejbStore() {}

    public void ejbActivate() {}

    public void ejbPassivate() {}

    public void ejbRemove() {}

    public void setEntityContext(EntityContext ctx) {}

    public void unsetEntityContext() {}
```

The order provides two versions of its create() function. Although they take the same information, one version accepts the String name of a product and the other accepts a remote reference. The version that takes the String name uses a helper method to convert this into an actual product. If the name doesn't match to a product, a CreateException is thrown:

```
// Lifecycle and framework methods

public OrderPK ejbCreate(int salesDivision, int orderNumber,
                         Product productOrdered,
                         Date dateDue) throws CreateException {
  this.salesDivision = salesDivision;
  this.orderNumber = orderNumber;
  this.productOrdered = productOrdered;
  this.dateDue = dateDue;
  status = DEFAULT_STATUS;

  return null;    // For container-managed persistence
}

public void ejbPostCreate(int salesDivision, int orderNumber,
                          Product productOrdered, Date dateDue) {}

public OrderPK ejbCreate(int salesDivision, int orderNumber,
                         String product,
                         Date dateDue) throws CreateException {
  this.salesDivision = salesDivision;
  this.orderNumber = orderNumber;
  this.dateDue = dateDue;
  status = DEFAULT_STATUS;

  try {
    ProductHome productHome = getProductHome();
    this.productOrdered = productHome.findByPrimaryKey(product);
  } catch (RemoteException re) {
    re.printStackTrace();
    throw new EJBException(re);
  } catch (FinderException fe) {
    fe.printStackTrace();
    throw new CreateException("Product does not exist");
  }
```

```
      return null;    // For container-managed persistence
    }

    public void ejbPostCreate(int salesDivision, int orderNumber,
                              String product, Date dateDue) {}

    // Implementation helpers

    private ProductHome getProductHome() {
      try {
        InitialContext initial = new InitialContext();
        ProductHome home =
          (ProductHome) javax.rmi.PortableRemoteObject
            .narrow(initial.lookup("java:comp/env/ejb/Product"),
                    ProductHome.class);
        return home;
      } catch (NamingException ne) {
        ne.printStackTrace();
        throw new EJBException(ne);
      }
    }
  }
}
```

create() methods must have at least enough information to specify the primary key of the new entity. In practice, they will usually have more. There are two possible patterns to initialize a new instance with a set of data:

❑   Call the create() method with that set of data

❑   Call a create() method, and then call update methods on the instance

If the second method is used, you should make sure that the update method calls all take place in the same transaction as the call to create(). Otherwise, if something happens in between your create() call and the updates (e.g. your client crashes), your database might be left with a half-initialized entity lying around.

The create() methods and the finder methods are declared in the home interface:

```
package factory.order;

import javax.ejb.*;
import java.rmi.RemoteException;
import factory.product.Product;
import java.util.Date;
import java.util.Collection;

public interface OrderHome extends EJBHome {

  Order create(int salesDivision, int orderNumber,
               Product productOrdered,
               Date dateDue) throws RemoteException, CreateException;

  Order create(int salesDivision, int orderNumber,
```

```
                String productOrdered,
                Date dateDue) throws RemoteException, CreateException;

    Order findByPrimaryKey(OrderPK order)
            throws RemoteException, FinderException;

    Collection findOpenOrders() throws RemoteException, FinderException;

    Collection findUncompletedOrders()
            throws RemoteException, FinderException;

}
```

The finder methods are specified in a format that is currently proprietary to each EJB container. Here is how I specified their functionality for the Orion application server:

```
<finder-method query="$status starting with 'o'">
  <method>
    <ejb-name>Orders</ejb-name>
    <method-name>findOpenOrders</method-name>
    <method-params>
    </method-params>
  </method>
</finder-method>
<finder-method query="$status not starting with 'c' and
                      $status not starting with 'f'">
  <method>
    <ejb-name>Orders</ejb-name>
    <method-name>findUncompletedOrders</method-name>
    <method-params>
    </method-params>
  </method>
</finder-method>
```

For an example of how these queries would look using the new EJB Query Language defined in EJB 2.0, see Chapter 23.

The Product Bean

The Product bean has three state properties. Two are strings: product (which is the key) and name (which is the human-readable name of the product), and the third is a list of routing instructions. A routing instruction is defined as follows:

```
package factory.product;

import java.io.Serializable;

public class RoutingInstruction implements Serializable, Comparable {
  public int sequence;
  public String instruction;

  public RoutingInstruction() {}
```

```
public RoutingInstruction(int sequence, String instruction) {
  this.sequence = sequence;
  this.instruction = instruction;
}

public int compareTo(Object o) {
  RoutingInstruction ri = (RoutingInstruction) o;
  if (sequence < ri.sequence) {
    return -1;
  } else if (sequence == ri.sequence) {
    return 0;
  } else {
    return 1;
  }
}
}
```

Note that this could have been modeled as a set of related entity beans. Why did we choose to make routing instructions an attribute?

❏ The lifecycle of a routing instruction is completely controlled by the product in which it is contained. A routing instruction is created for a particular product, and it should be deleted if the corresponding product is deleted.

❏ No entity other than a product will ever link to this routing instruction independently. If, hypothetically, some 'work station' needed to have a reference to all its associated routing steps, it might be worth while to make the routing a first class entity object to support this association.

❏ A routing is a lightweight object, and would suffer from the overhead of being a first class entity.

Here is the state of our product entity bean:

```
package factory.product;

import javax.ejb.*;
import java.util.List;
import java.util.LinkedList;
import java.util.Arrays;
import java.util.Iterator;

public class ProductEJB implements EntityBean
{
  // Properties

  public String product;
  public String name;
  public LinkedList routingInstructions;
```

Note that to be spec-compliant, the concrete implementation of that list and all its contents will need to be serializable.

The business methods of the product entity bean are defined as follows in the remote interface:

```
package factory.product;

import javax.ejb.*;
import java.rmi.RemoteException;

public interface Product extends EJBObject {
  public String getProduct() throws RemoteException;

  public String getName() throws RemoteException;

  public void setName(String name) throws RemoteException;

  public RoutingInstruction[] getRoutingInstructions()
        throws RemoteException;

  public void addRoutingInstruction(int sequence, String instruction)
        throws RemoteException;

  public void deleteRoutingInstruction(int sequence)
        throws RemoteException, NoSuchRoutingInstruction;

  public void replaceRoutingInstructions(RoutingInstruction[]
newRoutingInstructions)
        throws RemoteException;
}
```

Their implementations in `ProductEJB.java` are relatively simple to understand: they are all getter and setter methods. The only interesting thing about them is their handling of the dependent routing instruction list:

```
// Business methods

public String getProduct() {
  return product;
}

public String getName() {
  return name;
}

public void setName(String name) {
  this.name = name;
}

public RoutingInstruction[] getRoutingInstructions() {
  RoutingInstruction[] routingArray =
    new RoutingInstruction[routingInstructions.size()];
  return (RoutingInstruction[])
        routingInstructions.toArray(routingArray);
}

public void addRoutingInstruction(int sequence, String instruction) {
```

```
                  routingInstructions.add(new RoutingInstruction(sequence,
                                                          instruction));
      }

      public void deleteRoutingInstruction(int sequence)
              throws NoSuchRoutingInstruction {
        Iterator iter = routingInstructions.iterator();
        while (iter.hasNext()) {
          RoutingInstruction ri = (RoutingInstruction) iter.next();
          if (ri.sequence == sequence) {
            iter.remove();
            return;
          }
        }
        throw new NoSuchRoutingInstruction();
      }

      public void replaceRoutingInstructions(RoutingInstruction[]
                  newRoutingInstructions) {
        routingInstructions.clear();
        routingInstructions.addAll(Arrays.asList(newRoutingInstructions));
      }
```

The callbacks are mostly empty, because the container provides most of the functionality for us. The create() method takes as parameters a complete description of the object's state: product, name, and routing instructions:

```
      // Framework and lifecycle methods

      public String ejbCreate(String product, String name,
                          RoutingInstruction[] routingInstructions) {
        this.product = product;
        this.name = name;
        this.routingInstructions = new LinkedList();
        this.routingInstructions.addAll(Arrays.asList(routingInstructions));
        return null;
      }

      public void ejbPostCreate(String product, String name,
                            RoutingInstruction[] routingInstructions) {}

      public void ejbActivate() {}

      public void ejbLoad() {}

      public void ejbPassivate() {}

      public void ejbRemove() {}

      public void ejbStore() {}

      public void setEntityContext(EntityContext ctx) {}

      public void unsetEntityContext() {}
    }
```

Once again, the exception class defined in this package (NoSuchRoutingInstruction) is rather unremarkable:

```
package factory.product;

public class NoSuchRoutingInstruction extends Exception {

  public NoSuchRoutingInstruction() {}
}
```

Finally, here's the home interface:

```
package factory.product;

import javax.ejb.*;
import java.rmi.RemoteException;

public interface ProductHome extends EJBHome {

  Product create(String product, String name,
                 RoutingInstruction[] routingInstructions)
         throws RemoteException, CreateException;

  Product findByPrimaryKey(String product)
         throws RemoteException, FinderException;
}
```

The implementations of the Product and Order entity beans are quite simple. Their focus is on business logic, and not system-level concerns such as persistence.

The Complete Deployment Descriptor

We've seen a few bits and pieces of the XML deployment descriptor for this example as we examined the Java code. Here is the completed deployment descriptor for all four beans (a stateless session bean for managing orders, a stateful session bean for manufacturing a product, an order entity, and a product entity):

```
<?xml version="1.0"?>

<ejb-jar>
 <enterprise-beans>
```

Deployment information for the bean for managing orders:

```
    <session>
        <ejb-name>ManageOrders</ejb-name>
        <home>factory.manage_orders.ManageOrdersHome</home>
        <remote>factory.manage_orders.ManageOrders</remote>
        <ejb-class>factory.manage_orders.ManageOrdersEJB</ejb-class>
        <session-type>Stateless</session-type>
        <transaction-type>Container</transaction-type>
        <ejb-ref>
```

```
        <ejb-ref-name>ejb/Order</ejb-ref-name>
        <ejb-ref-type>Entity</ejb-ref-type>
        <home>factory.order.OrderHome</home>
        <remote>factory.order.Order</remote>
        <ejb-link>Orders</ejb-link>
    </ejb-ref>
    <ejb-ref>
        <ejb-ref-name>ejb/Product</ejb-ref-name>
        <ejb-ref-type>Entity</ejb-ref-type>
        <home>factory.product.ProductHome</home>
        <remote>factory.product.Product</remote>
        <ejb-link>Product</ejb-link>
    </ejb-ref>
    <env-entry>
        <env-entry-name>lead_time</env-entry-name>
        <env-entry-type>java.lang.Integer</env-entry-type>
        <env-entry-value>3</env-entry-value>
    </env-entry>
    <env-entry>
        <env-entry-name>max_inventory_time</env-entry-name>
        <env-entry-type>java.lang.Integer</env-entry-type>
        <env-entry-value>10</env-entry-value>
    </env-entry>
</session>
```

Deployment information for the bean for manufacturing products:

```
<session>
    <ejb-name>Manufacture</ejb-name>
    <home>factory.manufacture.ManufactureHome</home>
    <remote>factory.manufacture.Manufacture</remote>
    <ejb-class>factory.manufacture.ManufactureEJB</ejb-class>
    <session-type>Stateful</session-type>
    <transaction-type>Container</transaction-type>
    <ejb-ref>
        <ejb-ref-name>ejb/Order</ejb-ref-name>
        <ejb-ref-type>Entity</ejb-ref-type>
        <home>factory.order.OrderHome</home>
        <remote>factory.order.Order</remote>
        <ejb-link>Orders</ejb-link>
    </ejb-ref>
    <ejb-ref>
        <ejb-ref-name>ejb/ManageOrders</ejb-ref-name>
        <ejb-ref-type>Session</ejb-ref-type>
        <home>factory.manage_orders.ManageOrdersHome</home>
        <remote>factory.manage_orders.ManageOrders</remote>
        <ejb-link>ManageOrders</ejb-link>
    </ejb-ref>
    <env-entry>
        <env-entry-name>shipmentSQL</env-entry-name>
        <env-entry-type>java.lang.String</env-entry-type>
        <env-entry-value>INSERT INTO shipments (division, order_number,
                         carrier, loading_dock, date_completed,
```

```
                          manufactured_by ) VALUES (?, ?, ?, ?, ?, ?)
        </env-entry-value>
    </env-entry>
    <resource-ref>
        <res-ref-name>jdbc/shipDB</res-ref-name>
        <res-type>javax.sql.DataSource</res-type>
        <res-auth>Container</res-auth>
    </resource-ref>
</session>
```

Deployment information for the Order entity bean:

```
<entity>
    <ejb-name>Orders</ejb-name>
    <home>factory.order.OrderHome</home>
    <remote>factory.order.Order</remote>
    <ejb-class>factory.order.OrderEJB</ejb-class>
        <prim-key-class>factory.order.OrderPK</prim-key-class>
        <reentrant>False</reentrant>
        <persistence-type>Container</persistence-type>
        <cmp-field><field-name>salesDivision</field-name></cmp-field>
        <cmp-field><field-name>orderNumber</field-name></cmp-field>
        <cmp-field><field-name>productOrdered</field-name></cmp-field>
        <cmp-field><field-name>status</field-name></cmp-field>
        <cmp-field><field-name>dateDue</field-name></cmp-field>
    <ejb-ref>
      <ejb-ref-name>ejb/Product</ejb-ref-name>
      <ejb-ref-type>Entity</ejb-ref-type>
      <home>factory.product.ProductHome</home>
      <remote>factory.product.Product</remote>
      <ejb-link>Product</ejb-link>
    </ejb-ref>
</entity>
```

Deployment information for the Product entity bean:

```
<entity>
    <ejb-name>Product</ejb-name>
    <home>factory.product.ProductHome</home>
    <remote>factory.product.Product</remote>
    <ejb-class>factory.product.ProductEJB</ejb-class>
        <prim-key-class>java.lang.String</prim-key-class>
        <primkey-field>product</primkey-field>
        <reentrant>False</reentrant>
        <persistence-type>Container</persistence-type>
        <cmp-field><field-name>product</field-name></cmp-field>
        <cmp-field><field-name>name</field-name></cmp-field>
        <cmp-field><field-name>routingInstructions</field-name>
        </cmp-field>
    </entity>

</enterprise-beans>
```

Assembly information for the application as a whole; specifically, declarative transactions:

```
<assembly-descriptor>
  <container-transaction>
    <method>
        <ejb-name>Orders</ejb-name>
        <method-name>*</method-name>
    </method>
    <trans-attribute>Required</trans-attribute>
  </container-transaction>
  <container-transaction>
    <method>
        <ejb-name>Product</ejb-name>
        <method-name>*</method-name>
    </method>
    <trans-attribute>Required</trans-attribute>
  </container-transaction>
  <container-transaction>
    <method>
        <ejb-name>ManageOrders</ejb-name>
        <method-name>*</method-name>
    </method>
    <trans-attribute>Required</trans-attribute>
  </container-transaction>
  <container-transaction>
    <method>
        <ejb-name>Manufacture</ejb-name>
        <method-name>*</method-name>
    </method>
    <trans-attribute>Required</trans-attribute>
  </container-transaction>
</assembly-descriptor>
</ejb-jar>
```

Running the Manufacturing Application

At this point, you have enough information to run the manufacturing sample application. You should have the following classes in your EJB JAR (or directory structure, if your EJB container supports this format):

```
factory/
        clients/
                BeginManufacture.class
                CompleteManufacture.class
                ContextPropertiesFactory.class
                CreateProducts.class
                ManageSampleOrders.class
                PlaceSampleOrders.class
        manage_orders/
                DuplicateOrderException.class
                ManageOrders.class
                ManageOrdersEJB.class
                ManageOrdersHome.class
                NoSuchOrderException.class
```

```
                        NoSuchProductException.class
                        OpenOrderView.class
                        OverdueOrderView.class
                        ProductCreationHelper.class
            manufacture/
                        BadStatusException.class
                        Manufacture.class
                        ManufactureEJB.class
                        ManufactureHome.class
                        NoSelectionException.class
            order/
                    Order.class
                    OrderEJB.class
                    OrderHome.class
                    OrderNotCancelableException.class
                    OrderPK.class
                    StatusStrings.class
            product/
                    NoSuchRoutingException.class
                    Product.class
                    ProductEJB.class
                    ProductHome.class
                    RoutingInstruction.class
      META-INF/
                ejb-jar.xml
```

You also need to create the database table used by the manufacturing session bean for recording shipments. This was discussed in the previous chapter; as a refresher, here is the SQL to create the table:

```
CREATE TABLE SHIPMENTS (DIVISION INTEGER NOT NULL,
                        ORDER_NUMBER INTEGER NOT NULL,
                        CARRIER CHAR(50),
                        LOADING_DOCK INTEGER,
                        DATE_COMPLETED DATE,
                        MANUFACTURED_BY CHAR(50),
                        PRIMARY KEY (DIVISION, ORDER_NUMBER));
```

I developed and tested this example on the Orion application server. Some instructions on how to deploy an application on this server were provided earlier in this chapter. To summarize the steps required, you must:

Configure Orion to work with your data source. In the `config` directory under the main installation directory, there will be a file called `data-sources.xml`. Specify the correct values for the username, password, database url, connection driver, and schema.

Add a directory called `factory` to the applications directory below the Orion installation directory (the name 'factory' is arbitrary, but the other steps in my directions use it as well). Set up the directory structure to conform to the J2EE EAR format. I used the following directory structure (the first META-INF is for the application, and the second is for the EJB JAR):

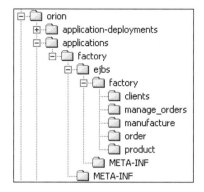

The `application.xml` file looks like this:

```
<?xml version="1.0"?>
<!DOCTYPE application PUBLIC "-//Sun Microsystems, Inc.//DTD J2EE Application
1.2//EN" "http://java.sun.com/j2ee/dtds/application_1_2.dtd">

<application>
    <display-name>Factory sample</display-name>
    <module>
        <ejb>ejbs</ejb>
    </module>
</application>
```

Add the application to Orion's `server.xml` file (located in Orion's `config` directory), as follows:

```
<?xml version="1.0"?>
<!DOCTYPE application-server PUBLIC "Orion Application Server Config"
"http://www.orionserver.com/dtds/application-server.dtd">

<application-server
   application-directory="../applications"
   deployment-directory="../application-deployments"
>
   <!-- Path to the libraries that are installed on this server. These will be
   accesable for the servlets etc -->
   <library path="../lib" />
   <rmi-config path="./rmi.xml" />
   <!-- JMS-server config link, uncomment to activate the JMS service -->
   <!-- <jms-config path="./jms.xml" /> -->
   <principals path="./principals.xml" />
   <log>
       <file path="../log/server.log" />
   </log>

   <global-application name="default" path="application.xml" />

   <global-web-app-config path="global-web-application.xml" />
   <web-site path="./default-web-site.xml" />
```

```
        <application name="factory" path="../applications/factory" />

    <!-- Compiler, activate this to specify an alternative compiler such
        as jikes for EJB/JSP compiling. -->
    <!-- <compiler executable="jikes" classpath="/myjdkdir/jre/lib/rt.jar" /> -->
</application-server>
```

After deploying the application, configure the finder methods in the generated `orion-ejb-jar.xml` file located in the `application-deployments/factory/ejbs/` directory off of Orion's root directory, as follows:

```
<?xml version="1.0"?>
<!DOCTYPE orion-ejb-jar PUBLIC "-//Evermind//DTD Enterprise JavaBeans 1.1
runtime//EN" "http://www.orionserver.com/dtds/orion-ejb-jar.dtd">

<orion-ejb-jar deployment-version="1.0rc1" deployment-time="e078d779e2">
    <enterprise-beans>
        <session-deployment name="ManageOrders" location="ManageOrders"
                            wrapper="SessionHomeWrapper1" timeout="1200"
                            persistence-filename="ManageOrders">
            <ejb-ref-mapping name="ejb/Order" />
            <ejb-ref-mapping name="ejb/Product" />
        </session-deployment>
        <session-deployment name="Manufacture" location="Manufacture"
                            wrapper="SessionHomeWrapper3" timeout="1200"
                            persistence-filename="Manufacture">
            <ejb-ref-mapping name="ejb/Order" />
            <ejb-ref-mapping name="ejb/ManageOrders" />
            <resource-ref-mapping name="jdbc/shipDB" />
        </session-deployment>
        <entity-deployment name="Orders" location="Orders"
                            wrapper="EntityHomeWrapper5" table="Orders"
                            data-source="jdbc/DefaultEJBDS">
            <primkey-mapping>
                <cmp-field-mapping>
                    <fields>
                        <cmp-field-mapping name="salesDivision"
                            persistence-name="salesDivision" />
                        <cmp-field-mapping name="orderNumber"
                            persistence-name="orderNumber" />
                    </fields>
                </cmp-field-mapping>
            </primkey-mapping>
            <cmp-field-mapping name="productOrdered">
                <entity-ref home="Product">
                    <cmp-field-mapping name="productOrdered"
                        persistence-name="productOrdered" />
                </entity-ref>
            </cmp-field-mapping>
            <cmp-field-mapping name="status" persistence-name="status" />
            <cmp-field-mapping name="dateDue" persistence-name="dateDue" />
            <finder-method query="$status like 'o%'">
```

```
            <!-- Generated SQL: "select salesDivision, orderNumber,
                 productOrdered, status, dateDue from Orders where status
                 starting with 'o'" -->
          <method>
             <ejb-name>Orders</ejb-name>
             <method-name>findOpenOrders</method-name>
             <method-params>
             </method-params>
          </method>
       </finder-method>
       <finder-method query="$status not like 'c%' and $status
                             not like 'f%'">
          <!-- Generated SQL: "select salesDivision, orderNumber,
               productOrdered, status, dateDue from Orders where status
               not starting with 'c' and status not starting with 'f'"
            -->
          <method>
             <ejb-name>Orders</ejb-name>
             <method-name>findUncompletedOrders</method-name>
             <method-params>
             </method-params>
          </method>
       </finder-method>
       <ejb-ref-mapping name="ejb/Product" />
    </entity-deployment>
    <entity-deployment name="Product" location="Product"
                       wrapper="EntityHomeWrapper13" table="Product"
                       data-source="jdbc/DefaultEJBDS">
       <primkey-mapping>
          <cmp-field-mapping name="product" persistence-name="product" />
       </primkey-mapping>
       <cmp-field-mapping name="name" persistence-name="name" />
       <cmp-field-mapping name="routingInstructions"
                          persistence-name="routingInstructions" />
    </entity-deployment>
 </enterprise-beans>
 <assembly-descriptor>
    <default-method-access>
       <security-role-mapping impliesAll="true" />
    </default-method-access>
 </assembly-descriptor>
</orion-ejb-jar>
```

Add the following application client deployment descriptor to a META-INF directory somewhere on your clients's CLASSPATH (the same application-client.xml file can be used for all the sample manufacturing clients):

```
<?xml version="1.0"?>
<!DOCTYPE application-client PUBLIC "-//Sun Microsystems, Inc.//DTD J2EE
Application Client 1.2//EN" "http://java.sun.com/j2ee/dtds/application-
client_1_2.dtd">


<application-client>
   <display-name>wrox</display-name>
```

```
        <ejb-ref>
            <ejb-ref-name>ManageOrders</ejb-ref-name>
            <ejb-ref-type>Session</ejb-ref-type>
            <home>factory.manage_orders.ManageOrdersHome</home>
            <remote>factory.manage_orders.ManageOrders</remote>
        </ejb-ref>
        <ejb-ref>
            <ejb-ref-name>Manufacture</ejb-ref-name>
            <ejb-ref-type>Session</ejb-ref-type>
            <home>factory.manufacture.ManufactureHome</home>
            <remote>factory.manufacture.Manufacture</remote>
        </ejb-ref>
    </application-client>
```

Now you should be able to run the clients that were described in Chapter 19. These clients just provide a simple test of the functionality provided by our EJBs:

❑   Run `CreateProducts` first to create some sample products.

❑   Next run `PlaceSampleOrders`. (Running either of these programs a second time without deleting the appropriate records from the database will result in harmless error messages.)

❑   Run `ManageSampleOrders` next; it will select an overdue order and cancel it:

❑   Run `BeginManufacture` next; it will use a stateful session bean to select an appropriate order for manufacture and serialize a handle to that bean. (The handle will be stored in `c:/current_product.ser`. If this is not an appropriate name on your computer you should change it in `BeginManufacture.java` and `CompleteManufacture.java`.)

❑   Finally, run `CompleteManufacture`; it will deserialize the handle, print out the instructions for manufacture, and ship the product. (Note that in this case, the only reason we've broken up the manufacturing process into two sample applications is to demonstrate how to serialize the handle.)

In Chapter 22, we will provide a more flexible web interface to these EJBs.

Summary

In this chapter we discussed entity beans in depth. The main points were:

- Entity beans represent the shared, transactional data in your application

- The persistence of entity beans can be managed by the bean programmer or by the container

- Container-managed persistence can boost productivity, but may not be capable enough for your needs

- Third party object/relational mapping tools may provide capable persistence services, but are proprietary and potentially expensive

- Bean-managed persistence forces the bean programmer to assume the burden of transferring state from the object to the data store

- Caching data within a transaction is supported by the container and data store

- Caching data between transactions may provide a boost in performance if your application and environment allow this

- Finder methods allow a client to locate shared object state corresponding to a particular identity or particular criteria

- Relationships can be managed by entity beans, but the exact mechanisms are not provided in the EJB-1.1 specification

- Reentrant entity beans are allowed, but can prevent the container from catching a particular class of error

In the next chapter, we examine four of the fundamental services that an EJB container can provide: declarative transactions, declarative security, support for remote communications, and an exception handling framework. Although every EJB container provides these services, you must have some understanding of each topic – and how it relates to EJB technology – to develop and deploy your EJB components effectively.

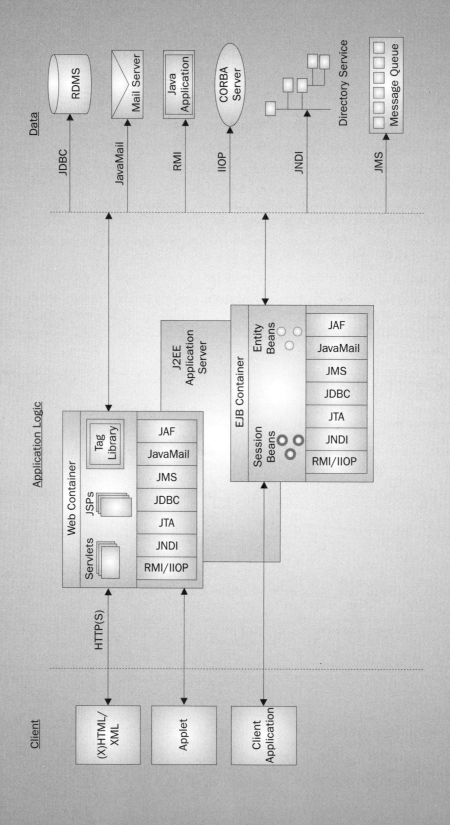

21

EJB Container Services

Although the intent of Enterprise JavaBeans technology is to free business logic programmers from having to develop system-level services, we must still understand how these services work in the context of EJB. Every significant enterprise application will need to provide support for transactions to protect the integrity of its data. Similarly, it will need to protect its resources against unauthorized access. It will need to provide support for remote access of its data and business logic and to handle exceptional conditions in a robust way.

Every EJB container provides support for transactions, security, communications, and exception handling. Although the implementation will differ between EJB containers, the EJB specification is written so that an enterprise bean may take advantage of these services in a portable manner. Programmers may write their business logic to take advantage of these container services without sacrificing the ability to run their beans in multiple containers.

For the most part, the EJB programmer will take advantage of these services without writing any Java code at all. One of the goals of the Enterprise JavaBeans specification is to allow us to simply declare our intent as to how services such as transactions and security should operate in a particular application, where possible. Another is to allow the application to be deployed to an arbitrary execution environment using only the tools provided by the application server vendor, with no additional programming required.

This is a more flexible approach than programming, and it is also easier, cheaper, and more robust.

> **The presence of declarative container services does not absolve the programmer, or the deployer, from understanding how transactions, security, communications, and exception handling work in the context of Enterprise JavaBeans technology.**

It will also require that the person or persons deploying the application understand the environment to which they are deploying: database, app server, security system, etc. This is less true of the application developer, who is insulated from the target deployment environment as much as possible.

You will notice that the emphasis of this chapter is to understand issues related to these often declarative or automatic services. This means that as you follow along in this chapter, you may be using your application server's deployment tools, rather than your code editor. Some of the examples that are code oriented demonstrate techniques that are for special cases (such as access to the security principal) or that I discourage in general (such as use of the `UserTransaction` interface). This is how it should be: Enterprise JavaBeans technology seeks to take system level services out of the user's code.

Just because the emphasis is on declarative techniques doesn't mean that you should read this chapter like a novel. You will want to see how each of these topics applies to your chosen application server and EJB container, so:

❑   Take the code samples from the last few chapters and configure the transactional attributes and security framework using the deployment tools that your vendor provides

❑   Look at your vendor's documentation regarding the communication services that it provides

❑   Examine the logging that your EJB container does when a system exception is thrown

❑   Take a look at the vendor-specific XML files that your container probably generates

The Enterprise JavaBeans technology attempts to separate system level concerns from the domain of the business logic programmer, and also to provide portability between different environments. As a result, it is bound to make significant demands on the person who needs to configure an EJB application to fit a particular environment. This chapter's goal is to help you understand the basic services that the EJB container provides, so that you can make intelligent decisions during application development, and equally important, during application deployment.

Because application servers and EJB containers vary so much, you must also read the documentation that comes with your chosen tools. This is really unavoidable, because of the numerous target environments for EJB technology, the sweeping aims, and the variety of implementations. The information in this chapter will apply to every EJB container, and will help you to understand the options with which you will be presented.

The topics we will cover are as follows:

❑   Transactions: A comparison of traditional programmatic transaction support and declarative transaction support. We will also look at specific declarative transaction situations and the existing options.

❑   Security: We will discuss Enterprise level security considerations and where Roles and Permissions come in. We will also look at situations where programmatic access control is necessary.

❑   Exception handling: We will examine our responsibility with regards to exceptions, both system and application related, the consequences of these and the resulting action by the containers in which our code resides.

❑   Communication between heterogeneous application servers.

Transactions

A transaction is a set of operations that must be processed as a single unit. To be considered transactional, the set of operations comprising this single unit of work must exhibit certain well-defined characteristics, often referred to by their mnemonic acronym A.C.I.D. This stands for **atomic, consistent, isolated**, and **durable**. It is quite easy to see the reason that these A.C.I.D. properties are desirable for your software in many circumstances:

- ❏ **Atomic** means that the operations in the set must succeed or fail as a group. If you debit one account and credit the other in a transaction, you must never have the situation where the debit failed and the credit succeeded, or vice versa. Either both must succeed and the money will be transferred, or both must fail and the accounting system must have neither stolen money from the customer, nor given money away.

- ❏ **Consistent** means that the database must be left in a state that does not compromise the business logic, regardless of the success or failure of any transaction. As a result, the business logic programmer will not have to undo the effects of a failed transaction in their code. It also means that a database administrator won't need to clean up orphaned records or mismatched data from operations that fail to complete.

- ❏ **Isolated** means that the business logic can proceed without consideration for the other activities of the system. For instance, while an EJB is checking to make sure that there is enough money in the account before transferring it, another process may be withdrawing money from this account to satisfy an ATM withdrawal. If the two processes aren't kept isolated from each other's effects, it's possible that both the transfer and the withdrawal will both succeed – using the same money. Due to the isolation property of transactions, the business logic programmer doesn't need to defend against this situation.

- ❏ **Durable** means that once a transaction has succeeded (has been **committed**); the results will be reflected in the persistent data store. As a result, the business logic programmer will not need to worry about a subsequent error of some kind causing their data to become inconsistent.

A transaction has a discrete starting point. After that starting point, changes made through any resource that is enlisted (participating) in the transaction – such as a database connection – will have the A.C.I.D. properties I just described. The transaction will also have a discrete endpoint. At the endpoint, the transaction can commit (make all its changes permanent) or rollback (undo all the changes that it has made in this transaction). There are two key points. First, these changes are all or nothing. Second, changes that other transactions are making won't interfere with these changes (subject to the isolation policy, described below).

Transactions can simplify application development by freeing the business-logic programmer from writing code to deal with the system-level and complex issues of failure recovery and concurrent access from a multi-user system. An EJB container will provide support managing these transactions without the application programmer needing to implement this logic in Java code.

Of course, transactions come at a cost in performance and scalability. Ensuring that these A.C.I.D. properties are applied to a set of operations requires the coordination of the relevant resources (such as a database) and the application server. More importantly, it may require that accesses to data be serialized, rather than being allowed to occur simultaneously. Applications may want some of their operation to occur outside of the control of a transaction for these reasons.

Additionally, some resources do not support transactions managed by an external transaction coordinator. The EJB container cannot manage the transactions for beans that use such a resource. In such a case, the bean developer should use container-managed transactions and indicate that the bean's methods do not operate in a transaction.

The EJB programmer may choose between using a simple API to demarcate transaction boundaries, and providing information in the XML deployment descriptor to allow the container to manage the boundaries of the transaction. The first option is called **bean-managed transaction demarcation**, and the second **container-managed transaction demarcation**. Both options shield the programmer from the true complexity of the implementation of a transaction processing system, upholding the basic principle of deferring to the container where possible. It is much less likely that you will need to use bean-managed transactions than you would need to use, say, bean-managed persistence. I strongly recommend that you use the declarative semantics available with container-managed transactions.

> **Bean-managed transactions are only possible for session beans; entity beans must use container-managed transactions.**

The developer of a session bean must declare the type of transaction demarcation in the XML deployment descriptor. Typically, this information will be edited by a tool; however, it can also be edited by hand. Here are example entries declaring each type of transaction demarcation:

```
<transaction-type>Bean</transaction-type>
```

or:

```
<transaction-type>Container</transaction-type>
```

Transactions Without a Container

The EJB container takes responsibility for managing your transactions, but of course it's possible to have transactions without Enterprise JavaBeans. To help make the concept of a transaction clearer, let's look at transactions in a stand-alone Java program. We'll examine an account object that updates the database by a connection that is passed as a parameter. The `java.sql.Connection` class provides basic transaction management that we'll use in our simple example (but you are not allowed to use in an application server). We'll look at two clients: one that does not use transactions and one that does. We'll see how transactions are necessary for data integrity. The database table is defined with two integrity constraints, to provide a minimum and maximum value for an account:

```
CREATE TABLE ACCOUNT (ACCOUNTID VARCHAR(25) NOT NULL,
       CUSTOMERNAME VARCHAR(25),
     . AMOUNT DOUBLE PRECISION,
       PRIMARY KEY (ACCOUNTID),
       CHECK (AMOUNT > 0),
       CHECK (AMOUNT < 15000)
);
```

Here is the definition of the account object. It has getter and setter methods, and create, read, update, and delete lifecycle methods:

```java
import java.sql.Connection;
import java.sql.PreparedStatement;
import java.sql.ResultSet;
import java.sql.SQLException;

public class Account {
  private String accountID;
  private String customerName;
  private double amount;

  public String getAccountID() {
    return accountID;
  }

  public String getCustomerName() {
    return customerName;
  }

  public void setCustomerName(String customerName) {
    this.customerName = customerName;
  }

  public double getAmount() {
    return amount;
  }

  public void setAmount(double amount) {
    this.amount = amount;
  }

  public void create(String accountID, String customerName,
                     double amount,
                     Connection con) throws SQLException {
    this.accountID = accountID;
    this.customerName = customerName;
    this.amount = amount;

    PreparedStatement statement = null;

    try {
      statement =
        con
          .prepareStatement("INSERT INTO ACCOUNT (ACCOUNTID,"
                            + "CUSTOMERNAME, AMOUNT ) "
                            + "VALUES ( ?, ?, ? )");
      statement.setString(1, accountID);
      statement.setString(2, customerName);
      statement.setDouble(3, amount);

      statement.executeUpdate();
    }
```

```
      finally {
        if (statement != null) {
          statement.close();
        }
      }
    }

  public void read(String accountID, Connection con)
          throws SQLException, RecordNotFoundException {
    PreparedStatement statement = null;

    try {
      statement =
        con
          .prepareStatement("SELECT CUSTOMERNAME, AMOUNT FROM ACCOUNT"
                            + " WHERE ACCOUNTID = ?");
      statement.setString(1," accountID);

      ResultSet result = statement.executeQuery();
      if (result.next()) {
        this.accountID = accountID;
        this.customerName = result.getString(1);
        this.amount = result.getDouble(2);
      } else {
        throw new RecordNotFoundException();
      }
    }
    finally {
      if (statement != null) {
        statement.close();
      }
    }
  }

  public void update(Connection con) throws SQLException {
    PreparedStatement statement = null;

    try {
      statement =
        con
          .prepareStatement("UPDATE ACCOUNT SET CUSTOMERNAME=?,"
                            + "AMOUNT=? WHERE ACCOUNTID = ?");
      statement.setString(1, customerName);
      statement.setDouble(2, amount);
      statement.setString(3, accountID);

      statement.executeUpdate();
    }
    finally {
      if (statement != null) {
        statement.close();
      }
    }
  }
}
```

```
public void delete(Connection con) throws SQLException {
  PreparedStatement statement = null;

  try {
    statement =
      con
        .prepareStatement("DELETE FROM ACCOUNT WHERE ACCOUNTID = ?");
    statement.setString(1, accountID);

    statement.executeUpdate();
  }
  finally {
    if (statement != null) {
      statement.close();
    }
  }
}
}
```

Here is the exception class that this account class uses:

```
public class RecordNotFoundException extends Exception  {
  public RecordNotFoundException() {}
}
```

The client will create two accounts, and transfer money between them. With the first set of values, the transfer will go smoothly. But if you comment out the first set of values, uncomment the second set of values, and run the client again, a constraint will be violated during the transfer. Unfortunately, the first account has been debited, but the second account can't be credited as the resulting account balance will equal more than the maximum allowable value. When the client exits, the bank will have stolen money from the customer. Here is that client:

```
import java.sql.Connection;
import java.sql.DriverManager;

public class Client1 {
  private static final String ACCOUNT1 = "A32-116";
  private static final String NAME1 = "Lynne Older";
  private static final double AMOUNT1 = 10000.0;

  private static final String ACCOUNT2 = "A32-117";
  private static final String NAME2 = "Patricia Mahar";
  private static final double AMOUNT2 = 12000.0;

  private static final double TRANSFER_AMOUNT = 1000.0;

  /*
   * Mary has 14000 in her account, therefore a credit
   * of 2000 will fail to go through.
   * private static final String ACCOUNT1 = "B32-116";
   * private static final String NAME1 = "Christina Couglin";
   *  private static final double AMOUNT1 = 10000.0;
```

```
 * private static final String ACCOUNT2 = "B32-117";
 * private static final String NAME2 = "Mary Klopot";
 * private static final double AMOUNT2 = 14000.0;
 * private static final double TRANSFER_AMOUNT = 2000.0;
 */

static {
  try {
    Class.forName("COM.cloudscape.core.JDBCDriver");

  } catch (Exception e) {
    System.out.println(e);
  }
}

public static void main(String[] args) {
  createAccounts();
  transfer(ACCOUNT1, ACCOUNT2, TRANSFER_AMOUNT);
}

private static void createAccounts() {
  Connection con = null;

  try {
    con = DriverManager.getConnection(
        "jdbc:cloudscape:C:/ProJavaServer/Chapter21/tx");

    Account account1 = new Account();
    account1.create(ACCOUNT1, NAME1, AMOUNT1, con);

    Account account2 = new Account();
    account2.create(ACCOUNT2, NAME2, AMOUNT2, con);

    System.out.println("Accounts created.");
  } catch (Exception e) {
    e.printStackTrace();
  }
  finally {
    try {
      if (con != null) {
        con.close();
      }
    } catch (Exception e) {}
  }
}

private static void transfer(String accountIDFrom,
                             String accountIDTo, double amount) {
  Connection con = null;

  try {
    con = DriverManager.getConnection(
        "jdbc:cloudscape:C:/ProJavaServer/Chapter21/tx");
```

```
         Account accountFrom = new Account();
         accountFrom.read(accountIDFrom, con);

         Account accountTo = new Account();
         accountTo.read(accountIDTo, con);

         accountFrom.setAmount(accountFrom.getAmount() - amount);
         accountTo.setAmount(accountTo.getAmount() + amount);

         accountFrom.update(con);
         accountTo.update(con);

         System.out.println("Funds transferred.");

      } catch (Exception e) {
        e.printStackTrace();
      }
      finally {
        try {
          if (con != null) {
            con.close();
          }
        } catch (Exception e) {}
      }
    }
  }
```

The code permanently records changes at each stage until it encounters an exception, whether driven by the business logic or by the system. At this point it will fast forward to the end of the file printing out any error message and bypassing all other operations. In this case, in the first example it should be fine, however, in the second there will be a loss of data integrity.

Here is an improved version of the client that uses transactions. When the database constraint is violated and the client exits, the first account will not have been debited (i.e. the transaction will have been rolled back) and the bank's accounts will still balance:

```
import java.sql.Connection;
import java.sql.DriverManager;

public class Client2 {
  private static final String ACCOUNT1 = "A32-116";
  private static final String NAME1 = "Lynne Olden";
  private static final double AMOUNT1 = 10000.0;

  private static final String ACCOUNT2 = "A32-117";
  private static final String NAME2 = "Patricia Maher";
  private static final double AMOUNT2 = 14000.0;

  private static final double TRANSFER_AMOUNT = 2000.0;

  static {
    try {
      Class.forName("COM.cloudscape.core.JDBCDriver");
```

```
      } catch (Exception e) {
        System.out.println(e);
      }
  }

  public static void main(String[] args) {
    createAccounts();
    transfer(ACCOUNT1, ACCOUNT2, TRANSFER_AMOUNT);
  }

  private static void createAccounts() {
    Connection con = null;

    try {
      con = DriverManager.getConnection(
           "jdbc:cloudscape:C:/ProJavaServer/Chapter21/tx");

      Account account1 = new Account();
      account1.create(ACCOUNT1, NAME1, AMOUNT1, con);

      Account account2 = new Account();
      account2.create(ACCOUNT2, NAME2, AMOUNT2, con);

      System.out.println("Accounts created.");
    } catch (Exception e) {
      e.printStackTrace();
    }
    finally {
      try {
        if (con != null) {
          con.close();
        }
      } catch (Exception e) {}
    }
  }

  private static void transfer(String accountIDFrom,
                               String accountIDTo, double amount) {
    Connection con = null;

    try {
      con = DriverManager.getConnection(
           "jdbc:cloudscape:C:/ProJavaServer/Chapter21/tx");

      con.setAutoCommit(false);

      Account accountFrom = new Account();
      accountFrom.read(accountIDFrom, con);

      Account accountTo = new Account();
      accountTo.read(accountIDTo, con);

      accountFrom.setAmount(accountFrom.getAmount() - amount);
      accountTo.setAmount(accountTo.getAmount() + amount);
```

```
            accountFrom.update(con);
            accountTo.update(con);

            System.out.println("Funds transferred.");

            con.commit();

        } catch (Exception e) {
          try {
            con.rollback();
          } catch (Exception re) {}
          e.printStackTrace();
        }
        finally {
          try {
            if (con != null) {
              con.close();
            }
          } catch (Exception e) {}
        }
      }
    }
```

One value of allowing the EJB container to manage transactions for you is that you can develop components without worrying about when you should commit or rollback a transaction. In a sense, the EJB container acts as the client does in this example, by figuring out when the business logic begins and when it ends and managing transactions accordingly. (It does this by examining the transactional attributes of your EJB methods that you declare in the deployment descriptor. Before and after each business method, it ensures that any necessary transaction is started, committed, or rolled back.)

Of course, it's quite easy to add transaction management for this simple case. In a more complicated application, with many possible method sequences, application exceptions, and business object types, it's more difficult to keep all the balls in the air. Not impossible, but difficult.

That difficulty increases by orders of magnitude for a distributed transaction, i.e. when there is more than one database being updated. If the account to be debited and the account to be credited are in different databases, it's no longer possible for the application programmer to use the `java.sql.Connection` class's simple transactional capabilities. Instead, you must manage a complicated process known as a 'two-phase commit'. A two-phase commit involves a transaction manager polling resources about their ability to commit changes, and then telling them to go ahead if every enlisted resource votes to commit. The implementation of this process is very complicated and error prone; the details are beyond the scope of this book.

Your EJB container may manage this complexity for you (some do not). If it does not and you absolutely need this functionality, you must find a different application server as there is really no workaround. A distributed transaction also needs the cooperation of your JDBC drivers. A JDBC driver that participates in a distributed transaction must implement a special interface that the transaction manager will use to communicate with it during the transaction. This interface is an industry standard and is known as XA, the Java version of which is defined as part of the JDBC Optional Package. Before you use a JDBC driver in a distributed transaction, you must ensure that it supports the XA interface. A list of JDBC drivers that support distributed transactions is available on Sun's web site at `http://industry.java.sun.com/products/jdbc/drivers`.

Declarative Semantics for Transactions

The bean developer must declare how a particular method in an EJB with container-managed transactions works with those transactions, by specifying this in the XML deployment descriptor. The Enterprise JavaBeans specification provides six options: **NotSupported**, **Supports**, **RequiresNew**, **Required**, **Mandatory**, and **Never**.

The 'NotSupported' Transactional Attribute

The first option for a method's transactional attribute is **NotSupported**. When a method with a transaction attribute of NotSupported is called, it operates in an "unspecified transaction context". (A transaction context is simply the state that needs to be maintained so that the set of related operations can operate as a group.) The specification gives the EJB container wide latitude in how to access resources in the case of an unspecified transaction context. The possible ways that those resources may be accessed, as suggested (but not mandated) by the EJB 1.1 specification, are:

- ❑ The container may execute the method and access the underlying resource managers without a transaction context. ('Resource manager' is the generic term for any Java 'driver' class that interacts with an asset in the execution environment. For instance, a java.sql.Connection instance is a 'resource manager' for a database. Another example of a resource manager is a JMS connection.)

- ❑ The container may treat each call of an instance to a resource manager as a single transaction (e.g. the container may set the auto-commit option on a JDBC API connection).

- ❑ The container may merge multiple calls of an instance to a resource manager into a single transaction.

- ❑ The container may merge multiple calls of an instance to multiple resource managers into a single transaction.

- ❑ If an instance invokes methods on other enterprise beans, and the invoked methods are also designated to run with an unspecified transaction context, the Container may merge the resource manager calls from the multiple instances into a single transaction.

- ❑ Any combination of the above.

Whenever a business method is executed outside of an application-specified transaction, there is a danger that the resources accessed by that business method may become inconsistent. The variety of techniques that the EJB container can use in this case indicates even more strongly how much caution must be used, and how conservatively the bean developer must code.

If a method with an attribute of NotSupported is called by another method with a specified transactional context, the EJB container will suspend this transaction while the method with the NotSupported attribute is executed. No transaction context is ever passed to a client or a resource from a business method with the NotSupported attribute. However, once the method returns, any suspended transaction is restarted.

The 'Supports' Transactional Attribute

If a method with the transactional attribute **Supports** is called by a client with a valid transaction context, the container acts the same as if the transactional attribute were Required. If this method is called without an existing transaction context, the container acts the same as if the transactional attribute were NotSupported. In other words, the EJB component developer must be prepared for either situation: transactional or non-transactional execution.

The 'RequiresNew' Transactional Attribute

The **RequiresNew** transactional attribute specifies that if a method with this attribute is called with an existing transaction context, the container will suspend that transaction and start a new one. This new transaction will be used for any resource access or other business method calls from that method. However, once the method completes, any suspended transaction will be resumed. If the method is called without an existing transaction, a new one will also be created. The transaction will commit when the method returns and the EJB container has completed its 'housekeeping.'

The 'Required' Transactional Attribute

If a method's transactional attribute is **Required**, the EJB container will always invoke this method with a valid transaction context. If the method is called from a client (e.g. another bean) with an existing transaction context, that context will be used. If the method is called without an existing transaction context, the EJB container will create a new one automatically. In this case, the transaction will commit after the method returns and the EJB container has completed its 'housekeeping,' such as calling `ejbStore()`.

The 'Mandatory' Transactional Attribute

If a method with the **Mandatory** transactional attribute is called with an existing transaction context, the container will use that context. If a method with this attribute is called without a valid existing transaction context, the container throws an exception (`javax.transaction.TransactionRequiredException`).

The 'Never' Transactional Attribute

The final option for a method's transactional attribute is **Never**. If a client calls with an existing transaction context, the container throws an exception (`java.rmi.RemoteException`). The client must call without a transaction context, in which case the container behaves as in the case of `NotSupported`.

Specifying Transactional Attributes

The transactional attributes for a method are specified in the XML deployment descriptor. The deployment descriptor uses `<container-transaction>` elements to indicate which transaction attribute apply to the various methods. Each `<container-transaction>` element has two child elements: a method, and the transactional attribute. There are three legal ways to specify the method element.

The first way is to specify a default transaction attribute for all the methods in a particular bean. This default attribute would only apply if there were no more specific transaction attribute in the descriptor (by one of the next two methods). An example of this is:

```
<container-transaction>
  <method>
    <ejb-name>Product</ejb-name>
    <method-name>*</method-name>
  </method>
  <trans-attribute>Required</trans-attribute>
</container-transaction>
```

The `<ejb-name>` element refers to the name of one of the EJBs declared in that same deployment descriptor. The `*` in the `<method-name>` element is a 'wild-card' that indicates the transaction attribute should apply to all the methods.

The second way is to specify a transaction attribute for methods in a particular bean, for example:

```
<container-transaction>
  <method>
    <ejb-name>Product</ejb-name>
    <method-name>getName</method-name>
  </method>
  <trans-attribute>Supports</trans-attribute>
</container-transaction>
```

If there are methods with the same name but different parameter lists, and they require different transaction attributes, this third method can be used that specifies the parameters:

```
<container-transaction>
  <method>
    <ejb-name>Product</ejb-name>
    <method-name>getTaxes</method-name>
    <method-params>
      <method-param>java.lang.String</method-param>
      <method-param>int</method-param>
    </method-params>
  </method>
  <trans-attribute>Supports</trans-attribute>
</container-transaction>
```

To set the transaction attribute for a method with no parameters, use a `<method-params>` element with no child `<method-param>` element. If there is an array passed as a parameter, it can be specified by the array elements' type, followed by one or more pairs of square brackets.

Choosing Transaction Attributes

Which of the available transaction attributes should you use? This will depend on the requirements of your business methods for the ACID properties (atomicity, consistency, isolation, and durability). It will also depend on the support for transactions provided by your persistent resources.

❏   If you have a method that modifies data in a relational database, you will almost certainly want it to participate in a transaction. However, you probably wouldn't have any special circumstances that required a new transaction. The best attribute would probably be `Required`.

❏   If you had a business method that retrieved a single piece of data, you wouldn't necessarily have circumstances that required you to manage a transaction, and could leave the determination up to the EJB container. However, if this data access took place in the context of some other operation that modified data, you would want to have a consistent view of the database. The attribute that would allow both these things is `Supports`.

❏   If the resource that your enterprise bean accesses does not support management by an external transaction coordinator, you should use the attribute `NotSupported` for all the methods of the bean.

The remaining transaction attributes are more esoteric, but they give the container's declarative transaction service the ability to manage most situations.

An entity bean's persistence callback methods ejbLoad() and ejbStore() are called with the same transactional attributes as the business method that triggered the ejbLoad() or ejbStore(). This makes sense, because the transactional attributes of a business method primarily relate to the resources that the business method accesses, either directly (via SQL calls, for example) or indirectly, via the read and update logic of the bean or container associated with those callback methods. The ejbStore() method is also guaranteed to be called on the transaction's commit boundary.

However, the situation is more complicated in the cases where the business method is called without a transaction, which can happen with the transaction attributes of NotSupported, Never, or Supports. The EJB container's management of state caching works well only if the container can use transaction boundaries to drive the ejbLoad() and ejbStore() methods. There are only two guarantees that the specification makes about when these callback methods are called for a business method that operates outside of a transaction:

❑ The container calls ejbLoad() at least once between the time that the EJB is first associated with an object identity and the time that the business method is called. (Note that this association with an identity is marked by the ejbActivate() callback.)

❑ The container calls ejbStore() at least once between the time that the business method is called and the time that the EJB is disassociated with an object identity. (Note that this disassociation with an identity is marked by the ejbPassivate() callback.)

> **The guarantees given by the specification makes regarding when ejbLoad() and ejbStore() are called are not enough to support correct caching of state.**

In between the time that ejbLoad() is called and the business method executes, the data in the persistent data store could have changed, and the EJB could potentially be operating on stale data. Of course, if the EJB has exclusive access to the database, or if the data does not have absolute requirements for freshness, this problem can be mitigated.

The more serious problem is that in between the time the business method executes and the ejbStore() method is called by the container, something could have happened to the EJB that caused the cached data to disappear without ever having been written to the database. For instance, a subsequent business method could cause an error in the EJB that forced the application server to eject that bean instance from the container. It's even possible that the EJB container could crash. The client would assume that its data changes had been made successfully, because the business method that it had called had returned without error. But in reality, the underlying resources would never be updated.

The easiest solution to this problem of non-transactional data access is to avoid using ejbLoad() and ejbStore() to control the caching of state in the EJB. Typically, the business method should access the state of the underlying resource directly (such as via SQL statements), and the callback methods ejbLoad() and ejbStore() should be left empty. However, if your bean's methods are read-only and your bean has exclusive access to the database or does not need absolutely fresh data, you can probably cache state in a non-transactional bean as you normally would. In other words, you may implement ejbLoad(), but ejbStore() should still be a no-op.

To summarize, caching data with ejbLoad() is an appropriate solution if (1) you want to represent non-transactional data as an EJB entity; (2) you want to avoid repeated reads of this data; (3) you do not need to update the data; and (4) you are not concerned about cached data getting out of sync with the persistent store.

User-Controlled Transactions

It is possible for a session bean to control its own transaction demarcation, via the `javax.transaction.UserTransaction` interface. The `UserTransaction` interface is defined as follows:

```
public interface UserTransaction {
  public void begin() throws NotSupportedException, SystemException;

  public void commit()
          throws RollbackException, HeuristicMixedException,
                 HeuristicRollbackException, SecurityException,
                 IllegalStateException, SystemException;

  public int getStatus() throws SystemException;

  public void rollback()
          throws IllegalStateException, SecurityException,
                 SystemException;

  public void setRollbackOnly()
          throws IllegalStateException, SystemException;

  public void setTransactionTimeout(int timeOut)
          throws SystemException;
}
```

This interface was discussed in Chapter 3. Briefly, a client or session bean calls the `begin()` method to programmatically start a new transaction. This transaction can be completed successfully by calling `commit()`, or unsuccessfully by calling `rollback()`. Rather than simply rolling back a transaction, a business method can also mark the transaction so that the only possible outcome is a rollback. This would make sense if subsequent methods that should be part of this transaction might still be called. The `getStatus()` method can be used to determine if the transaction has been marked for rollback.

A compliant EJB container or J2EE application server is not required to make the `UserTransaction` interface available to all clients. It must make it available to session beans, servlets, and JSPs, and can optionally make it available to other types of clients – such as a stand-alone Java client – and remain compliant.

A client that wants to use this interface should retrieve it from the JNDI namespace. An appropriate implementation of the `UserTransaction` interface will be available under the name `java:comp/UserTransaction`. (Note that session beans can also use a legacy method of retrieving the `UserTransaction` interface – the `SessionContext`.)

To mark the start of a transaction, the client (a session bean, servlet, JSP, or other) calls the `begin()` method, and to mark the successful end of a transaction it calls `commit()`. Consider the case where a servlet wants to call business methods in two different beans as part of the same transaction. Assume the following session bean business methods:

```
public class SampleSessionA implements SessionBean {

  public void someBusinessMethod() {
    // some business logic
  }

  // ... callbacks, etc.
}
```

and:

```
public class SampleSessionB implements SessionBean {

  public void otherBusinessMethod() {
    // other business logic
  }

  // ... callbacks, etc.
}
```

Assuming a J2EE application server, the servlet might have code that looked something like this:

```
try {
  InitialContext initial = new InitialContext();

  UserTransaction userTransaction =
      (UserTransaction)initial.lookup("java:comp/UserTransaction");

  SampleSessionAHome homeA =
    (SampleSessionAHome)javax.rmi.PortableRemoteObject.narrow(
      initial.lookup("java:comp/env/ejb/SampleA"), SampleSessionAHome.class);

  SampleSessionA sampleSessionA = homeA.create();

  SampleSessionBHome homeB =
    (SampleSessionBHome)javax.rmi.PortableRemoteObject.narrow(
      initial.lookup("java:comp/env/ejb/SampleB"), SampleSessionBHome.class);

  SampleSessionB sampleSessionB = homeB.create();

  try {
    userTransaction.begin();

    sampleSessionA.someBusinessMethod();
    sampleSessionB.otherBusinessMethod();

    userTransaction.commit();

  } catch (Exception e) {
    userTransaction.rollback();
  }

} catch (Exception e) {
  //…
}
```

1045

One disadvantage of this approach is that the client is taking responsibility for managing the transaction, rather than leaving that to the EJB container. A second disadvantage is that changes to the transaction management strategy of the application must be made to Java code, rather than to an XML file by a tool.

Note that in the above example, the same effect could have been achieved by defining a new session bean method with a transaction attribute of `Required`. The servlet could call the new session bean method, and that new session bean method could then call `someBusinessMethod()` and `otherBusinessMethod()`. Then `UserTransaction` interface need not be used at all.

Isolation Levels

Keeping one transaction isolated from the effects of other transactions against the same data can be an expensive operation. For many situations, less-than-perfect isolation is acceptable in terms of the business logic, and may yield a significant increase in performance and a decrease in the potential for deadlocks between conflicting transactions. Most multi-user databases offer some support for making trade-offs in isolation *versus* performance, and JDBC provides a standard interface to control this functionality.

The Enterprise JavaBeans specification is not relational-database specific, however; it attempts to be a general-purpose technology that is useful for accessing many different resources, such as ERP systems, sales management systems, object databases, relational databases, and more. APIs for managing isolation levels are resource specific, and so the EJB architecture does not define a general API for managing the isolation level of transactions. Regardless, such management may be important for a large-scale production system, or for a system with very strict data-correctness requirements.

EJBs that manage their own access to resources, such as session beans or entity beans with bean-managed persistence, can specify the isolation level of those resources programmatically. JDBC provides two methods in the `java.sql.Connection` interface to set and get the isolation level:

```
void setTransactionIsolation(int level) throws SQLException;
int getTransactionIsolation() throws SQLException;
```

It is likely that an EJB developer will know the target database or databases and be able to determine an appropriate isolation level by consulting the documentation for that database. However, it is also possible to programmatically discover whether or not a particular isolation level can be set for the data source referenced by a particular connection by calling the `getMetaData()` method of the `Connection` interface. This returns an object that implements the `DatabaseMetaData` interface. There are two relevant methods in this interface:

```
int getDefaultTransactionIsolation() throws SQLException;
boolean supportsTransactionIsolationLevel(int level) throws SQLException;
```

The first returns the default isolation level that the resource uses within a transaction, and the second indicates if the resource supports an isolation level with particular characteristics.

EJBs that depend on the container to mediate access to their resources – or in other words, entity beans with container-managed persistence – do not manage isolation levels themselves. However, the EJB container may provide proprietary mechanisms to allow the deployer to adjust isolation levels when the application is deployed.

Regardless of whether the EJB or the container manages isolation levels, care must be taken that all accesses to a particular database or other resource within a single transaction use the same isolation level. In other words, bean A can't do a select using one isolation level after bean B has done an update in the same transaction using a different isolation level. (If an EJB accesses more than one resource within a transaction, each resource may use a different isolation level.)

> *Technically, the requirement to use a consistent isolation level for a particular resource within a transaction is mandated by the resource, not the Enterprise JavaBeans specification. Most resources require that all accesses within a transaction be done using the same isolation levels. An attempt to change the isolation level in the middle of a transaction may cause undesirable behavior, such as an implicit commit of the changes done up to that point. The* `java.sql.Connection` *interface specifically forbids changing an isolation level in the middle of a transaction. If this does not apply to a particular resource you are using, by all means take advantage of this if you can, and if the requirements of your application justify the additional complexity – which in my opinion is unlikely.*

A resource such as a database can define arbitrary degrees of isolation with which a transaction can operate. However, the `java.sql.Connection` interface operates with four predefined isolation levels (these are integer constants defined in the `Connection` class):

- ❑   TRANSACTION_READ_UNCOMMITTED

- ❑   TRANSACTION_READ_COMMITTED

- ❑   TRANSACTION_REPEATABLE_READ

- ❑   TRANSACTION_SERIALIZABLE

These constants refer to specific levels of transaction isolation that deal with three well-defined problems of increasing difficulty: 'dirty reads', 'non-repeatable reads', and 'phantom reads':

- ❑   A **dirty read** allows a row changed by one transaction to be read by another transaction before any changes in the row have been committed. Setting an isolation level that allows this much interference is pretty permissive, and while it may improve performance, it is often inappropriate from the standpoint of maintaining data integrity. Take an example of a simultaneous account balance transfer and ATM withdrawal. A user of our software tries to transfer funds from a savings account to a checking account. At the same time, the user's spouse tries to withdraw money from the ATM. Let's say that the transfer operation fails after it had incremented the checking account, so the operation will be undone by the database. However, if the current isolation level for the ATM withdrawal allows dirty reads, it may have read the uncommitted balance-transfer data and allowed the withdrawal to succeed – even if there were not really enough money in the account. Oops!

- ❑   A **non-repeatable read** is where one transaction reads a row, a second transaction alters or deletes the row, and the first transaction re-reads the row, getting different values the second time. Exactly how this is prevented depends on your database, and may influence your choice of isolation settings. It may be that updates to the relevant data are prevented by an isolation level that ensures repeatable reads, or it may be that updates to relevant data are hidden by this isolation level. Unfortunately, all I can tell you is to understand the database to which you are deploying, if this is relevant to your application.

- ❑   A **phantom read** is where one transaction reads all rows that satisfy a WHERE condition, a second transaction inserts a row that satisfies that WHERE condition, and the first transaction rereads for the same condition, retrieving the additional 'phantom' row in the second read.

Again, the exact influence that this isolation level has depends on how your database implements the isolation level, either by locking or by hiding changes (probably by making copies of the data). Once again, you must understand the database to which you are deploying.

Each isolation level prevents a different set of these problems. The most permissive isolation level, TRANSACTION_READ_UNCOMMITTED, actually prevents none of them. Caution should be used with this isolation level. It is appropriate in situations where absolute data integrity is a lower priority than performance. An example might be an e-commerce site that was providing recommendations to customers based on purchase patterns by other visitors to the site. It would be important to respond quickly, to avoid irritating or losing a customer, but it might not be important to have the exactly correct set of recommendations.

The isolation level TRANSACTION_READ_COMMITTED prevents dirty reads, but allows non-repeatable and phantom reads. Although any decision about isolation levels must take into account application data integrity requirements, the target database, and performance and scaling needs, a simple generic recommendation for many situations is to use this isolation level.

The isolation level TRANSACTION_REPEATABLE_READ prevents dirty reads and non-repeatable reads. Phantom reads are not prevented.

The isolation level TRANSACTION_SERIALIZABLE prevents dirty, non-repeatable and phantom reads. This is a very restrictive isolation level that is probably going to affect performance, but will guarantee correct results.

The table below summarizes the different isolation levels available through the JDBC API:

Isolation Level	Problems Prevented
TRANSACTION_READ_UNCOMMITTED	none
TRANSACTION_READ_COMMITTED	dirty read
TRANSACTION_REPEATABLE_READ	dirty read non-repeatable read
TRANSACTION_SERIALIZABLE	dirty read non-repeatable read phantom read

Long Transactions

Enterprise JavaBeans technology, along with the capabilities of a transactional resource, can ensure that your business logic operates with the advantages of a transaction. But maintaining a transaction is expensive, primarily because of the locking and/or copying that a data resource must do to ensure that the ACID qualities of a transaction apply. As a result, transactions should be kept short. That means that the data should be read, updated, and written in one logical operation.

Unfortunately, the reality of most applications is that the data will be read, presented to the user, edited, sent back to the server, and written to the database. In a perfect world with unlimited resources and no contention for data, this would all happen in one transaction. But the user may work on this data for an arbitrarily long period of time. Imagine a scenario where a user opens an application, begins editing some data, and leaves for a three-week vacation without committing their changes to the database. It is not usually appropriate to leave a transaction open through any user-interface action.

How would you even be able to leave a transaction open? Using container-managed transactions, it isn't possible. However, you can leave a transaction open across business method calls using the UserTransaction interface discussed earlier. For instance, during one business method, you could acquire the UserTransaction interface and begin the transaction. During a subsequent business method, you would reacquire the UserTransaction and automatically continue in that transaction. All further business methods on that session bean would occur in the same transaction until you called commit(). Note that this is possible only for stateful session beans. A stateless session bean must commit the transaction before the business method in which it was started returns. If it does not, the transaction is 'lost' and will never be committed. Eventually, it will time out. Here is how the code might look for a transaction that remained open between business methods:

```
class LongTransactionSessionBean implements SessionBean {
  public void method1() throws Exception {
    UserTransaction userTransaction =
      (UserTransaction) initial.lookup("java:comp/UserTransaction");
    userTransaction.begin();

    performBusinessLogic();
  }

  public void method2() throws Exception {
    performBusinessLogic2();
  }

  public void method3() throws Exception {
    performBusinessLogic3();

    UserTransaction userTransaction =
      (UserTransaction) initial.lookup("java:comp/UserTransaction");
    userTransaction.commit();
  }

  // ... callback methods, etc.
}
```

In general, don't take advantage of the ability to use a single transaction across multiple business method calls. Instead, you should use application-specific strategies that are more conservative of resources to achieve a similar effect to a transaction. The two main approaches are implementations of either **optimistic locking** or **pessimistic locking**.

Optimistic Locking

The optimistic locking strategy allows multiple clients to use the same data. However, when the data is sent back to the server in a business method call of an EJB, some checking is done to ensure that the state data of the EJB can be updated without conflict. For instance, the date of the last modification may be compared to what it was when the client first retrieved the data. If they match, the update is allowed to proceed. If they do not, the client is notified that it must refresh the data and redo the modifications. A possible way to implement this strategy is to add a last-modified timestamp field to the database.

Pessimistic Locking

The optimistic strategy is the most scalable, because multiple clients can read the data without interfering with an individual client that wants to update. However, if an update involves a lot of work, it may be

1049

inappropriate to tell a second client that it must discard this work because someone else was making a modification. In this case, a pessimistic locking approach can be used. A client that wants to make modifications must 'check out' the right to modify the data. While this token is checked out, no other client can modify the data. If another client has checked out the right to modify the data, an exception is thrown. A possible way to implement this strategy is to add a time-checked-out field to the database. If this field is null, the check out can succeed, whereas if the field has a checked-out time within a certain timeout period, the check-out fails. The period is adjustable, based on how long a client can keep the data checked-out before the lock expires.

Two-Phase Commit

As discussed earlier in this chapter and in Chapter 3, a two-phase commit is a protocol that allows multiple transaction managers to participate in a single transaction. There are two scenarios where this will occur:

❑ Application logic accesses multiple resources (such as two databases) within a single transaction

❑ Enterprise JavaBeans in multiple application servers participate in the same transaction

Either of these scenarios is quite likely in an enterprise with heterogeneous transactional computer systems. It's easy to imagine an application that needs to update a sales database and a manufacturing database being maintained on two different machines. It's also easy to imagine two application servers being run in different departments, with the need to use common business logic.

A business logic programmer does not need to write special code to handle a scenario where a two-phase commit will occur: the burden of implementing transaction management is placed by the EJB specification on the EJB container and application server. However, because not all JDBC drivers and application servers support two-phase commits, the application architect needs to be aware of situations where this can occur, and the limitations of the technology.

As of May 20, 2000, there were fifteen JDBC drivers with support for distributed transactions either announced or implemented. To support two-phase commits, a driver needs to support the JDBC 2.0 Optional Package APIs – specifically, the XA support.

The EJB container/application server also needs to have support for distributed transactions, in the form of a transaction manager that can manage two-phase commits. Support for this was not present in any of the major commercial servers at the time of this writing, but it should appear as more JDBC 2.0 drivers appear.

Security

Most enterprises have a requirement to protect their data and processes from improper access, both from within the enterprise and without. Protecting data and processes requires the following four services:

❑ **Identification**
Every user of a secure system must be mapped onto an identifier. In Java security APIs, this identifier is known as a **principal**. An identifier is often expressed to the user as a 'user ID' during a log in process.

❑ **Authentication**
When a user claims that they have a particular identity, they must be able to present credentials to prove it. Frequently, these credentials will be in the form of a password. However, there are numerous other possibilities for credentials, such as a swipe card, retinal scan, fingerprint, or digital certificate stored on the users computer.

❑ **Access control**
Every secure system must limit access to particular users. When a user attempts to access a resource, such as a database, an application, or even a particular function, a security service must validate the right of that user to that resource. The most common way to enforce access control is by maintaining lists of users with the privilege to access particular resources (known as Access Control Lists).

❑ **Data confidentiality**
This is actually a type of access control, but is different enough in practice that it deserves its own category. Confidentiality of data is maintained by encryption of some sort. It doesn't do any good to protect your data by enforcing authentication when a user logs onto a system, if others can read the password or other authentication information as it is transmitted across the network.

The Enterprise JavaBeans specification concerns itself exclusively with **access control**. Data confidentiality is outside its scope, although a common approach for secure communication is to use the secure sockets layer (SSL) protocol. Identification and authentication are also not currently part of the Enterprise JavaBeans specification. In fact, until recently, they weren't part of any Java API.

Java security is somewhat unusual, because at first its security concentrated on where code came from, rather than who was running it. For instance, code that ran off your hard drive typically has greater permission to perform various actions than code that came from the Web. This reflects its early use providing dynamic downloadable functionality in the form of applets.

As there hasn't been a standard Java method for determining who is running code, application servers must resort to authenticating a user through proprietary means. For instance, some require a client application to provide a user-name parameter and a password parameter in the JNDI initial context, before looking up a home interface of an EJB. Others forward to the EJB container the identity provided by an implementation of the secure sockets layer protocol. Any technique that the application server chooses to use is legal; this issue is not addressed by Enterprise JavaBeans technology in any way.

A new API, **Java Authentication and Authorization Service (JAAS)**, adds a standard for security, based on who is running the code, to supplement the security based on the code's origin. Part of this new API provides for pluggable authentication modules. A client using JAAS can be configured to use different login techniques, such as a simple user-name/password dialog or a smart card reader plugged into the computer's USB; a server using JAAS can be configured to authenticate the user's identity and credentials using different back-end security services. Any possible security technique could be used, as long as a pluggable module existed. It's likely that many application servers and application clients will standardize on this API in the future.

Authentication for a particular identity can be provided by a Netware server, an Oracle database, Windows NT, a Unix server, or a simple application-server-specific XML file. All that is required is that the vendor's application server support the method you choose. Once the application server validates the user's credentials against their claimed identity, it will map that identity onto a logical role that the EJB application developer or deployer defines.

> This mapping of a user's actual security identity onto a logical security role is the key to understanding Enterprise JavaBeans security.

You can develop your EJB application without consideration for the actual security systems, groups, identities, or credentials in use by your enterprise. When you determine the security requirements of your application, you are working in an ideal world, and you can specify security requirements at an abstract level. However, when the application is actually deployed into a container, the abstract security requirements must then be mapped onto real-world security identities in a manner specific to your application server and security implementation.

An application using EJBs can specify, in a standard, portable, and abstract way, who is allowed access to business methods. The EJB container is responsible for the following actions:

❑   Examining the identity of the caller of a business method

❑   Examine the EJB's deployment information to see if the identity is a member of a role that has been granted the right to call this business method

❑   Throw a `java.rmi.RemoteException` if the access is illegal

❑   Make the identity and role information available to the EJB for additional fine-grained security checks

❑   Optionally log any illegal accesses

Specifying the Security Requirements

There are only two types of information that the Enterprise JavaBeans developer needs to define in order to specify the security requirements for their application. They are **security roles** and **method permissions**.

Security Roles

A **security role** is the mechanism by which caller identities are mapped onto logical, abstract types that can be used in any security environment. The specification defines a security role as a "semantic grouping of permissions that a given type of users of the application must have in order to successfully use the application". In other words, similar types of activities – such as opening an account, closing an account, and increasing an account's overdraft allowance – may be grouped under a single name, such as 'Account Manager'.

The application server will provide deployment tools that map these abstract roles to users or groups of users that actually exist in the enterprise's security environment. For example, the `account_manager` role might be mapped to everyone who is a member of the NT security group 'Bank Manager'. In this example, whenever a member of the 'Bank Manager' group calls an EJB business method, they would have all the permissions available to the `account_manager` role.

The EJB-specific security roles are defined in the XML deployment descriptor. Each XML element to define a security role can have two child elements. The first, the name of the role, is mandatory, whereas the second, the role description, is optional. However, because it will be necessary at deployment time to map this role to groups or individuals in the runtime environment's security implementation, I highly recommend that you provide a description.

For example, here are some roles that might be defined in a banking application:

```
<security-role>
  <description>
    This role includes every bank employee who
    is allowed to access the banking application.
    An employee in this role may make deposits
    and withdrawals on behalf of a third party.
    They may also make read-only inquiries for
    any information in the account.
  </description>
  <role-name>teller</role-name>
</security-role>
<security-role>
  <description>
    This role is allowed to open and close accounts,
    and increase an accounts overdraft allowance.
  </description>
  <role-name>account_manager</role-name>
</security-role>
<security-role>
  <description>
    A user in this role is allowed to close
    existing accounts, withdraw and deposit
    money, and make inquiries about their
    own account only.
  </description>
  <role-name>customer</role-name>
</security-role>
<security-role>
  <description>
    To protect the integrity of the data, a
    user in this role is allowed read-only
    access to accounts only.
  </description>
  <role-name>executive</role-name>
</security-role>
```

Remember that these roles don't necessarily have the exact equivalent in the enterprise's security environment. When the application is deployed, some mapping between existing security identities (either users or groups in most security schemes) and these EJB security roles must be made. This is done in an application server-specific manner, and independently of the development of the EJB application. The application developer need only define the exact roles that are required to secure the business logic in a consistent and appropriate manner.

There is a many-to-many relationship between the EJB-specific roles that are defined in the deployment descriptor and the roles that exist in the target environment's security system. For instance, there might be three groups and two other individuals that need to be mapped to the 'executive' role defined in the above example: 'Bank Manager', 'Vice President', 'Assistant VP', 'John Q. Smith', and 'Katherine Heigl'.

Method Permissions

A **method permission** is the granting to a particular security role of the right to call a business method. Once a security role has been defined, the activities that are allowed to that role must also be defined. Consider our `account_manager` example. That role is intended to represent permission to perform activities such as opening and closing an account. But the 'opening an account' and 'closing an account' activities need to be mapped to specific business methods, such as `openAccount()` or `closeAccount()`. This mapping is done using entries, known as method permissions, in the XML deployment descriptor.

There is a many-to-many relationship between roles and business method permissions. A single role may have permission to use many methods, and a single method may be accessible to many roles. The mapping between roles and business methods in the deployment descriptor is done using method permission XML elements. Every method permission element has one or more security role references, and one or more EJB business method references. Additionally, a method permission element may include an optional description element.

The following diagram represents a possible mapping of security roles to business methods. These roles and methods will actually be implemented (along with others) in Chapter 22:

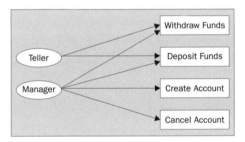

Business method references are specified for security using the same syntax as is used for transactions (see the section in this chapter on transactions for more information). You can specify that the roles in a particular method permission apply to all the methods in an EJB, just the methods with a particular name, or methods with a particular name and parameter list.

Here is an example of some method permissions that might be defined in our banking example. Notice that we only reference the logical roles that we have created in this same deployment descriptor, rather than actual entities in an actual security system implementation:

```xml
<method-permission>
  <role-name>teller</role-name>
  <role-name>account_manager</role-name>
  <method>
    <ejb-name>AccountManager</ejb-name>
    <method-name>findByPrimaryKey</method-name>
  </method>
  <method>
    <ejb-name>AccountManager</ejb-name>
    <method-name>deposit</method-name>
  </method>
  <method>
    <ejb-name>AccountManager</ejb-name>
    <method-name>withdraw</method-name>
```

```
        </method>
        <method>
          <ejb-name>AccountManager</ejb-name>
          <method-name>getAccountStatus</method-name>
        </method>
        <method>
          <ejb-name>AccountManager</ejb-name>
          <method-name>getRecentTransactions</method-name>
        </method>
      </method-permission>

      <method-permission>
        <role-name>account_manager</role-name>
        <method>
          <ejb-name>AccountManager</ejb-name>
          <method-name>create</method-name>
        </method>
        <method>
          <ejb-name>AccountManager</ejb-name>
          <method-name>closeAccount</method-name>
        </method>
        <method>
          <ejb-name>AccountManager</ejb-name>
          <method-name>extendOverdraftAllowance</method-name>
        </method>
      </method-permission>
```

The combination of roles plus method permissions establishes the basic security framework for an application that depends on Enterprise JavaBeans technology. This framework can be mapped into any arbitrary combination of real-world users, groups, and authentication techniques, without changing the application at all. The EJB container will enforce the method access rules that are declared in the deployment descriptor without any further intervention on the business logic programmer's part.

Programmatic Access Control

In some situations, the security policies of the application cannot be expressed using the method permissions in the deployment descriptor. Sometimes, whether or not an operation should be allowed depends on the data being manipulated, rather than on the operation being performed. For example, an account manager may be allowed to close the account of any individual, but not any corporation or governmental entity. Another case might be a division manager who can order raw material for their own division, but not for any other. The reality is that a large enterprise with significant operational and business logic requirements will probably need this kind of data-driven access control.

In other situations, the business logic may need to know the actual identity of the caller of a method, rather than simply the role that the caller plays in the enterprise. This might be necessary for auditing financial transactions, or for limiting database access to only those records associated with the caller.

For these cases, there is a simple API that allows the business logic programmer to provide fine-grained security control below the business method level. The `javax.ejb.EJBContext` interface, available as either the entity context or the session context, has the following two methods:

```
java.security.Principal getCallerPrincipal();
boolean isCallerInRole(String roleName);
```

getCallerPrincipal() is used to determine the actual identity of the caller of the method. The Principal() interface, which represents the underlying identity of that caller, is relatively opaque. Besides overloading equals(), toString(), and hashCode(), its only method is getName(). You should understand that the exact value of the Principal depends on the operational environment. If the underlying security mechanism were changed, the name returned from getName() on the Principal might also change.

Furthermore, it may be necessary for the EJB container to translate from one Principal to another before calling a business method. Although there is no API for a business logic programmer to control the value of a Principal, it is possible for an EJB 1.1-compliant container to provide proprietary tools to set up such translations at runtime. An EJB 2.0 compliant container provides a deployment descriptor element (<run-as-specified-identity>) that can also be used in simple cases. (For more information about EJB 2.0, see chapter 22.) This might be necessary in a diverse enterprise environment with multiple authentication systems. For instance, a telecommuter may be identified by a user and a password on the company's web site that would then be mapped to an identity in an Oracle database or an NT domain, before the application server could be accessed.

It is possible to use the Principal returned from getCallerPrincipal() to provide additional access control to business logic. As a rule, this is a bad idea. By examining the Principal directly in your code, you may be creating a dependency on a particular security implementation. Probably the most justifiable version of this is making sure that a particular user only alters their own information. If the underlying security system changed, only the database keys for individuals' records would need to change. The worst case scenario would be hard-coded values in the business logic like this:

```
if (principal.getName() == "SMITH_076") {
  // ...
}
```

The isCallerInRole() method is the best way to determine if the caller of a particular method has access to functionality based on the data they are trying to read or modify. You can use this method without introducing any dependencies whatsoever on the underlying security implementation. It works by programmatically applying additional screening criteria after the EJB container has allowed the function to be invoked.

Consider the case where an account manager or an executive can close an individual's account, but only an executive can close the account of a corporation. In the deployment descriptor, both would be given access to the closeAccount() method of the AccountManager bean, regardless of the type of account. There is no way to indicate to the EJB container that the closeAccount() method should be available to both roles for an individual, but only one of those roles for a corporation. However, in the business logic of the EJB, the programmer can write code that will check the type of account, and ensure that anyone trying to close a corporate account is authorized to do so. This is not complicated. The code would probably look something like this:

```
public class AccountManager implements SessionBean {
  private static final String CORPORATE_ACCOUNT_MANAGER =
    "corporate_account_manager";

  public void closeAccount(int customerNumber, int accountNumber) {
```

```
    Customer customer = getCustomer(customerNumber);
    if (customer.getType() == CustomerTypes.CORPORATE) {
      if (!isCallerInRole(CORPORATE_ACCOUNT_MANAGER)) {
        throw new java.lang.SecurityException(
          "Not authorized to close this account");
      }
    }
    CustomerAccount account = getCustomerAccount(accountNumber);
    account.close();
  }

  // ...

}
```

The application programmer may design an application to throw any exception in the event of an illegal access. One possibility is throwing `java.lang.SecurityException`, derived from `RuntimeException`. That means that any executing transaction will be rolled back, the instance will be discarded (probably overkill in this case), and the exception will be logged by the container. Some EJB containers can be configured to notify the system administrator when certain system exceptions, such as `SecurityException`, are thrown. If someone is trying to access the system inappropriately, it makes sense that the system administrator be notified immediately.

Just as we must declare the resources (such as database connections) and other EJBs that we reference in our code, we must also declare the roles that we reference in our code. The declaration of a role used in code is made in the deployment descriptor information relevant to that EJB. That role is then linked to a role defined as a `<security-role>` element in the deployment descriptor. This extra level of indirection allows the declarative security framework to change, without changing the code. Note that in the above sample code, we checked to see if the caller was in the role of `corporate_account_manager`, but this is not one of the roles which we have been using (`teller`, `account_manager`, `customer`, or `executive`). Our current policy is that only an executive may close a corporate account, so we would use the level of indirection in the security reference declaration to link `corporate_account_manager` to the `executive` role. The deployment descriptor information would probably look like this:

```
<security-role-ref>
  <description>
    The corporate account manager role is
    authorized to open, close, and change
    the terms and conditions of a corporate
    account.
  </description>
  <role-name>corporate_account_manager</role-name>
  <role-link>executive</role-link>
</security-role-ref>
```

Note that the `role-link` element must be used even if the `role-name` is the same as the `security-role` element that was declared as part of the application's security framework.

Security and Application Design

As a rule, it's bad application design to enable user interface access to functionality that will be disallowed by the business logic. If an account manager logs into our system and opens up a record of a corporate customer, the Open Account, Close Account, and Change Terms of Account menu items should be inaccessible or disabled. On the other hand, if an executive logs into our system and opens up that same record, the menu items should be accessible and enabled.

This is a book on server-side Java programming, so you may wonder why I'm mentioning this client-side design issue. Actually, this user-interface issue is a *server-side* Java programming issue as well, and not just if the user interface is a browser application using JSP. The problem is that deciding when to enable and disable user-interface access to a particular function requires business logic. For example, we may decide that a manager can close a corporate account if the corporation does less than $50,000/year banking with our bank; otherwise, only an executive can close the account. This is a business rule, and business logic is rightly the province of the server.

Consider the problem if we have distributed a Java Swing GUI to our 5,000 bank branches, and have hard-coded the menu items to be enabled or disabled based on the previously stated business rule. Now what happens if our policy changes, and a corporate account can only be closed by a manager if the corporation does less than $250,000/year banking with our bank? We need to reinstall all our client applications, perhaps at great trouble and expense.

If business logic in the application is limited to the server tiers, it can be changed quickly and easily. One possible solution is for the user interface code to query the server about the actions that are appropriate. The session bean that implements the analysis model's interface object for the application could have methods such as:

```
public boolean canOpenAccount(int customerNumber)
public boolean canCloseAccount(int customerNumber)
public boolean canChangeTerms(int customerNumber)
```

However, all these remote method calls would result in a lot of network traffic and sluggish performance. It's probably better to have a method that gets all the information at once, as long as some latency in the user interface is acceptable:

```
HashMap getCapabilities(int customerNumber, List whichActivities)
```

The business logic for the getCapabilities() method could combine the isCallerInRole() method with the customer data to determine a boolean value for each operation added to the query list of activities.

Exceptions

Although designing an application error-handling strategy is the responsibility of the business logic programmer, the EJB container provides a certain amount of support for the task. Specifically, there are two primary goals of the Enterprise JavaBeans specification regarding exception handling:

❑   An **application exception** thrown by the EJB or related code should be handled by business logic

❑   An **unexpected exception** or **system exception** thrown by the EJB or related code should be handled by the EJB container

Typical handling for an exception is a call to commit() or rollback() the relevant transaction. In addition, resources specific to that bean instance need to be kept consistent. The business logic is responsible for resource consistency with application exceptions, and the container is responsible for unexpected exceptions.

Application Exceptions

An application exception is any exception that is declared in the throws clause of a method in the home or remote interface of an EJB, except for java.rmi.RemoteException. An application exception must not be derived from java.lang.RuntimeException or java.rmi.RemoteException, because these are defined as system exceptions and will be treated differently by the EJB container. It can be derived from java.lang.Exception, or from other exception classes in an exception-handling hierarchy. Exactly how exceptions are used in an application is left to the architects of that application. There are, however, several application exceptions predefined in the Enterprise JavaBeans specification related to various container callbacks: CreateException, DuplicateKeyException, FinderException, ObjectNotFoundException, and RemoveException. These exceptions were mentioned in the previous two chapters, and are summarized at the end of this section.

To ensure that an application exception can be handled by EJB or client code, the Enterprise JavaBeans specification requires that an application exception thrown by an EJB instance should be reported to the client precisely. In other words, the client gets exactly the same exception that the EJB threw. This may seem obvious; what other exception might it get? However, we will see that this rule does not hold for unexpected (non-application) exceptions. Remember that there is an interposition layer between the client and the EJB, and the EJB's code is never called directly. So it is possible for the EJB container to arbitrarily transform exceptions from one type to another. The specification makes this option illegal.

> *Note that this means that any application exception declared in the EJB implementation class must also be declared in the bean's remote interface. The reverse, however, is not true. Just because a bean's remote interface declares that it throws an exception does not mean that the implementation class must do likewise.*

An application exception thrown from a method participating in a transaction does not necessarily roll that transaction back. Again, this is to give the caller's business logic a chance to take steps to recover. If the developer of the code that throws the exception knows that recovery is impossible, they can mark the transaction so that it is rolled back.

Let's consider a concrete example. Take the case of a customer session bean that calls a debitAccount() method of another session bean in one transaction. Assume that the debit method throws an application exception called InsufficientFundsException if the account does not have enough money to cover the debit. Due to the rules of the Java programming language, the method must either catch the exception or declare that it throws it. Either might be appropriate, depending on the requirements of the application. Let's first consider the case where the application might want to try to recover from the exception, by attempting a smaller debit:

```
private double attemptDebit(double amount, String customer) {
  AccountManager accountManager = getAccountManagerBean();
  try {
    accountManager.debitFunds( amount, customer );
  } catch (InsufficientFundsException insufficient) {
    try {
      amount /= 2;
      accountManager.debitFunds(amount, customer);
```

```
      } catch (Exception e) {
        throw new EJBException(e);
      }
    } catch (RemoteException re) {
      throw new EJBException(re);
    }
    return amount;
  }
```

If an `InsufficientFundsException` is thrown by the `AccountManager` business method `debitFunds()`, we try a second debit at half the original amount. This new attempt may succeed, if there are sufficient funds in the account to cover the new request. The business logic in this method is not realistic, but it's easy to extrapolate to a real situation. Note the results: an exception was thrown, but the business logic handled the recovery. Assuming that sufficient funds existed to cover the new debit amount, the transaction can commit successfully at the end of processing. (If sufficient funds don't exist to cover the new debit amount, an `EJBException` is thrown. This is a system exception, covered in the next section. I structured this example to show the full range of exception-handling options). In practice, a business method should usually rethrow the application exception if it can't recover, to give the calling function a chance to recover, as is demonstrated below.

Rather than attempt to recover from the exception in the business logic, the `attemptDebit()` method may be declare itself as throwing the `InsufficientFundsException` exception. The method would look like this:

```
private double attemptDebit(double amount, String customer)
        throws InsufficientFundsException
{
  AccountManager accountManager = getAccountManagerBean();

  try {
    accountManager.debitFunds(amount, customer);
  } catch (RemoteException re) {
    throw new EJBException(re);
  }
  return amount;
}
```

If the `amount` parameter is greater than the funds available, the `AccountManager` bean will throw the `InsufficientFundsException`. Rather than catching it, the `attemptDebit()` method declares in its signature that it throws that exception.

If this `attemptDebit()` method were called in the context of an existing transaction, it is the caller's responsibility to either recover from the exception or rethrow it. This is the same situation we saw with `debitFunds()` in the previous version of `attemptDebit()`. We could choose to attempt to recover from the exception or pass it up the call chain.

If the container started a new transaction directly before calling `attemptDebit()`, that transaction should complete when `attemptDebit()` returns. At this point, any necessary `ejbStore()` methods would be called and the changes would be committed to the persistent store. What happens in this case, when an exception is thrown by the business method for which the transaction was started? The EJB container will still attempt to commit all the changes to the database, and of course, the client will get the exception that was thrown.

This may be a little unintuitive, but it is an important point to understand. Even if you throw an application exception that isn't caught before being passed on to the client, the EJB container will still try to commit your transaction.

> **Throwing an exception does not equate to rolling back all your changes.**

It may be that under certain circumstances, the debitFunds() method has made changes to the database that make it mandatory for the transaction to be rolled back. In other words, it does not want the attemptDebit() business method or any other caller to be able to complete successfully.

Using the EJBContext interface (through either the SessionContext or EntityContext sub-interface), the bean throwing the application exception can mark the transaction for rollback, through the setRollbackOnly() method. The client code that catches the exception can determine if the transaction has been marked for rollback by calling the EJBContext method getRollbackOnly(). (There are equivalent methods in the UserTransaction for beans with bean-managed transactions: getStatus() and setRollbackOnly().)

Let's imagine that before we attempt to debit the funds, we may impose a fee on the customer for account usage. We need to do this first, because if the fee is going to be imposed, there needs to be enough money in the account for both the debit and the fee. However, if the debit fails, we need to make sure that the transaction up to that point isn't committed, or else we'll be charging the fee for activity that never occurred. The business logic for the debitFunds() method might look like this:

```
public class AccountManagerEJB implements SessionBean {
  public SessionContext ctx;

  public void debitFunds(double amount, String customer)
        throws InsufficientFundsException {
    try {
      BankCustomer bankCustomer = getBankCustomer(customer);
      bankCustomer.imposeFeeForActivity();
      bankCustomer.withdrawFunds();
    } catch (InsufficientFundsException ife) {
      ctx.setRollbackOnly();
      throw ife;
    } catch (RemoteException e) {
      throw new EJBException(e);
    }
  }

  public void setSessionContext(SessionContext ctx) {
    this.ctx = ctx;
  }

  // ...

}
```

Even if the `InsufficientFundsException` is caught by a business method higher up on the call chain and an attempt at recovery is made, the transaction will never commit once `setRollbackOnly()` is called. As a result, the fee for activity in this example will never be applied, even though we've already called the `imposeFeeForActivity()` method. Of course, this makes any further processing in this transaction futile. If it is possible that a business method that throws an application exception may have marked a transaction for rollback, clients of that method (e.g. other EJBs) in that same transaction should check via `getRollbackOnly()` to see if this is the case, before continuing with processing.

Predefined Application Exceptions

There are five predefined application exceptions used in Enterprise JavaBeans technology:

❑ A `CreateException` or any subclass indicates that an application-level exception occurred during a `create()` operation on a home interface. This can be thrown by the EJB developer from `ejbCreate()` or (for entity beans) from `ejbPostCreate()`. In bean-managed persistence and container-managed persistence, the EJB can throw `CreateException` for beans. For an entity bean with container-managed persistence, or for a session bean, it may also be thrown by the container. A typical use for a `CreateException` might be if invalid parameters were supplied to the `create()` method. The usual rules for application exceptions apply to the `CreateException`: the transaction should be marked for rollback if data integrity is threatened, otherwise, client code should be given an opportunity to recover.

❑ The `DuplicateKeyException` is a subclass of the `CreateException`. It indicates that a data constraint such as a primary key or foreign key was violated. As the underlying database is typically protected from updates that violate a key constraint, there is usually no reason to mark the transaction for rollback.

❑ A `FinderException` or any subclass indicates that an application-level exception occurred during a `findXXX()` operation on a home interface. In the case of bean-managed persistence, this exception is thrown from the `ejbFindXXX()` methods of the implementation class. In the case of container-managed persistence, the exception will be thrown if necessary by the EJB container. As finder methods do not change any data, there is usually no reason to mark the transaction for rollback.

❑ The `ObjectNotFoundException` is a subclass of `FinderException`. It indicates that the entity requested by the find method does not exist. Note that finder methods that return a `Collection` or `Enumeration` should not use this exception, but should instead return an empty `Collection` or `Enumeration`. As finder methods do not change data, there is usually no reason to mark the transaction for rollback.

❑ The `RemoveException` indicates that an application-level exception occurred while trying to remove the bean. This can be thrown by the EJB developer from the `ejbRemove()` method, or by the container. The usual rules for application exceptions apply to the `CreateException`: the transaction should be marked for rollback if data integrity is threatened; otherwise, client code should be given an opportunity to recover.

System Exceptions

A system exception is one from which an application does not expect to recover. The EJB specification lists several examples of situations where this might be the case:

❑ Failure to obtain a database connection

- ❏ JNDI API exceptions
- ❏ Unexpected `RuntimeException` (such as a `NullPointerException`)
- ❏ JVM error
- ❏ Unexpected `RemoteException` from invocation of other EJBs

Although the business logic is free to have recovery code for any of these situations, it is quite likely that recovery is not possible. For instance, failing to obtain a database connection or getting an exception from the JNDI API most likely means that the application was misconfigured at deployment time. There is no portable way for an EJB to adjust its deployment in the EJB container, even if a strategy could be determined for a particular environment – which is unlikely anyway. Writing code to recover from an unexpected `RuntimeException` is often a wasteful approach, because such recovery code can almost always be translated into precondition checking. Rather than throwing a `NullPointerException`, catching it, and figuring out what went wrong, you could instead simply check the parameters to the business logic to ensure that they are not `null`. If you still get an unexpected exception, something is wrong with the code and recovery is not appropriate.

Whenever a system exception is thrown, the EJB container must log the exception. This is because a system exception often indicates a problem that requires the attention of a system administrator. For instance, the failure to acquire a database connection may be because of a configuration error with the EJB container, a licensing problem with the database, an authentication problem for the connection, etc. Only if the problem is recorded in some log can the system administrator deal with it effectively. Optionally, an application server can provide services such as e-mail or pager notification when certain system exceptions occur.

The EJB container provides two recovery services to help ensure that the application's state remains consistent in the face of a system exception:

Firstly, **the current transaction is rolled back**. This is different from an application exception, where the EJB container attempts to commit the transaction regardless of the exception handling. If a business method throws a system exception, no changes or database updates associated with that transaction are committed, regardless of client attempts at recovery.

The EJB container rolls back the current transaction when a system exception occurs so that the business logic programmer doesn't need to surround every single business method with error recovery code. In the case of an application exception, the bean developer can indicate whether or not a transaction should be rolled back by setting `setRollbackOnly()`. To have the same ability for a system exception, every single business method would have to catch any exception derived from `java.lang.Throwable` and determine in the `catch` block whether or not to mark the transaction for rollback. To make matters worse, there would not necessarily be enough semantic information in the exception to decide whether or not recovery is possible by another business method. Did that `NullPointerException` happen before or after the database was updated? There's no way to tell, without adding even more exception handling code.

The second recovery service that the container provides to help ensure that the application's state remains consistent in the face of a system exception is to **discard the EJB instance**. In other words, once a bean throws a system exception, no other business methods or callback methods will be called on that Java class instance.

The benefit of having the container discard the instance is that the business logic programmer does not need to ensure that the non-transactional state of that bean is consistent. For instance, imagine a stateless session bean that used a socket connection to do some work. Rather than create a new connection for every business method call, we instead might create a single reusable socket connection in each stateless session bean

1063

instance's `ejbCreate()` method. If an unexpected exception interrupted us in the middle of processing, that socket might be left with unread data from a previous request. If we were to reuse this instance for another business method call, that business method call might fail because the socket connection was out of sync. This is just an example; there are many ways in which the state of an EJB can become corrupted by an unexpected system exception. Since the EJB specification places great value on the virtues of reliability and stability, the safest course of action – discarding the instance – is made mandatory.

You may wonder what happens from the client's point of view after an instance is discarded. Can the client continue to use its remote reference to that bean? For an entity bean or a stateless session bean, the answer is yes. This behavior is mandated by the specification, and all compliant EJB containers will allow it. This is because for entity beans or stateless session beans, the container can simply delegate future calls to a different instance of the EJB. However, a stateful session bean whose business method throws a system exception will cease to exist from the client's point of view. Any subsequent invocations through the remote interface must result in a `java.rmi.NoSuchObjectException`. This can result in a significant amount of lost work, so a programmer using a stateful session bean should be particularly careful about the circumstances under which he or she will allow a system exception to be thrown.

You may also wonder what happens to the resources of the discarded bean, since the bean developer does not get a chance to call any cleanup code after a system exception is thrown. What happens to open sockets, database connections, and so on after a system exception is thrown? The EJB container should take responsibility and immediately close any resource that was obtained through a resource factory using the JNDI namespace. Unfortunately, the container probably cannot close any resources that you obtained using the JDK APIs, such as a TCP/IP connection. These resources will eventually be closed during the normal garbage collection process.

A user-defined system exception must be derived from `java.lang.RuntimeException` or `java.rmi.RemoteException`. Additionally, exceptions derived from `java.lang.Error` are considered system exceptions, although `java.lang.Error` is not intended for application programmer use. Programmers should follow three basic rules to determine which system exception to throw:

❑ If the EJB encounters an exception derived from `RuntimeException` or `Error`, it should just propagate that exception or error to the container. In other words, the business logic programmer shouldn't worry about catching these errors (unless they expect them and has a recovery strategy).

❑ If the EJB encounters a checked exception from which it cannot recover, it should wrap the original exception in the `javax.ejb.EJBException` class (by passing the original exception as a parameter to the constructor of `EJBException`). Since `EJBException` is derived from `RuntimeException`, it does not need to be declared in the `throws` clause of a business method. Remember that throwing `EJBException`, or any other class derived from `RuntimeException`, will cause the transaction to be rolled back and the bean instance to be garbage collected. If the EJB can recover by marking the transaction for rollback and throwing an application exception, this is the preferred strategy.

❑ If the EJB encounters any other error condition from which it cannot recover, it should simply throw an instance of `javax.ejb.EJBException`, which can wrap the original exception or error message.

Unlike application exceptions, a client does not receive a system exception as it was thrown by the EJB: the container translates every system exception into a `java.rmi.RemoteException` or a subclass. This greatly simplifies the error handling for the client. Rather than worrying about catching stray `IllegalArgumentExceptions` or `IndexOutOfBoundsExceptions` coming back from a call to the server, the client need only deal with one checked exception: `RemoteException`.

If the EJB that throws the exception is participating in a client's transaction, it will notify that client that further processing of that transaction is futile by throwing a subclass of `java.rmi.RemoteException` called `javax.transaction.TransactionRolledbackException`. If there is an unspecified transaction context, or if the container began the current transaction right before that business method was called, the container will throw a simple `RemoteException`.

To facilitate backwards compatibility with the 1.0 version of the Enterprise JavaBeans specification, an EJB may throw a `RemoteException` that will then be treated as a system exception. This is the only checked exception that is treated as a system exception. This practice is deprecated and you should therefore not do it. As a rule, never throw `RemoteException` from any method in your implementation class. That said there are currently no consequences if you do.

Communication

The Enterprise JavaBean specification enforces rules that are designed to support distributed access to EJB components. The most important rule is that the home and remote interfaces are defined as RMI interfaces. This makes it simple to use an implementation of RMI as a remote access protocol. Another rule is that method parameter and return types must be legal values for RMI/IIOP, which makes it possible to use an implementation of RMI over IIOP. A rule with a similar purpose is that casting of home and remote interfaces must use `javax.rmi.PortableRemoteObject.narrow()` for RMI/IIOP compatibility. Finally, to keep the programming model consistent with remote access, all parameters must be passed by value and not reference, even for method calls within the same virtual machine.

One of the more interesting features of the EJB 1.1 specification is that it does not mandate that RMI, or any other particular distributed communication interface or implementation, actually be used. One choice is to use the 'native' JRMP (Java Remote Method Protocol) version of RMI, although in the JDKs up to (and including) 1.3, this would impose limitations on the number of remote clients because of the way JRMP is implemented. Several EJB container vendors have implemented their own version of RMI. Other container vendors have chosen to use a version of RMI that runs over IIOP. There is actually no requirement, anywhere in the EJB 1.1 specification, that a compliant EJB container provide for distributed access at all. This is not as unlikely as it sounds; an EJB container might be designed for access exclusively by JSP and servlet containers that run in the same Java Virtual Machine.

> *The EJB 2.0 draft specification requires that vendors provide support for RMI/IIOP. This is to ensure that EJB containers can interoperate at a basic level. EJB container vendors may offer other protocols as well.*

Communication Between Heterogeneous Servers

Communication between heterogeneous application servers is more difficult to achieve than it might seem at first glance. The problem is that there is *state* associated with every method call, such as the transaction context and the security identity of the caller. How to move this state from the client EJB to the server EJB isn't defined in the Enterprise JavaBeans 1.1 specification or the RMI specification. This lack of runtime compatibility between EJB containers is considered a weakness of the current situation.

The EJB 1.1 specification warns that future specification versions might require support for RMI/IIOP. Here is the relevant passage:

> **The EJB 1.1 specification does not require container vendors to use RMI-IIOP. A later release of the J2EE platform is likely to require implementations of J2EE platforms to implement the RMI-IIOP protocol for EJB interoperability in heterogeneous server environments.**

The EJB 2.0 draft specification does specify RMI/IIOP and other CORBA protocols as the solution to the interoperability problem. However, the 2.0 specifications made transaction interoperability and certain aspects of security interoperability optional. In other words, the situation is still not completely resolved, although significant progress has been made.

*One of the advantages of the RMI/IIOP protocol is that it can provide access to EJBs from non-Java clients. An excellent example of the non-Java client access that RMI/IIOP can facilitate is the Client Access Services COM Bridge that was available in pre-release form at the time of this writing. This bridge lets developers create native MS-Windows clients that access EJBs directly. (COM is Microsoft's **Component Object Model**.) It provides a standard object model that serves as the basis for everything from Windows platform services such as drag and drop, to distributed communications, to transaction monitoring and load balancing. The bridge provides a set of COM objects that let Windows client applications establish a connection to an application server and find or create references to EJBs. The references to EJBs are themselves presented to the client as COM objects.*

There are four types of CORBA-EJB mappings implicit or explicit in the draft EJB 2.0 specification: distribution, naming, transactions, and security.

- ❑ The **distribution mapping** describes the CORBA IDL for the interfaces and classes. This mapping is implicit from the application programmer's point of view when a Java client is used.

- ❑ The **naming mapping** mandates that the OMG COSNaming service be used for publishing and resolving EJBHome objects. A typical Java client – including server-side Java components such as other EJBs, servlets, and JSPs – would still use the standard Java JNDI interfaces to access that COS NameService. The deployer of a client application would obtain the host address and port number of the server's COSNaming service and the COSNaming name of each referenced home interface, and configure the client container accordingly using application-server specific tools. The client programmer and EJB developer need do nothing to comply with the EJB-CORBA name mapping.

- ❑ The **transaction mapping** provides rules for an EJB runtime that wishes to use an implementation of the CORBA Object Transaction Service (OTS) version 1.1 for transaction support. Transaction propagation is defined completely in an OMG specification; the mapping only specifies the rules that allow transaction context propagation to occur for EJBs, based on the OTS. Transaction propagation between heterogeneous EJB containers is not mandatory in the EJB 2.0 draft specification. There are rules that EJB container vendors must follow if they choose not to provide transaction interoperability.

- ❑ The final mapping is the **security mapping**. Secure communications is provided through mandatory support for the Secure Sockets Layer protocol. Interoperable propagation of the caller's identity is provided through RMI/IIOP according to the CORBA standard Common Secure Interoperability version 2 (CSIv2). However, support for the propagation of authentication data between heterogeneous containers is not mandatory. Instead, it is possible to set up 'trust relationships' between EJB or web containers that make further authentication unnecessary.

The bottom line is that CORBA does not provide perfect interoperability between different ORB-based application servers yet, and of course does not provide any help for interoperability with an EJB 1.1 non-ORB-based application server. It is likely that future versions of the specification will attempt to more completely specify the CORBA/EJB mapping to allow complete interoperability between all EJB containers. However, the interoperability that will be available for compliant EJB 2.0 containers may be enough to meet your needs.

In-VM Method Calls

If a method call from one EJB to another takes place in a single Java virtual machine, there is no need to use all the 'machinery' of remote communication, such as the marshalling of parameters and context state for network transport. The specification does mandate that arguments to methods that are passed by value must be copied as if the method were called remotely, even if they are in the same JVM. This is to ensure consistency of behavior, regardless of how EJBs are deployed.

Copying these parameters can be expensive, however. Some EJB containers will make an optimization available for in-VM parameter passing. This may improve performance, and won't necessarily compromise portability if the programmer is careful. In such a case, you must ensure that you treat every parameter in every method as a value object. In other words, you must not use a parameter to pass information back to the caller (even accidentally).

The costs of distributed communication can affect the architecture of your application. It's common for a high-volume web site to distribute processing across multiple web servers. For an application that depends on Enterprise JavaBeans technology, one question is where to locate the EJB containers. Although a common impulse is to place them on their own dedicated machines, it may be better to co-locate them with the servlets and JSPs that are generating the dynamic web pages. This can mean the difference between an in-VM call and a remote call (which will have more overhead, even across a dedicated network connection).

Summary

In this chapter we have examined four specific services that an EJB container will provide: transactional support, security, exception handling, and communications. Although the intent of Enterprise JavaBeans technology is to free the business logic programmer from having to develop system-level services, we must still understand how these services work in the context of EJB.

❑ The complete isolation of a transaction will often be traded off for an increase in performance

❑ The behavior of business methods in a transaction can be controlled declaratively (the preferred method) or programmatically

❑ Security is an important requirement for most enterprise applications, comprising identification, authentication, access control, and data confidentiality. The EJB specification concerns itself with access control.

❑ Security is specified declaratively in the deployment descriptor, using security roles and method permissions

❑ Business logic code can access the identity of the caller of a business method, and can also determine if he or she participates in a particular role

❑ There are two types of exceptions: application exceptions and system exceptions

❑ The business logic programmer is responsible for recovery from application exceptions. The current transaction will attempt to commit despite an application exception, unless the transaction is set for rollback only.

❑ The EJB container is responsible for recovery from system exceptions. Any current transaction will be rolled back and the bean instance will be discarded.

❑ The EJB specification provides rules that are designed to facilitate remote communication

❑ The rules for communication between servers from different vendors are not adequately specified in this version of the EJB specification

In the next chapter, we will look at the development process for Enterprise JavaBeans. The EJB specifications (versions 1.1 and 2.0) define various roles that are played in producing and using an application based on EJB components. Understanding these roles will help you to understand the reasons behind the design decisions of EJB technology, and will assist you in your application development and use. We'll look at Sun's reference server as a baseline for examining these various roles, as we develop a simple banking application. We'll also add a web interface to our manufacturing application as a way of exploring the full J2EE application development process.

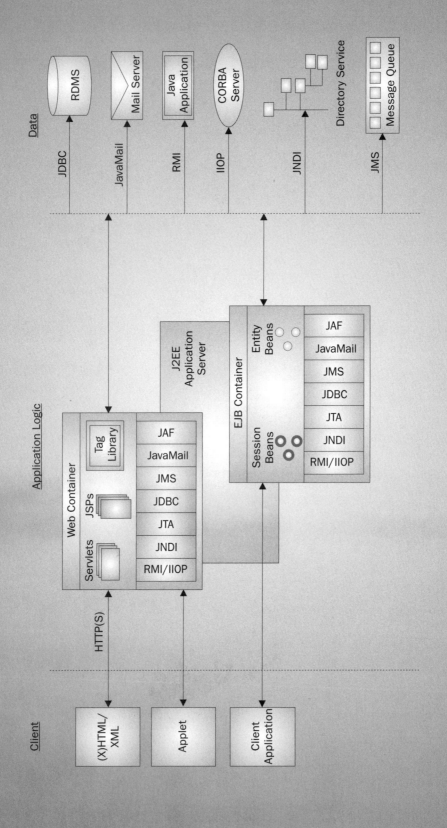

22

Development and Deployment Roles

The Enterprise JavaBeans 1.1 specification defines five distinct roles in the application development and deployment life cycle:

❑ Enterprise bean providers, who develop EJB components.

❑ Application assemblers, who combine the EJB components with other software, (for example, client programs or web components) to make a complete application.

❑ Deployers, who take the application and install it on an application server, resolving any resource references to existing resources in the target environment.

❑ Application server/EJB container vendors (which are sometimes separated into two roles in theory, but almost never in practice – with the exception of the open source container OpenEJB), who provide the application server on which the application is deployed.

❑ System administrators, who manage the application after it has been deployed into a target environment.

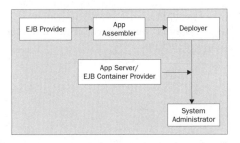

The Enterprise JavaBeans 2.0 specification adds an additional role, persistence manager provider. (For more information on EJB 2.0 and the persistence manager, see Chapter 23.)

These roles are not the product of a particular software engineering process or philosophy; instead, they are a natural outgrowth of the goals of Enterprise JavaBeans technology. Understanding the roles will help you understand the technology and how it can fit into your enterprise's software process, whether you have hundreds of people working on a project or just one. (These roles do not necessarily match up with people. For instance, the bean developer can be the same person as the application assembler and the application deployer.)

In the last chapter we occasionally referred to a hypothetical banking application to discuss services such as security, transactions, or exception handling. A point of emphasis in that chapter was that the developer of an EJB need not concern themselves with the actual implementation of these services, but could take advantage of them in a portable and consistent manner. One of the implications of this is that when the application is deployed, these services need to be configured for the target environment. In this chapter, we will be examining this banking application in terms of the division of labor among the various roles. We'll take the banking example and make it slightly less hypothetical. We'll look at two EJBs:

❑   An entity bean that represents an account

❑   A session bean that provides a façade to that entity

In order to provide a concrete example of the division of responsibilities provided for in the Enterprise JavaBeans specification, we'll need to use an actual application server. I've selected the reference implementation of the J2EE platform, provided by Sun and freely available for development, prototyping, and research from `http://java.sun.com/j2ee/j2sdkee/`.

The reference implementation's primary role is to supplement the various J2EE specifications (including the Enterprise JavaBeans specification) by providing a working model. It can be used by commercial and open source vendors to determine what their implementation must do under various circumstances. It can be used by developers to verify the portability of their application. It is also the standard platform for constructing the official J2EE compatibility tests.

A secondary role is to provide a compliant platform for J2EE technologies that developers can use without purchasing expensive commercial products. Not too long ago it may have been the best choice for the purposes of experimenting or prototyping. In Chapter 18, we discussed reasons why several currently available alternatives are probably better for these purposes. However, the reference implementation still is important as a reference point for J2EE application servers, and that is the capacity in which we will be using it as we explore the roles defined in the EJB specification.

The next five major sections of this chapter correspond to the five roles (bean provider, application assembler, deployer, system administrator, and application server provider). Each section has a description of the corresponding role. Along with this description, the account example and the reference implementation together provide a 'case study' by which we can examine a concrete example of the activities of that role. Please note that this material is not intended to replace the documentation that comes with the reference implementation.

The Enterprise Bean Provider

The Enterprise JavaBeans specification provides a component architecture. In other words, the data and business logic that comprise an application is organized into discrete units called components. It is the responsibility of the **enterprise bean provider** to provide the EJB components.

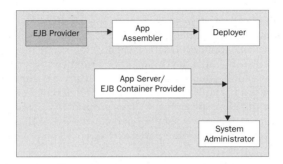

This role of enterprise bean provider is a personnel role, not a suggested job title. The 'provider' may be a single person; a team of people each having a separate role as analyst, programmer, or quality assurance specialist; or an outside vendor that you can treat as a black box. The important point to understand is that because EJBs are software components, they can be developed with minimal dependencies on other EJBs or other aspects of the application development process. The home and remote interfaces (and their documentation) should provide a sufficient contract to allow dependent parts of the application to be built.

The bean provider is typically an expert in the business logic that an enterprise requires. Someone with this skill set is often referred to as an 'application domain expert'. The EJBs they are developing are typically reusable components that implement workflow, process, or business entities.

The bean provider does not need to be an expert in system-level programming. They do not need to write code to support transactions, concurrency, security, communication, error handling beyond an application exception framework, load balancing, fail-over, or even persistence, if the services of the EJB container are used. They do not even need to understand the details of the target environment. The main requirement is that they can express business logic using Java code. You could make the argument that Enterprise JavaBeans technology exists only to enable the enterprise bean provider to write their business logic at this high level of abstraction.

There is a well-defined product that the enterprise bean provider produces – a JAR file containing:

❑   The bean's home interface

❑   The bean's remote interface

❑   The bean's implementation class and supporting classes

❑   In some cases, the bean's primary key class

❑   A partially-complete deployment descriptor

The structure of this JAR file has been discussed in previous chapters. To review, the classes are all placed in directories corresponding to their packages (which is standard procedure for Java JARs). The deployment descriptor is placed in a directory named META-INF, and must have the name ejb-jar.xml.

The first four items – home interface, remote interface, implementation classes, and primary key class – are not subject to change by the application assembler or deployer (and of course wouldn't be changed by the container vendor or the system administrator). The XML deployment descriptor, on the other hand, will be changed by the application assembler. (The responsibilities of the application assembler will be described in the next section.) Let's look at each of these products, in terms of their abstraction from the target environment for the enterprise bean provider.

Note that the tool you will use to build these items (with the possible exception of the deployment descriptor) is your development environment. This is important to note, because the focus will later switch to tools provided by your application server vendor. Of course it's possible that your application server vendor will provide an integrated development environment, or your development environment will have support for various application servers. The basic truth remains, however, that in every application using EJB there is a portable core (Java classes and deployment descriptor) and a proprietary mapping to a particular environment. (This proprietary mapping is ultimately just a set of instructions for how the application server should interact with your EJB. It is produced by the deployer and affects neither the code you write nor the portability of your component.)

The home and remote interfaces of the EJBs represent the business logic to the client (whether that client be a server-side component such as a servlet or JSP, or an actual component on the client tier). They are standard RMI interfaces that introduce no requirements for a communication method, database, security system, or application server.

Let's look at the remote and home interfaces in our example application, starting with the remote interface for the entity bean:

```
package wrox.some_isv;

import java.rmi.RemoteException;
import javax.ejb.*;

public interface Account extends EJBObject {
  void withdraw(double amount)
          throws InsufficientFundsException, RemoteException;

  void deposit(double amount) throws RemoteException;

  String getCustomerType() throws RemoteException;
}
```

Next, here's the home interface for the entity bean:

```
package wrox.some_isv;

import javax.ejb.*;
import java.rmi.RemoteException;

public interface AccountHome extends EJBHome {
  public Account create(int accountID, String customerName,
                        String customerType, double initialBalance)
                throws CreateException, RemoteException;

  public Account findByPrimaryKey(Integer accountID)
                throws FinderException, RemoteException;
}
```

The session bean's remote interface is as follows:

```
package wrox.some_isv;

import javax.ejb.*;
import java.rmi.RemoteException;

public interface AccountManager extends EJBObject {
  void createAccount(int accountID, String customerName,
                     String customerType, double initialBalance)
        throws NoAccountCreatedException, RemoteException;

  void withdraw(int accountID, double amount)
          throws InsufficientFundsException, NoSuchAccountException,
               RemoteException;

  void deposit(int accountID, double amount)
         throws NoSuchAccountException, RemoteException;

  public void cancel(int accountID) throws RemoteException;
}
```

The home interface for the session bean looks like this:

```
package wrox.some_isv;

import javax.ejb.*;
import java.rmi.RemoteException;

public interface AccountManagerHome extends EJBHome {
  AccountManager create() throws CreateException, RemoteException;
}
```

Finally, here are the exception classes we need:

```
package wrox.some_isv;

public class InsufficientFundsException extends Exception {
  public InsufficientFundsException() {}
}
```

```
package wrox.some_isv;

public class NoAccountCreatedException extends Exception
{

  public NoAccountCreatedException( String reason )
  {
    super( reason );
  }

  public String getReason()
  {
    return getMessage();
  }
}
```

```
package wrox.some_isv;

public class NoSuchAccountException extends Exception {
  public NoSuchAccountException() {}
}
```

For your component to be portable, it must avoid any dependencies on a particular implementation environment. It's easy to keep a simple interface separate from an implementation environment, so it's no surprise that the home and remote interfaces don't introduce any particular dependencies. The implementation classes provide a sterner test. There are all sorts of opportunities to create dependencies on a particular security implementation, a particular database, a particular set of requirements for transactional behavior, etc. The rules that the Enterprise JavaBeans specification imposes on the bean developer attempt to reduce these dependencies.

To understand how this works, let me provide a summary of Enterprise JavaBeans technology that removes all the details. The 'central idea' of EJB is to provide an abstract environment for business logic programming, free of concerns about system-level issues or the target environment. The most basic implementation strategy for the EJB container is to interpose on business method calls (that is, to wrap them in container code to handle security, transactions, data access, etc.). Now, the last piece of the puzzle: the fundamental relationship between the EJB developer/application assembler roles and the finished, running product is **indirection**. Indirection is the use of a 'placeholder' in your Java code or deployment descriptor, rather than a reference to an actual entity in the implementation environment. If you understand these three things – abstraction, interposition, and indirection – the details will fall into place.

This indirection happens at two levels: that of the EJB, and that of the application. To understand the difference, imagine that you have a banking account bean that uses the isCallerInRole() method to determine if the caller is using the permissions of an Automated Teller Machine. (We'll see an example of this shortly.) The bean may have a hard-coded role name of ATM, like in the following code:

```
if ((amount > 250)
        && account.getCustomerType().equals(CustomerTypes.INDIVIDUAL)
        && ctx.isCallerInRole("ATM")) {
   throw new SecurityException();
}
```

However, this hard-coded role name may not be consistent with the security framework of other EJBs in our application. We may have purchased this account management bean from an independent software vendor, and want to mix it with other EJBs we wrote or purchased from other sources. As a result, the specification provides a level of indirection at the EJB level; we map this role reference in the EJB to a security role defined in the deployment descriptor. If our security framework defines a role named UnmediatedAccess that refers to any access from the web or an ATM, the mapping might look like this (the complete text of both this EJB and the deployment descriptor follow shortly):

```
<security-role-ref>
  <description>
    This role refers to automated customer withdrawals
    from the account; no bank intermediary is involved.
  </description>
  <role-name>ATM</role-name>
  <role-link>UnmediatedAccess</role-link>
</security-role-ref>
```

If you are writing all your EJBs yourself, and combining them into an application for your own use, this constant indirection may seem unnecessary. You could just use the role-name UnmediatedAccess in your EJB and rid yourself of this bean-specific security-role-ref. However, this system is designed to maximize code portability and reuse of every enterprise bean.

There are three types of reference that an EJB provider may code and which must be declared in the bean-specific part of the deployment descriptor:

❑ References to other EJBs

❑ References to resources (such as a JDBC connection)

❑ References to security roles

Whenever you use any of these references in your code, you should think of them as 'virtual' references. You can develop your EJB without worrying about the details of what should be referenced (for example, the specific data-source mapping you must use, the security roles that will exist in the assembled application, or the final JNDI deployment name of a particular EJB). You must, however, supply in the deployment descriptor, either a security-role-ref, a resource-ref, or an ejb-ref. We have encountered all of these reference types in the preceding chapters. Whenever we developed a sample EJB that used a database connection, another EJB, or a security role, we declared that resource use in the deployment descriptor.

A <resource-ref> element describes a resource reference used in the Java code of the EJB. It has an optional <description> sub-element, and three mandatory sub-elements: <res-ref-name>, <res-type>, and <res-auth>. The res-ref-name element contains the name by which the Java implementation code looks up the resource in the EJB's JNDI context. The res-type element contains the Java type of the connection factory used to gain access to a resource connection. Standard types are javax.sql.DataSource (for JDBC connections), javax.jms.QueueConnectionFactory and javax.jms.TopicConnectionFactory (for JMS connections), javax.mail.Session (for JavaMail connections), and java.net.URL (for URL connections). The res-auth element allows the EJB developer to indicate who provides a name and password for the connection: the container or the EJB developer. Valid values are Application or Container.

An <ejb-ref> element describes a reference to another EJB used in the Java code of the EJB. It has an optional <description> sub-element, an optional <ejb-link> sub-element, and four mandatory sub-elements: <ejb-ref-name>, <ejb-ref-type>, <home>, and <remote>. The ejb-ref-name element contains the name by which the Java implementation code looks up the EJB in its JNDI context. The ejb-ref-type element indicates the type of bean. Valid values are Entity and Session. (This is true even in EJB 2.0, where a new type of bean called a message-driven bean is added. Message-driven beans do not have home and remote interfaces, but instead receive asynchronous messages. To communicate with a message-driven bean, a resource reference to a topic or queue would be used.) The home element indicates the fully qualified class name of the referenced EJB's home interface. The remote element indicates the fully qualified class name of the referenced EJB's remote interface. The optional ejb-link reference can contain an EJB name, to indicate a particular EJB deployment to which this ejb-ref should refer. Later in the chapter, an example of using an ejb-link element is demonstrated.

The deployer, using the application server's tools, can create a map between real resources (such as database connections) and the resource reference placeholders listed in the deployment descriptor. Of course, if it's obvious what is meant by a particular placeholder (for example, there is only one database connection type available, so all database resource references must be to that), a smart application server can do this mapping without asking for any more information. We've seen this when discussing the deployment of our earlier examples on Orion and jBoss.

Along with this EJB-level indirection, there is also application-level indirection. The security role that a particular EJB references with the isCallerInRole() method is linked to an application-level role declared in the deployment descriptor. But this application-level role is still an abstraction, and not an actual, real-world security system object. At deployment time, this indirection will finally be resolved. So here is the indirection that exists for our ATM role that was referenced in code:

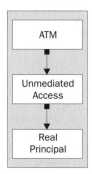

The "ATM" security role refers to the "UnmediatedAccess" security role, which at deployment time will be matched up to one or more real groups or principals in some security implementation. Neither the bean developer nor the application assembler need worry about the actual security implementation.

Another example of a similar indirection would be an EJB that referenced a JDBC Connection object in code. The EJB could use an arbitrary name to refer to the JDBC connection, without considering the rest of the application or the deployment environment. At deployment time, this arbitrary name would be linked to an actual DataSource connection factory that the application server had bound into its namespace.

Here is our implementation class for the AccountManager session bean. It uses two references, which it must declare: one to a security role, and one to the Account entity bean. For demonstration purposes, I'm making full use of the indirection by using different names for both the role and the bean:

```
package wrox.some_isv;

import javax.ejb.*;
import javax.naming.*;
import java.rmi.RemoteException;

public class AccountManagerEJB implements SessionBean {
  public SessionContext ctx;

  public void createAccount(int accountID, String customerName,
                    String customerType, double initialBalance)
        throws NoAccountCreatedException {
    try {
      AccountHome accountHome = getAccountHome();
      accountHome.create(accountID, customerName, customerType,
                   initialBalance);
    } catch (CreateException ce) {
      throw new NoAccountCreatedException(ce.getMessage());
```

```
      } catch (RemoteException re) {
        throw new EJBException(re);
      }
    }

    public void withdraw(int accountID, double amount)
          throws InsufficientFundsException, NoSuchAccountException {
      try {
        Account account = getAccount(accountID);

        if ((amount > 250)
              && account.getCustomerType().equals(CustomerTypes.INDIVIDUAL)
              && ctx.isCallerInRole("ATM")) {
          throw new SecurityException();

        }
        account.withdraw(amount);
      } catch (RemoteException re) {
        throw new EJBException(re);
      }
    }

    public void deposit(int accountID,
                          double amount) throws NoSuchAccountException {
      try {
        Account account = getAccount(accountID);
        account.deposit(amount);
      } catch (RemoteException re) {
        throw new EJBException(re);
      }
    }

    public void cancel(int accountID) {
      try {
        Account account = getAccount(accountID);
        account.remove();
      } catch (NoSuchAccountException nsae) {

        // great, already done
      } catch (Exception e) {
        throw new EJBException(e);
      }
    }

    private Account getAccount(int accountID) throws NoSuchAccountException {
      try {
        AccountHome home = getAccountHome();
        return home.findByPrimaryKey(new Integer(accountID));
      } catch (RemoteException re) {
        throw new EJBException(re);
      } catch (FinderException fe) {
        throw new NoSuchAccountException();
      }
    }
```

```
    private AccountHome getAccountHome() {
      try {
        InitialContext initial = new InitialContext();
        AccountHome home =
          (AccountHome) javax.rmi.PortableRemoteObject
            .narrow(initial.lookup("java:comp/env/ejb/GenericAccount"),
                    AccountHome.class);
        return home;
      } catch (NamingException ne) {
        throw new EJBException(ne);
      }
    }

  public void ejbCreate() {}
  public void ejbActivate() {}
  public void ejbPassivate() {}
  public void ejbRemove() {}
  public void setSessionContext(SessionContext ctx) {
    this.ctx = ctx;
  }
}
```

Here are the relevant resource declarations from the deployment descriptor (complete versions of which follow in a few pages, for the EJB development stage and the application assembly stage):

```
<ejb-ref>
  <ejb-ref-name>ejb/GenericAccount</ejb-ref-name>
  <ejb-ref-type>Entity</ejb-ref-type>
  <home>wrox.some_isv.AccountHome</home>
  <remote>wrox.some_isv.Account</remote>
  <ejb-link>Account</ejb-link>
</ejb-ref>
<security-role-ref>
  <description>
  This role refers to automated customer withdrawals
  from the account; no bank intermediary is involved.
  </description>
  <role-name>ATM</role-name>
  <role-link>UnmediatedAccess</role-link>
</security-role-ref>
```

An entity bean using container-managed persistence can automatically provide us with yet another type of indirection: the mapping of the bean's state data to fields in a persistent store. My account bean has four data fields: accountID, customerName, customerType, and accountBalance. These four fields could be mapped to fields with any name in a table in any type of database, and depending on the object/relational mapping capabilities of my application server could also be mapped to fields in different tables. If your application server and JDBC driver support distributed two-phase commits, they could even be mapped to fields in different databases. This capability is especially important when EJB applications must co-exist with legacy data.

Here is the implementation class for the Account entity bean. Note that I'm providing flexibility for my bean in the form of an environment parameter. In practice, this particular piece of information (the account minimum balance) probably belongs in a database where it can be changed without re-deploying the bean, but the technique is generally applicable to more stable information:

```
package wrox.some_isv;

import javax.ejb.*;
import javax.naming.*;

public class AccountEJB implements EntityBean {
  public Integer accountID;
  public String customerName;
  public String customerType;
  public double accountBalance;

  public void withdraw(double amount) throws InsufficientFundsException {
    if (accountBalance - amount < 0) {
      throw new InsufficientFundsException();
    }
    accountBalance -= amount;
  }

  public void deposit(double amount) {
    accountBalance += amount;
  }

  public String getCustomerType() {
    return customerType;
  }

  public Integer ejbCreate(int accountID, String customerName,
                      String customerType,
                      double initialBalance) throws CreateException {
    if (!customerType.equals(CustomerTypes.CORPORATION)
          && !customerType.equals(CustomerTypes.INDIVIDUAL)) {
      throw new CreateException("Unknown customer type.");
    }
    double minimumBalance = getMinimumBalance();
    if (initialBalance < minimumBalance) {
      throw new CreateException("Minimum balance required.");
    }
    this.accountID = new Integer(accountID);
    this.customerName = customerName;
    this.customerType = customerType;
    this.accountBalance = initialBalance;
    return this.accountID;
  }

  public void ejbPostCreate(int accountID, String customerName,
                      String customerType,
                      double initialBalance) throws CreateException {}

  private double getMinimumBalance() {
    try {
      InitialContext initial = new InitialContext();
      Double minimumBalance =
        (Double) initial.lookup("java:comp/env/minimumBalance");
      return minimumBalance.doubleValue();
```

```
    } catch (NamingException ne) {
      throw new EJBException(ne);
    }
  }

  public void ejbActivate() {}
  public void ejbLoad() {}
  public void ejbPassivate() {}
  public void ejbRemove() {}
  public void ejbStore() {}
  public void setEntityContext(EntityContext ctx) {}
  public void unsetEntityContext() {}
}
```

The final implementation class is a simple interface to provide some string constants:

```
package wrox.some_isv;

public interface CustomerTypes {
  public static final String CORPORATION = "corporation";
  public static final String INDIVIDUAL = "individual";
}
```

The deployment descriptor is the repository of information about the EJBs in an application. The application server's tools will use this information to understand what instances of indirection need to be resolved at deployment time. We have examined small parts of the deployment descriptor in isolation while discussing other features of Enterprise JavaBeans technology: it's time now to look at the deployment descriptor as a whole. There are two types of information contained within a deployment descriptor:

❑ **Structural information related to particular EJBs**
   This type of information relates to the Java coding that the bean provider performed, such as fully-qualified class names, references used, and transaction demarcation type (container-managed or bean-managed).

❑ **Application Assembly Information**
   This describes how the EJBs in a JAR are composed into a larger application deployment unit. Examples of such information could be defining security roles and method permissions, binding enterprise bean references to other beans, and defining transaction attributes on methods.

The top level element of a deployment descriptor is <ejb-jar>. There are two elements underneath this:

❑ <enterprise-beans> contains structural information relevant to particular EJBs.

❑ <assembly-descriptor> contains the information about how the EJBs are composed into a larger application deployment unit.

It's quite possible, even likely, that the same person or persons developing EJBs will also be responsible for assembling them into an application. In this case the division of responsibilities between the EJB developer and the application assembler may seem unimportant. However, with reuse and component resale by Independent Software Vendors (ISVs) in mind, the specification clearly specifies who is responsible for which entries in the deployment descriptor, and even indicates which entries can be specified by the bean developer and later changed by the application assembler. As a rough rule of thumb, the bean developer is responsible for the entries that are children of the <enterprise-beans> element, and the application assembler is responsible for the entries that are children of the <assembly-descriptor> element, although there are exceptions to this.

According to the specification, the bean provider must ensure the deployment descriptor contains the following information for each bean:

❑ **Enterprise bean's type: session or entity**
  The <session> or <entity> element will be the immediate child of the <enterprise-beans> element.

❑ **Enterprise bean's name**
  This is just a way to identify the EJB. The name doesn't have any relationship to the JNDI name under which the EJB will be deployed or accessible to clients, nor does it relate to the name that other beans will use to find this bean. The bean provider specifies the name in the <ejb-name> element.

❑ **Enterprise bean's implementation class**
  The fully qualified Java class name of the enterprise bean's implementation class is specified using the <ejb-class> element.

❑ **Enterprise bean's home and remote interfaces**
  The bean provider must specify the fully-qualified name of the enterprise bean's home and remote interfaces in the <home> element and <remote> element.

❑ **Whether an entity bean is re-entrant or not**
  The <reentrant> element is used, with a value of True or False. (Session beans are never re-entrant.)

❑ **Whether a session bean is stateful or stateless**
  The <session-type> element is used, with a value of Stateful or Stateless.

❑ **Whether or not a session bean manages its own transactions**
  The <transaction-type> element is used, with a value of Bean or Container.

❑ **Whether an entity bean uses BMP or CMP**
  The <persistence-type> element is used with a value of Bean or Container.

❑ **Enterprise bean's primary key class**
  The fully-qualified Java class name of an entity bean's primary key class is specified using the <prim-key-class> element. Technically, this is only mandatory for an entity bean with bean-managed persistence. To maximize indirection, this time of the primary key fields of the entity, an entity bean using container-managed persistence may defer the definition of its primary key until deployment. How to do this is beyond the scope of this book. If the primary key class is specified for an entity with container-managed persistence and the primary key maps to a single field in the entity, the <primkey-field> element should also probably be specified at this time.

❑ If the enterprise bean is an entity bean with container-managed persistence, the container-managed fields must be listed using <cmp-field> elements.

❑ Any environment entries, using the <env-entry> element.

❏ Any resource manager connection factory references in the Java code, such as a JDBC `DataSource` reference.

❏ Any references in the code to other EJBs.

❏ Any references in the code to security roles.

Keep in mind that this information will typically be specified using a tool. However, this is not required; the deployment descriptor is a simple XML file that can be edited by hand. Here is what our deployment descriptor looks like, as produced by the bean developer. Remember that this is not the completed product that we will deploy; it will be edited later by the application assembler:

```xml
<?xml version="1.0"?>

<ejb-jar>
  <enterprise-beans>
```

The name, state management type, Java classes, and transaction type of the `AccountManager` bean:

```xml
    <session>
      <ejb-name>AccountManager</ejb-name>
      <home>wrox.some_isv.AccountManagerHome</home>
      <remote>wrox.some_isv.AccountManager</remote>
      <ejb-class>wrox.some_isv.AccountManagerEJB</ejb-class>
      <session-type>Stateless</session-type>
      <transaction-type>Container</transaction-type>
```

Declaring our use of a reference to another EJB:

```xml
      <ejb-ref>
        <ejb-ref-name>ejb/GenericAccount</ejb-ref-name>
        <ejb-ref-type>Entity</ejb-ref-type>
        <home>wrox.some_isv.AccountHome</home>
        <remote>wrox.some_isv.Account</remote>
      </ejb-ref>
```

Declaring our use of a security role:

```xml
      <security-role-ref>
        <description>
        This role refers to automated customer withdrawals
        from the account; no bank intermediary is involved.
        </description>
        <role-name>ATM</role-name>
      </security-role-ref>
    </session>
```

The name, persistence type, Java classes (including the primary key class), and reentrancy of the Account bean:

```xml
<entity>
  <ejb-name>Account</ejb-name>
  <home>wrox.some_isv.AccountHome</home>
  <remote>wrox.some_isv.Account</remote>
  <ejb-class>wrox.some_isv.AccountEJB</ejb-class>
  <persistence-type>Container</persistence-type>
  <prim-key-class>java.lang.Integer</prim-key-class>
  <reentrant>False</reentrant>
```

The declaration of the fields for container-managed persistence:

```xml
<cmp-field>
  <field-name>customerType</field-name>
</cmp-field>
<cmp-field>
  <field-name>accountID</field-name>
</cmp-field>
<cmp-field>
  <field-name>accountBalance</field-name>
</cmp-field>
<cmp-field>
  <field-name>customerName</field-name>
</cmp-field>
  <primkey-field>accountID</primkey-field>
```

The declaration of an environment entry:

```xml
<env-entry>
  <env-entry-name>env/minimumBalance</env-entry-name>
  <env-entry-type>java.lang.Double</env-entry-type>
  <env-entry-value>150</env-entry-value>
</env-entry>
</entity>

</enterprise-beans>

</ejb-jar>
```

The Application Assembler

The application assembler combines EJBs (one or more EJB JAR files, which were the output of the bean developer) into a deployable application. This means that the XML deployment descriptor is edited so that application level information (such as security roles and references between beans) is added. The application assembler may also add other types of application components, such as servlets, JSPs, or client apps. A person in the role of application assembler does not need to understand the implementation of any EJBs; they just need to understand the home and remote interfaces, and the business logic that the methods in the interface represent.

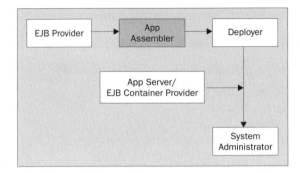

In the banking application that we have been discussing, the application assembler will have two roles:

❑ To complete the editing of the deployment descriptor.

❑ To provide some client applications. These client applications will simply test the functionality of the server-side components; a real application would obviously need some real client interface to the business functionality that the server components provided.

According to the specification, the following information in the deployment descriptor is relevant to this stage of the development of an application using EJBs:

❑ The application assembler may use the `<ejb-link>` element to indicate which EJB in a JAR file should be mapped to an enterprise bean reference declared by an EJB in the `<enterprise-beans>` section.

❑ The application assembler may define one or more security roles, as discussed in Chapter 21.

❑ The application assembler may define method permissions, as discussed in Chapter 21.

❑ The application assembler must link any security role references declared by an EJB to a security role that they have defined.

❑ The application assembler must define the transactional properties of the business methods defined in an EJB's home and remote interfaces, if the EJB uses container-managed transactions.

In addition, the following information that was provided by the EJB developer may be modified:

❑ In EJB 1.1, the enterprise bean's name. (In EJB 2.0, this rule was changed to accommodate the use of an EJB name in the EJB query language. For more information on EJB QL, please see Chapter 23.)

❑ The values of the environment entries.

❑ The description field for any entry.

Here is the final version of our application's deployment descriptor:

```
<?xml version="1.0"?>

<ejb-jar>
  <enterprise-beans>
```

```
<session>
  <ejb-name>AccountManager</ejb-name>
  <home>wrox.some_isv.AccountManagerHome</home>
  <remote>wrox.some_isv.AccountManager</remote>
  <ejb-class>wrox.some_isv.AccountManagerEJB</ejb-class>
  <session-type>Stateless</session-type>
  <transaction-type>Container</transaction-type>
```

The `ejb-ref` element now links to the `Account` bean:

```
<ejb-ref>
  <ejb-ref-name>ejb/GenericAccount</ejb-ref-name>
  <ejb-ref-type>Entity</ejb-ref-type>
  <home>wrox.some_isv.AccountHome</home>
  <remote>wrox.some_isv.Account</remote>
  <ejb-link>Account</ejb-link>
</ejb-ref>
<security-role-ref>
  <description>
  This role refers to automated customer withdrawals
  from the account; no bank intermediary is involved.
  </description>
  <role-name>ATM</role-name>
```

The role reference now links to a particular role defined in this deployment descriptor:

```
    <role-link>UnmediatedAccess</role-link>
  </security-role-ref>
</session>

<entity>
  <ejb-name>Account</ejb-name>
  <home>wrox.some_isv.AccountHome</home>
  <remote>wrox.some_isv.Account</remote>
  <ejb-class>wrox.some_isv.AccountEJB</ejb-class>
  <persistence-type>Container</persistence-type>
  <prim-key-class>java.lang.Integer</prim-key-class>
  <reentrant>False</reentrant>
  <cmp-field>
    <field-name>customerType</field-name>
  </cmp-field>
  <cmp-field>
    <field-name>accountID</field-name>
  </cmp-field>
  <cmp-field>
    <field-name>accountBalance</field-name>
  </cmp-field>
  <cmp-field>
    <field-name>customerName</field-name>
  </cmp-field>
    <primkey-field>accountID</primkey-field>
  <env-entry>
    <env-entry-name>minimumBalance</env-entry-name>
```

```
            <env-entry-type>java.lang.Double</env-entry-type>
            <env-entry-value>150</env-entry-value>
        </env-entry>
    </entity>

</enterprise-beans>
```

The assembly descriptor portion of the deployment descriptor may be omitted in the highly unlikely event that you have no security roles, method permissions, or transaction attributes to declare:

```
<assembly-descriptor>
```

We are declaring that all methods in both classes require a new or existing transaction context:

```
<container-transaction>
  <method>
      <ejb-name>AccountManager</ejb-name>
      <method-name>*</method-name>
  </method>
  <trans-attribute>Required</trans-attribute>
</container-transaction>
<container-transaction>
  <method>
      <ejb-name>Account</ejb-name>
      <method-name>*</method-name>
  </method>
  <trans-attribute>Required</trans-attribute>
</container-transaction>
```

Definition of security roles:

```
<security-role>
  <description>
  This role is performed by any account access
  in which a bank employee is not involved, such
  as an internet transaction or ATM withdrawal.
  </description>
  <role-name>UnmediatedAccess</role-name>
</security-role>
<security-role>
  <description>
  This role is peformed by any customer-service
  representative who does not have account-manager
  status.  They will be able to handle deposits and
  withdrawals, but not account management.
  </description>
  <role-name>Teller</role-name>
</security-role>
<security-role>
```

```
        <description>
        This role is performed by professionals who
        are allowed to manage an account (open, close).
        </description>
        <role-name>Manager</role-name>
    </security-role>
```

Definition of method permissions:

```
    <method-permission>
      <role-name>Manager</role-name>
      <method>
        <ejb-name>Account</ejb-name>
        <method-name>*</method-name>
      </method>
      <method>
        <ejb-name>AccountManager</ejb-name>
        <method-name>*</method-name>
      </method>
    </method-permission>

    <method-permission>
      <role-name>Teller</role-name>
      <role-name>UnmediatedAccess</role-name>
      <method>
        <ejb-name>Account</ejb-name>
        <method-name>withdraw</method-name>
      </method>
      <method>
        <ejb-name>Account</ejb-name>
        <method-name>deposit</method-name>
      </method>
      <method>
        <ejb-name>Account</ejb-name>
        <method-name>getCustomerType</method-name>
      </method>
      <method>
        <ejb-name>Account</ejb-name>
        <method-name>findByPrimaryKey</method-name>
      </method>
      <method>
        <ejb-name>AccountManager</ejb-name>
        <method-name>withdraw</method-name>
      </method>
      <method>
        <ejb-name>AccountManager</ejb-name>
        <method-name>deposit</method-name>
      </method>
    </method-permission>
  </assembly-descriptor>
</ejb-jar>
```

As an application assembler, I added everything that is a child of the <assembly-descriptor> element. For the container-managed transactions, I specified that all methods need to execute in a transactional context. For any business method call, if there is no current transaction the container will create one. For security, I defined three roles: UnmediatedAccess, Teller, and Manager. The manager has access to all the methods; the teller and 'unmediated access' (that is, the Web or an ATM) can only deposit and withdraw funds.

In addition, I added two things to the children of the <enterprise-beans> element:

❑ A <role-link> element to the security role reference in the session bean. Remember that the code (perhaps obtained from an independent software vendor) referred to a security role of ATM. Our application wants to be more general, and use the role UnmediatedAccess. The indirection of a reference allows us to do this; the <role-link> element closes the loop.

❑ A similar resolution of a reference, in this case to another bean. In the Java code, the account manager bean refers to the account bean as ejb/GenericAccount. However, the actual name of the bean is simply Account. I link the two together with the <ejb-link> element.

I have now linked the EJBs together to form a single, deployable application unit. With my first duty as an application assembler done, I now add other application elements. In this case, that means my test clients. I provide three; the first one is intended to be run with the security identity of a manager, and it creates a couple of accounts and does a deposit and withdrawal:

```
package wrox.some_isv;

import java.rmi.RemoteException;
import javax.ejb.*;
import javax.naming.*;
import javax.rmi.PortableRemoteObject;

public class TestClient {

  public static void main(String[] args) {

    try {
      InitialContext initial = new InitialContext();
      Object objref = initial.lookup("java:comp/env/ejb/AccountAccess");

      AccountManagerHome home =
        (AccountManagerHome) PortableRemoteObject.narrow(objref,
            AccountManagerHome.class);

      AccountManager accountManager = home.create();

      System.out.println("create individual account");
      accountManager.createAccount(1, "Dan OConnor",
                        CustomerTypes.INDIVIDUAL, 1500.0);

      System.out.println("deposit");
      accountManager.deposit(1, 550.0);

      System.out.println("withdraw");
      accountManager.withdraw(1, 75.0);

      System.out.println("create corporate account");
      accountManager.createAccount(2, "Wrox Press",
```

```
                                       CustomerTypes.CORPORATION, 150000.0);
      } catch (Exception e) {
        e.printStackTrace();
      }
    }
  }
}
```

The second client is intended to be run with the security identity of either an ATM machine or a web client. It will not succeed in its attempt to create an account, because the EJB container will prevent access to the method based on our declarative security permissions in the deployment descriptor:

```
package wrox.some_isv;

import java.rmi.RemoteException;
import javax.ejb.*;
import javax.naming.*;
import javax.rmi.PortableRemoteObject;

public class TestClient2 {
  public static void main(String[] args) {
    try {
      InitialContext initial = new InitialContext();
      Object objref = initial.lookup("java:comp/env/ejb/AccountAccess");

      AccountManagerHome home =
        (AccountManagerHome) PortableRemoteObject.narrow(objref,
            AccountManagerHome.class);

      AccountManager accountManager = home.create();

      System.out.println("create");
      accountManager.createAccount(2, "John Smith",
                                   CustomerTypes.INDIVIDUAL, 500.0);
    } catch (Exception e) {
      e.printStackTrace();
    }
  }
}
```

The third client is also intended to be run with the security identity of either an ATM machine or a web client. It will succeed in withdrawing a small amount of money from the individual account and a large amount of money from the corporate account. Because of the security check we wrote in Java, however, the attempt to withdraw a large amount of money from an individual account will fail.

```
package wrox.some_isv;

import java.rmi.RemoteException;
import javax.ejb.*;
import javax.naming.*;
import javax.rmi.PortableRemoteObject;

public class TestClient3 {
  public static void main(String[] args) {
    try {
      InitialContext initial = new InitialContext();
      Object objref = initial.lookup("java:comp/env/ejb/AccountAccess");
```

```
            AccountManagerHome home =
              (AccountManagerHome) PortableRemoteObject.narrow(objref,
                  AccountManagerHome.class);

            AccountManager accountManager = home.create();

            System.out
              .println("withdrawing small amount from individual account");
            accountManager.withdraw(1, 100.0);

            System.out.println("withdrawing large amount from corporate account");
            accountManager.withdraw(2, 1000.0);

            System.out
              .println("withdrawing large amount from individual account");
            accountManager.withdraw(1, 1000.0);

            System.out.println("done");
        } catch (Exception e) {
        e.printStackTrace();
        }
    }
}
```

Remember that there is no standard procedure for authenticating the client in the Enterprise JavaBeans specification. However, along with the stand-alone client, the J2EE specification provides for the concept of a client executing in a container. This container provides system level services, just as an EJB or a servlet executes in a container that provides system level services.

Although authentication techniques are still not specified for the client container, some sort of authentication is mandatory and the reference implementation provides it automatically for its clients that are executing in its 'client container'. (A client container is just a standard application that 'wraps' your application. You call it, passing your application name as a parameter, and it will call your application's main() *method for you.) Security was discussed at length in Chapter 21.*

Although there is no authentication code in these three examples, when they are executed a window will come up asking for a user name and password:

At the end of the application assembly stage, we have a completed application ready for deployment into an application server. As we have with other examples, you should package up your EJB components in a JAR file. The directory structure should be as follows:

```
wrox/
    some_isv/
            Account.class
            AccountEJB.class
            AccountHome.class
            AccountManager.class
            AccountManagerEJB.class
            AccountManagerHome.class
            CustomerTypes.class
            InsufficientFundsException.class
            NoAccountCreatedException.class
            NoSuchAccountException.class
META-INF/
            ejb-jar.xml
```

The Deployer

Once the application is completed, it must be inserted into the target environment. Remember that the business logic programmer does not need to worry about the target database or security system. The EJB component developer does not need to consider how to find other referenced components, or how clients will find the EJB. But these issues eventually need to be considered; the logical references that the enterprise bean provider uses must be mapped onto actual resources or identities. How this is done is completely specific to your application server vendor. Responsibility for doing it rests with the role of deployer. A deployer does not need to be a domain expert (an expert in the business); a person in this role must instead be an expert in the environment in which the application will execute (an expert in the company's database, security system, application server, operating systems, and network):

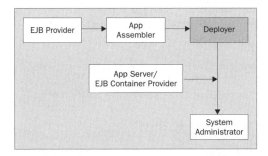

Let's consider what we need to do to deploy our application to the J2EE reference application server. To deploy the application into our configured environment, we use a reference implementation-specific GUI tool called deploytool, which is part of the reference implementation and can be downloaded from Sun's web site. The first thing that we will do is map the logical security roles, that we defined when we assembled the application, to actual users or groups in the underlying security system. We will use a simple security system that comes with the reference application server as a demonstration. Note that although this security system is included with the reference implementation, it is in no way part of the J2EE platform. The only requirement on a J2EE server or EJB container is that it map to some security system – the reference implementation includes this simple security system to fulfill this requirement. (Actually, there are two security systems that come with the J2EE platform; along with the simple security system we will use, there is also a certificate-based system for browser clients using the HTTPS protocol.)

The J2EE deployment tool's screen for mapping logical roles (such as `UnmediatedAccess`, `Manager`, and `Teller`) to the actual users and groups of the security system (such as `WebGroup` and `ATMGroup`) looks like this:

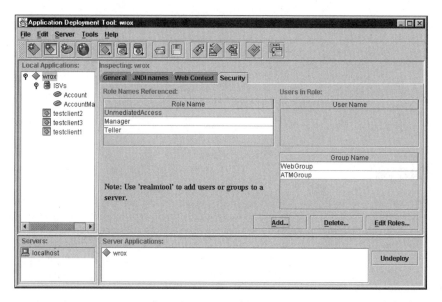

According to the EJB specification, adding users and groups to the operational environment is a system administrator's task. To allow the deployer to select some from the list, we'll briefly look at how they are added using the reference implementation. The J2EE server allows you to add and subtract users and groups using a command-line tool called `realmtool`. `realmtool` is documented in the file `doc\guides\ejb\html\Tools8.html`.

For this example, I added four groups: `TellerGroup`, `ATMGroup`, `ManagerGroup`, and `WebGroup`. Each group got one user: `SampleTeller`, `SampleATMUser`, `SampleManager`, and `SampleWebUser`. These are the 'real' security groups that I mapped to the abstract roles in the banking application.

The commands that I used to do this are as follows:

```
realmtool -addGroup TellerGroup
realmtool -addGroup ATMGroup
realmtool -addGroup ManagerGroup
realmtool -addGroup WebGroup
realmtool -add SampleTeller password1 TellerGroup
realmtool -add SampleATMUser password2 ATMGroup
realmtool -add SampleManager password3 ManagerGroup
realmtool -add SampleWebUser password4 WebGroup
```

To map a user or group to a role, we can just select it from the available options using the Add... button. To map an actual user or group to a logical role in the J2EE reference implementation, we just select it using the dialog that the Add... button displays:

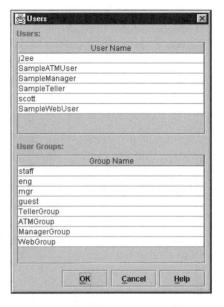

For the unmediatedAccess role, add the ATMGroup and WebGroup groups with the corresponding SampleATMUser and SampleWebUser users.

For the Manager role, add the ManagerGroup group and the SampleManager user.

For the Teller role, add the TellerGroup group and the SampleTeller user.

Now we need to map our logical database accesses to an actual database. I've only set up one database in my environment: the default Cloudscape database that comes with the J2EE reference implementation, which is bound to the arbitrary JNDI name jdbc/Cloudscape. In addition, we will need to map the properties of my account entity bean container-managed persistence to actual fields in the database. I will actually accept a default mapping and allow the application server to create my database table when I deploy my bean. Although this probably wouldn't be possible in a production environment, it's a great convenience when you are experimenting with the platform.

The next screen allows us to map our entity's state to a particular database bound into the global JNDI namespace; it also allows us to specify mappings to a particular table or columns (You can get to this by selecting your account bean, then selecting the Entity tag, then Deployment Settings...):

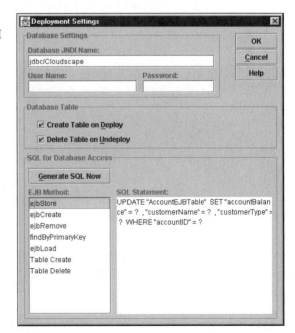

Note that a commercial application server (or an open source server) would probably provide more sophisticated object/relational mapping capabilities. The current limitations in this regard of the reference server are quite severe. The following information is taken verbatim from Sun's release notes:

❑   The entity bean class may be mapped to only one table in the database.

❑   A container-managed field may be mapped to only one column in the table.

❑   When the container loads the container-managed fields from the underlying database, it loads all of them.

❑   If the amount of data loaded is large, this approach may be inefficient because a business method may not need all of the container-managed fields.

❑   If the container-managed field of multiple entity beans map to the same data item in a database, and if these beans are invoked in the same transaction, they may see an inconsistent view of the data item.

❑   The Application Deployment Tool generates SQL statements for the `ejbCreate()`, `ejbRemove()`, `ejbLoad()`, and `ejbStore()` methods. You may modify only the table and column names of these SQL statements. You may not modify the number and order of the question marks, which are placeholders for the input parameters.

❑   You cannot call stored procedures in the generated SQL statements.

❑   In the 'Create Table' SQL statement, you may change the SQL type of a table column, provided the SQL type is compatible with its corresponding instance variable.

❑   The table and column names in all of the SQL statements must be consistent.

❑   The generated SQL statements have been tested with these types of databases: Cloudscape, Oracle, and Microsoft SQL Server. You may need to edit the generated SQL statements to satisfy the requirements of your database.

Finally, we need to map all the beans and references into the JNDI namespace. Note that the deployment tool will respect any links between beans that the application assembler declared using the `<ejb-link>` element. Here is the screen with which we do this:

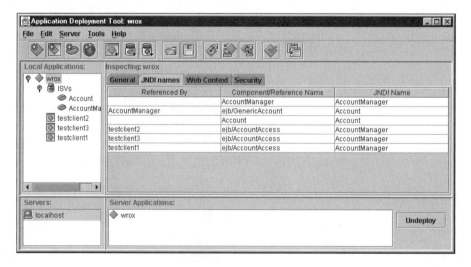

In this example, the `AccountManager` bean is bound to the global namespace under the name `AccountManager`. The `Account` bean is bound to the global namespace under the name `Account`. It's convenient to use the same name for the bean and the namespace, but it isn't required at all. A client that isn't executing in a 'client container' will use this JNDI name to find the bean from the JNDI initial context. The `ejb/GenericAccount` reference that the `AccountManager` bean uses is automatically mapped to `Account`, because the `<ejb-link>` forces them to be the same. The three clients I have defined as J2EE application clients (that will execute in a client container) use the same sort of link that an EJB reference would. In their code, they look up `ejb/AccountAccess` from the initial context, which is bound here to the `AccountManager` bean.

The Enterprise JavaBeans specification requires that an application server provide tools with which to do this mapping. It does not require that the tools have a GUI; they may simply be XML files that you need to edit by hand.

The System Administrator

The system administrator role is responsible for configuring the application server, EJB container, and the environment in which they execute – including the database, network, and security systems. The system administrator is also responsible for the 'well-being' of the EJBs that are executing in the container; a person in that role must monitor logs for system problems, security problems, etc.

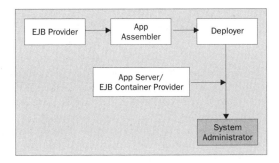

As a system administrator, we need to configure the application server environment. The reference application, although not intended to be a commercial system, does provide a certain amount of configurability. In particular, the following items can be configured by manually editing configuration files that reside in the `config` directory and are documented in `doc\release\ConfigGuide.html`:

- ❏ JDBC Drivers
- ❏ Transactions
- ❏ Port Numbers
- ❏ Log Files
- ❏ Security
- ❏ Memory Threshold for Passivation
- ❏ HTTP Document Root

The JDBC driver you use will depend on the database you use. For some databases, more than one JDBC driver may be available. The J2EE reference implementation can work with drivers that have XA support for two-phase commit, but will also work with older drivers that do not have this feature. You can also configure the user ID and password for your connections to the database (unless you obtain and authenticate a connection in code). To add a JDBC driver, you configure it in the `default.properties` property file and add that driver to the CLASSPATH of the server. Once again, you can find detailed instructions in the configuration guide cited above.

Distributed transactions can be configured to recover or to not be recovered in the event of a server crash. For enterprise beans with container-managed transactions, the period for transaction time-outs can be set in `default.properties`.

The J2EE reference implementation uses four TCP/IP ports:

- ❑   The EJB service uses one to download stub classes to the client

- ❑   The HTTP service uses one to service requests

- ❑   The HTTPS service uses another to service requests

- ❑   Finally, the ORB underlying the JNDI name server uses a port

The port numbers used for downloading EJB stub classes can be set in `ejb.properties`. The other ports can be set in `web.properties`.

The J2EE server produces several log files. You can change the default directory or name for these files in `default.properties`.

You can configure several security options. The keystore password by default is "changeit". You can change this by editing a property file (change the `keystore.password` entries in the `web.properties` file). When an authenticated web client makes a method call on an EJB, it gets a principal of a generic user. You can modify the name of the unauthenticated user by editing `auth.properties`. In the reference edition's deployment tool, methods are assigned a default role named ANYONE, which represents the set of all users and groups. You can change the name of this default role in `auth.properties`.

Passivation was discussed in Chapter 19 on session beans. By default, the server will passivate session beans when memory usage exceeds 128 megabytes. You can change this threshold in `default.properties`.

The J2EE specification includes servlets and JSPs, and the reference implementation contains a web server with a default document root of `public_html`; you can change this in `web.properties`.

These configurations are specific to the J2EE reference implementation, and other application servers will have a different set of configurations. This configuration may be done in a property file, as with the reference implementation, or using a GUI tool. Regardless, you will always need to configure your chosen application server to fit your particular environment.

The system administrator must also monitor the execution environment using application-server specific tools. The only tool that is mandated by the EJB specification is a log in which a record of system exceptions can be made. Logs are, in fact, the only monitoring tools provided by the reference implementation.

There is a new Java specification for application and network management called the Java Management Extensions (JMX, `http://java.sun.com/products/JavaManagement/`), which at the time of this writing is available through early access from the Java Developer Connection at Sun. This is a comprehensive framework that includes monitoring of properties, pluggable and dynamic management services, support for various management protocols such as SNMP, and the ability to be managed through the web via HTML browsers. At least one of the open source EJB containers, jBoss, is being designed completely around JMX. It is quite likely that Java-based application servers will standardize around these management extensions in the future. This will allow an EJB developer to make their application manageable in a standard and portable way. It will not, however, remove management tools from the arena of competition among application vendors. This will continue to be an area where vendors can differentiate themselves.

Container/Application Server Vendor

This is the final role defined by the EJB specification. It is the only role that you, the reader of this book, are unlikely to play. This book is not addressed to the provider of an application server, but rather to the user of one.

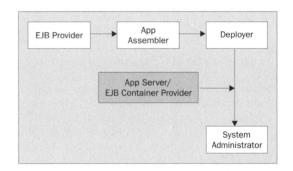

Nevertheless, you still need to choose an application server/EJB container. Because that EJB container will be responsible for all your system-level services, this choice will be very important to the success of your project. There are more than 35 products supporting EJB on the market right now, with capabilities ranging from 'barely working' to scaleable and reliable. They have prices ranging from $35,000/processor to free. Choosing among them can be quite difficult.

The first thing to consider is that you don't necessarily need to use the same application server for development and deployment. You can defer the decision about the application server on which to deploy until you have a prototype against which you can test the products from various vendors. Most vendors will let you evaluate their application server for a certain amount of time before purchasing it. If you've developed on a product that is free – or at least free or inexpensive for development – you can then deploy on a commercial (and possibly expensive) product that meets your runtime needs. The reference implementation, the three open source J2EE projects, and the Orion application server (free for development) are all possible choices for low-cost development. (If you already know your target application server, you may want to develop on this platform to gain experience with it and to receive early warning about things that might not work.)

Don't be fooled into thinking that a higher price means a better product. There's no substitute for evaluating a product in your environment. You can carry this too far, of course. No one should spend the time and money it would take to evaluate 35 different products that support EJBs in a quest to find the perfect one for their situation.

Understand what your requirements are before making a choice; the following criteria will probably be important to consider:

❑ Do you need an ORB-based product to communicate with non-Java clients or for vendor interoperability?

❑ What object/relational mapping capabilities do you require? Do you need (and does the vendor support) mapping an entity to multiple tables? What are the performance characteristics of a vendor's solution?

❑ If you aren't happy with a vendor's object/relational mapping capabilities, is there a third party product that will integrate with the application server?

❑ What kind of development and deployment tools are supported by a vendor's application server? Some products come from a background of providing productive toolsets.

❑ What are the performance characteristics of a particular product? Does it support clustering for performance and high availability?

❑ What version of the Enterprise JavaBeans specification does the application server support? Some well-known products always seem to lag behind.

❑ What platform(s) does the application server run on?

❑ How much does the product you are considering cost?

❑ What kind of support for the product is available?

It was quite tempting to mention particular products' strengths and weaknesses in this section, but the truth is that new versions come out fairly regularly that erase the weaknesses of the old. Any specific advice I gave you would probably be out of date by the time you read it. The only product-specific advice that I will give you is to give serious consideration to the three major open source products that are under development. It is quite likely that one or more of these products will end up giving you the features that you need, and that the J2EE platform, complete with clustering, management tools, object/relational mapping, and other high-end services, will become a commodity. Seems unlikely? Consider the success of Linux and Apache, and the sophisticated functionality that they provide.

A Web Interface for the Manufacturing App

As a further example of how EJB components can be used to create a complete J2EE application, I'm going to provide a simple web interface for the manufacturing application that we developed in Chapters 18, 19, and 20. (Like most sample applications, it will be light on error handling and robust behavior, to keep things simple and clear.) The web application will present a menu of choices to the user that allows them to create a sample product, place a sample order, manage orders, or manufacture a product for an order. The menu screen will look like this:

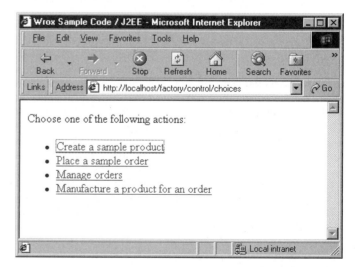

In Chapter 18, we discussed the model-view-controller architecture and its applicability to web applications. Recall the diagram that represented a possible model-view-controller design:

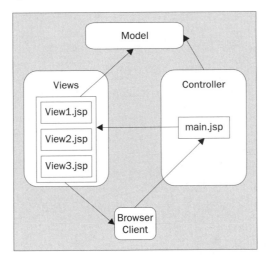

Our application will implement this design. The model will be our existing EJB façades (the ManageOrders and Manufacture session beans), plus a JavaBean class called ModelManager that will act as a proxy to the EJBs. The controller will be a front class, called main.jsp, which will forward processing to a JavaBean called RequestProcessor. RequestProcessor will update the model and then return the appropriate view to main.jsp. The main.jsp JSP will forward processing to the view that the RequestProcessor returned, which will also be a JSP component. Here is a diagram of the implementation:

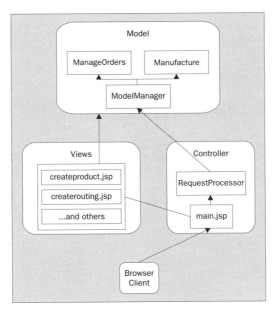

Let's look at the source code for these classes. (One thing to note is that I'm not using `tablibs` in my JSPs, which is more maintainable than scripting but involves some up-front work that would distract from the focus of this chapter.) First, `main.jsp`:

```
<%--
% The entry point for the manufacturing application
--%>
```

The model and request processor are at `session` scope:

```
<jsp:useBean
    id="modelManager"
    class="ModelManager"
    scope="session"
>
<%
    modelManager.init(config.getServletContext(), session);
%>
</jsp:useBean>

<jsp:useBean
    id="rp"
    class="RequestProcessor"
    scope="session"
>
<%
    rp.init(config.getServletContext(), session);
%>
</jsp:useBean>
```

We forward the request to the `RequestProcessor` class, which updates the model and returns the next view in the application sequence:

```
<%
    String targetView = rp.processRequest(request);
```

Now we dispatch the request to the appropriate view:

```
    getServletConfig().getServletContext().
    getRequestDispatcher(targetView).forward(request, response);
%>
```

Here is the code for the `RequestProcessor` class. For each request, it updates the model and decides on the next view in the sequence:

```
import java.text.DateFormat;
import java.util.Date;
import javax.servlet.ServletContext;
import javax.servlet.http.HttpServletRequest;
import javax.servlet.http.HttpServletResponse;
import javax.servlet.http.HttpSession;
import factory.manage_orders.NoSuchOrderException;
```

```
import factory.manage_orders.NoSuchProductException;
import factory.manage_orders.DuplicateOrderException;
import factory.manufacture.BadStatusException;
import factory.order.OrderNotCancelableException;

public class RequestProcessor {
  private ModelManager mm;
  private HttpSession session;
  private ServletContext context;
  private String stackURL;

  private DateFormat dateFormat = DateFormat.getDateInstance(DateFormat.SHORT);
```

In the `init()` method, we get a copy of the model proxy:

```
public void init(ServletContext context, HttpSession session) {
  this.session = session;
  this.context = context;
  mm = (ModelManager)session.getAttribute("modelManager");
}
```

The rest of the class is dedicated to processing the request. This may involve getting parameters from the request and updating the model accordingly, or setting attributes in the request that a subsequent view may examine. The screen flow is implicit in the code. A more complex application would need a more elegant mechanism; perhaps a generic finite state machine processor, with the state transitions defined in the database:

```
public String processRequest(HttpServletRequest req) {
  String selectedURL = req.getPathInfo();

  if ((selectedURL == null) || selectedURL.equals( ScreenNames.CHOICES )) {
    return ScreenNames.CHOICES_URL;
  } else if (selectedURL.equals( ScreenNames.CHOOSE_FOR_MANUFACTURE )) {
    String cellName = mm.getCurrentCell();
    if (cellName == null) {
      // requires "log on"
      stackURL = ScreenNames.CHOOSE_FOR_MANUFACTURE_URL;
      return ScreenNames.CHOOSE_CELL_URL;
    }
    return ScreenNames.CHOOSE_FOR_MANUFACTURE_URL;

  } else if (selectedURL.equals( ScreenNames.ORDER_CHOSEN )) {
    try {
      String salesDiv = req.getParameter( ScreenNames.SALES_DIVISION_PARAM );
      String orderID = req.getParameter( ScreenNames.ORDER_NUMBER_PARAM );
      mm.selectForManufacture( Integer.parseInt( salesDiv ),
        Integer.parseInt( orderID ));
      if (mm.hasNextRouting())
        return ScreenNames.ROUTE_FOR_MANUFACTURE_URL;
      else
```

```
          return ScreenNames.SHIP_URL;
      } catch (NoSuchOrderException nsoe) {
        req.setAttribute( ScreenNames.MESSAGE_ATTRIB,
          "The order does not exist in the system." );
        return ScreenNames.MESSAGE_URL;
      } catch (BadStatusException bse) {
        req.setAttribute( ScreenNames.MESSAGE_ATTRIB,
          "The order is not eligible for manufacture." );
        return ScreenNames.MESSAGE_URL;
      }

    } else if (selectedURL.equals( ScreenNames.CREATE_PRODUCT )) {
      return ScreenNames.CREATE_PRODUCT_URL;

    } else if (selectedURL.equals( ScreenNames.CELL_CHOSEN )) {
      String cellName = req.getParameter( ScreenNames.CELL_PARAM );
      mm.setCurrentCell( cellName );
      return stackURL;

    } else if (selectedURL.equals( ScreenNames.PRODUCT_CREATED )) {
      String prodID = req.getParameter( ScreenNames.PRODUCT_ID_PARAM );
      String prodName = req.getParameter( ScreenNames.PRODUCT_NAME_PARAM );
      mm.createProduct( prodID, prodName );
      return ScreenNames.CREATE_ROUTING_URL;

    } else if (selectedURL.equals( ScreenNames.CREATE_ROUTING )) {
      return ScreenNames.CREATE_ROUTING_URL;

    } else if (selectedURL.equals( ScreenNames.ROUTING_CREATED )) {
      String sequence = req.getParameter( ScreenNames.ROUTING_SEQUENCE_PARAM );
      String action = req.getParameter( ScreenNames.ROUTING_ACTION_STEP_PARAM );
      mm.addRouting( Integer.parseInt(sequence), action );
      return ScreenNames.CREATE_ROUTING_URL;

    } else if (selectedURL.equals( ScreenNames.CANCEL_ORDER )) {
      String salesDivision =
        req.getParameter( ScreenNames.SALES_DIVISION_PARAM );
      String orderNumber =
        req.getParameter( ScreenNames.ORDER_NUMBER_PARAM );
      String orderType = (req.getParameter(ScreenNames.ORDER_TYPE_PARAM));
      try {
        mm.cancelOrder( Integer.parseInt(salesDivision),
          Integer.parseInt(orderNumber) );
        prepareManageOrdersRequest( orderType, req );
        return ScreenNames.MANAGE_ORDERS_URL;
      } catch (OrderNotCancelableException once) {
        req.setAttribute( ScreenNames.MESSAGE_ATTRIB,
          "This order is not cancelable." );
        return ScreenNames.MESSAGE_URL;
      } catch (NoSuchOrderException nsoe) {
        req.setAttribute( ScreenNames.MESSAGE_ATTRIB,
          "This order does not exist." );
        return ScreenNames.MESSAGE_URL;
      }
```

1104

```
    } else if (selectedURL.equals( ScreenNames.MANAGE_ORDERS )) {
      String orderType = (req.getParameter(ScreenNames.ORDER_TYPE_PARAM));
      prepareManageOrdersRequest( orderType, req );
      return ScreenNames.MANAGE_ORDERS_URL;

    } else if (selectedURL.equals( ScreenNames.PLACE_ORDER )) {
      return ScreenNames.PLACE_ORDER_URL;

    } else if (selectedURL.equals( ScreenNames.ORDER_PLACED )) {
      try {
        String salesDiv = req.getParameter( ScreenNames.ORDER_SALES_DIV_PARAM );
        String orderNum = req.getParameter( ScreenNames.ORDER_NUM_PARAM );
        String productID = req.getParameter( ScreenNames.ORDER_PROD_PARAM );
        String dateDueString =
                        req.getParameter( ScreenNames.ORDER_DUE_DATE_PARAM );

        Date dateDue = dateFormat.parse( dateDueString );

        mm.placeOrder(Integer.parseInt(salesDiv), Integer.parseInt(orderNum),
                  productID, dateDue );

        req.setAttribute(ScreenNames.MESSAGE_ATTRIB,
                      "Thank you for placing this order." );

      } catch (NoSuchProductException nspe) {
        req.setAttribute( ScreenNames.MESSAGE_ATTRIB,
          "There is no such product." );
      } catch (DuplicateOrderException doe) {
        req.setAttribute( ScreenNames.MESSAGE_ATTRIB,
          "There is already an order in that sales division with that number." );
      } catch (java.text.ParseException pe) {
        req.setAttribute( ScreenNames.MESSAGE_ATTRIB,
          "That is not a valid date." );
      }
      return ScreenNames.MESSAGE_URL;

    } else if (selectedURL.equals( ScreenNames.ROUTE_FOR_MANUFACTURE )) {
      if (mm.hasNextRouting())
        return ScreenNames.ROUTE_FOR_MANUFACTURE_URL;
      else
        return ScreenNames.SHIP_URL;

    } else if (selectedURL.equals( ScreenNames.SHIP_PRODUCT )) {
      String loadingDock = req.getParameter(
        ScreenNames.SHIP_LOADING_DOCK_PARAM );
      String carrier = req.getParameter(ScreenNames.SHIP_METHOD_PARAM );
      mm.shipProduct( carrier, Integer.parseInt(loadingDock) );
      return ScreenNames.CHOICES_URL;

    } else {
      return ScreenNames.CHOICES_URL;
    }
  }
```

The `prepareManageOrdersRequest()` method is just a helper method to abstract out some functionality that was used twice:

```
private void prepareManageOrdersRequest(String orderType,
                                        HttpServletRequest req) {
  if (orderType.equals(ScreenNames.ORDER_TYPE_OVERDUE)) {
    req.setAttribute(ScreenNames.ORDER_URL_ATTRIB,
      ScreenNames.ORDER_TYPE_OVERDUE);
    req.setAttribute(ScreenNames.ORDER_ALT_URL_ATTRIB,
      ScreenNames.ORDER_TYPE_OPEN);
    req.setAttribute(ScreenNames.ORDER_ALT_VIEW_ATTRIB,
      ScreenNames.ORDER_TYPE_OPEN_TEXT);
    req.setAttribute(ScreenNames.ORDER_VIEW_ATTRIB,
      ScreenNames.ORDER_TYPE_OVERDUE_TEXT);

  } else // orderType.equals(ScreenNames.ORDER_TYPE_OPEN) )
  {
    req.setAttribute(ScreenNames.ORDER_URL_ATTRIB,
      ScreenNames.ORDER_TYPE_OPEN);
    req.setAttribute(ScreenNames.ORDER_ALT_URL_ATTRIB,
      ScreenNames.ORDER_TYPE_OVERDUE);
    req.setAttribute(ScreenNames.ORDER_ALT_VIEW_ATTRIB,
      ScreenNames.ORDER_TYPE_OVERDUE_TEXT);
    req.setAttribute(ScreenNames.ORDER_VIEW_ATTRIB,
      ScreenNames.ORDER_TYPE_OPEN_TEXT);
  }
 }
}
```

The constants that the application uses are defined in the `ScreenNames` class:

```
public interface ScreenNames {
  // paths
  public static final String CHOICES = "/choices";
  public static final String CREATE_PRODUCT = "/createproduct";
  public static final String CREATE_ROUTING = "/createrouting";
  public static final String MANAGE_ORDERS = "/manageorders";
  public static final String CHOOSE_FOR_MANUFACTURE = "/manufacturechoose";
  public static final String ROUTE_FOR_MANUFACTURE = "/manufactureroute";
  public static final String PLACE_ORDER = "/placeorder";
  public static final String ORDER_PLACED = "/order_placed";
  public static final String PRODUCT_CREATED = "/product_created";
  public static final String ROUTING_CREATED = "/routing_created";
  public static final String ORDER_CHOSEN = "/order_chosen";
  public static final String CANCEL_ORDER = "/cancelorder";
  public static final String CELL_CHOSEN = "/cell_chosen";
  public static final String SHIP_PRODUCT = "/ship_product";

  // jsps
  public static final String CHOICES_URL = "/choices.jsp";
  public static final String CREATE_PRODUCT_URL = "/createproduct.jsp";
  public static final String CREATE_ROUTING_URL = "/createrouting.jsp";
  public static final String MANAGE_ORDERS_URL = "/manageorders.jsp";
```

```
        public static final String CHOOSE_FOR_MANUFACTURE_URL =
                                            "/manufacturechoose.jsp";
        public static final String ROUTE_FOR_MANUFACTURE_URL =
                                            "/manufactureroute.jsp";
        public static final String PLACE_ORDER_URL = "/placeorder.jsp";
        public static final String MESSAGE_URL = "/message.jsp";
        public static final String CHOOSE_CELL_URL = "/cellid.jsp";
        public static final String SHIP_URL = "/ship.jsp";

        // parameters
        public static final String ORDER_TYPE_PARAM = "ordertype";
        public static final String ORDER_VIEW_ATTRIB = "order_view";
        public static final String ORDER_ALT_VIEW_ATTRIB = "order_alt_view";
        public static final String ORDER_ALT_URL_ATTRIB = "order_alt_url";
        public static final String ORDER_URL_ATTRIB = "order_url";
        public static final String ORDER_TYPE_OPEN = "openorders";
        public static final String ORDER_TYPE_OVERDUE = "overdueorders";
        public static final String ORDER_TYPE_OPEN_TEXT = "open orders";
        public static final String ORDER_TYPE_OVERDUE_TEXT = "overdue orders";

        public static final String SALES_DIVISION_PARAM = "salesdivision";
        public static final String ORDER_NUMBER_PARAM = "ordernumber";

        public static final String MESSAGE_ATTRIB = "message";

        public static final String PRODUCT_ID_PARAM = "product_id";
        public static final String PRODUCT_NAME_PARAM = "product_name";

        public static final String ROUTING_SEQUENCE_PARAM = "sequence";
        public static final String ROUTING_ACTION_STEP_PARAM = "routing";

        public static final String ORDER_SALES_DIV_PARAM = "sales_div";
        public static final String ORDER_NUM_PARAM = "order_num";
        public static final String ORDER_PROD_PARAM = "prod";
        public static final String ORDER_DUE_DATE_PARAM = "due_date";

        public static final String CELL_PARAM = "cell";

        public static final String SHIP_METHOD_PARAM = "shipping_company";
        public static final String SHIP_LOADING_DOCK_PARAM = "loading_dock";

}
```

ModelManager is the web-tier proxy for the EJB-tier model:

```
import javax.ejb.EJBException;
import javax.naming.InitialContext;
import javax.naming.NamingException;
import javax.rmi.PortableRemoteObject;
import javax.servlet.http.HttpSession;
import javax.servlet.ServletContext;

import java.util.Date;
import java.util.Iterator;
```

```
import java.util.LinkedList;

import factory.manage_orders.DuplicateOrderException;
import factory.manage_orders.OpenOrderView;
import factory.manage_orders.OverdueOrderView;
import factory.manage_orders.ManageOrders;
import factory.manage_orders.ManageOrdersHome;
import factory.manage_orders.NoSuchOrderException;
import factory.manage_orders.NoSuchProductException;
import factory.manufacture.BadStatusException;
import factory.manufacture.Manufacture;
import factory.manufacture.ManufactureHome;

import factory.order.OrderNotCancelableException;

public class ModelManager {
  private ServletContext context;
  private HttpSession session;
```

The model manager maintains references to the two session bean façade objects in our application.
Obviously we need to save a persistent Manufacture reference, because it is a stateful session bean.
We could reacquire the ManageOrders interface every time we use it. This might add some overhead,
but might also allow the EJB container to perform load balancing more effectively, depending on the
load-balancing implementation:

```
  private ManageOrders manageOrders;
  private Manufacture manufacture;

  private String currentCellID;
  private String currentProductID;

  public void init(ServletContext context, HttpSession session) {
    this.session = session;
    this.context = context;

    manageOrders = getManageOrdersEJB();
  }

  public void createProduct( String productID, String productName ) {
    try {
      manageOrders.createProduct( productID, productName );
      currentProductID = productID;
    } catch (java.rmi.RemoteException re ) {
      throw new EJBException( re );
    }
  }

  public String getCurrentCell() {
    return currentCellID;
  }

  public void setCurrentCell( String currentCell ) {
    currentCellID = currentCell;
```

```
    }

    public String getCurrentProductID() {
      return currentProductID;
    }

    public void addRouting( int sequence, String action ) {
      try {
        manageOrders.addRoutingInstruction( currentProductID, sequence, action );
      } catch (java.rmi.RemoteException re ) {
        throw new EJBException( re );
      }
    }

    public void placeOrder(int salesDivision, int orderNumber,
                           String product, Date dateDue )
              throws NoSuchProductException, DuplicateOrderException {
      try {
        manageOrders.placeOrder( salesDivision, orderNumber, product, dateDue );
      } catch (java.rmi.RemoteException re ) {
        throw new EJBException( re );
      }
    }

    public void cancelOrder( int salesDivision, int orderNumber )
      throws NoSuchOrderException, OrderNotCancelableException {
      try {
        manageOrders.cancelOrder( salesDivision, orderNumber );
      } catch (java.rmi.RemoteException re) {
        throw new EJBException( re );
      }
    }
```

Methods that access the stateful session bean must be synchronized, because illegal multiple concurrent accesses would otherwise be possible. This is not necessary for methods that access the stateless session bean, because each access could be directed to a different EJB instance:

```
    public synchronized Iterator getOrdersToManufacture() {
      try {
        LinkedList list = new LinkedList();
        manufacture = getManufactureEJB();
        OpenOrderView[] openOrders = manufacture.getOpenOrders();
        for (int iter=0; iter<openOrders.length; iter++) {
          list.add( new OrderView(openOrders[iter]) );
        }
        return list.iterator();
      } catch (java.rmi.RemoteException re ) {
        throw new EJBException( re );
      }
    }

    public synchronized void selectForManufacture(int salesDiv, int orderNum )
                        throws NoSuchOrderException, BadStatusException {
      try {
        manufacture.selectForManufacture( salesDiv, orderNum );
      } catch (java.rmi.RemoteException re) {
        throw new EJBException( re );
      }
    }
```

```
public synchronized boolean hasNextRouting() {
  try {
    return manufacture.hasNextRouting();
  } catch (factory.manufacture.NoSelectionException nse) {
    throw new EJBException( nse );
  } catch (java.rmi.RemoteException re) {
    throw new EJBException( re );
  }
}

public synchronized String getNextRouting() {
  try {
    return manufacture.getNextRouting();
  } catch (factory.manufacture.NoSelectionException nse) {
    throw new EJBException( nse );
  } catch (java.rmi.RemoteException re) {
    throw new EJBException( re );
  }
}

public synchronized void shipProduct( String carrier, int loadingDock ) {
  try {
    manufacture.ship( carrier, loadingDock );
  } catch (factory.manufacture.NoSelectionException nse) {
    throw new EJBException( nse );
  } catch (java.rmi.RemoteException re) {
    throw new EJBException( re );
  }
}

public Iterator getOrders(String type) {
  try {
    LinkedList list = new LinkedList();
    if (type.equals( ScreenNames.ORDER_TYPE_OPEN_TEXT )) {
      OpenOrderView[] openOrders = manageOrders.getSchedulableOrders();
      for (int iter=0; iter<openOrders.length; iter++) {
        list.add( new OrderView(openOrders[iter]) );
      }
    } else if (type.equals( ScreenNames.ORDER_TYPE_OVERDUE_TEXT )) {
      OverdueOrderView[] overdueOrders = manageOrders.getOverdueOrders();
      for (int iter=0; iter<overdueOrders.length; iter++) {
        list.add( new OrderView(overdueOrders[iter]) );
      }
    } else throw new IllegalStateException();
    return list.iterator();
  } catch (java.rmi.RemoteException re) {
    throw new EJBException( re );
  }
}
```

Finally, some helper methods:

```
private ManageOrders getManageOrdersEJB() {
  try {
    InitialContext initial = new InitialContext();
    Object objref = initial.lookup( "java:comp/env/ejb/ManageOrders" );
    ManageOrdersHome home = (ManageOrdersHome) PortableRemoteObject.narrow(
      objref, ManageOrdersHome.class );
    return home.create();
```

```
        } catch (NamingException ne) {
          throw new EJBException(ne);
        } catch (java.rmi.RemoteException re) {
          throw new EJBException(re);
        } catch (javax.ejb.CreateException ce) {
          throw new EJBException(ce);
        }
    }

    private Manufacture getManufactureEJB() {
        try {
          InitialContext initial = new InitialContext();
          Object objref = initial.lookup( "java:comp/env/ejb/Manufacture" );
          ManufactureHome home = (ManufactureHome) PortableRemoteObject.narrow(
            objref, ManufactureHome.class );
          return home.create(currentCellID);
        } catch (NamingException ne) {
          throw new EJBException(ne);
        } catch (java.rmi.RemoteException re) {
          throw new EJBException(re);
        } catch (javax.ejb.CreateException ce) {
          throw new EJBException(ce);
        }
    }
}
```

I use a view class to return information from the model to the various JSP views. The view is basically just a container for the information:

```
import java.util.Date;
import factory.manage_orders.OpenOrderView;
import factory.manage_orders.OverdueOrderView;

public class OrderView {
  private int salesDivision;
  private int orderNumber;
  private String product;
  private String status;
  private Date dateDue;

  public OrderView(int salesDivision, int orderNumber,
                   String product, String status, Date dateDue ) {
    this.salesDivision = salesDivision;
    this.orderNumber = orderNumber;
    this.product = product;
    this.status = status;
    this.dateDue = dateDue;
  }

  public OrderView(OpenOrderView view) {
    this(view.salesDivision, view.orderNumber, view.product,
        "open", view.dateDue );
  }

  public OrderView(OverdueOrderView view) {
    this(view.salesDivision, view.orderNumber, view.product,
      view.status, view.dateDue );
  }

  public OrderView() {}
```

```
  public int getSalesDivision() {
    return salesDivision;
  }

  public int getOrderNumber() {
    return orderNumber;
  }

  public String getProduct() {
    return product;
  }

  public String getStatus() {
    return status;
  }

  public Date getDateDue() {
    return dateDue;
  }
}
```

The 'main menu' view is provided by `choices.jsp`:

```html
<html>
<head>
<title>Wrox Sample Code / J2EE</title>
<meta http-equiv="Content-Type" content="text/html; charset=iso-8859-1">
</head>

<body bgcolor="#FFFFFF">
<p>Choose one of the following actions:</p>
<ul>
  <li><a href="createproduct">Create a sample product</a></li>
  <li><a href="placeorder">Place a sample order</a></li>
  <li><a href="manageorders?ordertype=openorders">Manage orders</a></li>
  <li><a href="manufacturechoose">Manufacture a product for an order</a></li>
</ul>
<p> </p>
</body>
</html>
```

The main 'create product' view looks like this:

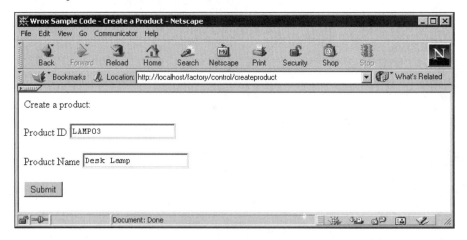

This view is provided by `createproduct.jsp`:

```html
<html>
<head>
<title>Wrox Sample Code - Create a Product</title>
<meta http-equiv="Content-Type" content="text/html; charset=iso-8859-1">
</head>

<body bgcolor="#FFFFFF">
<p>Create a product:</p>
<form method="post" action="product_created">
  <p>Product ID
    <input type="text" name="product_id">
  </p>
  <p>Product Name
    <input type="text" name="product_name">
  </p>
  <p>
    <input type="submit" name="Submit" value="Submit">
  </p>
</form>
<p>  </p>
</body>
</html>
```

After adding a product you can add routing steps:

This view for adding the routing steps is provided by `createrouting.jsp`:

```jsp
<jsp:useBean
   id="modelManager"
   class="ModelManager"
   scope="session"
 />

<html>
<head>
<title>Wrox Sample Code - Create a Routing</title>
<meta http-equiv="Content-Type" content="text/html; charset=iso-8859-1">
```

```
</head>

<body bgcolor="#FFFFFF">
<p>Create a routing for product <%= modelManager.getCurrentProductID()%>:</p>
<form method="post" action="routing_created">
  <p>Sequence
    <input type="text" name="sequence">
  </p>
  <p>Routing
    <textarea name="routing" cols="75" rows="10"></textarea>
  </p>
  <p>
    <input type="submit" name="Submit" value="Submit">
  </p>
</form>
<p>or you can be <a href="choices">finished with creating
  routings for this product</a>.</p>
</body>
</html>
```

You can place an order:

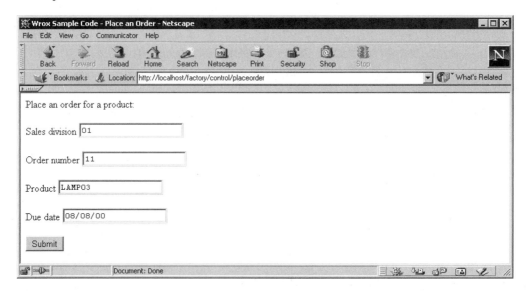

This is provided by `placeorder.jsp`:

```
<html>
<head>
<title>Wrox Sample Code - Place an Order</title>
<meta http-equiv="Content-Type" content="text/html; charset=iso-8859-1">
</head>

<body bgcolor="#FFFFFF">
<p>Place an order for a product:</p>
<form method="post" action="order_placed" name="PlaceOrder">
```

```
    <p>Sales division
      <input type="text" name="sales_div">
    </p>
    <p>Order number
      <input type="text" name="order_num">
    </p>
    <p>Product
      <input type="text" name="prod">
    </p>
    <p>Due date
      <input type="text" name="due_date">
    </p>
    <p>
      <input type="submit" name="Submit" value="Submit">
    </p>
  </form>
  <p> </p>
  </body>
  </html>
```

After the order has been placed, a thank-you message is shown, provided by `message.jsp`

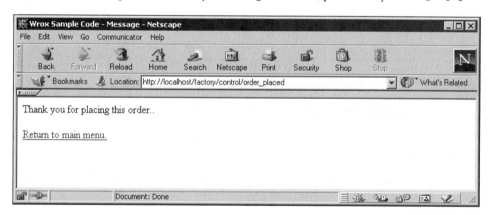

```
<html>
<head>
<title>Wrox Sample Code - Message</title>
<meta http-equiv="Content-Type" content="text/html; charset=iso-8859-1">
</head>

<body bgcolor="#FFFFFF">
<p>
<%= request.getAttribute("message")%>.
</p>

<p><a href="choices">Return to main menu.</a></p>
</body>
</html>
```

There are two versions of the order-management view, one for open orders and one for overdue orders. Any listed order can be canceled by clicking on a hyperlink. Here is the open order view:

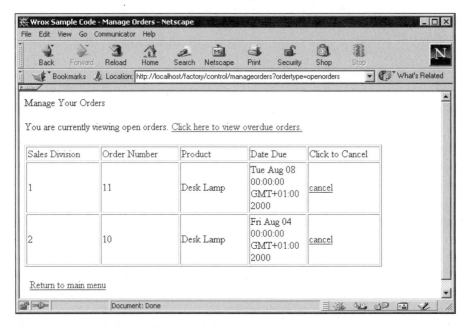

Here is the overdue order view:

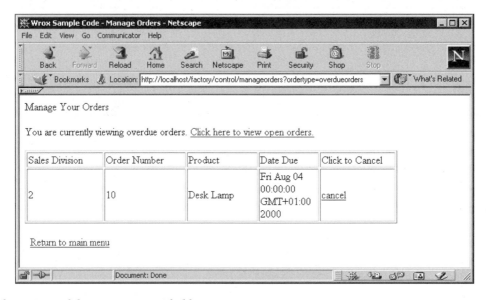

Both versions of the view are provided by `manageorders.jsp`:

```jsp
<jsp:useBean
  id="modelManager"
  class="ModelManager"
  scope="session"
/>

<%@ page import="java.util.Iterator" %>
<%@ page import="OrderView" %>

<html>
<head>
<title>Wrox Sample Code - Manage Orders</title>
<meta http-equiv="Content-Type" content="text/html; charset=iso-8859-1">
</head>

<body bgcolor="#FFFFFF">
<p>Manage Your Orders</p>

<p>You are currently viewing <%= request.getAttribute("order_view")%>. <a
href="manageorders?ordertype=<%= request.getAttribute("order_alt_url")%>">Click
  here to view <%= request.getAttribute("order_alt_view") %>.</a></p>

<table width="87%" border="1">
  <tr>
    <td width="21%">Sales Division</td>
    <td width="23%">Order Number</td>
    <td width="19%">Product</td>
    <td width="16%">Date Due</td>
    <td width="21%">Click to Cancel</td>
  </tr>
  <%
    String orderView = (String) request.getAttribute("order_view");
    Iterator iter = modelManager.getOrders( orderView );
    while (iter.hasNext()) {
      OrderView view = (OrderView) iter.next();
  %>
    <tr>
    <td width="21%"><%=view.getSalesDivision()%></td>
    <td width="23%"><%=view.getOrderNumber()%></td>
    <td width="19%"><%=view.getProduct()%></td>
    <td width="16%"><%=view.getDateDue()%></td>
    <td width="21%"><a href="cancelorder?salesdivision=<%=view.
    getSalesDivision()%>&ordernumber=<%=view.getOrderNumber()
    %>&ordertype=<%=request.getAttribute("order_url")%>">cancel</a></td>
    </tr>
  <%    }%>
</table>
<p>  <a href="choices">Return to main menu</a></p>
</body>
</html>
```

An order can be chosen for manufacture in the following view:

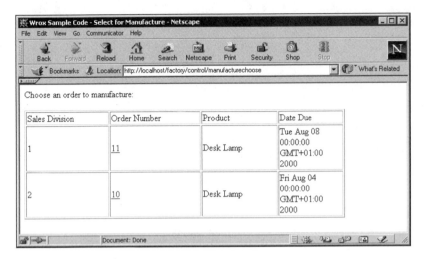

This view is provided by `manufacturechoose.jsp`:

```
<jsp:useBean
    id="modelManager"
    class="ModelManager"
    scope="session"
 />

<%@ page import="java.util.Iterator" %>
<%@ page import="OrderView" %>

<html>
<head>
<title>Wrox Sample Code - Select for Manufacture</title>
<meta http-equiv="Content-Type" content="text/html; charset=iso-8859-1">
</head>

<body bgcolor="#FFFFFF">
<p>Choose an order to manufacture:</p>
<table width="87%" border="1">
  <tr>
    <td width="21%">Sales Division</td>
    <td width="23%">Order Number</td>
    <td width="19%">Product</td>
    <td width="16%">Date Due</td>
  </tr>
  <%
    Iterator iter = modelManager.getOrdersToManufacture();
    while (iter.hasNext()) {
      OrderView view = (OrderView) iter.next();
  %>
    <tr>
    <td width="21%"><%=view.getSalesDivision()%></td>
```

```
        <td width="23%"><a href="order_chosen?salesdivision=<%=view.
                       getSalesDivision()%>&ordernumber=<%=view.getOrderNumber()
    %>"><%=view.getOrderNumber()%></a></td>
        <td width="19%"><%=view.getProduct()%></td>
        <td width="16%"><%=view.getDateDue()%></td>
        </tr>
<%     }%>
</table>
</body>
</html>
```

The first time that the user tries to choose an order for manufacture, they will be asked to enter a cell ID number to identify the area in which the product is being manufactured (to log in):

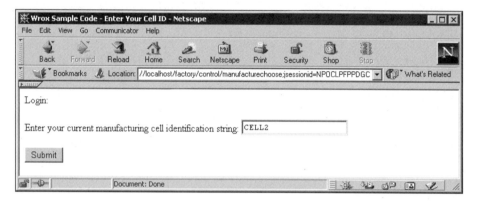

The ease with which I implemented this functionality is one of the advantages of using a front component. The view is provided by `cellid.jsp`:

```
<html>
<head>
<title>Wrox Sample Code - Enter Your Cell ID</title>
<meta http-equiv="Content-Type" content="text/html; charset=iso-8859-1">
</head>

<body bgcolor="#FFFFFF">
<p>Login:</p>
<form method="post" action="cell_chosen">
  <p>Enter your current manufacturing cell identification string:
    <input type="text" name="cell">
  </p>
  <p>
    <input type="submit" name="Submit" value="Submit">
  </p>
</form>
<p>  </p>
</body>
</html>
```

Once the order has been chosen for manufacture, the routing steps are displayed one at a time:

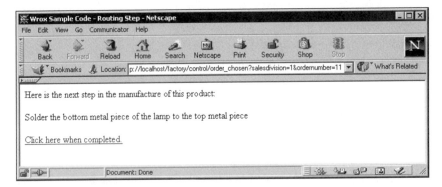

The view is provided by `manufactureroute.jsp`:

```
<jsp:useBean
   id="modelManager"
   class="ModelManager"
   scope="session"
 />

<html>
<head>
<title>Wrox Sample Code - Routing Step</title>
<meta http-equiv="Content-Type" content="text/html; charset=iso-8859-1">
</head>

<body bgcolor="#FFFFFF">
<p>Here is the next step in the manufacture of this product:</p>
<p><jsp:getProperty name="modelManager" property="nextRouting"/></p>
<p><a href="manufactureroute">Click here when completed.</a></p>
<p>  </p>
<p>  </p>
</body>
</html>
```

Finally, after all the routing steps have been displayed, the shipping information is entered:

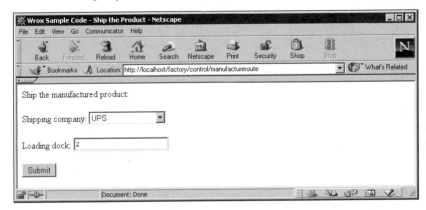

The view is provided by `ship.jsp`:

```html
<html>
<head>
<title>Wrox Sample Code - Ship the Product</title>
<meta http-equiv="Content-Type" content="text/html; charset=iso-8859-1">
</head>

<body bgcolor="#FFFFFF">
<p>Ship the manufactured product:</p>
<form method="post" action="ship_product">
  <p>Shipping company:
    <select name="shipping_company">
      <option>UPS</option>
      <option>Federal Express</option>
      <option>US Postal Service</option>
      <option>Private Carrier</option>
    </select>
  </p>
  <p>Loading dock:
    <input type="text" name="loading_dock">
  </p>
  <p>
    <input type="submit" name="Submit" value="Submit">
  </p>
</form>
<p>  </p>
</body>
</html>
```

I provide an HTML file that can be used as the 'welcome file' for this application, called `index.html`:

```html
<html>
  <head>
    <title>Wrox Sample Code - Manufacturing Application</title>
  </head>
  <body text="#000000" bgcolor="#FFFFFF"
    link="#0000EE" vlink="#551A8B" alink="#FF0000">
    <center>
      <h1>Factory Demo for JSPs and EJBs</h1>
    </center>
    <center><hr width="100%"></center>

    <p>This web site provides a simple interface to the manufacturing
        example that we developed for the chapters on Enterprise JavaBeans
        in the Wrox Server Side Java book.</p>

    <p><a href="control/choices">See the demo...</a>

  </body>
</html>
```

The welcome screen looks like this:

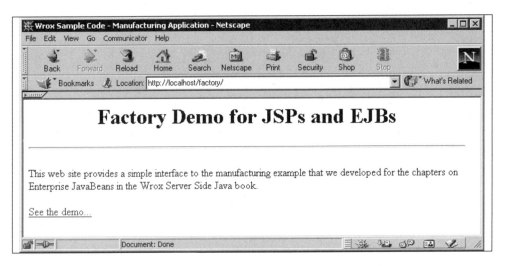

The web components are collected into a Java JAR with a .war extension, known as a web archive. This web archive has a web.xml deployment descriptor, located in the WEB-INF directory that specifies the welcome file, the servlet(s), the mapping of URLs to servlets, and the references to Enterprise JavaBeans. Here is the web.xml file:

```xml
<?xml version="1.0" encoding="UTF-8"?>

<!DOCTYPE web-app PUBLIC '-//Sun Microsystems, Inc.//DTD Web Application 2.2//EN'
'http://java.sun.com/j2ee/dtds/web-app_2.2.dtd'>

<web-app>
  <display-name>factoryWeb</display-name>
  <description>no description</description>
  <servlet>
    <servlet-name>entryPoint</servlet-name>
    <display-name>centralJsp</display-name>
    <description>no description</description>
    <jsp-file>main.jsp</jsp-file>
  </servlet>
  <servlet-mapping>
    <servlet-name>entryPoint</servlet-name>
    <url-pattern>/control/*</url-pattern>
  </servlet-mapping>
  <welcome-file-list>
    <welcome-file>/index.html</welcome-file>
  </welcome-file-list>
  <ejb-ref>
    <ejb-ref-name>ejb/ManageOrders</ejb-ref-name>
    <ejb-ref-type>Session</ejb-ref-type>
    <home>factory.manage_orders.ManageOrdersHome</home>
    <remote>factory.manage_orders.ManageOrders</remote>
  </ejb-ref>
  <ejb-ref>
```

```
        <ejb-ref-name>ejb/Manufacture</ejb-ref-name>
        <ejb-ref-type>Session</ejb-ref-type>
        <home>factory.manufacture.ManufactureHome</home>
        <remote>factory.manufacture.Manufacture</remote>
    </ejb-ref>
</web-app>
```

The directory structure of the web archive is as follows:

```
cellid.jsp
choices.jsp
createproduct.jsp
createrouting.jsp
index.html
main.jsp
manageorders.jsp
manufacturechoose.jsp
manufactureroute.jsp
message.jsp
placeorder.jsp
ship.jsp
WEB-INF/
        web.xml
        classes/
                ModelManager.class
                OrderView.class
                RequestProcessor.class
                ScreenNames.class
```

This web archive is added at the same level as the EJB archive in the EAR file. It must also be added to the J2EE-standard file `application.xml`. Assuming that the EJB JAR (or directory, if your application server supports this format) is named `ejbs`, and the web archive (or directory) is named `jsps` (note that these names are arbitrary), the `application.xml` file will look like this:

```
<?xml version="1.0"?>
<!DOCTYPE application PUBLIC "-//Sun Microsystems, Inc.//DTD J2EE Application
1.2//EN" "http://java.sun.com/j2ee/dtds/application_1_2.dtd">

<application>
  <display-name>Factory sample</display-name>
    <module>
      <ejb>ejbs</ejb>
    </module>
    <module>
      <web>
        <web-uri>jsps</web-uri>
        <context-root>/factory</context-root>
      </web>
    </module>
</application>
```

This application is (of course) portable and can be deployed on any J2EE-compliant server. Assuming that you are deploying it on Orion application server, the steps for deployment are basically the same as they were to deploy the EJB-only version, as described in Chapter 20. However, the web application needs to be added to a web site that Orion serves. The simplest way is to edit the `default-web-site.xml` file in the `config` directory. Add a `<web-app>` element. Specify an 'application' element property to be the same as that which you provided in Orion's `server.xml` file – in this case, factory. Specify a 'name' element property to be the same as the web module name that you specified in the J2EE `application.xml` file, in this case `jsps`. Specify a 'root' element property to be the web site path to which the application should be bound. In this case, I have specified '`/factory`.' Here is the entry in context:

```
<?xml version="1.0"?>
<!DOCTYPE web-site PUBLIC "Orion Web-site" "http://www.orionserver.com/dtds/web-site.dtd">

<web-site host="[ALL]" port="80" display-name="Default Orion WebSite">
  <!-- The default web-app for this site, bound to the root -->
  <default-web-app application="default" name="defaultWebApp" />
  <web-app application="factory" name="jsps" root="/factory" />
  <!-- Access Log, where requests are logged to -->
  <access-log path="../log/default-web-access.log" />
</web-site>
```

Once the application has been deployed, you can test it by directing your browser to `http://localhost/factory/`.

Troubleshooting Tips

Writing enterprise software is difficult, regardless of the tools and techniques that you use. It's almost inevitable that sooner rather than later, you'll come across an application server you can't get to work, an EJB you can't deploy, or an application that won't work how you designed it, and you'll spend hours or days trying to fix the problem. I've put together a few thoughts on how to approach these problems, although there still isn't a magic bullet for the software development process.

Regardless of whether you are writing a complete application or a single EJB component for resale, you will need to engage in a repeated develop-assemble-deploy-test cycle. If any stage of this process is slow, you will eventually be driven mad. Automate this process with a good IDE and/or tools such as Ant, the all-Java build system from the Jakarta Project (available from `http://jakarta.apache.org/ant/index.html`). Try not to develop on an application server that has a slow deployment process.

Read the documentation that comes with your application server. There's no substitute for knowing what you're doing.

You can still get your component to run in a debugger, by running your application server in the debugger. Most application servers will let you do this, although it's possible that some might not. If yours doesn't, simply use a different application server for debugging.

That doesn't mean your debugger is the first place you should turn. Your first option should be attempting to understand the code through inspection and thought, and not to use the debugger as a crutch. If you attempt to solve every problem with a debugger, you will bog down in the mechanics of the debugging process instead of improving your mental map of the code.

A debugger has other problems when you are using EJB components. Stepping through your code can change the behavior of your component in multiple ways, from 'fixing' timing bugs to causing a transaction to time out. Writing information to a log is often a less-invasive way to see what's happening in your code.

Some application servers provide proprietary optimizations, such as checking an is-modified method before synchronizing the state of an entity bean with the database. Try turning these optimizations off to see if you have made a mistake in their use.

Look at the logs. More than one time, I've started hunting around for the solution to a problem when the answer was perfectly visible in the application server's logs, as a clear error message or obvious stack trace.

At places in the code where you catch an exception that you didn't expect, print a stack trace before re-throwing an exception. This will cause an entry to be made in the application server's logs, from which you may be able to solve your problem.

If your problem is that your EJB JAR fails to deploy, take comfort, as this type of issue is often much easier to solve than a runtime error. Your application server should provide you with an error message that helps you pin it down. Solutions to a few common problems: make sure your callback methods and CMP entity data are declared as public, and make sure your deployment descriptor is in the META-INF directory (all caps).

When all else fails, try deploying your JAR on a different application server. Maybe the problem you're having is not your fault.

Summary

There are five roles defined in the Enterprise JavaBeans specification, corresponding to activities that must be performed for the successful development, deployment, and maintenance of an EJB-based application:

❑ The bean developer provides the EJB components for an application. They do not need to write code to support transactions, concurrency, security, communication, error handling beyond an application exception framework, load balancing, fail-over, or even persistence. They do not even need to be an expert in the target operational environment.

❑ The application assembler combines EJBs into a deployable application. The deployment descriptor is edited so that application level information is added. The application assembler may also add other types of application components, such as servlets, JSPs, or client apps. A person in the role of application assembler does not need to understand the implementation of any EJBs; they just need to understand the home and remote interfaces, and the business logic that the methods in the interface represent.

❑ Once the application is completed, the deployer must insert it into the target environment. The logical references that the enterprise bean provider uses must be mapped onto actual resources or identities. How this is done is completely specific to your application server vendor. A deployer does not need to be a domain expert; a person in this role must instead be an expert in the environment in which the application will execute.

❑ The system administrator role is responsible for configuring the application server, EJB container, and the environment in which they execute. The system administrator is also responsible for monitoring logs for system problems, security problems, etc.

❑ The application server/EJB container will be provided by a third-party vendor. The selection of an appropriate application server for development and deployment is important to the success of your software. Various factors such as cost, support, specification compliance, and optional features must be considered.

In the next chapter, we'll look at the draft EJB 2.0 specification. There are several important new topics, such as an improved model for container-managed persistence and a new type of EJB that responds to asynchronous messages. Among other topics, I'll show what you need to do to convert our manufacturing sample entity beans from EJB 1.1 persistence to EJB 2.0 persistence.

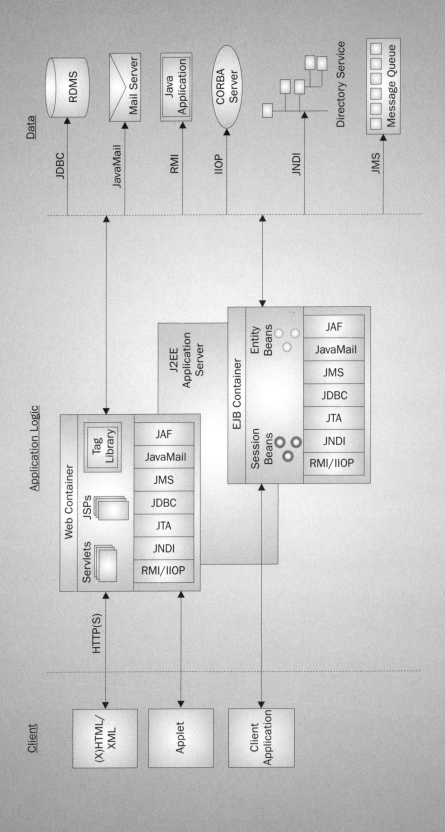

23

Enterprise JavaBeans 2.0

As this book's final revisions are made, a draft specification for version 2.0 of Enterprise JavaBeans has been released from Sun's Java Community Process. The information in that draft is subject to change. Small differences in the specification will certainly require you to make changes to the sample code before it will run in an EJB 2.0-compliant container (one of the more likely ones is the addition of primary keys to dependent objects). However, it is likely that it will be fundamentally similar to the final version of Enterprise JavaBeans 2.0. The material presented here is a hybrid of this draft specification and the most likely changes to that specification. (You can find the final version of the specification when it is available from Sun's web site at http://www.javasoft.com to clarify any differences.)

Many developers will be glad to hear that everything they know about Enterprise JavaBeans 1.1 still applies to EJB 2.0. Nothing has been deprecated. This is in stark contrast to the change from EJB 1.0 to EJB 1.1, when many major changes were made resulting in incompatibility.

If you have developed EJBs to the Enterprise JavaBeans 1.1 specification, they will deploy – unchanged – to a compliant EJB 2.0 container. The motivation for this is obvious: to be a credible enterprise technology, J2EE-compliant application servers cannot require an enterprise to redevelop its business components every time a new version is released. Sun had a little more flexibility moving from EJB 1.0 to EJB 1.1, because Enterprise JavaBeans technology was still in its infancy. The installed base of components and application servers was small compared to what it is today.

Although a bean developed to the EJB 1.1 specification will still work in an EJB 2.0 container, there are new capabilities that are available to application developers that will make them more productive, and their work more portable.

Note that it is assumed in the text that you have read the previous four chapters. The following aspects of the EJB2.0 specifications will be discussed:

- A new type of Container-Managed Persistence for entity beans, and specifying relationships and fields with relation to both development and deployment.

- The new EJB 2.0 Query Language, EJB QL

- Integration of EJBs with JMS

- The inclusion of business methods in the Home interface

New Features of EJB 2.0

The first new feature of the EJB 2.0 specification is a new type of **Container-Managed Persistence** (CMP) for entity beans. As discussed earlier in this book, there are many advantages to using container-managed persistence over bean-managed persistence. But the EJB 1.1 CMP contract had some weaknesses, too:

- First, there was no explicit support for managing relationships among entity beans.

- Second, there was no standard, portable way to manage dependent objects.

- Third, it was difficult for EJB container vendors to implement lazy loading mechanisms, dirty object detection, and similar value-added features.

These features – when provided at all – may need the cooperation of the EJB developer. Coding to the proprietary requirements of a particular EJB container could lead to non-portable code. Rather than make major changes to the existing CMP model, EJB 2.0 introduces an entirely new version of container-managed persistence. No changes were made to the 1.1 CMP model. Although the EJB 1.1 version of container-managed persistence has not been deprecated, I expect (as did the writers of the specification) that most new development will use the 2.0 version of container-managed persistence.

The second new feature is a **standard query language for container-managed persistence**. Remember, in the EJB 1.1 version of the specification, the EJB developer of a bean with container-managed persistence would provide a description to the deployer of what a finder method should do. The deployer was then responsible for providing the target application server with a query using server-specific syntax. This new standard query language will allow the bean developer, rather than the deployer, to develop the query syntax. This is good for two reasons:

- First, the query need only be developed and tested once, rather than in each operational environment. (As each EJB container has its own query syntax for EJB 1.1 CMP entities, a new version of every query needs to be developed and tested for every EJB container to which the entity is deployed.)

- Second, the EJB developer (who is an expert in business logic and a programmer) is more likely to have the appropriate skills than the deployer (who is an expert in the operational environment).

Note that the standard query language depends on features introduced to CMP entity beans in the 2.0 specifications, and will only work with EJB 2.0 CMP entity beans.

The third new feature is an **integration of Enterprise JavaBeans with the Java Message Service (JMS)**. The container can, as a result of the arrival of a JMS message, invoke a new type of stateless session bean, called a message-driven bean. Prior to the addition of the message-driven bean to the specification, an EJB that needed to respond to incoming JMS was "front-ended" by a client that consumed the asynchronous messages and forwarded them to an EJB by way of a synchronous method call. This was not ideal, either from an application-development perspective or from a deployment and management perspective.

The fourth new feature is to allow **business methods in the home interface**, rather than just the lifecycle methods that the EJB 1.1 specification allows. These business methods would support functionality that was independent of a specific entity identity – for instance, a method that needed to operate on a set of EJBs of that entity type. The equivalent functionality in EJB 1.1 would need to be placed in a stateless session bean. This new feature is a convenience that allows functionality related to a particular entity type to be grouped together in one EJB (the entity) rather than two EJBs (the entity and a session bean).

Finally, the EJB 2.0 specification defines an **interoperability protocol based on RMI/IIOP and CORBA**. This interoperability protocol should allow J2EE applications deployed on different servers to interact without any additional requirements placed on the EJB developer. However, transaction interoperability between containers is optional in this version of the specification. Developers of Enterprise JavaBeans do not need to do anything to take advantage of this interoperability.

This chapter will review these new features of the EJB 2.0 specification, both in terms of how to use them and when they are helpful and appropriate for your design.

One thing that you will want to consider is the state of the market. When will your target application server or application servers support EJB 2.0? In the highly competitive J2EE application server market, I suspect that implementations will lag the final version of the specification by at most six months or so, and some vendors will try to capture market share by releasing a product much sooner.

Container-Managed Persistence in EJB 2.0

In EJB 1.1, container-managed persistence was based on fields that were declared in the entity bean. For example, the Order bean from the manufacturing example in Chapter 20 of this book looks like this:

```
public class OrderEJB implements EntityBean {
  public int salesDivision;
  public int orderNumber;
  public Product productOrdered;
  public String status;
  public Date dateDue;
```

The EJB container would save the state of the EJB by copying these programmer-declared fields into persistent storage (for example by introspecting the bean, retrieving the values, and updating a SQL database). But this approach had its flaws. Many of these flaws stemmed from the lack of control that the EJB container had over these fields. For instance, the value of a field for a list with dependent objects might be replaced by the container with a special version of a list that loaded those objects only when necessary, and tracked which dependent objects were added, deleted, and modified. But what was to prevent the programmer from assigning a new `java.util.List` instance to the field? Only a convention specified by the container vendor.

Rather than try to improve this approach by specifying consistent rules that the bean developer needed to follow, the authors of the EJB 2.0 specification rejected this field-based approach entirely. Instead, the entity-bean developer specifies abstract accessor methods for the properties, dependent objects, and relationships in their EJB 2.0 CMP entity bean. Since access to the object's state is hidden behind these accessor methods, the EJB container can easily load data when it is used, track when data is modified, and use its own classes for tracking collections and relationships. The `OrderEJB` example above might look like this:

```
public abstract class OrderEJB2 implements EntityBean {

  // Exposed getter/setter business methods

  abstract public int getSalesDivision();
  abstract protected void setSalesDivision(int salesDivision);

  abstract public int getOrderNumber();
  abstract protected void setOrderNumber(int orderNumber);
  abstract public Product getProductOrdered();
  abstract protected void setProductOrdered(Product productOrdered);

  abstract public Date getDateDue();
  abstract protected void setDateDue(Date dateDue);

  abstract protected String getStatus();
  abstract protected void setStatus(String status);
```

Here's the key point. Nowhere in this class does the programmer define state fields for that entity. All they do is define abstract accessor methods, using the same convention that is familiar to programmers of regular (not enterprise) JavaBeans. Each item in the entity's state is represented by a `get<logical-item-name>` and `set<logical-item-name>` accessor method. (The programmer can define member variables in the entity, but such fields cannot represent container-managed state.)

Who implements these abstract methods? Your application server does – specifically, a new part of the application server called the **persistence manager**. The persistence manager's relationship to the EJB container is roughly akin to the EJB container's relationship with the application server. Someday, there may be a standard way to use an application server from one vendor, an EJB container from a second vendor, and a persistence manager from a third. Until standard APIs are developed that define these relationships, however, you can, in general, think of them all as the "application server."

Note that there can be exceptions to this, in the form of proprietary, but published, APIs. For instance, the open source OpenEJB project is intended to be a container that can be plugged into multiple application servers. Similarly, some EJB containers will probably provide APIs to plug in various persistence managers from established object/relational mapping companies.

Finally, it is much more likely that you will see portable persistence managers in the near future than it is that you will see portable EJB containers. While there is no standard contract whatsoever between the application server and the EJB container, much of the contract between the persistence manager and the EJB container is already defined in two ways: first, because much of this contract consists of the callback methods defined by the EJB 2.0 specification for entity beans; and second, because some other parts of the contract (such as access by the persistence manager to the transaction manager) were addressed in the specification. Officially, pluggable persistence managers are listed as a feature deferred to a future release. In practice, we're already 90% of the way there, and maybe the vendors will take us the rest of the way. Time will tell.

The bean developer is responsible for providing two components in the persistence model. The first is the Java code defining the bean, including all its dependent objects. The second is a description of the entity bean's persistence schema, including all the container-managed fields of the EJB and dependent objects, and the relationships between this bean, other entity beans, and dependent objects.

The bean deployer will provide the final piece of the puzzle to the persistence manager: a mapping of those fields and relationships to a persistence storage mechanism (likely a database). Exactly how this mapping occurs is specific to each persistence manager. However, the new design of entity bean persistence in EJB 2.0 almost guarantees that your vendor will support, at the very least, arbitrary mappings of dependent objects and relationships to a normalized database schema. You can program with dependent objects and relationships without concern for the target application server for your project.

There are four types of state that can exist in an entity bean using the 2.0 version of container-managed persistence:

❑ The first comprises **simple types**, such as int, Integer, float, Float, String, and Date. These types will typically be mapped to single columns in a relational database.

❑ The second is what the specification refers to as **dependent value classes**. These are any concrete class, other than a simple type, that is part of the state of your entity bean. A dependent value class must be serializable. It is quite likely that many application servers will save the state of dependent value classes in serializable form in a single column in your database, although nothing in the specification prevents them from providing a more sophisticated object/relational mapping, such as could be found for CMP entities in EJB 1.1. However, a dependent value class may not participate in any EJB 2.0 relationships, as we discuss shortly.

❑ The third type of state is **dependent object classes**. A dependent object class is defined in much the same way as the CMP entity bean itself. It is an abstract class with abstract accessor methods that are implemented by the persistence manager. It may have further dependent object classes, dependent value classes, and entity bean relationships (for example a dependent line item may have a relationship with a product entity bean). This is the preferred way to represent dependent objects.

❑ The fourth type of state is **related entity beans**. Unlike with EJB 1.1 CMP, EJB developers do not need to write the code to manage these relationships themselves. The persistence manager handles them automatically. A bean with EJB 2.0 container-managed persistence may have a relationship with an entity bean using any type of persistence: EJB 2.0 container-managed persistence, EJB 1.1 container-managed persistence, or bean-managed persistence.

The bean developer uses these four types of state without ever declaring member variables to represent state. They use abstract accessors that are then implemented by the persistence manager. In addition, the bean developer must provide information about the state and relationships of the bean in the XML deployment descriptor. At deployment time, the deployer will provide a mapping of the state information to the underlying persistent store.

In the deployment descriptor, there are only two types of state information: **cmp-field**s and **cmr-field**s (these are XML elements that refer to Container-Managed Persistence fields, and Container-Managed Relationship fields). A cmp-field can refer to a simple type (such as int, Double, String) or dependent value classes (such as com.wrox.AuthorContract). A cmr-field can refer to a dependent object class or a related entity bean. A dependent object class must not be used with a cmp-field, nor may a dependent value class be used with a cmr-field. The table overleaf highlights the differences between dependent object classes and dependent value classes:

Dependent Object Class	Dependent Value Class
Abstract	Concrete and serializable
State data retrieved and modified through abstract accessor methods	State data in member variables
Probably mapped to multiple columns in one or more database tables	Probably serialized into one database column
State data (cmp-fields) described in the deployment descriptor in a <dependent> sub-element of the <dependents> element	State data opaque to EJB container
Referenced by a <cmr-field> entry in the deployment descriptor	Referenced by a <cmp-field> in the deployment descriptor

The cmp-field Type

A cmp-field represents actual values in the state information in your entity bean and its dependent objects. It is helpful to think of a cmp-field as representing a column in a database table. Note that you do not necessarily need to use a relational database as your persistent store. Many applications will, but credible alternatives, such as object databases, do exist. More generally, you should understand that an entity that uses a relational database as its persistent store will not necessarily map to a single database table in that database.

The cmp-field element in the XML deployment descriptor is carried over from the EJB 1.1 version of the deployment descriptor. It plays exactly the same role that it did in that version of the specification. The cmp-field deployment descriptor elements enumerate the container-managed persistence values in the entity bean. The big difference between the specifications is that in EJB 2.0, the value is represented by accessor methods, rather than Java-language fields in the bean implementation. The cmp-field elements declare "virtual" variables, rather than concrete variables.

Here is the relevant part of the EJB 2.0 deployment descriptor for the manufacturing example used in previous chapters. This part of the deployment descriptor is identical to the EJB 1.1 version:

```
<entity>
    <ejb-name>Product</ejb-name>
    <home>factory.product.ProductHome</home>
    <remote>factory.product.Product</remote>
    <ejb-class>factory.product.ProductEJB</ejb-class>
<prim-key-class>java.lang.String</prim-key-class>
    <primkey-field>product</primkey-field>
<reentrant>False</reentrant>
<persistence-type>Container</persistence-type>
<cmp-field><field-name>product</field-name></cmp-field>
<cmp-field><field-name>name</field-name></cmp-field>
    ...
</entity>
```

A declaration of cmp-fields must be made for the state of all dependent object classes, as well as the main bean class. Here, there is no correspondence to the EJB 1.1 specification, because there was no such thing as dependent object classes. A dependent object is declared in the deployment descriptor underneath the new <dependents> element. There can be any number of child <dependent> elements. Each of those dependent elements can (and should) have a description. It must have the class name of the abstract class that the bean developer wrote, with the appropriate abstract accessor methods for that class' state. It must also have a name that is unique to that J2EE application (as the <dependent-name> element). This unique name is never referenced in the bean developer's code, but it is used to specify relationships and queries.

Here is what a declaration of a dependent object might look like. I have converted the manufacturing sample's routing instruction to be a dependent object class according to the EJB 2.0 specification. Here is how I would declare that dependent class in the deployment descriptor (this is the <dependents> element for the product EJB):

```
<dependents>
  <dependent>
    <description>Routing instruction dependent class </description>
    <dependent-class>
      factory.product.RoutingInstruction2
    </dependent-class>
    <dependent-name>RoutingInstruction</dependent-name>
    <cmp-field>sequence</cmp-field>
    <cmp-field>instruction</cmp-field>
  </dependent>
<dependents>
```

Keep in mind the important distinction between dependent object classes and dependent value classes. You cannot break down a dependent value class into individual cmp-field elements in the deployment descriptor. As far as the specification goes, dependent value classes are a single, indivisible unit. They must be serializable to give the EJB container the option of saving their state to a single database column (or similar persistence mechanism). Individual application servers may provide a more sophisticated treatment of dependent value classes, but you cannot portably rely on this behavior.

If I wanted to use the original RoutingInstruction class in this EJB, rather than the new RoutingInstruction2 class that conforms to the standards for a dependent object class, I could still do so. I would not need to (nor would I be allowed to) make a <dependent> element that described it in the deployment descriptor. Rather, I would simply add a <cmp-field> to the product section of the deployment descriptor for the list that contained those routing instructions:

```
<entity>
  <ejb-name>Product</ejb-name>
  <home>factory.product.ProductHome</home>
  <remote>factory.product.Product</remote>
  <ejb-class>factory.product.ProductEJB</ejb-class>
  <prim-key-class>java.lang.String</prim-key-class>
  <primkey-field>product</primkey-field>
  <reentrant>False</reentrant>
  <persistence-type>Container</persistence-type>
  <cmp-field><field-name>product</field-name></cmp-field>
  <cmp-field><field-name>name</field-name></cmp-field>
  <cmp-field><field-name>routingInstructions</field-name></cmp-field>
  ...
</entity>
```

If I used this approach, it is possible that the entire list would be serialized into a single column of the database, which would make it impossible for other applications (such as reporting tools) to access the data. It is also quite likely that my EJB would not benefit from such features as tuned updates and load-on-demand. The only compensating benefit for using a dependent value class is that a dependent value class might be reusable in other contexts (such as on the application client), or might already have been written.

The cmr-field Type

A `cmr-field` represents a relationship between an entity bean and another entity bean or a dependent object. In the EJB 1.1 specification, it was the responsibility of the bean developer to manage the relationships with other entity beans, and there was no standard way defined whatsoever for the bean developer to manage relationships to the EJB's dependent objects. In EJB 2.0 – and if you use the new version of container-managed persistence – the container will manage these relationships for you.

In keeping with the tradition of preferring declarative semantics to code, you give the EJB container information in the XML deployment descriptor about the relationships you want it to manage. It will use this information to perform this task on behalf of the business logic programmer. This is similar to the situation with transactions or access control. From the beginning, it has been the philosophy of Enterprise JavaBeans technology that if the container can perform a system-level task, it should. Now, with EJB 2.0, the task of maintaining relationships between logical groupings of state data has been made into one of these system-level tasks.

This is a quite logical extension of the persistence services that the EJB container already provided. An entity bean that used container-managed persistence could always have its member variables kept in sync with an underlying persistence store. But the state of an entity bean is not just its immediate member variables; it is the combination of those member variables and the relationships that the entity bean maintains.

A relationship is a common software development idiom. Relationships are often defined as the ability to navigate from instances of one class to instances of another class that have some common use based on their identity. Relationships are said to have **multiplicity** (or cardinality) and **direction**. The concept of multiplicity will most likely be familiar to anyone reading this text. Basically, each class in the relationship is allowed a certain minimum and maximum number of participating instances. The EJB container will only enforce four broad categories of multiplicity: one-many, many-one, one-one, and many-many. The concept of direction is also simple to understand. A relationship may be one-way, that is only one of the participants may be able to navigate it, or it may be bi-directional – either participant may be able to navigate it. The multiplicity and and direction of a relationship will always depend on the business rules and implementation techniques of your software, but here are some examples that may help to clarify these terms:

	One Way	Bi-Directional
One-to-one	Driver -> Automobile	Husband <-> Wife
One-to-many	Order -> Line-items	Boss <-> Employees
Many-to-many	Students -> Classrooms	Teachers <-> Students

Information about an entity bean's relationships is specified in the XML deployment descriptor, under the `<relationships>` element. Each relationship is represented by an `<ejb-relation>` element, which is a child of the `<relationships>` element. One endpoint of the relationship is an entity bean. The other endpoint of the relationship is another entity bean or a dependent object class.

If the endpoint is a dependent object class...

We have already seen how a dependent object is specified in the XML deployment descriptor, during the discussion of `cmp-field` entries, above. To recap, each dependent object must be specified as a `<dependent>` element under a `<dependents>` element. Each entry contains a description, an implementation class, a name, and the relevant `cmp-field` elements. The name of the dependent object is used to specify that dependent object in relationships or in queries.

If the endpoint is an entity bean...

When the endpoint of the relationship is an entity bean, there are two cases. The first case is that the related entity bean's schema is available. (It is available if the entity bean uses EJB 2.0 container-managed persistence, and is defined in the same `ejb-jar`.) In this case, no additional information needs to be provided about the entity. The second case is that the schema is not available (the entity bean is defined in a different `ejb-jar` or uses the EJB 1.1 persistence model). In this case, additional information about the entity bean needs to be provided in the form of an `<ejb-entity-ref>` element underneath the `<relationships>` element.

The motivation for making the bean developer provide this additional information is two-fold. First, entity references for any purpose in Enterprise JavaBeans technology are always made with a level of indirection to provide more flexibility in assembling applications. The `<ejb-entity-ref>` entry in the deployment descriptor serves as a placeholder for some deployed entity bean of the correct type. Second, the `<ejb-entity-ref>` element provides a unique name for use in relationships and queries. Although names within a single JAR must be unique, nothing in the Enterprise JavaBeans specifications forces a name to be unique across all deployed JARs, and in fact name clashes can easily occur. (Note that I'm talking about bean names, not JNDI entries, which will, in fact, be unique. But these are established at deployment time, too late to help us during development.)

If an `<ejb-entity-ref>` is necessary (that is, if the referenced entity bean is outside the immediate JAR), it will look similar to a resource reference declaration for EJBs. For instance, if in our manufacturing example we were deploying the order bean and the product bean in separate JARs, the reference might be declared as follows in the order bean's deployment descriptor:

```
<ejb-entity-ref>
  <description>
    This example is for the case where the product is deployed in a different
    jar from order. A product contains manufacturing instructions.
  </description>
  <remote-ejb-name>Product</remote-ejb-name>
  <ejb-ref-name>ejb/Product</ejb-ref-name>
  <home>factory.product.ProductHome</home>
  <remote>factory.product.Product</remote>
  <ejb-link>../product/product.jar#Product</ejb-link>
</ejb-entity-ref>
```

The description is an optional element that provides human-readable text regarding the referenced EJB. The `remote-ejb-name` provides a name for the referenced bean that is unique to this JAR. This is the name that will be used in relationships or finder queries to refer to the EJB. The home and remote interfaces specify the interface classes for the appropriate type of EJB. The optional `ejb-link` element serves the same role here as it does for a resource reference to an EJB – it allows the bean developer to indicate by EJB name which bean is being referenced.

If there is no `ejb-link` specified by the bean developer or application assembler, the reference must be resolved by the application deployer to point to a bean within the JNDI name space. This will be done using application-server specific tools.

Overcoming Name Conflicts in EJB Names Within a J2EE Application

If the bean developer or application assembler wants to use the `ejb-link` element to specify how the link should be resolved, they must use the EJB name of the linked bean. However, unlike with the deployed name in the JNDI namespace, there is no guarantee that the bean name will be distinct throughout the J2EE application. The Enterprise JavaBeans 2.0 specification introduces a new syntax for the `ejb-link` element for the case where there is a name conflict. A J2EE application is contained in a single JAR with an `.ear` extension. Within this EAR JAR, there might be multiple JARs containing Enterprise JavaBeans. In the case of a name conflict, the application assembler can indicate a particular EJB by specifying the path name of the `ejb-jar` file containing the referenced enterprise bean, relative to the current JAR. The name itself comes at the end of the path, separated from the path by #.

It's not necessary to use this new syntax if the bean's name is unique to the J2EE application (which will often be the case.) However, the syntax is not complicated. Assume that in our manufacturing EAR file, the directory and JAR structure was as follows:

```
/manufacturing/product/product.jar
/manufacturing/orders/order.jar
```

The `ejb-link` element for an `ejb-entity-ref` element from the order entity bean to the Product entity bean might be as follows:

```
<ejb-link>../product/product.jar#Product</ejb-link>
```

How to Specify the Relationship in the Deployment Descriptor

Each relationship between an entity bean and a dependent object, an entity bean and another entity bean, or a dependent object and another dependent object is specified in the deployment descriptor as a pair of `ejb-relationship-role` elements. One of those `ejb-relationship-role` elements will describe the relationship between the first entity bean or dependent object and its related entity or object, and the other element will describe the relationship in the other direction – from the related entity or object back to it.

Each `ejb-relationship-role` element declares that relationship role's name, its multiplicity, its navigability, and the name of the "virtual" field that represents the relationship (in other words, the name that will be appended to the "get" and "set" methods that the bean developer uses to access the relationship data). Each relationship role refers to a related entity bean or a dependent object by means of a dependent object name, an entity bean name, or the name of a remote reference to an entity bean, using the `<role-source>` element. The bean provider must ensure that the role-source refers to an actual, existing related object.

In our sample manufacturing application, the order bean has a one-to-one relationship with a product bean defined in the same JAR file of the same J2EE application. The relationship might be defined in the XML deployment descriptor as follows:

```
<relationships>
  <ejb-relation>
    <ejb-relation-name>Orders-Product</ejb-relation-name>
    <ejb-relationship-role>
      <ejb-relationship-role-name>
    order-has-product
```

```
        </ejb-relationship-role-name>
        <multiplicity>one</multiplicity>
        <role-source>
          <ejb-name>Orders</ejb-name>
        </role-source>
        <cmr-field>
          <cmr-field-name>product</cmr-field-name>
        </cmr-field>
      </ejb-relationship-role>

      <ejb-relationship-role>
        <ejb-relationship-role-name>
          product-in-order
        </ejb-relationship-role-name>
        <multiplicity>one</multiplicity>
        <role-source>
          <ejb-name>Product</ejb-name>
        </role-source>
      </ejb-relationship-role>
    </ejb-relation>
</relationships>
```

I have given the relationship the somewhat arbitrary name of Orders-Product. This name is never used anywhere in the code or referred to elsewhere by the deployment descriptor. It should be descriptive of the relationship for documentation purposes, but the only absolute requirement is that it be unique to this ejb-jar file.

There are always exactly two ejb-relationship-roles for every relationship, representing each direction that the relationship runs. These ejb-relationship-roles also have names, and these names are also arbitrary and unused (but required). There are no requirements on the ejb-relationship-role-names, not even for uniqueness. Again, however, they should be descriptive for documentation purposes. For this example, I have named the relationship from the order to the product as "order-has-product". I have named the reverse relationship "product-in-order".

That example from the manufacturing application demonstrates a one-to-one relationship with another entity bean. Here is an example from that project of a one-to-many relationship with a dependent object:

```
<relationships>
  <ejb-relation>
    <ejb-relation-name>Product-RoutingInstruction</ejb-relation-name>
    <ejb-relationship-role>
      <ejb-relationship-role-name>
        product-has-routing
      </ejb-relationship-role-name>
      <multiplicity>one</multiplicity>
      <role-source>
        <ejb-name>Product</ejb-name>
      </role-source>
      <cmr-field>
        <cmr-field-name>routingInstructions</cmr-field-name>
        <cmr-field-type>java.util.Collection</cmr-field-type>
      </cmr-field>
    </ejb-relationship-role>
```

```
    <ejb-relationship-role>
      <ejb-relationship-role-name>
        routing-for-product
      </ejb-relationship-role-name>
      <multiplicity>many</multiplicity>
      <role-source>
        <dependent-name>RoutingInstruction<dependent-name>
      </role-source>
    </ejb-relationship-role>
  </ejb-relation>
<relationships>
```

Note that this relationship, like the last one, is one-way. There is no way to navigate from the dependent object (the routing instruction) to its product, because there is no `cmr-field` defined for that dependent object.

Multiplicity of Relationships

Each relationship role needs to have a multiplicity (cardinality) specified. There are three valid choices for multiplicity: one-to-one, one-to-many, and many-to-many. Due to the limited number of choices, it really isn't that difficult to choose an appropriate multiplicity for your beans. But you absolutely need to have an understanding of what each of these choices means.

The easiest way to gain an understanding of the implications of each of these choices is to consider what they mean from the standpoint of relational database design. Although it is true that the Enterprise JavaBeans specification generalizes the database layer of an application to be a "persistent store", the truth is that many of the changes to the container-managed persistence model seem to have been made with the relational database model in mind.

The mapping of entity fields and relationships to particular tables is beyond the scope of the specification. However, it is easy to see how a basic mapping to a normalized database schema would be done for each type of relationship. A dependent object with a potential multiplicity greater than one would be saved in a row of a related database table. Relationship data is saved to a database by having columns that refer to the primary key of another table. The central question that we will consider is where those columns should be located: in the main database table for the persistence of the class declaring the relationship (as a foreign key); in the database table for the persistence of the class representing the other endpoint of the relationship; or in a table that exists for the sole purpose of tracking the relationship between those two classes.

In the case of a one-to-one relationship, the appropriate place to put the key reference is in the table for the persistence of the object that declares the relationship. For example, consider the case where an employee has a dependent object class representing his or her spouse. (This example does not attempt to fully, or even accurately, design the data model.) The "spouse" table might look like this:

table SPOUSE
integer spouse_id
varchar(25) fname
varchar(25) lname

The "employee" table would then refer to the `spouse_id` to maintain this one-to-one relation. This implicitly enforces the cardinality of the association (because there is only room for one `spouse_id` value in the employee table). It might look like this:

table EMPLOYEE
integer employee_id
varchar(25) fname
varchar(25) lname
integer spouse_id

In the case of a one-to-many relationship, the appropriate place to put the key reference is in the table for the persistence of the object other than the declarer of the relationship. For example, consider the case where an employee has a dependent object class representing his or her children. There can be many children related to a single employee. However, each child is related to exactly one employee. (For each employee, there may be any number of children.)

table CHILDREN
integer child_id
integer employee_id
varchar(25) fname
varchar(25) lname

The "children" table would refer to the `employee_id` to maintain this one-to-many relation. Many rows in the "children" table could refer to the same row in the employee table. Once again, the cardinality is implicitly enforced.

In the case of a many-to-many relationship, the key references to the related tables need to be maintained in a table created just for the relationship. For example, consider the case where an employee can be assigned to many projects, and a project can have many employees. (Again, I'd like to mention that this relational design model ignores many real-world complexities – like dates between which an employee is associated to a project.)

The project table might look like this:

table PROJECT
integer project_id
varchar(50) project_description

There would be a relationship table that might look like this (there would be an entry for each employee/project combination):

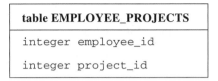

table EMPLOYEE_PROJECTS
integer employee_id
integer project_id

The design represented by these tables is as follows:

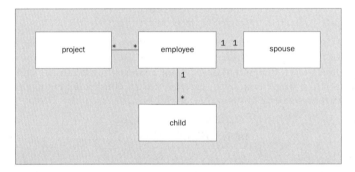

If you keep in mind these simple mappings of various multiplicities to relational database models, it will help you to understand which multiplicity is appropriate to a particular situation. It will also help you to understand various rules that we will encounter later about assignment of dependent objects.

Navigability and the <cmr-field>

Every `ejb-relationship-role` must have a role source. This role source simply identifies the perspective from which this relationship role is declared. The role source will have as its child element one of the following elements: `ejb-name`, `remote-ejb-name`, or `dependent-name`.

If this relationship role has a `cmr-field` (and the schema of the object is available) it is considered navigable. In other words, code in that `ejb` or dependent object may use the accessors associated with that `cmr-field` to navigate the relationship.

You have the option to make a relationship bi-directional for dependent objects, or for CMP 2.0 entity beans that are defined in the same `ejb-jar` file. When does it make sense to do it? Well, because at this point there aren't even any complete implementations of this preliminary specification, there is no general body of knowledge and experience to draw on for recommendations. I'll make a recommendation... just be willing to make your own judgment based on your experience and perhaps from sources such as the `ejb-interest` mailing list from Sun. (To join the list or see its archives, go to `http://archives.java.sun.com/archives/ejb-interest.html`) It seems to me that one of the main reasons to have a bi-directional relationship is when you have a many-to-many relationship between entity beans and dependent objects. The business logic in the dependent object might need to notify its other related entities about a particular change made through one entity. This situation could arise with many-to-many entity beans as well, although the specification discourages situations where a reentrant callback might be made on an entity.

The Complete CMP 2.0 Deployment Descriptor

To put the information about container-managed persistence fields and container-managed relationships in context, here is the complete EJB 2.0 deployment descriptor for the manufacturing sample application (ignore the <query> elements until the next section):

```xml
<?xml version="1.0"?>

<ejb-jar>
 <enterprise-beans>
```

(The session bean entries are the same as the EJB 1.1 deployment descriptors that we examined in Chapter 22, except for the updated home and remote interface references.)

```xml
    <session>
      <ejb-name>ManageOrders</ejb-name>
      <home>factory.manage_orders.ManageOrdersHome</home>
      <remote>factory.manage_orders.ManageOrders</remote>
      <ejb-class>factory.manage_orders.ManageOrdersEJB</ejb-class>
      <session-type>Stateless</session-type>
      <transaction-type>Container</transaction-type>
      <ejb-ref>
        <ejb-ref-name>ejb/Order</ejb-ref-name>
        <ejb-ref-type>Entity</ejb-ref-type>
        <home>factory.order.OrderHome2</home>
        <remote>factory.order.Order2</remote>
        <ejb-link>Orders</ejb-link>
      </ejb-ref>
      <ejb-ref>
        <ejb-ref-name>ejb/Product</ejb-ref-name>
        <ejb-ref-type>Entity</ejb-ref-type>
        <home>factory.product.ProductHome2</home>
        <remote>factory.product.Product2</remote>
        <ejb-link>Product</ejb-link>
      </ejb-ref>
      <env-entry>
        <env-entry-name>lead_time</env-entry-name>
        <env-entry-type>java.lang.Integer</env-entry-type>
        <env-entry-value>3</env-entry-value>
      </env-entry>
      <env-entry>
        <env-entry-name>max_inventory_time</env-entry-name>
        <env-entry-type>java.lang.Integer</env-entry-type>
        <env-entry-value>10</env-entry-value>
      </env-entry>
    </session>
    <session>
      <ejb-name>Manufacture</ejb-name>
      <home>factory.manufacture.ManufactureHome</home>
      <remote>factory.manufacture.Manufacture</remote>
      <ejb-class>factory.manufacture.ManufactureEJB</ejb-class>
      <session-type>Stateful</session-type>
      <transaction-type>Container</transaction-type>
```

```
<ejb-ref>
  <ejb-ref-name>ejb/Order</ejb-ref-name>
  <ejb-ref-type>Entity</ejb-ref-type>
  <home>factory.order.OrderHome2</home>
  <remote>factory.order.Order2</remote>
  <ejb-link>Orders</ejb-link>
</ejb-ref>
<ejb-ref>
  <ejb-ref-name>ejb/ManageOrders</ejb-ref-name>
  <ejb-ref-type>Session</ejb-ref-type>
  <home>factory.manage_orders.ManageOrdersHome</home>
  <remote>factory.manage_orders.ManageOrders</remote>
  <ejb-link>ManageOrders</ejb-link>
</ejb-ref>
<env-entry>
  <env-entry-name>shipmentSQL</env-entry-name>
  <env-entry-type>java.lang.String</env-entry-type>
  <env-entry-value>
    insert into shipments (division, order_number, carrier, loading_dock,
    date_completed, manufactured_by ) values (?, ?, ?, ?, ?, ?)
  </env-entry-value>
</env-entry>
<resource-ref>
  <res-ref-name>jdbc/shipDB</res-ref-name>
  <res-type>javax.sql.DataSource</res-type>
  <res-auth>Container</res-auth>
</resource-ref>
</session>

<entity>
  <ejb-name>Orders</ejb-name>
  <abstract-schema-name>OrderHome2</abstract-schema-name>
  <home>factory.order.OrderHome2</home>
  <remote>factory.order.Order2</remote>
  <ejb-class>factory.order.OrderEJB2</ejb-class>
  <prim-key-class>factory.order.OrderPK</prim-key-class>
  <reentrant>False</reentrant>
  <persistence-type>Container</persistence-type>
```

The <cmp-field> element is unchanged from EJB 1.1's CMP model:

```
<cmp-field><field-name>salesDivision</field-name></cmp-field>
<cmp-field><field-name>orderNumber</field-name></cmp-field>
<cmp-field><field-name>status</field-name></cmp-field>
<cmp-field><field-name>dateDue</field-name></cmp-field>
```

The finder queries for CMP entities are a new addition to the deployment descriptor. Previously, they were specified in an application server-specific format during deployment:

```
<query>
  <query-method>
    <method-name>findOpenOrders</method-name>
    <method-params/>
  </query-method>
```

```
    <ejb-ql>WHERE status LIKE 'o%'</ejb-ql>
  </query>

  <query>
    <query-method>
      <method-name>findUncompletedOrders</method-name>
      <method-params/>
    </query-method>
    <ejb-ql>WHERE status NOT LIKE 'c%' AND status NOT LIKE 'f%'</ejb-ql>
  </query>
```

The `<ejb-ref>` element is unchanged from EJB 1.1:

```
    <ejb-ref>
      <ejb-ref-name>ejb/Product</ejb-ref-name>
      <ejb-ref-type>Entity</ejb-ref-type>
      <home>factory.product.ProductHome2</home>
      <remote>factory.product.Product2</remote>
      <ejb-link>Product</ejb-link>
    </ejb-ref>
  </entity>

<entity>
  <ejb-name>Product</ejb-name>
  <home>factory.product.ProductHome2</home>
  <remote>factory.product.Product2</remote>
  <ejb-class>factory.product.ProductEJB2</ejb-class>
    <abstract-schema-name>OrderEJB2</abstract-schema-name>
    <prim-key-class>java.lang.String</prim-key-class>
    <primkey-field>product</primkey-field>
    <reentrant>False</reentrant>
    <persistence-type>Container</persistence-type>
    <cmp-field><field-name>product</field-name></cmp-field>
    <cmp-field><field-name>name</field-name></cmp-field>
  </entity>
</enterprise-beans>
```

Dependent objects have `cmp-field` and `cmr-field` values, just like entity beans:

```
<dependents>
  <dependent>
    <description>Routing instruction dependent class </description>
    <dependent-class>
      factory.product.RoutingInstruction2
    </dependent-class>
    <dependent-name>RoutingInstruction</dependent-name>
    <cmp-field>sequence</cmp-field>
    <cmp-field>instruction</cmp-field>
  </dependent>
</dependents>
```

Each relationship consists of two relationship roles. The participants can be two entities, two dependent objects, or one of each:

```
<relationships>
  <ejb-relation>
  <ejb-relation-name>Orders-Product</ejb-relation-name>
  <ejb-relationship-role>
    <ejb-relationship-role-name>order-has-product</ejb-relationship-role-name>
    <multiplicity>one</multiplicity>
    <role-source>
      <ejb-name>Orders</ejb-name>
    </role-source>
    <cmr-field>
      <cmr-field-name>product</cmr-field-name>
    </cmr-field>
  </ejb-relationship-role>

  <ejb-relationship-role>
    <ejb-relationship-role-name>product-in-order</ejb-relationship-role-name>
    <multiplicity>one</multiplicity>
    <role-source>
      <ejb-name>Product</ejb-name>
    </role-source>
  </ejb-relationship-role>
  </ejb-relation>

  <ejb-relation>
    <ejb-relation-name>Product-RoutingInstruction</ejb-relation-name>

    <ejb-relationship-role>
      <ejb-relationship-role-name>
        product-has-routing</ejb-relationship-role-name>
      <multiplicity>one</multiplicity>
      <role-source>
        <ejb-name>Product</ejb-name>
      </role-source>
      <cmr-field>
        <cmr-field-name>routingInstructions</cmr-field-name>
        <cmr-field-type>java.util.Collection</cmr-field-type>
      </cmr-field>
    </ejb-relationship-role>

    <ejb-relationship-role>
      <ejb-relationship-role-name>
        routing-for-product
      </ejb-relationship-role-name>
      <multiplicity>many</multiplicity>
      <role-source>
        <dependent-name>RoutingInstruction<dependent-name>
      </role-source>
    </ejb-relationship-role>
  </ejb-relation>
</relationships>
```

The assembly descriptor hasn't changed from our EJB 1.1 version:

```
<assembly-descriptor>
  <container-transaction>
    <method>
      <ejb-name>Orders</ejb-name>
      <method-name>*</method-name>
    </method>
    <trans-attribute>Required</trans-attribute>
  </container-transaction>
  <container-transaction>
    <method>
      <ejb-name>Product</ejb-name>
      <method-name>*</method-name>
    </method>
    <trans-attribute>Required</trans-attribute>
  </container-transaction>
  <container-transaction>
    <method>
      <ejb-name>ManageOrders</ejb-name>
      <method-name>*</method-name>
    </method>
    <trans-attribute>Required</trans-attribute>
  </container-transaction>
  <container-transaction>
    <method>
      <ejb-name>Manufacture</ejb-name>
      <method-name>*</method-name>
    </method>
    <trans-attribute>Required</trans-attribute>
  </container-transaction>
</assembly-descriptor>
</ejb-jar>
```

Coding CMP 2.0 Beans

At this point, you've been introduced to the basic concepts of the new EJB 2.0 container-managed persistence model for entity beans. Now we'll look at how this translates into the Java code of your EJB. There are a few details of which you should be aware, especially for dependent objects and relationships.

Fields

We have already seen the code for simple accessor methods for cmp-fields in an entity bean or a dependent object class. There is absolutely no complexity here; you simply provide an abstract getXXX() method and an abstract setXXX() method where before you would have used a field.

You may make these abstract accessors accessible to the client by putting them in the bean's remote interface. One disadvantage of this is that you cannot put data validation or transformation logic in an abstract method. If you need validation or transformation, you may want to expose different access methods to the client, which will perform the required function but delegate data access to the accessor.

Relationships

The code for relationships, however, will have a few details that need to be considered. The bean developer navigates or changes an entity bean's relationships the same way they access or manipulate a bean's member variables: by using abstract accessor methods that they declared in the bean. The return or parameter types of those methods with a one-to-one relationship will be the type of the related class. The return or parameter types of those methods with a one-to-many relationship will be either a `java.util.Collection` or a `java.util.Set` interface, containing zero or more instances of the related class. (The return type will never be `null`; if there are no instances of the related class, a collection or set with zero items will be returned instead of `null`. If the programmer passes a null parameter, the persistence manager will empty the collection, that is delete all the related element references.)

The collections used for one-to-many or many-to-many relationships are instantiated and managed by the persistence manager. The bean developer is not allowed to create them, or to assign a different collection as a `cmr-field` value. If the bean developer sets a collection `cmr-field` value to `null`, the persistence manager will set it to be an empty collection instead.

The collection classes and dependent value classes defined by the persistence manager may not be returned to a client. The persistence manager might be using a data-management strategy such as load-on-demand, and the state of the collection or value class may not be appropriate for serialization. The only `cmr-field` type that can be exposed as getter and setter methods in the remote interface of the bean is one that has a single entity bean as its return/parameter type.

Instead of returning container-defined collection classes or dependent value classes, the bean developer should simply use their own container class (such as one of the ones defined in the `java.util` package) and their own view class, to which they can copy the information retrieved from the accessor methods.

Creation of Dependent Objects

Dependent object classes are abstract classes. When you need a new one, you can't just instantiate one – because you can't instantiate an abstract class. The implementation of an abstract class is completely hidden from the EJB developer. The application server (and specifically, the persistence manager) gets to implement this class however it would like, when the EJB is deployed. To solve this problem, the designers of the EJB specification used the factory pattern. They require the bean developer to provide a "factory method" for each dependent object class that takes part in a relationship, of the form create<type>, where <type> is the name of the dependent object type.

Assignment of Dependent Objects

The semantics of assignment of dependent objects is a little complicated, although easy to understand when you consider the underlying reasons for the rules. The complication comes when a dependent object is already in a relationship with an entity bean, and it is assigned to a different relationship. The assignment has different meanings, depending on the type of relationship.

In the case of a **one-to-one** relationship, if a dependent object class instance is assigned from one EJB `cmr-field` to the same relationship type for another `cmr-field`, it will be moved (not copied), and the value of the source `cmr-field` is set to `null`.

In the case of a **one-to-many** relationship, if the collection class of dependent objects is assigned from one EJB `cmr-field` to the same relationship type in another `cmr-field`, it will be moved (not copied), and the value of the source `cmr-field` will be set equal to an empty collection.

Additionally, the bean developer may also manipulate individual members of a collection for a one-to-many relationship. However, they must respect the concept that assignment of a dependent object from one EJB to another represents a move, not a copy. If they assign an existing dependent object to a new EJB, they must already have deleted it from its original collection in the source EJB. The persistence manager will detect any attempt to share a dependent object in two different one-to-many relationships, and it will throw a `java.lang.IllegalArgumentException`.

In the case of a **many-to-many** relationship, if a dependent object class instance or collection is assigned from one EJB `cmr-field` to the same relationship type in another `cmr-field`, the object or objects of the first instance are assigned to the second instance, without being removed from the first instance. If the collection of one is assigned to the other, the objects contained in the two collections will be the same. However, the collections themselves are not the same, and subsequent additions to and removals from one collection will not result in changes to the other.

Why does the assignment of a dependent object have "move" semantics for one-to-one and one-to-many relationships, but "copy" semantics for many-to-many relationships? The reason is implicit in the various multiplicity constraints. The "one" in one-to-one and one-to-many indicates that an instance can participate in only a single relationship at a time. If assignment for these relationships had "copy" semantics, it would always result in an illegal state – and so would be worthless. In the case of a many-to-many relationship, it is legal for all the objects in a relationship to have multiple related instances, and so "copy" semantics make sense.

The Manufacturing Sample Application

It was simple to port the manufacturing application's two CMP entity beans to the EJB 2.0 model. The Order entity begins the same way by defining some constants:

```
public abstract class OrderEJB2 implements EntityBean {
   // Properties
   private static final String OPEN_STATUS = "o";
   private static final String DEFAULT_STATUS = OPEN_STATUS;
   private static final String CANCELED_STATUS = "c";
   private static final String IN_PROCESS_STATUS = "m";
   private static final String COMPLETED_STATUS = "f";
```

The state variables are redefined as abstract getter and setter methods. Some of these are exposed to the client, and therefore declared as `public`. Some are internal to the implementation, and so are declared as `protected`:

```
// Exposed getter/setter business methods

   abstract public int getSalesDivision();
   abstract public int getOrderNumber();
   abstract public Product getProductOrdered();
   abstract public Date getDateDue();

   // Non-exposed getter/setter methods

   abstract protected String getStatus();
   abstract protected void setSalesDivision(int salesDivision);
   abstract protected void setOrderNumber(int orderNumber);
   abstract protected void setProductOrdered(Product productOrdered);
   abstract protected void setDateDue(Date dateDue);
   abstract protected void setStatus(String status);
```

The following are the other exposed business methods:

```
// Other business methods

public String getOrderStatus() {
  String status = getStatus();

  if (status.equals(OPEN_STATUS))
    return StatusStrings.OPEN;
  else if (status.equals(CANCELED_STATUS))
    return StatusStrings.CANCELED;
  else if (status.equals(IN_PROCESS_STATUS))
    return StatusStrings.IN_PROCESS;
  else if (status.equals(COMPLETED_STATUS))
    return StatusStrings.COMPLETED;
  throw new EJBException("Unknown status");
}

public void cancelOrder() throws OrderNotCancelableException {
  String status = getStatus();
  if (
    status.equals(IN_PROCESS_STATUS)
      ||
    status.equals(COMPLETED_STATUS)
      )
    throw new OrderNotCancelableException();
  setStatus(CANCELED_STATUS);
}

public void beginManufacture() {
  setStatus(IN_PROCESS_STATUS);
}

public void completeManufacture() {
  setStatus(COMPLETED_STATUS);
}
```

In the EJB 1.1 version of this entity, the getStatus() method did the translation of the status string for the client. In the EJB 2.0 version, this translation is done by a new getOrderStatus() method. This is necessary because the naming convention for state accessor methods requires us to make getStatus an abstract method. We change the remote interface to reflect the new method:

```
public interface Order2 extends EJBObject {

public int getSalesDivision()
  throws RemoteException;

public int getOrderNumber()
  throws RemoteException;

public Product getProductOrdered()
  throws RemoteException;
```

```
    public String getOrderStatus()
      throws RemoteException;

    public void cancelOrder()
      throws RemoteException, OrderNotCancelableException;

    public void beginManufacture()
      throws RemoteException;

    public void completeManufacture()
      throws RemoteException;

    public Date getDateDue()
      throws RemoteException;
}
```

The lifecycle methods are similar to the EJB 1.1 version of the entity. They are rewritten to use the accessor methods to read or modify the entity's state:

```
// Lifecycle and framework methods

    public OrderPK ejbCreate(int salesDivision, int orderNumber,
      Product productOrdered, Date dateDue)
      throws CreateException
    {
      setSalesDivision(salesDivision);
      setOrderNumber(orderNumber);
      setProductOrdered(productOrdered);
      setDateDue(dateDue);
      setStatus(DEFAULT_STATUS);

      return null; // For container-managed persistence
    }

    public void ejbPostCreate(int salesDivision, int orderNumber,
      Product productOrdered, Date dateDue) {}

    public OrderPK ejbCreate(int salesDivision, int orderNumber,
      String product, Date dateDue)
      throws CreateException
    {
      setSalesDivision(salesDivision);
      setOrderNumber(orderNumber);
      setDateDue(dateDue);
      setStatus(DEFAULT_STATUS);

      try {
        ProductHome productHome = getProductHome();
        setProductOrdered(productHome.findByPrimaryKey(product));
      } catch (RemoteException re) {
        re.printStackTrace();
        throw new EJBException(re);
      } catch (FinderException fe) {
```

```
        fe.printStackTrace();
        throw new CreateException("Product does not exist");
    }

    return null; // For container-managed persistence
}

public void ejbPostCreate(int salesDivision, int orderNumber,
    String product, Date dateDue) {}

public void ejbLoad() {}
public void ejbStore() {}
public void ejbActivate() {}
public void ejbPassivate(){}
public void ejbRemove() {}

public void setEntityContext(EntityContext ctx) {}

public void unsetEntityContext() {}
```

The helper method to retrieve the product's home interface is identical to the previous version:

```
// Implementation helpers

private ProductHome getProductHome() {
    try {
        InitialContext initial = new InitialContext();
        ProductHome home = (ProductHome) javax.rmi.PortableRemoteObject.narrow(
            initial.lookup( "java:comp/env/ejb/Product" ), ProductHome.class );
        return home;
    } catch (NamingException ne) {
        ne.printStackTrace();
        throw new EJBException(ne);
    }
}
```

The Product entity bean also needs to change its interface because of a conflict with the state accessor naming convention. The getRoutingInstructions() method must become a getProductRoutingInstructions() method:

```
public interface Product2 extends EJBObject
{
    public String getProduct()
        throws RemoteException;

    public String getName()
        throws RemoteException;

    public void setName( String name )
        throws RemoteException;
```

```
    public RoutingInstruction[] getProductRoutingInstructions()
        throws RemoteException;

    public void addRoutingInstruction( int sequence, String instruction )
        throws RemoteException;

    public void deleteRoutingInstruction( int sequence )
        throws RemoteException, NoSuchRoutingInstruction;

    public void replaceRoutingInstructions(
        RoutingInstruction[] newRoutingInstructions )
        throws RemoteException;
}
```

The RoutingInstruction class is exactly the same as it was for the EJB 1.1 version. However, it is no longer used in the entity's persistent state. Instead, it is now a client view class. For the persistent state, a new dependent object class is defined: RoutingInstruction2:

```
public abstract class RoutingInstruction2
{
    public abstract int getSequence();
    public abstract void setSequence( int sequence );

    public abstract String getInstruction();
    public abstract void setInstruction( String instruction );
}
```

The product entity bean begins with abstract state accessors. Some of them are exposed to the client, and some are not. Note that there are two factors that influence the choice of which methods to expose. First, of course, there is the consideration of what information your clients need to perform their business function. Second, there is the rule that neither dependent object classes nor container-managed collections may be provided to the client:

```
public abstract class ProductEJB2 implements EntityBean {
    // Exposed getter/setter business methods
    public abstract String getProduct();
    public abstract String getName();
    public abstract void setName( String name );

    // Non-exposed getter/setter methods
    protected abstract void setProduct(String product);
    protected abstract Collection getRoutingInstructions();
    protected abstract void setRoutingInstructions(Collection collection);
```

The Product entity bean must also provide an abstract create method that the persistence manager will implement and that can be used to create a new RoutingInstruction2 instance:

```
    protected abstract RoutingInstruction2 createRoutingInstruction();
```

The business methods in the product entity are all related to the manipulation of routing instructions. The parameters or return values of these methods will use the RoutingInstruction class, because they are exposed to the client. The entity's state, however, uses the dependent object class RoutingInstruction2. Look at how this first business method translates between the two:

```
// Other business methods

  public RoutingInstruction[] getProductRoutingInstructions()
  {
    Collection routingInstructions = getRoutingInstructions();

    RoutingInstruction[] routingArray =
      new RoutingInstruction[routingInstructions.size()];

    Iterator iter = routingInstructions.iterator();
    int iterCount=0;
    while (iter.hasNext()) {
        RoutingInstruction2 ri2 = (RoutingInstruction2) iter.next();
        routingArray[iterCount++] = new RoutingInstruction(
          ri2.getSequence(), ri2.getInstruction());
    }
    return routingArray;
  }
```

When a routing instruction is added, the create method must be used to instantiate a new
RoutingInstruction2 implementation, since RoutingInstruction2 is an abstract class whose
implementing class is unknown to the bean developer (and will vary between persistence managers):

```
public void addRoutingInstruction(int sequence, String instruction)
{
  Collection routingInstructions = getRoutingInstructions();
  RoutingInstruction2 ri = this.createRoutingInstruction();
  ri.setSequence(sequence);
  ri.setInstruction(instruction);
  routingInstructions.add(ri);
}
```

To delete a routing instruction, simply remove it from its collection:

```
public void deleteRoutingInstruction(int sequence)
    throws NoSuchRoutingInstruction
  {
    Collection routingInstructions = getRoutingInstructions();
    Iterator iter = routingInstructions.iterator();
    while (iter.hasNext())
    {
      RoutingInstruction2 ri = (RoutingInstruction2) iter.next();
      if (ri.getSequence() == sequence)
      {
        iter.remove();
        return;
      }
    }
    throw new NoSuchRoutingInstruction();
  }
```

The last business method replaces all the routing instructions. Note that we can't simply replace the existing collection with one of our own; we need to use the persistence manager's implementation:

```
public void replaceRoutingInstructions(
    RoutingInstruction[] newRoutingInstructions)
{
    Collection routingInstructions = getRoutingInstructions();
    routingInstructions.clear();

    for (int iter=0; iter<newRoutingInstructions.length; iter++)
    {
        RoutingInstruction ri = newRoutingInstructions[iter];
        RoutingInstruction2 ri2 = createRoutingInstruction();
        ri2.setSequence(ri.sequence);
        ri2.setInstruction(ri.instruction);
        routingInstructions.add(ri2);
    }
}
```

And finally, the lifecycle and framework methods:

```
// Framework and lifecycle methods

    public String ejbCreate(String product, String name,
        RoutingInstruction[] routingInstructions)
    {
        setProduct(product);
        setName(name);
        replaceRoutingInstructions(routingInstructions);
        return null;
    }

    public void ejbPostCreate(String product, String name,
        RoutingInstruction[] routingInstructions) {}

    public void ejbActivate() {}
    public void ejbLoad() {}
    public void ejbPassivate() {}
    public void ejbRemove() {}
    public void ejbStore() {}

    public void setEntityContext(EntityContext ctx) {}

    public void unsetEntityContext() {}
}
```

The EJB 2.0 Query Language

The bean developer uses the new EJB query language to define finder methods for entity beans that use the EJB 2.0 version of container-managed persistence. **EJB QL** is a declarative language similar in many respects to SQL, and is intended to be portable to all EJB 2.0-compliant containers and persistence managers. EJB QL is defined in such a way as to make it possible for implementations to "compile" the finder queries to a target language – such as SQL – of a persistent store as a performance optimization. In other words, your EJB QL query might be translated to an equivalent SQL statement when your entity bean is deployed. At runtime, the container need not even parse the query.

Along with finder methods, EJB 2.0 defines two new types of methods that use the query language, known as "**select**" methods. Unlike finder methods, these select methods are not exposed to clients. They are used in the implementation class alone. They allow the programmer to retrieve dependent objects, values, or related EJBs based on relevant search criteria. One advantage of using a select method rather than trying to accomplish the retrieval with Java programming is that a select method can be more efficient, since a SQL query is more efficient than loading all the data and iterating through it. A second advantage is that a declarative approach is more maintainable and less error prone. These select methods are declared as abstract methods of the bean class, and are implemented by the persistence manager.

There are two types of select methods. One is similar to a finder method, in that it operates on all instances of that entity type. The pattern for these methods is `ejbSelect<METHOD>()`, where `<METHOD>` represents a descriptive name for the activity of the method. However, unlike finder methods, select methods of the form `ejbSelect<METHOD>()` can return individual instances or collections of any type represented by a `cmp-field`, as well as remote interfaces represented by a `cmr-field`. This type of select statement solves a difficult problem from EJB 1.1: how to efficiently work with a set of data without resorting to SQL statements in a session bean. For instance, a program that manages a college's alumni organization may want to get a list of all the cities with at least x alumni. An `ejbSelect<METHOD>()` method can implement this logic in a database-independent manner.

The second type of select method is associated with a particular entity identity. (Note that this means it cannot be used from the implementation of a home-interface business method.) The pattern for these methods is `ejbSelect<METHOD>InEntity()`. They can return individual instances or collections of any arbitrary type represented in that entity. This type of select method was introduced as a way of efficiently navigating the EJBs relationships with other entity beans and with its dependent objects. It may seem unnecessary for a simple bean, for which the Java code to locate and use dependent objects and related entities does not seem complicated, difficult, or inefficient. Consider, however, the case where an entity has thousands of dependent objects or related entities. It would be inefficient at runtime for the persistence manager to load all those dependent objects for a method that only needed to manipulate a few. Furthermore, it is clearer and less error-prone if the relationship navigation can be specified declaratively.

Where Does the Programmer Specify a Query?

A query of any of the three types – finder, `ejbSelect<METHOD>()`, or `ejbSelect<METHOD>InEntity()` – is specified in two parts. First, there is the **method declaration**. For a finder method, this is located in the home interface – just as it is for EJB 1.1 CMP entities. For either type of select, the method is declared as abstract in the bean's main implementation class. For example, an entity bean that represents an order might have a select method that returns the city to which the shipment should be sent:

```
public abstract class SportTeamEJB implements EntityBean
{
  // …

  abstract public String ejbSelectShipToCityInEntity()
    throws FinderException;

  // …
}
```

The method implementation must obey the appropriate naming convention. For a finder method, this means that the method must be declared in the home interface as returning the remote interface type, and must have a name of the form findByXXX(), where XXX is descriptive of the method's purpose. For a select method, the method must be declared in the bean's implementation class, and must have a name of the form ejbSelect<METHOD>() or ejbSelect<METHOD>InEntity(), as described above. The method must always be declared to throw javax.ejb.FinderException.

The return type of a select statement can be individual instances or collections of any type represented by a cmp-field, as well as remote interfaces represented by a cmr-field. The collection class must be either java.util.Collection or java.util.Set. One important difference between the two is that java.util.Collection will return duplicates, whereas java.util.Set will not (similar to the SQL keyword "distinct").

Second, there is the **query language** specified in the XML deployment descriptor. A query is defined as a <query> element as a child of the relevant <entity> element. A query has an optional description, the method to which it applies, and the query language string.

The method is specified using the <query-method> element. A query-method element has two sub-elements: <method-name> and <method-params>. Unlike when specifying method permissions and transaction semantics for a <method> element, the <method-params> element is mandatory. The same syntax is used.

The actual query language is in an <ejb-ql> element. Ignoring for now the content of the query, here is a possible example of an entry in the deployment descriptor:

```
<query>
  <query-method>
    <method-name>ejbSelectOverdueLibraryBooksInEntity</method-name>
    <method-params/>
  </query-method>
  <ejb-ql>SELECT b FROM b in books WHERE overdue is TRUE</ejb-ql>
</query>
```

How Does the Programmer Specify a Query?

An EJB QL string, depending on the context and use, may have up to three clauses: "SELECT," "FROM," and "WHERE." A **SELECT** clause indicates the return type of the query (or of the instances in a returned collection). A "select" method should always have one. A **FROM** clause declares variables that represent navigation paths in your schema, known as correlation variables. These variables are used in the WHERE clause or SELECT clause. This is a different concept from the "FROM" clause in SQL, and will be explained shortly. A **WHERE** clause is a conditional expression that limits the results of your query. It can include parameters from the finder or select method.

As we discuss the format of the EJB QL string, we'll consider the example of an entity bean implementing the concept of an order. (This ubiquitous example is used by the authors of the EJB 2.0 specification themselves in discussing EJB QL.) The Order entity bean has a one-to-many relationship with a dependent object representing line items. Each line item refers to a Product entity bean. An order also has a ship-to and a bill-to address.

The Concept of the Schema

The schema of an entity bean or a dependent object is the definition of its `cmp-fields` and `cmr-fields`. In this respect, it is similar to the schema of a relational database (consisting of its fields and its relationship constraints). A schema type has a name. For an entity bean, this schema type name is specified by the bean developer in the deployment descriptor with the element `<abstract-schema-name>`. For a dependent object, the schema type name is the same as the dependent object name.

The schema plays a central role in the EJB QL. Every query in an entity bean must use that bean's schema, or the schema of related objects in the same `ejb-jar`, for navigation.

It's important to understand the difference between a bean's schema and its remote interface. The remote interface is an actual, instantiable Java class that can be returned from a select method. The schema is a logical view on the bean, with no instantiable Java class. It may not be used as the return type from a select method. However, within the query, it can be used for navigation to follow relationships or retrieve state variables.

You cannot refer to a schema of an entity or dependent object that is defined outside your `ejb-jar`. You may call finder methods on entities outside your JAR, but you may not navigate to their dependent objects or refer to their state.

The schema of the example order entity would, of course, be expressed as an XML deployment descriptor. Its name (such as `OrderBean`) would also be specified in the deployment descriptor. I'll summarize the state variables of our sample schema here (the relationships were summarized above):

OrderBean	address dependent object
number custname lineitems order_date shipping_address billing_address	street city state postal_code

lineitem dependent object	ProductBean
product quantity shipped	name description type

Understanding the Context

Don't forget the difference between an `ejbSelect<METHOD>InEntity()` method and an `ejbSelect<METHOD>()` method. The first relates to a single entity, its state, and its relationships. The second will query all entities of the appropriate type.

Some EJB QL queries will be valid for either type of method. However, they will get very different results. Keep this distinction in mind when you are considering what a particular query means.

Navigation Operator "."

Within a query, you can navigate the entity's abstract schema in the WHERE clause – or in the FROM clause when you declare correlation variables. You use the **navigation operator** "." to traverse cmp- and cmr-fields. For instance, here is an example of a simple but valid EJB QL query:

```
SELECT shipping_address.city
```

The navigation operator is very similar to the "." operator in Java that allows the programmer to navigate state variables in a class.

This particular query does one of three things, depending on the select method to which it is attached. If the select method is declared as follows:

```
String ejbSelectShipToCityInEntity()
        throws FinderException
```

This query will simply return the name of the city to which the order should be shipped. The select method will only examine the shipping_address associated with the current entity. If the select method is declared as follows:

```
java.util.Collection ejbSelectShipToCity()
        throws FinderException
```

It will return a collection with one member for every single order in the persistent store. If there were one million orders in the database, this collection will have one million cities in it (including, probably, many duplicates). You would probably not have a query like this without a WHERE clause to limit the results. If the select method were to be declared as follows:

```
java.util.Set ejbSelectShipToCity()
        throws FinderException
```

It would return a collection with one member for every **unique** city in the orders table of the persistent store. A query like this might be used to retrieve a list of cities in which any items have ever been sold.

Here are some other examples of using the navigation operator. This one returns a dependent object of type address:

```
SELECT shipping_address WHERE shipping_address.state = 'NY'
```

This next example must be from a finder method, because it does not have a SELECT clause. Remember that SELECT clauses are mandatory for select methods, but illegal for finder methods:

```
WHERE billing_address.state = 'MA'
```

Navigating Over Collections

You cannot use the navigation operator to navigate into a many-valued relationship. For instance, the following is illegal:

```
SELECT lineitems.product.name WHERE lineitems.shipped = TRUE
```

To accomplish the goal of this query (a list of names of products whose orders have been shipped), you need to **declare a correlation variable in the FROM clause**. Assigning the correlation variable results in an implicit iteration. You use the "in" keyword to do the assignment/iteration.

The legal version of the query that provides a list of products whose orders have been shipped is as follows:

```
SELECT l.product.name FROM l in lineitems WHERE l.shipped = TRUE
```

This query will implicitly iterate over every lineitem. (You should understand that, depending on your persistence manager, this is probably done in the database using SQL that was created when your query was compiled. In other words, it is a very efficient operation compared to actually instantiating all these objects in your application server.) For each lineitem, the "shipped" flag will be checked. If it is TRUE, the name of the product in that lineitem will be added to the result.

Input Parameters

Many finder methods and select queries will need to be parameterized at runtime. To parameterize a query, add the appropriate parameters to the method declaration. Then refer to those parameters in the WHERE clause with a question mark, followed by a one-based index of the parameter in the method declaration. When the programmer calls a finder method or select query, the parameters that he or she passes to the method are matched up to the parameters in the query. For example, for the method:

```
OrderEJB findByCustomerName(String custname)
       throws FinderException
```

The query might be as follows:

```
WHERE custname = ?1
```

Date formats are always tricky when they need to be expressed in String form, because of the wide variety of formats and their meanings. The creators of EJB QL bypassed this nicely: date literals need to be expressed as a standard Java long millisecond value.

Other Entity Beans

Query references to entity beans that are within the same ejb-jar and use the EJB 2.0 persistence model represent a schema. Query references to entity beans that are outside the ejb-jar or use the EJB 1.1 persistence model represent the remote interface of the entity bean. For instance, assume (as we have done all along) that the Product bean is defined in the same JAR as the order bean. This query is illegal, because you cannot return a schema:

```
SELECT l.product FROM l in lineitems WHERE l.shipped = TRUE
```

If the product bean were defined in a different ejb-jar file, the query would be legal, because you would be returning the remote interface of a product bean from the select method. (On the other hand, in this second scenario, the following query would be illegal, because you don't have access to the schema of the product bean: SELECT l.product.name FROM l in lineitems WHERE l.shipped = TRUE.)

You can reference a remote interface, rather than a schema, for a locally defined bean by using **the remote interface navigation operation** =>. To make the above query legal, we would write it as follows:

```
SELECT l=>product FROM l in lineitems WHERE l.shipped = TRUE
```

You can also call an entity bean's finder method by using a **finder expression**. A finder expression has the following syntax:

```
EjbName>>finder_method(arguments)
```

Where `EjbName` is either the `<ejb-name>` element of an entity bean or the `<remote-ejb-name>` element of an entity bean reference. The arguments must match those in the signature of the entity bean reference. A finder variable (such as ?1 or ?2) can be used as an argument. Otherwise, the arguments must be literals: numeric values (6.2, 5), strings ('NY', 'purchased'), or boolean (TRUE or FALSE).

WHERE Clause Options

A WHERE clause in EJB QL is somewhat similar to a WHERE clause in SQL. You have many of the same options for comparison operators:

Logical operators: NOT, AND, OR

Comparison operators: =, >, >=, <, <=, <>
You can only compare like types: numbers with numbers, strings with strings, booleans with booleans, and an object type with another instance of that exact type. Comparisons for entity bean remote references or schemas are done by comparing their primary key values. Comparisons for dependent objects will probably also be done using primary keys, although this was not in the original draft specification.

Arithmetic operators: +, -, *, /

BETWEEN expression: [NOT] BETWEEN x AND y

IN expression: [NOT] IN (string, string, ...)
Or `entity-reference` [NOT] IN (finder-expression)

LIKE expression: [NOT] LIKE pattern [ESCAPE character]
Where the pattern is a string literal with an underscore representing any single character, a percent sign representing any sequence of zero or more characters, and all other characters representing themselves. The optional escape character is used to escape the meaning of one of the special characters, when it is necessary to represent a literal underscore or percent sign.

Null test: IS [NOT] NULL
Conditional expressions containing a NULL are evaluated in EJB QL just as they would be in SQL 92. Here is a brief description of the semantics of NULL values, taken from the draft EJB 2.0 specification:

❑ SQL treats a NULL value as unknown. Comparison or arithmetic operations with an unknown value always yield an unknown value.

❑ Path expressions that contain NULL values during evaluation return NULL values.

❑ The IS NULL and IS NOT NULL operators convert a NULL cmp-field or cmr-field value into the respective TRUE or FALSE value.

❑ Boolean operators use three valued logic, defined by the following tables for the AND, OR, and NOT operators:

AND OPERATOR	T	F	NULL
T	T	F	NULL
F	F	F	F
NULL	NULL	F	NULL

OR OPERATOR	T	F	NULL
T	T	T	T
F	T	F	NULL
NULL	T	NULL	NULL

NOT OPERATOR	
T	F
F	T
NULL	NULL

Queries from the Manufacturing Application

A findByPrimaryKey method does not need to have its query specified with EJB QL (because the container already has enough information to figure it out). In addition to the findByPrimaryKey methods, there are two custom finder methods in the sample manufacturing application. In the chapter on entity beans, we specified their query in an application-server specific file. We also used an application-server specific format. For the Orion server, it was as follows:

```
<finder-method query="$status LIKE 'o%'">
  <method>
    <ejb-name>Orders</ejb-name>
    <method-name>findOpenOrders</method-name>
    <method-params>
    </method-params>
  </method>
</finder-method>
<finder-method
    query="$status NOT LIKE 'c%' AND $status NOT LIKE 'f%'">
  <method>
    <ejb-name>Orders</ejb-name>
```

```
      <method-name>findUncompletedOrders</method-name>
      <method-params>
      </method-params>
    </method>
  </finder-method>
```

The queries are now specified in the deployment descriptor, and in a standard format (EJB QL). They look like this:

```
<query>
  <query-method>
    <method-name>findOpenOrders</method-name>
    <method-params/>
  </query-method>
  <ejb-ql>WHERE status LIKE 'o%'</ejb-ql>
</query>

<query>
  <query-method>
    <method-name>findUncompletedOrders</method-name>
    <method-params/>
  </query-method>
  <ejb-ql>WHERE status NOT LIKE 'c%' AND status NOT LIKE 'f%'</ejb-ql>
</query>
```

Message-Driven Beans

In the EJB 1.1 specification, it was possible for an EJB to send a message using JMS. However, it was not possible for an EJB to be the target of a JMS message unless an intermediate non-EJB message consumer forwarded it for processing. The Enterprise JavaBeans 2.0 specification adds a new type of EJB, called a **message-driven bean**, which can receive a JMS message.

Messaging is similar to RMI/JRMP or RMI/IIOP in that it is a mechanism for programs to communicate. You may wonder why it is important to add messaging to the RMI-based communication protocols that clients can already use with Enterprise JavaBeans. There are several advantages that messaging can provide:

❏   First, messaging can provide reliable, asynchronous delivery of information from the client to the server. A client application might be disconnected from the network (for example on a laptop on an airplane) when it sends a message. A messaging service can store this message and send it to the application server when the client is reconnected to the network.

❏   Second, messaging can be a simple way to provide interoperability with other enterprise components. Although there are other ways for components of a distributed software system to interoperate (such as CORBA and IIOP), messaging is often a good choice because it is simple and flexible.

❏   Third, messaging can be used to implement a publish-subscribe architecture. A client (which could be anything from a Java applet to an SAP installation) can send a message without considering what other components need the information. A message-driven bean can be a component that listens for messages on a particular topic.

Having said that, in many, even most, cases some flavor of RMI (or IIOP for non-Java clients) is the appropriate way to communicate with an EJB component. Unless you find that you require the functionality messaging provides, you should not introduce an additional layer between your client and the EJB component.

Another perspective from which to look at the situation is to consider the advantages that Enterprise JavaBeans technology can provide to a software architecture already committed to using messaging. JMS clients may also want to update a database through JDBC. The use of JMS and JDBC can be covered in the same transaction by implementing the consumer of a JMS message as an EJB.

The use of JMS is covered in Chapter 28, and an explanation of JMS will not be repeated in this chapter. However, there is some EJB-specific material regarding how to write and configure a message-driven bean.

A message-driven bean is similar to a stateless session bean in terms of the role it will play in your architecture. It will be used exclusively as a "boundary object," in that it is an entry point into your business logic from a client. From this object, methods on stateless session EJBs and on entity EJBs may be called. (Since a message-driven bean is stateless, it will never make sense to call from it to a stateful session bean.) Updates to resources such as a database can be made in the same transaction as message acknowledgement. If the transaction were rolled-back, the message would not be acknowledged and it would be redelivered (depending on the policy set by the administrator of the system).

In other ways, a message-driven bean is quite different from other types of EJBs. It has neither a home nor a remote interface. Instead, its public interface consists of a single onMessage() method that is called by the EJB container when an appropriate message arrives. The onMessage() method has a single argument: the message that is being delivered.

Exception handling is different for message-driven beans as well. The onMessage() method must not be declared to throw any checked exception (including java.rmi.RemoteException). It is also considered a programming error for a message-driven bean to throw an unchecked (run time) exception – as is the case with any listener for JMS messages, and unlike session or entity beans. If a run time exception is thrown anyway, the event is logged, the instance of the bean is discarded, and any existing transaction is rolled back. (The container will still be able to handle JMS messages using another instance of the bean.)

Message-driven beans do not have a client security context, because that information is not propagated with a message. This means that it does not make sense to apply standard access-control security to a message-driven bean, nor does it make sense to obtain the message-driven bean's Principal in the business logic. The EJB 2.0 specification allows for a deployer to select the Principal under which a bean's methods are executed. This applies to entity beans, session beans, and message-driven beans. The primary use for this will probably be to specify a Principal for message-driven beans, to use when calling other entity and session beans. The bean developer specifies the appropriate role in the deployment descriptor, and the deployer identifies a particular "run-as" principal, appropriate for the specified role, using container-specific tools. The deployment descriptor entry to specify a "run-as" principal would be as follows:

```
<security-identity>
  <run-as-specified-identity>
    <role-name>some-role</role-name>
  </run-as-specified-identity>
</security-identity>
```

Message-driven beans can execute in the context of a transaction as explained in earlier chapters. Like session beans, the transaction can be bean-managed (which I do not recommend) or container-managed. As there is no way to propagate an existing transactional context, a container-managed transaction must be newly created. Since there cannot be an existing transaction, the only legal values for the onMessage() business method of a message-driven bean with container-managed transactions are Required or NotSupported.

Regardless of the transactional context, the EJB container handles message acknowledgement. The bean developer should not use the JMS API for message acknowledgement. Assuming that the message-driven bean is using container-managed transactions, message acknowledgement occurs when the transaction commits.

A message-driven bean must implement the javax.ejb.MessageDrivenBean interface. Besides the onMessage() method (inherited by MessageDrivenBean through javax.jms.MessageListener), there are three lifecycle methods:

- ❏ **setMessageDrivenContext(MessageDrivenContext mdc)**
  After the bean has been constructed, this method is called by the container. The MessageDrivenContext is similar to the EntityContext or SessionContext both in the way it is used by the developer and because it inherits from EJBContext. The operation of the following methods in MessageDrivenContext is the same as for the methods in EntityContext or SessionContext: setRollbackOnly, getRollbackOnly, and getUserTransaction. The getCallerPrincipal and isCallerInRole methods cannot be used, because there is no client security context. The getEJBHome() method cannot be used, because there is no home interface for message-driven beans.

- ❏ **ejbCreate()**
  After the setMessageDrivenContext method is called and before any messages are received, the ejbCreate method is called. The bean developer can use this method to acquire any resources that are required per-instance. In general, resources should be acquired right before their use, and this method should be empty.

- ❏ **ejbRemove()**
  Before the instance is removed from the container (except in the case of a run time exception), the ejbRemove method will be called. The bean developer can use this method to release any resources that are required per-instance. In general, resources should be released right after their use, and this method should be empty.

Like session beans and entity beans, a message-driven bean instance is single-threaded. Therefore, a message-driven bean does not have to be coded as reentrant. A container may instantiate multiple instances of message-driven beans to process messages concurrently.

A message-driven bean is associated with a single JMS topic or queue. The deployer associates the bean with a particular topic or queue when the bean is deployed into the enterprise's environment. The bean developer does not specify a particular JMS destination, any more than they specify particular security principals or database connection information. Doing so would limit a bean's portability from environment to environment.

It may make sense for the deployer to associate more than one message-driven bean type with a topic subscription. Topics are used to implement publish-subscribe architectures, where any number of subscribers may exist. However, because JMS queues are used for point-to-point architectures, the bean deployer should not associate more than one message-driven bean type with a single queue.

The bean developer can also use the `<jms-message-selector>` element to specify the JMS message selector that determines which messages the bean receives. See the chapter on JMS for more information about JMS message selectors.

The usage of a message-driven bean is not significantly different from the usage of a stateless session bean. Here is an example of a message-driven bean, minus the business logic, that you can use as a template for your own development. (You can also compile, assemble, and deploy this as-is, so it is a complete example... although it doesn't do anything.)

```
package somepackage;

import javax.ejb.*;
import javax.jms.*;

public class SampleMessageBean implements MessageDrivenBean {
  public MessageDrivenContext mdc;

  public void onMessage(Message msg) {

    // Business logic
  }

  public void setMessageDrivenContext(MessageDrivenContext mdc) {
    this.mdc = mdc;
  }

  public void ejbCreate() {

    // Often empty
  }

  public void ejbRemove() {

    // Often empty
  }
}
```

Business Methods in the Home Interface

The last significant change from the point of view of the server-side programmer in the EJB 2.0 specification is that it allows business methods in the home interface of an entity bean. These business methods will execute without being associated with a particular object identity. The functionality of such business methods is intended to apply to that class of entity beans as a whole, rather than to a particular entity bean. In that sense, they are like class (static) methods in a Java object.

Using this new capability is simple:

❑   Declare your business method in the home interface. *Don't* begin your method name with `create`, `find`, or `remove`, which would conflict with naming schemes for create methods, find methods, or remove methods.

❑   Implement your business method in the bean implementation class, in a method with the name `ejbHome<METHOD>()`, where `<METHOD>` is the declared method name in the home interface. Don't use any method (`ejbSelect<METHOD>InEntity()`, `getEJBObject()`, or `getPrimaryKey()`) that requires a particular identity.

❏ Declare transactional and security semantics in the deployment descriptor exactly as you do for any other business method.

❏ And finally, call the method from a client using a reference to the home interface, exactly as you would call a create method, remove method, or finder method.

Until this addition to the specification, an entity EJB often needed to be paired with a stateless session EJB to provide it with aggregate methods related to that entity. This wasn't very clean from an architectural point of view. Now, those aggregate methods can be associated directly with the component that represents that entity. Allowing business methods in the home interface doesn't extend the capabilities of Enterprise JavaBeans technology so much as it provides a semantic convenience for improved design.

Home interface business methods shouldn't be used to replace session beans acting as façade objects for a non-EJB client. Façade objects are still useful for all the reasons listed in the chapter on session beans. However, business functionality relating to groups of entities can be moved from session beans to home-interface methods in entity bean components.

For example, our manufacturing example had an Order entity bean that represented an individual order. It also had a `ManageOrders` session bean that served two purposes: as a façade to certain clients, and as a services-layer session bean that operated on orders as an aggregate. The business logic that provided these services on collections of orders (in the `getOverdueOrders()` and `getSchedulableOrders()` methods) can now be moved to the order entity bean, which simplifies the architecture.

Here is what the new home interface would look like for the order bean (the last two methods are the new ones):

```
package factory.order;

import javax.ejb.*;
import java.rmi.RemoteException;
import factory.product.Product;
import java.util.Date;
import java.util.Collection;
import factory.manage_orders.OpenOrderView;
import factory.manage_orders.OverdueOrderView;

public interface OrderHome3 extends EJBHome {
   Order create(int salesDivision, int orderNumber,
             Product productOrdered,
             Date dateDue) throws RemoteException, CreateException;

   Order create(int salesDivision, int orderNumber,
             String productOrdered,
             Date dateDue) throws RemoteException, CreateException;

   Order findByPrimaryKey(OrderPK order)
         throws RemoteException, FinderException;

   Collection findOpenOrders() throws RemoteException, FinderException;

   Collection findUncompletedOrders()
```

```
              throws RemoteException, FinderException;

    OverdueOrderView[] getOverdueOrders() throws RemoteException;

    OpenOrderView[] getSchedulableOrders() throws RemoteException;

}
```

Here is the implementation class. It is very similar to `OrderEJB2`. The implementation methods for `getOverdueOrders()` and `getSchedulableOrders()` are named `ejbHomeGetOverdueOrders()` and `ejbHomeGetSchedulableOrders()`, respectively. Of course we need to add the environment information about the lead time and maximum inventory time for our calculations. We also need to save the entity context so that we can retrieve the home interface. Other than that, there are no differences:

```
package factory.order;

import javax.ejb.*;
import javax.naming.*;
import java.rmi.RemoteException;
import factory.product.Product;
import factory.product.ProductHome;
import java.util.Date;
import java.util.LinkedList;
import java.util.Collection;
import java.util.Iterator;
import factory.manage_orders.OpenOrderView;
import factory.manage_orders.OverdueOrderView;

public abstract class OrderEJB3 implements EntityBean {

    // Properties
    private static final String OPEN_STATUS = "o";
    private static final String DEFAULT_STATUS = OPEN_STATUS;
    private static final String CANCELED_STATUS = "c";
    private static final String IN_PROCESS_STATUS = "m";
    private static final String COMPLETED_STATUS = "f";

    public EntityContext ctx;

    // Exposed getter/setter business methods

    abstract public int getSalesDivision();
    abstract public int getOrderNumber();
    abstract public Product getProductOrdered();
    abstract public Date getDateDue();

    // Non-exposed getter/setter methods

    abstract protected String getStatus();
    abstract protected void setSalesDivision(int salesDivision);
    abstract protected void setOrderNumber(int orderNumber);
    abstract protected void setProductOrdered(Product productOrdered);
    abstract protected void setDateDue(Date dateDue);
    abstract protected void setStatus(String status);
```

```
// Other business methods

public String getOrderStatus() {
  String status = getStatus();

  if (status.equals(OPEN_STATUS)) {
    return StatusStrings.OPEN;
  } else if (status.equals(CANCELED_STATUS)) {
    return StatusStrings.CANCELED;
  } else if (status.equals(IN_PROCESS_STATUS)) {
    return StatusStrings.IN_PROCESS;
  } else if (status.equals(COMPLETED_STATUS)) {
    return StatusStrings.COMPLETED;
  }
  throw new EJBException("Unknown status");
}

public void cancelOrder() throws OrderNotCancelableException {
  String status = getStatus();
  if (status.equals(IN_PROCESS_STATUS)
          || status.equals(COMPLETED_STATUS)) {
    throw new OrderNotCancelableException();
  }
  setStatus(CANCELED_STATUS);
}

public void beginManufacture() {
  setStatus(IN_PROCESS_STATUS);
}

public void completeManufacture() {
  setStatus(COMPLETED_STATUS);
}

// Lifecycle and framework methods

public OrderPK ejbCreate(int salesDivision, int orderNumber,
                         Product productOrdered,
                         Date dateDue) throws CreateException {
  setSalesDivision(salesDivision);
  setOrderNumber(orderNumber);
  setProductOrdered(productOrdered);
  setDateDue(dateDue);
  setStatus(DEFAULT_STATUS);

  return null;    // for container-managed persistence
}

public void ejbPostCreate(int salesDivision, int orderNumber,
                          Product productOrdered, Date dateDue) {}

public OrderPK ejbCreate(int salesDivision, int orderNumber,
                         String product,
```

```
                             Date dateDue) throws CreateException {
    setSalesDivision(salesDivision);
    setOrderNumber(orderNumber);
    setDateDue(dateDue);
    setStatus(DEFAULT_STATUS);

    try {
      ProductHome productHome = getProductHome();
      setProductOrdered(productHome.findByPrimaryKey(product));
    } catch (RemoteException re) {
      re.printStackTrace();
      throw new EJBException(re);
    } catch (FinderException fe) {
      fe.printStackTrace();
      throw new CreateException("Product does not exist");
    }

    return null;   // for container-managed persistence
  }

  public void ejbPostCreate(int salesDivision, int orderNumber,
                            String product, Date dateDue) {}

// Implementation helpers

  private ProductHome getProductHome() {
    try {
      InitialContext initial = new InitialContext();
      ProductHome home =
        (ProductHome) javax.rmi.PortableRemoteObject
          .narrow(initial.lookup("java:comp/env/ejb/Product"),
                  ProductHome.class);
      return home;
    } catch (NamingException ne) {
      ne.printStackTrace();
      throw new EJBException(ne);
    }
  }

  public void ejbLoad() {}
  public void ejbStore() {}
  public void ejbActivate() {}
  public void ejbPassivate() {}
  public void ejbRemove() {}

  public void setEntityContext(EntityContext ctx) {
    this.ctx = ctx;
  }

  public void unsetEntityContext() {
    this.ctx = null;
  }

  public OverdueOrderView[] ejbHomeGetOverdueOrders() {
```

```
  try {
    LinkedList overdueOrders = new LinkedList();
    Date today = new Date();
    long todayMillis = today.getTime();
    long leadTimeMillis = getLeadTimeDays() * MILLIS_IN_DAYS;
    OrderHome3 orderHome = getOrderHome();
    Collection uncompletedOrders =
      orderHome.findUncompletedOrders();
    Iterator iterUncompletedOrders = uncompletedOrders.iterator();
    while (iterUncompletedOrders.hasNext()) {
      Order2 uncompletedOrder =
        (Order2) PortableRemoteObject
          .narrow(iterUncompletedOrders.next(), Order2.class);
      Date dateDue = uncompletedOrder.getDateDue();
      String status = uncompletedOrder.getOrderStatus();
      long dueDateMillis = dateDue.getTime();
      if ((status.equals(StatusStrings.OPEN) &&
           (todayMillis + leadTimeMillis > dueDateMillis))
              ||
          (status.equals(StatusStrings.IN_PROCESS) &&
           (todayMillis > dueDateMillis))) {
        OverdueOrderView view =
          new OverdueOrderView(uncompletedOrder
            .getSalesDivision(), uncompletedOrder
              .getOrderNumber(), uncompletedOrder
                .getProductOrdered().getName(), status, dateDue);
        overdueOrders.add(view);
      }
    }
    OverdueOrderView[] overdue =
      new OverdueOrderView[overdueOrders.size()];
    return (OverdueOrderView[]) overdueOrders.toArray(overdue);
  } catch (NamingException ne) {
    throw new EJBException(ne);
  } catch (RemoteException re) {
    throw new EJBException(re);
  } catch (FinderException fe) {
    throw new EJBException(fe);
  }
}

public OpenOrderView[] ejbHomeGetSchedulableOrders() {
  try {
    LinkedList schedulableOrders = new LinkedList();
    Date today = new Date();
    long todayMillis = today.getTime();
    long maxInventoryTimeMillis = getMaxInventoryTimeDays()
                                    * MILLIS_IN_DAYS;
    long leadTimeMillis = getLeadTimeDays() * MILLIS_IN_DAYS;
    OrderHome3 orderHome = getOrderHome();
    Collection openOrders = orderHome.findOpenOrders();
    Iterator iterOpenOrders = openOrders.iterator();

    while (iterOpenOrders.hasNext()) {
```

```
      Order2 openOrder =
        (Order2) PortableRemoteObject.narrow(iterOpenOrders.next(),
                                   Order2.class);
      Date dateDue = openOrder.getDateDue();
      long dueDateMillis = dateDue.getTime();
      if (todayMillis
            >= dueDateMillis - leadTimeMillis
              - maxInventoryTimeMillis) {
        OpenOrderView view =
          new OpenOrderView(openOrder.getSalesDivision(),
                       openOrder.getOrderNumber(),
                       openOrder.getProductOrdered().getName(),
                       dateDue);
        schedulableOrders.add(view);
      }
    }
    OpenOrderView[] schedulable =
      new OpenOrderView[schedulableOrders.size()];
    return (OpenOrderView[]) schedulableOrders.toArray(schedulable);
  } catch (NamingException ne) {
    throw new EJBException(ne);
  } catch (RemoteException re) {
    throw new EJBException(re);
  } catch (FinderException fe) {
    throw new EJBException(fe);
  }
}

private int getLeadTimeDays() throws NamingException {
  InitialContext initial = new InitialContext();
  Integer leadTimeDays =
    (Integer) initial.lookup("java:comp/env/lead_time");

  // a null pointer will roll back the transaction
  return leadTimeDays.intValue();
}

private int getMaxInventoryTimeDays() throws NamingException {
  InitialContext initial = new InitialContext();
  Integer inventoryTimeDays =
    (Integer) initial.lookup("java:comp/env/max_inventory_time");

  // a null pointer will roll back the transaction
  return inventoryTimeDays.intValue();
}

private OrderHome3 getOrderHome() throws NamingException {
  return (OrderHome3) ctx.getEJBHome();
}
```

As an example of how a home method would be used, the getSchedulableOrders() method in the ManageOrders session bean would now look like this:

```
public OpenOrderView[] getSchedulableOrders()
{
  try {
   OrderHome3 orderHome = getOrderHome();
   return orderHome.getSchedulableOrders();
  } catch (NamingException ne)  {
   throw new EJBException( ne );
  } catch (RemoteException re)  {
   throw new EJBException( re );
  }
}
```

Changes in Public Draft 2

The second draft of the EJB 2.0 specification is out, and there are several changes from the material presented in this chapter. Most of these changes relate to the new persistence model, dependent objects, and the new EJB query language.

First, the ejbSelect<method>InEntity() version of select methods has been eliminated in this draft. You can get the same effect by passing the primary key of the entity as a parameter to the select method. You can now, however, declare ejbSelect() methods in dependent objects.

The deepCopy() method has been eliminated; you must create and initialize a new instance using a create() method. Initialization methods have been added to the dependent object that are called when the corresponding create method is called. Just as with the entity bean itself, these methods are named ejbCreate() and ejbPostCreate() and are matched up by parameter lists. The requirement was added to declare an abstract delete() method on dependent objects; calling this method will remove the object from the database and from any relationships in which it participates. (Removing a dependent object from a relationship now does not remove it from the database.) A dependent object can be deleted directly using this delete() method, or indirectly if the new deployment descriptor element cascade-delete is specified for the relationship role.

As expected, primary keys were added to dependent objects. They can be specified in the deployment descriptor as one or more persistent fields of the dependent object class, or the definition of the keys can be deferred to the persistence manager if necessary for deployment on different back ends. You must be sure to initialize any key fields in your dependent object's ejbCreate() methods.

The EJB query language has been tightened. For instance, equality for dependent objects is now based on their primary keys. There are also some clarifications of the EJB QL type system, naming, and path expression semantics. Finally, it is possible to have a dependent object that does not participate in any relationship (known as a "detached" dependent object). The EJB QL now provides the ability to range over all instances of a dependent object abstract schema type to select dependent objects regardless of whether they can be reached using navigation.

There may be further changes yet, but the material presented in this chapter should go a long way to helping you understand the goals and the main constructs of EJB 2.0.

Summary

This chapter discussed the changes from version 1.1 to version 2.0 of the Enterprise JavaBeans specification. The biggest change was the introduction of a new persistence model for container-managed persistence:

❑ The CMP model in EJB 1.1 still exists, and has not been deprecated. Beans that executed in an EJB 1.1 compliant container should still execute in an EJB 2.0 compliant container.

❑ The EJB 2.0 CMP model substitutes abstract accessor methods for state variables.

❑ The container will manage dependent objects and relationships to other entity beans for an EJB 2.0 CMP entity.

❑ A persistence manager (introduced in this version of the specification) is responsible for providing a concrete representation of your abstract EJB 2.0 CMP entity bean.

❑ Most new development should use this new model.

Along with this new persistence model, the specification introduced a standard query language for EJB 2.0 CMP entity beans, and two new ways to use it (`ejbSelect<METHOD>()` and `ejbSelect<METHOD>InEntity()`):

❑ There are three parts to a query in EJB QL: the `SELECT` clause, the `FROM` clause, and the `WHERE` clause.

❑ The `SELECT` clause indicates the returned type from the method. It is illegal in finder methods, and mandatory in select methods.

❑ The `FROM` clause specifies correlation variables. These are necessary for iterating collections. They are available for convenience for single-valued expressions.

❑ The `WHERE` clause indicates which values should be selected. Its syntax is similar to SQL 92.

A new type of bean, the message-driven bean, was introduced. This allows an EJB to be a client of an asynchronous JMS message:

❑ A message-driven bean is associated with a single JMS topic or queue by the deployer. The bean developer can specify the type of JMS destination with which the message-driven bean should be associated.

❑ A message-driven bean has no remote or home interface. Its processing is done in the `onMessage()` method.

❑ A message driven bean can use bean-managed transactions or container-managed transactions. Since JMS messages cannot carry a context for transactions, the only appropriate values for container-managed transactions are `Required` and `NotSupported`.

❑ If a message-driven bean is participating in a container-managed transaction, acknowledgement of the receipt of the message will take place as part of that transaction.

❑ A message-driven bean has no client security context.

Finally, the bean developer is allowed to add business methods to the home interface of an entity. These methods are used to implement business logic that applies to that type of entity in the aggregate, rather than to a particular entity identity.

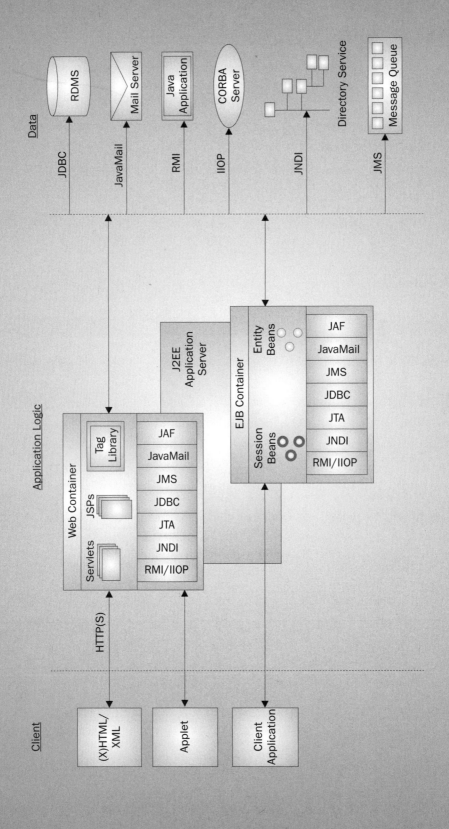

24

Design Considerations for J2EE Applications

The Java 2 Platform, Enterprise Edition (J2EE) delivers a whole range of useful technologies. So far in this book we have spent a great deal of time covering what these technologies are and how they should be applied.

> However, the key to creating usable, flexible, and maintainable applications is to apply technologies that are appropriate to the *context* of the problem being solved.

In this chapter we will look at some common ways of applying J2EE technologies to solve design issues in particular contexts. We will look at:

- ❑ What we mean by design and architecture

- ❑ The relationship between design and the context in which it occurs

- ❑ The forces at work when designing a typical e-commerce application for the J2EE platform

- ❑ Strategies for dealing with issues such as distribution, state management and transactions in J2EE application design

- ❑ The advantages and disadvantages of various J2EE technologies when applied in certain design contexts

The World is Changing

When software vendors who are usually at war agree on something, is this a good omen, or a bad one? Consider the 'enterprise' application platforms promoted by Sun and Microsoft. From a high level, the Java 2 Platform, Enterprise Edition (J2EE) and the Windows Distributed interNet Architecture (DNA) look very similar. Both combine multiple tiers, thin or thick clients, distributed object protocols, standard data access APIs, messaging services, middle-tier component environments, and transactions.

Is it a part of a secret joint marketing strategy, or is it simply that the world has changed and the changes are being reflected in the products on offer? The arrival of e-commerce and Internet timescales has changed the way that most business applications are defined and developed. The requirements are higher than before, and the timescales shorter. There is an increasing need for adaptability, since tomorrow's business requirements will almost certainly not be the same as today's. To design and develop applications under these conditions, you need serious (some would say 'professional') help.

From my perspective, this help takes two forms:

❑ A **standardized framework** on which applications can be built and deployed. The framework should provide appropriate levels of functionality and should also help to automate the creation of standard 'plumbing'.

❑ A set of **best practices** for using that framework. Most software developers do not have an infinite amount of time to spend on contemplating the philosophy of design or learning the most efficient ways of using certain APIs. What they need are guidelines to help them write good applications using the framework.

> In Java terms, the framework for development of distributed business applications is J2EE. The features and functionality of the platform allow for the creation of flexible, scalable, distributed, multi-tier, component-based applications.

In fact, the buzzwords listed above are just a few of those regularly applied to J2EE in an average marketing document. Basically, J2EE provides the landscape for the development of modern, Java-based enterprise and e-commerce applications.

Even the vendors now understand that developers need help in exploiting the ocean of functionality that has been delivered. Microsoft has provided, amongst other things, the Duwamish Books sample application to illustrate DNA best practices (http://msdn.microsoft.com/voices/). Sun Microsystems has recently issued the Sun Blueprints Design Guidelines for J2EE (formerly the J2EE Application Programming Model) and the associated Java Pet Store application to provide the same type of assistance (these can be found at http://java.sun.com/j2ee/blueprints/).

Obtaining the knowledge for effective application design on an enterprise platform does not come cheaply. The Sun Blueprints Design Guidelines for J2EE (hereafter referred to as the 'J2EE Blueprints') version 1.0 runs to around 350 pages. In addition, there is also a multitude of other resources, such as books, e-mail and news groups, newsletters, and articles that provide insights, discussion, advice, and sometimes controversial opinions on the creation of enterprise applications. Some of these are listed below:

❑ *Software Architecture in Practice*, Bass, Clements, and Kazman (ISBN 0-201-19930-0)

- ❏ *Client/Server Programming with Java and CORBA*, Orfali and Harkey, Published by John Wiley and Sons (ISBN 0-471-24578-X)

- ❏ *Programming with Enterprise JavaBeans, JTS and OTS*, Vogel and Rangarao, Published by John Wiley and Sons (ISBN 0-471-31972-4)

- ❏ *The Java 2 Enterprise Edition Developer's Guide* (referenced from the J2EE documentation page at `http://java.sun.com/j2ee/docs.html`)

- ❏ J2EE Patterns discussion e-mail list at Sun (`J2EEPATTERNS-INTEREST@JAVA.SUN.COM`)

- ❏ Interesting opinion in the ObjectWatch newsletter (`http://www.objectwatch.com`)

The combined thoughts and opinions found in these sources (and many more besides) cannot all be condensed into one chapter, hence the remainder of this chapter examines some of the main issues in enterprise development and the type of solutions that apply in a J2EE environment.

Design Context

Software is developed to solve a problem. That problem may be of a business nature, such as how to reduce the amount of time it takes an organization to process a customer's order, or it may be more technical, such as ensuring that a satellite control system responds correctly when instructed to change course. In either case, you cannot make an absolute judgment of the quality of the proposed solution. You can only judge the solution in terms of the context provided by the problem to be solved.

Consider the design for an airplane. Conventional wisdom would say that stability is a very important factor for an airplane design. However, many modern fighter aircraft are intentionally designed to be unstable, since this improves their maneuverability. This is a good design decision for a fighter plane, since a slight improvement in maneuverability can mean the difference between success and failure. Also, the organizations that use such planes are willing to pay for the expensive computer systems that help turn the unstable machine into something that can be controlled by a human pilot.

If you change the context of the problem, for example by looking at a passenger aircraft, safety considerations are paramount. Suddenly stability becomes very important – much more so than maneuverability. For such a plane, the extra maneuverability is not worth the risk to safety or the cost of the extra computer systems to control an inherently unstable plane. Hence, the same design decision in a slightly different context can be the wrong thing to do. No design decision is inherently good or inherently bad: it all depends on the context and the forces acting on the design. This applies both to the modeling of the proposed solution and the mapping of the model onto the underlying platform.

To discuss specific aspects of design then, it is useful to have a context in which to judge decisions. In this chapter, this context is provided by a simple e-commerce purchasing application. A first-pass UML model for the system is shown overleaf:

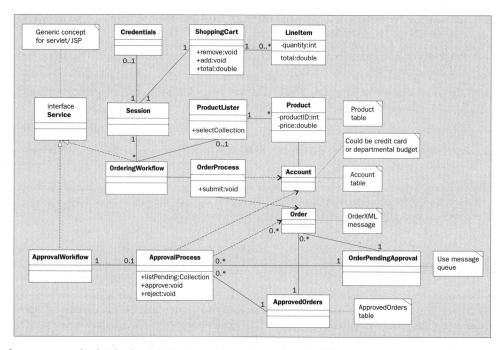

This is by no means the finished article, but provides a basis around which design decisions can be discussed. Indeed, some of the design decisions will affect how the model evolves. The initial stages of analysis and design involve the creation of a model that maps the problem to be solved. The inputs to the creation of this model are the use cases or user stories that describe the desired system functionality. These inputs can be crystallized in UML notation such as class diagrams and sequence diagrams. This initial problem domain model, which reflects 'real' things (people, documents, etc.), is then used as the basis on which to create a model of the proposed solution (the classes, components and interactions that will make up the software system). This solution will be shaped to a degree by the environment into which it will be deployed. In our case, this environment is the J2EE platform.

Consider a 'real' architect designing a house. The architect is given a set of requirements stating that the house must contain four bedrooms, a bathroom, living room, garage, and so on. If the house is to be built on the side of a hill, the design will differ from a house designed for a flat piece of ground. The design may make use of the slope of the ground to site the garage underneath the rest of the house, or it may build parts of the house into the hillside to improve the thermodynamic efficiency of the house.

Similarly in software, the solution that evolves from a basic model will differ depending on the *terrain* onto which it will be deployed. A pattern that is prevalent in this environment may suggest a convenient solution to a particular problem (such as the ground-floor garage described above). In this way, the environment will shape the model in the same way that the requirements do.

The evolved model can give us useful information about the system, such as the relationships between the different classes. This information is very useful when deciding some deployment issues such as componentization and packaging. Again, if there is a known constraint relating to the deployment of different parts of the system (for example, if one component must live on a particular database server) then this may mean that two related components cannot be packaged together. This in turn affects the relationship between the classes involved and thus affects the shape of the model. In this case, the interface of one or more of the classes involved may need to be altered to allow for the effects of distribution, or a proxy class may be introduced.

Before discussing the design decisions relating to our sample application for this chapter, let's first outline how the application is intended to work. The application will be referred to as the POSystem. Employees on a corporate intranet will use it to fill out purchase orders online. The user will select from the available products and build up an order, much like the usual web shopping cart. Once the user has selected the products they require, they will submit the order. At this point, the application diverges from web-based shopping since the user does not actually purchase the contents of their cart using a credit card. Instead, the purchase order that they have built up is sent to the appropriate departmental manager for approval. This approval will not happen in real time, since the manager may not be available. The second part to the application involves the manager processing the purchase orders that have been submitted and either approving or rejecting them. Another aspect of the context is that this system is intended for Acme Multinational Inc., and hence it has potentially thousands of concurrent users.

The design shown above for the system is reasonably simplistic and does not take into account the underlying technology landscape on which it will be implemented (although the comments do contain some thoughts and opinions). There are doubtless many aspects of the system that you might elaborate on, or where you may design things somewhat differently. Remember, however, that all solutions reflect the context of their design, and one of the main forces in this case is that the model is simple enough to be readily understood. The intention is to capture the *essence* of the system and not necessarily the detail. This is sufficient to discuss the move from model to system architecture. We do not need to build a completely working model, and hence become bogged down in the domain detail of purchasing systems. You can see a more involved, or evolved, solution for this type of problem in the Java Pet Store provided as part of the J2EE Blueprints.

A quick look at the model shows that the part of the system that builds the purchase order revolves around the `Product` class. `Products` can be listed on some basis (product code, category) and presented to the user. The `Products` selected by the user will be stored in a `ShoppingCart`, represented by a series of `LineItems`. The interaction with the user will be governed by the `OrderingWorkflow`, which encapsulates the user interface logic for displaying products, selecting products, and submitting a purchase order. As part of the ordering process, the purchase order must be sent to the appropriate manager. This will require some form of identification of the user and also of the manager. Credentials can be gathered from the user for this purpose. When the purchase order is submitted, it could be checked against departmental limits of various sorts, including how much money is left in the departmental budget.

The purchase order produced will be stored somewhere, pending retrieval by the manager. The manager will progress through the `ApprovalWorkflow` user interface logic to view and approve or reject purchase orders that have been submitted.

This, in essence, is the application to be implemented. There are many decisions that must be taken to evolve this model into an implementation using J2EE technologies.

On Architecture and Design

Some astute readers will have noticed that I have rarely used the word *architecture* so far. This is entirely intentional, since the use of the terms 'architect' and 'architecture' in the world of software is the subject of much debate. In building terms, the role of an architect is reasonably well understood. In software terms, application architecture can mean different things to different people. This then leads to the question of where architecture stops and where design begins. Are they, in fact, separate concepts, or just two facets of the same one?

The word 'architect' is derived from the ancient Greek for 'master builder'. If we take this at face value, there is the implication that an architect has mastered the craft of building to the degree that they can identify best practices and common patterns. It also implies that they understand many of the constraints imposed by the real world of bricks, stone, and concrete. This would be a good analogy to use in our current context, with the J2EE platform APIs providing the bricks.

I do not want to get bogged down in 'religious' discussion about software architecture. However, discussion of the term tends to revolve around certain aspects of a system and these are important for us to consider, namely:

- ❑ The system components that perform the business tasks of the system

- ❑ The type of interaction between those system components

- ❑ The services used by those system components

- ❑ The underlying platform that delivers or supports those services

- ❑ The style or idiom reflected by the system or its parts

- ❑ Other characteristics or capabilities (such as scalability) which address the non-functional requirements of the system

> **When considering these topics I will use architecture in its general meaning of structure or form.**

Architectural Styles

People will refer to 'Service-Based' architectures and 'Layered' or 'Tiered' architectures. However, it is not a case of making a straight choice between them. Many systems use aspects of multiple architectural styles in order to solve different parts of their overall problem.

Layered and tiered architectures have much in common. In many senses, tiered architectures can be viewed as a particular form of layered architecture. The main aim is to abstract some elements of a system in order to simplify the overall structure. A layer represents a cluster of functionality, or components that have similar characteristics (for example, type of function or physical location). Each layer provides functionality to the layers around it.

When discussing layered architectures, many people will think of top-to-bottom layers, such as those seen in a network stack. In the ISO model of a network stack, for example, the transport layer makes use of functionality provided by the network layer, which in turn uses the functionality of the data-link layer. Such layering provides abstraction of the underlying layers to allow for substitution. In terms of our application, the J2EE platform provides multiple layers – hardware, operating system, and J2EE itself – as shown in this diagram:

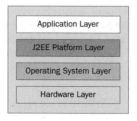

Since the application sits on top of the J2EE platform, the underlying hardware or operating system can be changed to provide better characteristics (faster, cheaper, more stable, etc.) without the need to re-write parts of the application.

Tiered architectures are a specific type of layered architecture based on a user-focused view of the system. This leads to a front-to-back partitioning with the user at the front and the underlying data etc. at the back. In a typical 3-tiered architecture, the user interface components will be in a separate tier from the business logic components, which in turn are in a separate tier from the data access components. The tiers reflect some form of physical partitioning, so that the three sets of components will exist in different processes, and typically on different machines. Communication will flow between the various tiers as the application goes about its work. A web-based 3-tier architecture can be seen below:

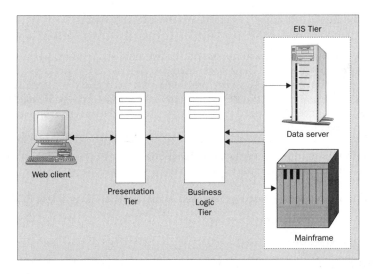

The POSystem application would use a tiered architecture for flexibility and scalability reasons. The separation of the user interface, business logic, and data access allows us to substitute better products or techniques at each tier without disturbing the others. The decoupling between the tiers allows us to add more capability to each tier as the system scales. An example would be adding more web servers at the user interface tier to service more clients. This would not automatically require more database servers on the data tier (although it might!).

A service-based architecture views the components of a system in terms of black-box services. An example from the system level would be a transaction service, such as the **Java Transaction API (JTA)** provided by J2EE. In this case, the user of the service is solely concerned with the interface to and characteristics of the service, not its implementation. Service-based architectures can be viewed as a larger form of component architectures, since applications will be created by writing programs or scripts that call upon various services to perform their required tasks. The concept of a service starts to get away from the concept of fixed clients and servers, since services will call other services to perform their tasks. There is no implicit requirement for calls to flow in a particular direction.

In terms of the POSystem, we could define a catalog service, a PO submission service, an account service, an ordering service, and so on. The user would use the ordering service, which would in turn use the catalog, account, and PO submission services to perform its workflow.

Forces, Patterns, and Iteration

From the discussion so far, it should be clear that the architecture of an application needs to be designed. Design can be considered as the solution to a given problem, in a given context. The context will consist of a series of forces that must be understood and balanced by the designer. There will be various forces at work constraining enterprise architecture, such as:

❑ The business problem being modeled

❑ Required technologies, including legacy systems

❑ System capabilities (scalability, availability, etc.)

❑ Reach of the application (usually embodied as thick vs. thin clients)

All of these forces, and many more, will impact on the eventual shape of the system and the architecture that best suits it. As discussed earlier, good architecture is specific to the situation. Its usefulness depends entirely on its context; that is, on the problems addressed and the forces at work in the system. When defining the requirements for the POSystem earlier, various forces were specified such as the potential for thousands of users, the need to process purchase orders asynchronously, and the desire to implement the system on top of J2EE.

The forces on the evolution of the system can be functional or non-functional, and can vary from high- to low-level. As this implies, design must occur at many levels and stages:

❑ The solution model (although it may be called 'elaboration' of the problem model)

❑ The broad system architecture

❑ Interfaces of system components

❑ Interactions between system components

❑ Internals of system components

Does this imply that architecture is an output of design? Hopefully, the answer to this is 'yes'. However, architecture can evolve rather than be designed, but designing an architecture implies intent.

Note also that **patterns** of varying forms appear at all these different levels. A pattern is a proven solution to a problem in a given context. In software terms, patterns are essentially the distillation of the 'wisdom' gained by practitioners of what works well when specifying, designing, and implementing software. The patterns movement was initially popularized by the book *Design Patterns – Elements of Reusable Object-Oriented Software*, Gamma *et. al.*, Addison-Wesley, ISBN 0-201-63361-2. However, patterns are not solely applied in the realms of micro-architecture as described in this book.

Patterns can be found in many areas of software and systems. At a high level, patterns can be found when performing analysis in specific domains. The entities and relationships discovered during such analysis will be repeated across a business sector, and this repetition leads to the discovery of such patterns. This type of pattern is discussed in detail in Martin Fowler's book on analysis patterns (*Analysis Patterns – Reusable Object Models*, Fowler, Addison-Wesley, ISBN 0-201-89542-0). If you are working in a specific domain, such as finance or telecommunications, it would be worthwhile investigating the existence of domain-specific patterns to save time and effort. In UML, as in XML, the world does not need another purchase order.

At the architectural level, work is currently being done investigating patterns that apply specifically to J2EE. Sun has an e-mail discussion forum for such patterns (J2EEPATTERNS-INTEREST@JAVA.SUN.COM) and has delivered some of their own material on this subject (see the slides for session TS-1341 *Prototyping Patterns for the J2EE(TM) Platform* at JavaOne 2000, http://java.sun.com/javaone). Other, Java-specific patterns exist at a variety of levels all the way down to language idioms. There are various Java patterns books on the market and some good discussions and articles, such as JavaReport's *Patterns in Java* column (archive versions of these are due to be available at http://www.curbralan.com). Although not specifically Java-oriented, the book *Pattern Oriented Software Architecture: A System of Patterns*, Buschmann *et. al.*, Published by John Wiley and Sons ISBN 0-471-95869-7 gives a good view of patterns at different levels of a system.

As we discuss the options for the design of the POSystem, various patterns will present themselves as suitable solutions for some of the problems we will encounter. An example of this is the use of the Model-View-Controller (MVC) pattern for the separation of user interface from data, we will see later in the chapter.

The effects of high-level architectural decisions cascade down through the design. If the need for scalability is translated into the use of a stateless model (as in the example we will see later), then this in itself may affect lower-level design decisions (such as the use of stateless session EJBs). Semi-functional requirements such as extensibility may have a wide-ranging impact on design decisions throughout the system. Taking the example of extensibility, if a system currently uses two possible data exchange mechanisms but it is anticipated that more will be required, an extra layer could be created to accommodate the required extensions.

Similarly, other decisions will be made further down in the application hierarchy for reasons of efficiency or suitability to the underlying platform. These decisions can require changes to higher-level parts of the architecture and hence feedback loops will form. Most mainstream formal development processes, such as the Rational Unified Process (http://www.rational.com/products/rup/), now encompass an idea of iteration and feedback between the phases of a software development. Implementation issues or changing technologies may generate valid feedback into the higher-level design or analysis.

Remember that most problems have multiple solutions. If the feedback changes the forces in operation at a certain point, a different decision may well be more appropriate. For example, it may be found that the need for a LineItem to refer to a Product in order to retrieve the item price leads to inefficiencies that slow the system down. It may be decided to replicate this price information in the LineItem itself in order to reduce these inefficiencies. This will change the model of the POSystem shown previously, but the overall functionality is unchanged.

Many practicing software developers will not have time to keep track of informed debate about the nature of design and architecture. Even if they do, the hope is to extract something of concrete use which will help the developer make better or more informed choices next time they sit down to design a system.

At what level does this chapter cover design issues? Essentially, it is a reflection of some considerations, trade offs, best practices, and rules of thumb commonly encountered when mapping some form of higher-level model onto the J2EE platform. This, then, is the design that sits between analysis and implementation.

Some of this design can be independent of implementation technology. As a UML model is refined, some of those refinements work well across all potential architectures. Other refinements must be informed by the platform onto which they will be deployed. The design of the system must take into consideration the idioms of the platform. It must also try not to fight the platform, going "against the grain". This, for me, is the main issue in this type of discussion.

> **The key challenge for many projects is performing this evolution from the 'pictures' to the code.**

We can now look at some general design considerations for J2EE-style environments and at some J2EE-specific idioms for design. One of the non-functional requirements stated above for our POSystem is that the implementation must be Java-based and must use the J2EE platform. This does at least provide us with some stakes in the ground.

Distributed Design

Distribution lies at the heart of J2EE applications, and distributing functionality provides much of the flexibility in the J2EE platform. However, analysis and high-level design frequently does not consider distribution, seeking first to create the correct business components. In this ideal world, all access between clients and servers would be transparent, as if the services were located on the same machine. Distribution also introduces complexity in the form of additional method calls and different programming paradigms. This much should become clear from reading Chapters 2, 4 and 22. In a distributed environment method calls are no longer deterministic, as they are in local processing. For example:

- ❑ A call may fail due to a network-related error

- ❑ Partial failure of a networked operation can cause problems, and this must be detected and corrected by the application

- ❑ Timing and sequencing issues arise and there is no guarantee of the order in which a sequence of calls from multiple processes will be received

Other factors must also be considered:

- ❑ Many orders of magnitude increase in the overhead of method calls

- ❑ The potential for communication to dominate computation

- ❑ Implicit concurrency in the system

- ❑ The need to repeatedly locate remote components as they migrate between servers over time

- ❑ The levels of unpredictability make it difficult or impossible to guarantee the consistency of all the data in the system at any one time

These and other issues must be considered when designing solutions for distributed environments. A good, if slightly dated, discussion of the issues with distribution can be found in the paper *A Note on Distributed Computing*, Jim Waldo *et. al.*, 1994, http://www.sun.com/research/techrep/1994/abstract-29.html.

In the context of our POSystem application, we must ensure that we take the following steps:

- ❑ Partition the system well so that components that communicate frequently and in bulk are co-located on the same machine where possible. Since communication over a network is comparatively slow, complex, and expensive we should seek to remove it where possible.

In the POSystem, it would not make sense for the `ShoppingCart` to be on a different machine from the `OrderingWorkflow`. This would unnecessarily increase the complexity of the interaction between these components.

❑ Where communication over a network is unavoidable, the interactions and method calls must be designed in a network-friendly way.

If our system is large, it is almost certain that the `OrderingWorkflow` will be on a different machine to the `ProductLister`. Some of the steps that can be taken to improve the communication between these components, such as batched methods or the use of serialized JavaBeans to hold data snapshots, are discussed later in this chapter.

Developing distributed systems is hard. Don't believe any product vendor who tells you otherwise. It is important to have a good understanding of what is going on in the system and what sorts of tradeoffs are being made. However, this does not necessarily mean that you need to write every line of code yourself. The type of distributed middleware typified by J2EE helps the designer and developer by providing much of the infrastructure and 'glue code' required when developing distributed systems. The benefits of these contracts, services and the use of interposition are discussed in Chapter 18.

The need to deliver performance, scalability, and data integrity in distributed systems underlies much of the functionality delivered in J2EE. Some examples are:

❑ Containers that can control concurrency and optimize performance while maintaining isolation

❑ Distributed transactions for data integrity

❑ Message passing to improve performance, scalability, and fault tolerance

❑ A naming service that provides location-independence

Start at the Beginning

Since we must start somewhere, let us start with the first thing the user needs: the listed products. All of the product listing functionality could be encapsulated within one or more JavaServer Pages or servlets. I will try to avoid discussion of any of the basics of JSPs and servlets since these have been well covered in Chapters 7 to 15. However, let's look at some aspects again from a design viewpoint.

Using JSPs or servlets would satisfy the requirements for this part of the system, since the product data could be accessed directly in the database via JDBC. JSPs and servlets give us the ability to implement the user workflow associated with selecting categories and products to list. Even at this simple stage, design choices can be made to create a more flexible and maintainable system. One aspect is the use of database connection pools to aid scalability. The whole issue of scalability and resource recycling is discussed in later in this chapter.

As we discussed in Chapter 14, the main design imperative for JSPs is to remove as much of the code as possible from the page. This separation of the presentation and the code has many benefits, such as:

❑ Code can be used in multiple pages

❑   Good design should mean that the page designer does not have to work around chunks of Java code

❑   Changes to the workings of the code do not require the pages that use that code to be edited

This guarantees that any use of JSPs beyond the most simplistic will involve such partitioning of HTML and Java code. As we saw, this partitioning can take various forms:

❑   The code for the page can be implemented as JavaBean components. Some logic remains in the page to drive the JavaBeans at the appropriate points.

❑   Code can be further abstracted into tag libraries. (For more information, see Chapters 12 and 13.) Use of custom tags makes it easier for a UI designer to manipulate the page.

❑   Functionality can be concentrated into one or more servlets (or JSPs) that are not involved in display. These will forward the results of their processing to JSPs that are dedicated to display.

While all of these mechanisms will reduce the amount of code required in our JSPs, from a design perspective, the last one, involving the use of **front components**, is the most interesting. A front component is a JSP or servlet whose sole task in life is to process user input (sometimes called user gestures). It contains no code to generate output for the user, however it captures data from the user, processes it, and decides what should be done next. The processed data is then passed to an appropriate JSP that is entirely concerned with formatting and presenting the data it is given.

Use of front components is part of the way towards the classic Model-View-Controller (MVC) architecture, with the front component acting as the controller, the presentation component as the view, and the data or state part of the system as the model:

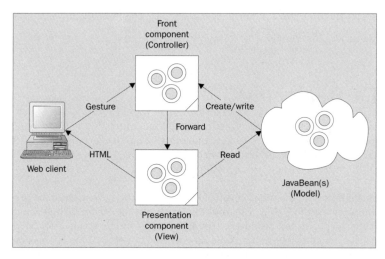

Using this architecture gives us some worthwhile advantages. Changes to the user workflow would not necessarily require changes to the view or model. Similarly, changes to the data access mechanism can be transparent to the view and controller. The three way separation gives a large number of options should changes be required in the style or location of the user interface. If the client had to be re-implemented as a Swing UI, the model could remain the same and simply be relocated to the client. If the workflow logic of the controller were implemented as a separate class from the servlet, then this too would be relocatable quite easily. Alternatively, a proxy could be created for use on the client that would map the Swing input to the appropriate user gestures expected by the JSP/servlet controller. The view could then be substituted for one that generated XML instead of HTML. The proxy on the client could then use this output to update its local model.

There is, of course, one slight problem with one of the suggested strategies above. Moving the model to the client is not quite the simple task that some 'draggy-droppy-pointy-clicky' tools would have you believe. If our model is accessing the database via JDBC, moving this functionality from server to client has some serious accessibility and security issues. Indeed, even moving it from server-to-server may cause such problems. This is just one of the issues with a JavaBeans-based model. If we were creating an application that had to be highly scalable, then this architecture would generally prove to be sub-optimal.

Holding state on the server on behalf of a client is a tricky business. In this case, the model will contain data and, potentially, a JDBC connection to the underlying database through which it can refresh its contents. By now, you should be well aware that this is simply not scalable. Consider the following issues associated with this scenario:

❑   To solve the memory problems, it may be possible to keep adding more memory. As the physical memory limit of the hardware is reached, another server can be added to handle some of the clients. The immediate problem here is that we then get lock-in between clients and servers. A particular server will hold the model for a particular client. This can potentially work against any load-balancing strategies used by the system.

❑   Physical memory is only one of the resources used by an application. In the case of the model, it also requires a database connection to access its underlying data. While memory may be relatively cheap, database licenses tend not to be. If each model holds one of these resources, they will be exhausted fairly quickly. If it must create one every time it needs to refresh or update its data, performance will be impaired.

If you have read the earlier chapters on EJB (Chapters 18 to 23), you will probably know where this is leading. To achieve serious scalability for most J2EE applications you should introduce EJB into the architecture, as shown below:

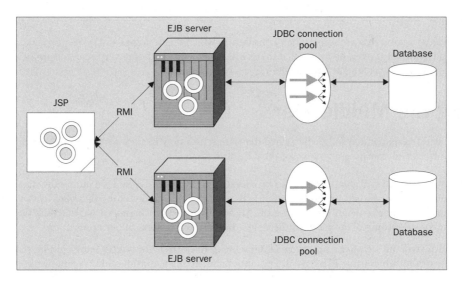

The J2EE Blueprints acknowledge that some applications will begin from a simple base HTML/JSP and then evolve as the requirements on the system change. In fact, they provide what might be thought of as a 'maturity model' for web-based J2EE applications, as shown here:

Application Type	Technologies	Complexity	Functionality	Robustness
HTML Pages	HTML pages	Very low	Very low	High
Basic JSP Pages and Servlets	HTML pages JSP pages Servlets	Low	Low	Low
JSP Pages with Modular Components	HTML pages JSP pages Servlets JavaBeans components Custom tags	Medium	Medium	Medium
JSP Pages with Modular Components and Enterprise JavaBeans	HTML pages JSP pages Servlets JavaBeans components Custom tags Templates Enterprise JavaBeans	High	High	High

This model acts as a good rule of thumb when considering which technologies will be required to implement a particular application. However, be aware that there will be exceptions. Some very scalable applications can be built simply with servlets, as long as you use the right server products.

Adding the Middle Tier

Our MVC system has expanded somewhat, since the state it uses now resides on the middle tier in an EJB. This presents us with several new design issues that must be addressed:

❑ What type of EJB should we use to provide the data access? Should we model the database as an entity EJB, or should we use a session EJB and fire SQL queries at the database from there? The pros and cons of the different types of EJB are discussed in Chapters 18 to 20. What we need to do is consider some of the patterns discussed there, in the context of our application.

❑ How will the web-tier components interact with the EJBs? Although we are gaining scalability and flexibility when using EJBs, we are potentially incurring a considerable communication overhead.

Think back to the application being used as the context for this design consideration. As a first pass, we might want to model our Product data as entity EJBs. This would mean that we could take advantage of Container-Managed Persistence (CMP) to save us writing some JDBC code and allow the container to optimize data access. Our web-tier components would then use the entity's home interface to search for appropriate Products to display, based on the user's preferences.

The immediate danger here is that this will degenerate into a frenzy of network-unfriendly property-based programming. Use of multiple getter or setter methods on distributed objects leads to an ugly 'sawtooth' effect in which communication dominates computation. It also increases the risk of partial failure should there be a problem part way through the getter/setter sequence. The first step to combat this is to use a `Serializable` JavaBean, say `ProductDetails`, to represent a snapshot of the data held in the entity. This use of the 'Combined Attributes' pattern (or distributed programming idiom) means that only a single method call is needed to retrieve all the data from the EJB.

`ProductDetails` would provide us a certain amount of optimization; however, the 'sawtooth' will quickly reappear if we have a `Collection` of `Product`s returned to the web-tier, from which data must be extracted. We quickly arrive at a commonly found EJB form of the Façade pattern. This has a session bean act as a façade or controller for a particular type of entity bean. Our web-tier components will converse with the session bean, `ProductLister`, which interacts with entities behind it. It will perform any entity searches and method calls on our behalf and will return to us just a collection of `ProductDetails` beans. This means that not only is no data access performed across the network, but the iteration is local to the web-tier also. All calls to the entities can be performed from within the same EJB server for optimization. The use of a session bean façade is shown below:

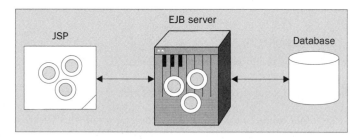

There are still certain considerations here. The `ProductDetails` bean need not contain the whole of the data in the `Product`. As a general rule, the data in such beans should be read-only. Since it represents a snapshot of the data, there may be limited value in including volatile data in the bean. If, for example, the `Product` contained the current stock level for that product, it may not be appropriate to include it in the `ProductDetails` bean since such information may be out of date by the time it is used. Such information should be retrieved 'fresh' directly from the `Product` (or its session façade) when needed. Another thing to bear in mind when using this data bean paradigm is that of interoperability. In the Java-to-Java scenario, it is easy to pass such serialized beans through an RMI interface. However, if any of your clients are potentially CORBA clients, then this interface could potentially be off-limits to them. Even if the client ORB implements the objects-by-value functionality required by CORBA 3, it still implies that more work needs to be done when unmarshaling the bean on the client. Integration issues with CORBA are discussed in detail in Chapter 29.

The use of a data bean to represent the EJB on the client points to a common pattern of design for J2EE. This involves the splitting of 'logical' data or functionality between tiers. For data, this means the use of a data bean on the web-tier as a representation of the data in the EJB-tier. This is a good strategy for providing quick access to slow-moving data. Similarly, the processing of user gestures may be split between tiers. A servlet on the web-tier may perform initial processing on the user input and then hand its data back to a session EJB, which can encapsulate many of the workflow rules that govern the flow of the user through the application. In this way, multiple types of client on other tiers can easily use that same session EJB.

The final question relating to the `Product` is whether it should, in fact, be modeled as an entity at all. Given that clients will use its session façade to access its data, would we not be better off accessing the database directly from the session bean and forgetting about using an entity bean? There is no absolute right or wrong answer here, although there should be a preference for abstraction over direct access. Much will depend on the origin of the data, the efficiency of the database, the efficiency of the EJB container, whether the entity's data is used by multiple beans on the EJB-tier, and the communication overhead between the EJB container and the database. A big deciding factor here can be the need for transactions. Entity beans will provide transaction control over the data in a database-independent way. However, if the data in our `Product` bean cannot be updated, then there is no need for transaction support. So, for example, the decision about whether to include the stock level in the `Product` class in our UML model would be very relevant here.

Going Shopping

Well, that concludes the consideration of the issues surrounding the listing of the products in our catalog. Now we need to actually do something useful, like ordering some! Creating a purchase order has a particular workflow associated with it:

- ❏ Show list of products to user
- ❏ Allow user to select one or more products from the list
- ❏ Submit the order

This will have iterations and other conditions, but it captures the essence of what we are trying to do. This workflow is encapsulated by `OrderingWorkflow` on the POSystem UML class diagram, and forms the controller for the form of MVC described above. The `Product` (and its associated session bean) takes on the role of the model. The type of view will depend on whether we are using a thick or thin client.

Our workflow is best implemented as a session EJB. This provides the best solution for scalability and flexibility. As mentioned previously in the discussion on splitting functionality, the implementation of the controller will usually be split so that the layer nearest the client will handle the user gestures, including any input error handling. This role will be performed in the web-tier for a thin client and in the client itself for a thick client. The user gestures will then be translated into an associated 'logical event' and passed to the workflow session bean that will then perform the associated business logic.

> It is worth re-iterating here that this design is not prescriptive. The decisions I am making here are based on my own opinions of how best to solve the problem for my big Acme Multinational Inc. For Fred Bloggs Insurance Brokers Ltd. (your friendly local broker), encapsulating the workflow in a servlet may provide all the scalability and flexibility needed, while reducing the overall complexity of the system. One of the principles of Extreme Programming Explained – Embrace Change, Kent Beck, Addison-Wesley, ISBN 0-201-61641-6 is to design for today's needs and not prematurely anticipate requirements that may never come to pass. As another designer puts it:
>
> "A simple, inelegant design concept we've never been able to convey to some of our in-house customers is to let us develop an application that will satisfy 90% of their needs but takes only a tenth the time to develop, rather than one satisfying 100% of their needs but taking ten times the development effort. If they think one possible permutation of data won't be supported, that's the one element that Suddenly Becomes More Critical to Life than Oxygen."

Examination of the UML class diagram will show that the `OrderingWorkflow` class uses a `Session` class to hold the client's state, such as the contents of the shopping cart. Anyone who has worked with JSPs or servlets will immediately recognize this concept from the in-built session object provided by the servlet API, as described in Chapter 9. However, caution should be exercised here. The class represents the *concept* of a session, and does not necessarily map onto the servlet session implementation. When previously discussing the holding of state on the server, several issues were highlighted about storing state in this client-specific way. The management of memory, recycling of resources, and avoidance of server lock-in are trickier in the web container than in the EJB container. By using EJBs for our session and shopping cart functionality, we can ensure that resources are used efficiently. It is also more flexible, in that it can be used by both thick and thin clients.

Given that we are now potentially working with several session beans, it is worth quickly digressing into considerations of stateful versus stateless models. As we saw in Chapter 19, under the stateful model a server-side component instance is dedicated to one particular client, and holds its data in temporary storage for ease of access. Under the stateless model, on the other hand, there is no dedicated server-side component instance for the client and all data must be retrieved from persistent storage. Although it is the subject of many debates and arguments, it is commonly accepted that using a stateless model has better scalability characteristics than a stateful model. However, the stateless model requires more work on the part of the designer and client application. This impacts on our choice of session bean for our `OrderingWorkflow` and `ProductLister` classes. As it stands, the work of the `ProductLister` is entirely stateless – it is presented with a category and it lists the product within it. In accordance with good practice, the results would be returned as a collection of data beans leaving no state on the server. Hence, this would suggest that the `ProductLister` would work well as a stateless session bean.

`OrderingWorkflow`, on the other hand, must have some concept of state to understand where the client currently is in the ordering process. This opens up a key design question over where the state should be stored – with the client, in the EJB, or in a database:

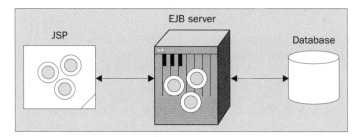

Each of these options has both benefits and issues:

❑ **State at the client**
The client must pass the state to each method call that needs it. This allows for stateless EJBs and so improves scalability. However, it puts more of a load on the client and the network, and can cause a security risk if done through cookies for thin clients. It also complicates the design of the EJB's remote interface.

❑ **State in the EJB**
By using a stateful session EJB, the required state can be loaded or acquired over time. This simplifies the design of the EJB's remote interface, and lightens the load on the client and network. However, it does reduce the ability of the EJB server to reuse beans and can also lead to the client being locked into one server.

If the system is to support thin clients, then some method of associating the client with the appropriate EJB must be provided. The client is then issued with a cookie that identifies the EJB containing its state. This mapping must be handled by the JSP providing the user interface.

❑ **State in a database**
The state for a stateless EJB can be stored in a database. The client is then issued with a cookie or identifier that identifies the state (usually the primary key of the state in the database). This has less of an impact in interface design than holding the state at the client, but has a small impact on the network load and client complexity. It does however retain the scalability of a stateless implementation, at the cost of more time spent looking up and retrieving the data from the database. Remember, though, that using the database cache or modeling the state as an entity bean could reduce this significantly. The term 'database' here really refers to any server-side repository, ideally a transactional one. However, if the state is not intended to be persistent then alternative storage, such as a JNDI-compliant directory service, would work well.

Scalability and performance requirements will have a large role to play in this decision. Once the state location is determined, it will have an impact on the design of the remote interface for the session EJB.

Submitting and Processing the Order

Once the user has progressed through the workflow for product selection, they will be ready to submit their completed purchase order for approval. The `OrderProcess` class, in our UML diagram, would have various responsibilities for checking the order. In addition to checking the validity of the order itself, it may also check to see whether the department has sufficient budget left for such an order or it may check to see if that particular user is allowed to raise purchase orders of that value. Since it is applying business rules to state that is passed to it, the `OrderProcess` class would be best mapped to a stateless session bean. Once the `OrderProcess` is satisfied with the order, it must forward it for approval.

At this point, a major issue in distributed design appears. The order must be approved by the user's manager, but it is not possible to include the manager in the system. At this point the system becomes **asynchronous**. The purchasing process cannot block on a synchronous call waiting for the manager to approve the purchase order. Rather, the purchase order must be captured and stored to wait until the manager can examine and approve it.

All of the interactions we have dealt with so far (RMI and HTTP) have been synchronous in nature, and the architecture for this asynchronous requirement will have to use a different technology or approach. The mechanism used will depend on the tightness of the coupling between the ordering system and the approval system. Three possibilities suggest themselves:

❑ **e-mail**
The application could use the JavaMail API to send an e-mail containing the purchase order to the manager. This would be very flexible for the manager, since they could even approve it from their web-based e-mail account while on vacation (or maybe not!). However, it does present more issues around the processing of the approval or rejection. Firstly, the application must be able to monitor the reply to the e-mail and process it when it arrives. The purchase order information must have been presented to the manager in human-readable form. To recover the original order information,

the application must either parse the e-mail message for all the order information or at least to recover some form of order identifier. An order identifier would refer to the original order data stored in a database somewhere. To provide authentication, the manager would have to use a digital certificate to sign the e-mail reply.

This solution gives good 'reach' and is very loosely coupled. However, it is somewhat unwieldy and potentially insecure.

❑ **Database**

The order could be stored in a database within the system. The manager would then have to access some form of application that queried the database for orders awaiting that manager's approval. The manager would then interact with that application to approve or reject the orders. Since all of the information is stored in a database, there would be no issue with handling a return value as with e-mail. However, some way would be required of indicating that the order had been approved or rejected, such as a flag in the database or by moving it to another table. Security would be provided by authenticating the manager before they used the application.

This solution has less 'reach', since it ties the two parts of the application to a common database (this may be required anyway to access product and budgetary information). This is the least asynchronous solution since the manager will have to go and access the data in the database, even if they are notified by e mail of its arrival. It is also tightly coupled to the order representation. However, it has good security and maintains a common development paradigm.

❑ **Messaging System**

The Java Message Service (JMS) could be used to send an asynchronous message to the manager via a dedicated messaging system. This message would wait on an appropriate queue until it could be delivered to (or was retrieved by) the approval application. Since the message is not intended to be human readable, it could be encoded in a convenient form, such as XML or a serialized JavaBean. The serialized bean would be more convenient to use for completely Java solutions, but XML is more flexible and aids integration as described in Chapter 28. The arrival of XML Data Binding functionality should make XML an even better choice here, as shown below:

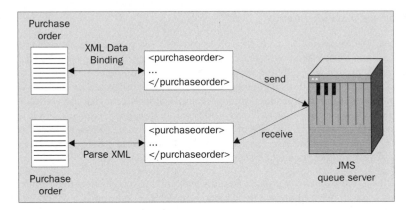

Once the order is approved or rejected, it could be moved to a specific 'approved' or 'rejected' queue. The design choice here is between the status of the purchase order being signified by its location (that is, which queue it is in) or by a flag in the message itself. Note that use of transacted queues would make sure that no message was left in limbo should the operation fail for whatever reason. Once in the appropriate queue, it would be available for further processing.

This solution has a reasonable 'reach', since messages can potentially even cross boundaries between organizations. The flexible message format provides low coupling between the applications and security is included as part of the messaging system. Downsides include the need for the developer to learn a new API and paradigm for programming.

Again, the precise requirement of the application would govern the forces on this decision. Given the requirements of the POSystem, I would probably choose the JMS-based messaging solution with XML-encoded messages for a balance between ease of processing, integration characteristics, and potentially global reach for Acme Corp.'s remote sites.

As we have seen, the timeframe between the submission of the purchase order and its approval or rejection by the manager can be very long (a matter of weeks if they are on vacation). This is obviously unacceptable in terms of an e-commerce application. Indeed, for the typical transactional e-commerce system, a delay in the order of minutes or tens of seconds during the possessing of a user order can lead to backlogs and 'system busy' screens. For this reason, even some things that might intuitively be thought of as synchronous may be performed asynchronously. Take online credit card processing as an example. Since the credit card must be checked and approved by a credit card processor (typically a third party company), this approval call can be queued for later delivery. Calls can be made in a batch, or when the system has spare capacity. On the positive side this can improve the performance and scalability of the system immensely, since no waiting is involved. The only real downside is for any credit card holder whose verification fails. In this case, they must be informed later (typically via e-mail) that their transaction could not proceed.

As you can see, there are some advantages to using asynchronous operation and messaging systems. There are, however, several downsides. The first is that there is no return value from an asynchronous operation. If an output is needed, the sender and receiver must agree that the result will be posted on a particular queue. They must also agree to an identifier for the particular message to which it is a response. Finally, the sender of the original message must listen for message deliveries or poll the queue to await the arrival of their response. Another downside is that transactions effectively stop at asynchronous boundaries. While this makes a lot of sense (transactions must complete as quickly as possible), it does mean that other mechanisms are required to handle any failure of the task that the message represents. In the credit card case, the order must be cancelled and an e mail message sent to the user. Both of these actions take place outside the scope of the transaction within which the user ordered their goods.

Back at the POSystem, the `ApprovalWorkflow` and `ApprovalProcess` are analogous to the `OrderingWorkflow` and `OrderProcess`. They are subject to many of the same forces on their design and hence would be implemented in generally the same way. One major difference is that there is only one type of data being handled (`Orders`). All of the data being worked on is to be processed by this part of the application. There is no 'constant' data, such as the product catalog. Another difference is that the workflow associated with accepting or rejecting an order is very linear. There is no separate iteration phase, as there is when loading the shopping cart, followed by submission. Because of these factors, `ApprovalProcess` includes control of the data used during approval. To facilitate this, it has a method to list the purchase orders currently awaiting the manager's approval. This simplifies the overall shape of this part of the system.

The `Account` class used in the approval process would check any requests against departmental limits and rules to ensure that the manager conformed to, say, their maximum debit. The `Account` would be modeled as an entity bean. This is justifiable since `Account` contains business logic as well as data. The debit of funds from the department's account would be coupled with the approval of the order. In a more closely coupled system, the approval process may also decrement the stock level of each product held in a database. In both cases `Account` will form part of a transaction, since the debit must only happen if the order is successfully approved (that is, moved onto the 'approved' queue).

The need for a transaction by the approval process could usually be discovered from the associated use case when modeling the system:

1. User logs on to approval system

2. User views list of pending purchase orders awaiting their approval

3. User selects a purchase order and views detail

4. User approves purchase order

5. System debits the departmental account by the amount on the purchase order

6. System forwards purchase order for fulfillment

Alternatives here would be for the user to reject the purchase order, for the debit to fail, or for the forwarding of the purchase order to fail. Steps 5 and 6 suggest a transactional relationship between them, hence requiring their mapping in the solution domain to use a transaction. In the case of `ApprovalProcess`, the `approve()` method would need to be marked as requiring a transaction, as would the `Account`'s `debit()` method. Use of transactional message queues would ensure that the move of the purchase order between the 'pending' and 'approved' queues formed an atomic operation with the debit.

The key to transactions is to keep them as short as possible. There is no need for all of the processing performed by `ApprovalWorkflow` or `ApprovalProcess` to be transactional. Indeed, this would have the effect of slowing down the system unnecessarily. The primary goal of transactions is to maintain data integrity. This requires that changes are isolated from each other and is essentially achieved by locking some of the underlying data. The more data is locked, the more likely it is that another transaction will have to wait until that lock is released. Although you can play many games with isolation levels, the bottom line is that more transaction use increases resource contention. Down this road lie timeouts and unhappy users. The only real solution to this is to keep transactions as short as possible. Therefore you should only use transactions where required, and ensure that transactional methods do not perform lots of unnecessary processing. Short transactions and rapid resource recycling are the two major factors in middle-tier scalability.

Lessons Learned

We could potentially follow the POSystem application through to the delivery of the order to the supplier system and so on. However, this would not really bring in any major new design issues. At this point, we can take stock of the main points to be drawn from the scenario and expand on these where appropriate.

Use Model-View-Controller (MVC) for User Interaction

MVC provides us with a very good micro-architecture for separating data from presentation and presentation from workflow. Although there are other architectures possible here, MVC is flexible and robust. Also, since it is widely understood, use of it will aid maintainability of your application.

JSP Design Principles

Ironically, as discussed in Chapter 14, the key to JSP design is to include as little of the 'J' element (Java) as possible. Any JSP that produces output should have its Java content minimized, to make it editable by the ordinary human beings who deal with page design and layout. Like normal HTML pages, JSPs should make use of directives to include other files (JSP or HTML) to create a common look to the site of which they form a part. This type of JSP, which forms an output template, is often called a **presentation component**. The only Java content in this type of page should be code for formatting data to be output as part of the page (for example catalogue listing). Even then, this should be minimized using one of the approved code 'outsourcing' methods.

Most Java code should be 'outsourced' to JavaBeans or servlets. User input should be handled by a front component that will process it and encapsulate the results in a JavaBean; this front component can be either a servlet or another JSP. This processing can include access to databases or EJBs, to generate any data that will form part of the output to the client. The data can be passed to the presentation component as part of the session or request. The front component then passes control to the presentation component. This mechanism is a specific use of a convenient filtering technique. Servlets and JSPs can be chained together with each one processing the user's request before it is forwarded to the next level. This type of design can be used to address issues such as those found in the 'Decorator' or 'Chain of Responsibility' patterns.

> Note that JavaBeans can also be used as wrappers for EJBs. This allows you to encapsulate all the EJB access code within a JSP-friendly package.

You can also use custom tags to remove code from JSPs, as described in Chapters 12 and 13. Although they require more work than using servlets and JavaBeans, they are more reusable and it is easier for page designers and their tools to handle the tags.

Choosing an Appropriate Data Format

Different formats can be used when passing data between different layers and components. In the POSystem, serialized JavaBeans were used to pass data between the EJB tier and the web tier, while XML was the chosen format when building messages to pass via JMS. Both of these choices could be reversed if other forces were at work on the system. If we knew that the application would have CORBA clients, or might need to interact with external systems, then XML would be a better choice for passing back data-snapshots from EJBs. Similarly, in an all-Java system there is no real reason (apart from future-proofing) not to use serialized JavaBeans as a standard data format.

One option not covered so far is the use of the RowSets as seen in Chapter 3. RowSets were introduced in JDBC 2.0 as a handy way of representing tabular data. A RowSet appears as a JavaBean, and can be used while disconnected from the database. It is also Serializable, so that it can be passed in an RMI method call. While it can be very useful in certain circumstances, passing a RowSet is not compatible with creating typesafe methods. Similarly, a field in a RowSet is potentially more open to incorrect interpretation than a property of a JavaBean or an element or attribute in XML. Passing data in RowSets mirrors the popular use of RecordSet in ADO (ActiveX Data Objects) in Microsoft Windows DNA applications. In both cases, it tends to lock the architecture into one technology.

Reduce the Amount of Data Passed

One way to improve performance is to reduce the amount of data passed between components. We have seen that property-based programming is inadvisable. Even when using best practices such as returning a `Collection` of JavaBeans containing a snapshot of entity bean data, care should be taken to pass back only that data which is required by the client.

Using a session façade for entity beans also presents an opportunity to use the 'Batch Method' distributed pattern/idiom. Rather than the session bean returning a set of JavaBeans to be operated on by the client, the operation that the client wishes to perform can be migrated into the session bean. The iteration through the beans then takes place on the server, with only the results being passed back to the client. This reduces network traffic, albeit at the cost of some server processing overhead.

When using a session façade, it is always worth asking what you gain from the underlying entity bean. Would it be better to access the database directly if no other class in the system uses it?

Design Interfaces for Distribution

The design of interfaces between components is an art in and of itself, though there are common guidelines that help to shape good interfaces. The methods in an interface should form a cohesive set, rather than a disparate collection. The methods themselves should be meaningful operations, not just a set of property accessors. As in all good design, minimalism is a good principle, as long as it does not create too much extra work for the user of the interface. (A certain amount of de-normalization is allowed!) An example of this could be where there is a single method that takes many parameters. If you can identify a set of common tasks for which there are various default values, you could create a method for each of these tasks. From a purist point of view, these extra methods may seem wasteful, but from a practical point of view it can save much unnecessary client code for creating or specifying empty or standard parameters.

When creating distributed systems, such as J2EE applications, you must design the interfaces between components to take the distribution into account. Care must be taken when deciding whether to pass objects by reference or by value. Passing by reference is flexible, but can lead to increased overhead through remote calls. Passing by value makes for local interaction, but is not always the solution since it can cause problems for non-Java clients. If only a small part of the data is required, passing an object by value can lead to more overhead than a handful of distributed calls. In addition, passing by value is not appropriate for fast-changing data.

One issue that is seldom highlighted in interface design is the use of exceptions. Exceptions should be designed at the same time as the rest of the application, to reflect anticipated error conditions (`BudgetLimitExceeded`, `ProductNotFound`, etc.). These business-level exceptions should be thrown, rather than low-level ones. It is particularly important not to bundle everything as a `RemoteException`. Exceptions should be layered, so that different tiers throw exceptions that are relevant to them, and the tiers that catch them should either handle the exception or generate an exception that makes sense to *their* clients, as shown:

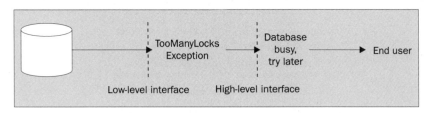

Use Messaging for Asynchronous Operations

In many applications, certain operations will take a long time to complete, and for the application to move on the operation must be made asynchronous. The messaging paradigm provides a simple way to design asynchronous operations. The use of messaging to defer slow operations is a distinct benefit for scalability. Obviously this must be used with care, since it is no good having a very scalable system that does the wrong thing!

Messaging is also a useful tool at times when the target server is not available, either by accident (server crash) or design (maintenance). In this way it brings a level of robustness to the application that is difficult to achieve when using exclusively synchronous mechanisms. Messaging does have downsides: it is more difficult to obtain a return value from the asynchronous processing, and transactions do not pass through the messaging system.

Messaging is not the only way of achieving asynchronous operations, since e mail and shared databases can also be used. However it does provide a common and flexible paradigm that is useful for integration with other systems.

Plan Transactions

Systems should only use transactions as required; they can be discovered from use cases and designed in as appropriate. The time spent in transactions should be minimized as far as possible, to avoid resource contention. Failure to plan transactional requirements can lead to buggy or slow systems.

Beyond the Purchase Order System

Design always occurs within a context. The context we have used so far has been the purchase order system shown at the start of the chapter. However, there are many mechanisms and patterns that are useful in the design of J2EE systems that are not required or not used in the scenario. In this section, we will look at some of these and the contexts in which they may apply.

EJB Interface Design

When writing an Enterprise JavaBean, it is a bad idea for the bean to implement its remote (business) interface. This would allow a reference to the bean itself to be accidentally passed back to a client, rather than passing the associated EJBObject. However implementing the remote interface is tempting, since it allows you to pick up any incorrect method signatures on the bean before the container's introspector does. To achieve this end, you can define a non-remote version of your business interface that can be implemented by the bean, and then create your bean's remote interface by inheriting from both the non-remote business interface and from EJBObject. The diagram below shows the inheritance hierarchy of the interfaces. Note that the methods on your non-remote business interface will still have to be declared to throw RemoteException in order to work correctly in the remote version:

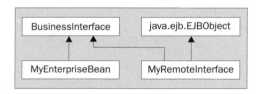

Unlike Microsoft's COM, or the forthcoming CORBA Components environment, Enterprise JavaBeans have only a single business interface. This means that there are issues with the design of EJBs that must be worked around. If the design of the bean suggests that it should implement two separate interfaces then this requirement can be addressed by using inheritance.

The next figure shows a potential inheritance hierarchy for two account interfaces, `CurrentAccount` and `SavingsAccount`. Both will have some common administrative operations, but they may well differ in the rest of their operations. Rather than just grafting a list of administrative methods into each interface and risking them getting out of sync, each interface can inherit from two others – the `AccountAdmin` interface containing the common methods, and an interface containing the account-specific methods, such as `CurrentOperations`. This would allow a client to narrow a `CurrentAccount` reference to either type `AccountAdmin` or `CurrentOperations`. The rest of the client code could then be written as if these were separate interfaces, and so type safety could be assured:

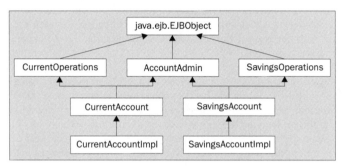

Note that this can only be done for the remote interfaces of EJBs. Home interfaces will need to return different types from their methods, and hence cannot be used in this way.

A final consideration for EJB interfaces is the consequence of using role-based discovery of interfaces. The identification of a role during analysis will often lead to the discovery of an interface containing methods specific to that role. An example of such an interface is the `AccountAdmin` interface in the figure above, which should be restricted to an administrator role. There are two possible routes here:

- ❏ You could implement the interface on an entirely separate bean. However, this would not be desirable if the methods on `AccountAdmin` and `CurrentOperations` acted on the same underlying data.

- ❏ Alternatively, you could implement the type of inheritance hierarchy shown above, and use the security attributes in the deployment descriptor to apply the correct security to this virtual interface. Although this is slightly unwieldy, it is the only safe alternative in the absence of multiple interfaces.

Distributed Events

As discussed previously, efficient operation is achieved by splitting most state between the Web and EJB tiers. A data bean can act as a read-only representative of the data in the associated EJB. One consideration here is what to do when the data being represented changes. The MVC pattern relies on the model to inform the view when its data changes. When the data is manipulated locally (in the same JVM), the delegation event model works fine for this: the model can fire some form of change event to the view, which would implement the appropriate listener interface for that event. The Swing API uses this form of event mechanism as part of its MVC implementation.

The issue here is that the data model is not local to the view: the view is in the web (or client) tier, and the model is in the EJB tier. There is no pre-supplied Java distributed event mechanism. However, there is enough of a framework to create your own. RMI allows you to set up callbacks from server to client, and these can be used as the basis for a distributed version of the delegation event model, with the server implementing a registration interface and the client (or view) adding itself as a listener. When its data changes, the server can inform all of its listeners of the change, and the views can update themselves based on this new data. If you wish to implement this type of framework, the Jini Distributed Event Specification, available from Sun's web site, provides a good basis.

One thing to note here for web-based interfaces is that they cannot change the browser's screen in an unsolicited fashion. Only when the user next submits a form or clicks on a link will the server have a chance to update the screen contents. (I am intentionally ignoring 'timed pull' here.) The Java Pet Store that comes with the J2EE Blueprints provides an interesting slant here. It allows web tier components to register their interest in particular data models with an instance of a local class called the `ModelManager`. The models themselves live on the EJB tier. Rather than setting up a distributed event system, each logical action submitted to the workflow on the EJB tier will return a list of the models that it has updated. The `ModelManager` instance will then inform the appropriate listeners in the web tier of these changes, and this ensures that the data beans in the web tier are up to date the next time the view is refreshed.

Another alternative for a distributed event system is to use asynchronous messages. Currently (pre-EJB 2.0) this has some issues when used with EJBs. If your EJB is the target of the event, it must wait for event messages to appear on the queue by implementing a listener interface. However this is not a good idea, since the EJB may have timed out by the time the message arrives. Therefore the event must actually be delivered to a helper object that can be stored via JNDI and retrieved later if required, and this helper object must be able to invoke the EJB and deliver the message to an appropriate method. This is rather inelegant and does not scale too well without a lot of work. EJB 2.0 promises message-driven EJBs, which will address this problem.

JMS itself can be used to implement various message-based or event-based patterns, though the functionality of interest will depend very much on the forces at work on the particular sub-system you are trying to design. A message queue can be used to pass messages from a producer to one or more consumers. Using point-to-point messages ensures a 1-to-1 relationship between the producer and consumer (although the behavior in the case where multiple consumers are silly enough to register for messages from the same queue is somewhat vague). Point-to-point would be good where a producer is creating items of work that must be processed by a consumer. Alternatively, when dealing with the distribution of information (such as the ubiquitous stock quotes), a publish-and-subscribe model can be used. In this case, multiple clients will receive the same information by registering for messages on a specific topic.

Messages can be made persistent if the application will have problems should they be lost in transit. Similarly, consumers can request that a server retain a copy of any publish-and-subscribe messages that have arrived for them when they were disconnected. These will be delivered when the consumer reappears. All of this helps the robustness of an application.

Working with Databases

There are many clever things you can do with databases that are beyond the scope of this chapter. If you are seriously into Java and database interaction you should read Chapter 3 or refer to something like *Database Magic*, with Ken North, Prentice Hall, ISBN 0-13-647199-4. However, from an overall design standpoint there are one or two principles to consider.

Firstly, don't be a Java snob. EJBs are great and they do a fine job of providing scalable data and business workflow. However, if performance is a high priority, why not let the database do as much work as possible? It is more efficient to run code inside the database than it is to extract the data, work on it and then put it back. Although embedding a stored procedure in your database and calling it to perform the work may not be as flexible, portable, or as cool using an entity EJB, you may find that it works many times faster and so could be a better fit for the forces on your application.

If you are using entity EJBs, try to avoid fighting the database. If you find you are querying many tables to build your entity's state then you may have a serious impedance mismatch between your bean and database. You might want to consider denormalizing your database somewhat to ease the fit with your entity, or creating one or more views that are a better match.

In general, it is worth spending a lot of time on your data design, as this tends to move a lot more slowly than the middle tier or client tier. If you get it wrong it can require serious rework of the other tiers.

State Management

State management is sometimes confused with transactions, especially if people have read some of the documentation on Microsoft Transaction Server (MTS). In MTS there is a tight coupling between transactions and stateless operation. This led many people to imply that transactions were the key to scalability. While transactions certainly help, the key aspect for scalability is state management.

State management has two parts to it:

❏   Synchronization (in the sense of consistency and persistence) of data

❏   Recycling of resources

EJBs make data synchronization reasonably simple; if you correctly handle the lifecycle methods of your chosen EJB type you cannot go far wrong. In the web and client tier, data tends to be more disposable, so you must take more responsibility for its persistence if this is required.

Much is spoken and written about the choice between stateless and stateful middle tier components. Each type of component has its own uses, and it would be foolish to use one particular type simply to conform to dogma. At the end of the day, you could model a typical `Account` bean either as an entity or as a stateless session bean that retrieves its data from a database at the start of each method. Only the interface will change to protect the innocent!

The final word is on recycling of resources; this is an important concept in all tiers. If you have an infinite number of resources available, then it does not matter how long a component holds on to a particular resource since other components can retrieve another one out of the infinite pool. As the number of resources drops, the amount of time a component holds the resource becomes more critical. This relationship is shown below:

Most of our applications have more than one resource, but it is still important to recycle resources as quickly as possible to aid scalability. The key is to use resources from resource pools, since these are allocated quickly. That means that you do not have to 'take the hit' of resource acquisition at initialization time, but can acquire and release resources when you need them throughout your component code. You should acquire a resource just before you need it, and release it as soon as possible afterwards. It may even be possible that another component you call could reuse a resource you have released earlier in the method.

In the EJB tier, there is a tendency to be less concerned about resource recycling, since it is presumed that the container will handle all of this for you. However, the principle of releasing resources as quickly as possible still applies. See the next chapter for more discussion on performance and scalability.

On Architecture and Process

Throughout this chapter I have stressed the need to judge architecture and design in context. The requirements that different types of application make on their application architecture will vary, for example:

❑ **e-Commerce apps:** Many clients, lots of reading, less updating, low contention, large working set

❑ **Banks and ATMs:** Many clients, low concurrency, high isolation level, no working set

The requirements of your application will depend very much on the functionality you are delivering, and this in turn will have a large influence on the decisions you make about your architecture. The most common application types give rise to architectural templates. The architecture used by the POSystem (3 tiers, thin client, etc.) is one of the most common, since it fits the web-based e-commerce style applications currently in vogue. Other architectural templates exist for differing types of application.

One of the most common non-functional requirements for systems is 'short time to market'. Systems are required 'yesterday', but with higher functionality, scalability, availability, etc. than ever before.
One concession to this is the increased use of common off-the-shelf (COTS) components where available. Build versus buy has always been a tradeoff to be made, but these days few organizations have the ability to build everything from scratch in the required timeframe. What is required is a solid architectural base on which to build applications.

In the past the application was king, to the extent that it relied only on the basic functionality of its underlying operating system or environment. This could be seen from the efforts required to port applications between platforms. Environments such as J2EE help to raise the bar in this respect. Much of the functionality that was previously part of the application can now be delegated elsewhere – to horizontal layers or vertical services. This gives rise to the 'tear off application', since the application code itself forms only a small part of the overall functionality. Since there is a lower investment in the application it can be re-written more often, and thrown away more easily when it becomes outdated. e-Commerce applications are typical of this sort of application (or should be). This transition is shown in the figure below:

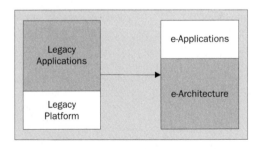

Another area where 'Internet time' has imposed time constraints is the development process. Before I go further, let me state here and now that I am not a great process person. I tend to focus on the technologies and architecture, rather than the finer points of the journey from requirements capture to implementation. However, it is interesting to observe how the approach to the development cycle has changed in the face of the Web and how this relates to design.

In one report on e-commerce, Gartner states that the transition to e-commerce is, "a programme, not a project". This reflects the realities in a world of rapidly changing business requirements. In such an environment, a commercial application cannot remain largely the same for two or three years after delivery. The changes required of the application in that timeframe will be significant – not simply bug fixes and usability improvements. In order to avoid becoming a legacy application, it must constantly evolve to meet changing demands.

All developers are familiar with the multiple iterations of code-compile-test that take place during implementation. To evolve the application, all parts of the analysis and development process become iterative. This has been taken on board by all forms of process, from high ceremony to low, from the Rational Unified Process (RUP) through the Microsoft Solutions Framework (MSF) and on to eXtreme Programming (XP).

So what does this mean for design? It means that you should approach design as an ongoing process, not as a once-only event. Approaching it as such can actually reduce the cost and impacts of incorrect design decisions. Over the life of any application, the technological landscape will change. This landscape is part of the context in which design decisions are made, and decisions made on the basis of a previous technology landscape may look stupid in a new one. What is needed is an acceptance that change will occur, and that it must be factored into the application lifecycle.

The acceptance of change leads to projects where functionality is handed off in stages, where the design evolves as the project progresses, and where refactoring is a part of everyday life (see *Refactoring: Improving the Design of Existing Code*, Fowler *et. al.*, by Addison-Wesley Publishing Co. ISBN 0-201-48567-2). Changes in technology and implementation issues should feed back up the chain, so that their implications can be taken into account in the mapping of the problem model onto the solution model. (Frank Buschmann uses a yo-yo as an analogy for this effect.) Although an open and flexible architecture is a good asset, take care not to spend too much time turning simple classes into libraries or frameworks that may never be exploited. When considering such exercises it is useful to bear in mind the eXtreme Programming principle of YAGNI, or "You Ain't Gonna Need It".

Summary

For many years I have been involved in the evaluation of new technologies. At the beginning, I tended to focus on the technology itself and the various bells and whistles it provided. Over time, it dawned on me that 90% of the developers in the world would never use these bells and whistles.

> **What they wanted to do was to use the technology to solve their business problems.**

To do that, they needed to understand the technology and apply it in their own particular context. The key really is to ensure that programmers use the core features of the particular technology appropriate to their context. The technology itself is of little use unless it is correctly applied. I hope that you have found some familiar context in this chapter, and will be able to apply some of the principles described.

In this chapter we have examined aspects of J2EE design, specifically:

❑ The relationship between design and architecture

❑ How the context provided by a particular type of application can affect the design decisions made

❑ Some of the issues typically found when designing a common J2EE-based application

❑ Some strategies for dealing with issues such as distribution, state management, and transactions in J2EE application design

❑ How different J2EE technologies may be applied to solve different design problems

The next chapter looks at the vital topics of performance and scalability in J2EE applications.

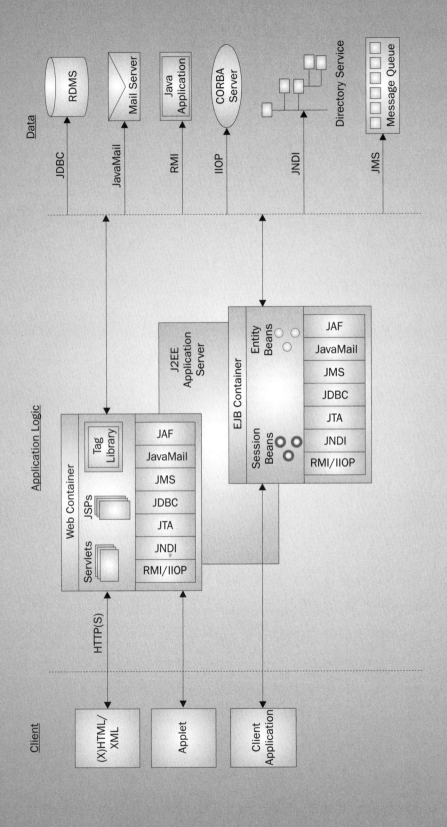

25

Performance and Scalability

It is not often that you will find a whole chapter devoted to the issues of performance in a book on Java technology. It is even more rare to find a serious and practical discussion of scalability and the issues that lead systems into deeper trouble the more popular they become. This is strange when you consider that performance and scalability are currently thought of as the biggest issues facing medium to large-scale deployed Java server systems.

In terms of being a significant risk to the overall success of a development project, performance and scalability has overtaken the issues of security and 'time-to-market' or developer productivity in the minds of many system architects and senior developers. This chapter aims to put this right with some practical advice on how to avoid, or identify and resolve, the common issues that negatively affect the performance and scalability of J2EE based systems.

Firstly, a word of warning for those of you who are very code-centric and value books in terms of the number of lines of code listed. This section contains information of practical value to system architects, developers and project managers alike, but be assured that by far and away the biggest problems come from poor architecture, not bad coding. The best approach to solving performance and scalability problems is to avoid them in the first place, not to fix them after the fact; hence this chapter is heavy on advice on how to avoid big problems and devoid of listings showing how to code around little ones.

Let's start our investigation by taking a look at why performance is such a common problem, why so many J2EE based systems end up with near-fatal scalability flaws and why these issues are so important in today's commercial world. Having explained how and why we find ourselves where we are today, I will consider the root causes of common performance and scalability related problems, what solutions are available, and when it is appropriate to use them.

Although they are related, it is important to consider performance and scalability separately, as they are fundamentally separate problems with different causes and, on the whole, different resolutions. So I will cover performance and scalability problems in separate sections and note when a particular factor may affect both. Within each section it is best to consider the issues into two broad categories:

- ❏ **Tuning** issues – those that can be identified and fixed during the 'tuning phase' of your project.

- ❏ **Design** issues – those that are endemic to the chosen system architecture and design approach.

These two categories of problem need to be addressed in different ways and at different times during the project. Design issues should, of course, be identified during the early phases of the project, by the use of prototypes or better still, avoided through the skill and experience of the designers. Tuning issues, on the other hand, are identified by testing, either during or after the main development phases of the project. I will address them in what seems like reverse order (tuning issues first) but this is because issues in the tuning category are generally much easier to explain and some discussion of architecture and the internals of J2EE technologies will be necessary before due consideration can be given to the design issues.

Previously I stated that performance and scalability are different parameters of a system's behavior, so I should define what that difference is before we proceed to look at each in detail. Performance and scalability often seem strongly related and indeed, in any real system, they do have some common elements. It is not surprising, therefore, that many people are confused as to what the difference between them is. They find it hard to see where factors that affect performance differ from those affecting scalability – so let's define that difference.

- ❏ **Performance** is that which affects the end-to-end response time of your system to requests from a single user at a time.

- ❏ **Scalability** is the ability of your system to maintain response times as the number of simultaneous users increases.

It is tempting to think that most aspects of your system will affect both performance and scalability in the same way at the same time, and this is where much of the confusion arises. In fact, these common factors are much rarer than you might think, and there are several things that you might do to increase scalability that will have a negative effect on single-user performance. With that in mind, let's now look at why problems in these areas arise so commonly.

Life is a Compromise

Nearly all real systems based on Java and J2EE (excepting the most trivial applications), experience some form of performance problem that must be overcome before the system can cope with the demands expected of it. In some cases the problems are small and easily overcome, but in others they cause serious delays in deployment.

Unfortunately, and far too often, systems are sometimes deployed with significant performance problems remaining, leading to the need for serious remedial action later in the life of that system. This often occurs at great expense, both monetarily and in terms of the loss of faith in the technical team. This is not a pleasant thought, but it does reflect the current reality. Why is this? Is there something

fundamentally wrong with the technologies we are using to build Java servers? Are system architects and software engineers lacking in the skills and experience necessary to build effective, complex systems, which perform and scale well?

There is some truth in both of these possibilities, but fortunately it's not as bad as that might sound. There is clearly a global skill shortage in areas needed to develop complex Java based servers, but, even more so, there is a lack of experienced architects and developers who have a proven track record of successfully implementing such systems.

This is a problem which is getting steadily worse as the demand for ever more complex systems intensifies due to the rise of Internet start-up companies and the progression of Java from an 'early adopter' technology into the mainstream. In most companies a developer with two years experience of Java and related technologies is regarded as an expert and will quickly get promoted to be an architect and lead teams of even less experienced people building complex systems.

In many ways this problem is normal for a new technology, but in the case of server-side Java skills the scale of the problem is becoming massive. Given this environment, it should be no surprise that problems will occur. I hope that through the use of experienced consultants and books like this, the transfer of experience will reduce this problem in future.

J2EE was, at least in part, designed to help overcome these skill shortages and increase productivity, and it is without doubt a massive improvement on what went before. However, one of the ways in which is achieves this is by hiding the underlying complexity, whether this be the garbage collector hiding the complexity of memory management that drove developers to distraction in C++ or the Enterprise JavaBeans container hiding the complexity of security, persistency, and transactions that are such an overt problem in most distributed systems.

Both Java and J2EE have been very successful in allowing people to build complex n-tier, object-oriented systems much faster than ever before, but in hiding the complexity they can lead naive designers and developers into serious performance traps. If you know where those traps are you can avoid them; that is the information I hope to impart in the main body of this chapter. It would seem crazy to provide a technology that has these potential pitfalls; clearly there are good reasons why J2EE is the way it is.

Time-to-Market

The time taken to bring the next 'killer' e-commerce idea to fruition as a real web site is a critical factor in the success of an Internet start-up company. It can often mean the difference between massive success and total failure. In these days of increasing similarity of products and greater competition among companies in the same market sector the need to gain competitive advantage and increased market share by bringing an enhanced service to market before your competitors is vital. Take, for example, a very competitive arena like the telecommunications market, where nimble providers who can bring enhanced discount options like 'Friends and Families' to the market quickly increase their market share dramatically. This, of course, is at the expense of their more sluggish competitors whose ancient billing systems cannot cope with such changes in much less than a year.

So you can see there is great advantage to be gained for companies (both small start-ups and large established organizations) from bringing systems to market quickly. The complexity of the basic technologies required to develop large-scale, n-tier, distributed systems or web enabled e-commerce systems has been steadily increasing at the same time as demand for these systems and the sophistication of the functions they must perform has grown exponentially. Just to compound the problem, the skills and experience needed by architects and designers to be effective in this highly distributed environment are different from more traditional systems. Most software engineers reading this book are probably embarking on their first major project with this technology. Clearly there is a major problem here that must be fixed if real-world systems are to benefit from n-tier distributed technology on a large scale.

The Upside and Downside of Delegation

There have been several attempts to solve this problem, CORBA and COM+ being among the most established and well known of the alternatives, and J2EE is another more recent attempt to solve the same problem. These all share a similar basic approach: each has tried to solve the problem by hiding the complexity of distributed programming, network protocols, component location, differing languages, and machine data representations, to name but a few.

Hiding complexity and achieving portability is achieved by providing high-level abstractions (generally, class-based interfaces) above the low-level technology. This technique is proven by the success of high-level languages, which saved us from the horror of programming in low-level machine specific code, and by the Java Virtual Machine itself, which is a celebrated example of abstraction to achieve portability. The developer's logic is implemented as components, which do not need to be aware of the location or the implementational detail of other components in the system. These components are invoked on demand through abstraction layers, which a hide the complexity of the network and hardware platforms and are provided as a library, or generated (through tools like IDL compilers), or a combination of both.

This technique is well proven, and I will refer to it as **delegation**. Several layers of abstraction may be involved, each one fulfilling its function (for example converting a parameter of a method to a network neutral format) and delegating on to the next layer until the user's code is reached and invoked. Each layer is more portable and simple because of this approach, but there is clearly a cost associated with traversing each level of delegation – this is a minor source of performance degradation.

The idea of 'location transparency' is also fundamental to distributed object technologies like CORBA and J2EE. The idea is that when you want to call on another component, you do not need to know where that component 'lives' to be able to call it. The syntax of how to call the component is the same whether it is in the same process as the caller, in a different process on the same machine, or even on a different machine several thousand miles away across a WAN. This is a very powerful notion, but at the same time it can lead naive developers down the road to big problems – into the 'Object Soup', as I tend to call it – but more of this later. These object distribution technologies also promote a component-based approach, through the support of well-defined interfaces, as another way to promote productivity and improve maintainability.

Despite being good attempts, both CORBA and COM+ have serious flaws, which caused the developer community at large to demand a better solution – a demand that gave an opportunity for J2EE to prove itself. J2EE is another attempt to promote better developer productivity and therefore improved time-to-market through similar delegation and abstraction techniques. It benefits greatly from the natural simplicity of the Java language, and in particular its native support for threads, garbage collection and built-in support for distributed computing through interfaces. At the risk of appearing glib and incensing people's sensibilities, I will try to summarize the reasons why neither CORBA nor COM+ has made the grade.

So What's Up With CORBA and COM+?

CORBA is a truly independent (of any one vendor) standard, supported on as many platforms as J2EE. It provides a very solid foundation for object based distributed computing, a foundation which J2EE has largely adopted and built upon. CORBA is however, a rather raw technology, too raw in fact for most developers to cope with comfortably. The complexities are so apparent that the learning curve is steep. The packaging (the manner in which CORBA technology is made available to the developer) was, and still is, poor, and only the fundamental problems of distributed programming were solved. There is, for example, no available implementation of a standard way to persist object state, and a persisting state in a relational database is almost an essential element of any real system.

This gave CORBA a deserved reputation for being difficult to use and leaving too much work to the developer. Although the OMG (the Object Management Group – a consortium of around 800 organizations who develop and agree the CORBA standards) does provide definition of many services (object persistence, distributed transactions, event notification, and so on) to flesh out the core distribution facilities available, it is very difficult to find good quality implementations of these services.

To illustrate, it has to be said that some of the service definitions were horrendously impractical. One such was the ill-fated Persistent Object Service, which was dropped – not to be confused with the new Persistent State Service, which seems far more realistic. Sadly though, this service is still not available to buy. CORBA does not address the issues of what the internals of a server should look like. For example, there is no standardized support for multi-threading – an essential for scalable servers – and this is deemed to be an issue of the implementation language chosen. While this may be a perfectly valid viewpoint (especially given the multi-language support of CORBA), it neither aids developer productivity nor portability.

Although it is specifically designed to support a variety of programming languages, CORBA was clearly focused on C++; just take a look at CORBA IDL to see what I mean. This was natural and not at all surprising, as C++ was the foremost OO language during the formative years of CORBA. The consequence of this is that although bindings from CORBA IDL exist to many languages (including COBOL), the mapping for C++ is the most natural to use and those for Java and other languages can be rather cumbersome, especially when compared to the RMI mechanism used by J2EE.

To be fair, the OMG has tried to rectify many of these problems in the most recent standards. The component model looks likely to be a major step forward, but unfortunately, due to the protracted nature of the OMG standards, much of this has come too late. The accelerating demands of the market place and the lengthy cycle for the ratification of an OMG standard means that the gap between what CORBA offers and what developers building systems for the real world need is more likely to grow, not narrow.

I hope that from my comments you can appreciate that I have used CORBA for many years on many projects with a good degree of success and despite having the reservations expressed above I would maintain that CORBA is almost certainly the best choice for server development in a non-Java environment. However, J2EE takes things to higher plane.

Having commented on the flaws in CORBA it is appropriate to comment on COM+. In true Microsoft style, COM+ makes a really excellent job of packaging the technology, presenting it to the developer with good tool support and a small but established set of ready-made components. The related technology of MTS (Microsoft Transaction Server), which is more directly comparable to J2EE than COM+, was possibly another influence on J2EE and has several good points. Unfortunately, poor scalability and lack of a real persistency mechanism leaves it well behind J2EE. In summary, the flaws in this technology are:

❑   It is in reality a closed-standard available from essentially one vendor – instant lock-in

❑   It offers very limited server platform availability – Windows NT or 2000

❑   It has a non-scalable distributed garbage collection model (delta pings)

It should be noted that J2EE only narrowly avoided falling into this last pitfall, saved by the adoption of a more CORBA like distribution model and IIOP as the underlying protocol for RMI. There are several other flaws in COM+, but this is enough to indicate the problems that have limited its success and acceptance.

I realize immediately that these comments may have inflamed the staunch supporters of both COM+ and CORBA, but I think that this just serves to demonstrate that they have become the first choice for only devoted followers. Neither of these technologies has truly managed to attract sufficient mainstream backing in a reasonable timeframe for them to be counted as truly successful solutions.

My comments on CORBA and COM+ should not be interpreted as a complete dismissal of these technologies. Nor are they a blanket endorsement of J2EE – it too is built on much the same concepts of delegation and location transparency. These are proven concepts but can be costly in performance terms if used without some care.

J2EE has flaws, as we will see, and this chapter is about how to avoid some of them. Having comprehensive support for server-side resources and a very natural integration with Java with all of its native support for important server-side programming features, threading, interfaces, and garbage collection gives J2EE an advantage.

You may feel that these matters don't concern you and that performance considerations are something best left to the Quality Assurance people after the development is complete, but I hope to convince you otherwise. As an architect, designer or developer, the decisions you make during every phase of a development project will carry an impact in performance terms and the earlier performance problems are rectified (or, even better, avoided) the less the impact to your project in terms of cost, time, and stress.

This section has tried to emphasize the ways in which J2EE and indeed Java itself represent a tradeoff between developer productivity, quality, and convenience on the one hand and system performance on the other. Delegation and distribution are powerful capabilities, but they carry a cost. Having put forward the essential need for good performance and countered that with the time-to-market benefits of J2EE, it is pertinent to ask a question: Where should the balance lie, and how can we reduce the impact of the unavoidable overheads? This will be revealed in the body of this chapter, but before we do that let's complete the big picture and consider why scalability is so important.

The Importance of Being Scalable

As stated earlier, scalability is the ability of your system to maintain good response times as the user population increases. This may seem like a fairly minor characteristic of your system – after all what's the problem? You decide how many users the system has to support and design it appropriately. If it fails to perform adequately, just throw extra hardware at the problem – simple, no? This is an unbelievably naïve approach, but it is the way many real systems come about. You may think that this is a valid approach, but consider two potentially serious problems with it:

❑ What do you do if you cannot accurately predict the number of users your system must support?

❑ What happens if applying the biggest hardware you can afford does not cure the problem?

It is comforting to make estimates of the expected numbers of users who will access your system and, in a closed user community, this should result in a useful scalability target for you to aim at. However, if your system will be exposed to the Internet, it becomes virtually impossible to make meaningful predictions about peak loads. Ironically, the more successful the site, the bigger the risk of scalability problems.

Recently there have been several instances of high-profile web sites being overwhelmed by huge numbers of users trying to access the site. The system is unable to cope with the demand and response times grow dramatically until eventually the site grinds to a halt and the users eventually give up and take their business to your competitors.

This problem may be seen as little more than unfortunate, but the risk is much greater than that. News travels fast on the Web and sites can very quickly gain a reputation for unbearable response times. Remembering that your customers are highly mobile and have plenty of choice is the first rule of e-commerce; you must retain their loyalty by making their experience of your site a good one if they are not to desert your site in favor of one that offers better response times.

The usual reaction to this problem is to throw ever more powerful and costly hardware at it, justified by the fact that the problem caused by the increased popularity of your site should also provide the profit to fund the solution. This seems a sensible solution and to some degree it is, but there are always limits and, depending mainly on the architecture chosen, sometimes a low ceiling on when it becomes ineffective.

It would be nice to think that you can always dig yourself out of scalability hole by beefing up the hardware, but the truth is that all architectures have some fundamental limits. Beyond a certain point, as you harness bigger and bigger machines you just end up with more idle hardware as other parts of the system glow white hot trying to cope with the load. These limits are caused by bottlenecks between system components and points of contention, which throttle the throughput of your system.

I will identify the usual culprits for these 'hot spots' later in this chapter and show how to avoid them through good design. If you need any proof of this behavior, just go and talk to someone who has had the experience of designing a large, fat-client, client-server system. Many of these work perfectly well for 50 or a few hundred users, but just try to scale them up to 2000 users and you will see exactly what I mean as the network and the database become bottlenecks that effectively restrict the flow of requests through the system. It is highly likely that the target for the number of simultaneous users your system must handle will be greatly in excess of 1000, so please don't rely totally on ever bigger and faster hardware to make your scalability problems disappear. There is only one infallible solution to scalability problems in n-tier systems – good design and appropriate architecture.

Denial of Service?

Scalability problems from legitimate use are not the only worry; to compound the problem you may also have to contend with a much more malicious threat – denial of service attacks. These are fortunately still rare occurrences, but these deliberate attempts to bring your web site to its knees by overloading it with requests, could cost you dearly. Recent estimates by the Giga Group suggest that the cost of web site outage for one hour could cost a B2B site about 0.3% of its annual revenue, while the same one-hour downtime for a B2C site at peak time can cost 1.5% of annual revenue. These frightening numbers are not intended to scare you, but they should emphasize how important good scalability is. Good scalability can protect your site from the normal usage peaks, which are often between 10 – 50 times the average load and will also minimize the effects of any denial of service attacks, should your site be unlucky enough to become a target.

Good scalability is even more about architecture and design than performance is. Unfortunately that means if you get it wrong first time and don't build prototypes to detect the problem in the early project phases, then fixing it could be expensive – in terms of both time and money – as it will mean significant changes to your system. If you had any doubts at the start, you should now feel strong justification for spending the time to improve the performance and scalability of your system. Let's move on to look at specific, commonly encountered problems; firstly for performance, and then for scalability.

Performance

By now you should understand that good performance is important, even if you didn't already before starting this book. Let's get into the technical detail that will give you the ability to improve your own projects by either avoiding performance problems or, if that's not possible, by identifying and resolving them quickly. In the following sections I will consider the technical issues related to performance in some detail. To do this I have split them into three categories according to when in the project lifecycle the issues are best considered.

The categories covered are:

❑   Coding issues

❑   Performance tuning

❑   Design-time issues

Clearly, they are not considered in project chronological order, but rather in order of increasing complexity and importance; for this reason it is also in order of size – I have tried to spend more time on the more important problems. The final part of this chapter on performance and scalability problems contains some recommendations on how to organize your project to best avoid the problems and some simple tips you can try out to reduce the risks of these problems.

Coding Issues

This section considers performance issues that can be handled during the coding phase of your project. At this stage, when you implement your business logic, the analysis is generally complete; design and prototyping cycles are homing in on the best solution, so the object model(s), system design and architecture have been substantially established. Functional testing and performance tuning remain to be done.

The way you code your business logic will clearly have an effect on the performance of your system, but as always in software engineering, the choice of algorithms, design and architecture will, for the most part, have a much larger effect on system performance than how individual chunks of logic are coded.

Issues of coding style and efficiency should be addressed by producing coding guidelines. Java programming style to promote good performance is one performance related topic that already seems to be covered adequately (for example the Java Report Magazine for January 1999 is full of good articles and specialist web sites like `http://patrick.net/jpt/index.html` are well worth a look), so I will use the limited space of this chapter to cover the more complex issues that are rarely mentioned.

One issue worthy of note, while we are talking of low-level issues, relates to garbage collection. This is both an immensely powerful feature of the Java VM and a potential headache, especially for server-side applications. On the plus side, the garbage collector means we don't have to worry about memory leaks – the perennial nightmare for programmers of other languages. A memory leak in a client is annoying, but a memory leak in a server-side component will eventually be fatal and may affect hundreds or thousands of clients; the moment of failure is just a matter of time, depending on the size of the memory leak and the frequency with which the leaking component is invoked.

Garbage collection is one of the features that make Java such a powerful server-side language, but it is also a double-edged sword. On the minus side, current implementations of Java garbage collection tend to halt every thread in the VM while the GC does its work, which can take anything from a few microseconds up to several seconds for a large, busy VM, handling the requests of hundreds or thousands of users. The effect on system performance when the garbage collector kicks in will be substantial and will significantly increase response times for the unfortunate users who's requests are interrupted by a GC cycle.

While it is not possible for developers to control this activity completely, setting the correct initial and maximum heap sizes and invoking the garbage collector at quiet times from your server code can improve matters. It is rumoured that extensions are being considered that would provide for a form of thread-local storage which could be garbage-collected a thread at-a-time, allowing the other threads to operate normally, thus minimising the impact of garbage collection on the overall server responsiveness. There is also a simple coding technique that can help: nulling references when you are finished with the object referred to by them can make the operation of the GC more efficient.

Performance Testing and Tuning

The process of performance testing is very similar to that for scalability testing as scalability tests are generally a superset of performance tests. Due to this, many of the things that are important and need to be said regarding performance testing will be covered in the section on testing later in this chapter, and I shall not repeat them here. That section will deal with both performance and scalability testing together. If you are thinking of carrying out performance tests, please remember to consult that section.

Testing performance is an activity that should take place throughout the lifecycle of a project. It is such an important aspect of n-tier and especially J2EE systems that it should start very early in the project, with prototypes to test the performance of the proposed architecture and component-level design. These are vital. Each component (typically a servlet, JSP, or Enterprise JavaBean) should be tested within a simulation of the final system framework to optimize its performance during the development phase.

There is another phase of the project devoted to assessing and improving the overall performance of the system – what I refer to as performance tuning, or what you might know as integrated testing and tuning. This is an occasion when performance and scalability should be considered together, as by the time you reach this stage the system must be considered as an integrated whole. As I mentioned above, the process of testing and collecting the results will be covered in the scalability testing section, but now let's look at the analysis of performance tuning data and what kinds of issue we can identify and resolve during this phase.

Performance Analysis

You will always have some 'gut-feeling' about where performance problems are likely to occur in your system, but try to avoid the temptation to assume too much about what the tests will reveal. Analyze the results carefully and objectively, before proceeding to fix the problems. It is likely that your guesses as to where the bottlenecks will be lurking may be broadly correct, but experience shows that complex systems are notoriously unpredictable and 'gut-feeling' can be misleading. If you follow it blindly you may miss a serious problem. If a problem is so obvious, ask yourself why it wasn't avoided during the design phase.

Many of the load testing tools that provide support during the performance test runs will also assist in capturing and analyzing the test results. Others are focused on capturing and presenting the information on where in your code the time was spent. Profiling tools such as J-Probe (`http://ww.klgroup.com/jprobe`) and Optimize-it (`http://www.optimizeit.com`) are good examples of this. They capture very detailed information and present it in flexible and useful ways allowing you to quickly pinpoint where most time is spent and why. These tools generally work by 'instrumenting' your code, adding extra code to acquire the timing data and other information to help relate it to what your code is doing.

While this is clearly very useful, a good tip is to remember that this will inevitably affect the absolute times produced. So don't try to capture real performance data while running profilers on the system. Carry out multiple runs, firstly to capture the raw performance data and establish the big picture, then apply the profiling tools to get detailed information on suspected system components. The tools available today allow you to get profiling data very easily, but it still takes some time to analyze and understand it – you don't necessarily need to cover your whole system in this level of detail.

Prioritize

You can never allocate as much time to testing or performance tuning as you would like. The development phase of most complex projects typically overruns and eats into any contingency time you will have allowed, so you must use the time for fixing performance problems wisely, where it is most likely to give good returns. You should carefully analyse the results of the tests and make sure you focus on those areas of the system that consume the most time overall. It is futile trying to shave a few milliseconds off calculating the value of a shopping basket, when it is taking several seconds to add each item to the basket.

Look at the total time spent in each part of the system, allowing for the number of times that each function is used. Reducing the time taken to display a page of the catalogue by 0.1 of a second will give much better returns than reducing the time taken to process credit card details by 0.5 second when the former operation is executed 10,000 times more often than the latter.

Corrective Action

This is the primary reason for doing performance testing in the first place – fixing performance problems. If you have done a good job on testing and analysis, corrective action is often the simplest part of the whole exercise. If you have an accurate pinpoint on a performance problem, fixing it is often straightforward, but this is definitely not true of scalability problems.

There will of course be a variety of potential performance problems and therefore a variety of solutions. Often, the solution is a simple re-write of your code to be a little smarter. Sometimes your code is already optimal and therefore you must enlist the help of a tool, or optimize the configuration of a system component (database, messaging layer) to overcome the problem. Sometimes, hopefully infrequently, you will have reached a fundamental limitation of your design. These problems are always costly to fix, in terms of time and money, so they are best avoided by good design and prototyping in the early phases of a project.

Earlier, I mentioned some tools that can help to capture performance data and analyze the results, but it's worth remembering that they do not automatically implement solutions to the problems – we still require skilled software engineers to do that. Having said that, there are two types of tool that can help us. The first type improves performance in a general way; the second type is designed to solve particular performance bottlenecks. Tools that require significant changes to your design cannot be used effectively in a corrective action phase of a project and so they will be deferred to the next section.

The very nature of the Java language itself gives rise to potential performance issues, being an interpreted language with a run-time system – the Java Virtual Machine that abstracts away from the hardware for portability reasons. Both these features bring benefits to the language, but also a performance downside relative to a language system that compiles directly to native code.

Optimizing Tools

In the first category we have tools such as **Just In Time (JIT)** compilers and optimized Java Virtual Machines. JIT compilers work by compiling (and caching) the Java byte code ahead of the VM needing it for execution. This will be faster than the VM interpreting the byte code. If the JIT compiler compiles code that will be executed many times, this will give you a big gain (around a five fold improvement in execution time), but there is a risk here. The JIT will try to work out what code will be needed and compile it, but it may get this wrong and spend time compiling code that is either not needed at all, or only executed once – this can actually degrade performance.

Perhaps the best well know JIT (now included in the standard Javasoft JDK) is that from Inprise, formerly Borland (`http://www.borland.com/jbuilder`). The optimizing VMs bring improvement by addressing some of the performance shortcomings of the Java language itself and can provide a significant overall performance improvement in much the same way as optimizing compilers did for C++ applications. They generally provide a variety of accelerators; from modifying your byte code to apply optimizations to highly tuned thread management.

Two examples of this type of tool are Hotspot (`http://Java.sun.com/products/hotspot`) and JRockit (`http://www.jrocket.com`). These tools are easy to apply and therefore to evaluate and choose, but the results will vary enormously, depending on the nature of your code and the frequency with which you use certain types of operation, so do evaluate before you buy. Plan to try these performance accelerators during the performance-testing phase to get quantitative evidence on what improvements they can make – then it is a simple matter of balancing the cost of the tool against the benefit it brings.

Performance Enhancing Tools

The second type of tool is focused on solving specific common performance bottlenecks. Good examples of tools in this category are web server accelerators. The performance of your web server is an important parameter and has a significant effect on the response times of your system. A clean and simple way to accelerate the speed of serving web pages is to add a memory-based page cache in front of or even behind the web server.

Requests for cached pages can be intercepted by the cache and served from memory without requiring the web server to access disk bound files and regenerate the page, and this can clearly give significant performance improvements. Of course, not all pages will be cached, so focus your attention where the major gains can be made. Only the frequently requested pages should be cached, thus optimizing the memory requirement and cost of the page cache against the overall performance benefit.

The first generation of these tools, products like Inktomi (`http://www.inktomi.com`) and Akamai (`http://www.akamai.com`), deal only with static pages; requests for dynamically generated pages which require results from the execution of business logic or access to a database must still go through the web server and the rest of your architecture. This is unfortunate, as increasingly the major content, certainly the most frequently accessed content, consists of dynamic pages. Even so, significant improvements can be gained from these caches.

This deficiency has already been recognized by some vendors and second-generation products, like Dynamai (`http://www.dynamai.com`) are now appearing that can cache dynamic pages. At first sight, caching dynamic pages may seem a strange concept; the whole basis of dynamic web pages is that the underlying data, making up the interesting content of the page, changes – so why bother caching it?

The key to understanding the benefit of a dynamic page cache is to realize that dynamic data changes, but often with a frequency such that the page may be requested many times before the underlying data changes and the cached version becomes invalid. To be effective and not risk presenting invalid information, dynamic page caches like Dynamai provide a set of rules by which the cached version of a page can be invalidated and regenerated on demand. These rules are 'dependencies' that describe which pages depend on which 'events'.

Just as for the first category, these tools are often simple to apply and don't require significant change to the system design or architecture. So again, you should plan to test these tools during performance tuning, evaluate the improvements they bring, and assess the cost against the benefit.

Design-Time Issues

Now it is time to consider the most influential set of issues with respect to performance, those that need to be addressed at design time. I cannot stress enough how important good design is to the performance of an n-tier J2EE system, and by that I do not mean the micro-level design of how the business logic is coded. Just as the choice of a good algorithm has more impact on the performance of a component than how you code it, selecting a good architecture and component granularity is much more influential to the performance of a system than the detail of how you implement it. This is a big topic to cover and to make it more manageable; I will split it into two main parts.

The first will consider what I refer to as the component-level architecture, meaning the way in which the required business logic is partitioned over a set of components and the way these components interact within the context of a container, with particular reference to the scope of transactions. The second part comprises the service-level architecture, which considers the deployment of components and services between containers, server instances, and system processes.

Component-level Architecture

J2EE is, to a minor degree, prescriptive about these matters – at the very least it encourages a considered approach to partitioning the logic of your system across a number of different component types (servlets, JSPs, session beans, and entity beans), each with different roles and responsibilities. This is important for the promotion of well-designed, maintainable systems and was a serious omission from the CORBA standards until the component model was introduced recently. Having said that, the J2EE standards that describe the various component technologies still leave an awful lot to the imagination of the developer when it comes to deciding which logic should go in which component type, and even the J2EE programming blueprint only gives simple examples of ways of partitioning. A more thorough look at these design decisions is covered in Chapter 24, but we will consider them from the standpoint of the effect they have on the performance of your system, and this will bring a different balance to the fore.

In the introduction to this chapter we saw that an objective of J2EE component technologies was the need to reduce the skill levels required by developers to successfully produce complex n-tier systems and to increase their productivity to improve time-to-market. This has resulted in high-level component technologies that encapsulate the complexities of the underlying technology and make heavy use of delegation in their implementation. This did indeed allow the ease-of-use objective to be met, but at the cost of some performance penalties. Taking this to the opposite extreme, ultimate performance would be obtained by developing in-line, hand-optimized code with no software abstraction layers wasting CPU cycles. Undoubtedly this would result in systems that were very fast, but totally non-portable, and impossible to extend or maintain without retaining the original development team. As a result, the typical e-commerce system would require thousands of developer years of effort to build.

Clearly there is a balance to be struck. The potential benefits that Java and J2EE bring in terms of portability, developer productivity and support for component reuse are massive. They are well worth the potential performance implications that come from using a language that is interpreted and containers that use several levels of delegation to simplify the implementation of business logic without concern for low-level technology issues. This does not, in any way, mean that all J2EE based systems are doomed to suffer bad performance, nor does it mean that you have to break the 'rules' of component behavior described in the various J2EE component standards to achieve good performance. What it does mean is that if you want to produce systems that perform well, it is essential that you, as a responsible system architect or developer:

❑ Understand the nature of the various J2EE component technologies and what the performance implications and overheads are so you can apply them without compromising system performance

❑ Understand where the right balance lies, between letting the tools do the work for you and taking control yourself

❑ Select vendor tools and implementations of J2EE that meet your performance/scalability criteria as well as meeting your functional requirements

We will return to the tool selection process later. In the remainder of this section I hope to consolidate the knowledge you will need to achieve success in the first two of these endeavors.

J2EE defines a number of technologies with which you can build components that encapsulate the logic for your system. Their characteristics and roles within the Model-View-Controller paradigm are as follows:

Component	Type	Location	MVC Role	Purpose
Application client	Client	Client	View	Non-web based, display logic
Applet	Client	Client	View	Web based, client-side display logic
Servlet	Web	Server	Control/ View	Web based, display controller
JSP	Web	Server	View	Web based, display logic
Session EJB	Enterprise	Server	Controller	Core business logic host
Entity EJB	Enterprise	Server	Model	Data mapping

Bearing in mind the title of this book, we will pay no further heed to the client-side components, other than to strongly suggest that you should stick closely to the thin-client approach and not be tempted to put true business logic in the client.

When implementing your server-side logic there are two important 'partitioning' choices to make:

❑ Should this functionality be implemented as a servlet, JSP, session bean, or entity bean?

❑ Which container or server process should it run in?

The latter choice we will consider under service-level architecture, but the choice of component technology needs to be established now. There will always be flexibility over this decision and sometimes you may even change your mind as the true purpose of the logic becomes clear, but when designing a complex system it is important to have a clear idea of what your approach to partitioning the logic is. If not, your system may perform badly, and will certainly be difficult to understand, extend, and maintain at the very least.

The table on the previous page indicates some reasonable guidelines for these decisions, based on the Model-View-Controller paradigm – without doubt, the most successful design pattern of all time. In an MVC architecture the logic and therefore components fall into one of three categories:

❑ **View components** – display the results of requests appropriately to the client.
Their function is purely display logic and they may well depend on the nature of the client. Avoid the temptation to implement business or application logic in these components. In a system with Java applications for clients, these will probably be client-side, visible components using swing widgets for presentation (possibly Java beans). In web-enabled applications these

may instead be downloaded to the client as an applet or achieve a similar effect from the server-side by formatting HTML and sending this back to the client via the web server (servlets and JSPs).

❑ **Model components** – represent the core business logic and state.
The model components come from the enterprise object model, so they will be good candidates for reuse in many applications within the enterprise. They commonly (although not exclusively) map to data in the corporate databases and will also contain the core business logic that belongs with that data. These are typically long-lived, persistent components that map nicely to entity beans in a J2EE system.

❑ **Controller components** – are application specific components that define the process or workflow. Controllers contain the application logic that achieves the functionality of your system by manipulating combinations of the model components. These components are typically session beans, though they may be servlets.

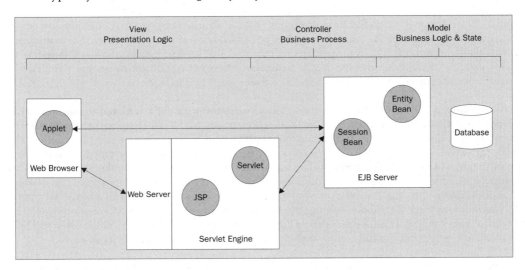

In essence servlets and JSPs are connectivity and display logic components, whereas the enterprise components (the Enterprise JavaBeans) are good containers for business logic and business state. Think of the servlet as a proxy for a web browser request on the server side – it represents that request and channels it into the rest of the architecture. The whole rationale behind partitioning is a big subject and outside the scope of this chapter (see guidelines on the recommended approach elsewhere in this book), so I will offer one more rule of thumb to help and then assume that you have decided your approach to partitioning at the component level.

Servlet or EJB?

The typical problem is in deciding if a particular piece of logic should be a servlet or an EJB. All too often the servlet wins, as it is typically the more familiar technology and seen as easier to implement. It is a mistake to choose a servlet for these reasons.

If you are struggling to make this decision, imagine that your system is not web-enabled (in other words your client is a Java application not a browser). If you would have put the logic on the client side then it should be a servlet/JSP, but if you would have put the logic on the server side, it should probably be an EJB. This rule is somewhat simplistic but none the less, useful. Remember that there is always a major overhead associated with calling 'across' the architecture for example from a servlet engine into an EJB application server – this performance hit should be minimized by carefully partitioning your logic to optimize the number of calls across the architecture for each client request.

As we will see, advanced architectures that combine the servlet engine and application server into one process will reduce the cost of calls across these containers, but this adds other complications and should not be seen as an excuse to avoid our primary directive, which is to avoid performance problems by good design wherever possible, not fix them later. To understand the performance implications that should be borne in mind when designing components, there is a very important concept that must be mastered – that of **granularity**.

Granularity

Granularity is essentially a measure of the 'size' or 'scope' of a component and its methods. It is particularly important for container based component technologies, such as J2EE, because there is a significant performance overhead from the container (the abstraction layer that hides the low-level technical issues) whenever the path of execution passes into or out of a component. There are some other, equally important, system properties that can be considered to have a scope and therefore a level of granularity – transactions and security in particular. These are important issues that significantly affect the performance of your system, so let's consider them in detail.

I have mentioned that there is significant overhead associated with entry into and exit from a J2EE component. Of course, calling any Java method represents an overhead compared to the sequential execution of in-line code, particularly when late-binding is considered, but we can safely ignore these small, high-level, language factors. When you consider what benefits object oriented programming brings in terms of productivity, extensibility, and maintainability compared to the procedural software monoliths resulting from previous programming paradigms, there is no need to defend this overhead. I am more concerned by the overhead attributable to the container/server than that of the Java language. Let's consider, as a good example, calling into and returning from a method on a session bean. The overhead comes mainly from the fact that calling an EJB component requires you to enter and leave via the container, which has 'housekeeping' tasks to perform and an RMI stub/skeleton as well.

Remember that EJBs achieve improved developer productivity by hiding the implementation complexity associated with distributed n-tier systems, for example, those of security, transactions, object distribution, and persistence. In deference to the EJB specification, the container in which your bean runs promises to ensure your bean will operate correctly in a multi-threaded, n-tier distributed, secure, transactional environment, even though the code in your bean was written with none of this in mind. In addition it may well provide automated (or container-managed as the terminology has it) persistency of the attributes. In other words, you just write the business logic (in the case of a session bean or perhaps entity bean), interact with other components using the J2EE APIs such as JNDI, JTS, and JMS and leave the complexities of n-tier architecture to the container. This seems to be pure magic and addresses most of the issues that caused CORBA programmers many headaches and much lost sleep; but most of us know by now that there is no such magic – unless it is the magic of delegation.

In EJBs this is achieved by providing container managed wrappers (the home and remote implementations) that intercept all calls to the component – the Enterprise JavaBean in this case – prepare the environment, and then delegate down to logic within the bean class – the actual implementation. This is a very effective mechanism for improving productivity but imposes a significant, mainly unavoidable overhead, and in fact the full process of calling an EJB is even more complex than that:

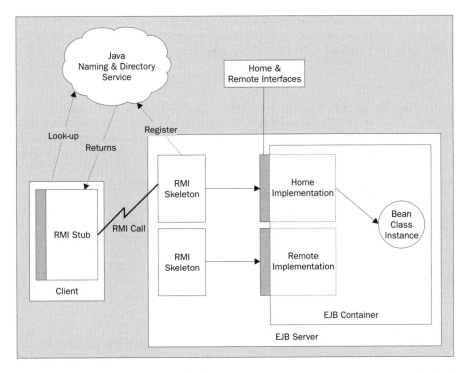

Let's walk through the steps necessary to invoke a method on a session bean to see where the overheads come from. The first time we call an EJB component we begin by finding it. This requires a call to the name service through the Java Naming and Directory Interface. If we know the name of the bean, or, more likely, its type or the service it provides, we can look up in the name service to get a reference to the bean or probably to its home. This normally requires a call out of process, across the network, to the distributed name service, often provided by an LDAP server or COS Name Service. When calling through JNDI you pass the name of the component or its home and the result is a reference to the bean or to the bean's home implementation.

Remember at this point that, at least in theory, all the references we get are distributed ones, meaning that RMI is being used to maintain location transparency. Each time we call on this reference we don't have to worry where (in which JVM process on which machine) in the system the component actually executes or even if it is not currently executing at all, RMI and the container will look after this complexity for us.

However, there is a price for this convenience – the reference is a distributed or RMI reference which means that the client (or caller) is first invoking the RMI stub for the component; this causes the server-side (the callee) skeleton to be called, which will then delegate to the home or remote implementation for the bean and finally into the bean class itself to invoke the active code. The first delegation (from stub to skeleton) may, in the worst case involve a network traversal; even if it does not, it may still involve data marshalling (converting any parameters to a network-neutral data format), traversing the TCP/IP stack, and then converting the parameter data back to the local machine format, (unmarshalling). This depends on how dumb or intelligent your particular RMI ORB and container is. Some will now even recognise a co-located (within the same JVM) caller/callee pair and return a regular Java (non-distributed and therefore more efficient) reference to the appropriate home/remote implementation.

So you can see that already, just to hide the complexity of calling between components in potentially remote locations, we may have amassed a pretty significant overhead on the call and we haven't even looked at the container overhead yet!

Container Overheads

The container must live up to its promise to provide your component a suitably secure, transactionally sound environment in which to do its work and the way the container achieves this is to insist that all calls to the component **must** go via the appropriate home or remote implementation. Think of the implementation as a container-provided wrapper around your bean class, which is the core of your component that you provide and that contains your logic. Another way to think of the home/remote implementation is as a little part of the omnipresent container that wraps your component to protect it from the problems of the n-tier world.

Either way, any call to your component must go through this implementation as is it the container's only chance to intercept the call and check the environment so it can live up to its promises. So, from the RMI skeleton, the implementation is invoked. This goes through its housekeeping activities (see below) and finally delegates to your component an instance of the bean class itself. Similarly, on the way out (after the required method on your bean class has been executed) the return must hand control back to the implementation that called it so that any housekeeping activities can be done, then finally back through the skeleton and stub to the original caller.

> *Notice that J2EE ensures that this process will work regardless of the nature of the caller (client), be it a Java application, applet, servlet, JSP, or another EJB bean either in the same container as the callee or in some remote location across the network – real location transparency.*

This whole story may sound horrendously complex and make you wonder how any EJB systems can perform effectively at all; and I haven't really begun to describe the work that goes on inside the container implementations! Fear not; be assured that many J2EE and EJB systems that perform very acceptably do exist. Many simple systems rely purely on a powerful hardware platform executing instructions at rates in the region of thousands of millions per second to make light work of this overhead. Even very complex EJB systems can still achieve remarkable performance; in fact I have worked on some that out perform their C++ equivalents by more than an order of magnitude, without requiring a hardware platform of monumental proportions and developed in a small fraction of the time taken for the C++ version.

All this is achieved through awareness of the nature of J2EE and the good technique of the designers, minimising the downside, maximising the upside. Sadly, there are also a large number of systems built on J2EE that perform very badly and require a huge hardware platform to produce acceptable results. This is mainly through ignorance of the techniques I will now describe.

The Art of Component Granularity

Clearly, the overhead incurred each time a component is called needs to be avoided as much as possible. At this point, some experienced object-orientated programmers may throw up their hands in horror and accuse me of heresy, so to avoid any misinterpretation, let me be very clear what I mean by this. Firstly this advice should not be taken as an invitation to do either of the following:

Produce a Few Huge Components Containing all the Code for a Large Proportion of the System

This is a level of granularity that is too coarse and results in systems that are very hard to comprehend and therefore debug and maintain. This is really procedural programming with a few object wrappers; the objects will tend to have little meaning as they incorporate many responsibilities. The ultimate form of this bad habit is to abandon components completely and produce reams of monolithic code. Do this and you will find it very hard to implement using J2EE; you can also kiss goodbye to any chance of achieving an efficient service-based architecture (see below).

Abandon J2EE Components and Use Myriads of Regular Java Classes

Productivity will be poor and you will lose the significant benefits of J2EE by trying to avoid the downside – this is a bad place to end up.

Sadly, too many developers new to J2EE adopt a rather naïve approach, making every tiny object a full-blown J2EE component. Having faced a system that will inevitably perform very badly and consume huge amounts of memory, they overreact and commit one of the above sins. As you will have guessed, the best solution lies somewhere between these two extremes. The difficult art, one that requires some experience and probably several mistakes before you acquire it, is that of finding the right balance. This is currently an art, not an exact science; but at least we can apply some guidelines to help, so let me cover these now and in so doing, try to explain what I do mean by my initial statement in this section.

The first part of the art is in understanding which of the classes in your system design to make into full-blown components. Just because you are implementing using J2EE, don't feel obliged to make true J2EE components out of every single Java class you have. In some cases you will be forced into a decision because of the nature of the component or its position in the architecture, but in many cases you will have a choice and the choices can be complex. I would like to offer two pieces of advice, which will hopefully make your life easier:

Don't Agonize for Hours Over These Decisions (Avoid Paralysis by Analysis!)

Make a decision based on some consideration of the following guidelines and go for it, but *do* build prototypes to prove the correctness of your decisions – remember that your initial choices are unlikely to be spot-on, but they are not irreversible and you will get much better as you get more experienced.

If you choose good tools and put together a flexible, productive development environment then changing your mind need not be costly nor set you back very far – as long as these experiments are done early in the life of the project. You do not want to be playing these games when your components have been populated with significant amounts of business logic. Once you have established an overall pattern for the designation of components within your project, future decisions will be much easier.

Be Lazy!

Just for once, life seems to be kind to us, and the best approach seems to be to not do any more work than you have to, and to follow the 'grain' that your tools establish. This may be a result of the hard work and experience that has gone into producing the various J2EE specifications and the tools and products that implement them.

At one end of the spectrum we have the small, very fine-grained objects. Typically these are utility or 'helper' classes and they will often be your own or third party pre-existing Java classes and will not be formally modeled – but leave them alone. Just because they are simple Java classes does not mean that they cannot function correctly in any part of a J2EE system. Conversely, the fundamental business data will need to be modelled to understand the relationships between these entities, and they should all be initially implemented as full components, entity beans, to get the transactional protection of the EJB container.

A good EJB product will come with tools that will take your entity model and automatically generate entity beans, preferably with container-managed persistence, for each of your modelled components leaving you nothing to code – this is the ultimate lazy approach! There are other overheads to take into account, especially when considering entity beans (see below), but you can identify where these become too much by prototyping and back off these objects from full entity beans to become dependent objects (see the EJB 2.0 specification).

The same general rule applies to the 'business logic controllers.' The bulk of the objects that will contain business logic and achieve their results by manipulating entity beans will be destined to become session beans. If you are using a good CASE tool to model your components, this or perhaps your IDE can be used to generate the framework of each session bean, to which you should add minimal logic to produce a prototype that will allow you to carry out performance tests. If you do not have the appropriate tools, either get them, or start with simple Java classes and convert only those you need to into session beans.

The second part of the art is to make correct decisions about what type of J2EE component your class is to become. The best guideline here is to ensure a clean partitioning of your logic over the component types available along the lines of the MVC (model-view-controller) pattern, the table on page 1222 will give you some good clues as to which type to choose and there is detailed advice in the previous chapter.

In summary, use servlets and JSPs to implement the display logic for browser clients – avoid the temptation to implement any business logic or business state in these component types – use EJB components for this. session beans are the principal controllers in the MVC scheme, containing application-specific logic and achieving changes in business state by manipulating combinations of entity beans. Entity beans are designed to contain business state and the core business methods associated with that state.

The third part is not to make the scope of your components too small, nor too large – the granularity needs to be just right to minimize the number of interactions among components within any use-case, but not to compromise maintainability or re-use potential. Most of this will come from good design and object modeling, the rest from interaction studies and prototypes. The closest we can currently get to an analytical approach to this problem is to study object interaction diagrams mapping the calls between your proposed components.

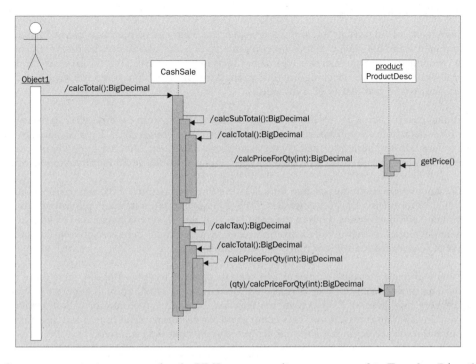

The diagram opposite is an example of a UML sequence diagram captured in Together/J (available from www.togethersoft.com), it shows in detail all the interactions between the components for a use-case. You don't need a full sequence diagram for this purpose, you only need to see the number of interactions, but the additional information in the sequence diagram will come in useful during the development phase.

Carry out this analysis for frequently used and particularly for performance-critical use-cases. The diagrams do not have to be captured in a CASE tool – a diagram on the back of a beer mat works just fine – but the CASE tool will make it easier and contribute to your system documentation. Look at the number of interactions between the components and optimise this by: reducing the number of components, moving the logic around among them, or where the interactions cannot be sensibly decreased, ensuring that they will be co-located.

Finally, use good container implementations and tools that will help to minimize the overheads associated with components. Using a smart container that provides a local finder can avoid a lot of JNDI lookups over the network and ensure that components are co-located for good performance. This will automatically minimize the impact of calling to another component if the container can identify co-located components and return a reference direct to the local home or remote implementation, this will avoid the RMI stub skeleton and therefore the possibility of marshalling/un-marshalling and traversing the TCP/IP stack. As an improvement gained by making a good product selection and not requiring any programming effort, this is an improvement well worth having!

Follow these guidelines and, given some experience and plenty of prototyping to test, even complex applications will be easy to implement and perform very adequately.

Transactional Granularity

As we have seen, it is important to carefully consider the manner in which you map your business logic over components and between methods on components in order to balance the overhead calling between components. We can call this logical or functional granularity, but there are other dimensions that we must consider when checking the total granularity of the system to optimize performance. We will now consider the granularity of transactions.

Transactional granularity is a very important parameter of the system because writing to persistent, transactional, data stores is an important element of virtually every system. Let's be honest – for 99% of systems we are talking about interfacing your system to a relational database and, when a relational database is involved, transactions will have a major impact on both data integrity and performance.

The J2EE way of representing persistent data is in the form of an entity EJB, which offers full transactional support from the container and, for a good container, automatic persistency through container-managed persistence. One of the promises that the EJB container makes to you, as a component developer, is that it will ensure the correct transactional behavior of your component regardless of your component's ignorance of transactions.

By now you will realise that the container will keep its promise to you – but of course there is a possible downside. The downside in this case is that the transactions the container will generate for you by default are very fine-grained. Every create method and every attribute mutator will, in principle, execute within separate transactions. This is not good for performance at the underlying database, as every transaction has a very significant impact in terms of database resources:

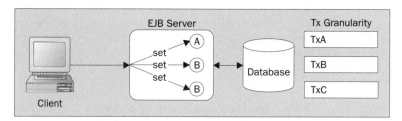

Apart from the performance implications of fine-grained transactions, another disadvantage of this behavior is that all these attribute changes and bean creations may need to be carried out atomically, and not as separate transactions to preserve the logical integrity of the data. To control this usage of database resources, we need to control the transactional granularity of our components.

The immediate reaction of some developers is to assume that this means using explicit transactions to override the default operation of the container by using programmer defined transaction boundaries – after all, you (the programmer) know that you intend to create a particular number of beans and change a particular number of attributes within a particular transaction. This is an incorrect assumption, as controlling the transactional granularity does not necessarily mean that you must implement explicit transactions – EJB is not that naïve!

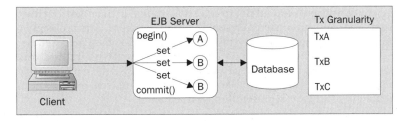

Explicit transactions require that you find the transaction service (though JNDI or a local finder) and then call begin(), commit(), or rollback() on that transaction instance as necessary. There is a much better way that not only solves the issue of controlling transactional granularity, but also ensures that your logic is partitioned in a safe way with respect to the distribution of transactions. This involves the use of a session bean to scope the transaction to that of a method on the bean. The container can control implicit transactions for both entity and session beans, but only at the scope of an individual method. If you organize the logic within a bean method (probably a session bean) so that it corresponds to the transactional granularity you require, you can allow the container to control the transaction by setting the transaction attribute for the method in the bean's deployment descriptor. The entity bean methods called within this method (attribute mutators for example) will normally have transactional attributes that allow them to use the existing transaction (TX_REQUIRED) established by the container on the call into this method:

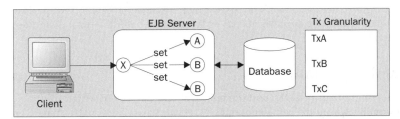

The use of explicit transactions should be reserved for those rare occasions when it is just not possible or convenient to devise a bean method that corresponds to the same scope as the desired transaction granularity.

Persistence Granularity

The J2EE components designed to provide persistency by mapping onto data sources such as relational databases are entity beans. As we have seen, each bean is not a simple Java object but a conspiracy of objects, each of which contributes to the bean overhead both in terms of execution performance, and the total size of the bean. This overhead is much more an issue of size (memory footprint) than one of performance, but it is included here as it is an issue of granularity that is increasingly important for systems comprising a large number of beans.

The overhead is often in the range of 1 to 2 Kb per bean. If your bean is coarse grained, it may well encapsulate several kilobytes of data, in which case the overhead is proportionately not too bad; a 1 Kb overhead on 2 Kb of data gives a 50% overhead. However, if your bean is very fine-grained, representing a simple date, or an integer, the effective data content is very small, a few bytes – in which case the relative bean overhead is enormous; the 1 Kb overhead is 200 times the data of a bean representing 5 bytes, or a 20,000% overhead. If your design calls for a lot of fine-grained beans with this kind of overhead, and typically fine-grained objects come in very high numbers, don't be surprised if you end up devoting tens or even hundreds of megabytes of memory to pure overhead. This is clearly undesirable.

When designing entity beans, be careful not to have a lot of fine-grained beans; choose them so they encapsulate a significant amount of data to justify the bean overhead. The problem here is that you may not have a completely free choice of granularity, given that the database may well be an existing one and the ability of your EJB container to support beans that map over several tables may be very limited or even non-existent. The draft EJB 2.0 specification has formalized the concept of dependent objects to address this problem. Dependent objects are persistent Java objects (not full beans) that 'belong' to a bean and are used to efficiently represent fine-grained data.

Security and Performance

Another function that the container can perform for you when an EJB method is called is to check the authority of the caller to access this method through a potentially complex set of security information based on roles. When considering security and its effect on performance we see yet again the recurring pattern of granularity. For reasons that should be clear by now, you really don't want to suffer the overhead of checking authority unnecessarily on every method call. J2EE offers us a variety of ways and places to implement security with great flexibility, but security is dealt with in considerable detail elsewhere in this book, so I will limit this section to the bare essentials.

Decide on your basic approach to security early in the design process. Determine where in the system it will be handled, and don't do security checks repetitively throughout the architecture, or performance will suffer in a big way. In my experience it is better to establish the credentials of a user early in the architecture, at the web server in fact, and allow only authorised access to the application server layer. Keep sensitive data within the application server layer safely behind a firewall and don't allow servlets to hold this data.

Service-Level Architecture

Having considered granularity at the component level and the way in which splitting logic across different components within the same container/server process affects performance, now let's step back even further to look at a much broader slice of the architecture to see the ways in which functionality (components) can be partitioned over physical processes and machines, and how this affects the end-to-end performance of the system.

Taking a service-based approach to systems architecture can result in systems that are very easily extended, managed, and maintained and promotes reuse in the purest form (i.e. using an existing service to gain functionality instead of re-implementing it within another process) but like all good ideas, it needs handling with a little care and appreciation:

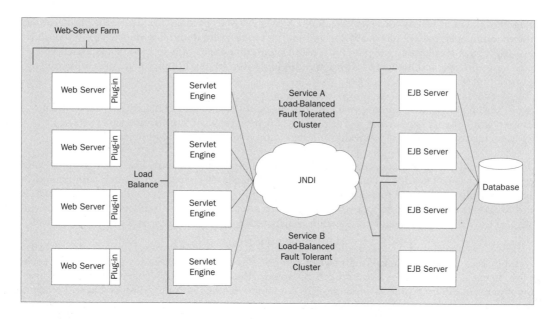

The Object Soup

Earlier in this chapter I mentioned the dangers of drowning in the 'object soup', and now the time has come to explain this term and show you how to survive. J2EE defines a number of component types and provides for these components to communicate when distributed over a multi-tier architecture, principally via RMI. Just like CORBA and DCOM, RMI supports the concept of 'location transparency'. Location transparency means that components (beans in the case of EJB) are always addressed in the same way, regardless of whether they are local or remote, whatever their physical platform or location on the network.

Through the use of JNDI, home interfaces to search for components, and the RMI interfaces that reflect exactly the syntax of the public interface presented by each component, you can easily locate and communicate with a component, without requiring any special code to allow for the fact that the component may well be implemented on some remote machine, or even move its location occasionally. In fact it is possible to get load-balanced over several different instances of the component type within a user session.

The literature often describes this capability, but also tends to go on to promote the idea that your system is a collection of components floating around. All you need to know is how to find them and what interfaces they present, and you do not need be concerned with where they actually execute or how they achieve their results. In other words your system is like a big bowl of soup with the components floating around like peas in this soup.

This is true in principle and location transparency is undoubtedly a very powerful capability, but in practice this simplistic 'object soup' approach can lead to systems that consume considerable network resources, perform poorly, and are hard to maintain. The problem is that for many reasons, including performance, scalability, and manageability, you often do care where a component you are about to call on physically resides.

Imagine a situation where your logic located in server A needs to make frequent calls on the services of other components that are physically located in different servers B and C somewhere out over the network. I have emphasised the potential cost of inter-component calls in EJB; this is higher when the call is inter-process and highest of all when those processes are on different machines separated by a network (inter-machine).

To put this in perspective, an inter-machine call is about three orders of magnitude slower than a call between components in the same server process. Clearly you want to be aware when you are experiencing this overhead if you want to design your system so that it will perform well.

Another consideration is that of manageability and maintenance. It is quite likely that at some stage server machines will need to be taken down for maintenance. If your logic is calling components in many other physical servers then it finds itself in a complex web of interdependencies that makes it very hard to assess and allow for the effect of taking down a server – even with the magic of transparent fail-over. So use the powerful feature of location transparency with a little care and things will go well.

In theory, the object soup factor should be considered at the component-level as well as at the service-level, but because the cost of calling between components across processes or machines is so much higher than calling within the same process the major effect is at the service level (that is, between components in different processes). Some EJB containers implement smart finders that will recognise when components are co-located (caller and callee are in the same process) and return a regular Java reference to the home or remote implementation, not an RMI reference. In this way the caller avoids the cost of going through the RMI stubs and skeletons and it reduces even further the cost of calls between co-located components.

Component Partitioning

So how do we go about partitioning our components between servers for maximum performance? Well, we have touched on this before – prepare and study simple object interaction diagrams showing the dynamics of how the components interact, and the calls between them. Consider the frequency of interactions – where the number of interactions between any pair of components is high and cannot be sensibly decreased without compromising good design, ensure that they will be co-located. Where there are zero interactions between components they are clearly candidates for different services that can safely exist in different server processes. In the middle ground, where there is one or a small number of interactions, then it is best to let other factors such as maintainability dictate the partitioning.

The results of this type of analysis can only be a guide. Remember the golden rule – always prototype and test to confirm your suspicions. If you apply these techniques, you should end up with a well-partitioned system, but there is always scope for the naïve approach to take over. This will lead to a design where all your components end up in the same server process. This is not good for scalability and you must avoid it.

Caching Strategies

I have already mentioned the way in which various web page caching products can dramatically improve apparent performance by allowing requests for frequently used pages to be intercepted before the web server and served by a memory-based cache. It is also possible to apply similar caching techniques within other parts of the architecture such as the application server caching information normally requiring a database access. These caching techniques are very effective and can sometimes produce orders of magnitude improvement in response times. However, providing these caches have multi-threaded capability, they also contribute even more significantly to the scalability of the system. For that reason I will defer discussion of them until later.

Scalability

If you remember, our definitions go like this: the performance of your system is what affects the response time for requests to a single user at a time, whereas scalability is the ability of your system to maintain the same response times as the number of users increases. We have already looked at how to maximize the single-user performance of our systems. Now let's consider how to achieve good scalability.

To start with, let's look at how we will recognize good scalability when we have it. Ideally, we would like to exactly maintain the excellent response times we have lovingly crafted our system to achieve for a single user as the number of users grows from one to infinity. In the real world, you cannot expect the response times to stay exactly the same as you increase from one to 1,000,000 users, even on the most powerful hardware platform. You should also not expect quite such good response times even for a single user from a system designed to support 100,000 users as those from a single-user system – but more of this later. So what can we expect a well-behaved, scalable system to do? Essentially, we can expect it to do two things:

❑ Show linear, small increases in response time with increasing simultaneous users

❑ Avoid software bottlenecks that limit hardware utilization

What the first point says is that we can expect a scalable system to demonstrate response times that will slowly increase as the user load increases (compared to single requests) but in a predictable, linear fashion. Conversely, the response times from a non-scalable system will quickly reach a point where the increase in response time with number of users becomes exponential. Plotting the average response time against the number of simultaneous requests best shows this. The high-scalability system (System A) shows pretty much a straight-line plot:

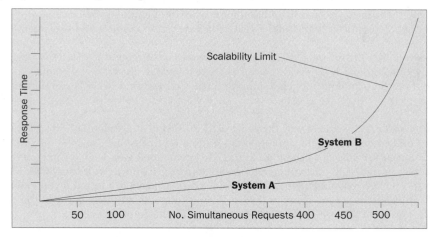

The number of users at which a 'dog-leg' appears in the scalability curve represents the scalability limit of the system for the given hardware platform. In the diagram above, system B shows a scalability limit at around 450 simultaneous requests. The plot becomes very non-linear at this point and response times grow rapidly with every new user that enters the system. This is the point at which users tend to give up and go to a competitor's web site.

It should be noted that I'm using the phrases 'simultaneous users' and 'simultaneous requests' synonymously. This is not quite accurate, but real users are inconvenient for testing purposes as they do not submit requests at regular time intervals. We require a more uniform load for testing purposes to make the capture of meaningful response time statistics easier, and to allow for reproducible testing. This is important so that you can measure the effect of your tuning and improvements. It is therefore traditional to work with client simulators that inject requests into the system at a regular, known frequency.

Typically the automated clients inject requests much more rapidly than a real user, but then you can scale up the resulting figures to give a user equivalent figure. If your real users tend to submit one request every 10 seconds on average, then a client emulator injecting the system with 10 requests per second is applying a system loading of 100 user equivalents. But beware – the client simulator must be multi-threaded, spinning off a thread for each emulated user that will submit a request, wait for the response and then make the next request, or it must pause the 10 seconds before making the next request (a good testing tool will do this for you – see below for some examples). Otherwise, you will get figures that are very misleading.

The second point, maximizing the hardware utilization, is crucial but often overlooked. Some systems give an initial appearance of good scalability, but in reality it is far below the results that should be expected for the power of the hardware platform being used. The reason is that a contention point in the architecture is causing a logjam of requests to form around a particular system resource; these hot spots or bottlenecks cause a significant proportion of the hardware to be idle. I give some typical examples of these bottlenecks and how to remove them below, but a simple example is where a system is I/O bound, causing most CPUs to be idle as they service block requests, awaiting the return of a disk access operation.

The result of a system like this is that the cost of deployment will be much higher than it should be – I exclude these systems from achieving good scalability status. Use the tools provided with your operating system to monitor hardware resource utilization; UNIX systems should come with SAG and SAR, the system activity reporting tools, and in addition most modern operating systems come with a reasonably sophisticated set of 'perfmeter' type utilities that will allow you to monitor and log system usage.

The inability to utilize the full capabilities of the hardware as the request load rises is a classic symptom of a system with a bottleneck. These will occur to some degree in all systems eventually as the load increases, but careful planning can help minimize them. You will find that a law of diminishing returns operates, just as in performance testing, so focus on the large problems first.

System bottlenecks are the reason why throwing extra hardware at a scalability problem often works, but only to a limited degree. Again a point of diminishing returns is met. Imagine the situation where your application server does not handle multi-threaded contention very well (a common problem for some EJB server products). By providing a powerful hardware platform with many CPUs for your application servers you may extend the point at which performance drops, but if you look carefully you will see that at any point in time many of the CPUs are sitting idle, as the majority of the threads in the system block on some common contention point such as the heap manager.

Some vendors recommend an architecture consisting of a large number of essentially single threaded server processes for this very reason. Check carefully to see that your software can make good use of the machine resources available – if not, there is probably a scalability bottleneck somewhere in the system that will cause you to buy more hardware than necessary.

A final rider on this subject is to ensure that your application servers, database, and operating system are configured correctly for the load you are applying – it would be embarrassing to blame your server vendor for poor scalability, only to find that you artificially limited the server's ability to handle requests by forgetting to allow a suitable number of database connections or threads in the thread-pool!

Scalability and Performance Testing

The process of scalability testing is similar to that for performance testing. Scalability tests will require everything that performance tests do, but, in addition, a more substantial hardware platform and a mechanism to emulate large numbers of client requests is required. The schedule for scalability tests is also similar to that for performance testing, so they are often combined sessions, but performance tests are performed more frequently, so it is good that they require less effort, equipment and planning. Just like performance testing, medium-scale tests should be carried out early in the project, to validate the scalability of your architecture and to confirm your product selections, web and application server, servlet engine, database, messaging middleware, and indeed your hardware choice.

Further small-scale tests should be carried out at regular intervals during the project, as you start to layer the business logic into your chosen architectural framework. The final scalability testing session will have to be a very large-scale affair; you should aim to take your system well beyond the maximum number of simultaneous sessions that you intend it to service. This may entail acquiring a very large hardware platform, which could be a problem if your deployment hardware is not yet available, or if you intend an initial deployment on a small configuration which will be scaled up as demand increases. I would suggest that you investigate renting a benchmarking center as run by most good hardware vendors, you never know, if you are planning a very significant expenditure on hardware, you may be able to talk your vendor into some free testing time – it's worth a try.

Tips, Tools, and Techniques

As with any job, having the right tools can make performance and scalability testing much easier and more productive, but not many developers seem familiar with using them. The paragraphs below go through the essential stages of a good scalability test cycle and point out some tips, techniques, and pitfalls whether you automate the testing process or stick to the manual approach.

Tools can greatly assist in the testing, analysis, and correction phases of the testing exercise, but there is a wide variation in the quality and effectiveness of the tools available in today's market. I have already mentioned several tools in the performance testing section, so now I will consider some generic categories of tool to help in scalability testing and explain how they can help in the various phases of the exercise. I will mention some of the market-leading tools that you should almost certainly consider using and some that I have personally found useful, but this is not meant to be a comprehensive review of testing tools. Given the rate at which vendors release new products, you should scan the web and magazine reviews before making a selection.

Let's go through the phases of a well-run scalability test and consider what types of tool can make a useful contribution. As we go I'll also try to mention some tips and techniques that I have learnt, sometimes by making mistakes, or just from the benefit of hindsight. Hopefully they may save you some time and make your testing more successful.

Planning

Good scalability testing is not at all easy to do. The more complex the system, or the greater the scalability requirements, the harder it is. To justify that statement, imagine how difficult it is to emulate the load equivalent to 150,000 simultaneous users to a high degree of fidelity, especially given limited hardware to host the clients. If you don't find that daunting then you probably don't appreciate what is involved! Finding 150,000 people and the equipment necessary to support them is clearly impossible, so some form of emulation is required.

As soon as you get into this territory, you start to quickly appreciate how difficult it is to attain an accurate emulation of even 1000 users given limited hardware. Scalability testing for large scale or complex systems has to be planned like a military exercise to be effective; a seemingly insignificant detail can turn out to be very influential. For example, the cost of losing a whole day's testing at an expensive benchmarking center, of having several Sun E10000 class machines sitting idle because an incorrect version of JDK or database was procured makes for an uncomfortable experience.

Although some tools do provide features to help with test scenario planning and maintenance, I have not found tools, other than the usual project planning tools, particularly useful in this phase. Attention to detail is important. Ensure that you asses the hardware and software required carefully and, especially if you are doing the testing in a rented test center, allow good time for installation and preparing the environment before testing can begin. Remember that you may need to carry out several cycles of testing before you reach your performance and scalability goals; the test, analyze, fix cycle that you expect in quality assurance applies equally in performance and scalability testing. If you make significant changes to the system, it is essential to re-test. The changes applied to improve performance in one area of the system may cause the opposite effect in others.

Performance and Scalability Testing

This is where commercial testing tools can be a big help. Writing your own test framework, although possible, is rarely the most cost effective or accurate and method of testing. It is not uncommon for lengthy and expensive testing exercises to produce completely meaningless results because the whole test architecture was actually limited by the performance of the TCP/IP stack on the machine running all the simulated clients, and not by the performance of the server systems.

Whether you use off-the-shelf tools or write your own test framework, it is essential that the tests provide a realistic emulation of user activity. If not, the results will be meaningless, regardless of how accurately you measure them. If you can capture the way real users operate the system (some tools provide scripting or capture/replay features to aid this), this is clearly preferable to some synthesized approximation of user activity.

Some tools offer comprehensive facilities to cover the test case preparation through scripting or capture and replay, load testing, results capture, and analysis (such as LoadRunner from Mercury Interactive – http://www.mercury.com). These tools can save you much time in the testing and analysis phases and may be the only way you can obtain realistic test results in a reasonable time frame.

Even when using tools specifically designed to emulate user loads, you must still keep your wits about you. Remember to monitor the vital signs of the servers and systems upon which your application is running. You may find that you are in fact measuring the limitations of your client emulator program or the platform on which it runs, rather than those of the system under test! Equally as important is to check that the operating systems, database, web, and application servers are correctly configured for the load that you are trying to apply. Most of these vital subsystems use a configuration file to control the resources they can use.

The default configuration as shipped by the vendor tends to be optimized for small deployments, so it doesn't hog too much in the way of machine resources. This may be perfectly satisfactory for development purposes, but almost certainly woefully inadequate for large-scale scalability testing where you are pushing each component to the limit. The particular parameters to pay particular attention to will vary from system to system, but here is a shortlist of common offenders:

❑ **Application server database connection pool size**
Try an initial allocation equal to the number of simultaneous requests your server is expected to handle. Monitor system response times and connection usage either via your application server tools or database administration tools, as you increase the number of simultaneous requests. Experiment with the pool size to optimize the response times; remember to make allowance for peak loads when calculating values for deployment.

❑ **Thread pool size**
Most thread pools expand and contract (give threads back to the system after an idle period) automatically based on the level of requests so there is nothing to tune, but some do not. Again, try an initial allocation equal to the number of simultaneous requests your server is expected to handle and try adjustments to optimize the response times for the target number of users.

❑ **Application server object cache size**

❑ **Database locks, indices, and cache sizes**
For these two categories I strongly recommend that you get help from your company DBAs or hire consultants from your vendor for the final scalability tests. Most products have tools to help monitor and tune these parameters.

❑ **JVM initial heap size**
Find out what the 'steady state' size of the VM is from tests and set the initial size to be that, plus about 10% extra. Use Java–XMS size.

❑ **Operating system parameters**
This includes file handles, process size limits, shared memory segments, process priorities, CPU allocations, and TCP/IP configuration parameters (especially packet size). Read the manuals that came with your operating system and products, if this isn't covered than contact your vendor. It can make a big difference. If you really don't know how to tune these, get some expert help, it can get pretty complicated as some of these actually interact with each other.

❑ **Logging, profiling, and debugging options**
Remember to switch OFF all debugging or profiling options and disable all unnecessary logging activities. It's quite surprising how many people forget this.

Designing for Good Scalability

We have seen that good performance is dependant on good design and architecture; this is even truer of scalability. High scalability is almost entirely the result of a good architecture. It is very rare that you can improve scalability by a quick re-write of a piece of code (unless the code was staggeringly bad in the first place). Let's look at some of the common factors and techniques that have a very significant effect on scalability: concurrency, data caching, and server replication.

Concurrency

By our very definition, scalability is linked to handling multiple, simultaneous user requests very efficiently. Each user request typically requires computing power from the system to drive the business logic and rapid access to the correct data, for the logic to operate on. Those of us who experienced them have seen flaws in older architectures, such as two-tier client-server computing. In these cases, the computing power for the logic was severely limited by running on a low-power client platform (PC) and access to the data was severely restricted by restrictive locking schemes and having to ship the data over the network to the client and then back to the database constantly.

1239

The key to scalability is concurrency – handling many requests at the same time, but there are a number of barriers to achieving high levels of concurrency; some of these are traditional problems of large-scale systems, but some emanate from the typical J2EE architectures.

Multi-Threading Issues

To be scalable, we need to handle multiple, simultaneous (concurrent) user requests efficiently. These requests require computing power to drive the business logic, so the issue is how to gain access to sufficient computing power efficiently without requiring an over-sized machine.

The traditional approach to this has been to have several single threaded processes, which take turns to get their slice of processor time to handle user requests. This seems to make sense because at any one time a number of requests will be blocking on some event, like waiting for a reply from the database. The problem here is that processes are relatively heavyweight creatures for the operating system to support and manage; each requires its own memory image, it takes significant system resource to switch between them, and a single CPU can still only actually do one thing at a time, even if it is very fast.

The modern approach is to use a hardware platform with many CPUs and several multi-threaded processes; this tends to give better responsiveness, scalability, and resilience. This is at least partly due to the fact that modern middle-tier hardware platforms and operating systems are optimized to provide a very effective environment for multi-threaded applications to prosper. Threads within a process are relatively lightweight creatures: they don't need their own memory image – they share one – and switches between them are fast. This is particularly effective when caching techniques are used, as the memory used by the cache (the cost of using this technique) can be shared over several threads.

The Java language provides native support for threads and although good thread programming requires some skill, it is now much easier and safer than with C++ for instance. The J2EE specs themselves don't mandate multi-threaded implementations, but it is clear that they expect it.

My comments above should not be construed to mean that I recommend using a single highly multi-threaded process; I do not. That approach is not resilient – one rogue thread can bring down your whole system. It also encourages poor n-tier design where everything resides in the same process, often called the software mainframe or monolith, and will not give the best scalability due to contention. The best approach is to have a small number (2 to 5 is a good range, assuming that your chosen server product handles threads well. If not, you will need a much larger number to get the required scalability) of multi-threaded, replicated servers per service cluster operating in a load-balanced, resilient cluster configuration. So why not have a single process running a massive number of threads? Apart from the problems I mention above; resilience and flexible design, you will not get the best scalability this way.

Contention Problems

There are several contention problems that negatively affect the scalability of very highly threaded processes, be they web servers, servlet engines, or EJB application servers. Contention results when a number of requests (each is typically, but not always, allocated to a thread) demand the use of the same limited resource, which does not allow multi-threaded access. An example of contention on this kind of resource, which is simple to understand and resolve, is that of database connection pools.

The idea of a pool is that it provides an efficient sharing mechanism for a scarce or expensive resource. Each pool is normally configured to contain a maximum number of items (in this case, connections to the database) so that the total resource consumed by this server can be limited. As requests arrive the pool manager issues connections and when the request has finished it returns the connection to the pool, so that it can be re-issued to the next request.

This is a very efficient way to manage resources like database connections that are expensive to open and close in terms of the amount of work done and time taken by the RDBMS. The resources are normally allocated on a first-come, first-served basis, although some pools may also use a priority ranking. When all the connections have been allocated and the pool is empty, the next request will block, waiting for a connection to be returned to the pool. We have reached the point of contention on that resource.

In this case it is easy to fix the problem (just increase the size of the pool) but you should be careful not to do this without some thought. Sometimes it is actually better for overall performance if you have fewer connections open to the database – some requests will block, but the active ones may have their queries handled much faster. You therefore need to experiment with this.

Your server will probably allocate connections to requests automatically; in which case, make sure it does this intelligently. Some servers blindly allocate a database connection to a request whether it needs it or not. Clearly this is potentially wasteful and ties up connections unnecessarily, requiring you to allocate more connections to get the same throughput as a server that allocates connections intelligently. Deferring the allocation of a connection until it is needed can improve scalability quite a lot, especially with a small connection pool. If your server does not support automatic allocation, you will be manually coding the request for a connection from the pool. To get the best scalability, emulate the deferred allocation technique and request it as late as possible and return it as early as possible in your code, because this will increase the availability of the connections.

There are some resources that are equally influential but are much more difficult, or even impossible, to control than database connections. These resources can be severe points of contention, a typical example being that of the heap memory manager. This is usually a major contention problem in multi-threaded Java servers. Java is a language that, by its very nature, makes a lot of calls to allocate and free memory. Anyone who knows how Java manages strings will understand the amount of copying and therefore memory allocation/deallocation that goes on.

The Heap Manager as a Bottleneck

When large numbers of components are frequently created in multiple threads, the heap manager can become a crucial bottleneck. This is because the regular heap managers provided with language systems are not good at allocating memory efficiently in a multi-threaded environment. In general they have come from a single threaded heritage and still contain many critical code sections that must be mutexed (allowing only one thread in at a time) to protect their fundamentally single-threaded nature. This will almost certainly be a major limitation on the scalability of your servers, as at any one time, many threads will be blocked waiting their turn to get some memory allocated.

By replacing the regular heap manager with one that is optimized for multi-threaded operation you will see a marked improvement in the effective number of threads that can run in parallel (Sun has mtmalloc, and SmartHeap, at `http://www.microquill.com`, is a third party product that works very well). The classic symptom of this problem can be seen by monitoring the CPU utilization of a single, multi-threaded server process running on a multi-CPU machine with a regular heap manager and trying to handle a large number (more than the number of CPUs) of requests simultaneously. Because many of the threads are blocking on access to the heap manager, you will see many CPUs are underutilized, or even almost completely idle. This means that the server is unable to take advantage of all the CPUs available, even when there are plenty of requests pending. Replacing the heap manager with a thread optimized heap manager can make a huge difference.

1241

The heap manager is a common contention point for Java based servers, but it is not the only resource that can cause problems. The design of the server itself can cause problems; often there are internal hashtables used for housekeeping that can cause contention. The standard Hashtable implementation from `Java.utils` has poor multi-threaded performance as the synchronization is rather brutal and many threads will be locked out of the table unnecessarily. The EJB server product that I use by preference has been extensively tested and improved to promote high scalability and for that reason a thread hot Hashtable was developed to minimize this contention. Check with your vendor to make sure that they are aware of these problems and have taken action to overcome them, or you may get disappointing scalability results even when your components are not to blame.

Data Concurrency

Another source of concurrency problems so common that it deserves special mention accessing data in a database, because it is accessed by pretty much every request in every server in your system. Just like in the discussions above for a J2EE server, the RDBMS has resources (such as indices and tables) that it must share, but also protect. The centralized nature of most databases makes them a prime candidate for becoming a scalability bottleneck.

One solution to this problem is data partitioning; spreading your data over several database server instances, thus spreading the load and reducing the contention on any individual server instance:

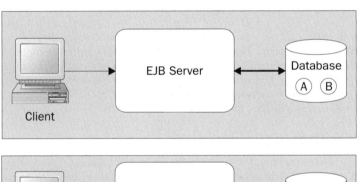

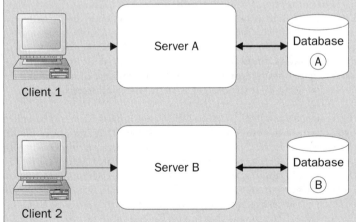

However, there are some problems with this technique:

❑ **Data Access Pattern**
It assumes that the pattern of access to the data will follow the way the data has been partitioned. If not then potentially every application server ends up having to contact every database for each request, thus degrading the intended benefit. If each request requires data from only one source, you will win big time.

❑ **Data 'Routing'**
Your application code will have to figure out which database to read/write the data from/to. Remember that you may end up with entity beans of the same (say 'orders') in several different databases.

❑ **Two-Phase Commit**
If you do end up writing data to different database servers in the same transaction then you will need a distributed transaction with a two-phase commit, to ensure the atomic properties of that transaction. Put simply, this really is not a place you want to be and any performance gains you may have expected will be lost in the overhead of the two-phase transaction.

The manner in which the data is partitioned over the servers is crucial to the effectiveness of this method. Typically you will want any one data item to be 'owned by' or 'homed to' one and only one database server. This preserves the important aspect of having a unique master that can resolve conflicts regarding any data items it owns (see optimistic locking below), but deciding the best owner is not always easy. Sometimes there is a strong departmental or geographical sense of ownership such as for currency: all the US $ trades are homed in New York while all ε (Euro) trades are homed in London. You must ensure that the partitioning scheme roughly matches the patterns of data access:

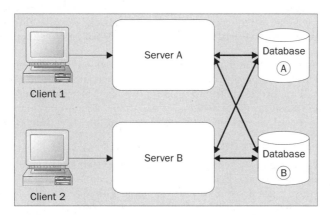

There are systems in which the data is copied into several physically separate databases to provide local copies of a master database for better scalability, but this can lead to terrible problems of data synchronization. There will be regular points at which the data must be rationalized (probably against the master) to ensure consistency. Another similar, but slightly more sophisticated, approach is that of database replication; this uses database copies as above, but adds a scheme for transmitting updates from each database to the others:

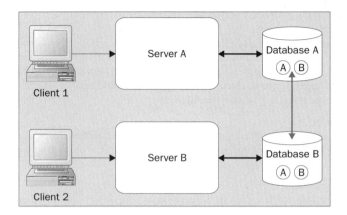

Again you can get into all manner of problems relating to who has the latest copy of the data. In my experience most of these schemes end up being more trouble than the benefit they bring. We will consider better solutions to this problem in the caching section below, but for now we will continue to assume that the database is centralized and consider a another major contention issue: locking.

Optimistic and Pessimistic Locking

An important role for a database management system like a relational database server is to protect the data from corruption. A common cause of corruption would be the effect of two requests updating the same record at effectively the same time, were it not for the locking capabilities of the database. Two servers (or even two requests in the same server) would fetch the record, make changes, and write back the record. But of course, whichever request writes the new data back last will obliterate the changes made by the first update, as both changes were based on the original record before either request started.

Traditional locking techniques would attempt to stop this problem by locking the record as soon as the first request declared an intention to update the record. This would prohibit the second request from reading the record until the first request had released its lock. This simple and historically effective technique is often known as **pessimistic locking**. It makes the assumption that someone probably will attempt to change the record you are intending to change, at the same time as you, so it must be protected with a hard lock.

The problems with this approach in terms of modern n-tier systems are twofold. Firstly the notion of refusing access to a data item (making the user wait) because someone else is 'using' it is no longer acceptable and, secondly, it just does not protect the data. You may wish to debate the first point, but in truth this is increasingly the case – would any modern airline reservations system refuse a potential customer the chance to view a seat because someone else is looking at it? 'Ha!' I hear you say – the second user would be able to see the seat because the system would not lock the seat record until another user has decided to reserve it. This brings me neatly to the second point.

Let me first introduce the notion of record versioning, implying that each record has a version number associated with it. The version is zero when the record is created, but gets incremented each time the record is changed. Now suppose two servers (lets call them A and B) read a record currently at version 1 at essentially the same time. Server A then decides to lock the record as its user wants to update it. Server A changes the record and completes its transaction, so the lock it took out must now be released, as the scope of a lock is defined by the transaction within which it was taken out.

The record is now at version 2 in the database. This now leaves the way clear (no lock is held) for Server B, which read the record at version 1, to lock the record, make different changes to the data and go and overwrite the record, removing the effect of the changes made by Server A.

This is a simple argument and some databases provide for different levels of locking 'strength' in an attempt to solve the problem, but in reality none of these measures are effective in most modern systems. In n-tier systems with replicated servers, pessimistic locking is not effective unless you operate a strict no-caching policy.

The solution we are looking for is, like most good solutions, remarkably simple – it is called **Optimistic Locking**. The tacit assumption now is that although another user may try to update the same data item as us, at the same time, the probability is that they will not – usually this is a good assumption for most systems. So how does it work? Remember those version numbers we introduced above, they are known as optimistic controls and form the foundation of this mechanism, which requires them to be checked every time an update is attempted. Lets go back to our Server A and B example and replay it, this time using optimistic locking. So both Server A and Server B read the record from the database at version 1:

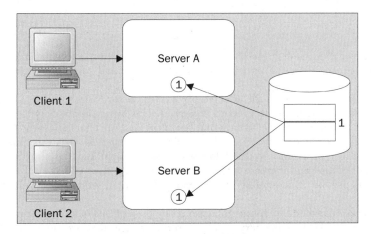

Server A changes the data and attempts to write it away to the database, the version check (version in the database against version the in server) is done and in this case passes, so the update succeeds and the version number increments to 2, and finally the transaction completes:

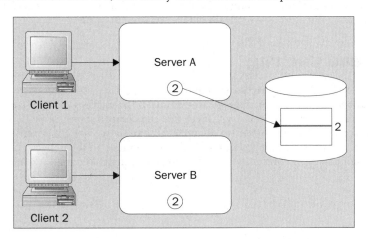

Meanwhile, Server B, which also read the record at version 1, changes the data and attempts to update the record. The database version is 2, but Server B has version 1, so the optimistic check will fail and the Server B's transaction will also fail:

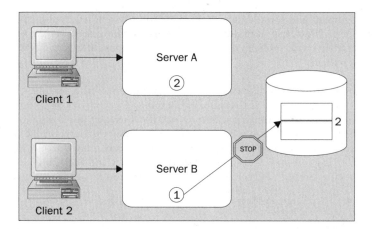

So what does Server B do now? Preferably, the failure of the optimistic check is reflected as an optimistic failure exception in the server, which will be caught and corrective action taken.

The simplest recovery is to re-read the affected objects (the record will be represented by an entity bean in an EJB server environment), so the record is re-read. This brings in not only the latest version of the data, but also the current optimistic version number. Provided the change information from the client request is still available, the transaction can be 're-played' and should work this time. When choosing an EJB application server, remember to check to see if it supports automatic optimistic locking. If it does, it will save you a lot of time and increase scalability dramatically, especially if your database is one of those few that still use the coarse-grained page level locks as opposed to row-level locks.

There will be occasions when the optimism assumed by the optimistic locking approach is unjustified; for example when data is changing very rapidly and the chances that two requests will attempt to change the same record at the same time are high. In this case, optimistic locking will result in lots of optimistic failures, which will degrade performance as lots of re-reads and replayed transactions will ensue. Two possible solutions to this problem are to use pessimistic locking and operate a strict no-caching policy (bad for performance and scalability), or a technique known as cache synchronization – but more of this later. We must learn to walk before we attempt to run.

Data Flow and Caching

In a typical (non-caching) system each user request will require access to the correct data, for the business logic to operate and produce the desired result. If the data resides in the database and the business logic lives in the application server layer this can create a lot of traffic between the database and application servers. This was never more apparent than in two-tier client server systems where access to the data was restricted by pessimistic locking schemes and the network became a serious bottleneck through having to constantly send data over it to the client and then back to the database.

It is blindingly obvious, but important to realize, that the bringing together of the business logic and business data or state is vital to allow the system to operate. We should also recognize that although 3-tier or n-tier architectures have allowed the business logic to exist on a platform more suited to providing the power it needs (the middle-tier server, typically a multi-processor UNIX or Windows NT machine), it has not fundamentally solved the problem of having to move the data from a database to meet with the logic and then put it back again. All we have done is move that bottleneck from between the client and the database, to between the middle-tier and the database.

In fact in some ways we have made the problem worse. Continually fetching records from a database, turning them into a J2EE components (typically entity beans), processing them, writing the data back to the database, throwing away the components, and then doing exactly the same all over again ad infinitum for subsequent requests is a great way to load down your system and limit your scalability. Just as in the two-tier case, the database, or the network between the database and the middle-tier servers, will become a significant scalability bottleneck.

Read to Write Ratios

This problem of the data access bottleneck is bad enough in a typical transaction processing application where the number of reads from the database is roughly equal to the number of writes to it, but things get much worse when the ratio of reads to write increases. In a traditional transaction processing application the records you wish to process are selected and retrieved from the database; these are processed in some way and finally they are written back to the to the database and the transaction completed. This is a read/write ratio of ~1; only the records requiring to be modified are retrieved, and then each is written. But the nature of data processing has changed significantly, especially with the advent of the Web; a browser is so called for a very good reason – users browse, read, or view large amounts of information. This compounds our data access problems.

The nature of using a typical web site involves browsing large amounts of information and then causing a much smaller amount of information to be created or changed. For example, buying a few CDs from a web shop after browsing, searching, and sampling 30 to 40 possible options. This behavior has lead to typical read/write ratios in the region of 10 to 100, which exacerbates the data flow problems in the system and makes the database an even more likely candidate to be a critical bottleneck. A database will tend to struggle if it is trying to handle the update/create load while at the same time the number of query operations has just gone up by a factor of 100.

This is particularly a problem for object-oriented or component systems, be they based on DCOM, CORBA or J2EE, because of the overhead associated with reading a relational record and constructing it into an object or component with the associated object/relational mapping process that must take place. If the object is to be processed and written back, then the overhead is more easily justified as the benefits of having the data in component form are clearer, but if it is just read, displayed, and dispensed with, then the overhead seems rather out of proportion to the benefit. How can we justify the overhead of object to relational mapping and help to minimize the effect of the database as a bottleneck?

An obvious way is to get more out of the data when in object form, that is, make the components do more, hold the data in the form of objects inside the middle-tier servers for longer, and make them participate in several requests before dispensing with them. This means that records will be less frequently fetched from the database and built into objects that get destroyed less often, which reduces the number of database accesses required, reduces the effective overhead of object/relational mapping, and maximizes the benefits of having components. This technique is generally known as **object caching** and has been around for at least ten years, well before the advent of J2EE – it just goes to show that there are very few new problems!

Object Caching

The idea of object caching is that your server will manage a cache of stateful components (entity beans in the case of EJB) that mirror and synchronize with the records in your database. Due to this, an automated object/relational mapping such as that termed 'container managed persistence' in the EJB specification is required. Note that although the objects reflect the state of the database, this cache exists within the middle-tier servers, not on the database tier.

A good object caching server will actually support object networks; caching not only the attribute data for the objects, but also the relationship information as described in an object model that relates components to one another. This allows for very rapid traversal of the object network as the relationships are typically represented as pointers and collections of pointers, depending on the cardinality of the relationship. Traversing relationships via pointers based within the server's memory is much faster than calling over the network to a database and carrying out the required joins to achieve the same effect.

When components (beans) are queried for (using a finder method on the home interface), they can be retrieved from the database and established within the server cache. Relationship navigations will initially require a database join to resolve the objects on the other side of the relationship, but thereafter the relationship pointers will be established in the cache (a process known as **pointer swizzling**) and can be navigated in lieu of a database join.

The cache must be transactional to be truly useful in most systems and the cache manager will ensure that transactions executed within the cache will be reflected onto the database – indeed, successful committal of the transaction on the database (after the required optimistic control checks of course) is a prerequisite for the cache based transaction to succeed. In caching EJB servers all of this is transparent and can be driven by our protective friend the container.

The object cache is conveniently described as being equivalent to an in-memory object database living within the confines of the middle-tier server, but without the associated legacy integration problems that an object database usually brings. This analogy is not strictly accurate, but useful nonetheless; indeed some caching servers also provide an object query language to search over the cached population of objects in much the same way that an object database would.

Object caches are very useful, but it's not all upside. The cache itself will take up memory, sometimes lots of memory. Practical object caching requires management capabilities, so that the cached population of objects can be configured, controlled, and monitored. These days however, memory is relatively cheap (compared to the real cost of developing ever more complex software it is almost free), and modern middle-tier platforms (especially the 64-bit variety) support huge amounts of it.

Another downside relates to the extra complexity that your systems may experience when object caching is used for multi-server or clustered architectures in particular. Optimistic locking becomes essential and the caches may need to be synchronized – more of this later in the server replication section below. Object caches, like any other powerful facility, need to be used with care to get the maximum benefit for the lowest cost and complexity. Used wisely they can improve the performance and scalability of your systems beyond all recognition, used naïvely they will become a millstone around your neck.

Cache Organization and Management

So how do we use the object cache effectively to help solve performance and scalability problems? – Let's look at an example to see the answer – the typical e-commerce site, as a web-shop should provide a good illustration. The first thing to understand is what to cache and what not to cache; you will be dealing with a number of different 'categories' of data, from the perspective of caching suitability. Let's call these reference data, core business data, and transactional data:

Category	Characteristics		
	Rate of Change	**Access Rate**	**Volume**
Reference Data	Low	High	Low
Core Business Data	Medium	Medium	Medium
Transactional Data	High	Low	High

❏   **Reference Data**

Reference data is characterized by the fact that it changes infrequently, is accessed with a very high frequency, and is present in low to medium volumes. An example of this is the catalogue – the items for sale in the shop – which will change, but for the usual web shop only a small part (perhaps 1%) will change on a daily basis. Another example is that of conversion and translation tables, for currencies, etc. This type of data is ideal for caching as it is accessed frequently. Every visitor to the site looks through the catalogue, which means that its presence in the cache is easily justified; the reduction of read traffic on the database will be significant and the performance boost will be substantial if the cache satisfies requests. The catalogue may well be pre-loaded into the cache when the server starts up, before it starts taking requests, and held for the lifetime of the server – or at least until a maintenance application changes it.

❏   **Transactional Data**

At the opposite end of the spectrum, transactional data changes frequently. Any particular item is accessed only a few times in its life cycle and there is a large amount of it. An example of this is the shopping baskets and the items within them. There is little point in holding them in the cache beyond that user's session, as, unlike the catalogue, they will not be required by other user's requests. The best way to treat this data is to load it on demand, fetch it into the cache when the appropriate user logs-in, and flush it from the cache when they logout or the session expires. This gives fast response times for that data while the user is active in the system, but does not clutter the cache up with unwanted data after the session terminates.

❏   **Core Business Data**

Core business data varies in its rate of change. Some is very static, some quite dynamic and it is accessed with medium to high frequency. For our example web shop this would be customer records, addresses, supplier information, stock levels, and accounting information. This type of data is not a clear-cut area for caching. Whether a particular set of objects is cached or not will depend on the memory available and the benefit to be gained by caching. The best approach is to experiment during scalability testing to optimize response times while minimizing cache size.

Relational Database Cache

Most people, when introduced to the idea of object caching, raise the question of the relational database cache: "I already have a large cache on my relational database, so why do I need an object cache?"

The database cache is usually an asset to performance and, rather conveniently, it still will be whether or not you use object caching as well. The objects in the cache must be created from selected database records and membership of associations determined by joins; the database cache will enhance the speed of both these operations. However, once established the object cache should (if decently implemented) outperform the database cache by a good margin. There are several reasons for this, but the most important ones are:

❑ The database cache holds pages of tables and indices, not objects, so there is still an object/relational overhead. The object cache is holding ready-formed objects.

❑ The object cache can navigate using pointers, and this will always be faster than the database, which must use joins, even if the indices are held in a memory-based cache rather than on disc.

❑ The database cache will be on the same machine as the RDBMS. This is usually the back tier so at least one extra network hop is involved before the data is available to the logic, compared to the object cache, which is in process with the EJB server and therefore the business logic.

Results will vary from server to server and application to application of course, but tests carried out with the EJB application server product that I know best – Persistence PowerTier (http://www.persistence.com) – indicate that a fully populated object cache will provide in the region of a ten-fold performance improvement above that provided by a fully populated relational database cache (meaning that the whole database is cached). This is an improvement well worth having!

It is simple to see that finding an object in the cache and avoiding a database query and a network hop will improve response times and therefore performance, but what about scalability?

To see significant scalability gains, the cache must offer multi-threaded access. When the cached components can be shared among multiple requests that can access the same components simultaneously without significant contention, then not only is it possible to get significant scalability gains, but also substantial saving in memory and database accesses from not having to read a copy of the object for each request.

Imagine the savings if 1000 simultaneous requests to view the special offers in the web shop can be satisfied from one set of objects that constitute the page. Multiple requests simultaneously reading a component in a shared fashion is not so tricky, but what happens when at least one request wants to write the objects?

Transactional Multi-threading

To be effective in a multiple request read/write environment the shared object cache needs to be not only multi-threaded but also transactional. Not surprisingly, this is known as transactional multi-threading. The essential properties of transactions are normally expressed by the acronym ACID, indicating that transactions must be Atomic, Consistent, Isolated, and Durable. The regular behavior of the transaction service and the underlying database ensure most of these even in a shared cache environment, but it is worth mentioning a concept called **Transactional Isolation**.

This is particularly important for a shared cache, as the isolation properties are difficult to maintain. If a request starts a transaction and begins to change a shared object, it is essential that other requests do not see the effects (state changes to the object) of this partial transaction until it is properly committed.

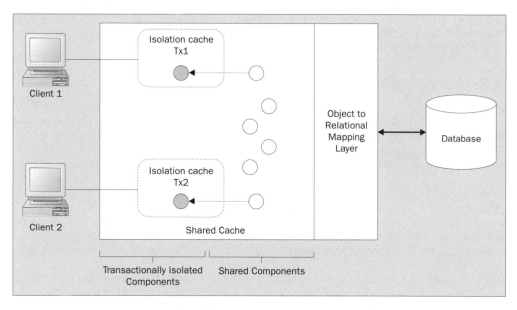

This is normally handled by establishing an isolation cache for each transactional context supported by the server. Objects are copied from the shared cache into the isolation cache that 'belongs' to the transaction, as they are touched within the transaction boundaries. This preserves a consistent view of objects during the transaction and ensures that any changes are isolated from the shared view of the objects. When the transaction completes, if optimistic control checks pass and the database is happy to accept committal (durable), then the isolation cache is folded back into the shared cache and all other users finally see the results of this committed transaction. Of course, if the transaction is rolled-back the isolation cache can be thrown away, thus maintaining the atomic nature of the transaction.

So we have seen that access to data within a system can frequently become a bottleneck that will limit scalability, and how techniques such as optimistic locking, data partitioning, and object caching can improve this situation. These techniques are not without their own issues, but in general, they work well to alleviate the common problem of scalability being throttled by a database. Most of our discussions so far have required us to consider the situation of only a single (albeit multi-threaded) instance of web server, servlet engine, and application server. The most powerful systems use clusters of servers to achieve vary large scalability.

Scalability Through Replication

All systems have some limitations on their scalability. It might be a database bottleneck, network bandwidth, throughput of your messaging software, the scalability of your application server, or (if you are lucky as this is the easiest to fix) it will be the power of your hardware platform. The ideal situation to attain is that of incremental scalability. In this scenario application services are based on clusters of servers. Adding more servers to each cluster, initially on existing hardware, can increase overall scalability and when that runs out of steam, additional or more powerful hardware can be added.

In addition to great scalability, this strategy offers the extra benefit of allowing you to deploy a system of modest scalability on a hardware platform of modest cost. As the loads on the system rise through increased usage, you can expand the hardware to gain increased scalability. One rider I would add to this pay-as-you-go expansion scheme, is that if you intend to end up with very large machines (such as Sun E6500 or E10000s) buy these machines early, but in small configurations, and expand by adding additional CPUs and memory. This will cause minimal disruption as you grow and will work out much cheaper in the long term.

Server Replication and Clustering

A key element in achieving the goal of incremental scalability is efficient server clustering and management. The technique of clustering is proven and has been around for several years in military and high-end systems, but now it is becoming available to mainstream commercial applications through J2EE technology. A slightly different approach to scalability through parallel execution is a recent advance from Sun called the Jini program.

Jini technology is based on the concept of building very flexible, resilient systems by federating (loose-coupling) together a number of component based distributed services or devices. An important element of Jini is the JavaSpace service, which provides for communication and sharing of common persistent objects between collaborating agents. This is currently a parallel initiative to J2EE aimed initially at the device level market. However the notions are equally applicable to enterprise level computing.

A (software) cluster is a group of server processes, which act in concert to provide the same logical service. Each server in the cluster may execute on the same or different server machines. We are considering a software clustering technique, not to be confused with hardware clusters, and the mapping to the hardware is not relevant (apart from possible performance and resilience implications). Usually the servers within a cluster act as peers. Each one is active (handles requests) and has the same status within the cluster, although in special circumstances it may be necessary to employ master/slave clustering.

Incoming requests are shared amongst the active servers in the cluster according to some algorithm, a technique called **load balancing**. Clusters are logical collections of servers and the configuration of servers participating in a cluster is normally dynamic; servers can be added or removed from clusters on-the-fly making maintenance much simpler. In some cases servers may even participate in more than one cluster, although I do not suggest you do this just for the hell of it! This flexibility very beneficial to incremental scalability; new servers can be added to help cope with increased loads without disrupting the system.

All this used to be a real challenge only a few years ago, but there now there are several good server products that support clustering and load balancing on the market; this is true of web servers, servlet engines, and EJB application servers.

A word of warning: although modern server products make clustering and the implementation of replicated servers quite easy, this does not remove all responsibility from the architect and designers. It is all too easy to fall into the trap of using logic and techniques that do not work in a replicated server environment and will cause problems, especially where data integrity is concerned – remember the need for optimistic locking for example. If you have even the slightest intention to deploy in replicated or clustered configurations, decide this early on and take it into account when architecting and designing the system. I have seen all manner of database corruption result from a rash decision to cluster servers containing logic that assumes it is executing as a system-wide unique instance.

Better scalability is not the only reason to deploy clusters. Increased resilience is an equally valid reason, but may result in slightly different deployment configurations, as we will discuss in the next section.

Load-Balancing and Fail-over

If you aim to increase scalability by replicating the functional units in your architecture, you need to ensure that the increased system load resulting from an expanding user population can actually take advantage of the new servers in your system. They need to share the load and typically this requires some form of load balancing. Load balancing is a simple concept, but more complex to get right in practice.

The simple explanation is that as each request enters the system some software or device will direct it to the most appropriate server in the cluster according to a load balancing strategy or algorithm. Most products provide for a number of built-in load balancing strategies and, in addition, user defined algorithms where you can supply the code to calculate the most eligible server in the cluster to receive the current request. Web servers and page caches may load-balance according to some characteristic of the requested URL, and servlet engine plug-ins may use 'zones' or a similar partitioning. In the case of load balancing over application servers, some strategies attempt to calculate the current load on each server and direct the request to the least loaded server.

In my experience, unless the requests are long lived or very intensive of resources the load balancing calculation may consume more resources than the request itself, so it is best to stick to very simple strategies like random or each server in sequence. In cases where servers in the same cluster are running on hardware platforms of considerably different capabilities, a weighted-random algorithm might be appropriate.

As I mentioned above, it is currently possible to implement load balancing at a bewildering number of places in the architecture and now that layer 5 to 7 switches and firewall load balancers are becoming reliable and affordable much of it can be done by intelligent network hardware and need not involve the J2EE containers and servers at all. Having said that, it is still most common to load-balance either between the web server's servlet plug-in and the servlet engines, or between the servlet engines and the EJB application servers. In practice the latter form of load balancing is implemented through the name service; the cluster provides a logical service to clients, which is identified within the naming service by a unique service or cluster name, 'pricing' for example.

Within the context of the cluster each server will usually have a name identifying it as a part of the cluster, 'pricing.1' or 'pricing.2' for example. It is neither necessary nor desirable for a specific server within the cluster to be addressed directly by its name; the client requests the service by name using JNDI and the load-balancing algorithm will select the most appropriate server instance within the cluster. This brings us to yet another of those granularity issues – the granularity of load balancing.

It would be possible to load-balance every request as it enters the system, but this may result in a lot of work for no reason and makes it hard to make effective use of stateful components like session beans. Often it is more efficient and gives better performance to load-balance at the session granularity, not at per request granularity. The initial request of a client into the system will result in the selection of a server from the requested cluster name via load balancing. This establishes a session within the chosen server and thereafter (for the duration of the session) the same session bean will be called by the client. This allows session state to be established within the session bean that can be used on each subsequent request from that particular client. Only in the event of server failure or a request to a different cluster would load balancing be involved again.

A typical cluster contains servers that act as peers: each one handles requests and has the same status. In some special circumstances it may be necessary to employ master/slave clustering. This is the case where special requirements of the application demand that only one active server may exist at any point in time for each processing element (like a book in a trading or auction system). This form of clustering is more often used for overcoming resilience problems rather than scalability issues, but demonstrates that server replication can also provide a very cost-effective form of failure resilience. If a server in a cluster dies, the others will carry on and may even take over the sessions belonging to clients of the failed server – a process known as **fail-over**.

A typical fail-over scenario involves the client having to catch the 'com failure' exception resulting from the failure of its allocated server. Code in the client would have to re-bind to a new server through JNDI. However, some vendors provide a sophisticated form of fail-over known as transparent fail-over where the client does not even have know that the server has failed as the client-side RMI stub will detect the failure and establish a connection to an alternative server without the need for error trapping code in the client.

Data Integrity in Replicated Systems

Before we leave our discussion of replicated and clustered servers, there is a subject of vital importance we must address – that of data integrity and currency. It is all very well building a system that performs very well and maintains good response times under the load of 200,000 active users, but if the information that is being presented and processed is out of date, inconsistent, or in danger of becoming corrupted, you have a major problem on your hands. Complex n-tier environments with clusters of replicated servers can lead to race conditions, which are very difficult to trace even if you are very careful. I strongly recommend the use of well tried and tested techniques such as optimistic locking to maintain data integrity. If you are using object caching in a clustered environment, then you may well need to resort to cache synchronisation techniques as well. Otherwise an inordinately large number of optimistic failures may ensue, which will not help performance. Good server products will provide these features for you.

Project Planning for Good Performance and Scalability

Before we leave the subjects of performance and scalability and to help pull it all together, let's see how we might encourage the application of the things we have learnt, by briefly considering some activities and guidelines that should help on a typical project.

I've said it before and I'll say it again – the best way to solve performance and scalability problems is to avoid them in the first place. This requires very early and continual consideration of the issues. Start thinking about performance and scalability during the initial phases of the project, and don't leave it until the end as many people do – remember that hitting a problem late in a project will be costly and stressful, especially if you don't find the problem until a few weeks before you need to deploy! Here are a few simple steps you can take to help your project be successful and deliver a well performing and highly scalable system, on-time and within budget:

- ❑ Consider performance and scalability when prototyping your system, and make them criteria of your design and architecture.

- ❑ Ensure that performance and scalability are on your list of non-functional requirements.

- ❑ Select tools and products with performance and scalability criteria in mind, not just functionality.

- ❑ Carry out performance tests when integrating each set of components.

- ❑ Plan a three-phase approach to scalability tests during the project:

  - ❑ A small/medium-scale test early in the project to confirm the architecture prototypes.

  - ❑ A medium-scale test approximately half-way through the development phase.

  - ❑ A very large-scale test at least two months prior to deployment.

- ❑ Solving scalability problems is often complex, so if you are not confident get expert help – particularly during scalability testing.

The above tips are not rules and are not guaranteed to ensure the success of your project, but I have found them be useful in many projects.

Summary

I started this chapter by stating that performance and scalability are currently rated as the biggest issues facing medium to large-scale, deployed Java server systems. I went on to say that performance and scalability problems are very common in many J2EE based systems. I'd like to finish by putting things in perspective and offering a hopeful view of the future with J2EE.

The first point to make is that J2EE itself is not responsible for this situation, at least, no more so than say CORBA or DCOM is at fault; it is more our lack of understanding and inexperience in the problems of complex distributed systems that causes the problem. I have been building high-performance distributed systems for many years now, trading systems and more recently large-scale e-commerce sites in both C++ and Java with CORBA and over the last three years EJB and then J2EE. At first I was skeptical about the ability of Java to perform sufficiently well to really satisfy these demanding applications. Since realizing that a slightly different approach – one that plays to the strengths of Java by making good use of multi-threading – is required, I have become confident that even the most demanding commercial applications can be satisfactorily implemented using J2EE.

Well, we have come quite a long way. If this chapter has opened your eyes to the fact that good performance and scalability is not something that just happens by chance, but needs as much effort and good design as the functionality your system provides, then it has achieved its purpose. If you have learnt a useful tip or two along the way then this is an added bonus. I'll leave you with the golden rule one final time and that still won't be once too many: the best way to solve performance and scalability problems is to avoid them in the first place.

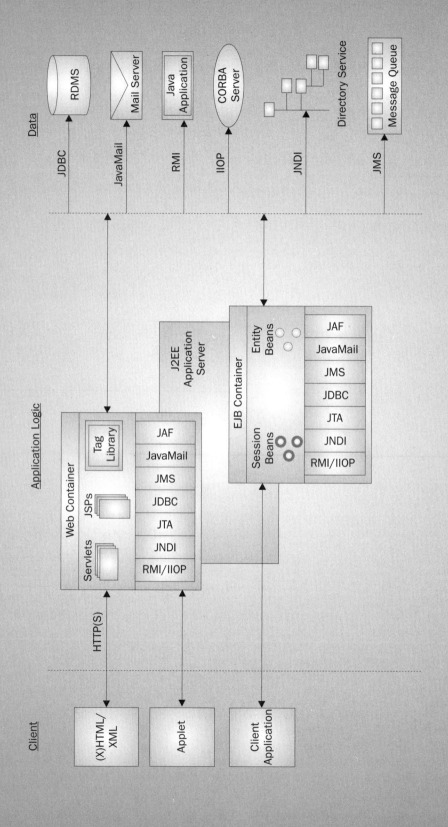

26

Debugging Java Server Applications

Debugging distributed, server-side applications isn't easy. Of course, that's one of the biggest clichés about this topic and doesn't really help us. In the first place we ought to take a look at what's different about Java server programming compared with other types of Java applications and what impact this has on the debugging process.

This chapter will not give a single debugging solution because, most probably, there isn't one. Debugging is as much a mental issue as a strict computational one. A bug is a part of a program that doesn't exactly do what it's supposed to. This 'supposed' stresses the human aspect of debugging. From the computer's point of view, there are no bugs. Oh yes, there are errors and exceptions, and these are somehow related to bugs, but that is not the same. Some serious bugs never throw an exception and, vice versa, an exception doesn't always mean there's a bug. The specifications of an application are typically interpreted in several ways. A problem for the end-user isn't always seen as problematic by a developer. That's where the expression 'it's not a bug, it's a feature' comes from. Debugging is the process of correcting or minimizing these problems.

In a strict sense, debugging can be seen as locating and fixing the 'wrong' code. Finding out there is a bug, or coding in a way that avoids certain problems, can also be seen as part of the debugging process as a whole.

In this chapter we will look at:

- ❑ What makes Java server programming different, and how this relates to debugging
- ❑ What type of problems can we expect, and what to do to avoid or find / correct them
- ❑ What tools and techniques we can use in the debugging process

Differences of Java Server Programming

What makes programming for the Java server different? Well, it differs from writing applets and applications in Java, but it also differs from writing CGI scripts and ActiveX objects in VB, etc. Of course it has some points in common with these alternatives as well, but Java server programming typically exhibits the following characteristics:

- ❑ Java is used as the programming language
- ❑ The application runs mainly on the server
- ❑ Processes often run for a very long time

The applications should:

- ❑ Be stable and robust
- ❑ Run in a multi-user / multi-threaded / multi-server environment
- ❑ Be able to handle heavy loads with reasonable performance

Let's see how these points relate to debugging.

The Java Language

Java itself is a very clean language and helps us to apply correct OO techniques. To make the debugging process as easy as possible we should create small, clear components and, where possible, follow the guidelines for creating beans: use get/set methods instead of directly accessing member variables, implement the serializable interface, and provide a 'no-argument' constructor. We don't need a reason to make a certain class a bean, we need a reason NOT to make it a bean. Just following the get/set naming conventions could already reduce the number of bugs just by making it easier to recognize and remember API's.

Small, neatly defined components make it easier to locate and isolate a problem and allow us to test our complete application on a low level by using unit tests for each component (see Chapter 27). It is important to make sure our beans are not coupled to a specific environment or usage. For example, do not import the `javax.servlet` package in a bean, even if we plan to use them only in our servlets, because that means they can only be debugged and tested inside a servlet context. The first time we'll want to use our beans in another setting is most probably while debugging.

One of the aids to debugging that relates to the Java language specifically is **Java Debugger (JDB)** included with the SDK. This is the standard Java debugging tool that, in a very basic low-level style, allows us to set breakpoints and step through the code line by line while the application is running.

More details on JDB and how it can be used can be found at
`http://java.sun.com/products/jdk/1.2/docs/tooldocs/win32/jdb.html`.

The Application Runs on the Server

This might seem obvious at first, but it has a very important implication on the debugging process. We use the term 'server' – as well as 'client' – mainly as a software concept (like in web server or database server) and not to denote some piece of hardware (like in file server or backup server). Of course, in many cases the two meanings go together. In contrast to applets and other applications, server applications generally run in a non-visual environment. As non-visual processes are less apparent, they are difficult to envisage. This makes them difficult to debug.

One of the main difficulties is that there is no obvious place where errors and other messages can be displayed. In addition programmers do not always know what to do when an error occurs, often exceptions are ignored using an empty catch clause:

```
try {
    // Problematic code
} catch (Exception e) {}
```

Since exception handling is present in almost every class, there should be a simple, easy to use, and correct alternative. One possible approach is to send error information to a log file. Although it's a good idea to log the errors, it's not enough. An error isn't handled just by logging it, where it might disappear amongst several megabytes of other information.

A server process is also physically further away from the developer. It usually doesn't run on the developer's own computer. Of course, many of the components and architectures can be run on a single PC and we should try to catch as many bugs as possible on our own system, but some problems only appear when they're run on the server. If we develop on our own single computer a complex system with, for example, Jini services to be run on five different servers, we may not be 100% confident that everything will immediately run smoothly when we deploy this.

These errors might be related to the network setup, incorrectly written property files, the servers' operating system, or simply because of the deployment itself. The network itself is one of the most critical factors and adds a lot to the total complexity of a system. It's a good idea to have a test server that mirrors the production environment, but it's not always easy to create a true copy. For example, when your application needs to send e-mails, it's not easy to test and debug this, even if you have a test server. In debug mode we use other e-mail addresses than in production, so we do not test exactly as it will be used. We should also be prepared to monitor the application when testing is as complete as it can be. This could be done by setting relevant monitors throughout. We'll discuss some of these tools at the end of the chapter.

Long Running Processes

Server-side Java processes typically run for a long time when compared with CGI scripts, as they don't start a new process with every request. Some problems might never occur in an application/applet context, just because these are typically stopped and restarted quite often. Which is obviously not something normally done on server-side applications.

One of the potential problems caused by long running processes is running out of system memory resources. Java's garbage collector takes care of many potential memory leaks; compared to C++ this saves the Java developer from some hard to debug problems. However, this doesn't mean that we can forget about memory issues altogether. The garbage collector destroys all objects that are no longer referenced. However, we can still have object instances that are no longer required but somehow still have a reference to them, and cannot be cleaned. Since these objects can keep references to other objects, we might keep a lot of memory space occupied. These objects are called 'loiterers'. (See http://www.ddj.com/articles/2000/0002/00021/00021.htm for some more details on memory leaks in Java).

At first we can use our OS to monitor the memory usage of the JVM. There are also tools like JProbe profiler (http://www.klgroup.com) and OptimizeIt (http://www.optimizeit.com) that give we a very detailed overview of how much memory our objects occupy and can help debugging these problems. The implementation of the garbage collector depends on the JVM. Some are better than others, this might lead to bugs or problems that only occur on a certain OS.

Most server-side applications use caching on several layers to speed up processing. In long running processes it's important that this cache doesn't grow to unlimited size. Since there's no 'sizeOf' in Java to measure how much memory an object uses, it's not easy to create a cache that is strictly memory limited. Most caches simply allow a fixed number of objects, regardless of their size. Although not very sophisticated, this might give good results, provided we base our cache size on tests and not on some wild guess. Also keep in mind that an object in the cache might keep a reference to other objects, preventing these instances from being garbage collected. In which case, a cache with a rather small number of objects can still occupy a lot of memory.

Even when resources are container managed it is important to hold on to resources for as little time as possible and to clean up other resources. We often see code like this:

```
try {
    FileInputStream in = new FileInputStream
    // Do something that can throw an IOException
    in.close();
} catch (IOException e) {
    // We don't have a handle here to the InputStream
}
```

When an error occurs, the InputStream isn't properly closed. We might just rely on the garbage collector to close the file, but the correct code should declare the FileInputStream outside the try block and close the FileInputStream in a finally block. In any case, the OS will, when the program finishes, close the file. Therefore, this code might not be a big problem for normal applications. Server-side applications, however, are meant to run for days (months) without restarting, so its proper cleanup becomes much more important.

The situation is even more complex in the case of JDBC connections. Especially when we use connection pooling. Some JDBC drivers not only keep resources occupied when a connection isn't closed, but also with open Statements and ResultSets. Normally we could expect the closing connection to take care of closing Statements and ResultSets, but this isn't always the case. Besides, when we use connection pooling, we don't close the connection at all. Therefore, the garbage collector cannot help us in any way.

If we use JDBC code similar to our file example:

```
try {
    Connection conn = // Get a connection from the pool
    Statement stmt = conn.createStatement();
    ResultSet rs = stmt.executeQuery("SELECT COLUMNS FROM TABLE");
    // Get the values
    // or update the database
    rs.close();
    stmt.close();
    return conn to the pool();
} catch (SQLException e) {
    System.out.println(e.getMessage());
}
```

There are several potential problems in this example:

- ❏ If something goes wrong the `Connection` is never returned to the pool, but also the `ResultSet` and `Statement` aren't closed properly and could keep open resources on the database.

- ❏ If we don't use `AutoCommit`, we should do a rollback in case of failure.

- ❏ Another thing that's often forgotten, we only use the first `SQLException`. `SQLExceptions` have a special feature that allows them to have several error messages linked to a single exception. We'll come back to this feature later. In our example, valuable information contained in the errors that are chained to the first exception is lost.

To avoid these problems, we should code it like this:

```
Connection conn = null;
Statement stmt = null;
ResultSet rs = null;
try {
  conn = get connection from the pool
  conn.setAutoCommit(false);
  Statement stmt = conn.createStatement();
  ResultSet rs = stmt.executeQuery("SELECT COLUMNS FROM TABLE");
  // Get the values
  // or update the database
  conn.commit();
} catch (SQLException e) {
  System.out.println(e.getMessage());
  while ((e=e.getNextException()) != null) {
    System.out.println(" next "+ e.getMessage());
  }
} finally {
  try {
    if (rs != null) {
      rs.close();
    }
    if (stmt != null) {
      stmt.close();
    }
    if (conn != null) {
      conn.rollback();
      return the conn to the pool
    }
  } catch (SQLException e) {
    System.out.println(e.getMessage());
    while ((e = e.getNextException ()) != null){
      System.out.println("  next "+ e.getMessage());
    }
  }
}
```

And even this code isn't bullet proof, but it certainly becomes ugly. OK, we might choose to ignore handling the exceptions that are thrown by the closing and rollback statements, but we still have more error handling than actual database code. Are we really writing code like this everywhere we access the database? Probably not, unless you're a very disciplined programmer

This illustrates that there are limitations to writing robust code and we sometimes have to make a tradeoff. For example, we may write in favor of the coding style or just simply because we often tend to write code with a minimum of keystrokes.

The difficulty with these memory- or resource-related bugs is that they only show up after a certain time and that they are difficult to reproduce, especially on our development computer.

Robustness and Stability

Server-side applications should not fail, but when they do, they should do so gracefully with a minimal impact on other components and the server. A server application crashing due to component failure can affect many users in addition to other applications running in the same VM.

Built-in range checking, memory management, and exception handling plus the absence of pointers prevent Java code from producing the types of system crashes associated with languages such as C++. It remains the developers responsibility to follow the specifications for API's carefully to avoid threading issues and other programmatic failure.

To test the robustness of our setup under heavy load we could use tools like Apache JMeter (`http://Java.apache.org/jmeter`) that simulate a number of concurrent users requesting information, these tools are normally used to measure performance. These tools will be covered later in the chapter. Stress testing the system can highlight weaknesses and look for performance bottlenecks. To provide stability at the hardware level, an application might be deployed on multiple servers. When one of them goes down, the others take over. Such a fail-over setup adds complexity to the total system. Due to this complexity, using a fail-over backup server might, oddly enough, introduce new bugs. For example, if we store non-serializable objects in a session or if the application server doesn't support distributed sessions we could lose information while switching over to the backup server. The same problem can arise if we use multiple servers in parallel to provide better performance (known as load balancing).

In a typical setup the interface to the user is made up of JSPs and servlets. This is an appropriate place to use an error page to inform the user about the error. Exceptions move up the call stack up to the point where they are caught. Eventually they reach the try-catch block around the body of the JSP-servlet (the servlet that's automatically created by the JSP engine) and the user is redirected to the error page.

In complex systems, the exception can originate from a distant low-level component. The end user shouldn't be bothered with these low-level details. A user should be shown an error like "user registration failed" instead of "SQLError: X03805: Primary key for table reg_usr is not unique".

In a clean setup, the higher components should catch exceptions (like `IOExceptions` or `SQLExceptions`) thrown by the components they use, and in turn, throw a higher-level exception (like `LoginException` or `EmployeeException`) themselves. If these higher-level components just pass on the low-level exceptions, all possible exceptions would have to be specified in the interface. This not only looks bad, but it also means our classes aren't properly encapsulated.

Of course it would be ideal if we could somehow show the higher-level error messages to the end user, but keep the option of seeing all the details of the original errors. To achieve this we can use nested (or chained) exceptions. Using nested exceptions means that an exception contains a handle to another exception (which might in turn have a reference to another, creating a chain of exceptions). This is a technique that's used in the JDK classes too, such as in `java.sql.SQLException` or `java.rmi.RemoteException`. Unfortunately, this isn't always implemented in the same way and it might have been better if this chaining mechanism were provided by the root exception object.

Exceptions normally have two constructors, the default constructor, and one where we can specify a `String` error message. In order to create nested exceptions, we make a third constructor that takes the message `String` and another object of type `Exception` that's stored in a member variable:

```
public class NestedException extends Exception {
  private Exception nested;

  public NestedException(){}

  public NestedException(String msg) {
    super(msg);
  }

  public NestedException(String msg, Exception nested) {
    super(msg);
    this.nested=nested;
  }

  public Exception getNestedException() {
    return nested;
  }
}
```

To use this technique, we must inherit our own custom exceptions from `NestedException` instead of from the root `Exception` class.

In our components that throw the higher-level exceptions and catch the lower-level ones, we typically use code like:

```
public boolean login(String userid, String password) throws LoginException {
  try {
    // Here we have code to validate the login
    // E.g. by looking it up in the database
  } catch (SQLException e) {
    // Log the error
    throw new LoginException("Could not validate login", e);
    // Constructor type 3 from NestedException
  }
}
```

Since we inherited our `LoginException` from `NestedException`, we can use the `LoginException` information to show the user what happened, and recursively check all exceptions that are chained to this `LoginException` to provide a more detailed error message for the developer. Since the chaining mechanism isn't built in the standard exception object, probably the safest way to recursively get all the information from a `NestedException` is to override the `getMessage()` method:

```
public String getMessage() {
  StringBuffer msg = new StringBuffer (super.getMessage());
  if (nested !=null) {
    msg.append("\r\n"); // or <BR /> for display in browser
    msg.append(nested.getMessage());
  }
  return msg.toString();
}
```

The standard `SQLException` doesn't use this technique to show the messages of the contained exceptions automatically in their `getMessage` method. As a result, most nested exceptions in `SQLexceptions` are never used and the information is just thrown away.

1265

The article at `http://www.javaworld.com/javaworld/javatips/f_jw-javatip91_p.html` gives a more detailed explanation of nested exceptions and shows how to get the stack trace from the nested exception, even if that exception is thrown on a remote RMI server.

Multi-User / Multi-Thread

Unlike some other technologies, server applications are inherently multi-threaded. Every request creates a new thread that executes the service method of a single servlet instance. While this technique offers good performance and easy solutions to some specific problems, it also introduces a certain complexity. Developers not familiar with multi-threaded systems might miss code that is not thread-safe. To make sure a piece of code is only executed by one thread at a time, we can use the `synchronized` keyword.

Let's give an example of a servlet that is not thread safe. We first create a very simple hit counter like this:

```
import java.io.*;
import javax.servlet.*;
import javax.servlet.http.*;

public class HitCounter extends HttpServlet {
  int hits = 0;

  public void doGet(HttpServletRequest req, HttpServletResponse res)
            throws ServletException, IOException {
    PrintWriter out = res.getWriter();
    res.setContentType("text/html");
    hits++;

    out.println("<html><head><title>Run command</title></head>");
    out.println("<body><h1>You are visitor # ");
    out.println(hits);
    out.println("</h1></body></html>");
  }
}
```

At first we might see nothing wrong with this code. However, consider two requests at almost exactly the same moment. Assume the current number of hits is 78. The first thread starts executing the `doGet()` method but when it reaches line 11 (hits is now 79), the OS switches to the second request and this new thread processes the complete method and displays "You are visitor # 80". Immediately after that the first thread can continue and also shows "You are visitor # 80". The following table clearly shows the execution of the two concurrent requests.

Thread 1	Thread 2	Hits
res.setContentType("text...		78
hits++;		79
out.println("<html><head>...		79
	res.setContentType("text...	79
	hits++;	**80**
	out.println("<html><head>...	80

Thread 1	Thread 2	Hits
	out.println("<body><h1>...	80
	out.println(hits);	80
	out.println("</h1></body>...	80
out.println("<body><h1>...		80
out.println(hits);		**80**
out.println("</h1></body>...		80

There's never been a number 79 and twice a number 80. Of course, if it's only a hit counter, we don't really care much about this. However, the same problem can occur in code that is more critical as well.

Think about the consequences if we want to give a prize for the 1000th visitor. We run the risk of having zero or two winners.

In our hit counter example, we might try to combine lines 11 and 15 to:

```
out.println(++hits);
```

The probability of still having the concurrency problem will be much lower, but it still exists. Besides, it isn't always possible to put the related lines that close together.

That's where we would need to synchronize to make sure no two threads will execute a single block of lines at the same time:

```
public void doGet(HttpServletRequest req, HttpServletResponse res)
            throws ServletException, IOException {

    PrintWriter out = res.getWriter();
    res.setContentType("text/html");

    out.println("<html><head><title>Run command</title></head>");
    out.println("<body><h1>Number of hits: ");

    synchronized(this){
      hits++;
      out.println(hits);
    }

    out.println("</h1></body></html>");
}
```

However, synchronizing can have a serious impact on execution speed. First of all, the action of locking an object itself takes some time, but obviously, when a thread has to wait on another thread to finish a piece of code, that time is just wasted. That's why we had better not synchronize the complete doGet() method by using:

```
public synchronized void doGet(HttpServletRequest req, HttpServletResponse res)
                throws ServletException, IOException {
```

as the chances of having one thread waiting for another would become much higher.

If it weren't for this performance penalty, the easiest solution would be to synchronize every method. It's also not easy to decide which parts to synchronize. If the question, "What to synchronize?" could be answered rigidly, this would most probably be done automatically for you by the Java compiler. Instead, we need to decide carefully ourselves which parts of our code needs synchronization and which parts will not cause problems.

Performance isn't the only issue in considering where to use synchronization. In fact, synchronizing too much can cause deadlock problems. Especially in a distributed environment this can become quite complicated. If we have an RMI server that calls back to the original calling object and both methods are synchronized, we end up with two servers waiting for each other and the system hangs.

Where can we expect concurrency problems?

❏   Servlet member variables like in the `HitCounter` example. Since there's normally only one instance of a servlet and every request uses that same servlet instance, every method that changes member variables should use synchronized blocks. The same is true for variable declarations between `<%! %>` JSP tags. We often see code where people use `<%! %>` to declare variables, where a (thread safe) `<% %>` scriptlet would give the same results. In fact, I hardly ever need to use `<%! %>` declarations in JSP.

Instead of writing:

```
<%! String myPage; %>
<% myPage = request.getParamter("target"); %>
<%@ include file="<%=myPage%>" %>
```

you could simply use:

```
<% String myPage = request.getParamter("target"); %>
<%@ include file="<%=myPage%>" %>
```

This at first sight does exactly the same thing, and if you try it out, gives exactly the same results. But with the first code, the requested page might be mixed up when two users try this at the same moment.

❏   Objects stored in the `ServletContext` (the JSP application scope). It should be obvious that these objects can be used by several threads at the same time.

❏   Objects stored in a session. Although at first, it might seem strange to have multiple concurrent requests using an object in a session. We might imagine a screen with several browser windows and a user clicking the mouse as fast as he can, but it's less spectacular. A single request for a page that uses frames can easily cause multiple requests that result in concurrent threads on the server. The fact that these multiple threads originate from a single user doesn't make it less problematic.

❑ To speed up our application, we often implement a caching mechanism. Instead of recreating certain objects every time we need them, we could put objects that take some time to be instantiated in a cache and use the same instance again later. An instance stored in such a cache can be retrieved and used by multiple requests at the same time. Ideally, the decision whether you're using a cache or not should be transparent to the programmer that uses the beans. Performance optimizations should be done near the end of the development cycle. But, by simply starting to use a cache, new concurrency bugs can suddenly appear in code that always ran fine.

❑ Singleton patterns and static methods that access static variables. The reason to use a Singleton pattern and static methods is to have a single instance of an object available to the whole VM so, obviously, we can have concurrent requests.

❑ RMI remote objects member variables are subject to concurrency in a similar way that servlet member variables are. But, as we said, be careful for locking problems when we synchronize too much.

Once again, we must conclude that concurrency errors are hard to debug. The bugs are difficult to reproduce on a development server and almost impossible to isolate properly. It's very likely that they show up only when the application is being used at full speed. Step (JDB-like) debugging probably won't help very much in locating the problem since the timing of the different threads is so crucial for the error to occur. This is where logging is very important, as it may be the only way to locate these errors.

Some multi-threading issues like deadlocks and race conditions can be investigated with tools like JProbe ThreadAnalyzer (http://www.klgroup.com)

The Stress-test tools we mentioned before, like JMeter, can help us reproduce concurrency problems.

Performance

Trying to produce clean, readable code doesn't always show the fastest results. Although performance can be a serious concern during development, we should try not to sacrifice good coding practice in favor of faster code. It turns out that, without proper profiling, developers often make wrong guesses about how to improve performance. Hackers' code that's supposed to make use of the last CPU cycle can make debugging a real nightmare.

Using a `StringBuffer` instead of concatenating `Strings` is a classical example where it's easy to improve the performance without making the code much more complex. Since we typically use a lot of `String` concatenation in servlets, you might get a significant performance boost by changing code like:

```
out.print("Hey, "+ username + " <P>");
out.print("you chose item # "+ itemNr + " <BR>");
```

into:

```
out.print("Hey, ");
out.print(userName);
out.print("<P>");
out.print("you chose item # ");
out.print(itemNr);
out.print(" <BR>");
```

or

```
StringBuffer responseLine = new StringBuffer();
responseLine.append("Hey, ");
responseLine.append (userName);
responseLine.append ("<P>");
responseLine.append ("you chose item # ");
responseLine.append (itemNr);
responseLine.append (" <BR>");
out.println(responseLine.toString());
```

Moreover, at the same time, make the code more readable.

However, the time we win by inlining code instead of calling another method, or by being too sparing with temporary variables, is probably not really worth the reduction of readability.

Debugging Tools and Techniques

The tools we should use for debugging our server-side applications depend on several factors. Some companies standardize on a single product or vendor and expect us to use the tools they provide for debugging. A more important factor is the developer's attitude and habits. Some developers like working with a slick editor that does a lot behind the scenes and lets us focus on the real programming issues. Others will argue that these editors mean that we lose control over vital parameters and that 'real programmers' prefer a simple text editor and use the command line to compile their classes. Most probably both approaches are correct in their own respect. The same attitudes determine the tools and techniques a developer will use for debugging.

Integrated Debuggers

Most of the popular Java IDE's (IBM's VisualAge for Java, JBuilder, Visual Café etc.) have debugging facilities for server-side Java that integrate nicely with the rest of the development environment. Other tools like JProbe offer additional debugging facilities. Although these debuggers can be helpful, they're not always the perfect and complete solution as they often seem to suggest:

❑   The debugging process is mostly reduced to setting breakpoints, stepping through the code and inspecting variables at runtime. However, debugging is much more than that. If we look at our overview of what's special about Java server-side programming, we see that many problems (like concurrency bugs) cannot be caught by this type of debugging. In fact, integrated IDE debuggers often introduce problems that either mask real application bugs, or introduce their own complexities that make their results unreliable when compared with real runtime behavior.

❑   If we can run everything on our development machine, debugging is rather more straightforward, but this doesn't always resolve errors. Even if the debugger is capable of doing 'remote debugging' this is always more difficult. The VM's on the different servers need to be started in some sort of 'debug mode'. This isn't always easy and sometimes even impossible. The effort and impact of restarting servers makes it much harder to switch to debug mode, so should only be used for errors that are difficult to find.

- The debugger is often linked to a specific application server and even to a certain platform. In OO-terminology: the lack of encapsulation creates a tight coupling between the development/debugging practices and the deployment possibilities. Independence and "Write Once Run Anywhere" is one of the most important features of Java.

- No matter how fancy and advanced our tool is, debugging a server-side application will never be easy. Saying "debugging is no problem because we use an advanced integrated debugger" is like "we don't have to bother with security anymore, because we use Java". In reality, keeping track of a distributed system with multiple threads on multiple systems will always be a complex task.

- Some of these tools aren't bug free themselves. The bigger the tool, the more bugs they have. Even if the tool is working fine, some developers don't like to depend on them and feel that they don't have total control over what's happening.

- These tools can be rather expensive. Especially when they force us to use specific servlet engines or web servers.

Do-It-Yourself, the JDB

Although it's more low-level and doesn't have a point-and-click interface, the standard Java debugger, JDB, also allows remote debugging. In a standard debugging session, an application is started with the JDB command instead of Java as a rule, we should try to debug our applications on our local machine whenever possible. Most server components can be started on our development computer, like the standalone webserver/servlet runner that is included in the JSDK, or have a standalone counterpart that can be used to simulate the server version.

For the JSDK server or Tomcat, the server is started with a batch file or startup script. Open a copy of this startup script in a text editor and look for the line where the server itself is started. In my version of Tomcat on Windows NT, this would be the line in tomcat.bat:

```
start java org.apache.Tomcat.shell.Startup %2 %3 %4 %5 %6 %7 %8 %9
```

Changing "java" to JDB, we have an alternative startup script that starts the server in debug mode.

Others application servers allow us to specify a JVM startup path and additional options to achieve the same results. It might take some time to figure out how to start a particular servlet engine in debug mode but in most cases it is possible.

An important feature of JDB is that it allows us the option to connect to an already running JVM, which may be on another computer. This might be easier than the normal JDB use we just described, especially in a server environment. First, the VM we want to debug, must be started in debug mode with the -XDebug switch. We also have to disable the JIT compiler by adding Djava.compiler=NONE to the command line and make a few extra classes available to the debugger. The server's complete startup command becomes something like:

```
java -Xdebug -Djava.compiler=NONE -Xbootclasspath:
$INSTALL_DIR\jre\lib\rt.jar;$INSTALL_DIR\lib\tools.jar <class>
```

The JVM starts as usual but displays a password on the screen that we need to connect to this VM. This password is necessary to identify the VM correctly, since there can be more than one running on the same server. Also, because you can connect to this debug VM from another host, the password provides additional security. The biggest problem is that it's not always possible to start the JVM visually in order to get the password.

Here's how I used this approach with the Apache JServ 1.1 (http://java.apache.org) servlet engine on Windows NT. Normally the JServ VM is started automatically for us by the JServ apache module (mod_jserv), but when using 'manual mode' ("ApJServManual on" in the JServ.conf configuration file) we must do this ourselves manually. I created a set of batch files to start this VM in several different modes.

The first one (JServ_normal.bat) starts JServ in normal mode. I can close the window that pops up on my screen and the engine is running invisible in the background

```
SET CP="D:\Java\jsdk2.0\lib\jsdk.jar";
SET CP=%CP%"D:\Apache Group\Apache JServ\ApacheJserv.jar";
SET CP=%CP%"F:\Java\classes";
SET CP=%CP%"D:\Java\jdk1.2.2\lib\tools.jar";
SET CP=%CP%"F:\Java\servlets\lib\jsp.jar";
SET CP=%CP%"F:\Java\servlets\lib\gnujsp10.jar";

D:\%JAVA_HOME%\bin\Javaw -classpath %CP% org.apache.jserv.JServ "D:\Apache
Group\Apache JServ\conf\jserv.properties"
pause
```

Another batch file (JServ_visual.bat) starts the engine in 'visual mode' by using Java instead of Javaw. By using this command I can see all messages that are printed to System.out on a console window. The engine remains visible on my screen (If I close the console window the engine is shut down):

```
...
SET CP=%CP%"F:\Java\servlets\lib\jsp.jar";
SET CP=%CP%"F:\Java\servlets\lib\gnujsp10.jar";
D:\%JAVA_HOME%\bin\Java -classpath %CP% org.apache.jserv.JServ "D:\Apache
Group\Apache JServ\conf\jserv.properties"
```

The third option (JServ_debug.bat) is to start in debug mode. This batch file shows me the password I need to connect to the JVM:

```
...
SET CP=%CP%"F:\Java\servlets\lib\jsp.jar";
SET CP=%CP%"F:\Java\servlets\lib\gnujsp10.jar";
D:\%JAVA_HOME%\bin\Java -Xdebug -DJava.compiler=NONE -
Xbootclasspath:D:\%JAVA_HOME%\jre\lib\rt.jar;D:\%JAVA_HOME%\lib\tools.jar   -
classpath %CP% org.apache.jserv.JServ "D:\Apache Group\Apache
JServ\conf\jserv.properties"
```

During development, I mostly use the second approach, which gives me immediate feedback on what's happening. When I need more debugging power, I use the JServ_debug.bat.

A similar setup is also possible for RMI servers. When using RMI, you have on the server-side a java application that instantiates server objects and registers them in the RMI registry. (With Naming.bind or Naming.rebind) We just have to start this application with the -XDebug switch as we showed with JServ.

When the server is running, we can use JDB as we do on our local computer, but instead of specifying the class to run, we specify the host name and password.

```
JDB -host rmi.myserver.com -password 5a32ix
```

Some text editors like JPadPro (http://www.modelworks.com) have a simple interface to JDB, so that we can use the editor to set breakpoints and step through the code. When we choose the option **Debug Class** JPadPro prompts us for a classname. Now, instead of entering the classname, we can specify -hostname *hyphen needs to stay with the hostname "-hostname"* and -password and connect the debugger to the remote VM. With other editors, it might not always be possible to fool the built-in debugger this easily but it's worth trying it out.

Again, this is a very narrow interpretation of the debugging concept. As we said before, debugging is much more than setting breakpoints and stepping through the code. Most of the remarks mentioned, regarding the fancy integrated IDE's are also valid with this low level JDB approach. But if you are the kind of developer who edits their code with notepad or vi and uses the command line to compile their classes, you might prefer this JDB command-line technique.

A Broader View

In our discussion about breakpoints and step debugging, whether using hardcore JDB or a nice point and click interface, we already mentioned that this approach simply isn't always good enough. Debugging is much more than that. It's everything that allows us to avoid, trace, or correct bugs in our code.

Eyeballing

As simple as eyeballing or code walkthrough may seem, just looking at the code is one of the most important and most used techniques for finding bugs. In fact, eyeballing is almost always part of the total debugging process. It happens quite often that we're using JDB-type debugging, and while stepping through the code we suddenly see the bug in one of the lines that is not processed yet. This mechanism can be extended to what we may call "peer eyeballing". The ability of someone not involved in the code development instantly to pick out an error you have been spending hours trying to find. We can become so consumed by the project that we develop a forest-and-trees syndrome that only a fresh set of eyeballs can overcome.

In order to enhance the visual inspection, we should keep our code clean and adhere to good standards and practices whether widely accepted or those set by our organization. (I can recommend *Jeff Langr "Essential Java Style" Prentice Hall, ISBN:0-13-085086-1*). Here are a few guidelines:

- ❑ Keep methods small and clear
- ❑ Try to make the code self-explanatory. Use intuitive variable and method names
- ❑ Use proper indentation. Whatever style we use for aligning braces, be consistent
- ❑ A nice list of how not to do it can be found at http://mindprod.com/unmain.html

The success of eyeballing depends very much on the expertise of our developer and how familiar they are with the code.

Although it appears that this is just a technique, there are also tools that can make the eyeballing easier. A good code editor has features like syntax coloring, bookmarks, and commands for locating matching braces. Use these options and take some time to learn or install the necessary shortcuts.

System.out.println()

Using the standard output or error stream is an obvious and often used debugging technique. It doesn't look very sophisticated at first, but its simplicity is also its power.

In most server components it's very unlikely that the standard output will be used in the core processing of the object. This leaves it available for outputting debug messages.

❑ Since the System object is part of the core Java objects, it can be used everywhere without the need to install any extra classes. This includes servlets, JSP, RMI, EJB's, ordinary beans and classes, and standalone applications

❑ Compared with stopping at breakpoints, writing to System.out doesn't interfere much with the normal execution flow of the application, which makes it very valuable when timing is crucial. For example, when debugging concurrency issues or when stopping at a breakpoint could cause a timeout in other components.

System.out.println() is easy to use as a marker to test whether a certain piece of code is being executed or not. Of course, we can print out variable values as well, but then its inflexibility becomes more apparent. I use it mostly with String constants such as System.out.println("debug: end of calculate method"). If we print out variables appended to a String message like in System.out.println("debug: loop counter=" + i); frequently, we're using a relatively expensive string concatenation just for debugging. Since the debugging overhead should be as low as possible, it might be better to use two statements if we are concerned about this:

```
System.out.println("debug: loop counter=");
System.out.println(i);
```

The most important problem is that it isn't always clear where the information is printed. Depending on the application server, our messages might be written to a file, a terminal window on the server, or they might be directed to Null and just vanish into thin air.

Most application servers and servlet engines start the JVM without a visual presence, like a console window. But even if we have the option of displaying a terminal window, (for example, by using Java instead of Javaw, as we did when starting the server in debug mode), the messages still show up on the server instead of on our PC.

Luckily, System.setOut() lets us change the OutputStream that is used by System at runtime. The following Debug class uses that technique to redirect the standard out to a ServerSocket at a specified port. The class extends OutputStream and registers itself as the standard output. It also starts a thread that listens to incoming connections. When a client connects, the standard out is redirected to that client socket. Since we keep a reference to the previous standard output we can keep sending all messages to the old Stream as well. To keep things simple, this class only supports a single connection:

```
import java.io.*;
import java.util.*;
import java.net.*;

public class Debug extends OutputStream implements Runnable {
    int port;
    ServerSocket server;
```

```
boolean active;
Socket client;
OutputStream clientStream;
Thread listener;
PrintStream old;

public Debug(int port) {
  this.port = port;

  try {
    server = new ServerSocket(port);
  } catch(IOException e) {
    System.out.println("could not create server");
  }
}

public boolean isActive() {
  return active;
}

public void startServer() {
  if (!active) {
    old = System.out;
    System.setOut(new PrintStream(this));
    active = true;
    listener = new Thread(this );
    listener.start();
    System.out.println("debug server started");
  }
}

public void stopServer() {
  active = false;
  System.setOut(old);
  System.out.println("debug server stopping");
  if (client!=null) {
    try {
      client.close();
    } catch (IOException e) {}
  }
}

public void run() {
  Socket localSocket = null;
  try {
    while (active) {
      localSocket = server.accept();
      if (client == null) {
        client = localSocket;
        clientStream = client.getOutputStream();
        new PrintStream(clientStream).println("Welcome to the Debug Server");
      } else {
        PrintWriter second = new PrintWriter(localSocket.getOutputStream());
        second.print("already connected");
        localSocket.close();
```

```
          }
        }
        System.out.println("debug server stopped");
      } catch(IOException e) {
        System.out.println("debug server crashed");
        System.out.println(e.getMessage());
        active = false;
      } finally {
        if (server!=null) {
          try {
            server.close();
          } catch (IOException e) {}
        }
      }
    }

    protected void clearClient() {
      if (client != null) {
        try {
          client.close();
        } catch (IOException ioe) {}
      }
      client = null;
      clientStream = null;
    }

    public void write(byte[] b) throws IOException {
      if (old != null) {
        old.write(b);
      }
      if (clientStream!= null) {
        try {
          clientStream.write(b);
        } catch (IOException e) {
          clearClient();
        }
      }
    }

    public void write(byte[] b, int off, int len) throws IOException {
      if (old != null) {
        old.write(b,off,len);
      }
      if (clientStream!= null) {
        try {
          clientStream.write(b, off, len);
        } catch (IOException e) {
          clearClient();
        }
      }
    }

    public void write(int b) throws IOException {
      if (old != null) {
        old.write(b);
```

```
      }
      if (clientStream!= null) {
        try {
          clientStream.write(b);
        } catch (IOException e) {
          clearClient();
        }
      }
    }
  }
```

So how do we use this `Debug` class? We simply use `System.out.println()` to send debug messages. The nice thing is that there is no direct connection between the class we want to debug and this `Debug` server. We don't additionally have to import anything. The `Debug` server makes sure that these messages are sent to the developer's machine.

To use this class to debug servlets and JSP, we can create a `DebugServlet` that switches debugging on and off like this:

```
import java.io.*;
import javax.servlet.*;
import javax.servlet.http.*;

public class DebugServlet extends HttpServlet {
  Debug debugger ;

  public void service(HttpServletRequest req, HttpServletResponse res)
            throws ServletException, IOException {

    String option = req.getParameter("option");
    res.setContentType("text/html");
    PrintWriter out = res.getWriter();
    out.println("<html><head><title>Debug servlet</title></head><body>");
    out.println("<h1>Debug servlet</h1>");
    if ("socket".equals(option)) {
      if (debugger == null) {
        debugger = new Debug(9999);
      }
      debugger.startServer();
    }
    if ("closesocket".equals(option)) {
      if (debugger != null) {
        debugger.stopServer();
      }
    }
    String testValue = req.getParameter("test");
    if (testValue != null) {
      System.out.println("Debug test: " +testValue);
    }

    if ((debugger != null) && (debugger.isActive())) {
      out.print("<a href=\"telnet://");
      out.print(req.getServerName());
```

```
        out.println(":9999\" target=\"_blank\"> Connect to the debugger </a><p>");

        out.print("<a href=");
        out.print(req.getRequestURI());
        out.println("?option=closesocket> Shut down debugger </a ><p>");
    } else {
        out.print("<a href=\"");
        out.print(req.getRequestURI());
        out.println("?option=socket\"> Start remote debugger </A><p>");
    }
    out.println("<form method=\"post\" >");
    out.println("Test <input type=\"text\" name=\"test\">");
    out.println("<input type=\"submit\">");
    out.println("</form> </body> </html>");
    }
}
```

By specifying the 'option' parameter, the servlet controls starting, and stopping of the remote debugger, the servlet itself shows the correct hyperlinks to perform these commands. We could create a 'debug client' as an application or an applet that opens a socket connection to out debug server. But, the only thing this client has to do is display to the user what was sent over the socket connection. On most OSs there is already a tool that does exactly that. It's called Telnet, and it's mostly used to control a server or interact with a certain service, but in our case, we just use it as an ultra-thin client solution to connect to port 9999 and see the debug messages. To make this even more convenient, the servlet presents a hyperlink that tries to open Telnet with the correct host and port. Any string that's entered into the form is printed to System.out, so this immediately allows us to check if everything is working, as is shown in the next screenshot.

The Telnet window not only shows the messages sent by servlets or JSP, but also those from any other object or bean that runs in the same VM:

Using the same approach, we can remotely debug RMI servers. We could easily start the Debug server in the application where we bind the remote objects to the naming server but we'll probably need to change some security settings before we can redirect standard out. Normally an RMI server is not allowed to redirect System.out, but we can (temporarily) enable this by adding:

```
permission java.lang.RuntimePermission "setIO";
```

to our Java.policy file (in the /lib/security directory):

```
Debug socket = new Debug(9999);
socket.startServer(); // start the debugging server
SomeObject testObject = new SomeObject(); // instantiate remote object
Naming.rebind(name,testObject);  // make it available through the registry
Naming.rebind( ...
```

Just as with the servlet implementation we can use telnet to connect to the debugging server.

Some DBMSs, like Oracle and Sybase ASA (Adaptive Server Anywhere) can have a JVM running inside the database server so that we can embed database logic, written in Java, inside the database itself. As a test I installed the Debug class in an ASA database and after a few tries managed to start the Debug server. As with other implementations, I was able to view the standard out from the VM that was running inside my database server in a Telnet window. You can probably think of lots of other opportunities to use this debugging technique.

The current Debug class is already very powerful, but it would be a good idea to:

❑   Add security like asking for a password or restricting access to certain IP addresses.

❑   Allow multiple telnet sessions to connect to a single server.

❑   Allow the client to specify filters. When there are lots of debugging messages, it might be better to send only the messages that contain a specified 'filter' string.

❑   Add an optional timestamp to each message.

❑   Allow the client to enter certain commands, like asking for memory usage, or shutting down the debug server through the telnet session.

❑   The JDBC DriverManager has a method SetLogWriter that works just like System.setOut. We could try to change the Debug class so that this JDBC log information is sent over the network instead of System.out.

Unit Testing

A consistent use of unit tests for every piece of code can help us catch certain bugs much quicker. See Chapter 27 for an in-depth look at unit testing. Testing by itself doesn't directly help us find bugs, but it makes it easier to detect whether there are problems or not. Note, however, that given the complexity of server programming, even these tests cannot guarantee that there will be no problems. Tests can also provide an easy environment where we can go through the same code process time after time, until it runs fine. Concurrency issues and bugs caused by the deployment server or the network can still slip through the net. However, most of the more obvious problems can be easily detected if we have a tight test procedure. The extra effort it takes to write tests for every piece of code is largely compensated by the time saved in debugging. If we don't use a framework to contain and run our tests (such as JUnit) we can also write test scripts in our object's main method. Of course this isn't very elaborate and doesn't offer us automation, but it can still help us to debug a class. It also shows how a particular class should be used in order to work properly.

For example, if we have a bean to send e-mails we could add the following to the main method:

```
public static void main(String[] args) {

    sendEmail instance = new sendEmail("localhost");

    System.out.println(instance.send("hercule.poirot@xyz.be",
                                     "hercule.poirot@xyz.be",
                                     "testmail",
                             "hi, this is a mail to test the sendmail bean"));
}
```

Self-Made Monitoring Tools

A simple way to create our own custom monitoring tools is by creating servlets (these should be protected by a password!) to keep an eye on the status of various critical components. Since most of these monitor servlets depend on our specific implementation, we cannot give detailed code for all of them.

Cache

One way to speed up a system is to cache frequently used data or objects in memory instead of creating or retrieving them every time we need them. If we created our own caching mechanism, we could make a servlet that shows how many items are in the cache and, if possible, show the names and type and provide a command to clear the cache completely.

The code we'll see later for monitoring objects stored in a session can be used as a starting point for a cache monitor.

Sessions

The following servlet allows us to check out all objects stored in the Session. We might also provide mechanisms to change the values of the objects or to delete them from the session:

```
import java.io.*;
import java.util.*;
import java.lang.reflect.*;
import javax.servlet.*;
import javax.servlet.http.*;

public class SessionMonitor extends HttpServlet {
  public void doGet(HttpServletRequest req, HttpServletResponse res)
                throws ServletException, IOException {
    res.setContentType("text/html");
    PrintWriter out = res.getWriter();
    HttpSession session = req.getSession(true);
    out.println("<HTML><HEAD><TITLE>session monitor</title></head>");
    out.println("<BODY><H1>SessionMonitor</H1>");
    out.println("This form allows us to add new string values to the current
                session to check out this servlet<br />");
    out.println("<FORM>add string key <INPUT TYPE=\"text\" NAME=\"key\"><br/>");
    out.println("add string value<INPUT TYPE=\"text\" NAME=\"value\"><br/>");
    out.println("<INPUT TYPE=\"submit\"></FORM><P>");

    testInit(req,session);
```

```
    String beanName = req.getParameter("name");
  . if (beanName == null) {
      showBeanList(req, session, out);
    } else {
      showSingleInstance(beanName, session, out);
    }
    out.println("</BODY></HTML>");
  }

  private void testInit(HttpServletRequest req, HttpSession session) {
    String newKey = req.getParameter("key");
    String newValue = req.getParameter("value");
    if ((newKey !=null) && (newValue != null)){
      TestBean test= new TestBean();
      test.setValue1(newValue);
      test.setValue2("fixed text");
      test.setValue3(newKey+"-->"+newValue);
      session.putValue(newKey, test);
      // for servlet API < 2.2  use setValue instead of setAttribute
    }
  }

  private void showBeanList(HttpServletRequest req,
                            HttpSession session,
                            PrintWriter out) {
    String URI = req.getRequestURI();
    String[] names = session.getValueNames();
    // For servlet API < 2.2  use getValueNames instead of getAttributeNames
    for (int i=0;i<names.length;i++){
      String attributeName= names[i];
      out.print("<A HREF=");
      out.print(URI);
      out.print("?name=");
      out.print(attributeName);
      out.print(">");
      out.println(attributeName);
      out.print("</A><BR />");
    }
  }

  private void showSingleInstance(String beanName,
                                  HttpSession session,
                                  PrintWriter out) {
    Object check = session.getValue(beanName);
    // For servlet API < 2.2  use getValue instead of getAttribute
    out.println("<H2> Checking object ");
    out.println(beanName);
    out.println("</H2><UL>");
    try {
      Class checkClass = check.getClass();
      Field[] fields = checkClass.getFields();
      for (int i = 0; i < fields.length; i++) {
        out.println("<LI>");
        out.println(fields[i].getName());
        out.println(" (");
```

```
            out.println(fields[i].getType().toString());
            out.println("): ");
            try {
              out.println(fields[i].get(check).toString());
            } catch (Exception e) {
              out.println(" ! Cannot be displayed !");
            }
          }
        }
      } catch (NullPointerException e) {
        out.println("null pointer Exception");
      }
    }
  }

  private class TestBean {
    public String value1;
    public String value2;
    public String value3;
    public String getValue1() {
      return value1;
    }
    public void setValue1(String value) {
      value1 = value;
    }
    public String getValue2() {
      return value2;
    }
    public void setValue2(String value) {
      value2 = value;
    }
    public String getValue3() {
      return value3;
    }
    public void setValue3(String value) {
      value3 = value;
    }
  }
}
```

Files

This is a servlet that allows us to read specific files (like a log file) that are not under the document root of the web server. Since these files can be long, I have provided options so we can view only a specific part of the file (for example the last 5K):

```
import java.io.*;
import java.util.*;
import javax.servlet.*;
import javax.servlet.http.*;

public class FileViewer extends HttpServlet {

  public void doGet(HttpServletRequest req, HttpServletResponse res)
            throws ServletException, IOException {
    String fileName = (req.getParameter("fileName"));
```

```
        if (fileName != null) {
          doView(req, res, fileName);
        } else {
          PrintWriter out = res.getWriter();
          out.println("<HTML><HEAD><TITLE> File viewer</TITLE></HEAD><BOdy>");
          out.println("<FORM> filename<INPUT TYPE=text NAME=fileName SIZE=50><br />");
          out.println(" skip first <INPUT TYPE=text Name=first Size=4> and show ");
          out.println(" <INPUT TYPE=text NAME=size SIZE=4 /> bytes<br />");
          out.println("Or Show last <INPUT TYPE=text NAME=last SIZE=4 /> bytes<p>");
          out.println("<INPUT TYPE=submit /></FORM> </BODY></HTML>");
        }
    }

    public void doView(HttpServletRequest req,
                       HttpServletResponse res,
                       String fileName)
               throws ServletException, IOException {
        PrintWriter out = res.getWriter();
        out.println("<HTML><HEAD><TITLE>View file</TITLE></HEAD>
                    <BODY BGCOLOR=silver>");
        out.println("<P><Pre>");
        if (fileName != null) {
          RandomAccessFile in = null;
          try {
            in = new RandomAccessFile (fileName, "r");
            int len = 0;
            try {
              len = Integer.parseInt(req.getParameter("last"));
              in.seek(in.length() - len);
            } catch (NumberFormatException e) {}
              try {
                len = Integer.parseInt(req.getParameter("first"));
                in.seek(len);
              } catch (NumberFormatException e) {}
              int size = 0;
              try {
                size = Integer.parseInt(req.getParameter("size"));
              } catch (NumberFormatException e) {}
              String line = null;
              int runningSize = 0;
              while ((line=in.readLine()) != null) {
                out.print(line);
                runningSize += line.length();
              if (size > 0 && runningSize > size) {
                break;
              }
              out.println("</PRE><BR />");
            }
          } catch (IOException e) {
            out.println(e.getMessage());
          }
          finally {
            if (in != null) {
              in.close ();
```

```
          }
        }
      }
    out.println("<P>");
    out.println("</BODY></HTML>");
  }
}
```

For security reasons, it's best not to give complete freedom to which file is read. We could create a `Properties` object with the files that are allowed and have them requested by their logical names instead of their real file names. This servlet should never be permanently placed on a production server; it is a debugging tool only.

Commands

If our servlets are allowed to execute commands we can use this simple but very powerful (and **dangerous**) servlet. The following code allows us to specify an executable file, execute it, and show the results. Servlets like this can help us a lot during development and debugging, but we should never keep them on our real server. As with the FileViewer, we could make it a bit safer by restricting the possible commands to a predefined list of executables:

```
import java.io.*;
import javax.servlet.*;
import javax.servlet.http.*;

public class RunBatch extends HttpServlet {

  public void doGet(HttpServletRequest req, HttpServletResponse res)
              throws ServletException, IOException {
    String command = req.getParameter("command");
    if (command == null) {
      PrintWriter out = res.getWriter();
      res.setContentType("text/html");
      out.println("<HTML><HEAD><TITLE>Run command</TITLE></HEAD>");
      out.println("<BODY><FORM><INPUT TYPE=text SIZE=80 NAME=command>
                  <INPUT TYPE=submit>");
      out.println("</FORM></BODY></HTML>");
    } else {
      Process proc = Runtime.getRuntime().exec(command);
      InputStream procOut = proc.getInputStream();
      byte[] buf = new byte[4096];
      int bytesRead;
      OutputStream out = res.getOutputStream();
      res.setContentType("text/html");
      out.write("<HTML><HEAD><TITLE>Run command</TITLE></HEAD>
                          <BODY><PRE>".getbytes());
      while((bytesRead=procOut.read(buf)) != -1) {
        out.write(buf,0,bytesRead);
      }
      procOut.close();
      out.write("</PRE></BODY></HTML>".getbyte());
    }
  }
}
```

Summary

In this chapter, we looked at what's typical in Java server programming, and how that complicates or helps debugging.

We then covered using Java to create applications that run mainly on the server, with processes often running for long periods of time. That they should be stable and robust, in a multi-user / multi-threaded / multi-server environment and they should be able to handle heavy loads with reasonable performance.

When looking at the tools and techniques, we found out that step debugging is possible. There are different ways in which people like to debug their code; there are those that like using big integrated debuggers and those with a hardcore, command line attitude, using plain JDB.

We saw that looking at the code carefully is an important technique on it's own.

For a number of reasons, 'old style' debugging, by sending messages to the standard out stream is often used in a server environment and we explained how to make best use of it.

At the end of the chapter, we showed how we could create servlets to monitor what's happening in the different components.

In the next chapter, we will look at how to write applications that don't have any bugs in the first place by employing unit testing.

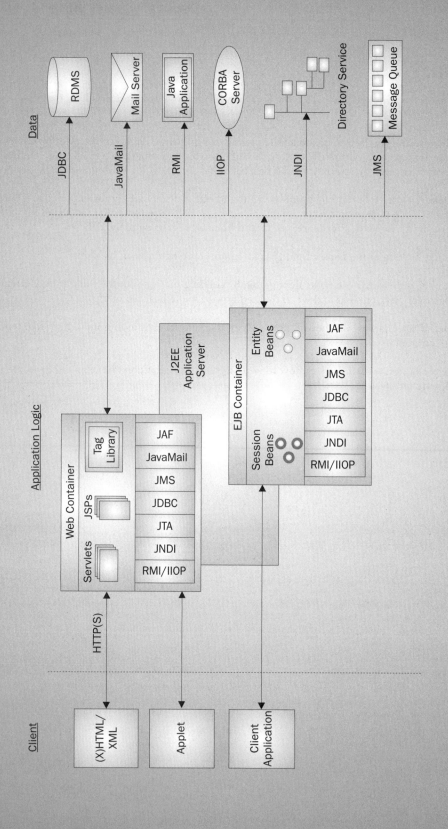

27

Unit Testing J2EE Applications

As programmers, our ideal is to make our programs perform 100% correctly, 100% of the time. This is a lofty and idealistic goal, but in reality programmers can only strive to get as close to this goal as possible. Unfortunately, its realization is limited by time and resources creating a tendency to code at the expense of design, testing, and other aspects of development, leading to buggy code and programs that perform less than ideally.

The reality of writing code is that even the best programmers make mistakes. As the project schedule gets more demanding, programmers become overworked and even less likely to catch their mistakes. The solution is to give programmers the tools they need to catch their mistakes. Programmers simply need tools that will help them to meet and document requirements, to help ensure that the code does what it is supposed to do. In this chapter we will discuss a tool that can give all these benefits to a programmer – **unit testing**.

If you are not experienced with unit testing, the concept of 'test first design' may be new to you. If so, this chapter will introduce this concept and discuss the benefits, during which we shall look at unit testing techniques for a variety of J2EE components.

We will look at:

❑   What unit testing is and why you should do it

❑   Using the JUnit framework for unit testing

❑   How to incorporate unit testing into your development cycle

❑   How to unit test simple objects, servlets and EJBs

First, let's take a closer look at what unit testing is really all about.

What is Unit Testing?

Many programmers do not view testing as a tool. They may see testing as another burden required by management, or as an added responsibility that cuts into programming time. While there are organizations and projects that embrace testing, and programmers who enjoy testing, this is not the norm. The first step is to think of unit testing as something that makes development easier. Unit testing, as distinguished from other types of testing, is always done by the programmer and is primarily for the programmer's benefit. Making this type of mindset switch is not easy, but it is important to approach unit testing with an open mind.

Unit testing only benefits the programmer if used correctly. You can tell if you are using unit testing correctly if you examine its impact on your work. Does it make code integration faster? Does it make you code better? Does it cut down on the time taken on other types of testing? Effective unit testing should never feel like a barrier or a chore. It should streamline your programming and make you more effective at your work.

While this sounds good, the challenge lies in finding a way to make unit testing a part of your process. First let's define exactly what unit testing is.

> **Unit testing is a method of white box testing that should be an important part of the development process.**

White box testing is distinguished from black box testing, in that it focuses on the implementation details and should be performed by someone familiar with the implementation.

When you are white box testing you are making sure your code works correctly. Black box testing, on the other hand, is concerned with testing the system from the user's perspective; the focus is on whether or not the requirements have been met, and the actual implementation is not relevant. Both white box and black box testing are necessary in order to make sure your application works correctly: however, only unit testing will be addressed in this chapter.

Unit testing focuses on small pieces of the system, and these individual components, or **units**, are tested independently of other units. Unit tests should put the component through a series of drills, including both valid and invalid inputs, to determine whether the component passed or failed each test. As a general rule, a white-box tester should have a view of the implementation, but in practice the best person to do unit testing is the programmer. Since no one but the programmer interacts with the code at this very low level, unit testing is most successful when it is the responsibility of the programmer. Some organizations may attempt to pass this responsibility to the quality assurance team. While this is possible, it takes away one of the most important features of unit testing – the benefits to the programmer. In this chapter you will see a variety of benefits that emerge when unit testing is used as a tool for the programmer.

As with any testing, unit tests are best written so that they are automated and can be easily repeated. Given the constraint that the tests should be written by the programmers and should be automated it makes sense in the context of this book to write the unit tests in Java. Although some organizations try to add written documentation to unit tests, the process works best when the unit tests are allowed to stand alone and do not require outside documentation. This is best done within a framework and, while you could write a framework yourself, there are a variety of frameworks already available for this purpose. The premier framework for unit testing in Java is **JUnit**, written by Erich Gamma and Kent Beck.

The examples in this chapter will use JUnit (available from `http://www.junit.org` – you need `junit.jar` from XPTest for TogetherJ), however any other well-implemented framework could be substituted. The important point is that the components need to be tested in a consistent and effective way.

Essentially, a unit test is a piece of code that takes a predefined unit of code and manipulates it.

> This manipulation is a simulation of various inputs to the unit. A unit test's purpose is to determine whether the unit works as designed.

A unit test should never focus on integration between components, only on verifying the integrity of the unit in question. In this case we are not concerned with architecture, or the integration of the various components: we are merely checking the specific behavior of the unit.

What is a Unit?

We defined unit testing as testing components of code. In an object-oriented language like Java, a unit almost always corresponds to a class. If you encounter a case where you feel more than one class constitutes a unit, first make sure that you are really focusing on their purpose, and not on integration or interaction between those components. You should find that a class can usually be tested by itself.

There are two major cases that confuse the issue:

❑　The first confusing case is interfaces. If a unit is usually a class, does that mean that an interface is also a unit? Think about what behavior an interface has – none. Since an interface is just a definition of a contract and has no actual behavior, there is no need to test it

❑　The second case is inheritance. If you have a superclass and several subclasses, there are a couple of options. You could test the superclass directly, or you could instead fully test each subclass. By fully testing each subclass, you would implicitly be testing the behavior of the superclass. The benefit of not testing the superclass is that you don't have to find a way to test a class that might be abstract. However, the down side is that you end up duplicating the tests of the superclass methods in each subclass test. This is exactly what hierarchies are designed to avoid.

The best approach is to test methods in the class they are defined in. If the superclass is abstract, you can simply define a concrete subclass for testing purposes that does nothing except implement the abstract methods with no behavior. This is a little risky, however. The subclass for testing needs to be changed if you change the structure of the superclass, and that may not be something the compiler or the test cases catch.

The tests that you write will relate directly to the methods of your class. Deciding exactly what to test and how best to test it takes some practice, but there are some general guidelines to follow:

❑　You don't need to write tests for getters and setters unless they do something besides simply get or set their property. The rationale for this is that they are so simple and sometimes are even generated by the development environment; it is a bad use of your time to test them. That doesn't mean you can't test them if it makes you more confident in the code, it just means that you have a finite amount of time to write tests, and there are more important areas to focus on.

1289

- ❏ As a general rule, you'll need at least one test per method. In reality, you'll need enough tests per method to ensure that you're testing all the possible inputs and outputs. While you will soon develop instincts about how much to test where you simply can't test everything, the key is to test a wide variety of inputs.

- ❏ The various access modifiers also affect how you write tests. Obviously, public methods need to be tested since they are accessed by outside code. Private methods do not need to be tested directly by your test cases since they are tested implicitly by your tests of public methods. Protected and packaged access methods need to be tested if they will be called by any class other than the class they exist in. Your baseline is that if another class calls the method, it needs to be tested.

If you don't think you need to test code, ask yourself why. With the exception of getters and setters, all your code needs to be tested either explicitly or implicitly. There is also a very important need to document the testing and any changes made to the code on that basis.

Introduction to the JUnit Framework

Before we actually begin writing unit tests, we need to understand a little bit about the JUnit framework and how it works. What's important to understand is not the details of JUnit, but the basic idea behind what you're doing. In the most general sense, you are writing a small program for each class that you want to test. The program you write will execute various pieces of code, divided into methods, that test your class. Each behavior of your class that you want to test will have a method in the program dedicated to it. It is important to note that each method that you want to test in your class might actually have many methods in the program since you want to test it in many ways.

How do the methods of your program actually test your class? First, the method manipulates an instance of the class being tested. This might mean calling a method or series of methods and passing in specific inputs. Once the object has been manipulated, the methods of the program issue assertions about the expected state of the object. An assertion is a statement that must be true if the code is working correctly. For example, `product.getId()==7` and `cart.getItems()!=null` are examples of assertions. In these examples, the test case would be saying that the product id must be 7 and the cart must have some items in it. If an assertion is not true, we say that the assertion has failed, and we know that the program has an error in it.

We said that a test is a small program. In Java terms, this means that you are writing a class with a `main()` method. The `main()` method, when executed, invokes the various methods in order to put the class you are testing through its paces.

Using the JUnit Framework

The JUnit framework is a great framework for writing unit tests; you will soon develop your own favorite way to use it. Let's look at an example of how the JUnit framework might be applied to a class. In this example, let's assume we want to test a class called `StringUtility` that has one method, `parse()`, which takes a `String` as an argument.

For the class `StringUtility` the test case might be called `StringUtilityTest`. (The test case is the actual implementation of the program that we will run to test the `StringUtility` class.) With JUnit, a test case extends the `junit.framework.TestCase` class. For each test you want to write within the test case, you create a public, no argument method whose name starts with `test`. In this example, we might create methods called `testParse()`, `testParseWithNullString()`, and `testParseWithEmptyString()`. The test case should have a `main()` method that invokes the `run()` method on a `TestRunner`. JUnit has both textual and graphical test runners, so you can choose whichever option you prefer. Many people find that choosing a textual user interface is faster when running multiple tests very frequently, but admittedly a graphical user interface is more impressive when showing a client or manager. The examples in this chapter use the textual interface; you can refer to the JUnit documentation for information on how to use the graphical user interface.

When you create your `testX()` methods, have each method `throw Exception`. This will allow all unexpected exceptions to flow up to the calling environment and be displayed as errors in the console. In addition, don't hesitate to make your method names as long as necessary to explain what you are testing.

Within the `testX()` method, you should have a variety of assertions. We already discussed that an assertion is a statement about the expected state of an object. When translating this into code, there are a variety of `assert()` methods built into `TestCase` that you can use. The easiest is `assert()`, which takes an optional `String` followed by a `boolean`. If you include the `String`, it will be printed if the assertion fails. This is helpful for debugging your code, and it is a good idea to include it. The `boolean` value that you pass in can be anything. If the `boolean` evaluates to `true`, the assertion passes. If the `boolean` evaluates to `false`, the assertion, and thus the test, fails. The examples we looked at above would look something like this:

```
Product product = new Product();

/* Call the method of the Product object that you are testing */

assert("Id of the product should be 7", product.getId()==7);
```

The idea in the above code is that the statement `product.getId()==7` should evaluate to `true`. If it does, `true` will be passed into the `assert()` method and the assertion will pass. If the expression evaluates to `false`, the assertion will fail.

This type of assertion where you are testing for equality is very common. To accommodate this, `TestCase` also has a method called `assertEquals()`, which basically takes two parameters and then determines if they are equal. The result of the test for equality is then the parameter to the assertion. The first parameter is the optional `String` that works the same way as with `assert()`. The other two parameters are the expected value and the actual value; the expected value is compared to the actual value to see if they're equal.

The other important assertions are `assertNull()` which returns `true` if what is passed in is `null`, `assertNotNull()` which passes if the argument is not `null`, and `assertSame()` which checks to see if two arguments passed in are references to the same object. All three of these assertions are also overloaded so that can also take the optional leading `String` parameter.

How to Approach Unit Testing

There are many schools of thought regarding how and when to integrate unit testing into a software development project. Some methodologies have the programmer write unit tests after they have written the code. This approach stems from the fact that testing usually takes place after the code is written. However, while other types of testing by nature cannot happen until the code is written, unit testing is not bound by this constraint. Unit testing is most effective when it takes place at the same time as development. In fact, the optimal situation is to write the unit test *before* you write the code.

At first, writing the tests first might seem counterintuitive. In actuality, writing the code first really doesn't make sense. How do you even know what to code? Perhaps you have an idea in your head of what the component should be, but very rarely is this completely developed. Writing the unit tests before the code is a way to gain focus. In a unit test you are defining the contract with the object. You implicitly define the API, but you also define all the requirements of the component. For example, suppose you are writing a component that takes HTML and converts it to plain text. You might have a conversation with a business analyst or with another programmer about this component. You know that it should take in a string and look through that string to find any HTML tags. It then returns a new string with all the HTML tags removed. You might think this is a pretty clear definition of the requirements for this object. You sit down and write the component. Then you or another programmer integrates it with the system. What happens when another component passes in a `null` string? Does your component throw a `NullPointerException`? Does it return `null`? Or does it return an empty string? And more importantly, which is the appropriate response as far as the system is concerned?

If you had written unit tests before the component, you would have been forced to consider various inputs to the component, including `null`. When you're writing the unit test, you are not immersed in code. Instead, you are focused on defining the behavior of the component. So, you are more likely to stop and ask the appropriate person what the expected behavior is.

Steps of Unit Testing

The following steps describe the basic process that you would go through in unit testing code. This process is intentionally very circular because unit testing is an ongoing process.

1. Determine the functionality of the component
This might be done by defining the requirements of the application as a whole and then breaking the system down into objects. Regardless of how you get there, when you sit down to begin a component you need to be clear on what function it is responsible for. The great thing about this is that unit testing will help you refine the requirements for the component. In this case, unit testing is really a part of the design process.

2. Design the behavior of the component
Depending on your overriding process, you might do this through a formal process or you might do it informally. Whether you have a UML diagram of the class or just a rough idea in your head, you need to have a fairly good idea of what the design of the component is.

3. Write the unit test to confirm the behavior of the component
Focus on capturing the intent of the component, not the implementation. Essentially, you should write the test as if the component were already written and working perfectly. What would you need to test to make sure it does what it should? Make sure to consider

expected and unexpected inputs. It is perfectly acceptable to use a test to make sure a particular method will throw an exception. You just need to ensure it is the expected behavior. Writing these tests without the class is hard the first few times. At first, the tests will not compile, since the code they test is not yet written. It is also easy to get drawn into the implementation details. You are literally playing a different role when you write tests, so try to focus on that.

4. Code the component so that all the tests will pass

Sometimes it is helpful to write the component in phases. First, simply create the class and any method signatures it needs so that the test case will compile. Run the test cases. In most instances they will all fail. Sometimes, what is expected is that the method will do nothing at this stage, so some test cases might pass right off the bat. The challenge is to make sure they keep passing. Go through each test case and write just enough code to make sure that case passes. Then rerun the tests. Continue with this process until all your tests pass. When all the tests pass, stop coding. This sound simplistic, but it is critical that you literally stop coding as soon as the tests pass. If you keep coding, you are adding code that really isn't needed. If you didn't define the behavior as something that needs to be tested, then it is not behavior you need. In other words, if more code is needed, we will need to do more unit testing.

5. Test the alternatives

Now that you have some experience with the component under your belt, consider other ways the component might behave. Maybe there was an input you didn't consider or an error condition that you didn't think about. Write test cases to capture these new conditions and then add or modify the code to make these tests pass.

6. Refactor the code

In step 4, you were told to stop coding after all the tests pass. This is true, but it doesn't mean that you can't even improve the design of the code. As needed, refactor your code to make it more efficient or better structured. As you learn about the code, use your knowledge to improve it. After each change you make, rerun your unit tests to verify that you haven't broken anything.

7. Write new test cases when something new happens

Every time a bug is discovered in the component, write a test case to replicate the bug. Then, modify the component so that the test case passes. Likewise, every time a new requirement is discovered or an existing requirement is changed, write or modify your tests cases to reflect the change. Then change your code.

8. Rerun all tests when the code changes

Every time you change the code for any reason, rerun all your tests to make sure you haven't inadvertently broken something.

Writing Testable Code

One of the most important steps to effective testing is to write code that is structured in a way that makes it testable. That doesn't mean you corrupt your design to fit the unit tests. Fortunately, the things that make code testable are also the things that make good object-oriented code. Small, modular methods and clearly defined object roles make code much easier to test.

The best way to make sure your code is easily testable is to write the test cases first. As we already mentioned, when you write the test cases first you are focusing on the purpose of the object, but you are also by definition focusing on how to test the component. This approach leads to simpler, better-structured code. You will find a dramatic difference between code where you write the test cases first and code you write without test cases. You will notice that you componentize your code better, that your code is simpler, and that it is more understandable. What's more, you will find that you are writing code that is of a much higher quality.

If you decide to implement unit tests on a project that already has an existing code base, you will find the process of writing unit tests much more difficult. This is because the code wasn't written to satisfy tests; it was written with a different frame of reference. You may also be overwhelmed by the amount of code that already exists that doesn't have test cases written. In this case, you simply have to take it one piece at a time. It is often better to write test cases for code that you need to change or new code that you add. As you maintain and modify the code, you slowly build a suite of test cases.

Why Unit Test?

Now that you understand what unit testing is and how to do it, it is important to understand why we should unit test. Unit testing is important in your software process for a variety of reasons.

Writing unit tests before you code gives you clarity about the requirements of the object. Since you define both the API of the object and all the expected behavior, your implementation is much easier. Writing the tests is also an incentive to explore the required behavior of the object for both good and bad inputs.

Unit tests document the requirements for an object. It is important for the developer to understand the requirements for an object, but it is even more important to capture them. Unit tests provide documentation for the requirements of the object. Only one thing is guaranteed to last as long as the code – the code itself. Since the requirements for the code are documented in code as opposed to an elusive Word or HTML document, the requirements stay with the code. Additionally, because the unit tests are used as a tool throughout the lifetime of the code, the tests evolve with the code. Even a thorough requirements document rarely gets updated to reflect the state of the system at every point in time.

Unit tests give you a measurable confidence in the quality of the code. At any time, you can run your suite of unit tests and get immediate feedback on how much of your code meets requirements. If your unit tests run at 100%, you have concrete feedback that your code has met all the requirements, as you understand them. Unit tests give your client a measure of the quality of the code. Just as unit tests give you immediate feedback, they also allow you to provide immediate feedback. Saying to a client, "I have 200 unit tests for the system and they all run at 100%" is a great way to give your client confidence in the code you are writing.

Writing comprehensive unit tests allows you to make changes to the system with confidence. The one certainty about requirements is that they will change. Without unit tests, you always run the risk of inadvertently breaking the code when you make changes. But with a suite of unit tests you are free to make changes to the code as the requirements change without worry. If you do break code, the unit tests will let you know.

Unit tests give you the freedom to learn from the system. Even the most experienced developer learns about the system as he codes. By the end, or even the middle, of a project you have a much better idea about how the application should work. Since you now have a suite of unit tests, you are free to improve the code as you learn about the application without having to worry about breaking something.

Unit tests extend the life of the code and help maintain the code. Code is hard enough to change when the person making modifications is the original programmer. But the reality is that through the life of the code many people make modifications. A suite of comprehensive unit tests makes it easy for someone unfamiliar with the code to make changes with confidence. Even if changes are made months or years later, there is no need to rely on someone remembering how the system is supposed to work.

Unit tests are a great way to share knowledge about the code in a way that is easy for programmers to digest, as they are easier to read, and so it is easier to share code. When learning about an object, it is often easier to understand the unit tests, which talk about the code, rather than understanding the code itself.

Unit tests provide a framework for confirming reported bugs. When a bug is reported on the system, the first step is to determine what component contains the erroneous code. Once you have identified that component, you simply need to write a unit test that confirms that behavior. The component should, of course, fail that unit test. We can then modify the code so that the new tests and all preexisting tests pass. We now have clearly reproduced the bug as well as integrated the documentation of the bug into your requirements. We can be confident that if that bug ever reappears in that component, the test will catch it.

These are some of the benefits of unit testing in general, but the specific benefits will vary slightly from project to project. In addition, some benefits are more valuable in the context of some organizations than others.

Unit Testing of Simple Objects

Two of the simplest types of objects to test are business objects and utility objects. Utility objects carry out operations that are largely independent of the system, normally low-level operations used by many objects. For example, if you need a string parsing utility for your application, you might create a utility class to carry out this function. A business object is a simple object whose main purpose is to store some data and represent an object in a system; a user object is an example.

Utility objects and business objects are the easiest objects to test because they are fundamentally the simplest in function of the objects in a system.

Unit Testing a Utility Object

Let's take a look at an example of unit testing a utility object. The first step is to figure out what the component will do. For our example, we have an application that retrieves data from a database. We have found that when we retrieve data from the database, it sometimes contains characters that don't display well when shown in an HTML page. Specifically, the data we retrieve from the database contains greater than and less than symbols, which can interfere with the display of the HTML page. To fix this, we need to write a utility class that replaces each occurrence of > and < with > and < respectively.

Now that we know the basic requirements of the component, we need to design the component. For this example, we will informally design the component, but we could create an object model at this point if we needed to. Since the only thing that this component will do is scrub `String`s to remove the greater than and less than signs, we can assume it will have one method that will take an input `String` and return the `String` scrubbed. We'll call this method `scrub()`, and we'll call the component `HTMLScrubber`.

Now that we know what the component will do and we have a rough idea of the structure, the next step is to write the unit tests. Since the class we are testing is `HTMLScrubber`, the test case will be called `HTMLScrubberTest`. `HTMLScrubberTest` extends `TestCase` and uses `junit.textui.TestRunner`. Note that `TestRunner` takes an argument of type `Test`. The use of the `suite()` method to provide that `Test` is a common practice. The basic format of the test case looks like this:

```
package com.wrox.simple;

import junit.framework.*;

public class HTMLScrubberTest extends TestCase {

  public HTMLScrubberTest(String arg1) {
    super(arg1);
  }

  public static void main(String[] args) {
    //Invoke the run method of the textual test runner.
    //Pass into this method a Test created by the Suite() method
    junit.textui.TestRunner.run(suite());
  }

  public static Test suite() {
    //Construct a TestSuite using the .class property of
    //the TestCase.
    return new TestSuite(HTMLScrubberTest.class);
  }

  // ...

}
```

The next step is to add test methods to the test case. You can either add a test and write it, or add all the tests and then code them. The later approach is better because it forces you to consider all the things you need to test at once and usually gives a more complete test. In this case, we need to test that the component can replace > with `&gt;`, that it can replace < with `&lt;`, and that it can handle inputs such as an empty string or `null`.

We'll define the following test methods at this point and add them to the test case:

```
public void testAlreadyScrubbed() throws Exception {}

public void testEmptyString() throws Exception {}

public void testGreaterThanAndLessThanScrubbing() throws Exception {}

public void testGreaterThanScrubbing() throws Exception {}

public void testLessThanScrubbing() throws Exception {}

public void testMultipleGreaterThanScrubbing() throws Exception {}
```

```
public void testMultipleLessThanScrubbing() throws Exception {}

public void testMultipleGreaterThanScrubbing() throws Exception{}

public void testNull() throws Exception {}
```

Notice that each test has a very descriptive name, is `public`, and throws an exception of type `Exception`. We now need to define each test further and give it some body. Let's start with `testLessThanScrubbing()`, which is a simple example. It is best to start with a simple case and slowly build to the more complex cases. This makes it easier to debug the more complex tests and better prepares you to write them. With these tests, we're testing various permutations of the original tests. We want to make sure the component can handle more than one greater than or less than sign, and that it can handle a combination of the two signs.

We want to create a string with a less than symbol in it, and pass it into an instance of `TestScrubber`'s scrub method. Then we need to examine the string we get out of the `scrub()` method and make sure that the less than sign was replaced with `&lt;`. Our test looks like this:

```java
public void testLessThanScrubbing() throws Exception {
    //Construct an instance of HTMLScrubber to use in the test
    HTMLScrubber scrubber = new HTMLScrubber();

    //Construct the string to pass into scrub
    String before = "test < test";

    //Construct a string equal to the expected results
    String after = "test &lt; test";

    //Assert that the after string should be equal to the results of
    //passing the before String into scrubber's scrub method
    assertEquals("Strings should be equal", after, scrubber.scrub(before));
}
```

The string `before` represents the value we are going to send into the scrub method, while the string `after` represents the expected outcome and will be used to test against the output. In the `assertEquals()` method, the first parameter is a descriptive string, the second parameter is the expected value, and the third value is the actual value from the component. This test will pass if the actual value (the value returned from the scrub method) matches the expected value. If these values are not identical, the test will fail.

Now that the `testLessThanScrubbing()` test has been defined, it will be easy to define the `testGreaterThanScrubbing()` method. In most cases, you'll find that tests build on each other like this. The first one is often the hardest to write. The `testGreaterThanScrubbing()` method looks like this:

```java
public void testGreaterThanScrubbing() throws Exception {
    HTMLScrubber scrubber = new HTMLScrubber();
    String before = "test > test";
    String after = "test &gt; test";
    assertEquals("Strings should be equal", after, scrubber.scrub(before));
}
```

1297

This should be self-explanatory. Now that two of the methods are written, the next few tests should be very easy to finish:

```
public void testGreaterThanAndLessThanScrubbing() throws Exception {
    HTMLScrubber scrubber = new HTMLScrubber();
    String before = "test1 > test2 < test3";
    String after = "test1 &gt; test2 &lt; test3";
    assertEquals("Strings should be equal", after, scrubber.scrub(before));
}

public void testMultipleGreaterThanAndLessThanScrubbing()
        throws Exception {
    HTMLScrubber scrubber = new HTMLScrubber();
    String before = "test1 >>> test2 <<< test3";
    String after = "test1 &gt;&gt;&gt; test2 &lt;&lt;&lt; test3";
    assertEquals("Strings should be equal", after, scrubber.scrub(before));
}

public void testMultipleGreaterThanScrubbing() throws Exception {
    HTMLScrubber scrubber = new HTMLScrubber();
    String before = "test >>> test";
    String after = "test &gt;&gt;&gt; test";
    assertEquals("Strings should be equal", after, scrubber.scrub(before));
}

public void testMultipleLessThanScrubbing() throws Exception {
    HTMLScrubber scrubber = new HTMLScrubber();
    String before = "test <<< test";
    String after = "test &lt;&lt;&lt; test";
    assertEquals("Strings should be equal", after, scrubber.scrub(before));
}
```

These test cases could easily be extended to process multiple input strings if that was needed. There are still a few tests left to write. The easiest is testAlreadyScrubbed(). This test is just like the ones we have already written, except that we want to make sure if a string already has > and < characters in it, they are not disturbed:

```
public void testAlreadyScrubbed() throws Exception {
    HTMLScrubber scrubber = new HTMLScrubber();
    String before = "test &lt; &gt; test";
    assertEquals("Strings should be equal", before, scrubber.scrub(before));
}
```

We've now tested all the normal conditions where a string gets passed into the scrub() method. We now need to consider inputs that we wouldn't expect. This is a very important part of the unit testing process. We've identified two cases where unexpected inputs could occur – an empty String, and null. When we defined the requirements for this object, we didn't determine the expected behavior in these cases. Already the unit test has forced us to consider cases we might not have thought of. By talking to other programmers who will use our component or simply by possibilities ourselves, we'll determine that when an empty string is passed in, it should return an empty string. If null is passed in, the method should throw a NullPointerException. We need to write tests to confirm that behavior:

```
public void testEmptyStringReturnsEmptyString() throws Exception {
  HTMLScrubber scrubber = new HTMLScrubber();
  assertEquals("Strings should be equal", "", scrubber.scrub(""));
}

public void testNullThrowsException() throws Exception {
  HTMLScrubber scrubber = new HTMLScrubber();

  try {
    scrubber.scrub(null);
    assert(false);
  } catch (NullPointerException e) {
    //We expect a NullPointerException to occur. Since this is what
    // we want to happen, there is no need for any code here.
  }
}
```

Notice that the names of both methods were changed to be more descriptive now that we know what the expected behavior is. Also notice that `testNullThrowsException()` doesn't have any asserts that compare values. Instead, the `scrub()` method is called and followed by the `assert(false)` line. This line will only be executed if the call to `scrub()` does not throw an exception; since we expect it to throw an exception, if it does not the test will fail.

At this point, we are done defining tests. The test case will not even compile since `HTMLScrubber` doesn't exist. In order to run the tests, we'll create the class with a `scrub()` method, but we won't define any behavior:

```
package com.wrox.simple;

public class HTMLScrubber {

  public HTMLScrubber() {
    super();
  }

  public String scrub(String s) {
    return null;
  }
}
```

We can now run the unit test. The output is displayed in text form, as shown overleaf:

```
Command Prompt                                                    _ □ ✕
C:\ProJavaServer\Chapter28>java com.wrox.simple.HTMLScrubberTest
.F.F.F.F.F.F.F.F.F
Time: 0.01

FAILURES!!!
Test Results:
Run: 9 Failures: 9 Errors: 0
There were 9 failures:
1) testLessThanScrubbing(com.wrox.simple.HTMLScrubberTest) "Strings should be eq
ual expected:<test &lt; test> but was:<null>"
2) testGreaterThanScrubbing(com.wrox.simple.HTMLScrubberTest) "Strings should be
 equal expected:<test &gt; test> but was:<null>"
3) testGreaterThanAndLessThanScrubbing(com.wrox.simple.HTMLScrubberTest) "String
s should be equal expected:<test1 &gt; test2 &lt; test3> but was:<null>"
4) testMultipleGreaterThanAndLessThanScrubbing(com.wrox.simple.HTMLScrubberTest)
 "Strings should be equal expected:<test1 &gt;&gt;&gt; test2 &lt;&lt;&lt; test3>
 b..."
5) testMultipleGreaterThanScrubbing(com.wrox.simple.HTMLScrubberTest) "Strings s
hould be equal expected:<test &gt;&gt;&gt; test> but was:<null>"
6) testMultipleLessThanScrubbing(com.wrox.simple.HTMLScrubberTest) "Strings shou
ld be equal expected:<test &lt;&lt;&lt; test> but was:<null>"
7) testAlreadyScrubbed(com.wrox.simple.HTMLScrubberTest) "Strings should be equa
l expected:<test &gt; test> but was:<null>"
8) testEmptyStringReturnsEmptyString(com.wrox.simple.HTMLScrubberTest) "Strings
should be equal expected:<> but was:<null>"
9) testNullThrowsException(com.wrox.simple.HTMLScrubberTest)
junit.framework.AssertionFailedError
        at junit.framework.Assert.fail(Assert.java:143)
        at junit.framework.Assert.assert(Assert.java:19)
        at junit.framework.Assert.assert(Assert.java:26)
        at com.wrox.simple.HTMLScrubberTest.testNullThrowsException(HTMLScrubber
Test.java:94)
        at java.lang.reflect.Method.invoke(Native Method)
        at junit.framework.TestCase.runTest(TestCase.java:155)
        at junit.framework.TestCase.runBare(TestCase.java:129)
        at junit.framework.TestResult$1.protect(TestResult.java:100)
        at junit.framework.TestResult.runProtected(TestResult.java:117)
        at junit.framework.TestResult.run(TestResult.java:103)
        at junit.framework.TestCase.run(TestCase.java:120)
        at junit.framework.TestSuite.run(TestSuite.java:144)
        at junit.textui.TestRunner.doRun(TestRunner.java:61)
        at junit.textui.TestRunner.run(TestRunner.java:181)
        at com.wrox.simple.HTMLScrubberTest.main(HTMLScrubberTest.java:14)

C:\ProJavaServer\Chapter28>
```

The dots and the Fs at the top represent each test run and the result. Each time a test is executed, a dot is displayed. If the test throws an exception, an E is printed, whereas if an assertion fails an F is printed. The rest of the output gives details about the number of tests that were run, the number that failed, and the number that threw exceptions. JUnit also provides detail on each failure and error.

In this case, every one of the nine tests failed, which is expected since we didn't implement the object. We need to write the object so that our tests will pass. Since the vast majority of the tests focus on the replacing of the greater than and less than signs with the HTML equivalents, we'll focus on that. The scrub() method can be modified as follows:

```
package com.wrox.simple;

public class HTMLScrubber {

    private static final char LESS_THAN = '<';
    private static final char GREATER_THAN = '>';
    private static final String LESS_THAN_SCRUB = "&lt;";
    private static final String GREATER_THAN_SCRUB = "&gt;";
    public HTMLScrubber() {
```

```
        super();
    }

    public String scrub(String s) {
        StringBuffer buf = new StringBuffer();

        for (int x = 0; x < s.length(); x++) {

            char c = s.charAt(x);

            if (c == LESS_THAN)
                buf.append(LESS_THAN_SCRUB);
            else {
                if (c == GREATER_THAN)
                    buf.append(GREATER_THAN_SCRUB);
                else
                    buf.append(c);
            }
        } // end for

        return buf.toString();
    }
}
```

In the `scrub()` method, we iterate through each character and check if it is a greater than or less than sign. If it is, we replace it with the HTML equivalent. We now need to rerun the test case to see how successful we were in coding the `scrub()` method:

```
Command Prompt                                                    _ □ ×

C:\ProJavaServer\Chapter28>java com.wrox.simple.HTMLScrubberTest
.........
Time: 0.01

OK (9 tests)


C:\ProJavaServer\Chapter28>
```

Every one of the test cases passed. We didn't even have to explicitly code the fact that a `null` passed in would throw a `NullPointerException`, since calling the `length()` method throws a `NullPointerException`. Since we now have tests that pass, we have the freedom to restructure the code. The `if` statement in the `scrub()` method is a little long and confusing. In addition, we are creating a lot of garbage. However, because we now have a test case, we are free to refactor the code as follows:

```
package com.wrox.simple;

public class HTMLScrubber {

    private static final char LESS_THAN = '<';
    private static final char GREATER_THAN = '>';
    private static final String LESS_THAN_SCRUB = "&lt;";
    private static final String GREATER_THAN_SCRUB = "&gt;";
```

```
public HTMLScrubber() {
  super();
}

private String scrub(char c) {
  if (c == LESS_THAN) {
    return LESS_THAN_SCRUB;
  }
  if (c == GREATER_THAN) {
    return GREATER_THAN_SCRUB;
  }
  return String.valueOf(c);
}

public String scrub(String s) {
  StringBuffer buf = new StringBuffer();
  for (int x = 0; x < s.length(); x++) {
    buf.append(scrub(s.charAt(x)));
  }
  return buf.toString();
}
}
```

Breaking the if statement out to the second scrub() method makes the code a little easier to read, and certainly more modular. However, we need to make sure we didn't break anything by moving the code around. We rerun the test case and find that all the tests still pass. Since the new scrub() method is private, we don't need to add tests for it.

We now know that the component is working as we've designed it and that it will handle unexpected input appropriately. The next step is one of the hardest for programmers to adjust to – stop coding. This is difficult because so many programmers fall in to the, "We're gonna need..." trap. The important thing is not to guess at future requirements. You now have a robust test case that will allow you to make changes with confidence. So simply stop coding until you actually need more functionality.

Unit Testing a Business Object

The next example we'll look at is a business object. Once we rule out the simple getter and setter methods, there is usually very little left in a business object. Some business objects do have a little more logic, however, and should be unit tested.

Let's look at one example. Suppose as part of your application you want to create a User object. This object is responsible for storing the user's name, as well as a Vector of Strings, representing the ids of pages in the application the user has visited. In addition, the User object must be able to present the Vector of Strings as one comma delimited string. It must also take in a String of this format and convert it to a Vector.

As before, we'll begin by designing the component informally. Since we have the requirements, we can assume that name is a simple property with a getter and a setter. We can also assume that the Vector of Strings is a property with a getter and a setter. These parts of the object we do not need to test. The other functionality, namely translating to and from the comma delimited string, will need test cases.

Next we define the test case. It will be called `UserTest`, and has a very similar structure to our previous test:

```java
package com.wrox.simple;

import junit.framework.*;

public class UserTest extends TestCase {

  public UserTest(String arg1) {
    super(arg1);
  }

  public static void main(String[] args) {
    junit.textui.TestRunner.run(suite());
  }

  public static Test suite() {
    return new TestSuite(UserTest.class);
  }

  // ...

}
```

Now that we have the basic format of the test case, let's think about what we need to test. We want to make sure that we can pass in a `String` and it will be converted to a `Vector`. We also need to make sure that when we ask for the `String` representation, the `Vector` is correctly converted to a `String`. Lets define a test method to make sure that when we pass in a `String`, the same `String` comes out:

```java
public void testStringPathInEqualsStringPathOut() throws Exception {
  User u = new User();
  String in = "1,2,3,4,5,6,7";
  u.setPathString(in);

  assertEquals(in, u.getPathString());
}
```

Notice that in this test, we create a new instance of `User`. We then pass in a path string of `"1,2,3,4,5,6,7"`. The assumption is that when we get the path string out via the `getPathString()` method, it will be the same string regardless of the transformations it has gone through.

Now let's consider inputs that are not expected. What should the method do if I pass in an empty string? In this case, we'll define the expected behavior when we pass in an empty string as returning an empty string. So we'll write a test to verify that behavior:

```java
public void testStringPathEmptyStringIn() throws Exception {
  User u = new User();
  u.setPathString("");

  assertEquals("", u.getPathString());
}
```

1303

We then need to consider the expected behavior if `null` is passed into the method. In this case, if `null` is passed in it should be treated as an empty string. This is an arbitrary decision for this example; in a real scenario you would have requirements guiding this decision, or you would need to determine the requirements for this object. So, we verify that if we pass in `null`, we get out an empty string:

```
public void testStringPathNullIn() throws Exception {
  User u = new User();
  u.setPathString(null);

  assertEquals("", u.getPathString());
}
```

We've now defined the basic tests for this simple object. Our next step will be to define the `User` object. As before, to begin with, just create the `User` object and enough methods so that the `UserTest` class can compile:

```
package com.wrox.simple;

import java.util.*;

public class User {

  public User() {
    super();
  }

  public String getPathString() {
    return null;
  }

  public void setPathString(String newPathString) {}
}
```

We can now compile and run `UserTest`. The results are as follows:

```
C:\ProJavaServer\Chapter28>java com.wrox.simple.UserTest
.F.F.F
Time: 0.01

FAILURES!!!
Test Results:
Run: 3 Failures: 3 Errors: 0
There were 3 failures:
1) testStringPathInEqualsStringPathOut(com.wrox.simple.UserTest) "expected:<1,2,
3,4,5,6,7> but was:<null>"
2) testStringPathEmptyStringIn(com.wrox.simple.UserTest) "expected:<> but was:<n
ull>"
3) testStringPathNullIn(com.wrox.simple.UserTest) "expected:<> but was:<null>"

C:\ProJavaServer\Chapter28>
```

This is of course expected since we have no behavior in our methods.

We'll continue by taking the unit tests one at a time and writing code to make each test pass. Before we do that, lets put in our two properties with getters and setters – name and path. The class then looks like this:

```
package com.wrox.simple;

import java.util.*;

public class User {
  private String name;
  private Vector path;

  public User() {
    super();
  }

  public String getName() {
    return name;
  }

  public Vector getPath() {
    return path;
  }

  public void setName(String newName) {
    name = newName;
  }

  public void setPath(Vector newPath) {
    path = newPath;
  }

  public String getPathString() {
    return null;
  }

  public void setPathString(String newPathString) {
  }
}
```

The unit tests still won't pass, so let's pick one test and make it pass. Sometimes it is easiest to start with the incorrect inputs, so let's take the test case, `testStringPathNullIn()`, and modify User to make this test run:

```
public String getPathString() {
  if (getPath() == null) {
    return "";
  }
  return null;
}

public void setPathString(String newPathString) {
  if (newPathString == null) {
    setPath(null);
  }
}
```

Here `setPathString()` and `getPathString()` have been modified so that they can handle a `null`. Let's rerun the test case and see if we made our one test pass:

```
Command Prompt                                              _ □ ×

C:\ProJavaServer\Chapter28>java com.wrox.simple.UserTest
.F..
Time: 0.01

FAILURES!!!
Test Results:
Run: 3 Failures: 1 Errors: 0
There was 1 failure:
1) testStringPathInEqualsStringPathOut(com.wrox.simple.UserTest) "expected:<1,2,
3,4,5,6,7> but was:<>"

C:\ProJavaServer\Chapter28>_
```

We actually fixed two test cases, and are left with only our main case. Because we have all three test cases, we are free to modify `setPathString()` and `getPathString()` without worry. Let's modify those methods as follows:

```java
public void setPathString(String newPathString) {
  //create a StringTokenizer to divide the String at the commas
  StringTokenizer t = new StringTokenizer(newPathString, ",");

  //create the Vector that holds the resulting path
  Vector v = new Vector();

  //iterate through the tokens (the individual Strings) and add
  //them to the Vector
  while (t.hasMoreTokens()) {
    v.addElement(t.nextToken());
  }

  //set the path to the vector
  setPath(v);
}

public String getPathString() {
  //retrieve the vector of path elements
  Vector v = getPath();

  //if the vector is null, represent it by returning an empty String
  if (v == null) {
    return "";
  }

  //create a string buffer for our result
  StringBuffer b = new StringBuffer();
  //iterate through each element in the vector and
  //append it to the StringBuffer
  for (int x = 0; x < v.size(); x++) {
    b.append(v.elementAt(x));
    //if it is not the last element, add a comma after it
    if (x + 1 != v.size()) {
```

```
        b.append(",");
      }
    }
    //return the StringBuffer as a String
    return b.toString();
  }
```

Notice that `setPathString()` now uses a `StringTokenizer` to parse the string and populate the `Vector`, and `getPathString()` uses a `StringBuffer` to construct the string. Let's rerun the test case to see if we fixed everything:

Although the test case we were trying to fix is okay, we broke one of the tests we had already fixed. When we look at the code, we can see that we are no longer handling `null` as a special case, and this is why we are getting the `NullPointerException`. Let's modify `setPathString()` as follows:

```
public void setPathString(String newPathString) {
  //add a special if statement to catch a null String
  //before we start to parse it
  if (newPathString == null) {
    //if the string is null, set the path to null and return
    setPath(null);
    return;
  }

  StringTokenizer t = new StringTokenizer(newPathString, ",");
  Vector v = new Vector();
  while (t.hasMoreTokens()) {
    v.addElement(t.nextToken());
  }
  setPath(v);
}
```

Now we can rerun the test case and see if we're done:

```
Command Prompt                                                    _ □ ×

C:\ProJavaServer\Chapter28>java com.wrox.simple.UserTest
...
Time: 0.01

OK (3 tests)

C:\ProJavaServer\Chapter28>_
```

All our tests pass. We are done with this component, and can be confident that it works as designed. The test cases also give us a framework for future changes. Once again, the final and hardest step is to stop coding.

Unit Testing Servlets

There are some unique challenges to testing servlets, since by definition a servlet functions in a request/response environment. Although some people may advocate running the servlet and writing HTML pages or using URLs to test it, this unnecessarily ties the servlet tests to the deployment environment. Any complex setup you add to a unit test makes it harder for you to run your tests quickly and often. In addition, it is harder to isolate the cause of the problem: it is not in our mandate to test environment errors. Instead, a servlet can be treated the same way as any other component. With the simple examples, we focused our test cases around the methods of the component. We wrote tests with specific inputs and then examined the output of the method to make sure it met our expectations.

Servlets are no different from any other component and can be approached in the same way. The service() method of a servlet takes a request object and a response. Rather than running the components in a web container where the request and response objects are created for us, we can create these objects ourselves and pass them into the service() method. You can populate the request object with any parameters that should be present, and then examine the response object to make sure that whatever is expected is present.

This approach will most likely require sub classing the request and response objects, and adding some support for testing in your subclasses. For example, if a servlet gets the output stream from a response and writes to it, you want to make sure that it is actually writing the appropriate data, so you could override the response to provide an output stream that is then stored in the response object where you can examine it in your test method. This is complex – but it really is the only way to unit test servlets. It may console you to know that once you have done this for the first time, it is much simpler to do again – the key thing is that having made this for one servlet, you can use it as a basis for testing any other servlet. Lots of up-front overhead, but in the end you have an excellent servlet test environment.

In this example, we will write a servlet that takes in one parameter, called id, which corresponds to the id of a product we want to display. The servlet will then output the appropriate HTML to display the product information for the specified id. Only the ids 1, 2, and 3 are valid for this servlet.

In general, we will create an instance of a request and a response. We need these because they are the required parameters to a servlet's service() method. Then we will create a PrintWriter class that will help us in capturing data output by the servlet. The fake response will use this print writer. When we execute the test case, we will pass our fake request and response into the service() method. Two of the first things we'll create are the request and response classes. We want to be able to set parameters on the request object, so that when the servlet calls request.getParameter() it will return the value that we set. We'll create a class called TestRequest that implements the ServletRequest interface:

```
package com.wrox.servlet;

import java.io.*;
import java.util.*;
import javax.servlet.*;

public class TestRequest implements ServletRequest {
  HashMap paramMap = new HashMap();
  public TestRequest() {
    super();
  }
  public String getParameter(String key) {
    return (String) paramMap.get(key);
  }
  public void setParameter(String key, String value) {
    paramMap.put(key, value);
  }

  // these methods we are not interested in for this test
  public Object getAttribute(String arg1) { return null; }
  public Enumeration getAttributeNames() { return null; }
  public String getCharacterEncoding() { return null; }
  public int getContentLength() { return 0; }
  public String getContentType() { return null; }
  public Locale getLocale() {return null; }
  public Enumeration getLocales() {return null; }
  public Enumeration getParameterNames() { return null; }
  public String[] getParameterValues(String arg1) { return null; }
  public String getProtocol() {    return null; }
  public BufferedReader getReader() throws IOException { return null; }
  public String getRealPath(String arg1) { return null; }
  public String getRemoteAddr() { return null; }
  public String getRemoteHost() { return null; }
  public String getScheme() { return null; }
  public String getServerName() { return null; }
  public int getServerPort() { return 0; }
  public boolean isSecure() { return false; }
  public void removeAttribute(String s) { }
  public void setAttribute(String arg1, Object arg2) { }
  public ServletInputStream getInputStream() throws IOException {
    return null;
  }
  public RequestDispatcher getRequestDispatcher(String s) {
    return null;
  }
}
```

Note that almost every method is empty, or returns either null or 0. For this example, we don't need most of the methods. In reality, you could turn your TestRequest and TestResponse objects into a complete tool for testing all the objects in your application. For now, though, getParameter() has been implemented to read from a hash map and setParameter() will add values to that hash map. This allows you to add a name value pair to the request (such as id = 7) and retrieve that value using the name only.

Next, we need to implement the `TestResponse` class. The only functionality we need here is we need to have `getWriter()` return an instance of `TestWriter`, which we will implement later:

```java
package com.wrox.servlet;

import java.io.*;
import java.util.*;
import javax.servlet.*;

public class TestResponse implements ServletResponse {
  TestWriter writer = new TestWriter();
  public TestResponse() {
    super();
  }
  public PrintWriter getWriter() throws IOException {
    return writer;
  }
  public void flushBuffer() throws IOException { }
  public int getBufferSize() { return 0; }
  public String getCharacterEncoding() { return null; }
  public Locale getLocale() {   return null; }
  public boolean isCommitted() { return false; }
  public void reset() { }
  public void setBufferSize(int i) { }
  public void setContentLength(int arg1) { }
  public void setContentType(String arg1) { }
  public void setLocale(Locale locale) { }
  public ServletOutputStream getOutputStream() throws IOException {
    return null;
  }
}
```

Notice that again most of the methods aren't implemented, but you would certainly add to the functionality if you intended to use it to test a variety of servlets.

Now we need to implement the functionality of `TestWriter`. A typical writer would output the data somewhere, probably to an HTML page. That is not helpful here – what we really want is to examine the output in the test case. In order to be able to do that, the writer won't output the data but will simply hold onto it so that we can examine it later in the test method:

```java
package com.wrox.servlet;

import java.io.*;
import javax.servlet.*;

public class TestWriter extends PrintWriter {

  private String output=new String();

  public TestWriter() {

  /* We really want to have a default constructor for TestWriter
     to make it easy to construct in the test case. Unfortunately,
```

```
        the API dictates that PrintWriter's constructer needs an
        OutputStream or Writer.  Fortunately, in a test case, we are not
        bound by the rules that govern "real" IO. In order to get our
        default constructor, we'll just fake out an OutputStream to
        satisfy the constructor.

        This type of sneaky behavior can be useful when you need a
        particular type of object to satisfy typing requirements, but
        you want to circumvent the API.
    */
    super(new OutputStream() {
      public void write(int b) throws IOException {
      }
    });
  }

  public String getOutput() {
    return output;
  }

  public void println(String x) {
    setOutput(getOutput() + x);
  }

  public void setOutput(String newOutput) {
    output = newOutput;
  }
}
```

Take a look at the constructor of the TestWriter. Normally, a writer serves as a wrapper for an output stream or another writer. For this test, we want to be able to construct the writer independently of an OutputStream or another Writer. You'll notice in the constructor, we're creating an empty subclass of OutputStream just to satisfy the requirements of the superclass's constructor. Basically what TestWriter does is add the data to an internal string that can be examined later.

Now that we've got the classes we need to test the servlet, we can go ahead and write the test case. There are three basic cases to test. We need to test that the servlet behaves appropriately with a valid id, an invalid id, and no id at all. Those will be our three tests:

```
package com.wrox.servlet;

import junit.framework.*;

public class DisplayProductInfoServletTest extends TestCase {
  public DisplayProductInfoServletTest(String arg1) {
    super(arg1);
  }

  public static void main(String[] args) {
    junit.textui.TestRunner.run(suite());
  }

  public static Test suite() {
    return new TestSuite(DisplayProductInfoServletTest.class);
```

```
    }

    public void testInValidId() throws Exception {}

    public void testNoId() throws Exception {}

    public void testValidId() throws Exception {}
}
```

Now that we have the basic structure of the class, let's write the first test – `testInValidId()`. We want to test that if we put in an invalid id, we get an appropriate error message. We'll create the `TestRequest` and the `TestResponse` objects, and put the parameter id into the request with a value of 7. If you recall, only the ids 1-3 are valid, so 7 constitutes an invalid id. Next we'll instantiate the servlet and call the `service()` method. Lastly we'll make sure that the value that the writer has saved for us in the output field is what we expect to see:

```
public void testInValidId() throws Exception {

    //create the request object to pass in
    TestRequest request = new TestRequest();

    //give the request a parameter called id with value 7
    //(roughly the equivalent of ?id=7 on a URL)
    request.setParameter("id","7");

    //create the response object to pass in
    TestResponse response = new TestResponse();

    //create the servlet and call the service() method with
    //test request and response
    DisplayProductInfoServlet servlet = new DisplayProductInfoServlet();
    servlet.service(request, response);

    //construct String of expected output
    String expected="<html><head><title>Invalid Product</title></head>" +
                    "<body>The product id is invalid.</body></html>";

    //compare the expected output to the actual output
    //of the servlet stored in the response's writer's output property
    assertEquals(expected, ((TestWriter)response.getWriter()).getOutput());
}
```

Next we'll test for no id. This test is exactly like the test for an invalid id, except that we'll set the id to an empty string instead of 7. We'll also expect a different message:

```
public void testNoId() throws Exception {
    TestRequest request = new TestRequest();
    request.setParameter("id","");
    TestResponse response = new TestResponse();

    DisplayProductInfoServlet servlet = new DisplayProductInfoServlet();
    servlet.service(request, response);
```

```
    String expected = "<html><head><title>Missing Parameter</title></head>"
            + "<body>You must specify a product id.</body></html>";

    assertEquals(expected, ((TestWriter) response.getWriter()).getOutput());
}
```

Finally, we'll test with a valid id. In this case we'll pass in 2. In this case the expected message should include information about the product:

```
public void testValidId() throws Exception {

    TestRequest request = new TestRequest();
    request.setParameter("id","2");
    TestResponse response = new TestResponse();



    DisplayProductInfoServlet servlet = new DisplayProductInfoServlet();
    servlet.service(request, response);

    String expected="<html><head><title>null</title></head>" +
            "<body><h1>Product Number 2</h1><p>" +
            "This is the description of product 2</p></body></html>";

    assertEquals(expected, ((TestWriter)response.getWriter()).getOutput());
}
```

It is not necessary to test for null inputs for the request and response, since we can be pretty sure that this will never happen in a real application server. Since we now have the tests, let's write just enough code to make the test case compile. As you can see, we're extending the HttpServlet class and implementing the service() method:

```
package com.wrox.servlet;

import javax.servlet.*;
import javax.servlet.http.*;
import java.io.*;

public class DisplayProductInfoServlet extends HttpServlet {

  public DisplayProductInfoServlet() {
    super();
  }

  public void service(ServletRequest request, ServletResponse response)
          throws ServletException, IOException {

  }

}
```

We'll run the test case, we should find that all three tests failed, since the `service()` method doesn't do anything yet:

```
Command Prompt                                                      _ □ ×
C:\ProJavaServer\Chapter28>java com.wrox.servlet.DisplayProductInfoServletTest
.F.F.F
Time: 0.101

FAILURES!!!
Test Results:
Run: 3 Failures: 3 Errors: 0
There were 3 failures:
1) testInValidId(com.wrox.servlet.DisplayProductInfoServletTest) "expected:<<htm
l><head><title>Invalid  Product</title></head><body>The product id..."
2) testNoId(com.wrox.servlet.DisplayProductInfoServletTest) "expected:<<html><he
ad><title>Missing Parameter</title></head><body>You must spec..."
3) testValidId(com.wrox.servlet.DisplayProductInfoServletTest) "expected:<<html>
<head><title>null</title></head><body><h1>Product Number 2</h1><..."

C:\ProJavaServer\Chapter28>_
```

We'll pick a test and write code to make it successful. We'll start with the `testNoId()` test and modify the `service()` method of the servlet so that it tries to retrieve the id from the request and convert it to an int. If it fails, we'll know that the id was either not a number or was not provided. To do this, we'll modify the `service()` method as follows:

```java
public void service(ServletRequest request, ServletResponse response)
          throws ServletException, IOException {

   String title = null;
   String body = null;
   int prodId = 0;

   try {
      prodId = Integer.parseInt(request.getParameter("id"));
   } catch (NumberFormatException e) {
      title = "Missing Parameter";
      body = "You must specify a product id.";
   }

   PrintWriter out = response.getWriter();
   out.println("<html><head><title>" + title + "</title></head><body>");
   out.println(body);
   out.println("</body></html>");
}
```

When we rerun the unit test, we see that we did in fact fix one of the tests:

```
Command Prompt                                                      _ □ ×
C:\ProJavaServer\Chapter28>java com.wrox.servlet.DisplayProductInfoServletTest
.F..F
Time: 0.091

FAILURES!!!
Test Results:
Run: 3 Failures: 2 Errors: 0
There were 2 failures:
1) testInValidId(com.wrox.servlet.DisplayProductInfoServletTest) "expected:<<htm
l><head><title>Invalid  Product</title></head><body>The product id..."
2) testValidId(com.wrox.servlet.DisplayProductInfoServletTest) "expected:<<html>
<head><title>null</title></head><body><h1>Product Number 2</h1><..."

C:\ProJavaServer\Chapter28>_
```

The next test to try to fix is testValidId(). We'll modify the service() method as follows; notice that if an id is retrieved from the request, then the code checks to see if it is between 1 and 3, and if it is it outputs the product information:

```
public void service(ServletRequest request, ServletResponse response)
        throws ServletException, IOException {

  String title = null;
  String body = null;
  int prodId = 0;

  try {
    prodId = Integer.parseInt(request.getParameter("id"));
  } catch (NumberFormatException e) {
    title = "Missing Parameter";
    body = "You must specify a product id.";
  }

  if (prodId > 1 && prodId < 3) {
    String prodName = "Product Number " + prodId;
    String prodDesc = "This is the description of product " + prodId;
    StringBuffer b = new StringBuffer("<h1>");
    b.append(prodName);
    b.append("</h1><p>");
    b.append(prodDesc);
    b.append("</p>");
    body = b.toString();
  }
  PrintWriter out = response.getWriter();
  out.println("<html><head><title>" + title + "</title></head><body>");
  out.println(body);
  out.println("</body></html>");
}
```

The test reruns with the following results:

```
Command Prompt                                                    _□X

C:\ProJavaServer\Chapter28>java com.wrox.servlet.DisplayProductInfoServletTest
.F..
Time: 0.09

FAILURES!!!
Test Results:
Run: 3 Failures: 1 Errors: 0
There was 1 failure:
1) testInValidId(com.wrox.servlet.DisplayProductInfoServletTest) "expected:<<htm
l><head><title>Invalid Product</title></head><body>The product id..."

C:\ProJavaServer\Chapter28>
```

We're now down to one test to fix. The service() method needs to be modified in order to handle the testInvalidId() test. We're adding an else to the if statement that outputs the appropriate information if the id is invalid:

```
public void service(ServletRequest request, ServletResponse response)
        throws ServletException, IOException {

  String title = null;
  String body = null;
  int prodId = 0;

  try {
    prodId = Integer.parseInt(request.getParameter("id"));
  } catch (NumberFormatException e) {
    title = "Missing Parameter";
    body = "You must specify a product id.";
  }

  if (prodId > 1 && prodId < 3) {
    String prodName = "Product Number " + prodId;
    String prodDesc = "This is the description of product " + prodId;
    StringBuffer b = new StringBuffer("<h1>");
    b.append(prodName);
    b.append("</h1><p>");
    b.append(prodDesc);
    b.append("</p>");
    body = b.toString();
  } else {
    if (prodId != 0) {
      title = "Invalid Product";
      body = "The product id is invalid.";
    }
  }

  PrintWriter out = response.getWriter();
  out.println("<html><head><title>" + title + "</title></head><body>");
  out.println(body);
  out.println("</body></html>");
}
```

We can now see that all three tests pass successfully:

```
C:\ProJavaServer\Chapter28>javac com\wrox\servlet\DisplayProductInfoServletTest.
java

C:\ProJavaServer\Chapter28>java com.wrox.servlet.DisplayProductInfoServletTest
...
Time: 0.09

OK (3 tests)

C:\ProJavaServer\Chapter28>
```

However, there is still a bug in this code! We considered both valid and invalid ids as well as an empty id, but we used an id of 0 as a special case. In reality, an id of 0 is invalid and we should test for it. We'll add the following test to the test case class:

```
public void testZeroId() throws Exception {
  TestRequest request = new TestRequest();
  request.setParameter("id","0");
  TestResponse response = new TestResponse();

  DisplayProductInfoServlet servlet = new DisplayProductInfoServlet();
  servlet.service(request, response);

  String expected="<html><head><title>Invalid Product</title></head>" +
                  "<body>The product id is invalid.</body></html>";
  assertEquals(expected, ((TestWriter)response.getWriter()).getOutput());
}
```

When we run the tests, we find that this test fails. This is a good example of why it is so important to try to consider every possible input. This is also a case where changing the code to fix this problem, could easily break other code. We'll fix this test case by modifying the servlet as follows:

```
package com.wrox.servlet;

import javax.servlet.*;
import javax.servlet.http.*;
import java.io.*;

public class DisplayProductInfoServlet extends HttpServlet {
  public DisplayProductInfoServlet() {
    super();
  }

  public void service(ServletRequest request, ServletResponse response)
          throws ServletException, IOException {
    String title = null;
    String body = null;
    int prodId = 0;
    try {
      prodId = Integer.parseInt(request.getParameter("id"));
    } catch (NumberFormatException e) {
      writePage(response.getWriter(), "Missing Parameter",
                "You must specify a product id.");
      return;
    }
    if (prodId > 1 && prodId < 3) {
      String prodName = "Product Number " + prodId;
      String prodDesc = "This is the description of product " + prodId;
      StringBuffer b = new StringBuffer("<h1>");
      b.append(prodName);
      b.append("</h1><p>");
      b.append(prodDesc);
      b.append("</p>");
      body = b.toString();
    } else {
      title = "Invalid Product";
      body = "The product id is invalid.";
    }
```

```
        writePage(response.getWriter(), title, body);
    }

    protected void writePage(PrintWriter out, String title, String body) {
        out.println("<html><head><title>" + title + "</title></head><body>");
        out.println(body);
        out.println("</body></html>");
    }
}
```

Now, all the tests pass. However, the reality is that the way this servlet was written is really not very good code. There are too many if statements to make the code easy to read, and it would be better if the HTML code was read from a file rather than being embedded in the code where it is difficult to change. However, that's why it is so important to write the test cases. If you had written the code without test cases, it would be difficult to change the code, because you would have no way of knowing if something was broken. Now, you are free to change the implementation of the code, and your tests will highlight any problems.

Servlets vary a great deal in their implementations, but this basic approach will work for any kind of servlet. If the servlet connects to another Java component, perhaps to retrieve data, you can also create a test version of that component much like the test version of the request and response.

Unit Testing the Database Access Layer

There are probably as many ways to test database access code as there are strategies for database access. From JDBC with SQL statements embedded in the code to third-party software solutions, there are a multitude of approaches to writing a database access layer. This section will address some general approaches to testing this type of code, and prepare you to approach your unique situation appropriately.

In a typical application, a certain amount of code is dedicated to performing database access; this means code that reads and writes from a database and any code that facilitates the process. Unit testing this type of code is difficult because of the external dependency on a database and software such as JDBC drivers. In addition, some projects choose to use a prepackaged software solution for their object to relational mapping and caching. Using an object database is also an option some applications choose. All these options make testing difficult, but the code can still be effectively tested.

The first step to effective unit testing of this layer in your application is to determine which components actually access the database and which components are just utilities to help the process. Any component that does not access the database can be unit tested the same way as a business object or utility. Once you separate out the objects that don't touch the database, you can focus on the database access components themselves.

One important consideration is making your methods modular. This of course is true for all code, but it is especially important for testing something as complex as database code. Another great advantage to unit testing or any kind of testing is to have a test database. This is a specific database that you can write to and read from without having to worry about harming critical data. It is also helpful for keeping standardized data that can be a baseline for your test cases.

One approach to unit testing is to have a test database with one row for each scenario you need to test. This means that you'll have rows with null or empty values in columns, as well as rows for good data. When you add a test, you'll probably have to add a row to the table. This works great for testing methods that read from the database, since you can hard code the expected results in your test cases and compare the data that is retrieved with the expected results. However, this approach doesn't really address testing methods that write data to the database. In this scenario, you might have a method that writes a row in a database. To test that method, you would write your test so that it calls the method and then uses a SQL call through JDBC to see if the data was actually written to the database.

This approach is pretty good if you have a test database. However, sometimes you do not have that luxury. The realities of a project sometimes mean you have to test against databases that you do not completely own. You can still write to the database for your tests, but there is always the concern that between the time you write the data and the time you remove it, something will happen such as a system crash, and cause the database to be in a bad state. JUnit provides two methods that run before and after a test is run: `setUp()` and `tearDown()`. The `setUp()` method runs right before each `testX()` method, and `tearDown()` runs right after. Using these methods you can start a transaction in `setUp()`, and do a `rollback()` in `tearDown()`. This ensures that no data will ever be written to the database. If there is an error and `tearDown()` isn't called, the data is never committed either.

Another option deals with using a prepackaged software solution. You don't have to test a third-party product, as you can assume this code works. But you do need to test the code that accesses the third-party code. If the product has an API that you access, you may be able to implement an interface with some test code and then implement a stub object that acts like the software package. This would give you the ability to control the outputs from the software package so that you can effectively test the interface between it and your code.

One important thing to understand is that writing the code and doing the setup for testing database access code is one of the hardest parts of writing unit tests. If unit tests are new for you, or even if just writing the unit tests themselves is new, don't start with database access code. Don't get discouraged by the setup around database access. You're essentially building a framework you can reuse to test different parts of the database access layer.

Unit Testing JSPs

Unit testing JavaServer Pages is either very easy or very difficult, depending on how you write your JSPs. If you embed a great deal of Java code in your JSPs, then testing them is very difficult. Since the JSP isn't a Java object, you can't test it with JUnit. This is a small distinction, really. The actual JSP file is a text file and not a Java object. However, once the JSP is compiled into a servlet, it really is a Java component. The obvious question is: why not unit test that file with JUnit?

The answer is that the class file that is generated doesn't necessarily have a corresponding Java source file, so it is really hard to write code against. Moreover, a change to the JSP would require you to recompile the servlet in the JSP engine and then run the unit test against that. It would be cumbersome to follow this process. However, regardless of all this, the most convincing argument for not writing the unit tests against these class files is that they are usually one really, really big method. The sheer logistics of constructing a reasonable test are very daunting.

There is even an argument to be made that testing a JSP isn't even really unit testing, since a great deal of the functionality of a JSP is interacting with other Java components. Consider the following example JSP:

```
<%@ page import = "com.wrox.jsp.BackgroundColorBean" %>

<jsp:useBean id="bgcolor" class="com.wrox.jsp.BackgroundColorBean"
 scope="session"/>
<jsp:setProperty name="bgcolor" property="*"/>

<html>
  <head><title>Set Background Color</title></head>
    <body bgcolor=<%= bgcolor.getBgcolor() %>>

      <% if ("white".equals(bgcolor.getBgcolor())) { %>
        Welcome to pick a color!<BR>
      <% } else { %>
        Excellent Choice! - Go Again<BR>
      <% } %>
      Pick a background color:  
      <form method=get>
      <input type=text name=bgcolor />
      <input type=button value="Submit" />
      </form>
    </body>
  </html>
```

and the bean it uses:

```
package com.wrox.jsp;

import java.util.*;

public class BackgroundColorBean {

  private String bgcolor="white";

  public BackgroundColorBean() {
  }

  public String getBgcolor() {
    return bgcolor;
  }
  public void setBgcolor(String newBgcolor) {
    bgcolor = newBgcolor;
  }
}
```

This JSP page could easily have contained all the code that is encapsulated in the Java code. However, by breaking it out, we are making this page easier to manage. We also have basically eliminated the need to unit test this page and the component. The Java component has only getters and setters, which we do not need to test. The JSP only calls properties of the Java component and sets one, so basically it functions as a getter and setter and there is nothing to test here either.

Certainly, we would want to test the interaction between the JSP and the Java code, but that falls under integration testing rather than unit testing. For example, we want to make sure that the appropriate HTML is displayed based on the bgcolor property of the Java component. However, this is clearly a point of integration between the JSP and the Java code, rather than a function of a unit.

One technique for unit testing an aspect of JSP is to run some type of HTML validator on the output HTML code. This is a way of ensuring the quality of your output, but is not really effective in testing that what is displayed is what should be displayed. The best way to do this is to use an automated tool that can examine HTML pages according to predetermined scripts. This is far outside the realm of unit testing, but it is important to understand unit testing's limits. Unit tests are never meant to test integration so, if you find testing something particularly difficult, stop to ensure that you are testing a unit and not integration.

It is not always possible to make the JSP and Java code as simple as in this example. However, you can always strive to put the Java code into Java objects and write unit tests for those objects, and you can then use the techniques already mentioned to test the HTML output. Since this is the recommended style of programming JSPs this should hopefully not be too difficult to do.

Unit Testing EJBs and RMI Objects

Enterprise JavaBeans are difficult to test, because often EJBs get a lot of context from the application server. They rely on this context heavily, and are not meant to be constructed outside of this context. You could use the techniques we've seen to 'stub-out' the behavior of the application server, but this is extremely difficult for something as complex as an application server. There are other types of components that also gain context from the application server such as RMI objects. The techniques described in this section will work equally well for any other component that requires context from the application server. In finding a solution to this problem, it is critical that we do not sacrifice the fact that we want our unit test to run quickly and in isolation. The answer is to run the tests cases so that they can access the units within the context of the application server.

Depending on the type of application and the application server, you can look up your unit within the application server. For example, if the component is an EJB, you can use JNDI to lookup the component. If the component is an RMI object, you can do a lookup using its RMI URL. Once you have a reference to the component running within the application server, you can execute your tests on the component the same way you would on a component outside of the application server. You may also find in helpful in some cases to run the test cases from within the application server. JUnit is just Java code. That means JUnit tests can certainly run within an application server if you choose. You might also find it helpful to build as servlet interface to help you run the tests.Consider the following example, a session bean that represents a shopping cart. The cart contains items and can calculate the total of the items in the cart. Its remote interface is:

```
package com.wrox.ejb;

import javax.ejb.EJBObject;
import java.rmi.RemoteException;

public interface ShoppingCart extends EJBObject {
    public double getTotal() throws RemoteException;
    public void setCartItems(Item[] newCartItems) throws RemoteException;
}
```

The bean implementation class is quite straightforward:

```java
package com.wrox.ejb;

import javax.ejb.*;

public class ShoppingCartEJB implements SessionBean {
  private Item[] cartItems;
  // A no-argument constructor is necessary
  public ShoppingCartEJB() { }

  public void ejbActivate() { }

  // This is the actual create method used by the container
  public void ejbCreate() throws CreateException {
  }

  public void ejbPassivate() {  }

  // These methods are required for the session bean interface
  public void ejbRemove() {  }

  public Item[] getCartItems() {
    return cartItems;
  }

  public double getTotal() {
    double total = 0;
    if (getCartItems() == null || getCartItems().length == 0) {
      return total;
    }
    for (int x = 0; x < getCartItems().length; x++) {
      total = total + getCartItems()[x].getPrice();
    }
    return total;
  }

  public void setCartItems(Item[] newCartItems) {
    cartItems = newCartItems;
  }

  public void setSessionContext(SessionContext sc) {}
}
```

The home interface is also simple:

```java
package com.wrox.ejb;

import javax.ejb.CreateException;
import javax.ejb.EJBHome;
import java.rmi.RemoteException;

public interface ShoppingCartHome extends EJBHome {
  public ShoppingCart create() throws RemoteException, CreateException;
}
```

The structure for the `Item` class is as follows:

```
package com.wrox.ejb;

public class Item implements java.io.Serializable {

  private String name;
  private double price;

  public Item() {
    super();
  }

  public Item(String name, double price) {
    super();
    setName(name);
    setPrice(price);
  }

  public String getName() {
    return name;
  }

  public double getPrice() {
    return price;
  }

  public void setName(String newName) {
    name = newName;
  }

  public void setPrice(double newPrice) {
    price = newPrice;
  }
}
```

Finally, here is the deployment descriptor:

```
<?xml version="1.0" encoding="Cp1252"?>

<!DOCTYPE ejb-jar PUBLIC '-//Sun Microsystems, Inc.//DTD Enterprise JavaBeans
1.1//EN' 'http://java.sun.com/j2ee/dtds/ejb-jar_1_1.dtd'>

<ejb-jar>
  <description>no description</description>
  <display-name>Ejb1</display-name>
  <enterprise-beans>
    <session>
      <description>no description</description>
      <display-name>ShoppingCart</display-name>
      <ejb-name>ShoppingCart</ejb-name>
      <home>com.wrox.ejb.ShoppingCartHome</home>
      <remote>com.wrox.ejb.ShoppingCart</remote>
      <ejb-class>com.wrox.ejb.ShoppingCartEJB</ejb-class>
      <session-type>Stateful</session-type>
      <transaction-type>Bean</transaction-type>
    </session>
  </enterprise-beans>
</ejb-jar>
```

The shopping cart unit could be tested outside of an application server, but you'd miss the home interface and the ShoppingCart interface in the testing. You would also lose the context gained by the application server. Instead, let's run the unit test inside the application server. It might look something like this:

```java
package com.wrox.ejb;

import javax.ejb.*;
import javax.naming.*;
import javax.rmi.*;
import java.rmi.*;

import junit.framework.*;

public class ShoppingCartTests extends TestCase {
  private ShoppingCartHome home;

  public ShoppingCartTests(String testname) {
    super(testname);
  }

  protected ShoppingCart createShoppingCart()
            throws RemoteException, CreateException {
    return home.create();
  }

  public void setUp() throws Exception {
    Context initial = new InitialContext();
    Object objRef = initial.lookup("ShoppingCart");

    home = (ShoppingCartHome)PortableRemoteObject.narrow(objRef,
                  ShoppingCartHome.class);
  }

  public static void main(String[] args) {
    junit.textui.TestRunner.run(suite());
  }

  public static TestSuite suite() {
    return new TestSuite(ShoppingCartTests.class);
  }

  public void testEmptyCart() throws Exception {
    ShoppingCart cart = createShoppingCart();

    assert("Total should add up to 0", 0==cart.getTotal());
  }

  public void testNormalCart() throws Exception {
    ShoppingCart cart = createShoppingCart();
    Item item1 = new Item("Item 1", 12.00);
    Item item2 = new Item("Item 2", 5.99);
    Item item3 = new Item("Item 3", 25.25);
    Item[] items = {item1, item2, item3};

    cart.setCartItems(items);

    assert("Total should add up to 43.24", 43.24==cart.getTotal());
  }
}
```

In this example, each test does not directly instantiate the shopping cart, but instead it defers to the `createShoppingCart()` method, which creates the object from the home interface. Notice that the home interface is set through the code in the `setUp()` method. Remember that this code is called before each test is executed.

The remaining issue is how to run the unit test within the application server. The way this is done will most likely vary by application server. However, one approach is to write a servlet that can call your test case and execute it within the application server environment. You may also be able to find a way to run your test cases from the command line and do a lookup into the application server; a main() method is included in `ShoppingCartTests` for this purpose.

Beyond these hints for executing your tests, writing tests for EJBs and RMI objects is really no different from writing tests for any other component You focus on the purpose of the object and not on the integration between components. You can also ignore interfaces and do not need to test getters and setters.

Summary

Hopefully you now understand some of the reasons for unit testing. Unit testing is a very powerful tool for programmers and can make your development faster and of higher quality. If unit testing was new to you and you remain unconvinced of the merits, the best thing you can do is simply to try it. Unit testing is one of those practices that is best understood by experiencing it.

If you have previous experience with unit testing, but not 'test first' design, the chapter should have shown you some of the merits of writing the tests first. By no means is this an easy process; it is essentially a transformation of perspective. It is, however, very much worth the effort that it takes to make such a change.

For those of you already using unit testing techniques as described in this chapter, hopefully you have gotten some new ideas on how to approach J2EE components. The key is to focus on the object itself rather than the details of the implementation. EJBs, servlets, business objects, or any other Java objects all need to be tested in the same way.

This chapter has presented some techniques for unit testing the types of components that you commonly encounter in J2EE applications. However, every situation is unique. You'll find challenges in testing the components in your code that will require you to use your imagination to find a suitable solution. It is critical that you not only capture and repeat the practices in this chapter, but that you feel comfortable extending and adapting the practices for your organization and applications.

There are no hard and fast rules that dictate how unit testing must be done. Instead, there are basic guidelines that make it more effective and beneficial. Every programmer who writes unit tests puts his own spin on the process and that's a good thing. Recall that unit testing is a tool and, like any tool, people choose to use it in slightly different ways.

The most important thing you can do to make unit testing a part of your software development practice is to start doing it. There is no need to be at 100% from day one. Start small and aim for a complete testing framework of all of your code.

The next chapter covers the Java Message Service (JMS) and its use in message-based integration.

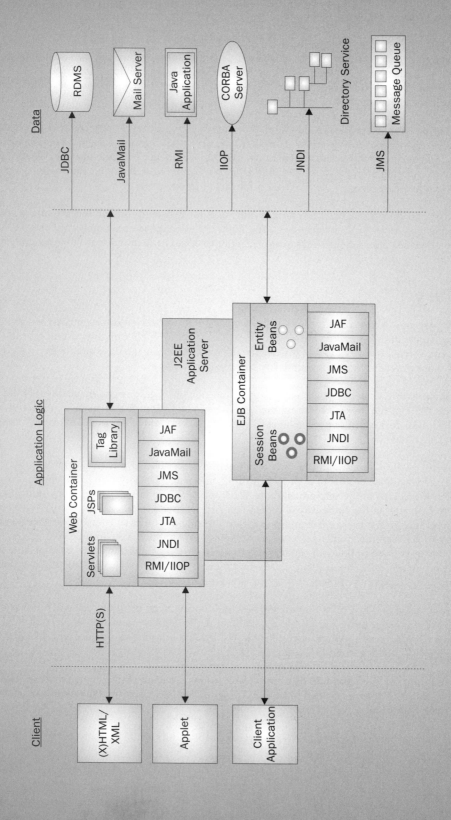

The Java Message Service

In this chapter we will look at the **Java Messaging Service (JMS)**. Messaging services provide for enterprise-wide asynchronous exchange of business data and events, and the JMS API provides an API and provider framework to allow portable, message-based applications to be developed in Java.

We will be covering:

- ❑   What messaging systems are
- ❑   The concepts of JMS programming and useful techniques
- ❑   A brief look at the available JMS implementations
- ❑   A sample JMS application
- ❑   Using JMS for message-based integration

Messaging Systems

Message-oriented Middleware (MOM) has provided the basis for data exchange within and between enterprises for decades.

> **MOM is generally defined as a software infrastructure that asynchronously connects multiple systems through the production and consumption of data messages. A message may be a request, a report, or an event sent from one part of an enterprise application to another.**

MOM facilitates building distributed systems through:

- ❑ Abstracting application interfaces into data descriptions

- ❑ Abstracting the underlying communication transports employed in distributed systems

- ❑ Providing a number of communication models that can be employed to solve different integration problems

- ❑ Facilitating communication among large numbers of application nodes

- ❑ Eliminating the need for all systems to be available simultaneously

- ❑ Ensuring that transactions are carried out within a specified Quality of Service (QoS)

Until recently, MOM implementations – such as IBM's MQSeries – have been proprietary systems. This has changed with JavaSoft's release of the **Java Message Service (JMS)** specification and its widespread adoption by developers of messaging infrastructures and application servers. The Java Message Service specification represents the leading approach to standards-based messaging middleware. JMS comprises an API (the `javax.jms` package), and semantics for a messaging service that provides capabilities such as persistence, verification, and transactions. Largely through the work of Mark Hapner at JavaSoft, the JMS specification supports a universal messaging model that supports a variety of asynchronous and synchronous communication mechanisms.

> **The JMS specification provides a solid, adaptable foundation for the construction of a messaging infrastructure that can be applied to a wide range of application domains.**

Like other J2EE APIs, JMS is not an implementation but rather the *specification* of an API into a messaging system with compliant semantics. The JMS specification refers to a **JMS provider** that implements the JMS API and semantics. Although one could implement a JMS provider in any number of ways, the most common commercial implementation is that of a **client library** and a **message broker**. Other possibilities include a JMS interface into an existing messaging infrastructure, or JMS services as part of a larger J2EE implementation, such as an application server. As it's helpful to visualize some specific form of provider when discussing JMS, we will use the purest form, the message broker model, within this chapter. Also note that the scope of this chapter is to discuss the *use* of a JMS provider, not how to implement one.

JMS Programming

The JMS specification offers the two most common models for messaging:

- ❑ **Publish/subscribe**
  Publish/subscribe (or 'pub/sub') is a *one-to-many* publishing model where client applications publish messages to **topics**, which are in turn subscribed to by other clients that are 'interested' in those topics. All subscribed clients will receive each message (subject to quality of service, connectivity, and selection).

- ❑ **Point-to-Point**
  Point-to-Point provides a traditional queuing mechanism where a client application sends messages, through a queue, to (typically) one receiving client that obtains the messages sequentially. A **JMS message queue** is an administered object that represents the destination for a message sender and a data source for a message receiver.

Many, if not all, real-world JMS applications use a mix of these two models; both pub/sub and point-to-point messaging use the same format of **JMS message.** We will discuss JMS messages themselves later in this chapter, but first we will examine the programming model behind JMS.

The two JMS messaging models employ a common programming model. Quality of service (QoS), security, acknowledgement modes (indicating how and when the messaging system is informed that a client has received a message), and the like are all handled in a uniform manner for both messaging models. While the logical routing of pub/sub messages is quite different from that of point-to-point, both models share a hub-and-spoke architecture between clients and the broker:

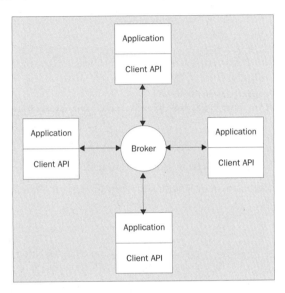

The broker is the heart of the messaging service, acting as a hub through which all messages are routed. Multiple brokers (for those JMS implementations that offer this feature) may be clustered, facilitating scalability and offering a higher level of fault tolerance. Clustered brokers also allow for centralized maintenance of security functions.

Clients access the broker through the JMS API, although this access is highly abstracted. Typically, clients call a messaging client runtime library, which implements the JMS interface and communicates with the broker. The manner in which this communication occurs – in other words, the over-the-wire protocol employed – is not specified by the JMS specification. In practice, most JMS implementations perform some form of proprietary marshalling over one or more protocols, including TCP/IP, HTTP, or SSL. Indeed, a primary intention of JMS is to shield the application developer from the implementation details of these lower-level transports, while providing a more capable set of messaging semantics then these protocols provide by themselves.

Publish and Subscribe Programming

Let's start by walking through the process of connecting to a broker and exchanging messages using the pub/sub model.

Connections and Sessions

Each client application opens a single **connection** to the message broker, regardless of the mix of messaging models it intends to use. The TopicConnection object provides the logical conduit for communication with the messaging system. In JMS multiple connections are allowed, but typically are only used when connecting to multiple distinct message brokers, as connections are relatively heavy in terms of memory use when compared with sessions. (We will discuss sessions shortly.) Typically, a client will locate a broker through JNDI, and then establish a connection through its **connection factory**.

Within the context of a connection, the client application establishes one or more **sessions**, each with its own transactional characteristics and acknowledgement modes. All actual messaging activity is performed via the TopicSession object.

The JMS syntax for creating a TopicSession on an established TopicConnection is:

```
public javax.jms.[Topic|Queue]Session
create[Topic|Queue]Session(boolean transacted, int acknowledgeMode)
```

where the method parameters are:

❑   transacted – if true, the session will be transacted

❑   acknowledgeMode – indicates whether the consumer or the client will acknowledge any messages it receives

Acknowledgement Modes

JMS supports formalized *acknowledgment* of message receipt. Like handshaking in a low-level communications protocol, acknowledgment informs the message broker when a client has successfully received a message.

> *JMS also provides a ReplyTo mechanism for application-level requests and replies; we will discuss this higher level 'acknowledgement' later in this chapter.*

Acknowledgment modes are controlled at the session level. The following acknowledgement modes are supported:

❑   **AUTO_ACKNOWLEDGE**
The session automatically acknowledges receipt of each message. In synchronous mode, this indicates a successful return from a call to receive(). In asynchronous mode, it indicates that the asynchronous message handler indicated a successful return.

❑   **CLIENT_ACKNOWLEDGE**
Allows the client application to indicate that it received the message successfully, possibly delaying the acknowledgement. The application must invoke the acknowledge() method on each message successfully received.

❑   **DUPS_OK_ACKNOWLEDGE**
A variation of AUTO_ACKNOWLEDGE that provides a 'lazy' mechanism that can result in duplicate message deliveries in failure situations. While this mode is only appropriate for insensitive data, it can provide increased efficiency within the messaging system. For example,

in a stock ticker application it may be acceptable for a client application to receive duplicate price updates, whereas in an order processing application it would not be appropriate to receive duplicate orders.

JMS also supports transactional behavior at the session level. We will discuss this later when we look at JMS programming techniques.

Topics

In pub/sub, each session **publishes** and/or **subscribes** to one or more **topics**. An authorized publisher produces messages through a specified topic, and authorized subscribers receive messages by subscribing to that topic. Topics may be static or dynamic objects, and can be temporary for transitory or anonymous uses.

Publishing a Message

In order to publish messages, a session must create a `TopicPublisher` object for the selected topic. Likewise, to consume messages published to a topic, a session must create a `TopicSubscriber` object that subscribes to the desired topic. In the figure below, the pub/sub session contains a publisher object producing messages to topics maintained by the message broker, and a subscriber consuming messages from topics to which the session is subscribed:

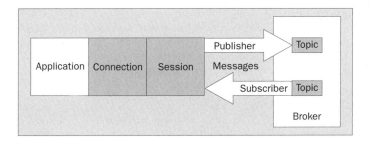

The following code sample illustrates the basic steps required to create a publisher and a subscriber for a sample topic, and publish a message:

```
String APP_TOPIC = "sample_topic";

// The session method is used to create the topic
javax.jms.Topic topic = session.createTopic(APP_TOPIC);

//The publisher uses the session method to create a publisher
publisher = session.createPublisher(topic);

// Publish a message to the topic
private void jmsPublish(String aMessage) {
  try {
    javax.jms.TextMessage msg = session.createTextMessage();
    msg.setText(user + ": " + aMessage);
    publisher.publish(msg);
  }
  catch (javax.jms.JMSException jmse) {
    jmse.printStackTrace();
  }
}
```

Let's look at the publishing of the message in more detail. When publishing a message, the publishing application can specify the quality of service to be used (delivery mode, time-to-live, and priority) as well as whether a reply is requested from the subscriber:

```
publish(Message message, int deliveryMode, int priority, long timeToLive)
```

where the method parameters are:

- ❑ `message` is a JMS `Message` object
- ❑ `deliveryMode` is either `NON_PERSISTENT` or `PERSISTENT`
- ❑ `priority` is between 0 and 9, where 0 is lowest and 9 is highest
- ❑ `timeToLive` is zero or a positive integer, where 0 is 'forever' and any other positive value is 'n milliseconds'

Delivery Modes

The **delivery mode** is one of several aspects that determine quality of service for message delivery and receipt:

- ❑ **NON_PERSISTENT**
  This is the most efficient delivery mode, because it does not require that the message be logged to stable storage. The JMS specification indicates that a JMS provider must deliver a `NON_PERSISTENT` message with an at-most-once guarantee, meaning that the broker may lose the message (due to a power outage, etc.) but it must not deliver it twice

- ❑ **PERSISTENT**
  This mode instructs the broker to place the message in a data store as an extension of the client's send operation. This insures the message will survive power and other system failures The JMS specification indicates that a JMS provider must deliver a `PERSISTENT` message with a once-and-only-once guarantee. It must not lose it, and it must not deliver it twice.

Priority

Normally, messages are received in **FIFO** (or 'first in, first out') order. When several messages await consumption by a subscriber, however, higher priority messages are presented to the client before those of lower priority, resulting in non-FIFO behavior.

Time-to-Live

The time-to-live parameter specifies how long the message broker should retain the message in order to ensure that all subscribers receive it. If, after initial delivery, any durable subscribers did not acknowledge delivery, the message is retained for the time-to-live duration in anticipation that a durable subscriber will connect to the message broker and accept delivery. (We will discuss durable subscriptions in the next section.)

If the time-to-live is specified as zero, the message will not expire. When a message's time-to-live is reached, the broker will typically discard it. The JMS specification does not define any form of notification of message expiration. Clients should not receive messages that have expired; however, the JMS specification does not guarantee that message brokers do not allow this to happen. Typically, a message set to live forever will be discarded as soon as delivery to all current subscribers and all durable subscribers is complete (that is, all subscribed clients have acknowledged receipt of the message).

Subscribing to Topics

We discussed topics earlier, and then created one so that we could send a message. There are a few more things to consider when subscribing to topics, such as whether the subscription is durable or not, and the concept of message selection.

Durable Subscriptions

A **durable** subscription indicates that the client wants to receive all the messages published to a topic, including messages published when the client connection is not active. The messaging system ensures that all messages published to the topic are retained until the durable subscriber acknowledges them or the messages have expired. For example, a seller in a trading community could go offline for an extended period and still receive bid requests that were broadcast during that time. Actual receipt of such messages also requires that they be sent as persistent, and that the time-to-live for each message is not exceeded.

To create a durable subscription to a topic, the client application invokes the following method provided by the session object:

```
TopicSubscriber createDurableSubscriber(Topic topic, String name,
                                        String messageSelector,
                                        boolean noLocal)
```

The method parameters here are:

- ❏ `topic` is a `Topic` object that specifies the topic we want to subscribe to
- ❏ `name` is a `String` (not necessarily the username, although that is not uncommon) that indicates the name under which to maintain the durable subscription to the specified topic
- ❏ `messageSelector` is a `String` that defines selection criteria (we will discuss message selectors shortly)
- ❏ `noLocal` is a `boolean`; if this is `true`, the subscriber will not receive messages that were published by the client application from subscribed topics

Non-Durable Subscriptions

To create a non-durable subscription to a topic, the client application invokes the following method provided by the session object:

```
TopicSubscriber createSubscriber(Topic topic, String messageSelector,
                                 boolean noLocal)
```

The parameters are:

- ❏ `topic`: a `Topic` object that specifies the desired topic
- ❏ `messageSelector`: a `String` that defines selection criteria
- ❏ `noLocal`: a `boolean`; if this is `true`, the subscriber will not receive messages that were published by the client application from subscribed topics

Message Selection

Subscribers can ask the messaging system to filter the messages they receive by qualifying their subscriptions with **message selectors**. Message selectors cause the JMS provider to evaluate message headers and properties before sending messages to the client application. Message selectors employ a syntax based on a subset of SQL-92 conditional expressions. Because the JMS provider handles the filtering, the application itself is more efficient, and the messaging traffic imposes less bandwidth use.

The following message selector might filter a subscription on a `Bidders` topic to retrieve only high-priority quotes that are requesting a reply:

```
"Property_Priority > 7 AND Property_Type='Quote' AND
        Property_Reply is NOT NULL"
```

We will discuss message selection within the greater scope of message routing in a later section of this chapter.

Receiving Messages

Once a client application has subscribed to a topic, it can receive messages either synchronously or asynchronously (the publishing of a message is always synchronous). To obtain messages asynchronously, the client application registers a `MessageListener` for the subscriber object:

setMessageListener(MessageListener listener)

where `listener` is the message listener to associate with this session. The listener is often assigned just after creating the topic subscriber from the session, so that the listener is bound to the topic to which a subscription was just made:

```
javax.jms.TopicSubscriber subscriber =
   session.createDurableSubscriber(topic, username);
subscriber.setMessageListener(myListener);
```

The listener object must implement the `onMessage()` method from the `MessageListener` interface. This method will be invoked by the JMS provider whenever a message is produced for this subscriber:

```
// Handle an asynchronously received message
public void onMessage(javax.jms.Message aMessage) {
  // Cast the message as a text message.
  javax.jms.TextMessage textMessage = (javax.jms.TextMessage) aMessage;

  // Read a single String from the message, print to stdout.
  String string = textMessage.getText();
}
```

A received message could potentially be of any message type supported by the JMS implementation (we will discuss message types later), but in the above example the code assumes that the message is a text message. In a full application, we would most likely want to check for other message types and take appropriate action, such as output an error message for types that are not supported by the application. Also, the above example simply sends the message payload to the console window. In a real application we would perform some action based upon the message contents.

Synchronous Message Receipt

The `receive()` methods of the subscriber provide synchronous calls to fetch messages. The various methods manage the potential blocking semantics associated with synchronous message receipt.

Message receive()

This method is a synchronous, blocking call to receive the next message produced for this subscriber. Note that this may not be the next message published for the subscribed *topic*, as the client application may have specified that filtering be applied to message receipt. This call blocks indefinitely until a message is produced. The return value is the next message produced for this subscriber; if a session is closed while blocking, the return value is `null`.

Message receive(long timeOut)

This call blocks until either a message arrives, or the specified timeout expires. The return value is either the next message produced for this subscriber, or `null` if no message is produced within the timeout interval. The `timeOut` value is specified in milliseconds.

Message receiveNoWait()

The `receiveNoWait()` method is effectively a blocking receive call with an instantaneous timeout. That is, it returns immediately whether a message is available or not, and receives the next message if one is available. The return value is the next message produced for this subscriber, or `null` if none is available. It is worth noting that this method is unlikely to provide useful message consumption when employed in the pub/sub model. The odds of some other client publishing a message to the topic at the precise instant that the receiver invokes `receiveNoWait()` are remote in the extreme. This method is, however, useful in the point-to-point model where messages wait on a static queue until consumed by a receiver.

Unsubscribing From a Durable Subscription

The `unsubscribe()` method unsubscribes a durable subscription that has been created by the client. This deletes the state maintained by the messaging system on behalf of the subscriber:

unsubscribe(String name)

The `name` string is the name used to identify this subscription at the time that it was made.

It is always a good idea to unsubscribe from topics when the client application is no longer interested in receiving messages. While a client application *can* stop listening to a topic while it remains subscribed, this incurs the messaging system overhead associated with the subscription. For example, the messaging system will continue to attempt delivery of messages to the client, even causing them to be placed in a non-volatile message store if the messages are persistent and the subscriber durable.

Point-to-Point Programming

In the point-to-point model (PTP), each session object **sends** and/or **receives** through one or more **queues**. The first message received by the broker is the first message delivered to a consumer. Consumers can either receive the message that is first in line, thus removing it from the queue, or browse through all the messages in the queue, causing no changes.

In the figure below, the PTP session employs **sender** objects that send messages to queues maintained by the JMS provider, and **receivers** that receive messages sent through specific queues:

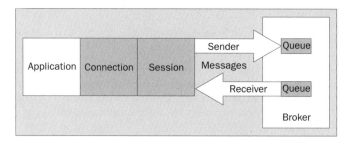

The FIFO nature of the PTP model requires that the JMS provider retains the second through nth messages until the first message is consumed. Even when there are no clients associated with a queue, messages are retained. Hence, unlike the pub/sub semantics, durability and persistence are implicit in PTP. There is only one message consumer for a given message.

Many of the concepts we saw with the pub/sub model remain applicable with the point-to-point model, and we will be using similarly-named classes: QueueConnection instead of TopicConnection, QueueSession in place of TopicSession, QueueSender rather than TopicPublisher, and QueueReceiver instead of TopicSubscriber.

Sending Messages

The act of sending a message in the PTP model is accomplished in a very similar fashion to publishing messages in the pub/sub model, even though the actual semantics of sending and receiving are strikingly dissimilar. To send a message to a queue, the client application first creates a queue, and then creates a queue sender:

```
javax.jms.Queue sendQueue = session.createQueue(sQueue);
javax.jms.QueueSender qSender = session.createSender(sendQueue);
```

Receiving Messages

To receive messages sent to a queue, the client application first creates a queue object, and then establishes a QueueReceiver:

```
javax.jms.Queue receiveQueue = session.createQueue ( rQueue);
javax.jms.QueueReceiver qReceiver = session.createReceiver( receiveQueue);
```

Once a client application has established a receiver for a particular queue, it can receive messages either synchronously or asynchronously. As in the pub/sub model, the client application establishes a message listener in order to obtain messages asynchronously:

```
qReceiver.setMessageListener(myListener);
```

The QueueReceiver object also uses a set of receive() methods for synchronous message receipt analogous to those provided by the subscriber objects found in the pub/sub model:

```
Message receive()
Message receive(long timeOut)
Message receiveNoWait()
```

These methods exhibit the same behavior as their counterparts in the pub/sub model.

Queue Browsing

JMS specifies a **queue browser** mechanism. A queue browser allows authorized clients to examine queues, counting messages for example, without destroying the examined messages. The `QueueBrowser` object is created with a session method:

```
session.createBrowser(Queue queue)
```

A message selector can be added to qualify the messages that are browsed. The syntax for message selectors was discussed earlier when we looked at message selection in the pub/sub model.

```
session.createBrowser(QueueSession session, Queue queue,
                      String messageSelector)
```

To browse the messages currently on the queue, in the sequence that they would be retrieved, the client application obtains an `Enumeration` by calling the queue browser's `getEnumeration()` method. Once the client application is through browsing the queue, resources associated with the browser can be dispensed with by calling `close()`.

Queue Browser Code Sample

The following code excerpt uses a queue browser to display the current contents of a queue:

```
// Create a browser and show the messages waiting on the queue q
System.out.println("Browsing queue \"" + q.getQueueName() + "\"...");
javax.jms.QueueBrowser browser = session.createBrowser(q);

// Get the enumeration
int cnt = 0;
Enumeration e = browser.getEnumeration();

if(!e.hasMoreElements()) {
  System.out.println("No messages in queue");
} else {
  // Walk the queue
  while (e.hasMoreElements()) {
    System.out.print("Message " + String.valueOf(++cnt) + "...");
    javax.jms.Message message = (javax.jms.Message) e.nextElement();
    System.out.println("[" + message + "]");
  }
}
```

Messages

The message is the core object of JMS. In addition to carrying the information payload, the message itself plays a key role in influencing routing, reliability, and other aspects of message delivery. As in virtually all other messaging systems, a JMS message is a package of bytes that encapsulates the message body as a payload and then exposes metadata that identifies, at a minimum, the message, its timestamp, its priority, its destination, and the type of message enclosed.

Message Format

All JMS messages contain all of the following three sections:

❑ **Header Fields**
All messages support the same set of header fields. Header fields contain values used by both client applications and JMS providers to identify and route messages.

❑ **Properties**
Contains JMS-specified and user-defined name-value pairs that can be used for message filtering/routing, and for application requirements. These are the properties which are used by the message selector mechanism available to message consumers. The JMS specification does not require the use of any message properties, even those defined by the specification. Property names must obey the rules for a message selector identifier, and are set before sending a message.

❑ **Body**
The body section contains the application-specific portion of the message. JMS defines several types of message bodies that correspond with the JMS-supported message types.

Message Types

The JMS specification defines five types of messages, all derived from the `Message` interface, which also defines message headers and the `acknowledge()` method used by all JMS messages:

❑ `BytesMessage` – A stream of uninterpreted bytes

❑ `MapMessage` – A set of name-value pairs where the names are strings and the values are Java primitive types. The entries can be accessed sequentially or by name

❑ `TextMessage` – A message containing a `java.util.StringBuffer`

❑ `StreamMessage` – A stream of Java primitive types, filled and read sequentially

❑ `ObjectMessage` – A message that contains a serializable Java object

Creating a Message

We've already witnessed simple cases of creating a messages in previous sections of this chapter, but let's look at it in a little more detail. A message is created from a session method, based on the desired message type:

```
javax.jms.Message          createMessage()
javax.jms.BytesMessage     createBytesMessage()
javax.jms.MapMessage       createMapMessage()
javax.jms.TextMessage      createTextMessage()
javax.jms.StreamMessage    createStreamMessage()
javax.jms.ObjectMessage    createObjectMessage()
```

Header Fields

The message header fields are defined and used by the sender and the broker to convey basic routing and delivery information. When using the simplest form of message creation (for example, a simple call to `publisher.publish(Message message)` in the pub/sub model), the JMS provider will insert default values into the three header fields essential for message delivery:

```
DEFAULT_DELIVERY_MODE = NON_PERSISTENT
DEFAULT_PRIORITY = 0
DEFAULT_TIME_TO_LIVE = 0
```

The default header field values can be overridden within the signature of the `publish()` or `send()` method. For example, in the pub/sub model:

```
publisher.publish(Message message,
                  int deliveryMode,
                  int priority,
                  long timeToLive)
```

or in the point-to-point model:

```
sender.send(Message message,
            int deliveryMode,
            int priority,
            long timeToLive)
```

Setting Message Properties

Properties are optional fields contained in a message, but distinct from the header and body. The property values are used by the message selection mechanism, as well as to carry any data required by applications or other messaging infrastructures. Property names must obey the rules for message selector identifiers. Property values can be `boolean`, `byte`, `short`, `int`, `long`, `float`, `double`, `String`, or `Object`. Property values are set prior to sending a message. When a client receives a message, its properties are in read-only mode. The JMS specification reserves the `JMSX` property name prefix for JMS defined properties. Support for these properties is optional – not all JMS providers implement their use.

The `Message` interface provides a number of methods for manipulating and examining properties. To iterate through a message's property values, the client application calls `getPropertyNames()` to retrieve a property name enumeration, and then uses the various property getter methods to retrieve their respective values:

```
public [type] get[type]Property(String name)
```

where `[type]` is one of `boolean`, `byte`, `short`, `int`, `long`, `float`, `double`, `Object`, or `String`. For example:

```
public boolean getBooleanProperty("reconciled");
```

1339

The getObjectProperty() method returns, in object format, an object that had been stored as a property in the message with the equivalent setObject() method call or its equivalent primitive set method. getStringProperty() and getObjectProperty() return null when attempting to access a non-existent property; other property get methods throw a NullPointerException when attempting to get a nonexistent property.

To set property values, the client application calls the various property set methods:

```
set[type]Property(String name, [type] value)
```

where [type] is again one of boolean, byte, short, int, long, float, double, Object, or String. For example:

```
setBooleanProperty("reconciled", true);
```

A message's properties are deleted by the clearProperties() method. This leaves the message with an empty set of properties:

```
public void clearProperties()
```

To check if a property value exists we can use propertyExists():

```
public boolean propertyExists(String name)
```

where name is the name of the property to test. This will return true if the property exists.

Setting the Message Body

Client applications use the setXXX() methods specified by JMS for all message types unless the message is read-only (in which case you'll need to copy or reset the received message). For example, for a TextMessage we use the setText() method.

JMS Programming Techniques and Issues

Now that we've learned how to produce and consume messages using the JMS programming model, as well as taken a look at the components of a message, we're ready to explore some additional JMS programming techniques, and some important JMS issues you need to be aware of.

Transactions

JMS provides a simple transaction mechanism, allowing a group of messages to act as a single unit of work. Among other uses, this is particularly handy for transmission of large XML documents as JMS messages, with the client application marshalling a large document through JMS as a transacted message set. Transactional behavior is controlled at the session level, and is optionally enabled when the session is created. When a session is transacted, message traffic is staged within the JMS provider until the client application either commits or rolls back the transaction. The completion of a session's current transaction automatically begins a new transaction.

The client application determines when the transaction is complete, and either commits or rolls back the transaction:

❏ The session `commit()` method tells the messaging system to sequentially release each of the messages that have been staged since the logical transaction began

❏ The `rollback()` method tells the broker to flush all the messages that have been staged since the logical transaction began

The use of transactions affects producers and consumers of messages in the following manner:

❏ **Producer**
On commit, the broker sends the set of staged messages
On rollback, the broker disposes the set of staged messages

❏ **Consumer**
On commit, the broker disposes the set of staged messages
On rollback, the broker resends the set of staged messages

When a rollback is performed in a session that is both a producer and a consumer, its produced messages are destroyed, and its consumed messages are resent.

Programmatic Message Acknowledgement

The JMS message acknowledgement mechanism is the fundamental wiring that supports several important messaging system semantics, such as guaranteed delivery and transaction management. Acknowledgement is the means by which the messaging system is informed that a particular client has consumed a specific message.

Earlier, when discussing sessions, we saw that JMS supports a number of different acknowledgement modes. One of the modes we discussed was `CLIENT_ACKNOWLEDGE`, wherein the client application explicitly must indicate that it has received a message successfully. The client application invokes the message `acknowledge()` method to make this indication. Invoking this method acknowledges receipt of the current message, as well as all previous messages received by the session. Client applications may individually acknowledge messages or they may choose to acknowledge messages in application-defined groups, by acknowledging the last received message in the group.

JMS specifies that the default acknowledgement mode for a session is implicit message acknowledgement, in which case calls to `acknowledge()` are ignored by the messaging system.

Message Routing

Most JMS implementations provide two primary mechanisms for intelligently routing message traffic between client applications: hierarchical topics, and message selection. Distributed applications typically employ a mix of these two mechanisms.

Routing via Hierarchical Topics

Many JMS implementations allow topics to be defined in a hierarchical fashion, so that topics can be nested under other topics. Issues such as the syntax for specifying hierarchical topic names – as well as the semantics of wildcarding – are largely unspecified within the JMS spec. When using implementations that support hierarchical topic namespaces, client applications can subscribe to the appropriate topic level to receive the most relevant information for the application or user. This technique provides a more granular approach to topic subscriptions, which can substantially reduce the amount of coding needed to filter unwanted messages, while supporting highly flexible subject-based routing.

Let's take the example of an online trading community to illustrate how hierarchical topics could be used. In such a community each buyer might send out bid requests by publishing messages to a topic named `bid_request`, using the pub/sub model. We use the pub/sub model as each buyer wants to inform any and all interested sellers of the bid request. In a large community that serves many buyers and sellers in a variety of product categories, we may want to break the `bid_request` topic into several subtopics, with one subtopic for each product category. These subtopics could further be divided into more granular categories. For example, a given topic hierarchy might be:

```
bid_request
bid_request.vehicles
bid_request.vehicles.cars
bid_request.vehicles.bicycles
bid_request.vehicles.motorcycles
bid_request.realestate
bid_request.realestate.rentals
bid_request.realestate.rentals.condos
bid_request.realestate.rentals.apartments
bid_request.realestate.rentals.houses
```

Each supplier could then subscribe to the topic, or set of topics, that it was interested in. For example, a supplier could subscribe to `bid_request.vehicles.*` if it was interested in bid requests for all kinds of vehicles.

> **The JMS specification does not provide a syntax for specifying hierarchical topic names, nor does it specify how hierarchical topics should behave. That said, hierarchical topics are an increasingly common feature in JMS implementations, and typically behave as described above. Be sure to check the documentation for a particular JMS implementation to see how and if it supports hierarchical topics.**

Routing via Message Selection

We discussed message selection in JMS earlier. Using this mechanism, consumers in both the pub/sub and point-to-point models can limit the specific messages that the client application will receive by qualifying their topic subscriptions or queue receivers with message selectors. As you'll recall, a selector tells the JMS provider to evaluate message properties according to the rules expressed in the selector, prior to sending messages to the client application.

In the trading community example above, each seller could request that the messaging system send it only bid requests that adhere to specified criteria. For example, a seller could subscribe to the `bid_request.vehicles.bicycles` topic, but indicate that it only wants to receive bid requests for mountain bikes. The seller could also opt to receive bid requests only when the buyer doesn't require overnight shipment. These filters would be created using the message selector mechanism discussed earlier:

```
"Property_MerchType = 'Mountain Bike' AND Property_ReqOvernight is NULL
```

Selecting a Routing Approach

Generally, hierarchical topics are used for routing situations that are relatively static, while message selection is used for *ad hoc* or programmatic routing. Hierarchical topics require that the topic namespace schema be both well defined and universally understood. Message selectors are more flexible, and can provide significantly more advanced routing criteria, but also incur additional processing overhead as each message must be examined and the filtering rules applied. Both approaches require that the client application knows how it should filter messages at the time that it creates a consumer, and both can be used together as demonstrated in the above example.

Messaging Reliability

There are several factors that affect the assurance that a consumer will receive a produced message. The specific factors vary for the two primary JMS messaging models; the key factors to contemplate when considering messaging system reliability are:

❑ **Publish/Subscribe:**
A publisher has no guarantee that any subscribers exist for a particular topic.

Subscriber message selectors inherently limit the number of messages that a client will receive. Regular subscriptions and durable subscriptions with a message selector definition that excludes a message will cause the consumer never to get that message.

Message destruction can occur due to expiry of the timeout set for the message, or due to an administrator action that permanently disposes of stored messages.

❑ **Point-to-Point:**
Since multiple receivers can share the queue message load, reliability can only be assured by the set of active receivers on a queue at any point in time.

Receiver message selectors inherently limit the number of messages that a client will receive. A queue would appear empty to any receiver that effectively deselects all the existing messages in the queue. At the same time, messages can stay on a queue until a receiver either provides a liberal message selector or no message selector at all.

Message destruction can occur due to expiry of the message, or due to an administrator action that permanently disposes of stored messages.

Using JMS to Transport XML

JMS was not designed specifically for carrying XML payloads, but in practice it provides an excellent means for transporting XML due to its support for the high-level semantics required. Already, JMS vendors have begun to provide XML handling as part of their product offerings, and solution providers are layering a wide range of XML applications – from EAI to B2B supply chain integrations – on top of JMS messaging infrastructures.

In this section we will examine some techniques for transporting XML using JMS. As of version 1.02, JMS does not yet contain a specific message type for XML data. Since we can't assume that the application developer will be using such an implementation, we will make do with the standard message types specified by JMS. In practice, the body of a `TextMessage` makes an appropriate vessel for transporting XML, so that's what we will use. We will use JAXP to manipulate our XML messages. We assume that you are familiar with XML in general and Java-based XML programming concepts, such as using parsers and working with DOMs.

For background on these subjects, please refer to Chapters 5 and 6.

Creating XML Messages

The process of creating and sending an XML message is quite straightforward: we simply construct the XML payload within a text buffer, and then encode into a text stream for placement in a normal `TextMessage` body. Once the payload has been constructed, the message is sent via the normal JMS connection/session/producer model:

```
StringBuffer body = new StringBuffer();
body.append ("<?xml version=\"1.0\"?>\n");
body.append ("<message>\n");
body.append ("  <sender>" + username + "</sender>\n");
body.append ("  <content>" + s + "</content>\n");
body.append ("</message>\n");
msg.setText(body.toString());
publisher.publish(msg);
```

Consuming XML Messages

Consuming XML messages is equally straightforward. Upon message receipt, the client application has three options for processing the XML message:

❑   Work with the XML payload as a text stream

❑   Work with the XML payload through the DOM

❑   Use SAX to process the XML in an event-based manner

In the following example, we will receive a message through a `MessageListener`, and then extract an element from the DOM representing the XML payload:

```
public void onMessage(javax.jms.Message aMessage) {
  try {

    // Cast the message as a text message.
    javax.jms.TextMessage textMessage = (javax.jms.TextMessage) aMessage;

    // This handler reads a single String from the
    // message and prints it to the standard output.
    try {

      // Create a stream from the message body
      // (we need a stream to hand to the parser)
      String string = textMessage.getText();
      StringReader reader = new StringReader(string);

      // Using JAXP, create a DOM from the text message payload
      try {

        // Get a JAXP document builder
        DocumentBuilderFactory dbf = DocumentBuilderFactory.newInstance();
        DocumentBuilder db = dbf.newDocumentBuilder();

        // Create a SAX InputSource for the stream
```

```
            InputSource source = new InputSource(reader);

            // Parse the XML and generate a DOM
            Document doc = db.parse(source);

            // Get the sender and content from the DOM
            org.w3c.dom.NodeList nodes = null;
            nodes = doc.getElementsByTagName("itemname");
            String itemname = (nodes.getLength() > 0)
                            ? nodes.item(0).getFirstChild().getNodeValue()
                            : null;
        } catch (Throwable te) {
            te.printStackTrace(System.err);
        }
    } catch (javax.jms.JMSException jmse) {
        jmse.printStackTrace();
    }
} catch (java.lang.RuntimeException rte) {
    rte.printStackTrace();
}
}
```

Performing XML-based Routing

Earlier, we discussed how routing of messages within a JMS messaging system could be achieved by using message selectors in conjunction with message properties. An XML application can utilize this mechanism to provide content-based routing within the messaging system. JMS does not yet have a way for the messaging system to route messages based upon the payload of the message, which would be required for XML content-based routing without application intervention.

Instead, the client application must programmatically search the XML message content for the desired data, and place it within the message properties. Once the relevant data has been copied to the message properties, subscribers can use the property values in message selectors, resulting in content-based routing.

The sample application documented at the end of this chapter contains a fully-functional application that uses JAXP and JMS to send and receive XML messages.

Request-Reply Programming

JMS provides a request-reply mechanism, allowing client applications to request that actions be carried out on their behalf by other applications. Request-reply can be thought of as an RMI-type mechanism where the interface is abstracted into a data message. Replies in the request-reply model are distinctly different from message acknowledgements:

❑ Replies are sent as full JMS messages in response to incoming messages, typically following some processing in the 'called' client

❑ Acknowledgements are a lower-level indication to the messaging system that a message has been received by a consumer

Messages that use the JMSreplyTo field are called **requests**. Such messages typically expect that the consumer will perform some appropriate action based upon receipt of the message, and then provide a mutually understood message – or **reply** – in response. The JMSreplyTo message header field contains the temporary destination where a reply to the current message should be sent. If the JMSreplyTo value is null, no reply is expected. Message replies often use the JMSCorrelationID to ensure that replies match their requests. A JMSCorrelationID would typically contain the JMSMessageID of the request message.

The destination can be either a queue or a topic, and could be structured into a requestor helper class, as shown in the following table:

Reply-To Mechanism	Destination	Helper class
Publish and Subscribe	TemporaryTopic	TopicRequestor
Point-to-Point	TemporaryQueue	QueueRequestor

Temporary Destinations Managed by a Requestor Helper Class

In the pub/sub model, the TopicRequestor uses the session and topic that were instantiated from the session methods. Notice that the code below never actually manipulates the TemporaryTopic object; instead it uses the helper class TopicRequestor:

```
javax.jms.TopicRequestor requestor =
   new javax.jms.TopicRequestor(session, topic);
javax.jms.Message response = requestor.request(msg);
javax.jms.TextMessage textMessage = (javax.jms.TextMessage) response;
```

Replier Application

Synchronous requests leave the originator of a request waiting for a reply. To prevent a requestor from waiting, a well-designed application uses the following flow technique.

First, get the message:

```
public void onMessage( javax.jms.Message aMessage) {
   javax.jms.TextMessage textMessage = (javax.jms.TextMessage) aMessage;
   String string = textMessage.getText();
```

Then, look for to see if the header specifies JMSReplyTo:

```
javax.jms.Topic replyTopic = (javax.jms.Topic) aMessage.getJMSReplyTo();
if (replyTopic != null) {
   // ...
```

If it does, send a reply to the topic specified in JMSReplyTo:

```
javax.jms.TextMessage reply = session.createTextMessage();
   // ...
}
```

Design for Handling Requests

The final steps taken by the message handler represent good programming style, but are not required by the JMS requests-reply mechanism:

```
// Set the JMSCorrelationID, tying the response back to the
// original request
reply.setJMSCorrelationID(aMessage.getJMSMessageID());

replier.publish(replyTopic, reply);

// Use transacted session commit so that the request will not be
// received without the reply being sent.
session.commit();
```

Writing a Topic Requestor

The default JMS `TopicRequestor` implementation blocks when waiting for a reply. You can write your own `TopicRequestor` class that will timeout (using `receive(long timeOut)`) or listen to the temporary topic as a `Subscriber`, thereby avoiding the blocking situation. The `javax.jms.TopicRequestor` class provides a good foundation for creating your own `TopicRequestor` class.

Using Queues to Load Balance Between Servers

An interesting use of queues is that of automatic load balancing. In some JMS implementations, multiple prospective receivers can attach to a queue, but only one takes delivery of each message. When each message is acknowledged as delivered, the broker disposes of it. No other client sees it and no other client can receive it. This behavior can provide the basis for simplistic load balancing at the application level. To do so, we would create multiple instances of the receiving application, each running on its own server:

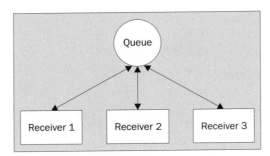

Whenever the broker receives a message on the queue, it will deliver it to the first receiver that is ready to receive a message. Servers that are busy processing other requests will not be ready to receive, and the queue therefore automatically balances the load between the multiple servers.

JMS Implementations

Programmers may elect to build their own Java messaging middleware from the JMS specification or to obtain this functionality from a third party. JMS implementations can be broadly classified as follows:

❑   Commercial offerings

❑　Full Java implementations

❑　Hybrid Java/C++ implementations

❑　JMS wrappers around existing messaging systems (such as IBM MQSeries)

❑　Open source implementations

There is also a reference implementation available from JavaSoft, although it is generally considered to be unsuitable for serious development.

JMS implementations are provided either as standalone messaging servers or as JMS services embedded within other environments such as an application server. A standalone server provides some advantages over an embedded messaging service by allowing the developer to:

❑　Place broker(s) where needed to optimize network topology, control traffic loads, provide fail-safe operation and/or leverage existing hardware

❑　Embed the messaging system within an application or platform

On the other hand, having the messaging service built into another environment offers the convenience of a single – if less flexible – solution, especially for organizations that have standardized on an application server and know their needs will not change. In addition to this, future versions of J2EE will merge messaging functionality with EJB invocation, requiring that application servers embed JMS functionality. Also, while many JMS implementations use the broker model referred to in this chapter, a few are implemented as peer-to-peer solutions that do not rely upon a broker.

While discussing JMS implementations, it should also be mentioned that the JMS specification leaves a number of significant features and issues to the JMS implementer to resolve. Since these aspects of the messaging system are unspecified their availability, and implementation details, will vary from implementation to implementation:

❑　Topic naming

❑　Hierarchical topic support

❑　Wire protocols

❑　Broker clustering

❑　Administration Tools

For an up-to-date list of commercial and open source JMS implementations, refer to `http://www.javasoft.com/products/jms/vendors.html`.

A Sample Application

Now let's look at a complete JMS messaging application. This is a simple command-line chat type application that:

❑　Uses the publish and subscribe model to send and receive messages

❑　Employs asynchronous messaging

- ❏ Encodes messages in XML
- ❏ Demonstrates using JAXP to create a DOM tree from the message payload
- ❏ Extracts elements from the DOM and displays them

Code Overview

The JMSChat application does not use any vendor-specific extensions to JMS, and should run on any JMS 1.0.2-compliant JMS messaging system.

Initialization

First, we obtain command line parameters that specify:

- ❏ The broker to use
- ❏ The username (used to identify chat participants and to connect to the broker)
- ❏ The user's password

```
import java.io.*;
import javax.xml.parsers.DocumentBuilderFactory;
import javax.xml.parsers.DocumentBuilder;
import javax.xml.parsers.ParserConfigurationException;
import org.w3c.dom.*;
import org.xml.sax.InputSource;

public class JMSChat implements javax.jms.MessageListener {

    private static final String APP_TOPIC = "JMSChat";
    private static final String DEFAULT_BROKER_NAME = "localhost:2506";
    private static final String DEFAULT_PASSWORD = "password";

    private javax.jms.TopicConnection connect = null;
    private javax.jms.TopicSession session = null;
    private javax.jms.TopicPublisher publisher = null;

    public static void main(String argv[]) {
      // Is there anything to do?
      if (argv.length == 0) {
        // Output usage information
        StringBuffer use = new StringBuffer();
        use.append("usage: java JMSChat (options) ...\n\n");
        use.append("options:\n");
        use.append("  -b name:port Specify name:port of broker.\n");
        use.append("                Default broker: " + DEFAULT_BROKER_NAME
                + "\n");
        use.append("  -u name      Specify unique user name. (Required)\n");
        use.append("  -p password  Specify password for user.\n");
        use.append("                Default password: " + DEFAULT_PASSWORD
                + "\n");
        use.append("  -h           This help screen.\n");
```

```java
      System.err.println(use);
      System.exit(1);
    }

    // Values to be read from parameters
    String broker = DEFAULT_BROKER_NAME;
    String username = null;
    String password = DEFAULT_PASSWORD;

    // Parse parameters
    for (int i = 0; i < argv.length; i++) {
      String arg = argv[i];
      if (arg.equals("-b")) {
        if (i == argv.length - 1 || argv[i + 1].startsWith("-")) {
          System.err.println("error: missing broker name:port");
          System.exit(1);
        }
        broker = argv[++i];
        continue;
      }
      if (arg.equals("-u")) {
        if (i == argv.length - 1 || argv[i + 1].startsWith("-")) {
          System.err.println("error: missing user name");
          System.exit(1);
        }
        username = argv[++i];
        continue;
      }
      if (arg.equals("-p")) {
        if (i == argv.length - 1 || argv[i + 1].startsWith("-")) {
          System.err.println("error: missing password");
          System.exit(1);
        }
        password = argv[++i];
        continue;
      }
    }
    // We must have a username
    if (username == null) {
      System.err.println("error: username must be supplied");
      System.exit(1);
    }

    // Start the JMS client
    JMSChat chat = new JMSChat();
    chat.pubandsub(broker, username, password);
  }

  // ...
}
```

Once we have obtained these, we create a connection to the broker, and a session to use for publishing and subscribing. We do this in the pubandsub() method:

```
      private void pubandsub(String broker, String username, String password) {

        // Create a connection
        try {
          javax.jms.TopicConnectionFactory factory;
          factory =
            (new progress.message.jclient.TopicConnectionFactory(broker));
          connect = factory.createTopicConnection(username, password);
          session =
            connect.createTopicSession(false,
                                       javax.jms.Session.AUTO_ACKNOWLEDGE);
        } catch (javax.jms.JMSException jmse) {
          System.err.println("error: Cannot connect to broker - " + broker);
          jmse.printStackTrace();
          System.exit(1);
        }
        // ...
```

We specified AUTO_ACKNOWLEDGE as the acknowledgement mode, meaning that the JMS provider will respond automatically any time our sample application obtains a message. We also specify that the session should not be transacted – messages will be sent to all subscribed clients as soon as they are received from our sample application. We catch the exception that will be thrown if we can't connect to the specified broker.

Next, we create a topic, based upon a hard-coded topic name, and then create a publisher and a subscriber for the topic:

```
      // Create Publisher and Subscriber to 'JMSChat' topic
      try {
        javax.jms.Topic topic = session.createTopic(APP_TOPIC);
        javax.jms.TopicSubscriber subscriber =
          session.createSubscriber(topic);
        subscriber.setMessageListener(this);
        publisher = session.createPublisher(topic);

        // Now that setup is complete, start the Connection
        connect.start();
      } catch (javax.jms.JMSException jmse) {
        jmse.printStackTrace();
      }
      // ...
```

After we created the subscriber, we used setMessageListener() to indicate that we want to receive messages asynchronously and that the listener object should be set to ourselves. Note that you must start the connection before JMS will send or receive messages on that connection.

Input Loop

We then go into a loop, waiting for messages to be entered by the user. We can go into this loop because we know that our message handler (described in a moment) will be invoked by the JMS provider whenever a message is received for our sample application.

Whenever the user enters a message, it is encoded along with the username into an XML document that is then sent through the publisher as a text message:

```
try {
   // Read standard input and send it as an XML message
   java.io
      .BufferedReader stdin =
         new java.io
            .BufferedReader(new java.io.InputStreamReader(System.in));
   System.out.println("\nEnter text messages. Press Enter to publish "
                      + "each message.\n");
   System.out.println("    (type EXIT to terminate application)\n");
   while (true) {
      String s = stdin.readLine();
      if (s == null) {
         exit();
      } else if (s.equalsIgnoreCase("EXIT")) {
         System.out.println("\nStopping client.\n>");
         exit();
      } else if (s.length() > 0) {
         // Create a text message to contain the XML
         javax.jms.TextMessage msg = session.createTextMessage();

         // Build an XML message from the username and message text
         StringBuffer body = new StringBuffer();
         body.append("<?xml version=\"1.0\"?>\n");
         body.append("<message>\n");
         body.append("  <sender>" + username + "</sender>\n");
         body.append("  <content>" + s + "</content>\n");
         body.append("</message>\n");

         // Place the XML in the body of the message
         msg.setText(body.toString());

         // Publish message to topic
         publisher.publish(msg);
      }
   }
} catch (java.io.IOException ioe) {
   ioe.printStackTrace();
} catch (javax.jms.JMSException jmse) {
   jmse.printStackTrace();
}
}
```

In this case, we rely upon all the default values in the message header. If the user enters *EXIT* as the message text, we close the connection and exit the program using the exit() method:

```
private void exit() {
   try {
      // Close the connection to the broker
      connect.close();
   } catch (javax.jms.JMSException jmse) {
      jmse.printStackTrace();
   }

   System.exit(0);
}
```

Message Handler

The onMessage() method will be invoked by the JMS provider whenever a message is produced for the topic to which we are subscribed. In our message handler, we use JAXP to parse the XML message and produce a DOM tree. We then extract the username and the message typed by the user from the tree, and output them:

```java
// Handle an incoming message
// (as specified in the javax.jms.MessageListener interface).
//
public void onMessage(javax.jms.Message aMessage) {
  try {

    // Cast the message as a text message.
    javax.jms.TextMessage textMessage = (javax.jms.TextMessage) aMessage;

    // This handler reads a single String from the
    // message and the parses it into a DOM.
    try {
      // Create a stream from the message body
      // (we need a stream to hand to the parser)
      String string = textMessage.getText();
      StringReader reader = new StringReader(string);

      // Using JAXP, create a DOM from the text message payload
      try {
        // Get a JAXP document builder
        DocumentBuilderFactory dbf = DocumentBuilderFactory.newInstance();
        DocumentBuilder db = dbf.newDocumentBuilder();

        // Create a SAX InputSource for the stream
        // (the JAXP document builder knows how to use InputSource)
        InputSource source = new InputSource(reader);

        // Parse the XML and generate a DOM
        Document doc = db.parse(source);

        // Get the sender and content from the DOM
        org.w3c.dom.NodeList nodes = null;
        nodes = doc.getElementsByTagName("sender");
        String sender = (nodes.getLength() > 0)
                        ? nodes.item(0).getFirstChild().getNodeValue()
                        : "unknown";
        nodes = doc.getElementsByTagName("content");
        String content = (nodes.getLength() > 0)
                        ? nodes.item(0).getFirstChild().getNodeValue()
                        : null;

        // Show the message
        System.out.println("[XML content from '" + sender + "'] "
                          + content);
      } catch (Throwable te) {
        te.printStackTrace(System.err);
      }
    } catch (javax.jms.JMSException jmse) {
```

```
        jmse.printStackTrace();
    }
} catch (java.lang.RuntimeException rte) {
    rte.printStackTrace();
}
}
```

Running the Application

The sample application should run with any JMS 1.0.2-compliant JMS implementation. It was developed and tested with Progress SonicMQ, but it does not employ SonicMQ's XML message type. You can download a free developer copy of SonicMQ from the Progress web site at http://www.sonicmq.com/. You need SonicMQ's client.jar in the CLASSPATH to compile JMSChat. In addition to a JMS implementation, you will need to download and install the JAXP package from JavaSoft, available at http://java.sun.com/xml/.

With SonicMQ running, start up a number of command prompts and start the JMSChat application in each, using the syntax:

```
java SampleApp -b <broker:port> -u <username> -p <password>
```

If SonicMQ is running on the same machine, and at the default port, you only need the -u option.

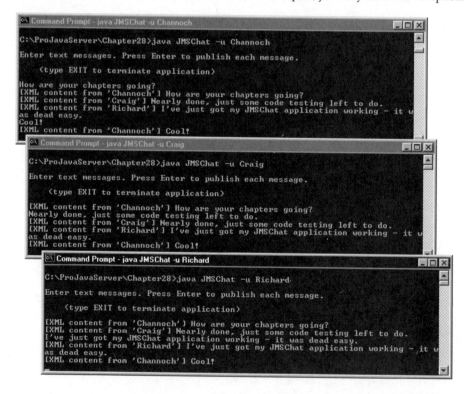

Message-Based Integration with JMS

One of the important uses of JMS lies with application integration: the notion of causing two applications to work in concert in order to carry out some new form of transaction. Today, more and more demands are being made to integrate applications, due to business drivers such as business-to-business commerce, deeper customer relationship management initiatives, and the streamlining of internal business processes. Application integration refers not only to coordinating transactions among a few points within an organization, but also to extending these transactions to external organizations to support a new breed of Internet-based applications, such as supply chain integration and automated trading communities.

Dynamic and extensible technologies such as the Java Message Service (JMS) and XML are now supplanting the relatively brittle and arcane client/server technologies that had until recently dominated the integration landscape, marking a healthy trend toward open, flexible infrastructures as well as promoting reusable integration strategies that can be applied to a wide variety of integration projects.

JMS and XML as an Integration Platform

Integration work can be broadly classified into two different approaches:

- **Data integration**
  Data integration bypasses application logic in order to directly manipulate data held within enterprise databases. This approach is typically employed for the speed and relative simplicity of its implementation.

  The simplest form is where data is extracted from multiple sources and combined to produce an aggregate data set. Data integration can however extend to manipulating and moving enterprise data housed in multiple stores. Database-oriented tools allow the integrator to extract, transform, and insert data as needed, to implement a new transaction between systems, performed automatically and in real time. Not all systems can be bridged in this manner, however, and there are clearly limitations on the scope and complexity of transactions that can be performed without business logic awareness.

- **Procedural or process integration**
  Procedural integration, on the other hand, effectively inserts new business logic between applications to coordinate and invoke existing functions programmatically.

  The primary disadvantage of procedural integration is that it is almost always an invasive approach. The applications to be integrated either need to be modified or 'wrapped' in such a way that the integration can access their business logic.

In practice, many integration projects contain a mix of both data and procedural integration. Traditional application integration uses proprietary integration products, which are rather complex and a study unto themselves. At their core, integration products frequently employ something of a messaging infrastructure, along with data transformation and migration tools. JMS and XML provide an open, standards-based toolkit for facilitating integration.

If we agree that messaging simplifies application integration and, further, that interfaces are best described as data, the question remains how should we encode these interfaces or, in other words, what should the message format be? In the Java world, passing serialized objects through JMS would at first glance seem a good idea. However, upon closer examination, passing objects has two severe shortcomings:

❏ First, the interface once again becomes quite rigid. To correctly interpret and respond to a message, the consuming application must have semantic knowledge of the payload that the object itself simply can't impart.

❏ Second, in the case of application integration between enterprises – say, across the Internet – passing objects requires that all parties be Java-based.

In fact, XML proves to be an optimal format for describing the interfaces within and between applications. The key to XML's success in this regard is the ability for an XML document or message to provide its own *semantic context*.

Often it is necessary not only to parse an XML message and perform some task based upon its contents, but also to transform a message, or a series of messages, into a different XML structure. Although XML messages are inherently self-describing, a particular application or system may require that the XML documents it receives be held in a vocabulary represented by a specific DTD, while another application might require a different vocabulary. This is especially likely to occur when performing integrations between multiple parties in a business-to-business supply chain or trading community. Fortunately, such transformations are easily performed on XML data using XSLT, or by manipulating a DOM tree.

Architectural Patterns for Integration

Jeffrey C. Lutz of BoldTech Systems has developed some **architectural patterns** for integration, in an attempt to provide a solid foundation for application integration work. They effectively incorporate the work of many in the field into a codified format that supports efficient design and clear communication, and they are in many ways analogous to the popular analysis and design patterns that assist the design and development of software in general. They offer a way to begin a discussion of application integration that runs deeper than the generalities and vagaries that are often employed, and will supply you with a solid grounding for your integration projects using JMS and XML. We highly recommend applying this conceptual toolkit when designing new integration scenarios.

A primary goal of application integration – and hence its architecture – is to promote decoupling in order to minimize dependencies between applications, or functions of applications. The patterns presented have been developed with this in mind, and offer alternative efficiencies:

Pattern	Description	Minimizes...
Integration Adapter	Converts existing interfaces into new interfaces	Dependencies on rigid legacy interfaces
Integration Messenger	Abstracts interactions between applications by using messaging communication models	Communication dependencies between applications
Integration Façade	Simplifies interfaces into legacy applications	Dependencies between client and server tiers
Integration Mediator	Encapsulates and choreographs application interactions	Application logic dependencies
Process Automator	Complex integration involving abstraction and sequencing of human and system activities	Dependencies between process automation logic and applications

Many of these patterns offer (variations or specialties) of the base pattern. Our look at patterns will primarily focus on those patterns and variations that leverage messaging. Not coincidentally, this is the majority of integration architecture patterns.

❑ **Integration Adapter**
This pattern is applied when providing legacy application services to other applications or systems. It converts custom interfaces into open interfaces that can be easily used by multiple applications, by invoking the adapter interface. The implementation of this pattern may or may not be intrusive to the legacy application. If the legacy system provides some form of API for the service, the implementation can avoid being intrusive.

One variation on this is the Message Broker Adapter. In this pattern, the message broker intelligently brokers the flow of messages between applications, offering a messaging interface into the back-end legacy system's interface. The Message Broker Adapter is typically referred to as an 'adapter' or 'connector'. When using JMS, we can easily create these connectors ourselves. Typically, such an adapter would use the JMS request-reply mechanism in the new messaging interface to the legacy service:

❑ **Integration Messenger**
The Integration Messenger pattern leverages the range of communication models typically available in messaging infrastructures to abstract the interactions between participants in the pattern: 'publish and subscribe' with a single service and multiple subscriber applications, 'point to point' with a single service and a calling application which doesn't block while the request is performed, and 'request-reply' where the single calling application does block during the request.

This pattern minimizes communication dependencies by employing a messaging system to carry out the delivery of messages, while abstracting the communication transport(s) used to marshal the messages and providing location transparency for the participants.

❑ **Integration Façade**
Whereas the Integration Messenger pattern abstracts access to legacy services, the Integration Façade pattern concerns itself with simplifying legacy interfaces through the creation of new, simpler interfaces that hide unnecessary complexity from calling applications. The Integration Façade may be used to provide such an interface for multiple calling applications, and may provide a single interface into multiple back-end systems.

❑ **Integration Mediator**
The Integration Mediator pattern represents an approach where the interaction is encapsulated inside the mediator itself. Unlike the Integration Messenger, whose sole charge is ensuring that a legacy service is invoked on behalf of a calling application, the mediator contains implicit knowledge of the application services it employs and actually choreographs the interaction of these services to provide a new transaction.

Integration Mediators may be either stateless or stateful. Stateless Integration Mediators perform their tasks in direct response to a single request; typical uses for stateless integration mediation include content transformation or mapping, and intelligent routing. Stateful Integration Mediators, on the other hand, are required when the task to be performed is based not only on the invocation of the mediator, but also by some pre-existing application or system state, for example, when accumulating messages and then performing an action when certain conditions are met.

❑   **Process Automator**
We will not discuss the Process Automator here, beyond saying that like the Integration Façade and the Integration Mediator, the Process Automator encapsulates integration logic that can be reused by any number of calling applications. The aim is to provide activity abstractions that shield process controllers from the details of system and human interactions.

Let's take one last high-level look at how to perform application integration using JMS and XML:

❑   Examine the integration at hand, and consider how to apply the various integration architecture patterns at your disposal

❑   Abstract service interfaces into flexible XML messages

❑   Map the elements of the selected architecture patterns into JMS messaging model constructs

❑   Perform any needed XML transformations, using either XSLT or programmatic DOM manipulation

❑   Layer in additional logic required for integration façades or integration mediators

Although the above process sounds harder than hard-coding a quick-and-dirty socket-based point integration, you will be well-rewarded with a more reliable, flexible, and reusable service.

Beyond Integration – Designing Open Applications

The main emphasis in this section has been on using JMS and XML to bridge existing applications in order to provide new functionality. But these technologies can also be employed as the foundation of *new* distributed system design, making future integrations and system extensions radically easier. In a new system, designed from the ground up with interfaces made from XML and JMS constructs, we can provide abstracted data interfaces, asynchronously invoked using JMS, instead of relying upon rigidly defined interfaces accessed via a synchronous mechanism such as RMI.

When we discussed integration techniques, we observed that procedural integration of traditional client/server applications is invasive. Note that this is *not* the case in messaging-based applications. Instead, adding new capabilities into a system comprised of messaging-based applications becomes completely organic.

Summary

In this chapter, we introduced the Java Message Service (JMS):

❑ The JMS specification offers a common Java API and semantics for an abstracted messaging system that can be used to create distributed applications.

❑ It offers a unified programming model for two primary messaging models: a publish/subscribe model for distributing data to multiple client applications, and a traditional point-to-point queuing model.

❑ JMS offers a high degree of control over messaging system behavior. We can programmatically specify how messages should be acknowledged, the quality of service to be used, register a 'durable' interest in messages produced for a given topic. Message properties can be used to provide intelligent routing of messages based on filters specified by client applications.

❑ We discussed JMS implementations, and examined a simple application that produces and consumes XML messages using the pub/sub messaging model.

❑ Finally, we looked at how JMS and XML can be used for integration with legacy systems.

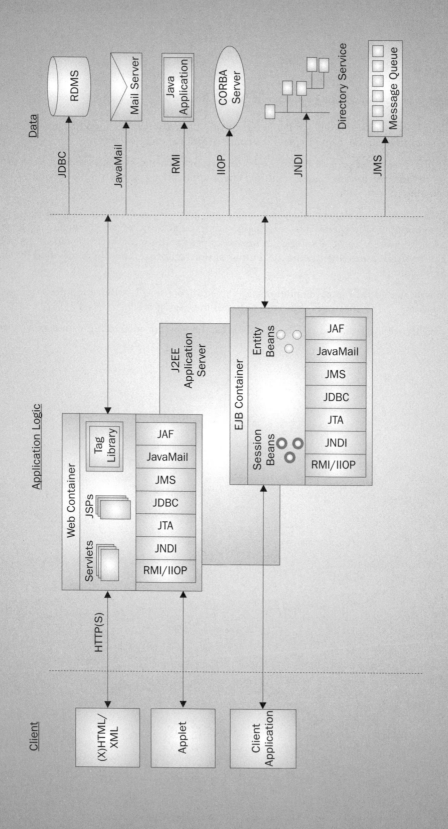

29

Integration with CORBA

Throughout this book, the focus has been on discovering the various parts that make up the J2EE architecture and using these Java-based technologies to facilitate the development of n-tier applications. In this chapter we are going to shift our focus slightly and introduce another type of distributed component architecture commonly used in n-tier applications, one based on a specification that is not part of the Java 2 platform. This architecture, as you probably have already deduced from the title of this chapter, is the **Common Object Request Broker Architecture (CORBA)**. As we shall see, CORBA provides several benefits not available when using Java's RMI, most notably that client applications, and objects can be written in different programming languages. By eliminating the restriction of a pure Java solution, programmers can more easily integrate legacy applications and components into their distributed applications.

In this chapter we will:

❑   Give an overview so that programmers new to CORBA can develop an understanding of its fundamental concepts

❑   Utilize our understanding of CORBA as we examine how the J2EE architecture and CORBA can be integrated together, allowing us to build n-tier applications that are easily accessible to a wider variety of clients, while leveraging existing investments in software components

❑   See how the lines between CORBA and Java's native RMI have blurred with the introduction of **RMI-IIOP (Remote Method Invocation over Internet Inter-ORB Protocol)**

Tools Used in this Chapter

The Java 2 SDK, Standard Edition includes a basic, CORBA/IIOP 2.0 compliant ORB product called JavaIDL that we will use throughout the chapter. Version 1.3 of the SDK is also bundled with an IDL to Java compiler, `idlj`. If you choose to use a previous version of the SDK, you will also need to download either the `idltojava` compiler or preferably the RMI-IIOP 1.0.1 package that includes the `idlj` compiler. Versions before 1.3 that do not also have the RMI-IIOP package added will not work successfully with the RMI-IIOP examples later in the chapter.

The Java 2 SDK also includes a Naming Service called `tnameserv` that can be used by the CORBA examples. In addition, the `j2ee` server bundled with the J2EE SDK includes a Java Naming and Directory service that functions as a CORBA Naming Service.

Throughout the examples, notes specific to the use of these packages will be made where applicable.

CORBA Overview

CORBA is a specification for a distributed application framework. Developed by the Object Management Group (OMG), CORBA, along with other OMG specifications such as CORBA's "over-the-wire" protocol, the Internet Inter-ORB Protocol (IIOP), provides a vendor-independent architecture for distributed object computing. At the time of writing, the current specification version is 2.3.1: CORBA 3.0 is expected to be complete in late 2000. The complete specifications are available from the OMG at `http://www.omg.org/technology/documents/formal`.

There are a few common misconceptions that tend to make learning and understanding CORBA much more difficult than it needs to be, so let's dispel them right away. Firstly, CORBA is not a programming language like Java or C++. CORBA is a specification, a definition of an application framework that was designed to simplify and standardize distributed object development. When building an application using CORBA, client and object development is still done in your programming language of choice.

> There is one restriction: the language you choose must have a mapping defined between itself and the OMG's Interface Definition Language, which we will see shortly.

Secondly, CORBA is not a product of a particular vendor. In fact, it is quite the opposite. The OMG consists of over 800 member companies. Currently, there are both commercial and public domain implementations of CORBA available from many different vendors.

Another popular misconception is that CORBA is strictly a competitor of Java's RMI. As we shall see in the final section of this chapter, CORBA and RMI used in combination can provide a more powerful application framework than is achievable using either one on its own.

In general, distributed applications built using the CORBA architecture enjoy several benefits:

❑ **Language independence**
Clients and objects can interact regardless of the programming language used to implement each, provided that the programming languages have defined mappings to the OMG's Interface Definition Language. Currently the OMG has defined mappings for Java, C, C++, SmallTalk, Ada, Lisp and COBOL.

- **Location transparency**
  Clients and objects are not directly aware of each others locations within the network, allowing relocation of one (or both) with no impact on the other

- **Support for heterogeneous networks**
  Due to the platform-independence of the CORBA architecture and support from many different vendors, CORBA-compliant products and frameworks exist for most operating systems and hardware platforms, allowing CORBA applications to span many different types of systems, from small, handheld devices to mainframes

- **Interoperability**
  Clients and objects running within different vendors' ORBs can communicate just as if they were located within the same ORB

Before we discuss the CORBA architecture, let's first consider an object that resides within an application. The object provides access to its functionality through its **interface**. The object's interface is simply the collection of public methods and attributes that the object implements to expose its functionality to clients. Any client that makes use of the object will do so through its interface, by invoking the object's public methods and accessing the object's public attributes:

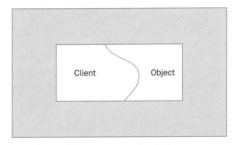

To create distributed objects in an n-tier application, we need to separate our objects from the client applications that contain them. Most distributed object frameworks use the same approach to enable this separation, which is based on the object's interface. Using the interface of the object, two new pieces of code are generated:

- A **stub** or **client stub** used in place of the object in the client application

- A **skeleton** or **server stub** included in a new server-side application that the programmer will create to contain the object

This new code effectively sits between the client and object and passes invocations on the object's interface back and forth between the client application and the new server application:

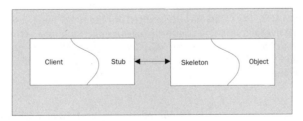

On the client side, the stub exposes the same interface as the original object. As a result, the client is unaware that the object now resides in a different process. When the client interacts with the stub through the interface, the stub takes the details of the interaction (which method was invoked, what parameters were provided, etc.) packages them into a message, called a **request**, and sends it across the network to the skeleton. The stub then waits for a return message, called a **reply**, from the skeleton.

On the server side, the server skeleton receives the request message and extracts the details of the client's interaction with the stub. Once this is complete, the skeleton invokes the correct method on the object, passing the parameters that were extracted from the request message. Any return values or exceptions thrown from the object are packaged into a new message, the reply. The reply is then sent back to the client stub. The client stub extracts the information from the reply message and returns it back to the client application:

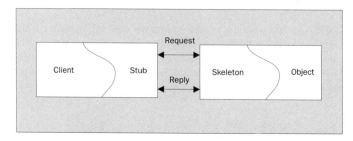

The key to the success of the interaction is that the client stub and the object expose the same interface. This allows the stub and skeleton to process any method invocations that the object can handle, passing the correct parameters. This also allows the skeleton and stub to return the correct return types and possible exceptions that the client is expecting.

CORBA follows basically the same approach with a few modifications. Let's first look at the different parts of the CORBA framework. The CORBA framework consists of three major parts:

❏   The **Interface Definition Language (IDL)**

❏   The **Object Request Broker (ORB)**

❏   The **Internet Inter-ORB Protocol (IIOP)**

The Interface Definition Language (IDL) is a language created by the Object Management Group for defining interfaces of distributed objects. IDL is programming-language independent, meaning that an interface defined in IDL does not require that a specific programming language, such as Java or C++, be used when implementing clients that use this interface, and objects exposing it.

> In conjunction with IDL, the OMG has defined IDL-to-language mappings, allowing an IDL interface to be mapped into a particular programming language. Once an IDL interface has been defined, the interface is compiled using an IDL to language compiler, generally provided by the ORB vendor, to generate the stub and/or skeleton in the target programming language.

With these mappings, a given IDL interface can be compiled using an **IDL compiler** to generate client stubs and server skeletons in a target programming language. Using IDL compilers for different target languages, interfaces defined in IDL along with the IDL-to-language mappings permit clients written in one programming language to access objects written in different programming languages.

The Object Request Broker (ORB) is the CORBA software product that is used when constructing distributed application components. The ORB's primary responsibility is to facilitate the creation and transmission of request and reply messages that occur between clients and objects. The ORB also provides functionality to the client and object directly for manipulating references to remote objects and bootstrapping commonly used services. The ORB is usually implemented as a set of libraries (or packages) included within each distributed application client and object server. In addition, some ORB implementations also include daemon processes that are used for object location and/or launching of remote server processes. One of the most important properties of an ORB product is the level of CORBA specification compliance that is provided. This level of compliance guarantees the functionality that the ORB provides.

The Internet Inter-ORB Protocol (IIOP) is a protocol, defined by the Object Management Group, which is used by ORBs to send messages back and forth between clients and objects. IIOP is actually the TCP/IP version of a more generic OMG-defined protocol named GIOP, the General Inter-ORB Protocol. All CORBA 2.0 compliant ORBs must have the ability to communicate using IIOP. Since IIOP is a vendor-independent protocol, any two ORB products that are 2.0 compliant can communicate with each other. This feature of the 2.0 specifications, known as **interoperability**, allows a client using one ORB product to use objects running within a different ORB product.

Using CORBA as our distributed object framework, our theoretical example presented above would resemble the following:

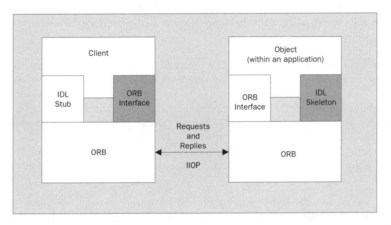

As in the approach described at the beginning of the chapter, the client and object communicate via a stub and skeleton. However, in CORBA, the stub and skeleton are generated from an IDL-defined interface, which provides us with an **IDL stub** and an **IDL skeleton**, commonly referred to as the stub and the skeleton. Also new to our conceptual view is the introduction of the ORB, which sits between the stub and skeleton and is responsible for the transmission of requests and responses as IIOP messages between client and server processes. The ORB also exposes an interface directly to the client and object for ORB initialization, bootstrapping of commonly used services such as the Naming Service, and manipulation of CORBA object references, which are described below.

To create a distributed object using CORBA, the object's interface is first defined in IDL. From this IDL definition, the stub and skeleton source code are generated in the client's, and object's, programming language(s). For example, below is a simple interface named *Test* consisting of two methods, *method1* and *method2*, each taking two parameters, a short named *param1* and a string named *param2*. *Method1* returns a short and *method2* returns a string. As you may have noticed, each parameter below is qualified with an 'in' label. We will examine this in detail later:

```
interface Test
{
  short method1( in short param1, in string param2 );
  string method2( in short param1, in string param2 );
};
```

When a client wants to invoke methods on the remote object, it first obtains an **interoperable object reference**, also called an **IOR** or simply an **object reference**, for the remote object, also known as a **CORBA object**. (We discuss how an object reference is obtained in the 'Object Location' section.) The object reference will be represented within the client as a local object (an instance of a class in the client's programming language), containing data that is used by the ORB to locate the remote object in the network. The data within the object reference is considered *opaque*, meaning that its format and value is unimportant to the client's application-level code. The actual contents and format of the object reference data is defined by the OMG in the CORBA/IIOP specification to ensure that an object reference is *interoperable*, meaning that an IOR can be used to access the remote object from within any ORB framework, regardless of where the IOR was created. As mentioned above, the actual type of the object reference is defined in the client's programming language within the IDL client stub. The object reference will expose an interface that maps directly to the interface defined in the IDL (using the IDL to language mapping).

It may be helpful to think of an object reference as a proxy object for the remote object. Once obtained, the client application can invoke methods on the object reference (proxy object) just as if it was the actual object:

- ❑ For each invocation on the object reference by the client, the stub-defined object creates a CORBA-defined request object, providing any parameter data that is necessary, and passes the request object to the ORB. The process of inserting parameters into the request for transmission is known as **marshalling**. The ORB examines the object reference to locate the remote object's containing application, creates an IIOP message, and sends it via the network to the server application.

- ❑ On the server side, the server application, on startup, creates an instance of the actual object and notifies the ORB that the object exists. The server application's ORB then waits for incoming client requests.

- ❑ When an IIOP message is received by the server application, the ORB extracts the method invocation data from the message. From the message, the ORB identifies the object that is to be the target of the method invocation and hands off the invocation information to the IDL-generated skeleton of the CORBA object. The object skeleton reads the message data, extracting (or **unmarshalling**) the parameter data, and then invokes the correct method, passing the parameters. The skeleton receives any return values or exceptions and creates the reply information including these return types and/or exceptions. This reply information is then returned to the ORB, which creates an IIOP message and sends it back to the client.

- ❑ The ORB at the client side, upon receiving the reply message, extracts the data from the IIOP message and passes it back to the stub-defined object reference. The stub then extracts the return data or exception from the reply and returns it back to the client application through the original IDL-to-language mapped interface.

We'll look at this in more detail below as we trace through a CORBA method invocation using a simple CORBA object and client.

Object Location

Before we can invoke operations on our CORBA object, our client must first obtain the CORBA object's object reference. The CORBA architecture provides several mechanisms that CORBA objects and their server applications can use to make their object references available to potential clients, namely:

- ❏ Using an object location service, such as the OMG Naming Service

- ❏ Recreating an object reference from its 'stringified' form

- ❏ Receiving an object reference from another CORBA object, commonly referred to as a factory object

To begin with, let's discuss object location services.

In general, an object location service is a software product that provides the ability to publish and retrieve object references. The most commonly used object location service is the OMG-defined Naming Service.

> *The OMG has defined a set of object services that are commonly used within distributed object systems. This set of services is called the CORBAServices. One of the most commonly used of these services is the Naming Service.*

Simply put, the Naming Service is a repository for storing CORBA object references. When a server application inserts an object reference into the Naming Service, it is required to provide a name that will be used to identify that object reference. This object reference-name association is called a *binding*. Once the object reference is bound, client applications can query the Naming Service, providing a name and receiving the associated object reference, if one exists.

The Naming Service stores its object reference bindings in *naming contexts*. A naming context is a CORBA object that maintains a collection of zero or more object reference bindings and zero or more naming contexts. The recursive nature of the naming context allows the creation of a hierarchy of naming contexts, much like the directory structure of a file system where each directory can contain files and additional directories. By creating new naming contexts within existing contexts, it allows developers to segment the global object namespace, helping to alleviate the problem of name collisions. To begin with, the Naming Service contains a single naming context, called the *root* or *initial context*. When you first obtain an object reference for the Naming Service, it is actually the object reference of the root context. From there, additional contexts and object reference bindings can be added. When querying the Naming Service for an object reference, we will provide a list of names describing the navigation through the hierarchy of naming contexts of names, the last name in the list being the name of the object.

For example, consider two types of CORBA objects, one that represents a checking account and one that represents a savings account. By creating separate naming contexts within the Naming Service, several checking account objects and savings account objects can exist without having to create and maintain unique names for each. So, to access Mary Smith's checking account, we would query the Naming Service (from the root context), providing a list containing two names, first "Mary_Smith" and next "Checking". Alternatively, if we started at the "Mary_Smith" context we could query directly for the "Checking" object:

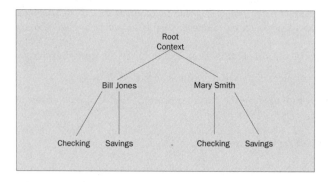

So, how is an object reference inserted into the Naming Service? Typically, the server application that contains the CORBA object is responsible for inserting it into the Naming Service. To do this, the server application must first obtain the object reference of the Naming Service's root context. It does this using a "bootstrap" mechanism of the ORB, namely the *resolve_initial_references* method. Using this method, the server can obtain object references to several commonly used services, one of which is the Naming Service. The actual object references returned are determined within the configuration of the ORB product.

The client, using the same "bootstrap" mechanism as the server, can now obtain the object reference of the Naming Service's root context and look up the object reference of its intended target CORBA object.

> *Note that the ORB only provides bootstrapping capability to a single Naming Service. If access to additional Naming Services, possibly running on different hosts, is required, the root naming context (or some sub-context) of each of these additional Naming Services must be bound within the Naming Service your client application can access. This is called a* federated *naming graph.*

> *CORBA 3 will introduce a new Interoperable Name Service that will provide a URL based method of accessing defined services on remote hosts. For example, a client application can obtain the object reference for a service, such as the Naming Service, running at* `http://www.abc.com` *by specifying the following URL:* `iioploc://www.abc.com/NameService`.

> *Alternatively, queries can be made to a remote Naming Service directly through a second URL format. For example, to obtain the IOR of an object named* `CheckingAccount` *from the Naming Service running on* http://www.abc.com, *client applications can specify the following URL:* `iiopname://www.abc.com/CheckingAccount`.

The second method that we can use to publish and retrieve object references is to store our CORBA object's object references in a data store in their 'stringified' form. An object reference's 'stringified' form is the contents of its internal data serialized into a string data type. An object reference is 'stringified' using a method in the ORB's interface called `object_to_string()`. Once stringified, the object references can be stored in some form of data storage, such as a database record or file. When adding the object reference to the data store, it should be associated with some sort of a label, making it possible to retrieve it by querying the data store for that label. When a client needs an object reference, it can obtain the object reference from the data store using the label and reconstruct the object reference from the string using another method of the ORB's interface, `string_to_object()`.

It is important at this point to make a distinction between stringified object references and object serialization. Object serialization is commonly used to store an object in a data store, such as a database, or for migrating an object from one process to another across the network. When serializing an object, all of the data that is necessary to reinstantiate the object in its exact state is captured. The goal is to create an exact copy of the object at a later time or in another location. On the other hand, stringified object references are most commonly used to convey the object reference of a particular CORBA object from one application to another. Since these applications may not be written in the same programming language, the actual objects instantiated in the applications may not be the same. The goal of "stringification" of an object reference is not to make a duplicate of the original object in another process but to ensure that an object instantiated within another application references the same CORBA object.

The third mechanism that a client may use to obtain an object reference is to invoke a method on a CORBA object that returns another object reference. This is possible because IDL interfaces can define attributes, parameter types, and return types that are themselves object references. This type of CORBA object, one that provides object references to other CORBA objects, is commonly referred to as a **factory object**, since it appears from the perspective of the client to create objects on demand. Obviously, this mechanism cannot be used unless the client has already obtained the object reference of the factory object, presumably through some other mechanism.

In addition to these methods, many CORBA implementations provide their own non-CORBA-compliant object location mechanisms that will provide clients with object references. Although these are certainly acceptable, they are not CORBA-compliant, and therefore cause our source code to become ORB vendor-specific. It could be difficult to port between different vendor's CORBA products.

This is a good time to point out a benefit of CORBA object references. Since the object reference is an opaque data type, the client is unaware of and unconcerned with the actual contents. The content, however, is the location of the remote object in the network. Because of this, the CORBA architecture provides the benefit of *location transparency* of CORBA objects. If a CORBA object and its containing server application are moved to a different host in the network, it is only necessary to update the CORBA object's object reference in the above mentioned object location mechanisms. The next time a client obtains the object reference, it will pick up the new object reference and use it just as it did the previous one.

A Simple CORBA Object and Client

Let's take a closer look at CORBA by building a simple example. We will then be able to trace the path of a method invocation from the client to the object and back.

There are several steps necessary to build a CORBA object and client. We will begin by examining the steps involved in developing the CORBA object and its containing application.

Defining the Interface

Before we can build the client or server applications, we must first define the IDL interface for the CORBA object. We'll use the simple IDL interface we saw earlier consisting of two methods, method1() and method2():

```
interface Test
{
    short method1( in short param1, in string param2 );
    string method2( in short param1, in string param2 );
};
```

If you recall the first method, method1(), takes two parameters, a short called param1 and a string called param2, and returns a value of type short. The second method, method2(), takes the same parameters and returns a value of type string.

To generate the stub and skeleton, we can use the IDL to Java compiler, idlj. See the 'Tools' section at the beginning of the chapter for more information on acquiring the compiler.

To compile the IDL interface, assuming the IDL file is named Test.idl, perform the following:

```
idlj -fall Test.idl
```

The option -fall instructs the compiler to generate both the client stub and server skeleton. To create only one or the other, use the -fclient or -fserver options.

Compiling the IDL interface will generate several java source files:

Source File	Description
Test.java	Defines a Java interface, Test, which is the object reference of our CORBA object (remote object). As with all CORBA object references is Java, Test extends the CORBA object reference base interface, org.omg.CORBA.Object. Interface Test is an empty interface, but extends the TestOperations interface below.
TestOperations.java	The TestOperations interface defines the IDL to Java mapped operations of the IDL interface
_TestStub.java	The client stub. The _TestStub class is the actual data type of an object reference in the client application. It extends org.omg.CORBA.portable.ObjectImpl, which provides the default implementation for all object references, and implements interface Test, described above.
_TestImplBase.java	The server skeleton. The _TestImplBase class provides an abstract base class for object implementations in the server side application. Using the _TestImplBase base class, the ORB component within the server can directly invoke methods on implementation objects derived from it. This class also implements the Test interface, forcing derived classes to provide an implementation for each of the IDL-defined methods.
TestHelper.java	Provides utility-type static methods for objects of type Test. Utilities include insertion and removal from CORBA types, input and output streams, etc. Also provides a narrow() function which is useful for downcasting object references to type Test.
TestHolder.java	Acts as a container for streaming objects of type Test to and from input and output streams

We'll see how this source code is used as we build our client and server applications.

Creating the CORBA Object and Server

Once the IDL skeleton is created, we can build our CORBA object implementation and server applications. Note that there are two common methods for creating object implementations, the ImplBase approach and the Tie approach.

The ImplBase approach involves using an IDL compiler generated class as the base class of our object implementation.

For instance, given an interface named Account, the IDL to Java compiler provided as part of the J2SE SDK will generate a class called _AccountImplBase, an abstract class we can use as the base class of our object implementation. This base class implements a Java interface created from our IDL interface, ensuring that our object will provide an implementation of every method in the CORBA object's interface. We will use the ImplBase approach throughout this chapter.

The Tie approach is useful when our intended object implementation already extends another class, since Java does not support multiple inheritance. The Tie approach creates a secondary object that extends the skeleton generated class just as the ImplBase base class does. By associating this tie object with our object implementation, all CORBA invocations are invoked on the tie object which in turn delegates these invocations to our actual implementation object. Use the –ftie option of the IDL compiler to generate the necessary Tie classes.

To create the CORBA object using the ImplBase approach:

❑ Create a new class, extending from the ImplBase class, _TestImplBase that we generated using the IDL compiler

❑ Within our new class, implement each of the methods in the Java interface that was generated by the IDL compiler (in our case, the interface Test)

To implement a CORBA server application, perform the following steps:

1. Import the following packages:

```
org.omg.CORBA.*

org.omg.CosNaming.*
```

2. In the main method of the application, initialize the ORB by calling ORB.init(). Parameters can be sent to the init() method either as a String array, such as from the command line, or as a java.util.Properties object. The most common of these parameters are:

Property Name	Description of Value
org.omg.CORBA.ORBInitialPort	The port that the Naming Service is using (defaults to 900)
org.omg.CORBA.ORBInitialHost	The host where the Naming Service is running (defaults to the localhost)
org.omg.CORBA.ORBClass	Class name of an ORB implementation
org.omg.CORBA.ORBSingletonClass	Class name of an ORB implementation that is returned by the init() method with no parameters

The last two, ORBClass and ORBSingletonClass are used to 'plug in' a new ORB implementation in place of the default JavaIDL implementation.

3. Create an instance of the object implementation with the server's `main()` method

4. Use the ORB's `resolve_initial_references()` method, passing in `"NameService"` as a parameter, to obtain an object reference to the Naming Service's initial context

5. Insert the CORBA object's object reference into the Naming Service, binding it to a name. In our case we'll use `"Test"`

6. Wait for incoming requests from clients

Here is an implementation of the `Test` object:

```
// Object implementation

public class TestObject extends _TestImplBase {
  public short method1(short param1, String param2) {
    return param1;
  }

  public String method2(short param1, String param2) {
    return param2;
  }
}
```

The server implementation is as follows (cross-referenced to the numbered steps above):

```
// Server Implementation

import org.omg.CORBA.*;                                      // Step 1
import org.omg.CosNaming.*;

public class TestServer {
  public static void main(String args[]) {
    try {

      // Initialize the ORB
      ORB orb = ORB.init(args, null);                        // Step 2

      // Create the Test object
      TestObject impl = new TestObject();                    // Step 3

      // Connect to the Naming Service
      org.omg.CORBA.Object contextObj =                      // Step 4
            orb.resolve_initial_references("NameService");
      NamingContext rootContext = NamingContextHelper.narrow(contextObj);

      // Insert the Test object reference in the Naming Service
      NameComponent name = new NameComponent("Test", "");    // Step 5
```

```
        NameComponent path[] = {
          name
        };

        rootContext.rebind(path, impl);

        // Wait for incoming requests
        java.lang.Object sync = new java.lang.Object();        // Step 6
        synchronized (sync) {
          sync.wait();
        }

      } catch (Exception e) {
        System.err.println("Exception : " + e);
        e.printStackTrace(System.err);
      }
    }
  }
}
```

Notice the call to `ORB.resolve_initial_references()` in step 4. The string `"NameService"` causes the method to return the object reference of the root context of the Naming Service. Also notice that the `resolve_initial_references()` method returns as a type a basic object reference, namely an `org.omg.CORBA.Object`. In order to use the object reference as a `NamingContext` object, we must narrow the object reference using the `NamingContextHelper`'s `narrow()` method, to yield a `NamingContext` object reference that we can use.

Once we have a valid `NamingContext` object reference, we must construct an array of `NameComponents` that describe the location of our `Test` object reference in the Naming Service. The reason that an array is required is to allow objects to be bound in the Naming Service in other than the root context that is returned by `resolve_initial_references()`. Each `NameComponent`, with the exception of the last one, identifies another sub-context under which the object will be located. For instance, if a Naming Service contained the following contexts:

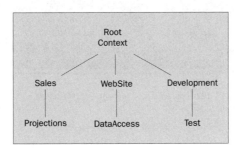

If we needed an object reference to the `Test` object in the `Development` context, we would create an array of `NameComponents` as follows:

```
NameComponent dev = new NameComponent("Development", "");
NameComponent test = new NameComponent("Test", "");
NameComponent path[] = {dev, test};
```

1Note that the second parameter of the NameComponent constructor is the *kind* parameter, a string that can be used to further describe the object. In our examples, we will leave the kind field blank.

We will insert our object reference in the root context. To do that, we will create a NameComponent array consisting of one NameComponent object that contains the name "Test". After defining the NameComponent array, we call the NamingContext object's rebind() method to insert the object reference. Using rebind() will overwrite any existing object reference in the context that has the same name. Alternatively, we could have used the NamingContext's bind() method, which would throw an AlreadyBound exception in the event that an object reference with the specified name already existed within the context. Since we may want to restart this server several times during testing, we'll use the rebind method.

At this point, all that is left to do is wait for incoming requests, as is done in Step 6.

To build the server, simply compile the classes we created, making sure that the IDL generated source files are in the CLASSPATH:

```
javac [ -classpath <location of generated source> ] *.java
```

To start the server, we must first start the Naming Service. To do this, run tnameserv from the command line. By default, the Naming Service will run on port 900. If you want (or need) to run the Naming Service on a different port, provide it on the command line like so:

```
tnameserv -ORBInitialPort x
```

where x is the new port that you want to use. Note that when providing parameters to the ORB on the command line, it is not necessary to fully qualify them as org.omg.CORBA.ORBInitialPort, etc.

Running the Naming Service should result in the following output, which contains the 'stringified' object reference of the initial Naming Context, the port used here is the default:

Once the Naming Service is up and running, start the server by typing:

```
java [classpath to generated files] TestServer
            [ -ORBInitialPort x ] [ -ORBInitialHost host ]
```

Where x is the port of the Naming Service, and host is the host where the Naming Service is running.

Creating the CORBA Client

The client application is similar to the server application, in that both initialize the ORB and retrieve the root context of the Naming Service from the ORB in the same manner.

To create the CORBA client application:

1. Import the following packages:

   ```
   org.omg.CORBA.*
   ```

   ```
   org.omg.CosNaming.*
   ```

2. Initialize the ORB by calling `ORB.init()` in the application's main method, just as we did in the server application

3. Using the ORB's `resolve_initial_references()` method, obtain an object reference to the Naming Service's initial context, just as in the server application

4. Retrieve the desired CORBA object's object reference from the Naming Service using its bound name, in our case `"Test"`

5. Invoke methods on the object reference

6. When finished using the object, call `_release()` on the object reference to indicate to the ORB that we no longer need the object. This allows the ORB to clean up any resources that it is using for that object reference.

Here is the source code for our test client application; again the numbered comments refer to the steps above:

```java
import org.omg.CORBA.*;                                        // Step 1
import org.omg.CosNaming.*;

public class TestClient {
  public static void main(String args[]) {
    try {
      ORB orb = ORB.init(args, null);                          // Step 2

      org.omg.CORBA.Object contextObj =                        // Step 3
      orb.resolve_initial_references("NameService");
      NamingContext rootContext = NamingContextHelper.narrow(contextObj);

      NameComponent name = new NameComponent("Test", "");
      NameComponent path[] = {
        name
      };

      org.omg.CORBA.Object obj = rootContext.resolve(path);    // Step 4
      Test testObj = TestHelper.narrow(obj);

      short result1 = testObj.method1((short) 1, "Test");      // Step 5
      String result2 = testObj.method2((short) 1, "Test");

      System.out.println("Result 1 is " + result1);
      System.out.println("Result 2 is " + result2);

      testObj._release();                                      // Step 6
    } catch (Exception e) {
      System.err.println("Exception : " + e);
      e.printStackTrace(System.err);
    }
  }
}
```

The ORB initialization and retrieval of the root `NamingContext` are done exactly as in the server application. In the case of the client, however, we call `resolve()` on the initial `NamingContext`, providing the path necessary to locate the object reference bound to the name `"Test"`. Just as with the `resolve_initial_references()` method, the `resolve()` method returns a basic object reference which we must narrow using the `TestHelper.narrow()` method defined in the `TestHelper` class generated by the IDL compiler. Once we have a valid object reference, we are free to invoke methods on it. When finished, we should always call `_release()` on the object reference to indicate that we are finished using it, allowing the ORB to cleanup any resources dedicated to that object reference.

To run the CORBA client, we do the following:

```
java TestClient [ -ORBInitialPort x ] [ -ORBInitialHost host ]
```

where the port and host are set just as in the server application.

The resulting output be as follows:

The Anatomy of a CORBA Object Invocation

Now that we have a working example, we are in a better position to understand what happens when we invoke a method on our `Test` object reference. To do this, let's trace the course of a CORBA object invocation from the client's object reference to the object implementation and back. We'll use the invocation of `method1()` as our example.

First, let's take another look at how we obtain the object reference in our client application. When we retrieve an object reference from one of the object location mechanisms discussed above, such as the Naming Service, we receive a generic object reference, in other words it is of type `org.omg.CORBA.Object`. In order to invoke operations defined in our interface, we'll need to downcast, or **narrow**, the object reference from the base `Object` interface to the Java-mapped IDL interface, namely interface `Test` defined in `Test.java`. This is performed using the `narrow()` method of class `TestHelper`. Let's look at the `TestHelper.narrow()` method and a few related definitions within `TestHelper` to see what happens during the narrow process:

```
abstract public class TestHelper {
  private static String _id = "IDL:Test:1.0";

  // ... some code removed

  public static String id() {
    return _id;
  }

  public static Test narrow(org.omg.CORBA.Object obj) {
    if (obj == null) {                              // Condition 1
      return null;
    } else if (obj instanceof Test) {               // Condition 2
```

```
                return (Test) obj;
            } else if (!obj._is_a(id())) {                 // Condition 3
                throw new org.omg.CORBA.BAD_PARAM();
            } else {                                       // Condition 4

                org.omg.CORBA.portable.Delegate delegate =
                    ((org.omg.CORBA.portable.ObjectImpl) obj)._get_delegate();

                return new _TestStub(delegate);
            }
        }
    }
}
```

Examining the conditions in narrow() will show us exactly what we retrieve back as the object reference in our client application. The four conditions have been labeled in the source code as 1-4:

- ❑ The first condition is straightforward. If a null object reference is narrowed, the method simply returns null.

- ❑ The second condition uses the instanceof operator to determine if the object passed to narrow is an object that directly implements the Test interface. If so, a simple cast is done and the cast object is returned. This allows clients of CORBA objects that are contained within the same application as the CORBA object to bypass the stub and skeleton and invoke its methods directly.

- ❑ The third condition uses the org.omg.CORBA.Object _is_a() method to ensure that the obj parameter is a class that implements the Test interface, designated by the id() method of TestHelper. In the event that the obj parameter doesn't implement our Test interface, a org.omg.CORBA. BAD_PARAM exception is thrown to indicate that the object passed to narrow does not implement the Test interface.

- ❑ The final condition creates a new _TestStub object from the obj parameter that was passed to narrow(). The delegate object reference that is extracted from the obj parameter and set into the stub object is for support of vendor-specific object reference implementations and is not important to us here. Note that _TestStub implements the Test interface, allowing us to invoke any of the methods defined in the Test interface (or its base interfaces) on the object returned from narrow().

Now, assuming that our CORBA object is located on a remote host, our client will receive a _TestStub object from the call to TestHelper.narrow(). Below is the source code for the _TestStub class:

```
public class _TestStub extends org.omg.CORBA.portable.ObjectImpl
    implements Test {

    // Constructors
    // NOTE:  If the default constructor is used, the
    // object is useless until _set_delegate (...)
    // is called.

    public _TestStub() {
        super();
    }
```

```
public _TestStub(org.omg.CORBA.portable.Delegate delegate) {
  super();
  _set_delegate(delegate);
}

// public methods
public short method1(short param1, String param2) {
  org.omg.CORBA.portable.InputStream _in = null;
  try {
    org.omg.CORBA.portable.OutputStream _out = _request("method1", true);
    _out.write_short(param1);
    _out.write_string(param2);
    _in = _invoke(_out);
    short __result = _in.read_short();
    return __result;
  } catch (org.omg.CORBA.portable.ApplicationException _ex) {
    _in = _ex.getInputStream();
    String _id = _ex.getId();
    throw new org.omg.CORBA.MARSHAL(_id);
  } catch (org.omg.CORBA.portable.RemarshalException _rm) {
    return method1(param1, param2);
  }
  finally {
    _releaseReply(_in);
  }
}   // method1

public String method2(short param1, String param2) {
  org.omg.CORBA.portable.InputStream _in = null;
  try {
    org.omg.CORBA.portable.OutputStream _out = _request("method2", true);
    _out.write_short(param1);
    _out.write_string(param2);
    _in = _invoke(_out);
    String __result = _in.read_string();
    return __result;
  } catch (org.omg.CORBA.portable.ApplicationException _ex) {
    _in = _ex.getInputStream();
    String _id = _ex.getId();
    throw new org.omg.CORBA.MARSHAL(_id);
  } catch (org.omg.CORBA.portable.RemarshalException _rm) {
    return method2(param1, param2);
  }
  finally {
    _releaseReply(_in);
  }
}   // method2

// ... remainder truncated

}     // class _TestStub
```

The stub class _TestStub provides a method for each of the methods defined in the IDL interface. These are the methods that are invoked when the client application uses the object reference returned from TestHelper.narrow(). Let's look at the implementation of method1 to see what occurs when an invocation is made on this object:

```
public short method1(short param1, String param2) {
    org.omg.CORBA.portable.InputStream _in = null;
    try {
        org.omg.CORBA.portable.OutputStream _out = _request("method1",
                    true);                              // Step 1
        _out.write_short(param1);                       // Step 2
        _out.write_string(param2);
        _in = _invoke(_out);                            // Step 3
        short __result = _in.read_short();              // Step 4
        return __result;                                // Step 5
    } catch (org.omg.CORBA.portable.ApplicationException _ex) {
        _in = _ex.getInputStream();
        String _id = _ex.getId();
        throw new org.omg.CORBA.MARSHAL(_id);
    } catch (org.omg.CORBA.portable.RemarshalException _rm) {
        return method1(param1, param2);
    }
    finally {
        _releaseReply(_in);
    }
}
```

So, what happens when this method is called?

❑ At Step 1, the stub object creates an org.omg.CORBA.portable.OutputStream object named _out, and inserts into it a request object with a method name of "method1". The org.omg.CORBA.portable.OutputStream object is used for marshalling method requests, parameters, exceptions, etc. in a platform-independent manner for transport across platforms.

❑ At Step 2, the parameters passed into the _TestStub method1() method are marshalled into the OutputStream object.

❑ At Step 3, _invoke() is called on the stub object passing the OutputStream object _out as a parameter. _invoke() is implemented by _TestStub's underlying base class, org.omg.CORBA.portable.ObjectImpl. At this point, the ORB takes over, using the OutputStream we've provided to construct an IIOP message. This message is then sent to the remote object using the network location of the remote object contained in the object reference.

❑ At this point, the client blocks waiting for the _invoke() method to return. When it does, the return type of the method1() invocation is unmarshalled from _invoke()'s InputStream return object (Step 4)

❑ Finally, the result is returned back to the caller (Step 5).

On the server side, the ORB will receive the IIOP method that has been sent by the client. When it does, it creates an org.omg.CORBA.portable.InputStream object using the data from the IIOP message. The InputStream object contains the information that our _TestStub object in the client inserted into its

`OutputStream`. The ORB then uses the information in the object reference to locate the correct CORBA object in its application and calls `_invoke()` on the CORBA object, providing the method name and the `InputStream` as parameters.

Below is the source code for the `Test` interface skeleton, `_TestImplBase`:

```
public abstract class _TestImplBase
    extends org.omg.CORBA.portable.ObjectImpl
      implements Test, org.omg.CORBA.portable.InvokeHandler {

  // Constructors
  public _TestImplBase() {}

  private static java.util.Hashtable _methods = new java.util.Hashtable();
  static {
    _methods.put("method1", new java.lang.Integer(0));
    _methods.put("method2", new java.lang.Integer(1));
  }

  public org.omg.CORBA.portable.OutputStream _invoke(String method,
          org.omg.CORBA.portable.InputStream in,
          org.omg.CORBA.portable.ResponseHandler rh) {
    org.omg.CORBA.portable.OutputStream out = null;
    java.lang.Integer __method =
      (java.lang.Integer) _methods.get(method);     // Point 1
    if (__method == null) {
      throw new org.omg.CORBA
        .BAD_OPERATION(0, org.omg.CORBA.CompletionStatus.COMPLETED_MAYBE);

    }
    switch (__method.intValue())               // Point 2
    {
    case 0:                                    // Point 3, Test/method1
      {
      short param1 = in.read_short();          // Point 4
      String param2 = in.read_string();
      short __result = (short) 0;              // Point 5
      __result = this.method1(param1, param2); // Point 6
      out = rh.createReply();                  // Point 7
      out.write_short(__result);               // Point 8
      break;
    }

    case 1:                                    // Test/method2
      {
      short param1 = in.read_short();
      String param2 = in.read_string();
      String __result = null;
      __result = this.method2(param1, param2);
      out = rh.createReply();
      out.write_string(__result);
      break;
    }
```

```
    default:
      throw new org.omg.CORBA
        .BAD_OPERATION(0, org.omg.CORBA.CompletionStatus.COMPLETED_MAYBE);
    }


    return out;                                    // Point 9
  }

  // Type-specific CORBA::Object operations
  private static String[] __ids = {
    "IDL:Test:1.0"
  };

  public String[] _ids() {
    return __ids;
  }


}   // class _TestImplBase
```

It is important to note here that our CORBA object implementation, TestObject, extends the
_TestImplBase class, so the _invoke() method that is invoked by the ORB is actually part of our
implementation object. Let's trace through the steps that occur in our CORBA object's _invoke() method:

- At Point 1, the method name passed to invoke is used to get the ordinal value of the method,
  as defined in the static hashtable _methods defined in _TestImplBase.

- This ordinal value, stored in the Integer variable __method, is applied to the switch
  statement in Point 2 to jump to the proper handler code for the specified method. In the case
  of an invocation on method1(), this code begins at Point 3.

- At Point 4, the input parameters are unmarshaled from the InputStream object and stored in
  temporary variables param1 and param2.

- Point 5 defines a temporary variable, __result, to contain the result of the method invocation.

- The invocation of the method is invoked at Point 6 as follows:

```
__result = this.method1(param1, param2);
```

  Notice that since our CORBA object is actually the _TestImplBase object, the object
  invokes the method on itself, passing the parameters it marshaled from the InputStream
  object, and storing the return value in the temporary __result variable.

- At Point 7, the actual method invocation has completed. The skeleton is now beginning to
  construct the OutputStream for return to the client. First, the skeleton uses the
  ReplyHandler object passed as a parameter to _invoke() to create the OutputStream,
  inserting a reply object into it.

- At Point 8, the return value is marshaled onto the output stream.

- We then break out of the switch statement to Point 9, where the completed OutputStream
  object is returned to the caller, namely the ORB. The ORB creates the IIOP reply message
  containing the OutputStream, and sends it back to the client.

When the message is received by the client, the ORB creates an `InputStream` object and populates it with the data from the message. Now the `_TestStub` object can unmarshal the return value and return it back to the client application, Points 4 and 5 in the `_TestStub` object. This completes the round trip of our CORBA method invocation.

An IDL Primer

To make use of CORBA servers, we'll need to invoke methods on their IDL interfaces, so let's now briefly examine the details of the IDL language. We will first look at the data types of the language and then proceed to the definition of interfaces. Note that this is not a complete specification for the language, but an abbreviated description designed to provide you with a good overview of the IDL language. For the complete specification, visit the OMG website at `http://www.omg.org`, where the specifications for the IDL language as well as the IDL to Java mapping are available for downloading.

Basic IDL Types

There are several basic data types in IDL that can be used to build up more complex structures in your IDL interface definitions. They include the usual integer and floating point numbers, such as [unsigned] short, [unsigned] long, etc. as we would expect. Non-numeric data types also are much like the java equivalents, char, bounded and unbounded strings (fixed and non-fixed length), the `boolean` type and `any`, a type that allows any IDL defined data type to be stored in it.

Complex IDL Types

In addition to these simple types, IDL provides a number of complex types.

Structures

A structure is probably the simplest of all the complex types and is much like the stuct in C and C++. A structure, declared as `struct`, is a data type that consists of one or more data elements of other types. Structs are convenient when an operation requires a number of parameters that can be logically grouped into one entity. The syntax for defining a structure is as follows:

```
interface Log
{
  struct date
  {
    unsigned short month;
    unsigned short day;
    unsigned short year;
  };

  struct logMessage
  {
    string msg;
    date msgDate;
  };

  void submitLogMsg( in logMessage msg );
};
```

Examining the above IDL definition, you can see that structures can contain not only basic types, but other structures as well. In fact, structures can also contain other types of complex types, enums, sequences, arrays, and even references to other objects.

Enums

An enumerated type, declared as enum, allows the definition of a set of values that can be referenced as a particular type. Once defined, the enumerated type can be used as a parameter or return value type. For example, let's say that we need to add to our previous IDL interface to accept log messages of varying severities. The IDL interface can define an enumerated type that specifies the legal values for the log message severity as follows:

```
enum Severity { INFO, WARNING, ERROR };
```

Unions

A union is another type of data structure, however; rather than containing several data elements, it contains only one element. The actual type of the element can be one of several different specified types, as specified in the enum's case statement. The actual type is controlled by a variable called a discriminator.

The discriminator, which is referenced after the union name, can be of integer, boolean, character, or enum type. Depending on the value of the discriminator, the correct data element will be referenced.

Arrays and Sequences

Arrays are declared in IDL as containing a fixed number of data elements. Arrays can also be declared as multi-dimensional. When declaring the array, the number specified indicates the total number of elements that can be contained within it. Note that the elements within the array are zero indexed, so an array of 10 elements is accessed as elements 0 through 9. Also note that in order for an array to be passed as a parameter or return type, a typedef must be created that identifies the array type and size. Once the typedef is defined, it is used in place of the complete array syntax, as seen below.

```
interface Log
{
    // ... interface as before

    typedef logMessage logMessageArray[ 10];

    void submitLogMsg( in logMessage msg );
    void submitLogMsgs( in logMessageArray msgArray );

};
```

Sequences are similar to arrays in that they define a list of elements. The sequence's elements are zero-indexed, meaning that the first element in the list is accessed as element 0. However, sequences differ from arrays in that they can be defined as bounded or unbounded. Unbounded sequences can contain any number of elements, constrained only by the available memory.

Modules

IDL interfaces may be defined within modules, providing a naming space that contains and isolates any names within it. The syntax of a module in IDL is as follows:

```
module OnlineBroker
{
  interface Account
  {
    // ...
  };
};
```

To access the `Account` interface from outside the module, it must be scoped using the module name and the scope resolution operator :: as such, `OnlineBroker:: Account`. Although using modules is not necessary when defining IDL interfaces, it does provide an isolated naming space. In this case, we will prevent any ambiguities with other IDL interfaces that happen to be named `Account`. Also note that IDL files can contain comments, denoted by the `//` symbol just as in Java.

Interfaces

Interfaces define the functionality of an object in a distributed system, and can contain several different types of definitions, each of which we will examine in turn. It is important to note that everything defined in an IDL interface is public. There is no concept of package, protected, or private access modifiers. Let's begin with attributes.

Attributes

Extending our example IDL, we now have:

```
module OnlineBroker
{
  interface Account
  {
    readonly attribute string accountNumber;
    attribute string accountHolderName;
  };
};
```

The interface now includes two attributes, namely `accountNumber` and `accountHolderName`. Each attribute usually has two implied operations associated with it, a get and a set operation. However, an attribute can be denoted as `readonly`, meaning that its value cannot be altered. Because of this, the `accountNumber` attribute will have only one operation defined in the IDL client stub, `getaccountNumber()`. In the case of the `accountHolderName` attribute, two operations, `getaccountHolderName()` and `setaccountHolderName()` will be created. We'll look at the contents of the client stub in more detail later.

Operations

Operations define methods on the remote object that can be invoked by clients. Remember that the only way clients can access the CORBA object is through its interface, so any functionality that the object wants to provide must be exposed through its interface as an attribute or operation.

Extending our example IDL, we have

```
module OnlineBroker
{
  interface Account
  {
    readonly attribute string accountNumber;
    attribute string accountHolderName;

    boolean buy( in string symbol, inout long quantity, out string cusip );

    boolean sell( in string symbol, out string cusip );
  };
};
```

Now we've added two operations, buy() and sell(), to our interface. These look very similar to methods defined in Java interfaces, however note that the parameters are preceeded by a modifier, namely in, out, or inout. This parameter modifier describes in which direction the parameter is passed:

❑　in parameters are set to a particular value by the client and passed to the server. The server receives the value and is free to alter it during the course of its processing; however, the client will not receive the updated value upon return of the operation invocation.

❑　out parameters work in the reverse manner: the server sets this value during its processing and returns the new value to the client

❑　inout parameters allow a client to pass a value to the server object: the server object is capable of altering this value, and the resulting value is returned to the client

One important note about operation names is that they cannot be overloaded, regardless of the operation's signature. Therefore, if you have two operations that have similar functionality but take different parameter types, you are forced to create two separate names for these operations. For example, an interface cannot include the following two operations:

```
void add( long num );
void add( float num );
```

Instead, the operations will require different names, such as addLong() and addFloat().

Exceptions

When defining operations for a distributed object, it may be beneficial to define exceptions that can be thrown during the course of processing. Exceptions in IDL are data structures that optionally can contain data elements, although including data elements is not necessary. Once defined, the exceptions that an operation can throw are identified in the operation's raises clause. Let's define a few exceptions in our example, and in conjunction with this we'll remove the rather vague boolean return types from the buy() and sell() operations and replace them with the current out parameters:

```
module OnlineBroker
{
  interface Account
```

```
    {
        readonly attribute string accountNumber;
        attribute string accountHolderName;

        exception InvalidSymbol()
        {
            string symbol;
        };

        exception ExceededBalance()
        {
            double currentBalance;
            double requiredBalance;
        };

        string cusip buy( in string symbol, inout long quantity )
            raises ( ExceededBalance, InvalidSymbol );

        string cusip sell( in string symbol )
            raises ( InvalidSymbol );
    };
};
```

Now, when the client invokes our buy() and sell() operations, they will expect that upon success, a cusip number will be returned which will identify the transaction. In the event of a problem, an exception will be thrown. When caught, the exception's data items can be examined to gain more information about the error that has occurred. Obviously, this interface would not be acceptable if this were a production system, since we don't want our client blocking during the buy() or sell() operations, which could possibly take minutes. The purpose of this interface is simply to demonstrate the different parts and syntax of an IDL interface.

A quick note, operations can also be defined as oneway, which causes them to be asynchronous. The invocation returns to the client immediately after the request is transmitted to the server. The syntax is as follows:

```
    oneway void doSomething( in string abc );
```

As a result of being asynchronous, oneway operations have several restrictions; they cannot have a non-void return type, they can only have in parameters, and no exceptions can be thrown.

Inheritance

Just like Java interfaces, IDL interfaces can inherit from other interfaces. In addition, all IDL interfaces implicitly inherit from the Object interface, making the Object interface the base interface of all CORBA objects. Again extending our example, let's create an interface for a margin account. The syntax for interface inheritance is as follows:

```
    module OnlineBroker
    {
        // ...interface Account

        interface MarginAccount : Account
        {
```

```
        readonly attribute double margin;
        void requestAdditionalMargin( in double additionalAmt );
    };
};
```

Multiple Inheritance

Unlike Java, it is also possible when defining an interface in IDL to inherit from more than one interface. This allows the new interface to inherit the attributes, operations, exceptions, etc. from each of its base interfaces. The listed interfaces are delimited by commas.

Let's now move on to integrating our CORBA objects and clients with various J2EE application components.

J2EE and CORBA

As you may have noticed in the previous section, the J2EE and CORBA architectures provide similar benefits to the programmer developing a distributed application. Each provides a framework that supports location transparency of distributed objects. Each enjoys multi-platform support and as a result permits applications to run in heterogeneous environments. The implementation language, however, is where these two architectures diverge.

J2EE makes development of distributed applications easier by allowing programmers to work entirely in Java. And since J2EE is based completely on the Java language, this allows the application components to benefit from Java's 'Write Once, Run Anywhere' model. However, making use of existing or third-party non-Java source code can be tedious. Making distributed components available to non-Java clients can also present difficulties.

CORBA on the other hand permits development in any one of a number of supported programming languages, addressing the use of APIs and legacy code written in different languages. In addition, performance-critical components can be isolated and developed in lower level, more performance oriented languages such as C++. On the downside, there is the learning curve of using IDL and understanding the IDL to-language mappings. In addition, no programming language ports as easily from platform to platform as Java, so moving non-Java CORBA components from one platform to another can present a significant expense in time and energy, as well as opening up the opportunity for new bugs. In summary, CORBA allows more flexibility, and possibly performance, at the expense of portability.

By integrating the CORBA and J2EE architectures, distributed applications can enjoy the above-mentioned benefits while many of the associated limitations can be reduced or even eliminated. As we will see, Java and CORBA work very well together. We can capitalize on this by hiding any non-Java application components such as thirdparty or legacy code behind IDL interfaces, making source code that was initially difficult to deal with from Java very accessible. Conversely, any functionality within our application that we want to make available to the world can be represented as CORBA objects, allowing many different types of clients to utilize it. When used properly, this integration provides the programmer with a very powerful toolset.

Our goal in this section is to demonstrate how components within the CORBA framework can be accessed from the J2EE framework. To demonstrate this, we will build a slightly more complex CORBA object and client, and then demonstrate how to interact with our new CORBA object from various J2EE application components.

The WroxQuotes CORBA Object

Our CORBA object will simulate a stock market quote retrieval service, allowing its clients to request the current volume, bid and ask prices, and the last transaction timestamp for one or more symbols. Obviously, we are not going to have a live data stream to provide market data, so for the purposes of these examples we will simulate fluctuations in the market conditions. We will build the server application containing the CORBA object, and a client application that we can use to test our CORBA object.

The first step is to define the interface that our CORBA object will expose. Below is the source code for the IDL interface:

```
module WroxStocks
{
  typedef string Symbol;
  typedef sequence<Symbol> SymbolList;

  exception UnknownSymbol
  {
    Symbol unknown;
  };

  interface WroxQuotes
  {
    struct Timestamp
    {
      unsigned short day;
      unsigned short month;
      unsigned short year;
      unsigned short hour;
      unsigned short minute;
      unsigned short second;
    };

    struct Quote
    {
      Symbol     symb;
      unsigned long volume;
      double     bid;
      double     ask;
      Timestamp  asOf;
    };

    typedef sequence<Quote> QuoteList;

    Quote getQuote( in Symbol symb )
        raises ( UnknownSymbol );

    QuoteList getQuoteList( in SymbolList symbList )
        raises ( UnknownSymbol );
  };
};
```

Our IDL interface is made up of several parts, so let's start from the outermost level and work our way in.

❑ Our interface and its supporting definitions are all defined within a module, namely WroxStocks. Since everything within the module must be referenced from outside using the module name, the IDL module provides us with a naming scope to prevent us from conflicting with other IDL definitions within our application.

❑ Within our module are two typedefs, an exception, and a single interface. The typedefs allow us to refer to a particular element of the interface through an alternate name. For example, the first typedef, Symbol, will now act as an alternate name for the string data type. The second typedef, SymbolList, is an alternate name for a sequence of Symbols. As we have seen, a sequence in IDL is similar to an array in Java. This sequence, since it doesn't contain a fixed size, is unbounded, meaning that there is no limitation placed on it as to how many items it can contain, within the limits of the hardware of course. Note the use of the Symbol typedef. These two elements of our module would have the identical structure if defined without the typedefs; this just provides a more convenient and descriptive means of defining the rest of our module.

One note however: in IDL, a sequence of elements must be expressed using a typedef when it is used as a parameter type or return type in operation definitions. You can see this further down in the interface definition in our operation definitions for getQuote() and getQuoteList().

❑ Also at the module level we have the definition of the exception UnknownSymbol. The UnknownSymbol exception contains a single Symbol item to indicate which of the possibly many symbols provided is in error.

❑ The last element defined in our module is the interface WroxQuotes. Within WroxQuotes, we have two structures defined to convey our output information. The first is a Timestamp structure. This is necessary since IDL does not have a date or timestamp structure or data type. Note that it is not important exactly how this information is expressed, whether it is broken down to basic data types as we did, or represented as the number of seconds from some reference point, as long as all clients that use the interface can understand and utilize the information as it is provided. Following the Timestamp structure is the Quote structure. This struct will be used to contain the information, including the timestamp, of each symbol that was provided as input. After the structs, we see another example of a sequence typedef, this time a list of Quotes.

❑ Lastly, the WroxQuotes contains two operations, getQuote() and getQuoteList(). The getQuoteList() operation makes use of the typedef'ed sequences we've defined above. Also, both of these operations can throw an UnknownSymbol exception, as indicated by the raises clause at the end of the operation signature definitions. It is these operations within our CORBA object that will perform the heavy lifting, retrieving the quote data from our (fictional) data stream and returning it to the client.

Now that we have the IDL definition, we can compile it to generate the IDL stub, skeleton, and supporting classes we'll need in the construction of our CORBA object and its containing server application. To compile the IDL, we'll use the idlj compiler provided by the J2SE 1.3.

> Tip : When creating the source files for the interface, server application and client application, it is best to create three subdirectories for the project, one for the interface, one for the server application and one for the client application. Depending on how your files are named, this may be necessary to prevent the **idlj** compiler from overwriting your own source files.
>
> As an example, for our WroxQuotes client, interface, and server, we can create three subdirectories within our project directory, like so:
>
> ```
> C:\ProJavaServer\Chapter29\WroxQuotes\Client
> C:\ProJavaServer\Chapter29\WroxQuotes\IDL
> C:\ProJavaServer\Chapter29\WroxQuotes\Server
> ```

To compile the IDL above, move to the IDL directory and invoke the IDL to Java compiler specifying the name of the IDL file, in our case we named it WroxStocks.idl, which contains the interface definition as follows:

```
idlj -fall WroxStocks.idl
```

The −fall option to the compiler will force the compiler to generate both stub and skeleton code, whereas the −fclient and −fserver options will restrict the output to the stub or skeleton respectively. Compiling this IDL definition will result in the following files:

File	Description
WroxStocks._ WroxQuotesImplBase	Abstract class that can be used as a base class for CORBA object implementations. It implements the WroxQuotes Java interface described below, forcing subclasses to implement every IDL-defined method.
WroxStocks._ WroxQuotesStub	Instances of this class will act as the proxy object in the client application. Invoking its methods will construct the requests that are forwarded to the remote object via the ORB. Note that it implements the WroxQuotes Java interface described below, ensuring that all defined methods will be accounted for and allowing indirect access to these objects.
WroxStocks.Symbol Helper	Helper class for Symbol string type (see below).
WroxStocks.Symbol ListHelper	Helper class for SymbolList string array (see below).
WroxStocks.Symbol ListHolder	Holder class for SymbolList string array (see below).
WroxStocks.Unknown Symbol	A final class extending org.omg.CORBA.UserException which represents any UnknownSymbol exceptions thrown.
WroxStocks.Unknown SymbolHelper	Helper class for UnknownSymbol objects (see below).
WroxStocks.Unknown SymbolHolder	Holder class for UnknownSymbol objects (see below).

File	Description
WroxStocks. WroxQuotes	This interface is the basis of the generated classes. It is through this Java interface that the client application will act on the proxy object, _WroxQuotesStub. It is also used to ensure that implementation objects built on top of _WroxQuotesImplBase provide a definition of each IDL defined interface. It is an empty Java interface that extends several other interfaces, namely WroxQuotesOperations (below), org.omg.CORBA.Object, the base interface of all CORBA objects, and org.omg.CORBA.portable.IDLEntity, an empty interface used to indicate that the implementing class is a Java value type (used by RMI IIOP for marshalling/unmarshalling).
WroxStocks. WroxQuotesHelper	Helper class for the WroxQuotes interface (see below).
WroxStocks. WroxQuotesHolder	Holder class for the WroxQuotes interface (see below).
WroxStocks. WroxQuotesOperations	An interface that defines the operations and attribute get/set operations defined in the IDL interface.
WroxStocks.WroxQuotes Package.Quote	A final class that represents a Quote structure in the IDL definition. This class implements the empty interface org.omg.CORBA.portable.IDLEntity, see WroxQuotes description for more detail.
WroxStocks.WroxQuotes Package.QuoteHelper	Helper class for the Quote class(see below).
WroxStocks.WroxQuotes Package.QuoteHolder	Holder class for the Quote class(see below).
WroxStocks.WroxQuotes Package.QuoteList Helper	Helper class for the QuoteList Quote object array(see below).
WroxStocks.WroxQuotes Package.QuoteList Holder	Holder class for the QuoteList Quote object array(see below).
WroxStocks.WroxQuotes Package.Timestamp	A final class that represents a Timestamp structure in the IDL definition. This class, like Quote, implements the empty interface org.omg.CORBA.portable.IDLEntity.
WroxStocks.WroxQuotes Package.Timestamp Helper	Helper class for the Timestamp class (see below).
WroxStocks.WroxQuotes Package.Timestamp Holder	Holder class for the Timestamp class (see below)

As you can see above, several `Helper` and `Holder` classes have been generated. In general, the `Helper` class is an abstract public class that contains public static methods used to assist the object type it is associated with. A `Helper` class contains methods for inserting and extracting its associated object into and from a CORBA `Any` object, a CORBA class that can represent any type. It also contains methods for reading from `org.omg.CORBA.portable.InputStream` objects and writing to `org.omg.CORBA.portable.OutputStream` objects. For interface types that extend `org.omg.CORBA.Object`, the Helper class will also contain a narrow method, allowing downcasting of references to `Object` types. Finally, the Helper class also provides support for CORBA Typecodes, containers for information about CORBA data types.

Holder classes are generated for object types that are themselves not streamable, that is, objects that don't implement the `org.omg.CORBA.portable.Streamable` interface. This is necessary to allow marshalling and unmarshalling of these types to and from the remote CORBA object.

Writing the CORBA Object and Server

So now that we have our IDL definition compiled, let's begin to build our CORBA object implementation and server.

The CORBA Object

The IDL compiler generates the `_WroxQuotesImplBase` abstract class that will act as the foundation for our implementation. Since it implements the `WroxQuotes` Java interface, which in turn extends the `WroxQuotesOperations` interface, our subclass will be required to define each method defined in the IDL interface.

Our implementation class, `WroxQuotesImpl`, extends `WroxStocks._WroxQuotesImplBase`, and therefore provides implementations of the two IDL-defined methods, `getQuote()` and `getQuoteList()`. Also note that you are free to provide any other methods that are needed as well, as we do by adding a method called `populateQuote()`. Of course, these additional methods will not be available to clients, only those contained (indirectly) in the `WroxQuotes` interface are exposed. The `populateQuote()` method is where our simulation of market data takes place. It simply generates a random volume, bid, and ask price. For the timestamp, we will simply use the current time. Here is our implementation object definition:

```
import java.util.Calendar;

class WroxQuotesImpl extends WroxStocks._WroxQuotesImplBase {

  protected void populateQuote(String symbol,
                               WroxStocks.WroxQuotesPackage.Quote quote)
  {
    long base = java.lang.Math.round(100 * java.lang.Math.random());
    long numerator = java.lang.Math.round(8 * java.lang.Math.random());
    long spread = java.lang.Math.round(8 * java.lang.Math.random());

    quote.symb = symbol.toUpperCase();
    quote.volume = (int) (1000000 * java.lang.Math.random());
    quote.bid = base + ((double) numerator / 8);
    quote.ask = quote.bid + ((double) spread / 8);

    Calendar cal = new java.util.GregorianCalendar();
    quote.asOf = new WroxStocks.WroxQuotesPackage.Timestamp();
    quote.asOf.day = (short) cal.get(Calendar.DATE);
    quote.asOf.month = (short) cal.get(Calendar.MONTH);
```

```
  quote.asOf.year = (short) cal.get(Calendar.YEAR);
  quote.asOf.hour = (short) cal.get(Calendar.HOUR_OF_DAY);
  quote.asOf.minute = (short) cal.get(Calendar.MINUTE);
  quote.asOf.second = (short) cal.get(Calendar.SECOND);
}

public WroxStocks.WroxQuotesPackage.Quote getQuote(String symb)
        throws WroxStocks.UnknownSymbol {
  WroxStocks.WroxQuotesPackage.Quote result = null;

  symb = symb.trim();

  // This is added to artificially create an Unknown Exception
  // so that we can test our error handling

  if (symb.equalsIgnoreCase("ABC")) {
    WroxStocks.UnknownSymbol us = new WroxStocks.UnknownSymbol();
    us.unknown = symb;
    throw us;
  }

  try {
    result = new WroxStocks.WroxQuotesPackage.Quote();
    populateQuote(symb, result);
  } catch (Exception e) {
    System.err.println(e);
    e.printStackTrace(System.err);
  }

  return result;
}

public WroxStocks.WroxQuotesPackage.Quote[]
        getQuoteList(String[] symbList)
        throws WroxStocks.UnknownSymbol
{
  WroxStocks.WroxQuotesPackage.Quote[] result = null;

  try {
    result = new WroxStocks.WroxQuotesPackage.Quote[symbList.length];

    for (int i = 0; i < symbList.length; i++) {
      symbList[i] = symbList[i].trim();

      // This is added to artificially create an Unknown Exception
      // so that we can test our error handling
      if (symbList[i].equalsIgnoreCase("ABC")) {
        WroxStocks.UnknownSymbol us = new WroxStocks.UnknownSymbol();
        us.unknown = symbList[i];
        throw us;
      }

      WroxStocks.WroxQuotesPackage.Quote quote =
```

```
                                new WroxStocks.WroxQuotesPackage.Quote();
        populateQuote(symbList[i], quote);
        result[i] = quote;
      }
    } catch (WroxStocks.UnknownSymbol us) {

      // Rethrow exception
      throw us;
    } catch (Exception e) {
      System.err.println(e);
      e.printStackTrace(System.err);
    }
    return result;
  }
}
```

Save this file in the server directory. Note that in the `getQuote()` and `getQuoteList()` method implementations, we throw an `UnknownSymbol` exception for symbol `"ABC"`. This has been added to allow us to generate exceptions on command to test our error handling from the various CORBA clients we will build.

The CORBA Server

Since we have our implementation class defined, we can now build the containing server application, which we'll call `WroxQuotesServer`. Our server implementation has several responsibilities. First, it must initialize the ORB object to enable communication with client processes. This is done with the following line of source code:

```
ORB orb = ORB.init(args, null);
```

The ORB has the ability to accept settings, either as command line arguments shown above, or as a `java.util.Properties` object passed as the second parameter. Among other things, these arguments can direct the ORB to the listening port of a Naming Service, as we will see below. In addition, the JavaIDL ORB provides the ability to 'plug in' a different ORB by providing the `ORB.init()` method with the class name of the new ORB.

Once the ORB is initialized, we can instantiate our implementation object and connect it to the ORB to allow the ORB to locate and direct requests to our implementation object as they are received:

```
WroxQuotesImpl impl = new WroxQuotesImpl();
orb.connect(impl);
```

Next, we must provide our CORBA object's object reference to the outside world so that we can receive and handle requests. Both the J2SE SDK and J2EE SDK provide a Naming Service, `tnameserv`, which we will use to associate our implementation's object reference with a name.

The first item of business is to obtain an object reference to the root context of the Naming Service, which can be retrieved from the ORB using its `resolve_initial_references()` method. This is why the ORB can take as a parameter the location of the Naming Service.

```
org.omg.CORBA.Object rootContextObj =
            orb.resolve_initial_references("NameService");
```

Note that `resolve_initial_references()`, since it can be used for many different types of objects, simply returns an `org.omg.CORBA.Object`, the base interface of all CORBA objects. Therefore, in the next step, we must cast this object reference into a `NamingContext` object. To do this, we can make use of the `NamingContext`'s Helper class method, `narrow()`.

```
NamingContext rootContext =
            NamingContextHelper.narrow(rootContextObj);
```

Once this is accomplished, we need to construct an array of `NameComponents` that will describe the name of our new CORBA object. The purpose of the array is to allow object names to be grouped in contexts. Each component in the array will identify a context in which the next component will be located. The last element in the array will define the object itself. If the array contains only one `NameComponent`, then the object will be contained within the root context. We will insert our object into the root context, so only one `NameComponent` will be necessary:

```
NameComponent name = new NameComponent("WroxQuotes", "");
NameComponent path[] = {
  name
};
```

The final step to making our object available is to bind the name, as described by the `NameComponent` array, to the object reference of our implementation object. This is done with the `bind()` or `rebind()` method of the `NamingContext`. `bind()` attempts to insert the object reference into the `NamingContext`, throwing an `AlreadyBound` exception if it already exists. To allow us to rerun the server multiple times without having to restart our `Naming Service`, we'll use `rebind()`, which inserts a new or replaces an existing object reference in the `NamingContext`. This can be done as follows:

```
rootContext.rebind(path, impl);
```

Our server's final step is to wait for incoming requests. Since the ORB is responsible for listening for requests, we only need to ensure that our server application does not exit. This can be done simply as follows:

```
java.lang.Object syncObj = new java.lang.Object();
synchronized (syncObj) {
  syncObj.wait();
}
```

Here is the complete source code for our CORBA object's server:

```
import org.omg.CORBA.*;
import org.omg.CosNaming.*;
import java.io.*;

class WroxQuotesServer {
  public static void main(String args[]) {
    try {
      ORB orb = ORB.init(args, null);

      System.out.println("Creating implementation object");
      WroxQuotesImpl impl = new WroxQuotesImpl();
      orb.connect(impl);
```

```
        System.out.println("Connecting to Naming Service");
        org.omg.CORBA.Object rootContextObj =
            orb.resolve_initial_references("NameService");
        NamingContext rootContext =
            NamingContextHelper.narrow(rootContextObj);

        NameComponent name = new NameComponent("WroxQuotes", "");
        NameComponent path[] = {
            name
        };

        System.out.println("Binding object to naming context");
        rootContext.rebind(path, impl);

        System.out.println("Ready to accept requests");
        java.lang.Object syncObj = new java.lang.Object();
        synchronized (syncObj) {
            syncObj.wait();
        }
    } catch (Exception e) {
        System.err.println("Exception caught : " + e);
        e.printStackTrace(System.err);
    }
  }
}
```

Coding the CORBA Client

Our CORBA client needs to perform three basic steps:

- ❑   Initialize the ORB
- ❑   Obtain the object reference of our CORBA object
- ❑   Invoke its methods to obtain the information it needs

The ORB initialization is performed just as in the server application, namely:

```
ORB orb = ORB.init(args, null);
```

Once this is accomplished, we need the object reference of our CORBA object. Since the server placed this object reference in the Naming Service under the name "WroxQuotes", we just need to access the Naming Service to retrieve it. The manner in which this is done is also very similar to the server:

```
WroxStocks.WroxQuotes quoteObj = null;

// ... as before

org.omg.CORBA.Object contextObj =
            orb.resolve_initial_references("NameService");
NamingContext rootContext = NamingContextHelper.narrow(contextObj);
```

```
NameComponent name = new NameComponent("WroxQuotes", "");
NameComponent path[] = {
  name
};

org.omg.CORBA.Object obj = rootContext.resolve(path);
quoteObj = WroxStocks.WroxQuotesHelper.narrow(obj);
```

The main difference between our server's handling of the Naming Service and our client's is that instead of binding (or rebinding), we need to call resolve() on the NamingContext, providing the NameComponent array to identify the object. This will return a basic object reference, of type org.omg.CORBA.Object. Using the narrow() method defined in our WroxQuotesHelper class, we can cast our generic object reference into a WroxQuotes object reference. Note that our quoteObj is actually a reference to the Java interface WroxQuotes, which in turn points to a _WroxQuotesStub object.

At this point, we are free to invoke methods on our remote object via the local stub object. Since we are actually invoking these methods on the stub object, these invocations are simply invocations on a local object, like so:

```
WroxStocks.WroxQuotesPackage.Quote quote = quoteObj.getQuote("MSFT");
System.out.println("SYMBOL\tVOLUME\tBID\tASK\tAS OF");
displayQuote(quote);
```

Below is the complete source code for our CORBA client, including several tests of the interface's methods:

```
import org.omg.CORBA.*;
import org.omg.CosNaming.*;
import java.util.GregorianCalendar;
import java.io.*;

class WroxQuotesClient {

  protected static void
  displayQuote(WroxStocks.WroxQuotesPackage.Quote quote) {
    if (quote != null) {
      GregorianCalendar cal = new GregorianCalendar(quote.asOf.year,
              quote.asOf.month, quote.asOf.day, quote.asOf.hour,
              quote.asOf.minute, quote.asOf.second);

      java.util.Date asOf = cal.getTime();
      System.out.println(quote.symb + "\t" + quote.volume + "\t"
                      + quote.bid + "\t" + quote.ask + "\t" + asOf);
    }
  }

  public static void main(String args[]) {
    WroxStocks.WroxQuotes quoteObj = null;

    try {
      System.out.println("Connecting to WroxQuotes CORBA object");
      ORB orb = ORB.init(args, null);

      org.omg.CORBA.Object contextObj =
```

```
                        orb.resolve_initial_references("NameService");
    NamingContext rootContext = NamingContextHelper.narrow(contextObj);

    NameComponent name = new NameComponent("WroxQuotes", "");
    NameComponent path[] = {
      name
    };

    org.omg.CORBA.Object obj = rootContext.resolve(path);
    quoteObj = WroxStocks.WroxQuotesHelper.narrow(obj);
  } catch (Exception e) {
    System.err.println(e.getMessage());
  }

  System.out.println("");

  try {
    System.out.println("Testing getQuote() method");

    WroxStocks.WroxQuotesPackage.Quote quote = quoteObj.getQuote("MSFT");
    System.out.println("SYMBOL\tVOLUME\tBID\tASK\tAS OF");
    displayQuote(quote);
  } catch (WroxStocks.UnknownSymbol us) {
    System.out.println("Exception caught : " + us);
    System.out.println("Unknown symbol -> " + us.unknown);
  } catch (Exception e) {
    System.err.println(e.getMessage());
  }

  System.out.println("");

  try {
    System.out.println("Testing getQuoteList() method");

    String symbols[] = {
      "MSFT", "AOL", "AMZN", "INTC", "SUNW"
    };

    WroxStocks.WroxQuotesPackage.Quote[] quoteList =
                              quoteObj.getQuoteList(symbols);
    System.out.println("SYMBOL\tVOLUME\tBID\tASK\tAS OF");
    if (quoteList != null) {
      for (int i = 0; i < quoteList.length; i++) {
        displayQuote(quoteList[i]);
      }
    }
  } catch (WroxStocks.UnknownSymbol us) {
    System.out.println("Exception caught : " + us);
    System.out.println("Unknown symbol -> " + us.unknown);
  } catch (Exception e) {
    System.err.println(e.getMessage());
  }

  System.out.println("");
```

```
    try {
      System.out.println("Testing UnknownSymbol exception with getQuote()");

      WroxStocks.WroxQuotesPackage.Quote newquote =
                                    quoteObj.getQuote("ABC");

      System.out.println("Exception test failed");
    } catch (WroxStocks.UnknownSymbol us) {
      System.out.println("Exception caught : " + us);
      System.out.println("Unknown symbol -> " + us.unknown);
    } catch (Exception e) {
      System.err.println(e.getMessage());
    }

    System.out.println("");

    try {
      System.out.println("Test UnknownSymbol exception with" +
                      "getQuoteList()");

      String symbols[] = {
        "MSFT", "AOL", "ABC", "INTC", "SUNW"
      };

      WroxStocks.WroxQuotesPackage.Quote[] quoteList =
                                  quoteObj.getQuoteList(symbols);

      System.out.println("Exception test failed");
    } catch (WroxStocks.UnknownSymbol us) {
      System.out.println("Exception caught : " + us);
      System.out.println("Unknown symbol -> " + us.unknown);
    } catch (Exception e) {
      System.err.println(e.getMessage());
    }

    quoteObj._release();
  }
}
```

Building and Running the Example

Now we can build our two applications, client and server, and execute them. Compile all of the `.java` files, including the files generated by the IDL compiler. When compiling the client and server applications, first make sure that the compiled IDL generated class files are in the CLASSPATH, like so:

From the client directory, perform the following:

```
    javac -classpath .;..\IDL *.java
```

Now from the server directory, and repeat this there:

```
    javac -classpath .;..\IDL *.java
```

Once the client and server applications are built, there are only three remaining steps.

First, we must start a Naming Service so that our server can publish its object reference for the client to use. To do this, simply run the `tnameserv` executable that can be found in the Java 2 SDK `bin` directory. The default listening port for `tnameserv` is 900. If this presents a conflict on your system, the listening port can be changed using the `-ORBInitialPort <port#>` command line arguments. For example, to start the Naming Service on port 1100, do the following:

```
tnameserv -ORBInitialPort 1100
```

Once the Naming Service is running, we can start our CORBA server application. Assuming that the Naming Service is running on port 1100, from the directory containing the server application's class files do the following:

```
java -classpath .;..\IDL WroxQuotesServer -ORBInitialPort 1100
```

Make sure that the IDL-compiler generated source is in the CLASSPATH. In the event that your Naming Service is running on a different source, the server application can be notified of this using the `-ORBInitialHost <host>` arguments.

Now all that is left to do is run our client application. Again assuming a Naming Service listening port of 1100, from the directory containing the client application's class files do the following:

```
java -classpath .;..\IDL WroxQuotesClient -ORBInitialPort 1100
```

As with the server application, if the Naming Service is running on a different source, the client application can be notified of this using the `-ORBInitialHost <host>` arguments.

The output of the client should resemble the following:

Integration with J2EE

Let's now take a look at how we can access our new CORBA object from the various J2EE application components:

❑ We'll start by creating a Java servlet that retrieves quotes from the `WroxQuotes` CORBA object

❑ From there, we will then construct a JavaServer Page that replicates this functionality to demonstrate the similarities and differences in accessing the CORBA object

❑ Finally, we'll construct an Enterprise JavaBean that 'wraps' the CORBA object, providing the same functionality to its clients

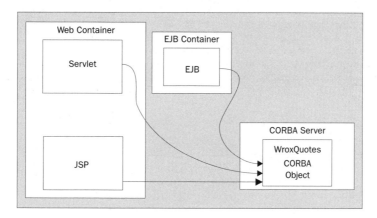

Servlets and CORBA Objects

First, let's examine how to build a Java servlet that accesses our CORBA object. To provide a list of stock symbols to our servlet, we will construct a simple HTML form that will request the stock symbols from the user and pass them, via the query string, to the servlet. The servlet will request the quotes for these symbols from our `WroxQuotes` CORBA object and display the results in tabular form. Since we will eventually deploy the new servlet into a web container, we will use the `HttpServlet` class as the foundation.

The servlet and other application components we will look at follow the same process for locating and accessing the CORBA object as our simple client application did. In fact, much of the code that we wrote in our client application could be reused as is. The only new task is to determine when in the servlet's lifecycle to perform each of the tasks that is necessary, namely initializing the ORB, accessing the Naming Service's root context, locating the object, and finally invoking the methods on the object. Since the servlet API guarantees us that the servlet's `init()` method will always be called and allowed to complete before any requests to its `service()` method are made, the `init()` method provides the opportunity to perform the ORB and object reference initialization tasks that are only required at startup, which in our case are the ORB initialization, accessing the Naming Service, and retrieval of the object reference. Therefore, let's define our servlet's `init()` method to perform our CORBA initialization steps:

```
public void init(ServletConfig config) throws ServletException {
    super.init(config);
```

```
        ORB orb = null;
        try {
          String[] args = {
            ""
          };
          String port =
                  getServletContext().getInitParameter("ORBInitialPort");
          String host =
                  getServletContext().getInitParameter("ORBInitialHost");

          Properties orbProps = new Properties();
          orbProps.put("org.omg.CORBA.ORBInitialPort", port);
          orbProps.put("org.omg.CORBA.ORBInitialHost", host);

          orb = org.omg.CORBA.ORB.init(args, orbProps);
        } catch (Exception e) {
          String msg = "Exception during ORB initialization";
          config.getServletContext().log(msg, e);
          ServletException se = new ServletException(msg, e);
          throw se;
        }

        try {
          org.omg.CORBA.Object contextObj =
            orb.resolve_initial_references("NameService");
          NamingContext rootContext = NamingContextHelper.narrow(contextObj);

          NameComponent name = new NameComponent("WroxQuotes", "");
          NameComponent namePath[] = {
            name
          };

          org.omg.CORBA.Object obj = rootContext.resolve(namePath);
          quoteObj = WroxStocks.WroxQuotesHelper.narrow(obj);
        } catch (Exception e) {
          String msg = "Exception while retrieving object reference";
          config.getServletContext().log(msg, e);
          ServletException se = new ServletException(msg, e);
          throw se;
        }
      } // end init
```

Basically, the init() method performs the same steps as our client application did, though there are several differences that stem from the fact that we are now performing these steps in a servlet rather than a client application. The first difference you may notice is how we provide the arguments to ORB.init(). Obviously, we don't have the benefit of command line arguments in the servlet, so instead we'll specify them in the application's deployment descriptor as initialization parameters, called ORBInitialPort and ORBInitialHost. This will allow is to retrieve them from our servlet and later on our JSP page. In init(), we obtain these from the context using the getServletContext().getInitParameter method, and construct a java.util.Properties object which will be passed to ORB.init().

> Note that we had to call super.init(config). We need to do this because we are overwriting the HttpServlet's init() method here, which is where the context information gets saved. If we didn't make this call, we would get a NullPointerException for the context.

The second difference we should point out is the handling of exceptions. Here, we will simply throw a servlet exception out to the servlet engine. Any exceptions that we catch as we initialize our object reference are caught, and a `ServletException` is created, initialized with the trapped exception, and thrown out of the `init()` method. This will stop the execution of the servlet initialization and will be passed up to the servlet engine. The servlet engine will log the error message (where depends on the configuration of the container) and send an error message to the browser, typically an internal server error message. We are certainly free to handle these errors more gracefully, but for our purposes here, this is sufficient.

The last difference is also related to error handling. When we trap an exception during our processing, before we throw the `ServletException`, we log the message using the `ServletContext`'s `log()` method. This will write the log message, and if provided the stack trace of the exception, to the container's event log. As with the error log, the actual location of this output is dependent on the container's configuration.

Once the servlet has initialized, and we have the object reference of our `WroxQuotes` object, we can begin to service requests, invoking methods on our CORBA object and constructing the HTML output. We will implement the `doGet()` method of our `HttpServlet`, since our HTML form will provide the input as part of the URL. Here is the implementation of our `doGet()` method and a supporting method, `parseSymbolList()`:

```
public void doGet(HttpServletRequest request,
                  HttpServletResponse response),
              throws ServletException, IOException {

  WroxStocks.WroxQuotesPackage.Quote[] quotes = null;

  String symbolList = request.getParameter("Symbols");
  String symbols[] = parseSymbolList(symbolList);
  try {
    if (quoteObj != null) {
      quotes = quoteObj.getQuoteList(symbols);
    }
    response.setContentType("text/html");
    try {
      PrintWriter out = response.getWriter();

      out.println("<html>");
      out.println("<head>");
      out.println("<title>");
      out.println("WroxStocks Quote Service");
      out.println("</title>");
      out.println("</head>");
      out.println("<body bgcolor=\"#CAFD90\">");
      out.println("<br/>");
      out.println("<table border align=\"center\">");
      out.println("<tr align=\"center\" bgcolor=\"FFFFFF\">");
      out.println("<td>");
      out.println("<table>");
      out.println("<caption align=\"top\" style=\"font:14pt\">");
      out.println("<b>WroxStocks Stock Quotes</b>");
      out.println("</caption>");
      out.println("<tr align=\"center\" bgcolor=Silver>");
      out.println("<th width=100>SYMBOL</th>");
      out.println("<th width=100>VOLUME</th>");
      out.println("<th width=100>BID</th>");
```

```java
        out.println("<th width=100>ASK</th>");
        out.println("<th width=260>AS OF</th>");
        out.println("</tr>");

        if (quotes != null) {
          for (int i = 0; i < quotes.length; i++) {
            if ((i % 2) == 0) {
              out.println("<tr align=\"right\" bgcolor=\"#FFFFFF\">");
            } else {
              out.println("<tr align=\"right\" bgcolor=\"#E0E0E0\">");
            }

            out.println("<td align=\"center\">" + quotes[i].symb + "</td>");
            out.println("<td>" + quotes[i].volume + "</td>");
            out.println("<td>" + quotes[i].bid + "</td>");
            out.println("<td>" + quotes[i].ask + "</td>");

            GregorianCalendar cal =
              new GregorianCalendar(quotes[i].asOf.year,
                                    quotes[i].asOf.month,
                                    quotes[i].asOf.day,
                                    quotes[i].asOf.hour,
                                    quotes[i].asOf.minute,
                                    quotes[i].asOf.second);
            Date ts = cal.getTime();
            out.println("<td align=\"center\">" + ts + "</td>");
            out.println("</tr>");
          }
        }
        out.println("</table>");
        out.println("</td>");
        out.println("</tr>");
        out.println("</table>");
        out.println("</body>");
        out.println("</ html>");
        out.close();

      } catch (IOException e) {
        String msg = "IOException caught";
        getServletContext().log(msg, e);
        ServletException se = new ServletException(msg, e);
        throw se;
      }

    } catch (WroxStocks.UnknownSymbol us) {
      response.sendError(202, "Unknown Symbol : " + us.unknown);
      return;

    } catch (Exception e) {
      String msg = "Exception caught";
      getServletContext().log(msg, e);
      ServletException se = new ServletException(msg, e);
      throw se;
    }
```

```
    }

    protected String[] parseSymbolList(String symbolList) {
      Vector tokens = new Vector();
      StringTokenizer tokenizer = new StringTokenizer(symbolList);
      while (tokenizer.hasMoreTokens()) {
        tokens.addElement(tokenizer.nextToken());
      }

      String[] result = new String[tokens.size()];
      for (int i = 0; i < tokens.size(); i++) {
        result[i] = (String) tokens.elementAt(i);
      }
      return result;
    }
```

Our `doGet()` method parses the input from the form, retrieved from the request object, parses it using our `parseSymbolList()` method, invokes the `getQuoteList()` method on our CORBA object via the object reference obtained in `init()`, and constructs the resulting HTML page, adding a row to the table for each quote that we received.

Notice that in all but one case, the exception handling is performed in the same manner as in `init()`, logging the error using the `ServletContext`'s `log()` method and throwing a `ServletException` in the event of a problem. The one case where we don't handle a trapped exception in this way is the `UnknownSymbol` exception that we may get from our CORBA object invocation. This is done simply because an invalid stock symbol is not a `ServletException`. Unknown or invalid stock symbols as input are an acceptable input, and should be handled differently. To provide a little more graceful mechanism, we can use the response object's `sendError()` method. This will return an HTTP error, in this case, 202 (`SC_ACCEPTED`) along with our error message back to the browser to indicate that the request was accepted but could not be completed. As with our `init()` error handling, we could construct a nice, well-designed error page to display to the user, but for our purposes here, this is sufficient.

Below is the remainder of the source code for our `WroxQuotesServlet`, these are the import statements we need:

```
import javax.servlet.*;
import javax.servlet.http.*;
import java.io.*;
import java.util.Properties;
import java.util.StringTokenizer;
import java.util.Vector;
import java.util.GregorianCalendar;
import java.util.Date;

import org.omg.CORBA.*;
import org.omg.CosNaming.*;
import WroxStocks.*;
import WroxStocks.WroxQuotesPackage.*;

public class WroxQuotesServlet extends HttpServlet {
  protected WroxStocks.WroxQuotes quoteObj = null;
```

We make sure that _release() is called by specifying this in the destroy() method:

```
public void destroy() {
  if (quoteObj != null) {
    quoteObj._release();
  }
  }
}
```

And that concludes the source code for the servlet. Now that we have our servlet completed, let's construct a simple HTML form, WroxQuotesForm.html, to provide input to our servlet:

```
<html>
<head>
<title>
WroxStocks Quote Service
</title>
</head>
<body bgcolor="#CAFD90">
<table border>
<tr align="center" bgcolor="FFFFFF">
<td>
<form method=GET action="servlet/WroxQuotesServlet">
<br/>
<h3>WroxStocks Quote Service</h3>
<p>Symbol(s): <input type="TEXT" name="Symbols" size=30>
<p><p><i>Enter stock symbol or multiple symbols delimited by spaces</i>
<p><input type="SUBMIT" name="SUBMIT" value="Get">
<input type="RESET" name="RESET" value="Reset">
</form>
</td>
</tr>
</table>
</body>
</html>
```

When compiling the servlet, be sure to include the directory containing the IDL-generated source files.

Deploying and Running the Servlet

Now that the HTML and servlet code is complete, we can deploy them and give it a try. Deployment of our CORBA client servlet is done in just the same manner as any other servlet.

We are going to be deploying our example servlet, JSP and EJB in Orion application server. In order to do this, create a new directory call WroxQuotes beneath the applications directory of the Orion install. Within this directory create an additional directory structure that looks like this:

```
applications/
            WroxQuotes/
                      ejbs/
                           META-INF/
                      META-INF/
```

```
Server/
webs/
        WEB-INF/
                classes/
```

For now we just want to concentrate on the `webs` directory. For simplicity, we will also move the necessary files from our CORBA server into this application. Move the `WroxQuotesServer` files into the corresponding `Server` directory here, and then copy the entire generated `WroxStocks` folder under the `WEB-INF` folder:

```
applications/
            WroxQuotes/
                    webs/
                        ...
                    WEB-INF/
                            classes/
                                    WroxStocks/
                                            WroxQuotesPackage/
```

Place the servlet in the `WEB-INF/classes` directory, and the `html` file under the `webs` directory.

Now we need to write the necessary deployement decriptors that Orion needs to set up our application. We'll start with the `web.xml` file for the `WEB-INF` directory:

```xml
<?xml version="1.0"?>
<!DOCTYPE web-app PUBLIC "-//Sun Microsystems, Inc.//DTD Web Application 2.2//EN"
"http://java.sun.com/j2ee/dtds/web-app_2_2.dtd">

<web-app>
    <servlet>
    <servlet-name>WroxQuotesServlet</servlet-name>
        <display-name>WroxQuotesServlet</display-name>
        <servlet-class>WroxQuotesServlet</servlet-class>
    </servlet>
    <welcome-file-list>
        <welcome-file>WroxQuotesForm.html</welcome-file>
    </welcome-file-list>
    <login-config>
        <auth-method>BASIC</auth-method>
    </login-config>

    <context-param>
        <param-name>ORBInitialHost</param-name>
        <param-value>localhost</param-value>
        <description></description>
    </context-param>
    <context-param>
        <param-name>ORBInitialPort</param-name>
        <param-value>1100</param-value>
        <description></description>
    </context-param>
</web-app>
```

This is where we are specifying the host and port settings that we need to connect to the CORBA Naming Service.

Next, we require the `application.xml` deployment descriptor for application that tells Orion that we are deploying a new web application:

```xml
<?xml version="1.0"?>
<!DOCTYPE application PUBLIC "-//Sun Microsystems, Inc.//DTD J2EE
Application 1.2//EN" "http://java.sun.com/j2ee/dtds/application_1_2.dtd">

<application>
    <display-name>Archive</display-name>
    <description></description>
    <module>
          <web>
                <web-uri>webs</web-uri>
                <context-root>/WroxQuotes</context-root>
          </web>
    </module>
</application>
```

Finally, before we can deploy the application in Orion we need to modify a couple of Orion's config descriptors to include our new application. Add the following line to `server.xml`, within the `application-server` tags:

```xml
<application name="WroxQuotes" path="../applications/WroxQuotes" />
```

Add this line to `default-web-site.xml` within the `web-site display-name` tag:

```xml
<web-app application="WroxQuotes" name="webs" root="/WroxQuotes" />
```

Now start Orion and your web application will be deployed for you.

Now our servlet is deployed and ready to test. First start, the `tnameserv` Naming Service using a port number of 1100:

```
tnameserv -ORBInitialPort 1100
```

Make sure that the CORBA server is running. You can run it from the original server location or the new one under the application. Either way make sure your provide the `WroxStocks` package in the `CLASSPATH`:

```
java -cp .;..\IDL WroxQuotesServer -ORBInitialPort 1100
java -cp .;..\webs\WEB-INF\classes\ WroxQuotesServer -ORBInitialPort 1100
```

Once the CORBA server has started, open a browser and enter the address of our HTML form, `http://localhost/WroxQuotes/`:

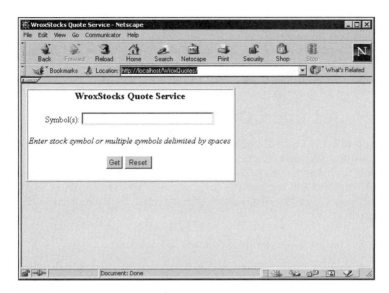

Providing an input string of MSFT AOL AMZN EBAY SUNW HWP DELL should yield the following:

SYMBOL	VOLUME	BID	ASK	AS OF
MSFT	537583	19.125	20.125	Fri Aug 04 21:46:23 GMT+01:00 2000
AOL	756060	35.5	35.625	Fri Aug 04 21:46:23 GMT+01:00 2000
AMZN	397942	44.75	45.0	Fri Aug 04 21:46:23 GMT+01:00 2000
EBAY	569641	17.75	18.5	Fri Aug 04 21:46:23 GMT+01:00 2000
SUNW	670445	25.0	25.625	Fri Aug 04 21:46:23 GMT+01:00 2000
HWP	473392	70.875	71.875	Fri Aug 04 21:46:23 GMT+01:00 2000
DELL	745463	65.25	65.625	Fri Aug 04 21:46:23 GMT+01:00 2000

Try experimenting with different inputs. Be sure to also try a few examples that will generate exceptions. For instance, shut down the J2EE and CORBA servers, restart the CORBA server with a different ORBInitialPort number, and retry the above example.

Remember that the servlet's init() method only runs once, so to retry init() related exceptions, restarting the Orion server is necessary. Also don't forget to attempt requests with our bogus ABC quote to see how the UnknownSymbol exception thrown from the CORBA server is handled by our code in the servlet's doGet() method.

It is worth pointing out that we could have also chosen to encapsulate the CORBA-related logic in a separate class, allowing us to decouple the servlet from the `WroxQuotes` object. However, I chose not to do this for the initial example in order to demonstrate more clearly the use of the CORBA object throughout the servlet lifecycle. In the next example, we will build a JavaBean that will encapsulate the access to our CORBA object and use it within a JavaServer Page.

JavaServer Pages and CORBA Objects

Now we'll examine how to use our CORBA object from a JavaServer Page. Much like the servlet above, the steps to access the CORBA object are very similar to that of our original client application. The differences we will see are in the use of the object within the framework of a JSP. To enable access to our CORBA object, we will first build a simple JavaBean that encapsulates our `WroxQuotes` CORBA object interaction. We can then use this bean in our JSP pages using the `<jsp:useBean>` tag without spreading the CORBA-related logic throughout the web application.

To begin with, let's define the JavaBean class to access the CORBA object:

```
import WroxStocks.WroxQuotesPackage.Quote;
import org.omg.CORBA.*;
import org.omg.CosNaming.*;

import java.util.Properties;
import java.util.Vector;
import java.util.StringTokenizer;

public class WroxQuotesBean {
  protected WroxStocks.WroxQuotes quoteObj = null;

  public WroxQuotesBean() {}

  public void finalize() throws Throwable {
    super.finalize();

    if (quoteObj != null) {
      quoteObj._release();
    }
  }

  public void init(String port, String host) {
    ORB orb = null;
    try {
      String[] args = {
        ""
      };
      System.out.println("orbProps: " + port + host);
      Properties orbProps = new Properties();
      orbProps.put("org.omg.CORBA.ORBInitialPort", port);
      orbProps.put("org.omg.CORBA.ORBInitialHost", host);
      System.out.println("orbProps: " + port + host);
      orb = org.omg.CORBA.ORB.init(args, orbProps);
    } catch (Exception e) {
      System.out.println("Exception during ORB initialization");
```

```
      System.out.println(e);
      e.printStackTrace(System.out);
    }

  try {
    org.omg.CORBA.Object contextObj =
      orb.resolve_initial_references("NameService");
    NamingContext rootContext = NamingContextHelper.narrow(contextObj);

    NameComponent name = new NameComponent("WroxQuotes", "");
    NameComponent namePath[] = {
      name
    };

    org.omg.CORBA.Object obj = rootContext.resolve(namePath);
    quoteObj = WroxStocks.WroxQuotesHelper.narrow(obj);
  } catch (Exception e) {
    System.out.println("Exception while accessing Naming Service");
    System.out.println(e);
    e.printStackTrace(System.out);
  }
}

public Quote[] getQuotes(String[] symbols)
        throws WroxStocks.UnknownSymbol {
  return quoteObj.getQuoteList(symbols);
}

public Quote[] getQuotes(String symbols)
        throws WroxStocks.UnknownSymbol {
  return getQuotes(parseSymbolList(symbols));
}

protected String[] parseSymbolList(String symbolList) {
  Vector tokens = new Vector();
  StringTokenizer tokenizer = new StringTokenizer(symbolList);
  while (tokenizer.hasMoreTokens()) {
    tokens.addElement(tokenizer.nextToken());
  }

  String[] result = new String[tokens.size()];
  for (int i = 0; i < tokens.size(); i++) {
    result[i] = (String) tokens.elementAt(i);
  }
  return result;
}
}
```

Keep in mind that to use the bean with the `<jsp:useBean>` tag, our class must be a public class and it must have a public constructor with no arguments. Now that the class has been written, let's define the JSP that uses it:

```
<!-- WroxQuotes.jsp -->
<html>
<head>
```

```
<title>
WroxStocks Quote Service
</title>
</head>
<body bgcolor="#CAFD90">

<%@ page import="WroxStocks.WroxQuotesPackage.Quote"
 errorPage="WroxQuotesError.jsp"%>

<jsp:useBean id="WroxQuotesBean" scope="application"
 class="WroxQuotesBean" >
<%
  String port = application.getInitParameter("ORBInitialPort" );
  String host = application.getInitParameter("ORBInitialHost" );
  WroxQuotesBean.init(port, host );
%>
</jsp:useBean>

<%
  String symbols = request.getParameter("Symbols");
  Quote[] quotes = null;

  try {
    quotes = WroxQuotesBean.getQuotes(symbols);
  } catch(WroxStocks.UnknownSymbol us)  {
    response.sendError(202, "Unknown symbol: " + us.unknown);
  }
%>

<br/>

<table border align="center">
<tr align="center" bgcolor="FFFFFF">
<td>
<table>
<caption align="top" style="font:14pt">
<b>WroxStocks Stock Quotes</b>
</caption>
<tr align="center" bgcolor=Silver>
<th width=100>SYMBOL</th>
<th width=100>VOLUME</th>
<th width=100>BID</th>
<th width=100>ASK</th>
<th width=260>AS OF</th>
</tr>
<%
   for(int i = 0; i < quotes.length; i++) {
     if( ( i % 2 ) == 0 ) {
%>
<tr align="right" bgcolor="#FFFFFF">
<%
   } else{
%>
<tr align="right" bgcolor="#E0E0E0">
```

```
<%
    }
%>
<td align="center"> <%= quotes[i].symb %> </td>
<td> <%= quotes[i].volume %> </td>
<td> <%= quotes[i].bid %> </td>
<td> <%= quotes[i].ask %> </td>
<td align="center">6/28/2000 19:59:00</td>
</tr>
<%
    } // END: for
%>
</table>
</td>
</tr>
</table>
</body>
</html>
```

Note that the JavaBean takes two parameters to its `init()` method, the port number and host name of the Naming Service. This allows us to specify these values at deployment time. Including the call to `init()` within the `<jsp:useBean>` tag ensures that our initialization function will only be called once, when the page is first loaded.

By default, any exceptions that occur will be caught in the servlet engine. To avoid this in the case of `UnknownSymbol` exceptions, we will add an exception handler to deal with these exceptions when thrown from the `getQuotes()` method. As with the servlet example, we are using the `sendError()` method of the response object. A more detailed error handling mechanism can be implemented, but for our examples this will be sufficient. With that in mind, we will also provide a very simple error page to handle any unhandled exceptions that are thrown. The error page is below:

```
<!-- WroxQuotesError.jsp -->
< html>
<head>
<title>
WroxStocks Quote Service Error
</title>
</head>
<body bgcolor="#CAFD90">
<%@ page language="java" isErrorPage="true" %>
<H2>Exception occurred</H2>
<br/>
<%= exception.toString() %>
<br/>
<%= exception.getMessage() %>
</body>
</ html>
```

Finally, we will need an HTML form to issue requests to the JSP we've created. To simplify things, we can use the same form as in the servlet example, as long as we make sure that the form's action is updated to point to the JSP's alias instead of the servlet's alias. Here is the updated HTML form.

```
<html>
<head>
```

```
<title>
WroxStocks Quote Service
</title>
</head>
<body bgcolor="#CAFD90">
<table border>
<tr align="center" bgcolor="FFFFFF">
<td>
<form method=GET action="WroxQuotes.jsp">
<br/>
<h3>WroxStocks Quote Service</h3>
<p>Symbol(s): <input type="TEXT" name="Symbols" size=30>
<p><p><i>Enter stock symbol or multiple symbols delimited by spaces</i>
<p><input type="SUBMIT" name="SUBMIT" value="Get">
<input type="RESET" name="RESET" value="Reset">
</form>
</td>
</tr>
</table>
</body>
</html>
```

Deploying and Running the JavaServer Page

Compile the bean and place it in the same directory as the servlet from earlier. In JSP pages reside in the webs directory with the html page.

Provided the class files are in the correct directories, all you need to do is stop and restart the Orion server. You use the web interface in exactly the same manner as for the servlet except that this time it's the JSP page (via the bean) instead of the servlet calling the CORBA server.

> It is advisably also to stop and restart the CORBA server object when you close down Orion. Start Orion up before you restart the CORBA server.

Enterprise JavaBeans and CORBA Objects

Continuing with our examination of different application components, let's now take a look at the integration of an Enterprise JavaBean and our CORBA object. In this example, we'll construct an EJB that takes requests for stock quotes and forwards them to our CORBA object, returning the results back to the client. Since our EJB doesn't maintain any state between invocations, we will implement it as a stateless session bean.

Let's start by defining the remote interface for our new EJB:

```
package ejbs;

import javax.ejb.EJBObject;
import java.rmi.RemoteException;

public interface WroxQuotes extends EJBObject {
  public StockQuote getQuote(String symbol)
```

```
        throws UnknownSymbolException, RemoteException;
    public StockQuote[] getQuoteList(String[] symbols)
            throws UnknownSymbolException, RemoteException;
}
```

This interface makes use of several other classes that we need to define, namely the StockQuote and UnknownSymbolException classes, defined below:

```
package ejbs;

import java.util.Date;
import java.io.Serializable;

public class StockQuote implements Serializable {
    public String symbol;
    public long volume;
    public double bid;
    public double ask;
    public Date timestamp;
}
```

We also define UnknownSymbolException:

```
package ejbs;

public class UnknownSymbolException extends Exception {
    protected String unknownSymbol = "";

    public UnknownSymbolException(String symbol) {
        unknownSymbol = symbol;
    }

    public String symbol() {
        return unknownSymbol;
    }
}
```

Now that we have the EJBObject-derived remote interface of our EJB, we can complete the definitions by creating our Home interface, WroxQuotesHome, and the actual class definition, WroxQuotesEJB:

```
package ejbs;

import javax.ejb.EJBHome;
import javax.ejb.CreateException;
import java.io.Serializable;
import java.rmi.RemoteException;

public interface WroxQuotesHome extends EJBHome {
    WroxQuotes create() throws RemoteException, CreateException;
}
```

To implement the CORBA logic in our session bean, we can make use of the WroxQuotesBean JavaBean that we developed in the last example. Here is the source code for our session bean, WroxQuotesEJB. Note that for convenience, I've hard-coded the parameters for the WroxQuotesBean's init() method. These could however be read from a configuration file, registry, etc when the EJB is first instantiated:

```java
package ejbs;

import java.rmi.RemoteException;
import javax.ejb.SessionBean;
import javax.ejb.SessionContext;
import javax.ejb.EJBException;
import java.util.Date;
import java.util.GregorianCalendar;

import WroxQuotesBean;

public class WroxQuotesEJB implements SessionBean {
  WroxQuotesBean quotesBean;

  public WroxQuotesEJB() {
    try {
      quotesBean = new WroxQuotesBean();
      quotesBean.init("2050", "localhost");  // Change if necessary
    } catch (Exception e) {

      // Throw a system-level exception to indicate that the
      // connection to the CORBA server failed
      EJBException ejbEx =
          new EJBException("WroxQuotes service initialization failed");
      throw ejbEx;
    }
  }

  public StockQuote getQuote(String symbol) throws UnknownSymbolException {
    StockQuote result = new StockQuote();

    String[] symbolList = {
      symbol
    };

    WroxStocks.WroxQuotesPackage.Quote[] q = null;
    try {
      q = quotesBean.getQuotes(symbolList);
    } catch (WroxStocks.UnknownSymbol us) {

      // Throw an application-level exception
      UnknownSymbolException usEx = new UnknownSymbolException(us.unknown);
      throw usEx;
    } catch (Exception e) {

    // Throw a system-level exception to indicate that the CORBA
    // invocation failed
      EJBException ejbEx =
        new EJBException("Failed to retrieve quote from WroxQuotes" +
```

```
                              "service");
      throw ejbEx;
   }

   result.symbol = q[0].symb;
   result.volume = q[0].volume;
   result.bid = q[0].bid;
   result.ask = q[0].ask;

   GregorianCalendar cal = new GregorianCalendar(q[0].asOf.year,
           q[0].asOf.month, q[0].asOf.day, q[0].asOf.hour,
           q[0].asOf.minute, q[0].asOf.second);

   result.timestamp = cal.getTime();

   return result;
}

public StockQuote[] getQuoteList(String[] symbols)
       throws UnknownSymbolException {
   WroxStocks.WroxQuotesPackage.Quote[] q = null;

   try {
     q = quotesBean.getQuotes(symbols);
   } catch (WroxStocks.UnknownSymbol us) {

     // Throw an application-level exception
     UnknownSymbolException usEx = new UnknownSymbolException(us.unknown);
     throw usEx;
   } catch (Exception e) {

     // Throw a system-level exception to indicate that the CORBA
     // invocation failed
     EJBException ejbEx =
       new EJBException("Failed to retrieve quote from WroxQuotes" +
                        "service");
     throw ejbEx;
   }

   StockQuote[] result = new StockQuote[q.length];
   GregorianCalendar cal = new GregorianCalendar();

   for (int i = 0; i < q.length; i++) {
     result[i] = new StockQuote();

     result[i].symbol = q[i].symb;
     result[i].volume = q[i].volume;
     result[i].bid = q[i].bid;
     result[i].ask = q[i].ask;

     cal.set(q[i].asOf.year, q[i].asOf.month, q[i].asOf.day,
             q[i].asOf.hour, q[i].asOf.minute, q[i].asOf.second);

     result[i].timestamp = cal.getTime();
   }
```

```
     return result;
   }

   public void ejbCreate() {}
   public void ejbRemove() {}
   public void ejbActivate() {}
   public void ejbPassivate() {}
   public void setSessionContext(SessionContext sc) {}
}
```

Building the Enterprise JavaBean

As the EJB requires both the `WroxStocks` package and the `WroxQuotesBean`, for simplicity copy both of these into the ejbs directory (where you should place the above EJB `java` files) before compiling the EJB.

Deploying the Enterprise JavaBean

In order to deploy the EJB in Orion, we need to write the `ejb-jar.xml` deployment descriptor:

```
<?xml version="1.0"?>

<ejb-jar>
  <enterprise-beans>
    <session>
        <ejb-name>WroxQuotes</ejb-name>
        <home>WroxQuotesHome</home>
        <remote>WroxQuotes</remote>
        <ejb-class>WroxQuotesEJB</ejb-class>
        <session-type>Stateless</session-type>
        <transaction-type>Container</transaction-type>
    </session>
  </enterprise-beans>

  <assembly-descriptor>
    <container-transaction>
      <method>
          <ejb-name>WroxQuotes</ejb-name>
          <method-name>*</method-name>
      </method>
      <trans-attribute>Supports</trans-attribute>
    </container-transaction>
  </assembly-descriptor>
</ejb-jar>
```

Save this in the META-INF directory under the ejbs directory. Now we need to modify the application.xml file to indicate that our application contains an EJB module:

```
<?xml version="1.0"?>
<!DOCTYPE application PUBLIC "-//Sun Microsystems, Inc.//DTD J2EE Application
1.2//EN" "http://java.sun.com/j2ee/dtds/application_1_2.dtd">

<application>
    <display-name>Archive</display-name>
    <description></description>
```

```
        <module>
                <web>
                        <web-uri>webs</web-uri>
                        <context-root>/WroxQuotes</context-root>
                </web>
        </module>
        <module>
                <ejb>ejbs</ejb>
        </module>
</application>
```

Testing the Enterprise JavaBean

Since our EJB is just like any other, it can be accessed by many types of clients, ranging from servlets to JSPs to other EJBs. For a change of pace, let's build a stand alone application that will act as a client to our new EJB to verify that it works correctly.

Below is the source code for a client that looks up our EJB in the JNDI Naming service and runs a small series of tests to exercise the functionality:

```java
import javax.naming.Context;
import javax.naming.InitialContext;
import javax.rmi.PortableRemoteObject;
import java.util.Properties;

public class WroxQuotesClient {

  public static void main(String[] args) {
    WroxQuotes quotesObj = null;
    try {
      System.out.println("Connecting to the WroxQuotes EJB");

      Properties prop = new Properties();
      prop.setProperty(Context.INITIAL_CONTEXT_FACTORY,
          "com.evermind.server.ApplicationClientInitialContextFactory");
      prop.setProperty(Context.PROVIDER_URL,
                      "ormi://localhost/WroxQuotes");
      prop.setProperty(Context.SECURITY_PRINCIPAL, "admin");
      prop.setProperty(Context.SECURITY_CREDENTIALS, "123");

      InitialContext initial = new InitialContext(prop);
      Object objref = initial.lookup("WroxQuotes");

      WroxQuotesHome home =
        (WroxQuotesHome) PortableRemoteObject.narrow(objref,
              WroxQuotesHome.class);

      quotesObj = home.create();

    } catch (Exception ex) {
      System.out.println("Exception: " + ex);
      System.exit(-1);
    }
```

```java
      System.out.println("");

      try {
        System.out.println("Testing single quote method");

        StockQuote quote = quotesObj.getQuote("MSFT");

        System.out.println("SYMBOL\tVOLUME\tBID\tASK\tASOF");
        System.out.println(quote.symbol + "\t" + quote.volume + "\t"
                            + quote.bid + "\t" + quote.ask + "\t"
                            + quote.timestamp);
      } catch (UnknownSymbolException usEx) {
        System.out.println("Exception: " + usEx);
        System.out.println("Unknown symbol is " + usEx.symbol());
      } catch (Exception ex) {
        System.out.println("Exception: " + ex);
      }

      System.out.println("");

      try {
        System.out.println("Testing multi quote method");

        String symbolList[] = {
          "MSFT", "AOL", "AMZN", "EBAY"
        };

        StockQuote[] quotes = quotesObj.getQuoteList(symbolList);

        System.out.println("SYMBOL\tVOLUME\tBID\tASK\tASOF");
        for (int i = 0; i < quotes.length; i++) {
          System.out.println(quotes[i].symbol + "\t" + quotes[i].volume
                              + "\t" + quotes[i].bid + "\t" + quotes[i].ask
                              + "\t" + quotes[i].timestamp);
        }
      } catch (UnknownSymbolException usEx) {
        System.out.println("Exception: " + usEx);
        System.out.println("Unknown symbol is " + usEx.symbol());
      } catch (Exception ex) {
        System.out.println("Exception: " + ex);
      }

      System.out.println("");

      try {
        System.out.println("Testing single quote method with invalid symbol");

        StockQuote quote = quotesObj.getQuote("ABC");

        System.out.println("SYMBOL\tVOLUME\tBID\tASK\tASOF");
        System.out.println(quote.symbol + "\t" + quote.volume + "\t"
                            + quote.bid + "\t" + quote.ask + "\t"
                            + quote.timestamp);
      } catch (UnknownSymbolException usEx) {
```

```
      System.out.println("Exception: " + usEx);
      System.out.println("Unknown symbol is " + usEx.symbol());
    } catch (Exception ex) {
      System.out.println("Exception: " + ex);
    }

    System.out.println("");

    try {
      System.out.println("Testing multi quote method with invalid symbol");

      String symbolList[] = {
        "MSFT", "AOL", "ABC", "AMZN", "EBAY"
      };

      StockQuote[] quotes = quotesObj.getQuoteList(symbolList);

      System.out.println("SYMBOL\tVOLUME\tBID\tASK\tASOF");
      for (int i = 0; i < quotes.length; i++) {
        System.out.println(quotes[i].symbol + "\t" + quotes[i].volume
                         + "\t" + quotes[i].bid + "\t" + quotes[i].ask
                         + "\t" + quotes[i].timestamp);
      }
    } catch (UnknownSymbolException usEx) {
      System.out.println("Exception: " + usEx);
      System.out.println("Unknown symbol is " + usEx.symbol());
    } catch (Exception ex) {
      System.out.println("Exception: " + ex);
    }

    try {
      if (quotesObj != null) {
        quotesObj.remove();
      }
    } catch (Exception ex) {
      System.out.println("Exception: " + ex);
    }
  }
}
```

Building this application in the normal manner will yield a small client application that will contact and use our EJB, in turn causing the EJB to invoke methods on our CORBA object.

However, before we can run the client, we need to provide the `application-client.xml` deployment descriptor (save this in the same place as `ejb-jar.xml`):

```
<?xml version="1.0"?>
<!DOCTYPE application-client PUBLIC "-//Sun Microsystems, Inc.//DTD J2EE
Application Client 1.2//EN" "http://java.sun.com/j2ee/dtds/application-
client_1_2.dtd">

<application-client>
    <display-name>WroxQuotes</display-name>
    <ejb-ref>
```

```
                    <ejb-ref-name>WroxQuotes</ejb-ref-name>
                    <ejb-ref-type>Session</ejb-ref-type>
                    <home>WroxQuotesHome</home>
                    <remote>WroxQuotes</remote>
        </ejb-ref>
</application-client>
```

Run the client, remembering to make sure the `orion.jar` file is on the `CLASSPATH`:

Here is a sample output from our test client:

J2EE as CORBA Clients Overview

Thus far, we have constructed a CORBA object residing in a server application and demonstrated how to access it from a variety of client types, namely a stand alone application, a servlet, a JavaServer Page and an Enterprise JavaBean. Looking over these examples you can see that the technique for acquiring the CORBA object's object reference and invoking methods on that object reference have remained pretty constant. The five basic steps that each CORBA-enabled client has followed are:

- ❑ Initialize the ORB
- ❑ Connect to the Naming Service
- ❑ Obtain an object reference from the Naming Service for a given name
- ❑ Narrow the object reference to the proper type
- ❑ Invoke methods on the remote object

Although our example CORBA object and its server application are implemented in Java, these same steps can be followed to access any CORBA object, regardless of its implementation language. And the reverse is true as well: we could easily build clients in C++, Smalltalk, etc. that access our WroxQuotes CORBA object.

Summary

In this chapter, we have examined several aspects of distributed programming with Java and CORBA:

- ❑ We discussed the principles of the Common Object Request Broker Architecture (CORBA) and discussed how to implement CORBA objects and clients using the JavaIDL ORB included in the Java 2 platform

- ❑ We walked through a typical CORBA invocation to see what happens within the IDL client stub and IDL skeleton as the invocation passes from one process to another

- ❑ We examined how to incorporate CORBA objects into our J2EE applications and developed a servlet, a JavaServer Page, and an EJB session bean that utilize our WroxQuotes CORBA object

- ❑ Finally, we showed how using RMI-IIOP allows our CORBA clients and objects to interoperate with our native Java RMI clients and objects as if they all were built and deployed in a common application framework

Using the information in this chapter, we can build n-tier applications where Java and non-Java clients and objects can seamlessly interact. By combining the benefits of CORBA and Java, our n-tier applications can now be both accessible to new clients and able to accommodate new distributed objects without concern for their implementation languages.

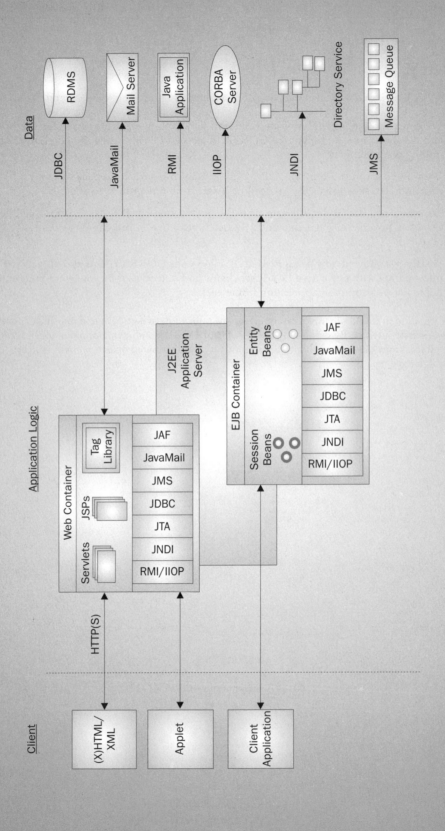

30

Putting It All Together – J2EE Applications

Now you have had an in-depth look at how to develop systems that make use of the different parts of the J2EE platform. This final chapter will focus on how the different components work together, and how you combine them into a complete J2EE application. We will look at:

❏ The concept of J2EE applications

❏ How you can fit different components together in one application

❏ An example of assembling a J2EE application step-by-step

In the example we will not explain thoroughly how to *build* the different components, but focus on *assembling* an application from individual components.

J2EE Applications

The Java 2 Platform, Enterprise Edition specification introduces the concept of **J2EE applications**. A J2EE application contains **J2EE modules,** which can be web applications, EJBs, or application clients. It also contains meta-information about the application, as well as shared libraries.

> **In other words, a J2EE application is a set of J2EE modules with some added 'glue' that binds them together into a complete integrated application. A J2EE application is a single Java Archive file with the `.ear` filename extension. When we talk about J2EE Applications in this chapter we do not mean just any application using J2EE technologies, but a J2EE application packaged as a single `.ear` file.**

Other chapters in this book discuss different J2EE components, like EJBs and servlets, thoroughly; this chapter will focus totally on the 'glue' that keeps the components together and makes them into a complete J2EE application.

Before showing how a J2EE application is composed in detail, let's revisit the concept of J2EE modules and consider the **application deployment descriptor**.

J2EE Modules

The different kinds of J2EE components have been discussed throughout the book but, to summarize, they are:

❑   Web Applications

❑   EJB JARs

❑   Client Applications

Web Applications

A web application consists of a web archive (WAR) file containing JSPs, servlets, tag libraries, and other content related to the web part of the application, together with a web deployment descriptor, web.xml. This kind of module is also referred to as a 'web' module, and is added to an application through the application deployment descriptor (which we will discuss later) using this XML syntax:

```
<module>
  <web>
    <web-uri>pathTo.war</web-uri>
    <context-root>thedir/</context-root>
  </web>
</module>
```

The `<web-uri>` element specifies the URI of the web application file relative to the context root of the application. The `<context-root>` element serves as a hint to the deployment tool that the web application is recommended to be put on a certain root on the web server; it does not have to reside under this root if the deployer wants it in another place.

EJB JARs

Enterprise JavaBeans can be packaged in an archive containing a set of EJBs and an `ejb-jar.xml` deployment descriptor. They are simply called 'ejb' modules, and the syntax for adding one to the application looks like this:

```
<module>
  <ejb>pathToEJB.jar</ejb>
</module>
```

The `<ejb>` tag specifies the URI of the EJB JAR relative to application's root context.

Application Clients

A Java application serving as a client to a J2EE application is packaged as a Java Archive (JAR) file including an `application-client.xml` deployment descriptor. An application client is normal Java application that runs inside an application client container, with the container providing the application with certain services. These are called 'java' modules, and are added to a J2EE application like this:

```
<module>
    <java>pathToClient.jar</java>
</module>
```

The `<module>` tag specifies the URI of the java application client relative to the application's root context.

The alt-dd Element

Every module definition may optionally include an `alt-dd` element, which specifies the URI to the post-assembly version of the deployment descriptor file for a particular J2EE module. The URI specifies the path of the deployment descriptor file relative to the application's root directory.

The Application Deployment Descriptor

The deployment descriptor for a J2EE application is called `application.xml`, and its DTD is available at `http://java.sun.com/j2ee/dtds/application_1_2.dtd`. It contains the meta-information for a J2EE application and specifies the following properties:

❑ Icons to use to represent the J2EE application in a GUI tool

❑ A name for the application

❑ A longer description of the application

❑ The modules of the application

❑ Security roles that the application uses

Here is a more detailed specification of the application deployment descriptor. Since the file is in XML format, like the other deployment descriptors, we will describe it using the actual tags, but with added annotations, and using:

❑ `<tag?>` to show that a tag is optional

❑ `<tag+>` to show that you need one or more of the tag

❑ `<tag*>` to show that you need 0 or more instances of the tag

```
<application>
    The root element of a J2EE application deployment descriptor.

    <icon?>
       Contains icon elements which specify the locations of the icons used
       to represent the application in a GUI tool.

       <small-icon?>path/to/icon.gif</small-icon>
          The small-icon must be a 16x16 pixel icon image of GIF or JPEG format.
```

```
        <large-icon?>path/to/icon.gif</large-icon>
           The large-icon must be a 32x32 pixel icon image of GIF or JPEG format.
    </icon>

    <display-name>The name</display-name>
        Specifies an application name.

    <description?>A description</description>
           Provides a human readable description of the application.

    <module+>
        Represents a single J2EE module. Contains specification of the module
        type a path to the module and an optional alt-dd element. The
        explanations of the J2EE modules were given in the previous section.

        <ejb>path/to/EJB.jar</ejb>
           OR
        <java>path/to/client.jar</java>
           OR
        <web>
           <web-uri>path/to/webapp.war</web-uri>
           <context-root>thedir/</context-root>
        </web>

        <alt-dd?>path/to/dd</alt-dd>
    </module>


    <security-role*>
        The security-role element contains the definition of a security role
        which is global to the application. The descriptions of the application
        security roles override those specified for a J2EE module.

        <description?>description</description>
        <role-name>name</role-name>
    </security-role>


</application>
```

A typical J2EE application deployment descriptor might look like this:

```
<?xml version="1.0"?>
<!DOCTYPE application PUBLIC "-//Sun Microsystems, Inc.//DTD J2EE Application
1.2//EN" "http://java.sun.com/j2ee/dtds/application_1_2.dtd">

<application>
  <display-name>My J2EE Application</display-name>

  <module>
     <ejb>my-ejb.jar</ejb>
  </module>

  <module>
```

```
      <web>
        <web-uri>my-web.war</web-uri>
        <context-root>/</context-root>
      </web>
    </module>

    <security-role>
      <role-name>users</role-name>
    </security-role>
</application>
```

The Structure of a J2EE Application

A J2EE application is a package built from other packages – J2EE modules – each of which contains J2EE components and a deployment descriptor. These modules, along with `application.xml`, together form the J2EE application:

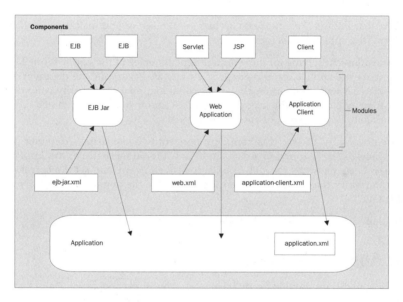

Enterprise Archive (EAR) Files

As with the other units in J2EE, a J2EE application is packaged into one distributable archive file. In the case of J2EE applications the archive is called an **Enterprise Archive** or **EAR** file, with the filename extension `.ear`. As with other Java archives, a `META-INF` directory contains information about the package; in this case, it contains the application deployment descriptor that we discussed above. A typical Enterprise Archive, in this case including an EJB JAR and a web application, could look like this:

```
META-INF/
          application.xml
application-ejb.jar
application-web.war
```

The Application Assembler Role

The **application assembler** is the person who takes a set of J2EE modules and assembles them into a complete J2EE application. To help them there are assembly tools provided by their application server vendor, or by a thirdparty J2EE tool vendor. Of course they don't have to use the GUI tools, but the application assembler should still know how the internals work and be able to assemble an application by hand using a text editor and the deployment descriptors.

They are also responsible for providing instructions describing external dependencies of the application, making it possible for the deployer to install the application into the production environment. Since this chapter is about assembling a J2EE application, we will focus on what a person with this role will have to know and do in the development process. We will also look at the role of the deployer, so as to be able to get all the way to a running application.

The Deployer Role

The **deployer** will take the packaged application and install it into the production environment. The deployer is usually an expert in a specific production environment; the job consists of three tasks:

❑ **Installation:** Putting the enterprise archive on the server and making it available to the J2EE platform (the application server).

❑ **Configuration:** Resolving all the external dependencies of the application. The deployer needs to configure the application server specific parts. For example, the deployer will often need to set up the user management for the application, mapping the security roles defined by the application assembler to the user groups and accounts that exist in the environment into which the application components are deployed.

The deployer may also need to configure how entity beans using Container Managed Persistence will be mapped to a data store, how the finder methods are implemented, where on the web site he wants the web applications to show up, and set the correct JNDI properties and manifest for the application clients. The tools of the application server will normally assist in this task.

❑ **Execution:** Starting up the newly installed and configured application.

Why J2EE Applications Matter

The benefits of J2EE applications should already be apparent, but some people will claim that they just add extra bloat and complexity. However they are of great importance, for two main reasons.

The J2EE specification states that the main goal of the J2EE application concept is "to provide scalable modular application assembly and portable deployment of J2EE applications into any J2EE product". What this means is that the two main goals are compatibility and making it easy to distribute prefabricated J2EE applications.

❑ **Compatibility:**
J2EE applications are said to be binary-compatible: the binary code can be used in any J2EE environment, and the procedure for deploying a J2EE application should be simple and similar across different implementations of the J2EE platform. This means that it is very easy to test that your application is really compatible with different platforms. It also means that the whole J2EE industry will be pressured to achieve higher compatibility, since users can easily

just plug an existing application into a different J2EE implementation from the one that it was built with. Any compatibility problems will become very visible.

❑ **Distribution:**
Before J2EE, distributing a complete enterprise application including EJBs, servlets, JSPs, stand-alone clients, etc. was usually difficult and problematic. There were a few different ways to do this, but none of them was really tempting. You could either zip it all up and write a text file saying how to deploy it in a certain environment, or just zip it up, explain the pieces, and hope that the person taking care of the installation knew how to deploy the different pieces in their environment. You could also write an installation program setting it up with a specific environment. To create a distributable package that would be easy to install in different environment meant a lot of trouble. Now there is a standard way to ship a complete application.

Future Development of J2EE Applications

J2EE is a very new concept, and the platform is set to continue changing at a high pace; J2EE 1.3 is currently in development. It introduces many concepts into the platform, but most of these things affect the different components of the platform, rather than the glue that holds them together. Since this chapter is solely discussing the glue (the J2EE application concept) we will not discuss all the changes happening to the J2EE platform, but rather try to find how it affects the usefulness of J2EE applications.

Many of the changes *will* affect the usefulness of J2EE applications, though. This is because many features that have until now been left to the vendor are being standardized. This makes J2EE applications more usable, since they will require less configuration when being moved to a new application server. The goal is to require less from the deployer, moving their job to the developers of the application. Specifically, the following will be standardized:

❑ **EJB CMP Finder query language (EJB QL)**
Until now, there has been no way to declare custom finders in a vendor-neutral way. This has moved the task to the application deployer, but the introduction of a new query language in EJB 2.0 will move the task to the more appropriate domain of the component developer.

❑ **OR-mapping features**
EJB 1.1 did not include facilities for generating complex object graphs with object relationships beyond a simple one to one mapping. This is being changed in EJB 2.0, and will let many more J2EE applications stay vendor-neutral.

❑ **JMS integration**
EJB 2.0 introduces a much-awaited third bean type, called message-driven beans. This will allow a whole new class of enterprise applications to work within the J2EE framework. Applications that need to listen to certain events will be able to use these beans, instead of having to solve this need outside the EJB container.

❑ **XML Parsing API**
With the inclusion of a standard API for XML parsing, fewer application will have external dependencies, which will make it easier to install J2EE applications that use XML.

It is also likely that many other changes are in the works for the Servlet 2.3 and JSP 1.2 specifications, but since these are still under development and are not available to the public, we could only guess what they will include. Areas that might be addressed include application events and servlet filters.

Many other concepts like Connectors, Management APIs, etc. are being added to J2EE 1.3, but how these new additions will affect the J2EE application concept is yet to be seen.

Designing a J2EE Application

In earlier chapters a great deal of effort has gone into showing you examples of good J2EE design patterns. Now we will see a design from the point of view of the J2EE application, rather than that of a specific J2EE module. There are many other resources for this available, and there is also an official 'J2EE blueprints' document available at http://java.sun.com/j2ee/blueprints/.

A common goal when designing applications is to separate different parts from each other, the MVC mantra mandates separating the Model, View, and Controller from each other. The MVC model is not always enough, and for many systems there is a need to go beyond this and separate the three layers into different sublayers. With J2EE there is also the issue of being able to do the same thing in many different ways, and this means that many design decisions have to be made.

As we have discussed before, the J2EE platform contains three main types of modules:

❑ EJB modules cover the data layer and part of the logic layer

❑ Web application modules cover part of the logic layer and the presentation layer

❑ Application client modules cover part of the logic layer, and the presentation layer

Web applications and application clients basically cover the same ground, but do so in distinctly different manners. A web application has a natural separation between its parts, with JSPs being suitable for presentation, servlets and beans being suitable for certain types of logic, and tag extensions being suitable for acting as a logic interface layer. In application clients the picture is more complex; there is an almost infinite number of ways to approach the separation issue, and a plethora of design patterns, with none of them a definite standard.

One possible design for a J2EE application is shown below. This is, of course, is not the only way to design your application, but it does provide reasonable separation between different aspects of your applications:

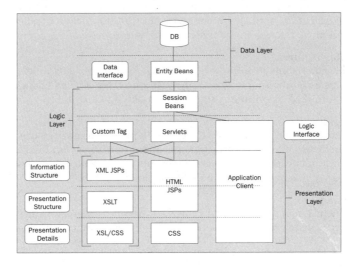

In this architecture, the layers are:

❑ **Presentation layer**
This is comprised of the presentation details (colors, fonts, etc.) using CSS (Cascading Style Sheets, see `http://www.w3.org/Style/CSS/`) or XSL (Extensible Stylesheet Language, `http://www.w3.org/Style/XSL/`); the presentation structure, using either XSLT or HTML JSPs; and the information structure.

The presentation structure means, for example, how tables and images are used in the page, whereas the information structure layer is where the *structure* of the contents is decided. For example, in a shopping-cart web page the information structure gathers the contents using the logic layers and provides it as information to the presentation structure layer. One way to do this is using JSPs to generate XML, and passing this to a presentation structure layer that uses XSLT to transform the information into a certain presentation structure.

You can also let the JSPs output normal HTML. In this case, your JSPs span the information structure and presentation structure layers. The information structure layer could be seen as an outsider, a fourth and rarely used layer: talking about an information layer is not very useful if you use straight HTML JSPs to convert content obtained from the logic layer into a complete presentation structure. In the example later in this chapter we will not design a separate information structure layer, but use HTML JSPs.

❑ **Logic layer**
The logic layer consists of tag extension libraries and servlets making up a logic interface and containing certain interface-related logic, and session beans where the real business logic is located.

❑ **Data layer**
This comprises entity beans (the data interface) and the database.

It might seem like overkill to use XML/XSL instead of plain HTML with this structure, since the use of tag extension libraries will almost fully separate the logic from the HTML pages. In this chapter, we will not use XML/XSL, since that would blur our focus on enterprise applications, and would require a lot of discussion on these concepts. However, besides separation there are some other advantages of using XML that might be applicable in some cases. Some of these are:

❑ In the future XML will be handled directly by clients, and it already is in some cases. This means that the XSL can live client-side, and the presentation can be changed without a round trip to the server.

❑ XSLT provides advanced transformation rules that can be performed without writing any code. Standard tag extension libraries will later make this possible in pure HTML JSPs.

The Application Development Lifecycle

The J2EE development model, with its different roles, is meant to be suitable for a software production line with distinctly defined phases. Of course theory often differs from practice, and it is not likely that many projects will follow the lifecycle very strictly; you will probably want to iterate over the cycle a few times during a large project. In theory, however, the lifecycle of your implementation phase (disregarding analysis, requirements specification, and other phases) should be:

❑ **Component Creation:**
First of all, the component provider creates components. This particular step is already done when the application assemblers enter the picture, and we will not dig into this subject any further. The different components have been extensively described in earlier chapters.

- ❑ **Component Packaging:**
  When the components have been developed they are packaged into J2EE modules. This is also something that is done before the application assemblers start their work it is also described thoroughly in earlier chapters.

- ❑ **Application Assembly**
  This is where application assemblers enters the picture. We have discussed how they are provided with complete J2EE modules which they will combine into one J2EE application. They do this by following certain steps:

  - ❑ Select which J2EE modules will be used for the application

  - ❑ Create the directory structure for the application

  - ❑ Place the modules in their correct places in the application structure

  - ❑ Edit J2EE module deployment parameters

  - ❑ Create the application deployment descriptor

  - ❑ Create documentation intended for application deployers

  - ❑ Package the application

  These steps will most likely be performed with assistance from an assembly tool; in a later section you will see an example of how this is done for our example application using the tools provided with the Orion application server.

- ❑ **Application Deployment:**
  When the application is assembled it is ready to be deployed in a J2EE application server. The deployer's tasks can be summarized as:

  - ❑ Installation of the application in the server

  - ❑ Configuration of external dependencies

  - ❑ Execution of the installed and configured application

Building a Complete J2EE Application

With this background, let's try to construct an application that is as simple as possible, yet that shows how to use different J2EE technologies together. We'll look at assembling and deploying the application in a variety of ways, using the J2EE Reference Implementation, the Orion application server, and some 'manual' techniques.

The purpose of this chapter is to show how different J2EE pieces fit together and how they are made into a complete application. Because of this, we will not expend much effort explaining the different parts of this application (EJBs, JSPs, servlets, etc.). Servlets are discussed in detail in Chapters 7-10, JSPs in Chapters 11-15, and EJBs in Chapters 18-23.

Requirements

The application we will devise is an extremely simple content management system, managing free-text articles. The system should provide the following functionality:

- ❏ Editors can add an article using an article entering application
- ❏ Everyone can view articles, and search articles based on the title of the article
- ❏ In the future, editors should be able to add and edit the articles from the web UI using the same user information as the article entering application, so we must prepare for this

Design

Using the J2EE application design we described earlier, let's start by identifying the different parts we need.

Obviously we need something defining the concept of an article. The articles will be persistent, and this persistence is part of the data layer of the application, so we model it as an entity bean. Attributes of an article that interests us are made into attributes in the bean:

- ❏ An id for the article
- ❏ The person who submitted the article
- ❏ The title/subject of the article
- ❏ The article's text/body
- ❏ The date the article was submitted

We also need something that will provide simple logic for handling articles: listing the articles, searching them, and adding new articles. This could easily be done within the article entity bean, but since we know this application will probably become larger in the future, we ought to make sure we have a nice separation between the data and application logic layers, just in case we want to change the data layer at a later time.

For this reason we need a session bean. It does not need to keep any conversational state, so we can let it be a stateless session bean, with the following methods:

- ❏ `getArticles()`
  This method is used to search the articles, or to list all the articles if `null` is sent as an argument
- ❏ `addArticle()`
  This method is used to add an article to the system; the attributes of the article are supplied as arguments

We now know how we will represent articles in the data layer, and how the application logic will be represented. The next question concerns how the user should interact with the system. From the requirements, we can see that we need to be able to present the articles and a simple article search in a web application. Specifically, we need a web page that allows us to list articles, and one that allows us to view an article. These pages only have to present information generated from the other parts of the system; they are part of the presentation layer, so we can make them JSP pages.

This means we have two JSPs, `article.jsp` and `articleviewer.jsp`. We want to use them within a simple HTML frameset, with a frame on the left containing simple commands to let us list all the articles, or search for specific articles. This can be done in pure HTML, with two pages: one to create the frameset and one to provide the contents of the left-hand frame.

We will also want some simple logic for the presentation layer. Specifically, we will probably want to store references to the session EJB's home interface for faster access. For this purpose we use a `ControllerServlet`.

Finally, we need to design the application client. This will be a simple GUI application that lets the user add a new article. An article consists of a title and a body, so we need two text input areas. The title can use a one-line text field, but the body needs a larger text area; we also need a button to click when adding the new article. We will not design this any further, since it will be a minimal Swing application and not of particular interest.

Implementing the Components

As with the design, we start our implementation with the EJBs. We will skip parts of the implementation, for reasons mentioned earlier, but the full source is available on the Wrox web site, `http://www.wrox.com/`.

EJB Module Implementation

In the design section we concluded that we want two EJBs: an entity bean and a stateless session bean. We start by implementing the entity bean. We do not need the explicit control that Bean Managed Persistence gives us, so we choose to implement the `Article` bean using Container Managed Persistence (CMP). Using CMP means:

- ❑ Better performance, since the container can optimize access to the database because it controls it
- ❑ Less development work
- ❑ A database-neutral data layer, since you never write any SQL

The article is designed as a dumb entity bean without any logic, which is trivial to implement. There are tools like Orion's EJBMaker that will automatically create CMP entity beans if you provide the fields you want it to have, but for now we will make it by hand. For simplicity I use an `Integer` as the primary key for the bean.

First we define the remote interface for the EJB, which just needs a get and a set method for every field, except for the `id` field, which we want to make read-only:

```
package com.wrox.cm.ejb;

import java.rmi.RemoteException;
import javax.ejb.*;
import java.util.*;

public interface Article extends EJBObject {

    public int getId() throws RemoteException;
```

```
    public String getTitle() throws RemoteException;
    public void setTitle(String value) throws RemoteException;

    public String getText() throws RemoteException;
    public void setText(String value) throws RemoteException;

    public java.util.Date getDate() throws RemoteException;
    public void setDate(Date value) throws RemoteException;

    public String getSubmitter() throws RemoteException;
    public void setSubmitter(String value) throws RemoteException;
}
```

Now the remote interface is done and we can go on to implement the actual bean class. This class is very uninteresting, since it basically just contains the mandatory methods for an `EntityBean`, and the access methods, which are all of the same shape:

```
public String getText() {
    return text;
}

public void setText(String value) {
    this.text = value;
}
```

However, we want to be able to create an article by specifying just the title and the text. This means we need to implement an `ejbCreate()` method that does some work. This method will need to:

❑   Get the current date to set the date field

❑   Get the submitter

❑   Calculate an id

The submitter can be obtained using `getCallerPrincipal().getName()` on the `EntityContext`, and we will make the id creation simple by using the time in milliseconds (since 1970) divided by 100. (This is not something you will want to use in a real case.) This makes the `ejbCreate()` method look like this:

```
public java.lang.Integer ejbCreate(String title,
                                    String text) throws CreateException {
    date = new Date();
    id = (int) (date.getTime() / 100);
    this.title = title;
    this.text = text;
    this.submitter = this.context.getCallerPrincipal().getName();
    return null;
}
```

We also match this method with an empty `ejbPostCreate()` method:

1437

```
public void ejbPostCreate(String title, String text) {}
```

The code for the rest of the bean implementation is rather lengthy but trivial, so we will not present it all here. Finally, we need a home interface for our `Article` bean. This will contain the `create()` method we defined, and the finders we need.

We want our finders to be able to:

❑   Find an article based on the ID: the default `findByPrimaryKey()` method

❑   Find all articles: `findAll()`

❑   Find all articles with a specific title: `findByTitle()`

This means that our home interface will look like this:

```
package com.wrox.cm.ejb;

import java.util.*;
import javax.ejb.*;
import java.rmi.RemoteException;

public interface ArticleHome extends EJBHome {

  public Article create(String subject, String text)
        throws CreateException, RemoteException;

  public Article findByPrimaryKey(int key)
        throws RemoteException, FinderException;

  public Collection findAll() throws RemoteException, FinderException;

  public Collection findByTitle(String text)
        throws RemoteException, FinderException;
}
```

Our `Article` EJB is now done and we move on to the session bean, the `ArticleHandler`.

`ArticleHandler` acts as a façade, and hides the data layer's entity beans. This means that the data layer could easily be changed if we for any reason wanted to do so. For it to act as a façade we need it to implement all the functionality our system needs, to avoid any need for the other components to use `ArticleHome`. This means we need to be able to:

❑   Create articles

❑   Find an article by title or id

❑   List all articles

This makes our remote interface look like this:

```
package com.wrox.cm.ejb;

import java.util.*;
```

```
import java.rmi.*;
import javax.ejb.*;

public interface ArticleHandler extends EJBObject {
  public Collection getArticles(String title)
        throws RemoteException, FinderException;
  public Article getArticle(int id) throws RemoteException, FinderException;
  public Article addArticle(String title, String text)
        throws RemoteException, CreateException, FinderException;
}
```

The implementation of this bean will also be pretty simple, since it is just a façade. The important methods are:

```
public void ejbCreate() throws CreateException {
  try {
    articles =
      (ArticleHome) new InitialContext()
        .lookup("java:comp/env/ejb/Article");
  } catch (NamingException e) {
    throw new CreateException("NamingException: " + e.getMessage());
  }
}

public Collection getArticles(String title)
        throws RemoteException, FinderException {
  Collection result = null;

  if (title == null || title.equals("")) {
    result = articles.findAll();
  } else {
    result = articles.findByTitle(title);
  }
  return result;
}

public Article getArticle(int id)
        throws RemoteException, FinderException {
  return articles.findByPrimaryKey(id);
}.

public Article addArticle(String title, String content)
        throws RemoteException, CreateException, FinderException {
  return articles.create(title, content);
}
```

Besides these, we need the mandatory methods from the SessionBean interface, but since we are not interested in the EJBs primarily we will not include them here.

Finally, we need to write the ArticleHome interface. All we need is our create() method; the interface looks like this:

```
package com.wrox.cm.ejb;
```

```
import java.rmi.RemoteException;
import javax.ejb.*;

public interface ArticleHandlerHome extends EJBHome {
  public ArticleHandler create() throws CreateException, RemoteException;
}
```

We have now implemented the EJB part; we would normally test the EJBs and assemble them into a J2EE module now. However, for this example we skip the testing and move the assembly to later.

Web Module Implementation

Let's move on to the web part of the application. We decided to use two JSPs in our design, article.jsp, which lists articles, and articleViewer.jsp, which displays a particular article.

article.jsp should list either all the available articles, or just the ones matching a certain title. We prepared for this need when we made our EJBs, and there is a getArticles(String title) method in our ArticleHandler bean that will do just this. If an empty title is provided, it lists all articles, so we can just invoke that method using the desired title if we are doing a search, or nothing otherwise.

Since we are listing articles, a JSP custom tag for iteration will be useful. There are many tag libraries which provide this ability, but I'm used to using the Orion tag libraries (http://www.orionserver.com/tags/) so let's use the Orion EJB tag library for the iteration, along with their utilities tag library:

```
<%@ taglib uri="utiltags" prefix="util" %>
<%@ taglib uri="ejbtags" prefix="ejb" %>
```

Using that, listing the articles will be simple. By doing

```
<ejb:iterate id="article" type="com.wrox.cm.ejb.Article"
             collection='<%= articleHandler.getArticles
                                (request.getParameter("content"))%>'
             max="40">
  <!-- Output the article information -->
</ejb:iterate>
```

we get access to the variable article, which we can use in the body of the <ejb:iterate> tag.

This assumes that we have access to the ArticleHandler through the variable articleHandler. To set this up, we rely on the ControllerServlet that we discussed earlier; to make sure that this is run, we include it from the JSP. The ControllerServlet will be mapped to the path Controller, and we also need a <jsp:useBean> to get access to the articleHandler variable in the page:

```
<jsp:include page="Controller" flush="true" />
<jsp:useBean id="articleHandler" type="com.wrox.cm.ejb.ArticleHandler"
  scope="session"/>
```

When we put these things together with the formatting HTML, and display the date and title of the article in a table, we get something like this:

```
<%@ page import="java.text.*" %>
<%@ page import="java.util.*" %>
<jsp:include page="Controller" flush="true" />
<jsp:useBean id="articleHandler" type="com.wrox.cm.ejb.ArticleHandler"
 scope="session"/>
<%-- Specify the use of the util taglib --%>
<%@ taglib uri="utiltags" prefix="util" %>
<%@ taglib uri="ejbtags" prefix="ejb" %>
<html>
  <head>
    <title>Articles</title>
  </head>
  <body bgcolor="#ffffff">
    <font size="5" face="Arial"><b>Articles</b></font><br>
    <table border="0" width="50%">
      <tr>
        <td bgcolor="#dd7777"><b>Date</b></td>
        <td bgcolor="#dd7777"><b>Subject</b></td>
      </tr>

      <%-- Iterate thru the articles, max x of them --%>
      <ejb:iterate id="article" type="com.wrox.cm.ejb.Article"
                collection='<%= articleHandler.getArticles
                                  (request.getParameter("content"))%>'
              max="40">
        <tr>
          <td bgcolor="#dddddd">
            <%=DateFormat.getDateInstance(DateFormat.LONG,
                                  request.getLocale())
                  .format(article.getDate())%></td>
          <td bgcolor="#dddddd">
            <jsp:getProperty name="article" property="title" />
            (<a href="articleviewer.jsp?id=<%=article.getId()%>">detail</a>)
          </td>
        </tr>
      </ejb:iterate>
    </table>
  </body>
</html>
```

Now that the article lister is complete, we want to make our article viewer JSP that will display the contents of an article. In this case we want somehow to have access to the details of an article; we defer setting this up to the `Controller` servlet, and just include the servlet and add a `<jsp:useBean>` to get access to the article details using a request-scope variable. Besides this we just have to add some HTML to format our output, and output the article contents. The finished JSP looks like this:

```
<%@ page import="java.text.*" %>
<%@ page import="java.util.*" %>

<jsp:include page="Controller" flush="true" />
```

```
<jsp:useBean id="detail" type="com.wrox.cm.ejb.Article" scope="request" />

<html>
  <head>
    <title>Article</title>
  </head>
  <body bgcolor="#ffffff">
    <font size="5" face="Arial"><b>Article -
    <jsp:getProperty name="detail" property="title" /></b></font><br>

    <table border="0" width="50%">
      <tr>
        <td bgcolor="#dd7777"><b>
          <%= DateFormat.getDateInstance(DateFormat.LONG,
                                  request.getLocale())
                          .format(detail.getDate())%> -
          <jsp:getProperty name="detail" property="title" />, by
          <jsp:getProperty name="detail" property="submitter" /></b></td>
      </tr>
      <tr>
        <td bgcolor="#dddddd"><jsp:getProperty name="detail"
            property="text" /></td>
      </tr>
    </table>
  </body>
</html>
```

We wanted to put this in a frame set, and so we need Two HTML pages, an index page that sets the frameset up, and a commands page that has a link to a page that lists all articles, and a form to search for articles. We will not discuss these HTML files here: they are available as part of the code download.

Now we have one final part missing, the `Controller` servlet. We have identified two tasks for it: setting up access to the `ArticleHandler`, and getting the article to be displayed. The article to displayed is obtained through a request parameter. We do all this in the servlet's `service()` method:

```
import javax.servlet.http.*;
import com.wrox.cm.ejb.*;
import javax.naming.*;
import java.text.*;

public class ControllerServlet extends HttpServlet {
  public void service(HttpServletRequest request,
                      HttpServletResponse response) {
    HttpSession session = request.getSession();

    ArticleHandler articleHandler =
      (ArticleHandler) session.getAttribute("articleHandler");

    if (articleHandler == null) {
      try {
        ArticleHandlerHome handlerHome =
          (ArticleHandlerHome) javax.rmi.PortableRemoteObject
            .narrow(new InitialContext()
```

```
                          .lookup("java:comp/env/ejb/ArticleHandler"),
                      ArticleHandlerHome.class);
      articleHandler = handlerHome.create();
      session.setAttribute("articleHandler", articleHandler);
      System.out.println("Added: " + articleHandler);
    } catch (Exception e) {
      e.printStackTrace();
    }
  }

  int articleID = 0;

  try {
    articleID = Integer.parseInt(request.getParameter("id"));
    request.setAttribute("detail", articleHandler.getArticle(articleID));
  } catch (Exception e) {}
  }
}
```

Now the web part is all done, and we move on to create the application client. It is a client-side Swing application, and we will not go through how it works – see the code download for details.

Component Packaging/Assembly

Now that the components are implemented we need to package them into J2EE modules; this can be done using the assembly tools your application server provides, by using thirdparty tools, or by simply assembling them without any special tools. I will not go into the fine details, since the concepts of the different modules have already been discussed.

Packaging the EJBs

Let us start at the same end as before, with the EJBs. To package them we need to create an `ejb-jar.xml` deployment descriptor, either by hand or using a graphical assembly tool. Its contents are as follows:

```xml
<?xml version="1.0"?>
<!DOCTYPE ejb-jar PUBLIC "-//Sun Microsystems, Inc.//DTD Enterprise JavaBeans
1.1//EN" "http://java.sun.com/j2ee/dtds/ejb-jar_1_1.dtd">

<ejb-jar>

  <description></description>
  <display-name>EJB-JAR for the articles</display-name>
  <enterprise-beans>
    <entity>
      <description></description>
      <display-name>com.wrox.cm.ejb.Article</display-name>
      <ejb-name>com.wrox.cm.ejb.Article</ejb-name>
      <home>com.wrox.cm.ejb.ArticleHome</home>
      <remote>com.wrox.cm.ejb.Article</remote>
      <ejb-class>com.wrox.cm.ejb.ArticleBean</ejb-class>
      <persistence-type>Container</persistence-type>
      <prim-key-class>java.lang.Integer</prim-key-class>
```

```
            <reentrant>False</reentrant>
            <cmp-field><field-name>submitter</field-name></cmp-field>
            <cmp-field><field-name>text</field-name></cmp-field>
            <cmp-field><field-name>id</field-name></cmp-field>
            <cmp-field><field-name>locale</field-name></cmp-field>
            <cmp-field><field-name>date</field-name></cmp-field>
            <cmp-field><field-name>title</field-name></cmp-field>
            <primkey-field>id</primkey-field>
        </entity>
        <session>
            <description></description>
            <display-name>com.wrox.cm.ejb.ArticleHandler</display-name>
            <ejb-name>com.wrox.cm.ejb.ArticleHandler</ejb-name>
            <home>com.wrox.cm.ejb.ArticleHandlerHome</home>
            <remote>com.wrox.cm.ejb.ArticleHandler</remote>
            <ejb-class>com.wrox.cm.ejb.ArticleHandlerBean</ejb-class>
            <session-type>Stateful</session-type>
            <transaction-type>Container</transaction-type>
            <ejb-ref>
                <description>The articles</description>
                <ejb-ref-name>ejb/Article</ejb-ref-name>
                <ejb-ref-type>Entity</ejb-ref-type>
                <home>com.wrox.cm.ejb.ArticleHome</home>
                <remote>com.wrox.cm.ejb.Article</remote>
            </ejb-ref>
        </session>
    </enterprise-beans>
    <assembly-descriptor>
        <security-role><role-name>users</role-name></security-role>
        <security-role><role-name>editors</role-name></security-role>
        <security-role><role-name>guest</role-name></security-role>
        <container-transaction>
            <description></description>
            <method>
                <ejb-name>com.wrox.cm.ejb.Article</ejb-name>
                <method-name>*</method-name>
            </method>
            <method>
                <ejb-name>com.wrox.cm.ejb.ArticleHandler</ejb-name>
                <method-name>*</method-name>
            </method>
            <trans-attribute>NotSupported</trans-attribute>
        </container-transaction>
    </assembly-descriptor>
</ejb-jar>
```

Call the resulting EJB JAR `cm-ejb.jar`.

Packaging the Web Module

From the JSPs, servlet, and referenced tag libraries we build a web application with the name `cm-web.war`, with references to the EJBs used. The `web.xml` file is as follows:

```xml
<?xml version="1.0"?>
<!DOCTYPE web-app PUBLIC "-//Sun Microsystems, Inc.//DTD Web Application 2.2//EN"
"http://java.sun.com/j2ee/dtds/web-app_2_2.dtd">

<web-app>
  <display-name>Article web app</display-name>
  <description>A web app listing articles</description>
  <welcome-file-list>
    <welcome-file>index.html</welcome-file>
  </welcome-file-list>
  <servlet>
    <servlet-name>Controller</servlet-name>
    <servlet-class>ControllerServlet</servlet-class>
  </servlet>

  <servlet-mapping>
    <servlet-name>Controller</servlet-name>
    <url-pattern>/Controller</url-pattern>
  </servlet-mapping>

  <taglib>
    <taglib-uri>ejbtags</taglib-uri>
    <taglib-location>/WEB-INF/lib/ejbtags.jar</taglib-location>
  </taglib>
  <taglib>
    <taglib-uri>utiltags</taglib-uri>
    <taglib-location>/WEB-INF/lib/utiltags.jar</taglib-location>
  </taglib>

  <ejb-ref>
    <ejb-ref-name>ejb/ArticleHandler</ejb-ref-name>
    <ejb-ref-type>Session</ejb-ref-type>
    <home>com.wrox.cm.ejb.ArticleHandlerHome</home>
    <remote>com.wrox.cm.ejb.ArticleHandler</remote>
  </ejb-ref>
  <ejb-ref>
    <ejb-ref-name>ejb/Article</ejb-ref-name>
    <ejb-ref-type>Entity</ejb-ref-type>
    <home>com.wrox.cm.ejb.ArticleHome</home>
    <remote>com.wrox.cm.ejb.Article</remote>
  </ejb-ref>
</web-app>
```

Packaging the Swing Client

We package the Swing application client, together with an `application-client.xml` file and a manifest declaring which is the main class (the one that will get executed when we execute the JAR). In this case, it is `com.wrox.cm.client.CMClient`. `application-client.xml` looks like this:

```xml
<?xml version="1.0"?>
```

```
<!DOCTYPE application-client PUBLIC "-//Sun Microsystems, Inc.//DTD J2EE
Application Client 1.2//EN" "http://java.sun.com/j2ee/dtds/application-
client_1_2.dtd">
<application-client>
  <display-name>Article client</display-name>
  <ejb-ref>
    <ejb-ref-name>ejb/ArticleHandler</ejb-ref-name>
    <ejb-ref-type>Session</ejb-ref-type>
    <home>com.wrox.cm.ejb.ArticleHandlerHome</home>
    <remote>com.wrox.cm.ejb.ArticleHandler</remote>
  </ejb-ref>
</application-client>
```

The manifest file contains the following:

```
Manifest-Version: 1.0
Main-Class: com.wrox.cm.client.CMClient
Name: "Pro Java Server Programming J2EE ed CM"
```

We call this JAR cm-client.jar.

Application Assembly

Now we are ready for the part that we particularly want to focus on: taking our assembled modules and building our J2EE application. As with the module assembly, we can assemble the application using vendor-provided or thirdparty tools, or we can just create the application deployment descriptor ourselves in a text editor. Since the focus of this chapter is on application assembly let's try doing this using the graphical tools supplied by both the J2EE Reference Implementation and Orion application server. We will also show how to assemble the application manually.

Assembling the Application Using the Reference Implementation

The J2EE Reference Implementation 1.2.1 comes with a deployment utility called deploytool. This actually covers both the assembly and the deployment parts of the process, and does separate the two phases very strictly. (Remember that the assembly phase is for generating a portable J2EE application, while the deployment phase is for deploying the application into a certain environment.) deploytool provides facilities for editing the assembly configuration (the generic part of the settings) as well as the RI-specific part of the configuration in the same view, and by default it stores the RI-specific information in the assembled application. This is, however, not a problem since it is named in a way that will not affect other J2EE implementations

First we need to create a new application: this is done from the File menu using New Application. You will be queried for a file name and a display name for the application. Fill in a suitable file name (such as C:\ProJavaServer\Chapter30\cm.ear) and a display name will be automatically suggested:

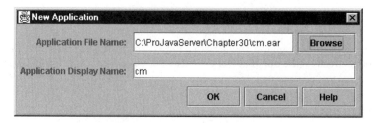

Now the application skeleton is in place so we can add our modules, starting with the EJB module. This too is done from the File menu, using the Add EJB JAR to Application... item.

This can also be done using the toolbar at the top of the deploytool:

After choosing this you will be asked to point out the location of your EJB JAR. Locate it and select Add EJB-JAR and it will be added to your application. It should now show up under Local Applications, and you can expand the EJB JAR to see your beans

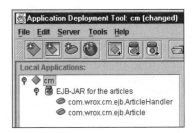

Add the web module and the application client module in the same way, using Add Web WAR to Application... and Add Application Client to Application... commands. After this you should see something like this:

Your application has now been assembled and is available as an EAR at the location you chose at the beginning. In this case, we will not provide any documentation about the application for the deployer, although that should normally be added here too.

Assembling the Application Using Orion

The Orion application server (http://www.orionserver.com/) comes with an application assembly tool called earassembler, which can be started by running

```
java -jar earassembler.jar
```

from the directory where Orion is installed. This will automatically open a new, unnamed enterprise application, to which we can add our modules. We'll start with the EJB module. To add this, go to the EAR menu, and from the Import submenu choose EJB Jar:

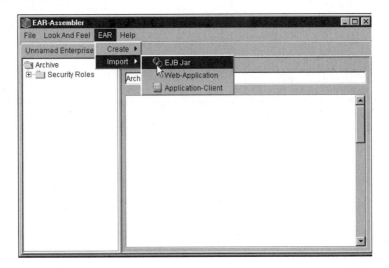

You will be asked to point out the location of your EJB JAR. Locate it and click **Open** to add it to your application. You will be asked whether you want to create a subdirectory; click **No**:

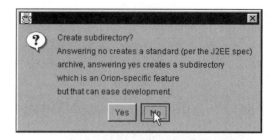

Finally, you will need to give the module a name. Click **OK** to accept the default value:

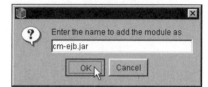

Add the web and application client modules in the same way, using the **Import Web-Application** and **Import Application-Client** commands. After this you should see something like the adjacent window:

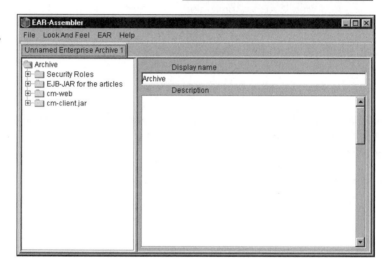

Your application has now been assembled. Save it as `C:\ProJavaServer\Chapter30\cm.ear`, then choose **Close Document** and finally **Exit**, both from the **File** menu.

Manual Application Assembly

You do not have to use any graphical assembly tool to assemble a J2EE Application. Earlier we looked at the Enterprise Archive file structure and the application deployment descriptor, and we can now use this knowledge to assemble our application. The structure of the application is decided by the application deployment descriptor. We have three modules:

❑ An EJB module, `cm-ejb.jar`

❑ A web module, `cm-web.war`

❑ An application client module, `cm-client.jar`

We define these in our descriptor, as follows:

```
<module>
  <web>
    <web-uri>cm-web.war</web-uri>
    <context-root></context-root>
  </web>
</module>
<module>
  <java>cm-client.jar</java>
</module>
<module>
  <ejb>cm-ejb.jar</ejb>
</module>
```

We also want to name our application; this is done using the `<display-name>` tag:

```
<display-name>Wrox Pro Java Server Programming J2EE ed CM</display-name>
```

Finally we want to specify the security roles the application uses. We need one role, `editors`, for specifying who is allowed to edit the article. This is just to show how it is added, and we will not actually consider security any further in this chapter:

```
<security-role>
  <role-name>editors</role-name>
</security-role>
```

Putting these things together, along with the deployment descriptor's mandatory items, we get the following:

```
<?xml version="1.0" encoding="Cp1252"?>

<!DOCTYPE application PUBLIC '-//Sun Microsystems, Inc.//DTD J2EE Application
1.2//EN' 'http://java.sun.com/j2ee/dtds/application_1_2.dtd'>

<application>
  <display-name>Wrox Pro Java Server Programming J2EE ed CM</display-name>
  <description>Application description</description>
  <module>
    <java>cm-client.jar</java>
  </module>
  <module>
    <web>
      <web-uri>cm-web.war</web-uri>
      <context-root></context-root>
    </web>
  </module>
  <module>
    <ejb>cm-ejb.jar</ejb>
  </module>
  <security-role>
    <role-name>editors</role-name>
  </security-role>
</application>
```

This file needs to go into the J2EE application file structure as `META-INF/application.xml`. If the three module files are in `C:\ProJavaServer\Chapter30\` and the `application.xml` deployment descriptor is in `C:\ProJavaServer\Chapter30\META-INF`, we can 'jar' this directory together to create `cm.ear`, a full J2EE Application that we can deploy in any J2EE environment.

Application Deployment

Having created our application archive file, we need finally to deploy it in our chosen J2EE application server. Since deployment is part of the focus for the chapter, it would be good to show how to deploy the application in a variety of ways; again, we will use a variety of tools, provided by the Reference Implementation and the Orion application server.

Deploying in the J2EE Reference Implementation

Let's first deploy the application in the J2EE RI, again using its deploytool.

> **Unfortunately, the application itself will not run successfully on the J2EE Reference Implementation, version 1.2.1, due to problems with using tag libraries. However, the deployment steps outlined here will be generally applicable to other J2EE applications.**

Make sure you have the J2EE RI server running, as well as the Cloudscape database that is provided with it, and then start deploytool. If the application doesn't show up in the Local Applications panel, open the `.ear` file from the location where you stored it, using Open Application... from the File menu.

Before trying to deploy the application we need to perform some initial configuration of the modules. We start with the EJB module, in which we need to define how the CMP mapping will work; specifically, we need to set up the data source and define the finder methods.

Choose the `Article` bean in the application tree and select the Entity tab to see the entity panel. In the panel, click Deployment Settings.... Choose `jdbc/Cloudscape` as the Database JNDI Name; you do not need a user name and password in this case:

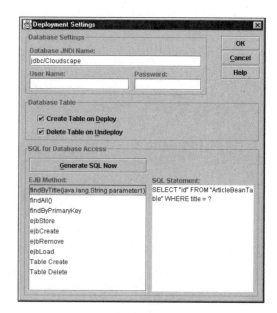

Click **Generate SQL Now** to generate the skeletons for your finders and other methods. You will be asked to supply the WHERE clauses for findAll() and findByTitle() yourself. Add WHERE title = ? to the SQL code for findByTitle(); findAll() doesn't need a WHERE clause, since it should just return all the articles.

Click **OK** to return to the deploytool. You can ignore the warning about the missing WHERE clause for the findAll() method.

The web application does not need any configuration at this stage, so we can now try to deploy the application into the server. Choose **Deploy Application...** from the **Tools** menu.

You will now be asked which server you want to deploy on. localhost should already be selected, and is correct if you want to install it on your local server. You can also choose if you want the client jar to be written: we want that, so select the checkbox indicating this:

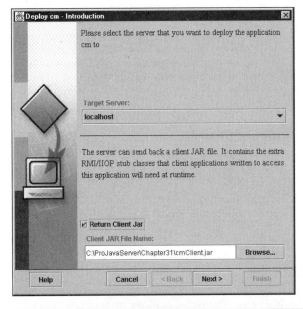

Next you will be asked to map the JNDI names: you need to specify what JNDI names to bind your EJBs to, and what JNDI names your ejb-refs will map to. Map your Article bean to the name Article and the ArticleHandler to ArticleHandler, and map the corresponding EJB references to the same:

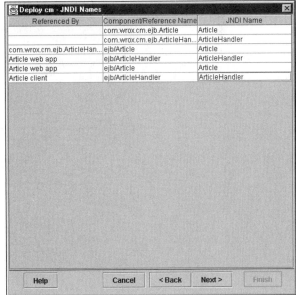

After specifying the JNDI names click Next, and you will be asked for the context root of your web application. Enter /cm to make the web application available under the /cm path on the web server. Click Next again.

The application is now ready to be deployed. Click Finish and the deployment will start. Hopefully the deployment process will succeed. If you get an error message, make sure that you completed all the above steps, and refer to the J2EE RI documentation to find out what might have gone wrong.

You should now be able to visit the web site at http://localhost:8000/cm (assuming port 8000 is used for the web server in your installation of the J2EE RI). We will discuss later how to run the client.

> Unfortunately, as we discussed earlier, the J2EE Reference Implementation 1.2.1 uses an old version of Tomcat as its Web Container, and is unable to execute the application's JSPs due to problems with the tag libraries.

Deploying in Orion

Let's now look at how to deploy the application in Orion, using its GUI and command-line tools, and by manually editing the configuration files.

To deploy an application in Orion using the GUI tools, we start the Management Console. In this case we do not need to connect to a remote server, but can start the console and the application server at the same time, by issuing the command

```
java -jar orion.jar -console
```

This will present us with the Service Console and the Hosts tree will show our local server. Right-click on this host, and in the popup menu choose Install application:

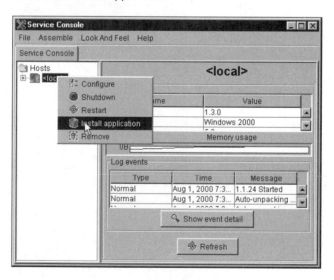

Navigate to and select the .ear file. You will be asked about what deployment name you want to choose; this is so that you can deploy the same application under different names. When you deploy it the first time, clicking OK is all you need to do. After this the EAR deployer window will open. All you need to do here is to select Deploy from the Installation menu.

Orion has auto-deployment features, which means that it will automatically find your data-sources, set up the JNDI references, and generate your finders. Of course, it cannot always guess exactly what your finders want to do but it does use certain heuristics:

❑ For findByX(param) finders, where X is a field in your bean and param is of the same type as X, Orion will generate a finder where the parameter is matched against the field X

❑ findAll() (and everything else) will be generated with empty WHERE clauses, thus returning all entities on a search

Of course ,the behavior of the finders can be modified, but in this case we will not need to do this, since the defaults work just fine. If any errors are found during deployment these will be shown. After a successful deployment you are asked if you want to bind the web app to a web site. Choose /cm as your root, and click Yes to have the web application automatically bound to the web site:

We could deploy the application into Orion using command line tools; this is done using the admin.jar program, which provides a way to do some of the things you do in the graphical console from the command line. admin.jar needs an URL pointing to the server you wish to operate on, and the user name and password of a user that is permitted to perform these tasks. The syntax for admin.jar is:

```
java -jar admin.jar ormi://host.domain.com{:port} user password [command]
```

To deploy an application you use the -deploy switch, with the following possible suboptions:

❑ -file: The Enterprise Archive to deploy

❑ -deploymentName: Name of the application deployment

❑ -targetPath: The path on the remote OS to place the archive at. If not specified the applications directory is used

In this case we will use the admin user and the password 123456. (The password you will use is the one you specified when you installed Orion.) Note that Orion needs to be running so that admin.jar can connect to it. The full line to deploy our application is:

```
java -jar admin.jar ormi://localhost admin 123456 -deploy -file /cm/cm.ear
-deploymentName cm
```

1453

This is what we need to have our application auto-deployed, but we also want to bind the web-application to the web site, and we do that using the -bindWebApp switch. This command has the syntax:

```
-bindWebApp [application deployment name] [web-app name] [web-site name] [context
root]
```

To bind our web application cm-web in the application deployed with the name cm under the web-site root /cm we would do:

```
java -jar admin.jar ormi://localhost admin 123456 -bindWebApp cm cm-web
default-web-site /cm
```

The third way to deploy an application in Orion is by editing the Orion configuration file. To add a J2EE Application you can add it to the server.xml configuration file (in Orion's config directory) like this:

```
<application name="cm" path="/path/to/cm.ear"/>
```

To add a web application to the default web site in Orion you edit default-web-site.xml. If you want to add the web application to our example, you just add:

```
<web-app application="cm" name="cm-web" root="/cm" />
```

Running the Application

Now let's run the application. We have two different interfaces to test:

❑ The article viewer web application

❑ The article entering Swing application

Running the web application is very simple. Just visit http://host:port/cm/ (with host and port being replaced with the host and port of your web server) and you will see the screen shown below. When you first start it, it will not contain any articles, but here we've entered a few using the client:

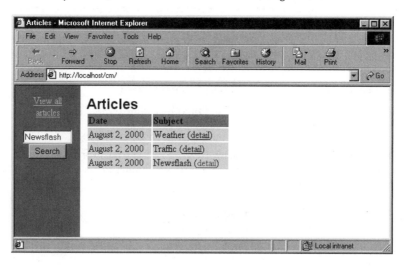

Running the article entering application is, however, somewhat more complex. There are many ways to do this, which differ between J2EE environments. Using Orion there are at least three ways:

- ❏ Running the client as an executable JAR (`java -jar cm-client.jar`). This requires the JNDI properties to be set correctly in the JAR

- ❏ Running the client using the application launcher (`applicationlauncher.jar`). Using this you can launch a local or remote application using the syntax:

```
java -jar applicationlauncher.jar ormi://thehost/cm/cm-client user password
```

- ❏ Running the client using the management console. In the graphical management console you can right-click the application client you want to execute and click Launch (Locally) to execute a client

Using the J2EE RI, the runclient utility can be used to launch the client application. runclient accepts the following syntax to launch an application:

```
runclient -client <appjar> [-name <name>] [application-arguments]
```

where <appjar> is the .ear file containing the application and <name> is the display name of the client.

Whichever way you launch the application, you should see something like this:

You can now use this to add articles, and the web application to read articles.

Using Other Application Servers

Deploying our example application, particularly in Orion, was easy, but you need to be aware that it is not always so. With BEA WebLogic Server, for example, you can't just drop the .ear file into the server; rather, you need to deploy the modules individually, using the supplied tools; you will also, of course, have to configure them, setting up the JNDI names and EJB references correctly, specifying finder methods and CMP options for entity EJBs, and so on. WebLogic's tool for deploying EJBs, DeployerTool, is seen overleaf:

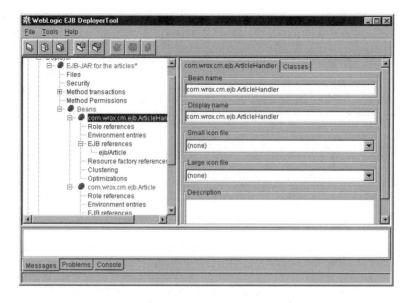

> The most important point is that you need to read your server documentation and find out
> its procedures for deploying modules and applications. Our discussion of the J2EE
> Reference Implementation and Orion should have given you a flavor of what to expect
> from other servers, but they all differ in subtle ways. Read the documentation!

Summary

This chapter covered J2EE Applications in depth, including:

- ❏ J2EE Applications, modules, and EAR files
- ❏ Design patterns for combining different J2EE components
- ❏ The process of J2EE application development
- ❏ Application assembly and deployment
- ❏ An example application

We've now seen the entire range of J2EE technologies, from the basic building-blocks of RMI, JDBC, JNDI, and JAXP, through the servlet and JSP web content APIs and Enterprise JavaBeans, to complete J2EE applications. We hope the book has inspired you to get stuck into creating your own J2EE applications – enjoy!

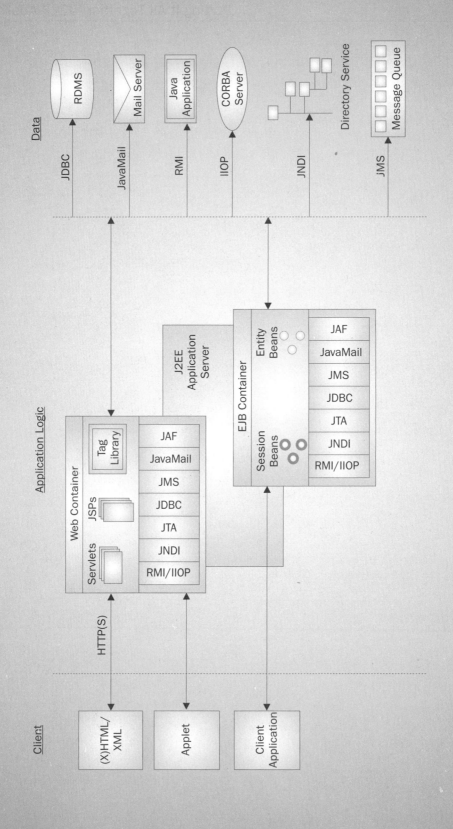

Configuring Tomcat and JRun

In this appendix we will go through typical installations of Tomcat and JRun, and highlight the interesting bits. It is organized into two sections: the Tomcat installation followed by a section on installing JRun.

Tomcat Installation and Configuration

Installing Tomcat

> See the Tomcat README (in the **jakarta-tomcat\docs** directory) for more details on installation and configuration.

Uncompress your download of `jakarta-tomcat` into some sensible place, like `C:\Program Files\Apache Group\`.

While configuring the system, bear these points in mind:

- ❑ You need to have a Java Development Kit installed (1.1.X, 1.2 or 1.3) – I have used JDK 1.3
- ❑ The CLASSPATH environment variable should include the `javac` compiler.
    - ❑ In Java 2, make sure that `tools.jar` is included in the CLASSPATH; this is typically somewhere like `C:\jdk1.3\lib\tools.jar`. Alternatively, set the JAVA_HOME environment variable to the path to your JDK installation, for example, `C:\jdk1.3`. Tomcat and ant use JAVA_HOME in their startup scripts to find `tools.jar`.
    - ❑ In JDK 1.1.x, the path to the `classes.zip` file is required instead.

❏ In Windows 9x, you may get DOS windows that say "**Out of environment space**". If this is the case, right-click on the offending DOS window, select **Properties**, go to the **Memory** tab, and set the initial environment to 4096 bytes.

❏ If you have multiple JDKs installed, you may need to edit the batch/script files to add full paths to `java` and other JDK tools.

I added this line to my `autoexec.bat` file:

```
set JAVA_HOME=C:\JDK1.3
```

although I could have used:

```
set CLASSPATH=C:\JDK1.3\LIB\TOOLS.jar;.
```

Some other things you may want to set are `ANT_HOME` and `TOMCAT_HOME`. We'll use these in the `build.xml` file later, and in the `jakarta-tomcat/bin` scripts. The startup script for ant tries `C:\Program Files\ant` or `C:\ant` and then gives up. I used:

```
set ANT_HOME= C:\progam files\apache group\jakarta-tomcat
set TOMCAT_HOME= C:\progam files\apache group\jakarta-tomcat
```

The `startup.bat` and `shutdown.bat` files try `TOMCAT_HOME` as the current or parent directory and then give up. We will refer to the installation directory for tomcat as `TOMCAT_HOME` for the remainder of this chapter, similarly for `ANT_HOME`.

Finally, run the `startup.bat` batch file found in the `TOMCAT_HOME\bin` directory. If the configuration is quite right, tomcat will print an error message and close the DOS window. To find out the problem try opening a DOS command window, `cd` to Tomcat's `bin` and type `startup` from there. This will mean that you can read the error message and try to correct it. The majority of problem relate to an incorrectly setup classpath.

Test the result by going to `http://localhost:8080/` in your browser. Run the `shutdown.bat` script when you're ready.

server.xml

For code that is provided as a WAR file you will not need to configure a new context as explained below. Simply copy the WAR file to the `\webapps` directory in TOMCAT_HOME.

If you are building the source code as you go along, you will need to establish a new context for each application we describe. Tomcat server is configured using the `server.xml` file in the `TOMCAAT_HOME\conf` directory.

In order to set up a new web application for the server, for example, myapp, you need to add a new Context tag within the ContextManager tag. Simply copy the sample used for the examples web application and paste and alter it to the following:

```
<Context path="/myapp " docBase="webapps/myfiles" debug="0"
 reloadable="true" >
</Context>
```

The Context tag allows us to alter a few attributes from their default settings. For example, here we:

❑ Set a path after the server name

❑ Point that to the relative directory in jakarta-tomcat, then set a debug level (0 the least, 9 providing the most information)

❑ Set reloadable to "true", so that beans and other classes are automatically reloaded into a running tomcat instance, speeding up the code-compile-test cycle for JSPs and Beans. This avoids the need for restarting Tomcat.

The contexts defined here are translated into tomcat-apache.conf when tomcat starts up.

web.xml

Your web application will now be visible to users of the site. The web-inf\web.xml file provides the configuration for the web application.

There's a web.xml file for server-wide configuration, in jakarta-tomcat\conf.

The web.xml file defines:

❑ Display name for general introduction to the application

❑ Context parameters for information on the deployed web application, for instance, the system admin's e-mail

❑ Servlet names and mappings

❑ Session configuration

❑ Tag library mappings (mapping the URL on the page to the actual .tld file)

❑ Supported mime types

❑ Welcome file list (the default page names that, if present, will be loaded when the URL does not include a file name)

Each tag library has a .tld file that describes the tags, their classes, body content type and attributes. This file needs to be available to the JSP container, when it comes across a JSP taglib directive. The mapping from taglib directive to actual file looks like this:

```
<taglib>
 <taglib-uri>
```

```
      /examples/taglib
   </taglib-uri>
   <taglib-location>
      /META-INF/Mylib.tld
   </taglib-location>
</taglib>
```

If you want to use a tag library that's wrapped as a JAR file, just point the URI to the JAR file, either directly from the JSP `taglib` directive URI, or through a `web.xml` mapping. For example:

```
<%@ taglib uri="/WEB-INF/lib/formtags-0.4-dev.jar" prefix="form" %>
```

or:

```
<taglib>
   <taglib-uri>
      http://localhost:8080/form/taglib
   </taglib-uri>
   <taglib-location>
      /WEB-INF/lib/formtags-0.4-dev.jar
   </taglib-location>
</taglib>
```

The key points are:

❑ The tag library descriptor is stored as the file `taglib.tld` in the `META-INF` directory or in a folder that is by convention named tlds within `WEB-INF`

❑ The class packages start from the root of the JAR file, so that classes can be accessed

It's worth noting that the URI is not the same as the `CLASSPATH` – so, although the JAR files in the `/WEB-INF/lib` folder are automatically added to the Tomcat server `CLASSPATH`, that doesn't mean that the URI can find them. You need to specify a relative URI to the JAR file. It doesn't have to be in any particular directory, but it seems sensible to keep it with the other libraries in your application, rather than with the template content.

Where to Put JSPs and Beans in a Web Application

We'll use the example application, views, developed in Chapter 12:

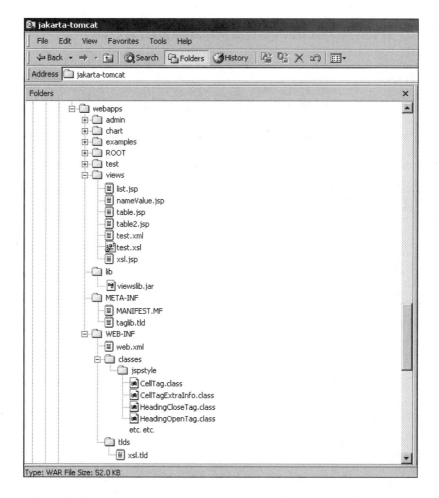

As you can see from the figure:

❑ JSPs and other template data in the `views` web application live in the `webapps/views` directory or a subdirectory of that folder

❑ The `CLASSPATH` for beans and other Java support classes starts in the `webapps/views/WEB-INF/classes` directory, so this is where the package names should start

❑ JAR files for support classes should go in the `WEB-INF/lib` directory, where they'll be added to the `CLASSPATH`

❑ The tag library descriptor files typically live in `webapps/views/META-INF` although they may also be within `WEB-INF/tlds`

❑ The `web.xml` configuration file for the web application is in `/webapps/views/WEB-INF`

JRun 3.0 Installation and Configuration

About JRun

JRun was the first servlet and JSP engine, and remains today the most widely adopted. The most recent release, JRun 3.0, includes an EJB server implementation with integrated transaction and messaging server. At the time of this publication, JRun 3.0 implements the most recent J2EE specifications including EJB 1.1, JTA 1.0, JMS 1.0, Servlet 2.2 and JSP 1.1. JRun was written by Live Software, which was purchased by the Allaire Corporation in 1999.

Obtaining JRun

JRun ships in the three product variations:

- ❏ **Developer**: Free, non-expiring copy for development. Includes full servlet/JSP and EJB/JTA/JMS functionality, unlimited number of JVM's but restricted to three concurrent connections. Not licensed for deployment.

- ❏ **Professional:** Includes full servlet/JSP functionality, unlimited number of JVM's and concurrent connections. Licensed for commercial deployment.

- ❏ **Enterprise:** Includes full servlet/JSP and EJB/JTA/JMS functionality, unlimited number of JVM's and concurrent connections, HTTP clustering. Licensed for commercial deployment.

You may download a copy from `http://commerce.allaire.com/download`. Choose the file that corresponds to your operating system. The main difference between them is that they have different installers.

Installation

JRun is written entirely in Java and has installers for Windows 95/98/NT/2000 (SP3 or greater), Solaris 2.6, 7, Red Hat Linux 6.x, HP-UX 11.0, IBM AIX 4.2, 4.3, SGI IRIX 6.5, Compaq UNIX Tru64 4.0. JRun is known to work on other platforms. This appendix will walk through the Windows installation: however, the install process is essentially the same for any operating system because all prompt for the same questions. In Windows, invoke either the `setup.exe` or `jr30.Exe` file which will kick-off the Windows install-shield. JRun will install by default to a `C:\Program Files\ Allaire\JRun`, choose the full-install option, which includes servlet/JSP and EJB/JTA/JMS servers, documentation and sample applications.

In Windows, JRun can be installed as either a service or application. It is recommended that you install JRun as an application on your development servers, and register it as a service on production servers. This is because there is no easy way to kill a service, which you may want to do during development. During the install, you will also be asked to select your Java runtime environment. On Windows platforms, Sun's JDK or JRE 1.3 is supported, as well as versions 1.2 and 1.1: however, note that the EJB/JTA/JMS functionality requires 1.2 or later. This is the case for most other vendors Java Virtual Machines as well. You will not be able to complete the install without a Java runtime.

You will be asked to specify the port number for the JRun Administration Server, so use port 8000, the default port number. (The default web site will run on port 8100) Next, create a password for the administrator account. Finally, you will be asked if you want to connect to an external web-server.

JRun can work as either a stand alone engine using its built-in HTTP server, or as an add-on to an existing HTTP server using a connector. The most common external web-servers are supported, including Microsoft IIS & PWS, Apache, Netscape Enterprise, Netscape FastTrack, Netscape iPlanet, Website Pro and Zeus Web Server. We will explain this later. Select I'll configure my web server later and click Finish. This should launch a new browser window which will prompt you to log into the JRun Management Console using the user name admin and whatever password you supplied during installation. To do this manually, open the browser window (use Internet Explorer or Netscape 4.0 or later) then open the page `http://localhost:8000/index.jsp`.

The figure below shows the JRun Administration Console, a web-based interface where you can manage your entire application. This includes WAR file deployment, configuring JDBC data sources, creating web apps, re starting the server, and much more. On the left side bar there is a tree-view controller that shows the different JRun server instances currently running, and for each server instance there are various configuration panels associated with the server, such as JDBC Data Sources, Java Settings, Web Applications, etc.

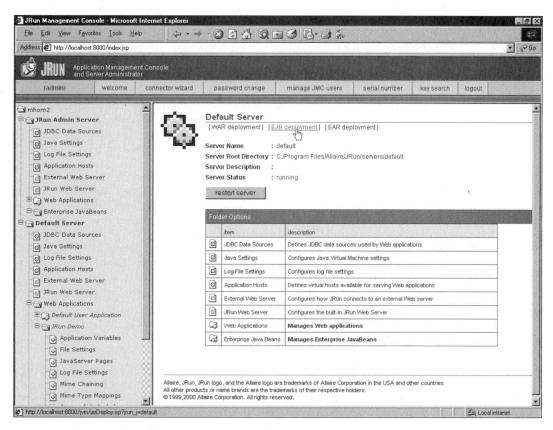

To understand the layout of the Administration Console, it's easiest to look at JRun architecture diagram shown below. JRun has multiple independent servers. Each JRun server instance runs within its on its own JVM. Within the JVM, there is an instance of an HTTP server, servlet, and JSP engine, as well as an EJB server with integrated transactions and messaging, all running in process:

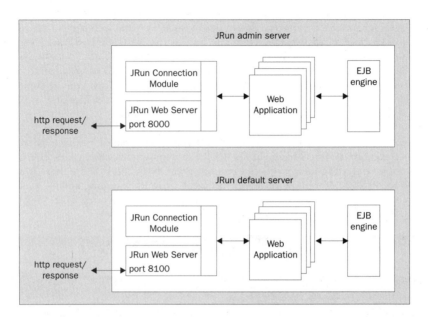

There are several reasons for this approach, including improved security and stability of the system. When you install JRun for the first time, two JRun servers are started up automatically, the Admin Server and the Default Server; you may create additional server instances at any time. The entire JRun Management Console is actually a web-application that is deployed on the Admin server; by default it listens for HTTP requests on port 8000.

The default server has several sample applications, and listens for HTTP requests on port 8100. You can quickly verify that the default server's servlet engine is running by invoking one of the sample servlets located at `http://localhost:8100/demo/index.html`. You should deploy your applications to the default server, or create new server instances and deploy on those servers. You should not deploy other applications on the Administration port, as you might want to consider restricting access to the Administration Console. This can be done by clicking on **JRun Web Server | Client IP Filter** on the Admin Server and listing out the IP addresses that should be granted access. Note that all HTTP listening port numbers can be changed in the Management Console by clicking on **JRun Web Server | Web Server Port** for the desired server instance.

Connecting to an External Web Server

As mentioned earlier, JRun includes connectors for the most common web servers. While some of these web servers may include support for servlets, one advantage of using JRun is that the servlet engine itself is portable. If you connect to an external web server, then are registering JRun as a filter to the external web server to figure out which requests JRun should service. JRun and the external web server communicate over a connector on some specified port. In this case we will connect to Microsoft IIS: however, it is a similar process for all web servers. A connector wizard that walks you through the basic steps facilitates the process of connecting to an external web server; this is shown on the opposite page. Be sure to install the connector to the server that hosts your application, usually the default server. In general, you should not connect an external web-server to the Admin Server because it is not supposed to be hosting your web applications.

Connector Wizard

Step 1 of 4

Configure connections between JRun and external web servers

This is the first of a four step wizard designed to guide you through the process of connecting your JRun server to third party webservers. Choose the JRun server and third-party Web server you would like to connect.

| Current Step | 1 | 2 | 3 | 4 |

JRun Server Information

JRun Server Name:
JRun Admin Server
JRun Default Server

Third-party Web Server Information

Web Server Type: Internet Information Server ▼

Web Server Version: 5.0 ▼

Web Server Platform: intel-win ▼

< back   next >   cancel

To start the connector wizard, from the left hand menu of the Management Console, expand a server tree and click on **External Web Server**. Follow the instructions on the screen – some tips are listed here:

❑ Shut down the external web server. In Windows, stop the WWW Publishing Service from the services panel; simply clicking the stop button from the Microsoft Management Console is not sufficient, as it does not unlock the dlls, resulting in a failed connection.

❑ Start the JRun Management Console (JMC)

❑ Run the JRun Connector Wizard to create a JRun Connection Module that manages the connection between the web server and the default JRun server. When asked to specify the server connector port, pick any unused port like 53001. This is the port that JRun and the external-web server use to communicate. If the JRun server and external web server are not on the same machine, make sure that the port isn't blocked by a firewall.

❑ You will need to choose a directory where the connection module is to be installed. The Wizard requests the scripts directory for IIS, which is normally `c:\Inetpub\Scripts` by default.

❑ Start the external web server and (restart) the default JRun server.

❑ Verify the connection between JRun and the web server by launching one of the sample servlets through the connector at `http://localhost/demo/index.html`.

While this is just a basic configuration, there are many other possibilities. The relationship between a JRun server and an external server can be 1:1, many:1, 1:many or many:many. See the advanced configuration guide for more details, available at `http://www.allaire.com/Documents/` under JRun Docs.

Where to Place Servlets, JSPs and Beans in a Web Application

The JRun 3.0 directory structure reflects changes in the servlet 2.2 specification, specifically the introduction of a standardized means of packaging applications. The JRun directory structure is shown below:

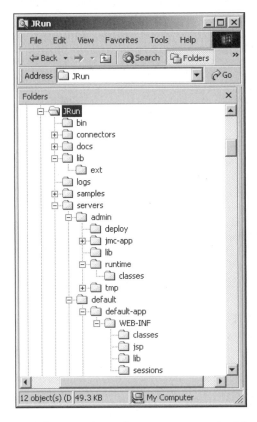

The /servers directory has a subdirectory for each server instance; in this case there are subdirectories for the Admin and Default servers. The servlet 2.2 specification introduces the notion of web applications, which map to a specified URL prefix. For example, all of the files in the demo application located at http://localhost:8100/demo/index.html are assigned the prefix of /demo followed by the relative path to the resource. Every web application root directory has a special directory called WEB-INF, which is not visible to external clients. Place all your class files (servlets, JavaBeans, etc.) associated with the current application in the WEB-INF/classes directory, or if they are package declared, re-create the directory structure using the WEB-INF/classes directory as the root.

Any class libraries packaged in jar files can be placed in the WEB-INF/lib directory. To invoke a servlet, use the /servlet invoker mapping. For example, http://localhost:8100/demo/servlet/SnoopServlet invokes the SnoopServlet class of the demo-app, located in JRun\servers\default\demo-app\WEB-INF\classes directory, belonging to the demo application. Alternatively you may create servlet mappings or aliases in either the Management Console by clicking Default Server | Web Applications | JRun Demo | Servlet URL Mappings, or by manually editing the web.xml file associated with the application, located in the WEB-INF directory for that application.

Creating an Application

The easiest way to create a new web application is to use the Create New Application wizard. Just specify which server you are creating the application for, the Application name, URL and root directory as illustrated in the figure below:

Note that JRun will automatically create a META-INF directory in the application root directory where you can place your class files and jar files.

Under the Hood

For those who prefer using property files rather than user interfaces to manage an application, we always have the option of modifying properties manually. It is always a good idea to back up your files first. JRun has a very simple property file hierarchy. In the /lib directory, there is a global.properties file which contains all of the default settings for all JRun server instances. These properties can be over-ridden at either a server-level in the local.properties file in the /servers/<server_name> directory, and again at the application level in the webapp.properties file located in the WEB-INF directory of the web-application. The following is an excerpt from the global.properties file. This is where you would configure JRun session management: for example, you can specify if you would like to persist session data to a file or relational database, specify the database drivers, the frequency of updates, etc. Any line that begins with a # mark is ignored:

```
############################################################################
## session services
############################################################################

# Session management service.
# to enable these deprecated methods:
#    Enumeration SessionContext.getIds()
#    HttpSession getSession(String id)
# use allaire.jrun.session.JRunSessionService instead.
session.class=allaire.jrun.session.WebappSessionService
# Invalidation time is the default session inactivity timeout.
```

```
# If the session is not accessed, it will be expired. This value
# can be set on each session by calling HttpSession.setMaxInactiveTime()
# specified in minutes.
session.invalidationtime=30

# true if sessions should be persisted when the server is terminated.
session.persistence=true

# What to do with session data when class files change. Values are
# reload, drop, or ignore. Only valid if session.persistence=true
session.persistence.classchange=reload

# true if sessions should be swapped out of memory to a storage service
session.swapping=false

# How often the session pool should be checked for sessions that should
# be swapped to a storage service, specified in seconds
session.swapinterval=10

# The approximate number of sessions that will be allowed in memory
# before swapping to a storage service. Due to delays in the swapinterval
# and sessions that may not be serializable, the actual maximum may
# differ. If 0, all session data will be written out immediately upon
# the completion of the request. session.swapping must be 'true' in order
# for this property to take effect.
session.maxresident=9999999

# The name of the storage service to use for session persistence
# and/or swapping
session.persistence.service=file
session.persistence.file.class=allaire.jrun.session.FileSessionStorage
session.persistence.file.path={webapp.rootdir}/WEB-INF/sessions

# JDBCSessionStorage provider
session.persistence.jdbc.class=allaire.jrun.session.JDBCSessionStorage
session.persistence.jdbc.JDBCDriver=sun.jdbc.odbc.JdbcOdbcDriver
session.persistence.jdbc.JDBCConnectionURL=jdbc:odbc:JRunSessions
# The table name to use
session.persistence.jdbc.JDBCSessionTable=sessions
# A key prefix to keep all server keys unique
session.persistence.jdbc.JDBCSessionIDPrefix={jrun.server.name}-
# The column names to use. The JDBCSessionIDColumn must be a VARCHAR
# type while the JDBCSessionDataColumn must be able to handle
# binary long data
session.persistence.jdbc.JDBCSessionIDColumn=id
session.persistence.jdbc.JDBCSessionDataColumn=data

# settings for cookie-based sesssion tracking
session.cookie.maxage=-1
session.cookie.secure=false
session.cookie.active=true
session.cookie.domain=
session.cookie.comment="JRun Session Tracking Cookie"
session.cookie.path=/
session.cookie.name=jsessionid
```

As you can see, the property files are self-explanatory and you are encouraged to look around at some of the highly configurable features such as a performance monitor that can be used to identify bottlenecks, a customizable logger, and much more.

Enterprise JavaBeans

As mentioned earlier, the most recent version of JRun includes a full EJB implementation with integrated transaction (JTA 1.0) and messaging (JMS 1.0) servers. The remarkable part of this is that the entire implementation is written in just 300 kB, and is thus very efficient. The easiest way to get EJBs working is to look at the ten sample EJB applications that are located in the `samples` directory. The samples cover Bean Managed Persistence, Container Managed Persistence, Transactions, Distributed Object Management, and numerous other advanced topics. They are easy to get started initially because you can optionally persist entity beans to regular files rather than setting up a database. All of the samples include the required make-files and there is a samples guide in the `docs` directory.

Technical Support

❑ JRun Support Forum:
   `http://forums.allaire.com/JRunconf/index.cfm`

❑ JRun Developer Center:
   `http://www.allaire.com/developer/jrunreferencedesk/`

❑ Knowledge Base:
   `http://www.allaire.com/Support/KnowledgeBase/SearchForm.cfm`

❑ Online Documentation:
   `http://www.allaire.com/Documents`

❑ JRun-Interest list:
   `http://www.egroups.com/group/jrun-interest/`

While this appendix highlights some of the key points in order to get started, complete product documentation is in the `docs` directory, and includes a setup guide, samples guide, and a comprehensive *Developing Applications in JRun* book in PDF format. An advanced configuration covering ISP and OEM installation and other advanced topics has been posted to the online documentation. The Knowledge base articles are highly recommended as JRun engineers mostly write them.

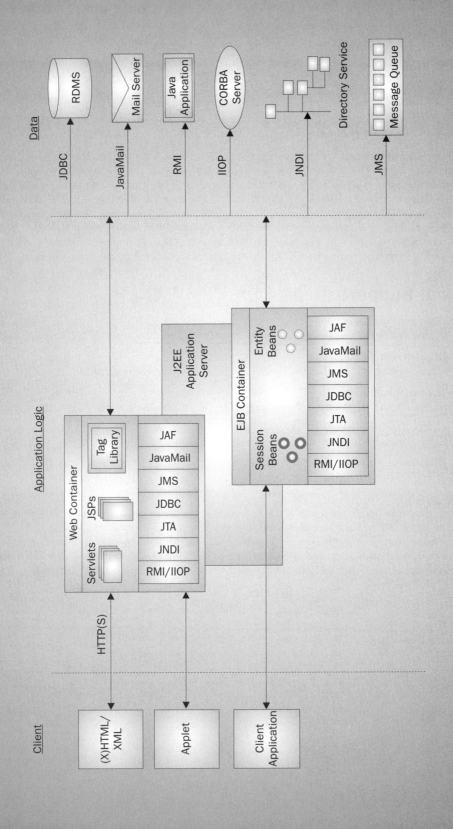

B

Setting Up Netscape's iPlanet Directory Server

This section will show you how to perform a simple installation of iPlanet Directory Server and load the server with the `airius.com` sample data used in Chapter 4. It is *not* a complete guide to iPlanet Directory Server – for that, see Netscape's documentation.

Before your start, make sure the machine you intend to install iPlanet Directory Server is listed in the DNS. Here we are installing on a machine called `richardh`.

Installation

❏ Run the file installation executable, and move through the first few screens

❏ After reading and accepting the license agreement, you will be presented with your first choice:

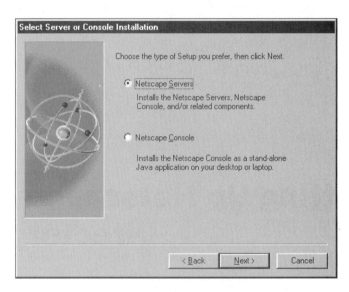

❏ Make sure Netscape Servers is selected, then click Next:

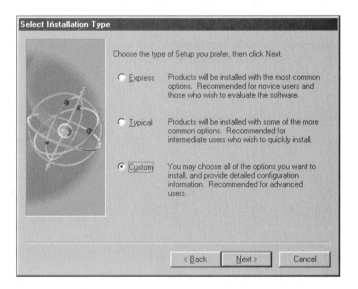

❏ Choose Custom, then click Next:

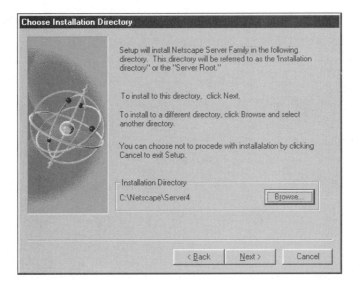

❏   Select your desired installation directory, or just use the default, then click Next:

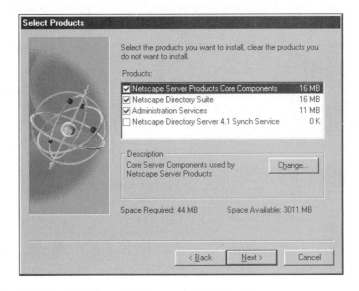

❏   Accept the default values shown above, and click Next:

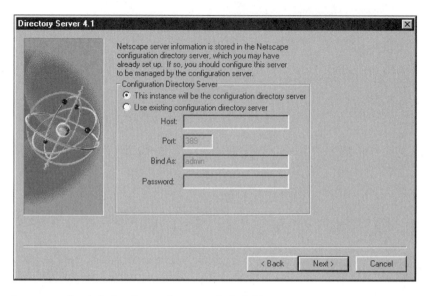

❏   Again, accept the defaults shown above, and click Next:

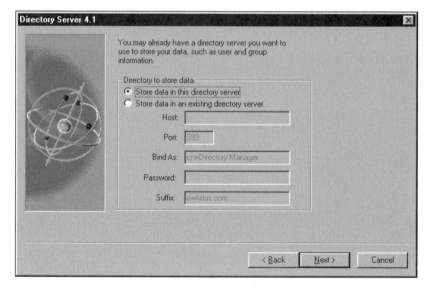

❏   Once more, accept the defaults shown above, and click Next:

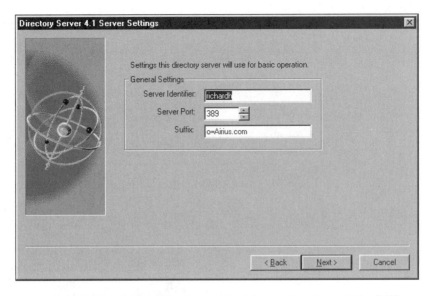

❏ Accept the default **Server Identifier, Server Port,** but we've changed the **Suffix** as we know we're going to be using the sample data for the `airius.com` domain

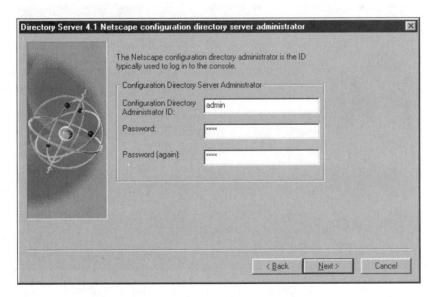

❏ Enter a password for the **Configuration Directory Server Administrator** (twice), and click **Next**:

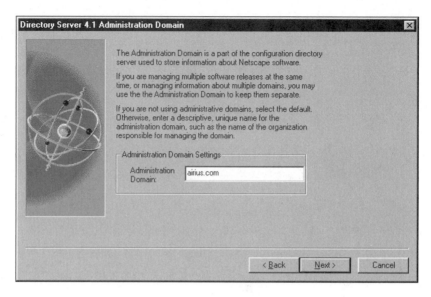

❏   Enter `airius.com` for the Administration Domain, and click **N**ext:

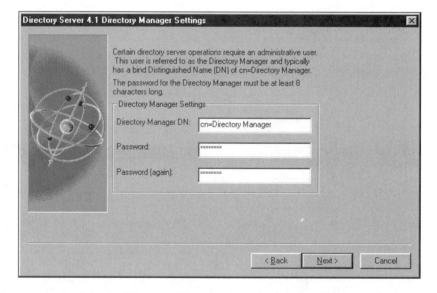

❏   Enter a password for the Directory Manager (twice), and click **N**ext:

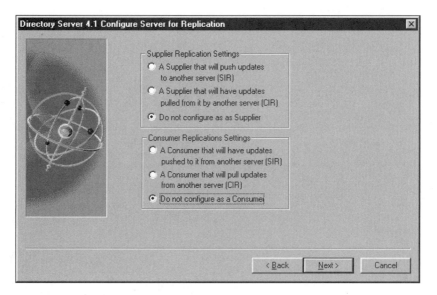

❑   Accept the defaults shown above, and click <u>N</u>ext:

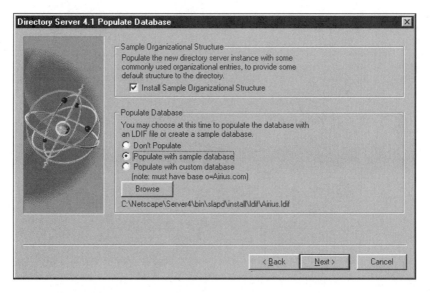

❑   Make sure the Install Sample Organizational Structure box is checked and select Populate
with sample database, before clicking <u>N</u>ext:

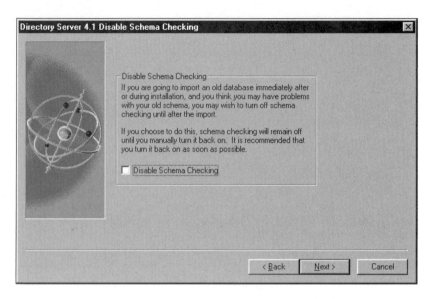

❏ Accept the default as shown above, and click Next:

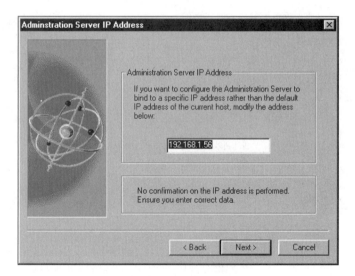

❏ Accept the default Server IP Address and click Next:

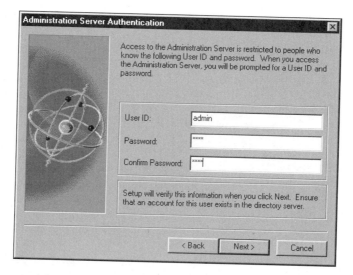

❑ Enter a password for access to the Administration Server (twice) and click **N**ext:

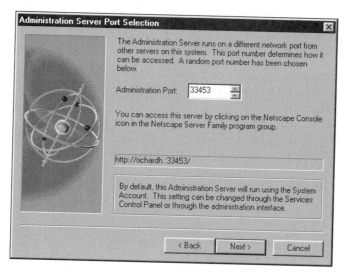

❑ Make a note of the Administration Port number, and click **N**ext:

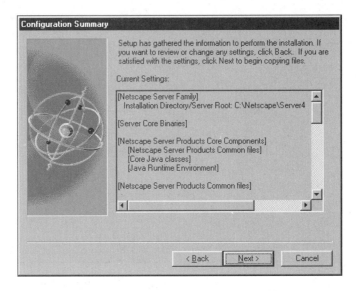

❑ Review the installation settings and click **N**ext to begin installing.

Using Netscape Console

Netscape Console is a Java application you can use to administer your Netscape Directory Server, view the data, and so on. Here we are using a directory server running on a machine called `btvs.VS2000` and with an administration port number of 23252.

❑ Choose Netscape Console 4.1 from the Start menu, under Programs/Netscape Server Products:

❑ Enter the configuration directory administrator user ID and password you chose earlier, and click OK:

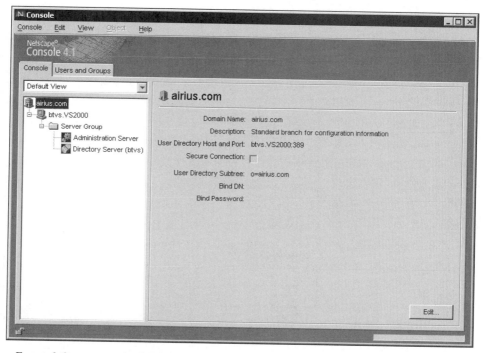

❑ Expand the tree on the left hand side, and double-click on the Directory Server node:

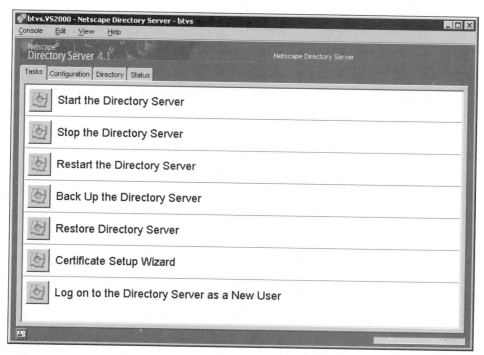

❑ This is the main screen for the Directory Server. To look at the actual data, click on the Directory tab:

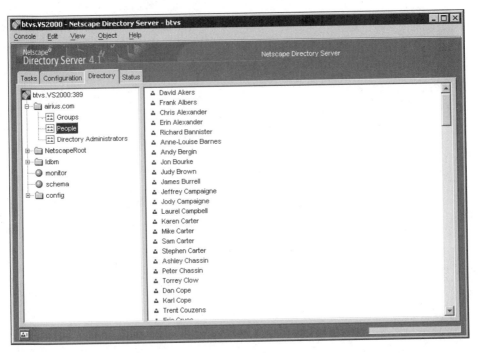

❏ Expand the airius.com node, and click on People. Double-click on Sam Carter, and his details will be displayed:

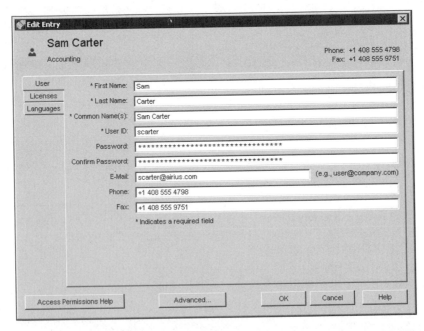

This has been a very quick tour of Netscape Directory Server. For more details on LDAP and Netscape Directory Server, see *Implementing LDAP*, Wrox Press, 1999, ISBN 1-861002-21-1.

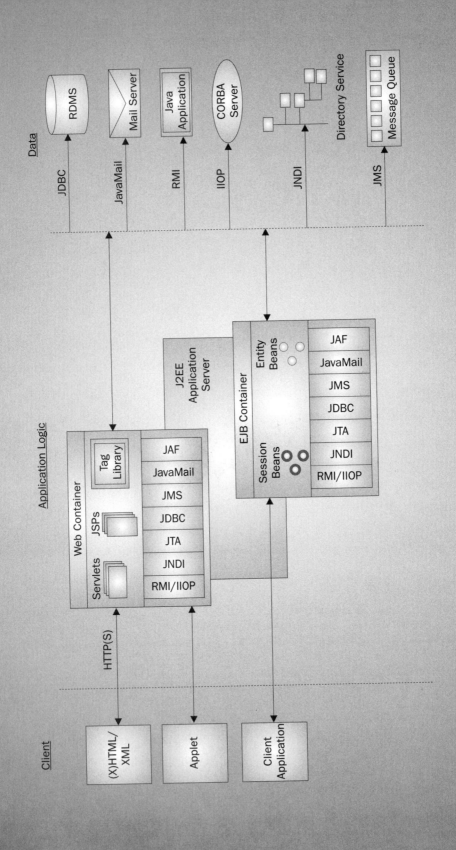

C

HTTP Reference

The Hypertext Transfer Protocol (HTTP) is an application-level protocol for distributed hypermedia information systems. It is a generic, stateless protocol, which can be used for many tasks beyond its use for hypertext. A feature of HTTP is the typing and negotiation of data representation, allowing systems to be built independently of the data being transferred.

The first version of HTTP, referred to as HTTP/0.9, was a simple protocol for raw data transfer across the Internet. HTTP/1.0, as defined by RFC 1945 improved the protocol by allowing messages to be in a MIME-like format, containing meta-information about the data transferred and modifiers on the request/response semantics. The current version HTTP/1.1, first defined in RFC 2068 and more recently in RFC 2616, made performance improvements by making all connections persistent and supporting absolute URLs in requests.

URL Request Protocols

A URL is a pointer to a particular resource on the Internet at a particular location and has a standard format as follows:

```
Protocol Servername Filepath
```

In order, the three elements are the protocol used to access the server, the name of the server, and the location of the resource on the server. For example:

```
http://www.mydomain.com/
https://www.mydomain.com:8080/
ftp://ftp.mydomain.com/example.txt
mailto:me@world.com
file:///c:|Windows/win.exe
```

The servername and filepath pieces of the URL are totally dependent on where files are stored on your server and what you have called it, but there are a standard collection of protocols, most of which you should be familiar with:

- ❑ **http**: Normal HTTP requests for documents

- ❑ **https**: Secure HTTP requests. The specific behavior of these depends on the security certificates and encryption keys you have set up

- ❑ **JavaScript**: Executes JavaScript code within the current document

- ❑ **ftp**: Retrieves documents from an FTP (File Transfer Protocol) server

- ❑ **file**: Loads a file stored on the local (Client) machine. It can refer to remote servers but specifies no particular access protocol to remote file systems

- ❑ **news**: Used to access Usenet newsgroups for articles

- ❑ **nntp**: More sophisticated access to news servers

- ❑ **mailto**: Allows mail to be sent from the browser. It may call in assistance from a helper app

- ❑ **telnet**: Opens an interactive session with the server

- ❑ **gopher**: A precursor to the World Wide Web.

This book exclusively deals with the first five of these

HTTP Basics

Each HTTP client (web browser) request and server response has three parts: the request or response line, a header section, and the entity body.

Client Request

The client initiates a web page transaction – client page request and server page response – as follows:

The client connects to an HTTP-based server at a designated port (by default, 80) and sends a request by specifying an HTTP command called a method, followed by a document address, and an HTTP version number. The format of the request line is:

```
Method        Request-URI    Protocol
```

For example,

```
GET    /index.html    HTTP/1.0
```

uses the GET method to request the document /index.html using version 1.0 of the protocol. We'll +come to a full list of HTTP Request Methods later.

Next, the client sends optional header information to the server about its configuration and the document formats it will accept. All header information is sent line by line, each with a header name and value in the form:

```
Keyword: Value
```

For example:

```
User-Agent:    Lynx/2.4 libwww/5.1k
Accept:        image/gif, image/x-xbitmap, image/jpeg, */*
```

The request line and the subsequent header lines are all terminated by a carriage return/linefeed ($\backslash$r$\backslash$n) sequence. The client sends a blank line to end the headers. We'll return with a full description of each HTTP Header value later on in the Appendix.

Finally, after sending the request and headers the client may send additional data. This data is mostly used by CGI programs using the POST method. This additional information is called a request entity. Finally a blank line ($\backslash$r$\backslash$n$\backslash$r$\backslash$n) terminates the request. A complete request might look like the following:

```
GET /index.html HTTP/1.0
Accept: */*
Connection: Keep-Alive
Host: www.w3.org
User-Agent: Generic
```

HTTP Request Methods

HTTP request methods should not be confused with URL protocols. The former are used to instruct a web server how to handle the incoming request, while the latter define how client and server talk to each other. In version 1.1 of the HTTP protocol there are seven basic HTTP request methods:

Method	Description
OPTIONS	Used to query a server about the capabilities it provides. Queries can be general or specific to a particular resource.
GET	Asks that the server return the body of the document identified in the Request-URI.
HEAD	Responds similarly to a GET, except that no content body is ever returned. It is a way of checking whether a document has been updated since the last request.
POST	This is used to transfer a block of data to the server in the content body of the request.
PUT	This is the complement of a GET request and stores the content body at the location specified by the Request-URI. It is similar to uploading a file with FTP.
DELETE	Provides a way to delete a document from the server. The document to be deleted is indicated in the Request-URI.
TRACE	This is used to track the path of a request through firewalls and multiple proxy servers. It is useful for debugging complex network problems and is similar to the traceroute tool.

Server Response

The HTTP response also contains three parts.

Firstly, the server replies with the status line containing three fields: the HTTP version, status code, and description of status code in the following format.

```
Protocol   Status-code   Description
```

For example, the status line

```
HTTP/1.0   200   OK
```

indicates that the server uses version 1.0 of the HTTP in its response. A status code of 200 means that the client request was successful.

After the response line, the server sends header information to the client about itself and the requested document. All header information is sent line by line, each with a header name and value in the form:

```
Keyword: Value
```

For example:

```
HTTP/1.1 200 OK
Date: Wed, 19 May 1999 18:20:56 GMT
Server: Apache/1.3.6 (Unix) PHP/3.0.7
Last-Modified: Mon, 17 May 1999 15:46:21 GMT
ETag: "2da0dc-2870-374039cd"
Accept-Ranges: bytes
Content-Length: 10352
Connection: close
Content-Type: text/html; charset=iso-8859-1
```

The response line and the subsequent header lines are all terminated by a carriage return/linefeed ($\r\n$) sequence. The server sends a blank line to end the headers. Again, we'll return to the exact meaning of these HTTP headers.

If the client's request is successful, the requested data is sent. This data may be a copy of a file, or the response from a CGI program. This result is called a **response entity**. If the client's request could not be fulfilled, additional data sent might be a human-readable explanation of why the server could not fulfill the request. The properties (type and length) of this data are sent in the headers. Finally, a blank line ($\r\n\r\n$) terminates the response. A complete response might look like the following:

```
HTTP/1.1 200 OK
Date: Wed, 19 May 1999 18:20:56 GMT
Server: Apache/1.3.6 (Unix) PHP/3.0.7
Last-Modified: Mon, 17 May 1999 15:46:21 GMT
ETag: "2da0dc-2870-374039cd"
Accept-Ranges: bytes
Content-Length: 10352
Connection: close
Content-Type: text/html; charset=iso-8859-1
```

```
<!DOCTYPE HTML PUBLIC "-//W3C//DTD HTML 4.0 Transitional//EN"
"http://www.w3.org/TR/REC-html140/loose.dtd">
<html>

    ...

</html>
```

In HTTP/1.0, after the server has finished sending the response, it disconnects from the client and the transaction is over unless the client sends a `Connection: KeepAlive` header. In HTTP/1.1 however, the connection is maintained so that the client can make additional requests, unless the client sends an explicit `Connection: Close header`. Since many HTML documents embed other documents as inline images, applets, and frames, for example, this persistent connection feature of HTTP/1.1 protocol will save the overhead of the client having to repeatedly connect to the same server just to retrieve a single page.

HTTP Headers

These headers can appear in requests or responses. Some control how the web server behaves, others are meant for proxy servers, and some will affect what your browser does with a response when it is received. You should refer to the HTTP 1.1 specification for a full description. You can download it from:

```
ftp://ftp.isi.edu/in-notes/rfc2616.txt
```

The authentication is covered in a little more detail in:

```
ftp://ftp.isi.edu/in-notes/rfc2617.txt
```

Other RFC documents from the same source may be useful and provide additional insights.

This table summarizes the headers you'll find most helpful. There are others in the specification but they control how the web server manages the requests and won't arrive in the CGI environment for you to access:

Header	Request	Response	Description
Accept:	•		Lists the types that the client can cope with
Accept-Charset:	•		Lists the character sets that the browser can cope with
Accept-Encoding:	•		List of acceptable encodings or none. Omitting this header signifies that all current encodings are acceptable
Accept-Language:	•		List of acceptable languages

Table Continued on Following Page

Header	Request	Response	Description
Age		•	A cache control header used to indicate the age of a response body
Allow:		•	Determines the available methods that the resource identified by the URI can respond to
Authorization:	•		Authorization credentials. Refer to RFC2617 for more information on Digest authentication
Cache-Control:	•	•	A sophisticated proxy-controlling header. Can be used to describe how proxies should handle requests and responses
Code:	•		Defines an encoding for the body data. This would normally be Base64
Content-Base:		•	Used to resolve relative URLs within the body of the document being returned. It overrides the value in the Content-Location header
Content-Encoding:		•	Specifies encodings that have been applied to the body prior to transmission
Content-Language:		•	This specifies the natural language of the response content
Content-Length:		•	The length of the body measured in bytes should be put here. CGI responses may defer to the web server and allow it to put this header in
Content-Location:		•	The actual location of the entity being returned in the response. This may be useful when deploying resources that can be resolved in several ways. The specifically selected version can be identified and requested directly
Content-MD5:		•	This is a way of computing a checksum for the entity body. The receiving browser can compare its computed value to be sure that the body has not been modified during transmission

Header	Request	Response	Description
Content-Type:		•	The type of data being returned in the response is specified with this header. These types are listed later in this appendix
Expires:		•	The date after which the response should be considered to be stale
From:	•		The client e-mail address is sent in this header
Host:	•		The target virtual host is defined in this header. The value is taken from the originating URL when the request is made
Last-Modified:		•	This indicates when the content being returned was last modified. For static files, the web server would use the file's timestamp. For a dynamically generated page, you might prefer to insert a value based on when a database entry was last changed. Other more sophisticated cache control headers are provided in the HTTP specification. Refer to RFC2616 for details
Location:		•	Used to redirect to a new location. This could be used as part of a smart error handling CGI
Referrer:	•		The source of the current request is indicated here. This would be the page that the request was linked from. You can determine whether the link was from outside your site and also pick up search engine parameters from this too, if your URI was requested via Yahoo, for example
User-Agent:	•		This is the signature field of the browser. You can code round limitations in browsers if you know this. Be aware of some of the weird values that can show up in this header now that developers are building their own web browsers and spiders
Warning:		•	This is used to carry additional information about the response and whether there are risks associated with it

Server Environment Variables

By and large, the headers in the request correspond with environment variables that are present when a CGI handler executes. Not all headers make it as far as the CGI environment. Some may be 'eaten up' by a proxy server, others by the target web server. Some environment variables are created as needed by the web server itself, without there having been a header value to convert.

Here is a summary of the environment variables you are likely to find available. There may be others if the web server administrator has configured them into the server or if the CGI adapter has been modified to pass them in. You can access them with the `Clib.getenv()` function. These are considered to be standard values and they should be present:

> *(Editor's Note: This list is written with respect to ScriptEase CGI scriptwriters. The server variables are also accessible from ASP as members of the* `Request.ServerVariables` *collection. The notes made here also apply to ASP scripts).*

AUTH_TYPE

The value in this environment variable depends on the kind of authentication used in the server and whether the script is even security protected by the server. This involves server configuration, and is server specific and also protocol specific. The value may not be defined if the page is insecure. If it is secure, the value indicating the type of authentication may only be set after the user is authenticated. An example value for AUTH_TYPE is BASIC.

CONTENT_LENGTH

If the request used the POST method, then it may have supplied additional information in the body. This is passed to the CGI handler on its standard input. However, ScriptEase will assimilate this for you, extract any query strings in the body, and decode them into variables that you can access more conveniently.

CONTENT_TYPE

The data type of any content delivered in the body of the request. With this, you could process the standard input for content bodies that are some type other than form data. This is relatively unexplored territory and likely to be very much server and platform dependent. If it works at all, you might choose a reading mechanism based on content type, and then use other headers to process the binary data in the body. If you are using this just to upload files, then the HTTP/1.1 protocol now supports a PUT method which is a better technique and is handled inside the server.

DOCUMENT_ROOT

This is the full path to the document root for the web server. If virtual hosts are being used and if they share the same CGI scripts, this document root may be different for each virtual host. It is a good idea to have separately owned cgi-bin directories unless the sites are closely related. For example, a movie site and a games site might have separate cgi-bin directories. Three differently branded versions of the movie site may have different document roots but could share the same cgi-bin functionality. In some servers, this may be a way to identify which one of several virtual hosts is being used.

FROM

If the user has configured their browser appropriately, this environment variable will contain their e-mail address. If it is present, then this is a good way to identify the user, given that they are the owner of the computer they are using.

GATEWAY_INTERFACE

You can determine the version number of the CGI interface being used. This would be useful if you depend on features available in a later version of the CGI interface, but you only want to maintain a single script to be used on several machines.

HTTP_ACCEPT

This is a list of acceptable MIME types that the browser will accept. The values are dependent on the browser being used and how it is configured, and are simply passed on by the web server. If you want to be particularly smart and do the right thing, check this value when you try to return any oddball data other than plain text or HTML. The browser doesn't say it can cope, it might just crash on the user when you try and give them some unexpected data.

HTTP_ACCEPT_LANGUAGE

There may not be a value specified in this environment variable. If there is, the list will be as defined by the browser.

HTTP_CONNECTION

This will indicate the disposition of the HTTP connection. It might contain the value "Keep-Alive" or "Close" but you don't really have many options from the ScriptEase:WSE-driven CGI point of view. You might need to know whether the connection to the browser will remain open but since SE:WSE won't currently support streaming tricks it won't matter much either way.

HTTP_COOKIE

The cookie values sent back by the browser are collected together and made available in this environment variable. You will need to make a cookie cutter to separate them and extract their values. Which particular cookies you receive depend on whereabouts in the site's document root you are and the scope of the cookie when it was created.

HTTP_HOST

On a multiple virtual host web server, this will tell you the host name that was used for the request. You can then adjust the output according to different variations of the sites. For example, you can present different logos and backgrounds for www.mydomain.com and test.mydomain.com. This can help solve a lot of issues when you set up a cooperative branding deal to present your content via several portal sites. They do like to have their logo and corporate image on the page sometimes.

HTTP_PRAGMA

This is somewhat deprecated these days, but will likely contain the value "no-cache". Cache control is handled more flexibly with the new response headers available in HTTP/1.1. Caching and proxy server activity can get extremely complex and you may want to study the HTTP specification for more info - ftp://ftp.isi.edu/in-notes/rfc2616.txt

HTTP_REFERER

This is the complete URL for the page that was being displayed in the browser and which contained the link being requested. If the page was a search engine, this may also contain some interesting query information that you could extract to see how people found your web site. There are some situations where there will be no referrer listed. When a user types a URL into a location box, there is no referrer. This may also be true when the link was on a page held in a file on the user's machine. There are some browser dependent issues as well. Some versions of Microsoft Internet Explorer do not report a referrer for HTML documents in framesets. If you have the referrer information it can be useful, but there are enough times when the referrer may be blank that you should have a fall back mechanism in place as well.

HTTP_USER_AGENT

The User Agent is a cute name for the browser. It is necessary because the page may not always be requested by a browser. It could be requested by a robot or so called web spider. It may be requested by offline readers or monitoring services and it's not uncommon for static page generators to be used on a site that was originally designed to be dynamic. Rather than try to cope with all variants of the browsers, you should focus on determining whether you have a browser or robot requesting your documents. That way, you can serve up a page that is more appropriate to a robot when necessary. There is no point in delivering a page that contains an advert, for example. You can make your site attractive to the sight-impaired user community by detecting the use of a text-only browser such as Lynx. You could then serve a graphically sparse but text rich page instead. When examining this value, be aware that there is much weirdness in the values being returned by some browsers. This may be intentional or accidental, but since the Netscape sources were released, developers have been busy writing customized browsers. Some of these will send User-Agent headers containing control characters and binary data. Whether this is an attempt to exploit bugs in web servers, CGI handlers, or log analysis software is arguable. You will encounter e-mail addresses, URLs, command line instructions, and even entire web pages in this header.

PATH

This is the list of directories that will be searched for commands that you may try and execute from within your CGI handler. It is inherited from the parent environment that spawned the handler. It is platform dependent and certainly applies to UNIX systems. It may not be present on all of the others.

PATH_INFO

This is a way of extracting additional path information from the request. Here is a URL as an example: `http://www.domain.com/cgi-bin/path.jsh/folder1/file`. This will run the SE:WSE script called `path.jsh` and store the value `/folder1/file` in the `PATH_INFO` environment variable. This can be an additional way of passing parameters from the HTML page into the server-side script.

PATH_TRANSLATED

This is only implemented on some servers and may be implemented under another environment variable name on others. It returns the full physical path to the script being executed. This might be useful if you have shared code that you include into several scripts.

QUERY_STRING

The query string is that text in the URL following a question mark. This environment variable will contain that text. SE:WSE will unwrap it and present the individual items as variables you can access directly.

REMOTE_ADDR

This is the remote IP address of the client machine that initiated the request. You might use this to control what is displayed or to deny access to users outside your domain.

REMOTE_HOST

It is very likely this value will be empty. It requires the web server to resolve the IP address to a name via the DNS. Whether that would even work depends on the remote user's machine even being listed in a DNS database. It is most often disabled because it imposes significant performance degradation if the web server needs to perform a DNS lookup on every request. You could engineer a local DNS and run that separately, only looking up IP addresses when you need to. Even so, that would still impose a turnaround delay on handling the request and time is definitely of the essence here.

REMOTE_IDENT

This is a deprecated feature. It relies on both the client and server supporting RFC 931 but, since the end user can define the value to be anything they like, the chances of it being useful are quite small. This is probably best avoided altogether and you will be very fortunate if you ever see a meaningful value in it. Of course, in a captive intranet situation where you have more control, you might make use of it.

REMOTE_USER

If the user has been authenticated and has passed the test, the authenticated username will be placed in this variable. Other than that, this variable and AUTH_TYPE are likely to be empty. Even after authentication, this value may be empty when the request is made for a document in a non-secured area.

REQUEST_METHOD

This is the HTTP request method. It is likely you will only ever see GET or POST in here. You usually don't need to deliver different versions of a document based on this value but it might be important to verify that the access was made correctly from your page via the correct method. Apart from the size of the data being larger with a POST, there is another more subtle difference between GET and POST. Using a GET more than once should always result in the same data being returned. Using POST more than once may result in multiple transactions to the back-end. For example, placing an order more than once due to reposting a form. This is one area where the back button on the browser works against you and you may want to interlock this somehow within your session-handling code to prevent duplicate financial transactions happening. You should be aware that this is happening when the browser displays an alert asking whether you want to repost the same form data.

SCRIPT_FILENAME

This is effectively the same as the PATH_TRANSLATED environment variable. It is the full path to the script being executed. Once you have established which of these your server provides (if any), you should be able to stick with it.

SCRIPT_NAME

This is the logical name of the script. It is basically the Request-URI portion of the URL that was originally sent. It is the full path of the script without the document root or script alias mapping. This would be portable across several virtual hosts where the SCRIPT_FILENAME/PATH_TRANSLATED values might not be. This is also useful for making scripts relocatable. You can use this value to rebuild a form so that it will call the same script again. The result is that the script does not then contain a hard coded path that will need to be edited if it is renamed or moved.

SERVER_ADMIN

If it is configured, the e-mail address of the server administrator is held in this environment variable. You could build this into the security mechanisms to alert the administrator when a potential break-in is detected. Be careful not to mailbomb the server administrator with thousands of messages though.

SERVER_NAME

This is the name of the server and may, on some systems, be equivalent to the HTTP_HOST value. This can be useful for manufacturing links elsewhere in a site or detecting the site name so you can build site-specific versions of a page.

SERVER_PORT

The port number that the request arrived on is stored here. Most web sites operate on port 80. Those that don't may be test sites or might operate inside a firewall. It is possible that ancillary servers for adverts and media may use other port numbers if they run on the same machine as the main web server. Most web servers allow you to configure any port number. In the case of the Apache web server you can set up individual virtual hosts on different ports. This means that you could develop a test site and use this value to activate additional debugging help knowing that it would be turned off if the script were run on the production site.

SERVER_PROTOCOL

This is the protocol level of the request being processed. This area is quite ambiguous in the specifications and previously published books. The browser can indicate a preferred protocol level that it can accommodate. This is the value it puts in the request line. However, the server may choose to override that and serve the request with a subset of the functionality that conforms to an earlier protocol level. The server configuration may determine a browser match and override it internally or the request may be simple enough so it can be served by HTTP/1.0 protocol even though the browser indicates that it could cope with HTTP/1.1 protocol. From a CGI scripting point of view, it is unlikely you would need to build alternate versions of a page according to this value. It might determine whether you could provide streaming media, but that technique is not currently supported by SE:WSE anyway.

SERVER_SOFTWARE

For example, Apache/1.3.6, but dependent on your server.

UNIQUE_ID

This is available in CGI environments running under an Apache web server that has been built with the unique_id module included. You could select the first one of these that arrives in a session, and use it as the session key thereafter, as another alternative way of generating unique session keys. It might also provide some useful user-tracking possibilities.

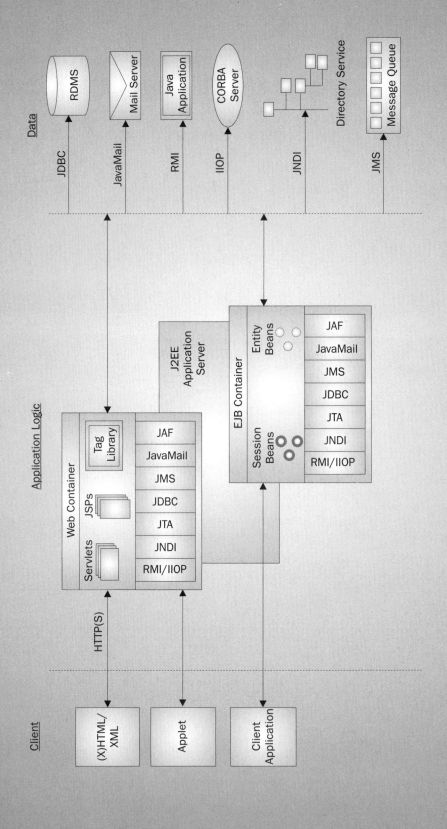

D

Internationalization

More than any business before, today's e-commerce world addresses a global market with customers from many different cultures and countries. For the web sites that are used as the presentation layer for e-commerce systems, this demands ways of supporting the many languages and writing systems that are used around the world. But internationalization is getting ever more important in other areas too. With the increasing use of web-based intranet systems by multi-national companies and organizations, the presentation of content in different languages is also required, or at least desired, in these systems.

In this chapter we will see how your web application can return content in different languages and character encodings as requested by a user. The following topics are covered in detail:

- ❑ Storing and sending text for different writing systems and character sets
- ❑ Character encoding support in the Java core API
- ❑ HTTP headers which show a user's preference for specific languages and character encodings
- ❑ Internationalization support in the servlet API
- ❑ Doing content negotiation based on languages and character encodings, and recoding documents as requested by a client

The servlet that we are going to develop will read text and binary files which are specified by a virtual path, and return them to the client in a similar fashion to the way a web server would return them without the use of the servlet. However, the servlet will be able to handle text files in multiple languages and transparently select a file in a language which is understood by the user.

Character Sets

Before we can start handling different languages we first have to know some details about the ways in which text in these languages is represented in a computer-readable form. In the USA, computers have mainly been using the **ASCII** (American Standard Code for Information Interchange, traditionally used on PCs and workstations) and **EBCDIC** (Extended Binary-Coded Decimal Interchange Code, used mainly on mainframe systems) characters sets in the past. Both character sets use 7-bit encodings, where each 7-bit **tuple** (an ordered sequence of 7 bits) represents one of 128 possible characters. These characters include the upper and lowercase Latin letters, Arabic numbers, and punctuation marks.

The ASCII character set was later used as a starting point for extended character sets with 256 characters encoded in bytes (tuples of 8 bits). Some of these extensions were of a proprietary nature, others are standardized by the ISO (International Standards Organization). One of the most common extended character sets is **ISO-8859-1**, also known as **Latin-1**, the first of the ISO-8859 family of 8-bit character sets. Latin-1 contains all the characters required to write text in many western European languages. Specifically, the languages Afrikaans, Basque, Catalan, Danish, Dutch, English, Faeroese, Finnish, French, Gaelic, Galician, German, Icelandic, Irish, Italian, Norwegian, Portuguese, Spanish, and Swedish are supported. Latin-1 is used as the primary character set for several Internet protocols, including HTTP.

There are other character sets that include the same characters (often with different character codes) and many others that contain characters for languages not covered by Latin-1, for example, the JIS (Japanese Industry Standard) character set for Japanese ideograms.

To solve the problem of having to work with many different character sets in an internationalized environment, the **Unicode standard** was created and is now available in version 3.0. Unicode is still evolving, so support for the missing languages and writing systems can be expected in the future. Unicode consists of 256 pages of 256 characters each, so each character can be represented by two bytes. The high byte contains the Unicode page number and the low byte contains the Unicode cell number that specifies the exact character in a page. The transition to Unicode is eased by the fact that the first page (characters 0x0000 to 0x00FF) is identical to Latin-1 which makes character conversion between Unicode and Latin-1 particularly easy because all Latin-1 characters (including all ASCII characters, the lower half of Latin-1) have the same character codes in Unicode. For example, the following table shows the character codes (in hexadecimal notation) of the different 'a' characters (with all kinds of accents) from the Latin-1 character set:

Character	ASCII	ISO-8859-1	Unicode
a	0x61	0x61	0x0061
à		0xE0	0x00E0
á		0xE1	0x00E1
â	The other characters are not available in ASCII	0xE2	0x00E2
ã		0xE3	0x00E3
ä		0xE4	0x00E4
å		0xE5	0x00E5

Unicode is the preferred character set for many new and evolving designs, including XML, HTML, and Java. More information on Unicode can be found at the official web site http://www.unicode.org.

Character Encodings

When working only with simple 7- or 8-bit character sets, such as Latin-1, for a limited set of languages, the distinction between character sets and character encodings does not usually come into play. Text files are written as a sequence of bytes, each one being the code of a single character. If more than 256 different characters are required (e.g., for Asian languages like Chinese or Japanese) this simple scheme cannot be used any more. Even when writing raw Unicode characters there are two natural encodings for writing characters as 16-bit numbers: when the 16-bit numbers are written to a byte stream either the high byte (in this case the Unicode page number) or the low byte (in this case the Unicode cell number) of the number can be writtten first. The former is called **big endian** byte order and was traditionally used on workstations, and the latter is consequently called **little endian** byte order and is used mainly on PCs.

Java uses Unicode internally to represent text in all kinds of data types, including:

- ❏   `char`, the 16-bit character type
- ❏   `java.lang.String`, the immutable string type
- ❏   `java.lang.StringBuffer`, the mutable string type
- ❏   `java.io.Reader`, the stream type for reading 16-bit characters
- ❏   `java.io.Writer`, the stream type for writing 16-bit characters

When exchanging data with other applications, characters have to be encoded with one of the standard Unicode encodings or an older encoding which supports a more limited set of characters. The following encodings are commonly used for Unicode:

- ❏   Raw Unicode data in network byte order (*big endian*).

- ❏   UTF-8: ASCII characters (those with a character code <= 127) are written as is, characters with a higher codes are encoded with escape sequences. This allows the use of single Unicode characters in ASCII text and keeps the ASCII parts readable for applications that don't support UTF-8. The resulting files are also smaller than raw Unicode files if they contain a lot of ASCII characters.

- ❏   UTF-7: Like UTF-8 but only the low seven bits of each octet are used. The resulting files are longer than UTF-8 files but they can be transmitted over channels that are not 8-bit clean (which means that transmitting a byte may set the eighth bit to zero regardless of its initial value). This is required for sending e-mail and news messages. On the other hand, HTTP is 8-bit clean, so it is not necessary to use UTF-7.

Character Encoding Support in the Java Core API

Some parts of the Java core API deal with character encodings. There are several ways to convert encoded text to the `char` and `java.lang.String` Unicode types and back:

- ❏   The `java.lang.String` constructors `String(byte[] bytes, int offset, int length, String encoding)` and `String(byte[] bytes, String encoding)` create a Unicode string from an array of bytes (or a part thereof) in the specified encoding.

- ❏   The `java.lang.String` method `getBytes(String encoding)` does the opposite of the previous methods. It returns a new byte array that represents a string in the specified encoding.

1503

❑ java.io.InputStreamReader has a constructor that takes an 'encoding' argument. An InputStreamReader can read text with the specified encoding from an underlying InputStream, e.g., a FileInputStream that has been constructed for a file on the local disk.

❑ java.io.OutputStreamWriter also has a constructor that takes an 'encoding' argument. This class does the opposite of InputStreamReader, which is encoding and writing text data to an OutputStream.

The encoding names used by all Java methods dealing with character encodings are specific to Java. The following table lists some Java encoding names:

Name	Description
UnicodeBig	Raw Unicode data in *big endian* (network) byte order
UnicodeLittle	Raw Unicode data in *little endian* byte order
UTF8	The 8 bit Unicode Transport Format
UTF7	The 7 bit Unicode Transport Format
8859_1	ISO 8859-1, also known as Latin-1, for West European languages
8859_2	ISO 8859-2, also known as Latin-2, for East European languages
8859_3	ISO 8859-3, also known as Latin-3, for Southeast European languages
8859_4	ISO 8859-4, also known as Latin-4, for Scandinavian and Baltic languages
8859_9	ISO 8859-9, also known as Latin-5, for Turkish, a modified version of Latin-1
JIS	JIS, a Japanese encoding

IANA Charset Names

By default, HTTP requests and responses containing a body of a text sub-type are assumed to be encoded in Latin-1. Alternative encodings have to be specified explicitly by appending a charset tag to the Content-Type header as in the following example:

```
Content-Type: text/html; charset=UTF-8
```

An HTTP response with such a Content-Type header contains HTML text encoded with UTF-8. The charset names for MIME documents are not identical to the encoding names used by Java. For Internet protocols like HTTP only the official encoding names published by the **Internet Assigned Numbers Authority (IANA)** should be used. The following table shows Java encoding names and the corresponding IANA names:

Java Name	IANA Names
UTF8	UTF-8
UTF7	UTF-7

Java Name	IANA Names
8859_1	ISO-8859-1 (preferred)
	ISO_8859-1:1987
	iso-ir-100
	ISO_8859-1
	latin1
	l1
	IBM819
	CP819
	csISOLatin1

Note that unlike the official IANA names, the Java encoding names are case-sensitive. They are actually parts of class names for byte to character and character to byte converter classes, and as such are bound to the naming rules for Java class names.

Content Negotiation

When a web server offers more than one variant of a resource (which includes offering text documents in different languages and character encodings) there needs to be a way to select the variant that is most appropriate for the user (e.g, when selecting languages) and the web client (e.g, displayable character encodings). This is called **content negotiation** and can be implemented in two ways:

❑ **Server-driven content negotiation:**
The server selects a variant based on information contained in the request. This can be one or more of the request headers, the requested URL or any other available information.

❑ **Client-driven content negotiation:**
When multiple variants of a resource are available, the server offers a list of choices from which the user can select one directly.

There are several HTTP 1.1 request headers that help in implementing server-driven content negotiation by giving the server hints as to what the user prefers. One such header that is used for internationalization is `Accept-Charset`, which contains a list of character encodings that are acceptable to the client. The list entries are separated by commas and can optionally contain quality values that specify the relative quality of the choices, for example:

```
Accept-Charset: UTF-8, ISO-8859-1, UTF-7;q=0.9
```

A client that sends this header indicates that it can display text encoded in UTF-8, UTF-7 and ISO-8859-1. The **quality values** that are appended as 'q' tags to the list entries must be between 0 and 1, with higher values meaning more preferable choices. The default for entries without 'q' tags is 1. For the example header this means that the UTF-7 encoding is acceptable to the client, but it prefers UTF-8 and ISO-8859-1 if the server can create them.

All clients should accept the default character set ISO-8859-1 even it is not explicitly listed in an `Accept-Charset` header.

A similar header exists for negotiating languages. The `Accept-Language` header contains a list of language names that are preferred by the user. The entries can also contain 'q' tags for relative quality values. Language names consist of one or more parts separated by hyphens. Usually a name consisting of one or two parts is used where the first part is a two-letter ISO 639 language abbreviation code and the optional second part a two-letter ISO 3166 country code. Registration of language names is also administered by the IANA. An example `Accept-Language` header is:

```
Accept-Language: en-US;q=1.0, en;q=0.5
```

This header indicates that the user prefers American English (quality 1.0) but will take any form of English as an alternative (quality 0.5).

Note that the absolute quality values are meaningless. They are only used to determine the order of the list entries. The following `Accept-Language` header has exactly the same meaning as the previous one because it also defines the order "en-US, en":

```
Accept-Language: en-US;q=0.1, en;q=0.01
```

Below is a list of some of the more common IANA Language/Country codes. For a complete list go to http://lcweb.loc.gov/standards/iso639-2/bibcodes.html:

Code	Language/Country Name	Code	Language/Country Name
af	Afrikaans	el	Greek
sq	Albanian	hu	Hungarian
eu	Basque	is	Icelandic
bg	Bulgarian	id	Indonesian
be	Byelorussian	ga	Irish
zh	Chinese	it	Italian
zh-CN	Chinese/China	ja	Japanese
zh-TW	Chinese/Taiwan	ko	Korean
hr	Croatian	mk	Macedonian
cs	Czech	no	Norwegian
da	Danish	pl	Polish
nl	Dutch	pt	Portuguese
nl-BE	Dutch/Belgium	pt-BR	Portuguese/Brazil
en	English	ro	Romanian
en-GB	English/United Kingdom	ru	Russian
en-US	English/United States	gd	Scots Gaelic
fo	Faeroese	sr	Serbian

Code	Language/Country Name	Code	Language/Country Name
fi	Finnish	sk	Slovak
fr	French	sl	Slovenian
fr-BE	French/Belgium	es	Spanish
fr-CA	French/Canada	es-AR	Spanish/Argentina
fr-CH	French/Switzerland	es-CO	Spanish/Colombia
gl	Galician	es-MX	Spanish/Mexico
de	German	es-ES	Spanish/Spain
de-AU	German/Austria	tr	Turkish
de-DE	German/Germany	uk	Ukrainian
de-CH	German/Switzerland		

Later in this chapter we are going to write an I18NServlet class ('I18N' means 'Internationalization': 'I' plus 18 letters plus 'N'), which should return localized content in a language that the user of a web site understands, and with a character encoding that the user's web browser can handle. In order to perform the server-driven content negotiation which is used by this servlet, we need to be able to parse Accept-style headers. This functionality is best implemented in an auxiliary class that can be used for all headers with the same structure (Accept, Accept-Language, Accept-Charset, etc.).

The assorted 'Accept' lists are managed by the AcceptList class, which keeps arrays of list entries and their quality values in private variables:

```
import java.util.*;

public class AcceptList {

    private String[] names;
    private double[] qualities;
```

These arrays are sorted by quality values, the highest of which is kept at index 0.

Accessor methods similar to those of java.util.Vector make it possible to iterate through an AcceptList or find entries:

size() returns the number of entries in the list:

```
public int size() {
    return names.length;
}
```

nameAt() and qualityAt() return the name and quality at the specified position. These methods are used when iterating through the list:

```
public String nameAt(int i) {
    return names[i];
}
```

```
public double qualityAt(int i) {
  return qualities[i];
}
```

indexOf() returns the index of an entry specified by its name or quality. If multiple entries have the same quality the first one is returned. Both methods return -1 if no matching entry is found:

```
public int indexOf(String name) {
  for(int i=0; i<names.length; i++) {
    if(names[i].equals(name)) {
      return i;
    }
    return -1;
  }
}

public int indexOf(double quality) {
  for(int i=0; i<qualities.length; i++) {
    if(qualities[i] == quality) {
      return i;
    }
    return -1;
  }
}
```

qualityOf() returns the quality associated with the given name, or a negative value if the name is not found. This is a convenience method which could also be implemented with the indexOf() and qualityAt() methods.

```
public double qualityOf(String name) {
  int idx = indexOf(name);

  if(idx == -1) {
    return -1.0;
  } else {
    return qualities[idx];
  }
}
```

AcceptList has a constructor that takes a String argument that is the value of an Accept-style header. The constructor consists of four parts:

❑ Check for a null reference

❑ Split the string into tokens

❑ Parse the tokens

❑ Sort by quality

If a null reference is passed to the constructor, an empty AcceptList is created. This makes it easier to create AcceptList objects from HTTP headers, because the constructor can be called without first having to check if the getHeader() method returned null because the header was not found:

```
   public AcceptList(String s) {
     if(s == null) {
       names = new String[0];
       qualities = new double[0];
       return;
     }
```

If a non-null reference was supplied, the string is split into the single list entries, separated by commas, using a `java.util.StringTokenizer`. The entries are added to a temporary `Vector` for further processing:

```
     ArrayList tokens = new ArrayList();
     StringTokenizer tok = new StringTokenizer(s, ",");
     while(tok.hasMoreTokens()) {
       tokens.add(tok.nextToken().trim());
     }
```

The `StringTokenizer` recognizes the comma-separated tokens and returns the next one on each call to the `nextToken()` method. Excessive white space at the beginning and end of each token is removed before adding it to the vector.

Now that the number of entries is known, the `names` and `qualities` arrays can be created and filled with the tokens. Each token is either only a name, in which case it is added to the arrays with a quality of 1.0, or it is a name plus a number of attributes, usually only a single quality value. In that case the attribute list is split off and separated into the single attributes. If one of these attributes is "q" its value is converted from a `String` to a `double` value by creating a temporary `java.lang.Double` object with `Double.valueOf`. If an illegal quality value is supplied that cannot be parsed as a number, the quality value 0.0 is assigned to the entry:

```
     names = new String[tokens.size()];
     qualities = new double[tokens.size()];
     for(int i=0; i<names.length; i++) {
       qualities[i] = 1.0;
       String t = (String)tokens.get(i);
       int sep = t.indexOf(";");
       if(sep == -1) {
         names[i] = t;
       } else {
         names[i] = t.substring(0,sep).trim();

         tok = new StringTokenizer(t, ";");
         while(tok.hasMoreTokens()) {
           String attr = tok.nextToken();
           int asep = attr.indexOf("=");
           if(asep != -1) {
             String aname = attr.substring(0,asep).trim();
             if(aname.equals("q")) {
               try {
                 qualities[i] =
                   Double.valueOf(attr.substring(asep+1).trim()).doubleValue();
               } catch(NumberFormatException nfe) {
                 qualities[i] = 0.0;
               }
```

```
                }
              }
            }
          }
        }

      sort();
    }
```

Finally, the arrays are sorted with a *Bubble Sort* algorithm that is implemented in a separate method:

```
    private void sort() {
      for(int i=0; i<qualities.length; i++) {
        for(int j=i+1; j<qualities.length; j++) {
          if(qualities[i] < qualities[j]) {
            double tmpq = qualities[i];
            qualities[i] = qualities[j];
            qualities[j] = tmpq;
            String tmpn = names[i];
            names[i] = names[j];
            names[j] = tmpn;
          }
        }
      }
    }
```

The *Bubble Sort* algorithm is rather inefficient, but straightforward and easy to implement. Efficiency is not an issue because an `AcceptList` contains only a small number of entries. The algorithm does not change the order of equal elements, so entries with the same quality will appear in the sorted list in the same order in which they appeared in the header from which the list was constructed. This is important because there are web browsers that do not send correct `Accept-Language` headers with quality tags but instead list all acceptable language codes without quality tags in the order of preference. For example, if the user prefers `de-DE`, `de`, `en-US`, and `en` in that order, the browser would send the following request header:

```
    Accept-Language: de-DE,de,en-US,en
```

An HTTP/1.1 conforming version of this header would be:

```
    Accept-Language: de-DE;q=1.0,de;q=0.9,en-US;q=0.8,en;q=0.7
```

By using a sorting algorithm that does not move elements that are already at a correct position in the list, both versions are equally acceptable to the `AcceptList` class.

Character Encoding Support in the Servlet API

When sending and receiving text data with a servlet you usually do not have to worry about character encodings. When you get a `Reader` object for reading text from the `ServletRequest getReader()` method, the reader is automatically constructed with the character encoding that was supplied by the client in the `Content-Type` header, or the default encoding ISO-8859-1 if no other encoding was specified.

For writing a text response you can obtain a `PrintWriter` object with the `ServletResponse` `getWriter()` method. All text that gets written to this writer is automatically encoded with the character encoding that was specified in the `Content-Type` header. As an alternative, the `setLocale()` method can be used to specify the character encoding and content language. Note that these methods should preferably be called before getting a `PrintWriter` object to write the body of the response. If no encoding was specified the servlet engine may find one automatically. In that case, all text written through the `PrintWriter` has to be buffered so that the servlet engine can know which characters are used in the body.

When the response is committed (either because it has been completely written, or because the buffer is full), the servlet engine examines the text to find a suitable encoding for it that is also acceptable to the client. Then it modifies the `Content-Type` header that you supplied to include a proper `charset` tag, and sends the buffered text encoded with the selected `charset`.

All this is completely transparent to the servlet developer. You only have to take a few points into consideration:

❑ Always use `Reader` and `Writer` objects that have been constructed by the servlet engine (or are wrapped around such objects) to handle text data. `ServletInputStream` and `ServletOutputStream` should only be used for binary data that must not be modified by the servlet engine, or if you want to encode text data yourself instead of letting the servlet engine do it for you.

❑ The servlet engine needs to buffer the response if you don't explicitly specify a character encoding via the `charset` tag of the content type, or a call to `setLocale()`. This makes it impossible to send *streaming* responses to a client. Note that the response may need to be buffered for other reasons as well, especially if you do not specify a content length before writing the response body. You can always call the `ServletResponse` method `flushBuffer()` to make sure all buffered data is sent immediately. Of course, calling this method for the first time will automatically commit the response.

The Internationalization Servlet

We can now move on to the actual `I18NServlet` class that should return localized documents in the user's preferred language. This servlet duplicates some of the core functionality of a web server – it returns documents from a directory tree on the local disk as requested by a virtual path. It does not have advanced features like file uploading or automatic creation of index pages but instead it can return documents with different variants that are selected dynamically. As usual, the `I18NServlet` extends `javax.servlet.http.HttpServlet`, the standard base class for HTTP servlets. Most of the functionality is implemented directly in the `doGet()` method.

First, we need to define a format for storing the documents on disk. The servlet API offers the `getPathTranslated()` method in the `HttpServletRequest` class to get the real path on disk for a document specified via a virtual path appended to the servlet name in a URL. Let's say the servlet is deployed at `/i18n/servlet/I18NServlet` on a local web server. The following URL could be used to access the file `i18n/hello.txt` relative to the server's document root:

```
http://localhost/i18n/hello.txt
```

If you want to access the same file via the servlet, you can use the following URL:

```
http://localhost/i18n/servlet/I18NServlet/i18n/hello.txt
```

The I18NServlet should be able to return files such as hello.txt that are only available in a single variant. These files are simply stored under their real name. Files with variants must be stored with a language code and an encoding name, so we have to make a naming scheme. If the test directory contains localized versions of hello.txt for English, German, French, and Japanese, these could be stored in the following files:

```
hello.txt--de
hello.txt--en.8859_1
hello.txt--fr.8859_1
hello.txt--ja.JIS
```

The file name is followed by a separator consisting of two dashes (--), then the language code in lower-case letters, followed by a dot and the Java encoding name. The encoding name can optionally be left out, in which case the default encoding ISO-8859-1 will be used, as shown above for the German version of hello.txt.

The I18NServlet getVariants() method is used to compile a list of variants for a file which is specified in this way:

```
private String[] getVariants(File file) {
   File dir = new File(file.getParent());
   final String prefix = file.getName() + "--";
   int prefixLength = prefix.length();
   String[] variants = listWithPrefix(dir, prefix);
   for (int i = 0; i < variants.length; i++) {
     variants[i] = variants[i].substring(prefixLength);
   }
   return variants;
}
```

The method uses an auxiliary method listWithPrefix() that returns the names of all files in a directory which start with a specified prefix:

```
private String[] listWithPrefix(File dir, final String prefix) {
   return dir.list(new FilenameFilter() {
     public boolean accept(File dir, String name) {
       return name.startsWith(prefix);
     }
   });
}
```

The method does its work in two steps:

❑ First, a list of file names for the variants is compiled by calling the list() method in java.io.File. This is then associated with the directory containing the file and its variants. An inner class which implements the java.io.FilenameFilter interface is used to restrict the files in the directory to only those which start with the right prefix, in other words, the original file name plus the two dashes.

❑ The entries in the array of file names are replaced with only the variant names, i.e, the file names without the prefix. When calling getVariants() for our hello.txt file, it will return the following array of strings (but not necessarily in order):

```
{
  "de",
  "en.8859_1",
  "fr.8859_1",
  "ja.JIS"
}
```

A second auxiliary method, `findVariant()`, is used to select the most appropriate variant from such an array. It takes an `AcceptList` object as a second argument. This object should have been created from an `Accept-Language` HTTP request header:

```
private String findVariant(String[] variants, AcceptList langs) {
  if (langs != null) {
    for (int i = 0; i < langs.size(); i++) {
      String lang = langs.nameAt(i).toLowerCase();
      for (int j = 0; j < variants.length; j++) {
        if (variants[j].toLowerCase().startsWith(lang)) {
          return variants[j];
        }
      }
    }
  }
  return null;
}
```

The method iterates through the entries of the `AcceptList`, starting with the most preferable one. If the `variants` array contains that entry or a longer name (for a more specialized language selection) that starts with that entry's name, it is returned. If all acceptable languages have been tried and there was no variant for any of them, `null` is returned to indicate the failure. Note that the language codes, both in the `variants` array and the `langs` list, are converted to lowercase before being compared, because they should be compared in a case-insensitive way.

By selecting an appropriate localized variant of the document, the `I18NServlet` can return different content for the same resource. A user who is using a web browser that is configured to prefer German-language text will see the following result when requesting the example resource `hello.txt`:

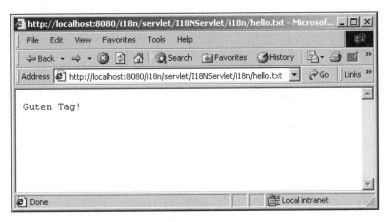

A user who prefers French will see this instead:

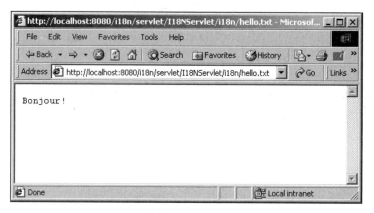

Note that the URL is the same in both cases.

The doGet() method, which should return the localized documents starts by finding the file to be returned to the client:

```
public void doGet(HttpServletRequest req, HttpServletResponse res)
        throws ServletException, IOException {
    String ctype;

    String fname = req.getPathTranslated();
    if (fname == null) {
      res.sendError(res.SC_FORBIDDEN);
      return;
    }
    File file = new File(fname);

    if (file.isDirectory()) {
      String url = req.getRequestURI();
      if (!url.endsWith("/")) {
        res.sendRedirect(url + '/');
        return;
      } else {
        file = new File(file, "index.html");
        ctype = "text/html";
      }
    } else {
      ctype = getServletContext().getMimeType(fname);
      if (ctype == null) {
        ctype = "text/plain";
      }
    }

    res.setContentType(ctype);
    // ...
```

If the virtual path cannot be mapped to a file name (in which case getPathTranslated() returns null) the servlet replies with a "Forbidden" response code. This can happen, for example, if the user tries to request a servlet or CGI script to be delivered through the I18NServlet instead of a regular file under the document root.

1514

Another feature traditionally implemented in web servers is also implemented in the `I18NServlet` for compatibility reasons. When a URL maps to a directory for which an index file is retrieved or created on the fly, the URL path must end with a slash (/), otherwise relative links would use the wrong base directory. For example, take our `test` directory that could contain an index file `index.html` with a link to `hello.txt`:

```
<A HREF="hello.txt">A greeting in your language</A>
```

To follow that link, a browser would strip off the last component of the URL path of the document in which the link appeared to find the base path. The relative link would then be appended to that path. If the index file was requested as `/test/index.html` or as `/test/` the base path (everything up to the last slash) is `/test/` and the relative link becomes `/test/hello.txt`. However, if the server would return the index file when `/test` (without a trailing slash) is requested, the browser would see the base path as `/` and create the wrong URL path `/hello.txt` for the relative link. So if the user provides a URL without a trailing slash, the servlet simply performs a behind-the-scenes redirect to the same URL with the trailing slash, so redirects all work as expected.

To implement this behavior, the `I18NServlet` first checks if the requested path maps to a directory. If this is the case and the slash is missing, the client is redirected. If the request maps to a directory and the URL path is already correct, the name `index.html` is appended and the content type set to `text/html`. If a file was requested instead of a directory, the `ServletContext` is queried for a MIME type for the file name with the `getMimeType()` method. If the server cannot provide a MIME type, `text/plain` is assumed.

It is important that the server is properly configured to return the right MIME types. If the server returns byte-identical files to the client, a content type could be incorrectly overridden and give the appearance of normal, successful completion, so that the wrong configuration does not even get noticed. This will fail when binary files are requested through the `I18NServlet`. If the server does not recognize them as binary files the default encoding `text/plain` is used and the files are copied as text data. Reading the files from disk is not a problem because the default character encoding ISO-8859-1 does not change the read data but the data can be destroyed when sending the response to the client because it may be encoded with a different charset which the client prefers over ISO-8859-1.

When the base file and its MIME type are determined there are three possibilities:

❑ The file to be returned is a text file (its content type starts with `text/`)

❑ The file exists (and is not a text file)

❑ The file does not exist

These cases are handled by a big `if` clause that spans most of the `doGet()` method:

```
if (ctype.startsWith("text/")) {
    // ...
} else if (file.exists()) {
    // ...
} else {
    res.sendError(res.SC_NOT_FOUND);
}
```

The case of a non-existent text file will be handled at a different place.

If a binary file does not exist, the servlet responds with a 404 ("Not Found") status code. If a binary file should be sent (second branch of the `if` clause) it is simply copied literally byte by byte from a `FileInputStream` to the `ServletOutputStream`:

```
InputStream in = new FileInputStream(file);
OutputStream out = res.getOutputStream();
copy(in, out);
in.close();
out.close();
```

The actual copying is implemented in the `copy()` method. Reading and writing single bytes is inefficient, so we use an array with a size of one kilobyte which is read and written as a whole:

```
private static final int BUF_SIZE = 1024;
```

```
private void copy(InputStream in,
                  OutputStream out) throws IOException {
  int num;
  byte[] ch = new byte[BUF_SIZE];
  while ((num = in.read(ch, 0, BUF_SIZE)) > 0) {
    out.write(ch, 0, num);
  }
}
```

The method continuously tries to read blocks of 1024 bytes and writes the read data to the `OutputStream`. A call to `read()` may read less than the requested number of bytes which needs to be taken into account when writing the block (or a part of the block). The method returns when the end of the `InputStream` has been reached. When reading a file from the local file system this means that the entire file has been copied.

We will later need a similar block-copy method that works on characters instead of bytes. It is almost identical to the previous method:

```
private void copy(Reader in, Writer out) throws IOException {
  int num;
  char[] ch = new char[BUF_SIZE];
  while ((num = in.read(ch, 0, BUF_SIZE)) > 0) {
    out.write(ch, 0, num);
  }
}
```

Returning a Variant of a Text File

The core of the `doGet()` method deals with returning text files. There should be two ways to select a specific variant of a file:

Server-Driven Content Negotiation

The servlet reads the `Accept-Language` header and finds a language for which the requested document is available.

Client-Driven Content Negotiation

If the client did not supply an `Accept-Language` header or there is no variant available for any of the acceptable languages, there needs to be a way for the client explicitly to request one of the available variants.

The client-driven content negotiation is handled with a `lang` parameter. A user who wants to see the French version of `hello.txt` would request the following URL:

```
http://localhost/i18n/servlet/I18NServlet/i18n/hello.txt?lang=fr
```

The auxiliary method `getSelectedVariant()` is used to find the first file that matches a selected base file and language:

```
private File getSelectedVariant(File file, String lang) {
   File dir = new File(file.getParent());
   final String prefix = file.getName() + "--" + lang.toLowerCase();
   String[] variants = listWithPrefix(dir, prefix);

   if (variants.length >= 1) {
     return new File(dir, variants[0]);
   } else {
     return null;
   }
}
```

This method works similar to the `getVariant()` method. It uses a custom file name filter that matches all files with the right base name and language code. If any such files were found, the first one is returned, otherwise the method returns `null`.

The method is used by `doGet()` in the following way:

```
String selectedLang = req.getParameter("lang");
File variant;
String encoding = "8859_1";

if (file.exists()) {
  variant = file;
} else if (selectedLang != null) {
  variant = getSelectedVariant(file, selectedLang);

  if (variant == null) {
    res.sendError(res.SC_NOT_FOUND);
    return;
  } else {
    String s = variant.getName();
    s = s.substring(s.indexOf("--"));
    int sep = s.lastIndexOf('.');
    if (sep != -1) {
      encoding = s.substring(sep + 1);
    }
  }
} else {
  // ...
```

First, the variables `variant` and `encoding` are declared and `encoding` is initialized with the default value. These variables are later filled with the right values. If the file exists under the requested name, it is assigned directly to the `variant` variable. The encoding is assumed to be the default encoding ISO-8859-1. Otherwise, if a variant has been selected with the `lang` parameter, the file for that variant is looked up with `getSelectedVariant()`. If the file name for the `variant` contains an encoding, it is extracted and assigned to the `encoding` variable.

If no variant could be determined up to this point, server-driven content negotiation is used to find one. A list of all variants is created with `getVariants()`. If no variants were found, the servlet returns a 404 ("Not Found") status code. Otherwise an `AcceptList` is created for the `Accept-Language` header and the previously described method, `findVariant()`, is used to select the best variant:

```
// ...
} else {
  String[] variants = getVariants(file);
  if (variants.length == 0) {
    res.sendError(res.SC_NOT_FOUND);
    return;
  }

  AcceptList langs =
    new AcceptList(req.getHeader("Accept-Language"));
  String variantName = findVariant(variants, langs);

  res.setHeader("Pragma", "no-cache");
  res.setHeader("Vary", "Accept-Language");

  if (variantName == null) {
    res.setStatus(res.SC_MULTIPLE_CHOICES);
    res.setContentType("text/html");
    PrintWriter out = res.getWriter();
    out.println("<html><head><title>"
                + "Select a language</title></head>"
                + "<body><h1>Select a language</h1><ul>");

    String url = URLEncoder.encode(file.getName());

    for (int i = 0; i < variants.length; i++) {
      String v = variants[i];
      int sep = v.lastIndexOf('.');
      if (sep != -1) {
        v = v.substring(0, sep);

      }
      out.println("<li><a href=\"" + url + "?lang=" + v + "\">"
                  + languageNameFor(v) + "</a>");
    }
    out.println("</ul></body></html>");
    out.close();
    return;
  } else {
    variant = new File(file.getParent(),
                       file.getName() + "--" + variantName);
    int sep = variantName.lastIndexOf('.');
    if (sep != -1) {
```

```
            encoding = variantName.substring(sep + 1);
        }
    }
}

Reader in = new InputStreamReader(new FileInputStream(variant),
                                  encoding);
Writer out = res.getWriter();
copy(in, out);
in.close();
out.close();
```

If `findVariant()` was successful, the `variant` and `encoding` variables are filled.

Finally, the selected file can be sent to the client. The code is similar to that for sending a binary file, except that a `Reader` and `Writer` pair are used to handle text data instead of an `InputStream` and `OutputStream`. An `InputStreamReader` is constructed with the encoding of the input file. It reads the file and converts all characters to Unicode. The `PrintWriter` object returned by `res.getWriter()` converts the Unicode characters to a suitable encoding which is determined automatically by the servlet engine.

Note that two cache control headers are set if a variant is selected on the server side. `Pragma: no-cache` instructs HTTP/1.0 clients and proxy servers not to cache the response at all. HTTP/1.1 has more sophisticated cache control methods. The `Vary: Accept-Language` response header tells HTTP/1.1-enabled software that the response depends on the `Accept-Language` request header. It may be stored in a proxy cache and subsequent requests can be answered directly by the proxy server as long as they have an equivalent `Accept-Language` header. If the header is different, the request must be forwarded to the origin server.

User-Driven Content Negotiation

One essential part of the `I18NServlet` is still missing. What happens if the client sends an `Accept-Language` header and the requested resource exists but no variant matches? In that case, the selection of one of the available variants should be left to the user. The following code in `doGet()` creates an HTML page with links to all variants of the requested document:

```
if (variantName == null) {
  res.setStatus(res.SC_MULTIPLE_CHOICES);
  res.setContentType("text/html");
  PrintWriter out = res.getWriter();
  out.println("<html><head><title>"
            + "Select a language</title></head>"
            + "<body><h1>Select a language</h1><ul>");

  String url = URLEncoder.encode(file.getName());

  for (int i = 0; i < variants.length; i++) {
    String v = variants[i];
    int sep = v.lastIndexOf('.');
    if (sep != -1) {
      v = v.substring(0, sep);
```

```
                   }
                   out.println("<li><a href=\"" + url + "?lang=" + v + "\">"
                               + languageNameFor(v) + "</a>");
               }
               out.println("</ul></body></html>");
               out.close();
               return;
           }
```

The HTTP status code 300 ("Multiple Choices") indicates that there is more than one variant of the requested resource. The details as to what a response with a "Multiple Choices" status should contain are not specified. If there is a default variant its absolute URL should be sent in a Location header, but this is not the case with our setup.

The variants are listed in the HTML page by iterating through the variants array and creating a link for each entry. The link leads back to the requested resource with an appended lang parameter to select that specific variant. Unlike a URL in a Location header (as used when redirecting a client), a link in an HTML page can be relative, so only the last component of the URL path (i.e. the file name) is used as a relative URL path. Note that the java.net.URLEncoder class is used to encode the file name in case it contains special characters (e.g, spaces) that may not be used as is in a URL. The reverse decoding process is implemented in the servlet engine. When a virtual path is resolved with the getPathTranslated() method, it is automatically decoded prior to translating it into a file name.

The language codes are not very comprehensible to most users, so they are replaced by spelled out names in the list. These names are generated by the languageNameFor() method, which looks them up in the languageNames hashtable:

```
private String languageNameFor(String code) {
  String name = (String) languageNames.get(code.toLowerCase());
  if (name != null) {
    return name;
  } else {
    return code;
  }
}
```

If no name was found for a language code, the code itself is returned as a makeshift solution. The language name table is filled in a static initializer block of the servlet:

```
private static final Hashtable languageNames = new Hashtable();

static {
  languageNames.put("af", "Afrikaans");
  languageNames.put("sq", "Albanian");
  languageNames.put("eu", "Basque");
  languageNames.put("bg", "Bulgarian");
  languageNames.put("be", "Byelorussian");
  languageNames.put("zh", "Chinese");
  languageNames.put("zh-cn", "Chinese/China");
  languageNames.put("zh-tw", "Chinese/Taiwan");
  // ...
  languageNames.put("tr", "Turkish");
  languageNames.put("uk", "Ukrainian");
}
```

When the example resource `hello.txt` is requested and none of the available variants is acceptable to the user, the following list is returned:

```
<ul>
    <li><a href="hello.txt?lang=fr">French</a>
    <li><a href="hello.txt?lang=ja">Japanese</a>
    <li><a href="hello.txt?lang=en">English</a>
    <li><a href="hello.txt?lang=de">German</a>
</ul>
```

Below is the full source code for the `I18NServlet`:

```java
import java.io.*;
import java.net.URLEncoder;
import java.util.*;

import javax.servlet.*;
import javax.servlet.http.*;

public final class I18NServlet extends HttpServlet {
  private static final Hashtable languageNames = new Hashtable();

  static {
    languageNames.put("af", "Afrikaans");
    languageNames.put("sq", "Albanian");
    languageNames.put("eu", "Basque");
    languageNames.put("bg", "Bulgarian");
    languageNames.put("be", "Byelorussian");
    languageNames.put("zh", "Chinese");
    languageNames.put("zh-cn", "Chinese/China");
    languageNames.put("zh-tw", "Chinese/Taiwan");
    languageNames.put("hr", "Croatian");
    languageNames.put("cs", "Czech");
    languageNames.put("da", "Danish");
    languageNames.put("nl", "Dutch");
    languageNames.put("nl-be", "Dutch/Belgium");
    languageNames.put("en", "English");
    languageNames.put("en-gb", "English/United Kingdom");
    languageNames.put("en-us", "English/United States");
    languageNames.put("fo", "Faeroese");
    languageNames.put("fi", "Finnish");
    languageNames.put("fr", "French");
    languageNames.put("fr-be", "French/Belgium");
    languageNames.put("fr-ca", "French/Canada");
    languageNames.put("fr-ch", "French/Switzerland");
    languageNames.put("gl", "Galician");
    languageNames.put("de", "German");
    languageNames.put("de-au", "German/Austria");
    languageNames.put("de-de", "German/Germany");
    languageNames.put("de-ch", "German/Switzerland");
    languageNames.put("el", "Greek");
    languageNames.put("hu", "Hungarian");
    languageNames.put("is", "Icelandic");
    languageNames.put("id", "Indonesian");
```

```
      languageNames.put("ga", "Irish");
      languageNames.put("it", "Italian");
      languageNames.put("ja", "Japanese");
      languageNames.put("ko", "Korean");
      languageNames.put("mk", "Macedonian");
      languageNames.put("no", "Norwegian");
      languageNames.put("pl", "Polish");
      languageNames.put("pt", "Portuguese");
      languageNames.put("pt-br", "Portuguese/Brazil");
      languageNames.put("ro", "Romanian");
      languageNames.put("ru", "Russian");
      languageNames.put("gd", "Scots Gaelic");
      languageNames.put("sr", "Serbian");
      languageNames.put("sk", "Slovak");
      languageNames.put("sl", "Slovenian");
      languageNames.put("es", "Spanish");
      languageNames.put("es-ar", "Spanish/Argentina");
      languageNames.put("es-co", "Spanish/Colombia");
      languageNames.put("es-mx", "Spanish/Mexico");
      languageNames.put("es-es", "Spanish/Spain");
      languageNames.put("sv", "Swedish");
      languageNames.put("tr", "Turkish");
      languageNames.put("uk", "Ukrainian");
  }

  private static final int BUF_SIZE = 1024;

  public void doGet(HttpServletRequest req, HttpServletResponse res)
          throws ServletException, IOException {
    String ctype;

    String fname = req.getPathTranslated();
    if (fname == null) {
      res.sendError(res.SC_FORBIDDEN);
      return;
    }
    File file = new File(fname);

    if (file.isDirectory()) {
      String url = req.getRequestURI();
      if (!url.endsWith("/")) {
        res.sendRedirect(url + '/');
        return;
      } else {
        file = new File(file, "index.html");
        ctype = "text/html";
      }
    } else {
      ctype = getServletContext().getMimeType(fname);
      if (ctype == null) {
        ctype = "text/plain";
      }
    }

    res.setContentType(ctype);
```

```
if (ctype.startsWith("text/")) {
  String selectedLang = req.getParameter("lang");
  File variant;
  String encoding = "8859_1";

  if (file.exists()) {
    variant = file;
  } else if (selectedLang != null) {
    variant = getSelectedVariant(file, selectedLang);

    if (variant == null) {
      res.sendError(res.SC_NOT_FOUND);
      return;
    } else {
      String s = variant.getName();
      s = s.substring(s.indexOf("--"));
      int sep = s.lastIndexOf('.');
      if (sep != -1) {
        encoding = s.substring(sep + 1);
      }
    }
  } else {
    String[] variants = getVariants(file);
    if (variants.length == 0) {
      res.sendError(res.SC_NOT_FOUND);
      return;
    }

    AcceptList langs =
      new AcceptList(req.getHeader("Accept-Language"));
    String variantName = findVariant(variants, langs);

    res.setHeader("Pragma", "no-cache");
    res.setHeader("Vary", "Accept-Language");

    if (variantName == null) {
      res.setStatus(res.SC_MULTIPLE_CHOICES);
      res.setContentType("text/html");
      PrintWriter out = res.getWriter();
      out.println("<html><head><title>"
                + "Select a language</title></head>"
                + "<body><h1>Select a language</h1><ul>");

      String url = URLEncoder.encode(file.getName());

      for (int i = 0; i < variants.length; i++) {
        String v = variants[i];
        int sep = v.lastIndexOf('.');
        if (sep != -1) {
          v = v.substring(0, sep);
        }

        out.println("<li><a href=\"" + url + "?lang=" + v + "\">"
                  + languageNameFor(v) + "</a>");
      }
```

```
          out.println("</ul></body></html>");
          out.close();
          return;
        } else {
          variant = new File(file.getParent(),
                          file.getName() + "--" + variantName);
          int sep = variantName.lastIndexOf('.');
          if (sep != -1) {
            encoding = variantName.substring(sep + 1);
          }
        }
      }

      Reader in = new InputStreamReader(new FileInputStream(variant),
                                        encoding);
      Writer out = res.getWriter();
      copy(in, out);
      in.close();
      out.close();
    } else if (file.exists()) {
      InputStream in = new FileInputStream(file);
      OutputStream out = res.getOutputStream();
      copy(in, out);
      in.close();
      out.close();
    } else {
      res.sendError(res.SC_NOT_FOUND);
    }
  }


  private void copy(InputStream in,
                    OutputStream out) throws IOException {
    int num;
    byte[] ch = new byte[BUF_SIZE];
    while ((num = in.read(ch, 0, BUF_SIZE)) > 0) {
      out.write(ch, 0, num);
    }
  }

  private void copy(Reader in, Writer out) throws IOException {
    int num;
    char[] ch = new char[BUF_SIZE];
    while ((num = in.read(ch, 0, BUF_SIZE)) > 0) {
      out.write(ch, 0, num);
    }
  }

  private String[] listWithPrefix(File dir, final String prefix) {
    return dir.list(new FilenameFilter() {
      public boolean accept(File dir, String name) {
        return name.startsWith(prefix);
      }
    });
  }
```

```
   private String[] getVariants(File file) {
     File dir = new File(file.getParent());
     final String prefix = file.getName() + "--";
     int prefixLength = prefix.length();
     String[] variants = listWithPrefix(dir, prefix);
     for (int i = 0; i < variants.length; i++) {
       variants[i] = variants[i].substring(prefixLength);
     }
     return variants;
   }

   private String findVariant(String[] variants, AcceptList langs) {
     if (langs != null) {
       for (int i = 0; i < langs.size(); i++) {
         String lang = langs.nameAt(i).toLowerCase();
         for (int j = 0; j < variants.length; j++) {
           if (variants[j].toLowerCase().startsWith(lang)) {
             return variants[j];
           }
         }
       }
     }
     return null;
   }

   private File getSelectedVariant(File file, String lang) {
     File dir = new File(file.getParent());
     final String prefix = file.getName() + "--" + lang.toLowerCase();
     String[] variants = listWithPrefix(dir, prefix);

     if (variants.length >= 1) {
       return new File(dir, variants[0]);
     } else {
       return null;
     }
   }

   private String languageNameFor(String code) {
     String name = (String) languageNames.get(code.toLowerCase());
     if (name != null) {
       return name;
     } else {
       return code;
     }
   }
}
```

The full code for the `AcceptList` class and all other source code can be downloaded from the Wrox website. If you deploy the supplied web application `i18n.war` at `http://localhost/i18n` you can access the file `hello.txt` through the URL `http://localhost/i18n/servlet/I18NServlet/i18n/hello.txt`.

Summary

The essence of internationalizing web sites is to allow anyone in the world to be able to visit a web site and automatically view it in a language of their choice. The ability to choose the language to be displayed is available via the use of `Accept-Language` headers for content negotiation. The `I18NServlet` that we developed returns localized documents and other resources that are stored in the web server's document tree to a client. When receiving a request for the base name of such a file, the `I18NServlet` goes through all variants to find the best match for the user's preferred languages and returns that variant with an acceptable character encoding. By making web sites totally international, the numbers of people to which the Web is available increases significantly. This, of course, is a perfect solution to any commercial web site that is looking for an increase in its market coverage.

In this appendix we have looked at:

❑   The differing character encodings and languages available to Java

❑   Content negotiation, a feature that allows a servlet to return text in the user's preferred language.

❑   Character coding support in the API.

❑   Introduction to concepts of character sets and character encodings.

❑   A servlet to allow text documents to have multiple variants, each in its own file.

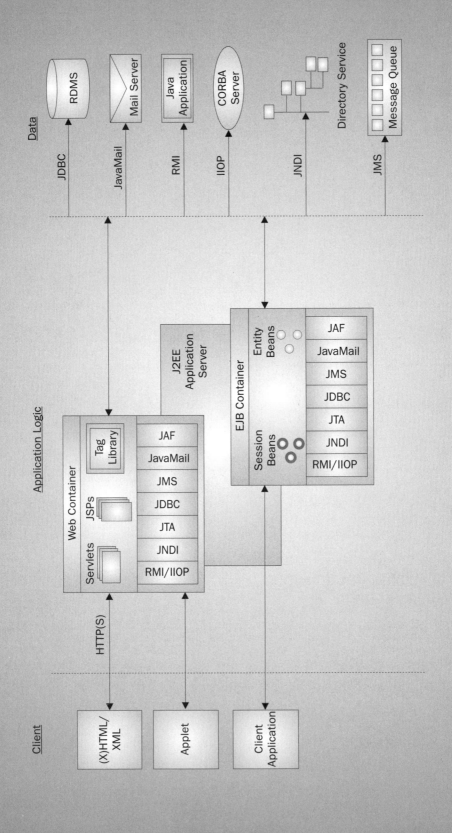

Swing HTML Generation

There is a great deal of discussion devoted to the relative benefits of Java servlets and JavaServer Pages and the situations where it is appropriate to use one rather than the other. This chapter will present another approach that attempts to facilitate the development of both JSPs and servlets.

In this chapter we will see how it is possible to use the Swing packages javax.swing.text and javax.swing.text.html to completely separate Java code from HTML, by parsing standard HTML files and creating representations of those files as Java objects. The core example will be based on HTML 3.2, as that is the level of support currently provided by Swing. Other alternatives, including XML, are possible depending on the parser API employed.

In this appendix, we will:

- ❑ First take a look at some of the important components of the packages javax.swing.text and javax.swing.text.html

- ❑ We will then employ then to create a simple HTML generator

- ❑ This will demonstrate how the generator allows us to set the values of HTML text fields, and select items from a servlet or a JSP page without writing any HTML statements

First, let's look at why we want to consider an alternative to JSP or servlets.

Problems with Servlets and JSP

Let's very briefly recap some of the most common issues.

While servlets provide a powerful option for web site implementation, one of the most limiting factors is that the HTML is written within the servlet *itself*. Anyone involved in even the smallest web site is aware of the continual need for change; content must be updated; links to other sites change; bugs have to be repaired. Editing the HTML statements within a section of Java code is tedious in the extreme and hence a highly inefficient and error prone process. Imagine picking through a very large servlet source code file and editing all these statements every time a new department is created or organizational focus is restructured:

```
out.println("<SELECT NAME="Department">);
out.println("<OPTION>Sales</OPTION>);
out.println("<OPTION SELECTED>Marketing</OPTION>);
out.println("<OPTION>Finance</OPTION>);
out.println("<OPTION>HR</OPTION>);
out.println("</SELECT>);
```

Add to this, the fact that, in most cases, the people who design the web pages are not those that write the servlet code. Thus web page creators would have to wait until a developer was available to make the required changes. To summarize potential servlet problems:

❑ HTML and Java code are combined in the same file, which is confusing and difficult to maintain

❑ As HTML and Java are combined in the same file, it is inevitable that more than one person becomes responsible for the file as both the HTML and logical aspects of the application become more sophisticated. This in turn, leads to further complications of maintenance and enhancement

❑ Writing servlets often demands a very in-depth knowledge of programming techniques. This is especially the case when addressing concurrency issues

❑ Debugging can be a very challenging (read painstaking) process where it is hard to envisage what is happening on a remote machine

The JSP specification certainly went a long way to resolving the problems inherent with servlets. Business logic could be created within a JavaBean, leaving only a minor coding effort to hook the logic to the JSP file. However, this minor coding may still prove to be a daunting task for a designer who is not conversant with Java. Take, for example, the following couple of lines:

```
<jsp:useBean id="miniParser" scope="session" class="test.MiniParser" />
<% miniParser.parseHTML("C:/Projects/Chapter2", "example.html"); %>
```

This may appear very mundane and trivial to the experienced Java developer, but completely incomprehensible to a graphic artist. Unfortunately in many cases, the developer will still need to be involved in editing the same files as a designer.

There are a number of other potential problems with JSP. On his web site, Jason Hunter, chief technology officer, K&A Software and author of Java Servlet Programming (O'Reilly) critically evaluates JSP (see http://www.servlets.com/soapbox/problems-jsp.html) and looks at some potential weaknesses:

- ❑ It is very hard to resist hacking the JSP with additional Java code even though this is considered bad design

- ❑ Certain simple activities may actually require that Java code be written

- ❑ Basic and repetitive tasks can be difficult to accomplish

- ❑ JSP provides poor support for looping

- ❑ Error messages are poor – when an error is generated, the output is cryptic and very hard to understand

- ❑ A Java compiler is a prerequisite for JSP to function

- ❑ JSP does not solve the servlet debugging problem

- ❑ While not a major issue, JSP essentially doubles the required disk space as there has to be a class file for every JSP file

As JSP and servlets are both Java-based, they share some of the problems inherent in Java. One of those being processing speed, as Java is interpreted not compiled. This problem, however, has been addressed by Just in Time (JIT) compilers that create object code at runtime. It is claimed that certain JITs can offer speeds almost equivalent to those of compiled languages such as C++.

> **The major disadvantages in using either JSP or servlets (and many other options such as ASP and server-side scripts) all arise from sharing HTML and programming logic in the same file.**

That the use of JSP and servlets does not provide the perfect solution should surprise no one, perfect solutions in computing do not exist and probably never will. The positive side is that many attempts are being made to address the problems.

Emerging Options

It seems that the use of servlets has gained general acceptance within the development community. They have been found to be efficient, work quickly, and on most platforms. Many organizations are now either implementing servlet type solutions or planning to do so – just take a look at the job ads. Equally, JSP as a development of the original servlet technology has won a lot of admiration and is increasingly seen as mainstream technology. Some of this is, of course, due to the high profile given to it by Sun, its Java web site being the first place developers go to for information.

However, the problems with both servlets and JSPs as discussed above, indicate that an ideal solution to the separation of content and logic has yet to be found. This is not to say that the current technology will cease to evolve. The current specifications of both servlets and JSP are under constant review and development.

Looking around the Web and reading various mail threads, it quickly becomes obvious that many people are aware of the problems, often as a result of personal experience. This presents an opportunity for someone somewhere to address this problem with a viable solution. It should, therefore, come as no surprise to anyone familiar with the IT industry, that there are a whole host of both commercial and non-commercial organizations competing to offer a solution to the conundrum.

For the developer, this is both good and bad news. Good news in that a number of new techniques are being created, one or more of which may provide a solution to their specific problem. Bad news because a great deal of time can be expended in evaluating the alternative approaches, then going through the process of learning the nuts and bolts of delivering on the selected approach.

One common idea is to encapsulate HTML or XML into templates and then use Java servlets to place data into the template. Another is to provide a Java API that allows programmers to build HTML or XML output with various constructors and methods. A list of some of the products and concepts follows plus where to find out more (note that many of these are designed to work with each other):

❑ **Cocoon** (http://xml.apache.org/cocoon/)
Part of the Apache Java project and relies on W3C technologies such as DOM, XML and XSL to provide web content

❑ **ECS** (http://java.apache.org/ecs)
Also part of the Apache Java project. ECS stands for **E**lement **C**onstruction **S**et and uses Java objects to generate HTML and XML

❑ **Enhydra** (http://www.enhydra.org)
An open source application framework sponsored by Lutris Technologies. Enhydra makes use of XMLC, Jolt or Java to create a Presentation object. The application data is stored in an Application object

❑ **FreeMaker** (http://freemarker.sourceforge.net)
Another open source product under GPL that provides an HTML template engine for Java servlets

❑ **JdJ** (http://www.inovista.com)
A Java GUI tool that parses HTML files into Java objects and generates a Java servlet that updates elements within the HTML with the results of SQL queries or HTTP parameter values

❑ **WebMacro** (http://www.webmacro.org)
Available under GPL, an HTML template engine and back-end servlet development framework. Page designers create HTML templates using a script language and developers use Java

❑ **XSLT** (http://www.xslt.com)
Extensible Stylesheet Language Transformations is a language for transforming XML documents into other XML documents. Stylesheet templates can include instructions to an XSLT engine to locate information in one or many input XML files. Sun currently offers an Alpha implementation of XSLT written in Java
(http://www.sun.com/xml/developers/xsltc)

Which Solution?

Do any of these newly emerging options provide a replacement for JSP? Are they complementary or do they provide a real alternative? What are the pitfalls? The short answer is that, at the moment, nobody knows.

Assume for an instant that the products and concepts actually work and are moderately bug-free; there are still a number of major hurdles to be surmounted. Software concepts need a core acceptance in order to build enough momentum to become accepted in the market. It is very difficult to convince developers to learn yet another set of techniques especially if they are not convinced that their job prospects are improved by doing so.

The HTML Generator Solution

The **HTML Generator**, which we will build in this chapter, reads an HTML file and combines it with the business logic that may or may not make use of a database. A JSP or servlet is then created that interacts between the HTML Generator and the data flowing to and from the client browser. The important point to note here is that the HTML file is not combined with any logic, it sits alone as a disk file. The design and structure of the file can be edited and modified without the need to touch any code!

The generator workflow is outlined below:

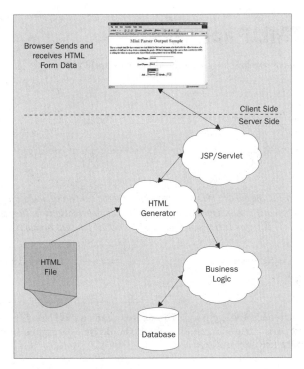

Among the many advantages to this approach are:

❑ The HTML is completely separated from any Java code, simplifying the delineation of the web designer's task and that of the Java developer

❑ Business logic is seperated from presentation code

❑ Presentation enhancements made by the web designer will be reflected in the output as the parser automatically updates the object with the new HTML. The Java developer has no need to touch or recompile any code

❑ Items within HTML tags such as form text fields and select items can be abstracted as Swing MVC (Model-View-Controller) type objects, which in turn, provides considerable capability to the developer

❑ Like any object, additional functionality can be added to the parser as, for example, support for multi-lingual applications

❑ Of course, a JSP or servlet can still employ the parsed object as required

Now let's move on and see how the various `javax.swing.text` packages can help us to create the HTML Generator.

It is worth noting before delving into the Swing packages that even at JDK 1.3, HTML support is still at 3.2. There are also certain weaknesses with the accompanying parser as will be seen later. A number of other API's may work better, especially some of the excellent XML parsers available. However, as Swing is familiar to most Java developers and will certainly evolve to solve these problems, it was chosen for this example.

The Swing HTML Packages

Swing provides a couple of sub-packages devoted entirely to HTML:

- `javax.swing.text.html`
- `javax.swing.text.html.parser`

These two packages are both part of the Swing `text` management hierarchy and make heavy use of the classes in that package.

Many of the classes in the Swing HTML package appear to be continually evolving, so it is worth checking the Javadoc for any enhancements, modifications or deprecations in the classes you wish to use. Even as of JDK1.3, it seems there is still a lot of potential for enhancement.

The HTML parser itself is `javax.swing.text.html.parser.Parser`. In the Javadoc for the parser, Sun describes it as follows:

> **"A simple DTD-driven HTML parser. The parser reads an HTML file from an InputStream and calls various methods (which should be overridden in a subclass) when tags and data are encountered."**

While there are many hooks provided within the parser for customization purposes, we are going to use it as it comes.

As we will see later in this chapter, the parser is not complete; for example, at the time of writing, it does not yet properly handle the HTML <FORM> and </FORM> tags. As the package is still being enhanced, we will use a hack to overcome this until the issue has been addressed by Sun. As Java is still relatively new, and has been subject to feverish enhancement, it is fairly common for developers to write a package of classes to solve a specific problem only to discover that a generic package that addresses the same problem is just about to be released. Unless you have a reason for writing your own solution, for example, in-house proprietary purposes, it is almost always better to rely on publicly available code. Reduce your overall workload, keep maintenance to a minimum!

As a brief aside, the HTML in this example is not making use of a stylesheet and is conforming to HTML 3.2. However, the Swing HTML parser does support the use of stylesheets and, in fact, supports scripting and any unknown tags you care to add.

Once parsed, HTML files are managed by a controlling class called `javax.swing.html.text.HTMLDocument`. `HTMLDocument` is a direct descendent of the Swing `text` package class, `DefaultStyledDocument`, an extension of `AbstractDocument`. This means that all public and protected methods in those classes, such as `getLength()` and `getText()` can equally be employed by `HTMLDocument`.

The parsed `HTMLDocument` is, in fact, an array of the text contained in the original document and a tree structure of elements representing HTML information about the text. So if we take a segment of HTML:

```
<B>
  <I>
    <FONT COLOR="#990000">
      Mini Parser
    </FONT>
  </I>
</B>
```

The parser will take the textual section, "Mini Parser", and then place it in a character array. If all we needed to do were to replicate a flat text file, this would already be sufficient. However, when it comes to regenerating more complex information, such as, Rich Text, XML, or HTML files, information about the text also must be stored. Java Swing handles this by placing that information in an implementation of the `Element` interface. In the above HTML, details about the font, such as its color and style, would have to be stored in such a structure. The parser then creates references from certain parts of the text array to certain elements which store the more complex information needed to re-create the original text. Elements can contain other elements and thus all the elements are stored as a tree structure with each element as a node.

The Swing HTML parser uses the `javax.swing.text.AbstractDocument.AstractElement` class to model elements. Within each element, information about the text is contained in `AttributeSets`. An `AttributeSet` is a collection of unique attributes or keys with values. In the following figure, we can see that the parser has taken the small snippet of HTML, placed the text into a simple character array, and linked it to an element which contains a set of attributes defining the HTML tag values:

One important point to note is that attribute sets are *immutable*, in other words, we cannot edit them. To update HTML information in a parsed document, therefore, we will have to copy the existing attributes into an implementation of `MutableAttributeSet`, edit that and then replace the original with the edited version. An example of this will be shown later.

Creating a Java Object from an HTML File

The next stage is to create an HTMLDocument, in fact a Java object, from the contents of an HTML file. The javax.swing.text.html package provides a tool, HTMLEditorKit, which manages the parser. While the HTMLDocument models the HTML, the Editor Kit is used to load and write HTML files, supports asynchronous loading, and attempts to keep as much of the original HTML as possible. As with other classes in the package, it has been designed to be extensible and, if necessary, the default parser can be replaced. So, to create an HTMLDocument:

```
HTMLEditorKit kit = new HTMLEditorKit();
HTMLDocument doc = (HTMLDocument)kit.createDefaultDocument();
```

When creating a new HTMLDocument with the createDefaultDocument() method, remember that the signature returns a Document, so a cast to HTMLDocument is required.

To load an HTML file, we can use the read() method. The signature is:

```
public void read(Reader in, Document doc, int pos)
                 throws IOException, BadLocationExecption
```

This method takes the content from the Reader and places it in the Document starting at the position specified in pos. If the Document is an instance of HTMLDocument, HTML 3.2 text will be read. Therefore, if we want to create an HTMLDocument from a file called C:\Temp\example.html on an MS Windows machine:

```
try {
  FileReader rd = new FileReader("C:/temp/example.html");

  // Create editor kit and use to create an empty HTMLDocument
  HTMLEditorKit kit = new HTMLEditorKit();
  HTMLDocument doc = (HTMLDocument)kit.createDefaultDocument();

  // Handle charset problems
  doc.putProperty("IgnoreCharsetDirective", new Boolean(true));

  // Load and parse the specified file
  kit.read(rd, doc, 0);

} catch(NullPointerException ex) {
  // Handle NullPointer
} catch(IOException ex) {
  // Handle IO exception
} catch(BadLocationException ex) {
  // Handle BadLocationException
}
```

Notice that a property, IgnoreCharsetDirective, has been set in the document. Using this helps to prevent certain exceptions such as ChangedCharSetException.

When we want to output the contents of an `HTMLDocument` to a disk file, we use the `write()` method in the Editor Kit:

```
public void write(Writer write, Document doc, int pos, int len)
                throws IOException, BadLocationExecption
```

For example, if we wish to output the contents of an `HTMLDocument` called `doc` to a file called `C:\Temp\dummy.html`:

```
try {
    File f = new File("C:/Temp", "dummy.html");
    FileOutputStream fos = new FileOutputStream(f);
    PrintWriter pw = new PrintWriter(fos);

    // Get the length of the file
    int len = doc.getLength();
    HTMLEditorKit kit = new HTMLEditorKit();

    kit.write(pw, doc, 0, len);

} catch(IOException ex) {
    // Handle IO exception
} catch(BadLocationException ex) {
    // Handle BadLocationException
} finally {
    if(fos != null)
        fos.close();
}
```

Handling HTML Form Items

When the parser encounters an HTML form item such as a text field or a list, it handles the item in an ingenious way; it uses a Swing model to represent the data. Thus data in a text field or a text area is stored in a `Document`, list items are held in a `DefaultListModel`, dropdown items are stored in a `DefaultComboBoxModel` and so on. So instead of a set of simple strings, we have access to the full range of Swing capabilities when dealing with the HTML form data. This is especially useful if, for example, we want to sort data in a list or insert an item at the middle of a combo box. The following diagram shows how the `HTMLDocument` views a very basic HTML file:

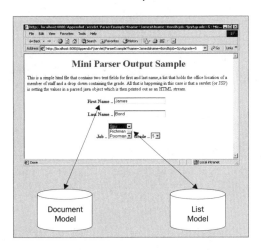

As is the case for other HTML tags, form items become `AbstractElements` once the file is parsed. The element attributes can be accessed by referencing the field name in the `HTML.Attribute` class. If we have an `AbstractElement`, `abstElmt`, and we need its name, we use the `NAME` constant:

```
String sName = (String)abstElmt.getAttribute(HTML.Attribute.NAME)
```

`HTML.Attribute`, as you would expect from the name, contains a type-safe enumeration of attribute names, some examples:

HTML.Attribute Field	HTML Attribute
HTML.Attribute.NAME	The name given to the element. For example, in the HTML `<INPUT TYPE="TEXT" NAME="FName">`, `"Fname"` is returned.
HTML.Attribute.VALUE	This can be used as an alternative method of retrieving the value contained within certain form items as opposed to using the Swing model.
HTML.Attribute.TYPE	References the HTML tag type. This is especially useful for distinguishing between the various form items, text fields, radios, checkboxes etc.
HTML.Attribute.ACTION	Applies to the `ACTION` part of the `FORM` tag.
HTML.Attribute.CHECKED	A Boolean type reference used with radio buttons and check boxes. The HTML, `<INPUT TYPE="RADIO" NAME="Radio" VALUE="Radio" CHECKED>` would contain a `CHECKED` attribute in its respective element.
HTML.Attribute.SELECTED	Another Boolean type reference used with select type items to indicate a data element that is selected as in, `<OPTION SELECTED>HELLO</OPTION>`

In addition to the `HTML.Attribute` constants, the `javax.swing.text.StyleConstants` class can be used to reference certain Swing specific attributes within the elements. `StyleConstants.ModelAttribute` to, for example, retrieve the data model.

Use field constants in the `HTML.Tag` class to test for the tag type. Important fields include:

HTML.Tag Field	Reference
HTML.Tag.INPUT	All Input tags such as text fields, hidden, and password fields
HTML.Tag.SELECT	Combo boxes and lists found with form tags
HTML.Tag.TEXTAREA	Text areas
HTML.Tag.TABLE	HTML tables
HTML.Tag.IMG	Images

Accessing and Editing the Elements

The `javax.text.ElementIterator` can be employed to access each element in turn in the whole element tree of a document. The `ElementIterator` also provides the capability to look at subsets of a document by beginning at and iterating through the children of a selected element. It is worth remembering that the underlying document is not locked when the iteration takes place, therefore any changes that happen to the document during the iteration will not be reflected. The class documentation states that it is the responsibility of the class user to track changes. In other words, it is up to you to handle multiple concurrency.

The class has two constructors:

```
public ElementIterator(Element root)

public ElementIterator(Document document)
```

Use the `Element` parameter to iterate only through the specified element and its children, and the `Document` parameter for the whole document.

`ElementIterator` is very similar to `Enumeration` in its functionality. The `next()` method will continue to return the next element until a null is returned indicating that the loop has completed. Access elements and their attributes are as follows:

```
ElementIterator elmtItr = new ElementIterator(doc);
Element elmt;

// Cycle through all elements
while((elmt = elmtIt.next()) != null) {

  // Retrieve the attribute set
  AttributeSet attSet = elmt.getAttributes();

  // Do something with the attributes
}
```

By iterating through a set of elements, we can test what type of element has been retrieved using the `HTML.Tag` constants as a basis for comparison. For example, if we want to know if `AbstractElement`, attr, is an `INPUT` tag:

```
String sName = attr.getName();

// Handle input items i.e. text fields, radios and cbs
if(sName.equalsIgnoreCase(HTML.Tag.INPUT.toString()))
  System.out.println("Got an INPUT tag");
```

Once the attribute set of an element is obtained, we can edit or update the attribute values. We can then programmatically change HTML file aspects, such as the data in a text field or the selected item of a list.

> **At the time of writing, programmatically updating HTML form items is still a fairly involved process. The standard functionality in the JDK 1.2.2 is cumbersome. JDK 1.3 offers a greatly enhanced set of methods: however, the vast majority of servlet engines do not yet provide support for 1.3, so we're stuck with the complexity for the time being.**

As already noted, the attributes of an element in an `HTMLDocument` cannot be edited. Therefore, to make any amendments, we have to copy them into an `AttributeSet` that can be updated or edited, remove the original set, and then replace it with the new one. Use the `AbstractElement.copyAttributes()` method to obtain a copy of the existing attributes:

```
public AttributeSet copyAttributes()
```

As an `AbstractElement` refers to sections of text in the document, it is important to be able to pinpoint the actual text. This is done by counting the number of characters from the start of the document where the referred text begins, to the number of characters from the start where the text ends. Two methods do that for us:

```
public abstract int getStartOffset()
```

```
public abstract int getEndOffset()
```

To create a set of attributes that can be edited, use the `SimpleAttributeSet` class. This is an implementation of the `MutableAttributeSet` interface based on `Hashtable`. If we pass an existing `AttributeSet` to its constructor, the `SimpleAttributeSet` will be based on those attributes, an empty set can also be created:

```
public SimpleAttributeSet(AttributeSet source)
```

```
public SimpleAttributeSet()
```

To add an attribute to the `SimpleAttributeSet`:

```
public void addAttribute(Object name, Object value)
```

The first parameter of the `addAttribute()` method will often correspond to the fields in the `HTML.Attribute` class discussed earlier. The second is the value that the attribute is to contain. Attributes can be accessed and removed in the same manner:

```
public Object getAttribute(Object name)
```

```
public void removeAttribute(Object name)
```

Setting Text Fields

If we have an `AbstractElement` called `abstElmt` that represents an HTML text field, we could set the text so the user sees 'HELLO' in the field as follows:

```
try {
  String sValue = "HELLO";

  int start = abstElmt.getStartOffset();
  int end = abstElmt.getEndOffset();

  AttributeSet attribset = abstElmt.copyAttributes();
```

```
    // Convert to mutable to add or remove data
    MutableAttributeSet mAttSet = new SimpleAttributeSet(attribset);

    mAttSet.removeAttribute(HTML.Attribute.VALUE);
    mAttSet.addAttribute( HTML.Attribute.VALUE, sValue);

    doc.remove(start, end - start);
    // "-" here is a dummy to force data entry
    doc.insertString(start, "-", mAttSet);

} catch( exception ex) {
    // Manage the errors
}
```

There are a couple of points to note in the above code. Firstly, the Swing model is not being used. Instead, we make a straight reference to the value of the field by using HTML.Attribute.VALUE. Setting the VALUE attribute will also update the model of the field, which is in fact a Document. The second point is that no text is actually inserted into the Document, the edit is done by adding a tag value so the resultant HTML will look something like <INPUT TYPE="TEXT" NAME="SALUTE" VALUE="HELLO"> Thus when we come to inserting a string into the document to update it, we have to pass a dummy string. The dummy will not be shown in the HTML text when it is eventually printed out. The AbstractDocument.insertString() method signature is:

```
public void insertString(int offs, String str, AttributeSet a)
                    throws BadLocationException
```

offs, is the offset where the text is to be inserted, str is the text to insert and a is the AttributeSet to be applied to the inserted text.

Setting Selects

Text fields and related form items such as hidden and password fields are relatively easy to handle. More effort is required when working with complex items such as selects (select items are HTML's answer to combo boxes and lists). In addition to containing multiple discrete values, it is also possible for one or more of the values to be selected. In this case, we are obliged to use the underlying data models, DefaultComboBoxModel for combos and DefaultListModel for lists. How this actually functions within a parsed HTMLDocument is that the values are stored as an instance of the javax.swing.text.html.Option class. The respective models contain arrays (or Vectors) of Options. To create an Option:

```
public Option(AttributeSet attr)
```

To set or retrieve the text for the Option:

```
public String getLabel()
```

```
public void setLabel(String label)
```

Options can also have a Value that may or may not be the same as the Label. When getting the Value, the Label is returned if there is no Value.

```
public String getValue()
```

We can also test whether or not the Option is selected; but annoyingly we cannot set the selection status:

```
public boolean isSelected()
```

To create a selected Option, therefore, we need to work with the Value attribute:

```
String sValue = "Test Value";
SimpleAttributeSet attribset = new SimpleAttributeSet();

if(True)  // Set selected if required
  attribset.addAttribute(HTML.Attribute.SELECTED, new Boolean(bSel));

// Wrap the label in quotes to avoid string truncation
set.addAttribute(HTML.Attribute.VALUE, "\"" + sValue + "\"" );
Option opt = new Option(attribset);

opt.setLabel(sValue);
```

Setting both the Label and the Value in the Option will result in a duplication in the eventual HTML, which will look like this:

```
<OPTION VALUE="Test Value" SELECTED>Test Value</OPTION>.
```

> While in many cases this usage creates additional unnecessary text, it can also be used to show meaningful text to a user, yet fire a code value when a Submit button is clicked. For example, LHR may be held in the value attribute while London Heathrow is what the user sees.

As the combo or list data is basically a Swing DefaultListModel containing Options as its elements, we simply add, retrieve, remove, or insert options using standard model methods:

```
public void addElement(Object anObject)
```

```
public Object getElementAt(int index)
```

```
public void insertElementAt(Object anObject, int index)
```

```
public void removeElementAt(int index)
```

So, to insert an Option, opt, to be the first element of a DefaultComboBoxModel, mod:

```
mod.insertElementAt(opt, 0);
```

When an element is to be added to a list or a combo, we first need access to its data model. Assuming that AbstractElement, attr is a select type object:

```
String sName = attr.getName();

if(sName.equals(HTML.Tag.SELECT.toString()) )
    // We've got a list or a combo
```

We can then retrieve the model using the `StyleConstants.ModelAttribute` constant:

```
int start = abstElmt.getStartOffset();
int end = abstElmt.getEndOffset();
AttributeSet attribset = abstElmt.copyAttributes();

// Convert to mutable to add/remove data
MutableAttributeSet mAttSet = new SimpleAttributeSet(attribset);

// Get the doc model for the select item
ListModel mod =
    (ListModel)mAttSet.getAttribute(StyleConstants.ModelAttribute);
```

Now we can create an unselected `Option` with 'New Item' as its text and add it to the list:

```
SimpleAttributeSet attSet = new SimpleAttributeSet();
attSet.addAttribute(HTML.Attribute.SELECTED, newBoolean(false));
attSet.addAttribute(HTML.Attribute.VALUE, "\"" + "New Item" + "\"" );

Option opt = new Option(attSet);
opt.setLabel("New Item");

// Put the option at the beginning of the list
mod.insertElementAt(opt, 0);
```

Finally, we replace the `AttributeSet` in the `HTMLDocument` exactly in the same manner as the text field:

```
doc.remove(start, end - start);

//The "-" here is a dummy to force data entry
doc.insertString(start, "-", mAttSet);
```

We will return to this topic and see how to toggle the `Selected` status of a list or combo value when putting together the demo servlet.

The Form Tag Hack

If up to this point you've tried to write some code to parse an HTML file containing form items and been disappointed to see that is hasn't worked, the reason is that as of JDK 1.2.2 (also 1.3), the parser does not handle the FORM tag. If we want to write a tool that programmatically updates form items from the server-side, then, it seems we have reached a dead end with the standard API. As the Java HTML parser has been designed with extension in mind, we could go ahead and extend it to meet our requirements. For the sake of this example, however, we will write a temporary class that renames the FORM tag before parsing to some dummy name and then finds that name and converts it back to form before final output.

The class effectively takes a char array, which can be created when initially reading in an HTML file and replaces the text of one tag type with a pre defined string. For example, if we read the data from an HTML file into a char array called ch and want to replace all <FORM> tags with <XXXX>:

```
ch = HtmlTagReplacer.repTag(ch, "form", "XXXX");
```

When we have completed what we want to do with the HTMLDocument object and to write it out to a browser, we can reset the tag back to its original value:

```
ch = HtmlTagReplacer.repTag(ch, "XXXX", "form");
```

A full listing of the class follows:

```
/**
 * ******************************
 * Class used primarily for the temporary renaming of an HTML tag
 * in a char array that represents the HTML file. The tag replacement
 * must be the same number of chars as the original.
 * This is used primarily to get around Swing's refusal to
 * print FORM tags - they can be temporarily replaced.
 * ******************************
 */

public class HtmlTagReplacer {

  /**
   * ********************
   * Static method that takes a char array representing an HTML
   * file and replaces all tags of the first param type with
   * tags of the second.
   * @param char[] the char array
   * @param String the original tag
   * @param String the rep tag
   * @return char[] the edited char array
   * ********************
   */

  public static char[] repTag(char[] chArray, String sTag1, String sTag2) {

    char[] chTag1 = sTag1.toCharArray();

    // Convert to upper
    chTag1 = convertToUpper(chTag1);
    char[] chTag2 = sTag2.toCharArray();

    // Convert to upper
    chTag2 = convertToUpper(chTag2);
    int iDocLength = chArray.length;
    int iTagLength = sTag1.length();
    for(int i = 0; i < iDocLength; i++) {
      char ch = chArray[i];
      if(ch == '<') {
        i++;
```

```
            // Get the next ch unless exceeds size of array
            if(i < iDocLength) {
              ch = chArray[i];
            } else {
              break;
            }

            // Remove spaces and slashes
            while(ch == ' ' || ch == '/') {
              i++;
              if(i < iDocLength) {
                ch = chArray[i];
              } else {
                break;
              }
            }

            // OK clean - so test string so can test if there is
            // enough space to hold a tag
            if((i + iTagLength + 1) > iDocLength) {
              break;            // Cannot be here
            }
            boolean match = true;
            int iLoc = i;     // Store the loc

            // Test if the current part is the same as the original tag
            for(int j = 0; j < iTagLength; j++) {
              if(Character.toUpperCase(chArray[i]) != chTag1[j]) {
                match = false;
                break;
              }
              i++;
            }

            // Now test for blank or slash
            if(match) {
              ch = chArray[i];
              if(ch != ' ' && ch != '>') {
                match = false;
              }
              if(match) {    // OK found it
                for (int j = 0; j < iTagLength; j++) {
                  chArray[iLoc] = chTag2[j];
                  iLoc++;
                }
              }
            }                       // End if (match)
          }                         // End ch = '<'
        }                           // End outside loop
      return chArray;
    }
/**
*****************
```

```
 * Convert a char array to upper case so that String comparisons can be made
 * @return char[] the converted array
 * @param char[] the array to convert
 * ****************
 */

private static char[] convertToUpper(char[] ch) {
  for(int i = 0; i < ch.length; i++) {
    ch[i] = Character.toUpperCase(ch[i]);
  }
  return ch;
}
}
```

A Simple HTML Generator

At this point, we have enough information to build a basic HTML generator. The goal of the generator will be to read in and parse an HTML file that contains form items, and permits the values of those form items to be set by a controlling class such as a servlet or JSP. The controlling class will then be able to write out the converted object as an HTML file that retains the original styling and format. In other words, the values in the form items will be set using some business logic on an object representing an HTML file. Each time the HTML is enhanced, it will be reflected by the parser as long as core details, such as form types and names, about <FORM> items do not change.

The HTML generator will be two classes MiniParser and a helper class, MiniParserHelper. MiniParser will reside on the server within a CLASSPATH and function in the same way as a JavaBean, although not conforming to the Bean specification.

First, we need to make some rules about the underlying HTML form items. As in components for a standard front-end application, written in say, Java or Visual Basic, the names of the components must be unique. This can easily be done by the web designer, who could create first and last name fields as follows:

```
<INPUT TYPE="TEXT" NAME="FName" SIZE="25">
<INPUT TYPE="TEXT" NAME="LName" SIZE="25">
```

As developers, we can now access the first name field as FName and the last name as LName.

We can divide the functionality of the generator into two main areas. One would be reading and parsing the HTML, the second editing and updating the values of the form items. Thus we can designate MiniParser for the first part and get the helper class to do the updating.

The MiniParser Class

The MiniParser class will make extensive use of HTMLEditorKit, so we can initialize this class when the object is instantiated:

```
import javax.swing.text.*;
import javax.swing.text.html.*;
```

```
import java.io.*;
import java.util.Hashtable;
import java.util.Vector;
import javax.swing.*;

public class MiniParser
{
   // Prepare doc and editor kit
   protected HTMLEditorKit kit = new HTMLEditorKit();
   protected HTMLDocument doc;

   // Instant. The helper class
   MiniParserHelper helper = new MiniParserHelper();
```

A method is needed to prepare the HTMLDocument and set any property options in that document:

```
public void initDoc() {
   // Re-init any doc
   doc = (HTMLDocument)kit.createDefaultDocument();

   // Store unknown tags
   doc.putProperty("IgnoreCharsetDirective", new Boolean(true));
   doc.setPreservesUnknownTags(true);
}
```

Setting setPreservesUnknownTags() to true means that the parser will store any tags that it is not familiar with. Setting to true here is important as we are going to replace <FORM> tags with ZZZZ.

A BufferedReader is used to read in the file from disk and convert it to a char array. A Boolean true is returned indicating a successful parse. Before actually parsing the file, the HtmlTagReplacer hack is be applied to remove the <form> tags (sFormRep is the String that will temporarily replace form):

```
private final static String FORM = "<form>";
private static String sFormRep = "ZZZZ";
```

When the HTML file is parsed, we have to store the form items we are interested in so that they can be accessed later. In this example, we are only interested in text fields and selects. However, as more functionality is added to the generator, we may need to store all aspects of the file, including textual sections, images, and tables.

Two Hashtables are defined (hashTextField and hashSelect), which use the name of the form item as the key and the AbstractElement that represents that form item as the value. When iterating through the parsed file, the constants in the HTML inner classes are used for comparison, these strings can also be prepared on instantiation:

```
// Prepare the component hashtables
private Hashtable hashTextField = new Hashtable();
private Hashtable hashSelect = new Hashtable();

// The FORM tag and attribute type descriptions
private String sInput = HTML.Tag.INPUT.toString();
private String sSelect = HTML.Tag.SELECT.toString();
private String sTextItem = HTML.Attribute.TEXT.toString();
```

The `Hashtables` are cleared (`reInitHashtables()`) and the iteration proceeds to find any form items:

```
private void updateHashtable() {
    reInitHashtables();
    ElementIterator elmtIt = new ElementIterator(doc);
    Element elmt;
    // Cycle through all elements
    while((elmt = elmtIt.next()) != null) {
        AttributeSet attSet = elmt.getAttributes();

        try {
            // Test to see if we have a form item
            if(attSet instanceof AbstractDocument.AbstractElement)
                addElement((AbstractDocument.AbstractElement)attSet);
        } catch(Error ex) {
            System.out.println("err " + ex);
        }
    }
}

public void reInitHashtables() {
  hashTextField.clear();
  hashSelect.clear();
}
```

When the `ElementIterator` stumbles across an `AbstractElement`, `addElement()` is called which in turn, tests if the name of the attribute is a tag that we are looking for; an `INPUT` or a `SELECT` tag:

```
protected void addElement(AbstractDocument.AbstractElement attr) {
    String sName = attr.getName();

    // Handle input items i.e. text fields
    if(sName.equals(sInput))
        updateInputs(attr);

    // Test for list and combos
    else if(sName.equals (sSelect))
        updateSelects(attr);
}
```

If an `INPUT` or a `SELECT` tag is successfully found, the relevant `Hashtable` is updated with the value of the name attribute (`HTML.Attribute.NAME`) and the `AbstractElement`. Depending on the tag type, this is accomplished with either `updateInputs()` or `updateSelects()`. While it would be good practice to use a single overloaded method to handle the form items, in practice this is difficult. Each form item contains some attributes specific to itself, so in the end it is easier to write a method to handle each individually:

```
private void updateInputs(AbstractDocument.AbstractElement attr){

    // First get the type variable by checking model type
    String sType = (String)attr.getAttribute(HTML.Attribute.TYPE);
```

```
    // Test model type is Text Field
    if(sType.equals(sTextItem)) {

      // Get the name
      String sName = (String)attr.getAttribute(HTML.Attribute.NAME);

      // Ensure not dupe
      if(isDupe(sName, hashTextField))
        hashTextField.put(sName, attr);
    }
  }

  private void updateSelects(AbstractDocument.AbstractElement attr) {

    // Get the name
    String sName = (String)attr.getAttribute(HTML.Attribute.NAME);

    // Ensure not dupe
    if(isDupe(sName, hashSelect))
      hashSelect.put(sName, attr);
  }
```

If, say, we want to find out about property and format settings of the 'LName' text field, we can access the element that represents by extracting the attributes of its `AbstractElement`:

```
AbstractDocument.AbstractElement abstElmt =
        (AbstractDocument.AbstractElement)hashTextField.get("LName");
```

The `isDupe()` method called when updating the Hashtables is used to force unique naming of form items and can also be used to inform a user of which items are in fact duplicates. The names of any duplicates are stored in a Vector, `vDupes`, which could be presented to a designer or developer depending on the development tool that is being used:

```
// The store to point out duplicate types
boolean bDupe = false;
```

```
// A vector of duplicate types
private Vector vDupes = new Vector(10,10);
```

```
private boolean isDupe(String sName, Hashtable hash) {
    boolean bOk = true;
    if(hash.containsKey(sName)) {
        bDupe = true;
        vDupes.addElement(sName);
        bOk = false;
    }
    return bOk;
}
```

To set up the parser, an overloaded method `parseHTML()` is employed to read in the HTML file, place the data into a char array, storing the array as a class variable. The overloading allows either a file or a pair of Strings defining the directory and file name to start the process. This method need only be called on initialization or when the underlying HTML file has been updated:

```
    protected char[] chars;
    protected File htmlFile;

public boolean parseHTML(String sDir, String sFile) {
    File f = new File(sDir, sFile);
    return parseHTML(f);
}

public boolean parseHTML(File f) {
    // Prepare doc
    initDoc();
    char[]ch = null;
    try {
        FileReader fr = new FileReader(f);
        BufferedReader br = new BufferedReader(fr);
        StringBuffer sb = new StringBuffer();
        boolean bRead = true;
        String s ="";
        // Read in each line of the html doc
        while(bRead) {
            s = br.readLine();
            if(s != null)
                sb.append(s);
            else
                bRead = false;
        }
        // Convert the string buffer to a char array
        try {
            ch = new char[sb.length()];
            sb.getChars(0, sb.length() - 1, ch, 0);
        }
        catch(Exception x) {
            System.out.println("HTMLParser: convert to char error when
                               parsing. " + x);
        }
        fr.close();
        // Keep a copy of the file
        htmlFile = f;
    }
    catch(Exception ex) {
        System.out.println("HTMLParser: error parsing HTML file " +
                           htmlFile + " : " + ex);
        return false;
    }
    // Store the parsed data
    chars = ch;
    return preparedParse(ch);
}
```

Another public method, preparedParse(char[] ch), is called by parseHTML() and, of course, can also be called externally. This is responsible for the temporary replacement of any FORM tags, placing the HTML into the HTMLEditorKit and finally calling the method that prepares the initial state of the parser:

```
public boolean preparedParse(char[] ch) {
    boolean bRet = true;
    bDupe = false;
    try {
        // Due to the current status of the java parser not handling
        // form tags we need this hack for that.
        // Replace this when API enhanced!
        // replace the form items
        ch = HtmlTagReplacer.repTag(ch, FORM, sFormRep);
        // Then read in the adapted array
        kit.read(new CharArrayReader(ch),doc,0);
        updateHashtable();
    }
    catch(Error ex) {
        ex.printStackTrace();
        bRet = false;
    }
    catch(Exception ex) {
        ex.printStackTrace();
        bRet = false;
    }
    return bRet;
}
```

The textual updating of the form items is to be undertaken in the MiniParserHelper class. However, so that users only need to deal with one class, we can add methods to the MiniParser that merely pass on update requests to the MiniParserHelper:

```
/***************************
 * Updates the text for a text field using the name to
 * locate the field.
 * @return boolean true on success
 * @param String the name of the field
 * @param String the value to update
 ***************************/

public boolean updateTextField(String sName, String sValue) {
    // Use the helper to set textfield values
    return helper.updateTextField(sName, sValue, hashTextField, doc);
}
```

```
/***************************
 * Sets the value of the item in the name as selected in
 * a select item and de-selects the others.
 * default is not checked.
 * @return boolean true on success
 * @param String the name of the select item
 * @param String the value to add
 ***************************/

public boolean updateSelectItem(String sName, String sValue) {
    // Use the helper to update the select item
    return helper.updateSelectItem(sName, sValue, hashSelect, doc);
}
```

```
/***************************
 * Adds an item to a combo or list html (select ) form item.
 * default is not checked.
 * @return boolean true on success
 * @param String the name of the select item
 * @param String the value to add
 * @param boolean checked status
 ***************************/

public boolean addSelectItem(String sName, String sValue,
                             boolean bChecked) {
    // Use the helper to update the select item
    return helper.addSelectItem(sName, sValue, bChecked, hashSelect, doc);
}
}
```

The final step is to write out the results as HTML using the writeHTML() method:

```
/***********************
 * Writes the current state of the document to the param stream
 * using the HTMLStreamWriter class.
 * @param Writer the output stream
 * @param boolean true to close the PrintWriter on completion
 ***********************/

public void writeHTML(Writer pw, boolean bClose) {
    String s ="";
    CharArrayWriter cw = new CharArrayWriter();
    HTMLWriter hw = new HTMLWriter(cw, doc);

    try {
        // First write to a char array
        hw.write();
        cw.flush();
        char[]ch = cw.toCharArray();

        // Replace the form items back to original
        ch = HtmlTagReplacer.repTag(ch, sFormRep, "FORM");

        // Now write it out
        pw.write(ch);
        cw.close();
        if(bClose)
            pw.close();

    } catch(IOException io) {
        System.out.println("MiniParser; writeHTML : " + io);
    } catch(javax.swing.text.BadLocationException bt) {
        System.out.println("MiniParser; writeHTML - BadLocation : " + bt );
    }
}
```

The Helper Class

As a design issue, it was decided that a helper class would be created to manage the update, editing, and insertion of new data into the parsed HTML object. This is, in fact, a fairly logical split, the main class being devoted to I/O and converting an HTML file into an `HTMLDocument`:

```java
import javax.swing.text.*;
import javax.swing.text.html.*;
import java.util.Hashtable;
import java.util.Vector;
import javax.swing.*;

public class MiniParserHelper
{
```

We have already seen how to set values for text fields and add options to select items. The most important methods in this class are for doing just that. The following methods are for text fields and selects respectively:

```java
/**
 * ************************
 * Updates the text for a text field using the name to
 * locate the field.
 * @return boolean true on success
 * @param String the name of the field
 * @param String the value to update
 * @param Hashtable the hashtable that holds details re textfields
 * @param AbstractDocument the parsed html file
 * ************************
 */

public boolean updateTextField(String sName, String sValue,
                               Hashtable hashTextField,
                               AbstractDocument doc) {
    if (doc == null)      // doc not ready
      return false;

    try {

      // Get the Abstract Element
      AbstractDocument.AbstractElement abstElmt =
            (AbstractDocument.AbstractElement) hashTextField.get(sName);
      if (sName == null)
        return false;

      int start = abstElmt.getStartOffset();
      int end = abstElmt.getEndOffset();
      AttributeSet attribset = abstElmt.copyAttributes();

      // Convert to mutable to add/remove data
      MutableAttributeSet mAttribs = new SimpleAttributeSet(attribset);
      mAttribs.removeAttribute(HTML.Attribute.VALUE);
```

```
      mAttribs.addAttribute(HTML.Attribute.VALUE, sValue);
      doc.remove(start, end - start);

      // The "-" here is a dummy to force data entry
      doc.insertString(start, "-", mAttribs);
    } catch (Exception ex) {
      return false;
    }
    return true;
}
```

```
/**
 * ************************
 * Adds an item to a combo or list html (select ) form item.
 * default is not checked.
 * @return boolean true on success
 * @param String the name of the select item
 * @param String the value to add
 * @param boolean checked status
 * @param Hashtable the hashtable that holds details re select items
 * @param AbstractDocument the parsed html file
 * ************************
 */

public boolean addSelectItem(String sName, String sValue,
                             boolean bChecked, Hashtable hashSelect,
                             AbstractDocument doc) {
  if (doc == null)      // doc not ready
    return false;

  try {

    // Get the Abstract Element
    AbstractDocument.AbstractElement abstElmt =
          (AbstractDocument.AbstractElement) hashSelect.get(sName);
    if (sName == null)
      return false;

    int start = abstElmt.getStartOffset();
    int end = abstElmt.getEndOffset();
    AttributeSet attribset = abstElmt.copyAttributes();

    // Convert to mutable to add/remove data
    MutableAttributeSet mAttribs = new SimpleAttributeSet(attribset);

    // get the doc model for the table
    ListModel mod =
        (ListModel) mAttribs.getAttribute(StyleConstants.ModelAttribute);

    // Create the option to add
    Option option = createOption(sValue, bChecked);

    // Handle combo model
    if(mod instanceof DefaultComboBoxModel) {
```

```
          ((DefaultComboBoxModel) mod).addElement(option);

          // Handle list model
        } else if(mod instanceof DefaultListModel) {
          ((DefaultListModel) mod).addElement(option);
        }
        doc.remove(start, end - start);

        // The "-" here is a dummy to force data entry
        doc.insertString(start, "-", mAttribs);

      } catch (Exception ex) {
        System.out.println("HTMLParser; addSelectItem; " + ex);
        return false;
      }
      return true;
    }
  }
```

Both methods require name, value, `Hashtable`, and `AbstractDocument` parameters. `sName` is the string value of the form item to be updated. As in the earlier example, if we want to set a value to the `LName` text field, we would pass "LName" into this parameter. `sValue` is what value we want the form item to contain, for example, we would put "Smith" here to show that name to a user. `Hashtable` is the relevant `Hashtable` we used in `MiniParser` to store String name key versus `AbstractElement`; for Text fields `hashTextField`, and `hashSelect` for the selects. The `AbstractDocument` is the current parsed HTMLDocument. The only difference is in `addSelectItem()` which requires a Boolean defining whether or not the option to be added to the list or combo is to be selected.

The major functionality not yet covered is the ability to change the selected item in a `Select` form item. This is handled by the `updateSelectItem()` method. All items that do not match the value of a string parameter are deselected. Let's look in a little more detail how this is done:

```
public boolean updateSelectItem(String sName, String sValue,
                                Hashtable hashSelect, AbstractDocument doc)
{

  if(doc == null )    //doc not ready
    return false;

  try {
    // Get the Abstract Element
    AbstractDocument.AbstractElement abstElmt =
        (AbstractDocument.AbstractElement)hashSelect.get(sName);

    if(sName == null|| sName.length() == 0)
      return false;

    int start = abstElmt.getStartOffset();
    int end = abstElmt.getEndOffset();
    AttributeSet attribset = abstElmt.copyAttributes();

    // Convert to mutable to add/remove data
    MutableAttributeSet mAttribs = new SimpleAttributeSet(attribset);
```

```
            // Get the doc model for the select item
            ListModel mod =
                (ListModel)mAttribs.getAttribute(StyleConstants.ModelAttribute);

            // Handle combo model
            int iSize = mod.getSize();
            for(int i = 0; i < iSize; i++) {
              Object obj = mod.getElementAt(i);

              if(obj instanceof Option)
                 handleOptionValue((Option)obj, mod, sValue, i);

              doc.remove(start, end - start);
            }
            // The "-" here is a dummy to force data entry
            doc.insertString(start, "-", mAttribs);

        } catch(Exception ex) {
          System.out.println("HTMLParser; addSelectItem; " + ex);
         return false;
        }
        return true;
    }
```

The parameter list is similar to the other set methods; only in this case the sValue parameter holds the value that is to be depicted to the user as the selected item. A Hashtable is queried for the relevant AbstractElement by matching the key passed in the name parameter. Then the ListModel holding the Options is extracted from the AttributeSet. Accessing each Option in turn in a loop, handleOptionValue() does the work of testing whether the Option value should be selected:

```
/*****************
 * Updates the selected item in a combo or list list model.
 * @param Option the option to test
 * @param ListModel the model
 * @param String the true value
 * @param int the index being edited/checked
 * @return ListModel the edited ListModel that was passed in
 ****************/

private ListModel handleOptionValue(Option opt, ListModel mod,
                                    String value, int iInd)
{
  // Not same label and not selected so leave alone
  if(!opt.getLabel().equals(value) && !opt.isSelected())
    return mod;

  // Not the same label and is selected so de-select
  else if(!opt.getLabel().equals(value) && opt.isSelected())
    return handleSelectModel(opt, mod, value, iInd, false);

  // Is the same label and not selected so select
  else if(opt.getLabel().equals(value) && !opt.isSelected())
```

```
        return handleSelectModel(opt, mod, value, iInd, true);

    // Already OK
    else
        return mod;
}
```

Using its parameter list, `handleOptionValue()` decides what to do with each `Option`. If the `Option` needs to be de selected because the values don't match or selected because the values match and the `Option` is not yet selected, the details are passed on to `handleSelectModel()` to adjust the `Option` settings:

```
/****************
 * Updates the select type model depending on what type of model.
 * @param Option the option to test
 * @param ListModel the model
 * @param String the true value
 * @param int the index being edited/checked
 * @param boolean the select status
 * @return ListModel the ListModel with Options edited
 ****************/

private ListModel handleSelectModel(Option opt, ListModel mod, String value,
                                    int iInd, boolean bState)
{
    // Handle combo model
    if(mod instanceof DefaultComboBoxModel) {
        DefaultComboBoxModel cmod =(DefaultComboBoxModel)mod;
        cmod.removeElementAt(iInd);
        cmod.insertElementAt(createOption(value, bState), iInd);
        return cmod;
    }

    // Handle list model
    else if(mod instanceof DefaultListModel) {
        DefaultListModel lmod =(DefaultListModel)mod;
        lmod.removeElementAt(iInd);
        lmod.insertElementAt( createOption(value, bState), iInd);
        return lmod;
    }
    return mod;
}
```

When dealing with the model types for selects, we may encounter either `DefaultComboBoxModel` or a `DefaultListModel` depending on the form item type, so we have to cater for both. There is no easy way of changing the selection in an `Option`, so we remove the `Option` we are dealing with from the model and replace it with a new one created with the attributes we want. `createOption` does this for us:

```
/****************
 * Creates an option item for a list or a combo
 * @return Option the list/combo item
 @param String the display name
```

```
    * @param boolean selected
    ************************/

   private Option createOption(String sValue, boolean bSel)
   {
     SimpleAttributeSet attSet = new SimpleAttributeSet();
     if(bSel)
       set.addAttribute(HTML.Attribute.SELECTED, new Boolean(bSel));

     set.addAttribute(HTML.Attribute.VALUE, "\"" + sValue + "\"" );
     Option opt = new Option(attSet);
     opt.setLabel(sValue);
     return opt;
   }
```

To get the correct Option selection setting, we simply add the HTML.Attribute.SELECTED attribute to the set if the Boolean parameter is true.

OK, using these two classes and for the time being, the HtmlTagReplacer hack, we've built a very basic HTML generator. While there is enormous scope for additional functionality, with what we already have, it is possible to create some interesting examples.

A Servlet Example

In the first example we'll make use of a very simple HTML file, basically some text and a number of form items, then write a servlet that loads HTTP parameters into the form fields.

Here is the HTML file called example.html:

```
<HTML>
<HEAD></HEAD>
<BODY>

<FORM ACTION="Nothing" METHOD="POST"
      ENCTYPE="application/x-www-form-urlencoded">

<H1 ALIGN="CENTER"><FONT COLOR="Red">Mini Parser Output Sample</FONT></H1>
<P><FONT COLOR="Black">
This is a simple html file that contains two text fields for first and last name,a
list that holds the office location of a member of staff and a drop down
containing the grade. All that is happening in this case is that a servlet (or
JSP) is setting the values in a parsed java object which is then printed out as an
HTML stream.
</FONT>
</P>

  <CENTER>
    <P>
      <B>
        <FONT COLOR="Black">
          First Name ..
```

```
            </FONT>
          </B>
          <FONT COLOR="black">
            <INPUT TYPE="TEXT" NAME="FName" Size="25" >
          </FONT>
        </P>
      </CENTER>

      <CENTER>
        <P>
          <B>
            <FONT COLOR="Black">
              Last Name ..
            </Font>
          </B>
          <FONT COLOR="black">
            <INPUT TYPE="TEXT" NAME="LName" SIZE="25" >
          </FONT>
        </P>
      </CENTER>

      <CENTER>
        <P>
          <B>
            <FONT COLOR="Black">
              Job ..
            </FONT>
          </B>
          <FONT COLOR="Black">
            <SELECT NAME="Jobs" SIZE="3" >
            </SELECT>
          </FONT>
          <B>
            <FONT COLOR="black">
              Grade ..
            </B>
          </FONT>
          <FONT COLOR="Black">
            <SELECT NAME="Grade">
            </SELECT>
          </FONT>
        <P>
      </CENTER>
    </FORM>
  </BODY>

</HTML>
```

Note that there are two input items (FName and LName), two selects, one list (Jobs), and one a drop down (Grade). These are the items that are going to be populated with the values of the incoming HTTP parameters.

The Servlet

Let's call the example servlet `ParserExample`, and have it extend `HttpServlet`. On instantiation, a number of objects are created, including the `MiniParser`:

```java
import java.io.*;
import javax.servlet.*;
import javax.servlet.http.*;

public class ParserExample extends HttpServlet {

  // Prepare the parser object
  MiniParser parser = new MiniParser();

  // the saved data read in from the html file
  char[] chars;
  String[] joblist = new String[] {
    "Soldier", "Sailor", "Tinker", "Tailor", "Spy", "Richman", "Poorman"
  };

  String[] gradelist = new String[] {
    "1", "2", "3", "4", "5", "6"
  };
```

There are also two string arrays initialized and populated which will be used to populate the list and combo.

As this is a simple example, most of the work will be done in the doGet() method. We start by reading in the HTTP parameters:

```java
public void doGet(HttpServletRequest req, HttpServletResponse resp)
        throws ServletException, IOException {

  // Get the http parameters - if null, replace with a blank to
  // Avoid null pointer type exceptions
  String sFName = req.getParameter("fname");
  if (sFName == null)
    sFName = "";

  String sLName = req.getParameter("lname");
  if (sLName == null)
    sLName = "";

  String sJob = req.getParameter("job");
  if (sJob == null)
    sJob = "";

  String sGrade = req.getParameter("grade");
  if (sGrade == null)
    sGrade = "";
```

All that is happening here is that the servlet is looking for some hard-coded parameter names; fname, lname, job, and grade. (To remove the problem of the hard coding here, with a little extra work, the field names could be defined in an external properties file that is read on servlet initialization.) When those are found, they are set to the relevant instance variable in the class. The next step in the method is to read-in and parse the HTML file, in this example, the filename is also hard-coded and is stored in the C:\Temp directory:

```
// Reset the parser with the original data
parser.parseHTML("C:/Temp", "example.html");
```

If you want to use a different directory to store the file, you will have to change the "C:/Temp" to your directory name and re compile. If you are using Linux and want to use the /usr/local directory, change this line to:

```
parser.parseHTML("/usr/local", "example.html");
```

As an aside here, a much more effective practice is to create a class variable for the directory (or any other variable that is likely to remain constant for the life of the servlet) and have it loaded in the init() method when the servlet is created:

```
public void init(ServletConfig sg) throws ServletException {
   super.init(sg);
   // Get html file and update the parser
   sDirectory = getInitParameter("directory");
}
```

Different servlet engines manage init variables in different ways. In Tomcat, they are stored in the web.xml file. We would need to add the following lines to that file, so that Tomcat would set the initialization parameter 'directory' with the value of '/usr/local' for a servlet called ParserExample:

```
<servlet>
  <servlet-name>
    ParserExample
  </servlet-name>
  <servlet-class>
    ParserExample
  </servlet-class>
  <init-param>
    <param-name>
      directory
    </param-name>
    <param-value>
      /usr/local
    </param-value>
  </init-param>
</servlet>
```

The parser setup line in doGet() would then read (not forgetting that sDirectory has to be a class variable and not local to any method):

```
parser.parseHTML(sDirectory, "example.html");
```

This is obviously much more flexible as no code needs to be changed and re compiled, the only change necessary is a quick edit of one line of the XML file.

1561

Right, back to doGet(). Setting the text field values with the respective parameter is now one line each:

```
// Put the data in the relevant components
parser.updateTextField("FName", sFName);
parser.updateTextField("LName", sLName);
```

All we do is pass the name of the text field and the HTTP parameter value we read in straight to the parser, which will in turn pass it to the helper class, if you recall how it works.

To simplify list and combo management, we write a method that takes a string array and populates the select item with the array data while setting each Option as not selected:

```
private void populateSelect(String sName, String[] list) {

    if (sName == null || list == null)
        return;    // cannot continue

    for (int i = 0; i < list.length; i++) {
        parser.addSelectItem(sName, list[i], false);
    }
}
```

The method loops through the array elements and then passes each one of them with the name of the select item to the MiniParser to append to the end of the list or combo. The lines in doGet() look like this:

```
// Setup the jobs
populateSelect("Jobs", joblist);

// And then grades
populateSelect("Grade", gradelist);
```

To highlight certain data options in select items that match what comes in from the HTTP parameters, we again resort to our MiniParser:

```
// Try and set the select values for the selects
parser.updateSelectItem("Jobs", sJob);
parser.updateSelectItem("Grade", sGrade);
```

Finally, get hold of the PrintWriter and fire the updated HTML back to the browser:

```
PrintWriter out = new PrintWriter(resp.getOutputStream());

parser.writeHTML(out, true);
out.close();
    }
}
```

Running the Servlet in Tomcat

Here is the web.xml deployment descriptor to set up the web application for the servlet example:

```
<?xml version="1.0" encoding="ISO-8859-1"?>

<!DOCTYPE web-app
    PUBLIC "-//Sun Microsystems, Inc.//DTD Web Application 2.2//EN"
    "http://java.sun.com/j2ee/dtds/web-app_2.2.dtd">

<web-app>
    <servlet>
        <servlet-name>Example</servlet-name>
        <servlet-class>ParserExample</servlet-class>
    </servlet>
</web-app>
```

Don't forget to copy example.html to C:\Temp or whatever directory you changed the code to reference.

While running Tomcat on the local machine in the Browser Address field enter the address to the ParserExample servlet providing arguments for the fname, lname, jobs, and grade parameters, i.e.:

```
http://localhost:8080/AppendixF/servlet/ParserExample?fname=Jame&lname=Bond&
job=Spy&grade=5
```

This should present HTML output as seen here:

In normal use, of course, this type of string would be the output generated when clicking the submit button of another HTML form.

Notice that in this example, we've output a complete HTML file (albeit a very basic one) and have not had to resort to writing a single line of HTML type code in the servlet.

A JSP Example

Let's repeat the servlet exercise, only this time use a JSP file to load the HTML and set the values. The code that comes with this chapter contains a file called JSPExample.jsp, which looks like this:

```
<jsp:useBean id="miniParser" scope="session" class="MiniParser" />

<%
     miniParser.parseHTML("C:/Temp","example.html");

     miniParser.updateTextField("FName", "John");
     miniParser.updateTextField("LName", "Hernandez");

     miniParser.addSelectItem("Jobs", "Soldier", false);
     miniParser.addSelectItem("Jobs", "Sailor", false);
     miniParser.addSelectItem("Jobs", "Tinker", true);
     miniParser.addSelectItem("Jobs", "Tailor", false);
     miniParser.addSelectItem("Jobs", "Spy", false);
     miniParser.addSelectItem("Jobs", "Richman", false);
     miniParser.addSelectItem("Jobs", "Poorman", false);

     miniParser.addSelectItem("Grade", "1", false);
     miniParser.addSelectItem("Grade", "2", false);
     miniParser.addSelectItem("Grade", "3", true);
     miniParser.addSelectItem("Grade", "4", false);
     miniParser.addSelectItem("Grade", "5", false);
     miniParser.addSelectItem("Grade", "6", false);

     miniParser.writeHTML(out, true);
%>
```

The JSP is, again, about as basic as it comes but it helps to illustrate the point. The class MiniParser is loaded just as a bean would be. It is then used to pump data into the HTML file and write it back to the user. Here there is no business logic, just hard-coded statements. There is no reason, though, why this data could not be sourced from a corporate database or some other form of data store using stored procedures located on yet another machine. HTTP input parameters could easily be used as selection criteria. However, note again that no HTML code is placed in a JSP file that writes HTML output to a client Browser.

If you have already set up all the files in the servlet example, all you need to do to view this JSP file in action is to place it in the web application:

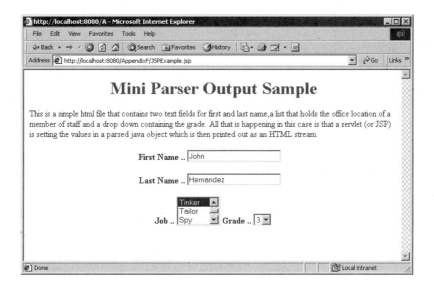

Problems and Development Potential

At this stage, we have a simple functioning object controller, `MiniParser` that can create a Java object from an HTML file and allow us to set the values of text fields and select items. To make this a really useful tool, though, we need to improve its efficiency and increase its range of functionality.

Many of the potential problems with the `MiniParser` approach will be apparent at this stage The most obvious is the current deficiency in the API functionality. Handling the hack to ensure that the `<FORM>` tag is kept is a real waste of system resources. However, this is likely to be addressed by Swing enhancements. Another solution would be to use an XML parser and re write the setter methods to work with that.

The other obvious problem is the overhead created by adding another layer of processing. Ignoring the 'hack' for the moment, given the assumption that the need for it will go away, the added overhead is surprisingly small. Real life implementations have been rather quick.

If we look at how the object works in both examples, it reads in and parses the HTML file each time it is referenced. This means repeating the same work every time. A better approach would be to parse the HTML file on object instantiation and store it in a separate location every time it is used. Thus we avoid the need to open a stream, read in the HTML, parse it, and create a `MiniParser` object. One obvious solution would be to serialize the finished object and then refer to that when necessary. Unfortunately, the current API makes it difficult for us. `HTMLDocuments` cannot yet be serialized as they contain objects such as CSS attributes that do not implement `Serializable`. If we clone the object after initialization, then re use the copy, this copy is in fact, a *shallow copy*; if we change one we change the other. This means the original object will contain any amendments made to the clone. The solution for the time being is to write a class that delves into the parsed object and creates a *deep copy* of the relevant data using the *new* operator. As we are likely to be developing the `MiniParser`, thus continually adding data structures, this is liable to be a time consuming and error prone process.

Concurrency is another issue to consider. When two users are accessing a web server at the same time, it is easy to imagine a text field receiving the correct information but for the wrong document. The JSDK 2.2 may help us here by ensuring the data integrity of instance variables. Synchronizing the class methods or groups of statements will also help. The downside to synchronization is that it slows the whole application while various threads await the completion of other threads. A fair amount of trial and error is generally needed to get this right. There are few hard and fast rules to concurrency management as each implementation differs from others in number of users and processing requirements.

The `MiniParser` is obviously only a mini solution. HTML radios and check boxes have to be added, as does capability to manage text areas and tables. Managing HTML tables, in particular, requires a significant amount of work. The textual parts of an HTML file can also be extracted and managed programmatically. This may be necessary when internationalizing applications, for example, providing different character sets to users. In fact, one of the real benefits of converting HTML items in the way described above is that the Model/View/Controller techniques can then be applied to the resultant objects.

Another useful addition would be to convert the `MiniParser` into a true JavaBean. A Customizer could then be created allowing users to set values in the HTML form items simply by entering values in a Graphical User Interface.

Summary

This chapter has looked at how various Swing packages can be employed to create an object that converts an HTML file into an object while allowing another object to edit or update items within the HTML. The editing and updating can be undertaken programmatically without needing any access to the actual HTML file. As long as certain rules are observed, the design and creation work is completely divorced from any business logic.

The HTML Generator offers a means of addressing the major problem created when writing server-side applications based on either JSP or Java servlets, the combination of HTML and Java code in the same file. HTML is stored in one file and the Java code in another. The HTML Generator does the work of combining the two, allowing web designers to concentrate on HTML structure and developers on business logic.

The purpose of this discussion is to suggest ways of facilitating and enhancing the usage of JSP and servlets rather than replacing them, the examples shown make use of both in turn. This approach has been proved to work in practical application. An enhanced version of the `MiniParser` created in this chapter has been successfully employed in a number of web sites. As is often the case, adding new layers to an application can increase processing requirements the trade off is ease of use and the simplification of project management.

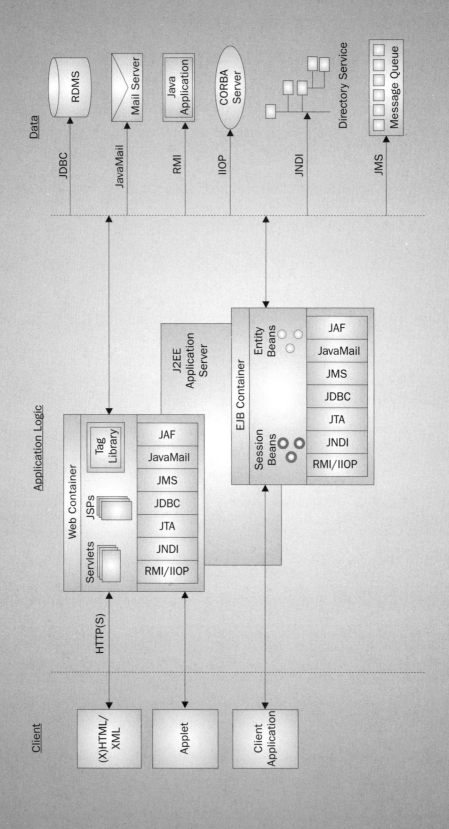

Support, Errata and P2P.Wrox.Com

One of the most irritating things about any programming book is when you find that bit of code you've just spent an hour typing simply doesn't work. You check it a hundred times to see if you've set it up correctly and then you notice the spelling mistake in the variable name on the book page. Of course, you can blame the authors for not taking enough care and testing the code, the editors for not doing their job properly, or the proofreaders for not being eagle-eyed enough, but this doesn't get around the fact that mistakes do happen.

We try hard to ensure no mistakes sneak out into the real world, but we can't promise that this book is 100% error free. What we can do is offer the next best thing by providing you with immediate support and feedback from experts who have worked on the book and try to ensure that future editions eliminate these gremlins. We also now commit to supporting you not just while you read the book, but once you start developing applications as well through our online forums where you can put your questions to the authors, reviewers, and fellow industry professionals.

In this appendix we'll look at how to:

- ❏ Enroll in the peer to peer forums at http://p2p.wrox.com
- ❏ Post and check for errata on our main site, http://www.wrox.com
- ❏ E-mail technical support a query or feedback on our books in general

Between all three support procedures, you should get an answer to your problem in no time flat.

The Online Forums at P2P.Wrox.Com

Join the Pro Java Server mailing list for author and peer support. Our system provides **Programmer To Programmer**™ support on mailing lists, forums, and newsgroups in addition to our one-to-one e mail system, which we'll look at in a minute. Be confident that your query is not just being examined by a support professional, but by the many Wrox authors and other industry experts present on our mailing lists.

How to Enroll for Support

Just follow this five-step system:

1. Go to p2p.wrox.com in your favorite browser.
Here you'll find any current announcements concerning P2P – new lists created, any removed, and so on:

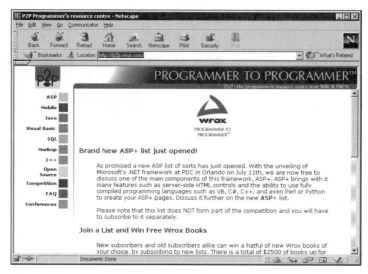

2. Click on the Java button in the left-hand column.

3. Choose to the list you want to access.

4. If you are not a member of the list, you can choose either to view the list without joining it or create an account in the list, by hitting the respective buttons.

5. If you wish to join, you'll be presented with a form in which you'll need to fill in your e mail address, name, and a password (of at least four digits). Choose how you would like to receive the messages from the list and then hit Save.

Why This System Offers the Best Support

You can choose to join the mailing lists to receive mails as they are contributed, as a daily digest, or you can receive them as a weekly digest. If you don't have the time or facility to receive the mailing list, then you can search our online archives. You'll find the ability to search on specific subject areas or keywords. As these lists are moderated, you can be confident of finding good, accurate information quickly. Mails can be edited or moved by the moderator into the correct place, making this a most efficient resource. Junk and spam mail are deleted, and your own e-mail address is protected by the unique Lyris system from web-bots that can automatically hoover up newsgroup mailing list addresses. Any queries about joining, leaving lists, or any query about the list should be sent to: `listsupport@p2p.wrox.com`.

Checking the Errata Online at www.wrox.com

The following section will take you step by step through the process of posting errata to our web site to get that help. The sections that follow, therefore, are:

- ❏ Wrox Developers Membership
- ❏ Finding a list of existing errata on the web site
- ❏ Adding your own errata to the existing list
- ❏ What happens to your errata once you've posted it (why doesn't it appear immediately)?

There is also a section covering how to e-mail a question for technical support. This comprises:

- ❏ What your e-mail should include
- ❏ What happens to your e-mail once it has been received by us

So that you only need to view information relevant to yourself, we ask that you register as a Wrox Developer Member. This is a quick and easy process that will save you time in the long run. If you are already a member, just update membership to include this book.

Wrox Developer's Membership

To get your FREE Wrox Developer's Membership click on **Membership** in the top navigation bar of our home site – http://www.wrox.com. This is shown in the following screenshot:

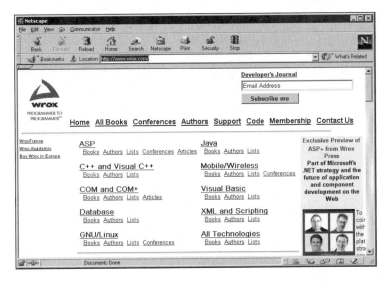

Then, on the next screen (not shown), click on **New User**. This will display a form. Fill in the details on the form and submit the details using the **Register** button at the bottom. Before you can say 'The best read books come in Wrox Red' you will get the following screen:

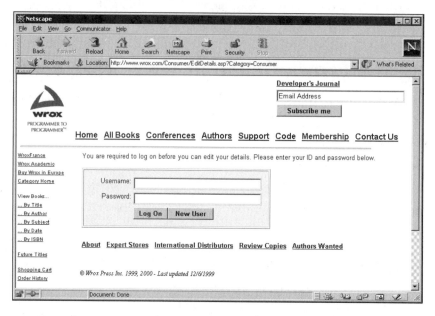

Type in your password once again and click **Log On**. The following page allows you to change your details if you need to, but now you're logged on, you have access to all the source code downloads and errata for the entire Wrox range of books.

Finding an Errata on the Web Site

Before you send in a query, you might be able to save time by finding the answer to your problem on our web site – http://www.wrox.com.

Each book we publish has its own page and its own errata sheet. You can get to any book's page by clicking on **Support** from the top navigation bar.

Halfway down the main support page is a dropdown box called **Title Support**. Simply scroll down the list until you find the book you want. Select it and then hit **Errata**:

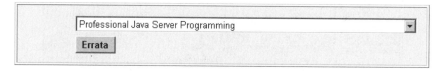

This will take you to the errata page for the book. Select the criteria by which you want to view the errata, and click the **Apply criteria** button. This will provide you with links to specific errata. For an initial search, you are advised to view the errata by page numbers. If you have looked for an error previously, then you may wish to limit your search using dates. We update these pages daily to ensure that you have the latest information on bugs and errors:

Add an Errata: E-mail Support

If you wish to point out an errata to put up on the web site, or directly query a problem in the book page with an expert who knows the book in detail, then e-mail support@wrox.com, with the title of the book and the last four numbers of the ISBN in the subject field of the e-mail. A typical e-mail should include the following things:

- ❏ The **name, last four digits of the ISBN,** and **page number** of the problem in the Subject field
- ❏ Your **name, contact info,** and the **problem** in the body of the message.

We won't send you junk mail. We need the details to save your time and ours. If we need to replace a disk or CD we'll be able to get it to you away. When you send an e-mail it will go through the following chain of support:

Customer Support

Your message is delivered to one of our customer support staff who are the first people to read it. They have files on most frequently asked questions and will answer anything general immediately. They answer general questions about the book and the web site.

Editorial

Deeper queries are forwarded to the technical editor responsible for that book. They have experience with the programming language or particular product and are able to answer detailed technical questions on the subject. Once an issue has been resolved, the editor can post the errata to the web site.

The Authors

Finally, in the unlikely event that the editor can't answer your problem, it will forwarded to the author. We try to protect the author against any distractions from writing. However, we are quite happy to forward specific requests to them. All Wrox authors help with the support on their books. They'll mail the customer and the editor with their response, and again all readers should benefit.

What We Can't Answer

Obviously with an ever-growing range of books and an ever-changing technology base, there is an increasing volume of data requiring support. While we endeavor to answer all questions about the book, we can't answer bugs in your own programs that you've adapted from our code. So, while you might have loved the chapters on file handling, don't expect too much sympathy if you cripple your company with a routine which deletes the contents of your hard drive. But do tell us if you're especially pleased with the routine you developed with our help.

How to Tell Us Exactly What You Think

We understand that errors can destroy the enjoyment of a book and can cause many wasted and frustrated hours, so we seek to minimize the distress that they can cause.

You might just wish to tell us how much you liked or loathed the book in question. Or you might have ideas about how this whole process could be improved. In which case, you should e-mail feedback@wrox.com. You'll always find a sympathetic ear, no matter what the problem is. Above all, you should remember that we do care about what you have to say and we will do our utmost to act upon it.

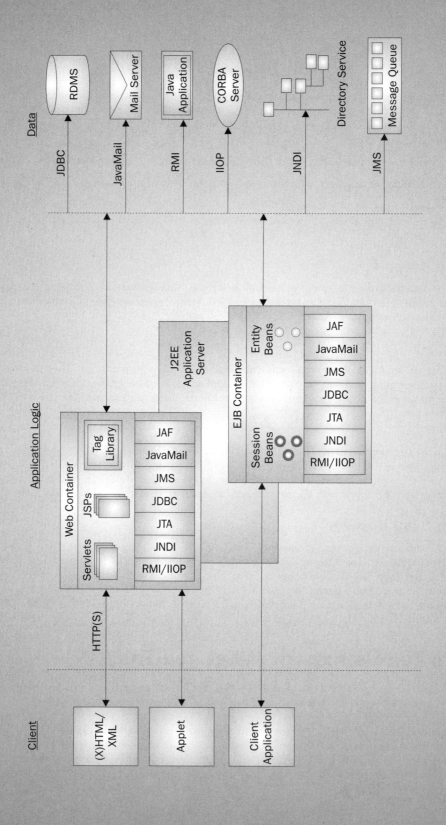

Index

A Guide to the Index

The index is arranged hierarchically, in alphabetical order, with symbols preceding the letter A. Most second-level entries and many third-level entries also occur as first-level entries. This is to ensure that users will find the information they require however they choose to search for it.

E

H

U

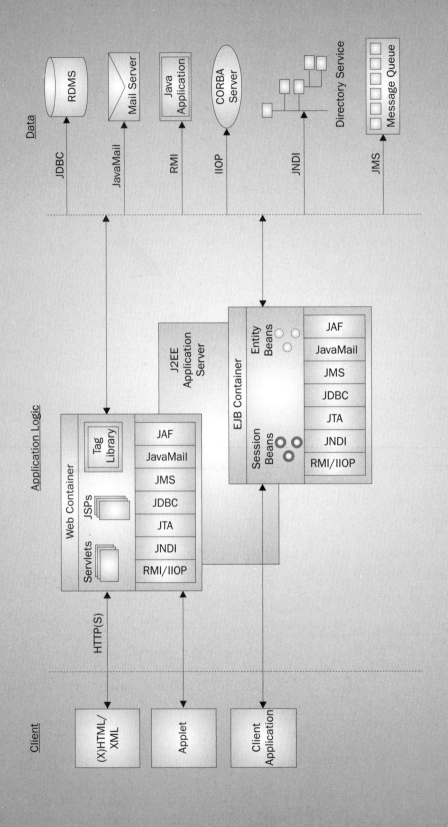

wrox
PROGRAMMER TO PROGRAMMER™

Wrox writes books for you. Any suggestions, or ideas about how you want information given in your ideal book will be studied by our team. Your comments are always valued at Wrox.

Free phone in USA 800-USE-WROX
Fax (312) 893 8001

UK Tel. (0121) 687 4100   Fax (0121) 687 4101

Professional Java Server Programming J2EE Edition- Registration Card

Name _____

Address _____

_____

_____

_____

City_____ State/Region _____

Country_____ Postcode/Zip _____

E-mail _____

Occupation _____

How did you hear about this book? _____

☐ Book review (name) _____

☐ Advertisement (name) _____

☐ Recommendation _____

☐ Catalog _____

☐ Other _____

Where did you buy this book? _____

☐ Bookstore (name)_____ City _____

☐ Computer Store (name)_____

☐ Mail Order _____

☐ Other _____

What influenced you in the purchase of this book?

☐ Cover Design

☐ Contents

☐ Other (please specify) _____

How did you rate the overall contents of this book?

☐ Excellent   ☐ Good

☐ Average   ☐ Poor

What did you find most useful about this book? _____

What did you find least useful about this book? _____

Please add any additional comments. _____

What other subjects will you buy a computer book on soon? _____

What is the best computer book you have used this year?

_____

wrox
PROGRAMMER TO PROGRAMMER™

NB. If you post the bounce back card below in the UK, please send it to:

Wrox Press Ltd., Arden House, 1102 Warwick Road,
Acocks Green, Birmingham B27 6BH. UK.

—— *Computer Book Publishers* ——

BUSINESS REPLY MAIL
FIRST CLASS MAIL   PERMIT#64   CHICAGO, IL

POSTAGE WILL BE PAID BY ADDRESSEE

WROX PRESS INC.
29 S. LA SALLE ST.
SUITE 520
CHICAGO IL 60603-USA